W9-CCU-887

THE DICTIONARY OF ANTIQUES

AND

THE DECORATIVE ARTS

THE DICTIONARY OF ANTIQUES AND THE DECORATIVE ARTS

A BOOK OF REFERENCE FOR GLASS, FURNITURE, CERAMICS, SILVER, PERIODS, STYLES, TECHNICAL TERMS, &c.

Compiled and Edited by

LOUISE ADE BOGER and H. BATTERSON BOGER

CHARLES SCRIBNER'S SONS   NEW YORK

Drawings by I. N. STEINBERG AND ASSOCIATES

COPYRIGHT© 1957, 1967 LOUISE ADE BOGER

*This book published simultaneously in the
United States of America and in Canada-
Copyright under the Berne Convention*

*All rights reserved. No part of this book may be reproduced in any form
without the permission of Charles Scribner's Sons.*

c-9.70[MJ]

PRINTED IN THE UNITED STATES OF AMERICA
LIBRARY OF CONGRESS CATALOG CARD NUMBER 67–18131

FOREWORD

The purpose of this work is to promote a fuller understanding and appreciation of the Decorative Arts. It should prove useful to the collector and to the student and also to the general reader and enquirer, because it has been designed to meet the practical needs of two semi-professional connoisseurs who have selected, defined and edited their list of essential terms during years of collecting objects of art at home and abroad. The work was started in America, expanded in Europe and finished in the Orient.

In the achievement of this work the writers have endeavored to embody the results of a study which over a period of years has occupied much of their leisure time as well as the working time of one of the collaborators. It has entailed visits to countless museums and galleries, churches and palaces, temples and shrines filled with the great works of art by the greatest artists that have ever lived. The authors have fashioned their material to the function and purpose of a dictionary—a concise, accurate book of reference giving an account of the meaning and significance of the words and terms most commonly encountered in the study of the Decorative Arts.

For special study and cross-reference the authors have appended a classified list of generic terms in which they have assembled, in alphabetical order within the alphabetically listed groups, items which are correlated within the particular categories. Items akin to more than one classification have necessarily been assigned to the group with which they are most commonly or most importantly associated.

LOUISE ADE BOGER
H. BATTERSON BOGER

Ashiya-shi
Hyōgō Prefecture
Japan

ACKNOWLEDGMENTS

We wish to acknowledge gratefully the courtesy and assistance afforded by different staff members of the Metropolitan Museum of Art, the Hispanic Society of America, the Frick Art Reference Library, the Frick Collection, Cooper Union Museum, and the art reference department at the New York Public Library. Grateful acknowledgment must also be made for the courtesy and cooperation extended to us by the Boston Museum of Fine Arts, the Philadelphia Museum of Art, the Corning Museum of Glass, the Henry Francis du Pont Winterthur Museum, the Musée du Louvre, the Honolulu Academy of Arts, the National Museum of Kyōto and the National Museum of Nara. The sincere desire to cooperate which we have encountered at museums whether in America, Europe or the Orient has been a heart-warming and rewarding experience.

We also wish to express our gratitude for the valuable help received from a wide circle of collector friends and acquaintances, extending over a period of almost two decades. Cordial thanks are also given to Mr. Frank Caro of C. T. Loo and to Mr. Milton Samuels of French and Company who have kindly helped us with some of our photographs. A special debt of gratitude is owed to Mr. K. Imai, curio dealer and collector of Kyōto, who permitted us to study rare pieces of Japanese porcelain in his collection.

Our thanks are also due to the following for their helpful criticism and suggestions relative to the original manuscript: Mrs. Yves Henry Buhler, Museum of Fine Arts, Boston; Randolph Bullock, Metropolitan Museum of Art; Miss Helen Comstock, *Antiques Magazine* and *The Connoisseur*; Carl C. Dauterman, Metropolitan Museum of Art; Leslie A. Hyam, president of the Parke-Bernet Galleries, New York; Paul N. Perrot, Corning Museum of Glass; F. St. George Spendlove, Royal Ontario Museum; and the late Fiske Kimball, Philadelphia Museum of Art.

We also most cordially thank Dr. Gustav Ecke of the Honolulu Academy of Arts for helpful suggestions, and Monsieur M. Florisoone, Conservateur des Musées Nationaux Adjoint du Directeur des Musées de France, and Dr. Kiichiro Kanda, director of the National Museum of Kyōto, who have kindly supplied us with particular information.

Above all we wish to acknowledge the many splendid books without which this dictionary could not have been compiled. Our modern knowledge of the Decorative Arts is founded on the pioneer research and scrupulous accuracy embodied in these scholarly works, which it has been our sincere effort to represent justly.

Finally our deep appreciation to Charles Scribner's Sons for the untiring interest they have given to every detail associated in the production of this book. In particular we are indebted to Elinor Parker whose warm appreciation and understanding of the Decorative Arts has helped to clarify the text in a number of the definitions.

CONTENTS

SUPPLEMENT

ILLUSTRATIONS

Color Plates opposite pages 54, 118, 182, 278, 342, 470

Full page Line Drawings

ILLUSTRATIONS

Abattant In French cabinetwork; a fall-front or drop-front panel. See *Secrétaire à Abattant*; *Drop-Front*.

Abricotier The wood of the apricot tree, *prunus armeniaca*, used in cabinetwork, especially by the French ébénistes. It is hard and compact, and its color is yellowish.

Abtsbessingen In German ceramics; a faïence manufactory is believed to have been in existence at Abtsbessingen, Thuringia, from around 1739, founded by the brother of the Prince of Schwarzburg; however, the earliest records are from 1753. The faïence produced here ranks among the best faïence of Germany. The wares are sometimes marked with a pitchfork taken from the Schwarzburg coat-of-arms, together with the painters' initials. Included among their productions were vases, tureens, carefully modelled flowers for table decoration, boxes in the form of pug dogs and cylindrical tankards. The painted decoration was in blue and in other high temperature colors. Enamel colors painted over the glaze in the style of porcelain were also used. The motifs for the painted decoration were in the Baroque and subsequent Rococo styles. Favorite Chinese subjects such as pavilions and Chinese flowers were also found.

Acacia Faux Wood The wood of the common locust tree, *robinia pseud-acacia*, used in cabinetwork. It is hard and its color is yellow and greenish striped.

Acacia Wood *Acacia pendula*. See *Violet Wood*.

Acajou A French term denoting the mahogany tree or any of many related trees. The woods from these trees are hard, and their color varies from brownish yellow to reddish brown. It was widely used in cabinetwork. Acajou was imported into France from the time of the Régence in ever-increasing quantities.

Acanthus In architecture and decoration; a term chiefly applied to the species *acanthus spinosus* native to the shores of the Mediterranean and notable for the elegance of its deeply cut and shiny large leaves. Conventionally treated acanthus foliage of the species *acanthus spinosus* is employed in the decoration of Corinthian and Composite capitals. Acanthus leafage conventionally represented has long been a favorite type of carved decoration in the ornamentation of furniture and has been freely used as a carved motif since the time of the Renaissance. It is probably one of the most popular of all carved leaf designs. After the introduction of mahogany in England and America it was especially fashionable as a carved motif on chairs and tables until towards the end of the 18th century.

ACANTHUS

Acorn In ornament; an ornament resembling an acorn. The acorn, as a carved decorative motif, was found during the 16th century and it continued in use during the 17th and 18th centuries. It was often used as a finial, such as on the uprights of a chair back, on the cover of a vase, and it was also used as a pendant, such as on a molding. This so-called acorn molding was sometimes employed in American cabinetwork on the upper part of a bookcase and on other similar tall articles of furniture. See *Acorn Chair*; *Acorn Spoon*.

Acorn Chair In English cabinetwork; the name given to a type of Jacobean oak chair which had a crossrail with acorn-shaped pendants.

Acorn Molding See *Acorn*.

Acorn Spoon In English silver; a silver spoon which had its stem terminating in the shape of an acorn. It was introduced around the 14th century. See *Spoon*.

Acroterium Or Acroter. In classic architecture; a pedestal for a figure or a similar decorative ornament placed at the apex or at each of the corners of a pediment. The term is applied by extension to the statue or other decorative feature placed on such a pedestal. When classic architectural details are incorporated in furniture design the term is used for a similar treatment, such as the plinth centered in a broken pediment of a secretary bookcase.

Act of Parliament Clock   The name originally given to an inexpensive English wall clock, which had a short plain wooden case, containing a pendulum, and a large open wooden dial usually painted black with gilt figures. The clock was so-called because in 1797, in accordance with an act of Parliament, a yearly tax of five shillings was imposed on all clocks, and innkeepers, foreseeing a shortage of clocks and watches among their patrons, hung these inexpensive clocks in their inns. The act was unpopular and was repealed in 1798. By extension the term is sometimes applied to all cheaply made wall clocks of this variety hung in public rooms, although it is correctly applied only to those made to meet the emergency which the new tax brought about. Wall clocks of this variety, generally weight-driven and with a trunk case and pendulum and unglazed dial, were made as early as 1760 in England. However, the earlier specimens were more elegantly and expensively finished.

Adam, Robert   1728–1792, famous English architect and designer of furniture. He was the second son of William Adam, who was a successful architect in Scotland. He was born at Kirkcaldy and had three brothers, John, James and William. He went to Italy in 1754 and, during the course of his itinerary, he visited the ruins of Diocletian's palace at Spalatro. In 1764 he published a splendid work entitled THE RUINS OF THE PALACE OF DIOCLETIAN. Much of his subsequent work reflected the influence of these studies and was to a large extent based upon them. In 1773, Robert and his brother, James, began

DESIGN
BY ROBERT ADAM

publishing WORKS IN ARCHITECTURE which contained designs of many of their more celebrated works and was instrumental in popularizing the Adam style of ornament. Robert Adam was able through his extraordinary ability to mold and adapt classic ornament in such a manner as to create a new treatment for classic ornament which was distinctive for its elegance and grace and for its refined and finished detail. Out of simple curvilinear forms of which he favored the oval he had the genius to evolve combinations of remarkable beauty and variety. He believed and successfully practiced that the smallest detail of decoration and furnishing was within the field of the architect and that only in this manner could a complete and accordant result be achieved. In his vast collection of drawings, in addition to designs for furniture, he illustrated designs for such pieces as carpets, lamps, andirons and articles of silver. He designed his furniture to form an essential part of his decorative scheme. His furniture designs were distinctive for their fine proportions, for the elegant simplicity of their classic form and for the delicate and graceful beauty of their classic ornament. Hepplewhite and Sheraton derived much from the work of Adam. The influence of Robert Adam prevailed upon decorative art from around 1760–1765 until his death in 1792. The furniture designed by Adam was essentially rectilinear in form and was inspired by classic models. After 1775 the influence of the Louis XVI style was evident in Adam's designs for furniture. The style of ornament used by Robert Adam was exceedingly rich in variety and was essentially borrowed from the ornament of the ancient Romans. The motifs were remarkable for their exquisite delicacy, their classic refinement and their elegance. Included among the favorite motifs were festoons of husks, drapery swags, a radiating design resembling a fan, the anthemion or honeysuckle, medallions, rosettes, delicate acanthus scrolling, trophies of armor, vases and urns of classical form, arabesques, the lyre motif, wheat sheafs, garlands, husk chains, classical figure subjects, masks and animal motifs such as the ram's head. Included among the different methods Adam employed to decorate his furniture were the following: carving, gilding, marquetry, veneering, painting, Wedgwood medallions, scagliola and occasionally bronze mounts in the classic taste. See *Classic Revival*; *Louis XVI*; *Kauffmann, Angelica*; *Cipriani, Giovanni*; *Pergolesi, Michele Angelo*; *Zucchi, Antonio Pietro*.

Adam Style   circa 1760–1765 to 1792. See *Adam, Robert*.

Adams, William   In English ceramics; one of a family of potters working in Staffordshire during the second half of the 18th and early 19th centuries. William Adams, d. 1805, of Greengates, Tunstall, working from 1787 made deep blue jasper ware and cream-colored earthenware. The marks, which were all impressed, were "Adams & Co"; "Adams B Adams"; "W. Adams & Co." William Adams, 1748–1831, of the Brick House, Burslem, and of Colbridge, was a general potter. A third branch of this family was that of William Adams of Stoke, b. 1772–d. 1829. The marks were "Adams", either impressed or printed, and "W. Adams & Sons", impressed. The blue printed wares made at their pottery for the American market during the early 19th century were commonly marked with an impressed eagle with a cartouche enclosing the name of the printed subject. Late in the 19th century descendants of this branch of the Adams family bought the Greengates pottery, which together with other kilns are still operated by them. See *Staffordshire*.

Adlerglas   Or Adlerhumpen. In German glass; a tall cylindrical-shaped enamelled German drinking glass either with or without a cover. The colored enamelled decoration portrayed the double eagle of the Holy Roman Empire having on its outstretched wings fifty-six armorial bearings of the different members composing the Holy Roman Empire. Each wing had six feathers and on each feather were four escutcheons

with the names of the Princes and cities to whom they belonged. In addition there were the escutcheons of the Seven Electors and that of the Pope. Enamelled glasses of imposing size were extremely popular in Germany from around the middle of the 16th century onwards. This subject of the double eagle was by far one of the most popular subjects for these large drinking glasses. The adlerglas is also called a Reichshumpen or Reichsadlerhumpen. See *Elector Glass*; *German Glass*; *Humpen*.

Affleck, Thomas   A Philadelphia cabinetmaker. He was born in Scotland and came to Philadelphia in 1763. At the present time he is commonly regarded to be the outstanding figure among Philadelphia cabinetmakers. It is generally agreed that the finest Chippendale-style furniture made in America was produced in Philadelphia. Affleck had a shop on Second Street. He died in 1795. See *Philadelphia Chippendale Style*.

Afghan Bokhara   An Oriental rug belonging to the Turkoman group. It is a product of Bokhara and is also woven by the dwellers in northern Afghanistan. The warp and weft are of dark wool or goats'-hair. The pile is of medium length, and is of goats'-fleece or fine wool. The ends are usually finished with a deep colored web and a long loose fringe. In its design it uses the octagon but much enlarged, and without the dividing lines which make the Tekke Bokhara look like a decorated checker-board. The Afghan Bokhara is more often after the order of the Khiva Bokhara and has often been sold under that name.   See *Turkoman Rugs*.

Afshar   An Oriental rug belonging to the Persian classification. It is generally classed as an inferior grade Shiraz. See *Shiraz*; *Persian Rugs*.

Agal Wood   See *Agalloch Wood*.

Agalloch Wood   An East Indian tree, *aquilaria agallocha*, the wood of which is used in cabinetwork, especially by the French ébénistes. It is soft, and its color varies. Also

ADLERGLAS

called aloeswood, agalwood and eaglewood. It is also burnt by the Orientals as a perfume.

Agalmatolite In minerals; a soft kind of compact stone usually having a yellowish, greyish or greenish color, used by the Chinese for carving images and grotesque figures. It is also called pagodite and figure-stone.

Agata A late 19th century American ornamental glass, shading from white to rose and having a mottled though always glossy surface. See *Art Glass*.

Agate Ware In English ceramics; the practice of mixing clays of two or more colors to produce an agate or marbled ware had its origin in antiquity. The solid agate ware made in Staffordshire around the second quarter of the 18th century was produced by mixing white, brown and blue stained clays. A little later the process was adopted by Wedgwood and he produced a material closely resembling natural agate which he made into vases and other similar objects. See *Marbled Ware*; *Staffordshire*.

Agra An Oriental rug woven at Agra, India; an important rug-weaving center during the reign of Akbar the Great, 1556–1605. The modern Agra rug is purely a commercial creation; it is one of the better grades of modern India Orientals. See *India Oriental*; *Oriental Rug*.

Aikuchi In Japanese arms; a knife or dagger without a guard. The hilt and scabbard of the aikuchi were frequently made of metal and were elaborately decorated. The aikuchi was carried, during the Tokugawa era, by persons of rank and retired fighting men, and was also used in committing hara-kiri, or ceremonial suicide. See *Tanto*.

Ailanto Or tree of heaven, *simaru ailante*. Its wood is used in cabinetwork, especially by the French ébénistes. It is native to East India and China. Its wood is hard and compact, and its color is reddish and veined.

Ailettes In armor; the protective plates

worn on the shoulders from the latter part of the 13th to the middle of the 14th centuries. They were of various shapes such as round, square, cross or shield-shaped, and frequently were decorated with a coat-of-arms.

Air Twist In glass; a spiral vein of air or a twisted air spiral formed by the extension of air bubbles or tears in the stem of a glass drinking vessel. The air twist stem, which was made in numerous variations, was fashionable in English glass from around 1740 to 1765. Originally the tears or bubbles were accidental, and because the effect was so pleasing they were later purposely put in the glass. See *Tear*.

Aiyin A coarse form of the Herat rug. See *Herat Rug*.

Ajouré A French term applied to metalwork which is pierced through, perforated or openworked, for example an ajouré silver fruit bowl or a bowl decorated with a pierced design.

Akbar the Great Emperor of India, 1556–1605. He established the Royal Factory at Lahore, India. His reign marked the beginning of the great Oriental rug weaving period in India, and continued through the reigns of Jahangir, 1605–1628, and Shah Jahan, 1628–1658. Some of these rugs compare favorably with the 16th century Persian rugs. See *India Oriental*.

Ak-Hissar Mohair Rug An Oriental rug belonging to the Turkish classification; so named after the town where it is made. The foundation is of a coarse wool and the pile is of mohair, sometimes mixed with wool. The ends are usually finished with a narrow web and loose warp threads. See *Turkish Rugs*.

Alabaster A compact variety of gypsum of fine texture; it is usually white and translucent. Sometimes it is veined, clouded or spotted. It is soft and can easily be scratched. It is carved into vases and other decorative objects and is used in figure sculpture. The

AIR TWIST STEM

other type of alabaster is a compact variety of calcite that is somewhat translucent. It is hard and cannot be scratched. This type, which is also called Oriental alabaster, was used by the ancients for making small vases for oils and perfumes. Sometimes it is beautifully banded and it is then known as onyx marble or simply onyx.

Alb In ecclesiastical costume; a vestment of white cloth, reaching to the feet and covering the entire person, having close sleeves, worn by priests in religious ceremonies and by some consecrated kings. Although some albs during the Middle Ages were of silk and sometimes of various colors, the alb is now white and it should be made of linen. The alb is either plain or decorated with apparels. These richly embroidered apparels were found at the wrist and at the bottom of the full robe. Especially typical were apparels of quadrangular form varying from twenty inches by nine inches to nine inches by six inches for the bottom and six inches by four inches to three inches square for the wrist. Apparels of this type were universally worn from the 13th to the 16th centuries and the religious ornament embroidered in silk and gold on these apparels was remarkably beautiful and appropriate. The alb is girded by a cord generally of white cotton about three yards long, which serves to adjust the alb to a convenient length. This cord which is called a girdle was formerly of various colors and made of rich materials. It was frequently beautifully worked and early records mention "girdles with gold and precious stones." See *Apparel*; *Chasuble*.

Albarello In ceramics; an Italian word for a variety of drug or apothecary jar. The form was practically cylindrical. Generally the center was slightly more narrow than the top and lower portions of the body. It had a wide round mouth and foot rim. Sometimes slight characteristic variations occurred in the form. The albarello form was found in Persian and in Mesopotamian wares from the 12th century, in Hispano-Moresque wares from the 15th century and in the Italian

Renaissance majolica wares. The albarello form was also used in other continental wares. One explanation for the derivation of the word is that the name is an Italian corruption of the Persian *el barani*, or a vase for drugs. It is also said that because of its supposed resemblance to a section of bamboo in which drugs were exported from the Orient, that it was given the Italian name of albarello or little tree. See *Pharmacy Vase*.

Albertolli, Giocondo 1742–1839. Italian designer of ornament and famous master of the Neo-Classicists in Italy. His decorative designs in the style of the antique were instrumental in developing and diffusing the Neo-Classic art in Italy. He was a director of the Academy of Milan, founded in 1775.

Alcora In ceramics; a pottery manufactory founded in Alcora, Valencia, Spain, around 1726 by Count Aranda. It was a leading manufactory for faïence in Spain during the 18th century, and the faïence produced there during the lifetime of its founder, c. 1726–1749, may be regarded as some of the finest of its kind made in Europe. Its production can be classified in three groups: the tin-glazed faïence from c. 1726–c. 1785, the porcelain first made around 1776 and the cream-colored earthenware made from around 1777. Of these three the faïence was the most important. Especially distinctive was the pictorial painting which was an original feature of Alcora faïence. Good figure modelling in the cream-colored ware is also worth noting. Other earthenware was in imitation of Wedgwood jasper ware and pottery in the English style, and displayed little originality. The manufactory mark of "A" was used after 1784.

ALBARELLO

Alcove Cupboard In English cabinetwork; in the early 18th century alcove and corner cupboards often formed a part of the wood panelling of rooms. The term appears in 18th century records. See *Buffet*; *Corner Cupboard*.

Alder Wood See *Aulne Wood*.

Ale Glass In English glass; a drinking vessel introduced during the 17th century and used for beer and ale. It consisted of a tall funnel-shaped bowl resting on a short stem, usually of baluster form, and a spreading foot. See *Yard of Ale*.

Alençon Point A French needlepoint lace sometimes referred to in lace literature as the Queen of Laces. It was made with a fine needle and the small pieces were later joined with invisible stitches. There were about twelve processes and each lace-maker was assigned one of these special branches. Due to its elaborate construction it was seldom made in large pieces, such as pillow covers. There were two kinds of grounds, namely, a hexagonal bride ground and a ground of meshes or réseau. In the 18th century the réseau ground was introduced and apparently entirely adopted. The designs were un-rivalled for their closeness and evenness. A distinctive feature was the cordonnet which had a foundation of horsehair placed around the edge of the design and closely worked over in fine buttonhole stitches. It is not known when the term *point d'Alençon* was first used; however, it is mentioned in an inventory of 1741 where it is stated to be *à réseau*. A strong resemblance existed between Alençon and Argentan which was the other French needlepoint lace. At the present time it is customary to regard Alençon as a lace with a fine réseau, with a mesh which is more frequently square rather than hex-agonal in form. The manufacture of Alençon was practically extinct, when it was revived under Napoleon, and it also flourished again under the Second Empire. Of more recent times it has been made at Burano, Brussels, and Bayeux, where it was introduced in 1855, and also at Alençon. See *Argentan Point*; *Argentella*; *Point de France*.

Aleyard An English drinking glass. See *Yard of Ale*.

Alicatados In Spanish ceramics; a Spanish term meaning cutwork given to a mosaic tilework made in the Near East, and also made in Spain from around the 14th century. See *Seville*; *Tiles*.

ALMORRATXA

Alisier Wood The wood of the whitebeam tree, *pyrus aria*, used in cabinetwork, espec-ially by the French ébénistes. It is hard, and its color is white.

Alla Castellana Ware In Italian ceramics; a lead-glazed earthenware with sgraffiato decoration. This type of ware was made in Italy from the early Renaissance in the 14th century onwards at many important pottery centers. However, the majority of centers producing this ware have not been conclus-ively identified, with the exception of Bo-logna and Pavia. It appears that Città di Castello near Perugia and neighboring La Fratta were important centers for producing lead-glazed earthenware with sgraffiato dec-oration.

Alla Porcellana In Italian ceramics; a con-temporary term given to a kind of Italian majolica decoration characterized by foliage and twisting stems executed in blue in the manner of 15th century Chinese porcelain.

Allecret In armor; the name given to a half suit of light plate armor similar to a corselet. Taces were also used with the allecret. It was especially used by the Swiss during the 16th century.

Allison, Michael American cabinetmaker working from around 1800 to 1845. He is listed at 42 and also at 46–48 Vesey Street, New York City.

Almond Wood See *Amandier Wood*.

Almoner's Cupboard In English cabinet-work; a livery cupboard used in the church in which bread was kept to be doled out to the poor. It is also called a dole cupboard. It was introduced around the beginning of the 16th century. See *Livery Cupboard*.

Almorratxa Or Morratxa. In Spanish glass; a variety of glass vessel which is principally a Catalan form. It is a rose-water sprinkler used on ceremonial occasions. The character-istic almorratxa has an ovoid or pear-shaped body resting on a high spreading foot. It has a short neck used for filling the vessel and four very slender upright spouts on the top of the shoulder for sprinkling. The almorratxa was used from about the 16th through the 18th centuries.

Alms Dish   An ecclesiastical dish or plate for the reception of alms, used in the Church. In English silver; it is usually in the form of a flat-shaped plate, with or without handles, used since medieval times. The greater number of the early alms dishes were of base metal plated, or of brass, pewter or latten. The later ones, many of which were made for secular use and then given to the Church, were made of finely wrought silver or gold, frequently with a print in the center depicting a religious subject or a coat-of-arms.

Aloes Wood   See *Agalloch Wood*.

Alpujarra   A distinctive kind of Spanish hand-loomed peasant rug deriving its name from the district of Alpujarra, in the province of Granada in the south of Spain, where it was woven. Frequently the date is woven into the rug, and extant examples bear the date of 1740. However, according to reliable sources, it seems that these rugs were woven at least from around the end of the 15th century. It is generally accepted that the Alpujarra rug was evolved and perfected by the Moors and that the technique was carried on by the Spanish peasants. In this rug the loops and weft are woven into the warp, with the raised loops giving a rather rough surface appearance. The loops are wound over an iron rod and when a row of loops is completed across the warp the customary rows of weft are woven in. As a rule the rug is rather coarse and heavy, and has about nine to twenty loops to every square inch. Originally the Alpujarra was used as a bedspread and not as a floor covering. The fringe is a distinctive feature and is woven separately of one of the principal colors. The colors and designs are relatively simple and possess a singular peasant charm. The majority of these rugs are woven in two colors; however, some display from three to as many as ten colors. Especially favored

as motifs are vases of flowers or the tree of life often with a bird on either side, stars and other similar geometric designs, as well as grapes and leaves and the pomegranate which is the symbol of Granada.

Alsace   In French Provincial; originally an old German province and later a French province. It lies between the Rhine River and the Vosges Mountains. The territory is now the departments of Haut-Rhin and Bas-Rhin in France. Much of the furniture made in the province of Alsace reflected the influence of the cabinetwork of Germany, Austria and Switzerland. This was particularly evident in their chair designs. One characteristic chair was similar to the type found throughout the Tyrol. This chair had a low wooden back and a rectangular wooden seat that rested on splayed legs. The back was shaped and pierced and was carved with different geometric motifs and emblems. The Alsatians always had a curious liking for colored decoration. This was revealed in their use of a simplified marquetry or inlay of different colored woods and in their taste for painted decoration and painted furniture. As a rule their furniture was inclined to be flowery and overloaded with ornament. See *French Provincial*.

ALSATIAN CHAIR

Altar Cup   In Chinese ceramics; a beautiful white porcelain cup of the Ming period that has the character T'an, which means altar, engraved inside. See *Ming*.

Altare   In Italian glass; during the Middle Ages glassmakers from Normandy settled at Altare near Genoa and developed an independent tradition similar to that of Venice. The Altare glass industry became the most important rival of the Venetian center and achieved a great importance, along with Venice, in the second half of the 15th century. It appears that with the exception of a few examples it is now impossible to make a distinction between the glassware of Venice and Altare.

Altissimo Marble   See *Statuary Marble*.

Alto-Rilievo   High relief. See *Relief*.

Amandier Wood   The wood of the almond tree, *amygdalus communis*, used in cabinetwork, especially by the French ébénistes. It is hard and compact, and its color is yellow.

Amaranth Wood   This wood, *amaranthus*, obtained from the amaranth tree or shrub in Guiana, was widely used in cabinetwork by the French ébénistes. It is hard, and its color is a purplish red.

Amberg   In German ceramics; a faïence pottery was founded at Amberg, Bavaria, Germany, in 1759 by Simon Hetzendörfer. The pottery began to manufacture cream-colored earthenware and porcelain in 1790. The manufactory was in existence until 1910. Much of the production was limited to useful wares in plain white or crudely painted in blue. The mark on the faïence was "AB" in monogram. The cream-colored ware was marked with the name of the town "Amberg", impressed.

Amberina   An ornamental colored glass made in America during the late 19th century. It is a clear glass with color tones from pale amber shading to ruby. Tablewares as well as ornamental pieces were made of amberina glass. The majority of these wares were patterned in molds. See *Art Glass*.

Amboina Wood   See *Amboyna Wood*.

Amboise   See *Amboyna Wood*.

Amboyna Wood   The wood of the amboyna tree, *pterospermum indicum*, of the Moluccas or Spice Islands, widely used in cabinetwork, especially by the French ébénistes. It is hard and its color is white-rose and yellow-brown. It is a beautifully curled and mottled wood. Also called amboise and amboina.

Ambry   Or Aumbry. In English furniture; an English term which has been obsolete since around 1600, but an occasionally used term in domestic and ecclesiastical antiquities that was also used to some degree as an archaism in different 16th century spellings. In the corrupt form *almery* it is confused with *almonry* as though it were a place for alms. In a general sense the term refers to a place to keep things such as a closet or a chest for implements, arms and similar possessions. It also refers to a cupboard, either built-in or movable. In a more specialized sense it refers to a place for keeping food. The term is also applied to a cupboard in a pantry, a store closet or a wall press. It is also used to describe a cupboard or closed recess in a wall for books and for ceremonial vessels belonging to the Church. A compartment of a cupboard was also occasionally called an ambry. In the second half of the 15th century "cubbordes with aumbreys" were mentioned in inventories, which it seems reasonable to assume implied that part of the open shelves was provided with doors. It appears that early in the reign of Henry VIII, 1509–1547, the term cupboard was given to what had been previously called an ambry and that around the end of the 16th century the terms ambries, cupboards and presses were more or less interchangeable. See *Cupboard*.

Amen Glass   In English glass; a type of Jacobite glass made to commemorate the rising of 1715, when James Stuart, 1688–1766, known as the Old Pretender and eldest son of James II, sought to establish himself as James III of England and James VIII of Scotland. These footed stem glasses are characterized by diamond point engraved prayers ending with Amen. They also bear the letters I.R. elaborately scrolled with a concealed figure eight and a crown. See *Jacobite Glass*.

American Colonial   1630–1789. The American styles of furniture are sometimes divided into two historical groups; namely the Colonial and the Federal. In American history the term *Colonial* refers to the thirteen original British Colonies which subsequently became the United States of America and to the period. Thus the term *Colonial* as applied to architecture and the decorative arts is used to cover that style which prevailed before and at the time of the American Revolution. In furniture it includes the

AMEN GLASS

Jacobean, William and Mary, Queen Anne and Chippendale styles. The earliest furniture made in America was in the Jacobean style, 1603–1688. Early Jacobean furniture was very scarce. Late Jacobean articles were slightly more plentiful. The Jacobean style was superseded by the William and Mary style, 1689–1702. In all of the different styles a number of years, probably five to ten years, intervened until the new styles became fashionable in America after they were adopted in England. In America many of the English designs were closely followed. This close similarity existing between the styles of England and America can be attributed to a great extent to the wide circulation of pattern books of engraved ornament and designs for furniture. Architectural publications and builders' handbooks were employed in a similar manner in architecture. These pattern books, which were a great formative influence both in England and in America, created a high standard of knowledge among the craftsmen, making the 18th century a period of remarkable achievement. Copies of these different publications appeared in America often within a few years of their original issue in England. In this manner the new English fashions were mirrored in America. Naturally the very elegant and ambitious cabinetwork made in England for the royalty and aristocracy was not found in America, since that class of society did not exist here. During the William and Mary style highboys and lowboys were introduced in America and remained in vogue for almost one hundred years. Gateleg tables became popular. The cabriole leg, which was introduced in England around 1700, was found in America early in the 18th century. It continued in vogue in America during the Queen Anne and Chippendale styles. However, straight quadrangular legs were employed on many chairs and tables and other articles of furniture designed in the Chippendale style. From around 1710 certain principles of the Queen Anne style occasionally appeared in American furniture design and the new style was adopted around

1720. The English Early Georgian style furniture with its characteristic phases, such as the lion mask and satyr mask, was seldom if ever found in America. Furniture of a pronounced architectural character was also limited, although numerous examples of secretary cabinets displayed pilasters or fluted columns. The elaborate carved and giltwood furniture in the taste of William Kent made for the English Palladian mansions was unknown. The Queen Anne style continued in vogue in America until around 1755–1760, when it was supplanted by the Chippendale style. However, from around 1745–1750 some of the American cabinetwork was executed in the early Chippendale style. The Queen Anne style was characterized by its graceful curvilinear lines. Many fine chairs, highboys, lowboys and other articles of furniture were made in America in the Queen Anne style. The cabriole leg commonly terminated in the Dutch or club foot. Although the claw and ball foot began to be used in America around 1735–1740, it is chiefly identified with the Chippendale style in America and was in general use from about 1750–1755 to 1785. Mahogany was introduced in the first quarter of the 18th century and was increasingly employed. Windsor chairs became popular from around 1725 onwards. The Chippendale style prevailed in America from around 1755 to 1785 and came into full expression around 1760. Undoubtedly the finest examples of the Chippendale style in America were made by the Philadelphia cabinetmakers. Philadelphia-style highboys and lowboys are renowned. Townsend and Goddard blockfront pieces in the Chippendale style are also celebrated. The Adam style, with the exception of a few articles such as mirrors, mantelpieces and fire-grates, was never developed in America. This was due to some extent to the suspension of commercial relations between the two countries during the Revolutionary War. By the time normal business was restored between the two countries the Hepplewhite style was the prevailing fashion in England and the American cabinetmakers

AMERICAN CHIPPENDALE
CHEST-ON-CHEST

changed from the Chippendale to the Hepplewhite style.

American Directoire At the present time literature pertaining to the history of American furniture often gives the name *American Directoire* to a style of furniture made in America from around 1805 to 1815. Occasionally this style is included in either the late Sheraton or in the early American Empire style. The American Directoire style is best exemplified in the chairs and sofas made by Duncan Phyfe and other contemporary American cabinetmakers. The characteristic American Directoire chair had its origin in the so-called Grecian chair, and the sofa, in which the Directoire style predominated, was inspired by the ancient Greek and Roman couches used for dining and reclining. In England this variety of chair and sofa designed in the Directoire style is considered to be in the style of the English Regency. Numerous American Empire chairs and sofas continued to display certain features of design which characterized these Directoire style pieces. See *Grecian Sofa*; *Grecian Chair*; *Greek Revival*.

American Eagle Pattern See *Ingrain Carpet*.

American Empire The name *American Empire* is commonly given to a style of furniture made in America from around 1810–1815 to 1830, while the term *Late Empire* is given to the furniture made from around 1830 to 1840. The furniture in this decade was coarsely designed and was characterized by its massive and cumbrous forms. The American Empire style was developed to a greater or lesser extent from the French Empire and English Regency styles. It displayed certain decorative features of the French Empire style, such as the round wood columns employed on sideboards, chests of drawers and other similar pieces, and the lion paw feet and the shaggy paw feet of other animals found on sofas and the splayed tetrapod bases of tables. The American cabinetmakers working in the Empire style showed a pronounced preference in their style of ornament

AMERICAN FEDERAL
DUNCAN PHYFE CARD TABLE

for eagles, fruits, flowers, foliage and horns of plenty signifying the abundance of this new land. The furniture was made of fine mahogany and displayed good workmanship.

American Federal 1789–1830. The term *Federal* includes those styles which were in vogue after the Federal government was established in 1789. Thus the Federal group includes the Hepplewhite, Sheraton and American Empire styles. The Hepplewhite style became fashionable in America shortly after 1785 and remained in vogue until about 1800. Carving and inlay were the principal methods used for decorating the American pieces made in the Hepplewhite style. Among the favorite motifs employed in inlay work were rosettes, festoons of flowers, husk pendants and acanthus foliage. As a rule the furniture in the Hepplewhite style was made of mahogany. The Sheraton style was the last of the great English furniture styles of the 18th century. It became increasingly popular in America after 1795. Practically every type of furniture that was in vogue in America from about 1795 to 1820 was made in the Sheraton style by Duncan Phyfe and other American cabinetmakers. Veneering was a pronounced feature of late 18th century cabinetwork. Mahogany was the principal wood. Satinwood, which was extensively used in England, was seldom used in America except for inlaid decorative bandings and stringing lines. The lyre form, which was a favorite decorative feature of Sheraton's, was used by Duncan Phyfe on his articles of furniture designed in the Sheraton style. Inlay work was extensively employed by Sheraton; included among the favorite motifs were rosettes, delicate festoons of flowers and husk pendants. Both large and small delicate inlaid ovals were especially typical. Reeding was widely used, especially on the legs of chairs and tables. See *Antique Furniture*.

American Glass Glassmaking in the American colonies, throughout the 18th century and early part of the 19th century, generally followed European glassmaking traditions, usually producing ordinary olive, amber, bluish and green glass similar to the German waldglas. The first glasshouse was at Jamestown, Virginia, in 1608 but it was forced to close due to pioneer conditions in the New World. The first glasshouse to establish successful operations was founded by Caspar Wistar, 1695–1752, and his son, at Wistarberg, Salem County, New Jersey, producing from 1739 to 1780. To Wistarberg, which made window panes and bottles, are ascribed bowls with covers, jugs and other vessels usually in colored glass, occasionally with impressed and trailed ornament as well as with colored and opaque white loops and stripes. Similar glass was undoubtedly made by other glasshouses and is referred to as South Jersey. Another prominent 18th century glasshouse was established at Manheim, Pennsylvania, in 1769 by Heinrich Wilhelm Stiegel. An important production of early American glasshouses was that of spirit flasks which were molded with portraits of famous persons, inscriptions and patterns. The development of the mechanical press for making pressed glass was the first American contribution to the glassmaking industry. The practical machine for pressing glass appeared in the later 1820's and within a few years was in general use for making tablewares. Although it was chiefly used to produce a rough imitation of cut glass it soon developed characteristic patterns and designs which were emphasized by lacy and beadwork combinations covering the entire surface. This so-called lacy period of pressed glass extends from around 1830 to 1850. See *Stiegel, Heinrich Wilhelm*; *Sandwich Glass*; *Paperweight*; *Flask*.

American Pottery Company In American ceramics; a pottery manufactory founded at Jersey City, New Jersey, in 1833. The various marks are a flag with "Am. Pottery Manufg. Co., Jersey City," printed; an elliptical design printed with the same name; and at a later date "American Pottery Co., 1840," impressed. The pottery closed in 1854. The wares included drug jars and boxes with printed labels, white pottery decorated with prints, and brown ware with colored enamels.

American Silver The early American silver was generally made from coin. Although there was no official regulation to control the actual fine silver content, as a whole, it was of a high quality due to the fact that some of the cities had guilds or societies by which the silversmiths regulated their silverware. Baltimore also had an assay office, carefully supervised by elected silversmiths. The mark appearing on silver was the maker's mark, usually in the form of his initials or full name, frequently combined with an emblem. During the early part of the 19th century the word "coin" was stamped on silverware to indicate that its fineness was equal to that of silver money; being 900 parts fine silver and 100 parts alloy in each 1000 parts. About the middle of the 19th century the word "sterling" was stamped on silverware to indicate its fineness; being 925 parts fine silver and 75 parts fine copper in each 1000 parts. By act of Congress on June 13, 1906, H.R. 14604; Public No. 226, stated that articles of silverware stamped "Coin, Coin Silver, Sterling and Sterling Silver, shall contain not less than the portions of fine silver mentioned above; however, when official tests are made, there shall be allowed a divergence in the fineness of four one thousandths parts from the foregoing standards."

American Tapestries The weaving of tapestries in America is particularly identified with the production of two manufactories. The first tapestry atelier in America was established by William Baumgarten in New York City in 1893. Skilled tapestry craftsmen were brought over from France, mostly from Aubusson, and under the management of M. Foussadier, a master craftsman from the Royal Windsor Tapestry Works in England, the factory soon gained an excellent reputation for its high standard of creative artistic work. The productions were mostly furniture coverings, hangings and curtains.

AMERICAN PRESSED GLASS
PITCHER

The other atelier producing tapestries of a high standard of workmanship was established by Albert Herter in 1908 on East 33rd Street in New York City. Herter was an accomplished designer as well as an artist-craftsman and he created many fine pieces inspired by the work of the Late Gothic style.

Amethystine Quartz A variety of quartz having the color of an amethyst or bluish-violet. See *Quartz*.

Amice In ecclesiastical vestments; an article of costume of religious orders comprising a rectangular piece of cloth made of linen or hemp first put on the head and then adjusted around the neck, hanging down over the shoulders and encompassing the chest. It is believed that the amice was originally an ordinary neck cloth for all classes of Roman citizens and that it was first used as an ecclesiastical vestment in Rome in the 8th century when it was worn with the dalmatic. It seems that the custom of wearing the amice as a hood dates from the end of the 9th century. In the 12th century it became customary to enrich the edge forming the front of the hood with a band of embroidery or apparel. When the amice with its apparels was turned down and fastened around the neck this border of embroidery formed a stiff collar which appeared above the dalmatic or chasuble. These embroidered or appareled amices of the medieval period were especially rich and elegant. The amice has varied at different times in character as well as in the manner of wearing.

Amorini In ornament; an Italian term given to infant cupids or cherubs. They were extensively used during the Italian Renaissance in painting, sculpture and cabinetmaking. They were also a favorite decorative motif in France. The singular is amorino. See *Putti*.

Amphora In Greek antiquities; a jar used for holding liquid or solid provisions, such as oil, wine or food. At the Panathenaic festival, which was celebrated once every four years

GLASS AMPULLA
WITH SILVER MOUNTS

in Athens, amphorae filled with oil were awarded as prizes. The amphora consisted of an ovoid-shaped body wide at the shoulder and tapering to and resting on a spreading foot. It had a short neck with a flaring lip rim, with two loop handles extending from the top of the shoulder to the lip rim.

Ampulla A small vessel or vial generally having a round body and a narrow neck containing liquids, especially oil and perfume, used in ancient times for toilet purposes and for anointing the bodies of the dead, when these vessels were also buried with them. Both the name and purpose of the ampulla were carried over in the Western Church, where it is used for holding consecrated oil or for other sacred uses. It seems that these vessels mentioned in medieval church inventories were most frequently made of glass and were mounted in silver and rested on a silver circular foot. The most famous ampulla in history was known as la Sainte Ampoule; it was used in anointing the kings of France at their coronation and was kept in the Abbey of St. Rémi at Reims. According to legend it was carried from heaven by a dove for the coronation of Clovis I, c. 466–511, who was king of the Salian Franks, 481–511. There was one period in French history when the kings of France claimed superiority over all rulers because of this vessel. It was unfortunately destroyed during the French Revolution. The words *ampul* and *ampulla* have the same ecclesiastical meaning; however, the latter is now more commonly used.

Amritsar An Oriental rug woven at Amritsar, in Punjab, India, which is an important modern rug weaving center. The rug is distinctly a commercial rug. See *India Oriental*; *Oriental Rug*.

Amstel In Dutch ceramics; see *Weesp*.

Amul Ware In ceramics; see *Persian and Near Eastern Pottery*.

Ananaspokal A German term referring to a pineapple cup. See *Pineapple Cup*.

Anathema Cup In English silver; the name given to a celebrated silver cup made in England in 1481 and which is now at Pembroke College, Cambridge. It is a plain silver gilt drinking cup with a bowl having double curve sides, resembling an inverted bell, that rests on a thick stem spreading into a base. The cup is so-called because of its inscription, QUI ALIENAVERIT ANATHEMA SIT.

Anatolian An Oriental rug belonging to the Turkish classification. It is named after the country of Anatolia, which is another name for Asia Minor. The foundation is usually wool, and the pile is of fine wool and very long. The ends are usually finished with a colored web and warp fringe. The antique Anatolian was made only in mat size. Some of these possess a fine quality of workmanship. The modern Anatolian is made in both large and mat size. The colors are usually harsh and the designs are widely varied. It is a serviceable rug. See *Turkish Rugs*.

Andaman Redwood A hard rose-colored wood, *pterocarpus dalbergioides*, found in the Andaman Islands, which was used by the French cabinetmakers during the 18th century. It is also called Andaman padouk. See *Padouk Wood*.

Andiers A French term for andirons. See *Andirons*.

Andirons The metal utensils used in a fireplace to support the wood or logs. Andirons are used in pairs. An andiron is a vertical standard or guard made of iron, brass, bronze, steel or silver, resting on a base or spreading foot; a horizontal bar is attached in the rear on which the logs rest. The vertical standard is usually decorated, often elaborately, with various classic motifs, heraldic devices or emblems; sometimes it is modeled in the form of a mythological figure, a caryatid or some other similar subject. Especially notable were the Italian bronze andirons made during the Renaissance. Andirons made in France during the 18th century by celebrated French ciseleurs were often artistic achievements. The French terms for andirons are *chenets*, *andiers* and *landiers*. Andirons for kitchen use, also called cobirons, are usually made of iron without decoration. Sometimes they are very tall and are fitted with hooks on the standards to hold the spits. Iron arms are attached to the standards to hold kettles and pots over the fire. An iron ring on the top of the standard in the form of a cup is used to hold a pot or kettle. Small andirons that are placed between the taller andirons are called creepers. Fire dogs and brand dogs are other names for andirons. See *Attelet*.

Anelace In arms; a 15th century dagger or small sword. The straight, double-edged blade is very wide at the hilt and tapers to a point. It was carried by civilians, usually horizontally at the back of the belt. *Cinquedea* is another name for the anelace.

Angel Bed See *Lit d'Ange*.

Angleterre In Flemish lace; a misnomer in common usage from the 17th century for much of the choicest laces made in Brussels. Due to the vogue for Flemish laces in England, the English Parliament passed an act in 1662 prohibiting the importation of foreign lace in order to protect their home industries. Flemish lace workers were invited to settle in England, but the venture was unsuccessful since England could not produce the quality of flax necessary to make fine Brussels lace. As a result the merchants bought the finest Brussels laces and smuggled them into England, selling them under the name of Point d'Angleterre or English Point. Gradually the term *Point de Bruxelles* was less used and was finally supplanted by the term *Point d'Angleterre*. There were distinctly varying types of Angleterre lace. It was notable for its beautiful fillings and openwork stitches. The outline of scrolls, festoons and leaves emphasized by a raised treatment gave a beautiful effect. Later the term was also applied to a combination needle and bobbin lace adding an additional definition to a term already confused in its meaning. See *Brussels Lace*.

RENAISSANCE ANDIRON

Angoumois In French Provincial; a former province of western France which now forms almost all of the department of Charente. The provincial furniture of Angoumois is similar in form and ornament to that of Vendée and Saintonge. See *Vendée*; *Saintonge*; *French Provincial*.

Angular Hook A design used in Oriental rugs, especially those in the Caucasian group. It is the same as one arm of the swastika.

Animal Cup A drinking cup usually made of silver ingeniously designed in the form of an animal, such as the lion, stag, fox, hare, hound, chamois, dragon or griffin. It is principally identified with old German silver and was introduced circa 1575.

SILVER ANIMAL CUP

Animal Rug A variety of fine Persian Oriental made around the 16th century. Except for the figures of horsemen and other hunters, animal rugs were similar in design and quality to the hunting rugs. See *Persian Rugs*.

Anise Wood The wood from the anise plant, *illicium anisatum*, obtained from China; it was widely used in cabinetwork by the French ébénistes. It is hard, and its color is grey.

Annealing In glass; the name given to the gradual cooling of hot glass whether it is made by hand or machinery. In this process the glass is placed in a heated chamber called a leer or lehr, during which time it is permitted to cool slowly. The process of annealing toughens glass and without it glass would be very brittle and not too serviceable.

Annular Clock In French furniture; an elaborate and richly decorated clock which has an annular or horizontal ring-shaped dial that is usually of white enamel with Roman numerals. A popular variety is urn-shaped on a square plinth, made of marble and mounted with bronze doré, with the dial rotating around the upper part of the body of the urn. Another type is orb-shaped with the dial around the center, supported by bronze figures resting on a marble base. The annular clock varied in height from about 15 inches to 35 inches. It was made extensively during the 18th century.

Ansbach In German pottery; a manufactory for producing faïence was started around 1708–1710 at Ansbach, Bavaria, Germany with the support of the Margrave Frederick William of Brandenburg by Mathias Bauer, d. 1725, manager. After 1747 it was under the management of the Popp family. It changed ownership in 1807 and closed in 1839. Ansbach faïence was not regularly marked. The mark was often signed by the chief painter, sometimes with the date and the name of the town being added. After 1769 the mark "A.P." was sometimes used. The mark, "On," which stands for Onolzbach, another name for the town, was occasionally found. Much of the early ware reflected the influence of Delft and Hanau and was painted in a clear full blue. The finest work was done from about 1729 to 1757. This ware was in imitation of the Japanese brocaded Imari pattern or imitated the Chinese Famille Verte coloring and design. Included among their wares were cylindrical tankards, enormous vases and faïence figures. Some of the finest German faïence was produced at this factory. After 1769, when the manufactory was entirely owned by the Popp family the wares were relatively unimportant.

Ansbach In German porcelain; around 1758 porcelain was produced in the faïence manufactory at Ansbach with the support of the Margrave Earl Alexander, d. 1791, and managed by Johann Friedrich Kaendler. In 1762 the porcelain kiln was moved to the Margrave's hunting castle at Bruckberg. It flourished until 1791, and in 1806 it ceased to operate as a state concern but survived privately until 1860. The mark was an "A" with or without an eagle of Brandenburg and the shield of arms of Ansbach in underglaze blue. On figures the shield mark was impressed. Much of the ware was not marked. Their finest productive period was from around 1767 to 1785. This porcelain ranks with the finest German porcelain. Many Ansbach figures were notable for their singular delicacy. Decorative and useful wares were distinctive for their finely molded designs and painted decoration.

Anthemion In ornament; a conventional design consisting of flower or leaf forms used by the Greeks. It is arranged in a radiating manner. A fine example of the anthemion design is on the Ionic columns of the Erechtheion. It is usually called the honeysuckle ornament because of its marked similarity to that flower. This classic ornament was employed in some of the styles of furniture. In English furniture; Robert Adam is usually regarded to be the first in England to use the anthemion. A fine treatment of the anthemion motif is the pierced splat in a type of chair back designed in the Hepplewhite style.

Antique Furniture In American furniture; the term *antique* as it is applied in American furniture has an interesting origin and meaning. In one sense the term *antique* refers to point of time. An early act of Congress which was passed to regulate the duties on foreign furniture stated that all furniture more than one hundred years old at the time of importation was regarded as antique and could enter duty free. Although this act did not refer to American furniture the popular conception of an American antique as an article of furniture over one hundred years old was undoubtedly based on this act. In 1930 the act was revised to read as follows, "Works of art (except rugs and carpets made after the year 1700), collections in illustration of the progress of the arts, works in bronze, marble, terra cotta, parian, pottery, or porcelain, artistic antiquities and objects of art of ornamental character or educational value which shall have been produced prior to the year 1830" shall be admitted duty free. Although this act did not refer to American furniture either, it became the popular conception in America to classify as antique almost all furniture made until about 1830. In the other and more correct sense the definition of the term *antique* has been decided by the connoisseurs who have studied the styles of furniture and understand what constitutes a true style. They regard as an antique any

article of furniture made in an approved style at the time that style was the prevailing fashion. The connoisseurs do not usually recognize any style beyond the Sheraton style which remained in fashion in America until around 1820–1825. And so they consider around 1825 as the fixed time which separates the antique furniture from the later cabinetwork. It should be remembered that in the 18th century and earlier all the furniture did not embody the requisites necessary for fine cabinetwork, namely, fine materials and workmanship and designs possessing artistic merit. This thought is conveyed in a Treasury decision of June 19th, 1930, that the article must have some artistic character, something more than mere mechanical skill, it must have an aesthetic appeal, age alone does not authorize free entry.

Antwerp Lace The laces made at Antwerp were essentially similar to those made in the neighboring Flemish towns. In the 17th century Antwerp exported to the Spanish Indies a variety of guipure consisting of large flowers joined with brides. After the loss of the Spanish markets, Antwerp continued to produce lace for her own consumption. The interest in Antwerp lace centered in one pattern, namely the potten kant pattern or pot lace, which had been worn on feminine caps from one generation to another. The pattern invariably had a vase, which displayed variations in its general treatment. See *Potten Kant*.

Aoi Tsuba In Japanese sword mounts; a form of sword guard that was popular during the 12th century. It is characterized by its four heart-shaped lobes resembling the leaves of the aoi, or four heart-shaped openings or indentations. Sometimes it combines both of these forms. See *Tsuba*.

Apostle Spoon The name given to a silver or silver gilt spoon which terminates in the figure of an Apostle, with the Apostle's emblem. A full set of the twelve Apostle spoons is rare and a set including the Master spoon is more rare. Apostle spoons are a

ANTHEMION MOTIF
ON ADAM ARMCHAIR

survival of the early English custom, from about 1495 to about 1660, of presenting a child at his christening a spoon adorned with the figure of an Apostle; it was usually given by the godparents.

Apparel In ecclesiastical costume; a decorative embroidery found on certain ecclesiastical vestments such as the alb and amice. The apparels were worked in silk and gold thread depicting ecclesiastical ornament and sacred imagery and occasionally they were further enhanced with pearls and jewels. Apparels of quadrangular form were often sewn on to the vestment. See *Alb*.

Apple Green In Chinese ceramics; a green transparent enamel, varying from a light to a dark emerald green, distinctive for its luster, iridescence and brilliancy, applied over a grayish or brownish crackled white glaze. It has shining white flakes, called by the French *ailes de mouches*, or fly's wings, which were caused by the internal breaking of the enamel over the crackle. Apple green wares, which are principally small pieces, were first made during the K'ang Hsi reign, 1662–1722. See *Ch'ing*.

Apple Wood The wood of the cultivated and wild apple tree, *pyrus malus*, was especially used in English and American cabinetwork. It is a hard wood with a fine grain and the tone is a light and warm pinkish-brown. Many well-designed articles, particularly country funiture, were made of this fruitwood during the 18th century. It was also used for turned members, applied carved decoration and for veneering and inlay work.

Application Lace In lace-making; see *Point Appliqué*; *Brussels Appliqué*.

Applied Decoration In cabinetwork; the name is given to a type of wood or metal decoration which is laid on the surface of furniture and is attached with either small nails or glue. Among the applied decorations most commonly employed are wood or metal mouldings, decorative motifs, such as scrolls and paterae. See *Mounts*.

CHEST OF DRAWERS
ON STAND WITH APRON

Appliqué In wall treatment; a French term generally given to an accessory piece applied to a surface for ornamentation; such as a candelabrum or a bracket fixed to a wall. In French cabinetwork; the term is frequently used for applied decoration; in particular for bronze doré ornaments such as are applied on commodes for ornamentation.

Appliqué or Applied Work In needlework; appliqué, which is the method of applying one material to another by means of decorative stitches, was known in ancient Egypt and it was much used during the Middle Ages. There are two kinds of appliqué, namely onlay and inlay. In the inlay form of appliqué, which was the earliest method, the design is cut out of the ground fabric and the pieces of contrasting color are sewn to the back of the material. In the later method or onlay appliqué the pieces forming the design are cut to their proper shape and are sewn upon the fabric ground.

Aprey A French faïence manufactory was founded in 1744 by Jacques Lallemant de Villehaut, Baron d'Aprey, and his brother, Joseph. The finest period of production was from around 1769 to 1792. Its best work was a type of painted colored enamel decoration in the style of Strasbourg. The manufactory closed for a period during the French Revolution and reopened in 1806. It operated under various changes of management until 1885. The accepted mark is "AP" or "APR" in a monogram, although it was not always used. Their finest work ranks with the best of French faïence decorated in painted enamels, and was notable for its charming and graceful forms and for its pleasing decoration.

Apricot Wood See *Abricotier Wood*.

Apron In cabinetwork; the horizontal decorative shaped piece which connects the upright supports or stiles beneath the drawers such as on a commode or on a chest of drawers. The name is also given to the horizontal piece under the top of a table that connects the legs and to the piece beneath the seat rail of a chair. See *Frieze*.

Apt In French ceramics; an important center for pottery making. The earliest pottery was established at Le Castelet near Apt in 1728 by César Moulin, and it remained in the Moulin family until 1852. Other pottery factories were founded in and around Apt. The finest Apt wares are of excellent quality and are distinctive for their finished workmanship and graceful forms. An early type was a yellow ware, the forms for which were molded after silver objects such as écuelles or porringers and ewers. Especially characteristic was a fine yellow and brown marbled pottery made into useful wares and figures. This marbled pottery was decorated with applied leaves and flowers and scrollwork in white or a light-colored clay.

Apulian Ware The ancient pottery found at Apulia, Italy; especially a type of Apulian vase having a black glaze or slip surface with red figures. White, yellow and other colors were also used to enhance the effect in this so-called red-figure variety.

Aquamanale The name given to a variety of metal ewer made during the 13th and 14th centuries used for washing hands, as the name implies. Handwashing during meals was important in the Middle Ages when forks were almost unknown and people ate with their fingers. The liturgical washing of the hands by the priest was also an essential part of the Roman ritual. This type of metal ewer was designed in fantastic forms of animals, human beings, buildings and other similar subjects. It is also spelled aquamanile. See *Ewer*.

Aquarelle A drawing done in water-color; particularly one done in thin water-color or ink.

Aquatint A form of etching, imitating wash tints done with a brush, or a water-color in sepia. Its most effective use is with soft ground etching which resembles the lines drawn with a lead pencil. The term also refers to the print reproduced from the plate done with this process.

Arabesque In ornament; a word simply meaning Arabian applied to a particular form of decorative design displaying a fantastic or intricate interweaving or interlacing of lines. It is applied to the grotesque decoration derived from Roman mural paintings and stucco work of the early Roman Empire and not to any form derived from Arabian or Moorish work with its richly colored geometrical designs in which representations of living creatures are excluded. The term is more or less restricted to the varieties of Italian Renaissance decorations which are a development derived from Greco-Roman grotesque designs revealed in ancient excavated buildings. With this in mind it seems that grotesque is a more appropriate name for these decorations than arabesque. A marked feature in this later Renaissance decoration is a floriated or foliated standard branching out with graceful and symmetrical intertwining lines of scrollwork, branches and leaves enriched with animals, birds, humans and fanciful figures. The arabesques of the Renaissance are elaborate and extravagant in their design with naturalistic and grotesque human and animal figures as well as trophies, armor and vases within the scrollwork. The arabesques in the Loggia of the Vatican executed by Raphael are said to have been inspired by those found in the ancient buildings of Rome and Pompeii. Later arabesques by such French designers of ornament as Bérain, Audran and Pierre Le Pautre are remarkable for their varied and fanciful composition. See *Grotesque*; *Raphaelesque*; *Bérain, Jean*.

ARABESQUE

Arak Rug See *Sultanabad Rug*.

Arbalest In arms; the medieval European crossbow. There are many varieties but all essentially consist of a heavy bow set on a stock with a channel for the arrow, and a device to hold and release the string. The earlier types were made of wood, and sometimes whalebone, while the later ones were of steel.

Arca In Spanish cabinetwork; the Spanish chest or arca was an important article of domestic furniture from early Gothic times. And, unlike in other countries where it was

supplanted at a later time by more specialized pieces for specific purposes, such as a
chest of drawers, its popularity continued
through the following centuries. Occasionally the inside of the lid of the chest was inlaid, carved or painted. This type of chest
was usually fitted with another plain lid
which covered the contents of the chest and
permitted the top lid to rest against the wall
in order to display its decoration. See *Chest*.

Arcaded   In furniture; the term is applied to
a kind of cabinetwork in which the design
resembled an arcade, i.e. a series of arches
with columns to support them. For example
during the Renaissance the Italian cabinetmakers designed a type of table with an
arcaded stretcher. Renaissance chests were
sometimes designed with an arcaded façade.

Arcanist   In ceramics; a workman claiming
knowledge of the secret of porcelain making
and other important pottery methods,
especially in the 18th century. Although
some arcanists did possess valuable knowledge many were imposters. The strict measures enforced at Meissen to prevent a leak-
age of Böttger's secret for making porcelain
proved an incentive for many runaway
workmen.

Archebanc   In French cabinetwork; a settle
or coffre bench introduced during the Gothic
period. It was a massive wooden bench with
wooden back and arms, and was made to
seat several persons. The part between the
seat and the floor was enclosed to form a
coffre. Also spelled archbanc. See *Settle*.

Architect's Table   In English cabinetwork;
the architect's or artist's table, introduced in
the first quarter of the 18th century, was
especially designed to serve the needs
of draftsmen, artists and architects. This
specialized table was suitable for drawing,
reading and writing. One characteristic
variety was designed with an oblong
molded top on a ratchet easel over a frieze
which rested on a turned standard and tripod
support. This table frequently displayed great
ingenuity in its construction. The more com-

ARCHEBANC

plex and elaborate specimens often had pull-
out fronts fitted with many small compartments and adjustable rising tops. It is also
called a reading and writing table.

Architrave   In classic architecture; the lowest
division of an entablature or that part which
rests directly on the columns of a building.
The term is also applied to any molded or
decorative band carried around a square
door or window. The term has a similar
meaning in cabinetwork when articles of
design are incorporated from classic architecture.

Ardebil Rug   A famous Persian Oriental rug
woven in the second quarter of the 16th
century, believed to have adorned the Ardebil mosque in Persia. It is generally regarded
as the finest Oriental ever woven. It is a
masterpiece in color, and its elaborate designs are executed with the greatest skill.
Many copies of this rug have been made.

Argand Lamp   A kind of lamp invented in
1782 by a Swiss, Aimé Argand; its wick is
tubular so that the air current is created
inside the flame and outside as well. See
Astral Lamp.

Argentan Point   In French lace-making;
the town of Argentan is renowned for its
needlepoint laces, which rivalled the laces
made at Alençon. There was a marked similarity between Alençon point and Argentan
point, but the latter is considered to have a
hexagonal bride ground with each side of
the hexagon worked in finest buttonhole
stitches. It is generally accepted that the
finest réseau was made at Alençon while
Argentan excelled in brides. Argentan designs were more striking and larger and bore
a closer resemblance to Venetian patterns.
A speciality of Argentan point was the bride
picotée ground consisting of a hexagonal
buttonhole bride with a minute row of three
or four picots or pearls on each side. Point
d'Argentan flourished during the reigns of
Louis XV and Louis XVI. In more recent
years Argentan has been successfully reproduced at Burano. See *Alençon Point*; *Point de
France*.

Argentella In lace-making; a needlepoint lace having a hexagonal mesh ground and within each hexagon is worked a small solid hexagon joined to the hexagon by six little ties or brides. When this form of ground is used on Alençon lace it is called Argentella. The origin of the name is not known. Some of the literature on lace implies that the lace was made in Venice or Genoa; however, at the present time there is no evidence to support this claim. See *Alençon Point*.

Argyle In English silver; a silver vessel, usually similar in shape to a coffee pot, used to hold hot gravy. It is fitted with an inner container to which the spout is joined, having a space between the container and the outside wall. By pouring hot water into an opening in the outside wall, such as a hinged lip, the gravy in the inner container is kept hot. There are several types, some having a hot-water container in the base. They were first made circa 1778.

Arita Ware In Japanese ceramics; Japanese porcelain was produced in the Hizen district from around the beginning of the 17th century. The Arita porcelain was sold and shipped from the town of Imari and became known as Imari or Imari-Yaki, *yaki* being the Japanese word for ware. See *Imari*; *Kakiemon*; *Nabeshima*; *Hirado*; *Hizen*.

Armadio In Italian cabinetwork; a tall, rectilinear, single-bodied, movable cupboard introduced during the Renaissance. It corresponded in its general design and use to the French armoire. See *Armoire*; *Cupboard*.

Armario In Spanish cabinetwork; a large movable cupboard generally fitted with two long cupboard doors. It was introduced during the Renaissance and was essentially similar to the Italian armadio, and to the French armoire. See *Armoire*; *Cupboard*.

Armet In armor; a helmet developed late in the 15th century that afforded complete protection to the head and neck. It was ovoid in shape and frequently had a comb. The armet had a pivoted visor and cheek pieces overlapping on the chin.

Armillary Sphere An early astronomical device. It consisted of an arrangement of rings that represented the positions of the more important celestial circles of the sphere. It was made so as to turn on its polar axis within a horizon and meridian. It was usually mounted on either a turned or elaborately carved wooden stand. See *Globe Stand*.

Armoire In French cabinetwork; the name given to a kind of domestic cupboard used during the Gothic period that was usually part of the wainscoting. It was originally a repository for arms, and was later used to store such things as clothes and other household possessions. During the Renaissance the tall rectilinear cupboard or armoire became more plentiful and was generally movable. One principal variety was single-bodied and was usually fitted with two long cupboard doors. It incorporated architectural features in its principles of design. In the 17th century this massive cupboard or wardrobe was found in many middle class homes. In the 18th century the armoire or cupboard was the pride of every provincial housewife and a visible sign of her prosperity. See *Armoire à Deux Corps*; *Cupboard*; *Wardrobe*.

Armoire à Deux Corps In French cabinetwork; during the second half of the 16th century the large double-bodied cupboard was extremely fashionable. It was rectangular and upright, and was of architectural design. The front and sides of the upper body were recessed; the lower body was mounted on ball feet. Each portion was fitted with two cupboard doors, divided and flanked by pilasters. The Henri II walnut armoire à deux corps with its architectural façade embodied the highest qualities of French Renaissance architecture. Also notable was the Burgundian Renaissance walnut armoire à deux corps with its richly sculptured carvings. Relatively few double-bodied cupboards were designed after the middle of the 17th century. See *Armoire*; *Cupboard*.

ARMILLARY SPHERE

Armoire d'Encoignure   See *Encoignure*.

Armorial Tapestry   A tapestry in which heraldic arms have been decoratively treated. This type of tapestry is without personages and without a story. See *Tapestry*.

Armorial Ware   In Chinese ceramics; the name given to a kind of Chinese Lowestoft decorated with the arms and crests of European families made during the Ch'ing dynasty. See *Chinese Lowestoft*.

Armpad   A small padded cushion on the arm of a chair covered with the same material as the seat and the back. The armpad was extensively used on French furniture, especially on chairs designed in the Louis XV and Louis XVI styles. See *Manchette*.

Arnheim or Arnhem   In Dutch ceramics; a faïence manufactory was founded at Arnheim in 1755 by Johannes van Kerckhoff. The wares were largely in the manner of Delft. Around 1756 it was taken over by J. Hanau, and it ceased to operate in 1773. Especially characteristic was painted decoration in deep blue or manganese of good quality. The accepted mark is a cock.

Arquebus   See *Harquebus*.

Arqueta   In Spanish furniture; a very small chest, especially one used as a receptacle for jewels. The Spanish fondness for table boxes was an old Moorish legacy. They were profusely placed on tables. They were rarely more than a foot in length and were richly ornamented.

Arras   In French ceramics; a French soft paste porcelain manufactory was founded in 1770 at Arras, Pas de Calais, by Joseph François Boussemaert of Lille. About a year later it was taken over by four ladies, Demoiselles Delemer, dealers in faïence. It ceased to operate in 1790. The wares were patently made in rivalry of the wares of Tournay. The wares made here during the 18th century were simply decorated. The accepted mark was "AR."

ARRETINE CUP

Arras Lace   The town of Arras, celebrated for its tapestries, was also an active center for all kinds of needlework. It is stated that the Emperor Charles V, 1516–1556, first introduced the manufacture of lace at Arras. Arras coarse thread bobbin-made laces of the 18th century enjoyed a good domestic market. Arras lace was not as fine as Lille lace; however, it was a strong and firm lace and flawlessly white. It appears that the gold lace of Arras enjoyed a good reputation, and it was found listed among the coronation expenses of George I, 1714–1727. See *Lille Lace*.

Arras Tapestry   The weaving of tapestries at Arras, France, dates from the 14th century, when it was one of the two great tapestry weaving centers, Paris being the other. In the 15th century it was the leading center of weaving until 1477 when the city was captured by Louis XI. By extension, the term *Arras* is now used as a general term for woven wall hangings because the city of Arras has long been famous for its tapestry weaving. See *Tapestry*.

Arretine Ware   In ancient ceramics; a Roman pottery made from about 200 B.C. to A.D. 100 in Arretine, in the ancient country of Etruria. The ware reflected the influence of metal work. The forms were simple and small and were borrowed from metal shapes, and much of the relief decoration was copied directly from embossed metal ware. The molded relief decoration was applied to a model bowl, which was then cast in a mold, and this mold was used to make the bowl. The body of the ware was usually of red clay; however, some of the earliest specimens were of black. The glaze had a fine lustrous quality which gave a deep richness to the color. The potter's signature almost always appeared on each piece. This ware is also called terra sigillata and Samian ware. After Arretine ware had degenerated, the production of ornamented pottery or terra sigillata was carried on in the Roman provinces; especially in Gaul in the country

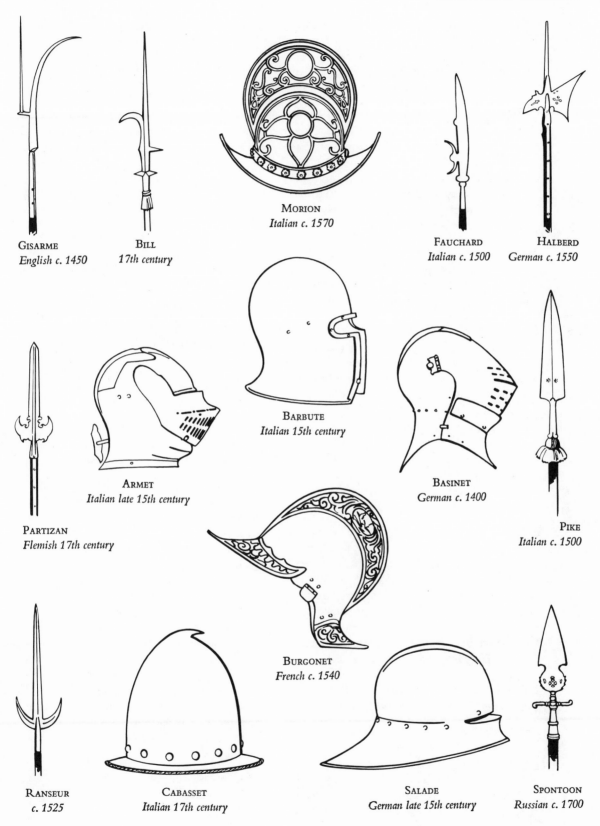

GISARME
English c. 1450

BILL
17th century

MORION
Italian c. 1570

FAUCHARD
Italian c. 1500

HALBERD
German c. 1550

ARMET
Italian late 15th century

BARBUTE
Italian 15th century

BASINET
German c. 1400

PARTIZAN
Flemish 17th century

PIKE
Italian c. 1500

BURGONET
French c. 1540

RANSEUR
c. 1525

CABASSET
Italian 17th century

SALADE
German late 15th century

SPONTOON
Russian c. 1700

bordering the Rhône and the Rhine where it was made until about A.D. 260. Barbotine was used to replace the molded designs on the Rhenish terra sigillata around the 3rd century. In another form of decoration medallions were applied to the bowls. See *Barbotine*; *Relief Decoration*.

Arrow Back In American cabinetwork; a form of Windsor chair having three or more arrow-shaped spindles in the back, made in the 19th century. Arrow back Windsor chairs were especially popular during the second quarter of the 19th century.

Artesonado In Spanish decorative art; the use of a pine panelled ceiling or artesonado was often the principal decorative feature in many Spanish Renaissance rooms. Its use was traditionally Moorish and indigenous to Spain. These ceilings displayed a pattern of minute divisions and intricate geometrical shapes and were generally enriched with painted and gilded decoration of Moorish inspiration. When the pine panelled ceilings were not embellished with carved and painted decoration they were simply oiled and were remarkable for their soft warm patina. Frequently the doors and window shutters were treated in a similar manner, but they were rarely enriched with carved and painted decoration. See *Yesería*.

Art Glass In American glass; a general name given to various kinds of late 19th century fancy or ornamental glass that was fabricated into free-blown, blown-molded or pressed tableware and decorative glassware. This so-called art glass satisfied a contemporary demand for fancy forms and various color effects. It was frequently made to imitate other materials, such as tortoise shell. See *Agata*; *Amberina*; *Aurene*; *Burmese*; *Favrile*; *Hobnail*; *Peachblow*; *Pomona*; *Satin Glass*; *Spangled Glass*; *Tortoise Shell*; *Vasa Murrhina*.

Artois In French Provincial cabinetwork; an old province in north-eastern France between Flandre and Picardy; now a part of the department of Pas-de-Calais. The provincial furniture of Artois has the same character-

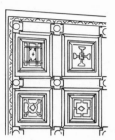

ARTESONADO

istics as that of Picardy. See *Picardy*; *French Provincial*.

Ash A hard wood, *fraxinus excelsior*, which is white in color with yellowish-brown streaks, was much in demand for English and American inexpensive country cabinetwork. It was principally used for the entire framework of chairs as well as for parts of chairs, such as the spindles of Windsor chairs. The wood was strong and elastic but not heavy. It was also used for drawer linings. It is also called frêne wood.

Ash, Gilbert 1717–1785. American chairmaker working in New York circa 1748–1785. His shop was on Wall Street.

Ashbury Metal In pewter; a very hard alloy of tin with antimony and zinc. It was principally used for snuff boxes, spoons and other similar articles. See *Pewter*.

Ashi In Japanese sword mounts; the loops on the scabbard of a tachi through which cords were passed so that it could be suspended from the belt. See *Tachi*.

Ashikaga The Ashikaga period in Japan, A.D. 1338–1573. See *Japanese Periods*.

Asparagus-Tongs In English silver; during the 18th century very large tongs of the bow-spring variety with wide grips were used for serving asparagus at the dining table. They were found with hall-marks as early as 1780. A later type of asparagus-server was the same as the fish-server. See *Fish-Server*.

Assay Cup A small cup used to assay wine or other drinks. Small gold and silver assay cups are mentioned in English records as early as 1530. In early times it was often the custom to assay the wine for the detection of poison before serving. This act of assay continued, but only in a complimentary manner, of tasting the food and drink before it was served to a distinguished personage.

Assisi Work In embroidery; this work, which is regarded as one of the most beautiful varieties of embroidery, originated in the convents at Assisi, Italy, during the Middle Ages. The designs, which are noteworthy for their charming simplicity, were generally inspired by the early paintings adorning the medieval churches. This work was done by outlining the design and filling in the background with cross-stitches. The finest work, which was done with cotton thread, was orange and black or blue and scarlet.

Astbury, John 1686–1743. In English ceramics; John Astbury and his son Thomas, who began producing wares around 1725, and other members of the same family were potters in Shelton and in other parts of Staffordshire in the 18th century. The name *Astbury* is generally applied to a type of earthenware covered with a lead glaze of yellowish tone. The color of the body varied from a red which became dark brown under the glaze, to a chamois color. The ware was decorated with applied reliefs, generally made of a white pipe clay, which were stamped, molded or modelled by hand. Birds, coats-of-arms, lions, vine leaves and grapes were included among the motifs. The reliefs were usually in white on a dark-colored ground; however, the color scheme was sometimes reversed. Occasionally a piece of Astbury ware was made in an almost white clay and can be considered among the earliest examples of cream-colored earthenware. However, the characteristic Astbury earthenware still consisted in part of colored clays. Some early pieces of Astbury ware date from around 1730 and some late pieces around 1745; its characteristic production flourished around 1739. The wares associated with the Astbury name were never marked. See *Portobello*; *Staffordshire*.

Aster Ornament In American furniture; the carved sunflower motif. It was sometimes used as a decorative motif in the center panel of the Connecticut chest. See *Connecticut Chest*.

Astragal Molding In cabinetwork; a small convex molding generally from one-half

to three-quarters of a circle. See *Torus*; *Molding*.

Astral Lamp A kind of Argand lamp. It was so made that the flattened ring-shaped cistern which held the oil did not interrupt the light on the table. See *Argand Lamp*.

Astrolabe Clock A clock that indicates the time in hours and minutes; the phases and position of the moon; the position and declination of the sun in the zodiac, and the azimuth and altitude of the sun, the moon and the principal planets.

Astronomical Clock A clock fitted with a mechanism designed to indicate the position of the sun, the phases of the moon, etc., together with its regular time indicator.

Ataujía A Spanish term applied to a kind of Moorish inlay work in which either gold or some other metal or various colored enamels were inlaid on a metal surface. See *Inlay*.

Athénienne In French cabinetwork; a small slender decorative round stand or table introduced late in the reign of Louis XVI. It was in the form of an antique tripod and was made of metal. Its form was copied from the tripods found at Pompeii and its decoration was similar to that of the classic originals. It had a bowl-shaped top made of onyx or some other similar material that rested on three incurvate metal supports. See *Tripod*.

Atlantes In ornament; the carved figures of men employed as supports. See *Caryatid*.

Attelet The French term applied to a small silver or iron skewer. The attelet made of iron was used by the kitchen maids to hold small birds and small fish while roasting over the fire. These were replaced by silver attelets for serving at the table. The handle end was usually in the form of a ring and often elaborately wrought. In the French provinces the terms *aste* and *haste* were applied to a skewer or spit of iron. These iron spits were mentioned as early as 1473 and were found on the great kitchen andirons or fire dogs called contre-hâtiers. See *Skewer*.

ASTER ORNAMENT
ON CONNECTICUT CHEST

Aubergine In Chinese ceramics; a pure purple enamel or glaze derived from manganese. It is generally accepted that the color aubergine was first used on porcelains made during the Ming dynasty, 1368–1644.

Aubusson Carpet A hand-woven carpet of tapestry weave, woven at Aubusson, France. Since this is the commercial center of the weaving of floor tapestries the term *Aubusson carpet* has become attached to tapestry carpets and they are called that even when woven elsewhere. A tapestry carpet is made exactly like a wall tapestry. See *Tapestry Carpet*; *Tapestry*.

DECORATIVE DESIGN
BY AUDRAN

Aubusson Tapestry The tapestry manufactories at the city of Aubusson in France were in full activity from the early part of the 16th century. Their finest works were produced during the 18th century. At the present time it is an important commercial center for real tapestry weaving. See *Tapestry*.

Audran, Claude 1658–1734. One of the foremost French decorative artists of his time. He is noted for his designs and compositions of figures, flowers, leaves, arabesques, grotesques and attributes which contributed in a large part to the creation of the Rococo style of ornament of the 18th century. The decorative designs of Watteau and Gillot were undoubtedly inspired to some extent by the work of Audran as well as by Bérain.

Audubon, John James 1785–1851. Artist and ornithologist. He was born at Aux Cayes, Haiti, and in 1789 his father took him to France where, during the course of his training, he studied drawing under Jacques Louis David for a short time. In 1804 he came to America and began his work of drawing and painting birds, which was done with minute detail. In 1827 Robert Havell of London began to publish BIRDS OF AMERICA in elephant folio size, in parts, and completed the work in 1838. The complete work consisted of 1065 drawings of birds in life size and 435 color plates. The AMERICAN ORNITHOLOGICAL BIOGRAPHY, in five volumes, which described the plates, was published in Edinburgh between 1831 and 1839. A popular edition of BIRDS OF AMERICA was published in America in 1844. The QUADRUPEDS OF AMERICA was published in 1842–1845 and the text in 1846–1854; this work was shared with John Bachman.

Aulne Wood The wood of the alder tree, *alnus glutinosa*, used in cabinetwork, especially by the French ébénistes. It is soft and its color is reddish.

Aumbry See *Ambry*.

Aumund In German ceramics; a faïence manufactory was founded at Aumund near Vegesack, Bremen, in Hanover, in 1751. It was in operation only until 1761. Included among its wares were tureens in the Rococo style and cylindrical tankards painted in blue or in high temperature polychrome. The wares were essentially without distinction. The marks were the initials of the various owners: "MTT"; "D & WT" and "AvE."

Aurene Glass In American glass; an iridescent ornamental glass created by Frederick Carder, at the Steuben Glass Works, which was established in 1903 at Corning, New York. See *Art Glass*.

Aurillac Lace It appears that rich laces of gold and silver were made at the French town of Aurillac long before the French minister Colbert established the so-called Points de France, in 1665, and they were frequently mentioned in early Church inventories. Extant examples of this early lace attributed to Aurillac consist of strips of metal twisted around silk. Contemporary records show that point d'Aurillac was highly regarded in the 17th century and it seems from these same records that it was a rich gold and silver lace similar to the point d'Espagne. Lace-making continued at Aurillac until the French Revolution.

Auvergne In French Provincial; a former mountainous province of south central France now in the departments of Haute-Loire, Puy-de-Dôme and Cantal. The provincial furniture of Auvergne is simple and massive. It is usually made of walnut or cherry. Louis XIII armoires are plentiful in this region. The Louis XV style flourished here as it did in almost all of the other provinces. Moldings were the only decoration employed on the Louis XV articles of furniture. Occasionally the moldings were enhanced with rather crudely carved geometrical motifs borrowed from the lace-making industry of that region. See *French Provincial*.

Aventurine A kind of Venetian glass first made around 1600 in Venice. In this glass many minute pieces of copper or gold-colored filings are scattered through a transparent yellow or brown-colored mass. It is also spelled avanturine. The name is also given to a work that resembles aventurine quartz, such as aventurine lacquer.

Avril, Etienne 1748-1791. A French ébéniste who was admitted as a master cabinetmaker in 1774. His work is chiefly identified with plain veneered pieces framed in very narrow bronze moldings. His cabinetwork was representative of the Louis XVI style which displayed large uniform unbroken surfaces and a closer affiliation with Roman architectural details in its style of decoration. See *Louis XVI*.

Awaji Ware In Japanese ceramics; pottery made on the island of Awaji. It was first made around 1831 by Kashü Mimpei who was ardently interested in ceramics. It has a brownish white clay body that is very smooth. It has a creamy colored glaze that varies sometimes to a light buff. It is occasionally crackled. It is characterized by its fine monochrome glazes of yellow, green, turquoise blue and blackish brown. Of especial interest is one glaze resembling tortoise shell. The decoration is molded in low relief. Articles made for the tea ceremony are of a soft pottery while the other wares have a dense and hard body of fine texture. The artistic pieces generally have painted designs in all colors and occasionally gold. The kiln also made a ware similar to the enamelled Awata pottery. It is also called Mimpei ware.

Awata Ware In Japanese ceramics; pottery was made in the Awata district in Kyōto from around 1651. Awata ware has a white clay body. The glaze is generally a deep cream color and occasionally a light buff. It is characterized by a network of very fine crackle. It has a rich enamelled decoration, and the colors comprise red, green and light blue. Occasionally gold is used. A feature of this ware is the use of underglaze blue and underglaze iron brown. The enamelled pottery of Iwakura and Omuro is similar to Awata ware. Ninsei worked for a short time at the Awata kilns. The Kinkōzan family and the Taizan family, the latter making wares for the Imperial family, are the outstanding artists for Awata ware. See *Ninsei*; *Iwakura Ware*; *Omuro Ware*.

Axminster In English carpets; Thomas Whitty began a manufactory for making hand-knotted pile carpets, using the same technique as employed in Oriental carpets, in the Court House, near the Church, at Axminster around 1755. Contemporary records of the second half of the 18th century show that his enterprise was successful and that Turkey carpets, which was an English name given to all Oriental carpets, woven at Axminster "were so very like in figure, colour and thickness not to be distinguished from the genuine article." It appears that the rugs were chiefly made by women. In 1835 the manufactory was closed and the looms were transferred to Wilton where these hand-tufted pile carpets continued to be woven. In the Victorian period the art of weaving hand-knotted carpets was reduced to a minimum; however, due to the efforts of William Morris, this craft was revived to some extent from around 1879.

AWAJI PLATE

Azulejos In Spanish interior decoration and ceramics; the term *azulejos*, which is the Spanish and Portuguese name for tiles, is derived from the Spanish *azul* meaning blue; however, the word was probably adopted at a later date because the early tiles were in polychrome. It is generally accepted that polychrome pottery tiles as a wall decoration originated in the Near East in the 9th century and were later made in Spain around the 14th century. These polychrome pottery tiles were used in Spanish interior decoration for dadoes and frequently for the facings of doorways, windows and window seats. They were also used to line the interior of niches, and for the enrichment of stairs, generally only the risers but occasally for the treads as well. The fashionable Dutch monochrome tiles in blue and white or in manganese purple and white were made during the 17th and 18th centuries in Spain; however, the traditional polychrome tiles continued to be made in the regional districts where the latest fashions were of little concern to the inhabitants. See *Yesería*; *Seville*; *Tiles*.

AZULEJOS

Baby Cage Or Baby Pen. In English cabinetwork; a utilitarian article of nursery furniture designed to teach a young child to walk. The upper frame was constructed to hold the child in a standing position, while the lower and wider frame was mounted on little wheels. The baby cage or going cart has been known on the Continent since the Middle Ages and in England since the 17th century. The piece was without artistic merit.

Baby Lace In English lace-making; a narrow bobbin-made lace, especially used for trimming infants' caps, which was an important part of the lace industry of Bedfordshire, Buckinghamshire and Northamptonshire. The lace, which was characterized by a delicate design and a fine clear net ground, was introduced around 1778. Baby lace was quite popular and it appears that large quantities were exported to America until the time of the Civil War. See *Northamptonshire Lace*.

Baccarat The name given to the fine crystal glass produced at the manufactory of La Compagnie des Cristalleries de Baccarat in the town of Baccarat, France. The Baccarat works were founded by D'Artigues in 1818. It is noted for its fine table service ware of crystal glass, and in particular for the beautiful crystal glass prisms and faceted lusters and drop lusters on handsome chandeliers. See *Glass*; *Flint Glass*; *Paperweight*.

Bachelor Chest In English cabinetwork; a form of a low chest of drawers with a folding top, occasionally designed in pairs, introduced early in the 18th century. As a rule the top, when open, was supported on runners and served as a writing board. Occasionally the bachelor chest was provided with candle brackets hinged at the corners.

Bacini In ceramics; the Italian term for painted and glazed earthenware plaques that were set into the walls of churches in different Italian cities as ornaments to the architecture. They were made in Italy, Spain, and more often in the Near East. Early majolica plaques served a similar decorative purpose.

Backgammon Board In English furniture; before the introduction of cards in the 15th century, backgammon, dice and chess were the popular medieval games of chance. The playing boards, which were placed on another piece of furniture, were often made with several folding leaves for the various games of chance. Many of the gaming boards used during the Tudor period were made on the Continent and imported to England. There are extant examples of backgammon and chess boards of inlaid oak or walnut made during the 17th century in England.

Backgammon Table In cabinetwork; see *Tric-Trac Table*; *Card Table*.

Backman, Jacob American cabinetmaker and carver who was born in Switzerland. He settled in Lancaster County, Pennsylvania, in 1766.

Back Plate In furniture; the decorative metal piece, usually made of bronze or brass, to which the handle is attached. See *Bail Handle*; *Handle and Back Plate*.

FAENZA BACINI

Backscratcher A term applied to a long slender rod of wood, tortoise shell or whalebone. It was fitted at one end with a carved human hand that was generally made of ivory; the other end usually had a knob. Sometimes a bird's claw or a rake was used in place of the hand. The backscratcher usually ranged in length from 10 to 20 inches. Frequently the more ornate ones had silver mountings. In addition to its original use, it was probably used to keep in order the elaborate coiffures of powdered hair worn by ladies of the 18th and 19th centuries. It is also called a scratchback.

Back Stool Chair In English cabinetwork; the name was found in contemporary English records from around the end of the 16th century to describe a chair without arms. The term still appeared in trade catalogues until about the middle of the 18th century.

Backsword A sword that has a blade with only one sharp edge; it is generally called a broadsword. See *Sword*.

Bacon Dish In English silver; an oblong covered dish fitted with a lower compartment for hot water. It has a long turned wood handle which screws into a socket at the back of the dish that serves as an opening through which hot water is poured into the compartment below the dish. It was introduced during the 18th century. See *Entrée Dish*.

Baden-Baden In German ceramics; after earlier and ineffectual attempts, a faïence and porcelain manufactory was established here in 1770 by Zacharias Pfalzer with private financial aid. It was active until 1778. All types of porcelain including busts and figures were made and were simply decorated with flowers of different colors. It was marked with the Baden coat-of-arms under an Electoral Hat. Glazed earthenware or faïence fine was also made and was decorated like the porcelain. Another and very active manufactory was founded in 1795. It made glazed earthenware or faïence fine in the English style. All types of wares were made including stoves. Relief decoration was especially characteristic and popular. The mark was "AA" impressed.

Bag Table In American cabinetwork; a colloquial term applied to the pouch variety of work table. See *Work Table*.

Bahut In French cabinetwork; originally the bahut, which is of medieval origin, was a rather shallow oblong box with a hinged lid and was attached to a coffre or chest. The combined piece was called a coffre à bahut and was used in traveling. The immediate articles needed for the trip were placed in

BAIL HANDLES
AND BACK PLATES

the bahut. Later the term *bahut* was applied to a coffre with an arched or convex lid used in traveling and finally to any coffre.

Baigneuse In French cabinetwork; a variety of upholstered day bed introduced in the French Empire style having a back which continued to form the two sides or ends of unequal height. The back and sides were upholstered in one continuous unit in a 'tub' manner and were characterized by a continuous down-curving line. See *Méridienne*.

Bail Handle In furniture mounts; a metal handle, generally of brass or bronze, more or less in the form of a half circle. In English furniture mounts; a bail type handle was the principal handle employed in 18th century English cabinetwork and superseded the drop handle. In the early examples the bail handle was attached to a shaped and flat solid back plate. After 1710–1715, by cutting away the center of the shaped back plate, it resembled a narrow band of scrollwork. From around 1750 the bail handle was commonly attached to two small circular back plates or rosettes. Occasionally the large shaped back plate occurred and it was elaborately pierced and chased in the Rococo style. Around 1775 the solid back plate was reintroduced and it was generally of oval or octagonal shape. The bail handle was conformingly shaped. While the earlier back plates were cut out by hand or cast in a mold these later back plates from around 1775 were stamped by dies. The escutcheon or keyhole plate was chiefly in the form of a cartouche during the 18th century. See *Knob Handle*; *Lion-and-Ring Handle*; *Loose-Ring Handle*; *Handle and Back Plate*; *Mounts*. The term *bail* is also given to the arched handle of a teakettle, a pail or some similar article. It is also spelled bale.

Bakhshis An Oriental rug belonging to the Persian classification. It is named after the village of Bakhshis, in the Herez district. It is referred to as a Herez fabric because it is woven by Herez weavers. The foundation is cotton and the pile which is rather short in length is wool. See *Persian Rugs*.

Bakhtiari An Oriental rug belonging to the Persian classification. It derived its name from the tribes of Bakhtiari, a semi-nomadic people, who weave them. The designs are usually large and forceful and include bold floral motifs and geometrical motifs. The colors are also strong. The ends are finished with either wool or goats' hair selvage and webbings laced with brightly colored yarns. This variety of rug is exceptionally sturdy. See *Persian Rugs*.

Baku An Oriental rug belonging to the Caucasian group. It is named after the city of Baku. The foundation is cotton or wool. The pile is wool with more or less camels' hair or goats' hair and is trimmed rather short. The principal motif is a large pear which is generally worked into a design of a rectilinear character. Frequently there is a central medallion with corners to match. See *Caucasian Rugs*.

Baldachin Or Baldaquin. A form of canopy projecting from a wall, suspended from the ceiling or supported by columns. It was usually placed above a throne or an altar. This form of canopy received its name from the fabric called baudekin or baldachin of which it was originally made. See *Baudekin*.

Bale Handle In furniture mounts; see *Bail Handle*.

Ball and Claw In cabinetwork; see *Claw and Ball*.

Ball-Flower In ornament; an English Gothic architectural motif introduced during the 13th century which was very popular during the early part of the 14th century. It was in the form of a conventionally treated open flower having a ball in the hollow center. It was generally used in the hollow of a concave molding and was placed at equal intervals.

Ball Foot In cabinetwork; a round or spherical-shaped foot. It was widely used in England during the 16th and 17th centuries on articles of furniture made of oak or walnut. See *Bun Foot*; *Foot*.

Balloon-Back In cabinetwork; see *Loop-Back*; *Windsor Chair*.

Balloon Clock The term applied to a type of bracket clock. It derived its name from the early ascension balloon which it is supposed to resemble. In English furniture; it was a popular type during the latter part of the 18th century. It has an enamelled or silvered circular dial which is either convex or flat. The short trunk is gracefully concave on each side and rests on a rectangular base with small bracket feet. It is principally made of either mahogany inlaid with exotic fruitwoods in the Sheraton style or ebonized pearwood with ormolu mounts. See *Bracket Clock*.

Balloon Glass In glassware; see *Brandy Snuffer*.

Balsamaria An Italian term applied to vases of various shapes, usually small, which were widely used in the nations of antiquity, such as Greece and Syria, to hold perfumes or unguents made from balsams. They were made of glass, pottery, horn, wood or metal and are found in large numbers in ancient tombs.

Baltimore Assay Marks See *American Silver*.

Baluster In cabinetwork; a short pillar or column of circular form and curving outline. The term is primarily applied to a typical classical form in which the shaft decidedly swells out near the bottom producing an elliptical or pear-shaped bulge. The term *baluster* is also applied to a post or pillar having a square, polygonal or circular outline which supports a rail. Baluster-turned members used as supports for chairs, tables, and other similar pieces were a feature of the French Louis XIII style and they were also popular during the Late Jacobean style in England from around 1650. In English cabinetwork split balusters, frequently stained black, were sometimes applied to the surfaces of oak furniture as a form of ornament. Baluster-turned galleries were occasionally found on mid-18th century English mahogany tripod tables. See *Turning*; *Spindle*; *Banister-Back Chair*.

GOTHIC BALL-FLOWER

Baluster Measure In pewter; a pewter vessel made for measuring liquids from a quarter of a gill to a gallon capacity. It derived its name from the form of the vessel. It is particularly identified with pewter made in the British Isles. See *Measures*.

GLASS GOBLET
WITH BALUSTER STEM

Baluster Stem In glass; the term *baluster stem* is applied to the stems of drinking vessels which resemble the form of a baluster. In English glass; the baluster-form, of Venetian origin, is the principal variety of stem found in the various types of English stemmed vessels. This form of stem is either in the shape of a proper baluster or one having an inverted baluster. At first the stems were rather short with a simple baluster outline; however, as the stems became longer the simple baluster-form appeared in a variety of complex outlines. The simple baluster-form stems became rare after 1710 although stems of various types resembling balusters continued to be made until the middle of the 18th century, some of which were combined with other forms of stems.

Bambocciata In painting; a grotesque scene from everyday life, such as a carousing spectacle in which people are eating and drinking to excess.

Bamboo-Turned In cabinetwork; a variety of turning that resembles bamboo. Some of the articles of furniture designed by Chippendale in the Chinese taste had bamboo-turned members, such as the legs of chairs and tea tables. See *Chinese Chippendale*. The taste for so-called bamboo furniture continued throughout the first quarter of the 19th century. It was chiefly made of beech and was most frequently painted to imitate the natural color of bamboo. It was especially popular for bedroom chairs and tables, particularly when the bedroom was decorated in the Chinese taste. The term *bamboo-turned* is also used for a type of American Windsor chair leg which was introduced around 1790.

Banc In French cabinetwork; a wooden bench. The banc, which is principally identified with Gothic and Early Renaissance furniture, was often so heavy that it was almost unmovable. It was generally placed in front of the fireplace and at mealtimes the long trestle-type dining table was placed in front of it. See *Archebanc*; *Bench*.

Bancelle In French cabinetwork; a small bench or banc. It was often designed with wooden side pieces and sometimes with a low wooden back. See *Banc*; *Form*.

Bancone In Italian cabinetwork; the term is applied to a variety of writing table with a flat top which usually extends well over two panelled front drawers beneath which is a panelled recessed section which has drawers let into the ends. It rests on runner feet. This writing table is identified with the cabinetwork of the 15th and 16th centuries.

Banded Or bandings. In English cabinetwork; the name *banding* was applied in veneering and inlay work to a band or a strip of wood which was laid in a wooden surface for decorative purposes. Its decorative effect was achieved either in the contrasting color or the grain of the band with the wooden surface. Finely inlaid bandings were much favored on drawers, cupboard doors and table tops on furniture designed in the Hepplewhite and Sheraton styles. See *Crossbanded*; *Veneer*; *Feather Banding*.

Banderole In ornament; a band or scroll suitable to receive an inscription used as a decorative motif. It was employed during the Renaissance and was a favorite motif in the Flemish Baroque style of ornament.

Bandwurm Glass In German glass; see *Passglas*.

Bandy Leg In cabinetwork; it is the same as a cabriole leg, although the term is seldom used. See *Cabriole Leg*.

Banister A corrupt form of the English word *baluster*.

Banister-Back Chair In English and American cabinetwork; the name given to a variety of tall open-back turned chair that was designed either as an armchair or a side chair. It was introduced in England around 1685 and came into general use in America between 1705–1725 when it enjoyed much popularity. The back consists of two vertical uprights and generally three or four vertical banisters which are usually split; the term *split* being used to describe one-half of a round banister. The banisters extend between a shaped top rail and a low cross rail which is several inches above the seat. The chair commonly has a rush seat. Usually the American banister-back chair was made of maple, while the English was of walnut. It is generally believed that the banister-back chair and the slat-back chair were variants of the elaborately turned and carved Restoration chair with its caned back panel and caned seat. The familiar shield-back chair in the Hepplewhite style was often designed with three, four or five banisters or bars. This type of shield-back chair is also called a banister-back or bar-back chair. Sheraton illustrated in his DRAWING BOOK designs for chair backs with delicate and slender banisters. These chair backs, with either a straight or shaped crest rail, were designed with three, four or five banisters or bars resting on a horizontal crosspiece raised several inches above the seat rail. See *Restoration Chair*; *Slat-Back Chair*; *Shield-Back*.

Banjo Clock A form of American wall clock. Simon Willard, 1753–1848, was the inventor of the banjo clock and he patented it in 1802. It has a circular dial over a flaring shaft which is flanked by brass open scroll brackets. Beneath the shaft is a rectangular pendulum door. It is frequently made with a fluted base finished with a pendant. The shaft and pendulum door are decorated with églomisé panels, and the dial is generally surmounted either with a gilded wood or brass cone or a brass eagle. Popular subjects for the glass panels were views of Mt. Vernon and Perry's Victory on Lake Erie.

Banko Ware In Japanese ceramics; a hard pottery ware first made during the second half of the 18th century by Numanami Gozayemon, a man of wealth who was interested in ceramics. His kiln was in Kuwana. In 1785 he worked in Tokyo, then called Edo, under the patronage of the shogun Iyenari. Here he made wares having a brown color clay body decorated with enamels in the Chinese style as well as imitations of Delft, Karatsu and Raku. About 1830 Mori Yusetsu working in Kuwana continued to produce similar wares from the original enamel formula and also purchased the original seal from a grandson of Gozayemon.

Banquette In French cabinetwork; a long upholstered bench or seat without arms or back. It was introduced during the Louis XIV style. See *Form*.

Baptismal Basin The name is given to any vessel of silver, pewter, porcelain or some similar material used in the rite of baptism. The basin was made in a variety of forms. One form commonly used was a shallow basin, sometimes having a deep depression with a domed center, with a wide flat brim and a molded flat base. Some basins were mounted on a low spreading foot. A great many early American silver baptismal basins were made since they were used in lieu of fonts.

Bar-Back In English and American cabinetwork; see *Banister-Back Chair*

Barbeaux In ceramics; a French term meaning cornflowers. It was a conventional decoration of sprigs of cornflowers widely used in French and English ceramics. It is reputed to have been designed in 1782 by Hettlinger of Sèvres for Marie Antoinette. However, it was commonly used on a number of French porcelains produced during the late 18th century and early 19th century.

Barberini Tapestries The Barberini tapestry manufactory was established in Rome shortly after 1630 by the Cardinal-Legate

AMERICAN
BANISTER-BACK CHAIR

Francesco Barberini, nephew of Pope Urban VIII, who assembled around him a number of Italian and other painters and a group of Flemish weavers under the directorship of Giacomo della Riviera. Upon the latter's death in 1639, he was succeeded by his son-in-law, Gasparo Rocci. The factory undertook many important series including the Life of Christ, the History of Constantine the Great and the Story of Apollo. The death of Urban VIII in 1644 arrested the production; however, some activity was resumed after 1660. See *Tapestry*.

Barberini Vase A celebrated Roman glass vase. See *Portland Vase*.

Barber-Pole Stripe A border design used in Oriental rugs; especially in the Caucasian group. It is an alternate arrangement of diagonal stripes. Sometimes the stripes have a small decorative pattern.

Barber's Basin In ceramics; an oval shallow pottery basin of the 18th century having the center portion of one side cut out in a semi-circular manner so that it could be held against the front of a person's neck. It is also made in other materials such as pewter. In English silver; extant examples date from 1690, and it is also called a shaving dish or basin.

Barber's Chair Or Shaving Chair. In English cabinetwork; during the 18th century different types of chairs were made for the use of barbers and for shaving. A characteristic variety resembled the Early Georgian corner chair with a triangular seat. This corner chair was provided with an additional shaped solid splat extending upward from the top rail presumably serving as a head rest.

Barbotine In ceramics; a slip or paste of clay which was first used on Rhenish pottery prior to the 3rd century to make such decorations as small flowers on the rims of flat dishes. By the 3rd century it began to replace the molded decoration which had formerly been used. It was applied by piping in the same manner as frosting is applied to a cake. See *Arretine Ware*; *Slip*.

Barbute In armor; a kind of helmet of Italian origin introduced in the 14th century. It is also a variety of salade of the 15th century. Its form, which was possibly influenced by ancient classical helmets, at first had a high, pointed crown, and at a later date was round. Large cheek pieces covered almost all of the face.

Barcheston Tapestries A tapestry manufactory was founded at Barcheston, Warwickshire, England, during the middle of the 16th century by Richard Hickes under the patronage of William Sheldon. It survived until the early part of the 17th century. See *Tapestry*.

Bar Foot In cabinetwork; the name is generally given to a horizontal bar that connects the front and rear legs. The legs terminate and rest on the bar. See *Foot*; *Runner Foot*; *Dantesca Chair*; *Savonarola Chair*.

Bargello In needlework; it is the same as Hungarian stitch or Hungarian work. See *Hungarian Work*.

Barley Sugar Turning In English cabinetwork; the name given to a twist-turned member, such as the leg of a chair, characterized by a deeply cut, closely spiralled twist. See *Twist Turning*.

Barometer Also called a Baroscope and Quick-Silver Weather-Glass. In English furniture; an instrument that indicates changes in the weather. The mercurial barometer consisted of a glass tube about a yard in length and a quarter of an inch in diameter, which was closed at one end and was filled with mercury, with the open end resting in a small cistern of mercury. It was invented by Torricelli, a student of Galileo, in 1643, and it was introduced into England after the Restoration in 1660. Of the various forms of early barometers there are three principal types. The Cistern barometer is based on the principles of Torricelli's apparatus employing a glass tube of mercury immersed in a cistern containing mercury. The mercury in the glass tube rises and falls according to the

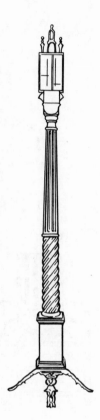

PORTABLE OR
STICK BAROMETER

atmospheric pressure on the mercury in the cistern and is read by means of an attached register-plate having a graduated scale. The Diagonal, Inclined, "Yard-Arm" or "Sign-Post" barometer, is a cistern barometer with a vertical tube of about 28 inches which then inclines horizontally about another 12 inches. This type was introduced around 1670. The Siphon barometer has a tube in the form of an inverted siphon, curved at the bottom, with one arm of the tube longer than the other. A type of siphon barometer was called a Wheel barometer and was first made about 1665. It contained a tiny float on the mercury in the longer tube attached to a thread passing over a pulley and almost balanced by a counterpoise in the shorter length of the tube. This operated an indicator hand on a dial. The siphon and wheel barometers were not in general use until about 1760-1770. The Portable or "Stick" barometer was in the form of a slender column about 36 inches in height and rested on the floor on a tripod base. The diagonal and long straight cistern varieties were popular during the first three-quarters of the 18th century. Many barometers were also fitted with a thermometer. The barometer cases were usually finely executed in mahogany or walnut, and at times elaborately carved and decorated. They were considered choice and important articles of domestic furniture.

Baroque   A French word meaning whimsical or irregularly shaped as applied to the arts, apparently taken from the Italian word *barocco* meaning a misshapen pearl. The word did not obtain any wide usage until around the middle of the 19th century when it was derisively used to describe a later phase of Renaissance art. It is commonly considered that Michelangelo led architecture and the decorative arts into the ways of the Baroque. It first became evident in Italy during the latter part of the 16th century, with Rome, which is called the Baroque city, being the fountainhead of Baroque art. The Italian architect and sculptor Bernini

is often regarded as the creator of the Roman Baroque. In Italy Baroque art was purely a continuation of the art of the late 16th century and reached its culmination around the middle of the 17th century. This later phase of Renaissance art was in reaction against the classical purity and pedantic perfection of the High Renaissance. Baroque art is characterized by a dynamic sense of movement, a dramatic planning and bold contrast, and very often massive forms. As a rule it has an air of splendid vitality and stateliness which offsets to a great extent its violation of High Renaissance design and ornament. Some Baroque art with grossly exaggerated and unsuitable ornament can best be described as a lapse in discretion. The classic ornament was of a sculpturesque and florid character and its plastic possibilities were completely exploited. Cartouches, large foliated scrolls, C-scrolls and S-scrolls, volutes, heraldic devices, banderoles, grotesques, human figures, and strapwork in intricate designs were all included among the favorite Baroque motifs. The Baroque style was known in France as the Louis XIV style. The French craftsmen removed from the Italian Baroque its excessive decoration. In the course of elimination, modification and assimilation they evolved the Louis XIV style. The Baroque style was so homogeneously developed by the craftsmen of France under the patronage of Louis XIV, 1643-1715, that Italy toward the end of the century along with the other countries of Europe accepted the French interpretation. Around 1720 the Rococo style of ornament was evolved and supplanted the Baroque. See *Michelangelo Buonarroti*; *Rubens, Peter Paul*; *Bernini, Giovanni*; *Louis XIV*; *Rococo*; *Renaissance, Italian*; *Louis XIII*; *Kent, William*; *Jacobean, Late*.

Barrel-Back Chair   In cabinetwork; the name given to a variety of a high-back upholstered armchair because of its supposed resemblance to the inside of a half barrel. The back is semi-circular in plan, and the back and arms are generally upholstered as

BAROQUE DESIGN
BY JEAN LE PAUTRE

one continuous unit. The name is chiefly identified with American cabinetwork. See *Tub Chair*.

Bartmann Jug Or Bartmannkrüge. In German ceramics; a Rhenish salt-glazed stoneware jug having a bearded mask molded on the front. It was first made toward the end of the 15th century onwards throughout the 17th century. Toward the end of the 16th century it was given the name of *bellarmine* because of the supposed resemblance of the bearded mask to the face of Cardinal Bellarmino who was intensely disliked in the Protestant countries. The English name of *greybeard* was also given to the globular Bartmann jug. See *Rhenish Stoneware*; *Frechen*.

Basalt Ware or Black Basaltes In English ceramics; the term *black basaltes* was the name given by Wedgwood to his black stoneware introduced around 1769. Essentially it was a refinement of a ware previously made at Staffordshire around 1740. The stoneware is a dense fine-grained material and is extremely hard. The black color is derived from iron and manganese. After its improvement by Wedgwood it was made by many contemporary potters in Staffordshire as well as in other places in England. It was also made on the Continent. Black basaltes was made by Wedgwood into vases, portrait medallions, panels in relief and other similar pieces. See *Wedgwood, Josiah*.

Bas d'Armoire In French cabinetwork; a French term, meaning a low cupboard, given to a variety of furniture essentially resembling the lower section of a cupboard or armoire made in two parts. The bas d'armoire was a fashionable piece of Louis XIV style furniture and was richly ornamented with gilded bronze mounts often combined with Boulle marquetry. It was generally provided with a marble top and was designed with either one or two cupboard doors. Also called an entre-deux, since it was designed as part of the architecture, filling the space left entre-deux, that

CHIPPENDALE BASIN STAND

is between two windows or doors; the height being decided by the dado. It was a popular and elegant piece in the 18th century.

Basilard In arms; a dagger or short sword carried by civilians during the Middle Ages. It had a short, straight, tapering blade, usually with a cross pommel and straight quillons. Some early basilards were chained to the breastplate to prevent loss if struck from the hand.

Basinet In armor; a form of helmet. The early basinet was simply a pointed iron cap. Later a basinet of light weight was worn under the battle helm. In the 14th century it was worn alone and consisted of a light headpiece, usually with a high pointed crown with a pointed visor and a chain mail piece or camail that hung to the shoulders to protect the neck and throat. In the 15th century it was fitted with a gorget instead of the camail.

Basin Stand In English cabinetwork; a piece of furniture used for holding a wash-basin. The basin stand was not designed as a special piece of furniture until around 1750. A principal variety is the circular tripod basin stand. It has a molded basin ring on three supports joined by a median trilateral shelf containing two narrow drawers and often surmounted by a covered urn. The lower three supports rest on a dished trilateral base with three legs. The top of the base is dished to receive the pitcher, and the covered urn is to hold the soap. Variations in design occur. Another smaller variety of basin stand was used for powdering the hair. It also was designed as a piece of harlequin furniture. The small mahogany basin stand of tripod form was also made in America and extant examples date from around 1760. See *Washstand*.

Basket In English silver; the cake basket and sweetmeat basket, which were favorite pieces of English silver, were introduced during the 17th century. Essentially the form and the style of ornament followed the prevailing fashions. Especially delicate and fanciful were the pierced baskets with bail handles designed in the Rococo taste. Occasionally the basket was made with a rounded bottom and rested on four ball and claw feet. Around the middle of the 18th century a basket resembling a large scallop shell resting on three feet, occasionally in the form of dolphins, was introduced.

Basket Stitch   A stitch in which the threads running one way alternately pass over and under the cross threads. In couching the basket stitch is worked over threads or cords to give the appearance of basket work. See *Couching*; *Embroidery*.

Basque   In French Provincial; the Basque country of France is situated in the southwestern section in the Pyrenees in the old province of Gascogne. The provincial furniture of the Basque country is distinctly French. Their cabinetwork was of good quality and was well proportioned. An outstanding feature was the carving which was in very low relief. The carved detail which had a flat quality was generally composed of geometrical motifs and sometimes of rather naïve designs of men and animals. Very often the carving covered the entire surface, and due to the skill of the carver the effect was almost always pleasing. See *French Provincial*.

Bas-Relief   Low relief. See *Relief*.

Basset   In French cabinetwork; a small round or square table similar in construction to a stool but taller. It was introduced during the Gothic period.

Basse-Taille   A process of enamelling. See *Enamel*.

Basso-Rilievo   Low relief. See *Relief*.

Bass Seat   In cabinetwork; see *Splint Seat*; *Rush Seat*; *Flag Seat*.

Basting Spoon   In English silver; a long-stemmed spoon with a correspondingly large bowl used for serving stew or hash. It was introduced late in the 17th century, and was also called a hash spoon.

Batavian Ware   In Chinese ceramics; a porcelain ware made during the K'ang Hsi period called Tzu Chin or lustrous brown. It derived its name from the Dutch East India Company who imported this ware into Europe. See *Tzu Chin*.

Batik   A form of resist dyeing originally done in Java. In this method wax is used to trace the design on the cloth and then the material is dyed, with the portions treated with wax remaining undyed. Then all the wax is removed. By repeating this process several or more times some intricate and multi-colored patterns can be obtained.

Bat Printing   In English ceramics; a variety of transfer printed decoration in which the impressions of the stipple engravings were taken on soft, flexible glue sheets or bats instead of the earlier method of taking the line engravings on thin sheets of paper. In this bat printing method the impressions are taken in oil and the transferred design is later dusted with enamel pigment. This method was introduced in England toward the end of the 18th century. See *Transfer Printed Decoration*.

Battersea   In English painted enamel; an enamel manufactory was started at York House in Battersea, a district in London, by Stephen Theodore Janssen around 1750. It was in operation for only a few years since Janssen declared bankruptcy in 1756. Painted enamels were later produced at Wednesbury and at Bilston in Staffordshire; however, as a rule, they are not as fine as those made at Battersea. In this work, which is a copper product, the copper base is completely covered with a soft white enamel, which, either in the natural color or as a reserve in a tinted pink or blue ground, affords a surface for the decoration painted by hand or by the process of transfer printing. The decorative motifs are greatly diversified and include such subjects as portraits of well-known persons,

GEORGE III
SILVER CAKE BASKET

landscapes, figures, birds, flowers and mottoes. This enamel decoration can be executed in full color when it is painted by hand; if transfer printing is used the color is largely confined to black or to sepia. However, if the transfer printing simply forms the outline of the design, it can be filled in with full color painting. The enamel decoration is often further enhanced with gilt Rococo foliation and scrollwork. Transfer printing done at Battersea is invariably distinct and clear. The Battersea pieces are generally very small and include such articles as snuff boxes, patch boxes and étuis. See *Enamel, in art*.

Battle-Axe A medieval weapon having a short shaft with a steel blade designed in different shapes. Sometimes opposite the blade are spikes or saw-teeth. A pole-axe is the same except it has a long shaft.

Baudekin In textiles; an exceedingly rich embroidered stuff originally woven with a warp of gold thread, the weft being silk. Later with a broader application the word was used for rich silk brocades. The city of Baghdad was associated with its earliest manufacture. It was used particularly for canopies or baldachins, for robes of state and for ecclesiastical copes and vestments of great value.

Bayeux Lace Lace was first made at Bayeux, which was an important French lace-making center, toward the end of the 17th century. Included among their 18th century fabrications were Mignonette and Marli. The black silk laces of Bayeux, Caën and Chantilly were so similar that it was practically impossible to determine in which town they were made. The so-called Blondes Mates for exportation were most successfully produced at Bayeux from around 1830. Throughout the 19th century Bayeux enjoyed an enviable reputation for producing fine laces both needle-made and bobbin-made. Point d'Alençon and Venetian point in high relief were included among their successful reproductions, which were praiseworthy for the

fineness of their designs and workmanship. See *Point de Raccroc*.

Bayeux Tapestry The name given to a celebrated embroidered hanging made in the 11th century. It consists of a piece of linen, 231 feet long and 20 inches wide on which worsted threads in eight colors have been embroidered with a needle. It comprises seventy-two scenes beginning with Harold's visit to Bosham on his way to Normandy and ending with the flight of the English at the battle of Hastings. Unfortunately the actual end of the work is no longer in existence. The decorative borders at the top and at the bottom depict figures of animals, scenes from fables of Aesop, from the hunt and other similar subjects, and sometimes scenes from the conquest of England by the Normans in 1066, under William the Conqueror. It is now generally accepted that it was executed for Odo, Bishop of Bayeux and half-brother of William the Conqueror, for the Cathedral of Bayeux where it was used to decorate the nave on certain feast days. It is invaluable as a historical document pertaining to early English history. It was originally known as the Toile de St. Jean and it is still displayed at Bayeux under glass.

Bayonet Fastener Or Bayonet Joint. In English silver; a particular and characteristic kind of device fastening the top to the body of such silver articles as dredgers and casters. It consists of two projecting ears or lugs attached to the lower part of the removable top, and when these two ears pass two notches in the grooved molding around the rim of the body the top becomes securely fastened to the body. The bayonet fastener was used on English casters as early as 1680.

Bayreuth In German ceramics; one of the most outstanding German manufactories of the late Baroque era was started at Bayreuth, Bavaria, around 1713–1714. It produced beautiful faïence and a fine brown glazed ware with gilt, silver and engraved decoration. It closed in 1852. Its finest work was from around 1728 to 1745. One variety of

BATTLE-AXE

faïence was painted in a pale mist-like tone of blue. Another variety of faïence consisted of fine pieces painted with coats-of-arms enclosed in rich Baroque strapwork borders. A third type of faïence comprised fine distinctive work of several well-known artists. After 1728 the ware was frequently marked. The mark consisted of the initials of the place and the owners, together with the painters' marks. They produced fine brown and yellow glazed ware. The Bayreuth brown glazed ware was not a stoneware but a reddish earthenware covered with a manganese brown or red glaze. The yellow glazed ware was practically the same except that it was lighter in body and was covered with a buff or pale yellow glaze. The typical decoration for this brown and yellow ware is in fired-on gold and silver and is often beautifully painted. Engraved decoration was also done. Porcelain was also produced at Bayreuth; however, not very much is known about the porcelain production. It apparently was first made around 1745–1748 and at later intervals.

Baywood   See *Campeche Wood*.

Bead   In cabinetwork; a small half round convex molding. See *Cockbeading*; *Flush Beading*. The term *bead molding* is also given to a small round molding designed as beads in a necklace. See *Molding*.

Bead and Reel   In cabinetwork; a round convex molding having oval beads alternating with disks that are treated singly or in pairs. See *Molding*.

Beaded   In silver; a pattern of engraved ornamentation used for edges and rims resembling a string of tiny beads.

Bead Work   In needlework; bead work, which has been a popular amateur pastime for quite a few centuries, was especially popular during the mid-Victorian era. Beads are made of various materials, such as glass, wood and metal, and are made in different shapes and sizes, some simulating the shape of gems. There are many kinds of bead work. Needle and thread bead work was used for making necklaces, evening bags, and as a trimming on dresses. Knitted and crochet bead work were employed for essentially the same purposes. Bracelets, necklaces, borders for table runners and other articles were made by working on the loom. A novelty type of bead work included bead embroidery work for dresses and other wearing apparel. Wooden beads in various shapes, such as round, oval, square and tube-shaped, were used extensively for making table mats and curtains for doorways and windows.

Beaker   A large drinking vessel with a wide mouth usually almost cylindrical, tapering slightly towards the bottom and resting on a flat or molded base. Some beakers have a slight flare at the lip and are made of various kinds of metal while those of glass having a pouring lip are used for scientific experiments. In silver; beakers date from about 1350 and were characteristic and popular pieces of secular plate during the 15th and 16th centuries when many were handsomely wrought and ornamented.

Bear Jug   In English ceramics; a stoneware vessel in the form of a sitting bear, frequently hugging a small dog. The head of the bear was detachable and formed a cup. The jug is identified with the wares made at Staffordshire and Nottingham during the 18th century. Essentially it was a rather awkward and clumsy jug.

Beau Brummel   In English and American cabinetwork; the name given to a variety of dressing table designed for a man. One characteristic variety was designed as an oblong table with a hinged lid that opened into a fitted interior with shaving and washing accessories and with a framed rising mirror. It was in vogue during the second half of the 18th century. See *Shaving Table*.

Beaujolais   In French Provincial; an old province in south-eastern France, now the department of Rhône. The provincial furniture of Beaujolais is related to and has the

STAFFORDSHIRE BEAR JUG

same general characteristics as the furniture of Bresse and Burgundy. See *Bresse*; *Burgundy*; *French Provincial*.

Beauvais The tapestry manufactory at Beauvais, near Paris, was founded by Louis Hinart in 1664 under the patronage of Jean Baptiste Colbert and subsidized by the French crown. It was established chiefly to produce tapestries for the general public and for the export trade. Especially notable are the 18th century tapestries woven at Beauvais from the cartoons of François Boucher. See *Tapestry*; *Tapestry Furniture Coverings*; *Gobelins*.

Beaver In armor; a piece of medieval armor that guarded the lower part of the face. Properly it moved upward. Later the term was used to include the visor which moved downward. See *Visor*.

CHIPPENDALE TESTER BED

Bed In English cabinetwork; prior to the 16th century the bed was simply a boarded box completely surrounded with curtains. Cords were attached to the ceiling to hold the draperies; however, sometimes a light framework was constructed for that purpose. During the 16th century the bed began to assume its characteristic contour, having wooden posts and a headboard. It is doubtful that the wooden tester was added until after the 16th century. And from that time all beds were designed with a tester until the 19th century. During the reign of Charles II the cornice which surmounted the tester was introduced and it remained in vogue as long as the tester. The Regency designers in addition to the popular tester bed introduced a variety of bed borrowed from the French Empire. It was of couch shape and was scrolled over at each end. The bed was always an important article of furniture in all homes and it was believed to reflect the affluence of its owner. Although a few high post beds were made in America in the Queen-Anne style, the high post bed with its tester and draperies was not made in any appreciable quantity until around the middle of the 18th century. The majority of fine

American tester beds were made of mahogany. The richly carved cornice surmounting the tester on English beds was seldom found on American beds. See *Field Bed*; *Tester*. In French cabinetwork; see *Lit en Tombeau*; *Lit à la Duchesse*; *Lit à la Polonaise*; *Lit d'Ange*; *Lit en Bateau*; *Lit Clos*; *Lit à Colonnes*; *Lit à la Turque*.

Bedfordshire Lace It is generally accepted that lace-making was introduced into the county of Bedfordshire, England, by émigré lace-workers from Flanders in the 16th century. The laces of Bedfordshire, Buckinghamshire and Northamptonshire were essentially similar in technique and in designs. See *Northamptonshire Lace*.

Bedstead The term given to the wood or metal framework on which the mattress or something of similar softness or springiness is raised. It supports the bed, which specifically refers to the mattress, on which are placed the bedclothes or the sheets and blankets. The name *bed* has come to be given to the entire structure, that is the bed or mattress, bedstead and bedclothes in its most elaborate form. The term *bedstead* may be used in this same complete sense instead of the term *bed*.

Bed Steps In English cabinetwork; bed steps were made in a variety of designs. One typical variety designed in the Sheraton style consisted of a set of three steps. The upper tread was hinged and opened to a well which was often fitted with a wash basin and a soap cup. Sometimes a drawer was constructed under the middle tread. The bed steps rested on four very short legs. Sheraton in his DRAWING BOOK gave two designs for bed steps. See *Library Steps*.

Beechwood The wood of the beech tree, *fagus sylvatica*, used for cabinetwork, especially by the French ébénistes. It is a semi-hard wood and its color is white.

Belgian Marble, Black A deep black marble of the finest quality quarried at St. Denis, Namur, Belgium. It is also called *Noir Fin*.

Bellarmine In German ceramics; see *Bartmann Jug*.

Belleek In ceramics; a glazed parian ware first popularized by McBirney and Armstrong of Belleek, Ireland, in 1863. It is characterized by a pearly luster. This luster is colorless or tinted, the most common colors being pastel pink or green. Belleek ware is very translucent. It has a natural ivory-color body that is easily scratched. It is decorated with gold or enamels. Recently it sometimes has a slip decoration. Of particular interest are the fine Belleek baskets made of evenly woven strands. The early mark is a round tower with an Irish harp on the left and an Irish wolfhound on the right. Under this is a ribbon having the name "*Belleek*" and a shamrock ornament. See *Parian*; *Luster Decoration*.

Bellevue A French faïence manufactory was founded at Bellevue around 1755 by Lefrançois. In 1771 the ownership passed to François Boyer and Charles Bayard who received permission to use Manufacture Royale. It is generally accepted that their most important wares were figures and groups in a chalk-like biscuit. Terra-cotta painted garden figures and wares for daily use in faïence and faïence fine were also made. Some of the excellent faïence fine tableware was distinctive for its charming decoration of landscapes painted in black or brown monochrome. The characteristic 18th century mark on biscuit figures was "*Bellevue Ban de Toul*," incised. The mark "*Bellevue*," impressed, was common on the excellent faïence fine tableware. Potteries are still active at Bellevue.

Bell Flower In American ornament; the name is sometimes applied to the husk-festoon which resembles open seed pods. See *Husk Festoon*.

Bellows A device for producing currents of air and used to aid the combustion of fires. The domestic hand bellows consists of two flat boards, usually pear-shaped, with a wide strip of leather, reinforced with several·wire rings, fastened around the edges. The bottom board is fitted with a hole with a flap of leather on the inside, through which the air enters and is then forced out through a nozzle at the narrow hinged end. The wide end of the bellows is fitted with two handles. Bellows were often ornamented to conform to the taste of the period. They are mentioned in English records as early as 1502.

Bell Pull A very long, narrow, decorative strip, elaborately worked, usually in petit-point, attached high on the wall to a lever that pulls the wire of the call bell in the pantry or kitchen.

Bell Salt, Standing A massive bell-shaped silver standing salt, usually having three compartments, the two lower compartments forming salt-cellars and the upper one serving as a pepper caster, with a small dome cover frequently fitted with a ring handle. It is principally identified with old English silver and was introduced around 1590 and was made until about 1615. See *Salt, Standing*.

Bell Seat In American cabinetwork; a colloquial term applied to a rounded, more or less bell-shaped seat frequently found on Queen Anne style walnut side chairs made during the second quarter of the 18th century.

Belter, John H. An eminent cabinetmaker working in New York from about 1840 to 1860. His pieces of furniture designed in the Victorian taste are very ornate. Especially characteristic of his work are the chairs and settees with their pronounced curves and with their elaborate openwork top rails and side rails. See *Victorian*.

Beluchistan Rug An Oriental rug belonging to the Turkoman group. It is woven by the nomadic tribes of Beluchistan and by the Beluches residing in Afghanistan and eastern Persia. The foundation is usually wool. The pile is of wool or goats' fleece and rather long and compact. The ends are usually very interesting. They have a deep

SILVER BELL SALT

web figured in colors or worked in a diaper pattern. The rugs are heavy in tone and the designs are usually based on geometrical patterns, hexagons and octagons. See *Turkoman Rugs*.

Beman, Reuben, Jr. American cabinetmaker of Kent, Connecticut. He was born in 1742.

Bench In cabinetwork; an oblong narrow seat made to accommodate several persons; with or without a back. During medieval times the different types of benches along with chests and stools were the principal forms of seats since chairs were relatively rare. See *Archebanc*; *Banc*; *Bancelle*; *Banquette*; *Dossier*; *Settle*; *Form*; *Cassapanca*.

Beneman, Guillaume A French ébéniste who was admitted as a master cabinetmaker in 1785. He was the principal cabinetmaker to the court of France, during the last years of the reign of Louis XVI. Toward the end of the reign of Louis XVI many pieces of furniture varied from the typical Louis XVI type. Much of the richly decorated furniture, especially such pieces as large commodes made for the royal palaces, displayed a striking resemblance in their quality of grandeur to the Louis XIV style of cabinetwork. Some of the work of Beneman illustrated the influence of this earlier period. Of particular interest were his large marble top mahogany commodes. The façade was divided into three shaped panels framed in bronze moldings. The large center panel which was in the form of an elliptical arch, shaped like the handle of a basket, extended practically the length of the commode. The frieze and the shaped panels were covered with bronze doré appliqués of classic motifs. The large center panel centered a figured medallion of biscuit ware. It had half-round cable-fluted pilasters over short vase-shaped legs. The panelled façade had two cupboard doors which enclosed two banks of six drawers. See *Louis XVI*.

Bennet Pottery In 1846, Edwin Bennet started a pottery manufactory in Baltimore

LOUIS XVI COMMODE
AFTER BENEMAN

with his brother William. The accepted marks are: "E. B"; "E. & W. Bennet, Canton Ave, Baltimore, Md." After William withdrew in 1856 the initials "E. B." were used. It made all types of articles from useful wares to decorative pieces. In particular it made pitchers in various forms which derived their name from the relief decoration such as hound-handled pitcher, stag hunt pitcher, and wild boar pitcher.

Bennington In American ceramics; a stoneware manufactory was started in 1842–1843 at Bennington, Vermont, by Julius Norton and Christopher Webber Fenton. During the period 1843–1847 the marks were "Norton & Fenton/Bennington, Vt." in an oval or circle; and "Norton & Fenton/East Bennington, Vt." It produced a variety of articles which during this period included hexagonal buff-colored stoneware pitchers with floral designs in relief. The glaze was of a rich brown color and is referred to as Rockingham since it was in imitation of the glaze made at the Rockingham kiln at Swinton, England. In 1847 Norton withdrew. During the period 1847–1848 the mark was "Fenton's Works/Bennington/Vermont," impressed. The wares included mottled Rockingham wares, parian wares, and wares for daily use. In 1849 Fenton secured a patent for a colored glaze. In this method metallic oxides were applied to the already fired body of the ware and then dipped in a clear flint enamel glaze. This ware was distinctive for its beautiful color of yellow, orange and blue, mottled or mingled with the Rockingham brown, The mark became "Lyman, Fenton & Co/Fentons/Enamel/Patented/1849/Bennington, Vt." In 1850 the United States Pottery was formed and in 1853 it was incorporated by five members including Fenton. The business closed in 1858. During the United States Pottery period two marks were used: "U. S. P." in a ribbon, impressed, with numerals for the pattern and size; and "United States Pottery Co/Bennington, Vt.," impressed in a raised medallion. Almost every type of article was made, including parian ware figures, doorknobs, doorplates, pitchers, cups, platters, large bowls and useful wares. Most of the forms and technique were copies of English wares since most of the potters were English; however, some typically American pieces were made such as the pitchers with relief decoration of waterfalls, called Niagara Falls pattern. Toby jugs of contemporary persons were very popular. The hound-handled pitchers, with mottled Rockingham glaze, were a distinctive Bennington production. The characteristic hound-handled pitcher had a handle in the form of a conventionalized hound, with relief decoration on one side of the body of a boar hunt scene and on the other side a stag hunt scene, with a border around the neck of leaves and grapes. An earlier kiln was started in Bennington in 1793 by Captain John Norton which produced red earthenware and bricks until about 1830. Before 1815 a stoneware kiln was added and the wares were marked with the Norton family name. In 1823 his two sons, Luman and John, became the owners. Luman's son, Julius, was the original partner of Fenton's from 1842–1843 until 1847. See *Rockingham*; *Parian Ware*.

Bent-Wood   Wood so shaped by bending into the desired form. Furniture made of bent-wood was widely used in Austria and pieces made for the export market were called Vienna furniture. It was introduced around the middle of the 19th century.

Bérain, Jean, the Elder   1638–1711. Belgian-born painter, designer and engraver of ornament living at the Louvre from 1677. His published designs greatly influenced contemporary decorative art. He was particularly gifted in assimilating the works of those who preceded him and in adapting those works to the prevailing Louis XIV style. He especially followed the work of Raphael. His delicate arabesques and playful grotesques which he treated in a Raphaelesque manner were very fine. His designs also served as an inspiration for the decoration of

furniture designed in the Louis XIV style. He executed the designs for court festivals and for the decoration and costumes employed in opera performances. He provided the designs for tapestries. He was much in demand to furnish the designs for wall panels and for ceilings. A large part of his collection of designs were published in three folio volumes. Bérain's later work is now generally regarded as an important factor in developing the style of the Régence. His delightful painted arabesques from around 1700 possessed a remarkable quality of French grace and lightness, and were distinctly French in feeling. He had a brother, Claude Bérain, who was also an engraver and who executed a number of plates of ornament, which included various kinds of arabesques. His son Jean Bérain, the Younger, 1678–1726, carried on the work of his gifted father. He is probably best known as an engraver. His style was remarkably similar to that of his father's. See *Louis XIV*; *Watteau, Antoine*; *Chinoiserie*; *Régence*.

Berdelik   A Perso-Turkish word meaning hanging. It refers to the handmade fabrics woven in the Orient not for floor coverings but for the adornment of walls.

Berettino   Or *bianco sopra azzurro*. In Italian ceramics; an Italian term applied to decorative designs executed in opaque white on a light or dark blue tin glaze ground. This style of decoration was used in Faenza, Venice, and other leading Italian majolica centers from the early 16th century.

Bergamo   An Oriental rug belonging to the Turkish classification. Bergamo is a corruption of the word *Pergamo*, which is the name of a village where this rug is woven. The warp and the weft are of wool and usually dyed. The pile is of fine wool and medium in length. The ends are usually finished with a wide red web, sometimes striped, and a short fringe. The antique Bergamo is of excellent workmanship; the modern ones try to imitate the old ones but as a rule they are inferior. See *Turkish Rugs*.

BENNINGTON
HOUND-HANDLED PITCHER

Bergère In French cabinetwork; a form of upholstered armchair perfected during the Louis XV style and characterized by its closed arms and a loose seat cushion. It was a comfortable chair and it was undoubtedly the most characteristic piece of Louis XV seat furniture. The bergère was made in a variety of forms; however, there were three principal types. One type was closely related to the contemporary fauteuil except that the seat was generally deeper and wider, the arms were closed and it was provided with a loose seat cushion. Another variety had an arched horseshoe-shaped back continuing to form the arms. The sides and back were rounded about the seat and were upholstered as one unit. This type of bergère is described as gondola-shaped and is often referred to as a bergère en gondole. The third type of bergère is called a bergère confessional. The back was higher and it was designed with shallow wings. It was essentially similar to the earlier confessional chair.

LOUIS XV BERGÈRE
EN GONDOLE

Berlin In German ceramics; a porcelain manufactory was started in 1751 by Wilhelm Kaspar Wegely with the permission of Frederick the Great. It closed in 1757. The factory mark was a "W" in underglaze blue. In 1761, Johann Ernst Gotzkowsky bought the manufactory. The porcelain was marked with a "G" in underglaze blue. In 1763 Frederick the Great, d. 1786, became the owner. It was called the Royal Berlin Porcelain Manufactory and it is still in operation. It is regarded as one of the seven outstanding German porcelain manufactories of the 18th century. The mark was a scepter in various forms. Its finest period was from 1761 to 1786. Table services made for the King and his friends were its outstanding productions, the finest being made prior to 1770 and featuring an entire new series of designs in the Rococo style. Vases in the Rococo taste with profusely applied modelled flowers also were made. Underglaze blue porcelain was also made for daily use. The artistic merit of the porcelain was lost when the Neo-Classic style was adopted around 1780. Figure

modelling practiced at Berlin was often very charming and distinctively painted in the Meissen style during its early and best period. Outstanding among the 19th century productions were the lithophanes or panels made from around 1830.

Berlin Wool Work In needlework; during the Victorian era, both in America and in Europe, Berlin wool work, also called tapestry needlework, was popular from about 1835 to 1870. It originated in Berlin at the beginning of the 19th century and its popularity was due to the printed patterns produced by Madame Wittich from about 1810. These patterns were clearly marked with the design and colors, and the stitches were plainly indicated. The later and better work, which was executed with a fine quality of wool yarn, was employed in upholstery work. Flower motifs and conventionalized designs were much favored, and their bright colors afforded a cheerful decorative effect for chairs, stools, cushions, settees, screens and many other articles. The designs were worked on canvas, generally in the tent or cross-stitch.

Bernini, Giovanni Lorenzo 1598–1680, celebrated Italian architect and sculptor. The art of Rome during the 17th century is closely connected with his work. Bernini's most famous work is the great colonnade of St. Peter's. He was greatly favored by the court at Rome. The decorations and furniture in all the great palaces built in Rome reflected his taste. He is generally regarded as the artistic dictator of Italian decorative art for the 17th century. See *Baroque*.

Berry Spoon In English silver; see *Sugar Sifter*.

Besaque In armor; a protective plate used during the 15th century to cover the opening of the armor at the armpits. It was either square, circular or oval and was attached with laces. It is also called a moton.

Beshire Rug An Oriental rug belonging to the Turkoman classification. The warp and weft are of wool, and the pile is wool and medium in length. The ends are usually finished with a deep striped web and long fringe. The rug is generally of brick-red color. The patterns which are rather of an Arabic character are arranged upon the field of the rug in the Turkoman manner. See *Turkoman Rugs*.

Betty Lamp An early American oil lamp extensively used during the 17th and 18th centuries. It is of European origin and is similar to the primitive cruzie lamp. It is a small, shallow pear-shaped vessel usually made of iron or tin with a wick laid in the small end. The Betty lamp was generally attached to a slender iron rod on a stand or to an iron ratchet hung from the ceiling. See *Cruzie Lamp*.

Bianco Sopra Azzurro In Italian ceramics; see *Berettino*.

Bianco Sopra Bianco In ceramics; an Italian term for a decorative design executed in opaque white on a very pale bluish or greyish white ground. It was much used on Italian majolica made from the early 16th century at Faenza, Castel Durante, and other leading ceramic centers. During the 18th century a similar decoration was used at English Delftware manufactories and at certain Continental manufactories such as Nevers and Marieberg.

Bibelot The French term *bibelot* is given to a small curio; a small object of virtù. The term is frequently used in the plural, *bibelots*, when it is applied to such articles placed on an étagère or what-not, or on a chimney piece.

Biberon In pewter; a drinking-water vessel of Swiss origin introduced during the 17th century. It resembles a kettle fitted with a lid and a short round spout near the top of the body. It was suspended by a bail handle to a bracket attached to the end of the sideboard in the living room or dining room in a Swiss house. The spout continued on the inside as a tube reaching almost to the bottom and drinking was effected by sucking. It is also called a *brunkessi*.

Bibik-Abad Rug See *Hamadan Rug*.

Bible Box In American cabinetwork; a small chest used as a Bible box, a desk box, as well as a general receptacle for many other possessions. These small boxes, fitted with hinged lids, were rather low and generally oblong, and were principally made of oak. They were either plain or enhanced with flat carving. Many were made with a slant-lid and occasionally were provided with a molding to secure a book, and thus they served as a desk or as a reading stand. They were principally made from about 1670 to 1720. See *Cumdach*.

Bibliothèque In French cabinetwork; the movable bookcase did not come into general use until the beginning of the 18th century. In one characteristic variety the length considerably exceeded the height. This bookcase, which was about 5 or 6 feet in length, had an oblong marble top with a three-quarter pierced metal gallery. The two or more long doors were generally designed with wire grille panels that were lined with silk. It had a molded base and was mounted on very short legs. It was designed in the successive 18th century styles. See *Bookcase*.

Bidri A form of inlay work practiced in India. The chief center of its production is Bidar, in Hyderabad, where it probably originated. Bidri articles are made for domestic use as well as for personal adornment. It consists of an alloy composed of tin or zinc, with smaller proportions of copper and lead. After the article is cast, an engraved design is worked on the surface and inlaid with silver. It is polished and then made black by applying a paste of sal ammoniac and saltpeter mixed with oil. This produces a dull black background which affords a fine contrast for the bright silver designs of geometrical or floral arrangement.

Biedermeier The term *Biedermeier* is applied to a style of furniture of German origin that was especially popular in Germany from about 1825 to 1860. The term is derived

BETTY LAMP WITH
IRON FLOOR STANDARD,
AMERICAN

from the name of a caricature in a German newspaper who typified a well-to-do middle class man without culture. The style, which is commonplace, is a potpourri of some of the features, but not the best ones, of Sheraton, Regency, Directoire and especially French Empire. Biedermeier was a fad rather than a decorative style. It was an incongruous assortment of several styles. Early Biedermeier furniture is quite simple in both form and ornament. It is characterized by a preference for curves, such as curved legs and curved chair backs. The favorite woods used in veneering are cherry, ash, pear, birch and particularly mahogany. In the later Biedermeier there is a marked tendency toward elaboration. Curves are more pronounced and exaggerated, and the ornament is enriched and more freely used. Realistic flowers and fruits became fashionable motifs. Rococo scrollwork began to appear and by 1840 much of the cabinetwork was in the Revived Rococo taste, which remained the principal inspiration until after the middle of the 19th century. See *Louis Philippe*; *Victorian*; *Charles X*.

BIEDERMEIER TABLE

Biggin In English silver; a kind of coffee pot in which the coffee is placed in a separate compartment and then fitted into a larger vessel which contains the water. It is in reality a percolator. It was so-named because a Mr. Biggin invented it around 1800.

Bijar Rug An Oriental rug belonging to the Persian group. It is woven in the town of Bijar and the surrounding country. The foundation is wool. The pile is wool and is short, sharp and erect. This variety of Oriental is thick and firm due to the fact that a coarse heavy two-strand yarn is used as an extra filling between the rows of knots. It is regarded as one of the best wearing of all Orientals. The designs cover a wide range of Persian patterns, and have plenty of strength and vigor in their execution. It is also called a Sarakh. See *Persian Rugs*.

Bilbao In American furniture; the name given to a wall mirror, around 1780–1800,

which is characterized by an elaborately carved and gilded openwork cresting over a rectangular upright frame made from pieces of various colored marbles. The rectangular mirror is enclosed in a gilt molding. It is generally accepted that the mirror derived its name from the Spanish city of Bilbao, from where it was originally shipped to the New England towns.

Bill In arms; a medieval weapon popular in the English infantry during the 15th and 16th centuries. It consisted of a long shaft having a broad blade with a cutting hook, and generally having a long spike at the tip and a short spike at the back. It is believed to have been inspired by the agricultural implement of the same name.

Billet In English pewter and silver; the terms *billet* and *purchase* are applied to the thumbpiece used to raise the lid on a tankard. See *Thumbpiece*.

Billiard Table A large oblong cloth-covered game table with raised padded sides. This game of skill, which is of uncertain origin, was mentioned in French records as early as the 15th century and by the 16th century French inventories included ivory balls and cues as well as tables with green cloth. It appears that by the middle of the 16th century billiards was firmly established in England. The execution of a billiard table due to its precision requirements was restricted to highly skilled cabinetmakers.

Bilsted In American cabinetwork; the wood of the American sweet gum tree, *liquidambar styraciflua*, also called bilsted, was used as a substitute for mahogany because of its pronounced similarity. It was much used during the Revolutionary War when mahogany from the West Indies was not available.

Bilston In English painted enamel; painted enamel work on copper was produced at Bilston as early as 1760 and perhaps earlier. By 1780 there were at least three manufactories operating at Bilston that made painted enamel articles. Bilston enamels were painted in all colors. As a rule the colors were not as refined as those employed at Battersea. A distinctive rose-color, called Rose Pompadour, was a fashionable color after 1760. Small flowers and gilt borders were typical decorations. The enameled articles made at Bilston included such pieces as snuff boxes and patch boxes, étuis, scent bottles, candlesticks and finely modelled toys in the form of birds, animals and fruit. See *Battersea*; *Mirror Knob*.

Binche   In lace-making; the town of Binche enjoyed from early times a fine reputation for lace-making. Due to the trade between the lace-makers of Brussels and Binche, the laces of these two towns had a marked resemblance. Occasionally the Binche laces lacked the lightness and richness of the Brussels laces, and the designs were often more intricate and not as well defined. Especially peculiar to Binche laces was either the omission of a cordonnet or simply one made of a thread scarcely thicker than the toile. Variations of the fond de neige ground were employed in place of the regular réseau ground. Binche laces were apparently quite fashionable in the 18th century. Unfortunately in the following century the lace industry at Binche rapidly declined and from around 1830 they principally produced bobbin-made sprigs of an inferior quality.

Birch   A hard close-grained wood, *betula alba*, which is whitish in color, used in English and American cabinetwork. It was principally used in provincial cabinetwork for legs and spindles as well as for the entire framework of chairs. It was also used to some extent for other articles of furniture. It seems that the North American variety was imported to England during the second half of the 18th century.

Bird Cage   The fashion for exotic birds was widespread in France among the wealthy classes from the time of the Renaissance. Undoubtedly his taste had its origin in Italy where aviaries were a marked feature in the gardens of the magnificent Italian villas.

Bird cages, which remained an important decorative accessory throughout the 19th century, were made of various materials, such as wood, wicker, brass or copper wire, and they were painted, gilded or enhanced with other kinds of decoration. Essentially they followed all the prevailing fashions in their style of ornament. Occasionally some of the very costly and elaborate bird cages simply contained stuffed birds. Of interest were the richly decorative bird cages made in France around the middle of the 18th century for mechanical singing birds.

Bird-Cage Clock   In English furniture; see *Lantern Clock*.

Bird-Cage Support   In English cabinetwork; the name given to a structural feature which was sometimes employed on the tripod tilting-top table that became fashionable in England around 1755. It consists of two small square pieces of wood joined together by four small baluster turned posts. Two parallel pieces of wood on the under side of the table top are attached to the upper part of the bird-cage by a pivot which allows the top to tilt, and the lower part fits over the columnar shaft of the base of the table by means of a round hole to allow the table to revolve. This structural feature also occurred in American cabinetmaking. See *Tea Table*; *Tripod Table*.

Bird-Cup   In German silver; a drinking vessel ingeniously designed in the likeness of a bird, such as a swan, owl, ostrich or partridge. It was introduced during the second half of the 16th century. Silver cups in the form of birds were also made in other countries. Jugs in the form of birds were also made of German stoneware. See *Siegburg*; *Owl Jug*.

Birdseye Maple   In American cabinetwork; *acer saccharinum*; see *Maple*.

Bird Tureen   In ceramics; tureens in the form of a duck, goose or other birds were fashionable during the Rococo style and were made

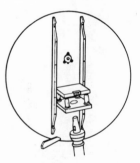

BIRD-CAGE SUPPORT

in faïence at such manufactories as Strasbourg and in porcelain at Meissen and Chelsea.

Biscuit In ceramics; the name applied to porcelain and pottery which has not been glazed, especially to the former. It is also called bisque.

Biscuit Figure In European ceramics; biscuit or unglazed porcelain figures were first made around 1751 at Vincennes and Sèvres. They became very fashionable and were made at many French porcelain manufactories during the latter part of the 18th century. They were also made in Germany. The principal manufactory for biscuit figures in England was Derby. Biscuit figures of soft paste or pâte tendre in distinction to biscuit figures of hard paste porcelain had a remarkable smoothness to the touch and a warm soft tone which gave them much of their charm. It is generally agreed that the soft paste biscuit figures of Sèvres and Vincennes were the most appealing in respect to the beauty of the material. The finest Derby soft paste biscuit dates from about 1790.

Bisette In lace-making; a narrow and coarse bobbin-made lace produced from around the 17th century in the neighborhood of Paris by the peasant women chiefly for their own use. It was made in three qualities, and although proverbially it possessed little value, it was a commercial article among traders.

Bishop Bowl In Danish ceramics; a popular form of pottery or porcelain bowl during the middle of the 18th century was called a bishop bowl. It was in the shape of a bishop's mitre and was often decorated with a drinking party scene. The term *bishop* has been applied in England since early in the 18th century to a sweet drink, of various formulas, the principal ingredients being wine, oranges or lemons and sugar; or mulled and spiced port.

Bisque In ceramics; see *Biscuit*.

Bizen In Japanese ceramics; pottery was produced as early as the 14th century in the old province of Bizen. In particular the name is given to a kind of unglazed hard red pottery much like the Chinese buccaro ware first made toward the end of the 16th century. The ware was made from a clay that fired smooth and hard, at times having a metallic sheen almost resembling bronze. Around the middle of the 17th century they also produced a bluish-brown or slate-colored ware made from a fine hard clay. Both the Ao or blue Bizen and the Aka or red Bizen were modelled into such objects as animals, birds, fishes, Japanese Gods and similar subjects. Realistic and excellent modelling has always been a feature of Bizen ware. The ware was also made into tea ceremony vessels. See *Buccaro*.

Blackamoor In English furniture; the English term applied to the guéridon or candlestand that originated in France around the middle of the 17th century. They were at first imported into England from the Continent and were mentioned in English records as blackamoor stands as early as 1679. See *Guéridon*.

Black Basaltes In English ceramics; see *Basalt Ware*.

Black Figure Ware In Grecian ceramics; the name given to a pottery ware made around 600 B.C. The ware is usually in the shape of one of the characteristic Grecian classical forms. It is characterized by figures painted in black on a light or dark red or yellowish ground and occasionally on a white slip ground. Around 520 B.C. the process was reversed and the ware became known as red figure ware.

Black Glass As a rule the name is given to a kind of glass that varies in color from a very dark green to a very dark purple. It was widely used for making bottles. There also was some black glass actually made. It was in imitation of jet and some of it was fabricated into buttons. In America the term *black glass* is generally given to the dark green variety; however, it is usually accepted that

BLACKAMOOR

some of the black variety was produced in America.

Black Gold Ware In Chinese ceramics; see *Mirror Black*.

Blacking Bottle In American glass; a small 18th and 19th century bottle that is generally four-sided with a short wide neck. It was used to hold blacking for shoes and boots.

Black Jack A large English leather vessel. See *Jack*.

Black Pewter In pewter; the name given to a variety of pewter because of its color. It contains 60 parts tin and 40 parts lead. It is a very cheap grade and is used for inexpensive articles such as candle molds. See *Pewter*.

Black Work In embroidery; the name given to a type of embroidery introduced during the reign of Henry VIII which remained fashionable throughout the Elizabethan era. It is reputed to have been introduced in England by Catherine of Aragon and is also called Spanish work. This work was generally done in a fine quality of black silk thread on a white linen ground in the back stitch, chain, satin or buttonhole stitch. Especially favored for the designs were scrolls of vine leaves and bunches of grapes. These designs were not drawn but were executed by the counted thread.

Blanc de Chine In Chinese ceramics; a beautiful white Chinese porcelain ware that is generally best known under its French name of *Blanc de Chine*. It was first made in the Ming period at Tê-Hua in Ch'üan-Chou in the province of Fukien. It is made into such articles as bowls, incense pots and religious figures. The beautifully modeled figures are generally considered to be its finest work. The Chinese goddess, Kwan Yin, was an especially favorite subject. The glaze in Blanc de Chine is united with the body in such a manner that it is difficult to perceive where the one stops and the other starts. The finest Blanc de Chine was made during the Ming dynasty. The glaze was thick and lustrous and had a rich warm glow.

The later glazes have a tendency to be glassy and the glaze is dead white and cold. The Chinese term is *Chien Yao* and also *Pai Tz'u*. See *Fukien*.

Blanket Chest In cabinetwork; see *Mule Chest*.

Blanket Stitch In embroidery; a stitch similar to the buttonhole stitch except that it is worked farther apart and lacks an extra twist of the thread.

Bleeding-Bowl The term *bleeding bowl* is applied in England to a small cup or bowl used in earlier times to receive the blood drawn by surgery. The drawing or letting of blood for medical reasons is mentioned in English records as early as 1430. In English silver; a small shallow bowl or cup about four and one-half inches in diameter with a single pierced flange handle. It resembles the porringer bowl made in America, but it is smaller in size. It was introduced in England around the second quarter of the 17th century. It is generally accepted that the bleeding bowl was made in pottery in England as early as the 16th century.

SILVER BLEEDING-BOWL

Bleu-de-Roi In French ceramics; the blue enamel color employed on Sèvres porcelain. It was invented at Sèvres prior to 1760 by Jean Hellot and supplanted the former underglaze gros bleu. This bleu-de-roi was the first of the family of enamel ground colors employed on porcelains.

Bleu Persan In French ceramics; a name given by a director of the Sèvres porcelain manufactory to the deep blue-ground faïence of Nevers because he thought it was of Persian origin. The color was imitated at Rouen, Delft, Lambeth and other manufactories. The color was probably originally inspired by 17th century Chinese porcelain.

Bleu Turquin Marble A marble from Seravezza, Tuscany. It is a variety of the Italian dove group of marbles. It consists of dove-colored tints and has numerous white markings.

Blind-Earl's Pattern In English ceramics; a pattern comprising rose leaves and birds executed in relief found on Worcester porcelain from around 1760. It was later named after the Earl of Coventry who became blind in 1780.

Blind Tooling A decorative method used in leather work and bookbinding in which designs or lettering are produced on the leather surface by stamping, embossing or by a tool. In this process, which is said to be blind or in blind, the impressions are plain and without any gold or color being added. See *Stamped Leather*.

Block-Front In American cabinetwork; the name *block-front* is given to certain articles of furniture made in America from about 1750 to 1780 that were distinguished by a singular feature of design. The pieces of furniture made with block-fronts were chiefly chests of drawers, slant-front desks, secretary cabinets, chests-on-chests and kneehole dressing tables or writing tables. In a block-front article of furniture the drawer was cut in such a manner as to form a raised flat surface at each end and a depressed flat surface in the center. As a rule the block-front was cut from a single thick piece of wood. However, the raised flat surface was sometimes attached by means of glue. Except for the block-front feature of design these articles essentially followed the style of the contemporary unblocked articles. The Chippendale style was in vogue in America from about 1755 to 1785. Practically all the block-front articles of furniture were made in New England and the finest in quality of design and workmanship were made in Newport, Rhode Island. It is generally accepted that the block-front furniture is an American innovation in design and that it was originally developed in the cabinet shops of John Townsend and John Goddard at Newport. As a rule block-front furniture was made of solid mahogany. See *Goddard, John*; *Townsend, John*.

Block-Tin Ware See White Iron Ware.

CHIPPENDALE BLOCK-FRONT
CHEST OF DRAWERS

Blonde de Caën In French lace-making; it is generally accepted that the bobbin-made silk blonde laces produced at Caën were remarkable for their workmanship, brilliance and lightness and were surpassed only by those made at Chantilly. The reputation of Caën blondes is due to the brilliant white silks which were first successfully prepared there. In the typical Blonde de Caën the design of flowers was worked in a different silk from that used for the mesh ground or réseau, which was the fond simple or Lille type of ground. The design was outlined in a thick silk thread. The lace-workers at Caën also made the Chantilly blondes. Due to the competition of machine-made blondes produced at Calais and Nottingham, the manufacture of white blondes was given up by the Caën lace-makers, who in more recent times made a black lace and also gold and silver blondes sometimes enriched with pearls. See *Chantilly*; *Blonde Lace*.

Blonde de Fil See *Mignonette Lace*.

Blonde Lace In French lace-making; blonde lace was first introduced in 1745. Since the silk originally used for these laces was of a natural or pale straw color they were known as blondes. These lustrous blonde laces were bobbin-made with a mesh ground. See *Blonde de Caën*; *Chantilly*.

Blonde Mate In French lace-making; the French term for the bobbin-made silk blonde laces characterized by rich and heavy floral designs on a mesh ground. They appealed especially to the Spanish taste and were widely exported to Spain and Mexico for mantillas in the 19th century. Blondes Mates were made at Chantilly, Bayeux and Caën. It is generally accepted that those made in Spain were inferior in workmanship and design.

Bloodstone See *Quartz*.

Bloodwood The wood of various kinds of trees; such as some *eucalypti* of Australia, the logwood of the West Indies and the crape-myrtle of the East Indies. The woods are hard and their color is red. It is used in cabinetwork.

Blown-Molded In glass; a term applied to articles of glass blown in a mold. The mold was used for giving shape to a glass vessel and for impressing a design on its surface. See *Free-Blown Glass*.

Blown Three Mold In American glass; the term *blown three mold* is applied to an article of glass produced by blowing in a mold which was approximately the size of the finished piece. The hinged metal mold, which contained a pattern in intaglio on the inside, consisted of two or more sections although the majority were of three sections. Some articles received their complete form from these molds but usually their final form was created after this process. A characteristic feature of this method is the indentations on the inner side of the glass which correspond to the convex portions of the pattern on the outer surface. These were caused by the force of blowing whereas in an article of pressed glass this inner surface is found to be smooth. This blown-molded process produces a more pleasing effect in the pattern impressions than those of pressed glass, as well as more brilliance. The force of blowing glass in a mold generally caused a thin line to form where the sections of the mold met and the number of these lines determines the number of sections in the mold.

Blue and White Ch'ing In Chinese ceramics; the Chinese technique in the production of blue and white on porcelain is unrivalled. The porcelain body of the Chinese ware to which underglaze blue is applied is only dried, while in other countries it is hardened in a kiln. The blue is mixed with water and painted on with a brush. Then the glaze is applied and the piece is placed in the kiln to be fired. The K'ang Hsi blue and white ware which is held in such high esteem is executed with the finest technical workmanship. The body of this ware is white and has a fine texture. It is finely potted. The blue pigment is carefully prepared and the glaze is made as clear as possible. The blue in the inferior pieces is not so fine. It is duller and generally reflects a trace of red or deep violet-blue tint. The painted decoration is first outlined faintly, and then is carefully filled in, in varying tones, which at times resemble marbling and ice crackling. Sometimes the design is in reserve on a blue ground. Blue and white wares were also produced in the Yung Chêng period, the Chien Lung, and the later eras, but the work was progressively inferior to the K'ang Hsi wares. See *Prunus*; *Ch'ing*; *Blue and White Ming*; *Chinese Soft Paste*.

Blue and White Ming In Chinese ceramics; the blue which was skillfully used by the Chinese in underglaze blue decoration was obtained from the cobaltiferous ore of manganese. Although this mineral was obtainable in certain sections of China it had been imported from the Near East since the time of the T'ang period. During the Ming dynasty the best quality of cobalt was imported from the Near East. The characteristic Chinese blue and white was porcelain. The designs were painted on the unglazed body which was then covered with a glaze and fired. Although Chinese records substantiate that underglaze blue decoration was used during the Sung dynasty, it did not become fashionable until the Ming dynasty. The Sung dynasty favored monochrome glazes. It is generally accepted that blue and white porcelain wares were produced from the beginning of the Ming dynasty, although Chinese records fail to make mention of them before the reign of Yung Lo, 1403–1424. During the Ming dynasty the finest blue and white was made from the imported blue known as Mohammedan blue. Supplies of Mohammedan blue were available during the Hsüan Te reign, 1426–1435, Chêng Tê reign, 1506–1521 and Chia Ching reign, 1522–1566. It is generally believed that the supplies of Mohammedan blue were very low during the Ch'êng Hua reign, 1465–1487, and during

MING BLUE AND WHITE VASE

the Wan Li reign, 1573–1619. See *Ming*; *Blue and White Ch'ing*; *Mohammedan Blue*.

Blue-Dash Charger In English ceramics; the name generally given to the faïence dishes painted in majolica colors made during the 17th and 18th centuries at Lambeth and Bristol. These dishes are generally characterized by a border of slanting lines or dashes.

Blue John A variety of colored fluorspar. See *Derbyshire Spar*.

Blunderbuss In arms; a short gun or pistol introduced into England from the Continent during the latter part of the 16th century. It was of large bore with a flaring trumpet-shaped mouth and could hold many balls at one time. It was used by civilians as a protection as well as by guards on stage coaches.

Boat Bed In French furniture; see *Lit en Bateau*.

Bobbin Lace Or Pillow Lace. The name given to lace made with the aid of small bobbins around which the thread is wound. The pillow, which is a round or oval board padded to form a cushion, rests on the knees of the lace-maker. A piece of parchment pricked through with small holes to form the design is fastened to the pillow and pins are stuck in some of these holes to guide the threads. The ground is formed by twisting and crossing the threads, and the pattern is formed by interweaving a thread much thicker than the ground thread. The work progresses very slowly since fifty bobbins are generally used in making one square inch and lace of one inch in width will have 625 meshes to every square inch. See *Lace*.

Bobbin Net A machine to make a plain thread net was invented in 1768, and the invention is generally credited to Hammond, a stocking framework knitter of Nottingham, England. Although improvements were made on the machine it was capable of knitting only a single thread, and if the thread broke the net unravelled. In 1809 John

CHELSEA-DERBY GROUP
WITH BOCAGE BACKGROUND

Heathcoat, of Longwhatton, invented the machine for making bobbin net. The machine produced a twisted net in place of the earlier looped net. The net was called bobbin net because the threads were wound upon bobbins. It is not to be confused with the earlier handmade bobbin or pillow net. In 1818 the first power machines were put in operation.

Bobêche The French name given to a round cup at the base of a candle, candlestick or chandelier, usually made of glass, to catch the candle drippings. It is also the socket of a candlestick that holds the candle.

Bobéchon A French term applied to a small flat iron disc fitted with a bobêche or candle socket. It has a flat piece of iron, joined horizontally to the disc, that tapers to a point so it could be used either as a handle or it could be stuck into a wall.

Bocage In ornament; the French word *bocage*, or little wood, is applied to a decorative design of trees, branches and foliage or a scene of wooded landscape such as was extensively used in tapestry work. In ceramics; it is also used to describe a background effect of foliage, trees and flowers affixed to porcelain figures or groups.

Boccaro See *Buccaro*.

Boggle The name given to a kind of Scotch vessel, generally a pitcher or a jug, shaped in the likeness of a man.

Bog Wood A variety of wood used in cabinetwork. It is characterized by a lustrous ebony or black color, having been preserved in a peat bog. Bog oak is usually the most common variety. Bog oak was one of the woods commonly used in inlay work in English furniture during the Elizabethan style. Holly and poplar were used for the lighter tones and bog oak for the darker tones.

Bohemian Glass The name given to a colorless potash-lime glass first made in the latter part of the 17th century. It was originally made to imitate Venetian glass; however, when it was finally developed, it was more colorless than Venetian glass. Bohemian glass was especially suitable for the reception of cut and engraved decoration in which German glassmakers rapidly excelled. The method of making ruby glass from gold chloride was rediscovered in the second half of the 17th century. See *Glass*; *Engraved Glass*; *Cut Glass*; *Doppelwandglas*; *Milch Glass*; *German Glass*; *Ruby Glass*.

Boîte à Farine   In French Provincial cabinetwork; see *Boîte à Sel*.

Boîte à Gaufre   The name given to a small rectangular French Provincial wood box used to hold honey-combs. In one characteristic variety the four sides are made of turned wood spindles and the top is of spindles with a finial in the center for a handle.

Boîte à Sel   In French Provincial cabinetwork; the small boîte à sel or salt box and the small boîte à farine or flour box with their naïve carved decoration executed in a peasant manner were often quite pleasing pieces of provincial work. Especially interesting were the different pairs of salt and flour boxes made in Provence in the Louis XV style designed with a high openwork cresting by which they were secured to the wall. The base was valanced and curved into very short cabriole legs. Each box was fitted with a hinged sloping lid and some had a narrow drawer directly above the base.

Bokhara   In Oriental rugs; the province of Bokhara in Turkestan is a great trade center as well as an important center for the weaving of rugs. See *Afghan Bokhara*; *Katchlie Bokhara*; *Khiva Bokhara*; *Tekke Bokhara*.

Bolection   In cabinetwork; a molding which projects above the surface of a panel. As a rule the term is generally applied to moldings which are characterized by an outward sweep and are of ogee contour.

Bombard   The name given to a large drinking vessel usually made of leather and extensively used in England during the 17th and 18th centuries. It has a leather handle and usually the body is round with the lower portion being bulbous-shaped. It is a kind of tankard, large jack or black jack.

Bombay Furniture   In cabinetwork; a term applied to the pieces of furniture made chiefly in Bombay, India, from the shisham wood or blackwood. Much of the furniture has been copied from the Dutch and it is often heavy in form. However, some of the smaller pieces, such as small tables, flower stands and boxes are well formed and have graceful lines. It is notable for the lace-like quality of its carving; for its geometrical patterns inlaid with ivory, ebony and wire, and for the suitability of the designs to the purpose of the article of furniture. Often the designs are handed down from father to son and sometimes a cabinetmaker knows only one design which he executes with consummate skill.

Bombé   In French cabinetwork; a French term applied to a vertical surface of an article of furniture, such as a commode, a chest of drawers, or other pieces of a similar variety, that has a rounded surface of convex form. A commode was sometimes both bombé and serpentine-shaped; that is, the body combined both horizontal and vertical curves. This bombé contour was introduced early in the Régence style. It was used throughout the Louis XV style and was gradually improved and perfected. During the Régence style the convex curve was too excessive and was usually placed too low. This bombé form was used in England during the Chippendale style, especially on commodes designed in the French taste. See *Kettle Shape*.

LOUIS XV BOMBÉ AND SERPENTINE-SHAPED COMMODE

Bonbonnière   A small decorative box used to hold sweetmeats or comfits derived from the French word *bonbon* meaning sweetmeat. In France these sweetmeat boxes were often elaborately designed in gold, silver or tortoise shell inlaid with gold and encrusted with jewels. Since about 1770 the name *bonbonnière* was generally applied to these boxes and as such they are mentioned in French records as early as 1772.

Bone China Or Bone Porcelain. In English ceramics; a ware having as an ingredient in its porcelain composition the ash of calcined bones, which is pure white in color. A patent for using bone ash was taken out by Thomas Frye of Bow in 1748, which date marks its first known actual use. Later bone ash was combined in England to form a hybrid paste containing china clay and stone. This hybrid bone ash paste was covered with a lead glaze and was introduced by Spode at Stoke-on-Trent and by Barr at Worcester late in the 18th century. This became the standard English body during the 19th century and is still being used at the present time. Bone porcelain or bone china is softer than hard paste. It is more durable and less expensive to make than soft paste. See *Soft Paste*; *Porcelain*.

Bone Glass A milky white-colored glass. The whitish color is caused by the presence of calcium phosphate or bone ash in the glass.

Bone Lace In English lace-making; the origin of the term *bone lace*, meaning pillow or bobbin-made lace, has never been conclusively ascertained, although it is generally accepted that the term was derived from the custom of using sheep's trotters before the introduction of wooden bobbins. Another theory based on Devonshire tradition states that the lace-workers being near the sea used fish bones for pins. In some 17th century inventories both bone lace and bobbin lace were listed in the same inventory. The term *bone lace* continued to be used in England until almost the end of the 18th century.

Bonheur du Jour In French cabinetwork; a French desk designed for feminine use. It was introduced about 1750 and was very fashionable during the Louis XVI period. It has a small oblong recessed superstructure designed with doors which are often of tambour construction and which open to a series of small drawers and compartments. The top is usually surmounted with marble and a three-quarter pierced metal gallery. The table generally has either a hinged writing lid or a pull-out writing board. Occasionally the narrow frieze drawer contains a writing panel in tooled leather. The table is designed with four slender legs.

Bonnetière In French Provincial cabinetwork; the name given to a form of tall and narrow wardrobe or armoire introduced around the middle of the 17th century, generally designed with a long panelled cupboard door. Essentially it resembled the characteristic armoire designed with two long panelled doors, but the bonnetière was only about one half as wide. Some of the early bonnetières were designed with two short cupboard doors, often having a narrow drawer separating the two doors. The bonnetière designed in the Louis XV style with a molded arched cornice and a valanced base curving into very short cabriole legs was especially popular. See *Armoire*; *Cupboard*.

Bonnet Top In American cabinetwork; the name often given to a form of hooded top having the contour of a scrolled or swan neck pediment. Its cleft extended partially or completely from the front to the rear. The opening centered a low plinth upon which was usually surmounted a decorative ornament. The bonnet top was a feature of the Queen Anne style. It was principally found on the highboy, the chest-on-chest and other articles of a similar nature. See *Hooded*.

Bookcase In English cabinetwork; an article of domestic furniture fitted with shelves and used for storing and displaying bound books. It was usually enclosed with glazed doors. Movable bookcases were rather rare until around the 18th century. Prior to that time the bookcases as a rule were built into the wall panelling of a room. A typical and popular 18th century bookcase had an upper section fitted with two glazed doors over a lower section fitted with two cupboard doors. This form of bookcase was essentially

BONNET TOP

similar in design to the typical 18th century china cabinet. One type of Early Georgian bookcase was very massive and was treated in a majestic architectural manner in the style of William Kent. *See Break-Front Bookcase; Break-Front Secretary Bookcase; Secretary Bookcase; Bibliothèque.*

Book-Rest In English cabinetwork; a portable book-rest to support a folio volume was an important accessory in the 18th century English library. It was of light framework with turned crosspieces and the upper bar was supported by a ratchet easel. As a rule the book-rest was made of mahogany and was relatively plain. A piece of similar construction was frequently incorporated in the design of the library table or architect's table.

Bordeaux In French ceramics; a faïence manufactory was started at Bordeaux by Jacques Fautier and Jacques Hustin in 1711 and was in operation until 1783. No factory mark was used. To a large extent the finest production of this manufactory was adopted versions of the faïence made at Moustiers, Nevers and Rouen. The greater part of the wares produced here was without distinction and consisted chiefly of dishes and plates painted in a simple manner.

Bordeaux A French porcelain manufactory was founded by Pierre Verneuilh in 1781 at Bordeaux. In 1787, it passed to the ownership of Alluaud and Vanier. The accepted marks are: two "V's" joined as a "W"; "AV" in monogram in circle, the upper part of which was enclosed in a semi-circle with the inscription "Bordeaux." It made a fine-quality ware for table service. The decorative motifs employed included foliage festoons in the style of Louis XVI, and strewn flowers, such as yellow daisies, cornflowers and pansies. The wares closely resembled those of Paris.

Bori In Japanese sword mounts; the name *bori* is applied to the art of carving. Various types of bori are used on the beautifully decorated sword fittings. These include relief carving in various forms, incised chisel-ling and engraving. See *Guri Bori; Kata-Kiri-Bori; Kebori; Niku-Bori; Sukashi-Bori.*

Borne In French cabinetwork; an upholstered round or oval French salon seat designed to accommodate several persons. It has a cone-shaped or cylinder-shaped backrest in the center.

Boss In ornament; a circular protuberant ornament applied on the surface as a decorative motif. It was often richly carved, generally with a conventional leaf or flower design. It was also called a turtle-back. A feature of Early Jacobean cabinetwork was the occasional use of split turnings and bosses applied to the surface of furniture for decorative purposes. They were often stained black. See *Prunt.*

Bosse, Abraham 1602-1676. A prominent French architect, designer, painter and engraver, noted particularly for his decorative work. Many of his compositions were inspired by the works of Callot.

Boston Rocking Chair In American cabinetwork; the name is applied to a variety of rocking chair. It has a wooden seat which has a downward curve along the front part and an upward curve along the back part. It has a high back fitted with vertical spindles surmounted by a flat crest rail. The chair was evolved from the Windsor chair. It is of American origin and was introduced about 1840.

Böttger, Johann Friedrich 1682-1719. Celebrated German alchemist and ceramic technician. In 1708 he started the Dresden faïence manufactory. He invented and perfected in 1708-1709 a fine red stoneware which was hard enough to be polished on the lapidary's wheel. It resembled the Chinese buccaro ware of Yi-hsing. The ware is known by his name. In 1708 he made the first true or hard paste porcelain in Europe and in 1709 he produced a suitable glaze for it. In 1710 the Elector of Saxony established the Meissen manufactory and appointed

BOSTON ROCKING CHAIR

Böttger as manager. See *Meissen*; *Porcelain*; *Buccaro Ware*, in Chinese Ceramics.

Bottle Glass A term applied to green glass. See *Green Glass*.

Boucher, François 1703–1770. A celebrated French painter and decorative designer. He was a principal exponent of the Rococo style and a prolific inventor of decorative fantasies in the Rococo manner. He also invented numerous fantastic chinoiseries which are closely related to the Rococo style and which were a favorite decoration on furniture, porcelains, lacquered woodwork, silver and fabrics. His designs were adapted for popular use through the works of contemporary engravers. See *Rococo*; *Louis XV*; *Tapestry*.

Boudeuse In French cabinetwork; an upholstered French salon seat designed to accommodate several persons. It has double seats with one back-rest joining them.

Bouffioulx In ceramics; much stoneware in imitation of the Rhenish stoneware was made at Bouffioulx, in Belgium, and at Châtelet, Namur, Dinant and other places in the Walloon country from the late 16th century. Among their earlier wares were the characteristic Bartmann jugs and distinctive flattened circular pilgrim flasks decorated with applied medallion reliefs. Later types of wares were in imitation of Westerwald wares. They included jugs and tankards with blue and purple coloring and cut decoration.

Bougeoir In French accessories; a small candlestick made in a variety of forms resting on a foot or base, or on a tray provided with a handle for carrying. The name is derived from the French word *bougie* meaning a wax candle. The term *bougeoir* as applied to a small candlestick appears as early as 1586 in the inventory of Marie Stuart as "un bougeoir d'argent doré," and in l'Inventaire de Gabrielle d'Estrées in 1599 as "a bougeoir of silver and silver gilt for attaching to the bedstead." See *Bougie Box*.

Bougie Box In silver; a small cylindrical container that holds a coil of wax taper, the

BOUILLOTTE LAMP

end of which passes through an opening in the lid of the box. The term *bougie* means a wax candle. It derived its name from a town in North Africa where these candles were made and exported to Europe. It was introduced during the 18th century. See *Bougeoir*.

Bouilloire Or *Bouillotte*. In French silver; the tea kettle or bouilloire mounted on a spirit burner or rechaud became popular in France when tea was introduced, which seems to coincide more or less with its introduction in England. However, tea drinking as a social custom was never developed to the same degree in France as in England. In the 19th century the term *bouillotte* was generally applied to a tea kettle of faïence or pottery, while the term *bouilloire* was reserved for a tea kettle made of metal.

Bouillotte A French tea kettle. See *Bouilloire*.

Bouillotte Lamp The name given to a variety of brass or bronze doré French table lamp. It has a dish-shaped base that supports a shaft fitted with two or three candle brackets and a metal shade which is often painted a very dark green. The shaft is surmounted with a finial. The height of the candle brackets and shade can be adjusted by means of screw keys. It was introduced late in the 18th century. The bouillotte lamp is depicted in the literature of French furniture placed in the center of a bouillotte table with persons seated around the table playing the card game of bouillotte.

Bouillotte Table In French cabinetwork; the name given to a kind of French card table which was used for playing the card game of bouillotte. It was introduced during the style of Louis XVI. It has a circular white marble top with a pierced brass gallery over a conforming narrow frieze fitted with two small drawers and two pull-out slides. It is mounted on four straight tapered legs. The diameter of the top averages about 26 inches. In addition to its use as a card and game table, it seems that the

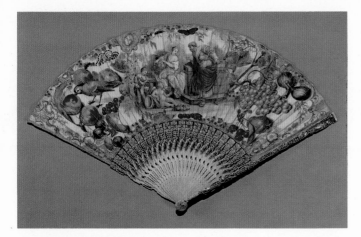

FAN—*Italian, 18th Century.*
The Metropolitan Museum of Art, gift of Mrs. William Randolph Hearst, 1963.

GILT BRONZE AND SÈVRES PORCELAIN CLOCK—*French, 18th Century.*
The Metropolitan Museum of Art, gift of The Samuel H. Kress Foundation, 1958.

COFFER ON STAND, WITH SÈVRES PORCELAIN PLAQUES—*French, 18th Century.*
The Metropolitan Museum of Art, gift of The Samuel H. Kress Foundation, 1958.

BATTERSEA ENAMEL SNUFF-BOX—*English, 18th Century.*
The Metropolitan Museum of Art, bequest of Mary Clark Thompson, 1924.

bouillotte table was also sometimes used as a tea table and probably for other serving purposes, since it was a very practical and adaptable table. *See Card Table.*

Boulle, André Charles 1642–1732. The leading cabinetmaker of the Louis XIV era and the most celebrated member of a distinguished family of ébénistes. The different members of this family are probably the best known of French marqueteurs. Their greatest artistic achievements were acquired in the marquetry of metals and tortoise shell combined with beautifully sculptured bronze mounts. Boulle did not originate this form of marquetry; however, he did bring this art to its highest perfection and his name is generally given to this kind of marquetry. In this work very thin layers of brass and tortoise shell of equal thickness were glued together and designs of arabesques and other motifs were traced on the surface. These ornaments were cut out with a fine saw and produced exact corresponding pieces in the two materials, which could then be counterchanged. In other words the ground was both in tortoise shell and brass and the ornament was also duplicated. The tortoise shell ground and the brass ornament were glued on the wooden foundation. This was described as inlay of "the first part," as distinct from the "counter inlay" which was the reverse combination of the materials. The inlay of "the first part" was regarded as the more artistic and was therefore the more desired. Usually on a piece of furniture both "the first part" and the "counter part" were combined. Occasionally Boulle placed gold leaf or a similar material beneath the tortoise shell to make it more brilliant. Sometimes in this form of marquetry very thin layers of wood of the exact thickness as the brass were used in place of the tortoise shell. This marquetry of brass and tortoise shell was particularly used on oblong tables, cabinets, commodes, tall case clocks and bracket clocks, and was admirably suited to the sumptuous Louis XIV style interiors. It seems that Boulle occupied twenty work-

shops at the Louvre. In addition to numerous contemporary imitators, his work was carried on by his four sons. Toward the end of the 18th century French ébénistes, such as Montigny and Jacob, made fine reproductions of the original models. The artistic perfection in the original Boulle work was never duplicated in any of the subsequent work, and authenticated pieces by Boulle are ranked among the furniture treasures of the world.

Boulton, Matthew 1728–1809. He was the outstanding English producer of fine articles and mounts in ormolu. He opened a manufactory at Soho, near Birmingham, in 1762 in partnership with John Fothergill. He supplied many of the wealthy homes with fine clocks, cassolettes, vases and candelabra all handsomely mounted in ormolu. He also produced large quantities of finely chased ormolu mounts which were applied to furniture. Due to his interest in other enterprises his work began to deteriorate early in the last quarter of the 18th century. At his manufactory at Soho, he also produced Sheffield and silver plate as well as ormolu clocks and other decorative articles. Although he did not introduce the principle of the silver thread edge, which concealed the copper between the layers of silver on Sheffield plate, he developed the technique to a great degree of perfection and excelled in its use. His Sheffield plate made in partnership with Fothergill is highly prized. See *Ormolu.*

Bourg-La-Reine In French ceramics; see *Mennecy.*

Bout de Pied In French cabinetwork; a French term, meaning foot end, is given to the lower part of the duchesse brisée. See *Duchesse Brisée.* The term in a general sense may be applied to any small article of furniture drawn up to a chair to form a chaise longue.

Bow In English ceramics; it is generally believed that the Bow manufactory in east London was established in 1744 by Thomas Frye and Edward Heylyn. Some of the best

LOUIS XIV CABINET
WITH MARQUETRY
BY BOULLE

English porcelain in a rather unsophisticated style was produced here around 1750 and 1760 and later. Frye was manager until 1759. Weatherby, d. 1762, and John Crowther became the owners; the latter declared bankruptcy in 1763. It is assumed that the manufactory was aided by William Duesbury who transferred the models and molds to Derby around 1775–1776. There was no factory mark on the early wares. From around 1760–1765 an anchor and a dagger in red is rather common on wares assumed to have been made at Bow. The wares believed to have been made before 1750 have little artistic merit. For the next ten years a soft paste porcelain, of varying quality, apparently having bone ash as an ingredient, was made. The best material was similar to Mennecy porcelain. The figures were chiefly copied from Meissen, as well as the useful wares. Vases in the Rococo style with applied leaves and flowers and with Rococo masks were most charming. Underglaze blue painting was practiced but it was without distinction. Figures of birds were notable for their fine coloring. The later productions, which were frequently marked with the anchor and dagger, reveal quite a decline in quality. The material was full of imperfections and of a dull tone. The figures, which were poorly painted, occasionally revealed good modelling. The figures, vases, and tablewares were mostly copied from other English factories as well as these factories' marks. See *Bone China*.

Bow-Back   In English and American cabinetwork; the name given to a type of Windsor chair. In this variety the back is a continuous bent piece of wood and is joined to the seat or to the horseshoe-shaped arm rail, and is fitted with several vertical slender spindles. It is also called a Hoop-Back. See *Windsor Chair*.

Bow-Front   In cabinetwork; a term given to a front of an article of furniture, such as a commode, chest of drawers or other pieces of a similar variety, that gently swells with a convex curve from one side to the other.

HEPPLEWHITE BOW-FRONT
CHEST OF DRAWERS

Sometimes it is also called swell front. See *Serpentine Front*.

Bowknot   In ornament; a decorative motif that consists of a knot with loops. Graceful bowknots of ribbons and streamers were very fashionable during the Louis XVI style and were effectively used to hold the flowers in position on panels.

Bowl   In Chinese ceramics; in useful or daily wares the bowl or wan is found in numerous sizes and shapes. Undoubtedly the most common is the small rice bowl or kung wan. A shallower form of bowl, called t'ang wan, was used for soup. The tea bowl or ch'a wan was furnished with a cover. When drinking tea, the cover was slightly tilted to form a narrow opening in order to keep the tea leaves in the bowl. After the introduction of the teapot, which apparently was not before the Ming dynasty, the tea cup or ch'a pei without a cover or handle was generally used. It seems that vessels with spouts and handles before the Ming dynasty were used as wine pots or for other liquids. A tiny bowl is the customary form for a wine cup, although goblets with deep bowls and with shallow or tazza-shaped bowls resting on tall stems were also used. Ceremonial wine cups used for weddings and libations were similar in shape to the bronze ritual vessels. See *Cup Stand*.

Box   A box is defined as a case or receptacle generally fitted with a lid. Originally the name was given to a small container made of any material for drugs, ointments or valuable possessions. From around 1700 the term was extended to include larger receptacles designed to contain different kinds of personal property. It is generally understood unless it is otherwise designated that a box is made of wood and has four sides. A box is one of the earliest forms of furniture and it probably came into existence about the same time as a chest, from which it is distinguished only by its size. The quality of workmanship found in a box varies from the most perfected craftsmanship of the goldsmith to the simplest kind of cabinetwork. Boxes were made in every conceivable material and their surface was enriched with every decorative art process as well as with precious stones. The uses of boxes during the 18th century were innumerable and they range from plain boxes for gloves to the exquisite gold nécessaire.

Box Stretcher   In cabinetwork; a continuous rectangular stretcher, generally near the floor, that connects the legs of chairs or tables. It is an early form of a stretcher. See *Wainscot Chair*; *Caquetoire*.

Boxwood   See *Buis Wood*.

Brace-Back Chair   In cabinetwork; the term is applied to a wooden chair, especially a Windsor chair, that has a portion of the rear of the wooden seat extending beyond the back to which is fitted two slender spindles that are secured in the crest rail of the back thus forming a brace or support.

Bracket   In English cabinetwork; see *Wall Bracket*.

Bracket Base   In cabinetwork; see *Bracket Foot*.

Bracket Clock   In English furniture; after the short pendulum was introduced in 1658 by Fromanteel small clocks of the so-called bracket or table variety appeared in ever increasing numbers. One principal variety around 1680 had a square-fronted squat case with a domed top of either wood or pierced metal. The dome top, which was fitted with a metal handle in order to facilitate carrying it about, was often referred to as a basket top. The case was wood and it was most often either ebony or walnut, and it was decorated with elaborately pierced mounts of brass. It was mounted on small feet. This variety, with some variations in design, was produced throughout the 18th century and early 19th century and was decorated in the contemporary style. Later models sometimes had a finial in place of the metal handle. It is said that the name was derived from the fact that some of the later

18th century models had separate brackets designed with the clock to be attached to the wall for the reception of the clock. See *Clock*; *Balloon Clock*.

Bracket Foot   In English and American cabinetwork; the bracket foot is so called because it somewhat resembled the shape of a bracket. There are three principal kinds of bracket feet. In their order of introduction in cabinetwork they are straight bracket, ogee bracket and French bracket. The straight bracket foot is characterized by a straight corner edge. The ogee bracket foot has the contour of a cyma curve with the convex curve at the top. In the French bracket foot the corner edge curves out slightly and the inner edge is designed in a long curve. Bracket feet are principally used on chests of drawers, secretary cabinets, slant-front desks, tall case clocks, bookcases and other pieces of a similar nature. See *Foot*.

Bradburn, John   d. 1781. English cabinetmaker to George III. He succeeded William Vile as cabinetmaker to the Crown in 1764 and held this position until he retired in 1777. Between the years of 1764 and 1777 in the capacity of cabinetmaker and carver he supplied considerable furniture to the Royal household. It can be deduced from his accounts that his speciality was carving with much decorative detail. Unfortunately it has been impossible to locate any of this elaborately carved work except for a clock case made for George III. His cabinet shop was located in Hemings Row in St. Martin's Lane and it seems that in 1767 he moved his shop to No. 8 Long Acre. See *Vile, William*.

Bradshaw, George Smith   English cabinetmaker and upholsterer working at Greek Street, Soho, in 1756. He was in partnership with Paul Saunders. This partnership was dissolved in 1756, and Saunders was later found in business at Soho Square at the corner of Sutton Street. John Mayhew, who later was a partner in the firm of Ince and Mayhew, served an apprenticeship with Mr. Bradshaw. He was working for him in 1756.

STRAIGHT BRACKET FOOT

OGEE BRACKET FOOT

FRENCH BRACKET FOOT

Bradshaw, William English cabinetmaker working around 1736 to 1750. He is regarded as an important and well-known cabinetmaker of the mid-Georgian era.

Braguette In armor; see *Brayette*.

Brand Dogs Another term for andirons. See *Andirons*.

Brandewijnkom In silver; an oval silver bowl designed with two handles. It was used on festive occasions when it was filled with raisins saturated in brandy. It is principally identified with old Dutch silver and was introduced in the 17th century.

Brandy Snuffer In glassware; a short stemmed, bulbous-shaped glass that tapers towards the rim, used for snuffing and drinking brandy. It is also called a balloon glass.

Brandy Warmer In English silver; a small cylindrical silver bowl resembling a small saucepan, fitted with a long straight handle with a turned wood hand grip. It was introduced around the beginning of the 18th century.

Brasses In furniture mounts; the handles, back plates and their fittings are frequently referred to collectively as brasses.

Bratina The name given to a Russian drinking cup that is generally globular in form with a contracted lip. It is designed either with or without a cover. It was often made of gold or silver and frequently enriched with precious stones. The bratina which the peasants used was usually made of wood or copper.

Brayette In armor; a piece attached to armor to protect the groin. It was in the form of a plate cod-piece or a breech of mail. Also called *Braguette*.

Brazier A metal pan or receptacle to hold burning charcoal that was used principally in the East and in southern Europe to provide heat. The brazier was often richly decorated. Braziers are first mentioned in England and France circa 1690.

GEORGE II
SILVER BRANDY WARMER

Brazilwood See *Sapan Wood*.

Bread and Cheese Cupboard In English cabinetwork; an early English bedroom cupboard. See *Livery Cupboard*.

Bread Trough In cabinetwork; a large oblong flaring bin or box that rests on short legs or feet. It is the same as a kneading table or trough, a maie or a pétrin. See *Maie*; *Hutch*.

Breakfast Table In English cabinetwork; the custom of having breakfast served in the bedroom led to the introduction of the small mahogany breakfast table around the middle of the 18th century. It was designed to correspond with the furniture in the bedroom. One characteristic variety had an oblong top with drop-leaves. The frieze was fitted with a narrow drawer and it rested on four slender straight legs. Essentially it was usually a rather plain piece of furniture. Its average length when the leaves were raised was slightly less than 3 feet. Later in the 18th century the Pembroke table was often used as a breakfast table. The slender legs were generally fitted with brass toe caps and casters. See *Pembroke Table*.

Break-Front In cabinetwork; the term is applied to a feature in cabinetwork in which the front is "broken" and extends slightly forward from the side sections, such as in a break-front bookcase.

Break-Front Bookcase In English cabinetwork; it is the same as a break-front secretary bookcase except that it is not designed with any writing facilities. See *Break-Front Secretary Bookcase*; *Break-Front*.

Break-Front Secretary Bookcase In English cabinetwork; the mahogany break-front secretary bookcase was a characteristic and popular piece of furniture during the second half of the 18th century. The upper section with its projecting central portion was fitted with four glazed doors which enclosed adjustable shelves for the reception of books. The lower section, which also had a projecting central portion, was designed with four wood cupboard doors which were surmounted by two lateral drawers and a central fall-front pull-out fitted writing drawer. This drawer when open had a tooled leather writing surface and the interior was fitted with small drawers and pigeonholes. The lower section rested on a molded plinth base. Variations in design occurred. Occasionally the underbody was designed with two banks of drawers in place of the two lateral cupboard doors. See *Break-Front*.

Breccia   The name is given to a variety of rock made of angular fragments embedded in a stony substance and often having many different colors. Breccia marble when made smooth is widely used for the tops of tables and commodes and also in ornamental work.

Brèche   See *Breccia*.

Bresse   In French Provincial; an old district in eastern France formed by the Saône River on the west and the Rhône River on the south. It originally formed a part of the feudal duchy of Burgundy. The furniture of Bresse like that of Burgundy was characterized by its rather massive construction, by its pronounced use of moldings and by its use of architectural details. A distinctive feature of their cabinetwork for such panelled articles as the buffet-vaisselier was the use of contrasting woods. The framework was often walnut and the panels were of ash or oak. The vaisselier-horloge is especially identified with Bressan cabinetwork. See *French Provincial*.

Bretagne   In French Provincial furniture. See *Brittany*.

Breton   In French Provincial furniture. See *Brittany*.

Breton Bed   In French Provincial furniture; see *Lit Clos*.

Brewster Chair   In American cabinetwork; an armchair belonging to William Brewster, 1560–1644, of the Plymouth Colony, which he is supposed to have brought over with him on the Mayflower. The chair, which is characterized by its turned members and vertical spindles, is now in Pilgrim Hall, Plymouth, Massachusetts. It is a heavy and massive chair of crude construction having an open back with two rows of spindles and four spindles in each row. Each open arm is also filled in with a row of four spindles. On one side there are two rows of four spindles each extending to the floor. In the front and also on the other side beneath the seat there are just the single upper rows of four spindles each. Literature on American furniture states that the chair should have forty spindles but that some are missing. The chair was probably made in England from a Dutch prototype. Chairs of this variety, which are called Brewster chairs, were made in America, particularly in New England, without much change in form except for the number of rows of spindles. The chief difference between the Brewster and Carver chair is that the former has more spindles. See *Carver Chair*.

Bric à Brac   A French term reputed to be formed from the French phrase *de bric et de broc* meaning by hook or by crook. The term is collectively given to old curiosities possessing an artistic quality, such as various antiquarian odds and ends as old furniture, porcelain, plate, glass and similar articles.

Bride Bouclée   In lace-making; see *Bride Picotée*.

Bride Epinglée   In lace-making; see *Bride Picotée*.

Bride Picotée   A French term in lace-making applied to a six-sided buttonhole bar decorated with a little row of three or four loops on each side. It is much used in Argentan lace. It is also called bride bouclée and bride épinglée.

Bride Tortillée   A French term in lace-making given to a bride or tie having a few threads twisted around each mesh instead of the more laborious buttonhole stitching.

Brides   The French name given to the ties in

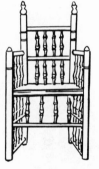

BREWSTER CHAIR

lace-making which connect the different parts of the pattern or toile. See *Ground.*

Brides Ornées A French term in lace-making applied to ties ornamented with picots, loops or pearls.

Bright-Cut In English silver; the name given to a type of engraved design. It is a narrow band consisting of a series of deeply cut zigzag lines engraved around the edge of an article made of silver. It was popular during the late 18th century.

Brinjal Bowl In Chinese ceramics; the name, which is of the same derivation as the word *aubergine*, given to a variety of K'ang Hsi porcelain bowl. The colors employed include both medium-fired glazes and low-fired enamel colors. Especially distinctive is a dark manganese purple glaze used as a ground color with incised flower sprays in leaf-green, pale green and yellow colored enamels. See *Three Color Ware.*

BRISTOL TIN-GLAZED
EARTHENWARE PLATE

Bristol In English porcelain; a soft paste porcelain manufactory was founded around 1750 at Lowdin's glass house and was transferred to Worcester in 1752. In 1770 a hard paste porcelain manufactory was established at Bristol by William Cookworthy, with Richard Champion as manager. It was a continuation of the previous porcelain manufactory at Plymouth. It was purchased by Richard Champion in 1773. Due to financial embarrassment Champion sold his patent for making hard paste porcelain to a group of Staffordshire potters, who continued the manufacture of simply decorated wares at New Hall. The mark while Cookworthy owned the factory was the same as the Plymouth mark, the alchemist's sign for tin; later a cross in blue enamel or gold and a capital "B" in blue were the marks commonly found on tableware. Figures and vases were not so often marked. The porcelain like that of Plymouth was technically imperfect and was often somewhat misshapen. Undoubtedly the best work was the productions by Champion. Many of these

pieces were obviously for presentation. In his work the style of Sèvres predominated. Figure modelling closely imitated Sèvres and Derby figures. Large vases, generally of hexagonal form, decorated with applied flowers were also made. The designs for fine tableware were in the Sèvres style.

Bristol In English pottery; it is generally believed that pottery was probably produced here from medieval times. However the chief claim to fame for Bristol pottery is due to the tin-glazed earthenware produced here during the second half of the 17th century and the 18th century. Several potteries were in operation at Bristol as well as at neighboring Brislington and Wincanton. Edward Ward started a pottery at Water Lane or Temple Back, Bristol, in 1683, which was operated by his family until 1741. It continued to operate at Temple Back under different proprietors until 1884, when new premises were taken, and is still in existence at Fishponds just outside the city of Bristol. No regular factory mark was used on Bristol pottery. It is practically impossible to separate the wares of the Bristol and Brislington potteries, which are in turn very often hard to separate from those of Lambeth of the earlier period and of Liverpool of the later period. The early tin-glazed wares which were made until around 1720 were of the majolica types. After 1720 they were largely supplanted by wares which imitated Chinese porcelains and Delft wares. The forms were similar to the Delft wares. Tiles were also made. Punch bowls painted with ships were made around the middle of the 18th century at Bristol and also at Liverpool. The wares produced at Wincanton were essentially similar to those of Bristol. Toward the last quarter of the 18th century the production of Delft ware types was largely succeeded by cream-colored earthenware. Brown stoneware with Bristol glaze was made in the 19th century.

Bristol In English glass; glassmaking at Bristol achieved its greatest success around 1760 when there were at least fifteen glasshouses in operation. They made all kinds of crystal glass tableware as well as decorative pieces such as vases, decanters and candlesticks in both white and colored glass. Of outstanding interest is the milk glass and the blue glass made at Bristol. The milk glass was made in imitation of porcelain and was painted in enamel colors. The glass was a rich milk white and was as translucent as porcelain. The surface was fine and smooth but not glassy. Especially characteristic of its painted decoration were motifs such as birds and figures treated in an oriental manner and flowers. Bristol milk glass was made into jars, vases, scent bottles, mugs, salt cellars and other similar articles. Michael Edkins, who was known for his painted decoration on Bristol pottery, was one of the artists working on Bristol milk glass from about 1762–1787. The fine blue glass made at Bristol was distinctive for its rich vivid blue coloring and for its brilliancy. Especially lovely was the blue glass decorated with gilding. Mixed colors were also used at Bristol, such as for mugs and flasks marbled with different colors, or splashed with various colored spots or threaded with opaque white to produce alternate stripes or spiral effects. Bristol glass has always been notable for the fine quality of its flint glass, its workmanship and its decoration. See *Glass*; *Paperweight*; *Milch Glass*.

Britannia Metal The term applied to a silver-white metal alloy, which is a pewter of good quality since it does not contain any lead. A good quality Britannia metal is made of 150 parts tins, 10 parts antimony and 3 parts copper; it frequently contains bismuth and zinc. By increasing the amount of tin and lessening the amount of antimony this alloy could be made very thin. Many articles of Britannia metal were made by a process known as spinning. In this process the metal was cast in flat sheets and the parts were formed by pressing the sheets with blunt tools over revolving blocks made in the shape in which the parts were to be finished. This method afforded greater production,

lessened the cost of equipment since no brass molds were needed, and the articles were lighter in weight and could be fashioned with sharper edges. When Britannia ware was cast and not spun and of a thicker grade than usual, it resembled fine pewter ware. It was introduced around 1769. See *Pewter*.

Britannia Standard In English silver; see *Hall-Marks, London*; *Sterling*.

Brittany In French Provincial; an old coastal province in north-western France on the English Channel and the Atlantic Ocean; now the departments of Finistère, Côtes-du-Nord, Morbihan, Ille-et-Vilaine and Loire Inférieure. Breton, the name applied to the natives of Brittany or the things of Brittany, is also the name of an old territory which covered the western half of Brittany, or what is now the departments of Finistère, half of Côtes-du-Nord and half of Morbihan. Much of the provincial furniture of Brittany was simply peasant pieces. As a rule the furniture of Brittany was of heavy proportions and was profusely ornamented with carving in low relief or with other forms of decoration. Turning was a favorite method of decoration. Turned spindles were much in evidence on Breton furniture; such as spindled backs for chairs and spindled galleries on the edge of open wall shelves. The favorite woods were oak, chestnut and cherry. The lit clos or lit demi-clos which is a variety of closed bed is especially characteristic of Breton furniture. It is also called Bretagne. See *French Provinical*; *Lit Clos*.

Broad Glass In glass; see *Crown Glass*.

Broadsword In arms; a sword with a broad, straight blade having only one cutting edge. It was the military sword of the 17th century, the civilian sword being the rapier. It had a basket hilt having a hand guard ornamented with rings and shells.

Brocade In Japanese ceramics; the so-called brocade pattern employed in the painted decoration of a variety of Imari porcelain. See *Nishiki-de*; *Imari*; *Chinese Imari*.

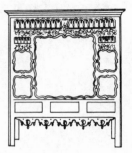

BRETON LIT DEMI-CLOS

Brocade In textiles; a woven silk fabric. The design gives the effect of having been embroidered on top of a rich silk fabric. This embroidery effect is made by floating weft threads on the surface of satin or other weaves. The figures appear to be in slight relief and are usually in several colors. Some of the more elaborate brocades are still woven on hand looms. See *Silk*; *Upholstery*.

Brocaded Damask In textiles; a woven silk fabric. It consists of embroidery effects produced by floating weft threads on the surface of damask, the pattern of which is made to appear in slight relief. See *Brocade*; *Damask*.

Brocatelle In textiles; a heavy damask type of fabric characterized by a firm texture and embossed figures. The figures, which are usually large and definite, are done in a satin weave against a twill background. The characteristic figures stand out in high relief from the background because of the coarse stiff linen or cotton weft threads that are buried beneath the surface. See *Upholstery*.

Broderie Anglaise In embroidery; a variety of beautiful white embroidery of Eastern European origin introduced in England during the Middle Ages. The designs contain an abundance of small and simple detail, and consist of oval and round eyelets executed in a chain stitch, satin stitch and overcast stitch.

BROKEN PEDIMENT

Broderie de Nancy In needlework; a kind of drawnwork often embroidered in colored silk. See *Drawnwork*.

Broken Arch In cabinetwork; see *Broken Pediment*; *Pediment*.

Broken Pediment In cabinetwork; the term is applied to a pediment in which the curved or straight lines are stopped before reaching the top center point. The center space between the broken lines generally has a low plinth surmounted with some decorative motif such as a vase. After the architectural influence began to affect English furniture during the early 18th century the broken pediment was frequently used on bookcases, wardrobes, cabinets and mirrors. See *Pediment*.

Broken Swirl In glassware; the name given to a decorative pattern which is a combination of a vertical-ribbed and a swirled-rib design. The molten glass is inserted into a rib-mold then removed and twisted to make the vertical rib lines oblique. It is then quickly replaced in the rib-mold to receive the vertical lines. The resulting design resembles broken swirled lines.

Bronze An alloy formed entirely of copper and tin or chiefly of copper and tin having small quantities of other elements, such as lead, zinc, phosphorus and silver. See *Sentoku*.

Bronze Doré A name given to gilt bronze. See *Ormolu*.

Bronzes, Chinese Chinese bronzes from earliest times are admirable for their high degree of artistic and technical workmanship. The Chinese were great collectors of bronzes. According to some archaeologists it is doubtful that any extant bronzes are of the Shang dynasty. It is generally accepted with some degree of certainty that bronzes of excellent workmanship were made as early as the 5th century B.C. Bronzes were used for both utilitarian and ceremonial purposes. The color of bronze, which is affected by the varying proportions, ranges from a copper red through lighter reds and golden yellow to nearly silver as is seen in the bronze mirrors. Included among the ceremonial bronzes of the Chou dynasty, 1122–255 B.C., are the ting, a kind of tripod vessel; ku, a form of beaker; chüeh, a tripod libation vessel, and others. The typical early bronze bells, which are flat in section like pointed ellipses, are decorated with projecting bosses. Of interest are the mirrors which seldom if ever are found before Han. The early ones are circular and are simply decorated with geometrical designs. As a rule the reflecting surface was slightly convex, and rarely concave. Some very fine mirrors are identified

CHINESE CERAMIC FORMS

POTICHE
K'ang Hsi

DOUBLE-GOURD VASE
Chia Ching

GINGER JAR
K'ang Hsi

GALLIPOT
K'ang Hsi

CLUB-SHAPED VASE
K'ang Hsi

CUP STAND
Sung

HILL JAR
Han

STEM CUP
Hsüan Tê

TS'UNG
Ming

CLUB-SHAPED SQUARE
VASE *K'ang Hsi*

COUPE
K'ang Hsi

BULB BOWL
Sung, Chün Yao

GRANARY URN
Han

CHINESE BRONZE FORMS

HU
Chou

CHUEH
Chou

TING
Chou

KU *Chou*

YU *Chou*

CHIA *Chou*

CHIU *Chou*

with the T'ang dynasty, A.D. 618–906, and are notable for their artistic workmanship. Bronze became more widely used during the Han dynasty, 206 B.C.–A.D. 220, and fine representations of animals were cast in bronze. During the Six Dynasties, A.D. 265–589, votive figures were cast in gilt bronze and the so-called hill jar was made in bronze from its ceramic prototype. The Chinese made reproductions of many early bronze forms during the Sung dynasty, A.D. 960–1279. Only a few bronzes made during the Ming dynasty, 1368–1644, are laudable. From the end of the Chou dynasty the tendency was to simplify bronze forms and to employ engraved and inlaid decoration in place of the earlier decoration executed in relief. Many bronzes bear inscriptions which in ancient times were cast in the surface like the ornament. The decoration on the early bronzes consisted of imaginary forms and representations, borrowed from the spiritual and animal world, and of a pattern of thin lines worked in the key or fret design. The forms were strongly modelled and were executed in rather high relief. The lines, which were closely spaced in sharp relief, were carved in the surface of the original model from which it was cast in bronze. Other line designs included the diamond or lozenge pattern. In the later bronzes which duplicated this form of decoration the designs were often applied by means of stamps to the molds. They lacked the crisp and sharp quality which was so typical of the earlier method of decoration. Delicate thread lines in relief were worked in bands around the vessels. The head of the ogre was a favorite decorative motif during the Chou dynasty. Decorative bosses or studs were frequently in the form of animal heads. During the Han dynasty and later dynasties gold lines were often inlaid. Confucian, Taoist and Buddhist subjects and emblems and animal figures were popular during the Sung and Ming dynasties. The patina which is acquired naturally over a period of centuries gives bronze a singular character both in color and in texture. Some collectors

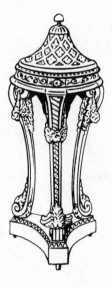

LOUIS XVI BRÛLE PARFUM

prefer the bronzes to remain in the state in which they were excavated. Other collectors prefer a surface which has been carefully worked over. If the patina is thick and is of good color the bronze object may be carefully ground down and polished. A favorite Chinese method is to polish bronze with the hand. Generations of such handling in China have given some bronzes in famous collections a peculiar and beautiful coloring.

Brûle Parfum A French term for perfume burner. See *Cassolette*.

Brummagem A common and unrefined form of the name of the town of Birmingham, England. It was used with disdain or scorn to describe an article made in Birmingham, especially counterfeit coins or groats, which were first coined in England in 1351 and last issued in 1662. Counterfeit groats coined at Birmingham are mentioned in 17th century records. The term was later extended to include plated and lacquered wares manufactured at Birmingham which were not genuine. Cheap and showy articles imitating similar articles of fine quality and material were also frequently described as brummagem. A record of 1853 refers to a work table inlaid with brass "in that peculiar taste which vulgarly is called brummagem."

Brunkessi A kind of drinking vessel. See *Biberon*.

Brunswick In German ceramics; a faïence manufactory was started by Duke Anton Ulrich of Brunswick with Johann Philipp Frantz as manager in 1707. In 1710 it was leased to von Horn who took von Hantelmann as a partner in 1711. This partnership continued until 1749 and the mark used was "VH" in a monogram. From 1749 to 1756 the proprietors were Reichard and Behling and the mark was "B & R" or "R & B". Duke Karl bought the manufactory in 1756 and leased it to Rabe, d. 1803, who bought it in 1766. It ceased to operate in 1807. The mark used was "B"; the mark "R & C" is also recorded.   The early productions were painted blue and were obviously in imitation of the Dutch. Around the middle of the 18th century the wares began to show some inventiveness and freshness in their style. Rococo molded vases and ewers were often distinctive for their delicate coloring and touch. A certain paleness in the color was especially typical. The successive contemporary vogues for faïence figures, tureens in the form of birds and vegetables, pierced baskets and classical vases were all followed at Brunswick. Another faïence manufactory was founded at Brunswick, in 1745, by Rudolph Anton Chely. It operated until 1757. The factory mark was a monogram of crossed "Cs". Included among their productions were vases of Chinese form painted with landscapes in the Delft style, tureens in forms of birds and figures of peasants.

Brush Jar In Chinese ceramics; a deep cylindrical porcelain jar used by the Chinese to hold their writing brushes.

Brussels Appliqué In lace-making; a more modern 19th century Brussels lace in which the pattern is worked either with a needle or with bobbins and is applied to a ground of machine-made net. Net was first made by machinery in 1768, and the machine for making bobbin net was invented in 1809.

Brussels Carpet In English textiles; in 1740 Lord Pembroke at Wilton introduced the method of weaving carpet with a pile using the same principles employed in weaving velvet. Carpet woven in this manner with an extra warp was known as Brussels carpet, deriving its name from the place of origin. The looped pile in these carpets was not cut. In 1749 the method was introduced at Kidderminster. Brussels carpets woven at Wilton and Kidderminster were very popular during the 18th and early 19th centuries. From around 1825 Jacquard's mechanical device for registering the pattern was introduced, and from around 1850 steam power was applied to the looms.

Brussels Lace The manufacture of Brussels lace was established from at least the beginning of the 16th century. Undoubtedly the most choice Flemish laces were made at Brussels, and their finest laces rivalled those made in Italy. Especially praiseworthy was the extraordinary fineness of the thread used in Brussels lace, which accounted for much of its beauty. There were two kinds of grounds, namely the bride and réseau. Although the former was made first it was discontinued except for special orders from around 1660. The réseau was made either with a needle or with bobbins. The needle-made net ground, which was three times as expensive as the bobbin ground, was worked from one design to another. The bobbin-made net ground or vrai réseau permitted the flowers to be made separately and worked in with the net later. With the development of machine-made net in the 19th century the vrai réseau was seldom made except for the aristocracy. The motifs were also made either with the needle or with bobbins, and were called point à l'aiguille or point plat respectively. The finest designs and flowers were made in Brussels where they achieved perfection in relief or point brodé. The beautiful fillings and openwork stitches were praiseworthy. The motifs for Brussels lace followed the prevailing fashions. The making of Brussels lace was so complex and specialized that sometimes as many as seven lace-workers were engaged in making one piece of lace. Application laces were not known until more recent times. See *Angleterre*; *Vrai Réseau*; *Flanders Lace*; *Point Gaze*; *Brussels Appliqué*.

CH'ING BRUSH JAR

Brussels Tapestries The weaving of tapestries at Brussels dates from the early 14th century. Brussels has always been an important tapestry center, and from 1465 through the 16th century it was the leading tapestry center. In the 17th century the finest tapestries were once again woven in France. Included among the great Renaissance tapestries woven at Brussels were those designed by Bernard Van Orley, the court painter. The world-renowned set of tapestries, the Acts of the Apostles, designed by Raphael for Pope Leo X, was woven in Brussels around 1519 by Peter Van Aelst, a Brussels tapestry manufacturer. See *Tapestry*.

Buccaro In ceramics; the term *buccaro* has through long usage become a general term for unglazed pottery. The term *buccaro* was given to a scented pottery made by the Indian population of Central and South America and imported into Spain and Portugal. The term *buccaro* was given to a type of unglazed pottery made in Spain and Portugal from the 16th to the 18th centuries. Its color was black, red or white, depending on the kind of clay that was used for the body.

BUCCARO TEAPOT, MING DYNASTY

Buccaro Ware Or Yi-hsing Yao. In Chinese ceramics; a Chinese unglazed red stoneware made at Yi-hsing. This ware from the earliest days of its importation into Europe has been known by the Portuguese name of *buccaro*. It was essentially a utility ware and consisted of such pieces as teapots, cups for tea and bowls for rice. This type of stoneware was the first Chinese ware to be successfully reproduced in Europe by Böttger of Meissen at the beginning of the 18th century. In England, John Dwight at Fulham made a stoneware of reddish color in imitation of buccaro. It was also imitated by Ary de Milde and other potters in Holland. See *Bizen*; *Buccaro*; *Yi-hsing Yao*; *Elers*.

Bucchero Ware In ceramics; the name given to an Etruscan black ware pottery made from about the 7th to the 5th centuries B.C. The decoration usually consists of crudely engraved geometrical designs and figures in relief imitating Greek, Egyptian and Asiatic ornament. There is a tendency in this ware both in form and ornament to imitate metal work. Some of this ware was also made in red. See *Buccaro*.

Buckinghamshire Lace Although bobbin-made lace was probably made earlier in the county of Bedfordshire than in the neighboring county of Buckinghamshire in England, it was in the latter that the manufacture flourished and gained an early reputation. Newport-Pagnell, in the central part of the county, was mentioned in the 18th century notices as one of the leading towns in England for bobbin-made laces. The designs were worked even with the net ground, and the reputation of these laces made in the midland counties was largely credited to the fine net ground. See *Northamptonshire Lace*.

Buckler In armor; a type of shield used from the 13th to the 17th centuries, especially a small, round shield held in the left hand when fencing.

Buddha In Chinese art; see *Chinese Gods*.

Buen Retiro In Spanish ceramics; the principal porcelain manufactory of Spain founded by Charles III, d. 1788, King of Naples, who, in 1759, inherited the crown of Spain and who transported with him the ceramic artists and workers from Capo-di-Monte. The wares began to decline after 1780 and it ceased to operate after 1808. La Moncloa, 1817–1850, was to some extent a continuation. The manufactory was established in the gardens of the royal palace of Buen Retiro, near Madrid. The mark of a fleur-de-lis, generally in blue or gold, was almost always used on the wares produced until 1804. After 1804 a crowned "M" was used, which was afterwards used at La Moncloa. The finest and most typical Buen Retiro porcelain was made from about 1765 to 1780 and differed in certain details from the Louis XVI style. It was as carefully finished as Sèvres, by which it was much influenced, and it was made of a beautiful soft paste material having a wax-like texture. Figures were the chief production and they merit high praise. The painted decoration at its best was remarkable for its fineness. Vases, tableware, bowls, jugs, mirror frames and other similar objects were all produced here and showed distinction and refinement. During the last two decades of the 18th century classical biscuit figures and biscuit vases with low relief decoration were characteristic productions.

Buffet In cabinetwork; the term *buffet*, from the French word *buffet*, meaning sideboard, dresser, refreshment table or room, is given to a category of furniture, especially a sideboard or side table or a cupboard in a recess, for the disposition of china, plate or glass. The buffet, which is of French origin, varied greatly in form and was either partly or completely opened or closed. The name is given to almost any dining room piece provided with one or more flat spaces or shelves for the reception of articles necessary in the dining service but not placed on the table. Until very recently the term *buffet* was applied in English furniture literature to an open three-tiered article of furniture introduced late in the 16th century. However, it has now been conclusively ascertained in contemporary English records that this article of furniture was described as a court cupboard by the English during the Elizabethan and Jacobean periods. Contemporary records of foreigners traveling in England reveal that they called it a buffet. In England during the 18th century an alcove in a panelled dining room fitted with shelves for the disposition of china and plate was described as a buffet. Sheraton in his CABINET DICTIONARY observes that the buffet was "anciently an apartment separated from the rest of the room by small pillars or balusters. Their use was for placing china and glassware, with other articles of a similar nature. In houses of persons of distinction, in France, the buffet is a detached room decorated with pictures suitable to the use of such apartments, as fountains, cisterns, vases, etc. These ancient buffets seem to be in some manner superseded by the use of modern sideboards, but not altogether, as china is seldom if ever placed upon them; and we therefore think, that a buffet may, with some propriety, be restored to modern use, and prove ornamental to a breakfast room, answering as the repository of a tea equipage." Sheraton illustrates a design for a buffet having open shelves in the upper portion and fitted with two cupboard doors in the lower portion. He states, "these suit well to be placed on each side of the fireplace of a breakfast room." See *Crédence*; *Court Cupboard*.

Buffet à Deux Corps   In French Provincial cabinetwork; a double-bodied buffet introduced during the Louis XIV period. It had a molded cornice over two panelled cupboard doors. The lower section, which usually projected slightly, was also fitted with two panelled cupboard doors, directly above which were occasionally two drawers. As a rule the upper section was distinctly longer than the lower section. Since it was principally designed in the Louis XV style it usually rested on a valanced and molded base which curved into short cabriole legs. These finely panelled buffets were especially found in Normandy, Brittany, Auvergne and Provence. They were also found in Parisian bourgeois homes.

Buffet à Glissants   In French Provincial cabinetwork; see *Buffet-Crédence*.

Buffet Bas   In French Provincial cabinetwork; the buffet bas was a characteristic piece of panelled provincial furniture. It was a kind of low sideboard cupboard, and was principally found in the dining room. The buffet bas had an oblong top over a frieze with two drawers which were directly above the two panelled cupboard doors. The length of the buffet bas greatly varied. It was sometimes designed with as many as five or six panelled cupboard doors when its length reached around 9 feet. Other variations in design occurred. It was often finely carved and the carved detail was in the prevailing style. The buffet bas was introduced during the Louis XIV style.

Buffet-Crédence   In French Provincial cabinetwork; the name *buffet-crédence* or *crédence sideboard* was generally given to a kind of panelled buffet that was identified with the regional furniture of Provence. The majority were made at Arles. It was usually designed in the Louis XV style. The buffet-crédence was made in two sections. The narrow and low panelled upper section was deeply recessed and was fitted with two sliding end panels, rather than doors, that flanked a center fixed panel. The projecting lower section was fitted with two

LOUIS XV
BUFFET-CRÉDENCE,
PROVENÇAL

panelled cupboard doors. It was mounted on a valanced base that curved into short cabriole legs. Variations in design occurred. It was finely carved with Rococo ornament and was fitted with fret-pierced steel escutcheons and large buttress hinges. It was a charming and original article of provincial furniture and was distinctive for the exuberance of its decoration. It was also called a *buffet à glissants* because of the sliding feature of its end panels in the small recessed superstructure.

Buffet-Vaisselier In French Provincial cabinetwork; during the Régence the buffet-vaisselier or dressoir was introduced. It was a favorite and characteristic piece of French provincial furniture. In Gascogne it was called an escudié; in Champagne a ménager; in Normandy a palier, and in Auvergne a vaisselier. Essentially the buffet-vaisselier was the same in all the provinces. As a rule it was designed in the Louis XV style. In a broad sense it consisted of a lower section fitted with two or three cupboard doors and a deeply recessed superstructure fitted with several rows of narrow open shelves. The shelves always had a back of solid wood and were frequently flanked by narrow lateral panelled cupboard doors. Each shelf was edged with either a small turned balustrade or a beading to secure the plates. The lower projecting portion was commonly designed with two small drawers over panelled cupboard doors. It rested on a molded and valanced base that curved into short cabriole legs. Variations in design occurred. Sometimes the longer models had four cupboard doors. It was always an interesting and well-designed piece of furniture. See *Dresser*; *Vaisselier-Horloge*.

Buhl In cabinetwork; the name is popularly applied to a process of metal inlay derived from the work of André Charles Boulle. In English cabinetwork; this technique was employed by the cabinetmaker Gerreit Jensen late in the 17th century and by other cabinetmakers working in the mid-Georgian era. Around 1815 a buhl manufactory was operated by a Frenchman, Louis Gaigneur, at No. 10 Queen Street, Edgware Road. Other contemporary firms also produced buhl work. See *Boulle, André Charles*.

Buis Wood The wood of the boxtree, *buxus sempervirens*, used for cabinetwork. It is very hard and its color is yellow.

Bulb Bowl In Chinese ceramics; a shallow bowl-shaped vessel of varying form, averaging around 9½ inches in diameter, principally used as a stand or saucer for a flower pot and often used individually as a bulb bowl. It is sometimes called a flower pot stand. It was mounted on three or four feet which were very often engraved in the form of cloud scrolls. The Chün yao bulb bowl was without decoration except for the bowl with a plain round body which had two bands of raised studs or bosses. Chün yao bulb bowls corresponded in shape to the flower pots which they held, and both were remarkable for the elegant simplicity of their forms and for the indescribable beauty of their glazes. It is generally believed that bulb bowls were very frequently used separately, such as the vessels of similar form made in celadon and Ming monochromes. See *Chün Yao*.

Bulbous In cabinetwork; a term given to a variety of leg or support that has a protuberant form. This type of leg was originally used on the furniture of the Low Countries. Heavy bulbous supports on tables, beds and buffets were a characteristic feature of Elizabethan furniture. The Elizabethan bulbous supports were richly carved and gadrooned. In the 17th century they were generally baluster-turned and their entire character was less pronounced. The term *bulbous* is also applied to anything which is bulb-like in shape. See *Cup and Cover*; *Melon Support*.

Bull's Eye In glass; the name is given to a glass with a convex center used in doors and windows to transmit light but not vision. See *Crown Glass*. In American furniture; the name is also popularly given to a round

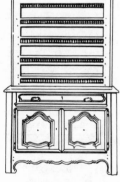

LOUIS XV
BUFFET-VAISSELIER,
BRETON

convex wall mirror. See *Convex Wall Mirror.*

Bull's Eye Lamp   An early kind of lamp having a bull's eye magnifying glass on each side of the flame or light.

Bull's Eye Mirror   In furniture accessories; the name frequently given to convex mirrors of crown glass made at Nuremberg and other places in southern Germany by at least the 15th century. See *Mirror.*

Bun Foot   In cabinetwork; a round flattened ball-shaped foot. It was introduced in English furniture about 1660 and was widely used on oak and walnut furniture, such as on cupboards and other pieces of a similar nature. See *Ball Foot*; *Foot.*

Bunzlau   In German ceramics; a distinctive variety of salt-glazed stoneware, having a peculiar bright and rich rust-brown and coffee-brown color, was made at Bunzlau, Silesia, or in that vicinity chiefly during the 18th and 19th centuries. It had a fine grey-brown body and it is believed that its color was due to a wash of a ferruginous material. Its principal wares were pear-shaped tankards and coffee pots, which were sometimes spirally reeded. Decorative motifs when used consisted of applied reliefs of yellowish clay of formal leaves and flowers and coats-of-arms. Sometimes the reliefs were painted in enamel colors of red, blue and black with touches of gilding. The manufactory has been active until modern times. No mark was found on the 18th century pieces.

Burano Lace   Lace-making on the island of Burano near Venice was mentioned in 17th century records and their Punto di Burano was highly esteemed. Much of the old Burano point lace was a coarser version of the Point de Venise à Réseau. In the 18th century they also made a point lace resembling Alençon. Late in the 19th century the art of lace-making was revived at Burano with excellent results. This modern Burano lace includes in addition to the traditional Punto di Burano many other designs of fine laces, such as Alençon, Argentan and Angleterre.

Bureau   In cabinetwork; the term *bureau* is the French generic name for a desk or writing table. The word is derived from the French word *bure*, a kind of coarse material, with which it was originally covered. The original English meaning was essentially the same since it referred to a desk or writing table having drawers for papers. The word *bureau* has never been too clearly defined in English writing furniture. Sheraton in his CABINET DICTIONARY of 1803 says that in England the term has usually been applied to common desks with drawers under them. In a broad sense the term *bureau* can be used interchangeably with the word *desk*. In a more limited denotation the term *bureau* is restricted to a slant-front desk resting on several rows of long drawers. In America the term *bureau* is used to describe a chest of drawers used as a receptacle for clothes. See *Writing Furniture.*

Bureau à Cylindre   In French cabinetwork; a variety of a large French desk introduced toward the middle of the 18th century. It had an oblong top over a solid wooden cylinder which when rolled back revealed a fitted interior and a pull-out leather-lined slide. Very often a three-quarter pierced metal gallery extended around the oblong top. The front was generally designed with five drawers which were arranged in two rows. It was mounted on four legs. The celebrated Bureau du Roi was designed as a cylinder desk. See *Cabinete-Secrétaire de Cylindre*; *Cylinder Desk*; *Writing Furniture*; *Bureau du Roi.*

LOUIS XVI
BUREAU À CYLINDRE

Bureau à Dos d'Ane   In French cabinetwork; a French slant-front desk designed for feminine use. It had a narrow oblong top and a hinged slant lid which opened to a fitted writing interior. The valanced frieze was fitted with a row of drawers and it was mounted on four cabriole legs. The bureau à dos d'âne was so called because the contour of the slanting front and the slightly slanting back resembled to some degree the device placed on a donkey's back for carrying things. It was introduced during the Louis

XV style and was distinctive for its graceful curves. It was decorated with either marquetry or lacquer work combined with finely chased bronze mounts. It was a variant form of the bureau à pente. See *Writing Furniture*.

Bureau à Pente In French cabinetwork; a French slant-front desk. It had an oblong top and a hinged slant lid which opened to an interior of small drawers and compartments. The frieze was fitted with a row of drawers and it was mounted on four legs. It was introduced during the Louis XV style. See *Writing Furniture*; *Slant-Front Writing Desk*.

Bureau Bookcase See *Secretary Bookcase*.

Bureau Cabinet See *Secretary Cabinet*.

Bureau Dressing Table In English cabinetwork; a variety of kneehole dressing table having the top drawer provided with a small hinged mirror and compartments for toilet equipage, introduced before the middle of the 18th century. In a variant form the entire top of the table lifted up revealing compartments for toilet accessories and a hinged mirror. The top drawer in the bureau dressing table was often provided with a writing board, while in other examples the top of the table was finished in baize. Occasionally the hinged mirror was reversible and served the dual purpose of a book-rest. The majority of these bureau dressing tables were made of either walnut or mahogany and some were occasionally japanned. Chippendale in the DIRECTOR refers to this variety as a "buroe dressing table" and remarks that "the recess should be of circular form as it looks more handsome." See *Bureau Table*.

EARLY GEORGIAN
BUREAU DRESSING TABLE

Bureau du Roi In French cabinetwork; a famous French desk, now at the Louvre, considered to be the finest piece of cabinetwork and bronze work executed in a piece of furniture. It was made for Louis XV by Oeben and Riesener with the assistance of several other artists. The original ideas for it were those of Oeben but the greater part of

the work was done by Riesener as Oeben died before 1767. It is signed, Riesener H. 1769 à L'Arsenal de Paris. It is a large cylinder-top desk magnificently inlaid with exotic woods and elaborately ornamented with chased and cast gilt bronze figures, plaques and other mountings. The bronze work was executed by Duplessis, Hervieux and Winant. The work of construction took nine years. It was ordered in 1760 and completed in 1769. See *Bureau à Cylindre*; *Oeben, Jean François*; *Riesener, Jean Henri*.

Bureau Ministre In French cabinetwork; the French term given to a kneehole writing table. It was introduced around the beginning of the 19th century and was designed with two tiers of drawers extending to the base in each of the prevailing French styles. See *Kneehole Writing Table*.

Bureau Plat In French cabinetwork; a large French writing table. It had an oblong top inset with leather and edged with bronze doré mouldings. The frieze was fitted with a row of three drawers. The bureau plat was notable for its fine cabinetwork and the quality of its bronze mounts. Especially outstanding were the bureaux plats made by Charles Cressent in the style of the Régence. See *Writing Furniture*; *Cressent, Charles*; *Serre-Papiers*.

Bureau Table In American cabinetwork; a contemporary term used by Townsend and Goddard to describe a kneehole desk of block-front construction serving as a dressing table. See *Bureau*; *Block-Front*.

Burette In pewter; a French term meaning cruet or vase. The name is given to a pewter cruet or pewter bottle which contains sacramental wine or water. It is usually made in pairs. One is marked A for aqua or water and the other V for vinum or wine. The term is also applied to vessels in glass.

Burgauté In Chinese ceramics; a term given to porcelain covered with black lacquer and inlaid with mother-of-pearl. Early specimens of this work were found in the Ming dynasty; however, the majority were in the Ch'ing dynasty. It is also called *lac-burgauté*.

Burgomaster Chair In English cabinetwork; a variety of chair of Dutch origin. It was introduced in England around 1700 and was popularly called the burgomaster chair. It was made first in walnut and later in mahogany. The chair has a circular frame. It has a flaring semi-circular back composed of four turned uprights and traverses enclosing three oval panels carved and pierced with leaf scrolls. It generally has a caned compass seat mounted on six legs usually of cabriole form. The six cabriole legs are connected with turned cross stretchers usually resembling in arrangement the spokes of a wheel. It is generally believed that the burgomaster chairs were the precursors of the Queen Anne and Georgian corner chairs.

Burgonet In armor; a light-weight helmet worn during the 16th and 17th centuries. The characteristic burgonet had a straight brim, cheek pieces and a guard for the back of the neck. It generally had a comb or crest and sometimes a visor and a chin piece. The essential difference between some burgonets and an armet is that the former always had a straight brim. See *Cabasset*; *Morion*.

Burgundy In French Provincial; a former dukedom from the 9th to the 15th centuries, and a former province in the Rhône Valley in eastern central France. The Burgundian furniture during the Renaissance was characterized by its massive construction, by its vigorous and bold carving in high relief, by its richly carved moldings and by a pronounced use of architectural features in its principles of design. Especially characteristic is the Renaissance double-bodied cupboard richly decorated with carved human and allegorical figures in high relief. This taste for opulence was evident in all their subsequent cabinetwork. Their furniture was always inclined to be rather massive, and the moldings and carved detail were of a heavy quality. See *French Provincial*; *Henri II*; *Sambin, Hughes*.

Burjier In English cabinetwork; a Hepplewhite term used to designate an armchair having a conforming stool. It is the same as a duchesse.

Burl Or Burr Wood. In cabinetwork; a burl is a malformation protruding on the trunk of a tree caused by some form of injury. It is a very dense piece of wood with an irregular and mottled grain. Since the 16th century it has been used in English cabinetwork for veneering and inlaying. Burl is usually obtained from the walnut, oak, elm, yew, alder and maple trees. Burl wood was used in American cabinetwork from early Colonial times.

Burling, Thomas American cabinetmaker working from around 1773–1801 at 36 Beekman Street, New York City.

Burmese In American glass; a late 19th century American ornamental glass having color tones shading from greenish-yellow to pink with either a dull or a glossy finish. See *Art Glass*.

Burse In ecclesiastical art; a receptacle or case for the linen corporal cloth which serves the purpose of covering the consecrated elements in the Eucharist. See *Corporal Case*.

Burujird Rug See *Hamadan Rug*.

Butler's Sideboard In American cabinetwork; the name given to a variety of Sheraton-style sideboard surmounted with a recessed china cabinet which was fitted with two glazed doors. In one characteristic type the center drawer in the lower projecting sideboard portion was designed with a fall-front writing flap which opened to reveal a fitted writing interior. This writing compartment was used by the butler for his household accounts. This type of butler's sideboard is also sometimes called a Salem secretary.

Butler's Table In English cabinetwork; a small movable tray-top table used for serving at tea time or in the dining room. One principal variety has an oblong top fitted with

BURGUNDIAN RENAISSANCE
ARMOIRE À DEUX CORPS

handles with either a molded edge or with narrow vertical leaves which can be let down level with the top. The legs are frequently finished with brass toe caps and casters. In some examples the tray top is movable and rests on an X-shaped stand. It was introduced during the middle of the 18th century.

Buttenmann A German drinking vessel. See *Tanzenmann*.

Butter Dish In Irish silver; a finely wrought ajouré silver dish fitted with a glass liner. The dish was oval and rather deep. It was designed with a pierced cover which was generally surmounted with a finial in the form of a cow. The dish was about 7 inches in length. Frequently the sides were pierced and chased with rustic scenes. It was introduced during the latter part of the 18th century.

Butterfly Table In American cabinetwork; a small plain drop-leaf table. It was found in the different New England states and was introduced during the first quarter of the 18th century. In this table the two leaves were supported by two large wooden wing brackets. The table has been so named because of the supposed resemblance in the shape of the solid wooden wing brackets to the shape of butterfly wings. The table was small and its average height was about 26 inches. The top of the table was usually of either maple or cherry and the rest of the table was of different woods. The table had a fixed oblong top and when the leaves were raised to its level the top was generally either oval or rectangular in shape. The oblong top rested on four either plain or turned splayed legs which generally terminated in small ball feet. The legs were usually connected with a plain continuous stretcher which was close to the floor. A small drawer was generally fitted beneath the top of the table, and the lower part of the drawer was wider than the upper part since it fitted between the splayed legs. Each of the two leaves was supported on a large wing bracket which was pivoted at the upper end to the under

BUTTERFLY TABLE

side of the top and at the lower end to the stretcher.

Buttonhole Stitch In embroidery; a closely made loop stitch which is generally used to make a firm finish on the edge of material. In lace-making; the buttonhole stitch is worked over a thread or group of threads. It is one of the principal stitches in needle-point lace.

Byrnie In armor; a medieval Anglo-Saxon term applied to a skirt of mail. The name is also given to Danish body armor of the 10th century.

Byzantine The art of the Eastern Roman Empire. It is a mixed art and is composed of Greco-Roman and Oriental elements. An important stimulus was given to the development of Byzantine art in A.D. 330 when the Emperor Constantine made the ancient city of Byzantium the new capital of the Roman Empire and moved his court and government to Constantinople, which was the new name for Byzantium. Christianity had also been established as the state religion. The final division of the Roman Empire into Eastern and Western became permanent in A.D. 395. The influence of Byzantine art, except for the interruption caused by iconoclasm, persisted until 1453 when the Moslems conquered Constantinople. While the West was in chaos, Greco-Roman civilization blended with Oriental influence was sustained by Byzantine art. The 6th century was a glorious period in Byzantine art. Mosaic work in both marble and glass attained its highest degree of perfection in Byzantine architecture. The acme of Byzantine mosaic work was achieved in the 6th century in churches at Ravenna. Byzantine art rose to a new period of great splendor under the Macedonian emperors, 867–1056. After this time a general deterioration became increasingly evident. All the decorative arts flourished at Constantinople such as weaving, working in metal and in ivory, enamelling, and the art of miniature painting on manuscripts. The influence of

Byzantine art spread throughout Europe. It was one of the principal elements in Romanesque art and architecture which attained its highest development in Europe in the 12th century. The city of Venice, which is rich in Byzantine architecture, kept Byzantine art alive in Italy and the architecture of this period in Venice is sometimes referred to as Byzantine-Romanesque. See *Romanesque*.

Byzantine In ceramics; some interesting varieties of pottery classed as Byzantine have been found in the territory of the old eastern Roman Empire, which covers a wide area of Eastern Europe. Undoubtedly the finest wares belong to medieval times and include green and yellow glazed pottery with sgraffiato and incised decoration. They date from the 10th to the 13th centuries. On the incised wares geometrical, radiating and small symmetrical foliate motifs were in predominance. Other wares displayed impressed design or were painted in yellow, brown, green, blue, red and manganese in the same motifs found on the incised wares. Probably dating from the 15th century are some interesting peasant wares with marbled slip decoration in green and brown, and other types showing Turkish and Spanish influence.

BYZANTINE BOWL
WITH SGRAFFIATO DECORATION

C

Cabaret A French term meaning tea or coffee service. The name is usually given to a matched set, generally made of silver or porcelain, comprising a teapot or coffee pot, sugar bowl, creamer, cups and saucers and tray, for one or two persons. Sometimes the silver spoons, knives and forks are included. During the 18th century finely worked gilded silver traveling cabarets in fitted cases were made by the silversmiths.

Cabaret In French cabinetwork; the term *cabaret* was used in the French language around the end of the 17th century to describe either a small table or plateau. Later it was applied to either a combination of a plateau mounted on a small table or to a plateau mounted on a plateau. The cabaret combining the table and plateau was used in the serving of coffee or tea. The top of the table and the top of the plateau were frequently of marble, and it was a fashionable piece of 18th century furniture. In a characteristic variety the plateau was similar in design to the table upon which it was mounted except that it was about one half of the size.

Cabasset In arms; a helmet worn by foot soldiers from the second half of the 16th century and during the 17th century. It is somewhat pear-shaped with a narrow brim. At the top of the helmet is a tiny horizontal point which is believed to resemble the stem of a pear.

Cabinet In cabinetwork; the name given to an article of furniture which was used as a receptacle for the owner's rarest possessions, such as enamelled boxes, jewels, pieces of carved ivory and other small objects of art. The cabinet was closed with two doors which when opened revealed an interior fitted with many small drawers, secret panels and small doors. The cabinet was always a choice article of furniture and the

ITALIAN RENAISSANCE
CABINET

cabinetmaker exerted all his skill in its decoration. The cabinet, which was often oblong, most frequently rested on a stand. Occasionally it rested on a lower cupboard section or on a chest of drawers. Especially distinctive were the Italian Renaissance cabinets inlaid with pietra dura. The cabinet during the 16th century enjoyed a great vogue. The demand for Flemish Renaissance cabinets was so great among French noblemen that Henri IV, 1589–1610, sent French cabinetmakers to the Netherlands to learn the art of decorating the cabinet, especially the art of carving in ebony. The interior of the cabinet was generally richly ornamented with carving, painting, gilding and inlay work. The French Renaissance cabinet was often decorated in characteristic Italian Renaissance style and the exterior was frequently enriched with inlays of exotic woods, semi-precious stones, metals, ivory, tortoise shell and mother-of-pearl. The cabinet was known in England as early as the reign of Henry VIII; however, it was not until after the Restoration in 1660 that it became a characteristic piece of furniture. One variety of walnut cabinet around 1680 was generally mounted on a stand and was finely decorated with floral marquetry or was veneered with oysterwood parquetry. Especially characteristic of Carolean furniture was the Oriental or European lacquer oblong cabinet generally mounted on an exuberantly carved and gilded stand. The doors of the lacquered cabinet opened to reveal a series of small drawers and doors all colorfully lacquered. There was much demand during the William and Mary style for lacquered cabinets and walnut cabinets beautifully decorated with seaweed marquetry. Cabinets were made in England throughout the 18th century and were decorated in accordance with the taste of the period. From around the middle of the 18th century the majority of cabinets were fitted with glazed doors. The writing cabinet with the fall-front is included in writing furniture. See *Writing Furniture*; *Writing Cabinet*; *China Cabinet*; *Vargueño*; *Hanging Wall Cabinet*.

Cabinete-Secrétaire de Cylindre   In French cabinetwork; the name is given to a variety of tall French desk having a cabinet section enclosed by two wood doors mounted on the oblong top of a bureau à cylindre or cylinder desk. See *Bureau à Cylindre*; *Writing Furniture*.

Cabinetmaker   The name applied to a craftsman skilled in the art of making fine furniture and interior woodwork and panelling, such as the finer kind of joiner's work. See *Joiner*.

Cabistan Rug   See *Kabistan Rug*.

Cabochon   In ornament; a convex oval ornament with a plain surface; the motif originated in the cutting of a precious stone. It was much used as a decorative motif during the 16th and 17th centuries, such as on the Burgundian, Flemish and François I armoires. The cabochon motif was popular in England from around 1740 to 1760. It was treated in the French Rococo taste and was kidney-shaped. A carved Rococo shell surrounding a cabochon was a fashionable motif around the middle of the 18th century.

Cabriole Leg   In cabinetwork; it is generally accepted that this distinctive form of leg originated in China. It seems that the word *cabriole*, which is a French dancing term meaning a leap, was taken from the Italian word *capriola* meaning a goat's leap. The leg is a decorative form of a four-footed animal's front leg from the knee downward. The top curves outward as a knee, and then curves inward toward the lower part just above the foot where it curves outward again and forms the foot. The cabriole leg has the contour of a cyma curve with the convex part at the top. It was introduced in French furniture late in the Louis XIV style. This early cabriole leg terminated in a cloven foot or pied de biche. It was introduced in England from the Continent around 1700. For the next fifty years all fashionable furniture both on the Continent and in England was designed with a cabriole leg. In England the cabriole leg most frequently terminated in a claw and ball foot, and in France in a French whorl foot. Due to the vogue for Gothic and Chinese ornament and detail in England from around 1750–1760 the straight leg supplanted the cabriole leg; however, the latter continued to be used on furniture designed in the French taste. As a result of Adam's influence the cabriole leg was generally discarded around 1770 in favor of the straight leg based on the Louis XVI style. Nevertheless Hepplewhite and his school occasionally employed it on a few fashionable chairs designed in the French taste. A decidedly attenuated cabriole leg persisted longest in France on the very small table or guéridon. See *American Colonial*; *Louis XV*.

CABRIOLE LEG

Cabriolet   In French cabinetwork; a French term applied to a chair having a concave back. It is especially identified with an open armchair or fauteuil designed in either the Louis XV or Louis XVI style.

Cachepot   In French ceramics; a French term for an ornamental container to hold a flower pot. Especially notable were the fine porcelain cachepots made at Vincennes and Sèvres. The cachepot was also made in other materials. Late in the 18th century the cachepot was sometimes made of tôle and was painted in the antique classic manner.

Caddy Spoon   In English silver; a variety of small silver spoon. The bowl was designed in the form of a shell, a scoop or some similar shape and it generally had a short, wide, fan-shaped stem. It was used to scoop the tea from the tea caddy and it remained inside the caddy. See *Tea Caddy*; *Tea Chest*.

Cadogan Teapot   In English ceramics; a variety of teapot or hot water pot having the form of a Chinese peach-shaped wine pot, filled through a hole in the base. It derived its name from the Hon. Mrs. Cadogan who had brought the original Chinese wine pot to England. It is believed that it was first made as a coffee pot at Swinton early in the 19th century and was later made by several Staffordshire potters.

Caelatura In metal art; the name given to the Roman art work executed in metal other than statuary produced during the classic times of the Roman Empire. It included work in relief, intaglio work, chasing and engraving. Repoussé work was one of its highly developed branches. See *Crustae*; *Repoussé*.

CADOGAN TEAPOT

Caen In French ceramics; a French porcelain manufactory that operated during the late 18th century. The accepted mark is "Caen" in red. Included among the wares were coffee pots, milk jugs, cups and bowls decorated with landscapes in black enclosed in small squares and suspended from wreaths and festoons painted in green and gold. Some of the wares were sent to Paris to be decorated in the style of Sèvres.

Caffaggiolo In Italian ceramics; during the first three decades of the 16th century some of the most beautiful of all Italian majolica was made at Caffaggiolo, near Florence. It is believed that the manufactory was under the patronage of the Medici family. Among the marks are "SPR" in monogram; a trident. Many pieces have no mark at all. Although Caffaggiolo majolica was influenced by the work at Faenza it revealed much originality in its design. An unusual dark cherry red was almost peculiar to this manufactory. A deep strong dark blue heavily laid on with a coarse brush was much used as a background. The green was clear and transparent and the orange and lemon yellows were excellent. The finest painting was from around 1508 to 1525. Attributed to Caffaggiolo are plates and dishes and large jugs.

Caffieri, Jacques 1678–1755. Caffieri and his son, Philippe Caffieri, 1714–1774, were undoubtedly the two great French metal workers during the Louis XV style. Their skill as decorative sculptors, bronze founders and metal chasers was unsurpassed. They held the title successively of Sculptor, Founder, and Chaser to the King. Their bronze mounts, which freely and boldly flowed into one another on a piece of furniture with consummate skill, were unrivalled for their vigorous curves and for the dexterity of their execution.

Cailloutages In ceramics; the French term for cream-colored earthenware. It was so called because calcined flints were included among its ingredients.

Caillouté In French ceramics; a decorative marbled colored ground used on Sèvres porcelain, marked with a pebble-shaped network.

Calambac Wood A kind of fragrant wood, *aquilaria agallocha*, from the East Indies, widely used in cabinetwork by the French ébénistes. It is hard and heavy and has a brown color. It is also called agalloch.

Calamus In ecclesiastical art; a silver tube through which the Communion of the chalice is received by the faithful. It is also called fistula and cannula, the latter being the Latin word for a small reed or pipe.

Caliatour Wood A red dyewood from the East Indies, similar to sandalwood, widely used in cabinetwork. It is very hard and heavy, and its color is bright red.

Calico In textiles; the name *calico*, derived from Calicut, a leading port city in India during the 16th century, is given in a general manner to cotton cloth of all varieties imported from the East. In particular the name was originally applied to a plain woven light-weight painted cotton cloth of East Indian origin. By extension the term was later given to various cotton fabrics made in Europe, some occasionally having a linen warp. There are many kinds of calicoes such as plain, painted, printed, dyed and stained. The terms *painted calicoes* and *chintz* had the same meaning in England and were used interchangeably. See *Chintz*.

Caliver   In arms; a 16th century matchlock gun smaller than the musket but larger than the carbine.

Callot Figure   In ceramics; a grotesque figure of a dwarf made of porcelain. It was so called because it was copied after designs by the French designer Jacques Callot, b. 1593–d. 1635. Callot figures were made at Meissen, Vienna and Chelsea.

Camagon Wood   The wood of the camagon tree of the Philippine Islands used in cabinetwork. It is hard and its color is black and brown veined.

Camail   In armor; a hood of chain mail worn under the helmet. Also a piece of mail fastened to the basinet to protect the neck and shoulders, made during the 14th century. Some camails had a triangular front piece to be fastened to the helmet to protect the face. The plate gorget and beaver replaced the camail in the 15th century.

Cambrian Pottery   See *Swansea*.

Camel-Back   In English furniture; a transitional chair chiefly in the Hepplewhite style and displaying some features of the Chippendale style. It is characterized by a triple-arched crest rail. Occasionally the center arch is more pronounced. The pierced splat, which extends to the seat rail, is commonly in the form of an anthemion palmette. It has straight, quadrangular, stretchered legs.

Cameo   Engraved relief work done on hard stones or gems. The work is in direct contrast to that of intaglio. The material selected for this type of engraving usually has layers of different colors; in this manner the figure is cut in relief in one layer, while another layer of a different color serves as a background. See *Intaglio*.

Cameo Glass   An ornamental glass having opaque white figures, foliage and other decoration executed in relief on a colored ground. Notable examples of cameo glass were made in the Roman Empire during the first century A.D. The technique consisted of casing a glass of one color, generally blue, with a second layer, generally opaque white. Portions of the outer layer were removed to form the background, remaining areas being used for the figures and other ornamentation which were cut or carved with a gem engraver's tools. Cameo glass though usually made in two layers can also be made in three or more layers. It is also called overlay glass and case glass. See *Portland Vase*; *Daum Frères*; *Gallé, Emile*; *Hochschnitt*.

Cameo Incrustation   In glass; the method of enclosing in cut crystal glass white porcelaneous cameos and medallions, which acquired a silver-like color when enclosed in the clear glass. It appears that this technique was a French invention and was developed around the beginning of the 19th century. Cameos of a porcelain-like material were sometimes found in glass paperweights in conjunction with other forms of decoration. Incrusted cameos are also known as sulphides.

Campagne   In lace-making; a narrow and fine white bobbin-made lace used as an edging on other laces primarily to widen them. Campagne, which was made from the 17th century, was worked in gold thread and colored silk thread, when it was used as a trimming on cloaks, scarfs and buttons.

Campanini   A French term for carrara marble.

Campan Marble   A term applied to the marbles found in the Hautes-Pyrénées district of France. The campan marbles are richly colored and many examples contain fossil shells embedded in the matrix. They were widely used in cabinetwork. French ébénistes designed tables and commodes with handsome marble tops. They were employed to enhance the splendor of stately mansions and palaces such as Versailles. There are several varieties. Vert: light and dark green with grey and white veins and

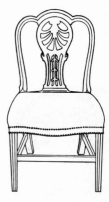

CAMEL-BACK CHAIR

almond-shaped markings. Rouge: beautifully colored with a mottling of red, violet and white. Rose: pink and white with thin veins of green and white. Mélange; green, pink and white bands between which are bands of dark red with green veins, the whole traversed by heavy white veins. Isabelle: pink with reddish-brown and white blotches, intersected with slender veins.

Campeche Wood The wood of the campeche tree, *haematoxylon campechianum*, of Campeche, Mexico. A kind of mahogany used for cabinetwork; it is very heavy and hard and has a brownish red color. Also called logwood and baywood.

Camphor Jade White jadeite; see *Jade*.

Can Or Cann. A vessel for holding liquids; formerly applied to vessels, including drinking vessels of various shapes and sizes, generally made of metal. Cann is an obsolete spelling. In American silver; the name generally given in America to the English silver mug. Apparently in America during the 18th century the characteristic can had a bulbous-shaped body mounted on a circular molded base and provided with a scroll handle in contrast to its predecessor, the straight-sided cylindrical mug. As the 18th century advanced the bulbous contour became more pronounced and the circular foot more defined. In the last decade of the 18th century Paul Revere recorded a "hooped cann" which had straight tapering sides and bands of applied "hoops" or moldings. See *Mug*.

Canadella In Spanish glass; the name applied to a variety of ewer which was typical of the province of Catalonia. The characteristic Catalan canadella consists of a very long wide cylindrical neck on a rather pear-shaped body resting on a flat molded base. A long slender loop handle is attached from the shoulder of the body to almost the top of the neck and a very long slender spout rises from the opposite shoulder of the body. Extant examples of this form of ewer date from the 14th century.

LOUIS XVI CANAPÉ

Canapé In French cabinetwork; a French settee which was generally upholstered and occasionally caned. It was introduced during the Louis XIV style. The principal features of design incorporated in the bergère and fauteuil in the different prevailing French styles were essentially found in the canapé for it was generally designed en suite with the chairs.

Canapé à Corbeille In French cabinetwork; the term *canapé à corbeille* is usually given to a characteristic variety of French upholstered settee introduced during the Louis XV period. It is so named because of its supposed resemblance to the shape of a round basket. It has a gracefully swept arched horseshoe-shaped back which continues to curve around the front, forming semi-circular ends. The back and arms are upholstered as one unit. The front seat rail is slightly rounded. It is also called an ottomane. See *Canapé*.

Canapé Dish In English silver; a covered silver entrée dish, usually resting on a spirit burner stand and sometimes fitted with a compartment for holding hot water. See *Entrée Dish*.

Candaliere In Italian ceramics; the Italian contemporary term, meaning candlestick, for a favorite decoration employed on Renaissance Italian majolica. It consisted of a symmetrically arranged design centering a vertical motif which was generally a candelabrum of fantastic form.

Candelabrum In Greek and Roman classic times the name was given to a candlestick generally of a decorative nature, and the term was also applied to a stand on which a lamp or candlestick was placed. It was generally made of bronze and sometimes of marble. The Romans favored a massive marble candelabrum. Occasionally the bronze or marble top was designed as a large shallow bowl in which the resinous wood was burnt. A candelabrum is now defined as a decorative candlestick with two or more arms or branches fitted with sockets for holding candles. At an earlier period the term *chandelier* was occasionally given to what is now understood to be a candelabrum. In ornament; the candelabrum was a favorite decorative classic motif, and it was often a part of the composition of an arabesque or a rinceau. See *Candaliere*.

Candlebeam In furniture; a form of hanging light or chandelier composed of cross-pieces of wood upon which candles are affixed. In England the medieval halls were lighted by coronas and candlebeams. See *Corona*.

Candle-Board In cabinetwork; the small sliding shelf in a desk or table used to hold the candlestick.

Candle Box A hanging wall box in which candles were kept. The candle box was introduced in England during the 17th century. It was either rectangular or cylindrical and it was generally made of oak, pewter, or brass.

Candle Extinguisher A device used to extinguish the flame of a candle. It was a small cone-shaped metal piece with a small knob or ring at the apex, and sometimes provided with a metal rod as a handle attached at right angles to the cone. The tray or stand to hold the candle snuffers was frequently provided with a hook or pin to hold the cone extinguisher. See *Snuffers*.

Candle Screen In English cabinetwork; around the middle of the 18th century small mahogany screens were frequently used to protect the lighted candle from the draft. The candle screen was usually designed either as a miniature tripod pole screen or as a cheval fire screen. Its height was slightly over one foot and it was made entirely of wood. See *Cheval Fire Screen*; *Pole Screen*; *Screen*.

Candle-Slide In cabinetwork; it is the same as a candle-board.

Candle-Snuffers In English silver; see *Snuffers*.

Candlestand In English cabinetwork; a slender stand having a small top designed to support a candlestick. It was used to augment the lighting arrangement in a room. It originated on the Continent, and was introduced in England after the Restoration, 1660. However, it did not come into general use in England until the 18th century. A principal and favorite variety was the tripod candlestand. This type generally had a small molded circular top supported on a carved or turned columnar shaft which rested on a tripod base. The majority of tripod candlestands found in America were made during the second half of the 18th century in the Chippendale style. See *Guéridon*; *Torchére*; *Tripod Table*; *Blackamoor*.

Candlestick The name is principally given to a movable stand or support for holding a candle. The candlestick is made of various materials, such as metal, wood, glass and pottery. It appears that candles did not come into general usage in England until the 16th century when secular candlesticks with sockets were introduced. Candles, which are closely associated with Church ritual, were made in England of wax or tallow in the Middle Ages, but it seems their usage was largely limited to churches. Candlesticks invariably provided with a pricket were used in churches prior to the socket type. It is generally accepted that the earliest English candlestick was made between 1560–1590. English silver candlesticks prior to the Restoration in 1660 were relatively simple, with the more elaborate specimens dating from 1660 onwards. See *Candelabrum*; *Pricket*.

Cane-Colored Ware In English ceramics; a buff or cane-colored stoneware made by Wedgwood and other contemporary Staffordshire potters which was occasionally enriched with enamel decoration. Chocolate-colored stonewares were also made. See *Wedgwood, Josiah*.

Caned In cabinetwork; a term applied to a piece of furniture such as a chair or settee that has a rattan-woven back and seat.

CANDLE SCREEN,
TRIPOD TYPE

Caning or rattan was introduced into Europe by the Dutch. Caned chairs and settees were extremely fashionable in France during the Louis XV period. They were made in the same shapes as the upholstered canapés, bergères and fauteuils. The frames were generally made of walnut, beech or cherry, and were often painted and sometimes gilded. When the frame was gilded the caning was also gilded. During the winter the caned furniture had cushions fastened to the seat and to the back. Caned fauteuils and side chairs were much used in the dining room. The chaise à poudreuse or the chaise à bureau was a characteristic piece of caned French furniture. An early caned English chair was the popular carved and turned Charles II chair or Restoration chair. It had a caned back panel and a caned seat. Due to the taste for brilliant and light color effects toward the end of the 18th century a number of caned chairs and settees were designed in the Sheraton style. They were generally made of satinwood, painted or lacquered wood and were decorated in accordance with the prevailing style of classic ornament.

Canephora In ornament; originally the name was given in Greek antiquities to a maiden who carried on her head a basket which contained the utensils and offerings for religious festivals. The term is applied in architecture to either a feminine or masculine figure who carries a basket or a similar object on his head. Canephorae or canephori are sometimes worked in a frieze. They were occasionally used in furniture design such as for supports or as decorative motifs especially during the Late Renaissance in Italy when different figure subjects were extensively employed. See *Caryatid*.

Canister In ecclesiastical art; the name given in the Roman Catholic Church to a metal vessel or case frequently of silver or silver gilt used to contain the wafers previous to consecration.

Canister The small container used as an alternative method to a partitioned tea caddy

CANEPHORA MOTIF

to hold tea. The tea was contained in two or more of these canisters made of metal, glass or earthenware, and as a rule the canisters were placed in a tea caddy. In English silver; undoubtedly the finest English tea canisters were made of silver. Extant examples date from the early 18th century. The majority of early examples were bottle-shaped with canted corners and were provided with a cap fitting over a narrow neck. Vase-shaped canisters were typical of the Neo-Classic style and were sometimes provided with two looped handles. See *Tea Caddy*.

Cann In American silver; see *Can*.

Cannelle Wood Also canella wood. Wood from a tree, *canellaceae alba*, of Ceylon and the West Indies, used in cabinetwork. It is hard and its color is white. It is also called cinnamon bark.

Cannula In ecclesiastical art; see *Calamus*.

Canopy An architectural term for a decorative or ornamental projection above a door, window or a similar opening. The canopy was often a part of the structure of medieval furniture, such as a chair, settle or dresser. Canopies or hangings of fabrics were often suspended above throne chairs, beds and couches. From around the middle of the 16th century onwards the canopy over a bed supported by the posts or suspended from the ceiling was commonly called a tester in England.

Cántaro In Spanish glass; the term *cántaro* is applied to a particular variety of glass vessel peculiar to many parts of Spain. It consists of a spherical or ovoid body resting on a spreading foot and always has two spouts which rise from opposite sides of the shoulder. One spout is used for filling and the other, which is very slender, is used for drinking. The body is surmounted with a bail handle attached crosswise between the two spouts. Extant examples date from the 17th century. See *Càntir*.

Canted In cabinetwork; to cut off the edge or corner of a square such as a canted stile on a commode; to give an oblique or slanting direction such as the canted sides of a commode which are not parallel or at right angles. See *Chamfered*.

Canterbury   In English cabinetwork; a stand or rack surmounted with upright openwork partitions, used for holding papers, music, etc. In the CABINET DICTIONARY of 1803, Sheraton says the term *canterbury* was then applied to some pieces of cabinetwork that the Archbishop of Canterbury was said to have ordered. One was a supper tray with a semi-circular end, and with three partitions crosswise, to hold knives, forks and plates. The other was a small music stand. See *Plate Stand*.

Càntir   In Spanish glass; the term *càntir* is applied to a characteristic 18th century glass vessel used for holding wine or water. The càntir consists of an ovoid, pyriform or spherical body resting on a high spreading foot. It is always fitted with two vertical spouts, one for filling the vessel and the other of small diameter for drinking. A ring-shaped handle surmounted with a flower or rooster finial is attached to the top of the body in a straight line between the two spouts. See *Cántaro*.

Canton   In Chinese ceramics; from as early as the 12th century stoneware articles, and possibly porcelain, were produced and exported by the many kilns in the province of Kuangtung, of which the city of Canton, the chief commercial center and port on the Pearl River, is the capital. The terms *Canton ware* and *Canton china* are often given to enamelled porcelain which was ordered by European traders and shipped from the port of Canton and other nearby ports on the Pearl River estuary. Most of this porcelain dates from about 1730 to 1770 and although it was all made in the kilns at the great ceramic center of Ching tê Chên much of it was decorated in Canton, especially in Famille Rose. The name *ruby back porcelain* is given to the finest examples of Canton enamelled ware having a body of egg-shell

thinness and colored on the inner side with crimson or rose-pink. See *Famille Rose*; *Ching tê Chên*.

Cantonnière   The narrow cantonnières were part of the hangings of a Louis XIV style bedstead. They served to keep out the air where the curtains came together at the bed posts. The term *cantonnière* is also sometimes given to a tall narrow corner cupboard with a swelled or rounded front identified with French provincial furniture.

Capo di Monte   In Italian ceramics; a porcelain manufactory was founded in the royal palace of Capo di Monte by King Charles III of Naples. It was active from 1743 to 1759, when Charles III inherited the Spanish throne and took with him the ceramic workers and established a new factory at Buen Retiro, near Madrid. Ferdinand IV reopened it in 1771 and at the same time removed it to the royal Villa di Portici. He transferred the works again in 1773 to the royal palace at Naples where it flourished until 1806. From 1807 to 1834 the factory and materials changed hands several times. The production of this last period had little artistic importance. Eventually the molds and models were acquired by the Doccia manufactory. The porcelain from 1743 to 1759 was often not marked; however, a fleur-de-lis impressed was commonly found on figures. During the second period the marks were a crowned "N" and "FR" or "RF" in monogram. The material for Capo di Monte porcelain was a creamy white color. Especially fine and ranking with the best made in Europe were some beautifully modelled figures marked with a fleur-de-lis and made of a slightly yellowish soft paste porcelain. Figures from the Italian Comedy were much favored. The majority of wares such as tableware and vases decorated in low relief and enamelled in harsh colors and very often marked with a crowned "N" are later Doccia reproductions and were made of a greyish paste. Classical figures in glazed or unglazed porcelain were made from around 1785 and figures of Neapolitan folk types appeared around 1800. In the final period,

SHERATON CANTERBURY

1807–1834, biscuit and white glazed figures in the style of the Empire were typical. The porcelain material after 1771 was generally of a pleasing ivory tone and the texture had much charm.

Captain Glass An English term applied to the large glass vessel, placed in the center of the comport or salver. It is a large bowl resting on a stem and its design and decoration conform to the smaller jelly and sweetmeat glasses that surround it.

Capucine A French term applied to the wooden furniture originally found in the monastery cells. There is an order of friars named Capuchins. See *Chaise à Capucine*.

Caquetoire In French cabinetwork; a distinctive type of wood armchair introduced around the middle of the 16th century deriving its name from the French word *caqueter*, meaning to chatter or gossip, or in other words a *chaise de femme*. It was designed with a high narrow upright panelled back, with the top of the open arms forming a U-shape. The arms rested on baluster-turned supports continuing to conformingly shaped legs, which were joined with a continuous stretcher close to the floor and were mounted on bun feet. The seat was much wider in front since it followed the curve of the arms. The width of the seat in the back was only as wide or slightly wider than the narrow back panel which joined the seat. The back legs were also much closer together than the front legs since they were a continuation of the back panel. Variations in design occurred. Many extant French examples are in walnut. Writers of French furniture literature also give the name to a form of small low chair that can be easily moved around the room for the convenience of feminine gossip or conversation. The name with its allusion to gossip has always made it a popular term and it is found in many inventories from the time of the Renaissance.

Carafe A French term referring to a decanter,

CARD-CUT FRETWORK

flagon or water bottle; especially one having a bulbous body with a long tapering neck that is used for wine or water at the table.

Carbine A small firearm first made late in the 16th century that is shorter than either the musket or the rifle. It was generally used by the cavalry.

Card-Cut In English cabinetwork; the term *card-cut* is usually given to fretwork patterns carved in low relief in the Chinese taste. See *Fretwork*; *Chinese Chippendale*.

Cardinal's Hat A name given to an early form of a pewter dish, because it resembled the shape of an inverted Cardinal's hat, which has a flat broad brim and a low crown. The name is found in English records dating from 1430.

Card Table In cabinetwork; probably the earliest form of a gaming table was simply a wooden board placed on a chest. Backgammon, chess, draughts and dice were all known in England before the 15th century when playing cards were introduced. During the Elizabethan era a small square table with folding leaves which when opened were supported by sliding bars served as a gaming table. The card table was an important and popular article of furniture due to the mania for playing cards which developed in France and England during the 18th century. In English cabinetwork the card table assumed its characteristic form during the reign of Queen Anne. The principal variety of Queen Anne style card table had an oblong hinged top with outset rounded corners over a frieze of conforming shape that rested on four legs. When opened the interior was fitted with four round dished candle discs, one at each corner, and four sunken counter wells or money pockets. The interior was usually lined with needlework, damask or green baize. The card table was designed in all the successive 18th century styles. During the Rococo the folding top was often of serpentine contour. The Sheraton style card table frequently had an oval-shaped folding top. In French cabinetwork; the principal

French card table introduced during the reign of Louis XV was designed with a folding top mounted on a pivot. Piquet, which is a card game played by two persons, inspired the designs for a number of small elegant tables. A triangular table was designed for tri or three-handed ombre. Quadrille was a fashionable card game for four persons and a number of square tables were especially made for that game. These tables often had circular dished corners for candlesticks. For five-handed reversi and brelan, tables with five sides were designed. The card table in America was first designed in the Queen Anne style. It seems that of all the extant American furniture designed in the Hepplewhite style that card tables are the most numerous. See *Tric-Trac Table*; *Bouillotte Table*; *Concertina Movement*.

Card Tray In silver; a small salver. See *Salver*.

Carlin, Martin c. 1730–1785. French cabinetmaker. He was admitted as a master cabinetmaker July 30, 1766. Carlin was a perfect exponent of the Louis XVI style and he is generally regarded as the best-known cabinetmaker working in the Louis XVI style. His furniture was perfectly proportioned and displayed exquisite taste in all its details. His marquetry and veneered furniture revealed his special talent for effectively combining the different colored woods and bronze mounts to achieve a maximum of beauty. He also worked in ebony. He admired the contrast of the delicate bronze mounts against the dark and polished ebony surface. He did much work for Madame du Barry.

Carlton House Desk In English furniture; the name *Carlton House* was given to a large type of English writing desk which was introduced during the last quarter of the 18th century and which was very popular during the last decade of the century. The origin of the design and the reason for its name have never been ascertained. It had an oblong top with rounded rear corners. The two sides and the back of the desk were sur-

mounted with a conformingly shaped plateau or superstructure of small drawers and cupboards, surmounted by a three-quarter ormolu gallery. The plateau was fitted with a small drawer at each end and with two central tiers of three small drawers each, flanked by incurvate cupboard doors. Frequently the plateau had a tier of three small drawers at each end and was of the same height as the back portion. The writing surface was panelled in leather and centered a rising easel rest. The frieze was fitted with three drawers. It was designed with four quadrangular tapered legs finished with ormolu toe caps and wheel casters. The drawers were commonly fitted with ormolu bail handles. The name *Carlton House* was given to this variety of desk by at least 1796, when the name appears in Gillow's cost book dated 1796. Sheraton gives a design dated 1793 in the Appendix to his DRAWING BOOK for this form of desk or writing table. He describes the desk as a Lady's Drawing and Writing Table and suggests that it be made of either mahogany or satinwood.

Carnet de Bal The terms *carnet de bal* and *dance program* are erroneously applied to a small French nécessaire fitted with writing accessories known as a *souvenir* since the 18th century. See *Souvenir*.

Carolean A term applied to the English style of ornament and furniture from 1660 to 1688. It is also called Late Jacobean, Late Stuart and Restoration. The name is derived from the Latin word *Carolus*, meaning Charles. See *Jacobean, Late*.

Carolean Chair In English cabinetwork; see *Flemish Chair*; *Restoration Chair*.

Carpet Bowls In ceramics; pottery balls of solid clay were made in England and Scotland for use in a game called carpet bowls. They were probably made during the first half of the 19th century. It was a favorite winter game played with six pairs of heavy pottery balls. The balls were decorated with

SILVER CARD TRAY

bands of various colors and the jack was a white ball.

Carquois, à la   In French ceramics; a characteristic polychrome Rococo painted decoration used on Rouen faïence from around the middle of the 18th century that was imitated elsewhere. The motifs included bows and arrows, flowers, quivers and other similar subjects. See *Rouen*.

Carrara Marble   A fine white marble chiefly found in the vicinity of Carrara and Massa, towns in Tuscany, Italy. The finest quality of this marble is much favored by sculptors. Michelangelo's most celebrated pieces of statuary were of Carrara marble.

Carriage Clock   See *Sedan Clock*.

Carrickmacross Lace   Appliqué lace was made in the vicinity of Carrickmacross, Ireland, from around 1820. The design was cut from fine cambric and was applied to a net ground with various needle stitches. This form of needlework was made in Italy in large quantities from around the 13th to the 17th centuries. Around 1850 some fine examples of Brussels and guipure lace were shown at the Bath and Shirley school, at Carrickmacross, and were given to the best lace-workers. As a result of this experiment cut cambric or linen work in the style of guipure became identified with Carrickmacross.

CARVER CHAIR

Cartel   In French furniture; a finely wrought mural clock or wall clock generally of bronze doré. The cartel designed in the Louis XV and Louis XVI styles was a veritable masterpiece of the ciseleur's art. The Louis XV cartel was remarkable for its capricious and fanciful sculptured bronze ornamentation. The round dial was sometimes framed in asymmetrical leaf scrolls and scrolling stems having realistically modelled flowers and leaves. Occasionally it was surmounted by the figure of a shepherd playing a flageolet and a shepherdess with an open book posed before two blossoming trees. The cartel was introduced in England from France early in the reign of George II. The English cartel emulating the French cartel was generally of carved and gilded wood.

Cartisane   In lace-making; a small strip of thin parchment or vellum entirely covered with silk, gold or silver thread and employed to produce the raised pattern, particularly in guipures. Cartisane was not a very satisfactory material, since dampness caused it to shrivel and it could not be washed. As a result it was later replaced by a cotton material.

Cartoon   A term applied in art work to a full-sized drawing to be used as a guide or model in making tapestries, fresco paintings, mosaics and other similar work. See *Tapestry*.

Cartouche   In ornament; a French term given to a decorative motif having the shape of a scroll of paper. It was especially used as a tablet in the form of a partly unrolled scroll of oval form on which could be placed a heraldic device or some inscription. The cartouche was a favorite motif in the Baroque style of ornament. Cartouche-shaped bronze escutcheons were occasionally employed on the drawers of French furniture.

Carver Chair   In American cabinetwork; an armchair belonging to John Carver, 1571–1621, the first governor of Plymouth Colony, which he is supposed to have brought over with him on the *Mayflower*. The chair, which is characterized by its turned members and vertical spindles, is now in Pilgrim Hall, Plymouth, Massachusetts. It is a heavy and massive chair of crude construction. The open back has a row of three spindles, and above the row of spindles is another turned crosspiece. The front legs are joined by two turned members and each side has two turned members joining the front with the rear leg. The chair was probably made in England from a Dutch prototype. Chairs of this type, which are called Carver chairs, were made in America, particularly in New England, without much change in form until at least the end of the 17th century. See *Brewster Chair*.

Carving In cabinetwork; the degree of relief or projection of carved ornament is generally designated by the terms *low relief* or *bas-relief*, *half relief* or *mezzo-rilievo* and *high relief* or *alto-rilievo*. Fully sculptured carving of figures is sometimes referred to as carving in the round. This kind of carving was occasionally employed on the stiles of Late Renaissance cabinets. The term *incised carving* is given to carved decoration which is made by cutting or carving into the wood. In chip carving the design is formed by chipping the surface of the wood. The name *pierced* or *openwork carving* is given to a variety of carved decoration which is carved entirely through, such as a pierced or open-work splat on a chair back. Carving has always been one of the favorite methods for decorating the surface of furniture. See *Relief*; *Pierced*.

Caryatid In ornament; a draped female figure used as a motif or as a decorative support. The pronounced use of boldly modelled caryatids was evident in Italian Renaissance furniture design from around the middle of the 16th century.

Case Bottle In English glass; the name given to a variety of glass bottle which became rather popular during the latter part of the 18th century. These bottles ranged from small drug and scent bottles to large wine and spirit bottles. They were generally made in sets and they were usually contained in an especially designed wooden box or case. See *Spirit Case*.

Case Glass See *Cameo Glass*.

Cash Pattern In Chinese ceramics; a Chinese round copper coin or disc having a square hole in the center. It is a symbol of prosperity and is used in decoration either singly or worked into a diaper pattern.

Casing In glass; see *Flashing*.

Casque In armor; a type of open helmet modelled on classical lines worn as early as the 12th century. It was conical in shape with a broad, straight, fixed nasal cover. It was popular during the 16th century and some of the finest helmets were of this type, especially the Italian ones with their elaborate designs which were embossed, chiselled and gilded.

Cassapanca In Italian cabinetwork; a long and massive combination bench and chest. It was introduced around the middle of the 15th century in Florence. It had a back and arms, and the seat was hinged so that the lower portion could be used as a storage chest. It was generally raised on a dais since it was used as a seat of honor. The cassapanca was distinctive for its fine carvings. See *Chest-Bench*.

TUSCAN CASSAPANCA

Cassel In German ceramics; there were four potteries in existence at Cassel, Hesse-Nassau, during the 18th century. A faïence manufactory from 1680 to 1786–1788; a porcelain manufactory 1766 to 1788; the Steitz vase and earthenware factory, 1771 to 1862 or later; and Le Fort's, later Hillebrecht's, earthenware factory, 1772 to 1805. All these factories were either owned or patronized by the Landgrave of Hesse-Cassel at some time or other. Of these four the most important was the one established in 1771 making marbled and agate ware and glazed earthenware. The faïence wares, 1680 to 1786, had little artistic merit. They were largely blue and white and at first were strongly influenced by the wares of Delft. The mark "HL" in monogram was sometimes used. The porcelain wares, 1766 to 1788, were chiefly blue and white wares for daily use. The mark is the lion of Hesse with a double tail, or "HC". The porcelain material was imperfect. Earthenware in the English style, 1771 to 1862, included marbled and agate ware and glazed earthenware, especially vases and figures. Vases modelled in the Neo-Classic style in imitation of Wedgwood vases were especially outstanding. The mark "Steitzische Vasenfabrik in

Cassel" was sometimes found on the vases. Another mark after 1788 was the Hessian lion impressed, but it is very seldom found. Useful wares were also made.

Cassel In German glass; it is recorded that glass was produced at Cassel, Germany, from the 16th century. In 1695 Franz Gondelach, born at Gross-Almerode in Hesse in 1663, was appointed chief glassmaker at the Court of the Landgrave Carl of Hesse-Cassel, which post he was still holding in 1716. Franz Gondelach was one of the foremost German glass engravers and his work represents the highest achievement attained in the Baroque style. Most of the identified work of Gondelach, produced at Cassel and Potsdam, was in hochschnitt or cameo relief and includes coats-of-arms, a portrait of the Landgrave Carl, bacchantes and similar subjects on goblets having the stems, feet and finials on the covers elaborately carved in foliage or shell motifs, and sometimes having monograms in openwork. See *Potsdam*, in German glass; *Hochschnitt*.

Cassolette In French furniture; a French term given to a perfume burner or essence vase in which various perfume-giving substances were burned. It was made in pairs and was introduced in France during the 17th century and was called a brûle parfum. Around the middle of the 18th century it became an elaborate decorative accessory. It was usually in the form of a classic urn or vase, with the body and cover made of marble, or some similar material, richly ornamented with ormolu or bronze doré mountings. The metal mount around the top of the body was perforated. Charcoal was placed in the body and sprinkled with a perfumed substance. Essence vases in the Neo-Classic style were widely used in England from around and after 1760. See *Boulton, Matthew*.

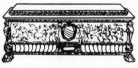

FLORENTINE CASSONE

Cassone In Italian cabinetwork; the name given to a variety of chest introduced during the Gothic period. The cassone had the greatest artistic value of all contemporary domestic furniture. Great Renaissance artists and the most skillful of craftsmen expended all their talent in creating cassoni which were veritable works of art. These cassoni were enriched or decorated with pastiglia work, painted panels, gilding, intarsia, certosina and carving. See *Chest*.

Castel Durante In Italian ceramics; the majolica made at Castel Durante, renamed Urbania in 1635, near Urbino, during the first three decades of the 16th century ranks among the world's most beautiful painted pottery. Its productions like those of Tuscany and Faenza had a great formative influence on the majolica styles adopted in Italy. Its painted decorations are especially associated with two great artists, Giovanni Maria and Nicola Pellipario, who later was at Urbino. Included among the characteristic decorative manner of Castel Durante as found on dishes and plates were borders of foliage and central medallions; fantastic subjects with cupids, grotesques and demons occasionally arranged symmetrically or a candaliere; bound and blindfolded figures; white ribbon streamers on a blue ground; borders composed of grotesques, cupids, masks, foliations and trophies. Bianco sopra bianco, particularly for inner borders, was a feature of Castel Durante. The so-called a trofeí decoration was much favored. It is generally believed that the full istoriato manner known as the Urbino style was the invention of Pellipario while still working at Castel Durante. Another familiar type of dish was the so-called bacile amatori, which was usually painted with portraits of ladies or helmeted warriors. Pellipario's best painting was remarkable for its beauty of color, for its delicate and sensitive drawing and for its skillful composition. He is generally regarded as the greatest of all majolica painters. The majolica workshops at Castel Durante flourished during the 16th century; however, in the succeeding century the work was very inferior. See *Istoriato*.

Castelli In Italian ceramics; a leading center for majolica during the 17th and 18th centuries. The productions of the neighboring centers· at Naples, Atri, Teramo and Bussi are generally included in the majolica of Castelli. Their productions were almost completely decorative works and were representative of the final revival of the art of Italian majolica. Especially characteristic are borders of putti or cupids among flowers and foliage, and pictorial panels of landscapes or of three-quarter length mythological subjects notable for their charming composition and delicate painting. Gilding was often used. Much of the fame of Castelli rests on the work of Carlo Antonio Grue, 1655–1723. After 1750 the quality of the painting declined. The potteries survived into the 19th century; however, the work had little artistic merit. See *Italian Majolica*.

Caster In English furniture; small solid wheels or casters permitting an article of furniture to be moved around without lifting were introduced in England around the end of the 17th century from the Continent, where they had been in general use from a much earlier time. The early English caster was made of wood. Around the middle of the 18th century leather casters were in common use, and from around 1770 brass casters became available. Many varieties of casters made of brass were illustrated in the late 18th century pattern books.

Caster Or Dredger. In English silver; a small container having a perforated top which was originally used for casting pepper. The pepper caster first appeared as the upper part of the bell-shaped salt circa 1600. It is not found as an individual piece until about 1680. The early casters were of cylindrical form with dome-shaped tops while the later ones were often vase-shaped and followed the prevailing taste in silver. Dredger is another name for a caster. See *Muffineer*; *Bell Salt, Standing*.

Castleford In English ceramics; a pottery was founded around 1790 by David Dunderdale at Castleford, Yorkshire, England, for making cream-colored earthenware similar

to that made at Leeds. The pottery also made black basaltes and other characteristic Leeds and Staffordshire wares. Especially typical was the white and cream-colored stoneware decorated in relief designs outlined in a brilliant blue made in the early 19th century.

Castor Ware An English pottery made with a slip decoration in the 3rd century in Castor, Northamptonshire, during the Roman occupation. Vases, jars and drinking cups were ornamented with hunting scenes, warriors, gladiators and other similar subjects. The method of slip painting employed to execute these designs was called barbotine. A similar ware with slip decoration was found in the Rhine district. See *Barbotine*.

Cat In English furniture; a tripod stand made of turned wood or metal used in the 18th century to support a plate to be kept warm in the fireplace. A characteristic wooden variety had three turned splayed members joined at each end of the upright shaft; because of this feature either end served as the top or feet. Its height was slightly more than a foot and its width was about a foot.

Catchpole A medieval weapon having a long shaft and generally double prongs at the head with reversed prongs inside. It was used to unhorse a knight by catching him at the throat.

Caucasian Rugs A general classification applied to a group of Oriental rugs woven in the Caucasus, which is the part of Russia between the Caspian and the Black Seas. Their patterns adhere to straight lines and mosaic effects. Their primitive designs are highly developed. Blue, red, ivory, yellow and green are the most frequently used colors. The colors are interestingly handled and well-balanced. Almost all the rugs in this group have no shading off from one hue to another. They make use of the angular hook, also called a latch hook, which gives a saw-tooth effect or spiky points to the designs. This hook does help to soften the color contrast between two fields of color. Caucasian rugs are usually made in small

SILVER CASTER

sizes. This group includes: Daghestan, Circassian, Mosul, Derbend, Karabagh, Genghis, Kabistan, Soumak, Mosul Kurd, Tchichi, Shirvan, Shemakha, Baku, Kazak, Kashmir. See *Oriental Rugs*.

Caudle Cup In English silver; the name given to a variety of two-handled cup generally fitted with a cover. It was used for drinking caudle, which is a warm drink made of gruel mixed with wine or ale and sweetened and spiced. It varied in shape and in decoration. One of the more familiar shapes was a bulbous pear-shaped cup, the lower half of which was elaborately worked. Each handle frequently represented the head of a woman merging into a decorative scrolled form. The average height was about 6 inches. Sometimes it had a saucer-like tray of conforming design. The caudle cup was introduced in the early 17th century.

Caughley In English ceramics; a manufactory was founded at Caughley, in Shropshire, shortly after 1750. Thomas Turner became the proprietor in 1772, and porcelain of the Worcester type began to be made. In 1799 it was purchased by John Rose of the Coalport manufactory. He produced biscuit ware at Caughley which he had glazed and finished at his Coalport manufactory. It closed in 1814. Caughley porcelain was of undistinguished quality and it chiefly imitated Worcester. A principal decoration was transfer printing in underglaze blue; however, painting in colors was also found. The familiar name for the wares was Salopian from the old Anglo-Saxon name for that part of the country. Much of the Salopian as well as early Coalport ware which it closely resembles was decorated in London. A bright hard quality of gilding was often added to the Salopian ware decorated in London. Among the marks were "S" in blue, "C" in blue or gold and "Salopian" in blue.

LOUIS XV CAUSEUSE

Causeuse In French cabinetwork; a French term meaning talkative or chatty given to an upholstered small settee designed for two persons. It was introduced early in the 18th century and was designed in the successive 18th century French styles.

Cavetto A concave molding; the curve is usually one-fourth of a circle in profile. In English furniture; it was widely used on the cornices of the chest-on-chest, china cabinet and similar pieces of furniture made of veneered walnut designed in the Queen Anne style. See *Molding*.

Cavetto A term applied to the center portion of a dish, saucer or plate. See *Marli*.

Cavo-Rilievo Hollow relief; see *Relief*.

Caylus, Anne Claude Philippe, Comte de 1692–1765. French archaeologist and man of letters. He was an enthusiastic admirer of Greco-Roman art and he devoted much of his time to the study and to the collection of antiquities. He traveled extensively in Italy, Greece, the Near East, England and Germany. Among his antiquarian works is the RECUEIL D'ANTIQUITÉS published over a period of years beginning in 1752. This publication along with numerous other publications appearing around and after 1750 hastened the development of the Classic movement in France and the final abandonment of the Rococo style. Comte de Caylus also wrote a treatise on the method of encaustic painting with wax. This method had been mentioned in Pliny; however, he said that he had rediscovered it. He was also an excellent engraver, and he made many engraved copies of the paintings of the greater masters. See *Classic Revival*.

Cedar The wood of the cedar is widely used for making chests due to its fragrance. It is a very durable wood and its color is reddish. The African cedar of wine-red color was used by the French ébénistes in cabinetwork. The Asiatic and Siberian cedar is a soft white mottled red.

Celadon In Chinese ceramics; a Chinese porcelain with a beautiful translucent green glaze having a velvet-like texture. The color of the green, which was developed to imitate jade, varies. The body varied from grey to white and burnt yellowish to reddish brown where exposed. The best-known kilns were at Lung-ch'üan in Chekiang. They were famed for their celadon during the Sung dynasty. The characteristic Lung-ch'üan celadon has a beautiful creamy and unctuous glaze of sea green or light grass green. Much of the existing ware is in the form of thick and heavy bowls, plates and jars. The decoration was carved with a knife, etched with a fine point or molded in low relief and was generally under the glaze. It is recorded that in the early Ming dynasty the Lung-ch'üan kilns were moved to nearby Ch'ü-chou Fu. However this is not to be interpreted that celadon was no longer made at Lung-ch'üan or that it was not made prior to early Ming at Ch'ü-chou Fu. This celadon is known as Ch'ü-chou ware. Spotted celadon, or Chinese, Pao-pie, or Japanese, Tobi Seiji, is so called because it had spots of reddish brown which were caused by iron that turned reddish brown in firing. There were also celadon kilns in northern provinces, such as the kilns in Honan, near the capital Kai-Feng Fu which was the eastern capital under Northern Sung before A.D. 1127. An important kiln for celadon was at Ch'ên-liu which is southeast of Kai-Feng-Fu. This is called Tung Yao or Eastern ware. They made a light and dark shade of celadon that was imitated during the Yung Chêng period at the Imperial manufactory. The name *celadon* is also given to early green Korean wares and to good imitations of Chinese celadon made in Japan. Green porcelain is called Ch'ing Tz'u in China and Seiji in Japan. It is said that this distinctive green was called celadon, which is a French word, after a character named Celadon in D'Urfé's romance of ASTRÉE. See *Korean Wares*.

Celestial Globe Stand   In cabinetwork; see *Globe Stand*.

Cellarette   Or Cellaret. In English furniture; the mahogany cellarette which was designed as a receptacle for the storage of wine bottles in the dining room was first used during the Early Georgian era. It was usually placed under the sideboard table. The interior had a lead lining and was divided into partitions for the bottles. It was fitted with side handles and a lock and key. Later it was often fitted with casters. It was designed in different forms; one characteristic variety was octagonal in form. The term is also applied to that part of a sideboard properly fitted to hold wine bottles. Generally one of the sideboard pedestals grouped with the sideboard table was used as a cellarette. The cellarette was also made in America and the earliest examples are in the Chippendale style. See *Pedestal Sideboard Table*; *Sideboard Pedestals*; *Sideboard*.

Cellini, Benvenuto   1500–1571. Celebrated Italian sculptor and metal worker, who is generally regarded as the most talented metal worker of that time. He produced many beautiful pieces in gold, silver and bronze as well as objects made of rock crystal richly mounted in metal and pieces made of gold and inset with enamel. Much of his finest work was produced under the patronage of Pope Clement VII at Rome and later for the court of François I in Paris. His work on such pieces as small boxes, jewel settings, medals, plate, vases, candlesticks and similar articles was executed in the highest quality of craftsmanship and was remarkable for its exquisite and intricate detail.

Censer   Or Thurible. In ecclesiastical art; a portable vessel in which burning incense can be carried, the aromatic substances being sprinkled on burning charcoal. It was used by the ancient Egyptians and consisted of a long handle with a bowl at one end and a box to hold incense at the other end. Roman censers were of elaborately wrought silver and bronze, sometimes in the form of a candelabrum surmounted with a small flat brazier. In Christian times the censer was in the form of a spherical bowl provided with a perforated lid, although censers of square or polygonal form were also made. It was carried and swung by three chains, with a

GEORGIAN CELLARETTE

fourth chain attached to the lid. Early censers or thuribles were of simple design while during medieval times many were of architectural form with tracery and lids with towers. The later variety of censer was generally finely and elaborately worked in gold, silver, champlevé enamel or gilt bronze and was sometimes encrusted with jewels. The term *thurible* is the proper ecclesiastical name for a censer in the Western Church.

NORMAN CENSER

Center Table In cabinetwork; a form of occasional table suitable for general use, and, as its name implies, usually found in the center of a room or in the center of a particular seating arrangement. If any distinction is made between a center table and an occasional table, the former appellation is reserved for a more important table displaying exceedingly fine cabinetwork, whose purpose is principally decorative rather than utilitarian. See *Occasional Table*.

Cerisier Wood The wood of the cherry tree, *prunus cerasus*, used in cabinetwork, especially by the French ébénistes. It is a hard wood and its color is reddish veined.

Certosina In Italian Renaissance cabinetwork; an intricate inlaid decoration of geometrical and conventionalized designs, made with minute pieces of ivory or bone laid in walnut. Venice is often credited with its origin, because its designs are strongly tinctured with Eastern influence. It was a favorite decorative process during the 15th century. See *Inlay*.

Chafing Dish In American silver; the term *chafing dish* is given to a brazier to hold burning charcoal for heating food placed upon it. It was introduced in America late in the 17th century, following a style used in France. The body was cylindrical and usually of ogee contour with pierced ornaments, and it rested on three brackets terminating in the form of a claw and a wooden ball foot. It was provided with a long turned wood handle fitted into a silver socket.

Chain In glass; see *Guilloche*; *Trailed Circuit*.

Chain Mail In armor; see *Mail*.

Chain Stitch A decorative stitch used in embroidery resembling the links of a chain.

Chair In cabinetwork; *chair* is now the common name given to a movable seat with a rest for the back, generally having four legs. It is designed either with or without arms and is often referred to as an armchair or side chair respectively. The chair was a familiar article of furniture in classical antiquity. Especially characteristic was the Grecian throne chair or thronos, a lofty seat for exalted persons, and the Grecian klismos, a variety of light side chair. The Roman sella curulis, or a folding stool of X-form, was often designed with a low back and its design was the inspiration for some of the earliest medieval European chairs. From the Middle Ages to the 19th century the development in chairs, like in all articles of furniture, has been from the simple to the complex, from scarcity to plenty and from crudely made to skillfully wrought. The chair during medieval times was a symbol of authority and its use was restricted to the master of the house and to distinguished guests. Chests, benches, settles and stools were generally used for seats. Gradually more chairs were made and finally during the 17th century the chair became a household necessity. No other article of furniture displays such a variety of design, and, as in all categories of cabinetwork, the 18th century was the great period in chairmaking. See *Klismos*; *Dantesca*; *Curule*.

Chair-Back Settee In English cabinetwork; a form of settee designed with open chair backs. This type of settee was made in England as early as 1680, and the back was similar to two tall banister-back chairs. The chair-back settee with an upholstered seat was reintroduced in the Queen Anne style and was extremely popular. It was designed with either two or three chair backs. The form of the open chair-back settee followed the

DANTESCA
Florentine c. 1450 - 1475

BURGOMASTER CHAIR
Dutch, early 18th century

LOUIS XVI
French c. 1780

**RESTORATION OR
CHARLES II CHAIR**
English c. 1675

HEPPLEWHITE
English c. 1785

SAVONAROLA
Tuscan c. 1490

HENRI II CAQUETOIRE
French, 2nd half 16th century

DIRECTOIRE
French c. 1795

QUEEN ANNE
English c. 1715

SHERATON
English c. 1795

HIGH RENAISSANCE
Tuscan c. 1525

LOUIS XIII
French, early 17th century

EMPIRE
French, early 19th century

CHIPPENDALE
English c. 1755

REGENCY
English c. 1810

FRAILERO
Spanish 16th century

LOUIS XIV
French c. 1675

RÉGENCE
French, early 18th century

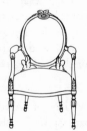

**ELIZABETHAN PANELLED
BACK OAK CHAIR**
English c. 1600

ADAM
English c. 1777

SLAT-BACK CHAIR
*American,
early 18th century*

**GOTHIC CHAIR
WITH COFFER SEAT**
French, 15th century

LOUIS XV *French c. 1740*

WILLIAM AND MARY
English c. 1695

DUNCAN PHYFE
American, early 19th century

design of the contemporary chair with an open back. The chair-back settee was designed in all the successive 18th century styles. Hepplewhite illustrates in the GUIDE a chair-back settee comprising four backs that are shield-shaped and are filled with bars or banisters. He called it a bar-back sofa. The chair-back settee was made in America in the Queen Anne, Chippendale, Hepplewhite and Sheraton styles.

Chairmaker In English furniture; in the Middle Ages and well into the 17th century practically all of the chairs for domestic use were made by carpenters and joiners. The craft of making chairs was not organized into a guild, such as that of the carpenters, joiners and turners, and records show that leading craftsmen making chairs in the period from around 1700 to 1750 refer to themselves as joiners and belonging to that company. The term *chairmaker* appears in early 18th century advertisements; however, present evidence does not support the belief that the work in the cabinetmaker's shop was rigidly subdivided in the Early Georgian period. It appears, however, that the making of caned chairs, which were so fashionable in the latter part of the 17th century, was considered to be a special trade. It seems that seat furniture in general was regarded as a special phase of cabinetmaking. This thought is supported by such large firms as Seddons where there was a department especially designated for the making of chairs, benches and settees.

Chair Rail A piece of wood running along the lower part of the walls of a room to prevent the backs of the chairs injuring the plastering when they are placed against it. This piece of wood is generally made to conform with the other woodwork of the room, and the wall space beneath is often decorated as a dado. See *Dado*.

Chair Table In English cabinetwork; the oak chair table was known as early as the middle of the 16th century. It was designed with a large circular or rectangular back

which extended beyond the uprights. The back worked on pivots and could be pulled forward to rest on the arms. When the back was let down in this manner it formed the top for a table. The chair table was made throughout the 17th century. It was sometimes called a monk's chair.

Chaise à Accoudoir In French cabinetwork; the French term *accoudoir*, meaning elbow rest or elbow cushion, is given to a distinctive variety of 18th century French chair characterized by an upholstered and thickly padded crest rail mounted on a shaped narrow back. In this form of chair the occupant sits in a reverse position and rests his arms upon the crest rail. It is similar in its principles of design to the voyeuse and fumeuse.

Chaise à Bec de Corbin In French Provincial cabinetwork; the name is given to a kind of Louis XIV provincial chair, having turned members. It was so named because of the supposed resemblance of the end of the arm to a crow's beak.

Chaise à Bureau In French cabinetwork; a desk chair. The principal variety was a kind of corner or roundabout chair with a low back. It was designed with an arched horseshoe-shaped back that continued to form the arms which rested on arm supports. The back could be described as gondola-shaped. The chair was sometimes designed with a circular revolving seat. It was generally caned and the seat was fitted with a leather cushion; frequently the front of the caned back was covered with leather. It was introduced during the Louis XV style. A characteristic and popular dressing table chair or chaise à poudreuse was of similar design.

Chaise à Capucine In French Provincial cabinetwork; a turned open armchair or side chair of marked simplicity with an open back and a straw or rush seat. It was originally found in the monastery cells and was adopted by the laity during the first half

CHAIR TABLE, ENGLISH

of the 17th century. After the middle of the 17th century the structure gradually became more refined. It was chiefly made of oak, cherry and occasionally of walnut, sometimes the wood was painted. The majority of these chairs owed their interest to the designs of their open backs. In some of the fine Louis XV examples, the uprights, open arms and armposts were designed with curved lines in place of the usual straight lines and the legs were cabriole in form. The straw seats were often provided with loose cushions covered in imported chintz or in printed cotton or linen. During the Louis XVI style the straw chairs gained much in refinement. The Directoire chaise à capucine often had a broad concave crest rail and a pierced splat. See *Capucine*.

Chaise à Poudreuse In French cabinetwork; see *Chaise à Bureau*.

Chaise à Sel In French cabinetwork; a French term meaning salt chair. It was a type of chest-bench introduced during the Gothic period. It comprised a wooden chest fitted with a panelled back and arms. The seat was hinged in order to give access to the salt which was kept in the section beneath the seat. The chaise à sel continued to be used in the French provinces.

Chaise à Vertugadin In French cabinetwork; the term is applied to a variety of 16th century small side chair similar to a farthingale chair. See *Farthingale Chair*.

Chaise de Femme In cabinetwork; a term frequently applied, especially in England, to a Caquetoire, which is a kind of French armchair. See *Caquetoire*.

Chaise Encoignure In French cabinetwork; a chair designed to stand in a corner of a room. In particular, a type of upholstered corner chair introduced during the Louis XV style. This chair designed in the Louis XV style had a gracefully curving valanced front seat rail which centered a cabriole leg. The term *marquise d'alcove* is now some-

times used to describe a very large type of corner chair.

Chaise Longue In French cabinetwork; a variety of day bed or long chair having one end designed in the form of a chair back. The chaise longue, which was upholstered and sometimes caned, was a fashionable piece of 18th century French furniture. It was constructed in either one, or in two or three pieces. See *Duchesse Brisée*; *Duchesse*; *Méridienne*; *Lit de Repos*.

Chaise Percée In French cabinetwork; a chair usually having a caned back and a hinged seat, which opens to a well fitted with an earthenware bowl.

Chalice In ecclesiastical art; a cup for wine used at the celebration of the Eucharist generally made of silver and occasionally of gold. In very early times it was also made of other materials, such as crystal and glass, and displayed variations in form. Early specimens were provided with handles, generally two but occasionally only one. In the 12th century when the cup was withdrawn from the laity the bowl of the chalice became smaller and the handles were no longer necessary. The chalice consists of a bowl, stem, knop and foot. The knop was often enriched with enamelling, precious stones, tracery or tabernacle work and the stem was frequently engraved and enamelled. The foot was designed in different shapes, such as circular and hexagonal, and generally extended considerably beyond the diameter of the bowl, which varied from about 3 inches to 6 inches and was of proportionate depth. See *Paten*; *Calamus*; *Communion Cup*.

Chamber-Candlestick In English silver; a tray candlestick in the form of a circular dish stand centering a candle-holder and fitted with an incurvate handle. It was provided with a cone-shaped device to extinguish the flame of the candle, as well as a pair of snuffers resting in a slot in the stem of the candle-holder. It was popular during the 18th century.

GOLD AND ENAMEL
CHALICE

Chambers, Sir William 1726–1796, English architect and designer. He was instrumental in developing the Chinese taste in England during the middle of the 18th century. In 1757 he published DESIGNS OF CHINESE BUILDINGS. He was appointed architect to King George III. He also designed the furniture for some of the buildings which he erected.

Chamfered In cabinetwork; the name given to the surface formed when the angle or edge has been cut away, such as a chamfered table leg. The chief distinction between canted and chamfered is the difference in degree of size; if it is cut off at an angle of 45° on a large scale it is referred to as being canted. The term *chamfer* is also applied to a small groove, furrow or channel, such as one cut in wood or stone.

Champagne In French Provincial; an old province in north-eastern France, bordering on Picardy, Lorraine and Burgundy. The furniture of Champagne was characterized by its simplicity in form and in ornament. As a rule the articles of furniture had well-balanced lines and little or no carving. Such woods as oak, walnut and cherry, which were not native to this region, were sparingly used. See *French Provincial*.

Champagne Glass In English glass; it is generally accepted that the champagne glass until around 1750 consisted of a wide open bowl of ogee contour which rested on a baluster or air twist stem and a conical-shaped foot. From around 1750 it had a tall funnel-shaped bowl with a plain, cut or air twist stem and resembled the ale glass. This shape remained fashionable through the early part of the 19th century when it was superseded by the saucer-shaped bowl with a hollow stem.

Champlevé Enamel See *Enamel*.

Chandelier Originally a French candle-holder. The name is now given to a lighting fixture, made of wood, metal, porcelain or glass, hanging from the ceiling; especially one having two or more branches. It was used as early as the 14th century. Especially remarkable are the 18th century German porcelain chandeliers made at Meissen and the French bronze doré chandeliers made by the celebrated French ciseleurs. See *Candlebeam*; *Corona*; *Candelabrum*.

Chandlee In American clockmaking; a famous family of American clockmakers working in Philadelphia, and Nottingham, Maryland. The first was Abel Cottey, 1655–1711, born in England, and working in Philadelphia circa 1682 and later. His son-in-law Benjamin Chandlee, Sr., 1685–1745, who was his apprentice, carried on the business and moved to Nottingham in 1711–1712. His son Benjamin Chandlee, Jr., 1723–1791, succeeded to his father's business. Several other members of this prominent family are noted clockmakers. They produced fine tall case clocks with eight-day movements and with finely engraved dials.

Chanfron In armor; the protective armor for a horse's head. It is generally a plate which covers the head, often with side plates attached.

Chantilly In French ceramics; a famous soft paste porcelain manufactory was founded at Chantilly by Louis-Henri de Bourbon, Prince de Condé, in 1725 under the direction of Ciquaire Cirou, d. 1751. It was in existence until about 1800, and after this date several independent manufactories were established making hard paste porcelain and earthenware. The finer Chantilly was made under Cirou's management and its distinctive glaze was made white and opaque with tin-ashes as in faïence. This early glaze with its milky whiteness and smoothness was unsurpassed in the history of porcelain. The glaze after 1750 during the second period was the usual lead glaze of a slightly yellowish warm tone; however, it was still of fine quality. The accepted mark is a hunting horn; red enamel in the earlier period and underglaze blue in the later period. Especially characteristic of Chantilly were the delicate painted designs

CHANTILLY PLATE

inspired by the Japanese Kakiemon porcelain which were in vogue from around 1725 to 1740. The painted colors were remarkable for their soft brilliance. Figure modelling of the early period was in the Japanese French taste and revealed an individual charm. The influence of Vincennes was apparent after the middle of the 18th century. During the later period quantities of simple and very often graceful tableware was produced. The plates were principally decorated in underglaze blue with slight floral patterns. During the last quarter of the 18th century there was evident an increasing amount of formalism in the designs which to a large extent detracted from their artistic interest.

Chantilly Lace Laces were made at Chantilly from the beginning of the 17th century. Chantilly is identified with the manufacture of bobbin-made black silk lace, which was created there and rightfully bears that name. Chantilly black lace, which was fashionable with the French aristocracy in the second half of the 18th century, is invariably made of silk; it is a grenadine and not a shiny silk. The designs and mesh ground were of the same silk and the cordonnet was a thicker strand of flat untwisted silk. Some of this lace was made of white blonde. A distinctive feature was the fond chant or six-pointed star réseau. Both black silk and white blonde Chantilly were fashionable during the French Empire. At this time the rich and large floral designs called by the French blondes mates became the prevailing style. Much of the black Chantilly was exported to Spain for mantillas. It is generally accepted that the French black silk laces and white blondes were unrivalled. See *Blonde Lace*; *Blonde de Caën*; *Bayeux Lace*.

Chantourné In French cabinetwork; a term, derived from the French word *chantourner* meaning to cut or carve in profile, applied particularly to a form of headboard characterized by its pronounced Baroque outline, chiefly comprising Baroque C-scrolls. This type of bed is called a chantourné de lit and is especially identified with a form of Louis XIV four-post tester bed or a lit à colonnes.

Chapin, Aaron American cabinetmaker working circa 1783–1838 first at East Windsor, and later at Hartford, Connecticut. Highboys and secretaries attributed to Chapin are fine examples of design and workmanship in the Chippendale style.

Charger A large flat dish or plate for carrying a large joint of meat to the table by the servant who, in medieval times in England, was also called a charger. Many early English chargers were made of silver. See *Blue-Dash Charger*.

Charka A small Russian drinking cup usually fitted with a single flange handle, used for drinking strong liquors. It was especially popular during the 17th century.

Charles II Chair See *Restoration Chair*.

Charles X King of France, 1824–1830. In French cabinetwork; in the literature on French furniture the name *Charles X style* is sometimes given to the furniture made during that monarch's reign and which continued into the reign of Louis Philippe, 1830–1848. The era was not marked by any new decorative movement; for it revealed no innovations in design. The French Empire style was continued in a more or less desultory fashion. Later in the 1820's a revival in the Gothic style with Gothic arches was essayed. This Neo-Gothic movement was introduced in connection with the Romantic literature so popular in Europe at that time. The furniture with its shapeless imitation of the Gothic was without artistic merit. Essentially it was a fad and was typical of the later French 19th century cabinetwork, which was principally an imitative art displaying no creative greatness. Renaissance, Louis XIV, with a predilection for Boulle work, and Louis XV were all reintroduced. The latter is especially identified with the Revived Rococo of Louis Philippe. The Empire style, stripped of all its former grandeur, kept growing more impoverished

LOUIS XIV
CHANTOURNÉ DE LIT

and heavy under Charles X. The furniture lacked character and vitality. It was marked, however, by fine materials and good craftsmanship, which were the outstanding and redeeming features of all the cabinetwork until around 1850. Some of the best work of this later Charles X phase was in chair design. Tables with lyre-shaped or X-shaped supports were also sometimes pleasing. In addition to mahogany, light colored woods also became fashionable. See *Empire; Louis Philippe; Louis XVIII.*

Charme Wood The wood of the hornbeam or yoke-elm trees, *carpinus betulus*, used in cabinetwork, especially by the French ébénistes. It is very hard and its color is white.

Chasing The art of making either raised or indented designs on a metal surface with particular steel tools or punches. Chasing is widely used as a decorative process by the silversmith.

Châsse A French term applied to a reliquary or shrine of a saint. It is usually in the form of a small rectangular metal box with a hinged gable cover. Châsses are generally ornamented with engraved figures of saints, and are frequently decorated with a ground of champlevé enamel.

Chasuble In ecclesiastical vestments; a form of mantle without sleeves covering the body and shoulders and put on over the alb and stole by the celebrant at Mass or the Eucharist. Originally it was worn by laymen as well as ecclesiastics, and in Saint Augustine's time around A.D. 400 it was called a casula, which is the diminutive form of the Latin *casa*, meaning a cottage or house. At that time it was simply a circular piece of cloth covering the entire body, with a hole in the center for the head. It was worn on cold and rainy days by peasants working in the fields and by travelers. During the Middle Ages the chasuble was probably the most graceful vestment of the Church. It was full, long and pointed and was gathered up over each

CHASUBLE

arm in a few graceful folds. Many writers on religious costumes deplore the change in form to the stiff and small chasuble dating from around 1700, which deprives the chasuble of its ancient beauty and dignity. From a very early period chasubles were richly decorated with embroidery and occasionally with jewels. The enrichments were remarkable for their symbolical beauty. Plain velvet is probably the best material for chasubles, since it enhances the striking richness of the embroidery of the orphreys.

Châtaignier Wood The wood of the chestnut tree, *castanea vesca*, used in cabinetwork, especially by the French ébénistes. It is hard and its color is yellow white.

Chatônes In Spanish furniture; a Spanish term applied to ingeniously designed ornamental nailheads used for decorating furniture. The use of decorative nailheads was a feature of Spanish cabinetwork.

Chauffe-Assiette In French furniture; a plate warmer. The principal type was generally of pedestal form and was about 35 inches high. The interior was metal lined and was fitted with shelves and a charcoal brazier. It was often made of tôle painted a dark color. It generally had a brass tray-shaped top with an ajouré gallery. The sides were fitted with brass handles; it rested on a plinth base which had casters. See *Plate Warmer; Chauffe-Plat.*

Chauffe-Plat In French furniture; a compartment over an oven or above the fireplace to keep the food hot. The term is also applied to an article of dining room furniture serving the same purpose. If the interior of the chauffe-assiette or plate warmer is not especially designed for the reception of plates only, it may also be used as a chauffe-plat, that is, to keep the food hot prior to serving. See *Chauffe-Assiette.*

Chauffeuse In French cabinetwork; a wooden chair introduced in the 16th century characterized by its very low seat. It was used by the mother or nurse in the dressing and care of babies and small children. Illustrations in French furniture literature show the mother sitting in this type of chair near the hearth. The chair with its low seat permitted the mother to reach conveniently all the things around her. The term was also applied to a form of lady's chair having a relatively high narrow back and characterized by a low seat. It seems that in an upholstered chair of this type the occupant could enjoy more warmth from the hearth when her chair was placed near it. See *Slipper Chair*; *Nursing Chair*.

Chausses In armor; the name applied to plate armor made to fit the legs closely. During the 13th century they were worn by nobles; however, at a later time they were also used by the other classes.

Checkered Diamond In glass; a decorative motif consisting of four small diamonds within a diamond. See *Diamond Pattern*.

Cheese Coaster An English piece of dining table service. It consists of a small wooden crescent-shaped piece which is mounted on a rectangular base fitted with casters. It was used to hold a head of cheese and was introduced around 1800.

Chelsea In English ceramics; the foremost English porcelain manufactory. It was established prior to 1745 at Chelsea, London, and was in existence until 1784. The early pieces marked with a triangle were generally in white and the forms were frequently taken from silver. It is assumed that Charles Gouyn was the manager during the "triangle" period. The next manager was Nicholas Sprimont. The manufactory seems to have been owned by Sir Everard Fawkener, secretary to the Duke of Cumberland who was a patron of the factory. Its first period was from around 1749 to the death of Fawkener in 1758. The manufactory seems then to have been closed for a couple of years. The mark for this period at first was a raised anchor or an anchor in relief and later a red anchor painted on the surface. The material for this period was a soft paste of exceptionally fine quality and the glaze which was slightly opaque was a cool white tone. The styles at first were influenced by Meissen; the Japanese brocaded Imari pattern and the Kakiemon designs were favored and borrowed from Meissen. The forms were in the Rococo taste. It is generally accepted that the Chelsea figures of this period are the finest ever made in England and rank among the best in European porcelain. Most of the figures were in the contemporary Meissen style and were simply and boldly modelled. Beautifully modelled figures of birds in natural colors were outstanding. Especially charming were the scent bottles, snuff boxes and other small objects, usually known as Chelsea toys and generally in the form of miniature figures. After Fawkener's death, Sprimont seems to have become proprietor as well as manager. The anchor mark was generally in gold. There was a noticeable change in the wares. Bone ash was included in the material and the glaze was more glassy. The general influence was Sèvres. Gilding was more profusely used and the decoration became more elaborate. Sprimont sold the manufactory to James Cox in 1769, who resold it in 1770 to William Duesbury and John Heath of Derby. The Chelsea factory was principally used by them for making tableware until it closed in 1784. The productions of this period, 1770–1784, are commonly called Chelsea-Derby and essentially follow the style of the Derby manufactory.

Chenets French andirons. See *Andirons*.

Ch'êng Hua The Ch'êng Hua reign of the Ming dynasty in China; 1465–1487. See *Chinese Dynasties*.

Chêng Tê The Chêng Tê reign of the Ming dynasty in China; 1506–1521. See *Chinese Dynasties*.

Chêng T'ung The Chêng T'ung reign of the Ming dynasty in China; 1436–1449. See *Chinese Dynasties*.

LOUIS XV CHAUFFEUSE

Chenille A variety of cord having a velvety texture resembling the skin of a caterpillar. Chenille cord or yarn has a center core of thread from which protrude, at right angles, short fibres of silk or wool. It was generally used for bordering and trimming on wearing apparel and furniture coverings.

Cherry Wood A hard close-grained fruit-wood, *prunus cerasus*, which is reddish in color, was used for general household furniture as early as 1680 in America. It was also used in England during the 17th century for inlay work and for small articles of furniture. See *Cerisier*; *Merisier*.

Cherub In ornament; a classical figure of a small child used extensively as a decorative motif. See *Amorini*; *Putti*.

Chest In cabinetwork; a large oblong box, generally made of wood, with a hinged lid. It was one of the earliest pieces of domestic furniture. During the medieval times the domestic chest was a very important article of furniture and served many purposes. It was used as a receptacle for storing clothes, wall hangings, fabrics and other possessions. It also served as a travelling box for carrying these possessions on a journey. In the medieval castle it was also one of the principal forms of seats, with benches and stools comprising the other characteristic seats. Cushions were often placed on the chest to provide a little comfort and some feeling of luxury. The chest also sometimes served as a bed and as a table. See *Cassone*; *Coffer*; *Coffre*; *Arca*; *Hutch*; *Tilting Chest*; *Bahut*; *Nonsuch Chest*; *Connecticut Chest*; *Hadley Chest*; *Pennsylvania Dutch Chest*; *Chinese Furniture*; *Grecian Furniture*; *Roman Furniture*.

Chest-Bench In cabinetwork; a wooden chest having a back and very often arms, used as a seat for two or more persons. It was introduced during the Gothic period. See *Archebanc*; *Cassapanca*; *Settle*.

Chestnut Bottle In American glass; a small 19th century American spirit bottle having

CHIPPENDALE YOKE-FRONT
CHEST OF DRAWERS

sides which are slightly flattened. It derived its name from its supposed resemblance to the shape of a chestnut.

Chestnut Wood See *Chataignier Wood*.

Chestnut Wood, French See *Marronnier Wood*.

Chest of Drawers In cabinetwork; the name given to an article of furniture having its entire front designed with a series of drawers. It was mounted on short legs and feet or simply on feet. The chest of drawers originated on the Continent. In English cabinetwork; the chest of drawers was fully developed around 1680-1685. The principal fronts found on the chest of drawers are serpentine, reverse serpentine, bow and straight front. The term *commode* was generally given in England to a chest of drawers designed in the French taste. In American furniture the chest of drawers is generally called a bureau. The American bureau or chest of drawers became a popular piece of furniture during the last quarter of the 18th century especially in the Chippendale, Hepplewhite and Sheraton styles. It appears that the popularity of the highboy and the lowboy in America essentially retarded the development of the chest of drawers until the Hepplewhite style. See *Commode*; *Block-Front*; *Kettle Shape*; *Bombé*.

Chest of Drawers on a Stand In English cabinetwork; the chest of drawers mounted on a stand was introduced around 1680. As a rule it was seldom more than five feet in height, which made the top drawers easily accessible. Unfortunately this feature of accessibility was lost in the later tallboys. Chests of drawers mounted on a stand were made into the early years of the 18th century, and the earlier turned legs were replaced by legs of cabriole form. The stretcher also disappeared. As a rule the chest of drawers mounted on a stand had a flat oblong molded top. The arrangement of drawers in the stand varied. This variety of furniture provided with drawers in the stand is called a highboy in America. See *Tallboy*; *Highboy*.

Chest-on-Chest In English and American cabinetwork; a chest of drawers resting on another chest of drawers; the upper chest, of conforming design, being slightly narrower. The upper section was designed with a row of two or three small drawers over three or four graduated long drawers. The slightly projecting lower section consisted of three or four long drawers and usually rested on bracket feet. It was introduced in England circa 1700 and was widely used in America during the second half of the 18th century. It is also called a double chest of drawers. It is more frequently called a chest-on-chest in America, while in England the terms *double chest* and *tallboy* are more commonly used to describe this type of chest of drawers. See *Tallboy*.

Chest-on-Frame In English and American cabinetwork; a chest mounted on a stand or frame. The name is especially applied to the 18th century chests mounted on a conformingly designed stand. See *Mule Chest*.

Cheval Fire Screen In English cabinetwork; the French term *cheval*, meaning horse or support, is given to a variety of fire screen having a vertical upright frame enclosing a panel sliding in grooves on the inner sides of the uprights which rest on arched supports. The cheval fire screen, which was introduced into England from the Continent, came into general use toward the end of the 17th century and continued in fashion throughout the 18th century. It was also called a horse fire screen. The majority of screens contained panels of needlework or tapestry. In some examples the panels were fixed. Both Chippendale and Hepplewhite illustrated the cheval type of fire screen in their pattern books. It derived its name from the frame or horse supporting the panel. See *Fire Screen*; *Écran à Coulisse*.

Cheval Mirror In English furniture; during the last quarter of the 18th century, a variety of mirror was introduced which had a mirror plate long enough to reflect a person's full length. This standing type of mirror was called a cheval dressing glass and sometimes a horse dressing glass. The mirror was enclosed in a rectangular frame which was attached to the uprights by swivel screws. The uprights rested on splayed bridge feet. Sometimes the cheval mirror was mechanically designed with lead weights so it could be raised or lowered. Frequently candle arms were attached to the uprights. The cheval mirror was illustrated in Sheraton's DRAWING BOOK and remained popular through the Regency style. The cheval or horse dressing glass derived its name from the framework or support on which it was suspended, since the French term *cheval* means horse or support. See *Psyché*.

Cheveret In English cabinetwork; a small table having an oblong top over a shallow frieze drawer mounted on four slender quadrangular and tapering legs joined with a shelf. This table, which was in common use late in the 18th century, was often made of satinwood. It was designed with a movable book stand having an open shelf for books over one or two rows of shallow drawers. It was provided with a bracket-like handle. This variety of table was called a cheveret in Gillow's cost book. See *Gillow, Robert*.

Chia In Chinese bronzes; a ritual cup used for libations. Its usual form consists of a round body with a loop handle and resting on three legs; however, some were square-bodied with four legs. The chia sometimes has a cover. On the top of the rim are two short posts, called chu-posts. These chu-posts represent the North star and have bell-shaped tops.

Chia Ching The Chia Ching reign of the Ming dynasty in China; 1522–1566. See *Chinese Dynasties*.

Chia Ch'ing The Chia Ch'ing reign of the Ch'ing dynasty in China; 1796–1820. See *Chinese Dynasties*.

Chiaroscuro An Italian term referring to an early process of wood-engraving prints done

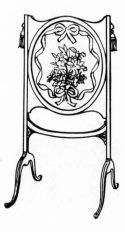

HEPPLEWHITE
CHEVAL FIRE SCREEN

from several blocks; also a term applied to the arrangement of light and shade in painting; also to a drawing or picture in brown and white or black and white.

Chichi   In Oriental rugs; it is another spelling for the name Tchichi. See *Tchichi*.

Chi Chou Yao   See *Kian Temmoku*.

Ch'ien Lung   The Ch'ien Lung reign of the Ch'ing dynasty in China; 1736–1795. See *Chinese Dynasties*.

Chien Wên   The Chien Wên reign of the Ming dynasty in China; 1399–1402. See *Chinese Dynasties*.

Chien Yao   In Chinese ceramics; the Chien ware, which was first made during the Sung dynasty, was so named because it was made in the province of Fukien, first at Chien-an and then at Chien-yang. This ware consists entirely of tea bowls. The characteristic Chien yao tea bowl is conical in shape and has a coarse reddish-black stoneware body. The glaze is blue-black streaked or mottled with a lustrous brown. Sometimes the brown is the strong color and the mottlings and streaks are in black. Especially fine is the Chien yao bowl with a shining black glaze having fine radial rust-colored streaks that resemble the fur of a hare or the markings of a partridge. See *Temmoku*; *Kian Temmoku*; *Honan Temmoku*. The term *Chien yao* is also the Chinese term for Blanc de Chine. See *Blanc de Chine*.

REGENCY CHIFFONNIER

Chiffonnier   In English furniture; it is generally accepted that the term *chiffonnier* was first applied during the Chippendale style to a shallow, rectangular, standing piece of furniture of open construction, designed in the Chinese taste and fitted with several shelves, which was commonly used for the display of china. During the Regency the term was given to a low shallow standing cupboard. The front was commonly fitted with two grill doors; occasionally the front was entirely open. The cupboard was fitted with adjustable shelves and was used to contain books. Its average height was about 25 to 40 inches and its length usually exceeded its height. It was often mounted on a plinth base. This low book cupboard was a very characteristic and popular piece of Regency furniture.

Chiffonnier   In French cabinetwork; the term is generally given to a tall chest of drawers which was essentially a feminine piece of furniture. The name, which is derived from *chiffonnier* meaning a collector of scraps or odds and ends was applied to this piece of furniture in which the ladies kept their work, such as needlework and cuttings of cloth. The chiffonnier, which rested on a base with very short legs, was about 4 to 5 feet in height, and was generally fitted with five and occasionally six drawers of equal depth. It was of costly workmanship and was made principally of rosewood or violet ebony. It was introduced around the middle of the 18th century. In America it is generally used as a piece of bedroom furniture.

Chiffonnière   In French cabinetwork; a small table introduced during the Louis XV period, generally used by ladies "to keep their needlework or trifles in." The principal variety was designed with a rectangular top over three small and narrow superimposed drawers. It rested on four long and slender legs which were sometimes joined with an undershelf. During the Louis XVI style the chiffonnière was very often classified as a work table, especially when the top was designed with a brass gallery to secure the balls of wool. See *Work Table*; *Table à Ouvrage*.

Chih   In Chinese bronzes; the name given to a drinking vase or vessel. It is in the form of a baluster-shaped vase having a domed cover with a finial.

Chi Hung   In Chinese ceramics; the name given to the brilliant red derived from copper. This sacrificial red is particularly identified with the reigns of Hsüan Tê and Ch'êng Hua during the Ming dynasty. During the K'ang Hsi reign of the Ch'ing dynasty an attempt was made to reproduce this Ming red. The attempt was not successful but the misfiring did result in the magnificent monochromes called Peach Bloom and Lang Yao or Sang de Bœuf. See *Ming*.

Child's Chair In English and American cabinetwork; there are two principal forms of chairs designed for children, namely one with very short legs and another with elevated supports. This latter type, which is often referred to as a high chair, facilitated the feeding of the child. The chair with the short legs was essentially a miniature form of the chair designed for adults. The chair, which was solidly constructed to withstand hard usage, was generally made entirely of wood, and occasionally it had a slip seat. The majority were relatively plain and their charm was in the simplicity of their design. Chairs were made for children in England at least as early as 1600 and they were made in America from early Colonial days.

Ch'i-Lin In Chinese art; a fabulous or mythical animal subject extensively used in painting, sculpture and ceramics. It has a dual nature and is both male and female. It is generally portrayed as having a head that resembles the head of a dragon, the body of a deer with slender legs and horse's hoofs, a curly and bushy tail like a lion's, and shoulders with flames. It is regarded as the noblest form of animal creation and it is reputed to live for one thousand years. It is symbolic of perfection and happiness and its appearance portends a virtuous ruler. It is also called a kylin. See *Chinese Animal Figures*.

Chimera In ornament; a mythical female monster emitting flames; generally having a lion's head, goat's body and dragon's tail. Also any fanciful conception of a monster with incongruous parts.

Chimney Glass In English furniture; the term *chimney glass* was sometimes applied in England to the overmantel mirror which was introduced at the end of the 17th century. See *Overmantel Mirror*.

China See *Porcelain*.

China Cabinet In English cabinetwork; a large rectangular cabinet having glazed doors and an interior fitted with shelves for displaying porcelains. Although the term *cabinet* is principally reserved for a piece of furniture fitted with small drawers, doors and secret compartments, it is also generally applied to an article of furniture having an upper portion that is glazed and is fitted with shelves for the display of porcelain. The characteristic Carolean china cabinet rested on a wooden stand. During William and Mary, due to the vogue for collecting Chinese porcelains, china cabinets became more plentiful. A characteristic 18th century china cabinet had two glazed doors in the upper portion, and the lower portion was generally designed with drawers and occasionally with two panelled cupboard doors in place of the drawers. It appears that the earliest extant examples of the china cabinet in America date from around 1790 and were in the Hepplewhite style. See *Corner Cupboard*.

China Clay In ceramics; the English term for kaolin. See *Kaolin*.

China Stone In ceramics; the English term for petuntse. See *Petuntse*.

China Table In English cabinetwork; Chippendale illustrates in the DIRECTOR, 1754, a form of oblong table designed with a gallery, a frieze and four legs. He states that these tables are "for holding each a set of china and may be used as tea tables." See *Tea Table*.

China Tree Wood The wood of the China tree, *melia azedarach*, from Guiana and China, was widely used in cabinetwork. It is hard and its color is red brown and black spotted.

Chinese Animal Figures In Chinese art; a variety of animal subjects were extensively used by the Chinese in painting, sculpture, textiles and ceramics. The animal subjects to a large extent represent mythical creatures; however, some were also borrowed from

GEORGE III CHINA CABINET

the animal kingdom. Among the animal motifs which played an important part in Chinese culture and art are the following: Dog of Fo; Ch'i-Lin; Fêng Huang, Lung, Lu, Hu; Ho; T'u and Fu. See *Chinese Gods*; *Chinese Symbols and Emblems*; *Chinese Four Season Flowers*.

Chinese Chippendale In English cabinet-work; Chippendale and other prominent mid-18th century furniture designers in their effort to conform to the prevailing fashion for chinoiseries produced many designs for furniture in the Chinese taste. The form of the furniture underwent little or no change; most of the time the carved enrichments were simply grafted on characteristic mid-18th century pieces. An assortment of Chinese detail was added to the prevailing Rococo style of ornament. Pagoda motifs and fret-work figured prominently. Carved pagoda tops were freely employed on many articles of furniture and a carved pagoda motif was introduced in a wide molding. Chinese figure subjects, birds, flowers and bells were introduced as carved enrichments to produce an oriental feeling. Chinese detail was frequently combined with Rococo motifs. Decorative appointments, such as mirrors, sconces and wall brackets, were light and fanciful and were often of a fantastic outline. The vogue for furniture in the Chinese taste reached its peak around 1760. See *Chippendale, Thomas*; *Chinoiserie*; *Bamboo-Turned*.

CHINESE CHIPPENDALE
MIRROR

Chinese Dynasties In Chinese art; the art work of China is designated by the dates of the dynasties and the reigns of the monarchs in each dynasty. The following is a chronological list of the dynasties and the reigns:

Chinese Dynastic Dates

Shang	1766–1122 B.C.
Chou	1122– 255 B.C.
Ch'in	255– 206 B.C.
Han	206 B.C.–A.D. 220
Six Dynasties:	A.D.
Chin	265– 420
Liu Sung	420– 479
Northern Wei	386– 535

Six Dynasties (continued)	
Chi	479– 502
Liang	502– 557
Ch'en	557– 589
Sui	589– 618
T'ang	618– 906
Five Dynasties	907– 960
Sung	960–1279
Yüan	1280–1368
Ming	1368–1644
Ch'ing	1644–1912

Reigns of the Ming Dynasty

Hung Wu	1368–1398
Chien Wên	1399–1402
Yung Lo	1403–1424
Hung Hsi	1425
Hsüan Tê	1426–1435
Chêng T'ung	1436–1449
Ching T'ai	1450–1456
T'ien Shun	1457–1464
Ch'eng Hua	1465–1487
Hung Chih	1488–1505
Chêng Tê	1506–1521
Chia Ching	1522–1566
Lung Ch'ing	1567–1572
Wan Li	1573–1619
T'ai Ch'ang	1620
T'ien Ch'i	1621–1627
Ch'ung Chêng	1628–1644

Reigns of the Ch'ing Dynasty (to 1850)

Shun Chih	1644–1661
K'ang Hsi	1662–1722
Yung Chêng	1723–1735
Ch'ien Lung	1736–1795
Chia Ch'ing	1796–1820
Tao Kuang	1821–1850

Chinese Embroidery The embroidery art of China is of very early origin and is celebrated for its skillful and delicate execution which is almost unsurpassed except for the work of the Japanese. Due to the dampness of the climate little early Chinese work survives but the ancient designs have been continuously reproduced. The work is produced by men as well as women and is remarkable for its elaborate execution in which the ground is entirely covered on such articles as state robes and screens. The Chinese embroidery work is done in many different ways and with a variety of stitches. In some of the work both sides of the piece are the same. It is executed by painting the design on a thin fabric, then stretching it, and working a satin stitch backward and forward so that the finished piece does not have a wrong side. The most notable Chinese embroidery is done with floss silk and gold and silver threads displaying an endless variety of designs which include dragons, mythological monsters, figures, symbolical devices, cherry blossoms, asters, and birds and butterflies all executed in a variety of oriental color tones.

Chinese Export Porcelain In ceramics; a collective term for porcelain made in China for the export market, such as Lowestoft, Armorial and Jesuit wares.

Chinese Four Season Flowers In Chinese art; the Chinese artist revealed great talent in floral painting. Some of the finest porcelain designs are of flowers. Flowers treated in a conventional manner occur in scrolls and in continuous running designs; especially favored were the lotus and peony scrolls. However the majority of floral designs are treated in a naturalistic manner and are admirable for their flowing and graceful qualities. Each flower is easily recognizable, but without a copied or studied character. The Chinese were great lovers of flowers and had a special flower for each month and one for each season. The peony was for spring, the lotus for summer, the chrysanthemum for fall and the plum blossom or prunus for winter. See *Chinese Gods*; *Chinese Animal Figures*; *Chinese Symbols and Emblems*.

Chinese Furniture Fine Chinese household furniture which once furnished prosperous Chinese homes from the 15th century onwards is characterized by simplicity of line unbroken by ornamentation. The designs of much of this furniture bear a striking resemblance to the best of contemporary Western furniture design. The furniture, which combines beauty and functional design, has an air of dignity and refinement and is well proportioned and balanced. Polished woods of superb quality, skillfully selected and handled, were an outstanding feature of this cabinetwork. The finest woods were largely imported. Much of the fine furniture was made of hua-li or rosewood, which is not too unlike the European rosewoods. The Chinese preferred above all other woods tzu-t'an or red sandalwood. Hua-mu or burl and wu-mu or ebony were especially used for inlay work. Altogether there were about twenty varieties of woods in common use. Among the lesser woods were pear, elm, cedar, oak, camphorwood, chestnut, pine and cypress. Teak wood was apparently never used traditionally in proper Chinese cabinetwork. Originally the Chinese lived on mats or platforms before and during the T'ang dynasty, 618–906. The Japanese who borrowed heavily from the Chinese culture and customs still live at the present time in the same manner. They sit or recline on flat surfaces covered with mats, often with various types of low supports for back or arm rests. This living platform is called in China a K'ang; it is either movable or built in. The built-in k'ang, which is lower than a chair seat, extends in the average home completely across one side of a room and it is generally deep enough to recline on. It is covered with a woven mat. In addition to the small low table which is the most characteristic piece of k'ang furniture, the other typical pieces are chests or very low cupboards which are used to hold quilts, cushions and bedding. They are generally in pairs and are placed against each side of the wall on the k'ang. It is generally accepted that the chair as a domestic article of furniture was introduced in Early Han, since Han tomb models are known. During the 17th and 18th centuries the chair was made in a great variety of forms and materials. As a rule the seat of the chair is slightly higher than the standard European chair. The stretcher served as a foot rest. Wooden footstools were also in general use. Cupboards both

CHINESE PLATE
WITH PEONY MOTIF

CHINESE CHAIR,
MING DYNASTY

large and small are an important variety of Chinese furniture. Small open shelves, designed with shelves at split levels for the reception of porcelain, were much used. They were placed on tables, chests or cupboards. A rather tall shallow rectangular piece of furniture designed with small cupboard doors and several shelves at split levels was an interesting article of Chinese furniture. Chests and boxes in tiers were preferred to chests of drawers. The Chinese always favored a round dining table, although square dining tables also were in general use. Stools rather than dining chairs were customary. They have always been a much used article of Chinese furniture. Writing tables or painting tables were made; desks or bureaus were relatively scarce. Side tables were an important and imposing article of Chinese furniture. They were long and narrow and were usually higher than the European side table. Small tables such as the lute table especially designed to hold the Chinese zither, semi-circular small tables, nests of tables and many other varieties of interesting and unusual shapes were a delightful category of Chinese furniture. The Chinese bed with its four posts and tester is not too unlike the 18th century European tester bed. Lacquered articles of furniture were usually reserved for a more elaborate setting. Entire rooms of lacquered furniture were generally found only in palaces. See *Tzu-T'an*.

Chinese Glass   The technique of melting and molding glass was practiced in China from at least the time of the Han dynasty, 206 B.C.–A.D. 220, but apparently glass blowing was not practiced to any appreciable extent until the reign of K'ang Hsi, 1662–1722. Although Chinese glass displays a high degree of workmanship, it seems that their chief interest in glass was only to imitate the texture of more precious materials, such as jade, emerald and other hard stones. The decoration was often lapidary in character and much was carved on the lapidary's wheel. In the 18th century they also tried to duplicate the texture of porcelain in their glass and they painted it in enamel colors in a manner generally restricted to porcelain. It is generally accepted that the most productive period in Chinese glassmaking began during the reign of Ch'ien Lung, 1736–1795. Intricately cut snuff bottles, belt buckles and other similar articles were especially typical. Cameo glass snuff bottles imitating carved stones were particularly praiseworthy, and marbled effects were also skillfully developed. See *Ku Yüeh Hsüan*; *Snuff Bottle*.

Chinese Gods   In Chinese art; there are four kinds of subjects recognized in Chinese art. They are figures; nature which includes birds, animals and flowers; landscapes; and miscellaneous subjects. The motifs borrowed from these four categories are endless. The figure subjects are deities and deified mortals borrowed from the three religions, namely Confucianism, Taosim and Buddhism. Taoism, which has the strongest hold on the Chinese imagination, has furnished the largest number of motifs for decorative art. Included among the favorite figure subjects are the following: Confucius, Buddha, K'uei Hsing, Kuan Ti, Kuan Yü, Shou Lao, Lu-hsing, Fu-hsing, Hsi Wang Mu, Kuan Yin, Pu-Tai Ho-Shang and the Eight Taoist Immortals or Pa Hsien. See *Chinese Animal Figures*; *Chinese Symbols and Emblems*; *Chinese Four Season Flowers*.

Chinese Hand-Tufted Carpet   See *Hand-Tufted Carpet*.

Chinese Imari   In Chinese ceramics; Chinese porcelain decorated with underglaze blue and overglaze colored enamels in the Japanese Imari style. It was made during the reign of K'ang Hsi, 1662–1722, and it is generally accepted that Japanese models continued to be used during the succeeding reign of Yung Chêng, 1723–1735. They copied the Kakiemon style and the characteristic old Imari wares. Especially characteristic of the old Imari was the porcelain with masses of a dark cloudy blue with a soft Indian red and gilding; these colors being supplemented by touches of green, aubergine and yellow enamels and a brownish black. The designs which consisted of asymmetrical panels and mixed brocade patterns had a bold decorative effect due to the prominence of the blue, red and gold. See *Imari*; *Kakiemon*.

Chinese Lacquer Lacquer correctly called as well as used both in China and in Japan is a natural product and is the sap of a tree, *rhus vernicifera*. The tree was indigenous to China, and was cultivated in Japan from at least the 6th century. The foundation for lacquer ware in both China and Japan is generally wood, although sometimes brass or porcelain was used. The process employed in producing lacquer in China was essentially the same as in Japan. Any slight variations in the process are relatively unimportant. Lacquer was engraved in both China and Japan. The Chinese carved lacquer work was highly esteemed. In this method the lacquer was built up of successive layers which were either of the same color or of different colors, depending upon the desired result. Then it was cut back from the surface into designs. The red lacquer which was so highly prized was colored with cinnabar. It is believed that all branches of lacquering now practiced in China were known at least as early as Sung. The use of gold lacquer in which the Japanese have never been rivalled was not developed in China. Gold was only used in China as a simple flat decoration, particularly on a black ground. Especially notable is the coromandel work. In this method the design is cut out in intaglio and then completed with different color or with gold. There was a great demand for coromandel screens in western Europe toward the end of the 17th century. They were chiefly imported by the East India Company. The art of lacquering in Japan was developed far beyond any Chinese conception. See *Japanese Lacquer*; *Burgauté*.

Chinese Lowestoft In Chinese ceramics; a hard paste porcelain ware made in China during the 18th century for the various English trading companies. It was known as Company Porcelain; it was also called East India porcelain because of the trading companies that handled it. It acquired the name *Lowestoft* in error as it was thought to have been made at a little factory at Lowestoft, England. It was a poor quality ware and has only a historical value. It is generally agreed that much of this porcelain was manufactured at Ching tê Chên and was sent to Canton to be decorated. The ware was decorated in accordance with the merchant's taste. The final destination of the ware in Europe such as France, England and Portugal was often revealed in the taste of its decoration. See *Armorial Ware*; *Jesuit Ware*.

Chinese Oriental Rug This rug is woven exactly like an Oriental rug. The weave is generally rather loose and coarse, and the foundation is usually cotton. The pile which is long is made of silk or wool. As a rule the colors are pale with blue and yellow predominating. The designs are indigenous to China and are usually broken or separated from each other by large areas of solid color. See *Oriental Rug*.

Chinese Railing In English cabinetwork; Chinese railing, which is lattice-work or trellis-work, was sometimes used to fill in the open backs and open arms of mahogany chairs designed in the Chinese taste during the Chippendale style.

Chinese Soft Paste In Chinese ceramics; a kind of porcelain compounded with a special clay that is described by the Chinese as Hua Shih or soapy rock. It seems to be a kind of pegmatite or steatite which makes the body of the ware especially receptive to painted designs executed in underglaze blue. The Chinese used their finest quality of cobalt blue on this ware as well as the most skillful brush work. It generally had a crackled glaze. This so-called soft paste blue and white ware was first made during the K'ang Hsi reign and in the succeeding reigns of Yung Chêng and Ch'ien Lung during the Ch'ing dynasty. Especially typical

CHIPPENDALE CHAIR WITH
CHINESE RAILING

of the ware are small pieces such as snuff bottles, small tea incense bottles and objects essential for writing. See *Ch'ing*; *Blue and White, Ch'ing*.

Chinese Symbols and Emblems In Chinese art; a great diversity of emblematical devices and symbols were often employed in Chinese art. A popular set was the Eight Precious Objects or Pa Pao. They are the pearl or chu that grants every wish, a copper coin or ch'ien for wealth, the lozenge or hua, the open lozenge or fang shêng symbol of victory, musical stone or ch'ing, a pair of books or shu, a pair of horn-like objects or chüeh, and a leaf of artemisia or ai yeh, a plant of good omen. Another favorite set was the Eight Happy Omens or Pa Chi Hsiang which were among the signs on Buddha's feet. They are the wheel or lun, knot of longevity or ch'ang, canopy or kai, umbrella of state or san, lotus or hua, twin fishes or yü, shell or lo and vase or p'ing. The eight attributes of the Eight Taoist Immortals were also much favored. See *Chinese Gods*; *Eight Taoist Immortals*; *Hundred Antiques*; *Eight Trigrams*.

EIGHT PRECIOUS OBJECTS
or PA PAO

Chinese Taste European decorative art has been influenced by the art of China for many years. Chinese porcelains have influenced European ceramics since the 16th century. From early in the 17th century the Dutch East India Company brought lacquered woodwork articles, especially screens, to Europe from the Orient and was largely responsible in creating a vogue for all kinds of lacquered articles. From the time of the Restoration, 1660, there was evident in England an ever-increasing appreciation for Chinese porcelains, lacquered work, embroideries and all kinds of Chinese bibelots, such as carved ivories, jade and Chinese bronzes. The reign of William and Mary was marked by a mania for china collecting and lacquered articles enjoyed great popularity. Another interesting feature resulting from the contact with the Orient was the custom of tea drinking. This custom, although not entirely new, became an accepted social custom during the reign of William and Mary. Apart from the direct influence of imported wares was the more diffused interest in the Orient to which can be attributed the fantastic chinoiseries depicting an imaginary world of pseudo-Chinese figures and scenes. Chinoiseries as a basis of design invaded all of the branches of the decorative arts; however, they were not as consistently developed in England as in France and in the other Continental countries. Chinese taste was less in evidence in England during the Early Georgian period until around the middle of the 18th century when a widespread revival in Chinese taste occurred. Chippendale and other contemporary designers included Chinese detail in their repertory of ornament which they introduced on pieces of furniture of essentially mid-Georgian contour. The mid-Georgian Chinese taste in interior decoration was generally confined to one or two rooms in the wealthy homes which were hung with Chinese wallpaper and with the carved and painted decoration conveying an oriental feeling. Before the end of the 18th century another revival in the Chinese taste occurred in England. This later Chinese interest is identified with the Regency style, and was partly due to the influence of George, Prince of Wales, who had his drawing room at Carlton House treated in the Chinese manner. The interest in Chinese art was also evident in America before 1700, and lacquered or japanned articles were made in America from around the beginning of the 18th century. The Chinese influence of the mid-eighteenth century in England was evident in American Colonial furniture designed in the Chippendale style, as well as in wallpaper, fabrics and other branches of the decorative arts. See *Chinese Chippendale*; *Chinoiserie*; *Japanning*; *Delft*; *Johnston, Thomas*.

Ch'ing In Chinese ceramics; a Chinese color word. It is generally described as the color of nature. It was used in early Chinese records in a comprehensive and vague manner. It was applied to the sea green in celadon, to the pale shades displayed in the Sung glazes and to certain other colors and neutral tints. See *Celadon*.

Ch'ing The Ch'ing dynasty of China, 1644–1912. The art of this period is referred to as Ch'ing. In Chinese ceramics; the splendid porcelains which are associated with the Ch'ing dynasty were not made during the early years of this period due to unsettled domestic conditions and spasmodic fighting. The Imperial manufactory at Ching tê Chên was destroyed during the rebellion of 1673. In 1680, after the rebellion was practically over, the Emperor ordered the rebuilding of the Imperial manufactory at Ching tê Chên, and a glorious age of Chinese porcelains which was to last almost one hundred years began. The great emperors K'ang Hsi, 1662–1722, Yung Chêng, 1723–1735, and Ch'ien Lung, 1736–1795, were all patrons of the arts. Essentially the period marked a renaissance in ceramics. There were several new developments in Ch'ing; however, the basic principles had already been established during the Ming dynasty. The processes are chiefly those of the preceding dynasty. The monochromes during the Ch'ing dynasty were widely diversified and numerous, and are representative of some of the most refined porcelain of this period. The Ch'ing monochromes were chiefly developments of Ming monochromes, imitations of Sung glazes and numerous innovations. The success of the Imperial manufactory is attributed to three remarkably talented superintendents. Ts'ang Ying-Hsüan was appointed in 1680 to reorganize the Imperial manufactory. He was followed in the Yung Chêng period by Nien Hsi-Yao. T'ang Ying, who was appointed to assist Nien Hsi-Yao in 1728 and who later succeeded to the position which he held until 1749, is generally considered to be the greatest of the three. Although the influence of the work of these three was felt for many years, the absence of inspired leadership gradually became apparent in subsequent

production. The final blow occurred during the T'ai P'ing rebellion, 1850–1875, when the Imperial manufactory was razed. See *Chinese Dynasties*; *Sung*; *Ming*; *Peach Bloom*; *Mirror Black*; *Sang de Bœuf*; *Clair de Lune*; *Flambé*; *Powder Blue*; *Apple Green*; *Imperial Yellow*; *Famille Verte*; *Blue and White, Ch'ing*; *Three Color Ware*; *Chinese Soft Paste*; *Ching tê Chên*.

Ch'ing Ho Hsien In Chinese ceramics; wares of the Tz'u Chou type were made at this site during the Sung dynasty. See *Tz'u Chou*.

Ching T'ai The Ching T'ai reign of the Ming dynasty of China, 1450–1456. See *Chinese Dynasties*.

Ching tê Chên A renowned ceramic center in China, usually considered to be the greatest pottery center in the world. It was located east of the large Po Yang lake in the northern Kiangsi province. In 1369, Hung Wu, 1368–1398, who was the founder of the Ming dynasty, rebuilt the various kilns already located there and made it the Imperial manufactory. The colored and painted porcelains of the great Ming dynasty were developed there. In the succeeding Ch'ing dynasty a veritable renaissance in Chinese porcelains was achieved at Ching tê Chên. This great ceramic center had about three thousand kilns. The many hundreds of private manufactories located there followed the work of the Imperial potteries.

Chinkinbori In Japanese lacquer; the term applied to engraved lacquer. See *Japanese Lacquer*.

Chinoiserie In ornament; a French word meaning Chinese art is particularly applied to the decorative designs which depict an imaginary world of pseudo-Chinese figures and scenes. These designs of fantastic composition became fashionable as a decoration at the end of the 17th and 18th centuries in Europe. The taste for imported Chinese wares, such as embroidered silks, lacquered articles and porcelains, received an important early stimulus through the Dutch East India

CHINOISERIE BY PILLEMENT

Company, who conducted a most lucrative trade with the Orient from early in the 17th century. In addition to the influence of imported Chinese wares in Europe there were certain travel books, especially those published by the Dutch about the third quarter of the 17th century, which played an important part in developing an interest in Chinese art. These books attempted to show Chinese customs and their manner of living. The designing of chinoiseries was particularly suited to the French genius. They first appeared mingled with Baroque ornament around the end of the 17th century. Jean Bérain was especially instrumental in dedeveloping the early phase of chinoiseries in France. French cabinetwork displaying this style of ornament from around 1700 to 1720 is considered to be in the style of Régence. Chinoiseries in the Rococo taste were principally attributed to the French school of decorative designers led by Antoine Watteau, François Boucher and Jean Pillement; the engraved designs of the latter were especially popular in England. Chinoiseries became a fashionable decoration on furniture, lacquered woodwork, silver, porcelain, pottery, wallpaper, cotton and linen textiles. The vogue for chinoiseries was not as consistently developed in England as on the Continent. See *Régence*; *Watteau, Antoine*; *Boucher, François*; *Louis XV*; *Vernis Martin*; *Chinese Chippendale*; *Regency*; *Chinese Taste*.

Chintz In textiles; the word *chintz*, which is the plural of chint, is a Hindu word derived from the Sanskrit *chitra*, meaning many-colored. The name is given to a cotton cloth painted or printed in different colors, a process originating many centuries ago in the East. It seems that imported chintz or painted calicoes first appeared in England early in the 17th century. During the last quarter of the 17th century calicoes with their designs already drawn were imported from India and later painted in England. From the beginning of the 18th century the vogue for chintz in all kinds of upholstery grew by leaps and bounds. The demand for chintz began to threaten the English industries of silk and wool, and, as a result, Parliament passed an act in 1722 forbidding the importation as well as the English manufacture of all calicoes. In 1774 part of the act was rescinded to permit the English manufacturing of chintz, but the ban on imported chintz was enforced until a later date. See *Calico*; *Cretonne*; *Upholstery*.

Chio In Chinese bronzes; the term applied to a libation cup. It consists of a small ovoid-shaped body resting on three legs. There are two elongated pouring lips arranged symmetrically on opposite sides of the mouth. A cover which extends over the mouth and pouring lips resembles the conventionalized heads and beaks of two birds.

Chip Carving A form of crude hand carving done by cutting chips out of the wood with a knife or chisel. See *Carving*.

Chippendale Style Circa 1740–1745 to 1780. See *Chippendale, Thomas*.

Chippendale, Thomas c. 1718–1779. English cabinetmaker and furniture designer. He was the son of Thomas Chippendale I, a cabinetmaker and wood carver of Worcester. He moved to London with his father about 1727 and opened his own shop in 1749; in 1753 he moved to No. 60 St. Martin's Lane where he remained for the rest of his life. He had as his first partner James Rannie, who died in 1766. His second partner was Thomas Haig. In 1754 he published the first edition of the GENTLEMAN AND CABINET MAKER'S DIRECTOR. A second edition was printed in 1755, which was virtually a reprint, and a third in 1762. The DIRECTOR contained one hundred and sixty engraved plates of designs for furniture. The third edition had two hundred engraved plates. The majority of the designs were in the French Rococo, the Chinese or the Gothic taste. Some of the designs were of a fantastic character and were not adaptable to be developed into actual furniture. Some of the finest designs were derived directly

CHIO

from the French. Many of the Chinese designs with their geometrical lattice-work were remarkable for their elegance and effectiveness. It is erroneous to believe that all these designs were to be executed in mahogany. Many were to be finished with lacquering, gilding or painting. The designs in the DIRECTOR displayed to a large extent the traditional style of the mid-Georgian period, upon which were grafted the different new and short-lived fashions. Chippendale's reputation was originally derived from this book, and the foundation of the popular acceptance of the Chippendale style was based upon this book. It should be remembered, however, that Chippendale was but one of the many designers of fine furniture around the middle of the 18th century. Trade publications of a similar type, but not on such a grand scale, were issued by Ince and Mayhew, 1759-1763; Robert Manwaring, 1765; Lock and Copland, 1740-1752 and 1768-1769, as well as by other designers. The designs in the DIRECTOR essentially established the English Rococo style. As a result of recent research Chippendale's place in English cabinetwork has been reappraised. It has now become patent that Chippendale was responsible for only a few, if any, of the designs in the DIRECTOR. Evidence now suggests that Lock and Copland were retained by Chippendale and that Chippendale was indebted to them for a large portion of the designs appearing in the DIRECTOR. Present evidence points out that Copland was responsible for a majority of the designs for carver's pieces in the DIRECTOR and that Lock made sketches for the same type of work commissioned by individual clients. Chippendale spent much of his career as the organizing head of a very large and successful business which undertook the entire furnishings of a house. In order to determine the merit of the cabinetwork executed at Chippendale's shop it is necessary to examine the finished pieces. In only a few cases has the furniture been conclusively identified as having been made at his shop; the two most valuable sources

being the furniture at Nostell Priory and that at Harewood House. The accounts for Nostell Priory date from 1766 to 1770 and include examples in the Rococo style. It can be ascertained from these invaluable accounts that the furniture made at Chippendale's shop was notable for the finely selected wood, for the fine constructional methods and the quality of craftsmanship in general, and for the use of refined moldings. The beautiful quality of the carving on some of these pieces establishes the fact that Chippendale employed highly skilled craftsmen. However, his work in the Rococo style is now considered to be inferior to that of Vile. The accounts from Harewood House in Yorkshire date from 1772 and represent the post-DIRECTOR phase of Chippendale's work, which is regarded as his most perfected work. It must be remembered, however, that some of these pieces were designed by Robert Adam and were executed by Chippendale's cabinetmakers. This furniture was designed in the Neo-Classic or Adam style and was frequently decorated with superb marquetry work and with handsome ormolu mounts. It was executed with the highest quality draftsmanship. And so Chippendale in his last phase, 1770-1779, under the influence of Robert Adam has achieved his eminence in a style which was the antithesis of the style with which his name is popularly identified. See *Rococo; Gothic, English; Chinese Chippendale; Pilaster; Marquetry; Adam, Robert; Vile, William; Ince and Mayhew; Lock and Copland; Mahogany; Cabriole Leg.*

CHIPPENDALE SETTEE

Chippendale, Thomas, Jr. 1749-1822. He succeeded to the business of his father at No. 60 St. Martin's Lane, and for some years the firm continued to trade under the name of Chippendale and Haig until the latter retired in 1796. In 1814 he had premises at No. 57 Haymarket and in 1821 he was found at No. 42 Jermyn Street. He became bankrupt in 1804, when his entire stock was sold at auction. Thomas Chippendale Jr., as his father had formerly been, was a member of the Society of Arts and exhibited five paintings at the Royal Academy between 1784 and 1801. The firm under his supervision enjoyed a good reputation despite his financial embarrassment and was very active at the end of the 18th century and the beginning of the 19th century. He maintained the high standard of workmanship which had been established by his father. He supplied furniture to both Harewood House in Yorkshire and Harewood House in Cavendish Square. Some of these pieces, executed in the style of the Regency, show the Regency style at its best and are of a less extravagant nature. See *Chippendale, Thomas*; *Regency*.

Chiu   In Chinese bronzes; the name given to a bowl for food which appears in a variety of forms. It is found with two or four handles or without handles. It rests on a base in the form of a low or high foot and at times on three short feet. The later variety occasionally had a cover in the form of an inverted bowl.

Chocolate Pot   A vessel in which hot chocolate is served. In English silver; the early chocolate pot was similar to the early coffee pot, the only difference being a small hole in the lid, covered with a removable cap, to allow a stick or brush to be inserted in order to stir the contents. Frequently the cap, which is usually surmounted with a finial, is attached to a chain which is fastened to the handle. The chocolate pot was made in several shapes, such as cylindrical and pear-shaped. Occasionally the chocolate pot had a lip spout, and as such was also used as a hot milk or hot water jug. It was introduced late in the 17th century.

Chopin   A Scottish liquid measure equal to $1\frac{1}{2}$ English pints. It is derived from the French word *chopine* which is equal to about $\frac{4}{5}$ths of an English pint. A vessel of this capacity was commonly made in pewter. See *Mutchkin*; *Measures*.

Chrismatory   In ecclesiastical art; a case to contain the holy oils and chrism, which is a consecrated oil deriving its name from the Latin *chrisma* meaning anointing or unction.

CHRYSANTHEMUM VASE

In the Roman Catholic Church the case contains three vessels or flasks of oil for baptism, confirmation and anointing the sick. Chrismatories are either small and portable or they are large when they are kept in the sacristy. Silver and gilt chrismatories occasionally enriched with enamelled sacred images are mentioned in medieval church inventories.

Christmas Nativity Art   See *Crèche Art*.

Chrysanthemum   In Japanese crests; the official emblem of the Imperial family of Japan is the kiku-no-go-mon or the august chrysanthemum crest. It is represented with sixteen petals. The chrysanthemum flower can also be used as a badge by other families or societies; but the petals must be either more or less than sixteen. The sixteen-petal chrysanthemum was widely used as a decorative motif on porcelains, lacquer ware and other similar pieces that were made only for the Imperial household. In Chinese art; the chrysanthemum is one of the flowers of the Chinese four seasons representing Autumn. See *Chinese Four Season Flowers*.

Chrysanthemum Vase   In Chinese ceramics; a vase with a long slender neck on an ovoid-shaped body having reeding around the lower portion resembling the petals of a chrysanthemum. In particular, one of the seven classic shapes of the Chinese Peach Bloom wares.

Ch'ü Chou   See *Celadon*.

Chueh   In Chinese bronzes; a small cup principally used for pouring libations. It has an ovoid-shaped bowl provided with a loop handle and rests on three legs and sometimes four legs. On one side the lip rim is extended in the form of a pointed lobe, while the opposite side is extended in the form of a wide trough-like pouring spout. Two chu-posts, representing the North star, are attached on the top of the rim.

Chü-Lü Hsien   In Chinese ceramics; wares of the Tz'u Chou type were made at this site during the Sung dynasty. See *Tz'u Chou*.

Ch'ung Chêng The Ch'ung Chêng reign of the Ming dynasty in China; 1628–1644. See *Chinese Dynasties*.

Chün Yao In Chinese ceramics; a large group of wares first made in the early part of the Sung dynasty in Honan province at Chün Chou or Chün T'ai. The ware was strong and durable, and was chiefly composed of bulb bowls, deep flower pots with plates, bowls and other similar useful pieces. Each piece of first quality generally had a Chinese numeral from 1 to 10 carved on the base. It had a hard glaze that was very thick and highly opalescent and that often flowed sluggishly. The colors were rich and variegated. The characteristic Chün glaze had a foundation of lavender-grey or blue-grey usually with a faint flush of red detected somewhere in the glaze. Sometimes this pale lavender flecked with greyish-white had a large splotch or splotches of dappled dark purple. In other bowls the red in the glaze suffused into a lilac-purple which sometimes shaded on to crimson. Sometimes the red almost dominated the grey on the outside of the bowl, while the inside was a lavender grey. Occasionally the grey formed an opaque greenish-grey layer over the lavender; this layer as a rule occurred inside the bowl and was often broken by Y-shaped or irregular lines which the Chinese called earthworm marks. The red and purple glazes were full of bubbles, which in bursting gave the surface a pitted appearance. These pin holes, which the Chinese called ant tracks, explained to a large extent the characteristic dappling and fine streaking. Often added to this blend of colors was an interesting brownish tint. This occurred at the edge of the rim and other similar projecting parts where the glaze was thin and was almost transparent and colorless. The crackle, which occasionally occurred, is generally regarded to be accidental. The body of the ware varied widely in texture and in quality. The ware having the incised numerals had a fine greyish white porcelaneous body. The glaze flowed with relative smoothness.

Another ware, which was always without numerals, usually had a coarse-grained buff-grey porcelaneous body. The glaze flowed unevenly and ended above the base, which was rough and unglazed, in a wavy roll or in heavy drops. Between these two Chün wares was another ware which has sometimes arbitrarily been called Kuan Chün, or Kuan ware of the Chün type. It is also regarded as a finer ware of the second category. It was without numerals, and was characterized by thinner potting and by a controlled glaze. Soft-Chün, which the Chinese called Ma-Chün, was a beautiful ware. It had a buff earthy-looking body and a thick opaque glaze. The glaze was finely crazed, and was more waxy than the characteristic Chün glaze. As a rule the color was pale lavender-blue and occasionally peacock blue, and generally there was a splash or two of crimson.

CHÜN YAO FLOWER POT

Chu-Posts In Chinese bronzes; the name given to a pair of short post-shaped appointments found on ancient Chinese libation vessels. The chu-posts represent the North or Polar star and are found on the lip rim of a libation vessel in the form of square or round short posts usually with bell-shaped tops.

Churrigueresque A Baroque style of architecture introduced in Spain late in the 17th century. It was so called from the name of the architect, José Churriguera, d. 1725, who was the chief leader of the movement. This style lasted for about one hundred years. See *Renaissance, Spanish*.

Ciborium In ecclesiastical art; the canopy over the altar resting on four columns, in the early Christian Church, from which was hung the receptacle containing the reserved sacrament. At a later time in the Western Church the canopy became known as a baldaquin and the vessel containing the reserved sacrament was called a ciborium. The ciborium was often elaborately wrought in gold, silver and champlevé enamel in a form resembling a chalice with a domed cover.

Cinnabar Lacquer A term applied to lacquer or lacquer work; the lacquer being colored with cinnabar which is a vermilion or red mercuric sulphide. See *Japanese Lacquer*; *Lacquer*; *Chinese Lacquer*.

Cinquecento An Italian term referring to the 16th century. It is particularly applied to the 16th century as a period, representing the highest development of Italian Renaissance art. It follows the quattrocento period.

Cinquedea In arms; see *Anelace*.

Cinquefoil In ornament; a decorative motif having five pointed lobes resembling the leaf of the cinquefoil. It was widely used in Gothic design. In architecture; an ornament composed of five leaves or sections formed by the spaces between a group of cusps in a pointed Gothic arch or in a circular ring. The ornament was suggested from the cinquefoil plant, *potentilla reptans*, which has compound leaves each having five leaflets. See *Quatrefoil*; *Trefoil*.

GOTHIC CINQUEFOIL

Cipriani, Giovanni Baptista 1727–1785. A Florentine artist who came to England in 1755. In a short time he became well known for his painted decoration in buildings and houses. Included among his more important works were four panels for the ante-room of Lansdowne House and the ceiling of the ballroom at Melbourne House. He was an excellent draftsman. It is generally believed that his Neo-Classic treatment of antique and mythological figures and subjects as well as of Renaissance motifs afforded an inspiration for much of the painted decoration on late 18th century furniture such as commodes and cabinets. See *Adam, Robert*.

Circassian Rug An Oriental rug belonging to the Caucasian group. The foundation is of wool, and the pile is of wool, and rather short in length. Its designs are Caucasian with some Persian patterns and they are rather crudely executed. Also called Tcherkess. See *Caucasian Rugs*.

Circassian Walnut A fine quality of walnut from the Circassia district in the Russian Black Sea area. It is brown with dark stripes.

Ciselé Velvet Ciselé is a French word meaning cut. It is applied to various kinds of cut silk velvet. Especially fine were the figured cut silk velvets on a satin ground made during the Italian Renaissance. See *Velvet*.

Cistercian Ware In English ceramics; a variety of English red ware almost having the hardness of stoneware made during the 16th century and found around the Cistercian abbeys. Some of the pottery bears dates prior to 1540 when the monasteries were dissolved. The ware has a black or dark brown glaze and occasionally has a trailed white slip decoration.

Cistern Or Wine Cistern. The name applied to various large vessels for holding liquor or water. In English silver; see *Wine Cistern*. In English cabinetwork; see *Wine Cooler*.

Citrine See *Quartz*.

Citron Wood The wood of the sandarac tree, *callitris quadrivalvis*, of Morocco, widely used in cabinetwork, especially by the French ébénistes. It is a hard, durable and fragrant wood, and its color is yellow red.

Citronnier Wood The wood of the citron tree, *citrus medica*, of Asia and Middle Europe, widely used in cabinetwork. Its wood is firm and durable, and its color is white veined.

Clair de Lune In Chinese ceramics; clair de lune or moon white is the name given to a Chinese ware having a beautiful glaze of the palest blue. It was first made during the K'ang Hsi reign at Ching tê Chên. It was made in the same forms as Peach Bloom with an additional few forms of its own. It is sometimes faintly tinged with lavender. The glaze is without crackle.

Classeur A small French open case placed upon a bureau, having vertical divisions for holding papers; also any other piece of furniture so used, such as a large one with leg supports used for holding prints.

Classic Revival Or Neo-Classic. The term is applied to the style of classic ornament which derived its inspiration from a revived interest in Greek and Roman art. It is generally accepted that the excavations begun at Pompeii and Herculaneum in 1738 resulted in discoveries of antique art that aroused a new interest in it. Publications on antiquities by Comte de Caylus and Sir William Hamilton and the archaeological researches by Johann Winkelmann and his eulogies on antique art were all important factors. The Adam brothers and Giovanni Piranesi were also noteworthy figures in this renewed revival of interest in antique culture. However, the success of the movement was undoubtedly largely due to a reaction against the Rococo, for France had begun to tire of her Rococo style around the middle of the 18th century. The light and graceful Louis XVI style is the early phase of the Neo-Classic and the pompous Empire style is the later phase. Between these two is the Directoire style which has essentially the qualities of a transitional style. During the Louis XVI style the classic ornament was borrowed from the Renaissance and antique art, and was interpreted in the lighter form of the 18th century. Gradually as antique art was better understood the taste for the antique became more exacting and its closer imitation was sought, which finally resulted in the Empire style. In England the principal genius of the Neo-Classic was Robert Adam. He is regarded as virtually the creator of a style which is known by his name. The subsequent classic styles of Hepplewhite and Sheraton reflected the spirit of the Adam style. In England the later phase of the Neo-Classic is called the Regency. Italian Neo-Classic furniture design was essentially an Italian interpretation of the contemporary French and English styles. See *Adam, Robert*; *Louis XVI*; *Empire*; *Regency*; *Directoire*; *American Federal*; *American Directoire*; *American Empire*; *David, Jacques Louis*; *Albertolli, Giocondo*; *Hamilton, Sir William*; *Caylus, Comte de*; *Piranesi, Giovanni*; *Rococo*.

Clavichord A rather small rectangular musical instrument having strings and a keyboard. It was placed upon a table or stand. The mechanism consists of tangents or metal wedge-shaped pieces attached in an upright position to the ends of the keys. The tones are produced by pressing the keys, causing the tangents to rise and strike the strings. It is the earliest form of keyboard stringed instrument and was evolved in the 13th century from the monochord which was used for teaching singing and the notes of the scale in medieval monasteries. Until the 18th century several tones were usually produced from the same string and clavichords varied as to the number of keys. Some are depicted in 15th century works of art with nine keys and six strings, and later examples have as many as twenty or more keys. In contrast to the Virginal, Spinet and Harpsichord whose strings are plucked to produce a tone, the strings of the clavichord are struck; it is thus the prototype of the modern piano.   See *Virginal*; *Spinet*; *Harpsichord*.

Claw and Ball Foot In cabinetwork; the design for this foot was derived from the oriental design of a dragon's claw holding a ball or a pearl. It was introduced in England about 1710. It succeeded the club foot; however, the latter continued to be used until around the middle of the 18th century. The claw and ball foot was in vogue until about 1765. It was the foot most commonly found on a cabriole leg. Also called Ball and Claw. See *Foot*; *Club Foot*; *Cabriole Leg*.

Clay, Charles d. 1740. English clockmaker. He excelled in producing elaborate and ingenious musical clocks. By 1723 he had become clockmaker to the Board of Works.

Claymore A large medieval two-edged sword with cross hilt used by the Scottish Highlanders. It is incorrectly applied to the broadsword with a basket hilt adopted in the 16th century as the full-dress sword in the Highland regiments.

LOUIS XVI BRONZE APPLIQUÉ

EMPIRE BRONZE APPLIQUÉ

Clay's Ware An English term applied to a form of papier-mâché patented by Henry Clay of Birmingham in 1772. Clay's manufactory made many panels for furniture of this papier-mâché, which was japanned and highly polished by hand. Also characteristic of this ware were tea caddies, trays, boxes and panels for coaches. Clay's ware was prepared from strong sheets of paper pasted together rather than from paper pulp, and was not papier-mâché in the strict sense of the word. Originally Clay's ware was called paper ware, but the commonplace name hampered the sale of the articles, so the firm of Jennens and Bettridge, who were the most successful makers of paper ware in the 19th century, revived the name of papier-mâché which immediately found favor with the public. English papier-mâché revealed a high standard of workmanship until around 1850 when a decline became increasingly evident. Undoubtedly the finest English work occurred from around 1825 to 1850. Furniture made entirely of papier-mâché was an Early Victorian product. See *Papier-Mâché*.

CLICHY PAPERWEIGHT

Clichy A French glass manufactory founded in 1840 at Clichy, a suburb of Paris. In addition to its fine crystal glass the manufactory is especially noted for its very fine paperweights. It closed in 1870. See *Paperweight*; *Flint Glass*.

Clignancourt In French ceramics; a porcelain manufactory founded at Clignancourt, Paris, in 1771 by Pierre Deruelle, under the patronage of Louis-Stanislas-Xavier, known as Monsieur, Comte de Provence, brother of Louis XV. It remained in existence until at least 1798. The porcelain was of a fine quality. Included among the accepted marks are a windmill; crowned "M"; "M"; "LSX" in a monogram.

Clock It is doubtful if the domestic clock was known much before the 16th century. The earliest domestic clock was driven by weights and was of the hanging variety. It required adequate space beneath the mechanism for the fall of the weights and it was generally a fixed clock and was large in size. Shortly after 1500 the domestic clock driven by springs was devised and was perfected around 1525. It was first made on the Continent and was later imported into England. The spring-driven clock resulted in a compact chamber clock. This spring-driven clock in a metal case did not remain in fashion in England for any great length of time. The majority of English domestic clocks from the time of Queen Elizabeth I until the last quarter of the 17th century were weight driven. They were enclosed in a metal case usually of brass and were hung against the wall or set upon a wall bracket with the chains and weights exposed and hanging down. This early clock in England was known as a lantern or bird cage clock. The introduction of the pendulum as a regulator marked a most important development in the science of measuring time. It is generally accepted that the first pendulum clock was made in Venice around the middle of the 17th century. With the introduction of the pendulum the clock assumed a different character. The use of the long pendulum resulted in the designing of the tall case clock which extended to the floor. The long case was originally designed to protect the weights from any outside interference. The tall case clock rapidly gained importance as a decorative article of furniture and the cabinetmaker expended all his skill in decorating the case. After the short pendulum was introduced in England in 1658 small clocks of the so-called bracket or table variety appeared in ever-increasing numbers. See *Tall Case Clock*; *Lantern Clock*; *Bracket Clock*; *Fromanteel, Ahasuerus*.

Clodion, Claude-Michel 1738–1814. French sculptor. He is particularly noted for his finely modelled terra-cotta statuettes of mythological figures as well as for his decorative friezes of cupids, nymphs and similar subjects. The early pieces were made

CLOCKS

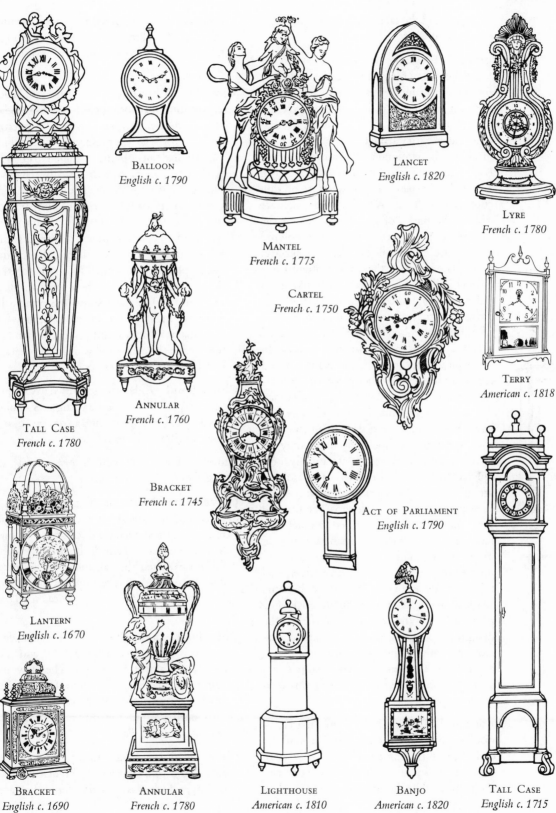

BALLOON
English c. 1790

LANCET
English c. 1820

LYRE
French c. 1780

MANTEL
French c. 1775

CARTEL
French c. 1750

TERRY
American c. 1818

TALL CASE
French c. 1780

ANNULAR
French c. 1760

BRACKET
French c. 1745

ACT OF PARLIAMENT
English c. 1790

LANTERN
English c. 1670

BRACKET
English c. 1690

ANNULAR
French c. 1780

LIGHTHOUSE
American c. 1810

BANJO
American c. 1820

TALL CASE
English c. 1715

at Nancy and the later pieces in biscuit were produced at Sèvres.

Cloisonné Enamel In Japanese art; cloisonné enamel, which is referred to in Europe simply as enamel, was developed during the 19th century. It is the work of covering the surface of bowls, vases and other decorative objects with vitrified compounds applied in either the cloisonné or champlevé style. Kaji Tsunekichi started this work in 1838. Generally the base of this work is of thin copper. The cloisons, which are delicate ribbon-like pieces of metal, are laid on the surface in the desired designs. The colored enamels are then applied to the open surface. In the later part of the 19th century three distinct schools developed, each having a different technique. The school of Namikawa Yasuyuki of Kyoto produced a work of soft rich colors in perfectly executed graceful designs on well-formed vases. In some pieces the decoration usually covered the entire surface; in other pieces the decoration was of pictorial designs on a soft-toned monochrome ground. The school of Namikawa Sosuke of Tokyo developed the cloisonless enamels, although at times they do have cloisons. The designs are usually outlined with thin metal ribbons. The cloisons are hidden as the work progresses, unless they are required in the design. The finished work has an entirely vitrified enamel surface. The work of the third school is that of monochrome and translucid enamels. In monochrome enamels the vitrified enamel is made to do as much as is possible the same work as a porcelain glaze in monochrome porcelains. In the translucid enamels the designs are chiselled or cut in the metal surface and are visible after the enamel is applied. Sometimes colored enamels are applied to the chiselled designs in this type of work. See *Enamel*.

Close-Stool In English furniture; the close-stool was found in England from around the end of the 15th century. The majority were of box form and the early ones were covered with fabric while the later ones were finished

CHIPPENDALE CLOTHESPRESS

in wood. They remained in general use until early in the 18th century when the night table and close-stool chair were introduced. See *Night Table*.

Clothespress In English furniture; an article of furniture for storing clothes. Chippendale and his contemporaries illustrated numerous designs for the clothespress. The typical variety had an oblong molded top over two long doors which usually enclosed sliding shelves and trays. The lower portion contained one or more rows of long drawers and rested on a molded base with short feet. The clothespress was much preferred to the tall wardrobe or press which had preceded it. Hepplewhite illustrated the clothespress in the GUIDE and stated it to be a necessary piece of furniture. The clothespress was principally designed in America in the Hepplewhite and Sheraton styles and, as in England, it superseded the earlier tall wardrobe generally fitted with two long cupboard doors.

Cloud-Band A design motif used in Oriental rugs, especially in Persian rugs. A cloud-band usually appears in a design like a floating ribbon of silk.

Clouté d'Or In French decorative art; see *Posé d'Or*.

Cloven Hoof Foot In cabinetwork; a type of carved foot used on a cabriole leg that resembled the cloven hoof foot of an animal. It is also called a pied de biche. In English furniture; when the cabriole leg was introduced around 1700 it terminated in a cloven hoof foot. See *Club Foot*; *Pied de Biche*; *Foot*.

Club Foot In English furniture; the club foot was introduced around 1705 and succeeded the cloven hoof foot. The claw and ball foot succeeded the club foot around 1710; however, the latter continued to be used until around the middle of the 18th century. See *Pad Foot*.

Cluny Guipure In lace-making; in the latter part of the 19th century the French town of Le Puy, which was an active center for lace-making in central France, named some of its coarse patterns guipure de Cluny, after the museum in Paris. The town of Mirecourt, an early and important lace center in the province of Lorraine, also in the later part of the 19th century produced a Cluny lace, which was so-called because the first patterns were copied from extant examples of early lace found at the Cluny museum. Both Le Puy and Mirecourt found these so-called Cluny laces extremely successful and profitable.

Cluster Leg In English furniture; a leg usually in the form of a triple cluster column. The cluster column was a feature of Gothic architecture. During the revival of the Gothic style the legs of tables and chairs were occasionally designed in the form of a cluster column. See *Chippendale, Thomas*; *Gothic, English*.

Coaching Glass A small English drinking glass; the small rounded bowl held one draft of liquor. It did not have a stem or a foot. The bowl was rounded at the bottom and had a knob attached at the center of the bottom. As a stage coach stopped at an inn, a waiter carried out a tray containing these glasses, which were placed on their rims. They were taken and held right end up and filled with liquor; when empty they were replaced on the tray with their rims down. The fuddling glass is similar to the coaching glass except that it is used indoors and is more decorative.

Coach Watch See *Sedan Clock*.

Coalbrookdale See *Coalport*.

Coalport Or Coalbrookdale. In English ceramics; a porcelain manufactory was founded at Coalport, Shropshire, by John Rose around 1796. It absorbed the factory at Caughley in 1799 and it acquired molds and material from Nantgarw and Swansea around 1822–1823. It is not possible to distinguish the early Coalport porcelain from that of Caughley. A large part of it was sent in white to London to be decorated. Later

between 1820 and 1850 all types of wares were produced and were chiefly imitative. Until recently the manufactory was in existence with works in Staffordshire. Included among the accepted marks are "CBD" in monogram and "CD".

Coaster In English silver; a decanter coaster; another name for decanter stand. See *Decanter Stand*.

Coat-of-Mail In armor; see *Mail*.

Cobb, John d. 1778. Celebrated English cabinetmaker. He was in partnership with William Vile at No. 72 St. Martin's Lane from 1750 to 1765. After Vile retired in 1765 Cobb carried on the business until his death in 1778. He supplied furniture to George III, the nobility and the aristocracy. See *Vile, William*; *Marquetry*.

Cobirons The name applied to andirons for use in the kitchen. The vertical shafts are fitted with hooks to support the spits. See *Andirons*.

Cochin, Charles-Nicholas, the Younger 1715–1790. Noted French designer, engraver and writer on art. He was appointed First Painter to the French court in 1755. Although his decorative designs were often executed in the Rococo style, he was a strenuous opponent of that style of art. Some of his work resembled the compositions of Boucher. He possessed a remarkable facility as a draftsman. In 1754 and 1755 he published two famous letters attacking the Rococo style of ornament and the extravagance into which it had fallen.

Cockbeading Or Cockbeaded. In English cabinetwork; a small projecting molding applied around the edge of a drawer front. It was introduced during the Early Georgian era. It was often used in the cabinetwork designed in the Chippendale style. See *Bead*; *Molding*.

Cockfighting Chair In English cabinetwork; an English chair similar to the reading chair. See *Reading Chair*.

COBIRONS

Coconut Cup In silver; a variety of decorative standing cup. The body of the cup, which was made of the shell of a coconut, was richly mounted in silver and rested on a silver stem that flared into a circular foot or base. Coconut cups were mentioned in medieval times and were popular in the 15th and 16th centuries. In English silver; the coconut cup was introduced into England from the Continent. Extant examples date from the first quarter of the 15th century. See *Standing Cup*.

Coelanaglyphic Hollow relief. See *Relief*.

Coffee Pot In English silver; coffee was first known in England about 1650, and the early silver coffee pot, of which extant examples date from about 1670, had straight sides tapering toward the top with a straight spout. It was fitted with a conical cover and a wooden handle, at a right angle to the spout, set in silver sockets. This form is sometimes called a lighthouse coffee pot. During the reigns of Queen Anne and George I the cover was shaped like a high dome. This form was succeeded by the coffee pot of octagonal shape. Both the coffee pot with a high dome-shaped cover and the one of octagonal form had a graceful swan neck spout frequently terminating in a bird's beak with a hinged flap used to conserve the heat. Evidence of the pear-shaped form appeared prior to about 1750 and evolved into the graceful pyriform coffee pot with a plain body and dome-shaped cover having a decorative finial. There were several variations of the pyriform in the latter part of the 18th century. In the last quarter of the 18th century the coffee pot assumed a classic form, borrowed from antique Roman vases, resting on a high foot. During the early 19th century the pear-shaped coffee pot was again adopted. See *Teapot*.

Coffer In cabinetwork; a kind of chest. The coffer was generally smaller in size than the domestic chest and was more strongly made since it was primarily intended to hold valuables and documents. Sometimes it was clamped by iron bands and furnished with an elaborate and intricate lock, the interior being fitted with secret receptacles. The distinction between the chest and the coffer is not always observed, with the result that the terms are frequently used interchangeably. See *Chest*.

SILVER-MOUNTED
COCONUT CUP

Coffered Panel An architectural term for a decorative, deeply sunk panel in a ceiling, generally centering a flower or some similar motif. The term is used in furniture for a similar panel treatment, such as on the façade of a chest. The opposite of a coffered panel is a fielded panel having bevelled edges and a flat field in the center.

Coffin-End Spoon In American silver; a spoon having a stem-end shaped on the top and on the sides in such a manner as to have a supposed resemblance to a coffin. It was introduced around 1800.

Coffre In French cabinetwork; the name given to a French chest. The coffre of the 13th century was crudely made of thick boards, held together by braces of wrought iron. The wood was generally either painted red or covered with hide or painted canvas, which provided a contrast for the ironwork. The 14th century coffre was decorated with carved designs which were borrowed from Gothic architecture. The iron fittings, such as the hasp and the case of the lock, were notable for their minute detail and for their artistic quality. See *Chest*; *Coffer*; *Bahut*.

Cogswell, John American cabinetmaker of Boston, Massachusetts, working circa 1760–1818. His shop was on Middle Street.

Coiffeuse In French cabinetwork; the term *coiffeuse* is generally given to the characteristic toilet or dressing table introduced at the beginning of the 19th century and designed in the Empire style. It had an oblong top, generally of white marble, over a frieze fitted with drawers, and was principally designed with either lyre-shaped or curving X-form end supports. Two slender uprights

DELFTWARE LION—*English, 18th Century.*
The Metropolitan Museum of Art, gift of Mrs. Russell S. Carter,
1945.

MAJOLICA TAZZA—*Italian, 16th Century.*
The Metropolitan Museum of Art, gift of V. Everit Macy,
in memory of his wife, Edith Carpenter Macy, 1927.

DETAIL FROM STONEWARE TANKARD—*German, 17th Century.*
The Metropolitan Museum of Art, gift of R. Thornton Wilson, 1954, in memory of Florence Ellsworth Wilson.

which were attached at the rear of the table, supported a framed rectangular, oval or circular mirror by means of swivel screws. The uprights were often of bronze and were frequently fitted with bronze candle arms. The width of the mirror varied from about one third to practically the entire length of the table. The name *coiffeuse* is also given to any side table fitted with toilet accessories in the frieze drawer and having a miniature psyché placed on the top of the table. See *Psyché*; *Poudreuse*.

Coin Glass The name given to a kind of 17th and 18th century drinking glass, which had a rounded bowl that rested on a stem with a base. A knop on the stem enclosed a coin of money. Sometimes the glass was designed with a cover surmounted with a knop that enclosed another coin.

Coin Silver See *American Silver*.

Cold Colors Or Cold Painted. A term used in ceramics and glass for unfired colors. It is generally believed that much of this form of painting has been lost by repeated cleaning or rubbing, while colors transmuted by heat or fire are in effect imperishable.

Colichemarde In arms; a type of sword blade frequently found on smallswords. It is triangular in section from near the hilt to a third of its length; then it tapers abruptly to a more narrow section, which is often four-sided, to the point. The term is a French corruption of the name of Count Otto Wilhelm Königsmark, 1639–1688. See *Smallsword*.

Cologne In German ceramics; the great production of Rhenish stoneware at Cologne and nearby Frechen had its origin in medieval times. The typical brown ware was made at least as early as the 15th century; however, it did not achieve artistic importance until around 1525 and it showed evidence of decline around 1600, when the potteries for making salt-glazed stoneware were transferred to Frechen. The material for the stoneware was grey and the color of the surface, which was achieved by a wash of ferruginous clay, varied in tone from a chestnut brown to a dull yellow. The color was invariably more or less speckled. After 1600 the coloring generally had irregular patches of blue. There were three principal manufactories in Cologne. The most active pottery was in the Maximinenstrasse. It produced pear-shaped jugs and the so-called Bartmann jugs with a bearded mask on the neck. A very fine variety of jugs was decorated with applied oak leaves on scrolled stems. The best production was from around 1520 to 1550. A smaller manufactory was in the Komoedienstrasse. A third and rather important manufactory was in the Eigelstein producing the characteristic stoneware jugs. See *Frechen*.

Colonial Style See *American Colonial*.

Colored Looping In American glass; an applied glass decoration developed in the 19th century which was borrowed from English and German glass. Parallel threads of one or more contrasting colors were applied and formed into parallel loops and then imbedded in the glass surface. It was a favorite method for decorating all kinds of glass in America. In English glass it is often called Trailed Ornament.

Colt In American arms; the first practical repeating gun with automatic revolution and cylinder locking operated by cocking the hammer was patented by Samuel Colt, 1814–1862, in 1836. Colt established his first manufactory for repeating firearms under his patent at Paterson, New Jersey, called the Patent Arms Mfg. Co. The company was active from 1836 to 1842 and then failed due to the lack of government and public support. The Mexican War stimulated a demand for arms and Colt secured a government contract for one thousand army revolvers which he had produced by Eli Whitney at Whitneyville, Connecticut. In 1847 Colt acquired additional contracts and established the Colt Patent Fire Arms Mfg. Co., at Hartford, Connecticut, where it has

EMPIRE COIFFEUSE

continued to operate. The Colt firearms, which included pistols, rifles, carbines and shotguns with the Colt revolving cylinder, were made in various types and calibers, and achieved great fame in the Civil War, Spanish American War and with the Indian fighters and famous characters of the West.

Comb In armor; the projecting ridge on the top of a helmet. This ridge or blade was especially characteristic of the morion and the burgonet. During the latter part of the 16th century the comb was frequently very large and high on these helmets.

Comb-Back Windsor Chair In cabinet-work; a type of high back Windsor chair; in which the center rear spindles continue upward through the horseshoe-shaped arm rail and terminate in a shaped crest rail. In a double comb-back a few of the center rear spindles pass through the high crest rail to form a second smaller shaped crest rail. In another form of comb-back the center rear spindles pass through the horseshoe-shaped arm rail and the bowed back, which is joined to the arm rail, to terminate in a shaped crest rail. See *Windsor Chair*.

COMB-BACK
WINDSOR CHAIR

Combed Ware In English ceramics; a method of marbling in which colored clay slips were combed on the surface to produce a marbled effect. Simple forms of combing were characteristic of peasant pottery. *Welsh ware* was an early English term for combed slip ware. From the late 17th century in England feathered patterns were made by combining white and brown slips and then later covering the combed surface with a yellow glaze. See *Marbled Ware*.

Commedia dell'Arte In decorative art and ornament; see *Italian Comedy Subjects*.

Commode In French cabinetwork; the commode was one of the most fashionable and characteristic pieces of 18th century French furniture. The marqueteur, the lacquer worker, the ciseleur and the cabinetmaker expended their greatest skill in its form and decoration. The commode almost always had a handsome marble top. The origin of the commode is not known. The early commode dates from the end of the 17th century. Its average height was about 32 inches and its length varied from about $2\frac{1}{2}$ to 5 feet. The characteristic Louis XV commode was of bombé form. The front and sides of the bombé commode were very often serpentine-shaped also. It was usually designed with two, three or four drawers, which were arranged in two or three rows. The division between the drawers was generally concealed as much as possible by either the marquetry or lacquer and by the bronze mounts. The characteristic Louis XVI commode had rectilinear lines. Another fashionable Louis XVI commode was of semi-circular plan. As a rule this type of commode was fitted with drawers and lateral cupboard doors. In English cabinetwork; during the second half of the 18th century the French commode was an important piece of English furniture. Chippendale made many finely carved mahogany commodes based on the Louis XV style. Contemporary with the mahogany commode was the lacquer commode of Louis XV contour decorated in the Chinese taste. Numerous satinwood marquetry commodes based on contemporary French models were made between 1760 and 1775. After 1775, painted decoration gradually supplanted marquetry. The painted decoration was largely influenced by the style of such decorative artists as Angelica Kauffmann.

Commode-Desserte In French cabinetwork; the term is generally given to a kind of commode fitted with drawers and open shelves which has an oblong top with quadrant-shaped returns or rounded ends. It was introduced during the Louis XVI style. Essentially its construction was similar to that of a rectangular commode to which had been added shelves in the shape of a quarter of a circle at each end. The panelled frieze was fitted with a long central drawer and usually lateral convex drawers. There were two deep long drawers beneath the

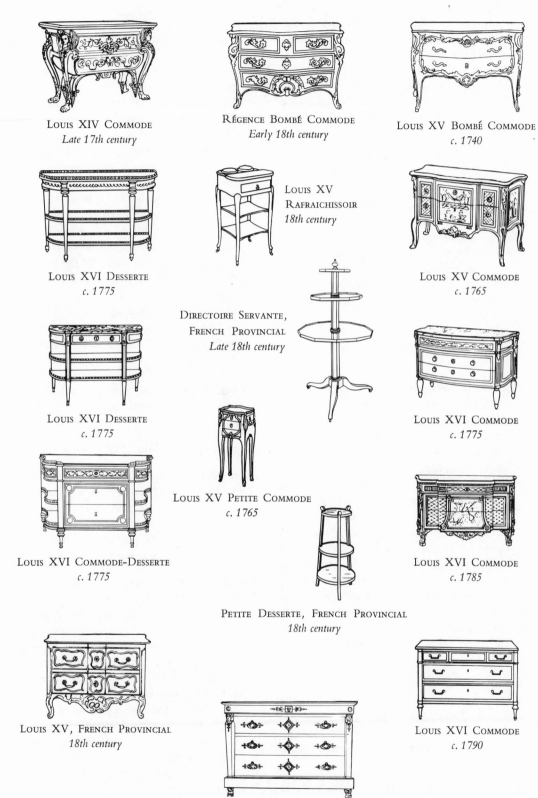

LOUIS XIV COMMODE
Late 17th century

RÉGENCE BOMBÉ COMMODE
Early 18th century

LOUIS XV BOMBÉ COMMODE
c. 1740

LOUIS XVI DESSERTE
c. 1775

LOUIS XV RAFRAICHISSOIR
18th century

LOUIS XV COMMODE
c. 1765

LOUIS XVI DESSERTE
c. 1775

DIRECTOIRE SERVANTE, FRENCH PROVINCIAL
Late 18th century

LOUIS XVI COMMODE
c. 1775

LOUIS XVI COMMODE-DESSERTE
c. 1775

LOUIS XV PETITE COMMODE
c. 1765

LOUIS XVI COMMODE
c. 1785

PETITE DESSERTE, FRENCH PROVINCIAL
18th century

LOUIS XV, FRENCH PROVINCIAL
18th century

LOUIS XVI COMMODE
c. 1790

EMPIRE COMMODE *c. 1810*

central frieze drawer and two open shelves under each lateral frieze drawer. It had a marble top and a pierced metal gallery and the shelves also had metal galleries. It was mounted on four short straight and tapering legs. It was usually veneered in mahogany; occasionally it was made of ebony. The façade was framed with bronze moldings. The commode-desserte was also designed with a demilune top. Its use is usually interpreted as a buffet. See *Desserte*.

HEPPLEWHITE
COMMODE DRESSING TABLE

Commode Dressing Table In English cabinetwork; an 18th century name given to a chest of drawers designed more or less in the French taste and provided with a rising framed mirror and compartments for toilet accessories in the top drawer. Several commode dressing tables were made by Chippendale from around 1767 to 1770 and Hepplewhite in the GUIDE, 1788, illustrated the commode dressing table with a serpentine front.

Commode Secretary In French provincial cabinetwork; the name given to a slant-front desk or bureau. The principal variety had an oblong top and a hinged slant lid opening to a fitted writing interior, over a bombé-shaped commode fitted with several rows of long drawers and mounted on feet or a bracket base. Occasionally the narrow top was surmounted with a cabinet portion fitted with two doors. This latter form was essentially similar to the Dutch and Flemish scribanne, which was undoubtedly the source of inspiration, since much furniture was imported to Bordeaux from the Netherlands around the end of the 17th century. It was introduced during the Régence and the early models were massive and rather cumbrous.

Commonwealth The term sometimes applied to the Cromwellian period of the English Renaissance, 1649–1660, a part of the Jacobean period, when Oliver Cromwell was Lord Protector of the Commonwealth. See *Jacobean*.

Communion Cup A cup used for wine in the communion service. In English ecclesiastical silver; during the reign of Edward VI, 1547–1553, the chalice was replaced by the communion cup which is used in the communion service of the Book of Common Prayer, first issued in 1548. At the same time the use of the cup was restored to the laity, which necessitated a cup having a more capacious bowl. It seems that in the 16th and 17th centuries the models for the communion cups were inspired by the plain domestic cups. The capacious bowl was mounted on a substantial stem and in the majority of examples the ornament was limited to an engraved band around the bowl. It appears that by the time of Elizabeth I the provision of a paten, which would also serve as a cover for a communion cup, became customary. For a short time around the middle of the 17th century there was a partial return to the more elaborate medieval style; however, it was not until the Gothic Revival of the 19th century that the communion cups and other church plate were decorated in the style of the medieval period. See *Chalice; Paten*.

Company Porcelain See *Chinese Lowestoft*.

Comport In English glass; the name given to an 18th century large glass stand or salver. It had a large, flat, disc-shaped top piece supported on a heavy stem mounted on a flaring foot. It was placed on a dining table to hold jelly glasses. See *Salver; Jelly Glass*.

Concertina Movement In English cabinetwork; the name given to a folding frame of a hinged top card table. The other characteristic form of construction for supporting the hinged top when extended was the swing-leg. Both forms of construction were used during the first half of the 18th century, with the concertina movement being the more characteristic form after 1715. It seems that in the second half of the 18th century the concertina movement was the prevailing form. During the Regency the card table was very frequently mounted on a central support. See *Swing Leg*.

Confessional In French cabinetwork; a large upholstered wing chair introduced during the style of Louis XIV. See *Easy Chair*.

Confidente In French cabinetwork; the name given to an unusual type of large upholstered sofa which had rounded-off ends separated from the main part by arms so that a small triangular seat was formed at each end. Identified with the styles of Louis XV and Louis XVI. Hepplewhite illustrates the confidente in THE GUIDE, 1788, which he spells confidante. He observes that "this piece of furniture is of French origin and is in pretty general request for large and spacious suits of apartments," and that "an elegant drawing room with modern furniture is scarce complete without a confidante: the extent of which may be about nine feet." He mentions that "this piece of furniture is sometimes so constructed that the ends take away and leave a regular sofa and the ends may be used as barjier chairs," barjier being an Anglicized spelling of the French bergère.

Confucius 551–478 B.C. The great Chinese philosopher and teacher. His Chinese name is Kung-Fu-Tse. See *Chinese Gods*.

Connecticut Chest In American cabinetwork; the name given to a variety of early rectangular oak chest which was made principally in Connecticut. The front of the chest was usually designed with three rectangular panels which were generally over two rows of drawers. The short legs were formed from a continuation of the stiles. The center panel was commonly decorated with three carved circular designs each enclosing conventional sunflowers or asters. The end panels were generally carved with a tulip design. The other distinctive features were the applied split banisters on the stiles and the applied circular or oval bosses on the drawers. It is also called a Connecticut Sunflower chest. See *Hadley Chest*.

Console Table In cabinetwork; the term *console* is used to describe a variety of side table whose top is supported by one or more brackets or consoles. The console table was fixed to the wall, very often under a mirror, and was without legs in the back. At the present time the term *console* is often applied, although erroneously, to any decorative side table, with supports in the form of brackets or legs, which is placed against the wall. It was introduced in France during the Louis XIV period and in England during the Early Georgian period. See *Eagle Console Table*.

Constable Glass In English glass; during the latter half of the 18th century drinking glasses bearing Masonic emblems and inscriptions became quite popular. These glasses usually had a very thick and heavy foot and were used for toasting. One variety of Masonic glass was called a constable glass and was used by the master and wardens on certain occasions. It was a large, tall glass, which held an English quart of liquor.

Constitution Clock In American furniture; a banjo clock having a scene of the naval battle of the Constitution and the Guerrière painted on the square glass pendulum door. See *Banjo Clock*.

Constitution Mirror In American furniture; the name sometimes given to a Chippendale architectural style of mirror, circa 1750–1775. It had a richly carved and parcel gilded rectangular frame surmounted with an elaborately carved and gilded swan neck or scrolled pediment which centered an eagle, phoenix, pheasant, vase or other ornament. See *Early Georgian Architectural Wall Mirror*.

Continental Silver A general term applied to the articles of silver, domestic and ecclesiastical, made on the continent of Europe. Many articles of silver were marked as to the actual fine silver content, especially those of France, Germany and Holland where very influential and strong guilds operated to protect the interests of the trade. See *Fine Silver*.

CONNECTICUT CHEST

REGENCY
CONVEX WALL MIRROR

Conversation Chair In English cabinet-work; Sheraton in his CABINET DICTIONARY, 1803, plate 27, illustrates a chair similar to the French voyeuse. He writes that "the manner of conversing amongst some of the highest circles of company on some occasions is copied from the French by lounging upon a chair. Hence we have the term conversation chair which is peculiarly adapted for this kind of idle position." In this type of chair the occupant placed himself with his back to the front of the chair in a straddle position and rested his elbows on the arm rest. See *Voyeuse*.

Convex Wall Mirror In English furniture; toward the end of the 18th century the Empire style circular convex mirror in a carved and molded gilt frame was introduced from France. It had a circular molded deep cavetto frame applied with gilt spherules or small balls. The convex mirror plate was encircled with an ebonized reeded fillet. The cresting was usually surmounted with a spread eagle. Frequently the base of the mirror was ornamented with a carved foliage pendant. It was often designed with lateral candle arms and was then called a girandole mirror. The convex wall mirror became extremely fashionable in England. It is also identified with the Federal style in America. Most of these mirrors found in America were imported from either England or France.

Copaïba Wood The wood of the copaïba tree, *copaifera*, of Brazil was widely used in cabinetwork, especially by the French ébénistes. It is hard, and its color is red spotted. Also called copaiva.

Cope In ecclesiastical costume; a vestment made of a semi-circular piece of silk or some other material similar to a long cloak and fastened across the chest by a clasp called a morse which was often exquisitely made of gold or silver and set with precious jewels. The cope was worn by ecclesiastics in processions and also at Vespers and at other ecclesiastical functions. It derives its name from cappa or hood which in early times hung loosely on the shoulders and could be pulled up to cover the head. Embroidered flat hoods attached to the back merely as a decorative feature date from around the 14th century and were praiseworthy for their beautifully worked sacred imagery. Copes were ornamented with embroidery and jewels from a very early period, and in the 13th century they became the most magnificent of all ecclesiastical vestments. Along the straight edge of all copes is a border or band of embroidery called the orphrey which hangs down from each shoulder. Perhaps the cope through the centuries has changed less in form than any of the ecclesiastical vestments.

Copeland See *Spode*.

Copenhagen In Danish ceramics; see *Kastrup*; *Store Kongensgade*; *Osterbro*; *Royal Copenhagen*.

Copland, Henry English designer of furniture. He collaborated with Lock on the publication of a number of books. In 1746 several engraved plates of ornament by Copland alone were brought out. The ornament is treated in the Rococo style and is among the earliest of the Rococo or Rocaille to appear in England. A few of Copland's designs appear in the CHAIR MAKERS' GUIDE published in 1766 by Robert Manwaring. There is no evidence at the present time that Copland was a cabinetmaker or a carver. See *Lock, Matthias*; *Chippendale, Thomas*.

Coquillage In ornament; the term, which means a shellfish, is derived from the French word *coquille* meaning a shell and is applied in cabinetwork to a carved Rococo motif of shell form. It was a popular motif, and a carved coquillage enclosing a cabochon was widely used by English cabinetmakers around the middle of the 18th century on the center of seat rails of chairs and settees made of mahogany.

Corail Wood The wood of the coral tree, *erythrina*, of the West Indies and East Indies, widely used in cabinetwork. It is soft and its color is fiery red veined.

Coraline Point A kind of Venetian Point lace; so named because of the branching coral-like lines which are worked through the designs. See *Needlepoint*; *Venetian Point*.

Coral Wood See *Corail Wood*.

Corbel An architectural term for a wall bracket of different forms which in Gothic architecture served as a support to build outward and upward. A similar treatment in cabinetwork is known by the same name. In a restricted sense a modillion is a corbel; the latter is particularly identified with medieval architecture, such as a bracket serving as a starting place for vaulting ribs.

Cordial Glass In English glass; the small glass drinking vessel for cordial was introduced in England about 1700. It is usually about 6 to 8 inches in height, and it is characterized by a very small flute-shaped bowl, tapering gently to form the stem and resting on a spreading foot. Another type consists of a very small cup-shaped bowl on an ornamented or plain stem resting on a spreading foot.

Cordonnet A French word meaning twist, edging. In lace-making; the name applied to the outline of the decorative design or pattern. It consisted of a single thread; several threads worked together to give the appearance of one, or a thread of horsehair closely worked over with the buttonhole stitch. In England it is called gimp.

Cormier Wood The wood of the service tree, *pyrus domestica*, used in cabinetwork, especially by the French ébénistes. It is very hard, and its color is reddish.

Corne, à la In French ceramics; a characteristic polychrome Rococo decoration used on Rouen faïence around the middle of the 18th century that was imitated elsewhere. The motifs included cornucopiae, butterflies, bees, flowers and other similar subjects. See *Rouen*.

Corner Cabinet In English cabinetwork; see *Corner Cupboard*; *China Cabinet*.

Corner Chair In English and American cabinetwork; the name *corner chair* or *roundabout chair* was given to an open-back armchair so designed that it could be placed in the corner of a room or could be used as an occasional chair. It was introduced during the early 18th century and was principally designed in the Queen Anne, Early Georgian and Chippendale styles. It was fitted with a slip seat. The characteristic variety usually had a semi-circular or horseshoe-shaped arm rail, which had a rear raised portion, over two pierced and vase-shaped splats, flanked by three supports which joined at the three corners and continued to the three rear legs. The seat rail rested on four legs, one at each corner. Variations in design occurred. The corner chair was fashionable in ·America from around 1725 to at least 1775 or later and it was principally designed in either the Queen Anne or Chippendale style. See *Writing Chair*.

Corner Cupboard In English cabinetwork; the name given to a cupboard, either built-in or movable, fitted with solid doors designed for the corner of a room. When the upper portion is glazed for the display of china it is classified as a cabinet. The earliest form of English corner cupboard was of the hanging variety. Its average height was almost four feet. The hanging cupboard was much used during the time of William and Mary as a receptacle for china. It was usually decorated with lacquer work. A characteristic Georgian built-in cupboard was the corner or alcove cupboard, with its shell niche, that formed a part of the panelling of a room. It was frequently constructed in two parts and each part was fitted with a pair of panelled cupboard doors. In American cabinetwork; the movable corner cupboard was made for almost one hundred years. The earliest dates from around 1725. The corner cupboard was found in the dining room and was used

GEORGE II
CORNER CHAIR

for the reception of china and glass. It was generally designed in two sections. Each section was fitted with either one or two cupboard doors. The doors in the upper section were almost always glazed. The plain undecorated corner cupboard made of a common wood was generally intended for kitchen use. See *Cupboard*; *Buffet*.

CORNUCOPIA LEG

Corner Table In American cabinetwork; the name is frequently given to a form of drop-leaf table with a triangular-shaped top over a conformingly shaped frieze. In all probability the design for this table was borrowed from an early 18th century English card table with a triangular folding top. The corner table had three stationary legs and a swing-leg supporting the drop-leaf which was triangular in form and was of the same size as the top. The corner table was made in the different 18th century styles. Essentially it was a plainer type of table and many were relatively small. See *Occasional Table*.

Cornflower In ceramics; see *Barbeaux*.

Cornice In classic architecture; the highest part of the three principal members of an entablature. The term has a similar meaning in cabinetwork when classic architectural features are incorporated in its principles of design. Cornices were employed on such articles as bookcases and secretary cabinets. The cornice was a feature on the tester bed from the reign of King Charles II through the 18th century. This richly carved cornice surmounting the tester on English beds was seldom found on American tester beds. The term is also used for the wooden frames from which the draperies were hung. Chippendale in the DIRECTOR and Hepplewhite in the GUIDE illustrated numerous designs for cornices in the prevailing style of ornament.

Cornucopia In ornament; a classic motif represented as a twisted horn filled to overflowing with fruits, flowers or vegetables. The term *cornucopia* means horn of plenty and it was used as a symbol of abundance.

Cornucopia Leg In cabinetwork; a type of short leg which gradually widens from the bottom to the top and resembles in form a cornucopia. This cornucopia-form support is chiefly identified with the Directoire type sofa. It was often reeded and was often shod with a brass paw foot and castered. See *Grecian Couch*; *Grecian Sofa*.

Coromandel Lacquer See *Chinese Lacquer*.

Corona The name given in England to an early variety of hanging light or chandelier generally in the form of one or more metal hoops or circles. Coronas of hammered iron were mentioned as early as the 13th century in ecclesiastical inventories. The corona was provided with either prickets or spikes for candles or cups for oil which were placed at regular intervals around the hoop. The corona greatly varied in size and some were extremely large in circumference. In the medieval palaces the coronas hanging in the great halls were sometimes made of gold and silver. See *Couronné*.

Corporal Case In ecclesiastical art; the case or box in which the linen corporal cloth is kept and is carried to the altar. The corporal cloth is laid on the altar and the consecrated elements are placed upon it during the celebration of the Mass. As a rule the corporal case was extremely rich in design and in material. Medieval English church inventories list corporal cases covered with silk, velvet or gold cloth elaborately embroidered with sacred imagery and occasionally further enriched with pearls.

Corselet In armor; a 16th century half armor consisting of the helmet, gorget, breast plate and back plate, tassets, arms and gauntlets. See *Cuirass*.

Cosmati Work A medieval Italian glass mosaic inlay work remarkable for the delicate and jewel-like quality of its brilliant and colorful designs which were chiefly geometrical and occasionally pictorial. Its name was derived from the Cosmati family who were artful workers in mosaic, sculptors, and architects, and who were producing this kind of work during the 13th and 14th centuries. Among their works are included altars and choir screens enriched with sculpture and glass mosaic.

Coster In ecclesiastical appointments; a hanging of rich fabric occasionally embroidered and placed on the sides of an altar or choir. The term is also found in English records dating from the 15th century for a hanging for a bed as well as for the walls of a room.

Costrel In English ceramics; a late Gothic variety of pilgrim's flask. It was generally in the form of a flattened elongated pear, having a tapering neck, with two or four loops attached to the shoulders or sides through which a cord was drawn. See *Pilgrim Bottle*.

Couch In cabinetwork; a kind of day bed intended to be used for reclining or for sleeping; especially one having a raised end or arm. See *Grecian Couch*; *Méridienne*.

Couching A kind of embroidery in which threads, cords, etc., are laid upon the surface of the material to create a design. These cords are secured by means of fine stitches called couching stitches. Couching is either relatively flat or raised, and is named according to the kind of couching stitch used, such as a basket stitch. The term is found in English records dating from the late 14th century. See *Embroidery*.

Counterpane Or Counterpoint. The latter term was used in England for a coverlet or bed-cover from around the 14th to the middle of the 17th centuries. It was derived from the French term *contre-pointer* or *courtepointe* meaning to quilt, or fabrics stitched through on both sides. In England, the term *counterpane* began to be used from around the end of the 17th century.

Counter Table In English cabinetwork; a variety of table or chest having its top divided into spaces with distinctive symbols for counting money. Until the 16th century the counting of money was primitive and was done with a counter table or counter board. A characteristic variety of counter table was designed with an oblong hinged top which was hinged at one end. The top extended well over an underframing that was enclosed to form a shallow cupboard fitted with a cupboard door. It was mounted on four legs connected either with a shelf close to the floor or with a continuous floor stretcher. In another variety the top was kept in position by means of sliding bars which permitted access into the interior without disturbing the counters.

Coupe In Chinese ceramics; a kind of jar or bowl to hold water for cleaning the brushes used in writing. The characteristic shape is of domical or beehive form with a small flaring mouth. The writer's coupe is a typical Peach Bloom form.

Courbaril Wood The wood of the locust tree, *hymenaea courbaril*, from Asia and America, widely used in cabinetwork. It is hard and solid and its color is pale red veined.

Couronné A French word meaning wreathed or crowned given to a medieval form of French hanging light or chandelier. See *Corona*.

Couronné A term in lace-making applied to the minute loops on the outer edge of a cordonnet.

Court Cupboard In English cabinetwork; the term *court cupboard* is now employed to describe an open structure of shelves for the display of plate introduced toward the end of the 16th century. Its form was inspired by a similar variety which had been designed earlier in France. It was rectangular and upright and was rarely above 4 feet in height. It was composed of three tiers and was entirely open. The uppermost tier had a frieze which rested on supports. The median tier or shelf also had a frieze and rested on four supports which were joined by a deep shelf at the base; it was mounted on feet. The two friezes were often fitted with drawers. The two pairs of front supports were bulbous in outline, while the rear supports were narrow and straight. It was made of oak and

DIRECTOIRE COUCH

was richly carved. The court cupboard was made throughout the Carolean era; however, the later ones lacked the fine quality of workmanship in both form and decoration which had characterized the Elizabethan examples. The court cupboard was largely supplanted at the beginning of the 18th century in the wealthy homes by the alcove cupboard or the buffet and by the long side table or sideboard table. See *Cupboard*; *Buffet*; *Dresser*; *Hall and Parlor Cupboard*.

Courting Chair Or Love Seat. In English cabinetwork; a form of seat furniture characterized by its very wide and deep seat. Essentially it resembles a chair wide enough to hold two persons and is occasionally described in English furniture literature as a double chair or very small settee. Some illustrations of the courting chair in English furniture literature give the length of the seat as 3 feet and 1 inch. It was a very popular 18th century type in England. The backs of these love seats were generally upholstered until around the middle of the 18th century, although some were made with open backs. Chairs of this type with very wide seats were also found in America. See *Marquise*.

Courting Mirror In American furniture; a type of rectangular mirror, circa 1800, characterized by a molded wooden frame which centers a continuous strip of small pieces of glass painted with leaves and flowers. The cresting is also covered with pieces of glass painted with flowers. It is generally accepted that the mirror originally came from China. Sometimes the mirror is enclosed in a shallow box which is supposed to represent its original shipping box. The average height for this mirror was about 18 inches.

Couter In armor; an elbow cop, a protection for the elbow. It first appeared in the latter part of the 14th century, and by the 15th century it became quite large and elaborately wrought.

Cow-Creamer In English silver; a small vessel to hold cream made in the shape of

COURTING MIRROR
ENCLOSED IN A SHALLOW BOX

a cow with its looped tail for a handle. The cream is poured through its mouth and is filled through an opening in the cow's back fitted with a cover, which is usually decorated with a band of minute flowers and a bee in full relief. It was introduced during the reign of George II, 1727-1760. It was also a characteristic form in English ceramics; in particular in Staffordshire ware. See *Cream Jug*.

Crab's Claw Crackle In ceramics; see *Crackle*.

Crabstock Ware In English ceramics; an 18th century pottery, especially teapots, cream jugs and mugs having handles and spouts made to resemble wood with twigs and branches wrapped about them. The decoration was the characteristic small leaves, tendrils and delicate vines in relief.

Crackle In ceramics; a glazed surface covered with a network of fine lines or cracks. It is generally agreed that crackle was originally accidental and later usually planned. Crackle was caused by the difference in the expansion and contraction of the body and the glaze under heat and cold. In Chinese ceramics; the name *crab's claw crackle* is given to a large crackle, and *fish roe* to a small and fine crackle. Often the two types were combined in one piece. See *Ko Yao*; *Kuan Yao*; *Sang de Bœuf*; *Sung*.

Cradle Or Berceau. In English and American cabinetwork; in a strict sense the term *cradle* refers to a little bed or crib for a baby mounted on rockers; by extension the term also includes a swing crib, a simple crib which does not rock or swing, and a basket bed. Essentially there are two principal types of. cradles, namely the low cradle mounted on rockers and the relatively high cradle suspended on posts called a swing crib. It appears that cradles were known in England from around the 15th century and that hooded cradles mounted on rockers were made in the early 17th century. Cradles varied from the simple to the elaborate. The elegant cradles reproduced the elaborateness of the costly state beds and were richly and completely draped. The more common cradles were made entirely of wood and were decorated with carved ornament. Toward the end of the 18th century the swing cradle supported on posts was regarded as the more fashionable form. It was frequently provided with a hood and the straight sides were often fitted with caned panels. Cradles were made in America from early Colonial days. It is doubtful if the richly draped examples found in England were made in America.

Crape-Myrtle *Lagerstraemia indica.* See *Bloodwood.*

Crazing In ceramics; the accidental splits in a glaze consisting of a mesh of fine cracks. In Chinese porcelains the term *crackle* is generally used to describe a glaze characterized by a mesh of fine cracks; particularly when the crazing was deliberately planned. See *Crackle.*

Cream-Colored Earthenware In English ceramics; the English name applied to a fine lead-glazed ware originally and principally made in Staffordshire. It has a hard light-colored body that generally contains flint. From around 1760 it began to supplant Delft ware and tin-glazed faïence for tableware in the world's markets and is still the standard material. It was known by different names in various countries; in France it was called faïence fine, in Germany steingut and in Sweden flintporslin. Plain cream-colored earthenware was virtually the creation of Josiah Wedgwood, and after securing the patronage of Queen Charlotte about 1765 he named it the now familiar "Queen's Ware." Its qualities of thinness, durability and dense hardness were soon recognized, and Wedgwood's cream-colored earthenware was immediately imitated by innumerable potteries in the vicinity as well as at potteries at Leeds, Liverpool, Bristol, Swansea and elsewhere. It quickly secured a wide European market. Cream-colored earthenware was made into every kind of tableware.

Wedgwood was constantly improving the utility of the forms such as the handles on teapots and cream jugs. The decoration was chiefly in imitation of silver and was largely confined to beaded and feather edged borders and pierced openwork. See *Pearl Ware.*

Cream Jug In English silver; the cream jug was introduced early in the 18th century. The early variety was helmet-form and sometimes rested on small feet. From the first part of the reign of George II, 1727–1760, the form of the cream jug followed the same variations in style as the pear-shaped teapot, and appeared as a bulbous pear-shaped jug resting on a low molded foot. This style was followed by the pear-shaped jug supported on three small feet. During the early part of the reign of George III, 1760–1820, the jug was made in pyriform with several variations resting on a short spreading circular foot. In the last quarter of the 18th century the jug of conical form appeared which rested on a spreading circular foot and square plinth. Many variations occurred in these principal types. See *Cow-Creamer.*

Cream-Pail In English silver; the name given to a silver vessel introduced during the latter part of the 18th century. It was placed on the table and the cream was served with a small ladle or spoon. One variety resembled a small bucket or pail with a bail handle. Another type was shaped like a classic bowl with a bail handle and rested on a spreading foot. Cream-pails were either chased or pierced and fitted with glass liners. It is also called a piggin.

Crèche Art The French term *crèche* meaning the crib, and which in Italian is called *presepe*, is applied to the art of reconstructing the scene of the Nativity which had been set up as early as the 8th century in Rome at the Basilica Liberii, known today as the Basilica of S. Maria Maggiore. From the 7th century onwards this basilica kept the relics of the Holy Manger of Bethlehem and it is believed that the 8th century scene had

HOODED CRADLE

been built in imitation of one which had long existed there. Sculptured scenes of the Nativity first appeared in the 13th century and by the second half of the 15th century sculptured scenes of a permanent nature became more frequent and as such have influenced the development of the Christmas crèche as it is generally understood today. It seems that the first crèche constructed especially for the Christmas season stood in the Jesuit church in Prague in 1562 and a few years later one presented to the Duchess of Amalfi, Constanza Piccolomini di Aragona, presents the character which the crèche was to retain in future centuries. The Nativity group varies as to the number of figures but chiefly consists of the Holy Family, the Wise Men, an ox and an ass, shepherds and other representative figures. The figures were made in a variety of materials such as wood, plaster, papier-mâché and wax, and in the 17th and 18th centuries, when it reached its highest and most elaborate development in Naples, great craftsmen devoted their skill to this art. Frequently these figures were dressed with the most costly of fabrics. Even to the present day woodcarvers with a true religious sentiment carry on this vigorous and colorful artistic tradition in some villages in Bavaria and Austria. In America; this traditional European custom was introduced by the early German settlers who emigrated to Pennsylvania in the 17th and 18th centuries. The proper German term for these scenes of the Nativity is *krippe*; although the term *putz*, derived from the German *putzen*, meaning to adorn, trim or brighten, is applied to this art by the Pennsylvania Germans. The putz is characteristic of all Pennsylvania German communities; however, the communities originally settled by the religious sect commonly known as Moravians are chiefly responsible for its regional form of development in America. These Moravian communities are in such places as Bethlehem, Nazareth, Lititz, Reading, Emmaus and Allentown. Every putz is an individual creation in which there is no

RENAISSANCE CRÉDENCE

restriction in the manner of religious or artistic expression. The putz does not follow the traditional European principles which restrict it to the scene of the Nativity. The subjects are frequently intermingled with popular local traditions or folk lore such as Indians performing everyday work tasks or the candle-light scene of the naming of the city of Bethlehem by Count Zinzendorf in 1741. The putz is an elaborate setting often decorated with gay colors and tinsel.

Crédence In French cabinetwork; the crédence during the Renaissance developed into an elaborate type of buffet and was chiefly used to hold valuable plate. The principal variety was designed with a massive oblong horizontal upper section which was usually panelled and carved and was generally fitted with one or more doors. It was mounted on a stand which had a carved frieze that rested on four heavy supports that were secured to a display shelf close to the floor. The traceried iron mounts were of lace-like quality and were frequently backed with red velvet in order to enhance the detail work. See *Credence Table*.

Credence Table In cabinetwork; originally the credence table was a small side table, placed near the dining table in the medieval palaces of royal and noble families. The food, ready to be served, was placed on this table for tasting, to guard against poisoning. This custom originated in Italy, where the tasting of the food and drink for poisons was done by an official of the household called the credentiarius. In France both the ceremony and table were called crédence, and in Italy, credenza. After the need for the ceremony had disappeared the name still survived. In England the term *credence* was used to describe a small altar table which held the bread and wine. It should be remembered that the credence table in England is identified as an article of ecclesiastical furniture. See *Crédence*; *Credenza*.

Credenza In Italian cabinetwork; the credenza was an important article of Renaissance furniture. As a rule its length exceeded its height. The principal and characteristic variety had an oblong top over a frieze which was fitted with two or three drawers that were separated by carved brackets. Beneath the frieze were two or three doors; the number of cupboard doors corresponded to the number of frieze drawers. Each door was divided by either a narrow vertical panel or a fluted pilaster that was directly under the frieze bracket or modillion. It rested on a carved and molded base which was often surmounted on carved lion's feet. See *Credence Table*; *Sacristy Cupboard*.

Credenzina In Italian cabinetwork; a credenzina or small credenza, was essentially similar to a credenza. In fact, it often resembled in appearance one section of the credenza. The credenzina was designed with one or two cupboard doors and had the corresponding number of frieze drawers. See *Credenza*.

Creepers The term applied to small andirons placed between the taller andirons. See *Andirons*.

Creese In arms and armor; see *Kris*.

Creil In French ceramics; a manufactory was founded at Creil, Oise, about 1794. It produced faïence fine and other wares of the English type. It was joined to the manufactory of Montereau early in the 19th century and was active until 1895. Much of the Creil earthenware was decorated with transfer printing which was generally in black and rarely in underglaze blue. The quality of the white earthenware was improved through the years. The mark "Creil" impressed was often used either with or without accompanying letters.

Cressent, Charles 1685-1768. The distinguished French cabinetmaker, sculptor and metal worker. His work is closely identified with the style of the Régence. Naturally during his long life his style changed in accordance with the dictates of fashion. He was also one of the outstanding craftsmen working in the Louis XV style. He not only designed and made the furniture but he also made the wax models for his bronze mounts which were so characteristic of his work. His work was inspired to a large extent by the decorative art work of Watteau. His bronze versions of busts of charming female figures, which were called espagnolettes, retained all the grace and refinement of the originals as done by Watteau and are considered to be among the artistic triumphs of French metal work. His talent for harmoniously combining wood and metal gave his cabinetwork a remarkable quality of unity. Especially outstanding were his bureaux plat or large writing tables having projecting cabriole legs headed with espagnolettes. See *Régence*.

Cresset The term applied in medieval times and later to a basket-shaped lamp made of iron in which various inflammable substances such as pitched rope or oil were burnt to furnish a light. As a rule the cresset was attached either to a pole or to a building.

Cresting In cabinetwork; the name given to a decorative carving surmounting the top rail of a chair back; to a decorative carving surmounting the front stretcher of a chair, such as the Restoration chair; to the ornamental carving on top of a mirror and to other similar carvings surmounting a top piece.

Crest Rail In cabinetwork; the term applied to the top rail on a chair back or settee.

Cretonne In textiles; the French name of uncertain origin given to a strong fabric of hempen warp and linen weft first made around Lisieux in the province of Normandy. Essentially it was used in the same manner as chintz for the coverings of chairs and sofas and for curtains. However, it is stronger than chintz. It is stated in French literature that around 1850 the printed designs, which somewhat resembled chintz, were remarkably striking and artistic, and that by 1860 cretonne had largely replaced chintz. In England the name is given to

TUSCAN CREDENZA

a strong unglazed cotton cloth having a colored printed design either on one or both sides. It seems that the manufacture of cretonne began in England around 1860–1870, and an English record of 1887 mentions the "pretty cretonne curtains."

CREWELWORK, ENGLISH
LATE 17TH CENTURY

Crewel Stitch A stitch used in embroidery which makes a line of rope-like appearance. It is worked from the bottom of the material towards the top always keeping the crewel yarn, which is a loosely twisted worsted yarn, to the right of the needle.

Crewelwork A kind of embroidery worked in the crewel stitch with crewel yarn, generally upon a plain material, such as linen. It is usually done in the nature of a spreading pattern covering only part of the ground; due to the varying length of stitches and the careful blending of colors, very interesting and decorative effects can be created. Some of the finest examples of crewelwork were done during the Jacobean era. See *Embroidery*; *Upholstery*.

Criblé A form of wood engraving first practiced in the middle of the 15th century. In this method light and dark effects were achieved from drilling into the wood many small round holes of different size which produced white in the printing.

Cricket Stool In English furniture; the name applied to a variety of plain stool having three splayed legs. It was first made during the Jacobean period.

Cricket Table In English furniture; the term given to a type of small and plain three-legged table, having a triangular top. It is principally identified with Jacobean furniture.

Cries of London The term applied to the series of 13 paintings executed by Francis Wheatley, R.A., English painter, 1747–1801, depicting the city peddlers of London crying their wares. The Wheatley series are considered to be the finest portrayal of this type of London life. Prints of the series were published by Colnaghi and Company,

of London, under the title, The Itinerant Traders of London. The following is a list of their titles, dates of publication and by whom engraved: 1. Two Bunches a Penny, Primrose, July 2, 1793, L. Schiavonetti; 2. Milk Below, Maids, July 2, 1793, L. Schiavonetti; 3. Sweet China Oranges, July 1794, L. Schiavonetti; 4. Do You Want Any Matches, July 1794, A. Cardon; 5. New Mach'rel, January 1, 1795, N. Schiavonetti, Jun.; 6. Knives, Scissors, and Razors to Grind, January 1, 1795, G. Vendramini; 7. Fresh Gathered Peas, Young Hastings, January 1795, G. Vendramini; 8. Round and Sound, Five Pence a Pound, Duke Cherries, June 25, 1795, A. Cardon; 9. Strawberries, Scarlet Strawberries, June 25, 1795, G. Vendramini; 10. Old China to Mend, September 1, 1795, G. Vendramini; 11. A New Love Song, Only a Ha'penny a Piece, March 1, 1796, A. Cardon; 12. Hot Spice Gingerbread, Smoking Hot, May 1, 1796, G. Vendramini; 13. Turnips and Carots, Ho, May 1, 1797, T. Gaugain.

Cries of Paris In German ceramics; the term *Cries of Paris* or *Cris de Paris* is given to a charming group or class of porcelain figures originally produced by Kaendler at Meissen in the 1740s. These figures of folk types were suggested from engravings by the Comte de Caylus published in 1737–1742. They portray such folk characters as a bird-seller, hurdy-gurdy player, and other similar subjects. About 1753 other folk subjects were made after contemporary English engravings.

Crimping In glass; an applied decoration consisting of dents or flutes shaped or tooled on various parts of a glass vessel and giving it a rather wavy effect. It was a favorite method for decorating American glass.

Crinet In armor; the protective steel plates in medieval armor covering the top part of a horse's neck; a mane guard.

Crinoline Group In German ceramics; the term *crinoline group* is applied to the small porcelain figures of ladies wearing wide spreading crinoline skirts. These figures which most frequently portray the ladies with their lovers first appeared in Meissen porcelain around 1737. They were modelled by Kaendler and his assistants after the works of such French artists as Watteau, Boucher and Lancret. Crinoline groups were also made by other factories such as Nymphenburg and Vienna.

Criseby In ceramics; see *Eckernförde*.

Crizzelling In glass; a term used to describe a fault or defect developing in glass. It is a network of fine cracks in the interior of glass producing a cloudy effect and a loss of transparency.

Crochet A variety of knitting worked with a hooked needle. The finest and most beautiful crochet work was of Irish origin where it was made as early as 1845 by the poor children in the schools of the Ursuline convent at Blackrock, County Cork. The principal centers were Cork in the south and Clones in the north of Ireland. With the introduction of machine-made work done in Switzerland, and in Nottingham in England, its production almost ceased. However, it was revived in the late 19th century and Clones became the most important center. Crochet is included as one of the seven types of Irish laces.

Crocket In ornament; a decorative motif derived from Gothic architecture in the form of a projecting piece of stone sculpture on the ridge of a spire or on the edge of a gable. It was frequently found in medieval woodwork such as on the top center panel of a cupboard or on the side pieces of a choir stall. It was principally in the form of a fantastically cut leaf with a strong stem or ribs worked in pronounced relief. The curved legs of the X-form chair during the 17th century were sometimes decorated with crockets.

Croft In English furniture; essentially a kind of filing cabinet, deriving its name from the inventor, Rev. Sir Herbert Croft, 1757–1816, who first directed one to be made to hold the papers for his dictionary. The oblong cabinet was of table height and the oblong top was provided with two drop-leaves with rounded ends. It was provided with a frieze drawer and a single door and was mounted on a plinth base. The door opened to reveal about six rows of drawers, with two drawers in each row. The sides were furnished with bail handles in order that it could be easily moved about. It was a relatively small piece of furniture, and its height exceeded its width. It was a rather plain piece since it was made simply for a utilitarian purpose.

Crolius In American ceramics; a family of potters working in New York City from around 1729. The kiln was on Potter's Hill and in 1812 it was moved to 65 Bayard Street where it continued to operate until 1848. Several existent pieces have a stoneware body with a salt-glaze.

Cromwellian The term applied to the period of English Renaissance from 1649 to 1660. Also called either the Commonwealth period or Protectorate period, since Oliver Cromwell was Lord Protector of the Commonwealth. See *Jacobean*.

Cromwellian Chair In English cabinetwork; during the Protectorate an angular oak chair of uncomfortable form was made. It was popularly known as the Cromwellian chair. The turned armposts, front legs and front stretchers were often knobbed. Two plain side stretchers and a rear stretcher connected the four legs. The seat and back panel were of leather and were secured to the frame with a row of brass-headed nails. The flat straight arms were often covered with leather. The chair was also designed without arms.

Cross-Banded In English cabinetwork; a band of veneer inlaid transversely to the grain in the main surface. Cross-banding was introduced during the Charles II style and was used throughout the 18th century.

GOTHIC CROCKETS

Crossbow In arms; a medieval weapon consisting essentially of a bow set cross-wise on a stock having a channel or groove in the top for the arrow. A mechanical device holds and releases the string. Crossbows are found in almost all countries and vary in size from those that are held in the hands and used to shoot from the shoulder to enormous pieces mounted on the ground. They are used to shoot arrows, darts, stones and huge rocks or balls. See *Arbalest*.

CROSSBOW

Cross-Guard In armor; the sword guard composed of quillons or arms at the base of the hilt on a sword.

Crossrail In cabinetwork; the term applied to a horizontal piece in an open chair back. It is the same as a slat.

Cross-Stitch A stitch which is used in embroidery. The stitches are diagonal and in pairs and the thread of one stitch crosses that of the other, thereby making a square or x-form. It is also a kind of needlework. See *Embroidery*.

Cross-Stitch Carpet See *Embroidered Rugs*.

Cross Stretcher In cabinetwork; the name given to a stretcher on a chair, table, etc., that extends from the front legs to the rear legs, crossing at the center. It is the same as an X-form stretcher. Also called a cruciform stretcher; saltire stretcher. See *X-form Stretcher*.

Crotch Mahogany In cabinetwork; the term applied to a piece of solid or veneer mahogany having an ornamental grain. This wood with its beautiful feathery or mottled markings is cut from the crotch or fork of the mahogany tree where it divides into two limbs or branches. Although crotch wood is obtained from many trees it is especially valuable in mahogany. The crotch or fork of these limbs is cut lengthwise to show the fiber direction to best advantage. Pieces of wood so cut are known in America as crotches and in England as curls.

Crouch Ware In English ceramics; the name given according to a doubtful tradition to a salt-glazed brownish or drab-colored stoneware, which derived its name from the use of a Derbyshire clay by that name, made in Staffordshire. It preceded the Staffordshire white stoneware. This supposed Crouch ware is believed to have been made before 1714. The typical drab stoneware having a grey body and decorated with white reliefs, which is often identified as belonging to the Crouch ware class, is a Staffordshire ware of a later date. It is probable that this problematical Staffordshire pottery known as Crouch ware may be found among the wares classified as Fulham and Nottingham.

Crown-Derby See *Derby*.

Crown Glass A variety of blown glass made in the form of a large flat disc by rapid spinning. A knob or lump of glass, which is called a bull's eye, is left in the center and is caused by the glassblower's punty or iron rod. This knob is often seen in old crown glass window panes. This kind of glass is also called bull's eye glass. Sheets of crown glass were sometimes as much as 4 feet in diameter. When these sheets were cut into small squares or diamonds they were marked by a slight rippling of concentric lines as well as a slight bulging. Distinct from the crown glass process, which is also referred to as the Normandy process, is a kind of cylinder process referred to as the broad or Lorraine process. In this method the glass cylinder is split and is then placed in a heated chamber and flattened. The slight ripples in broad glass are straight. Broad glass, as well as other kinds of split glass, was later made mechanically.

Crozier Or Crosier. In ecclesiastical art; the term *crozier*, derived from the Low Latin word *croce* meaning a crook, is mentioned as early as about the end of the 5th century as an episcopal ornament in the sacramentary of St. Gregory the Great. It is said that when St. Patrick went to Ireland to preach the gospel in the 5th century he carried with him a crozier which later became known as "the staff of Jesus." These earlier croziers were of small size and not larger than a walking stick and were still smaller in the 12th century. In the 13th century the bearer of a bishop's crook or pastoral staff was called a crozier and in the 14th century the name was applied to a cross-bearer or one who bears a cross before an archbishop. The term *crozier* is often applied erroneously to the cross of an archbishop. In the 16th century the terms *crozier's* or *crozier-staff* were commonly used for the episcopal crook which was borne by the crociarius and later the crook itself was called the crozier. The croziers of the 14th and 15th centuries are considered to be the most magnificent and most elaborately decorated articles of ecclesiastical ornament. They were most frequently made of gold and silver decorated with enamel and the section just below the scrolled top part was designed with intricate tabernacle work in tiers resembling medieval church architecture with figures of saints in niches.

Crozier-Back In cabinetwork; the term is sometimes applied to a chair back having the upper portion of the two uprights gently curving backward. It is so called because of its supposed resemblance to a bishop's staff or crozier. This type of chair back is identified with the French Directoire and Empire styles and with the English Sheraton and Regency styles.

Cruciform Stretcher See *Cross Stretcher*.

Cruet A small cut glass bottle used to hold oil or vinegar at the dining table. It is also an ecclesiastical term applied to a pair of vessels used in the Mass to hold water and wine.

Cruet Stand In English silver; a stand to hold cruets, or cruets, casters and muffineers. It was made in a variety of shapes. Especially fine were the 18th century ajouré silver cruet stands designed in the shape of a basket. It was introduced in the beginning of the 18th century.

Crunden, John An English architect and designer working around the middle of the 18th century. In 1765 he published THE JOYNER AND CABINET-MAKER'S DARLING OR POCKET DIRECTOR. It contained a number of Chinese designs and ornamental frets which were undoubtedly used by cabinetmakers making furniture in the Chinese taste. He published several other similar works, and in 1770 he published CONVENIENT AND ORNAMENTAL ARCHITECTURE.

Crustae In Roman decorative art; the term *crustae* was given to the repoussé metal plaques which were mounted on smooth silver cups or vases. The designing of these elaborately worked plaques was one of the specialized branches of caelatura work. See *Caelatura*; *Repoussé*.

Cruzie Lamp An early European oil lamp extensively used during the 17th century. It consisted of a shallow vessel or cup, usually of iron or tin, to contain the oil with a wick laid in the narrow end or spout. The cruzie lamp, which had its origin in antiquity, was generally attached to an iron ratchet hung from the ceiling or to an iron rod on a stand. See *Betty Lamp*.

Crystal Glass A brilliant colorless glass of fine quality containing a high proportion of lead oxide and deriving its name from its resemblance to rock crystal. It is used in the manufacture of tableware, vases and decorative pieces. Also called lead glass. See *Flint Glass*.

C-Scroll In ornament; see *Scrolls, C and S*.

Cubitiere In armor; the protective steel plate, in medieval armor, covering the elbow. See *Vambrace*; *Rerebrace*.

Cuenca In Spanish ceramics; see *Seville*.

Cuerda Seca In Spanish ceramics; see *Seville*.

Cuirass In armor; the name given to the breast plate and back plate worn during the Middle Ages. They were fastened together with straps and buckles or similar devices. The cuirass of the 16th century was musket-

AJOURÉ SILVER
CRUET STAND

proof whereas the corselet was pistol-proof. See *Corselet*.

Cuisse In armor; a medieval protective steel covering for the thigh; especially for the front of the thigh.

Cumdach The name given to a case designed to hold copies of the gospel or other religious writings. The cumdach, which is a fine example of Irish art, was made between the 10th and 16th centuries, and was richly worked in gold, enamel and precious jewels.

CUP AND COVER SUPPORT

Cup and Cover In English cabinetwork; a kind of heavy bulbous support designed to represent a tall silver cup and cover. It is also occasionally called a melon support. The heavy bulbous support was a characteristic feature of Elizabethan furniture. See *Bulbous*.

Cupboard In English cabinetwork; originally in medieval times the term *cupboard* was used to describe an open framework or an open structure fitted with boards or shelves to hold cups. Around the second quarter of the 16th century the term began to acquire its modern meaning and was used to describe a piece of furniture of similar structure fitted with shelves and enclosed with doors, being either fixed or movable. However the term was often still applied to designate a structure formed of superimposed shelves. It is a comprehensive term and generally describes a number of pieces of furniture which are most of the time entirely enclosed with doors and are fitted with shelves or have cupboard space to hold dishes, linens, food and clothes. Included among the principal types of cupboard are the ambry, armoire, food and livery cupboard, panetière, almoner's cupboard, wardrobe, press, kas, clothespress, court cupboard, corner cupboard, hall and parlor cupboard and encoignure. See also *Buffet and Dresser*. The term *cupboard* is also given to an enclosed unit or compartment in another piece of furniture; such as the cupboard compartments in a Sheraton sideboard.

Cupid's Bow In English and American cabinetwork; the name given to one of the two principal kinds of serpentine-shaped crest rails used in the open chair back designed in the Chippendale style. This serpentine-shaped top rail is so called because of its supposed resemblance to the bow used by Cupid in Roman mythology. A marked feature of this crest rail was the turned-up extremities, which sometimes extended one or more inches beyond the uprights. These ends were often twisted in a manner to form whorled terminals. Variations in design frequently occurred in this form of crest rail. The other kind of serpentine-shaped crest rail had the ends curving downward to form continuous rounded ends where they joined the uprights.

Cup Plate In glass; a small plate from about $2\frac{5}{8}$ inches to about $4\frac{1}{8}$ inches in diameter having a circular depression in the center to hold the teacup. It was used to hold the teacup after the hot tea was poured into the saucer from which it was drunk after it was sufficiently cooled. The cup plate was a 19th century innovation, and was popular from around 1827 to around and slightly after 1850. It is generally accepted that the cup plate was of European origin. It was first made in pottery and porcelain and later in pressed glass. In America it was almost always made of pressed glass. The impressed decoration included sunbursts, hearts, ships, log cabins, historical motifs, portraits of statesmen, eagles, and the usual 19th century pressed glass patterns.

Cup Stand In Chinese ceramics; a small circular stand of varying form characterized by a hollow ring in which the base of the tea bowl or wine cup was inserted. The cup stand is of early origin and fine Chün yao and Northern Sung celadon cup stands are found in private collections of Chinese porcelains. Chinese cups were later furnished with straight edged trays, and they served the same purpose as a saucer, since saucers in the European style were not used. See *Bowl*.

Curio A well-known abbreviation of the word *curiosity* given to an object of art possessing the value of a rarity or curiosity. The term is especially applied to an object of this type having its origin in the Far East, such as an article from China and Japan.

Curio Cabinet See *Vitrine*.

Curly Maple In American cabinetwork, *acer rubrum* and *acer saccharinum*, see *Maple*.

Curragh In Irish lace-making; the technique of making application flowers in the manner of Brussels lace from Brussels lace patterns was successfully developed at a school at Curragh, County Limerick, around the middle of the 19th century. It was known as Curragh Point or Irish Point. See *Irish Point*.

Currier and Ives American lithography printers of the 19th century. It was founded in 1834 by Nathaniel Currier, 1813–1888. At first it was a partnership called Currier and Stodart; this partnership was dissolved in 1835. The business was carried on as N. Currier. In 1852 James Merritt Ives joined the business, and in 1857 he became a partner. The firm was then known as Currier and Ives. The prints of the firm are famous not only as collectors' items but for their pictorial record of the principal events of the entire middle portion of the 19th century. The prints cover practically every subject of interest to the people; such as reproductions of the great works of art, folk pictures, seasonal scenes of city and rural life, current event pictures of battles, disasters, railroads and clipper ships and thrilling hunting pictures. They published over 7000 different titles; many of the works portrayed American life; such as those done by Arthur Fitzwilliam Tait, 1819–1905, Fanny Palmer (Mrs. Frances F. Palmer), George Henry Durrie, Louis Maurer, Thomas Worth and Charles Parsons.

Curtain Holder A decorative metal holder, generally gilded, used to draw window draperies or hangings back and to keep them in place. The earliest English examples date from the second half of the 18th century and were in the Neo-Classic taste. There were two principal varieties. One type was flat and U-shaped, while the other variety consisted of a rod with a rosette at one end over which the drapery was hung in soft folds.

Curule In cabinetwork; a term applied to a variety of armchair or stool, the supports or legs of which were curved and crossed each other in the front and in the rear in an X manner. The legs resembled the legs of a camp stool and generally could be folded like a camp stool. The curule stool had its origin in Egyptian antiquities. The first important armchair for domestic use made in Italy during the Gothic period was of ancient Roman curule form. The armchair of the curule type for domestic use was also found in England and in France during the Gothic period. It undoubtedly was copied from the Italian model. In France, around 1790, due to the prevailing fashion for a closer imitation of the antique, stools of ancient curule form were featured in collections of designs for furniture. See *Dantesca*; *Fauldesteuil*; *Savonarola*; *Dagobert*; *Glastonbury*; *Faldistorium*; *Empire*; *Chair*.

EMPIRE CURULE STOOL

Cushion Decorative cushions used to give support or ease to the body in a sitting or reclining position had their origin in classical antiquity. Illuminated manuscripts of the Middle Ages depicted round and square cushions, the latter having the corners gathered-in and finished with tassels, placed on chests and benches. Until the use of upholstery became more general, loose cushions were a necessity and they also gave the wooden chairs, settles and benches an air of luxury as well as a touch of color. Needlework, velvet, damask and brocade were included among the favorite materials for the cases, which were often further enhanced with fringes, braids and tassels. Day beds were often appointed with graduated sets of three or four cushions. When loose cushions were no longer a necessity the taste for them still continued for they provided an air of luxury and also contributed to comfort. Chippendale in the DIRECTOR recommended the use of cushions at the back and bolsters at each end even though they were not illustrated in his drawings for large and deep sofas. See *Squab*.

Cushion Frieze   In ornament; see *Pulvinated Frieze*.

Cusp   The term *cusp*, which means a point, is given in architecture to a point made by two intersecting curved lines. Cusps varying from simple to elaborate forms were employed in Gothic architecture, such as in windows and in tracery work. They were also used in contemporary medieval woodwork and furniture. Cusping was revived as a decorative feature during the English Gothic revival of the mid-18th century. Chippendale and other designers introduced cusping into the splats for chairs and lattice-work panels.

CUSPS IN GOTHIC TRACERY

Cut-Card Work   In English silver; a kind of silver work in which conventional designs of leaves and flowers are cut from thin sheet-silver and applied to a silver surface. It was a familiar decoration on English silver, such as caudle cups, during the late Stuart period.

Cut Glass   The name given to glass ornamented by cutting decorative designs into glass, principally the simple cutting of facets and grooves. The process of cutting is done by an iron wheel on a lathe with an abrasive of sand and water. It is then made smooth with an abrasive of powdered pumice and is finally polished by a wheel with a very fine powder. Essentially there is no difference between the process of glass cutting and engraving. However the art of the engraver requires more skill and judgment. Cut glass is principally the cutting of facets while engraved glass displays the finer pictorial and decorative work. In English cut glass; the craft of cutting glass was

brought to England from Germany. Since English flint glass surpassed Bohemian glass in brilliance the former was more desirable. Toward the end of the 18th century England produced her finest examples of cut glass. See *Bohemian Glass*; *Glass*; *Engraved Glass*.

Cutlass   In arms; a short heavy cutting sword having a single edge which was usually curved. It was used by naval men and was popular during the 18th and 19th centuries.

Cutwork   In needlework; a kind of open-work embroidery in which part of the cloth is cut away to form a decorative design. It is generally believed that the origin of lace was derived from the cut and drawnwork embroidery which was so extensively developed from around the 15th century. Cutwork and drawn linen work achieved a high standard of perfection in Italy in the 16th century. Cutwork was made in several methods. In one method a network of threads was fixed to a small frame. These threads were crossed and interlaced into intricate designs. Then a piece of fine cloth was fixed beneath the network, which was sewn with a needle to the cloth by edging around the parts of the design which were to remain. Finally the extra cloth was cut out. See *Embroidery*; *Reticella*. In cabinetwork; the terms *fretwork*, *cutwork* and *lattice-work* are practically interchangeable.

Cuvilliés, François de   1695–1768. A well-known designer of ornament working in the Rococo style, born at Hainaut. He received his training in France, although he worked entirely abroad. From 1725 he had the title of architect to the Court of Bavaria and held posts of increasing importance under the successive Electors until his death. He derived the inspiration for his ornament chiefly from the designs of Meissonier, Pineau and Lajoue, although he did not slavishly copy their work. His drawings were executed with much facility. The Rococo art at Würzburg, Nymphenburg and elsewhere in Bavaria from around 1730 onwards was largely inspired by Cuvilliés.

Cylinder Desk In English cabinetwork; a variety of desk or secretary with a tambour cylinder. The principal variety was designed with a narrow oblong top and a tambour cylinder over a frieze fitted with drawers. Frequently below the frieze there was an an arched apron piece flanked by two small lateral drawers. It rested on four legs. Sometimes the oblong top was surmounted with a bookcase fitted with two glazed doors. The tambour cylinder when rolled back revealed a fitted writing interior. Undoubtedly the design for this tambour cylinder desk was inspired by the French bureau à cylindre designed with a solid wood cylinder. Only occasionally was the cylinder made of a solid piece of wood in the English examples. Variations in design occurred. It was introduced during the Hepplewhite style. See *Writing Furniture*.

Cyma Curve In cabinetwork; a decorative continuous double curve employed more often in cabinetwork than any other ornamental curve. The English painter, William Hogarth, 1697–1764, referred to it as "the line of beauty." The cyma curve had its origin in architecture. It is technically called cyma recta when the upper part is concave and the lower part is convex, and cyma reversa when the upper part is convex and the lower is concave.

Cymaise In European pewter; a wine vessel frequently fitted with two handles used for ceremonial occasions from the 14th century onwards. One handle was fixed on the side for holding the vessel when the wine was being poured and the other handle was a swing handle of the bail type for carrying the vessel. The cymaise was provided with either a pouring lip or spout. An appointed deputation offered the cymaise to visiting noblemen as they approached the city. It seems that vessels of a similar type were later offered as prizes for shooting matches and bore the coat-of-arms of the town. The vessel is especially identified with the pewter of Germany, Switzerland and France. It is also spelled cymarre, cimaise and semaise.

Cypress The wood of the French cypress tree used in cabinetwork, especially by the French ébénistes. It is hard and compact, and its color is pale red with brown veins. The wood of the Asiatic cypress is hard and its color is greenish striped. This close-grained and compact wood was used in English cabinetwork as early as the 15th century for chests. It was particularly used in America from early Colonial days for general household furniture.

Cytise Wood The wood of the cytisus shrub, *medicago arborea*, used in cabinetwork by the French ébénistes. It is very hard and its color is greenish. It is also called ébénier des alpes.

PEWTER CYMAISE

D

Dado The block or cube-shaped part which forms the body of a pedestal between the cornice and the base moldings. In interior decoration; the term is applied to the lower part of the walls of a room which are finished in wood and resemble a continuous pedestal. A panelled wooden dado is usually called a wainscot. The name is also given to the lower part of the wall papered or painted, or of a different color or material from the upper part. See *Chair Rail*.

Dag In arms; a small pistol. The names *dag* and *pistol* were used interchangeably during the latter part of the 16th and throughout the 17th centuries. Sometimes the name *dag* is applied to all wheel-lock pistols.

Dagger In arms; a very short sword or hand weapon having a short blade, used for stabbing. It was made in a variety of forms and had many different names. It has been worn from early in the 14th century onwards, usually on the right hip. See *Basilard*; *Anelace*; *Kris*; *Miséricorde*; *Poniard*; *Dirk*; *Main Gauche*; *Kukri*; *Khuttar*.

Daghestan Rug An Oriental rug belonging to the Caucasian classification; so named after a district in Caucasian Russia. The foundation is of wool, and the pile is of a fine wool and short in length. The ends are usually finished with a narrow web and loose or knotted warp threads. It has a mosaic design softened by small primitive figures. In workmanship the Daghestan is one of the finest in the Caucasian group. See *Caucasian Rugs*.

Dagobert Chair In furniture; the name *chair of Dagobert* is given to an early bronze chair of the curule variety, having each leg or support headed with an animal's head and terminating in the foot of an animal. The seat, which was stretched between the two side rails and which was probably of leather, has disappeared. The chair derived its name from Dagobert who was King of the Franks. It is generally believed that the chair dates from the 7th century. The chair is in the Louvre. See *Curule*.

Daimyō Nanako In Japanese sword mounts; a form of nanako work having lines of dots separated by spaces of equal width in which the surface of the metal is left untouched. The name *daimyō nanako* is also given to a pattern or a series of orderly arranged tiny square pyramids. In this method the surface is cut diagonally with V grooves at right angles forming the pyramids. See *Nanako*.

Dai Seppa In Japanese sword mounts; see *Seppa*.

Dai-Shō In Japanese arms; a term given to the long and the short swords carried by the Japanese samurai or military men. The long, dai, was the fighting sword called the katana, and the shorter, shō, was the supplementary sword called the wakizashi. Very often a pair of these swords had identical or similar designs on their mountings. Frequently the mountings on the shorter sword were more elaborate, since it was the custom to leave the long sword at the entrance when entering a house and to place the shorter one on the mat floor beside its owner. See *Katana*; *Wakizashi*.

Dai-Shō-No-Soroimono In Japanese sword mounts; the term referring to a complete set of fittings for a pair of swords. Those for the longer, dai, fighting sword called katana, and those for the shorter, shō, supplementary sword called wakizashi. Such sets are very rare. See *Soroimono*; *Mitokoromono*; *Kodōgu*.

Daisy-in-Hexagon In glass; a pattern-molded design which has a flower similar to a daisy enclosed within a hexagon. It is one of the most elaborate pattern-molded designs used in the ornamentation of Ameri-

DAGHESTAN BORDER DESIGN

140

can glass. It is particularly identified with American glassware. See *Diamond Daisy*.

Dalmatic In ecclesiastical costume; a vestment with wide sleeves having a slit extending from the hem of the tunic on each side and characterized by two vertical stripes reaching from the shoulders to the hem. The dalmatic, which derives its name from from Dalmatia where it was first used, is worn in the Western Church by deacons and bishops on certain occasions. A similar robe is worn by emperors and kings at their coronation as well as at certain other solemn functions. It is believed that the dalmatic as a vestment was introduced by Pope Silvester I, 314–335. The early dalmatic was long and loose with wide sleeves. The opening for the head to pass through was slit a few inches on each side of the shoulder and these slits were laced with silk cords finished with tassels. Later the tassels hanging from either shoulder at the back became merely a decoration and were formerly much favored. In many European countries, such as England, France and Spain, the dalmatic and tunicle can no longer be described as a tunic since they resemble a scapular-like cloak with an opening for the head and with square lappets covering the upper part of the arms. In Italy the sleeve has still been retained and the dalmatic remains essentially a tunic. Dalmatics elaborately embroidered with rich orphreys and borders were especially magnificent in the Middle Ages, and sometimes the orphreys and edges of the sleeves were adorned with pearls and precious stones. See *Tunicle*.

Damascening The art of incrusting gold wire and occasionally silver or copper wire on a steel, iron or bronze surface. In this method the gold wire was beaten into the incised designs which had been finely cut with a graver and was then made smooth and polished. This form of ornamentation, which was much used on sword mounts and armor, was remarkable for its delicate and rich decoration. It is especially identified with Oriental metal work. It derived its name from Damascus, where this type of

metal work was widely practiced by the early goldsmiths and from which city it was exported.

Damask In textiles; a fine, lustrous, flat-figured fabric, the figures generally being large and continuous. Usually the warp and weft are of the same weight, quality and color, the difference in tone between the figures and the ground being produced by the contrasting lines in the weaves. It is commonly made with satin weaves; some of the combinations of weaves used in damask are taffeta, twill, grosgrain, or weft satin figures on a warp satin ground, or warp satin figures on a ground of contrasting weave. Always the lines of the figures run in one direction and the lines of the ground in another and it is this line contrast which makes the light and shade effects that are characteristic of damask. Originally damask was made of silk. See *Silk*; *Upholstery*.

Dantesca Chair In Italian cabinetwork; the first important armchair for domestic use was of ancient Roman curule form or a folding chair of X form. It was similar in construction to a camp stool with curved legs and was designed in two principal types, namely the Dantesca and the Savonarola. The Dantesca had two front and two rear supports of curule or curved X form. The front and rear lower supports were secured by runner feet and the upper supports by down-curving arms. The seat and back panel were of leather and were stretched between the supports and secured with ornamental nailheads. The early Dantesca chair was crude and plain; its surface was not enriched with intarsia, certosina or carving until late in the 15th century. See *Curule*; *Savonarola*.

Darly, Mathias English designer, publisher, engraver and caricaturist. In collaboration with George Edwards he published in 1754 A NEW BOOK OF CHINESE DESIGNS. He published in 1770 a book entitled THE COMPLEAT ARCHITECT, which was his most important work.

DALMATIC

Darn   In lace-making or embroidery; to sew with a stitch similar to the one used in darning; that is with interlacing stitches of thread.

Darned Netting   In needlework; one of the earliest forms of lace-fabric which was essentially a net embroidery. It was characterized by a net ground consisting of a network of square meshes. The design was generally darned with stitches, and since the stitches were controlled by counting the meshes distinctive geometrical designs were formed. It was known by different names, such as lacis, opus araneum, spider work and punto a Maglia Quadra. Modern survivals of this darned netting are known as filet guipure and filet brodé à reprises. See *Lacis*.

Date-Letter   In English silver; see *Hall-Marks, London*.

Daum Frères   A glassmaking firm founded in 1875 at Nancy, France. Their glass is particularly notable for its carving or cameo work. Some of their pieces were made with three or more layers of glass of various colors, which produced striking blended color effects by cutting through or partly through the different layers. The surface of the glass was generally processed with hydrofluoric acid, giving it a satin-like finish. They essentially adopted the same methods practiced by Emile Gallé, but unfortunately his highly individual style was lost in much of the work produced at their glass manufactory. See *Cameo Glass*.

Dauphiné   In French Provincial; a former province in southeastern France, now in the the departments of Isère, Drôme and Hautes-Alpes; it was bounded on the south by the old province of Provence. The provincial furniture of Dauphiné has the same general characteristics as that of Bresse with the earlier pieces being similar to those of Burgundy. See *Bresse*; *Burgundy*; *French Provincial*.

Davenport   In English cabinetwork; a variety of small desk having four sides that were more or less equal. It is reputed that

LATE GEORGIAN DAVENPORT

the name is derived from a desk originally made to order for a Captain Davenport by Gillow and Barton, a well-known firm of English cabinetmakers established by Robert Gillow in 1731. A principal form was designed with a sloping top fitted with a drawer and a writing slide at each side over four graduated drawers. It was mounted on four short tapered quadrangular legs that were finished with brass toe caps and casters.

Davenport   In English ceramics; John Davenport and his successors were potters at Longport, Staffordshire, from 1793 to 1882. They made cream-colored and blue-printed earthenware and porcelain. The wares were technically of good quality. They sometimes used an excellent dark blue ground color. The Davenport manufactory was one of the chief makers of porcelain in Staffordshire. Included among the marks were "Davenport" with an anchor and "Davenport" over "Longport". See *Staffordshire*.

David, Jacques Louis   1748–1825. French painter. David completely dominated the art of his time. He was the principal exponent of a more intense Classic Revival which endeavored to recapture the spirit of the antique through its closer imitation. David went to Rome to study around 1775, and during his stay in Rome his taste for severe classicism became fully matured. In 1789 he returned to Paris and was made painter to Louis XVI. He was an ardent admirer of Napoleon. After the downfall of Napoleon he was forced to spend the rest of his life in exile. David, who was an important political figure as well as an antiquarian and painter, gave the order for the furniture for the Convention to Georges Jacob and to two architects, Fontaine and Percier, who were then unknown. David depicted new forms for furniture in his paintings, in which he used antique models for the actual shapes. He was chiefly responsible for improving these new forms in furniture design. Especially typical was his celebrated portrait of Mme Recamier. The fashion for imitating the ancients was extended to the style of dress as is evident in studying the gown of Mme Recamier. See *Directoire*; *Denon, Baron*; *Empire*; *Recamier*; *Jacob, Georges*; *Louis XVI*; *Watteau, Antoine*; *Classic Revival*.

Day Bed In English furniture; the name given to a variety of couch used for reclining or sleeping. The French term *chaise longue* or long chair is descriptive of this variety of furniture. The characteristic variety had one end designed as a chair back and it had a very long seat, which resembled a narrow bench. As a rule it was upholstered, and occasionally caned. It is generally accepted that the day bed was introduced during the reign of Henry VIII, 1509–1547. The day bed lost much of its popularity in the Early Georgian period. In American cabinetwork; the day bed, which was made from about 1640 to 1780, was commonly known as a couch. It was designed in the Late Jacobean, William and Mary, Queen Anne and Chippendale styles. The so-called Grecian couch was often used for reclining during the early 19th century. See *Grecian Couch*.

Deal The name given to a sawn board generally less than 3 inches in thickness and less than 9 inches in width used in English cabinetwork as early as the middle of the 16th century. It seems that this wood was principally cut from pine or fir and was imported from the Baltic countries. From early in the 18th century it largely replaced oak in the wood panelling of early Georgian homes. It was also much used as a framework for furniture veneered in walnut or mahogany during the second half of the 17th and first half of the 18th centuries.

Decanter In English glass; the glass wine decanter with its glass stopper was introduced early in the 18th century. The name is derived from the word *decant* meaning to pour off gently from one vessel to another. The purpose of decanting was to separate the wine from the sediment in the original wine bottle. The decanter had an ovoid-shaped body with a neck long enough to grip with the hand. During the middle of the 18th century the decanter was finely engraved and was frequently designed to match the wine glasses. Later the decanter was richly cut and had rings designed around the neck to catch the drops of wine as well as to afford a firmer grip for an unsteady drinker. From around 1795 to 1820 the decanter was also made with a squat-shaped body.

Decanter Stand In English silver; the name given to a circular stand having a wood-turned base, covered with baize, and having either pierced or solid metal sides that were usually made of silver. It was used for moving the decanter around the dining table. Sometimes the decanter stand was mounted either on casters or on small silver wheels. The decanter stand was occasionally made with a silver base. It was introduced late in the 18th century.

Deception Bed In American cabinetwork; various forms of concealed beds were known in America in the 18th century. A form of half tester bed folding against a wall and concealed with a curtain was popular in New England early in the 18th century. Chests of drawers with removable fronts allowing a frame for the bedding to unfold were also made. William Martin, a Philadelphia upholsterer, advertised all kinds of chairs, couches, deception beds and other articles of furniture. Sheraton in his CABINET DICTIONARY refers to a deception table and observes it "is one made to imitate a Pembroke table, but to answer the purpose of a pot cupboard, or any other secret use, which we hide from eyes of a stranger." See *Press Bed*; *Harlequin*.

Décor Bois In ceramics; a style of painted decoration having a painted ground in imitation of grained wood. A decoration resembling a white sheet of paper or a card having a landscape painted in crimson, grey or black was made to appear as though attached to the ground. It is generally accepted that this style of decoration origi-

LATE JACOBEAN
CANED DAY BED

DELFT WIG STAND

nated on Niderviller faïence around 1770. The style was extensively imitated at many ceramic manufactories, such as Frankenthal, Vienna, Nymphenburg and Nove.

Delafosse, Jean-Charles 1734–1789. French architect and designer of ornament. Although some of his early designs were in the Rococo style, his decorative work is especially identified with the transitional phase from the Louis XV style to the Louis XVI style as well as the Louis XVI style, which represents the early phase of the Classic Revival in France.

Delanois, Louis 1731–1792. A noted French ébéniste who worked under the patronage of Madame du Barry. He received his master in 1761, and from his atelier he produced pieces of cabinetwork with such a high degree of finish, elegance and originality that he attracted many of the nobility to his workshop. One of his many distinctive pieces was a bedstead he made for Madame du Barry designed with columns and a domed canopy. This bedstead, which was to be placed in an alcove, was elegantly mounted in bronze doré modelled in the form of roses which were her favorite flowers.

Delft In Dutch ceramics; during the second quarter of the 17th century the town of Delft near Rotterdam assumed a leading position among the Dutch centers of faïence making, and became famous for its imitations of Chinese porcelains made in tin-glazed earthenware. Its finest period was from around 1640 to 1740. The material for Delft faïence was characterized by a whiteness and thinness of substance. Delft faïence in imitation of blue and white in the Chinese style bore the closest resemblance to the original of any of the European porcelain or faïence imitating Chinese prototypes. Perhaps the most typical early types of Delft blue and white faïence were in the designs of Wan Li, 1573–1619, and in the transitional period from the end of Ming to the beginning of

the reign of K'ang Hsi or from about 1644 to 1662. Practically every type of porcelain of the reign of K'ang Hsi, 1662–1722, was subsequently imitated. In another variety of Delft blue and white Dutch figures were occasionally intermingled with Chinese motifs and the forms were often adapted to the European taste. Another type of blue and white of much importance and dating from around 1650 was in the Dutch style of contemporary oil painting and was decorated only with European landscapes, figure and portrait subjects. Decorative designs in the Baroque taste were made from around 1675 and onwards. A more common blue and white ware was made from 1750 to 1800 and later. Polychrome wares in the Chinese and Japanese style, particularly the Famille Verte porcelain of the reign of K'ang Hsi, and Japanese brocaded Imari ware, were closely imitated from early in the 18th century. At first only high-temperature colors were used on this faïence. They also made a polychrome ware with a black ground which may have been inspired by the Chinese Famille Noire. Other colored grounds were also used. As the 18th century advanced muffle colors and gold replaced the high-temperature colors on the more ambitious pieces. From late in the 17th century onwards, polychrome wares in the Dutch style that were essentially original in design were made. Especially fine were the pieces with baskets and pots of flowers treated in a natural manner. Designs in the Baroque taste and in the Rococo taste subsequently followed; the latter being used until the 19th century, since the Neo-Classical style was never adopted. The Dutch were not skillful modellers, and as a result their figures and modelled wares, which they adopted from the Chinese and Meissen, were crude and were of little artistic importance. Delft faïence was often marked with the initials, the name or the mark of the owner. The owner's mark was usually the same as the sign of the factory such as a flower, star, peacock, three bells, rose or some other symbol. See *Faïence*.

Delftware In ceramics; the English name for tin-glazed earthenware. It is synonymous for faïence which is reserved for the later tin-glazed wares of the 17th century either in the more or less original styles made in France and in other countries or more often in the Dutch-Chinese or Delft tradition. See *Faïence*; *Delft*.

Delhi Rug An Oriental rug woven at Delhi, India, which was an important rug weaving center in India during the late 16th and early 17th centuries. The modern Delhi rug is purely a commercial creation. See *India Oriental*; *Oriental Rug*.

Della Robbia In ceramics; the tin-glazed terra cotta made by a celebrated Florentine family of sculptors. It was made by Lucca della Robbia, c. 1399–1482, his nephew Andrea, 1435–1525, and the latter's sons, Giovanni, 1469–c. 1529, and Girolamo, 1488–1566. Essentially the work belongs to the art of sculpture or modelling rather than to ceramics. Lucca della Robbia, who was a great sculptor in marble and bronze, made beautifully modelled terra-cotta reliefs on which he used colored glazes made with an admixture of tin ashes. The light blue and other tin glazes were often of remarkable beauty. It is erroneous to believe that Lucca della Robbia invented the process or was the first to use opaque tin glazes. His reliefs were notable for his excellent knowledge of anatomy and for his fine modelling of hands. Especially striking are his colorful wreathed borders of fruits naturalistically represented, which were extensively imitated by followers belonging to his school. Andrea della Robbia did many beautiful reliefs of the Madonna and the Child. His work is usually as highly regarded as the work done by Lucca della Robbia.

Demi Grand Feu In ceramics; the French term for medium fired glazes. These glazes are applied to porcelain that has been biscuited or already fired in the porcelain kiln, since these glazes melt at a medium temperature and cannot stand the heat required to fire porcelain. After they are applied to the biscuited porcelain they are melted in a second temperate fire. These glazes are alkali lead silicates colored with metallic oxides. They melt at a temperature higher than is required to fire enamels. See *Glaze*; *Grand Feu*.

Demilune In cabinetwork; crescent-shaped or half-moon-shaped. The term is frequently applied to describe a commode of semi-circular contour; such as the demilune satin-wood commodes designed by Adam which became fashionable after 1780.

Demirdji An Oriental rug belonging to the Turkish classification; so named after the town where it is woven. The warp and the weft are of a coarse wool. The pile is of wool and rather short in length. The Demirdji is a rather modern rug, being first woven toward the end of the 19th century. See *Turkish Rugs*.

Demoiselle à Atourner In French furniture; the name given to an early variety of wig stand that served as an early form of a dressing table. It usually had a round table top that supported a short columnar shaft surmounted by a feminine head of carved or painted wood on which the coiffure was placed. Occasionally it had arms fitted with circular shelves to hold toilet articles. It was used during the Gothic era.

Denon, Dominique Vivant, Baron de As a result of Napoleon's Egyptian campaign in 1798 and 1799 there was a vogue for Egyptian style of ornament. This was chiefly due to the archaeological studies of the French artist, architect and archaeologist, Baron Denon, 1747–1825. He was a friend of David's. Napoleon invited him to accompany the military expedition to Egypt. In 1802 he published his most important work which was entitled VOYAGE DANS LA BASSE ET LA HAUTE EGYPTE; it was in two volumes and contained 141 plates. Among the favorite motifs employed by the French were the Egyptian terminal figures, the

DELLA ROBBIA PLAQUE

sphinx, the lotus capital and the lion-headed supports for chairs and tables. See *David, Jacques Louis*; *Directoire*; *Empire*; *Egyptian Detail*.

Dentelle   A French term meaning lace, lacework; toward the end of the 16th century lace in France was generally called dentelle. Prior to that time the term *passement* was used.

Dentelle à la Vierge   In lace-making; a pretty bobbin-made lace having a double ground, principally made by the peasants in Dieppe, Normandy. This lace was much favored for caps and was probably first made in the 17th century.

Dentil   A small rectangular block used as a repetitive motif in the bed mold of a cornice. As a rule the projection of a dentil is equal to its width, and the space between to half its width. Dentils were frequently used on the cornices of furniture of architectural design, such as on bookcases and secretary cabinets designed in the Early Georgian style.

DERBY SUGAR BOWL
WITH IMARI PATTERN

Derbend Rug   An Oriental rug belonging to the Caucasian group, so named after a city in the province of Daghestan, in the neighborhood of which these rugs are made. The foundation is of wool and the pile is of a fine wool and rather long and has a silk luster. The ends of some are finished with a wide web, others have a short web and knotted fringe. This variety of rug uses a mosaic design. See *Caucasian Rugs*.

Derby   In English ceramics; it seems that porcelain was made around 1745 at Cockpit Hill in Derby. In 1756 a porcelain manufactory was established in Nottingham Road with William Duesbury as manager, who soon became sole owner. It is believed that Duesbury purchased the Longton Hall works in 1760 and secured control of Bow in 1762. He bought the Chelsea manufactory in 1770 and continued to operate it in association with Derby until 1784, when he closed it. Duesbury's son succeeded his father upon the latter's death in 1786. In 1811 it was pur-

chased by Robert Bloor and finally closed in 1848. A small factory was started on King Street by some of the workmen from about 1850 to 1870. An entirely new company opened a factory in 1876 and it was called the Royal Crown Derby Porcelain Company. The productions from 1786 to 1811 are generally known as Crown Derby and from 1811 to 1848 as Bloor-Derby due to the marks that were in general use. The early porcelain made at Derby was unmarked. After 1770 various marks were in regular use. A distinctive Derby mark is a crowned "D" with crossed batons and six dots between the "D" and the crown in blue, crimson or purple. An anchor traversing the "D" in red or gold is the usual Chelsea-Derby mark, 1770–1784. From about 1755 to 1770 figures were made in the Meissen style and the tablewares were in the style of the Chelsea wares marked with a red anchor and were often decorated with Meissen flowers. Painting in underglaze blue was relatively rare. During the Chelsea-Derby period, 1770–1784, the figure modelling as a rule revealed the influence of Sèvres. Biscuit figures were also made. The tablewares also showed the influence of Sèvres, but the interpretation was in the Chelsea tradition for taste, and as a result the wares had a singular English charm and simplicity. The material was a pleasing slightly warm white and the glaze was clear and brilliant but rather thick. The Crown Derby wares, 1784–1811, maintained the traditions of the Chelsea-Derby productions. The biscuit figures were of very good quality. The manufactory enjoyed a pre-eminent position in England during the last quarter of the 18th century. During the Bloor period, 1811 to 1848, a general artistic decline soon became evident that was to increase in the ensuing years.

Derbyshire Chair   In English cabinetwork; a variety of Jacobean oak side chair introduced around 1650 made in Derbyshire and Yorkshire. One variety had an arcaded top rail and a central crosspiece joined with turned spindles. The top rail and the crosspiece were ornamented with knobbed finials. The two uprights were surmounted with scrolled finials curving outward. The wooden seat was usually sunk or dished to hold a cushion. The legs were joined with stretchers. Another variety introduced a few years later had two or three broad, flat crosspieces connecting the two uprights. They were elaborately hooped and scalloped and vigorously carved, and were decorated with short pendants. The scrolled finials surmounting the two uprights were curved inward. Occasionally a mask with a pointed beard was carved in the center of the top rail. The Derbyshire chair was rarely designed with arms. It is also called a Yorkshire chair.

Derbyshire Spar   A colored crystalline stone found in the caverns of the Tray Cliff, Castleton, in Derbyshire, England. Although ordinary commercial fluorspar is found in many parts of the world, the colored varieties are confined to the Tray Cliff caverns. The colored varieties shade from blue, green and yellow to a rich amethyst purple; the latter being the most familiar and favorite shade. It was discovered in England in 1743, and by 1760 it was widely used in decorative work. Vases, cassolettes and candelabra were made of Derbyshire spar and were mounted in ormolu by Matthew Boulton at his Soho works between 1762 and 1765. It was exported to France where it was called Bleu Jaune, and as a result of this appellation it became popularly called Blue John in England.

Deringer   In American arms; Henry Deringer, born at Easton, Pennsylvania, in 1786 and died in 1868, was the son of Henry Deringer, Sr., a Colonial gunsmith and maker of Kentucky rifles. As a youth he was apprenticed to a maker of firearms at Richmond, Virginia, until 1806 when he settled in Philadelphia where he established his own arms manufactory. Deringer produced pistols of all sizes as well as rifles, carbines and swords. He became particularly

well known for his very small percussion pistols, especially one to which his name is attached, having a barrel usually about an inch and a half long with a large bore of 0·41 inch. It was with one of these Deringers that John Wilkes Booth assassinated Abraham Lincoln. Due to the popularity of these small pistols originated by Deringer several firearms competitors produced similar models which were called "Derringers" in order to circumvent lawsuits. And, as a result, the word Derringer spelled with two r's is used to include all pocket pistols having a short barrel and a large caliber.

Deruta   In Italian ceramics; some of the world's most beautiful painted majolica, both polychrome and lustered, was made at Deruta, Umbria, from about 1490 to 1550. Potteries still exist at Deruta. It is generally accepted that potters were working there late in the 14th century and that majolica having artistic importance was made at Deruta from the latter part of the 15th century. A most important variety was the polychrome ware, 1500–1520, of the petal-back class, which was so called because of a distinctive imbricated floral pattern decorated on the backs of plates and dishes. The coloring was unrivalled and the figure painting was of the highest quality and was remarkable for its extreme delicacy and refinement. Luster painting was done at Deruta from about 1500. The golden yellow or mother-of-pearl and the ruby luster were of uncommon beauty. The ruby luster seems to have disappeared from Deruta around 1515; however, the golden yellow with its nacreous reflections was used for almost a half a century longer. A very familiar variety, which ranks among the masterpieces of majolica, had lustered and polychrome decoration and was made from about 1515 to 1540; the finest being made prior to 1530. The plates, which were often very large, were boldly painted with busts and figure subjects in a linear style and were often broadly outlined and shadowed in blue, having simple borders of star-rays,

DERBYSHIRE CHAIR

foliage or gadroons. Sometimes the designs were in relief. This style of painting characterized by its bold simplicity is closely associated with the familiar Deruta manner, which became well established on their wares, and is in direct contrast to the very sensitive painting on the so-called petal-back variety. See *Italian Majolica*; *Luster Decoration*.

Deshilado   A Spanish term meaning cut and drawn thread linen work.

Desk   In English cabinetwork; an article of furniture for reading or writing having a table or board serving as a rest or support for the writing paper or book, for which purpose the table or board is generally conveniently sloped. The name is given to a variety of articles displaying a wide difference in their construction and accessories depending upon their use, such as for prayer, music, reading, school, studying and writing. The most distinctive feature is a sloping surface. The early English desks with a writing board and book-rest were derived from the ecclesiastical lectern and were very massive and cumbrous. After the invention of printing and the resultant smaller books, portable desks with a sloping surface came into general use, and they remained practically the only form of furniture designed for writing during the first half of the 17th century. With the introduction of bureaux toward the end of the 17th century, the small portable desk continued to be used, but the interior was fitted with writing accessories, such as pigeonholes and drawers, reproducing the plan of the large bureaux. Early in the 18th century the portable desk was sometimes mounted on a stand with cabriole legs. Portable desks were used throughout the 18th century although they were not regarded as fashionable, due to the many innovations in 18th century writing furniture. See *Writing Furniture*.

Desk-on-Frame   In English and American cabinetwork; a desk mounted on a stand or a frame; in particular the portable desk with

LUDWIGSBURG COFFEE POT
WITH DEUTSCHE BLUMEN

a sloping or slant-front mounted on a stand. See *Desk*.

Desmalter, Jacob   A French ébéniste; see *Jacob, Georges*.

Desserte   In French cabinetwork; the term *desserte* is usually given to a kind of side table having a demilune marble and galleried top over a conformingly shaped panelled frieze, mounted on four quadrangular or cylindrical tapered legs. It had two matching undershelves with pierced galleries. The desserte side table was sometimes designed with an oblong top and incurvate returns or ends that curved inward over a conformingly shaped frieze and a low and matching galleried undershelf. It was introduced during the Louis XVI period. The term *desserte* is also usually given to a variant form of the commode-desserte. It was similar to the commode-desserte with a demilune top except that it had two long open galleried shelves in place of the two long deep central drawers; that is, it had six open-shelf compartments. See *Commode-Desserte*; *Servante*.

Dessert Knife   In English silver; a knife usually having a silver blade and an ivory handle; introduced during the George III era, 1760–1820. See *Knife*.

Dessert Spoon   In English silver; a variety of spoon, intermediate in size between the teaspoon and tablespoon, usually conforming in shape to the tablespoon. It was introduced late in the 17th century. See *Spoon*; *Teaspoon*.

Deutsche Blumen   In ceramics; a contemporary German name given to flowers painted in a natural manner. This style of flower painting was introduced at Meissen around 1740. It rapidly became very fashionable and by the middle of the 18th century practically every existing porcelain factory was decorating its porcelain with the so-called deutsche blumen. Especially fine were the German flowers painted on the earliest Vincennes and Chelsea porcelain. The deutsche blumen supplanted the earlier and stylized Indian or Oriental flowers. See *Indian Flowers*.

Devil's Work In Chinese ceramics; see *Kuei Kung*; *Ling Lung*.

Devonshire Lace The name is given to all laces made in Devonshire since the 16th century. Included among the Devonshire laces are Honiton, Trolly lace, fine reproductions of rich and expensive Flemish laces and coarse laces resembling simple Torchon.

Dewdrop In American glass; see *Hobnail*.

Diamond Daisy In glass; a pattern-molded design having a flower resembling a daisy enclosed within a square which is set in a diamond motif. It is called occasionally Daisy-in-Square. It is one of the most elaborate pattern-molded designs employed in the decoration of American glass and it is especially identified with American glass. See *Daisy-in-Hexagon*.

Diamond Pattern In American glass; a pattern-molded design extensively employed in the decoration of American glass. There were three principal varieties of the diamond pattern used in America; namely rows of diamonds above vertical flutes, an all-over diamond pattern, and the checkered diamond pattern. It is also called the Ogival pattern and the Expanded Diamond pattern. In English glass it is often referred to as reticulated. See *Checkered Diamond*.

Diamond Point In French Provincial cabinetwork; a carved geometrical ornament framed in a rectangular panel consisting of a diamond-shaped pyramid flanked by four small triangular-shaped pyramids. Another combination of the diamond point consisted of eight elongated triangular pyramids of equal size. One group of four formed an elongated diamond, which was flanked by the remaining four. The diamond point was principally identified with the cabinetwork from the province of Gascogne and was a favorite decoration for armoires or cupboards. It was introduced early in the 17th century. See *Star Diamond Point*; *Gascogne*.

Diamond Point Engraving In glass; see *Engraved Glass*; *Dutch and Flemish Glass*.

Diamond-Point Spoon In English silver; a silver spoon having the stem terminating in a diamond-point. It was introduced around the end of the 14th century. See *Spoon*.

Diaper In ornament; a pattern characterized by the continuous repetition of any small conventional design which covers a surface uniformly. The pattern may be based on floral or geometrical designs. The name was also given to a silk fabric woven during the Middle Ages which was characterized by an elaborately embroidered over-all geometrical pattern. The fabric was also called diaspron.

Dimity A fine cotton material, deriving its name from two Greek words meaning twice and thread, since it was originally woven with two threads. It appears that it was first woven in Italy around the middle of the 16th century and that it was imported into the other European countries. Hepplewhite in the GUIDE recommends the use of white dimity for beds because it gives an "elegance and neatness truly agreeable."

Dinanderie The name given to articles or wares made of brass, in particular, the fine domestic and ecclesiastical brass work made from about the 11th century onwards at the towns of Dinant and Huy in Belgium. From the 12th to the middle of the 15th centuries Dinant and nearby towns produced magnificent works in brass such as lecterns, altar candlesticks, chandeliers, tabernacles and fonts for cathedrals and churches. In 1466 Dinant was sacked by Charles the Bold and the brass founders fled to Bruges, Tournay, Huy and Namur where they continued their craft.

Dining Table In English cabinetwork; the characteristic dining table during the Gothic period was made of oak and was of trestle construction, having a massive removable rectangular top. The dining table of perman-

DIAMOND POINT

ent structure was introduced around the middle of the 16th century. The characteristic Elizabethan table had a rectangular top over a carved apron and rested on four bulbous-shaped supports, which were joined with a continuous floor stretcher. Sometimes it was designed with a draw-top. This table remained in general use throughout the 17th century and was gradually superseded toward the end of the 17th century by the oval or round table. This table was made of walnut or oak and was generally of the gate-leg variety with two drop-leaves. The characteristic Early Georgian mahogany table had an oval or round top and cabriole legs. It was so constructed that one cabriole leg swung out at each side to support the flaps. It was occasionally made with square flaps so that two tables could be placed together. A variety of mahogany extension table which came into general use during the mid-Georgian era, circa 1750, consisted of a center table with two oblong drop-leaves and two semi-circular end tables, each generally having drop-leaves. This variety of extension table continued in favor until the 19th century. At the end of the 18th century the pedestal dining table became fashionable. It was designed in two or more sections with each section being supported on a turned pedestal with a molded and splayed tetrapod base. This type of table was in general use during the early 19th century. At the same time the round dining table, which was extensively employed in France during the Empire, was revived in England. In French cabinetwork; the 18th century French dining table was generally round or oval and was made with adjustable leaves. See *Draw-Top Table*; *Gate-Leg Table*; *Refectory Table*; *Swing-Leg*.

Dining Tray   In Japanese lacquer; traditionally the Japanese used individual dining trays or ozen rather than a large dining table. These trays are either flat or mounted on very short straight legs, since the Japanese sit on the matted floor or tatami. This custom of individual trays is still observed in some Japanese homes and hotels. Ozen are made in various sizes for the different courses. The ozen most commonly used is about one square foot. A very small ozen is used for tea and cake and also for sake or rice wine. Essentially the ozen is a very plain tray and is generally lacquered in black, deep red or dull orange monochrome. By extension the term *ozen* is now given to the large dining table, mounted on very low legs, around which a number of persons may sit at meal time.

Diptych   A term originally applied to a Roman two-part hinged tablet which could be closed by folding. It was originally used during the Roman Empire as a consular document. In the early Christian churches the names of contributors were listed on the two inside panels. Each outside panel generally had a painting of a religious character. As the list of names increased in size, a third fold or panel was added to the diptych and it was called a triptych. Around the 9th century it was used as an altar piece, and the inside panels as well as the outside were richly decorated. During the Middle Ages the painted decoration was often done by the outstanding contemporary painters.

Directoire   The name given to the style of ornament and furniture design developed in France from 1793 to 1804, during the time of the Convention, 1792–1795, the Directory, 1795–1799 and the Consulate, 1799–1804. Essentially it was a time of transition between the Louis XVI style and the Empire style. The form of much of the furniture was to a large extent a continuation of the Louis XVI style but more severely treated. Other articles of furniture were more or less exact copies of Greco-Roman art. These pieces displayed the prevailing fashion for a closer imitation of the antique in their many novelties of design and decoration. Gradually the French cabinetmakers discarded the exaggerations of these antique novelties, but retained their essence, gave their work uniformity and finally perfected the Empire style. Among the favorite ornaments were those symbolic

SHERATON DINING TABLE

of the Republic, such as the Phrygian caps of liberty, fasces, lictors' axes and oak and laurel crowns. Favorite classic motifs included the swan, lozenge, star, lyre and wreaths. During the Directoire style Greek art was paramount for decorative motifs and for models to be used for formulating the shapes of furniture. The Recamier sofa was characteristic of the Directoire style. The principal chair was of Grecian inspiration and was characterized by its rolled-over back or concave crest rail. The French Directoire style became fashionable in England about 1795 and many features of its designs were copied by the contemporary English cabinetmakers. Sheraton in his CABINET DICTIONARY adopted some of the features of the French Directoire style. In America Duncan Phyfe followed the later work of Sheraton, the French Directoire, and French Empire styles. See *Louis XVI*; *Empire*; *David, Jacques Louis*; *Classic Revival*; *Denon, Baron*; *Grecian Chair*.

Dirk In arms; a dagger, in particular one carried by the Scotch Highlanders. The Scottish dirk consists of a very heavy single-edge blade that is thick at the back and tapering to a point. The hand grip is of baluster shape and it is without a guard.

Disbrowe, Nicholas 1612–1683. American cabinetmaker working at Hartford, Connecticut, in 1639. Disbrowe was born at Waldon, Essex, England. He was the maker of chests and other oak furniture, and is one of the few 17th century American cabinetmakers whose names are known. See *Winslow, Kenelm*.

Disc Foot In cabinetwork; a rounded flat-shaped foot. See *Foot*; *Pad Foot*.

Dish Cover In English silver; a deep dome-shaped, oval cover made of silver or Sheffield. The top of the cover is surmounted with a handle. It was introduced circa 1800.

Dish Cross In English silver; a silver stand used on the table to hold silver and porcelain dishes. It was designed in the form of a cross with adjustable arms, the ends of which were incurvate to secure the dish. It rested on four feet. The center of the cross was formed by a circular piece which was high enough from the table to allow a movable spirit burner to be placed beneath. Some were fitted with burners. It was introduced during the last half of the 18th century.

Dished In cabinetwork; a concave depression cut in a surface, such as the wooden seat of a chair. See *Derbyshire Chair*.

Dish Ring In silver; a decorative silver stand particularly identified with Irish silver, and sometimes called a potato-ring. It is a spool-shaped ring varying from about 3 to 4 inches in height and from about 7 to 8 inches in diameter. A dish ring was used all through dinner to support, in succession, the earthenware soup bowl, the wooden potato bowl, the glass fruit dish and the silver punch bowl. It was made in Ireland from about 1750 to 1820.

Distemper The art of distemper painting is done with pigments tempered with gum, or size, mixed with pipe-clay, whitening or some similar substance, and used with a water medium. This method of painting is widely used for temporary decorative work on walls, such as theatrical scenery. It was used extensively for making the large tapestry cartoons. Due to the fact that the colors are lighter in tone when dried than at the time of application, considerable skill is necessary in mixing the colors. The French term for this method is *gouache*. See *Tempera*.

Divan The term *divan* is of Persian origin and is used throughout the Near East to describe a continuous bench-like structure or a raised part of the floor against the wall of a room. It is used as a place for sitting and reclining as a kind of sofa or couch, and is usually furnished with cushions.

Djijim A hand-woven embroidered rug made in the Orient; it is made by weaving a web, and upon this is embroidered with thread and needle the rug patterns in vogue in the locality where it is woven.

DIRECTOIRE
TÔLE WALL FOUNTAIN
WITH SWAN HANDLES

Djushaghan Rug   See *Joshaghan Rug*.

Dobbin   A small, 18th century, English drinking glass holding a gill of liquid.

Doccia   In Italian ceramics; a porcelain manufactory was founded in 1735–1737 by the Marquis Carlo Ginori and is still owned by the Ginori family. During the 19th century, the manufactory chiefly produced imitations of earlier wares, with the original marks often being added. The old Capo-di-Monte molds were bought by Doccia and they often copied Capo-di-Monte and sometimes marked it with a crowned "N" of Naples. It is sometimes difficult to distinguish Doccia porcelain from that of Venice and Capo-di-Monte. However some original and distinctive work is ascribed to this factory. The designs and colors of their painted decoration showed the influence of Vienna, Meissen and Sèvres. No mark was used on the early wares from 1737 to 1757. The mark of the star was used during the late 18th and first half of the 19th centuries. It is generally found on very translucent porcelain painted with figures and landscapes, the latter being views of Florence of exceptional quality. Modern Doccia marks include the name "Ginori".

Doctor's Lady   A Chinese carved figure. See *Physician's Model*.

TABLE
WITH DOLPHIN SUPPORTS

Dog of Fo   In Chinese art; a Chinese animal figure widely used in ceramics, sculpture and painting. He is a lion but is very gentle, and he is usually playing with a silk ball tied with a ribbon which he holds in his mouth. He is generally depicted in pairs, one playing with the ball and the other with a lion cub. The very large lion figures were placed as guardians at the entrance gate to a Buddhist temple; because of this duty they were called Dog of Fo or Buddha. The smaller lion figures were used as holders for incense sticks on the altars of Buddhist temples. See *Chinese Animal Figures*.

Dog Tooth   In ornament; an English Gothic motif originally carved in a cavetto mold-ing at the beginning of the 13th century. At first the motif was rather crude. It finally developed into a four-petal flower and was so called because of its supposed resemblance to a dogtooth violet. The four petals were grouped together in a conical manner and were joined at the point.

Dole Cupboard   See *Almoner's Cupboard*.

Doll House   Fine examples of doll houses were made on the Continent during the late 17th and 18th centuries. Undoubtedly the more elaborate examples, which were too valuable to be used as ordinary playthings, were made for the amusement and pleasure of adults. Such miniature houses still containing their original furniture and decoration are a valuable source in re-creating the polite domestic life of an age no longer in existence.

Dolphin   In ornament; the sea dolphin treated in a fanciful manner was used as a sculptured, painted or carved motif in decorative art. It is especially identified with the Italian Renaissance. Included among the other styles in which it was used are the Louis XIV and Louis XVI styles. In Early Christian art; the dolphin was used as a symbol of love, diligence and swiftness.

Domino Paper   In decorative papers; the name given to an early form of illuminated paper, which simply means the practice of coloring paper by hand, developed in France. These papers with their marbleized designs and occasionally small figures and grotesques crudely printed from wood blocks and colored by hand were especially used as the inside lining of book covers and around the chimneypieces of peasant cottages. The artisans engaged in this craft were known as Dominotiers. The coloring matter was principally colored inks or water colors mixed with glue which prevented the spreading and increased the durability of these colors. The method of marbleizing paper as developed by the Dominotiers was also used in England. See *Illuminated Paper*.

Don Pottery In English ceramics; the Don Pottery was started probably as early as 1790 at Swinton, Yorkshire. Around 1800 it was enlarged by John Green of Leeds, and in 1834 it was sold to Samuel Barker of the Mixborough Pottery. Included among the marks was "Don Pottery", impressed. Its principal productions were cream-colored earthenware and other wares in imitation of those made at Leeds.

Doppelwandglas In glass; the process of laying gold and silver leaf between two layers of glass is of early origin. It is believed to have originated in the neighborhood of Alexandria around the first century A.D. Occasionally designs were scratched on the gold leaf with a sharp point. The terms *doppelwandglas* and *zwischengoldglas* are given to this kind of glass in Germany. See *Bohemian Glass*; *Fondi d'Oro*.

Dopskal A Swedish term applied to a small drinking bowl, usually made of silver, fitted with one or two handles, with or without a cover. It is chiefly identified with the Scandinavian countries. It was introduced during the first half of the 17th century.

Dorotheenthal In German ceramics; a faïence manufactory was founded at Dorotheenthal near Arnstadt, Thuringia, around 1715 by Augusta Dorothea, daughter of a Duke of Brunswick, with Johann Philipp Frantz apparently being the first manager. The factory closed prior to 1806. The mark occasionally used was "AB" in monogram in combination with painters' marks. Especially characteristic of their work is the painted decoration of Baroque scrollwork, or laub-und-bandelwerk, which they treated in a distinctive manner. Included among their wares were cylindrical tankards and two-handled vases and figures. They were painted in high-temperature colors of great brightness of tone and the designs were vigorously executed.

Dossal Or Dossel. In ecclesiastical art; a decorative cloth hanging at the back of the altar deriving its name from the French *dos* meaning back. As a rule the dossal, which was of early origin, was richly embroidered with appropriate religious ornament and it was changed according to the festivals of the church year.

Dossier In English Gothic cabinetwork; a wooden bench with a high back and canopy built in the wainscot; it was elaborately panelled and carved. The bench was used primarily as a seat for dining, generally holding four persons. In French cabinetwork; the term *dossier* is also applied to the headboard and to the footboard of a bedstead.

Douai In French ceramics; a manufactory for making faïence fine was founded at Douai, Nord, in 1781 by two Englishmen, Charles and James Leigh, and was in existence until 1820. The firm was known as Houzé de l'Aulnoit & Cie. Other potteries making similar wares were also active at Douai. The most common production of Douai was cream-colored earthenware similar to that of Leeds, England. Decorative motifs pierced in openwork, handles in the form of twisted stems, reliefs in biscuit and marbled wares were characteristic and were in imitation of English wares. During the period of the French Revolution snuff boxes, plates and similar pieces made of white or cream-colored earthenware were decorated with current patriotic emblems and mottoes. The wares were occasionally marked "Leigh & Cie" or "Douai" impressed. Other marks such as "Martin Dammann" and "Halfort" belonged to another pottery operating here.

Double Chest In English cabinetwork; see *Chest-on-Chest*.

Double Cup In Renaissance silver; a tall decorative standing cup. It was in the form of twin cups, one of which can be inverted and fitted over the other. The body of the cup rested on a stem and spreading foot.

RENAISSANCE
SILVER DOUBLE CUP

It varied in height but was seldom less than 10 inches. See *Standing Cup*.

Double Scroll Handle In silver; see *Scroll Handle*.

Double Spoon In silver; a form of silver double spoon consisting of a stem, which is usually spirally turned, with a spoon bowl at each end. One spoon bowl was about the size of a teaspoon and the other about the size of a tablespoon. It is principally identified with Dutch silver and was used for measuring tea. It was introduced in the late 18th century.

Doublet Pattern A pattern in which the arrangement of the person or group on the right is exactly the same but reversed as the person or group on the left. This arrangement is found especially in Persian and Byzantine fabrics.

Dovetail In cabinetmaking; the term is applied to a feature in construction consisting of two pieces of wood, one of which has wedge-shaped openings cut on its edge, while the other has wedge-shaped projections on its edge. The projections fit tightly into the openings, making a strong union. See *Dowel*.

Dowel In cabinetmaking; a small cylindrical piece of wood used to join or connect two pieces of wood by being sunk in the edges of each. See *Dovetail*.

Dower Chest In American cabinetwork; more properly a dowry chest or bridal chest. It is the colloquial term applied to a Pennsylvania Dutch chest which bears the initials purporting to be the initials of the bride for whom the chest was made or the name of the man owner. See *Pennsylvania Dutch Chest*.

Dragon In Chinese art; see *Lung*.

Dragon In arms; a type of gun resembling a long barrel pistol. The barrel of the dragon is about 16 inches long and of full musket bore with either a flintlock or a snaphance. It was usually hooked to the belt of a

HENRI II DRAW-TOP TABLE

dragoon, or a mounted infantryman, as they were called.

Drake Foot See *Pad Foot*.

Dram Cup In American silver; the name generally given in America to a wine taster, although the actual term *wine taster* occasionally occurs. Silver dram cups are mentioned in 17th century American inventories.

Dram Glass In English glass; a small English drinking glass first made during the 17th century. The dram glass was made in a variety of forms. One early type of dram glass was in the form of a small tumbler. The dram glass is also called a Nip; Joey; Ginette; Gin Glass.

Drap d'Or A French term applied to cloth of gold; a rich fabric used in the 15th and 16th centuries. It usually was done in a plain weave of all gold thread, often combined with appliqué velvet and gold or silk embroidery.

Drawn Stem In glass; the stem of a vessel, generally a drinking glass, made by drawing or pulling out a gathering of metal at the base of the bowl to form the stem.

Drawnwork A kind of decorative needlework done in textile fabrics, especially linen; it is made by drawing out some of the threads from the fabric and joining the cross threads to obtain a design or pattern; also by drawing all into a new form, making various ornamental designs. There are three branches of drawnwork; plain drawnwork, embroidered drawnwork, and drawnwork with color effects. It was known in medieval times as opus tiratum and punto tirato, and later as Hamburg point, broderie de Nancy, Dresden point and Tonder lace. See *Needlework*.

Draw-Top Table In cabinetwork; an ingeniously devised table introduced during the Renaissance. It was a large massive oblong table. The top was made in three pieces, that is two lower sliding leaves under a center top. It was so designed that the main top was held in place by two blocks of wood and was not permanently fixed. The two leaves were fitted on two tapered runners, so that when they were drawn out the runners supported them and held them level with the center table top. In this manner the table was elongated to double its length. It is generally accepted that this table was first made in Italy. See *Dining Table*.

Dredger   In English silver; another name for a caster. See *Caster*.

Dresden   In ceramics; the term *Dresden China* was commonly used in England from the 18th century for Meissen porcelain. The marks "Dresden" and "D" under a crown are found on modern forgeries of Meissen.

Dresden   In German ceramics; a faïence manufactory was founded in 1708 at Dresden, Saxony, by Johann Friedrich Böttger, a year before he discovered porcelain and the consequent establishment of the Meissen manufactory. The factory closed in 1784 after several changes in management. The only Dresden faïence of artistic importance was made from around 1710 to 1738. No mark was used for that period. From 1768 onwards the mark "DH" was used. Included among the early productions are vases, flower pots and figures; the latter being inspired by figures from the Italian Comedy and also from Chinese art. From the beginning of the royal period in 1779 the forms became classical. A favorite painted decoration was medallion portrait heads in black silhouette or in grey monochrome on a light colored ground. An interesting and peculiar painted pattern consisted of a group of miscellaneous objects such as letters, scissors and other similar items arranged together; it was called quodlibetz or what you please. Blue and white porcelain for daily use was also made. The numerous figures were chiefly copies from other factories.

Dresser   In English cabinetwork; the dresser is of early origin. It was known during medieval times, when the name was gener-

ally applied to an open framework of shelves used to display the owner's fine plate, such as silver cups and silver tankards. The distinction between a cupboard and dresser was never too clearly made in early English times. After the Restoration the term *dresser* was usually applied to a long, shallow, oblong piece of oak furniture fitted with a row of drawers which rested on turned legs. At this time it was generally designed without a superstructure of shelves, although it is probable that shelves were sometimes secured to it. The oak dresser was gradually superseded in the wealthy homes by the long walnut side table. The dresser continued to be made for country use and in the 18th century was usually designed with a recessed superstructure of shelves. See *Welsh Dresser*; *Buffet-Vaisselier*.

Dressing Mirror   See *Toilet Mirror*.

Dressing Table   In cabinetwork; a table especially designed to hold various accessories of the toilet. In English cabinetwork; around 1690, when the swinging toilet mirror on a box stand became fashionable, a veneered walnut side table was introduced. It had a rectangular top over a valanced apron which was fitted with a row of drawers. This type of side table, since it was useful as a dressing table, was also called a dressing table and was in general use until around the middle of the 18th century when tables particularly designed for dressing became plentiful. The arrangement of the drawers varied. It most frequently had one long drawer over a row of three drawers, the two lateral drawers often being deeper. In America this form of dressing table is called a lowboy. A variety of dressing table designed in the Chippendale style was in the form of a kneehole writing table. The top drawer was fitted with a hinged mirror and was divided into compartments for toilet articles. The dressing table with a fitted interior was designed in other distinctive types by Chippendale and his contemporaries. The dressing table with a hinged

LATE JACOBEAN DRESSER

box lid was in vogue in the second half of the 18th century. When it was closed it resembled a table; however, when the lid was open the interior contained a rising framed mirror and compartments for toilet articles. Hepplewhite illustrated a dressing table essentially designed as a chest of drawers, with the top drawer enclosing the necessary toilet fittings. Many other designs for dressing tables were made in the second half of the 18th century. In American cabinetwork; the dressing table of kneehole form and the lowboy were especially characteristic. The dressing table with a hinged box lid was also made in limited numbers. See *Beau Brummel*; *Poudreuse*; *Bureau Dressing Table*; *Commode Dressing Table*; *Toilet*.

DROP HANDLE

Dressoir   See *Buffet-Vaisselier*.

Drinking Horn   A form of drinking vessel generally made of the horn of an ox, buffalo or the tusk of an elephant, and occasionally made of metal and shaped in the form of a horn. Horns mounted in silver represent some of the earliest work of the English silversmiths. It seems that the majority of silver-mounted drinking horns were made from around the 14th century through the 16th century.

Drinking Table   In English cabinetwork; the name *English wine table* or *drinking table* was given to a specialized table introduced toward the end of the 18th century to be used for after-dinner drinking. It was designed in various forms. One characteristic type had a horseshoe-shaped top which averaged about 6 feet in length. A metal rod was attached across the open center portion and was fitted with coasters to hold wine bottles. A long narrow network bag was also stretched across the open portion and was used to hold biscuits. The two ends of the table faced the fireplace and were sometimes fitted with a rod to hold a curtain to deflect the heat of the fire.

Drop   In silver; the slightly molded junction

between the stem and the back of the bowl of a silver spoon. It was used for reinforcement and could be either a single or double drop. It was introduced in England during the early part of the reign of George II, 1727–1760.

Drop-Front   In cabinetwork; the upright front on a cabinet or writing cabinet that is hinged and is opened by dropping forward. Also called a fall-front and in French an abattant. See *Writing Cabinet*; *Secrétaire à Abattant*; *Vargueño*.

Drop Handle   In furniture mounts; a decorative brass handle in the form of a bulbous drop or pendant, suspended from a square-shaped eye that was fastened through the back plate to the drawer by means of a split metal tang. Simpler varieties of the pendant type included the acorn, pear and tear drop, which were fitted with a small circular plate. In English furniture the drop handle was the principal type of handle used during the Carolean and William and Mary styles. In American furniture the drop handle was in fashion from about 1690 to 1720. See *Bail Handle*.

Drop-Leaf   In cabinetwork; the end or side leaves of a table that are hinged and dropped downward when not in use as an extension of the table top. See *Pembroke Table*; *Dining Table*.

Dropped Seat   In cabinetwork; a wooden chair seat having the entire center portion and front dished out in a concave manner so that it was slightly lower than the sides and rear.

Droschel   A Flemish term in lace-making applied to handmade bobbin net. See *Bobbin Lace*; *Vrai Réseau*.

Drum Table   In English cabinetwork; the term *drum table* is given to a form of mahogany library table which became popular in England at the end of the 18th century. It was designed with a circular top inset with a tooled leather panel over six or eight frieze

BIBERON, PEWTER
Swiss 18th century

CAUDLE CUP, SILVER
English 1660

CANTIR, GLASS
Spanish 18th century

COACHING GLASS
English 18th century

FLUTE, GLASS
Dutch c. 1650

CAN, SILVER
American c. 1780

GOBLET, SILVER
London 1610

PASSGLAS
German 17th century

MILKMAID CUP, SILVER
English 17th century

PORRO, GLASS
Spanish 18th century

POSSET POT, POTTERY
English 18th century

ROEMER, GLASS
German 17th century

TAZZA, SILVER
London 1582

THISTLE GLASS
Scottish 18th century

TANKARD, SILVER
London 1706

THUMB
GLASS
*German
17th century*

MÜHLENBECHER, SILVER
Dutch 17th century

JACK, LEATHER
English 16th century

TRICHTERBECHER,
SIEGBURG STONEWARE
c. 1540

ALE GLASS
English 18th century

CHARKA, GOLD
Russian 17th century

SCHNELLE, SIEGBURG STONEWARE
c. 1560

QUAICH, SILVER
Glasgow 1670

KOVSH, GOLD
Russian 16th century

drawers. Half the number of drawers were often mock drawers. The top revolved on a column with four splayed legs which were finished with brass toe caps and wheel casters. The frieze instead of being fitted with drawers was also designed with partitions for books. Other variations in design also occurred. In English furniture literature this table is commonly called a library table and is so mentioned in Gillow's Cost Books in 1798.

Dublin Tapestry Works A tapestry manufactory was established in 1728 by Robert Baille at Dublin. There is no record of this manufactory after 1768. See *Tapestry*.

DuBois, René 1737–1799. A distinguished French ébéniste to Marie-Antoinette. He received his master in 1755. Some of his finest work was executed in lacquer embellished with motifs in the Chinese taste. Among the many notable pieces which he produced was an important bureau for the Empress of Russia and a famous commode in black lacquer decorated in the Chinese taste and exquisitely mounted in bronze doré. This latter piece was made by request for the marriage of Marie Antoinette.

Du Cerceau, Jacques Androuet French architect, designer and engraver. The style of Henri II was greatly influenced by du Cerceau. His designs for furniture were remarkable for their elegance and originality of treatment. After studying in Italy he returned to the French court around 1558 where he remained until his retirement in 1580. His publications of engraved styles of ornament became available during the last quarter of the 16th century. See *Henri II*.

Duchesse In French cabinetwork; the name given to a kind of chaise longue which was fashionable in France from about 1740 to 1780. It was characterized by a gondola-shaped or tub-shaped back. Occasionally the foot of the long seat was also designed with a very low gondola-shaped end. The duchesse was constructed either in one piece or in two

LOUIS XVI DUCHESSE

or three pieces, when it was called a duchesse brisée. See *Bergère*; *Duchesse Brisée*; *Chaise Longue*.

Duchesse Brisée In French cabinetwork; the French term *brisée*, meaning broken in pieces, was applied to a variety of duchesse or chaise longue generally designed in three parts. It was composed of two gondola-shaped bergères and a stool. The one bergère serving as a foot-end or bout de pied was designed with a lower back. The duchesse brisée was also made in two pieces of equal length, each piece having a gondola-shaped back and an elongated seat. In another form the two pieces were of unequal length, with the one piece having a long seat. The duchesse brisée was in vogue from around 1740 to 1780 and was either upholstered or caned, the latter being fitted with loose cushions. See *Duchesse*; *Bergère*.

Duchesse Lace A name given to a Brussels bobbin lace of fine quality having sprigs resembling Honiton lace and joined by brides. The work resembles the guipure de Flandre made at Bruges in the 17th and 18th centuries, which was much favored for cravats, more than it resembles the early Brussels laces.

Duck Foot In American cabinetwork; a colloquial term applied loosely to a Dutch foot. Occasionally its meaning is restricted to a web foot. See *Pad Foot*; *Web Foot*.

Duelling Pistols A pair of pistols used for duelling; sometimes finely ornamented and engraved. The duelling pistol was a single barrelled pistol and it was especially accurate and reliable at twenty paces.

Dumb-Waiter In English cabinetwork; it is generally believed that the dumb-waiter was chiefly designed to take the place to some extent of that of a butler in the dining room. It is usually agreed that this type of dumb-waiter was an English innovation and that it was introduced late in the first half of the 18th century. The principal variety consisted of three circular trays increasing in size from top to bottom. The trays revolved on a shaft which rested on a tripod base. It served a number of purposes in the dining room. One of its main uses was to hold dessert plates, knives and forks as well as the dessert. It was also useful for after-dinner drinking. As a rule the mahogany dumb-waiter made in America was designed in the Chippendale style. See *Rafraîchissoir*; *Servante*.

Dunlap A family of American cabinetmakers working at Salisbury and Chester in New Hampshire during the 18th and early part of the 19th centuries. They were John I, John II and Samuel I, whose son Samuel II, 1751–1830, is the best known.

Durlach In German ceramics; a faïence manufactory was started at Durlach, Baden, in 1722 by Johann Heinrich Wachenfeld. A privilege was granted in 1723 by the Margrave of Baden. It closed in 1840 after having changed ownership several times. Its best and only distinctive work was from around 1775 to 1818. This group was composed of small pear-shaped jugs and coffee pots carefully painted with figure subjects taken from everyday life such as farm workers and craftsmen. The pieces were obviously meant for gifts and were almost always dated. They generally had rhymed inscriptions with the name of the recipient in black letters and were commonly decorated with borders of vine leaves. The manufactory enjoyed a large business but its other wares had little artistic merit. Toward the end of the 18th century they began to make a cream-colored earthenware which after 1818 was marked "Durlach", impressed. The only 18th century marks ever found were those of the painters.

Dutch and Flemish Glass Or Netherlands Glass. Although it is reasonable to assume that glass was made in the Netherlands prior to the 16th century, at the present time the earliest information concerning the industry

of glassmaking is recorded in 1541 at Antwerp where a glasshouse was being operated by a Venetian. It seems that from that time onwards Italian glassmakers were found in different parts of the Netherlands. Undoubtedly the fame of Netherlands glass depends upon the fine quality of engraving with a wheel and more importantly of engraving with a diamond point. In the latter medium the Dutch were unrivalled. Glass objects made in the Netherlands during the 17th and 18th centuries were more praiseworthy for their fine engraved decoration than for any originality in forms or in materials. At first glassmaking was influenced by Venetian work and later by German and English forms and technique. Diamond engraving was fashionable until around 1690 when it was largely supplanted by engraving with the wheel in the German manner. In the 18th century a new method of stippling with a diamond point was developed resulting in a delightful miniature style. Especially praiseworthy was an original calligraphic style of linear diamond engraving created around the second quarter of the 17th century by Anna Roemers Visscher, 1583–1651, depicting exquisite realistically treated flowers, fruit and insects, in conjunction with graceful and fluent calligraphy and inscriptions in Roman capital and Greek letters. Dutch wheel engraving in the German manner is especially associated with their productions from around the middle and latter 18th century. From around 1720 the Dutch achieved some work of remarkable beauty in stippled engraving, using it almost alone as a medium for pictorial work. The diamond stippled engraved portraits and still lifes often based on contemporary prints, executed by the glass engravers Franz Greenwood, 1680–1761, and David Wolff, were particularly noteworthy. See *Glass*; *Engraved Glass*.

Dutch Chair Or Dutch Model Chair. In cabinetwork; a distinctive type of splat-back walnut chair was introduced in England from Holland around or shortly after

DUTCH ROEMER

1700. It had curved uprights and a pierced and carved wide shaped splat extending to the seat rail. The legs, which were narrow, were cabriole in form and terminated in scroll or hoof-shaped feet. They were joined with a stretcher. The manner in which the uprights continued into the crest rail approximated a hoop-shape. The principles of design incorporated in this chair and another related type of Dutch origin were introduced in English chair design and were further developed in the characteristic Queen Anne walnut splat-back chair. In the reign of Queen Anne the foreign influence became less pronounced. See *Queen Anne Splat-Back Chair.*

Dutch Colonial A term applied to a style of building characterized by having a gambrel roof, or a double slope of two parts inclined unequally on each side, the upper part a flat slope, and the lower section a steep slope. The term is also applied to the style of some furniture used by the Dutch who settled principally in and around New York and along the Hudson Valley. It is usually wooden furniture of a heavy form, and is frequently confused with the style of the Pennsylvania Germans.

Dutch Foot See *Pad Foot.*

Dutch Furniture The Dutch cabinetmaker continued throughout the 16th century to stamp his cabinetwork with more and more Dutch peculiarities until it finally developed a distinctive Dutch character. This divergence in Dutch and Flemish furniture with the latter following the French styles and the former developing into a national Dutch style dates from around 1640. It must be remembered that the Dutch style was not entirely divorced from the French style, for later in the century, due to the Revocation of the Edict of Nantes in 1685, many highly skilled French craftsmen sought refuge in Holland, the foremost among whom was Daniel Marot. Marot's designs were based on the style of Louis XIV and his later work in Holland showed a blending of Dutch

DUTCH COLONIAL KAS
WITH PAINTED DECORATION

and French designs. Due to the close understanding existing between England and Holland, English furniture was more influenced by the Dutch than by any other European country during the 16th and 17th centuries. English walnut and marquetry furniture from the time of the Restoration in 1660 until about 1700 displayed the unmistakable imprint of Dutch influence. And although Dutch influence persisted in England as long as walnut remained the fashionable wood for cabinetwork the influence was less marked after 1700. The finest Dutch cabinetwork was made from around 1660 to 1690, after which date Dutch furniture gradually declined in quality. The English cabinetwork during that period was generally more restrained in character than the Dutch, which was often extremely ornate. Especially typical was the Dutch floral marquetry which they used profusely, almost covering the entire surface of an article of furniture. Dutch carving for that period was also more elaborate and revealed more intricate detail than the English. It was often more lavish and extravagant than the Flemish; however, they used it much less frequently than the Flemish. Furniture of lacquered woodwork in the oriental taste was also fashionable. A peculiar heaviness and ornateness characterized much of their fine furniture. The early 18th century Dutch furniture was essentially similar to the furniture designed in England during the Queen Anne and Early Georgian period. Like the Flemish, the remaining 18th century Dutch furniture designs were influenced by the great 18th century French furniture designers working in the Rococo and Neo-Classic styles. Dutch furniture in the Rococo taste was generally marred by exaggerated curving lines and excessive ornament. The Dutch, who were skillful marqueteurs, continued to use marquetry, generally of a floral design, throughout the 18th century. The Dutch East India Company formed in Holland early in the 17th century, with its vast trading activities, afforded a great impetus in developing Chinese influence in the European decorative arts. See *Marot, Daniel*; *Dutch Chair*; *Queen Anne Splat-Back Chair*; *Jacobean, Late*; *William and Mary*; *Chinoiserie*; *Renaissance, Netherlands.*

Dwight, John c. 1637–1703. English potter. He took out patents in 1671 and 1684 for the manufacture of stoneware at Fulham, Middlesex. See *Fulham.*

DUTCH SIDE TABLE

E

Eagle In ornament; the eagle motif has been employed as an emblem of sovereignty from the days of the Greeks and Romans. It was employed especially as a carved motif in different styles of furniture. The American eagle was a favorite patriotic design in American cabinetwork, especially after the adoption of the Constitution in 1788, when it became the national emblem. It was both carved and inlaid. The carved and gilded eagle attached as a finial to wall mirrors and clocks was much in evidence. Many brass eagles were imported for banjo clocks. When the eagle was used in inlay work it was generally in an oval medallion and often had streamers in its beak with marks representing stars. See *Queen Anne and Early Georgian*; *Eagle Console Table*; *Convex Wall Mirror*; *Early Georgian Architectural Wall Mirror*; *Constitution Mirror*; *Empire*.

EARLY GEORGIAN
ARCHITECTURAL
WALL MIRROR

Eagle Console Table In English cabinetwork; an elaborately carved and gilded console table of the Early Georgian style. It had an oblong marble top over a richly carved frieze which was supported by a finely executed spread eagle standing on a rock. It rested on a molded oblong or shaped ebonized plinth. Eagle console tables were often designed in pairs and were an important feature in the symmetrical architectural treatment of a drawing room.

Eaglewood See *Agalloch Wood*.

Early Georgian Architectural Wall Mirror In English furniture; the name given to a characteristic variety of mirror introduced during the Early Georgian style. It was so named because of the architectural treatment of its design. The frame was made of either walnut or mahogany and was parcel gilded. The upright mahogany frame, with its carved and gilded moldings, was surmounted by a pediment. The pediment was either broken or swan neck and centered a low plinth which was surmounted by a

gilded eagle, a shell or some other decorative carving. Occasionally the mirror was surmounted by a triangular pediment. The base of the frame was frequently valanced. Sometimes the base was fitted with two brass candle arms; this type with candle arms is called a girandole mirror. In America this architectural wall mirror was generally called a Chippendale style mirror. See *Queen Anne and Early Georgian*; *Elliott, John*; *Constitution Mirror*; *Girandole*.

Early Georgian Style See *Queen Anne and Early Georgian*; *Kent, William*.

Earthenware In ceramics; the term is used in England for pottery which has a body that is not vitrified. Majolica, faïence, delftware and slipware are all varieties of earthenware. The term is synonymous with pottery. See *Pottery*.

East, Edward Celebrated English watchmaker to Charles I. He was appointed to the office of "Chief Clockmaker and Keeper of the Privy Clocks" in 1662. Clocks capable of telling time by night were chiefly made by East. In a day and night table or bracket clock the top was removable in order to insert a lamp. There was a semi-circular opening above the dial which revealed perforated Roman numerals through which the light was reflected. A small slit above the opening served as a pointer.

Eastern Loom In Oriental rug weaving; the device on which an Oriental rug is woven. It consists of four poles held together by ropes according to the size of the rug to be woven. The warp threads are strung on these poles and kept at the proper tension by weights, which are attached to one of the cross poles. This frame either stands upright or is level with the ground. Because of its primitive construction it can easily be taken apart and put together; that is why so much of the weaving is done by wandering groups of weavers. See *Oriental Rug*.

East India Porcelain See *Chinese Lowestoft*.

Easy Chair In English cabinetwork; the large well-padded and upholstered wing chair which was introduced in England from the Continent around 1680, was called an "easie chair" in contemporary English inventories. In America the wing chair was popular from about 1700 to 1810 and was generally known as an easy chair during the period in which it was made. See *Confessional*; *Wing Chair*.

Ebénier des Alpes See *Cytise Wood*.

Ebéniste The name given to a French cabinetmaker; derived from menuisier en ébène or joiner in ebony as he was originally called at the beginning of the 17th century, at which time Henri IV sent cabinetmakers to Holland to study the work being done in ebony. The 18th century was the age of the great French ébénistes. In 1743 cabinetmaking was divided into two groups; namely, the menuisiers d'assemblage or makers of solid wooden furniture, and the menuisiers de placage et de marqueterie or veneerers and inlayers. This latter group a few years later adopted the name of ébéniste even though working in ebony had been discarded for the time being. The term *maître ébéniste* or *master cabinetmaker* was given to one who had been admitted into the Paris Communauté des Maîtres Menuisiers et Ebénistes or the Corporation of Master Joiners and Cabinetmakers. Prior to 1751 the master cabinetmaker was not required to sign his furniture. However in that same year a regulation was passed in Paris which decreed that the master cabinetmaker had to sign all his furniture and had to deposit an impression of his stamp on a sheet of lead at the town hall. As a rule he stamped his furniture on the underframing of chairs and tables and under the marble tops. There were over one thousand ébénistes in the 18th century in Paris who signed their work, all of whom produced cabinetwork of the finest workmanship.

Ebénisterie In French cabinetwork; the French term meaning cabinetmaking or cabinetwork given to the work of the ébéniste and the finished pieces which have been made by hand.

Ebonize The practice of staining an inferior wood to look like ebony was employed in cabinetwork from the time of the Renaissance. In English and American cabinetwork pear wood was often stained black to imitate ebony. Applied wood ornament such as split spindles, lozenge- and oval-shaped bosses were sometimes used as decoration on oak chests during the Early Jacobean era and provided an interesting contrast. Ebonized woods were more freely used during the English Regency and American Empire styles. They were also a feature of Victorian cabinetwork. See *Convex Wall Mirror*.

QUEEN ANNE WING CHAIR

Ebony A heavy, hard and durable wood, of various species, *ebenaceae*, from tropical Africa and Asia. The Madagascar ebony was widely used by the French ébénistes for cabinetwork; its color is black. They also used ébène de Portugal from the East Indies, which is black and white spotted; the ébène rouge, or ébène grenadille from Madagascar, which is reddish brown striped with black; the ébène verte from Madagascar, which is brown olive striped with green; the ébène blanche from the Moluccas, which is white.

Echinus A convex or rounded classic molding which was a part of the Doric column. The term is also given to the ovolo molding carved with the egg and tongue. See *Egg and Tongue*; *Ovolo*.

Eckernförde A faïence manufactory was founded at Eckernförde, Schleswig, Germany, in 1765 and was a continuation of one founded at Criseby in 1759 by Johann Nicolaus Otte. The only work of artistic importance was some attractive Rococo faïence made from around 1761 to about 1768. Included among the productions were tureens in the form of vegetables and other types of vessels decorated with modelled and applied flowers and leaves.

It is practically impossible to distinguish the wares made at Eckernförde from those made at Criseby. The marks used were the Scandinavian compound type and included the the names or initials of the owner, the various painters and the town.

Ecran à Coulisse In French cabinetwork; the French term *coulisse*, meaning a groove, is given to a variety of fire screen having a vertical upright frame enclosing a panel sliding in grooves on the inner sides of the uprights which rest on arched supports. It was introduced in the Louis XIV style and is similar in principle to the English cheval fire screen. The panel could be easily pulled up and down and in that manner the direct heat from the fireplace could be regulated. Frequently the fire screen had a shelf near the floor joining the two arched supports, serving as a foot rest. Occasionally the fire screen was designed with a shelf which could be let down by means of metal quadrants. This shelf was used to hold a cup of coffee or tea, an inkstand or a needlework case. The shelf could also be slanted to serve as a reading desk. This type of fire screen was sometimes provided with two adjustable metal candle arms. The sliding panel was made of different materials, such as tapestry, painted paper or canvas and lacquered wood. This form of fire screen was also designed with a fixed panel enclosed in an elaborately carved upright frame, when it is referred to as an écran. Both the écran and the écran à coulisse were in vogue in the 18th century. See *Cheval Fire Screen*; *Fire Screen*.

Ecran à Eclisse In French furniture; the French word *éclisse*, meaning split wood, was given to a tripod form of pole screen having a screen-stick or pole mounted on a tripod base and provided with a small adjustable panel. This pole screen of tripod form was of early origin; however, it seems that it never became a fashionable French model. See *Pole Screen*.

Ecran à Eventail In French furniture; a fan-shaped fire screen of bronze doré. The écran à éventail had a vertical fan-shaped case

LOUIS XV
ÉCRAN À ÉVENTAIL

on a decorative base that enclose nine pierced and pivoted foils or leaf-shaped parts. When the very thin pierced metal foils were opened it resembled an open fan. It was introduced during the Louis XV style. See *Fire Screen*.

Ecuelle In French silver; a French term meaning porringer. It was a shallow, covered bowl generally having a dome-shaped cover surmounted by a finial and two flat pierced handles that were horizontal to the rim. Sometimes the early écuelle had a flat cover surmounted by a handle. It was introduced in the 17th century. See *Porringer*.

Edo In Japanese historical periods; the Edo or Tokugawa period in Japan, 1615–1867. See *Japanese Periods*.

Egg and Dart A classic convex molding having a running design or a continuous pattern of an egg-shaped ornament alternating with a dart. See *Ovolo*; *Egg and Tongue*.

Egg and Spinach Glaze In Chinese ceramics; see *Hu P'i*; *Three-Color Ware*.

Egg and Tongue A classic convex molding having a continuous pattern of an egg-shaped motif alternating with a tongue. Classic running designs were a legacy of ancient architecture and they were much used in furniture design, especially in those styles which borrowed from antique ornament. See *Echinus*; *Ovolo*.

Egg Cup Frame In English silver; a wire pattern frame, or stand, usually of silver or Sheffield, used to hold two or more silver egg cups. In addition to the rack for egg cups it was sometimes fitted with a rack for toast, spoons and salt. It was introduced around 1780.

Eggshell In Chinese ceramics; eggshell porcelain is called T'o T'ai or bodyless by the Chinese because of its extreme thinness. It was first made during the Ming dynasty, and as early as the reign of Yung Lo, 1403–1424, it was highly regarded. In some of the very rare examples the body material seems almost non-existent; it seems to consist of glaze only. In the fine white specimens the delicate decoration is traced on the body in a white slip and is scarcely visible except when held to the light. Other pieces have colored designs and some have a colored ground.

Eglomisé A French term applied to a decorative method for ornamenting glass by drawing and painting on the underside and backing the ornamentation with metal foil, generally gold or silver leaf. The name is derived from Jean Baptiste Glomi, d. c. 1786, French designer, framer and collector who is generally given credit for inventing a method of framing prints with black and gold narrow bands painted from the back of the glass. However it is not known whether he ever employed a backing of gold or silver foil. This process of a metal foil backing was practiced at an early time in the Near East and was employed by the Italians during the Renaissance. Toward the end of the 17th century a vogue developed for wall mirrors with glass borders which were sometimes decorated in gold and silver foil against a ground of black, red and occasionally green. This was a characteristic and favorite French method. The designs were especially intricate such as arabesques and elaborate foliated scrolls.

Egouttoir In French Provincial furniture; a plate rack on which are piled freshly washed dishes placed there to drain. By extension the name *égouttoir* is given to an article of furniture that was designed with open rack shelves that could be used for that purpose. See *Etimier*.

Egyptian Detail In ornament; toward the end of the 18th century for a short space of time an attempt was made to introduce certain Egyptian ornamental features and symbolism in furniture and decoration. This fashion for Egyptian detail was established in France after Napoleon's Egyptian campaign in 1798, and it soon spread to England. See *Denon, Baron*; *Hope, Thomas*; *Smith, George*; *Regency*.

Eigelstein In German ceramics; see *Cologne*.

Eight Happy Omens or Pa Chi Hsiang See *Chinese Symbols and Emblems*.

Eight Precious Objects or Pa Pao See *Chinese Symbols and Emblems*.

Eight Taoist Immortals or Pa Hsien In Chinese art; Chung-li Ch'üan is represented as a fat man with a peach in one hand and a fan in the other with which he awakens the souls of the dead. Lü Tung-pin is depicted with a sword. He protects the world against evil. He is the patron of the barbers. Ts'ao Kuo-ch'iu carries a pair of castanets in his hand and is the patron of mummers and actors. Han Hsiang Tzǔ is represented as a young man playing a flute. He is the patron of musicians. Ho Hsien Ku is the patroness of housewives and is shown carrying a lotus. Chang Kuo Lao is the patron of artists and calligraphers. He is the god of literature and his attribute is a musical instrument composed of a drum and a pair of rods. Lan Ts'ai-ho is the patron of gardeners and florists and is seen carrying a hoe and a basket of flowers. Li T'ieh-kuai is portrayed as a lame beggar and has a pilgrim's gourd from which pour forth clouds and fanciful dreams. He is the patron of astrologers and musicians. These Eight Immortals are often seen in attendance to Shou Lao or are seen on the backs of mythical creatures crossing the sea to the Island of Everlasting Happiness. The eight attributes are among the favorite symbols employed in Chinese art. See *Chinese Gods*; *Chinese Symbols and Emblems*.

Eight Trigrams Or Pa Kua. In Chinese symbols; the pa kua or eight trigrams are represented by eight sets of straight lines. Each set consists of three parallel superimposed broken and unbroken straight lines. These eight trigrams are arranged symmetrically around a circular sign which is the symbol of Creation. This well-known disk-shaped symbol of Creation consists of two intertwining forms resembling commas which are the primary powers called yin

CHAIR
WITH SPHINX SUPPORTS

and yang. The eight trigrams are said to have been evolved from markings on the shell of a tortoise by the mythological Emperor Fu Hsi, 2852 B.C. It is also said that the eight trigrams were created from the two primary powers, the unbroken line (———) called yang or symbol of the male source, and the broken line (— —) called yin or female source. Each one of the eight cabalistic signs is composed of a different combination of the broken and unbroken lines. Wên Wang, 1231–1135 B.C., father of Wu Wang the founder of the Chou dynasty, applied his vast knowledge to an exhaustive study of the trigrams and attached to each of them certain interpretations which constitute the most sacred and abstruse work of the Chinese classics known as the Canon of Changes. The Canon of Changes serves as the fundamental work for the knowledge of the principles that control or cause the power of foreseeing and foretelling future events by means of lines or figures, philosophical mysteries and the secrets of creation.

EIGHT TRIGRAMS OR PA KUA

Eiraku Ware In Japanese ceramics; the name given to a variety of porcelain made in Kyōto. It derived its name from a ceramist called Eiraku whose real name was Zengoro Hozen, 1795–1854. He was skilled in imitating late Ming and early Ch'ing three-color ware, Ming gilded porcelain and blue and white Chinese wares. He also cleverly copied Ninsei's enamelled pottery. Of especial interest is a skillfully blended three-color ware of green, yellow and purple glazes, having ridges to outline the designs and to separate one glaze from another. His son, Wazen, was adept in making gilded porcelain having a rich coral red ground with finely executed decoration in gold. See *Kyōto Ware*; *Kairaku-en Ware*.

Elbow Chair In English cabinetwork; same as armchair.

Elder Wood See *Sureau Wood*.

Elector Glass Or Kurfürstenhumpen. In German glass; a cylindrical beaker of imposing size depicting in enamelled decoration the Emperor of the Holy Roman Empire and the Seven Electors. It seems that the majority of these drinking glasses were made from around the late 16th or beginning of the 17th centuries. This subject and the subject found on the adlerglas were very popular subjects for the enamelled decoration so frequently applied to large cylindrical German drinking vessels. See *Humpen*; *German Glass*; *Adlerglas*.

Elers In English ceramics; John Philip and David Elers who were potters and originally silversmiths came to England from Holland before 1686. According to evidence they made "brown mugs" and "red teapots" at Fulham for about three years prior to 1693. It seems that they moved to Staffordshire in 1693. By local tradition the Elers factory was at Bradwell Wood near Newcastle-under-Lyme. At the present time there is no authenticated specimen of their work. It is believed that they made a fine hard unglazed red stoneware in imitation of Chinese buccaro ware. Pieces of unglazed red stoneware attributed to them include small mugs, teapots, tea canisters, tea cups and other similar objects. They were delicately and thinly made and were often decorated with applied stamped reliefs. A plum blossom in the Chinese style was a favorite motif for the stamped reliefs. Numerous other pieces of unglazed Staffordshire red ware have been erroneously attributed to them.

Elfe, Thomas c. 1719–d. 1775. American cabinetmaker of Charleston, South Carolina, working circa 1747–1775.

Elizabethan The term applied to the English style of ornament and furniture design during the reign of Queen Elizabeth I, 1558–1603. Italian Renaissance influence which became evident in ornament from around 1530 onwards was supplanted during the reign of Queen Elizabeth by that of the Netherlands. This influence was largely due to the importation of Flemish pattern books, such as those by De Vries. German and French influences were also contributing factors. Irrespective of all these different influences the Elizabethan style possessed a genuine national character. The English cabinetmaker developed a style of furniture along native English lines characterized by simplicity of construction and by strong and serviceable qualities. The furniture was massive and rectilinear in form and was principally made of oak. Heavy bulbous supports on tables, bedsteads and court cupboards were a characteristic feature and were richly carved or gadrooned. The Elizabethan furniture was decorated with either carving or inlay, the former being by far the favorite method. Elizabethan carving was always vigorous and robust and often had a striking quality of barbaric richness. In ornament the Renaissance alphabet of classic motifs as principally interpreted in Flemish pattern books was substituted for the Gothic. Survivals of Gothic detail were still evident. Included among the favorite Elizabethan Renaissance motifs were intricate strapwork, acanthus leafage, vase forms, candelabra, swags, figure subjects, masks, grotesques, caryatids, arabesques and scrolls. Split baluster turnings were occasionally applied to the surface as a decorative detail late in the Elizabethan style. The furniture like the interior decoration was characterized by its wealth of ornament which was lacking in classic refinement and was inferior to the finished composition found in the contemporary Italian and French styles of ornament. The English had not been able up to this time to assimilate the principles of the Renaissance. This better understanding of the Classic Orders and forms was to be provided by Inigo Jones. See *Renaissance, English*; *Jacobean*; *Tudor*.

Elliott, John 1713–1791. A well-known American maker of mirrors. He came to Philadelphia from England in 1753. After his retirement from business in 1776, the business was carried on by his son, John Elliott, Jr., who was joined in the business by his two sons, in 1804. The business continued until 1809. Apparently from the labels which were often placed on the mirrors he first had a store on Chestnut Street and later on Walnut Street. The Elliott family made fretwork mirrors from around 1753 to 1809. They also made the Early Georgian architectural wall mirror which was called a Chippendale style mirror in America, and a few carved and gilded mirrors in the Chippendale style. Their advertisements stated that they also handled imported mirrors and sconces from London. Apparently the senior John Elliott had some experience in cabinetmaking, in all probability in England, for one of his early advertisements stated that he was a cabinetmaker.

Elmwood   See *Orme Wood*.

Embossing   The term applied to the art of making raised designs on the surface of metal, leather, fabrics, paper and other similar materials. In a strict sense the term can be given only to raised designs made by engraved plates or discs of a press which forcibly press the design into the surface of the material. Embossing is practiced extensively in the art of leather work and especially in bookbinding. The embossing of wallpapers, etc., is done by impressions from engraved cylinder rollers. See *Repoussé*.

Embroidered Rugs   Rugs upon which have been worked ornamental designs with the needle. Rugs of the 16th century were sometimes richly embroidered in gold, silver and silk, such as some of the Polonaise rugs. Spanish carpets of the 17th and 18th centuries were occasionally done in needlework in either the tent stitch or in the cross-stitch.

Embroidery   The art of working ornamental designs with a needle upon a woven fabric is of early origin and was practiced by the Egyptians. The countries of the Euphrates were celebrated in classical times for their magnificent embroidered fabrics. Phrygia was also famous for its needlework, and Asiatic and Babylonian embroideries were shipped to Greece and Italy from Phrygian ports. Of great historical value is the 11th

ELIZABETHAN
COURT CUPBOARD

century Bayeux tapestry or embroidery. From around the 10th century onwards in Europe the art of pictorial embroideries became widespread and was developed with rare skill. It is from the openwork embroidery, which is generally called cutwork and which was so extensively used in the 16th century, that the origin of lace is derived. Embroidery through the centuries has always been a fashionable as well as profitable pastime for women of all classes of society. The materials required for embroidery are needles, threads, scissors and a small frame to secure the material. There are many different stitches used in embroidery. Some of the more common forms of canvas stitch are cross-stitch, tent stitch, Gobelin stitch, Irish stitch and plaited stitch. Other principal stitches include crewel, couching, chain or tambour, herringbone, buttonhole, feather, rope, satin, darning, running, basket and blanket stitches.

Empire The term is applied to the style of ornament and furniture design in France from 1804 to 1825–1830. It attained its highest development during the time of Napoleon, 1804 to 1814–1815. This later phase of the Classic Revival fostered the cult of antiquity. It was essentially an archaeological revival in which antique Greek and Roman as well as Etruscan and Egyptian forms were exactly copied. The Empire style was largely created by two celebrated French architects, Fontaine and Percier. In 1785 Fontaine went to Rome to pursue his studies and he was accompanied by Percier. Upon their return they were engaged by Napoleon to remodel and redecorate the palace, Malmaison. Their designs established the official Empire style in Paris. Both Fontaine and Percier were fervent disciples of antiquity and their strong attachment to antique culture dominated the style. The Empire style had an air of austere and imposing grandeur that was admirably suited to Napoleon and Imperial France. The style was cold, exact and formal and was characterized by its elegant severity. The furniture, which was essentially massive and heavy, was chiefly rectangular in construction except for some pieces designed from ancient Roman curule models. It was generally made of solid or veneered mahogany. Symmetry was a pronounced principle of the style. Flat uniform surfaces of veneered mahogany with flat bronze doré appliqués remarkable for their jewel-like quality were typical of the style. Occasionally the surface was decorated with metal inlays of either bronze or silver. Marquetry and lacquering were completely discarded. Carving was sparingly employed and its use was generally restricted to chairs and settees. Exotic subjects such as swans, winged lions and winged sphinxes used as supports were a special feature of design. The classic ornament was principally borrowed from antique Greek and Roman art. In accordance with their dislike for anything associated with the Bourbon monarchs they discarded many of the earlier fashionable motifs and details. Included among the favorite Empire motifs were stiff and formal acanthus foliage, tightly woven wreaths, Greek palm leaves, winged classical figures in flowing gowns, Olympian gods and goddesses, emblems of victory, eagles, swans, lions, chimeras, caryatids and terms, Egyptian lotus capitals, sphinxes, antique musical instruments and vessels such as lyres and kraters, winged trumpets, flaming torches, thunderbolts, stars and many others. The Empire style was adopted to a greater or less extent throughout Continental Europe and next to France it was most successfully interpreted in Italy. After 1815 evidence of a gradual decline was increasingly apparent as the forms for furniture became more cumbrous and the composition of the ornament became more coarse. The end of the Napoleonic wars in 1815 marked the beginning of a new industrial era with the introduction of the factory method, resulting in a decided break with the old traditions of craftsmanship not only in cabinetwork but also in the other decorative arts. See *Classic Revival*; *Regency*; *Directoire*; *David, Jacques Louis*; *Denon, Baron*; *Fontaine, Pierre Fran-*

EMPIRE DECORATIVE DESIGN

çois *Léonard*; *American Empire*; *Charles X*; *Restoration*.

Enamel In art; the name given to the hard vitreous compound applied and fused on the surface of metallic articles at a low temperature. The name is also given to the metal article which is ornamented with enamel. The compound is a form of glass consisting of silica, minium and potash which is melted and mixed with metallic oxides to produce various colors. The art of enamelling had its origin in antiquity. The art of champlevé and cloisonné enamel work was carried on at Byzantium for centuries. During the 13th and 14th centuries it flourished at Cologne and Limoges. A process of enamelling called basse-taille was developed in Italy at the beginning of the 14th century. The method called plique-à-jour was also developed in the 14th century. Toward the end of the 15th century it was discovered that enamelling could be done without cloisons and that it was possible to superimpose another layer of enamel on the first layer of enamel. Shortly after these discoveries grisaille painted enamel was developed. The following are the different methods of enamelling. In champlevé enamel work depressions are cut in the metal plate with raised metal lines remaining between the depressions which form the outline of the design. The enamel is laid in these depressions and then fused. Afterward it is smoothed and polished. In cloisonné enamel the cloisons, which are delicate ribbon-like pieces of metal, are laid and fixed in the metal surface in the desired designs. The rest of the process is similar to champlevé. The plique-à-jour process is the same as cloisonné except that the cloisons are not attached to the base. A flat piece of metal is used as the base on which are placed the cloisons. After the transparent enamel is fused the base is removed and the finished work resembles that of transparent stained glass. In the basse-taille process the gold or silver metal is engraved with a design and carved into a base relief lower than the surface. When the enamel is fused it is level with the portion that is not carved and permits the design to show through the transparent enamel. In painted enamel the metal base is generally copper and the enamel is laid over the entire surface on both sides and then fused. The ground is generally dark and the subjects are laid on usually in a white enamel. The white having some translucency gives it light and shade. Subsequently grisaille painted enamel was developed. In grisaille the white is mixed with a medium of oil, turpentine or water and is painted on a dark ground. In the beginning grisaille was not practiced alone, and the designs were usually painted over in colored enamel. Colored painted enamels are first done in grisaille, then colored with transparent enamels and fused. The colored enamels are sometimes applied over a metal foil before fusing or over lines painted in gold to give additional brilliance. See *Cloisonné Enamel*; *Miniature*; *Grisaille*; *Battersea*.

LIMOGES ENAMEL

Enamel In ceramics; an enamel is a compound of glass tinted with mineral oxides to give various colors, such as copper for various shades of green, iron for yellow and manganese for a purplish brown. Vitreous enamels can stand only a relatively small amount of heat. Consequently they have to be applied on an already fired glaze or on an unglazed already fired body and fused or melted to it in another firing at a low temperature or petit feu in a muffle kiln. In order to obtain this low melting point a large amount of lead or other flux is added to make the enamels more fusible. Painting in enamels was found as early as the 13th century on the ceramic wares of China; however, the earliest pieces were simply done in red or green enamels. The so-called Rhages earthenware made by the Persians employed enamel colors during the 13th century or earlier. Although enamel decoration was first found on the European stoneware at Kreussen, Germany, around 1622, it was not until around 1660 that important specimens were made, when a full palette of enamel colors was used in decorating faïence in Germany. Hard paste porcelain with painted enamel decoration was first made at Meissen around 1710–1715. Enamel colors, which are available in a wide range, are also called overglaze colors, petit feu or muffle colors. See *Petit Feu*.

Enamel In glass; it is generally believed that the technique of applying solid or translucent enamels to the surface of glass was first practiced successfully by the Saracens in the 13th century, although earlier attempts had been made by the Romans and the Byzantine Greeks. The latter had chiefly employed washes of opaque paints. The Saracens perfected enamelling on glass and their pieces of enamelled glass produced during the 13th and the 14th centuries have never been surpassed. Enamelling was extensively done by the Venetians by around the middle of the 15th century. It was done in Spain toward the end of the 15th century. The technique of making fine enamelled glass as practiced by the Venetians was copied by the Germans around the middle of the 16th century. See *Glass*; *Venetian Glass*; *German Glass*; *Islamic Glass*.

Encaustic Painting The term *encaustic*, which is derived from the Greek word meaning to burn in, is applied to the ancient methods of painting in heated wax, as practiced by the Greeks, Egyptians and Romans. By extension, although not entirely correct, the term is applied to all methods of painting in wax.

Encoignure In French cabinetwork; a low corner cupboard which was often designed in pairs. It became fashionable after the middle of the 18th century as an article of drawing room furniture. The encoignure was generally richly decorated with either marquetry or lacquer work combined with bronze mounts. It usually had a marble top. The façade of the encoignure was either serpentine-shaped or bowed; it was designed with either one or two cupboard doors. It rested on a base and short legs. Variations

LOUIS XV ENCOIGNURE

in design occurred. It was also called an armoire d'encoignure. See *Cupboard*.

Encoignure à Deux Corps In French Provincial cabinetwork; a form of tall cupboard designed to stand in the corner of a room, made in two sections. Each section was fitted with either one or two doors. As a rule the upper section was slightly recessed. The majority of provincial corner cupboards were made in the Louis XV style, and were simply decorated with shaped molded panels. They were mounted on a valanced base curving into short cabriole legs. Occasionally when it was designed with a third recessed section it was called an encoignure à trois corps. See *Cupboard*.

Endive In ornament; the endive leaf treated as a decorative motif. It was especially used in Gothic ornament and later in the Louis XV style of ornament. Both of these styles showed a preference for leaf ornament selected from the native flora, such as endive, parsley and cress leaves.

Endive Pattern In English cabinetwork; see *Seaweed*.

Enfilade A French term meaning a suite of chambers. In French Provincial cabinetwork; the term is applied to a long, low buffet designed with four or more cupboard doors. It is essentially similar to the buffet bas.

Enghalskrug In German ceramics; a popular type of faïence jug with a long neck having a thick lip rim. It generally had a globular shaped body, which rested on a spreading circular foot, and a plaited rope handle. It was a popular 17th century form at Hanau and at the neighboring town of Frankfurt-on-Main. Sometimes it was mounted in pewter.

Enghien Tapestries Tapestries were woven at the town of Enghien, Belgium, a comparatively important weaving center during the 16th century. These tapestries were usually characterized by large leaf verdure designs. See *Tapestry*.

Engine Turned Decoration In ceramics; a design or pattern in relief which is made by cutting the surface of a dried but unfired article of pottery. Its most common form is that of irregular basket work or rose-engine turned. It was principally used as a decoration on Staffordshire unglazed red stoneware, especially that made by Wedgwood.

English Decorated Style See *Gothic*.

English Point In lace-making; see *Angleterre*.

English Porcelain In ceramics; the porcelain made in England during the 18th century is distinctive for its variety of composition. The French form of soft paste porcelain was made at Chelsea, Derby and Longton Hall. Soapstone pastes were made at Worcester, Caughley and Liverpool. The manufactories at Plymouth and Bristol made a hard paste porcelain. For several decades after 1750 Derby was a most productive manufactory, and a large number of the existent English porcelain figures were made there. A soft paste was made at Nantgarw and Swansea from about 1813 to 1823. A type of porcelain was developed at Bow, around the middle of the 18th century, in which bone ash was used as an ingredient. This variety of hybrid porcelain, in which part of the kaolin was replaced by bone ash, became by the end of the 18th century and still remains the standard type for English porcelain. The production at Lowestoft resembles that of Bow inasmuch as it contained bone ash in its composition. See *Porcelain*; *Soft Paste*; *Bone China*.

English Silver A general term given to the articles of silver, domestic and ecclesiastical, made in the British Isles conforming to the sterling standard. See *Sterling*; *Hall-Marks*; *London*, *Irish*, *English Provinces*, *Scottish*.

English Soft Paste In English ceramics; see *English Porcelain*.

Engobe In ceramics; the French term for a mixture of clay, that is usually white, thinned with water and applied as a coating over the body of pottery to conceal its natural color which is generally reddish or buff. It was much used on peasant pottery to imitate the whiteness of porcelain and to provide a more appropriate ground for painted decoration. It also served as a preliminary for sgraffiato or incised decoration in which the design was scratched through to the original color of the body.

Engraved Glass Engraving is one of the principal methods for decorating glass. It is done with a wheel or with a diamond point. Engraving with a wheel has been practiced since the time of the Romans. However, it is necessary to differentiate between deep carving and surface cutting. The former was practiced from the early days. Toward the end of the 17th century the Germans not only excelled in this work but they also developed and perfected surface cutting. Examples of this type of decorative engraving made by the Germans and the Bohemians from the end of the 17th century and by the Dutch during the following century are unrivalled. In this process of wheel engraving the designs are made on the glass by means of minute copper wheels which are fed a mixture of emery and oil. As a rule the incised parts remain unpolished and the small circular depressions are polished. Engraving with the diamond point seems to have originated in Venice during the 16th century. The culmination of this art was attained in the Low Countries during the 17th and 18th centuries. It is a process of scratching or stippling the surface of glass with a diamond point. In stippling the design is produced by means of minute dots made with a diamond point and a small hammer. Stippled engraving is very delicate and almost resembles frost on the glass. It was a favorite Dutch method for decorating glass. Engraving with a diamond point results in designs of gossamer-like quality. The fine cross lights created by the deeper incision of wheel engraving is not achieved. The method of scratching the surface of glass for decorative purposes is very old. It was used by the Romans as a decorative process; however,

DIAMOND POINT
ENGRAVED GLASS

instead of a diamond point, they probably used a piece of flint. See *Etched Glass*; *German Glass*; *Glass*; *Cut Glass*; *Dutch and Flemish Glass*; *Hochschnitt*.

Engraving The art or process of producing marks or designs by incising or cutting into a surface of metal, stone or glass; the art of making pictures by printing from an engraved surface. Pictures are made by one of four varieties of engraving; namely, etching, line engraving, mezzotint and wood engraving. The term *engraving* also refers to the impression of the picture made from the engraved plate.

Engrêlure In lace-making; the French term given to the footing or one of the two edges of lace, the other edge being the couronné. The engrêlure, which keeps the stitches of the ground firm, is used to sew the lace to the material which it is to enrich.

Enile Rug See *Oushak*.

Entablature In classic architecture; the horizontal structure resting on the top of the columns of a building, consisting of the architrave, frieze and cornice. This classical treatment was freely interpreted in some articles of cabinetwork incorporating architectural features in their principles of design, such as bookcases, from the time of the Renaissance.

GEORGE III
SILVER EPERGNE

Entrée Dish In English silver; a covered dish to hold vegetables or savories. It is usually oval, oblong or octagonal in shape. Sometimes it is fitted with a movable division for different vegetables. Occasionally the cover is made with a detachable handle, in order that it may be converted into an extra dish. The entrée dish is sometimes fitted in a separate base on feet in which hot water is kept. Occasionally the entrée dish is fitted with a spirit burner stand and this dish generally has a compartment for hot water. Another variety of entrée dish is called a bacon dish. Entrée dishes were introduced late in the Georgian period.

Entrelacs In ornament; a French architectural term meaning to interweave, twist or interlace, given to a decorative repetitive or continuous design. Entrelacs à rosaces or twisted bandings enclosing rosettes executed in gilded bronze were a favorite frieze decoration for furniture designed in the Louis XVI style and were applied to such articles as decorative tables and secrétaires à abattant.

Envelope Table In English cabinetwork; a small table with a square pivoting top provided with four segmental flaps and generally designed with a frieze drawer. As a rule it was mounted on four slender quadrangular tapered legs fitted with casters. It derived its name from the resemblance of the four folded flaps to the folds of an envelope. The envelope table was introduced early in the 19th century and was made by such firms as Gillow's and Seddon's.

Epaulière In medieval armor; the protective steel plates covering the shoulder; especially the part that connects the breastplate with the back covering.

Epergne The French name given to an elaborate centerpiece for the dining table, usually made of silver and beautifully wrought in openwork. The épergne usually has a finely wrought large dish or basket-shaped piece in the center, supported on a stand, having several arms or brackets that support smaller pieces which conform in shape and in decoration to the large piece in the center. It was fashionable in England from around the middle of the 18th century.

Epine-Vinette Wood The wood of the hawthorn tree, *crataegus oxyacantha*, used in cabinetwork, especially by the French ébénistes. It is hard and its color is yellow.

Eponge, Boîte à In French silver; see *Soap Box* and *Sponge Box*.

Equation Clock A tall case clock having equation dials to indicate the difference each day between true solar time as recorded by a sun dial and a clock's mean solar time. This clock was introduced during the late 17th century. It usually indicated the day of the month, the rising and setting of the sun, the sun's position in the zodiac and the age and phases of the moon.

Erable Wood   See *Maple*.

Erfurt   In German ceramics; from 1717 to about 1792 a productive faïence manufacture was carried on at Erfurt, Thuringia. The most activity and best work at the Erfurt factory owned by Johann Paul Stieglitz was from 1734 until about 1792. The factory mark, which was seldom used, was a wheel with six spokes taken from the arms of the Elector of Mayence. The wares were painted in the typical Thuringian high-temperature colors. Cylindrical tankards generally mounted in pewter were especially characteristic. They were decorated in a rough but effective manner with such motifs as figures, landscapes, flowers, animals and similar subjects. Dishes, bowls, jugs with narrow necks, and even some figures were included in their productions.

Escabeau   Or Escabelle. In French cabinetwork; the Gothic stool was of trestle form with two solid end supports. Since chairs were relatively rare during the Gothic period, stools, benches and chests were generally used for seats. The stool was still profusely made throughout the 16th century. It had a square, round, oblong, and sometimes triangular molded seat. *Placet* was another French term for a stool.

Escritoire   In English cabinetwork; the words *escritoire*, *scriptor* and *scrutoire* were different names applied to early forms of English writing furniture such as the writing cabinet with a fall-front. The term *scriptor* was still used during the Early Georgian period. See *Writing Furniture*.

Escudelles ab Orelles   In Spanish ceramics; the name given to a type of shallow Valencia luster pottery bowl with handles that was made during the 15th and 16th centuries. It usually had two handles and occasionally four handles. It was so called because of the supposed resemblance of the form of each handle to the shape of an ear.

Escudié   See *Buffet-Vaisselier*.

Escutcheon   In furniture mounts; the decorative metal plate or shield around a keyhole. The name is also applied in heraldry to a shield with armorial bearings.

Espagnolette   In French mounts; a bronze bust of a charming girl which was used as a mount on the stiles of commodes, on the tops of the cabriole legs of writing tables, and on other metal work, such as on bail handles and on escutcheons. Especially fine were the espagnolettes made by Charles Cressent, which were copied from the decorative art of Watteau. The espagnolette was identified with the style of the Régence and the Louis XV style. The French term *espagnolette* is given to a hasp or window fastener.

Espetera   In Spanish furniture; a wrought iron plaque, either solid or pierced, hung on a kitchen wall to hold such utensils as roasting forks, sauce pans and ladles. It was a characteristic Spanish kitchen article.

Essence Vase   See *Cassolette*.

Estagnié   In French Provincial cabinetwork; the term is generally given to a variety of hanging open shelves used for holding pewter utensils. It often had a drawer under the open shelves.

Estoc   In arms; a sword having a long, narrow, quadrangular blade used for thrusting during the 13th to the 17th centuries. The early estoc was without scabbard and was carried by rings on the belt of a footman or hung from the saddle of a horseman.

Etagère   In French cabinetwork; the name given to a set of open hanging wall shelves. It was frequently designed to fit in a corner of a room. Occasionally the étagère had a row of either two small drawers or doors beneath the two or three open shelves. The almost infinite variety of open hanging wall shelves was an outstanding feature of provincial cabinetwork. The name is also given to a small set of standing open shelves having

ESPAGNOLETTE BY
CRESSENT

several tiers for the reception of bric-a-brac. The name is found in French records from the 17th century onwards. See *What-Not*.

Etched Glass It seems that the method of engraving or etching a design on glass by means of hydrofluoric acid was first done by Henry Schwanhardt, the son of Johann Schwanhardt of Nuremberg, around 1670. In this process the parts that are not to be exposed to the acid are covered in a protective resinous paint or wax. The design is cut through the paint with a sharp steel point. The glass is exposed to the acid which affects the uncovered parts bared by the steel point. See *Engraved Glass*; *Glass*; *German Glass*.

Etching A method of engraving in which the cut out or incised marks are produced on a copper plate by the eating-away action of acid. The term *etching* also refers to the drawing so etched and reproduced by printing. The plate is covered with an acid-resisting compound, which is called the etching ground. A drawing or design is traced on the etching ground. An etching needle is used for incising the design through the ground; this cutting penetrates to the copper. The biting or eating away of the lines on the plate is done by applying the acid, which reacts on the exposed copper. The finished plate is then used to reproduce the drawing or etching by printing. See *Engraving*.

Etimier In French Provincial cabinetwork; the name sometimes given to a type of cupboard or an upright double-bodied buffet of marked simplicity. The upper portion was fitted with two cupboard doors, while the lower portion was open and consisted of two racks made of slender pieces of wood. These racks were generally used to hold the freshly washed pottery dishes and the pewter utensils. The étimier was usually found in the humble dwellings of the peasants.

Etruria In English ceramics; see *Wedgwood*.

ETUI

Etruscan In decorative art; Etruria, which was the name used by the Latins for the country of the Etruscans, flourished in the north-western and central part of Italy before the rise of the Romans. The Etruscans, who were of foreign origin, settled here about 800 B.C. and their civilization attained its highest phase of development about 500 B.C. Etruscan art in its early stage was influenced by Egyptian and Near Eastern art, but its later and principal inspiration was drawn heavily from Grecian art. Essentially it was a hybrid art which never succeeded in completely assimilating the classic principles as perfected by the Greeks. Etruscan furniture was basically similar to and almost entirely dependent on Grecian furniture. Some of the best Etruscan work was achieved in bronze, such as decorative reliefs, figures of men and animals and mirrors. They also produced fine goldwork and jewelry, terra cotta, pottery and the distinctive black and red bucchero ware. See *Bucchero Ware*.

Etui A French term meaning a small box or case. Etuis used for carrying toilet articles and other small personal utensils were mentioned in royal records in France from the 14th century. A special form of étui popular in the 17th century was called an étui à aiguille, étui à cure-dents, and étui à épingles, for needles, toothpicks and pins respectively. It was a small hollow cylinder with a lid, made of gold, silver, ivory and other material, and was used to carry small utensils for the toilet or for sewing. In the 18th century, a principal variety of étui especially identified with French objects of virtù was more or less cylindrical and about 5 or 6 inches in length and three-quarters of an inch in diameter. It was generally made in gold, silver, tortoise shell or enamel, and richly ornamented, frequently with precious jewels. See *Nécessaire*; *Souvenir*.

European Soft Paste In ceramics; see *Soft Paste*.

Evans, David An American cabinetmaker working in Philadelphia and producing pieces in the Chippendale style. See *Philadelphia Chippendale*.

Ewer The name is given to a form of jug or pitcher having a wide spout and a handle. It was usually mounted on a stem and flaring foot or on three feet. Generally a deep circular dish or basin decorated in a similar manner was placed beneath the ewer. The ewer was chiefly used during ancient times to pour water over the hands after eating.

Especially fine was the elaborately wrought silver ewer and dish made during the Renaissance. See *Aquamanale*; *Jug*.

Exercising Chair In English furniture; a wooden armchair, with a foot-rest and a high seat, used for exercising. The seat was covered in leather and its interior contained several boards with springs, which could be operated by the sitter's weight, in the manner of a concertina. It was introduced during the latter part of the 18th century.

RENAISSANCE
EWER AND DISH

F

Fabergé, Carl Gustavovich 1846–1920. Goldsmith and jeweller to the Russian Imperial Court. He is regarded as one of the finest goldsmiths and jewellers of all times. In 1870 he assumed control of his father's business in St. Petersburg. During the next three decades his exquisite gold and enamel bibelots won him international fame. Although he may have made several of these wonderful enamel fantasies, it is generally accepted that he confined his attention to the designing and guiding of these objects of virtù in every stage of creation. Because of the war in 1914 he eventually closed his workshops in which he had employed about five hundred artisans. Fabergé was a superb craftsman. Each piece was indelibly marked with his personality and showed the liveliness of his imagination. The Easter eggs which he made for the Russian Imperial family are perhaps his finest work. It is believed that he made the first Easter egg for the Tsarina in 1884. These eggs which always contained some delightful and exquisite surprise are a miracle of delicacy and inventiveness. His flowers cut from precious and semi-precious stones are remarkable for their delicate tracery and beauty of form. His animal figures are so skillfully cut that they seem almost alive. All his work revealed his minute attention to detail and his thorough knowledge of the subject.

FAENZA SPOUTED DRUG POT

Faenza In Italian ceramics; perhaps the leading productive center in Italy for majolica. From at least 1475 until the end of the 16th century its wares were equal in quality to those of any other Italian center producing majolica. Probably the majolica produced at Faenza from 1500 to 1530 may be regarded as the finest of all. Potteries still exist at Faenza. An early type of majolica with green and purple decoration was made at Faenza during the late 14th and 15th centuries as well as at Orvieto and Tuscany.

Extant 15th century specimens include plaques, tiles, vases, drug vases and globular jars with two handles in the form of winged dragons, drug pots with snake spouts and dishes and large plates. The work is distinctive for the quality of coloring which is clear and strong, for the admirable figure drawing and for the excellent proportions of the forms. A purely decorative treatment of Renaissance motifs was traditional to Faenza work. Earliest specimens with a berettino ground, which was a favorite type at Faenza, were made late in the 15th century. The carefully and elaborately painted pieces which belong to the great period from 1500 to 1530 may be recognized as the work of one or other of about eight artists of the highest accomplishments. Large plates with panel painting in the true Faenza tradition with religious and sometimes mythological figure subjects are among the most beautiful of all known majolica paintings. Majolica with fruit painting of a rich color was made at Faenza around the middle of the 16th century. It is probable that this style which is closely associated with Venice originated at Faenza. Around 1570 an attractive and original style of painting in which only yellow and blue were used was introduced at Faenza. See *Italian Majolica*.

Fagoting A decorative needlework, which is done by drawing out parallel threads from a fabric and fastening the remaining cross threads into hourglass-shaped groups. The name is also given to the work itself. It is also spelled faggoting. See *Needlework*.

Faïence In ceramics; a French term derived from the Italian town of Faenza which was a great center for Italian Renaissance majolica. This name is given on the continent of Europe to earthenware covered with a lead glaze which is made white and opaque by adding tin-ashes. The glaze is commonly called a tin glaze or a tin enamel glaze. In

England the term *faïence* is increasingly being used and has the same meaning as *delftware*. A distinction recognized as a helpful practice is generally made between the earlier Italian Renaissance wares called majolica and the later faïence wares. The term *faïence* is usually restricted in meaning to the Dutch and other wares imitating the Chinese in the 17th century and to the later more or less original tin-glazed productions of Germany, France and other countries. This limitation marks the historical and artistic distinction between the two main classes of tin-glazed or tin-enamelled earthenware. The essential difference in making Italian majolica and Delft faïence was that the latter used a more refined clay which made possible a finer manipulation of the paste. After the article was shaped it was fired without glaze and then dipped in the tin glaze and dried. Until around 1675 the painting was generally done on the unfired tin glaze and then both were fired in the grand feu. Thus the colors were limited to the so-called high-temperature colors or those few colors that could stand the heat of the grand feu. In some of the finer Italian majolica and Delft faïence an additional lead glaze was applied over the tin-glazed decorated surface which imparted a higher gloss and enriched the colors. This final glaze was either fired by itself or in one single operation. Due to the competition from porcelain, which began to develop late in the 18th century, with its overglaze painted enamel colors that permitted a wider range of colors, the makers of faïence began to employ the enamel colors over the glaze and to fire them in the petit feu or at low temperature in a muffle kiln. This change from high temperature or true faïence colors fired with the tin-glazed ground to muffle colors added later over the glaze was not employed on the more common faïence wares. See *Grand Feu*.

Faïence Fine   In ceramics; a French term used to describe lead-glazed white or cream-colored earthenware of the English type. See *Cream-Colored Earthenware*.

Faïence Parlante   In French ceramics; a collective term for the different pieces made at numerous French manufactories having inscriptions in their decorative designs. The term *faïence patronymique* is applied to a variety having pictures of saints frequently bearing a date given as a presentation on birthdays, christenings and other similar events. The faïence patriotique or faïence populaire was chiefly characterized by emblems and was especially popular during the French Revolution.

Falchion   In arms; a sword used during the Middle Ages. It had a short, broad, slightly curving, single-edged blade with its widest part near the point.

Faldistorium   In furniture; the name given to a variety of curule chair of ecclesiastical origin. It had a wrought iron curule frame with four upright supports, usually of turned brass, terminating in brass knob hand grips. The seat, which was of leather and frequently covered with velvet, was stretched between the two side rails. It was especially identified with the Late Renaissance in Italy. See *Curule*.

Faldstool   The name given to a folding seat of curule form or X-shape. The ecclesiastical faldstool, mentioned as early as the 11th century, is a seat without arms for the use of bishops and other prelates when not occupying the throne or when officiating at churches other than their own. The faldstool is also called a desk at which worshippers kneel in acts of devotion, especially one used by the sovereign of Great Britain at the coronation ceremony. The faldstool is also called a litany-stool at which the litany is appointed to be said or sung. In English cabinetwork; faldstools of a later period were made for secular use and were often covered and draped with costly fabrics richly embroidered and were the seats of princes and noblemen. See *Curule*.

Fall-Front   In cabinetwork; see *Drop-Front*.

False Topaz   See *Quartz*.

GOTHIC FALDSTOOL

CHINESE
ARGUS PHEASANT FAN

CHINESE HAND SCREEN

EARLY CHRISTIAN
FLABELLUM

SPANISH FAN

Famille Jaune In Chinese ceramics; see *Famille Verte*.

Famille Noire In Chinese ceramics; the black ground or famille noire is derived from manganese. The black ground is made by overlaying a dull black pigment with a coating of transparent green enamel which results in the rich greenish black color which is so highly esteemed. See *Famille Verte*; *Famille Rose*.

Famille Rose In Chinese ceramics; during the third decade of the 18th century the opaque colors of the rose family in which different shades of pink and carmine play a leading part largely supplanted in porcelain decoration the transparent Famille Verte enamels. Present evidence indicates that Famille Rose porcelains were in full production during the Yung Chêng reign, 1723–1735. See *Famille Verte*.

Famille Verte In Chinese ceramics; the enamelled polychrome porcelains in which green has a leading part first made during the K'ang Hsi reign, 1662–1722. They are a development of the Wan Li five-color ware or wu ts'ai yao. Much of the Famille Verte is distinguished by an overglaze blue enamel; although some of the ware has an underglaze blue and some combine both the underglaze blue and the overglaze blue enamel. The Famille Verte colors are known to the Chinese as the ying ts'ai or hard colors in distinction to the Famille Rose known as juan ts'ai or soft colors. Famille Verte is further divided into Famille Jaune and Famille Noire depending on the color of the background. The polychrome enamels are either painted over the glaze or are enamelled on the biscuit or unglazed porcelain. Some of the finest Ch'ing porcelains are enamelled on the biscuit. In addition to a variety of greens the other transparent enamel colors are yellow, aubergine and violet blue. The red, which is half pigment and half enamel, is of a coral tone. A dry brown black pigment is also used. See *Famille Rose*; *Famille Noire*; *Five-Color Ware*.

Fan The use of the fan dates from early times when it was frequently represented among the ancient Assyrians and Egyptians as well as on Greek vases as an emblem of authority or for utilitarian use. The fan of the ancients was often of large size on a long shaft and carried by slaves. In early Christian times the flabellum, or fan used to keep flies from the altar during the Mass, was in use from the 4th to the 14th century. There are two varieties of fans, the folding and the rigid types, the latter being reserved for ceremonial and state occasions. The varieties of fans comprise an endless diversity of forms, material and construction. In the folding fan the two principal parts are the sticks and the leaf or mount. The leaf consists of paper, parchment or a fine fabric of two pieces of equal size in the form of a segment of a circle and mounted so as to produce from twelve to twenty-four folds of equal dimensions. In China the fan is of ancient origin and its many traditions of introduction are based on mythology. Many early Chinese fans were made of the feathers of the ostrich, peacock, and argus pheasant, as well as grasses and leaves, with beautifully wrought handles of ivory, gold, silver or wood. The folding fan was introduced into China from Japan. In Japan the fan is regarded as an emblem of life and as such enters into almost every phase of Japanese life and ceremonial occasions. According to research authority the first folding fans were made in Japan by a fan-maker living near Kyōto in the Tenji period, 668–672. The importance of the fan in Japan is evidenced by the variety of categories comprising fans for special purposes such as war-fans, dancing-fans, court-fans, tea-fans and many others. Tea-fans consisting of three sticks are used at the tea ceremony on the first day of the New Year to commemorate the curing of the illness of Emperor Murakami, 947–967, with tea given to him by the Goddess Kuan Yin. In the early 16th century folding fans were introduced into Italy and Spain by Portuguese traders from the Far East and later in the same century they were made in Paris. In

1673 Louis XIV formed the corporation of the Maîtres Eventailistes. The French fans of the 18th century were often fine works of art produced by the decorative artists, carvers, jewelers and goldsmiths. In England during the reign of Henry VIII some fans were used with full dress and others for walking. Those used for walking had handles about 18 inches long and also served as sunshades. These walking sticks made of gold, silver or wood with peacock or ostrich feathers were elaborately wrought during the 16th century especially in the reign of Queen Elizabeth I. In America fans were extremely popular in the 18th century and were made in Boston as early as about 1730. See *Japanese Fan*.

Fan-Back Chair In cabinetwork; the name given to a form of wooden chair having spindles in the back arranged in a radiating or fan-shaped manner. The term fan-back is frequently applied to a Windsor chair whose spindles are so arranged.

Fancy Chair In American cabinetwork; the term *fancy chair* was given to an inexpensive painted open-back chair made of a light wood and enriched with either painted or stenciled decoration. It was popular from about 1800 to 1850 and was designed in the Sheraton style and later in the American Empire style. The majority of chairs were painted black and usually had a cane or rush seat. The front legs were generally cylindrical and ring-collared. The top rail, any design in the open back, such as banisters, the front of the seat rail, and the front stretchers were often enriched with a decorative painted panel. The painted decoration chiefly consisted of floral and leaf designs and was generally gilded. After 1820 these chairs instead of being hand-painted were chiefly decorated with stencil work. The cabinet-makers who specialized in these chairs were called fancy-chair makers.

Fan Motif In ornament; a decorative radiating motif resembling an open fan. The fan motif was much used in inlay work on

articles of furniture designed by Adam, and in the subsequent styles of Hepplewhite and Sheraton. The carved fan motif formed of radiating grooves in the segment of a circle was a characteristic decoration on New England highboys designed in the Queen Anne style.

Farthingale Chair In English cabinetwork; a small side chair introduced around the beginning of the 17th century that was popular during the Early Jacobean period. It was essentially a lady's chair and was designed so that she could sit comfortably in her voluminous hoop skirt or farthingale. The chair was rectangular in shape. The seat was noticeably high and the back was unusually low. The chair had an upholstered seat and back panel. Frequently the frame was entirely covered with fabric; in other examples it was sometimes painted and gilded. The French term is *Chaise à Vertugadin*.

Fasces A bundle of rods from which the head of an axe projected held together with a wide tape. It was used as a Roman symbol of authority. The imperial fasces was crowned with laurel. The fasces was sometimes used as a motif in decorative art. During the French Empire when emblems of victory and imperial emblems were in vogue the fasces was frequently employed.

Fathpur Rug An Oriental rug woven at Fathpur, India, which was an important rug weaving center during the reign of Akbar the Great, 1556–1605. See *India Oriental Rug*; *Oriental Rug*.

Faubourg St. Antoine Henri IV established a tapestry manufactory in the Faubourg St. Antoine in 1597, and in 1603 he transferred the workrooms to the Louvre. Maurice Dubourg and Henri Laurent were the head weavers. See *Tapestry*.

Faubourg Saint-Denis Or Faubourg Saint-Lazare. In French ceramics; a hard paste porcelain manufactory was established in Paris in 1771 by Pierre-Antoine Hannong

FAN-BACK WINDSOR CHAIR

who left before 1776. His porcelain was generally marked with a small "H" or crossed clay pipes. The mark "CP" was registered in 1779 showing the protection of Charles Philippe, Comte d'Artois, and was found until around 1793. Two new manufactories were active around 1798, apparently developing from the original. The early 19th century wares were often marked with the name *Schoelcher* who was one of the proprietors. The porcelain made by Hannong was extremely translucent and vitrified. The productions, which were principally tablewares, displayed the characteristic French refinement. The carefully painted decoration was similar in style to the contemporary styles in vogue at the different Paris porcelain manufactories during the late 18th and early 19th centuries. See *Paris Porcelain*.

Faubourg St. Germain Raphaël de la Planche established a tapestry manufactory at Paris in the Faubourg St. Germain around 1627. In 1662 it was merged with the Gobelins. See *Tapestry*; *Gobelins*.

Faubourg Saint-Lazare In French ceramics; see *Faubourg Saint-Denis*.

Faubourg St. Marceau See *Gobelins*.

Fauchard In arms; a 16th century pole arm. It is characterized by a long shaft mounted with a broad, single-edged blade that is curved on the cutting edge. An ornamental prong balances the blade on the back. The name *fauchard* is variously applied to different weapons. See *Glaive*.

Fauldesteuil Or Faudesteuil. In French cabinetwork; a medieval secular chair having its origin in the ancient Roman curule chair and essentially similar to the English faldstool. The chair with its curving X-shaped legs either actually folded or gave that impression. See *Curule*.

Fauteuil In French cabinetwork; a chair with arms. In 18th century French seat furniture the bergère and canapé were generally designed en suite with a fauteuil having open arms.

LOUIS XVI FAUTEUIL

Favrile A late 19th century American glass made by Louis C. Tiffany, and characterized by delicate iridescent effects. The glass was produced in a variety of colors, with beautifully executed decorative designs. See *Art Glass*.

Feather Banding In English cabinetwork; a banding of veneer consisting of two strips of wood laid together with the grain of each running diagonally to the other. The effect produced resembled a herringbone or feather design. Drawer fronts on walnut furniture were often inlaid with a border of feather banding during the late 17th and early 18th centuries. It is also called plume grain and herringbone banding.

Feather Edge In silver; a decorative engraved design. It is a narrow band consisting of engraved oblique lines which form a feather-like design around the edge. It was introduced during the second half of the 18th century.

Feathered Ware In English ceramics; see *Combed Ware*.

Feather Stitch A decorative embroidery stitch composed of blanket stitches which are worked in such a manner to form a branching zigzag line.

Federal Style In American cabinetwork; see *American Federal*.

Feeding Cup In English silver; see *Spout Cup*.

Fei-Ts'ui Jade See *Jade*.

Feldspar In ceramics; a variety of crystalline rocks from which clays were formed by decomposition. It was used in the manufacturing of porcelain as fluxes or fusible ingredients.

Feldspathic Glaze In ceramics; see *Glaze*.

Felletin Tapestries Tapestries were first woven at the town of Felletin, France, during the 16th century. As a rule the tapestries were of coarse verdure designs. See *Tapestry*.

Fender In English furniture; the low rail

or metal fireguard which is placed before the opening of a fireplace. It was introduced during the late 17th century. The 18th century fender was generally either a straight or a slightly bow-shaped strip of steel ornamented with pierced fretwork to conform in design with the grate. Around the middle of the 18th century the fender became more elaborate with finely pierced scroll designs. During the late 18th century and early 19th century the brass fender was more strongly constructed. The top and bottom were heavily molded and other moldings were used to strengthen the thin perforated strip. It rested on cast brass feet.

Fenestration In Gothic cabinetwork; the term *fenestration*, which had its origin in architecture, is used in furniture to describe an arcading or a simple blind arcade in which the mullions in the windows were replaced by moldings extending out from the surface. These moldings reproduced the mullions in decorative detail. Panels with fenestration were widely used on the façade of Gothic chests.

Fêng-Huang In Chinese art; an imaginary or mythical phoenix-like bird widely used in Chinese painting, textiles, sculpture and ceramics. It is commonly represented as having the head of a pheasant, the beak of a swallow, a long flexible neck, plumage of many brilliant colors and a flowing tail between an argus pheasant and a peacock, with long claws pointed backward as it flies. It has a dual nature, being both male and female. It was a special emblem of the Empress and was believed by the ancient Chinese to make its appearance when the country was ruled by a wise monarch. See *Chinese Animal Figures*.

Fên Ting In Chinese ceramics; see *Ting Yao*.

Feraghan Rug An Oriental rug belonging to the Persian classification. The warp and the weft are of cotton and the pile is of wool, short in length. The ends are finished with a narrow web and loose warp threads. Most of these rugs will have the Herati motif,

covering the field in one form or another. The other design most often found is the guli hinnai. The rug is notable for its fine workmanship. The modern Feraghan is inferior to the antique Feraghan in design and in fineness of texture.

Feretory In ecclesiastical art; a portable or stationary shrine in which was kept the remains or relics of saints. The word *feretrum* signifies a bier; however, since shrines containing relics of saints were often carried in solemn processions, the shrine itself gradually became known as a feretrum. The use of feretories or portable shrines dates from very early times. The earliest feretory was in the form of a chest having a ridged top with sloping sides resembling a slanting roof. This form was characteristic of the finest examples made in the 14th and 15th centuries when they were magnificently wrought with religious motifs and sacred imagery executed in high relief and surmounted with small spires of exquisite detail. Feretories were often made or adorned with the richest of materials, such as gold or silver set with precious stones, ivory or crystal mounted in gold or in gilded bronze, metal enriched with enamelling, and carved wood brilliantly painted and gilded.

Ferrara Tapestries Tapestries were woven at Ferrara, Italy, as early as the 15th century. The Duke Hercules II, 1508–1559, head of the house of Este, attempted to revive the industry and established a manufactory in 1536. He appointed two Flemish weavers, Hans and Nicholas Karcher, as master weaver and painter, and he appointed Battista Dosso as designer. Nicholas Karcher left in 1546 to go to the Medici tapestry works at Florence. The manufactory declined during the reign of Alphonso II, 1559–1597. See *Tapestry*.

Ferronnerie In European ceramics; a French term given to a variety of ornament having the appearance of wrought ironwork, consisting of scrolls and bands interpreted as pierced and as curling outward from the

FÊNG-HUANG

surface. It first appeared around the middle of the 16th century on majolica made in France and in the Netherlands. Occasionally the name is given to the scrolled designs found on some French faïence toward the end of the 17th and early 18th centuries.

Festoon In ornament; a conventional and graceful arrangement of flowers, leaves or fruit bound together and depending from a decorative bow-knot, patera, classic urn, etc. Festoons were much used by the Greeks and Romans on friezes and panels. The festoon was a favorite classic motif in decorative art and in furniture design. Drapery festoons, bow-knotted husk festoons, bead, leaf or flower festoons were all employed. Especially typical are the Adam style gilded mirrors with their delicate festoons. The festoon motif is also called the swag motif.

Fiat Glass In English glass; see *Jacobite Glass*.

Fiddle and Thread In silver; a fiddle pattern stem or handle designed on a spoon or fork having an engraved thread line outlining the stem. Frequently the top of the stem is ornamented with a shell motif. This type of stem is called a thread and shell. It was introduced in the early 19th century in England. See *Fiddle Pattern*; *Spoon*; *Fork*.

Fiddle Back In English cabinetwork; an open chair back having a solid splat which resembled a fiddle in outline. It was introduced around 1700 in the hoop-back chair. See *Queen Anne Splat-Back Chair*.

Fiddle Pattern In silver; a form of a stem or handle found on a spoon or fork. About half of the length of the handle is broad and flat and then it shapes inward and has small angular shoulders above the bowl or tines. It was introduced in English silver early in the 19th century. See *Spoon*; *Fork*.

Fiddle-Shaped Table In cabinetwork; the name sometimes given to an occasional table, because of the supposed resemblance of its top to the shape of a fiddle. The end portions are of equal width and the center portion on both sides is shaped and curves inward.

FIELD BED, AMERICAN

Field Bed In English cabinetwork; according to medieval records this type of bed was originally designed for use in war and traveling. The term was still used in the 18th century. Hepplewhite in the CABINET MAKER AND UPHOLSTERER'S GUIDE had one plate entitled "Sweeps for Field Bed Tops" which gave five ways in which the tester could be arched. Several of the designs were hinged in order that the framework could be folded. According to these drawings it seems that this type differs from the usual tester bed in that the latter has a more elaborate and elegant tester. The field bed simply has a light and plain framework of varying arched form secured to the tops of the four posts and covered with fabric. See *Bed*.

Fielded Panel See *Coffered Panel*.

Figuline In ceramics; a term applied to the earthenware vessels made by the potter and also to the potter's clay of which these vessels are fabricated. The rustiques figulines made by Bernard Palissy, c. 1510–1590, at Saintes undoubtedly were the foundation upon which his reputation as a potter later depended. These rustiques figulines made by Palissy were molded after nature and included such familiar objects as shells, leaves, fishes and lizards.

Figurestone See *Agalmatolite*.

Filet Brodé à Reprisés A kind of darned lace; a modern survival of opus filatorium or darned netting. See *Darned Netting*.

Filet Guipure A kind of darned lace; a modern survival of opus filatorium or darned netting. See *Darned Netting*.

Filigree The term given to a decorative work made of fine wire which is chiefly used to ornament gold and silver. The wire is soldered on the gold or silver in intricate and elaborate designs, such as on a sword hilt.

Filigree Glass In Venetian glass; see *Threaded Glass*.

Filigree Paper Decoration In English de-

PENDANT, GOLD, ENAMEL AND JEWELS—
Italian, 16th Century.
The Metropolitan Museum of Art, gift of
J. Pierpont Morgan, 1917.

THE ROSPIGLIOSI CUP, ATTRIBUTED TO BENVENUTO CELLINI—*Italian, 16th Century.*
The Metropolitan Museum of Art, bequest of Benjamin Altman, 1913.

corative arts; filigree paper decoration was originally inspired by gold and silver filigree work. It appears that the earliest work dates from around the 15th century. This craft was revived around the middle of the 17th century and it became a fashionable amateur hobby for ladies of the 18th century. This later work consisted of narrow strips of plain or wrinkled stiffened paper which was colored and gilded and made into twisted rolls. Occasionally small shells and metal threads were used in conjunction with the paper rolls and these different materials were worked into decorative designs which were used to ornament such articles as mirror frames and boxes. Sometimes mirror frames with stumpwork were further enhanced with this paper filigree decoration around the middle of the 17th century. Mosaic work was also imitated in paper filigree decoration.

Fillet An architectural term for a relatively small and narrow flat molding, usually in the form of a small plain band, to separate a group of moldings from each other. The term is also given to a flat surface included between other moldings. Fillets were employed in cabinetwork from the medieval period. Occasionally in fine spiral turning a narrow fillet or band was arranged in the bottom of a groove so that the deeper depressions were not too dark.

Fillings See *Jours*.

Fine Silver The number of parts out of 1000 which are pure silver, with the remaining number being the alloy. See *American Silver*; *Sterling*.

Finger Bowl A small bowl-shaped vessel for holding water, used at the table to rinse one's fingers. It is also called a finger glass, finger cup and finger basin. Early English finger bowls were sometimes larger, and were also used to cool wine glasses at the table. The term *finger bowl* or *finger glass* is also given to a vessel, usually made of glass having the general shape of a large jar, being rather bulbous-shaped, with a cover having a finial. The vessel usually has six deep round

indentations spaced irregularly around the body, slightly below the middle, so that the finger tips can be inserted to hold the vessel securely, taking the place of a handle. The vessel is of central European origin and was made as early as the 17th century.

Finger Glass See *Finger Bowl*.

Finger Vase In ceramics; a variety of flower vase with five tubular holders set side by side in a fan-shaped arrangement. The form was introduced at Delft and was copied at other ceramic manufactories.

Finial The name given to a carved ornament which is placed at the top of a piece of furniture, such as on the cornice of a tester bed, on bed-posts, or on the top of a mirror; or which is placed on the cover of a vase or urn, etc. Especially characteristic as finials are acorns, flaming torches and plumes. Other subjects for finials include vases, urns, flowers and birds, such as eagles.

Fior di Persica Marble See *Fleur de Pêcher Marble*.

Fireback The term applied to a cast-iron slab, which was widely used in England from the 16th century. It was placed in the back of a fireplace opening, and used as a protection for the stone and brick. It was cast in a mold and ornamented with various designs; such as allegorical figures, heraldic emblems, griffons, rosettes and fleur-de-lis. It is also called a fire-plate.

Fire Dogs See *Andirons*.

Fire-Grate An iron or steel container used in a fireplace to hold burning coal. The variety usually used in England during the 18th century resembled an oblong basket resting on supports rather high above the hearth. Many 18th century fire-grates were artistically wrought; such as those designed by the Adam brothers, having decorative motifs of festoons, acanthus leaves, paterae, radial fans and classic urns to conform with the interior architecture. Fine polished steel grates were widely used during the early 19th century.

FIREBACK WITH ROYAL ARMS

Firelock The name given to a variety of hand firearm that came into general use during the second half of the 17th century. This type of musket belonged to the group of firearms provided with a mechanism for striking a spark to ignite the powder charge. In the firelock the mechanism was much improved over the earlier forms, such as the snaphance. The flintlock is also called a firelock. This firelock or flintlock was the well-known Brown Bess of the British army. See *Wheel Lock*.

Fire Mark A molded metal plate having the insignia or name of a fire insurance company. In 1667, the year after the Great Fire of London, the first fire insurance company was founded and a few years later formed a brigade of their own firemen. To enable its firemen to identify insured properties a lead plate in the form of a phoenix rising from the flames was used as a fire mark. Fire marks were usually placed about level with the second story windows. Each fire insurance company's brigade answered an alarm but only the brigade whose mark appeared on the house fought the fire. In America, the first fire insurance company was formed in 1752 called the Philadelphia Contributionship whose fire mark was four crossed hands each clasping the wrist of the other. Volunteer fire brigades received their reward for fighting a fire from the company whose mark was on the house. Fire marks were used in America until the middle of the 19th century.

SILVER FISH-SLICE

Fire Pan A flat metal pan used for holding burning coals; a brazier. During the 16th and 17th centuries in England the fire pan was sometimes made of silver and was finely wrought.

Fire-Plate See *Fireback*.

Fire Screen In English furniture; there are two principal types of fire screen; namely, the cheval fire screen and the pole screen. See *Cheval Fire Screen*; *Pole Screen*; *Screen*. In French furniture; see *Ecran à Coulisse*; *Ecran à Eventail*.

Fire Tools The utility pieces made of iron, steel or brass, used for attending a fire in a fireplace. They usually consist of a shovel, poker and tongs, and were often richly decorated. Especially notable were the 18th century French fire tools with their finely wrought bronze handles. Fire tools are mentioned in England as early as 1659 and in France in 1672.

Firing Glass An early English drinking glass having a round and sometimes ovoid shaped body resting on a stout stem and heavy flat foot which was wider than the body. This glass was strongly made in order that it could be knocked on the table after toasts. Firing glasses were used during the 18th century.

Fir Wood See *Sapin Wood*.

Fish Roe Crackle See *Crackle*.

Fish-Server In English silver; a silver serving piece introduced around 1800. It consisted of a fish-slice with a smaller blade of conforming design fitted above and attached with a spring. A thumbpiece on the handle raised the smaller blade in order to secure the piece of flat fish for serving. This variety of server was also used for asparagus. See *Asparagus-Tongs*; *Fish-Slice*.

Fish-Slice In English silver; a variety of fish-slicer and server was introduced around 1770. The early type was designed with a broad blade resembling a trowel which was diamond or triangular-shaped with pierced scrollwork. About 1780 the blade began to resemble the shape of a fish and by 1790 the blade was rectangular with rounded ends. From around 1800 the openwork design of the blade was in the form of the backbone and ribs of a fish. Other designs and shapes occurred. See *Fish-Server*.

Fish Tail In American cabinetwork; a colloquial term applied to the carved detail frequently found on the top rail of a banister-back chair because of its supposed resemblance to the tail of a fish.

Five-Color Ware Or Wu Ts'ai. In Chinese

ceramics; an enamelled polychrome porcelain supplemented with underglaze blue. Although enamelled porcelains combined with underglaze blue were made in the 15th century as early as Hsüan Tê, it was not until the 16th century that they were fully developed and perfected. They are often referred to as Wan Li wu ts'ai or Wan Li polychrome since it is generally accepted that the greatest quantity were made during that reign. They are also especially identified with the preceding reigns of Chêng Tê and Chia Ching. In this ware all the Ming enamels were combined with underglaze blue. The enamelled colors included various shades of green, amber yellow, a purplish brown or aubergine and a distinctive turquoise green. They also used a tomato red derived from iron sulphate and a dry brown or black derived from manganese. These last two are more or less dry pigments and were principally used in outlining the design. The violet blue enamel derived from cobalt did not come into general use until the K'ang Hsi period in the Ch'ing dynasty. During the Ming dynasty a distinctive turquoise green enamel was generally used in its place. These colors were all highly translucent except the tomato red and black. See *Ming*; *Famille Verte*.

Five Dynasties See *Chinese Dynasties*.

Flabellum In ecclesiastical art; during Early Christian times two fans or flabella were used to keep flies from the altar during Mass. Toward the end of the 14th century the use of fans was gradually abandoned. Flabella were later made of precious metals, champlevé enamel and gilded bronze and were used for other purposes. Sometimes they contained a relic and they were used in processions.

Flagon A large bottle for holding wine or other liquors. It was in use since early times, particularly a variety of flagon made of metal provided with a screw top such as was used by pilgrims. In more recent times the name has been given to a large glass wine bottle having a globular-shaped body with flattened sides and a short neck and holding about double the quantity of a regular size wine bottle. The name *flagon* is also applied to a large vessel holding wine for use at the table, especially a jug-shaped vessel fitted with a handle and spout and generally a lid.

Flag Seat In cabinetwork; the name applied to a chair seat made from the blades or leaves of the flag which is one of various indigenous plants chiefly growing in moist places. Although flag is sometimes applied to any reed or rush, it is now regarded as properly denoting a member of the genus *iris*. Flag seats were freely used in American cabinetwork for the plainer types of chairs. See *Rush Seat*; *Splint Seat*.

Flail A medieval weapon having a long shaft with a spiked metal ball attached to the end by a short piece of chain. This weapon was known as the morning star. In another form, which was known as the scorpion, the long shaft had several pieces of chain attached to the end.

Flambé In Chinese ceramics; a kind of red glaze marbled with grey and purple. It is generally believed that the glaze was intended to be Lang yao or Sang de Bœuf and that this transmutation in color was at first accidental. It was first made during the K'ang Hsi reign. Later the color was purposely sought and mastered. Fine flambé red glazes were completely controlled in the following reign of Yung Chêng in the Ch'ing dynasty. See *Sang de Bœuf*; *Chi Hung*.

SILVER FLAGON

Flamboyant The name given to the third and last phase of Gothic architecture in France. The term, which literally means flaming, was given to this Late Gothic style because of the resemblance of the flowing lines in window tracery to the curving lines of flames. The Flamboyant style corresponds in period to the English Perpendicular style. It is generally accepted that the Flamboyant style had its inception in the flowing curvilinear lines of the English Decorated style. See *Gothic, French*.

Flanchard In medieval armor; the protective steel covering for a horse's flank.

Flanders Lace The origin of lace is often claimed by both Italy and Flanders. It seems that the majority of lace writers give credit to Italy for the needlepoint laces, while Flanders is given preference for the bobbin-made laces. Although Flanders made fine needlepoint laces, it was in bobbin-made laces that she excelled. Bobbin-made laces were of early origin in Flanders and it seems that by the end of the 15th century the making of bobbin lace was a common occupation. These laces were highly prized in other European countries, and through émigré Flemish lace-workers their technique and designs became the source of lace-making in many European countries. Old Flemish laces possessed great beauty and some were of varied grounds. It is sometimes stated in lace literature that the earliest lace made in Flanders was a variety of a bobbin-made guipure, having the flowing designs made of tape and joined with brides and occasionally without brides, when in the latter case the edges of the pattern touch each other. The flax of Flanders was highly prized because it guaranteed the gossamer-like quality of the lace. See *Brussels Lace*; *Mechlin*; *Antwerp Lace*; *Valenciennes*; *Binche*; *Point de Gaze*; *Angleterre*; *Guipure de Flandres*.

EAGLE FLASK

Flandre Or Flanders. In French Provincial; an old coastal district of Europe now included in Belgium and France. The predominating influence of the provincial furniture of Flanders was that of the Netherlands. Much of their Renaissance furniture reflected the innate Flemish taste for opulence in its carved decoration. Some of their more ambitious 17th century pieces such as armoires decorated with floral marquetry reflected a Dutch feeling in their treatment. During the 18th century their cabinetwork followed the French styles. Especially typical of Flanders are the fine spinning wheels or rouets and the hand-looms made of elaborately turned spindles. See *French Provincial*.

Flâneuse In French furniture; a French term, derived from the French word *flâner* meaning to lounge about, given to a form of lounge chair provided with a foot-rest, used in the garden. This chair, as illustrated in French furniture literature, was of similar construction and was practically identical in appearance to a modern deck chair. The back, seat and foot-rest were caned.

Flashing Or Casing. In glass; the name given to the method by which the gathering is dipped in another color before it is blown into glass, resulting in a surface layer of glass in a different color from that of the object. This coating is later partially cut through to form a design of a contrasting color. This technique was used for cameo glass and other forms of glass having a similar decorative effect. It is also possible to obtain a similar effect by cutting through a stained glass surface, such as stained glass windows.

Flask In American glass; a pictorial glass whiskey flask was extensively produced by American glass manufactories from about 1820 to 1880. It was a narrow-necked, bottle-shaped vessel, especially with a broad flat body of varying form. It was made in different colors and held a half pint, pint or quart of liquid. The flask was ornamented with portraits of early American presidents, famous persons, inscriptions and decorative designs. The flask is classified according to the decoration or portrait impressed in the glass, such as George Washington, Franklin, Lafayette, Jenny Lind, Zachary Taylor, American Eagle, masonic emblems, cornucopia, sailing ship and frigate. The approximate date of a flask can frequently be identified since it sometimes has the name of the glasshouse where it was made impressed in the glass.

Flat Carving In cabinetwork; carving in which only the background is cut away or taken out, leaving the design flat and level with the surface. See *Carving*.

Flat Point In lace-making; a general term applied to laces, which are made without any raised work. They are in direct contrast to the raised point laces. The name is also sometimes applied to Brussels bobbin lace.

Flaxman, John 1755–1826. English sculptor. He is particularly well known in the decorative arts for his designs in the Neo-Classic style which were used by craftsmen working in the different branches of the decorative arts, such as Paul Storr, who used many of his designs in his elaborate silver work. From 1775 to 1787 Flaxman was working at Josiah Wedgwood's pottery where he created decorative classical designs for earthenware pieces. Much of this work, which was executed in low relief, is noteworthy for the purity of its classic composition and for its delicate and refined workmanship.

Flemish Chair In Flemish cabinetwork; the name given to a characteristic Flemish armchair showing strong Baroque influence, introduced around the middle of the 17th century. It was a tall upright chair and was finely turned and carved and pierced with leaf scrolls and foliations. The turned uprights were surmounted with finials and were connected with a crested carved top rail and a carved bottom cross-piece, several inches above the seat rail, between which extended a carved openwork panel with a caned center. The open arms were frequently carved and scrolled, with conforming armposts. The seat was frequently caned and was broader in the front. The two front Flemish scrolled legs were connected with a broad, ornately carved, arched front stretcher, while a serpentine X-shaped stretcher connected the four legs. It was also designed as a side chair. Many of the Baroque features characteristic of this chair were incorporated in the Charles II Restoration chair and Carolean chair. See *Restoration Chair*.

Flemish Furniture See *Renaissance, Netherlands*.

Flemish Glass See *Dutch and Flemish Glass*.

Flemish Scroll In ornament; a scroll consisting of two Baroque reverse C-scrolls joined together at an angle. The Flemish scroll was much in evidence in late 16th and 17th century Flemish cabinetwork. The front legs on the Flemish chair were generally designed in the form of Flemish scrolls. See *Flemish Chair*.

Flemish Tapestries Tapestries were woven in Flanders from the 14th to the 19th centuries. See *Brussels Tapestries*; *Tournay Tapestries*; *Oudenarde Tapestries*; *Tapestry*.

Fleur-de-Lis In ornament; the French term for flower of the lily; the iris. The name was given to the floral design selected by Charles V of France, 1364–1380, as the royal emblem. The fleur-de-lis was a characteristic French Gothic motif.

Fleur de Pêcher A marble obtained from Seravezza, Tuscany. The name, meaning peach blossom, is given to a violet-colored marble, having green and white veins. This is a rare marble, not to be confused with the French marble of the same name. This marble is obtained only in small blocks. It is also called fior di persica.

Fleuri Marble See *Griotte d'Italie Marble*.

Fleur Volante In lace-making; a French term meaning flying flower applied to the minute loops ornamenting the cordonnet in the body of the pattern.

Flint Glass Or Lead Glass. In English glass; flint glass derived its name from the calcined flints which were the original siliceous ingredient used in its composition. Sand was soon substituted for the calcined flints, but the name *flint glass* continued to be used and is still used for the English glass having potash as an alkali and lead oxide as a fluxing agent. This flint glass, lead glass or crystal glass was softer than the German potash-lime glass and was therefore less adaptable for fine engravings. Undoubtedly the beauty of the material of flint glass has never been surpassed. It is the most colorless and brilliant of all glass. It differs from German and other

FLEMISH CHAIR

fine glass in that it is partly formed of a considerable quantity of lead which permits the glass to reflect light in a singular manner. The introduction of flint glass, 1676, marks the beginning of the period of artistic achievement in the history of English glass. The European leadership in glass was shared by England and Germany until well in the 19th century. The brilliance of flint glass had a decided advantage over Bohemian glass for cutting. Due to the vogue for cut glass, English cut glass enjoyed an excellent Continental market by the 19th century. See *Ravenscroft, George*; *Cut Glass*; *Glass*.

Flintlock See *Wheel-Lock*; *Snaphance*; *Fire-lock*.

Flintporslin In ceramics; a Swedish term for lead-glazed white or cream-colored earthenware in the English manner. See *Cream-Colored Earthenware*.

Flip The name applied to a dram glass or a mug to hold flip. Flip is an English drink composed chiefly of ale, beer, or cider, sweetened, spiced, and sometimes made with eggs. A poker-shaped iron called a flip dog is plunged into the liquor while it is hot and the flip is then drunk hot.

Flock Paper In wallpaper; a variety of wallpaper originating in France around 1620. The designs were drawn or stenciled in an adhesive mordant and then a colored flock, which is the same as powdered wool, was scattered over the entire surface. After the adhesive had dried the flock was brushed from the untreated surface. In this manner almost perfect imitations of Italian figured velvets, which were fashionable as wall coverings during the first half of the 18th century, were achieved. Especially fine were the red flock designs on a white or ivory ground, distinctive for their velvet-like texture and slightly raised surface. Flock papers were found in England from around 1660 onwards and the finest were made in the period from about 1720 to 1750. The taste for flock papers did not develop in France until around 1750 when they became very

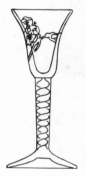

FLOWERED GLASS

fashionable until around 1780. Silk flock papers using a silk waste were made in France during that period. After 1780 flock papers were no longer in vogue. See *Wallpaper*.

Florence In Italian ceramics; see *Caffaggiolo*; *Tuscany*; *Medici Porcelain*.

Florida Porcelain See *La Moncloa*.

Flörsheim In German ceramics; a faïence manufactory which is still in existence was established at Flörsheim, near Frankfurt-on-Main, in 1765 by Georg Ludwig Müller. It was sold in 1773 to the Carthusian Monastery of Mayence and managed by Caspar Dreste. The monks leased the factory and finally sold it in 1797. The accepted mark on the faïence was "FH" in monogram. The production ranged from useful wares and jugs painted in a peasant manner in blue or in high-temperature colors to elaborate table centers decorated in openwork. Some of the faïence was also painted in enamel or muffle colors. Cream-colored earthenware was also made and bore the impressed mark of a bunch of grapes with "MIW"

Flower Box In English cabinetwork; a decorative wooden box or stand in which bulbs were raised, introduced during the reign of Charles II. The early flower box was frequently either lacquered or painted and enriched with carved gilded ornament. As a rule during the 18th century it was semi-circular in form and was either fitted with glasses for raising the bulbs or was lined with zinc. The decoration was in accordance with the successive 18th century styles of ornament.

Flowered Glass In English glass; a trade name given to a variety of crystal tableware made from about 1740 to 1780 that was engraved with realistic flowers on the bowl. The early flowered glass was generally decorated with a single engraved flower. After the middle of the 18th century the other side of the bowl was often engraved with a butterfly, a bird or some similar subject.

Flush Beading In cabinetwork; a bead molding or a small convex molding that is flush with the surface. See *Cockbeading*; *Bead*.

Flute In Venetian glass; a tall, slender, cone-shaped wine glass with the bowl attached to the foot by a circular knop. It was used especially for sparkling wines and it was introduced in England from the Continent during the 17th century.

Fluting In cabinetwork; parallel grooves or furrows cut out of the surface of a piece of wood. The grooves, which should be very close together, are usually half round or rectangular; the former being the more desirable shape. Fluting is the opposite of reeding. Fluting was a favorite decorative detail on furniture designed in the Adam style. As a rule the chair leg designed in the Louis XVI style was round and tapered and was fluted vertically and occasionally spirally.

Folding Spoon In English silver; a spoon which folds in half above the shoulders. Sometimes it has a finely wrought metal case which conforms in shape to the folded spoon. It was introduced during the 14th century.

Folwell, John An American cabinetmaker working in Philadelphia and producing fine pieces in the Chippendale style. See *Philadelphia Chippendale*.

Fond In lace-making; a French term meaning ground or groundwork given to the ground of needle-made or bobbin-made laces as distinct from the design or toile. Grounds are generally grouped into fond claire, bride claire and bride ornée. Included in the fond claire is the réseau or network ground.

Fond Chant In lace-making; the name given to a six-pointed star réseau or ground. It is a distinctive feature of Chantilly lace, *chant* being an abbreviation for Chantilly. This ground is sometimes more clearly described as diamond-shaped and crossed by two horizontal threads.

Fond de Neige A kind of ground used in lace-making, having a snow-like appearance. It is also known as Oeil de Perdrix.

Fond Ecaille In French ceramics; the French term given to a tortoise shell brown high-temperature glaze used on hard paste porcelain from about 1775 made at Sèvres.

Fondi d'Oro In glass; the Italian name given to a principal method of decorating glass by the use of gold foil. It was first employed during the Roman Empire. The technique consists of applying to a sheet of glass gold leaf which is cut out with a pointed instrument to form a design. A second layer of glass is then applied, permanently enclosing the design. German glassmakers during the 18th century successfully revived the technique, adding silver leaf and sometimes lacquer colors. In German the technique is also called zwischengoldgläser. See *Glass*; *Doppelwandglas*; *Venetian Glass*.

Fond Simple A ground in lace; it is the thinnest, simplest and most transparent of all grounds. It consists of a hexagonal mesh, four sides of which are made by twisting two threads around each other, and the other two sides by the crossing of the threads over each other. This ground was widely used in the laces made at Lille, France.

Fontaine, Pierre François Léonard 1762–1853, French architect. The French Empire style was established in Paris by Fontaine and Percier, who were engaged by Napoleon during the Consulate, 1799–1804, to remodel and redecorate the palace, Malmaison. Included among their publications were: PALAIS, MAISONS, ET AUTRES EDIFICES DE ROME MODERNE, 1802; RECUEIL DE DÉCORATIONS INTÉRIEURES, 1812. Fontaine as architect to Napoleon I, Louis XVIII and Louis Philippe, was engaged in the principal architectural works erected in Paris during that long time. See *Empire*; *David, Jacques Louis*.

Fontainebleau Tapestries Tapestries woven at Fontainebleau, France. In 1539, François I established a Royal Manufactory at Fon-

FOLDING SPOON

tainebleau. One of the principal designers was Claude Baudouin, and among the weavers were Jean and Pierre Lebries. See *Tapestry*.

Food Cupboard In cabinetwork; it is the same as a livery cupboard. See *Livery Cupboard*.

Foot A term applied in architecture, furniture, silver, etc., to that part of a piece that resembles a foot, due to its use or position. In architecture it is the lowest part or base of a column. In silver it is the base or bottom of a silver vessel such as the lowest part of a tankard, a jug or a teapot. In cabinetwork it is the lowest part or base of an article of furniture such as the lowest part of a chair leg, a cupboard or a chest of drawers. See *Claw and Ball*; *Ball Foot*; *Bar Foot*; *Bracket Foot*; *Bun Foot*; *Cloven Hoof Foot*; *Club Foot*; *Disc Foot*; *Drake Foot*; *Dutch Foot*; *French Whorl Foot*; *Hoof Foot*; *Melon Foot*; *Onion Foot*; *Pad Foot*; *Paw and Ball Foot*; *Paw Foot*; *Ribbed Foot*; *Runner Foot*; *Slipper Foot*; *Snake Foot*; *Spade Foot*; *Web Foot*; *Pied de Biche*; *Plinth Foot*.

Footman In English furniture; an oblong or oval metal stand usually made of brass or polished steel placed in front of a fireplace. It served to keep the dishes warm in the days before spirit burners and hot-water dishes came into general use.

Footrail In cabinetwork; the name sometimes given colloquially to a kind of plain heavy stretcher close to the floor that could be used to rest the feet upon. It was an early form of stretcher and was principally used during the Renaissance on chairs and tables. See *Box Stretcher*.

Footstool In cabinetwork; the footstool had its origin in antiquity. It was used in ancient Greek and Roman times to mount the couches which were relatively high, and as a foot-rest for the lofty throne chairs occupied by exalted personages. During the late Gothic era footstools began to replace the foot carpets and cushions which were

sometimes used as foot-rests. Footstools were used to a greater or less extent in all the succeeding centuries and they varied from relatively elaborate to simple utilitarian pieces. Of particular interest and characteristically Dutch were the many foot-warmers which could also serve as footstools.

Fork In silver; the fork as an instrument for manipulating food at the table was introduced in England around 1635, although it had been used in several of the Continental countries many years earlier. The early fork was small in size, and until the second quarter of the 18th century it was made with two, three or four prongs. The fork gradually grew larger and later in the 18th century in England the two sizes which are known as dinner and dessert forks were in use and generally had four prongs. The stem of the silver fork invariably followed the pattern of the contemporary spoon. See *Spoon*.

Form Or Forme. In cabinetwork; a long narrow wooden bench without a back. It was an important article of Gothic furniture and its primary function was to seat guests at the long dining table. The form was made throughout the Renaissance and it was still very often of Gothic construction, having an oblong molded top with traverses keyed through truss end supports.

Forme See *Form*.

Four-Poster In American cabinetwork; a colloquial term applied to a bed having four high posts. Sheraton states in his CABINET DICTIONARY, 1803, that a four-post bed is "a name for all such as are used in common lodging rooms that have feet and head posts." See *Bed*.

Fractur In decorative arts; a term applied, in a broad sense, to the various forms of decorative writing done by the Pennsylvania Germans, evolved from the European medieval art of illuminated handwritten manuscripts. The name is derived from *fraktur-schrift*, the German term for a decora-

TWO PRONG FORK 1709

THREE PRONG FORK 1683

FOUR PRONG FORK 1678

tive calligraphy which received its name from a 16th century type face called fractur, that succeeded the more rigid Gothic type face. This fractur art as practiced by the Pennsylvania Germans throughout the 18th century was done entirely by hand until about the end of the century when the text portion was produced by the printing press. The fractur writers or scribes practiced their individual style of calligraphy which ranged from a crude form to the extremely fine work usually done by schoolmasters and ministers. The decorative designs on these illuminated certificates and manuscripts include a wide variety of subjects and motifs executed in a naïve peasant manner. The most popular were conventionalized floral motifs, with the tulip as the predominating flower form. Included among the other favorite decorative motifs were birds, human and animal figures, angels and cherubs. The colors were strong and brilliant, with a marked preference for red. The Tree of Life motif was much used with birds perched on branches having leaves and flowers of various species on the same tree. The taufschein, a baptismal certificate, executed in the fractur art, displayed a great variety of decorative designs. A birth certificate is called a geburts-schein, and a marriage certificate is called a trauschein. The vorschrift is the beautifully handwritten manuscript executed by the country schoolmaster to teach children how to form the letters and numerals in fractur writing and German script. See *Tree of Life*.

Frailero In Spanish cabinetwork; the frailero or monk's chair was the most characteristic variety of Spanish Renaissance chair. It was a walnut rectangular armchair. It was made of plain quadrangular supports and had a broad front stretcher which was its most distinguishing feature. A leather back panel was stretched between the upright supports and a leather seat panel was stretched between the side rails; both the seat and back panel were securely fastened with decorative nailheads. In some of the more elaborate examples the leather was covered with

velvet. The upright supports were frequently surmounted with finials. The arms were usually straight and very wide. The frame of the earliest frailero was so constructed as to be collapsible so that it could be carried on a journey. Variations in design occurred.

Framea The name given to an ancient spear of German origin used both as a javelin and as a hand weapon. It was an iron lance set in a wooden shaft.

Franche-Comté In French Provincial; a former province in eastern France bordering on Switzerland. It is now in the departments of Jura, Doubs, Haute-Saône and part of Ain. The provincial furniture of Franche-Comté was essentially similar to that of Bresse, with the earlier Renaissance pieces being similar to those of Burgundy. See *Bresse*; *Burgundy*; *French Provincial*.

François I King of France from 1515 to 1547. The name is given to one of the three principal styles of ornament of the French Renaissance. The style was always varied and vivid with abundant decorative fancy which gave it a singular charm. The furniture of François I was notable for its exuberant and fanciful decoration; for the varied and graceful composition of its ornamentation and the fine detail work of its carvings. The furniture was characterized by the stability and simplicity of its construction. It was rectilinear and massive in form. The form remained essentially Gothic. Carving and inlay were the chief decorative processes, the former being by far the favorite method. The ornament was classic and was borrowed from the Italian Renaissance. In the beginning favorite Gothic motifs such as carved linen-fold panels and fenestrations were combined with the classic motifs. Included among the classic motifs commonly used were; the acanthus leaf, arabesques, rinceaux, foliated scrolls, cartouches, vase forms, candelabra, rosettes and shells. Figures in many various forms were used, such as human, animal and mythological figures, half figures terminating in

MOTIF
FROM BIRTH CERTIFICATE

scrolls, caryatids, winged cherubs and all kinds of fanciful conceptions such as chimeras, satyrs and griffons. The medallion motif was characteristic of François I; it was a head or a bust of a man or woman in profile or in full face and was carved in varying degrees of relief. See *Henri II*; *Louis XIII*; *Renaissance, French*.

Frankenthal In German ceramics; a porcelain manufactory regarded as one of the seven great 18th century German porcelain factories was established in 1755 by Paul-Antoine Hannong with a privilege from the Elector Palatine, Karl Theodor, at Frankenthal. It closed in 1799 after many changes in management, and the molds were removed to Grünstadt. The marks corresponded to the different periods in the history of the factory. From 1755 to 1759 the mark was "PH" and the lion or shield from the Elector's arms; from 1759 to 1762 "IH" incised or impressed, or "JAH" in blue with or without the lion; 1762 to 1793 the initials "CT" under an Electoral Hat in blue with the addition between 1770–1788, of a numeral for the year; and 1794 to 1799 the initials of the van Recums who were the last to operate the manufactory. Its finest period was from 1755 to 1775. The porcelain material was a hard paste of fine quality having a rather creamy white color. The glaze was thin and did not obscure the details of the modelling of figures which were the principal interest of the manufactory. The figures revealed exquisite workmanship, an admirable feeling for the plastic quality of a porcelain model and a lavish use of detail. As a rule the decorative pieces such as vases and also the tablewares were of fine quality. The flower and figure painting were notable; the latter was always a feature of Frankenthal decoration. The wares to a greater or less extent retained their highly individual character almost until 1780, after which the classical style as interpreted in Sèvres porcelain was the predominating influence.

Frankfurt-on-Main In German ceramics; a faïence manufactory, one of the oldest and most important in Germany, was established here in 1666 by Johann Simonet under the patronage of Johann Christoph Fehr. It changed ownership several times and finally closed around 1772. The letter "F" was used enough to be generally accepted as a factory mark. The factory's chief claim to fame is due to the faïence made from around 1666 to 1723. The early ware was in imitation of Delft faïence and has often been commonly mistaken for Delft. The finer varieties were painted in blue or in blue and purple with designs derived from the blue and white Chinese late Ming. From these were eventually developed original and beautiful designs that generally can be distinguished by the presence of a motif of prickly lotus leaves. They made large dishes with wide flat rims and deep wells frequently painted with Biblical or other figure subjects and jugs finely painted in purple occasionally with Biblical subjects. Some of the most characteristic types were similar to those of the neighboring town of Hanau such as lobed and reeded dishes, armorial jugs and jugs with narrow necks or the so-called Enghalskrug. See *Delft*; *Enghalskrug*.

Franklin Fly Whisk An 18th century device attached to a chair and used to whisk away flies. It is supposed to have been an invention of Benjamin Franklin. It is made of wood, and has a treadle attached to the front and rear stretchers of a chair. A long, slender, upright, wood shaft rises at the back of the chair, with a wooden arm at the top, which extends towards the front; this arm is fitted with a fan-like piece which moves by working the treadle with the foot.

Frechen In German ceramics; an important center for Rhenish stoneware. Late in the 16th century the potteries for making stoneware at Cologne were removed to nearby Frechen. Especially characteristic of their production from the late 16th century were globular Bartmann jugs decorated with the coats-of-arms of Cologne, Cleves, Amsterdam and other places. They continued to produce and export these Bartmann jugs

FRANKFURT-ON-MAIN
ENGHALSKRUG

throughout the 17th and into the 18th centuries. See *Cologne*.

Free-Blown Glass The name given to blown glass that is handled manually with shaping and measuring tools, in distinction to the blown glass which receives its shape in a mold. Free-blown glass is also called hand-blown glass. See *Blown-Molded*.

Freedom Box In English silver; a small shallow gold or silver box most frequently of either cylindrical or oval form. In the 18th century it was the custom in some boroughs to present to a person of distinction who was enrolled as a freeman, a vellum certificate recording his enrollment, enclosed within one of these boxes. The box usually was engraved with the arms of the borough.

Freiberg In German ceramics; a distinctive variety of grey stoneware jugs were made here in the latter part of the 17th century. They were decorated with bands or panels of carved ornament consisting of geometrical designs and rosettes enamelled in white, black, light blue and red. They were often enriched with contemporary finely embossed pewter mounts. Due to the combination of black and white the misleading name of *mourning jug* or *Trauerkruge* was applied to these jugs.

French Bracket Foot See *Bracket Foot*.

French Carpet See *Savonnerie Carpet*; *Aubusson Carpet*.

French Polish See *Polish*; *Varnish*.

French Porcelain In French ceramics; the earliest porcelain made in France is composed of the unsurpassable soft pastes first made at Rouen around 1673 and at Saint-Cloud perhaps as early as 1677, and later at Chantilly and Mennecy and the earliest Vincennes, 1738–1753. Probably the finest and most finished soft paste porcelain was produced at Sèvres from 1753 to 1772. It is generally accepted that the productions of Saint-Cloud, Chantilly, Mennecy, Vincennes and early Sèvres rank among the finest porcelains ever produced. The Duc de Brancas made the first French hard paste porcelain in his laboratory at the Château de Lassay about 1763 to 1768. Sèvres first produced hard paste porcelain in 1768. After 1770 and onwards the production of hard paste porcelain steadily increased. From about 1772 to 1800 both hard paste and soft paste porcelain were made concurrently in France. See *Soft Paste*; *Porcelain*.

French Provincial French provincial furniture was a more or less skillful interpretation of the prevailing fashions adopted in Paris. Household possessions were relatively few in the provinces until around the middle of the 17th century. The Louis XIII style was essentially the first French style developed in the provinces. Provincial cabinetmakers working in the Louis XIII style produced chairs with straw or wooden seats, stools, tables and cupboards. Turning was the principal method used for decorating the surfaces of this furniture. Spiral turning was the most common and baluster turning the most artistic. The cupboard was undoubtedly the most important article of 17th century provincial furniture. Geometrical carved ornament, especially the diamond point and star diamond point, was used to decorate the panelled cupboard doors. Furniture designed in the Louis XIII style was made for the middle classes for practically a century until it was supplanted by the Louis XV style. In certain regions, especially in Gascogne and Guienne, it lasted much longer. In fact in these two provinces it remained their favorite style. Although it is generally accepted that cabinetmakers working in the provinces were familiar with the Louis XIV style it was not adopted by the people in the country to any appreciable extent because of its sumptuous character. However, a large number of imposing Louis XIV style cupboards were found in the provincial dwellings of the middle classes as well as simpler armchairs with turned members having the general lines of the Louis XIV style. The Louis XV style, which could easily be modified to suit the needs of all classes of society,

LOUIS XIII CUPBOARD
GASCOGNE

flourished in almost every province. In fact it has always been the favorite provincial style. It retained its popularity in some provinces such as Provence into the early 19th century. Louis XV style provincial furniture was characterized by its graceful lines and flexible moldings, by its good constructional methods and materials and by the originality of its decoration. When the Louis XVI style came into fashion many provincial cabinetmakers never advanced beyond the transitional phase. In these pieces the influence of the Louis XVI style was evident only in the Louis XVI carved classic ornament, for the shapes retained their graceful curving lines of the Louis XV style. Many large provincial cities did completely adopt the Louis XVI style; this was especially evident in chair design. The Directoire style and particularly the French Empire style were not adopted in the provinces to any appreciable extent. The majority of provincial cabinetmakers continued to produce furniture designed in the Louis XV and Louis XVI styles until the machine age gradually forced the closing of their shops. The local originality found in the furniture was more pronounced in some provinces than in others. However, it is important to remember that the similarity existing in all provincial furniture was by far more marked than its differences. The diversity of regional tastes was found principally in the decorative details. The articles of furniture were much the same in all the provinces for the people in each respective social class. In some of the poorer provinces, such as Auvergne and Brittany, much of the furniture was so-called rustique, while in the wealthier provinces, such as Provence, Normandy and Saintonge, the bourgeois had many of the fashionable pieces originating in Paris, but more simply treated. Most of the furniture was made in native solid woods, such as walnut, oak, wild cherry, beech and fruit woods. Included among some of the characteristic regional pieces were the chaise à capucine, armoire, buffet-vaisselier, buffet bas, pétrin and panetière. The furniture was marked by good

LOUIS XV BUFFET BAS
NORMANDY

workmanship. Provincial furniture should display some provincial character generally held to be distinct from the national character in order to be classified as provincial. See *Alsace*; *Angoumois*; *Artois*; *Auvergne*; *Basque*; *Beaujolais*; *Bresse*; *Brittany*; *Burgundy*; *Champagne*; *Dauphiné*; *Flandre*; *Franche-Comté*; *Gascogne*; *Languedoc*; *Limousin*; *Lorraine*; *Lyonnais*; *Normandy*; *Périgord*; *Picardy*; *Poitou*; *Provence*; *Saintonge*; *Savoie*; *Vendée*; *Rustique*; *Regional Furniture*.

French Whorl Foot In French cabinetmaking; the name given to a kind of foot that swirled or whorled forward. It rested on a small plain piece of wood called a shoe. It was used on cabriole legs and was introduced during the Régence. As a rule English furniture such as chairs and settees designed in the French taste having cabriole legs terminated in a French whorl foot.

Frêne Wood The wood of the ash tree, *fraxinus excelsior*, used for cabinetwork, especially by the French ébénistes. It is hard, and its color is white and yellowish-brown striped.

Fresco In art; *fresco* is an Italian word meaning fresh; it refers to the method of painting on freshly applied plaster while it is still wet; specifically called buono fresco or true fresco. The pigments are put on with water, and the lime of the ground by penetrating the paint is changed by exposure into a carbonate which functions as a binding material. Another method, but not as satisfactory, specifically called fresco secco, permits the plaster to harden and to be practically dry before the painting is started. In this method lime water is used to mix the pigments and dampen the ground before beginning to paint. Fresco paintings are durable only in a dry and pure atmosphere. By extension the term is applied to painting on plaster in any method.

Fresquera In Spanish cabinetwork; a Spanish ventilated domestic food cupboard. A characteristic variety was rectangular in form and rather shallow and hung on the wall; the upper division in each of the two cupboard doors was designed with a row of turned spindles or lattice-work. It was a well-proportioned piece of furniture and was distinctive for its graceful simplicity.

Fret In ornament; the name given to a wide variety of decorative designs composed of small straight geometrical lines or bars. The Greek fret, which was much used by the Greeks and Romans, consists of a series of small straight lines or bands of various length placed at right angles to each other. The fret was also used in China and in Japan. In Japan, where the fret design was much used on lacquer and ceramic wares, the lines were placed obliquely forming acute and obtuse angles. It is also called key pattern.

Fretwork In cabinetwork; the term is applied to wood cut into decorative patterns which vary in intricacy from the simple to the complex. Fretwork was used either as a perforated ornament or on a solid ground. Both styles of fretwork were freely used either in the structure or in the ornament of mahogany furniture designed in either the Chinese or the Gothic taste by Chippendale. Occasionally both styles of fretwork were employed on the same piece of cabinetwork. See *Card-Cut*; *Lattice-Work*.

Fretwork Mirror It was a favorite wall mirror in America. The majority were made of mahogany during the second half of the 18th century. It had an upright molded frame with a fret-scrolled cresting, which was commonly arched and a conformingly shaped fret-cut base. Essentially it was a plainer type of mirror and the variations in shape and in decoration were slight. Occasionally there was a narrow gilded molding next to the mirror plate. Frequently the cresting and valanced base centered a carved motif such as a shell. The fretwork mirror is generally regarded as a Chippendale style mirror unless it displayed some characteristic design feature of a later style. See *Elliott, John*.

Friar's Chair See *Frailero*.

Friesian The name given to the wheel-form scratch carving used during Colonial days by the Pennsylvania Germans to ornament Bible boxes, chests and other similar articles.

Frieze In cabinetmaking; the term *frieze*, which is an architectural term, is applied to the flat band beneath the cornice of a bookcase, a cabinet or some other similar article of furniture, or to the flat band beneath the top of a table. As a rule it is enriched with carving or some other decorative process.

Fringe The use of fringe as a decorative bordering in upholstery work was widespread. It was found on valances for windows and tester bedsteads, on loose cushions, on draperies for windows, on chairs, settees, benches and stools, as well as on other similar pieces. Fringe consists of a narrow band to which are attached silk threads worked in different methods. An early form of fringe was a loose fringe having straight silk strands sometimes mixed with metal threads. Deep or narrow tasselled or tufted fringes having tassels or balls of silk floss were introduced in England from the Continent after the Restoration in 1660. These deep tasselled and tufted fringes were especially fashionable for the elaborate festooned valances found on the late 17th century tester bedsteads. It appears that the making of fringes was a fashionable recreation for ladies toward the end of the 17th century. The vogue for fringe seemed to disappear after the first decade of the 18th century, but was revived in the last years of the 18th century, when the fashion for fringe in France became especially pronounced. This taste for fringe during the Empire style was an unhappy omen of things to come in the Victorian era.

Frit In ceramics; the glassy ingredient of soft paste porcelain. Sometimes it is made of the separate ingredients of glass and sometimes it includes actual broken glass fused and powdered before it is mixed with the clay. In glass; the term *frit* is applied to

CHIPPENDALE
FRETWORK MIRROR

prepared materials ready for founding; also to those materials partially fused and set aside to be used later. See *Soft Paste*.

Frog Mug A small English earthenware drinking mug, having a figure of a frog modelled on the inside. It was made in the 18th century at Sunderland, Leeds and other potteries.

Fromanteel, Ahasuerus Eminent clockmaker. Although it has not been conclusively proven, it is generally believed that he was the first clockmaker to introduce pendulum clocks in England in 1658. It is said that Vincenzio Galilei, whose father Galileo Galilei discovered the pendulum as a regulator in 1639, set up the first pendulum clock in Venice in 1649. However, it seems that the invention never gained prominence until Christian Huygens van Zulichem, 1625–1695, the well-known Dutch mathematician, made a pendulum clock in 1657. His friend Fromanteel saw it and introduced it in England.

Frontal In ecclesiastical art; a hanging panel of silk or a decorative movable panel placed in front of an altar. There were three kinds of frontals; namely, a frontal of metal enriched with precious stones and enamels, a frontal of carved wood brilliantly painted and gilded and occasionally enhanced with crystal, and a frontal of a rich fabric, such as gold cloth, silk or velvet, elaborately embroidered with sacred imagery and occasionally enhanced with pearls. Frontals of either metal or carved wood were often exquisite specimens of Christian art. The frontals made of a rich fabric occurred most frequently and were remarkable for their magnificent needlework of sacred ornament suitable to the various seasons and festivals. It is said that the frontals of cloth had their origin in curtains drawn in front of the altar in reverence to the shrines generally kept there and that gradually the curtains were replaced by a hanging panel. Frontals were of an early date and medieval church inventories describe their rich designs and materials.

STAFFORDSHIRE
SET OF TEN CONJOINED
FUDDLING CUPS

Frothingham, Benjamin 1734–c. 1790. American cabinetmaker working in Charlestown, Massachusetts, circa 1756. He is recorded as a maker of Chippendale style pieces.

Fruitwood A general term applied to the various woods of fruit-bearing trees; such as lemon, lime, etc., that were used in cabinetmaking.

Fu In Chinese art; the Chinese bat which expresses happiness and good fortune was widely used as a decorative motif in Chinese ceramics, sculpture and painting. See *Chinese Animal Figures*.

Fuchi In Japanese sword mounts; the ornamental band on the hilt of a Japanese sword or dagger next to the tsuba or guard. The fuchi was usually elaborately ornamented like the other mountings and was generally ornamented to match the kashira. The fuchi and kashira were usually made by the same artist. See *Kashira*.

Fuddling Cup A name given to an English earthenware puzzle cup. It consists of a group of cups, joined together in such a manner that when all the cups are filled, all the liquid can be drunk from any one of the cups. The word *fuddle* means to tipple, to booze, or to have a drinking bout.

Fuddling Glass See *Coaching Glass*.

Fu-hsing In Chinese art; a Taoist deity. See *Lu-hsing*; *Chinese Gods*.

Fujiwara Late Heian period in Japan, A.D. 897–1185. See *Japanese Periods*.

Fukien In Chinese ceramics; the province of Fukien has been renowned for its potteries from early days. See *Chien Yao*; *Blanc de Chine*.

Fulda In German pottery; a faïence manufactory supported by the Prince-Bishop of Fulda was founded at Fulda, Hesse, in 1741 when the Meissen painter Adam Friedrich von Lowenfinck and his brother Karl Heinrich came from Bayreuth to Fulda. The manufactory achieved great distinction and closed in 1758 due to the troubles caused by the Seven Years War. The tin glaze was of a fine quality. The most typical decoration was in a Fulda-Chinese style and was painted in enamel colors and gold. It was distinctive for its fineness and brilliance. The Chinese Famille Verte porcelain was the principal inspiration for this decoration; however, the individual talent of the Fulda artists imbued it with some original quality. Painting in high temperature colors and painting in blue with manganese purple outlines was also done. Figure modelling was also practiced at Fulda. Factory marks were sometimes but not always used and included "FD" and "Fuld" with painters' marks.

Fulda In German porcelain; a porcelain manufatory of great distinction was founded at Fulda in 1765 under the patronage of the Prince-Bishop of Fulda at the request of Johann Philipp Schick, who also had a considerable share in the founding and directing of the Fulda faïence manufactory. It was active until 1790. The marks were in sequence a cross from the arms of the city; two "F's" in a monogram forming an "H" under an Electoral Hat and two crossed "F's" forming an "A". The principal qualities identified with Fulda porcelain are the remarkable fineness and flawlessness both in the paste and in the glaze, and the extraordinarily careful and finished workmanship. The figures made at Fulda are among the most costly and highly prized of all German porcelain. The finer figures and groups seem to have been made from around 1768 to 1775 and are generally marked with a cross. They are distinctive for their delicate modelling and for their lightly painted fresh and clean harmonious colors. Shepherds and shepherdesses, figures from the Italian Comedy, elegantly dressed ladies and gentlemen and many others are among the exquisite and doll-like figures and groups. The tablewares revealed the same fine quality in material and in workmanship as the figures. The decoration, which showed little originality, included Meissen flowers, landscapes and monochrome, and en grisaille figure painting.

Fulham In English ceramics; stoneware has been manufactured at Fulham, Middlesex, from 1671 until the present time. The establishment of a pottery at Fulham was due to John Dwight, d. 1703, who took out a patent in 1671 and renewed it in 1684 for the manufacture of stoneware. Especially noteworthy are a distinctive series of figures made at Fulham. The Fulham pottery remained in the hands of Dwight's family until 1864, when it was bought by C. I. Bailey. The productions by Dwight fall into two principal types or groups. One group consists of a series of busts and statues fabricated in salt-glazed stoneware. The other group is composed of useful wares which vary from small mugs made in a fine translucent stoneware to rather coarse imitations of the Rhenish Bartmann or Bellarmine stoneware jugs. The figures which rank among the best contemporary plastic art were of a greyish white or buff-colored stoneware. Since his wares were always unmarked it is difficult to conjecture the extent of his manufacture of useful wares. In addition to the Bellarmines other authenticated pieces include small mugs some of which are a plain slightly brownish white and others are mottled with patches of brown and blue. After Dwight's death it seems that only ordinary wares were made at Fulham such as beer jugs and heavy cylindrical tankards with a drab colored body, the upper part being covered with an iron brown and salt-glazed and commonly decorated with clumsy applied reliefs.

Fulham Tapestries Tapestries woven at Fulham, England, circa 1750. Père Parisot established a tapestry manufactory at Fulham circa 1750. See *Tapestry*.

Fu Lion In Chinese Art; the lion or shih or shih tzŭ. See *Dog of Fo*.

Fumed Oak Oak that has been darkened by the vapor of ammonia.

FULDA GROUP

Fumeuse In French cabinetwork; a distinctive form of 18th century chair similar in its principles of design to the voyeuse and chaise à accoudoir. It is characterized by a narrow shaped back and a broad crest rail, the latter being either provided with, or in the form of, a box-like compartment to hold pipes, tobacco and other smoking accessories. In this type of chair the occupant sits in a reverse position and rests his arms on the wide crest rail. See *Voyeuse*; *Chaise à Accoudoir*; *Ponteuse*.

Fundame In Japanese lacquer; fine gold and silver powder worked in the lacquer and rubbed to produce a flat, dull finish on the surface. See *Japanese Lacquer*.

Fürstenberg In German ceramics; a porcelain manufactory regarded as one of the seven most important in Germany during the 18th century was established in 1747 by Duke Carl I of Brunswick. It was scarcely active before 1753 and enjoyed its most flourishing period between 1770 and 1814. It is still in existence. The mark of a cursive "F" in underglaze blue was generally used on all but the very early wares; after and around 1770 a running horse impressed was used on the biscuit busts. The productions of the early period, 1753 to 1768, were characterized by the skillful use of numerous relief patterns such as Rococo scrollwork. Of particular interest were some well-modelled porcelain figures. Clock cases, candlesticks and vases were all modelled in the most fantastic Rococo forms. Vases were always an important feature of Fürstenberg productions. The best work as an entirety was done from 1768 to 1795. The painting was frequently copied from engraved designs and was often done in monochrome. Landscapes, figure subjects, groups of birds and flowers were favorite motifs for the painted decoration. Figures were made in considerable numbers. A specialty were the carefully modelled biscuit medallions and busts of illustrious French and German contemporary persons and of scholars and poets from antiquity. The last period of artistic interest, about 1795 to 1814, and often referred to as the Classical period, was marked by a more exacting devotion to the antique.

Fusain Wood The wood of the spindle tree, *euonymus europaeus*, used in cabinetwork, especially by the French ébénistes. It is also used for spindles and skewers. It is hard and its color is pale yellow.

FÜRSTENBERG VASE

Gabri Ware In ceramics; see *Persian and Near Eastern Pottery*.

Gadroon An architectural term which means a convex decoration. In cabinetwork; the term is applied to a running or continuous ornament that is generally convex and rarely concave. Essentially it is a pattern of ridges. It was frequently carved on the edges of furniture such as on the edge of a table top. Moldings carved with gadrooning were a feature of Italian Renaissance cabinetwork and were much used on the finely carved walnut cassoni. Gadrooning was first employed in England during the 16th century and was a characteristic form of decoration for the bulbous supports. In silver; gadrooning, either hammered or cast, was frequently used as a decorative treatment for the edge of a plate or for the rim of a bowl. Occasionally gadrooning radiated from the top center of the cover of a vase or from the bottom of the body of a silver vase. In glass; a molded gadrooning was occasionally employed as a decorative feature. It was impressed on a second thin layer of applied glass, and was a popular method for ornamenting English and American glass. In needlework; the term is applied to the raised part of the fabric which has been done by means of stitches. It is also spelled godroon.

Gallé, Emile 1846–1904. French artist glassmaker of Nancy, who ranks high on the list of artists using glass as a medium of artistic expression. In his style of indefinite cloudings of more or less opaque colors he rejected the use of clear glass. He employed as decorative processes flashing, etching, and wheel engraving and much less frequently enamel painting. His floral motifs were naturalistically treated and were imbued with a remarkable freedom and imagination. He is especially noted for his carved or cameo glass. Some of this work was executed with more than one layer of different colored glass, producing an unusual and effective blending of colors as the different colors were revealed by cutting.

Gallery In cabinetwork; a decorative railing around the edge of a table, a shelf, a tray or some other similar object. Delicately pierced wooden galleries of fretwork or of baluster-form spindles were much employed on tea tables of tripod form designed by Chippendale. Finely pierced metal galleries were a feature of the Louis XVI style, such as on a bouillotte table, the bureau à cylindre and the commode-desserte.

Gallipot In ceramics; the name given to a kind of jar that has a small mouth and a short neck. The elongated body is wider at the shoulders than at the base. The gallipot was a characteristic Chinese form.

Gama Ishime In Japanese sword mounts; a form of decoration covering the surface of the background of metal used for Japanese sword mounts. It is characterized by its resemblance to the skin of a toad. See *Ishime*; *Nanako*.

Gaming Table See *Card Table*; *Backgammon Board*; *Billiard Table*; *Tric-Trac Table*.

Garde-Manger In French cabinetwork; an upright, rectilinear, ventilated food cupboard. It was generally designed with one and occasionally with two long cupboard doors. Either the sides or the doors were spindled or pierced to provide the necessary ventilation. See *Livery Cupboard*; *Panetière*.

Garden Rug The general name given to a Persian Oriental made in the 16th and 17th centuries, having elaborately detailed designs depicting a Persian garden with its flowers, orchard and park, and with obvious axial avenues and paths. See *Persian Rugs*.

Garden Seat or Barrel-Shaped Seat In Chinese furniture; the barrel-shaped garden seat or liang tun meaning cool seat, in the

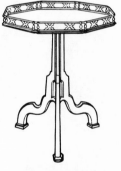

CHIPPENDALE TABLE
WITH GALLERY

form of an ancient drum, is of very early origin. It appears that barrel-shaped seats made of stone were placed around massive oblong stone altar tables from the early Sung dynasty and probably much earlier. Liang tun made of granite were also the customary garden seats from early times and were placed around stone garden tables with square tops. The sides of these stone garden seats generally had lion mask ring handles carved in relief or circular openings. Barrel-shaped seats made of porcelain were highly esteemed, for it is stated in the T'ao Shou, "We find that when, during the Sung dynasty, the Minister of State, Wang Kuei, had audience of the Emperor in the Jui-chu Hall of the Palace, he was given a porcelain barrel-shaped seat painted purple and commanded to be seated." Porcelain barrel-shaped seats were chiefly decorated in polychrome enamels, in openwork designs filled in with color, and in underglaze blue and white. The latter is especially characteristic of the Wan Li reign. An openwork barrel-shaped seat made of wood, frequently rosewood or hua-li, was also a fashionable article of furniture in the Chinese home. The openwork designs on these seats were remarkable for their refined and striking simplicity.

MING GARDEN SEAT

Garderobe See *Wardrobe*.

Garfagnana Marble, Rosso A marble from Tuscany, Italy. A pink and white ground variegated marble, having numerous dark reddish brown veins. Also called molina rosa.

Garnier, Pierre c. 1720–. A French ébéniste who received his master in 1742. He is regarded as one of the most famous cabinetmakers of his time and until 1789 he is known to have been producing the finest of work for the aristocracy. Especially praiseworthy were his veneered pieces decorated with a marquetry of flowers.

Gascogne In French Provincial; an old province in south-western France, formed by the Bay of Biscay on the west and on the south by the Pyrenees in the Basque country.

Gascogne or Gascogny and Guienne have always been the principal source for Louis XIII style provincial furniture. They made certain articles in the Louis XIII style throughout the 18th century. The Louis XIII style large double-bodied cupboard or armoire à deux corps having a slightly recessed upper section was a characteristic piece. The panelled doors which were flanked by spirally turned columns were carved with the diamond point or star diamond point ornament. Their carved geometrical ornament was remarkable for its clear-cut quality. Although many other provinces employed the diamond point ornament it was in these provinces that it achieved its highest degree of perfection. Périgord was an old division in the province of Guienne north of the Gargonne River. It is generally regarded that the finest examples of Louis XIII cabinetwork in these provinces were executed in Périgord. Périgourdin furniture was distinctive for its splendid proportions, for the purity of its lines and for the clear-cut quality of its carvings. The furniture made at Bordeaux and in that general vicinity which was also in the province of Gascogne followed the prevailing 18th century French styles. Mahogany was much used. Bordeaux was a wealthy city and her furniture resembled that of Saintonge and Poitou. See *Basque*; *French Provinical*.

Gate-Leg Table In English cabinetwork; the table of gate-leg construction was known in England as early as the middle of the 16th century. Although this type of table is made in a variety of sizes and is designed for different purposes, it always features the same special method of construction. It is characterized by a fixed top with flaps which are supported on extra pivoted legs. Each pair of pivoted legs is joined at the top and at the bottom by stretchers and swings outward in the manner of a gate to support the leaves when raised to the level of the table top. The earliest gate-leg tables were provided with a single drop-leaf and a single gate-leg and the gate-leg was attached by wooden hinges at the top and at the bottom rather than a pivot. The characteristic type with two drop-leaves and a gate-leg on either side was introduced around 1620. The gate-leg table was known in America from around 1650–1660. It retained its popularity in both England and in America during the early 18th century until it was superseded by the fashionable drop-leaf table with a swing-leg. It is generally accepted that the gate-leg table continued to be made in America until around 1750 or later in the country districts. See *Dining Table*; *Spider-Leg Table*; *Swing-Leg*.

Gates, William English cabinetmaker working around 1777 to 1783 for George III in Long Acre, London. It appears that in 1783 he was in partnership with Benjamin Parran, Jr., and after the beginning of the 19th century he had some kind of business arrangement with Charles Elliott. He succeeded John Bradburn as cabinetmaker to the King in 1777. It seems from the evidence of the Royal accounts, between the years 1777 to 1783, that he favored or specialized in inlaid furniture, such as satinwood inlaid commodes. It is apparent from the few pieces of work known to have been executed by Gates that he was one of the most capable marqueteurs working in England at that time. See *Marquetry*.

Gaudreau, Antoine-Robert c.1680–c.1751. A famous French ébéniste producing exquisite pieces of cabinetwork in the style of Louis XV. Sometime after 1726 he was attaché au service du Garde-meuble de la Couronne, as well as director of interior decoration of the Bibliothèque Royale and the palace of the Tuileries. Like other ébénistes of his time he neglected to sign his pieces. He produced the celebrated médaillier, or medal cabinet, for Louis XV which is in the Bibliothèque Nationale. Another noted piece is an elaborately executed large commode which was made for and is still in the chamber of the King at Versailles. This commode in the Rococo style with its handsomely wrought bronze doré mounts was designed by Slodtz but was made by

Gaudreau with the assistance of Jacques Caffieri. Gaudreau produced many fine pieces for the nobility, the Dauphin, Madame de Pompadour, as well as for the King.

Gaudy Dutch In ceramics; the name given to a particular type of English Staffordshire earthenware of the 18th century made especially for the rural trade among the Pennsylvania Germans as well as for some urban use. It was executed in a rather crude technique comprising flowers and splashes of green, yellow and red on a white ground in brilliant colors.

Gautier, Andrew 1720–1784. American cabinetmaker working in New York City. According to his advertisement appearing in 1765, he specialized in making Windsor chairs.

Geburtsschein A German term meaning birth certificate. It is frequently used when referring to such a record of the Pennsylvania Germans. See *Fractur*; *Taufschein*.

Gemel Bottle A glass bottle or flask, generally almond-shaped, consisting of two bottles fused together with two short necks bending in opposite directions. It is also called a twin bottle; the word being derived from the Latin word *gemellus*, the diminutive of *geminus* meaning twin.

Genghis Rug See *Guendje Rug*.

Genoa Lace Laces were fabricated in Genoa from the 15th century. The points of Genoa, or Points de Gênes, which were so highly esteemed in the 17th century, were all bobbin-made laces. Gold and silver plaited laces as well as the points of Genoa continued to enjoy an excellent reputation throughout the 18th century. The bobbin-made guipures of Genoa were worked in several distinctive varieties. Apparently they also made a kind of tape guipure. In more recent times in addition to their traditional laces they also made a black silk lace in imitation of Chantilly, and an embroidered lace having the designs worked in darning stitches on tulle. They also produced some

WILLIAM AND MARY
GATE-LEG TABLE

fine examples of Macramé which were exhibited at the Paris Exhibition of 1867. See *Italian Lace*.

Genoese Velvet A figured cut and uncut pile fabric. Around the 14th century the Genoese originated a kind of silk velvet which had a cut pile that contrasted with an uncut pile. Often the designs were woven in cut and uncut pile with the ground in satin, taffeta or some other similar weave. See *Velvet*.

Genouillière In medieval armor; the protective steel covering for the knee.

Genre In painting; a style of painting which simply portrays scenes from ordinary and everyday life without any other significance, as distinguished from the heroic, religious or historic in art. The term *genre* is derived from genre bas or low style or that which is without grandeur of subject or scale. The genre paintings are generally small in scale. The figures are in just proportion. The artist is required to paint the subject he selects within a limited field of vision and with minute objective accuracy. The artist's ability to distinguish values and tones give these pictures an indefinable quality of charm. The Dutch school furnished many paintings of genre which gave a glimpse of Dutch life that was entirely satisfying.

Georgian Period The era in English history during the reign of the four Georges. George I, 1714–1727; George II, 1727–1760; George III, 1760–1820; George IV, 1820–1830. The early Georgian period approximately extends from 1720 to 1760–1770, and the late Georgian period from 1760–1770 to 1820–1830. When the term *mid-Georgian* is used it applies to those years around the middle of the 18th century. In cabinetwork; the names *George I*, *George II* and *George III* are sometimes used to designate articles of furniture made in each one of the successive reigns that were more or less in accordance with the prevailing taste but did not possess the true characteristics of the prevailing style. In a still broader sense the term

GERMAN GLASS BEAKER
WITH COVER

Georgian is often applied to an article of furniture made in the 18th century but which cannot be identified except in a very general way.

Gera In German ceramics; a porcelain manufactory was founded at Gera, Thuringia, in 1779 and was sold shortly afterwards to two members of the Greiner family, who owned the Volkstedt factory. The wares were marked with "G", "Gera" or the crossed swords of Meissen. The useful wares made at Gera were imitated from the more ordinary types made at Meissen. They also made some presentation cups and saucers with carefully painted decoration consisting of views of Gera, inscriptions and mottoes and similar subjects. As a rule the figure modelling was of poor quality and roughly painted. Faïence was also made at Gera. A small manufactory was founded in 1752 that remained active at least until 1780. Some pieces still extant are marked with a "G" or "Gera". The wares were painted in high-temperature colors in a clear white tin enamel ground. Vases and cylindrical tankards were included in their productions.

German Flowers In German ceramics; see *Deutsche Blumen*.

German Glass Or German and Bohemian Glass. In Germany and Bohemia glassmaking has been a long established and productive industry. Glassmaking in the Rhineland has been carried on continuously from the time of the Roman Empire. Throughout the medieval period glasshouses located in the forests of Germany produced utilitarian vessels made from a common greenish colored glass known as *wald*, or forest glass. Dating from the 16th and 17th centuries Germany, as well as the other countries in Europe, largely imitated the Venetian Renaissance models. Although the Germans employed the Venetian technique of enamelling from around the middle of the 16th century, throughout the 17th century and even later their interpretation and selection of designs were distinctly German in feeling.

Armorial themes were especially typical. In addition to the enamel painting some of the painting on German glass, like the Venetian glass, was also done in oil. Almost concurrent with the development of English flint glass, in 1676, the Germans developed a fine crystal glass, which was a potash-lime glass, called Bohemian glass. Apparently it was first made in Bohemia. An important milestone in German and Bohemian glass history was the application of the technique of wheel engraving to this new Bohemian glass. Although the Germans had practiced wheel engraving as a decorative medium from around the beginning of the 17th century, it did not attain full development until the last quarter of the 17th century with the introduction of Bohemian glass, which was particularly suitable for engraved and cut decoration. Before the end of the 17th century they produced masterpieces of engraved glass of unrivalled beauty, which had not been seen since the medieval Islamic era. Engraved glass decoration flourished exceptionally well during the first half of the 18th century, especially in Bohemia, Silesia and Potsdam. Due to the vogue for brilliant cut crystal glass in England during the latter part of the 18th century, German cut glass remained more or less in fashion until around 1850. Certain new ideas in colored and stained glass were especially popular from around 1825 to 1850. Enamel painting in the Renaissance and Baroque styles was revived from around 1850, while engraved and cut decoration have continued popular methods to the present time. See *Glass*; *Engraved Glass*; *Enamel*; *Schäpergläser*; *Roemer*; *Waldglas*; *Ruby Glass*; *Mildner Glass*; *Adlerglas*.

German Porcelain In ceramics; soft paste porcelain was practically never made in Germany. Böttger of Meissen discovered the secret for making hard paste porcelain in 1708–1709, and the first hard paste porcelain in Europe was made in the royal Saxon factory at Meissen. The second manufactory for hard paste porcelain was established in Vienna in 1719. No other German manu-

factory succeeded in making true porcelain until after the second half of the 18th century when a number of manufactories were established in the different princedoms. Practically all the German porcelain of artistic importance and originality was made from around 1750 to 1775 with the exception of Meissen and Vienna. Five of the principal manufactories, Höchst, Nymphenburg, Frankenthal, Ludwigsburg and Fürstenberg were essentially creations of the middle of the 18th century. The porcelain manufactory at Berlin, due to the sustained patronage of Frederick the Great, King of Prussia, enjoyed a predominance which lasted into the 19th century. Minor manufactories under princely patronage were located at Fulda, Ansbach, Ottweiler, Cassel, Baden-Baden, Kelsterbach, Pfalz-Zweibrücken and Kloster-Veilsdorf. A number of private manufactories were started around 1770 in the forest region of Thuringia. Their wares were made by a cheaper process and were coarse and had relatively little artistic merit. The exceptions were the productions of Gotha and Kloster-Veilsdorf, both in the Thuringian group.

German Silver An alloy of copper, zinc and nickel. The usual proportions used for making imitation silver are 50% of copper with equal parts of nickel and zinc. Its color resembles that of silver but is slightly more greyish. It is also called nickel silver, white silver, and paktong, which is the Chinese alloy of different proportions.

German Stoneware In ceramics; see *Rhenish Stoneware*; *Kreussen*; *Bunzlau*; *Freiberg*; *Böttger, Johann Friedrich*; *Stoneware*.

Gesso An Italian term for plaster of Paris. It is applied to a surface prior to painting or gilding. It is also used for modelling and sculpture. In cabinetwork it was much used by the French on the carved frames of chairs and settees and on the carved legs of elaborate console tables with marble tops that were to be gilded. Ornament made from gesso pressed in molds was sometimes

FRANKENTHAL VASE

affixed to the surface of furniture or mirrors by means of glue or pins and then gilded or painted. Mirrors designed by Adam in his later work often had swags or festoons made of gesso or some similar composition strengthened by a wire core. In this manner an exceedingly delicate and fragile effect was achieved. See *Gilding*, in Furniture.

Ghiordes Knot It is also called the Turkish knot. It is one of the two types of knots used in tying the tufts of pile yarn upon the warp in Oriental rugs. It is so knotted that the two outstanding ends of each knot alternate with every two threads of the warp. It derived its name from the ancient town of Ghiordes in Asia Minor. The other type of knot is called the Sehna knot.

Ghiordes Rug An Oriental rug belonging to the Turkish classification; it derived its name from the city of Ghiordes where it was made. The warp is of fine wool, cotton or silk and the weft is of cotton, linen or single strand wool. The pile is a very fine selected wool and is comparatively short in length. Sometimes the ends are finished with a silk fringe which has been sewed on; others have the selvage and loose warp threads. This rug is notable for its beautiful designs and for the skillful blending of its colors. It was usually made in the size of prayer carpets, although some larger ones were made. See *Turkish Rugs*.

Gibbons, Grinling 1648–1720. English carver and designer. He was born in Rotterdam and came to England when he was about fifteen years old. By the time he was twenty-five years old his remarkable skill as a wood carver was well known. He was employed by Charles II and Sir Christopher Wren. His wood carvings adorn many of England's great churches, palaces and colleges, included among which are St. Paul's Cathedral and the church of St. James, Piccadilly, Trinity Colleges at both Oxford and Cambridge and St. George's Chapel at Windsor Castle. His carvings of flowers, fruit, birds and foliage have rarely been equalled. His work is unsur-

WOOD CARVING
BY GRINLING GIBBONS

passed for its minute detail, its delicate refinement and graceful realism. Although his carvings revealed real strength they were imbued with an airy lightness and lace-like quality. Gibbons is credited as the leader or a prominent member of a style of wood carving. However, much work which has been attributed to him has since been revealed to have been the work of other carvers. Gibbons was also an excellent draftsman, a fine designer and a skillful sculptor. Recent evidence reveals that he collaborated with Vanbrugh at Blenheim Palace and that some of the finest stone carving and sculpture on the exterior was his workmanship.

Gilded Leather Gold and silver leathers are made from the skins of calf, kid, or sheep, and although they seem gilded they are actually silvered. After the skins are softened and made smooth, they are cut to fit the engraver's block or die, which is about 16 by 23 inches. The hide is carefully sized and leaves of silver, about 3 inches square, are applied and beaten with a fox's tail. The parts of the surface which are to be gold, red, or other colors, are varnished with the correct lacquers. The one which makes the gold is a light brown lacquer. Gold leaf is rarely used because of its cost. Sometimes imitation gold leaf (copper) or imitation silver leaf (tin) are used. In addition to the reliefs received from the block or die in the press, other decoration is frequently tooled in with chisels or patterned punches called irons.

Gilding In furniture; the practice of gilding has its origin in antiquity. Ever since the Middle Ages the two principal methods of covering wood with gold leaf have been either water gilding or oil gilding. The latter method which is simpler and more durable cannot be burnished with a burnishing tool so it never has the luster of water gilding. In order to make the surface of the wood smooth and hard for water gilding the surface is prepared with a ground of gesso. This method can be and is sometimes used in oil gilding; however, a less laborious method can be used in which the ground can be composed of white lead or red ochre, ground in oil, or of paint-pot scrapings. Then a mordant or a substance to make the gold leaf adhere is applied. In oil gilding the mordant has to be sticky or tacky, while the mordant in water gilding must be made very wet with cold water. The surface is then ready for the application of the gold leaf. In oil gilding the gold surface is polished with a cloth, and in water gilding the gilt surface can be either matt-finished or burnished, depending upon the effect desired. Occasionally both methods are used on the same article of gilded furniture in order to achieve contrast in tones. Gilding was employed on furniture in Italy from the Gothic style on, and was probably introduced into France from Italy and later into England from the Continent. The practice of gilding furniture in England did not become common until after the Restoration in 1660, and then its use was restricted to the fine pieces of cabinet-work. It is generally believed that the finest gilding was done on English cabinetwork from around 1700 to 1750 at the time when the Palladian mansions were being built. The vogue for gilded furniture declined in England during the second half of the 18th century. Gilded furniture was fashionable in France during the reigns of Louis XIV, Louis XV and Louis XVI. In gilding glass the mordant is composed of isinglass. See *Eglomisé*; *Parcel Gilded*; *Gilded Leather*; *Pastiglia*; *Ormolu*.

Gilding   In ceramics; the practice of decorating pottery and glass with gold was known in ancient times. In European ceramics gilding was probably first used around the middle of the 16th century; however, it was not until about one hundred years later that gilding was regularly used, when it was found on German faïence jugs richly decorated in gold. Four different methods were used for applying added decoration in gold to porcelain, stoneware and pottery before the 19th century. In an early method a gold sizing was painted on with a brush and while it was still tacky the gold leaf was applied.

No firing was done. In this method the gilding easily wore off. In a second method known as lacquer gilding, the gold leaf was ground up with a lacquer varnish and applied with a brush. This gilding also wore off. The method apparently used in the 18th century for most of the fine porcelain gilding was done by grinding gold leaf in honey. The mixture was applied with a brush and secured by a light firing. This gilding was durable, soft and rich in tone and thick enough to permit chasing and tooling. In a fourth method introduced about 1780 an amalgam of gold and mercury was applied and the latter was evaporated in the muffle kiln. It resulted in a gold film that was burnished to a hard and brittle brightness. It was generally inferior to the earlier method. The commercial potter of the 19th century employed a liquid gold which did not require any burnishing and produced a thin film resembling luster painting. During the Middle Ages gilding was used in the Islamic East, as on the enamelled wares of Rhages in Persia. In Chinese porcelain gilding was used during the Ming dynasty, 1368–1644, and in the subsequent Ch'ing dynasty, 1644–1912. The gilding on 18th century Chinese porcelain was very thin and had little brilliance. Gilding was also used on Japanese porcelains, as on the enamelled Imari wares decorated in the brocade pattern. Gilding was regarded as indispensable on the finest European porcelain and its lavish use was a feature of the Baroque style. It continued to play an important part during the following Rococo style both on porcelain and faïence. During the Empire period the practice of gilding large surfaces to simulate gold became the fashion, which is generally regarded with disfavor since the feeling for porcelain was lost in this practice.

Gill   A liquid measure equal to one fourth of a pint. A vessel of this capacity was commonly made in pewter. See *Measures*.

Gillingham, James   An American cabinetmaker, who was born in 1736, was working

GILDED SIDE TABLE
WITH MARBLE TOP

around 1765–1770 in Philadelphia. He had his shop on Second Street between Walnut and Chesnut Streets and produced fine pieces in the Chippendale style. See *Philadelphia Chippendale*.

Gillot, Claude 1673–1722. French painter and decorative artist. See *Watteau, Antoine*.

Gillow, Robert English cabinetmaker. He was a son of Robert Gillow who founded a cabinetmaking firm in Lancaster in 1731. He opened a branch shop for his father in London at No. 176 Oxford Street around 1760 which was carried on by him and his brothers until 1817. The firm continued to operate after 1817 under the family name although no member of the family participated actively after that date. In 1757 Robert's son, Richard, was taken into the partnership when he was twenty-three years of age. In 1800 he invented the telescopic dining table. He died in 1811. The furniture for the London shop was made for many years at Lancaster. The firm enjoyed a good reputation. Their cabinetwork was of good quality and was well made; however, it lacked ingenuity in its designs and in its treatment of ornament. See *Telescopic Dining Table*.

Gimp The name given to a decorative trimming of twisted threads originally called guipure. See *Guipure*. In lace-making the term is given to the pattern resting on the ground. In laces made in the Midlands and at Honiton the term is given to the coarse glazed threads employed to give relief to some of the edges of the design. See *Cordonnet*.

Ginger Jar In Chinese ceramics; a porcelain jar having a wide mouth and a globular body tapering slightly toward the base and fitted with a cover. It is generally thought that these jars were filled with sweetmeats, ginger and tea and were given to relatives and friends during the Chinese New Year holiday as a present, with the jars being returned to the owners. See *Prunus*.

QUEEN ANNE
GIRANDOLE MIRROR

Gin Glass In English glass; see *Dram Glass*.

Girandole The name given to a decorative candelabrum or branched candlestick having several lights. It was generally made of metal, especially bronze doré or silver, and occasionally of gilt wood. It came into general use during the second half of the 17th century and was generally made in pairs. Especially notable are the 18th century bronze doré girandoles made by the celebrated French ciseleurs. In English records the term *girandole* taken from the French and derived from the Italian *girandola* meaning a kind of revolving firework or a revolving fountain jet is mentioned toward the end of the 17th century. It is a comprehensive term and includes both the branched candlestick and, more commonly, fixed wall appliqués provided with branched supports for candles. The term came into general use in the mid-18th century trade catalogues when French taste was especially dominant. These wall appliqués were designed with either an openwork background or a mirror, enclosed in scrollwork, to reflect the light. Chippendale illustrated both types in his DIRECTOR. Hepplewhite, who also gave designs for girandoles in the GUIDE, states that they "are usually executed of the best carved-work, gilt and burnished in parts. They may be carved and coloured suitable to the room". By extension the term was also given, in addition to wall-lights proper, to mirrors provided with candle-branches which supplemented the lighting of rooms. See *Girandole Mirror*.

Girandole Mirror The name given to a wall mirror designed with candle arms or candle-branches. It was generally fitted with two candle arms. See *Convex Wall Mirror*.

Gisarme A medieval weapon appearing in a great variety of forms but generally defined as having a broad cutting blade with a projection in the form of a hook on the end of a long shaft. It was used by foot soldiers to strike a cleaving blow or to pull down mounted men. See *Glaive*.

Glaive A medieval weapon consisting of a broad, slightly curved, heavy sword-blade at the end of a long shaft. It often had a projecting hook when it was combined with the gisarme and called a glaive-gisarme. It was used by foot soldiers to strike at horsemen.

Glass A compound in which the essential materials are silica in the form of sand, flint, or quartz, and an alkaline flux of either soda or potash fused in a furnace. To produce a glass of a sturdier and tougher quality small quantities of oxide of lead, chalk or limestone are added to the basic ingredients and are in practice essentially required. Glass is generally translucent but not always transparent. The earliest glass vessels are attributed to the Egyptians dating from around the 15th century B.C. They were made during the ensuing centuries by modelling the glass around a removable form. The art of coloring glass by adding metallic oxides, such as copper and iron, began almost at the same time. The Near East, with Alexandria as the great trade center, continued to be the most important source for glass until the Roman era. The Roman phase in glass history began around the first century B.C. when it is believed that the art of blowing glass was first introduced. It was also found that glass could be made transparent. Practically all the methods for decorating glass, such as blown-molded, engraving, and placing gold leaf between layers of glass, were used to a greater or less extent by the Romans during the first centuries of the Christian era. The Romans carried their art of glassmaking to all parts of Europe. From this early glass, articles for domestic use began to appear in which the common greenish waldglas of northern Europe played an important part during the medieval period. The art of glassmaking in the West rapidly declined from the 5th century onwards, with the exception of the magnificent medieval stained glass windows. In the Mohammedan countries from around the 9th century onwards decorative glass of remarkable refinement was made and the beautiful Islamic enamelled glass of the 13th and 14th centuries has never been surpassed. Much of the finest work was apparently done in Syria. Fine glassmaking was revived in the West at Venice and Murano from around the 13th century onwards, and from late 15th century for almost the next two hundred years, Venice, or more accurately Murano, was the source for the finest and most exquisite articles of glass produced in Europe. Dating from the 16th and 17th centuries Germany, as well as the other countries of Europe, largely imitated Venetian glass with the aid of emigrant Italian workmen. Toward the end of the 17th century the Germans developed the Bohemian or potash-lime glass which was more suitable for cutting and engraving than the Venetian soda-lime glass. Decorative engravings made by the Germans and the Dutch are unrivalled. The art of diamond engraving achieved its perfected development in the Netherlands during this time. In 1676 in England, George Ravenscroft developed English flint glass, a potash-lead glass, which was one of the most important contributions in the history of glassmaking. In America the first successful glass manufactory was the so-called Wistarberg Works, established in Salem County, New Jersey, in 1739 by Caspar Wistar, which produced free-blown pieces for domestic use as well as window panes and bottles. From the latter part of the 18th and early 19th centuries the American glasshouses produced pieces similar to the Continental prototypes usually from olive, amber and green glass. See *Venetian Glass*; *Bohemian Glass*; *Flint Glass*; *Engraved Glass*; *Enamel*, in glass; *Islamic Glass*; *German Glass*; *Dutch and Flemish Glass*, *American Glass*.

Glass Cane In glass; canes of glass are either colorless and transparent or are colored in various tints; the latter group includes the opaque white canes which are called latti-

VENETIAN GLASS GOBLET
WITH DRAGON STEM

cinio. A cane of colored glass which is about $\frac{1}{8}$ to $\frac{1}{4}$ of an inch in diameter is surrounded by a casing of ordinary clear glass. These canes form the simple threads of various width with which numerous Venetian vases are decorated. These canes are also the ingredients of the canes having different filigree patterns of which filigree vases and bowls are composed. The canes enclosing filigree patterns are of a more complicated character. Essentially a filigree glass cane is made of a number of colored glass canes which are reduced to threads of extreme tenuity that twist in various patterns and form a new cane. This new filigree cane has a diameter of about $\frac{1}{8}$ to $\frac{1}{4}$ of an inch and has a thin surface of transparent glass. See *Threaded Glass*; *Glass*.

Glass Sellers' Company   See *Sealed Glasses*.

Glastonbury Chair   In English cabinetwork; the name is frequently given to a variety of folding chair usually identified as a piece of ecclesiastical furniture. The chair was made of oak and had a panelled back which slanted slightly backward and extended to the seat rail. The arms, which were joined to the front seat rail, curved downward in the middle. The legs were X-shaped and a horizontal stretcher joined the X-shaped legs at the point of intersection. This chair was first designed around 1530. See *Curule*.

Glaze   In ceramics; the shiny and generally glass-like coating applied to the surface of porcelain, stoneware and pottery. The five principal glazes are alkaline, lead, tin, salt and feldspathic. The alkaline siliceous glazes are of the nature of soda-glass and are essentially composed of sand fused with some form of soda. They were principally used on the wares of ancient Egypt and on the wares of Syria and Persia. They had a distinctive transparent quality and by adding copper to the glazes rich colors of blue or turquoise were obtained. The lead glazes consist of a silica, such as sand, which is fused with the aid of the natural sulphide of lead or with an oxide of the same metal.

GLASTONBURY CHAIR

Sometimes potash was also used. Lead glazes were known to the ancient Romans and to the Chinese of the corresponding time. Lead glazes can be intentionally stained yellow or brown by the use of iron in some form, or green by the use of copper, blue by cobalt, purple and brown by manganese and black by manganese and iron. In contrast to the colored glazes is the refined and almost colorless lead glaze used on cream-colored earthenware. Lead glazes are the most extensively used of all the different kinds of glazes for ordinary glazing purposes. The white and opaque tin glazes are made by an admixture of ashes of tin to a lead glaze. Tin glazes, or tin enamel glazes, as they are sometimes called, are used on majolica and faïence. Lead glazes and tin glazes are the only glazes that can be used on soft paste porcelain. Salt glazes are produced on high-fired stoneware by throwing salt into the kiln when it has reached its highest temperature. They are thin and very hard. If coloring is desired, iron, cobalt or manganese is applied to the stoneware before it is fired. The feldspathic glazes are typically those associated with hard paste porcelain. They consist of fusible feldspathic rock or petuntse which is powdered and mixed with lime, sand, potash or quartz and other ingredients. They require a high temperature to fuse them and normally they are translucent and perfectly united with the hard paste material. They may be colored; cobalt gives blue, iron a range of greens and browns and copper gives lavender blues and reds. During modern times additional colored feldspathic glazes have been introduced. During the 19th century a leadless glaze was introduced for commercial pottery in which other fusible ingredients were used in place of lead in an otherwise lead glaze. This was done because of the injurious effect of lead upon the health of the potter.

Globe Cup   The name given to a decorative standing cup, usually of silver, made in the form of a celestial or terrestrial globe. Sometimes it was fitted with a mechanism which enabled the cup to move about the table. It was principally identified with German silver and was introduced around the 16th century. See *Standing Cup*.

Globe Stand In cabinetwork; the name applied to a stand designed to hold a celestial or terrestrial globe. The making of globes, especially celestial globes, had its origin in antiquity. During the Middle Ages globes were made for philosophers and nobles for the advancement of their studies, and in the Arab countries engraved brass globes were made for their highly developed astronomical science. The early maps were either drawn by hand and affixed to a wooden ball or were engraved on metal. During the 16th century maps precisely made to fit the surface of a globe were often printed on paper and ornamental stands were frequently found in the libraries of Continental houses. In England, until the end of the 16th century, Mercator's globes were extensively used while in 1592 Emery Molyneux produced the first English celestial and terrestrial globes. The early stands for globes were usually plain with turned legs while many of the later examples were richly and elaborately carved. These stands, which support the globe within a wooden ring called the horizon, are fitted with three legs, a tripod base or four or more legs. An orrery and an armillary sphere are frequently found among the furnishings in a large library and are also mounted on stands similar to globe stands. See *Orrery*; *Armillary Sphere*.

Go The game of go or wei ch'i meaning surrounding game, since the object of the game is to try to surround each player's go-stones, has always been a favorite Chinese diversion. The term *go* is translated in a broad sense as checkers. The game of go appears in two popular subjects for porcelain decoration. One concerns the story of a Chinese general who was unwilling to permit the news of a great victory to interfere with his game of go. In another legend two

old men, who are the spirits of the Pole Stars, are seated around a go-table and the game is being closely followed by the Taoist patriarch, Wang Chih. The game was introduced into Japan from China in the 8th century. The go-board has 19 lines lengthwise and 19 lines crosswise, making 361 crosses or me. The game, which is very complicated, is played with 180 white stones and the same number of black stones, the object being to occupy as many crosses as possible with stones.

Goat and Bee Jug In English ceramics; a cream jug introduced at Chelsea around 1745. The front of the jug was decorated with a reclining goat and bee modelled in relief. This curious shape of cream jug was also made in silver in the 18th century.

Gobelins The tapestry manufactory of the Gobelins was originally founded as a dye works at Faubourg Saint Marceau, Paris, during the middle of the 15th century, by Jean and Philibert Gobelin. During the 16th century the manufacturing of tapestries was also added. In 1601, Marc de Comans and François de la Planche, Flemish merchant weavers, established workrooms there, for the manufacture of tapestries, which enterprise was incorporated by Henri IV in 1607. In 1662, it was purchased by Jean Baptiste Colbert for Louis XIV, and under the directorship of Charles Lebrun, the royal painter, fine tapestries and furniture were produced there. It closed in 1694, and in 1697 it was reopened as a manufactory mostly for presentation pieces and those for royal use. It was again closed during the Revolution, and resumed work after 1814 under the patronage of the Bourbons. The manufacturing of handmade carpets was added in 1826. The Gobelin Works has continued to operate as a state enterprise. See *Tapestry*; *Manufacture Royale des Meubles de la Couronne*.

Gobelin Stitch A short upright stitch which is used in embroidery. It is also used in tapestry work, and is called a tapestry stitch. See *Embroidery*.

CHELSEA GOAT AND
BEE JUG

Goblet The term is applied to a kind of cup or drinking vessel without a handle. It consisted of a bowl mounted on a stem which rested on a foot. The bowl was large in relation to the height of the stem. Goblets were mentioned in English records as early as the late 13th century. In English glassware; the capacity of the bowl was a gill or more of liquid.

Goddard, John, I 1723-1785, American cabinetmaker. Originally John Goddard was regarded as the creator of the block-front furniture that was made from about 1750 to 1780 in New England. At the present time the credit for originating block-front furniture is shared by Goddard and John Townsend, who were cousins-in-law. These two men have given Newport, Rhode Island, its high position in American furniture history. See *Block-Front*.

Goddard, John, II 1789-1843. American cabinetmaker of Newport, Rhode Island. Much of his work was similar to that produced by Duncan Phyfe. He was the son of Stephen Goddard and grandson of John Goddard.

Godendag A medieval Flemish weapon similar to an early form of a halberd. See *Halberd*.

LOUIS XVI GONDOLA-BACK
CHAISE À BUREAU

Godroon See *Gadroon*.

Göggingen In German ceramics; a faïence manufactory was established at Göggingen, near Augsburg, Bavaria, in 1748 by Georg Michael Hofmann with a privilege from the Landgrave of Hesse-Darmstadt. Although it operated for only six years it was very productive. The faïence ware was generally marked with the name of the town in full or abbreviated. Their productions covered a wide variety of articles, including figures modelled in a porcelain style, and stove tiles. The Enghalskrug, or a narrow-necked jug, made at Göggingen had a distinctive pear-shaped body and a long slender graceful neck. Wavy-edged plates and Rococo moldings were typical and the wares were especially thin and light. The painted decoration which reflected both European and Chinese influences was carefully executed and was done in either blue or in high temperature colors. Figure painting in blue or purple monochrome was sometimes found on jugs.

Gold Thread The technique of making gold thread, which was known to the Etruscans, was developed in Italy in the 14th century. Genoa first made gold thread in imitation of the gold threads of Cyprus. Later Lucca, Venice and Milan followed Gold lace was also made of drawn metal wire. This was also of early origin and was known in the days of Herculaneum and Pompeii. For common purposes a tinsel was used in place of the real gold thread or wire.

Gomoku-Zōgan In Japanese sword mounts; a form of metal decoration used on tsuba and other mounts in which the surface is covered with tiny pieces of brass and copper wire inlaid on iron. It is supposed to resemble pine needles floating on a pond or lake. See *Zōgan*; *Ishime*; *Nanako*.

Gondelach, Franz In German glass; one of the foremost German glass engravers particularly noted for his hochschnitt or cameo relief work. See *Cassel*, in German Glass.

Gondola-Back Chair In French cabinetwork; a shape of chair back introduced during the style of Louis XV. It had an arched horseshoe-shaped frame which continued to form the arms and was characterized by its rounded appearance. See *Bergère*.

Gondola-Shape In French cabinetwork; the name given to a variety of bergère having the back and arms designed as one continuous unit. See *Bergère*.

Gonome Nanako In Japanese sword mounts; a form of nanako decoration on sword mounts. In this method the dots are orderly arranged in diagonal lines forming lozenges. In the center of each lozenge is a dot making a group of five dots to each lozenge. See *Nanako*.

Goodison, Benjamin English cabinetmaker working in London around 1727 to 1767 at the Golden Spread Eagle, Long Acre. He is regarded as one of the most outstanding cabinetmakers of the Georgian era. His name is frequently found in accounts for furniture ordered for the Royal palaces as well as for the mansions of the nobility. Authenticated pieces are distinctive for their vigorous design and excellent craftsmanship. He made his nephew, Benjamin Parran, a partner, who, with Benjamin Goodison Jr., continued the business until 1783.

Göppingen In German ceramics; a faïence manufactory was established at Göppingen, Württemberg, by Andreas Pliederhäuser and Johann Michael Stiefvater in 1741. It was active until about 1778. The factory mark was a stag's horn from the arms of Württemberg. The faïence definitely identified as Göppingen work is of a rather poor quality with a greyish tin glaze and coarsely painted.

Gorevan Rug An Oriental rug belonging to the Persian classification. The rug derived its name from the village of Gorevan, in the Herez district; it is referred to as a Herez fabric because it is woven by Herez weavers. The foundation is cotton and the pile is wool, rather short in length. The ends are usually finished with a narrow web and loose warp threads. See *Persian Rugs.*

Gorget In armor; the protective steel collar piece of a suit of armor. It was first used late in the 15th century. As a rule it consisted of small overlapping rings of plate and was joined either to the body armor or to the armet.

Gostelowe, Jonathan An American cabinetmaker working around 1744 to 1795. He had his cabinet shop on Church Alley between Second and Third Streets in Philadelphia. In 1790 his shop was at 66 Market Street. He produced fine furniture in the Chippendale style. See *Philadelphia Chippendale.*

Gotha In German ceramics; a porcelain manufactory was established at Gotha, Thuringia, in 1757 or later by Wilhelm von Rotberg, after earlier experiments by Nikolaus Paul. Prince Augustus of Gotha became the proprietor in 1802. The early mark was an "R" in underglaze blue or impressed; probably after 1783, "R-g"; probably after 1805, "Gotha" or "G" in blue or enamel color. From around 1830 and later a rebus mark of a hen on a mountain peak, impressed, was used in association with the place name. The Gotha wares were essentially different from the other wares produced in the manufactories in Thuringia. The material was very fine, although slightly creamy colored, and the painted decoration was very carefully executed. It seems that the factory produced little until around 1775, at which time the classical style was adopted. Figure painting and floral sprig patterns were typical and were probably derived from Fürstenberg. Medallion heads, especially silhouettes, were carefully painted, sometimes on a gold ground. The influence of Fürstenberg was evident in the vase forms, classical figures and busts which were usually in biscuit.

Gothic The Gothic style of ornament and architecture first began to develop in northern France after the middle of the 12th century and gradually spread over all of western Europe. Vertical line effects were a dominating feature of Gothic art except in Italy where more emphasis was placed on the horizontal effect. The great tracery windows were first developed in Gothic architecture. They were such an important influence in Gothic architecture that the character of the stone framing was chiefly instrumental in the name of the different Gothic periods, such as Lancet, Rayonnant, Perpendicular and Flamboyant. Domestic furniture during the Gothic period was of simple and crude construction. It was solid and massive and severe in character. The forms of the furniture were generally rectilinear with emphasis on the vertical. The use of curved lines was limited to the folding chair of

GOTHIC WOOD CARVING

ENGLISH DECORATED STYLE
WINDOW TRACERY

ENGLISH
PERPENDICULAR STYLE
WINDOW TRACERY

curule form. In the northern countries the furniture was chiefly made of oak. Walnut was also used in France and other local woods were used in each country to some extent. The craftsman who made the furniture was completely influenced by the architecture that surrounded him. The decorative details were borrowed from the architecture. Carving was the favorite process for decorating the surface of furniture. Foliage was much favored as a motif in Gothic ornament. The plants were always selected from the native plant life and included vine leaves with grapes, maple leaves and cress and parsley leaves. Tracery work either solid or pierced was extensively employed by the wood carver in decorating furniture and was copied from the great tracery windows. Panels with fenestrations were widely used on the façade of chests. Figure subjects, animals and birds in Gothic ornament were often treated in a grotesque manner. Chests, stools, benches and tables comprised the larger part of the household furniture. Chairs were extremely rare. The characteristic Gothic chair was made of oak and had a rectilinear, box-like form, with a high panelled back, sides and arms. The portion beneath the seat was usually enclosed to the floor, with the seat being hinged to give access to this box-like chest. Tables were primarily used for dining. Cupboards were both movable and built-in. Chests, stools and benches were generally used for seats. See *Chest*; *Chair*; *Dining Table*; *Bed*; *Cupboard*; *Romanesque*; *Neo-Gothic*.

Gothic Arch An arch introduced during the Gothic period; it rises to a point at its apex, instead of a keystone, as in the round arch.

Gothic, English The Gothic style of ornament and architecture in England is usually divided into the following periods. Early English, 1180–1280; the Decorated style, 1280–1380; the Perpendicular style, 1380–1530, and the Tudor style, 1485–1558. The Early English style was characterized by the use of the Lancet arch and the Lancet-shaped window. The Decorated style was

so called because of its rich decorative development. The tracery work was of flowing, curvilinear lines and the ornament was distinctive for its beauty of detail. The Ogee arch was used. The Perpendicular style was distinguished by the vigorous perpendicular lines in the tracery windows and the use of the Tudor arch. Prior to the late 15th century English furniture of any decorative quality was confined to the nobility. However from that time onwards more furniture was made and the ornament became more elaborate and more finished in detail. In the beginning these pieces were chiefly rather coarse reproductions of foreign models. It was not until around 1550 that furniture of a distinctive English character was produced in any quantity. Included among the favorite Gothic motifs were tracery work, linen-fold, Gothic trefoil and quatrefoil, heraldic devices, ball-flower, dog-tooth and foliated and floral scroll-work. From around 1530 Italian Renaissance motifs were sometimes found mingled with Gothic ornament. Carving was the favorite decorative process. Gilding and painting were also occasionally used; the painting was done in tempera or wax. See *Tudor*; *Renaissance, English*; *Gothic*; *Joint Stool*; *Form*; *Dossier*; *Settle*; *Prie-Dieu*; *Hutch*; *Dresser*; *Livery Cupboard*; *Wardrobe*; *Ambry*. There was an attempt made by a few in England around the middle of the 18th century to revive the Gothic style. Chippendale in order to conform with the fashion sometimes introduced Gothic detail in his furniture designs. He occasionally used the cluster leg on chairs and tables designed in the Gothic taste. Carved Gothic detail was in vogue from around 1750 to 1760. Another later effort was made to revive the Gothic style during the English Regency. See *Smith, George*; *Gothic Taste*.

Gothic, French Gothic architecture with its pointed arch originated in France and succeeded the Romanesque style of the 12th century with its rounded arches. The Gothic style of ornament and architecture in France is usually divided into the following periods, Early French, 1160–1275; Middle French or Rayonnant, 1275–1375, and Flamboyant, 1375–1515. The Rayonnant style was characterized by radiating lines in its designs, such as in the great tracery rose windows. The decoration was distinctive for its rich quality. The Flamboyant style was characterized by flame-like or waving lines and the ornament was minute in detail and profusely employed. From the 12th to the 14th centuries France assumed a leading role in the development of western Europe. It is generally accepted that the finest examples of Gothic furniture were made in France. French carving was notable for its precise, clean-cut detail which gave it a flat and finished effect. Foliage, tracery work, the fleur-de-lis, rosettes, real and fantastic birds and animals, grotesque figures were included among their favorite motifs. Polychromy was occasionally used to accent the delicate richness of the tracery designs. The metal mountings, hasps and lock cases were remarkable for the jewel-like quality of their workmanship. The term *Louis XII style* is often applied to any art exhibiting traces of Renaissance influence between the dates of 1498–1515, when Louis XII was king of France. This term is incorrectly used since this period did not possess the characteristics of a style. See *Flamboyant*; *Renaissance, French*; *Escabeau*; *Banc*; *Bancelle*; *Archebanc*; *Form*; *Huche*; *Buffet*; *Armoire*; *Coffre*; *Credence Table*; *Gothic*; *Tapestry*.

Gothic, German   The Gothic style of ornament and architecture in Germany is usually divided into the following periods, Early, 1175–1275; Middle, 1275–1380, and Late, 1380–1530. The early period was more of a time of transition for it was not until toward the end of the 13th century that the Romanesque style was entirely supplanted by the Gothic style. German Gothic was characterized by its profuse use of lines, which were geometrical and regular in form, by its desire to use geometrical figures, by its ingenuity of technique and its great elaboration of detail. Included among their favorite decorative motifs were elaborate tracery work, twisted spirals, strapwork, armorials, rosettes and birds, the latter generally worked in conjunction with leaf forms.

Gothic, Italian   The Gothic style was introduced in Italy in the 13th century from France. However, it never flourished to the same degree in Italy as it did in the other countries. Italy combined the Gothic style with her then flourishing Lombard, Tuscan and Byzantine-Romanesque styles. Especially notable were the fanciful Venetian Gothic palaces. Antique culture was so much a part of the Italian people that the Gothic style declined first in Italy. By the end of the 14th century Renaissance motifs were sometimes found mingled with Gothic motifs on Gothic or Romanesque forms. It was evident that Italy was preparing early for the Renaissance. An interesting feature of Italian furniture is the emphasis placed on the horizontal line effects both in the form of the furniture and in the composition of its decoration. For decorating the surface of furniture the Italians used intarsia, pastiglia, gilding, painting and carving. Tracery work was a favorite motif for carved detail. The painted decoration often depicted stories from mythology, romantic scenes and similar subjects. See *Dantesca*; *Savonarola*; *Cassone*; *Renaissance, Italian*; *Renaissance*; *Gothic*; *Romanesque*.

Gothic, Spanish   The Gothic style of ornament was first introduced into Spain from France during the first half of the 13th century. The ornament during the early period was characterized by strong Moorish influence. Architects were imported into Spain from France and the Low Countries who brought with them their own styles of Gothic ornament. During the late Gothic the ornament was largely influenced by the ecclesiastical architecture found in northern Europe, with Spanish flamboyant Gothic panelling and tracery being much in evidence.

FRENCH GOTHIC
FLAMBOYANT TRACERY

Gothic Taste The phrase *Gothic Taste* was used in England by the admirers of the pseudo-medieval forms which they attempted to introduce into architecture, interior decoration and furniture. Horace Walpole, 1717-1797, the English author and wit, was one of the leaders of this Gothic cult, and his home Strawberry Hill, Twickenham, is the most famous instance of this Gothic style. The effort to revive the Gothic style was restricted to a few. Designers of furniture in the Gothic taste made no pretense of adhering either to the form or to the materials actually employed by the makers of the original Gothic furniture. Leading designers, such as Chippendale, rarely did more than introduce details, which they regarded as Gothic, into pieces of furniture of essentially mid-Georgian contour. Tracery work, trefoil and quatrefoil motifs, Gothic cusping, and cluster columns were included in the repertory of ornament and detail reminiscent of the medieval style. The legs of chairs and tables designed in the form of a cluster column were a typical feature of this Georgian Gothic fashion. Carved Gothic detail enjoyed its greatest vogue from around 1750 to 1760, although it continued for some years after the introduction of the Neo-Classic style. Another later effort to revive the Gothic style occurred during the English Regency. The mid-Georgian Gothic taste in interior decoration was generally confined to one room, the exception being Strawberry Hill which was entirely decorated in the Gothic taste. Carved Gothic detail was also introduced in American cabinetwork designed in the Chippendale style. See *Gothic*; *Gothic, English*; *Regency*; *Smith, George*.

Gouache A French term applied to the art of distemper painting. See *Distemper*.

Gouthière, Pierre 1740-1806. Undoubtedly the two principal French metal workers during the Louis XVI period were Gouthière and Thomire. Gouthière executed a great quantity of metal work of the utmost variety. In addition to his furniture mounts, he

CHIPPENDALE CHAIR
IN THE GOTHIC TASTE

mounted in bronze such pieces as vases and bowls made of jasper and choice marbles. He executed many articles in bronze such as cartels, candelabra and andirons. Gouthière was selected by Madame du Barry to make the bronze fitments for her château at Louveciennes which was regarded as the most exquisite masterpiece of the Louis XVI style. Much of the fame of her château was due to the magnificent bronze embellishments by Gouthière. His best work was admirable for its delicacy, refinement and finish. His superlative work was unexcelled for its artistry and for its quality of workmanship.

Gouty Stool In English cabinetwork; the name given to a type of footstool having a ratchet, in order that the top can be adjusted to any angle. The gouty stool was in general use during the Georgian period, and was illustrated in Hepplewhite's GUIDE of 1788.

Governor Winthrop Desk Or Winthrop Desk. In American cabinetwork; a term erroneously applied to a slant-front writing desk designed in the Chippendale style. The dates for John Winthrop, 1588-1649, Governor of Massachusetts Colony, and John Winthrop, 1607-1676, Governor of Connecticut Colony, conclusively prove that their names cannot be associated with an article of furniture designed in the Chippendale style which did not flourish in America until around the middle of the 18th century. See *Slant-Front Writing Desk*.

Gozame Ishime In Japanese sword mounts; a form of ishime metal decoration used as a background on sword mounts. In this method the surface is made to resemble a Japanese straw floor mat, or tatami. See *Ishime*; *Bori*; *Nanako*; *Zōgan*.

Gradin In French cabinetwork; the name *gradin* is often used interchangeably with the term *serre-papiers*, especially when the serre-papiers were mounted on either end of the top of a writing table. *Table à Gradin* is the French term applied to a very small writing table designed for a lady. It was introduced during the Louis XV style and consisted of an oblong table with four slender cabriole legs. The rear portion of the top was surmounted with a small rectangular superstructure usually fitted with two doors which, when opened, revealed small drawers and pigeonholes. See *Serre-Papiers*.

Graffiato In ceramics; see *Sgraffiato*.

Graham, George 1673–1751. A foremost English horologist. He was assistant and successor to Thomas Tompion and one of his favorite students. He contributed outstanding and progressive ideas to the art of horology. During his later life he largely devoted his ingenuity to astronomy and astronomical instruments, particularly to perfecting an astronomical timekeeper.

Graining In cabinetwork; a process of painting furniture by means of which the color and figure of a more expensive wood is imitated in one of a less expensive kind. The graining of wood was practiced in England as early as the 17th century. It was widely practiced during the early 19th century in England and continued to be popular until the middle of the century. See *Marbling*.

Grains d'Orge In armor; see *Mail*.

Granary Urn In Chinese ceramics; an early cylindrical pottery vessel of the Han dynasty. As a rule it tapered slightly toward the base. It resembled a farmer's silo and had a top in the form of a tile roof with a hole in the center. It rested on three feet, each being shaped in the likeness of a seated bear.

Grandfather's Clock A name given to a tall case clock generally believed to have been prompted by a song which was popular around 1880. See *Tall Case Clock*.

Grand Feu In ceramics; the French term for the high-temperature kiln required to fire the body and glaze of porcelain, majolica, faïence and a few varieties of ware with a lead glaze. The temperature is generally from 1200° C. to 1400° C. The term *demi grand feu* is generally confined to Chinese ceramics, and is seldom used in European ceramics. See *Petit Feu*.

Grandmother's Clock A name for a tall case clock that was of much smaller proportions than the standard tall case clock. See *Miniature Tall Case Clock*; *Grandfather's Clock*.

Greave In armor; plate armor used on the leg between the knee and the ankle. It was worn in Europe from the 11th to the 17th centuries. The early type covered only the front part of the leg as it did in classical times and the later greave covered the front and back as well. The bronze greaves of the Greeks and Romans were beautifully wrought. It is also called a jamb or jambeau.

Grecian Chair In cabinetwork; the most characteristic Grecian chair was the klismos, a variety of light side chair. The klismos was the principal inspiration for the late 18th century and early 19th century European chair designed in the Directoire and Regency styles. The chair, which was a Grecian innovation, was perfected by the 5th century B.C., and was distinctive for its sweeping curving lines and for its elegant and graceful simplicity. In the principal variety the uprights of the splat-back and the rear legs generally formed one continuous graceful curve and were made from a single piece of wood. The front legs curved forward correspondingly. The solid splat chair back had a concave, broad and flat crest rail which extended beyond the uprights and was about the height of the shoulders. The seat rail, which was invariably straight in front, was generally slightly lower than the top of the legs. The seat was usually plaited. In an early variation the uprights rolled over and terminated in swans' heads or a similar motif. The principal features of design incorporated in this chair were found in American chair design from around 1805 to 1825. See *Grecian Furniture*.

Grecian Couch In English and American cabinetwork; the name used by Sheraton to describe a variety of couch the design for

GRECIAN KLISMOS

which was derived from those used in classical times for reclining on at meals. It was generally designed with an out-scrolled side which continued in an unbroken curve to form the seat rail. Sometimes the other side rail continued to curve upward and roll inward just above the seat cushion. It was often designed with a shaped back panel which extended about one half the length of the seat. It rested on legs of cornucopia form. It is identified with the style of the English Regency and American Directoire. See *Méridienne*; *Recamier*; *Grecian Sofa*.

Grecian Furniture Practically all knowledge of Grecian furniture is derived from references in literature and more importantly from innumerable scenes of Greek life found on vases and marbled reliefs. In the early archaic period Greek art was still very dependent on Egyptian and the great Oriental arts that preceded her own. This is evident in ornament in the use of the palmette, the anthemion and above all the sphinx which in its Greek form became a favorite Renaissance motif. It is also discernible in the use of Egyptian forms for furniture. However during the fully developed period of the 5th century B.C., which marked the acme of Greek creative genius, the Greeks evolved original creations and whatever they had borrowed they perfected and made their own. Perfection of form was achieved in every branch of Greek art. In furniture the forms became more pure and the proportions were perfected. In the ensuing 4th and 3rd centuries B.C., a general deterioration set in, and purity of line and simplicity of form yielded to over-elaboration. It is apparent that the same Greek conservatism found in architecture and sculpture was also found in furniture. Although Greek furniture is confined to a few pieces there is a wealth of detail which prevents monotony. Chairs, stools, couches, tables and chests were all the furniture they possessed. Throughout Greek classical times from the 7th century to the 2nd century B.C., there were three principal forms of seats, namely the throne chair,

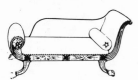

DUNCAN PHYFE
GRECIAN COUCH

chair and stool. The throne chair or thronos was always a dignified and stately chair and its use was reserved for gods and goddesses as depicted in sculpture and painting and for princes and other dignitaries. The Grecian couch or kline served as a combination bed, couch and sofa. The footstool was a necessary article for it was used as a foot-rest for the throne chair which was a lofty seat, and it was used to mount the couch which was quite high. The table was principally used in Greek classical times for the serving of meals. Each person generally had his own table and it was placed next to the couch on which the dinner guest was reclining. The chest either large or small was an indispensable household article and like so much of the Grecian furniture its form was evolved from the Egyptian chest. See *Grecian Chair*; *Classic Revival*; *Roman Furniture*.

Grecian Sofa In English and American cabinetwork; the name used by Sheraton in his CABINET DICTIONARY to describe a sofa of lyre form, the design for which was borrowed from antique classic models. It was characterized by out-scrolled sides which continued in an unbroken curve to form the seat rail. It was designed with legs of cornucopia form. The Grecian sofa is identified with the style of the English Regency and the American Directoire. Duncan Phyfe made many fine sofas of lyre form.

Greek Fret In ornament; see *Fret*.

Greek Lace See *Reticella*.

Greek Revival Toward the end of the 18th century there was apparent in England a general interest in Greek architecture and everything pertaining to Greek art. This was evident in the Grecian style of ornament employed in architecture. Grecian vases and other objects of art, as well as furniture copied from the same classic sources, were found in many wealthy English homes. In the first quarter of the 19th century not only were the forms of furniture changed to harmonize with antique classic ideals but the furniture designers adopted a new ideal of Grecian severity. In order to achieve this new ideal of Grecian severity in furniture, the ornament was restricted, the lines were simplified, and there was a partiality for large uninterrupted surfaces. Greek motifs were increasingly employed. The lyre, the lion monopodium, and the lion foot were all borrowed from classic antiquity. The word *Grecian* became an important word in the English cabinetmakers' vocabulary. Sheraton in his CABINET DICTIONARY illustrated Grecian couches and Grecian sofas. Early in the 19th century the so-called Grecian chair was introduced. In American cabinetwork this interest in Grecian taste and forms was evident in the work of Duncan Phyfe and other contemporary cabinetmakers. See *Regency*; *Holland, Henry*; *Hope, Thomas*; *Grecian Chair*; *Grecian Couch*; *Grecian Sofa*.

Green Glass A term applied to glass in its original color, having neither been colored nor made colorless. Its natural colors extend through shades of green, olive amber and amber. The color is accidental and is the result of certain metallic substances, such as iron, contained in the raw materials. The principal alkaline base is soda or potash and the secondary base is generally a kind of lime. It is commonly believed to be the first glass produced in America, and was made with potash from wood ashes. Green glass was used for window glass, for bottles and flasks and for early glass utensils for daily use. It is also referred to as bottle glass. European equivalents of the term are *waldglas* and *verre de fougère*.

Grendey, Giles 1693–1780. English cabinet and chair maker, of Aylesbury House, St. John's Square, Clerkenwell. He was Liveryman of the Joiners' Company in 1729 and was elected Master in 1766. He is known to have made various fine pieces of mahogany furniture and lacquered chairs and cabinets. He was also engaged in the export business.

Grenzhausen In German ceramics; see *Westerwald*.

Grès The French term for stoneware. See *Stoneware*.

Grès de Flandre In ceramics; the name formerly given to the salt-glazed stoneware which is now recognized to have been made in the Rhineland, Germany. See *Steinzeug*; *Rhenish Stoneware*.

Greybeard In ceramics; the English name for the Bartmann or Bellarmine jug identified with Rhenish salt-glazed stoneware made during the late 16th century and the 17th century. The front of the jug was decorated with a molded bearded mask. The so-called greybeard jugs were made at Fulham, England.

Griffon In ornament; an ancient four-footed mythical monster of the eagle variety. As a rule it was designed as half eagle and half lion, the front part resembling an eagle. It was sometimes used as a decorative motif in furniture design. It is also spelled griffin.

Griotte d'Italie Marble. A variety of marble from Carcassonne, Aude, France. It is dark brown, almost black, with bright cherry-colored patches distributed evenly and with pearly white eyes or spots, which enhance its beauty. The marble is also called oeil-de-perdrix or partridge eye, when these spots are more numerous. The variety without spots is called fleuri.

Griotte St. Rémy Marble A variety of marble from Rochefort, Namur, Belgium. This is the brightest colored of the St. Rémy marbles. It is a dull brownish red with small patches of white, and it is not as brilliantly colored as the French griotte called griotte d'Italie.

Grisaille In painting, the term *grisaille*, which is derived from the French word *gris* meaning grey, is applied to a style of painting in various tints of grey used to depict solid bodies in relief. In English cabinetwork; commodes designed in the Adam style were occasionally decorated with medallions of classical figure subjects painted en grisaille. Painting en grisaille was also employed in

GREYBEARD JUG

enamel work, ceramics and in other similar crafts.

Grog Lifter   In English glass; See *Punch Lifter*.

Gros Bleu   In French ceramics; an underglaze ground color of dark blue employed at Vincennes and Sèvres from around 1749 to 1760. The color, which was taken up by the glaze, was also copied at other manufactories, such as Chelsea, where it was known as mazarine blue in order to distinguish it from the gros bleu and where it was employed from around 1758 to 1769.

Gros Point   A needlework done with wools on a canvas or mesh ground. The method is the same as is used in petit point, the difference being that in gros point the stitches are made over four cross-threads instead of two and the yarn is coarser and heavier. See *Petit Point*; *Embroidery*.

Gros Point de Venise   See *Punto Tagliato a Fogliami*.

Groszbreitenbach   In German ceramics; a porcelain manufactory which is still operating, was started at Groszbreitenbach, Thuringia, around 1778 by Anton Friedrich von Hopfgarten. As a rule it is very difficult to distinguish their productions and marks from those of Limbach. It is believed that the factory principally made blue and white wares. It seems that from around 1788 the trefoil mark of the Limbach pottery was also adopted as their mark.

Grotesque   In ornament; a French term derived from the Italian applied to a distinctive form of decorative design employed in painting and in sculpture comprising representations of portions of human and animal figures fantastically portrayed and interwoven with foliage and flowers. This form of decorative design was found in the excavated ancient Greco-Roman buildings in Italy. This specialized meaning had its provenance in the statement that grotte was the popular name in Rome for these rooms in ancient buildings revealed by excavation

ITALIAN GROTESQUE

and which contained these mural paintings that were characteristic examples of "grotesque." In a broad sense the term is applied to a form of design characterized by unnatural combinations or distortions that are extravagant or treated in a bizarre or fantastic manner. See *Arabesque*; *Raphaelesque*.

Ground   In lace-making; the name given to the part of the lace connecting the ornaments which form the pattern or toile. There are two kinds of grounds, namely brides and réseaux. The bride ground is made of a few threads overcast with buttonhole stitches or of threads plaited or twisted together. The réseau ground is a net and is made with either a needle or bobbins. Net was first made by machinery in 1768, and the machine for making "bobbin" net was invented in 1809.

Guadamací   A Spanish term applied to finely tooled leather with elaborate designs brilliantly painted and gilded. The term *guadamací* is derived from the town of Gadamés, Tripoli, where fine leathers had been prepared for many years and from which town the Moors carried the art into Spain. The Spaniards were unrivalled in their leather work. See *Gilded Leather*.

Guaiac Wood   A French Guiana tree *guaiacum sanctum*. The wood was widely used by the French ébénistes in cabinetwork. It is very hard and its color is green and black stripes. It is also called holy-wood.

Guard Room Table   In Spanish cabinetwork; a characteristic variety of rectangular table introduced during the Renaissance. As a rule it was designed with splayed trestle end supports. It usually had a scrolled wrought-iron underbrace attached beneath the center of the table and joined at the stretchers of each trestle end support. The frequent use of ornamental wrought-iron underbraces for tables and benches was a unique feature of Spanish construction.

Gubbio   In Italian ceramics; the acclaim given to the majolica made at Gubbio, which is in the Duchy of Urbino, principally rests upon the rare and breath-taking beauty of its ruby and gold luster decoration rather than upon its originality in designs. The best work was achieved during the first thirty years of the 16th century. Around 1495 Giorgio Andreoli, who generally signed his work as Maestro Giorgio, settled at Gubbio. Due to his renown for luster painting it is generally believed that in addition to the original work that he lustered, he also added luster painting on other pieces made and painted elsewhere. The early pieces assigned to Maestro Giorgio have been the subject of much discussion. However from 1519 majolica dishes having his factory mark in luster pigment are not uncommon. Dated specimens with his mark continue until 1541. Included among the finest and most original work of the potters at Gubbio are vases and dishes with gadrooning and embossed decoration artfully designed to permit the fullest play of light to the brilliant luster coloring. A characteristic and popular design at Gubbio consisted of a central panel, frequently square in shape, with a cupid or a bust surrounded by palmettes, grotesques or foliation. The influence of Castel Durante was evident in much of this work. See *Italian Majolica*; *Luster Decoration*.

Guelder Rose Vase In German ceramics; the 18th century vogue for flowers realistically modelled in porcelain had its inception at Meissen around 1740, being either contained in or applied on vases. Especially praiseworthy were the guelder rose vases made for Louis XV around 1742. Flowers modelled as separate blossoms came into vogue around the middle of the 18th century. They were colored after nature, and were wired and mounted in gilded bronze. Modelled flowers in imitation of Meissen were an important part of the production at Vincennes where they were made in fine soft paste. One celebrated bouquet had at least 480 separate blossoms and was sent by the Dauphiness Marie-Josèphe to her father the Elector of Saxony. In addition to roses other flowers were also realistically modelled and colored, such as lilies, tulips and hyacinths.

Guendje Rug An Oriental rug belonging to the Caucasian group. As a rule it is rather coarsely woven. The foundation is wool and the pile is of a fine wool, medium in length. As a rule the designs are of geometrical forms, rather similar to the Karabagh and Kazak rugs. It is also spelled Genghis. Sometimes it was called a Turkman rug. See *Caucasian Rugs*.

Guéridon In French cabinetwork; a decorative candlestand which originated in France around the middle of the 17th century. In the beginning one characteristic stand was made in the form of a young negro and was called a guéridon, which was the name of the young Moor brought from Africa to serve as a page. The Moor in his brilliant costume was made either of carved wood which was painted and gilded, or of bronze, and he held a candle-holder in one hand. Sometimes he supported a small top on his head by his raised hands. The French craftsmen soon designed innumerable forms of guéridons of a more elegant and artistic quality inspired by the prevailing taste in decoration. The fashion for guéridons continued throughout the 18th century. The term guéridon was also given in France during the 18th century to a variety of very small occasional tables remarkable for their exquisite workmanship. See *Candlestand*; *Blackamoor*.

Guérite In French furniture; a French term, meaning a sentry box and also a hooded chair, given to a variety of wicker armchair with a high rounded back and closed sides continuing to form a hood. The part beneath the seat is rounded and extends to the floor. This type of chair was in general use in the 16th and 17th centuries in France and the high back served as a protection against drafts. From around the 18th century onwards the guérite became a fashionable piece of garden furniture. See *Wicker Chair*.

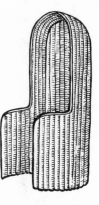

GUÉRITE

Guernsey In English pewter; the name given to a type of measure, of various sizes, used during the 18th century on the island of Guernsey. It was a pot-bellied vessel with the upper part of the body rising with straight sides to the mouth. It rested on a molded foot rim and the vessel was fitted with a modestly scrolled side handle. It was provided with a flat hinged lid, marked with the word Guernsey, and lifted by a billet. The Guernsey measure differed from the Jersey measure in that the former had molded bands around the upper part of the body.

Gueuse In lace-making; a French term meaning beggar, given to a lace of marked simplicity having a network ground with bobbin-made flowers worked in a loose and thick thread. Gueuse was extensively used in France in the 17th century; however, from the 18th century it was chiefly used by the lower classes.

Guienne In French Provincial cabinet-work; a former French province. See *Gascogne*.

Guilloche In ornament; a continuous or repetitive motif which was one of the principal decorative bands used in ancient classic times by the Greeks in architecture. It is composed of a series of circles all spaced the same distance from one another and enclosed in a band which interlaces or interweaves around them in a winding manner. The guilloche was worked as a single, double or triple band. The single guilloche was used as a carved classic motif in furniture design such as on the frieze band of a table or on classic moldings. It was used during the Italian Renaissance and later in the Louis XIV and Louis XVI styles. In glass; the guilloche was also applied on glass vessels and was also called a trailed circuit or chain. See *Trailed Circuit*.

Guipure In lace-making; a kind of lace or decorative gimp or passement made of cartisane and twisted silk. The work derived its name from a heavy thread covered in

GUILLOCHE

silk called guipure. Guipure lace was made with either a needle or with bobbins in different designs and widths. Guipure made of silk, gold or silver was very costly and was worn by the aristocracy in medieval and Renaissance times. It is not known when the term *guipure* was first applied to thread passements; however, they were of early origin and many have Renaissance designs. Guipure thread laces display a wide variation in their designs. Undoubtedly the finest were made in Flanders and in Italy. In some the striking and flowing designs are joined with brides while some feature a coarse réseau that is often round. At the present time the meaning of guipure has been considerably extended, and it includes designs joined by large coarse stitches as well as designs without any ground. See *Tape Guipure*.

Guipure de Flandre In lace-making; it is generally accepted that the finest thread guipures were made in Flanders and in Italy. They displayed many variations in their style. A remarkably rich and soft guipure de Flandre was made at Bruges in the 17th and 18th centuries and was much favored for cravats. A more modern Flemish guipure made at Bruges and executed in point plat resembles Honiton, but the workmanship is coarser. It is extremely white and consists of bobbin-made flowers generally joined with brides à picot.

Guli Hinnai Motif A design motif used in Oriental rugs, especially in Persian rugs. Guli Hinnai is the flower of the henna plant. It usually consists of a small yellow plant, set in rows and with profuse flower forms uniting them in diamond arrangement, somewhat after the manner of the Herati pattern.

Gulistan Rug See *Oushak Rug*.

Gumley, John English cabinetmaker and glass manufacturer working from around 1694 to 1729 at Salisbury Exchange in the Strand and also at the corner of Norfolk Street in the Strand, 1714. He was in partnership with James Moore in 1714 to 1726 and a little later for several years with William Turing. See *Moore, James*.

Guri A Japanese lacquer work in which several layers of colored lac are revealed by carving. In China the work is known as Tsui-Shiu.

Guri Bori In Japanese sword mounts; a decorative work consisting of carving and welding done on sword fittings in imitation of guri lacquer work. In this method several sheets of metal, usually alternating shakudo and copper, are welded together. Sometimes as many as fifteen or more of these very thin sheets are found in a tsuba which is slightly more than one eighth of an inch thick. The carving, which is done in V-shaped grooves or channels, with sloping sides, is cut through these layers. For example, when fifteen sheets are used, the channels are cut through seven layers on each side, revealing the black and red metals and leaving one layer of shakudo in the center. It is then pickled in order to show the black and red colors of the two metals. Sometimes the channels are rounded at the bottom producing a different effect from those having a sharp bottom. See *Bori*; *Nanako*; *Ishime*.

Gurkha A Hindu dagger. See *Kukri*.

GURI INCENSE TRAY

H

Habaner Ware In ceramics; a distinctive and important variety of peasant majolica made in Moravia and on the borders of Hungary from the end of the 16th century onwards. The earliest makers were German immigrants. Some of the earlier examples with their elaborate openwork borders strongly reflected the influence of Italian majolica. Especially characteristic of their productions are small globular jugs with short necks and dishes and plates with wide flat rims. The painting was executed in a remarkably vigorous and firm manner. Flowering plants and scrolls were typical decoration, while the plates were frequently painted with houses, animals, figures and similar motifs.

Hadley Chest In American cabinetwork; an early variety of chest that received its name from the town of Hadley, Massachusetts, where a number of chests of this type were found. It was a rectangular chest and had a hinged top. The front of the Hadley chest was designed with three sunken rectangular panels, beneath which were generally one, two, or three long drawers. The short legs were formed from a continuation of the stiles. The chest was decorated with an over-all flat carving of simple designs. The carved decoration, which was crudely executed, was generally composed of a tulip pattern with vines and leaves. As a rule the initials of the owner were carved in the design; very often they were inscribed in the center panel.

HADLEY CHEST

Hafner In German ceramics; a German term literally meaning stove-maker. The name was given to the potters, especially during the Renaissance, producing tile-work stoves, architectural ornaments and sometimes decorative objects and dishes from lead-glazed and other earthenware. The making of pottery stoves in Germany had its origin in Roman times and stove tiles were made at least from the middle of the 14th century. The principal type of late Gothic stove tiles were covered with a green glaze and were decorated in relief sometimes with figure subjects. Around 1500 the green glaze was supplemented with additional colored glazes and with a white tin glaze or tin enamel glaze. Stove tiles were made throughout the 16th century in many places in Germany, Austria, Switzerland and the Tyrol. The most important center in Germany was Nuremberg. The tiles were notable for their rich and strong coloring and for their freely executed and forceful designs. The tiles were molded in relief and were sometimes further enriched with figures in the round and with foliage appliqués either modelled by hand or pressed in molds. The subjects were chiefly religious, historical or allegorical. The colored glazes were roughly separated by the reliefs. Especially noticeable and effective were the appliqués of rolls and strips of white clay. Pottery dishes and vessels made in this technique rank highly in 16th century German ceramic art. In another distinctive type of tile stove these tiles with their colored glazes and relief decoration were combined with panels of majolica generally decorated with blue and yellow designs on a white tin glaze or tin enamel ground.

Hagi-Yaki In Japanese ceramics; a pottery made at Hagi in Nagato and at Rakuzan in Izumo. The artist was Rikei, a Korean, who used the name of Kōraizaemon. This ware, which was developed from a Korean stoneware, had a grey crackled glaze clouded with a salmon-pink color. The artist Gombei, who was a pupil of Rikei's, was working at Rakuzan around 1675.

Hague See *The Hague*.

Haguenau In French ceramics; a branch manufactory of the Hannong factory at

222

Strasbourg was active at Haguenau, Alsace, from 1724 to 1781. It seems probable that the wares may have been made here, since Haguenau was the source of the clay, and decorated at Strasbourg. Other minor faïence manufactories were active during the 18th century. Porcelain and cream-colored earthenware were also made at Haguenau; however, the reputation of Haguenau depends upon the branch Strasbourg factory.

Haig, Thomas English cabinetmaker. He became the partner of Thomas Chippendale, Sr., in 1771. Upon the latter's death in 1779, Haig became the partner of Chippendale Jr., until 1796.

Hains, Adam b. 1768. American cabinetmaker of Philadelphia who was working until about 1815. He had a shop at 135 North Third Street and later at 261 Market Street.

Halberd A medieval weapon consisting of an elongated pikehead having at its base an axe-blade on one side and a pick on the other affixed to the end of a shaft which was generally about 5 or 6 feet in length. The halberd was used by foot soldiers and was capable of striking a powerful cleaving blow against a horseman. The pike-head was used to keep the horseman at a distance. The bill, which originally was a form of scythe blade with a sharp concave side, was one of the early types of weapons from which the halberd, partizan and ranseur developed.

Halfpenny, W. and J. English architects and designers. In 1725 W. Halfpenny issued his first publication, entitled MARROW OF ARCHITECTURE. He and his son John published in parts, between the years 1750–1752, a book entitled NEW DESIGNS FOR CHINESE TEMPLES, GARDEN SEATS, BRIDGES, DOORS AND SIMILAR DESIGNS. The book included a few designs for chairs, mirrors and fireplaces. A similar book issued in 1751–1752 was entitled RURAL ARCHITECTURE IN THE CHINESE TASTE. Two other publications appeared in 1752, on Gothic taste and another on Chinese taste. Working in collaboration with his son John, later installments of NEW DESIGNS were issued.

Half-Pike See *Spontoon*.

Half-Relief See *Relief*.

Hali See *Kali*.

Hall and Parlor Cupboard In English cabinetwork; this term is now given to several forms of cupboards introduced during the 16th century that were known as cupboards by their original owners and that were intended by their obvious appearance for the hall or for the living room rather than for a bedroom. One variety introduced during the Elizabethan era had a closed upper portion while the lower portion formed a stand. The oblong rectangular upper portion was fitted with three panelled cupboard doors surmounted with a frieze and a cornice. The lower portion was designed with a frieze, sometimes fitted with drawers, resting on four legs which were joined to a heavy display shelf close to the floor. The two front legs were bulbous in form and the two rear supports were quadrangular and plain. It was richly decorated with carved and inlaid work. This variety is sometimes termed a credence; however, without any contemporary authority. Another variety of cupboard having the lower portion designed as a stand was introduced late in the reign of Queen Elizabeth I. In this type the upper portion was designed with a canted front. The upper section had three recessed panels, fitted with one or more cupboard doors, with the two end panels canted, surmounted with a projecting frieze and cornice which rested on two bulbous form supports. The lower portion had a frieze resting on four supports, the two front supports being bulbous in contour. The legs were joined to a deep display shelf that was mounted on feet. Both friezes were often fitted with drawers. It was handsomely carved. In another variety of hall cupboard both the upper and lower portions were closed. This type, which until recently has been called a Court Cupboard in the literature

ELIZABETHAN
HALL AND PARLOR
CUPBOARD

on English furniture, was introduced around the middle of the 16th century and retained its popularity until the Restoration in 1660. The principal variety of this type of cupboard during the 16th century was rectangular and upright. It had a projecting cornice above an upper cupboard section which contained three panels designed as one or more doors. The frieze of the cornice rested on two bulbous supports. The projecting lower body had a frieze band, sometimes fitted with drawers, over two panelled doors. The end stiles were lengthened to form feet. During the Elizabethan era the two end panels in the recessed upper section were often canted. Other variations in design occurred. Although this type of cupboard was no longer fashionable after the Restoration it was made by the village cabinetmaker along traditional English lines until early in the 18th century when it was gradually supplanted by the popular farmhouse dresser, with its superstructure of shelves. These oak cupboards were made in America from around 1650 to 1700 and they are generally regarded to be the earliest examples of fine cupboards found in America. See *Court Cupboard*; *Cupboard*; *Tridarn Cupboard*.

GEORGIAN HALL CHAIR

Hall Chair In English cabinetwork; a variety of wood chair introduced early in the 18th century found especially in the halls and corridors of the Palladian mansions. Chippendale in his third edition of the DIRECTOR in 1762 illustrates six designs for hall chairs. He also suggests their use for summer houses. These chairs, which generally had a wooden seat, were often made of mahogany, while some were painted. The family crest was very often colorfully painted in the center of the back panel. Sheraton in his CABINET DICTIONARY describes chairs of this type for the use of servants or strangers waiting to conduct some type of business transaction. See *Hall Settee*.

Hallett, William 1707–1781. English cabinetmaker working at Newport Street in 1732. He moved to St. Martin's Lane next door to William Vile at the corner of Long Acre in 1752 and he retired in 1769. He is regarded as one of the most eminent cabinetmakers working at that time and he is sometimes regarded as the most fashionable cabinetmaker during the reign of George II. Included among his clientele were such connoisseurs as the Earl of Leicester and Lord Folkestone.

Hall-Marks, English Provinces The silver plate produced in several provincial towns had special hall-marks as well as the regular hall-marks. The principal town mark for several of these more important silver centers is as follows: "Chester": until 1700 the word "Sterling"; until 1779 three lions dimidiated with three wheat-sheaves; after 1779 three wheat-sheaves and a sword; "Birmingham": an anchor; "Sheffield": a crown; "Exeter": a castle with three turreted towers; "Newcastle": three castles placed two above one; "York": five lions passant on a Greek cross.

Hall-Marks, Glass See *Sealed Glasses*.

Hall-Marks, Irish The Goldsmiths' Company of Dublin, incorporated by a charter from Charles I dated 1637, regulated the goldsmiths' and silversmiths' trade in Ireland, and the standard conformed to was identical to the English standard. "Dublin": the crowned harp, introduced in 1637, is used to signify silver made in Dublin. Until 1730 only three marks are found on Dublin silver: the harp crowned, the date letter and the maker's initials; in 1730, the figure of Hibernia was adopted to signify the payment of duty; from 1807–1890 the reigning sovereign's head was added in another punch. Cork: prior to 1710 this town used a number of marks on silver; however, after 1710, the word "Sterling," in various forms, is the principal punch used.

Hall-Marks, London Hall-marks were introduced in 1300 in England by royal decree so as to keep the purity of silver plate up to the required standard. Since the time silver was first marked in London, seven different marks have been used and with the exception of one, i.e. the sovereign's head, are in use with minor variations at the present time. The marks which are to be found on plate assayed in London in their chronological order are as follows: 1. The leopard's head. 2. The worker's or maker's mark. 3. The annual letter. 4. The lion passant. 5. (a) The lion's head erased and (b) the figure of Britannia. 6. The sovereign's head.

1. Edward I (1272–1307) established the first mark by statute in 1300; it is called the King's Mark and it is a crowned leopard's head. In reality it is a lion's head. In 1821 the crown was removed and it has remained uncrowned ever since.

2. The second mark established in 1363 was the maker's or worker's mark. Originally signs or symbols were used as maker's marks. Later one or more of his initials, sometimes in combination with the symbol, were used. In 1739 a law was passed which made it mandatory that the maker's mark consist of the initials of his Christian name and surname only.

3. The third mark is the date-letter or annual letter introduced circa 1478; it is the assayer's or warden's mark. The use of this mark was arranged in cycles of twenty years each, during which time the alphabet in proper sequence is used, omitting the letters J, V, W, X, Y, Z. The letter is changed regularly in the month of May in each year. With each new cycle the style of letters is changed, and, in addition to the changing of the style of the letters, the shape of the shield, in which it is placed, is sometimes varied. The shield enclosing the letter was introduced in 1560. This mark is used to determine the date the silver was made.

4. The lion passant was introduced as a standard mark circa 1545.

5. The lion's head erased and the full-length figure of Britannia were adopted in 1697, and replaced the crowned leopard's head and the lion passant until 1719. They were used to indicate a higher standard of silver than the old sterling standard. In 1719, when the old standard for sterling was re-stored and became operative in 1720, the leopard's head and lion passant marks reappeared; with Britannia and the lion's head erased being used for silver higher than the standard of sterling.

6. The reigning sovereign's head was introduced as a mark in 1784, to signify payment of duty; however the mark was discontinued in 1890 when the duty was abolished.

Hall-Marks, Scottish A number of town marks are used by the various towns in Scotland, in addition to the maker's mark, date letter, etc. The town mark of Edinburgh, introduced circa 1485, is a three-towered castle, and in 1759 the thistle was added in a separate punch. The town mark of Glasgow is a bird, a fish, a bell and a tree, all combined in one punch. After 1819 a lion rampant was added in a separate punch.

Hall Settee In English cabinetwork; the hall settee was similar in character to the hall chair which it supplemented. It was generally made entirely of wood, and the back panel very often centered a colorfully painted family crest. See *Hall Chair*.

Hamadan Rug An Oriental rug belonging to the Persian group; made in Hamadan, Persia. The foundation is of cotton. Goats'-hair, as well as camels'-hair and wool, are used in the pile, which is comparatively thick. One end is usually selvaged, the other has knotted fringe. Nearly all Hamadan rugs have an outside band of camels'-hair in natural color. The predominating colors are red, blue and yellow, all in strong, lustrous tones. Characteristic of the majority of Hamadan rugs is the use of compact diaper patterns, which are very complex and leave little ground space visible. The city of Hamadan has in recent years become an important commercial rug-weaving center. Rugs are also obtained for the Hamadan market from nearby villages of Kara-geuz, Oustri-Nan, Burujird and Bibik-Abad. Modern Hamadans are purely a commercial creation; their designs are Persian, but of a wider range. See *Persian Rugs*.

HALLMARKS, LONDON 1738

Hamilton, Sir William 1730–1803. British diplomat and archaeologist. In 1764 he was appointed envoy to the court of Naples, which post he held until 1800. He was greatly interested in science and art, and was a notable collector. His collection of Greek vases and Etruscan and Roman antiquities which was published in books, 1766–1767, provided decorative designs from the antique and were instrumental in developing the Neo-Classic style especially in England. See *Classic Revival*.

Hammered In pewter; hammering was a method used by pewterers to give additional toughness or strength to pewter. Sometimes no trace of the hammering shows on the finished product, although as a rule such marks are more or less present on all articles of good workmanship. See *Sadware*; *Pewter*.

SILVER HANAP

Han The Han dynasty of China, 206 B.C. to A.D. 220 was a period of great development of the arts and a time when China was one of the greatest nations. In Chinese ceramics; the pottery of the Han period is represented in collections by mortuary wares that were undoubtedly made especially for burial purposes and are found in tombs. It was a burial custom of the Chinese to place in the tomb models of the things which surrounded them in life to accompany them to the spirit world. Models made of pottery were much used during the Han and T'ang periods. The pottery models included a vast number of objects such as farm buildings, grain towers, farm animals, their dwellings, utensils for cooking, food and drink, images of members of the family and servants. A great deal of the tomb pottery is an unglazed grey ware modelled after the bronze utility vessels. At times un-fired designs are painted on the models or designs are stamped or molded. The glazed pottery is usually a red ware with a soft lead glaze which produces a reddish to a yellowish-brown tone. Occasionally the glaze was a green tint from copper oxide. The glaze is often mottled or streaked. Many pieces have a silvery or golden iri-

descence caused by being buried in the damp ground for so many centuries. Glazed Han ware is frequently decorated with relief appliqués which were stamped in molds and were fired on with a slip. Occasionally incised decoration was combined with the relief appliqués.

Hanap A medieval goblet or drinking cup having a thick stem and a molded foot; it was generally designed with a cover. It was chiefly made of silver and was used as a table or buffet ornament in the same manner as a loving cup was used.

Hanau In German ceramics; a faïence manufactory was started at Hanau, near Frankfurt-on-Main, in 1611 by Jacobus van de Walle and Daniel Behaghel, from Holland. It was one of the earliest and most active German faïence manufactories. There was no factory mark until 1740; however, a repairer's mark of an incised crescent was often found on jugs. From 1740 to 1786 the mark was an "HV" and a monogram of crossed "A's"; the mark "Hanau" was often used in this period and also until 1806, when the factory closed. The early faïence was similar to Delft. The motifs used in the painted decoration were chiefly borrowed from the Chinese and Dutch until about the second quarter of the 18th century. Although manganese and other high temperature colors were sometimes used, most of the painted decoration was done in blue and often on a distinctive ground strewn with small groups of dots. Included among their productions were decorative pieces of Chinese forms such as double gourd vases, the so-called Enghal-skrug or a jug with a narrow neck, lobed and radially ribbed dishes, inkstands, salt-cellars and similar pieces. Much of the Hanau ware both in form and in decoration was similar to that of Frankfurt-on-Main; however, the decoration on the Hanau ware was generally inferior. After 1725 the floral motifs reflected the influence of Meissen and were often done on the familiar Hanau dotted ground. From 1740 the manufactory began to show evidence of decline, and the wares were in the contemporary European taste.

Hand Block Printing A method of fabric printing in which a fabric is printed by hand with a series of wooden blocks having the design cut in relief. The larger surfaces are filled in with felt, and the fine details are done in wire strips, driven into the wood. After the pattern is laid out, the blocks are dipped in dye and set on the cloth. Each color must be thoroughly dry before the next is applied. There is no limit to the number of colors or the size of the patterns. Very rich and soft effects can be obtained by this method.

Hand-Blown Glass See *Free-Blown Glass*.

Handkerchief Table In American cabinet-work; the name sometimes given in recent American furniture literature to a drop-leaf table with a triangular-shaped top because of its supposed resemblance to a triangular-folded handkerchief. See *Corner Table*.

Handle and Back Plate In American furniture mounts; brass handles were employed on the drawers of practically all the better American cabinetwork from around 1685–1690 to 1825 when knobs, either of brass or later of glass, became the prevailing fashion. Many of the brass mounts, which also included the escutcheons as well as the handles and back plates, were imported from England. From around 1685–1690 to 1720 drop handles were in vogue and the small back plate, to which the handle was attached, was commonly circular, oval or lozenge-shaped. From around 1720 handles of the bail type superseded the earlier drop handles. Generally the bail handle, from around 1720 to 1780–1785, was attached to either a solid shaped brass back plate, which occasionally was pierced, or to two small rosettes; the latter type was especially identified with the Chippendale style. As a rule the back plates of Hepplewhite style furniture were oval in form and the bail handles, which were conformingly shaped, were attached on each side to the oval back plates. These back

plates were stamped out with dies and the impressed motifs included such favorite patriotic subjects as stars and eagles, as well as acorns, flowers, cornucopia and oak leaves. The drawers on Sheraton style furniture were also frequently mounted with oval bail handles and back plates. Another favorite handle for Sheraton style furniture was the loose-ring handle attached to a round back plate at the top. Oval and octagonal brass handles attached at the top to a conformingly shaped back plate were also sometimes used. Another form of handle was the lion-and-ring handle, with a ring suspended from the mouth of a lion mask. Although the Sheraton types of handles were used on the early Empire style furniture brass knob handles were more typical of the Empire style. Some Sheraton style furniture, especially the drawers of tables, was also fitted with brass knob handles. These knob handles were round and projected about an inch from the surface of the drawer and were frequently ornamented with decorative motifs of a patriotic character, such as eagles and the head of George Washington. They were much used by Duncan Phyfe for the drawers of tables and sewing stands. Glass knobs either of pressed or cut glass were much used from around 1815–1820 to 1840. Wooden knobs were especially identified with the Late Empire and Early Victorian cabinetwork. See *Bail Handle*.

Handrest In Chinese writing accessories; the handrest or chên shou, meaning a pillow for the hand, is used by calligraphists as a support for the wrist while writing. The earliest handrest was made of bamboo which was cut in such a manner so that the one side placed on the paper was flat and the other side was slightly convex. Since Chinese writing is written downwards the handrest also helped in alignment. Handrests were made of different materials such as porcelain, jade and ivory. Handrests made of jade were even more of a luxury item than those made of ivory. It seems that the finest ivory handrests were made in the 18th century

SHAPED BACK PLATE
AND BAIL HANDLE

OVAL BACK PLATE
AND BAIL HANDLE

LOOSE RING HANDLE

and were about 2 to 2½ inches in width and about 5½ to 16 inches in length. As a rule the carving on the slightly rounded side was rather simple and was executed in low relief, while the carving on the flat side was very elaborate and in hollow relief, depicting well-known legends and scenes from Chinese life. The ivory carvings were remarkable for their artistic merit and rank with the carvings found on such ivory objects as Buddhist figures and other religious figures, vases, plaques, brush pots, snuff bottles, trays and ink-screens. See *Writing Equipage*.

Hand-Screen A flat, rigid fan used in China since early times and introduced into Japan in the 6th century. Hand-screens were made of a variety of materials and were usually circular, pear-shaped or gourd-shaped in outline. They were affixed to a short rod or handle. See *Japanese Fan*.

Hand-Tufted Carpet A handmade cut pile carpet. It is of the same construction as an Oriental; however, it is not as finely woven, and it is made of heavier wool. See *Oriental Rug*.

Hanging Corner Cupboard In English cabinetwork; see *Corner Cupboard*; *Hanging Wall Cabinet*.

Hanging Shelves In English cabinetwork; the term is usually given to a piece of furniture made from two or more boards fastened in a frame and designed without doors. Crudely constructed hanging shelves for books were known as early as the Middle Ages. Hanging oak shelves for domestic use were made during the 16th century; however, it was not until the reign of William and Mary that shelves came into general use. The vogue for hanging shelves was largely due to the mania for collecting Oriental porcelain since they were principally used for the display of porcelain.

Hanging Wall Cabinet In English cabinetwork; there was a vogue for mahogany hanging wall cabinets designed in the

CHINESE CHIPPENDALE
HANGING WALL CABINET

Rococo or Chinese taste around 1750–1760. The majority were designed with glazed doors and were used for the reception of porcelain. Occasionally the hanging cabinets designed in the Chinese taste were enclosed with fretwork doors and sides. The hanging wall cabinet was made throughout the second half of the 18th century and was decorated in the contemporary taste. Hanging corner cabinets with glazed doors did not seem to be as popular as the hanging corner cupboard. See *Corner Cupboard*; *Vitrine*.

Hanoverian Glass An English drinking glass having an engraved decoration of loyal and patriotic mottoes to the House of Hanover or to its reigning monarchs.

Hanoverian Pattern In English silver; an early 18th century silver pattern evolved from one of the older styles. It was reproduced from the earlier spoon with an elliptical bowl designed with a rat-tail on the back, and the stem followed the style of the Old English pattern. See *Old English Pattern*; *Rat-Tail Spoon*.

Hansel in the Cellar See *Hansje in den Kelder*.

Hansje in den Kelder Or Hansel in the Cellar. A festive drinking cup, usually of silver, originally made in Holland around the 17th century. It consisted of a circular shallow bowl which rested on a stem and a base. The bowl was fitted with a perforated domed center containing the figure of a child which emerged when the dish was filled with wine. It was used to celebrate the arrival or expected arrival of a child in the family.

Hard Paste In ceramics; another term for kaolinic and feldspathic porcelain. See *Porcelain*.

Hardwood The name given to any hard, close-grained wood or timber as well as to the wood of deciduous trees as distinguished from the softwood of coniferous trees. Deciduous trees or shrubs are those that shed their leaves every year, and coniferous trees or shrubs are mostly evergreens which bear cones. Although this definition is used to describe hardwood many deciduous trees produce wood softer than many coniferous trees. Included among the many hardwoods are mahogany, ebony, maple, oak, walnut, and chestnut. Included among the softwoods which are relatively soft and easily cut are pines and firs.

Hare's Fur In Chinese ceramics; see *Chien Yao*.

Harewood A wood widely used as a veneer on English furniture during the second half of the 18th century. It is sycamore stained with oxide of iron. Its color is greenish grey.

Haricot In French cabinetwork; the name *haricot*, which means kidney bean, is applied to a small table introduced during the Louis XV style. It is characterized by a crescent- or bean-shaped top over a conformingly shaped frieze fitted with very small drawers and resting on very slender legs of cabriole form. Sometimes it is less elegantly called a kidney table. The haricot was also a favorite motif during the Louis XV style.

Hari Ishime In Japanese sword mounts; a form of ishime decoration on metal sword fittings. It is used as a background and is characterized by minute cuts resembling work done with a needle. See *Ishime*; *Nanako*.

Harland, Thomas 1735–1807. American clockmaker working circa 1773–1806 at Norwich, Connecticut. He is considered to be one of the most important American clockmakers. In an advertisement of 1800, he stated, "spring and eight-day clocks with enamelled and silvered faces completely finished and regulated, in mahogany and cherry cases."

Harlequin In English cabinetwork; the term is applied to a piece of furniture which is ingeniously designed to conceal its real purpose or an additional use; such as, certain washing stands by Sheraton which when closed resembled night tables. The dressing table was often designed as a piece of harle-quin furniture during the second half of the 18th century. See *Harlequin Pembroke*.

Harlequin China In ceramics; the name given to a service or set, such as a set of cups, characterized by different colors, deriving its name from Harlequin, the performer in a pantomime who wears a parti-colored costume. References to harlequin china are found in English literature and the following is quoted from a book published in 1871, "she had six lovely little harlequin cups on a side-shelf in her china closet . . . rose, and brown, and gray, and vermilion, and green, and blue."

Harlequin Pembroke In English cabinetwork; a variety of Pembroke table introduced around the last decade of the 18th century having an oblong superstructure which can be raised from the body of the table by means of weights. Sheraton illustrates a harlequin Pembroke table in his DRAWING BOOK and writes that the concealed box-like structure "can be raised to any height, gradually until at length the whole is out." This structure is fitted with small drawers and compartments containing such accessories needed for writing, drawing or needlework. Sheraton in observing about the name writes, "it is termed a harlequin table, for no other reason but because, in exhibitions of that sort, there is generally a great deal of machinery introduced in the scenery."

Harpsichord A musical stringed instrument which in form resembled the outline of the grand piano. It was larger than the spinet and the case was provided with legs. The mechanism of the harpsichord was essentially the same as the simpler virginal and spinet with their single strings except it was furnished with two keyboards, additional mechanical features and extra strings which were controlled by stops. The harpsichord was in use from the 16th to the 18th centuries. See *Clavichord*; *Virginal*; *Spinet*.

Harquebus A 16th century firearm which was the predecessor of the musket. It

HARPSICHORD

consisted of a heavy barrel and a short thick butt. The early type was very heavy and was usually fired from a support by means of a hook to which it was attached. It was operated by a trigger and matchlock. The later type was lighter and could be fired without a support. It was later operated by a wheel lock or flint lock. During the latter half of the 16th century the harquebus was gradually displaced by the musket. It was also called an arquebus.

Harvard Chair In cabinetwork; the name given to a wooden chair which has been used by the president of Harvard University when conferring degrees since the 18th century. It is a three-legged turned wooden chair with a triangular wooden seat. The base of the triangle forms the front of the seat. The heavy turned front supports continue to form the armposts and are connected to the back of the chair by four turned pieces. The rectangular back is constructed of many turned spindles. The crest rail is surmounted with small turned finials. This variety of chair due to its peculiarities of design is believed to have been of Byzantine origin. It was introduced in England in the 16th century from Scandinavia. The name *varangian* is sometimes given to this kind of chair in Europe.

HATCHMENT
FROM AN ENGLISH MAZER

Hatchment An escutcheon or armorial ensign. The term is especially applied to a square or lozenge-shaped plaque having the armorial bearings of a deceased person and which is fastened to the front of his house. A hatchment, or armorial ensign or escutcheon, was given for an act of achievement, from which word it was corrupted through such spellings as atcheament and hachement. The term *hatchment* is applied to armorial bearings engraved on articles of silver and other similar pieces.

Hauberk In English medieval armor; the name given by the Normans to the coat-of-mail worn at the time of the Norman conquest. It resembled a long tunic. The skirt was slit both in the front and in the rear to facilitate riding in the saddle. The sleeves which were loose only covered the elbow. The hauberk was most frequently made of woven rings or of rings sewn upon leather or upon a sturdy fabric. The hauberk was called a byrnie by the English.

Häufebecher A German term applied to a small cup, usually made of silver. They were made in nests of twelve, eight and lesser numbers, as well as in pairs and single cups, and they fitted into each other as far as the moldings encircling the center of the cup. The cups were engraved or embossed with religious, allegorical or other like subjects. The bowl was usually circular in shape and rested on a short and circular foot. It was usually about 4 inches high with the diameter of the mouth measuring about 3 inches. It was introduced about the middle of the 16th century and was principally identified with German silver. It is also called a setzbecher and monatsbecher.

Hausmalerei In German ceramics; a German term, literally meaning home painting, given to the independent faïence and porcelain painters of Germany, whose painting included some of the best ceramic art work as well as some of the poorest. At first in the latter part of the 17th century the work was done by a few talented artist-enamellers who sometimes changed from enamelling glass and metal to enamelling the faïence then being made in Germany. These Hausmaler also did some of the early enamelled decoration on Meissen and Vienna porcelain. The porcelain manufactories soon regarded this practice with disfavor and did everything possible to check the work of these independent artist-enamellers. After the middle of the 18th century it had practically degenerated to hackpainting, although the practice was partially revived during the Empire style.

Haut-Relief High-relief. See *Relief.*

Hawk's Beak Spout In silver; a spout on a pitcher that resembles a hawk's beak, having a slight downward curve.

Hawthorn   In Chinese ceramics; the prunus design is often miscalled hawthorn. See *Ginger Jar*; *Prunus*.

Hawthorn Wood   See *Epine-Vinette Wood*.

Hearth Rug   See *Odjaklik*.

Heart-Shaped Chair Back   In English cabinetwork; it was one of the two most characteristic shapes for the open-back chair designed in the Hepplewhite style. This type of back which resembled interlaced hearts evolved from the shield-back which was the other typical Hepplewhite style chair back.

Heaume   In armor; during the 12th century the heaume or great helm was introduced. It was a large flat-topped piece covering the entire head and face almost to the shoulders. In the 13th century the crown became conical in shape to afford a better glancing surface and by the 14th century it was superseded by the lighter-weight basinet.

Hehbehlik   A Perso-Turkish word meaning saddle-bag. It was a large bag or pouch woven exactly like an Oriental rug. It was thrown across the horse, camel or donkey behind the saddle and was used to carry articles. The hehbehlik was generally one of a pair and was joined by straps or a band.

Heian   A Japanese period; consisting of Jogan or Early Heian period A.D. 794–897 and the Fujiwara or Late Heian period A.D. 897–1185. See *Japanese Periods*.

Heliotrope   See *Quartz*.

Helm   In armor; see *Heaume*.

Helmet   In medieval armor; a metal headpiece having as a rule attached parts to cover and protect the face and neck. The earliest form of helmet was a casque which in its original form was simply a metal cap. The basinet, salade, armet and burgonet were developed in that order by the makers of armor. The burgonet was worn until armor finally disappeared from the battlefield around 1675. See *Casque*; *Basinet*; *Salade*; *Armet*; *Burgonet*; *Heaume*; *Cabasset*; *Morion*.

Helmet-Form Creamer   In English silver; a term applied to a silver cream jug so-called because the shape of the body was similar in form to an inverted helmet. The helmet-form was the earliest form of cream jug and extant examples date from about 1727. The helmet-form creamer or cream jug was also made in other materials, such as earthenware and porcelain. See *Cream Jug*.

Helmet-Form Ewer   In English silver; the design for this form of ewer, which resembled an inverted helmet, was introduced in England from the Continent by Huguenot silversmiths who sought refuge in England after the Revocation of the Edict of Nantes in 1685. It appears that the earliest extant example bears the date of 1697. Ewers of helmet-form often elaborately wrought with Rococo ornament date from around 1740, with the rose-water dishes being conformingly decorated. Helmet-form ewers were also made in other materials, such as faïence and earthenware.

Hemstitch   A decorative needlework done by drawing out a few parallel threads from a fabric and fastening the cross threads in successive small clusters. The name is also given to the stitch used in making it and the work itself.

Henri II   King of France from 1547 to 1559. The name is given to one of the three principal styles of ornament of the French Renaissance. The Henri II style was a style of refinement and restraint. Its finest work was achieved during the reign of Henri II. The ornament consisted of classic motifs such as the acanthus leaf, arabesques, rinceaux, scrollwork, vase forms, swags, shells and rosettes. Figures in many various forms were used, such as humans, animals, and all kinds of monstrous beings. Toward the middle of the 16th century changes in furniture design became apparent. Italian classic design began to exert its influence on the form. Many features of classical architecture were incorporated into the forms, such as slender columns, fluted pilasters,

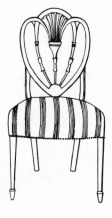

HEPPLEWHITE
HEART-SHAPED CHAIR BACK

arches, cornices and moldings. The forms were generally simple and severe. Classic proportions were perfected; the classic ornament and the moldings were in scale with the piece they decorated as well as with each other. The decoration was moderate and the motifs were well distributed. Carving and inlay were the principal decorative processes, and the former was by far the favorite method. The carvings were finely executed and were often in low relief. Walnut gradually supplanted oak. The furniture of this period fell into two principal schools of art. The style already described was characteristic of the furniture designed around Paris. The other principal school included the regions around Burgundy. This style was characterized by an over-abundance of ornament; by a profuse use of grotesques and of all kinds of human and animal figures; by the accentuated relief of its carvings, and by a lack of balance in its proportions. This school reflected the influence of Hughes Sambin. See *François I*; *Louis XIII*; *Renaissance, French*; *Sambin, Hughes*; *Burgundy*; *Du Cerceau, Jacques*.

Henri Deux Ware   In French ceramics; see *Saint-Porchaire*.

HEPPLEWHITE SHIELD BACKS

Hepplewhite, George d. 1786. English cabinetmaker and designer of the 18th century. Biographical information relating to Hepplewhite is exceedingly meager. He is known to have served an apprenticeship with the firm of Gillow of Lancaster, and later to have come to London where he conducted a business in Redcross Street, St. Giles, Cripplegate. After his death, his widow, Alice, continued the business under the name of A. Hepplewhite and Co. In 1788, the CABINET MAKER AND UPHOLSTERER'S GUIDE was published. It comprised almost three hundred unsigned designs from the drawings of A. Hepplewhite and Co. New editions of this folio volume were published in 1789 and 1794. No claim was made for originality in the GUIDE. The character of the Hepplewhite style is based on the designs in the GUIDE. These designs were not the creation of any one particular person, but represented collectively the prevailing taste in furniture designs. Consequently the name *Hepplewhite* is accepted as expressing the prevailing fashion rather than the individual. In fact there has never been a single piece of furniture which has been definitely known to have been made by Hepplewhite. The GUIDE gave a fine interpretation of Adam's style and adapted the style for the use of the cabinetmaker. Elegance was the keynote of the style. The designs were reasonable, consistent and simple and at the same time elegant and refined. They were marked by a lightness of touch and were distinctive for their delicacy and gracefulness. All the designs were not of the same high quality; some were mediocre and commonplace. The Hepplewhite style was in vogue from about 1780 to 1795. It is not known how long the A. Hepplewhite and Co. remained in business. The classic form of Robert Adam and the Louis XVI style essentially influenced the contour of Hepplewhite furniture. Although Hepplewhite adhered to straight structural lines he freely introduced curved lines into many pieces of furniture. He preferred a slender straight tapering leg which was commonly of quadrangular form and occasionally of cylindrical form. The woods most frequently used were mahogany and satinwood. The decorative processes employed included carving, gilding, marquetry, veneering, painting and lacquering or japanning. The style of ornament included all the classic motifs introduced by Robert Adam and the prevailing motifs of the Louis XVI style. Circular or oval paterae, rosettes, fans, pendants of husks, Prince of Wales feather badge, wheat-ear motif, acanthus scrolling, ovoid classic urns and medallions were among the favorite motifs. See *Classic Revival*; *Louis XVI*; *Adam, Robert*.

Hepplewhite Style   Circa 1780–1795. See *Hepplewhite, George*.

Herat Border   See *Herat Rug*.

Herati Motif   A design motif used in Oriental

rugs, especially in Persian rugs. It usually consists of a rosette between two long curved leaves. This pattern is also commonly called the fish pattern, because of the supposed resemblance of the leaves to the backbone of a fish.

Herat Rug An Oriental rug belonging to the Persian classification. The foundation is cotton, sometimes wool. The pile is of wool, medium in length. The ends are usually finished with a narrow web and loose warp threads. It is durable and heavy. The chief design is the Herat pattern, also called the fish pattern, worked in a diaper arrangement for the body of the rug and also in the border, known as the Herat border. Occasionally in the body of the rug is worked a diaper arrangement of the pear, all inclining in one direction. The Herat was also woven during the 16th and 17th centuries. See *Persian Rugs*.

Herculaneum In English ceramics; a manufactory was started near Liverpool on the right bank of the Mersey River by Richard Abbey, in 1793–1794. It was taken over in 1796 by Worthington, Humble and Holland, who called it Herculaneum. They made cream-colored earthenware, much of it being printed in blue or black, and other wares in the Staffordshire style. They also made an unimportant bone porcelain from about 1800 to 1841. The factory ceased to operate also in 1841. The mark was "Herculaneum", impressed.

Herek Rug An Oriental rug woven at Herek-Keui, Turkey. Around 1850 a rug factory was established there to fill the rug requirements of the Imperial court. The designs of the modern Herek are Persian, adapted to the American taste. See *Turkish Rugs*.

Herend In Hungarian ceramics; a porcelain manufactory was established by Maurice Fischer, 1800–1880, with the patronage of Count Charles Esterházy at Herend, a town in the Bakony forest, about 1839. Its wares, which were usually of very fine quality, were copies of Oriental and 18th century European porcelains, especially those of Vienna, Berlin, Meissen, Sèvres and Capo di Monte. Herend porcelain became well known throughout Europe and at the International Exhibition in London in 1851 Queen Victoria ordered a dinner service which was decorated with a conventional design of flowers and butterflies in the Chinese manner. When the Vienna factory closed in 1864 Emperor Franz Joseph ordered that his favorite models and patterns be given to Herend for future use. In 1867 Fischer was made a member of the Magyar nobility with the title of Fischer of Farkasháza. Fischer retired in 1873 and gave the factory to his five sons who carried on for one year and became bankrupt in 1874. There were several changes in ownership until 1926 when the factory was revived. The mark is "Herend" impressed; and at a later date a version of the Hungarian coat-of-arms was added in underglaze blue or enamel over the glaze.

Herez Rug An Oriental rug belonging to the Persian classification. It derived its name from the Herez district where it is woven. The foundation is cotton and the pile is wool trimmed short. Other Oriental rugs woven by the Herez weavers are: Serapi; Gorevan; Bakhshis. See *Persian Rugs*.

Herreboe In Norwegian ceramics; a faïence manufactory was founded here in 1757 by Peter Hofnagel. It operated until 1770. No regular factory mark was used; sometimes the full name of the factory or the name of one of the painters was used; however, much was unmarked. The painted decoration, which was almost always done in monochrome of blue or manganese purple, is a remarkable demonstration of the Rococo style. The motifs included Chinese Rococo subjects and characteristic Rococo motifs such as scrolls, foliage, shells and naturalistic flowers. The manner of painting, the selection of motifs and the twisting and wavy decoration in relief all contributed to give the finished work a spirit of restlessness and rhythm which was most unusual. Included

HERREBOE BISHOP BOWL

among their wares were wall fountains and lavabos, trays, tureens, bishop bowls and the customary tablewares.

Herrera, Juan de In Spanish Renaissance ornament and architecture; see *Renaissance, Spanish*.

Herringbone Banding See *Feather Banding*.

Herringbone Stitch A decorative embroidery stitch in which the threads are worked in a form of cross-stitch, and also a form of stitch in which the threads are worked obliquely and equidistant along both sides of a line.

Hêtre Wood See *Beechwood*.

H-Form Stretcher In cabinetwork; the name given to a form of stretcher which was similar to the letter H. It was composed of two side stretchers which joined the front and rear legs and one cross stretcher which joined the two side stretchers in the middle.

Hibachi The Japanese hibachi or brazier is made of wood, metal or pottery. The shape is chiefly round or rectangular. It holds a metal ash container in which charcoal is burned. It is the only heat-producing unit in a Japanese home.

Hickory An American hardwood tree, *carya alba*, having a brown color and widely used in cabinetwork. It is also the Australian acacia. It was especially used for certain articles which required a strong wood but not a heavy wood, such as the spindles of Windsor chairs.

Highboy In American cabinetwork; the highboy was introduced in America around 1700 and retained its popularity for almost one hundred years. It was designed in the form of a chest of drawers mounted on a stand that was always fitted with drawers. If the stand did not have drawers this article of furniture is referred to as a chest of drawers mounted on a stand. The upper section was usually designed with a row of three small drawers over three or four graduated long drawers. The arrangement of the drawers

QUEEN ANNE
BONNET TOP HIGHBOY

in the lower section varied. It most frequently had one long drawer over a row of three small drawers, with the two lateral drawers often being deeper. The stand, which as a rule was valanced, was mounted on four cabriole legs; however, the early highboy designed in the William and Mary style usually had turned legs with an additional two legs in the front. The design for this stand essentially followed the design for a type of side table which was called a dressing table in England and a lowboy in America. The highboy was designed in the William and Mary, Queen Anne and Chippendale styles. The William and Mary highboy was characterized by its flat top, its six inverted cup-turned legs and its flat, shaped stretcher. The characteristic Queen Anne highboy had either a flat or scroll top and had four slender cabriole legs terminating in club feet. The valanced stand, which was generally designed with one or two rows of drawers, often had acorn pendants. Sometimes the top central drawer and the bottom central drawer were carved with a fan or sunburst motif. The highboy designed in the Chippendale style commonly had a scroll top; however, some highboys were made with a flat top. The four cabriole legs, which were often shorter and acanthus carved, terminated in claw and ball feet. The claw and ball feet were the principal indication of the Chippendale style. The valanced apron frequently centered a carved recessed shell motif, and the top drawer was often decorated in a similar manner. See *Philadelphia Style Highboy*; *Chest of Drawers on a Stand*.

High Chest of Drawers See *Tall Chest of Drawers*.

Highdaddy In American furniture; it seems to be generally understood that the term refers to a high chest of drawers mounted on a frame that is designed without drawers.

High-Relief See *Relief*.

High Temperature Color Or Grand Feu Color. In ceramics; a term applied to the colors which can stand the heat of the high temperature kiln. See *Grand Feu*; *Petit Feu*.

Hill Jar   In Chinese ceramics; an early cylindrical pottery vessel of the Han dynasty. It invariably had a cover modelled in the shape of a mountain with waves at its base. It rested on three feet, each being shaped in the likeness of a bear. The circular body was usually ornamented with a band of relief decoration consisting of waves and exotic birds and animals. It is also called a Po Shan Lu.

Hilt   The handle of a sword or dagger. In the more complete type of hilt the component parts consist of a pommel which is a finial or knob at the end; a grip which is the part gripped by the hand; the quillons which are the projecting arms and together form the cross-guard; the knuckle bows which are the shaped pieces between the cross-guard and the pas d'âne. The heel of the blade is the blade part between the cross-guard and pas d'âne, and the pas d'âne is the piece or actual base part of the hilt.

Hinge   In English furniture mounts; the early wooden pin hinge commonly found on chests was superseded toward the end of the 13th century by the metal butterfly hinge, which was so named because of its supposed resemblance to a butterfly. This hinge was in general use until the 15th century when the half of the hinge attached to the door was elongated in the form of a strap and became more elaborate in outline. The butt hinge with only the barrel showing was in general use during the 16th century. In the following century the cock's-head hinge was extensively used. It was so named because the outline of the curved plates working on a central barrel more or less resembled the head of a cock. Another variety was the H-hinge, with its two vertical plates treated symmetrically, made in the 16th, 17th and 18th centuries. In American furniture mounts; the different forms of hinges found in America were essentially of English inspiration. The butterfly hinge was the earliest form of hinge used in America. The H-hinge made in the shape of a letter H was very popular. The HL-hinge, which was a variant of the H-hinge, was in the combined form of those two letters. Another principal form was the rat-tail hinge, which was so named because of the supposed resemblance of the lower part of the hinge to a rat's tail. This is not to be confused with the English rat-tail spoon. The strap hinge with its elongated strap terminating in either a point or a round end was also a favorite form for decorative hinges and was chiefly found on chests. It appears that all of these hinges with the exception of the butterfly hinge were used on cupboards.

Hirado Ware   In Japanese ceramics; a blue and white or white porcelain made at Mikawachi which is near Arita in the Hizen province. It enjoyed the patronage of the feudal prince of Hirado. The ware was always relatively scarce. Its finest period of production was from around the middle of the 18th century until around 1830. Hirado ware was decorated with delicate underglaze blue. The motifs included such subjects as children at play, landscapes and pagodas. The pure white ware, of which much less was produced, had designs which were incised or in relief. It was noted for its milk-white glaze and for its fine decorative designs.

Hira-Makie   See *Japanese Lacquer*.

Hirame   In Japanese lacquer; a variety of lacquer work having minute, irregularly shaped pieces of sheet gold or silver worked in the surface. See *Japanese Lacquer*.

Hira-Zōgan   In Japanese sword mounts; a term applied to Hon-Zōgan inlay work when it is flat. See *Zōgan*.

Hispano-Moresque   See *Mudéjar*.

Hispano-Moresque   In Spanish ceramics; the lustered ware made in Spain by Moorish potters both before and after the termination of Moorish rule in 1492. The term may also be given to some of the non-lustered pottery

BUTTERFLY HINGE

STRAP HINGE

COCK'S HEAD HINGE

H HINGE

made at Valencia, Granada and Seville. The origin of lustered pottery is not clear. It was found in the 9th century in Mesopotamia and almost as early in Egypt and Persia. It is generally believed that lustered wares were made in Spain by the end of the 14th century and that Malaga was an early productive center during the 15th century. The motifs for this ware were of Mohammedan inspiration such as interlacements and a variety of geometrical designs. The development of Spanish lustered pottery subsequently centered around Valencia. The beautiful blue and white and lustered pottery of Valencia reflected a distinctive European quality and motifs such as flowers were increasingly used in the painted decoration. Valencian pottery exerted a strong influence on the ceramic styles of Italy, to which country large quantities were exported after the middle of the 15th century. See *Luster Decoration*; *Valencia*.

HITCHCOCK CHAIR

Hitchcock Chair   In American cabinetwork; a type of small side chair made during the first part of the 19th century at Hitchcockville, Connecticut, circa 1826–1843. Although the chair sometimes varied slightly in design the characteristic Hitchcock chair had a turned crest rail with an enlarged center portion and a wide slat which was usually plain but sometimes cut in a design. At times a very narrow slat was placed below the wide one. The back supports, which continued to form the round rear legs, were flat on the front in order to allow sufficient surface for a painted design. The seat was of rush, but later chairs also had wooden and caned seats. The round front legs were often splayed and were sometimes tapered; in the case of the latter they frequently terminated in small ball feet. The legs were connected with a round stretcher in the rear, two on each side and a turned one in the front. The chair was commonly painted black and was embellished with bright colored floral and fruit stencil designs with touches of gilt or bronze. See *Hitchcock, Lambert*.

Hitchcock, Lambert   An American cabinetmaker working circa 1818–1843. He was born at Cheshire, Connecticut, and moved to Barkhamsted. At a later date the settlement around his shop was called Hitchcockville. The chairs produced at this factory carried the label "L. Hitchcock, Hitchcockville, Ct." In 1829, the label was changed to "Hitchcock, Alford and Company, Hitchcockville, Conn." After Hitchcock left the firm, the name was changed to Alford and Company. During the period from 1826 to 1843 the term *warranted* was also printed beneath the chair seat. See *Hitchcock Chair*.

Hizen Ware   In Japanese ceramics; a province famous in the ceramic history of Japan. Three principal varieties of porcelain were made here: the enamelled porcelain of Arita which is popularly called Ko Imari or old Imari and the fine enamelled Kakiemon style of Arita ware; the enamelled porcelain of Nabeshima; and the blue and white Hirado porcelain. See *Arita Ware*; *Kakiemon*; *Imari*; *Nabeshima*; *Hirado*.

Ho   In Chinese art; a bird subject symbolic of longevity. It was represented as a crane, a heron or a stork and was believed to live for many years. See *Chinese Animal Figures*.

Ho   Or Huo. In Chinese bronzes; the term applied to a ritual jug or vessel. It is usually in the form of a jug-shaped vessel resting on three or four legs and having a loop handle and cover. A straight pouring spout extended from the side of the body.

Hobnail   In American glass; a pressed glass characterized by an over-all pattern of bosses or studs that resemble the heads of hobnails. It was made in more than fifteen varieties and in different colors. It was first produced around 1850 and became very popular around 1880. It was originally called dewdrop or opalescent dewdrop since much of the glass had an opalescence. See *Art Glass*.

Ho Chou   In Chinese ceramics; it is generally accepted that there were four potteries located in the Shansi province as early as the T'ang dynasty and that the one at Ho Chou produced the finest ware. It is assumed that during the Sung dynasty at Ho Chou a grey ware was made that was similar to a type of t'zu chou incised slip ware. It was washed in a white slip and had excellent free-flowing incised designs and was covered in a finely crackled yellow-green glaze.

Hochschnitt In German glass; the German term *hochschnitt* or cameo relief is applied to a rare and intricate technique of engraving on glass. Glass engraved in the hochschnitt manner frequently combined with it the more usual tiefschnitt or intaglio work. The hochschnitt engraving was generally found on glasses having elaborately carved stems and knops in the Baroque style. From about 1690 to 1700 hochschnitt work was produced by many famous German glass engravers including Franz Gondelach working at Cassel and Potsdam. Much of this work was signed by the artists and the principal glasshouses whose production included hochschnitt were Potsdam, Cassel, Berlin and Petersdorf. See *Cassel*, in German Glass; and *Potsdam*, in German Glass.

Höchst In German ceramics; the town of Höchst, near Mayence, is known for its fine porcelain and also for some distinctive faïence made for a short time from around 1746 to 1757. The manufactory was established in 1746 with the support of the Elector of Mayence. From 1778 a rapid decline became evident and it finally closed in 1796. The factory mark for faïence was the mark of a wheel, generally with six spokes, taken from the arms of the Elector of Mayence. The influence of Meissen and Strasbourg was evident in the faïence wares, which were decorated only in enamel colors. It is doubtful if porcelain was made at Höchst before 1750. With the exception of the biscuit figures and reliefs which were not marked, the mark of the wheel was generally used. At first it was in red, some other enamel color or gold, and from about 1762 in underglaze blue. The Electoral Hat or crown over the wheel was probably used only from 1765

to 1774. An impressed or incised wheel was rarely found. Höchst is one of the seven important manufactories making porcelain during the 18th century in Germany. The glaze and the hard paste material were of a fine and distinctive quality. The tablewares reflected the influence of Meissen and Frankenthal and the painted decoration, which was done in delicate and clear enamel colors, was in accordance with the contemporary fashions, the Rococo motifs being later supplanted by the Neo-Classic motifs. The best known figures were made between 1767 and 1779 and were essentially German in style. However, some early figures inspired by Meissen models and in the style later developed at Frankenthal are praiseworthy.

Hocked Animal Leg In cabinetwork; a kind of support or leg which terminated in an animal's foot including that part of a leg which corresponds to an ankle. It was a feature of the English Regency style and was occasionally used on chairs and stools.

Hock Glass A tall, slender stemmed wine glass having a deep round bowl that curved slightly inward at the rim. The name is derived from hock or hockheimer which is a white Rhine wine.

Hogarth Chair In English furniture; the name frequently given to a Queen Anne splat-back chair characterized by its curving lines and cabriole legs. The well-known English painter William Hogarth, 1697–1764, referred to the cyma curve which is the distinguishing feature of the cabriole leg as "the line of beauty." Hogarth frequently depicted a Queen Anne splat-back chair with cabriole legs in his paintings in which cyma curves were also employed·in the undulating uprights, in the arm posts and in the shape of the solid splat. See *Cyma Curve*.

Hogarth Glass In English glass; the name given to a short and heavy footed stem drinking glass of firing glass proportions.

HOCKED ANIMAL LEG

The name is derived from the glasses seen in many paintings by William Hogarth, 1697–1764. They appear in such works as the Rake's Progress, Election pictures and others of a similar nature, and are considered to be the typical tavern glass of the times. See *Firing Glass*.

Höhr In German ceramics; an important center during the 16th century for the production of German stoneware with a salt glaze. See *Westerwald*.

Holitsch In Hungarian ceramics; a faïence manufactory was established here in 1743 at the request of Francis of Lorraine, the consort of the Empress Maria Theresa, and was continued as an imperial project until 1827. The wares were principally inspired by French faïence and to a large extent were painted in enamel colors and closely imitated the Strasbourg styles. The wares were generally marked with an "H". The motifs were also borrowed from the local peasant majolica. They also made wares in the Italian Castelli style which were painted in high temperature colors. After 1786 they principally made lead-glazed cream-colored and white earthenware in the English style bearing the mark of "Holitsch", "Holitsh" or "Holics", impressed. These wares until around 1810 were of admirable quality and workmanship, largely due to painters and workers brought here from the Vienna porcelain manufactory.

HOLY-WATER SPRINKLER

Holland, Henry English architect, 1746–1806. He was instrumental in developing the early phase of the Regency style in England. Holland developed his style in accordance with the contemporary French interpretation of classicism. He incorporated many of the features of the French Directoire style. His designs included drawings for furniture such as bookcases, pier tables and mirrors. Holland was a brilliant decorative artist and through his style of decoration he was influential in introducing certain Greek and Roman details in contemporary English decorative art. After his death the Regency designers largely borrowed from

the excavations at Pompeii. This phase of the Classic Revival was greatly influenced by the work of Thomas Hope. See *Regency*; *Hope, Thomas*; *Directoire*.

Hollie-Work In lace; a needle lace made in England from mid 16th century. The name is a corruption of holy point which was used to denote church laces. During the 18th century it was much used for babies' shirts and caps. It is made with a buttonhole stitch and the pattern is formed by skipping stitches, which leaves tiny holes in the work.

Hollins, Samuel English potter working at Shelton, Staffordshire, during the last quarter of the 18th century. He principally made colored stoneware, such as red and green, in the Wedgwood style. His wares were of good quality. The pottery was carried on by his sons. The marks were "S. Hollins" and "T. & J. Hollins", impressed.

Hollow Relief See *Relief*.

Hollow Ware A general term applied to all forms of articles made from silver, porcelain or some other similar material in the form of hollow vessels, such as mugs, ewers, tankards, bowls and pitchers, in direct contrast to flat ware. The term is now applied especially to hollow vessels made of metal.

Holly Wood See *Houx Wood*.

Holy-Water Sprinkler A medieval weapon consisting of a spiked metal ball attached to the end of a long shaft. Occasionally the ball was attached to the shaft by a short chain. It is also called a morning star. See *Flail*.

Holy-Wood See *Guaiac Wood*.

Honan Celadon In Chinese ceramics; see *Celadon*.

Honan Temmoku In Chinese ceramics; a tentative name, which through long usage is now generally given to a large variety of Chinese Sung black and tan glazed wares found in the province of Honan and in practically all the other provinces that made pottery with a dark brown glaze. The Honan ware consists of vases, jars and bottles as well as tea bowls. The principal colors are black and tan with brown markings. The black glaze is thick and rich and glossy. Occasionally examples are found with a smooth reddish brown glaze with scarcely any black and the surface is more or less mat. Some Honan wares have a body of buff or buff-white, or of white or grey-white which is more or less porcelaneous. The rare oil spot temmoku generally belongs to this group. Occasionally a rare tea bowl is found that is covered with small silver spots which are actually a silver-like reflection caused by the metallic luster of the brown. This is referred to by the Chinese as the oil spot glaze. See *Temmoku*; *Kian Temmoku*; *Chien Yao*.

Honey Pot In English glass; a variety of pot or jar, elaborately cut and made in different forms, introduced during the 18th century. Especially popular was the honey pot of urn shape with a beautifully cut lid and resting on a square foot. Occasionally it is also called a sweetmeat jar. In English silver; a similar variety of pot or jar was also made of silver toward the end of the 18th century. It was commonly of beehive shape resting on a circular flat foot and fitted with a cover.

Honeysuckle In ornament; see *Anthemion*.

Honiton Lace The earliest mention of Honiton lace in Devonshire, England, was around 1620 and it seems that the town was then an active lace center. Especially praiseworthy was the Honiton lace in which exquisite bobbin-made sprigs were formed separately and later worked in or sewn on a beautiful and regular net ground. The finest ground was made by the needle but it was much more expensive than the bobbin-made ground. In the 19th century machine-made net supplanted the hand-made net; the last example of the latter was in 1869. In more recent years the application of Honiton sprigs upon a net ground was largely supplanted by a distinctive Honiton guipure, in which the bobbin-made sprigs were joined by various needle-made stitches, by cutwork or by purlings. The embroidered reliefs were of remarkable delicacy and the work was admirable for its richness and fine workmanship.

Hon-Zōgan A Japanese inlay art similar to the art work practiced on the Chinese iron vases and censers inlaid with gold. It is a process of hammering gold or silver wire into grooves cut in the surface. When this inlay is flat it is called hira-zōgan, and when it is projected above the surface it is called taka-zōgan. See *Nunome-Zōgan*; *Zōgan*.

Hood In furniture; the upper part of a tall case clock that encloses the dial and movement. It rests on the trunk of the clock. See *Tall Case Clock*.

Hooded In English cabinetwork; the term *hooded* is applied to a top that is rounded or arched and covers the entire top from front to back. The hooded top was in either a single or a double arch. The hooded top outlined in a molded cornice was adopted during the last decade of the 17th century and was chiefly employed on the secretary cabinet. The boldly molded double-arched cornice was a characteristic feature of the secretary cabinet during the reign of William and Mary. It was also employed on some secretary cabinets designed in the Queen Anne style. See *Bonnet Top*.

Hoof Foot In cabinetwork; a cloven-hoof foot. It is also called a pied de biche. See *Cabriole Leg*; *Foot*.

Hookah See *Narghile*.

Hooked Rug A handmade rug formed by pulling narrow strips of cloth through a burlap or canvas backing by means of a wood or metal hook. Coarse wool yarns have now usually replaced the strips of cloth.

HOODED

Hoop-Back In cabinetwork; the name given to a type of Windsor chair back. It had a horseshoe-shaped arm rail upon which a bow or hoop-back made from a continuous piece of bent wood was joined at each end of the center rear portion of the arm rail. The center rear spindles extended through the horseshoe-shaped arm rail to the higher bow-back. It is also called a bow-back. See *Windsor Chair*. The term *hoop-back* is also given to a form of chair back in which the uprights and top rail form a continuous arch of varying form, such as the Queen Anne splat-back chair or Dutch chair. See *Queen Anne Splat-Back Chair*.

Hope, Thomas English architect. 1769–1831. He was the son of a wealthy Dutch banker and merchant. He settled in England in 1794. He was a close friend of Percier, the French designer and architect, and showed a strong predilection for his work. Thomas Hope was instrumental in developing the Empire style in England. He used a large part of his fortune in collecting paintings and antique sculptures and in designing the furniture and decorations for his London house and his country home in Surrey, called Deepdene. In 1807, he published his furniture designs for Deepdene in a book entitled HOUSEHOLD FURNITURE AND INTERIOR DECORATION. In these designs he displayed a certain talent for adapting the classical rudimentary principles to the use of furniture; however, his work lacked the grace of the contemporary French work of Fontaine and Percier. Hope's furniture designs were closely derived from the French Empire style. His designs were sometimes extravagant. His furniture was often massive and ponderous and was not practical for general use. His drawings were marred by a certain lifeless and uninspiring quality. Hope's book exerted considerable influence on contemporary English decorative art. Thomas Hope employed the Egyptian style of ornament as an appropriate background for his Egyptian antiquities. He also illustrated designs for furniture in the Egyptian taste in his book. In these designs for furni-

HOOP-BACK WINDSOR CHAIR

ture the Egyptian influence was restricted essentially to the Egyptian style of ornament. See *Regency*; *Empire*; *Egyptian Detail*.

Hôpital de la Trinité Henri II, King of France from 1547 to 1559, established a tapestry manufactory in Paris at the Hôpital de la Trinité, which was an asylum for orphans. It was part of the scheme to teach the children a trade. In 1662 it merged with the Gobelins. One of the principal weavers was Maurice Dubourg, and among the designers were Henri Lerambert and Antoine Carron. See *Tapestry*; *Gobelins*.

Horn-Beam Wood See *Charme Wood*.

Horse In Chinese art; the horse or ma is a favorite animal subject in Chinese ornamental design. The white horse or pai ma is one of the principal animals in Buddhist designs. The eight horses of the Emperor Mu Wang, 10th century B.C., who carried him to the palace of Hsi Wang Mu, the Queen Mother of the West, are associated with Taoist lore. They are generally seen at pasture gamboling about in playful frolic. There is also a dragon horse or lung ma connected with the Emperor Fu Hsi, 2852 B.C. Finally there are the sea horses who move rapidly over the waves in a flying gallop. See *Chinese Animal Figures*.

Horse Dressing Glass In English cabinetwork; an 18th century term for a form of dressing glass. See *Cheval Mirror*.

Horse Fire Screen In English furniture; an 18th century term for a form of fire screen. See *Cheval Fire Screen*.

Horsehair A cloth made partially of horsehair generally having a linen or cotton warp. It is a rather stiff and harsh fabric. Plain, striped and checkered horsehair was used as a covering for furniture in England from around 1775 onwards. Because of its durability it was much used for chairs subject to hard usage, such as dining room chairs.

Horseshoe-Back In cabinetwork; a term given to a hoop-back or bow-back chair which splays slightly outward at the bottom where it joins the seat. A good example can be found on some Windsor chairs. See *Bow-Back*. The term *horseshoe-shaped* is applied to a chair back which has the arms and crest rail designed in one continuous piece, such as a corner chair or roundabout chair and a chaise à bureau.

Hotei In Japanese art; one of the seven Japanese household gods of good fortune. He was the most popular one. See *Pu-Tai Ho-Shang*; *Chinese Gods*.

Hot Milk Jug In English silver; see *Jug, Hot Water*.

Hot Water Jug In English silver; see *Jug, Hot Water*.

Hot Water Vegetable Dish In English silver; a deep two-handled entrée dish having a cover with a finial. It was placed in a hot water stand of conforming design fitted with a metal liner to hold water. See *Entrée Dish*.

Hound-Handled Pitcher In ceramics; a stoneware pitcher having the handle modelled in the form of a fox, a dog, or a hound. It was originally made in Hungary and at a later date in England. They were first made in America during the second quarter of the 19th century. Of particular interest were those made at Bennington, Vermont. The glaze was a mottled Rockingham glaze of rich brown. The decoration was in relief and each side of the pitcher usually depicted a hunting scene or some animal of the chase. See *Bennington*; *Rockingham*.

Houx Wood The wood of the holly tree, *ilex aquifolium*, used in cabinetwork especially by the French ébénistes. It has a fine grain and its color is almost white. It was widely used in English marquetry and in American inlay work.

Hsiang In Chinese art; the elephant or hsiang was a favorite animal subject. It was symbolic of strength and power. See *Chinese Animal Figures*.

Hsien In Chinese bronzes; the name given to a vessel for ritual as well as domestic use for steaming cereals and vegetables. The hsien is composed of two parts. The upper section resembled a deep pot or cauldron with lobes on the rim through which a rod or pole could be passed for carrying the pot when it was hot. The bottom was perforated. The lower section was shaped like a li resting on three or four legs. See *Li*.

Hsi Wang Mu In Chinese art; a Taoist subject who was the goddess of long life. She is represented as a graceful slender young girl carrying a flower basket which at times was suspended on a cane over her shoulder. She is often seen under a peach tree in full blossom. See *Chinese Gods*.

Hsüan Tê The Hsüan Tê reign of the Ming dynasty in China; 1426–1435. See *Chinese Dynasties*.

Hu In Chinese art; a Chinese animal figure extensively used in Chinese sculpture, painting and ceramics. It is a tiger, which in China is regarded as the king of all animals. His image served many purposes, such as calling the men to battle and watching over the graves of the dead. See *Chinese Animal Figures*.

Hu In Chinese bronzes; a jug-shaped vessel used for holding beverage. The name is given to any of various forms of jug-shaped vessels provided with either a bail handle or handles on the sides. The covers of these vessels sometimes served as cups.

Hubble Bubble See *Narghile*.

Huche In French Gothic cabinetwork; the name given to a kneading-trough; a bin, such as a corn bin or bread bin; also a bread hutch. As early as the Gothic period the term *maie* or *pétrin* was used to describe a French kneading trough or kitchen huche having a hinged top. This early type was of crude construction. See *Pétrin*; *Hutch*.

Huet, Christopher d. 1759. French decorative painter and designer working in the

BRETON HUCHE
WITH TABLE TOP

Rococo style. His amusing singeries and delightful chinoiseries are remarkable for their airy and graceful delicacy. He undoubtedly belongs to the great line of decorative designers stemming from the work of Bérain and Audran.

Huet, Jean-Baptiste 1745–1811. A foremost French decorative artist of the 18th century. In 1790 he was attached to both the Gobelins and Beauvais tapestry manufactories where he executed designs of elegant compositions after the works of Boucher and d'Oudry. He executed many important compositions of animal studies.

Hull In English ceramics; a pottery was established in 1802 at Hull, Yorkshire, England, making earthenware in the Staffordshire style. From 1825 it was operated by William Bell, and the wares were frequently marked after that date with "Bellevue Pottery Hull", surrounding one or two bells.

Humpen In German glass; a large cylindrical beaker, which because of its imposing size it is reasonable to assume was to be shared by several convivial drinkers. German enamelling, particularly of armorial themes, was frequently applied to these vessels, which apparently were quite popular during the late 16th and 17th centuries.

SHERATON HUNT SIDEBOARD

Hundred Antiques or Pa Ku In Chinese art; the term is applied to a comprehensive group of symbols and symbolical motifs which were often grouped together in panel decoration. A popular set of Pa Ku emblems is the Pa Pao or Eight Precious Objects. See *Chinese Symbols and Emblems.*

Hungarian Work A kind of needlework of Italian origin. The designs, which completely cover the ground, are developed with upright stitches, generally consisting of parallel zigzag patterns producing a sawtooth effect. Although the design consists of diagonal lines, it is always worked in a long vertical stitch which overlaps. Each one of the designs is worked in a single color

with its intermediary graduated tones. It is also called bargello work. The stitch is called a Hungarian stitch or flame stitch.

Hung Chih The Hung Chih reign of the Ming dynasty in China; 1488–1505. See *Chinese Dynasties.*

Hung Hsi The Hung Hsi reign of the Ming dynasty in China, 1425. See *Chinese Dynasties.*

Hung Wu The Hung Wu reign of the Ming dynasty in China; 1368–1398. See *Chinese Dynasties.*

Hunter's Table See *Hunting Board.*

Hunting Board In American cabinetwork; the name *hunt board, hunter's table* or *hunting board* is often given in certain parts of the South to describe a form of sideboard table designed with a frieze and generally without drawers, or a form of sideboard designed with drawers or with cupboard doors used for the service of refreshments. This type of table varied considerably in design and in quality. Undoubtedly its most distinguishing feature was its height. The hunt table had to be tall enough so that the huntsmen could stand comfortably around it and enjoy their liquid refreshments. When fitted with drawers or cupboards it is usually called a hunt sideboard.

Hunting Chair In English cabinetwork; Sheraton writing in his CABINET DICTIONARY 1803, observes that these chairs "are stuffed all over except the legs which are of mahogany." He illustrates a chair designed with a frame that pulls out in front and upon which may be placed a cushion for resting the legs. Contemporary records, such as the accounts from Thomas Chippendale Jr., show that the name was given to a form of caned mahogany armchair that was quite masculine in appearance. It seems reasonable to assume that thick leather cushions were added to the seat and back to provide additional comfort.

Hunting Rug A Persian Oriental rug made during the 16th and 17th centuries. The elaborately detailed designs showed forests with figures of horsemen and other hunters with dogs pursuing animals of the chase. See *Persian Rugs*.

Hunt Sideboard   See *Hunting Board*.

Hu P'i   In Chinese ceramics; tiger skin or hu p'i is the name given to a variety of ware which combined several different colored glazes giving a splashed or spotted effect to this ware. This splashed effect was found on T'ang wares and later on K'ang Hsi wares; however, the glazes on the latter were thinner and the finished work was less effective.

Hurricane Glass   A tall, large cylindrical-shaped article of glass open at the top and at the bottom. It was placed over a candle-stick to protect the flame from the wind and the draft.

Hurricane Lamp   The name given to a candlestick fitted with a hurricane glass that rested on the rim of the candle-holder. See *Hurricane Glass*.

Husk Festoon   In ornament; a festoon, chain or garland of decoratively arranged husks suspended in a curved form between two points. The term *husk* is applied to the dry outer cover of certain seeds and fruit. Delicate husk festoons were extensively used on furniture designed in the Adam, Hepplewhite and Sheraton styles. Gilded mirror frames in the Adam style enriched with fragile husk festoons made of composition and strengthened by a core of wire were much favored. See *Festoon*.

Hutch   In English cabinetwork; the term *hutch* which is derived from the French word *huche* was applied during the Gothic period to a household chest of crude construction. The name was also usually given to an article of furniture having the general contour of a chest raised on supports or legs and having a fixed top with one or more doors in front. Undoubtedly the hutch was used for different purposes, such as for storing clothes and other possessions. It is generally accepted that the hutch of rough construction was used as a bin for storing grains and as a kneading-trough.

ADAM STYLE MIRROR
FESTOONED WITH HUSKS

I

I In Chinese bronzes; the I is a vessel used for holding grain. It is a square-shaped vessel having a cover with a finial. The cover resembles in form the hipped roof of a house.

Ice Glass In Venetian glass; a form of clear glass having a roughened ice-like or frozen appearance, made in Venice from around the 16th to the 18th centuries. This effect was achieved by dipping the warm glass in cold water, thus creating a multitude of minute cracks which were made smooth by further heating and slight blowing. See *Venetian Glass*.

If Wood The wood of the yew tree, *taxus baccata*, used in cabinetwork especially by the French ébénistes. It is hard and its color is reddish.

Igel In German glass; a short squat tumbler or a club-shaped vessel generally made of green glass, covered with prunts or glass studs. It was introduced during the 16th century. See *German Glass*; *Krautstrunk*; *Waldglas*.

Illuminated Manuscript In a strict sense the term is applied to the brilliant book decoration developed in the later Middle Ages. In a broad sense the term is given to all the early illustrated and decorated manuscripts. The art of illustrating a written text by means of pictures for the purpose of elucidation was practiced as early as the 15th century B.C. in Egypt. Around the 13th century A.D. the art of book ornamentation was well developed and it was practiced in more or less the same manner with some minor improvements for the next three hundred years. The illuminated MS of the Middle Ages was embellished with bright colors and with gold. The gold was applied in the form of gold leaf and was highly burnished. This method of burnished gold leaf gave a brilliant effect to the medieval

miniatures, which is the name given to a picture in an illuminated MS, to the initial letters and to the borders.

Illuminated Paper In wallpaper; an early form of decorative wallpaper originating in France toward the end of the 16th century. In this process engraved wood blocks outlined the design on the paper and the colors were painted in by hand. Illuminated papers became obsolete when the process of printing colors from several superimposed wood blocks directly on the paper was developed in France around the middle of the 18th century. The vogue for flock papers also hastened the decline for illuminated papers. See *Wallpaper*.

Ilmenau In German ceramics; a porcelain manufactory was started at Ilmenau, Thuringia, in 1777 by Christian Zacharias Gräbner. Apparently no mark was used until 1792 when the initial "I" was found; its use was relatively rare. From 1808 the mark is supposed to have been "N & R." The porcelain wares were largely in imitation of Meissen, even to the mark. Of particular interest were the white biscuit medallion reliefs on a pale blue ground in the style of Wedgwood's blue jasper ware, made from around 1792 to 1808. Contemporary persons and classical figures were the favorite subjects for these medallions.

Imari In Japanese ceramics; a kind of Japanese porcelain made at Arita in the Hizen province. Arita ware is popularly called Imari ware because in the Edo period it was shipped to various parts of the country from the port of Imari which is near Arita. The name Ko Imari or old Imari is well known in Japan and in Europe. Japanese porcelain made of native materials was first produced at the beginning of the 17th century when china clay of fine quality was discovered in Izumiyama, Arita, by Korean

ILLUMINATED BORDER
GERMAN 15TH CENTURY MS

potters. This early ware was simply decorated in blue under the glaze. Overglaze decoration of vitrified colored enamels was developed around the middle of the 17th century. Kakiemon and Goroshichi, two skilled ceramists, carried the art of color decoration to a high standard of excellence and the method was soon adopted in Arita ware. Colorful and brilliant overglaze decoration admirably suited the Japanese taste. At first the designs were influenced by the enamelled ware of the late Ming dynasty. Soon the patterns were borrowed from the prevailing Japanese designs in weaving. These designs became more elaborate, and finally developed into a characteristic style known as Imari Nishiki-de or porcelain having these classic Japanese colors and designs. Since Arita ware during the Edo period occupied the most important position of all enamelled porcelains the characteristics of Japanese porcelain are manifested in its style of decoration. The Imari Nishiki-de soon attracted the attention of the Dutch merchants, and after the middle of the 17th century it was exported to Europe where it won great admiration. Some Imari ware was especially made to order and reflected European influence in its decoration. Around 1730 in Europe it became very fashionable to imitate 17th century Imari wares, especially those decorated in the style of Kakiemon. Meissen, Chantilly and other Continental potteries, and Bow, Chelsea and Worcester in England all copied Imari designs. A large part of the wares of Worcester and Derby during the last quarter of the 18th century and first quarter of the 19th century were in the later Imari patterns heavily decorated in blue, red and gold. See *Hizen*; *Kakiemon*; *Chinese Imari*; *Nishiki-de*.

Imbricated In cabinetwork; the term applied to a molding carved with overlapping scales resembling the scales of a leaf bud or the scales of a fish.

Imperial Ware In Chinese ceramics; see *Kuan Yao*.

Imperial Yellow In Chinese ceramics; a distinctive clear and strong yellow color that was obtained and mastered during the K'ang Hsi period. The usual tint was a full deep color like the yolk of an egg. It appeared darker when applied on unglazed porcelain and lighter when applied on a white glazed porcelain. Occasionally a delicate engraved design was worked under the yellow glaze. The Imperial ware had five-clawed dragons engraved under the glaze. This imperial yellow also included variations such as lemon, mustard and primrose.

Ince, William and Mayhew, John English cabinetmakers and furniture designers working around 1758 to 1810 at Broad Street, Golden Square, Soho, and also in Marshall Street, Carnaby Market. William Ince served an apprenticeship with Mr. West who was a cabinetmaker in King Street, Covent Garden, and John Mayhew was in service with George Smith Bradshaw of Soho. The firm enjoyed an excellent reputation among cabinetmakers during the second half of the 18th century. However, Ince and Mayhew are chiefly remembered by their folio volume of designs. It was published in parts between 1759 and 1763 and was entitled THE UNIVERSAL SYSTEM OF HOUSEHOLD FURNITURE. This folio volume contained about three hundred designs and was predicated upon Chippendale's DIRECTOR. The notes were in English and in French. They included designs for tripod tables which had not been included in THE DIRECTOR. They also had a category of designs to be worked in bronze or in other metal at the end of the book. Some of the designs were blatantly copied from THE DIRECTOR. Although the work had merit it is generally considered to be much inferior to THE DIRECTOR. Sheraton in criticising the work said that Chippendale's DIRECTOR was "a real original as well as more extensive and masterly in design."

Incense Boat An ecclesiastical boat-shaped vessel in which the incense was kept for

IMARI PLATE

replenishing the censer. It is also called an incense ship. See *Censer*.

Incense Box In Japanese lacquer; the incense box or kogo in the form of a very small round or square case is one of the characteristic and choice articles of Japanese lacquer work. The incense box is very often of the same high quality of beautiful workmanship found on the inrō and suzuri bako, for the lacquer worker lavished on these pieces his most ingenious fancies and technical skill.

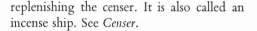

INCENSE BURNER
IN THE FORM OF A RABBIT

Incense Burning Accessories In Chinese ceramics; the equipage necessary for burning incense was regarded by the Chinese as an indispensable appointment in the library of a scholar. It comprised an incense box or hsiang ho, a vase or p'ing to hold the miniature tools, namely a poker, spade and a pair of tongs, and the urn or shao hsiang lu in which the incense was burned. It appears that the Chinese preferred a vase for the incense tools or chu p'ing which had a short neck and a narrow mouth and was heavy enough around the base to retain its balance. The incense burner was found in numerous forms, such as figures of animals and birds emitting the smoke through their nostrils and mouth or beak. However, the most common form was similar to the bronze tripod cauldron or ting with upright lobes on the rim. These accessories were also made in other fine materials such as lacquer and jade, while the tools were sometimes carved in jade, turquoise, lapis-lazuli or rock crystal.

Incising The decorative method of producing designs by cutting, carving or engraving into a surface of metal, wood, glass or pottery. See *Carving*; *Engraving*; *Sgraffiato*; *Engraved Glass*.

India Embroidery The embroidering of fabrics has been practiced in India since the 4th century B.C. The needlework displayed upon state occasions by Indian princes has exhibited some of the most elaborate and beautiful work ever produced. The Indian embroidery, with its unusual color combinations, requires the utmost patience and skill

in working out the elaborate designs which are worked in stitches in every conceivable form and color. Cashmere work is one of the principal embroideries of India and the shawls executed in this work have been highly prized in Europe. These shawls are made of a series of borders which almost cover the entire material and are worked in every shade of each color. Cashmere work is usually done on a very fine woollen or silk fabric with threads of green, red, black and white all used on the same piece. These borders are made separately and then joined together with invisible stitches, giving the appearance of a single piece of work.

Indian A comprehensive term extensively used from around the end of the 16th century to the middle of the 18th century to describe any oriental object imported into Europe. Contemporary inventories in England reveal such articles as Indian cabinets and screens. Oriental influence in contemporary design was often referred to as the Indian fashion. It is believed that this term used to describe anything pertaining to China or Japan had its origin in the name of the various East India importing companies.

Indian Flowers Or Indianische Blumen. In ceramics; a kind of floral decoration used on porcelain in which the flowers were treated in a formal or stylized manner. The design was of oriental origin and was chiefly inspired by the Japanese Kakiemon and the Chinese Famille Verte porcelain. It was introduced at Meissen around 1725. It was also a popular decoration for the dresses of figures. The Indian flowers were sometimes done in monochrome, especially rose-pink or purple. However they were more often done in polychrome, with an iron red as the predominating color. Indian flowers were imitated at the majority of porcelain manufactories. Later they were supplanted by the Deutsche Blumen, or flowers realistically treated. See *Deutsche Blumen*.

India Oriental Rugs Rug weaving became important in India during the last half of the 16th century when Persian weavers

CARVED WALNUT TABLE *Italian, 16th century*

CARVED WALNUT WRITING CABINET
(drop-front writing panel removed)
Florentine, late 16th century

CARVED WALNUT SACRISTY CUPBOARD
Tuscan, c. 1490-1500

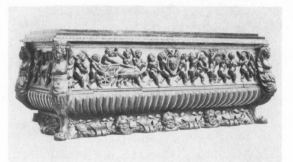

CARVED WALNUT CASSONE
Venetian, second half of 16th century

CARVED WALNUT CREDENZA
Florentine, 16th century

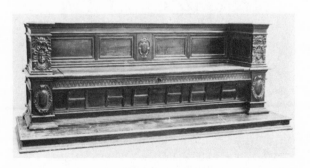

CARVED WALNUT CASSAPANCA *Florentine, mid 16th century*

Courtesy of the Metropolitan Museum of Art

RÉGENCE CARVED AND GILTWOOD CONSOLE
TABLE
Early 18th century

RÉGENCE MAHOGANY BUREAU PLAT
MOUNTED IN BRONZE DORÉ
Early 18th century

LOUIS XV CARVED AND PAINTED CANAPÉ
IN 18th CENTURY TAPESTRY
c. 1750

LOUIS XV TABLE À OUVRAGE
c. 1760

LOUIS XV CARVED AND
PAINTED FAUTEUIL IN
18TH CENTURY TAPESTRY
c. 1750

LOUIS XV MARQUETRY BUREAU A PENTE
MOUNTED IN BRONZE DORÉ
Mid 18th Century

Courtesy of the Metropolitan Museum of Art

LOUIS XVI VENEERED TINTED BEECHWOOD
TABLE À OUVRAGE WITH ADJUSTABLE READING
STAND, WITH SÈVRES PLAQUES AND MOUNTED
IN BRONZE DORÉ
Stamped M. Carlin (M.E. 1766)

LOUIS XVI VENEERED MAHOGANY COMMODE-
DESSERTE MOUNTED IN BRONZE DORÉ
Attributed to Jean Henri Riesener (M.E. 1768)

LOUIS XVI AMARANTH AND SATINWOOD
MARQUETRY SECRÉTAIRE À ABATTANT WITH
A MEDALLION PLAQUE, MOUNTED IN BRONZE
DORÉ
Stamped J. H. Riesener, 1790

LOUIS XV MAHOGANY COMMODE INLAID WITH
A TULIPWOOD AND SATINWOOD VENEER,
MOUNTED IN BRONZE DORÉ
Stamped P. Dupré (M.E. 1766)

Courtesy of the Frick Collection, New York

ENGLISH FURNITURE

WILLIAM AND MARY WALNUT CABINET WITH
SEAWEED MARQUETRY, ON A STAND
c. 1695–1700

CHIPPENDALE CARVED
MAHOGANY CARD TABLE
c. 1755

QUEEN ANNE PARCEL-
GILDED CARVED
WALNUT CHAIR
c. 1720

MAHOGANY COMMODE, SIMILAR IN DESIGN TO
EXAMPLES OF FURNITURE BY THE FIRM OF VILE
AND COBB
c. 1750

CHINESE CHIPPENDALE
CARVED MAHOGANY CHAIR
c. 1760

QUEEN ANNE LACQUERED
SECRETARY CABINET
c. 1700–1715

Courtesy of the Metropolitan Museum of Art

ADAM-HEPPLEWHITE CARVED
MAHOGANY WINDOW BENCH
c. 1780-1790

INLAID HAREWOOD
BONHEUR DU JOUR IN
THE FRENCH TASTE
c. 1770-1780

SATINWOOD MARQUETRY COMMODE
IN THE FRENCH TASTE WITH
ORMOLU MOUNTS
c. 1765-1770

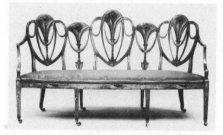

HEPPLEWHITE PAINTED SATINWOOD
CHAIR-BACK SETTEE
c. 1785

SHERATON PAINTED SATINWOOD CHAIRS
c. 1795

REGENCY ROSEWOOD
CHEVERET WITH
ORMOLU MOUNTS
Early 19th century

Courtesy of the Metropolitan Museum of Art

AMERICAN FURNITURE

QUEEN ANNE WALNUT CARD TABLE
Philadelphia, c. 1740-1750

QUEEN ANNE WALNUT AND CHERRY
TEA TABLE
Massachusetts, c. 1730-1740

CHIPPENDALE MAHOGANY
SETTEE
Philadelphia, c. 1775-1780

PHILADELPHIA STYLE CHIPPENDALE
MAHOGANY HIGHBOY
c. 1769

PHILADELPHIA STYLE MAHOGANY
LOWBOY
c. 1769

BLOCK-FRONT MAHOGANY
CHEST-ON-CHEST.
TOWNSEND-GODDARD SCHOOL,
POSSIBLY JOHN GODDARD
Newport, 1765-1780

Courtesy of the Henry Francis du Pont Winterthur Museum

SHERATON INLAID SATINWOOD
AND MAHOGANY BED
Massachusetts, c. 1800-1810

INLAID SATINWOOD AND
MAHOGANY CHEST OF DRAWERS
New England, c. 1790-1800

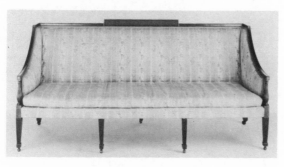

SHERATON MAHOGANY SETTEE *New York, c. 1795-1800*

INLAID SATINWOOD AND
MAHOGANY SECRETARY
BOOKCASE
Baltimore, c. 1790-1800

CHIPPENDALE MAHOGANY CHAIR
ATTRIBUTED TO
BENJAMIN RANDOLPH
Philadelphia, c. 1760-1775

DROP-LEAF MAHOGANY TABLE,
ATTRIBUTED TO DUNCAN PHYFE
New York, c. 1800-1810

Courtesy of the Henry Francis du Pont Winterthur Museum

SPANISH FURNITURE

CHESTNUT BENCH *17th century*

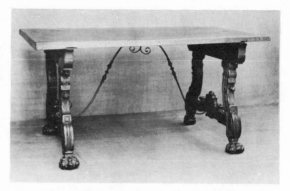

WALNUT TABLE *17th century*

WALNUT PAPELERA, *17th century*

WALNUT FRAILERO WITH EMBROIDERED
LEATHER BACK PANEL AND SEAT
Late 16th century

Left:
WALNUT VARGUEÑO WITH
GILDED IRON MOUNTS
BACKED BY RED VELVET AND
MOUNTED ON A TAQUILLÓN
17th century

Right:
WALNUT VARGUEÑO INLAID
WITH BOXWOOD AND IVORY
AND MOUNTED ON A
PUENTE STAND
16th century

Courtesy of the Hispanic Society of America

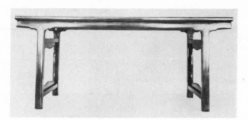

ROSEWOOD SIDE TABLE
c. 15th century, Ming
Owned by the Honolulu Academy of Arts

ROSEWOOD DOUBLE-BODIED
CUPBOARD OR WARDROBE
*c. 17th century, Late Ming to
Early Ch'ing*
Owned by Mr. and Mrs.
C. Wendell Carlsmith, Honolulu

ROSEWOOD ARMCHAIR
c. 16th century, Ming
Owned by the Honolulu Academy of Arts

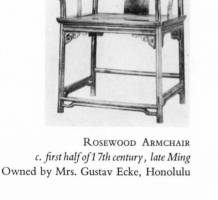

ROSEWOOD ARMCHAIR
c. first half of 17th century, late Ming
Owned by Mrs. Gustav Ecke, Honolulu

ROSEWOOD LOW CUPBOARD
c. 16th to 17th century, Ming
Owned by Mrs. James R. Judd, Honolulu

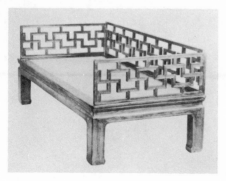

ROSEWOOD MOVABLE K'ANG OR COUCH
c. 15th century, Ming
Owned by Mrs. Gustav Ecke, Honolulu

Photographs by the Honolulu Academy of Arts

FRENCH CARPETS

AN 18TH CENTURY AUBUSSON CARPET

A 17TH CENTURY SAVONNERIE CARPET MADE FOR THE PALACE AT VERSAILLES

Courtesy of French & Company, New York

PERSIAN PRAYER RUG
WITH INSCRIPTIONS
16th century

GHIORDES PRAYER RUG
18th century

INDIA RUG
17th century

CHINESE RUG
18th century

Courtesy of French & Company, New York

ORIENTAL RUGS

POLONAISE CARPET
17th century

ISPAHAN CARPET
17th century

SAMARKAND RUG
18th century

JOSHAGHAN RUG
18th century

Courtesy of French & Company, New York

A 15TH CENTURY FLEMISH GOTHIC TAPESTRY DEPICTING AN EPISODE IN THE SIEGE OF JERUSALEM, WOVEN AT TOURNAY, 1460-1470. IT SHOWS THE EMPEROR VESPASIAN KNEELING BEFORE THE EMPEROR TIBERIUS AND RECEIVING HIS PERMISSION TO MARCH AGAINST JERUSALEM.

A 16TH CENTURY FLEMISH TAPESTRY WOVEN AFTER THE CARTOONS OF VAN ORLEY REPRESENTING THE MADONNA AND CHILD FLANKED BY SAINTS.

Courtesy of French & Company, New York

TAPESTRIES

AN 18TH CENTURY ROYAL BEAUVAIS TAPESTRY DEPICTING THE
ELOPEMENT OF HELEN, WOVEN AFTER THE CARTOONS OF J. B.
DESHAYS AND SIGNED BEAUVAIS

AN 18TH CENTURY ROYAL GOBELIN TAPESTRY DEPICTING
AN EPISODE IN THE STORY OF DON QUIXOTE, WOVEN IN 1755

Courtesy of French & Company, New York

SPANISH VELVET
Early 16th Century

SILK FABRIC BROCADED IN COLORED
SILK AND METAL
French, late 17th or early 18th century

SILK FABRIC BROCADED IN COLORED
SILK AND METAL
French, mid 18th century

PRINTED COTTON PROBABLY FROM A DESIGN
BY JEAN BAPTISTE PILLEMENT
Bromley Hall, England, c. 1765

Courtesy of the Cooper Union Museum

EUROPEAN FIREARMS

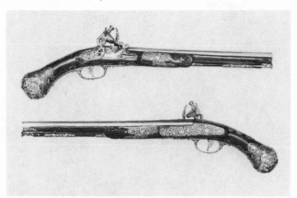

FLINTLOCK PISTOLS
Italian, c. 1690

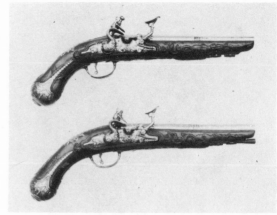

SNAPHANCE PISTOLS
Italian, c. 1675

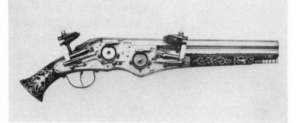

DOUBLE BARRELLED
WHEEL-LOCK PISTOL
Nuremberg c. 1580

DOUBLE BARRELLED WHEEL-LOCK
PISTOL MADE FOR EMPEROR CHARLES V
BY PETER PECH OF MUNICH
German c. 1540

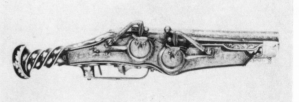

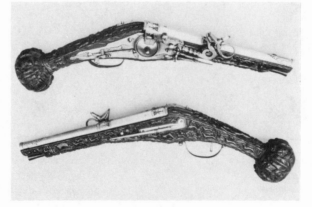

WHEEL-LOCK PISTOLS
German, late 16th century

Courtesy of the Metropolitan Museum of Art

were imported and Shah Akbar, 1556–1605, set up looms in his palace. Other Indian princes followed his example, and rugs of the finest workmanship were woven. The designs were of Persian origin. During the last half of the 19th century, due to the industrial development of India under English rule, and especially due to the introduction of rug weaving into jails. with the substitution of modern factory methods for primitive methods, the rugs in India became a factory product. These rugs were very inferior. In more recent years the quality of India rugs has greatly improved although they are distinctly a commercial creation. Persian designs and modified Persian designs still predominate in their patterns. See *Oriental Rug*; *Akbar the Great*.

Indiennes In textiles; the French term given to chintz and calicoes introduced into Europe from India. The French term *perse*, which is also given to chintz, was acquired through error because it was thought that these prints originated in Persia rather than in India. See *Chintz*.

Ingrain A variety of machine-made carpet with a flat surface. The plain ingrain is almost similar in weave to a rag carpet. The figured ingrain, which is either two-ply or three-ply, is bound together where the warp and the weft from the upper cloth are woven into the warp and the weft of the lower cloth, and vice versa. In the three-ply ingrain one of the cloths is always buried in the center. In the two-ply ingrain the face and back cloths are of different colors and the two cloths interchange positions according to the design, thus binding the structure together. In the two-ply ingrain the colors on the back of the carpet exactly reverse those on the face. The patterns included American Eagle, Martha Washington and Henry Clay. See *Wilton*.

Inkstand In English silver; see *Standish*.

Ink-Stone Box In Japanese art; see *Suzuri Bako*.

Inlay Or Inlaying. A decorative art. The use of inlay for decorative purposes is an ancient art. In this method the ground or surface is ornamented by inserting or sinking into spaces cut in the solid ground a material of a different color or substance. Included among the materials most commonly used for inlay work are cut and polished semi-precious stones such as amethyst, onyx, lapis lazuli, agate and jasper, exotic woods, ivory, mother-of-pearl, tortoise shell, marble, glass and various metals. In cabinetwork; inlay work has always been a favorite decorative process. Inlays of exotic woods are most frequently used. The term *marquetry* has a somewhat different meaning from the word *inlay*, however, they are sometimes used as if they were synonymous. See *Mosaic*; *Pietra Dura*; *Certosina*; *Intarsia*; *Niello*; *Bidri*; *Damascening*; *Zōgan*; *Korean Wares*.

In Memoriam Picture An American picture, circa 1800, usually depicting a cenotaph bearing an inscription to a deceased person, with one or more female figures under a tree. The picture was done in silk needlework but the faces and arms were painted in flesh color.

Inrō In Japanese art; a small case for holding different kinds of medicine. The word *inrō* originally signifies the vessel (rō) to hold seals (in). During the latter part of the 15th century a small article composed of a tier of three or four small boxes about 4 inches square containing seals was called an inrō and was usually placed on a shelf as an ornament. The majority of these inrō were imported from China and are believed to have been the inspiration for the inrō of Japanese design. Around the middle of the 16th century the inrō in its present form was first made. It is usually about $3\frac{1}{2}$ inches in length and about 2 inches in width. It is a rather flat article and is composed of a tier of four boxes joined together with a cord. A netsuke is attached to the end of the cord and serves as a button or catch to hold it between the girdle and the garment. A bead called an ojime runs along the cord which

LACQUERED INRŌ

links the inrō and the netsuke. The netsuke and the ojime are usually finely carved. As a rule the early inrō was simply covered with black lacquer; however, around the middle of the 17th century the inrō became more of a work of art. Many were covered with gold lacquer, multi-colored lacquer and raised work. These inrō were remarkable for their unrivalled workmanship and for their exquisite and delicate designs. See *Netsuke*.

Intaglio   The name given to a type of engraved, carved or incised figure or design cut into a very hard material. The design or figure is below the surface of the material on which it is cut. It is exactly opposite to cameo or a design in relief. The term is especially applied to incised gems. See *Cameo*.

Intaglio-Rilevato   Hollow relief. See *Relief*.

Intarsia   In Italian decorative art; intarsia or inlay work in multi-colored woods was one of Italy's great artistic achievements. Its finest period was from 1475 to 1525. The most elaborate designs such as landscapes, interiors of rooms, garden scenes and human figures, as well as decorative motifs such as arabesques, foliated scrolls and grotesques, were depicted in minute pieces of colored woods. It was principally used for the decoration of lecterns and choir stalls. It was also used in cabinetwork, in particular on the cassone. Designs in intarsia were also worked in minute and delicate bandings and were used to ornament furniture. Intarsia work enjoyed its greatest popularity during the 15th and early 16th centuries. See *Inlay*.

Iridescence   In glass and ceramics; the quality of showing a play of various and changing colors; the interchange and intermingling of colors as seen in mother-of-pearl, soap-bubbles, or a rainbow. In glass; much ancient Roman glass, as well as that of the countries of the Middle East, has a peculiar opalescence or iridescence due to its burial in damp soil. It is caused by a form of surface decay which is the result of being affected by dissolved carbonic acid in the soil moisture. Through the centuries this has drawn the alkali from the glass, leaving the surface in a disintegrated and laminated condition in which the light rays have been broken up in a prismatic manner. If a piece of this variety of ancient glass is immersed in water, which fills the minute spaces in the laminated surface, the iridescent coloring will disappear, but will reappear when it is again dry. In ceramics; the alkaline siliceous glazes on wares of ancient Egypt and the Middle East which have been buried for centuries are frequently found with the same iridescence. This was caused by the same conditions that affected the glass.

Irish Chippendale   A popular name given to the mahogany furniture made in Ireland during the Rococo era, circa 1750–1765, and marked by a rather flat and disconnected style of carving. The furniture was well constructed, and the inspiration for the pieces was chiefly derived from original models imported from England.

Irish Embroidery   A general term applied to the beautiful white embroidery work executed in Ireland. This needlework, which is done by the peasantry of Ireland and resembles the embroidery of Madeira, Saxony and Scotland, acquired a high reputation for the excellence of workmanship and delicate designs. Irish work is done on fine linen, muslin and cambric, principally with flat and raised satin stitches with the addition of dots, French knots and overcast stitches and a few eyelet holes. It differs from broderie Anglaise in that the eyelet holes do not form the principal part of the design.

Irish Point   In lace-making; Irish point lace owes its origin to the convent school at Youghal which was opened in 1852 for making needle-made laces and is also indebted to their lace-workers for spreading this art of fine needlework. An outstanding recipient of their teachings was the Convent of the Poor Clares at Kenmare, County Kerry, where lace-making was introduced

INTARSIA
FOLIATED SCROLLWORK

around 1861. They made principally flat needlepoint, appliqué and guipure laces. Equally outstanding was the Carmelite Convent at New Ross, County Wexford, where at first they made cutwork, net lace and flat needlepoint. Around 1865 they came into possession of some old Venetian Rose Point which they diligently studied and successfully reproduced. Their fine Rose Point earned them an enviable reputation. They were also known for their exquisite crochet work.

Irish Rose Point In lace-making; see *Irish Point*.

Irish Stitch In embroidery; a long vertical stitch chiefly used for groundings or patterns formed with graduating shades of colors. The Irish stitch is taken over five or more threads in an upright direction and worked on fine canvas. Its characteristic feature is in the method of being alternately started from the last or bottom row of canvas and the third row. This allows the stitches of one line to extend to the center of the stitches of the next line and produce an even-toned variation of the colors.

Iron Red In Chinese ceramics; a red color made from iron oxide. It was neither an underglaze color nor a glaze color and had to be fired at a low temperature over a glaze. It was used in the so-called Five-Color Ming wares and in the Famille Verte wares of the K'ang Hsi dynasty. The Ming iron red was duller and darker. From the beginning of the Ch'ing dynasty the color became lighter as it became more refined. Iron red used as a monochrome was usually found on wares made after K'ang Hsi.

Ironstone China In English ceramics; a dense hard earthenware patented by Charles James Mason in 1813, which he introduced at his pottery at Lane Delph, Staffordshire. Ironstone china which is greyish or bluish in tone is supposed to have pulverized slag of iron as an ingredient in its clay composition. Essentially it was similar to the stone china introduced by Spode around 1805. The painted decoration was generally composed of decadent Japanese patterns transfer printed in blue. See *Stone China*.

Isabelle Campan See *Campan Marble*.

Ishime In Japanese sword mounts; the term applied to a surface resembling the texture of stone. The backgrounds on metal sword mounts are decorated with nanako, raised dots; jimigaki, polished surface; or ishime. There are many varieties of ishime although the most characteristic form is a roughened surface produced by a blunt tool. Tatsuta ishime resembles stone; Nashi-ji ishime is like the skin of a pear; Hari ishime appears as though small holes were picked out by a needle; Zara Maki imitates stone; Gozame ishime resembles Japanese straw floor mats or tatami; and Gama ishime is like the skin of a toad.

Islamic Glass Or Near Eastern Glass. The art traditions of Egypt, Persia, Mesopotamia and Syria contributed to the development of a distinctive Islamic style of glass. Probably the most dominant feature of this Islamic style is the subordination of the individual motif to the general or over-all decorative effect, having the different motifs arranged in intricate patterns, stylistically treated with an emphasis on repetition. From the 8th or 9th century to the 11th century this new art in glass was well expressed in a group of carved and engraved glass objects displaying a singular splendor, vitality and refinement. The craftsmen cut and engraved many glass objects with the same technique and designs employed on the more costly rock crystal. The richly gilded and enamelled Islamic glass of the 13th and 14th centuries ranks among the great contributions to the art of glassmaking. Syria, especially Damascus and Aleppo, deserves credit for perfecting the technique of enamelling and gilding. The enamelled lamps made for the Egyptian mosques are especially praiseworthy. The sack of Damascus in 1400 brought to an end this glorious period of enamelled glass in Syria, although enamelled glass of artistic

PERSIAN MOSQUE LAMP

merit was made in the Near East for at least another century. See *Glass*; *Mosque Lamp*.

Ispahan   A Persian Oriental rug of the 16th century. It differed from the Persian garden, hunting, and animal rugs in that its elaborate designs were purely imaginative. Palmettes, cloud-bands, lancet leaves, spiral tendrils and arabesques were the principal motifs of the designs. The fine Ispahan of the 16th century was without medallion or decorated corner areas, the upper half was identical with the lower half, doubling from a suggested center. The border consisted chiefly of palmettes and arabesques. The colors were rich and beautifully blended. All 16th century Ispahans did not conform to this design. Ispahans of the 17th century were usually not as fine and their designs covered a much wider range. The pile in these rugs was of the finest wool and the foundation was of silk or linen. See *Persian Rugs*.

Istoriato   In Italian ceramics; an Italian term, literally meaning storied, given to a style of pictorial painting on Italian majolica, generally occupying the entire surface of a plate or dish. The figure subjects were depicted against distant landscapes, with buildings and arcades in the foreground. This style of painting was developed and perfected by Nicola Pellipario, probably the greatest of all majolica painters. Istoriato painting is especially associated with the majolica made at Urbino where Nicola was working after 1528. However he was working around 1515 at Castel Durante where he painted pieces in the istoriato manner. This style of painting was adopted at most of the Italian majolica centers around the middle of the 16th century and remained more or less in vogue until the end of the 16th century. Istoriato painting was also done at Lyons, France.

Italian Comedy Subjects   The name *commedia dell'arte* is given to the medieval Italian Comedy in which the main story or plot was well defined although the dialogue was impromptu and improvised by the actors. The characters of the Italian Comedy, wearing traditional costumes, were clearly identified as well as their plots and counterplots. The comedy includes such familiar names as Columbine, Harlequin, Cynthio, Pantalone and Isabella. The Italian Comedy became popular in France and other European countries around 1715 and its characters were portrayed in an endless series of charming porcelain figures. Superb modelling of these figures was produced at Nymphenburg, Höchst, Fürstenburg and Fulda. The influence of the Italian Comedy is reflected throughout European art and literature. The Italian Comedy was the inspiration for many designs by Antoine Watteau who introduced such characters as Gilles and the Troubadour from the contemporary French interpretation. See *Watteau, Antoine*; *Régence*; *Louis XV*.

Italian Lace   The credit for the origin of lace is a subject often disputed by Italy and Flanders. The Italians claim the invention of needlepoint lace. Although the subject has never been settled to everyone's satisfaction, Italy is generally given priority by most lace authorities for needlepoint lace, and Flanders is given preference for the bobbin-made laces in which the latter excelled. There seems to be sufficient evidence to support the belief that lace-fabric appeared in Italy as early as the 15th century. The source of this art of fine needlework has never been positively ascertained; however, lace literature sometimes suggests that it was derived from the Greeks who sought refuge in Italy. Early Italian lace was made chiefly by the nuns and expressly for the Church. The laces produced at Venice, Genoa and Milan were the best known commercially in the early period. Venice was renowned for her needlepoint laces and Genoa made almost exclusively bobbin-made laces. See *Venetian Point*; *Genoa Lace*; *Milan Lace*; *Burano Lace*.

Italian Majolica   In ceramics; the earliest decorated Italian pottery of any artistic interest was made toward the end of the 14th century. It was painted in copper green

NYMPHENBURG PANTALONE

and manganese purple on a rather imperfect white ground most frequently obtained by the use of oxide of tin. The principal centers making this green and purple decorated majolica were Orvieto, perhaps the earliest, Siena and Florence in Tuscany, Faenza, Rome, Padua and others. Throughout the 15th century the green and purple and the blue and white luster wares of Valencia, Spain, were very fashionable in Italy and influenced the work of the three great 15th century majolica centers, namely Tuscany, Faenza and Deruta. By the 16th century the vogue for majolica was firmly established. The art of majolica attained its acme of perfection between 1505 and 1525. The majolica was painted by a number of great individual artists whose paintings compare in beauty with the contemporary Italian masterpieces in oils. The fashionable and successive decorative styles in majolica were to a great extent employed at all the majolica manufactories. Each manufactory generally had its favorite type of decoration. The secret for metallic luster pigments which gave added beauty to the color was in the possession of several of the factories. From about 1500 onwards a golden or a mother-of-pearl and a ruby luster were being used at Deruta; the ruby luster seems to have disappeared from Deruta about 1515 and was found at Gubbio where it is associated with the work of Maestro Giorgio Andreoli. Included among the leading 16th century majolica centers were Faenza, Castel Durante, Caffaggiolo, Deruta, Gubbio, Urbino and Venice. During the 17th and 18th centuries the majolica tradition was more or less maintained, particularly at Castelli. Included among the typical decorative majolica pieces were the bacili or large dishes, scudelle or dishes on a low foot, scannellati or gadrooned dishes molded from examples in metal, albarellos or the more or less cylindrical pharmacy jars, spouted drug vases and confectionery vases and broth bowls. In addition many pieces were made for daily use, such as jugs and dishes. See *Majolica; Faïence.*

Itō Sukashi In Japanese sword mounts; a form of decorative work executed on the Japanese tsuba. It was produced by cutting intricate openwork designs through the metal with a fine saw. The finest and most remarkable work of this type was produced by the celebrated members of the Itō family.

Ivory Carving The earliest examples of the use of ivory for decorative pieces date from pre-historic times. Ivory carving was widely practiced during the earliest dynasties of Egypt and Assyria. During ancient Greek and Roman times many articles of carved ivory were produced, such as statuettes and especially diptychs for private and official persons. The ivory carvings of the Gothic period are generally considered to be the finest in western Europe, especially those during the 13th and 14th centuries. They are admirable for their elaborate composition, delicate openwork and minute detail. During the 17th and 18th centuries ivory carvings enjoyed great popularity in Germany and in the Netherlands. The ornament was executed in a Baroque manner and the objects included a diversity of religious and secular pieces. Articles were carved of ivory in China since ancient times. Decorative ivory pieces were made for the Imperial household during the Chou dynasty, 1122–255 B.C. As the demand for ivory carvings increased in China it became necessary to import ivory. An atelier was established at Pekin in 1263 to make ivory and rhinoceros-horn carvings for the Imperial household, such as for furniture, personal adornments and decorative objects. An ivory-carving atelier was included in the Imperial workshops at the palace in Pekin in 1680 during the K'ang Hsi reign, 1662–1722, and was in operation for more than one hundred years. The Chinese have produced some of the finest ivory carvings. They are highly esteemed for their technical skill and delicate workmanship. Carved figures of religious and philosophical subjects are remarkably beautiful and artistic. Great technical skill is necessary to produce the delicate and intricate work displayed in such articles as the

IVORY FIGURE
OF LI FU-JÊN

concentric spheres known as devil's work balls. These were first produced as early as the 14th century in Canton and are still being made there. The concentric balls are carved from one piece of ivory, one within the other. Each ball is carved with a delicate design in pierced work and some specimens have as many as fifteen balls carved one within another. See *Netsuke*.

Iwakura Ware In Japanese ceramics; a pottery made in the vicinity of Kyōto sometime after the middle of the 17th century. Awata ware, Omuro ware and Iwakura ware were all made a little north of Kyōto. These three wares were all similar and it is difficult, especially in the early days, to distinguish one from another. Iwakura pottery had a white clay body. The glaze, which as a rule had a very fine crackle, varied from a cream to a light buff. It was decorated with underglaze blue and bright overglaze enamels of red, green and light blue. Occasionally gold was used. The decoration was done by artists trained by the Kinkōzan family who were the outstanding artists for Awata ware. See *Awata Ware*.

Izumo Ware In Japanese ceramics; a pottery made at Izumo in the Totori Prefecture in north-west Japan. It had a sandy clay body with a brownish yellow glaze. Tea bowls were the principal article. An important kiln was established there about 1750. Porcelain resembling Awaji or Mimpei ware was made at Izumo at a later date.

IZUMO TEA BOWL

Jacaranda Wood   The wood of the Brazilian jacaranda, genus *jacaranda*, is widely used in cabinetwork. It is very hard and its color is a beautifully mottled black and white.

Jack   A medieval short leather coat for defense worn by the infantry. It was generally sleeveless and occasionally it had metal rings or plates sewn to it.

Jack   A large English leather vessel used for drinking or for holding liquor. It was also called a black jack; however, that term was not used until the 16th century. The early jack was often painted with armorial devices and initials. It was rarely mounted in silver. Toward the end of the 17th century a smaller variety resembling a drinking mug with a tapered cylindrical body and mounted in silver came into fashion for a short length of time. See *Bombard*.

Jackfield   In English ceramics; a red earthenware with a black glaze was made at a pottery in Jackfield, Shropshire, managed by Maurice Thursfield from around 1750 to 1775. Jacobite emblems, mottoes and inscriptions were characteristic decoration, and were done in oil-gilding and unfired painting.

Jacob, Georges, 1739–1814. French ébéniste, received master September 4, 1765. He was the founder of a celebrated family of cabinetmakers. He was instrumental in establishing many of the new forms introduced during the Directoire style. He retired from business in 1796 and gave his large workshop in the Rue Meslée to his sons. The one son, François Honoré, under the name of Jacob Desmalter, later became the outstanding cabinetmaker of the Empire style. See *David, Jacques Louis*; *Directoire*; *Empire*.

Jacobean   The term *Jacobean*, which is derived from *Jacobus*, the Latin word for James, refers to the things pertaining to James I, his reign and his times. It is especially applied to the style of ornament and furniture design employed in England during the early 17th century. Its accepted dates are 1603–1649. By extension the term is usually applied to the style of ornament and furniture design during the time of the Stuart kings, 1603–1688. Since England during this period experienced three distinct political changes, which in turn affected the decorative arts, the Jacobean period is generally divided into three phases, namely, the Early Stuart or Early Jacobean, 1603–1649, the Commonwealth, Cromwellian or Protectorate, 1649–1660, and the Late Stuart, Late Jacobean, Restoration or Carolean, 1660–1688. The term *Carolean* is derived from Carolus, the Latin word for Charles. After the Restoration in 1660 English furniture design began to reflect Baroque influence. The English Renaissance style of architecture became more correct during the reign of James I, due to a better understanding of classic principles. James I was the patron of Inigo Jones who studied in Italy and who introduced the Palladian Renaissance style of architecture into England. The Early Jacobean furniture was essentially a continuation of the Elizabethan style. Oak continued to be the principal wood. The furniture was characterized by its simplicity and solidity of construction. It was massive and essentially rectilinear in form. As the 17th century progressed the furniture began to lose some of its massiveness. The furniture became more plentiful and more decorative in quality. Carving was the principal and favorite method for decorating furniture; turning and inlay work were also used. The style of ornament was essentially the same as during the Elizabethan era. Strapwork was profusely used during the reign of James I. Human figures, animal figures, grotesques and masks were less frequently used than in the Elizabethan style. With the establishment of the Commonwealth there was a return to

EARLY JACOBEAN
FARTHINGALE CHAIR

simplicity and austerity. The production of furniture of a decorative character was brought practically to a standstill. Such furniture as was made was heavy in form and usually devoid of ornament. Furniture which could serve a double purpose was often favored, such as a combined chair-table. Puritan furniture was characterized by its severity and was designed for a purely utilitarian purpose. See *Jacobean, Late*; *Stuart, Early and Late*.

Jacobean, Late With the restoration of the monarchy an entirely new phase almost revolutionary in its scope invaded the field of furniture designing in England. Charles II and the other royalists having spent their exile on the Continent acquired a taste for luxury and foreign fashions. They rejected the older and more English types of solid oak furniture. Simple chairs, tables and cupboards were no longer adequate for the more elegant manner of living. Chests of drawers, cabinets, candlestands and tall case clocks were included among the new types of furniture introduced in England after the Restoration. French and Dutch cabinetwork exerted the strongest influence on English cabinetwork; however, the latter predominated. The furniture was chiefly rectilinear in form. During the reign of Charles II there was a growing tendency to introduce scrolls into the structure. Arms, armposts, legs and stretchers were often shaped in the form of scrolls. Scrolls were worked in a variety of combinations; the S-scroll, C-scroll and Flemish scroll being the most commonly employed. The cabinetmaker was constantly striving to obtain greater lightness and elegance in the structure and in the decoration of furniture. The taste for rich decorative effects was evident in the vogue for brilliant floral marquetry and for colorful lacquer work. Later during the reign of Charles II the carved woodwork was sometimes covered with gilt gesso. Especially typical were the elaborately carved gilt cabinet stands for the lacquer cabinets. Walnut was the principal wood. The Charles

CHARLES II
LACQUER CABINET

II furniture was characterized by its ornately decorated frames and floral leaf carving. The furniture, except for the traditional English oak pieces, was typically Baroque in both form and ornament. Included among the favorite motifs were pendants of fruit, flowers and foliage; foliated scrolls; S-scrolls, C-scrolls and Flemish scrolls; cartouches; vase forms; birds; masks; cherubs' heads; amorini; human figures terminating in scrolls and the coronet or crown. See *Jacobean*; *Dutch Furniture*; *Restoration Chair*; *Gibbons, Grinling*.

Jacobite Glass In English glass; a name given to different types of English drinking glasses made to commemorate the Old Pretender and the Young Pretender. They were used during the first half of the 18th century by the Jacobites to drink secretly to "their King across the water." The Old Pretender was James Stuart, 1688–1766, son of James II, and the Young Pretender was Charles Stuart, 1720–1788, son of James Stuart. The Fiat glass, Pretender glass and Rose glass are all forms of Jacobite glasses. These glasses are goblets and wine glasses with either plain stems having a tear, or air twist stems, and they are all diamond point engraved. The designs are portraits of the Old or Young Pretender, the conventional Stuart or Jacobite emblem of the rose and bud, and the star, oak leaf or the word *Fiat*, alone or combined. The so-called Rose glasses having the Stuart rose which usually has six petals, occasionally seven or eight, and either one or two buds, are symbolic of Charles. The word *Fiat*, meaning let it be done, was a password and toast among Jacobite sympathizers. See *Amen Glass*.

Jade, Chinese The term *jade* is given to two different mineral species, namely jadeite, which is a silicate of alumina and soda, and nephrite, which is a silicate of magnesia and lime. The Chinese classify jade under three headings: Yü, which is the general name; Pi Yü, which is the dark green variety, and Fei-ts'ui which is a beautiful emerald green variety. This last variety derived its name from the resemblance of the color to the bright color of the kingfisher. It is now applied to all colors of jadeite with the exception of the opaque dark green color. Jade is remarkable for its quality of tenacity. Jade is appraised in China for its resonancy, its freedom from cracks and its color. There are many different colors of jade. The Chinese especially admired the snow white, cinnabar red, beeswax yellow, kingfisher green and ink black. One rare kind had the appearance of mutton fat with vivid red spots and another was bright spinach green flecked with dots of gold. Lavender jadeite was highly esteemed and also a white jadeite streaked with patches of shaded green. When jade is polished it should have a soft greasy appearance. Absolutely pure jadeite as well as nephrite should be white without any tinge of color. The colors are due to the admixture of other bases in the composition. The green color of jadeite is due to chromium which is the coloring matter of the emerald, and the color of nephrite is due to iron. As a rule jadeite is more brilliant in color, is more translucent and is occasionally partially crystalized. Its fundamental colors seem to be lavender and bright apple green. Brilliant emerald green or white with patches of emerald green has the greatest value. Nephrite, which is fibrous, is usually some shade of green; it may be celadon, spinach green, grey green and many other greens. Other nephrite coloring includes reddish grey, blue grey, yellow, black, cream and a pure translucent white which is compared to mutton fat. There is also a black variety of jadeite known as chloromelanite. The Chinese have never been surpassed in the art of carving jade.

Jadeite   See *Jade, Chinese.*

Jalousie   A window shutter or blind composed of narrow horizontal wooden slats which slope upwards from without, in order to exclude the sun and rain but to allow the admission of some light and air. Although this form of blind is of uncertain origin and the word *jalousie* is of French

derivation, it is mentioned in Spanish literature in 1598 as a lattice window or drawing window and called a gelosia. In Europe it is also referred to as a Venetian jalousie and in Paris in 1757 a French craftsman advertised that he was offering a perfected type of jalousie. It seems that his improvements included the tapes and cords to adjust the slats to various angles to admit or exclude the light and air. During the latter part of the 18th century craftsmen in Philadelphia advertised themselves as makers of these blinds which they called Venetian blinds.

Jamb   In armor; see *Greave.*

Jambeau   In armor; see *Greave.*

Jambiya   In arms; the knife of the Arabs. In each Arabian country there are slight variations in the shape of the blade, the hilt and the scabbard; however, it is characterized by a curved, double-edged blade usually having a rib down the center.

James, Edward   An American cabinetmaker working in Philadelphia. He produced furniture in the Chippendale style. See *Philadelphia Chippendale.*

Japanese Embroidery   The embroidering of fabrics in Japan dates from very early times and displays some of the most elaborate achievement in needlework. Much of the Japanese work is symbolical and reveals unusual originality and force in its designs as well as the most skillful execution and management of color. Their fine work is done upon silk with colored silk, gold and silver threads, and much of it displays the same remarkable technique as in other Japanese works of art such as the manner in which they produce, with a few lines, a distant landscape or a foreground subject, in subordination to the principal theme. These rich and skillfully executed designs include birds with brilliant plumage, Japanese deities, mythological subjects, Japanese everyday life, cherry blossoms, plum blossoms and chrysanthemums. The finest pieces are Japanese heirlooms which include screens,

JADE BRONZE-FORM VASE
ON CARVED STAND ·

kimono, obi and covers used for wedding gifts.

Japanese Fan The fan is regarded by the Japanese as a symbol of life and appears in almost every phase of the life of the people from the Imperial and noble families to the peasants. The earliest fans were, as in other countries, made with feathers or palm leaves. The rigid fans or hand-screens were introduced from China at the end of the 6th century and consisted of various materials attached to a rod used as a handle. The folding fans are of Japanese origin and were first made by a fan-maker living near Kyōto in the Tenji period, 668-672. This earliest form was made of fifteen bamboo sticks having a divergence from the handle which keeps the fan end slightly open when the handle end is closed. The following varieties include some of the more important forms of Japanese fans. The chūkei, dating from the 7th century, is carried by priests and noblemen and is similar in form to the early folding fan. The suye hiro ogi, which was introduced in the 7th century, is used for dances in the Nō drama. It is of the early folding type and consists of from fifteen to twenty-four sticks. The akome ogi, or early court fan, dating from the 7th century, is composed of thirty-eight white painted sticks and is elaborately decorated with twelve long streamers of various colored silks. The hi ogi, or court fan dating from the 11th century, is made of hi wood having a lustrous golden brown color and soft velvety texture. The hi ogi with its twenty-four sticks is often borne by the Emperor and nobles at the Imperial court and held vertically in the right hand. The early war fans dating from the 11th century are the gumbai uchiwa, a rigid hand-screen which is the earlier type, and the gumbai ogi or folding type. Both varieties were usually made of iron. The gumbai uchiwa with its metal or bamboo handle was extremely heavy and was used by officers for offense or defense and for direction. In the 12th century the gun sen war fan appeared and was made

of from ten to fourteen slender sticks of finely wrought iron and sometimes of bamboo. The most characteristic gun sen had a red sun painted on the paper mount with little if any decoration. The purpose of the gun sen was to give signals. The tea fan, or rikiu, introduced in the 17th century, consists of only three sticks and is used at the tea ceremony on the first day of the New Year to hold little cakes. It is to commemorate the curing of the illness of Emperor Murakami, 947-967, by tea given to him by the Goddess Kuan Yin. See *Fan*.

Japanese Lacquer The art of lacquering in Japan dates from about the 6th century. Japan learned about lacquering from China but she later developed it far beyond the Chinese conception. The art of lacquering culminated in Japan toward the end of the 17th century. The work of that era, which represented the golden age in lacquer art, was of incomparable beauty. Flat decoration or hira-makie in which gold dust or mother-of-pearl was used was developed and practiced in Japan from about the 8th century. The motifs included flower and leaf designs, arabesques and scrolls. Although mother-of-pearl was used in the decoration of a lacquer ground, it was not used to make complete designs until the 17th century. This type of work in which ivory and mother-of-pearl were profusely used was developed for the European market and did not particularly appeal to the Japanese. Lacquer decoration in relief or taka-makie was developed around the middle of the 15th century. This technique was purely Japanese. The acme in this branch of lacquer work was achieved toward the end of the 17th century and remains unrivalled. The term *kin-makie* is applied to the gold lacquer which is remarkable for its magnificent luster. The finest examples of Japanese lacquer art are most frequently found on inrō and ink-stone boxes. Lacquer art has been employed on all kinds of objects, on the interior of buildings and on furniture. In addition to the previously mentioned forms of Japanese lacquer

GUMBAI UCHIWA FAN

GUN SEN FAN

SUYE HIRO OGI FAN

RIKIU FAN

processes there are: Chinkinbori, engraved lacquer; Fundame, fine gold and silver powder worked in the lacquer and rubbed to produce a flat, dull finish on the surface; Guri, alternate layers of colored lacquer revealed by carving; Hirame, tiny, irregularly shaped pieces of sheet gold or silver worked in the surface; Kiribame, small sheets of gold or silver inlaid in the surface of lacquer; Nashi-Ji, coats of lacquer at various depths sprinkled with gold or silver, resembling the skin of a pear; Raden, inlay of metal and shell in lacquer; Rōiro, highly polished black lacquer; Shu-Nuri, cinnabar or red lacquer; Togidashi, having the design built up with many coats of lacquer in gold or silver and colors and then rubbed down to reveal them. Among the great lacquer artists of Japan are Kōami, Igarashi, Hon'ami, and Kōrin. It seems that Michinaga Kōami, who flourished during the third quarter of the 15th century, created a new style in his lacquer work by employing the works of great painters of the day, such as Tosa Mitsunobu, Kanō Masanobu and Sōami, as under-paintings on his lacquer pieces. Many generations of the Kōami family continued to produce fine lacquer work. Shinsai Igarashi and his descendants as well as those of Kōami formed the creative force in lacquer work during the late Ashikaga period from about 1450 to 1568. Kōetsu Hon'ami, 1558–1637, was a great creative genius in painting and calligraphy and is famed for his lacquer pieces. Ogata Kōrin, 1658–1716, who worked in Kyōto, was an artist and lacquer worker of great talent, producing new mediums of technique and developing interesting compositions remarkable for their purity of design. The present-day technique of Japanese lacquer art is the same that has existed for centuries. After the lac is dried it is mixed with cinnabar, gamboge or some other colors. Thin flax cloth or Japanese paper is glued with lacquer and rice paste to the piece to be lacquered, which is generally made of white pine. It is then lacquered, sized, dried, rubbed down and polished. This work takes many days.

Then the artist selects the decoration. He makes an outline of the design with a white lead paste and then fills in the details of the designs with gold and colors. This is covered with a semi-transparent lacquer and then polished. When relief work is desired the designs are built up with a heavy paste of white lead, lampblack, camphor and black lacquer. The use of gold in fine lacquer work adds to its rich appearance. Especially fine and lustrous are the pieces having a gold ground. See *Lacquer*; *Japanning*; *Chinese Lacquer*.

Japanese Periods The dynastic and historical periods of Japan are referred to in the designation of their arts in the same manner as in the Chinese subjects. These periods are:

	A.D.
Asuka	552– 645
Nara or Tempyo	710– 794
Heian	794–1185
Jogan (Early Heian)	794– 897
Fujiwara (Late Heian)	897–1185
Kamakura	1185–1333
Muromachi or Ashikaga	1338–1573
Momoyama	1573–1615
Edo or Tokugawa	1615–1867
Meiji	1868–1912

Japanese Sword In Japanese arms; the characteristic and national swords of Japan are the katana having a long blade, and the wakizashi having a shorter blade. These two swords were carried at the same time by the samurai, or military men. See *Katana*; *Wakizashi*; *Dai-Shō*.

Japanese Sword Mounts The fittings or mounts on a Japanese sword are numerous and serve a constructive purpose. All the mounts are rather easily removed or attached, making it possible for them to be changed or placed on another hilt or scabbard. These mounts are generally elaborately decorated and the best represent the finest artistic work ever produced with metals. For the most important fittings see: *Dai-Shō-No-Soroimono*; *Fuchi*; *Kanamono*; *Kashira*; *Kodōgu*; *Kogai*; *Kojiri*; *Ko-Katana*; *Kozuka*; *Menuki*; *Mitokoromono*; *Seppa*; *Soroimono*; *Tsuba*.

1. WARI-KOGAI

2. KOJIRI

3. KOZUKA

4. TSUBA

5. MENUKI

Japanese Wood-Block Print See *Ukiyo-e*. "Pictures of the Drifting World."

Japanning The name given to the process of applying varnishes to the surface of wood, metal and similar materials, and then baking it on in an oven. It is a crude imitation of the Japanese lacquer art, which is executed in a different method and with different materials. Although japanning is most commonly done in black, it is also done in colors and transparent varnishes. Work done with several coats of black produces a deep, brilliant black; while black applied in thin coats produces a dark brown tone. Japanning produces a highly polished surface which is more durable than painted or varnished work. It was widely used on papier-mâché articles, clock dials and metal boxes for documents. In England the term *japanning* was commonly given to their lacquer work which was done by a different method from that practiced in the Orient. The vogue for lacquered furniture and other articles developed after the Restoration in 1660 and it continued to recur throughout the following century. Much of the work was done by amateurs since it developed into a fashionable hobby. The designs comprised an incongruous assortment of ornament and were executed on a black or colored ground. The decoration was in slight relief. Although this work had an attractive decorative effect it had little merit either in the quality of workmanship or in the composition of its designs. It could not be compared with the oriental lacquer work. Japanned furniture achieved its greatest popularity in England early in the 18th century. It again became fashionable around the mid-18th century and Chippendale in order to meet this revived interest stated in the DIRECTOR that some of his designs were suitable for japanning. He particularly favored bedroom pieces for this medium of decoration. Although some japanning around 1750 was still executed in the earlier method with a priming or undercoating, most of the japanning from the mid-18th century onwards could scarcely be distinguished from painting. As a rule it was simply paint and varnish. Frequently the colors were laid on with gum water in place of varnish. Japanned beechwood chairs and settees were characteristic of the Sheraton style. They were generally japanned in lamp black and enriched with painted decoration in either polychrome or en grisaille. This inexpensive furniture was colorful and it satisfied the prevailing fashionable taste for rich color effects. In America practically all the japanned furniture done in a manner similar to that found in England with raised designs was made in New England, especially in Boston. During the later 18th century the japanning in America was similar to the contemporary English work. See *Japanese Lacquer*; *Stalker and Parker*; *Johnston, Thomas*; *Chinese Taste*.

Jardinière In French cabinetwork; the name given to a form of table designed to hold plants and flowers. It was introduced during the Louis XVI style. The characteristic jardinière had a narrow oblong frieze fitted with a metal-lined frieze well and was mounted on four straight legs. It was finely veneered and it was often inset with Sèvres porcelain plaques. By extension the term is applied to any article of furniture designed to contain growing plants and flowers.

Jasper See *Quartz*.

Jasper Ware In English ceramics; the name was given by Wedgwood to a hard, fine-grained stoneware which he perfected in 1775. It was obtained by adding sulphate of barium to a semi-porcelain clay. It was slightly translucent and pure white when fired. By mixing metallic oxides to the white body various colored bodies were obtained. A pale blue body is undoubtedly the best known. Later, around 1780, the color was applied only in surface washes and this ware is known as jasper dip. Included among the colors finally used were the familiar light

LOUIS XVI JARDINIÈRE

blue or lavender, sage-green, olive green, pink-lilac, yellow and an intense black. Wedgwood's blue jasper ware with white reliefs was extensively imitated in other materials in England and on the Continent. A great diversity of articles were made from jasper ware, such as cameos and intaglios for seals, portrait-reliefs, beads and buttons, as well as vases, ewers, candlesticks and similar articles. Plaques of jasper ware were used by the cabinetmakers for the decoration of furniture. The classic composition of these plaques was in accord with the prevailing Neo-Classic style of decoration.

Jaune Jonquille In French ceramics; the yellow ground color introduced on Sèvres porcelain around 1752.

Jelly Glass In English glass; a glass vessel used for jellies as well as for other kinds of confections. It was made in a variety of shapes and sizes. An early kind of jelly glass was a little round glass with a folded lip. This form was made throughout the 18th century and was sometimes referred to as a patty pan. A favorite type of jelly glass had a bell-shaped bowl mounted on a circular foot. In this variety the bowl was often joined to the foot with one or more heavy moldings. It appears that a glass salver was often used in conjunction with jelly glasses. See *Comport*.

Jensen, Gerreit d. 1715. English cabinetmaker to the Royal Household from Charles II to Queen Anne, working from around 1680 to 1715, upon the Pavements in St. Martin's Lane. It can be deduced from the Crown accounts that much of Jensen's furniture was decorated with marquetry work or lacquer and in a few examples inlaid with metal. It seems that he was the only craftsman in England around the end of the 17th century who was practicing the Boulle technique of metal inlay. All the cabinetwork was of the finest quality.

Jersey In English pewter measures; see *Guernsey*.

Jersey Porcelain and Earthenware Company In American ceramics; a pottery located in Jersey City, New Jersey. The first porcelain made in America was produced there in 1825. It was a white porcelain principally decorated in gold. They also made a cream ware and a yellow ware. Due to the competition from imported cream ware they were forced to give up the production of true porcelain in 1828. The pottery was finally bought by Henderson and was known as D. & J. Henderson Co. They made yellow ware, cream ware and Rockingham. The ware was marked with the firm's name and with "Jersey City" impressed in a circular form.

Jesuit Ware In Chinese ceramics; a Chinese porcelain having enamelled color decoration of a religious nature. Its decoration was inspired by priests living in China. It is essentially the same sort of ware as Chinese Lowestoft; however, some examples are of a little better quality. See *Chinese Lowestoft*.

Jewelled Decoration In French ceramics; the term is generally reserved for the unusual Sèvres decoration used from around 1781 and later. In this process drops of colored enamel were applied and fused over gold or silver. Although this process is supposed to have been introduced at Sèvres a similar process was in use earlier in the 18th century especially at the Saint-Cloud manufactory.

Jimigaki In Japanese sword mounts; a term applied to the highly polished surface on Japanese metal work.

Joey Glass In English glass; a small tumbler-shaped drinking glass. The name was derived from the English fourpenny piece called a joey, which was the price of the drink. It is also called a dram glass.

Jogan The name given to the early Heian period in Japan, A.D. 794–897. See *Japanese Periods*.

Johnson, Thomas An English carver and designer of furniture working around 1755. His first book of designs was published in

JESUIT WARE BOWL

1755 and was entitled TWELVE GIRANDOLES. In 1758 he published THE BOOK OF THE CARVER which contained fifty-three engraved plates. Between the years of 1756 and 1758 he published in monthly parts ONE HUNDRED AND FIFTY NEW DESIGNS. It contained a diversity of designs such as carver's pieces, frames, tables, candlestands, sconces and similar articles. His designs are generally considered to have the least quality of any of the contemporary designers who issued trade publications. However a few carved pieces which may be assigned to him have been regarded with more favor. He gave his address as Queen Street near Seven Dials, and a later address was from The Golden Boy in Grafton Street, St. Ann's, Soho.

Johnston, Thomas   A well-known · American japanner and engraver working at Boston, Massachusetts, circa 1732–1767. His name is also spelled Johnson. His engraved advertising card states "japanner at the Golden Lyon in Ann Street Boston." The vogue for decorating furniture and other articles in the Chinese taste reached America around 1700, and Boston craftsmen produced numerous pieces in that medium. Virtually all the japanned furniture done in a manner similar to that found in England with raised designs was made in New England, especially in Boston where advertising appeared in newspapers at least as early as 1712 stating that several cabinetmakers specialized in japanning. See *Japanning*.

GOTHIC JOINT STOOL

Joined   In cabinetwork; the term refers to an article of furniture joined by mortise and tenon, secured by pegging in contrast to the use of glue.

Joiner   In English furniture; a joiner is a craftsman or artisan whose occupation is to construct things by fitting together or joining pieces of wood such as pieces of furniture, panelling in a room and similar work. His woodwork is more ornamental than that of a carpenter. In England the joiners' guild called the Joiners' Company was granted a charter in 1570, and included among its members joiners, carpenters and turners. The turners are those whose occupation is turning wood on a lathe for such things as spindles and balusters for chair backs, legs for chairs and tables and other similar articles. See *Cabinetmaker*.

Joint Stool   Or Joined Stool. In cabinetwork; a stool made by a joiner; a stool of mortise and tenon joinery. In English cabinetwork; extant examples of oak joined stools date from the late 15th or early 16th centuries. The early joined oak stool was of trestle form with an underframing keyed through the two solid splayed end supports. Around 1600 the plain oblong wooden seat rested on columnar splayed legs joined with a box stretcher close to the floor. Joined stools were in general use until late in the 17th century, and cushions were often placed on the wooden seats to provide a little comfort. They continued to be used in the outlying districts in the 18th century. Joined stools are frequently mentioned in English records from the 16th to the 18th centuries. In the early inventories they are often spelled joyned or joynt. A record of 1434 mentions, "a litil joyned stool for a child." The joint stool was an early article of American furniture and was in general usage from around 1650.

Jones, Inigo   1573–1652. Celebrated English architect who introduced in England the principles of classic design as interpreted by the illustrious Italian architect, Palladio. He visited Italy when he was quite young and again in 1613. Although his interest was architecture it is apparent that he devoted some time to the designing of furniture. It is probable that while serving in the office of Surveyor General of the Works he may have designed some furniture for the Crown. See *Palladio, Andrea*.

Jones, William   English architect and designer of furniture. He published in 1739 the GENTLEMAN'S AND BUILDERS' COMPANION in which he gave several designs for side tables, console tables and pier mirrors. His work was characteristic of the furniture designed for the Early Georgian Palladian mansions.

Joseph Jug In German ceramics; the name given to the well-known salt-glazed stoneware jugs made at Raeren. They were decorated with reliefs having as their subjects Joseph and his brothers. The original Joseph jug was made in 1587 by Jan Emens and was decorated with an arcaded frieze of reliefs depicting the story of Joseph.

Joshaghan Rug An Oriental rug belonging to the Persian classification. As a rule the foundation is of wool. The pile is of selected wool and medium in length. The ends are finished with a narrow web and loose warp threads. The rug is distinctive for the quality of its workmanship, for its pleasing designs and soft color tones. Also called a Djushaghan. See *Persian Rugs*.

Joubert, Gilles 1689–1775. A famous French ébéniste who worked for Louis XV. In 1758 he was appointed "ébéniste ordinaire du Garde-meuble de la Couronne." Among his many fine pieces of cabinetwork are included two superb clock cases for the chamber of Louis XV at Versailles, and an exquisite commode for the chamber of Marie-Antoinette. He produced many pieces for the Dauphin, Madame du Barry, and others.

Jours A term in lace-making applied to the decorative stitches used to fill in enclosed spaces. They are also called modes and fillings.

Jug A deep vessel for containing liquids varying in shape and size, commonly having a cylindrical or swelling body or a body tapering toward the top, provided with a handle on one side and often having a pouring spout. Frequently the term is preceded by a descriptive word explaining its purpose or kind, such as wine, cream, milk,

water or brown. The term is given in various localities with different extensions and limitations to vessels generally made of pottery, glass, metal and occasionally of leather and wood. Sometimes the jug, as in a hot water jug, is provided with a lid. See *Ewer; Aquamanale; Toby Jug*.

Jug, Hot Milk In English silver; see *Jug, Hot Water*.

Jug, Hot Water In English silver; the name given to a variety of jug with a lip spout, frequently having a pear-shaped body that rested on a low circular foot. It was fitted with a hinged cover and a scroll handle. Occasionally the lip spout had a separate hinged cover that was often perforated. It was introduced during the early Georgian era and was chiefly used to hold hot water or hot milk.

Ju-i In ornament; the name given to a conventionalized design widely used in Chinese ceramics. It was so called because a form of Chinese scepter, also called a ju-i, had a similar head, fungus-shaped and bent over like a hook. See *Ling Chih*.

Jungfrauenbecher A festive drinking cup in the form of a young girl, usually made of silver. Her long skirt formed a bell-shaped cup. She held in her uplifted arms a smaller cup on a swivel. The average height of the cup was from about 6 to 10 inches. The cup was used at a wedding feast, when both cups were filled with wine. First the bridegroom drank the wine in the larger cup, then he turned the figure right side up, without spilling any of the wine in the smaller cup which was for the bride. The cup was also called a wager cup, with the competitor having to drink the wine from both cups without spilling any of the contents. The cup is principally identified with German silver and was introduced around 1565.

Ju Ware In Chinese ceramics; a ware made at Ju Chou in central Honan. Toward the end of the Northern Sung period the Ju Chou potters were ordered to make their

HEAD OF A JU-I SCEPTER

ware for the Imperial court. It is generally believed that when the Sung court went south in A.D. 1127 the Ju Chou potters remained in the north. Existing Chinese records indicate that the ware had a pale blue or a bluish-green glaze and that it was some-times crackled. It is generally thought that the body was reddish brown. Coarser porcelains of the Ju type were made at T'ang Chou and T'êng Chou in Honan and at Yao Chou in Shensi. It is also called Ju Chou ware. See *Sung*; *Ying Ch'ing*.

JU WARE EWER

K

Kaba-Karaman An Oriental rug belonging to the Turkish group. It derived its name from the town of Karaman where it is woven. The foundation is of wool; the pile, which is rather long, is of a coarse wool. It is a coarse rug but durable. See *Turkish Rugs*.

Kabistan An Oriental rug belonging to the Caucasian classification. The warp is wool or cotton and the weft is usually of cotton. The pile, which is short, is of fine wool. The ends usually have a narrow web and a loose fringe. In workmanship the Kabistan is one of the finest in the Caucasian group. It has a mosaic design softened by small, primitive, floral motifs. See *Caucasian Rugs*.

Kabuto Gane In Japanese sword mounts; the name given to the pommel on a tachi, a state sword. It covers about 1½ inches of the hilt with a decorative opening on each side. The kabuto gane corresponds to the kashira on other Japanese swords or knives.

Kabuzuchi In Japanese sword mounts; the name sometimes applied to a knob or pommel. See *Kabuto Gane*; *Kashira*.

Kago-Ami In ornament; a Japanese diaper pattern that resembles woven bamboo. See *Diaper*.

Kairaku-en Ware In Japanese ceramics; porcelain made to order for the feudal chief of the province of Kishū by Eiraku. It derived its name from the Kairaku garden. The colored glazes completely cover the ware and comprise green, yellow and purple and sometimes white. Occasionally turquoise blue is used in place of one of the three colors. A slight ridge outlines the design and separates one glaze from another. The colors are skillfully blended. Four characters, kai-raku-en-sei, are impressed in a seal on the ware. See *Eiraku*.

Kaiserteller In pewter ware; an elaborately worked pewter platter or plate, usually having representations of one or more emperors. It is identified with German pewter of the 16th and 17th centuries.

Kakemono In Japanese art; a hanging scroll painting of early origin. The painting is done on either paper or silk and is generally mounted on a fine brocaded silk fabric. It is attached at the top and at the bottom to wooden rods which are generally tipped with ivory. The kakemono is hung in the tokonoma, which is a platform raised 4 or 5 inches higher than the matted floor. In the Japanese house the tokonoma is a place of honor. When the kakemono is not hanging in the tokonoma it is rolled up and kept in a box especially made for it and generally stored in a godown. A large Japanese house sometimes has a hundred or more kakemonos. Each kakemono has a special significance and is hung at the appropriate time. Ceremonial occasions, the advent of a new season and certain holiday periods are considered proper times for changing the kakemono. The painting is either a monochrome in india-ink often on a pretentious scale, or is in water colors. The subject is usually landscape, flower and bird studies, historical subjects of the religious and spiritual life of Japan, or a historical picture of the Tosa school. The kakemono scroll unrolls vertically, the makimono horizontally. See *Makimono*.

Kakiemon In Japanese ceramics; porcelain decorated in colored enamels made at the Nangawara kiln in Arita. Around 1650, Sakaida Kakiemon, 1596–1666, learned from a Chinese potter the technique of producing enamelled porcelain. The result was the ware known as Kakiemon. Essentially it is a refined type of Imari ware. It is decorated with underglaze blue and colored enamels of iron red, blue-green, violet, light blue and greyish yellow. Gold was rarely added.

KAKEMONO

The designs are tasteful, delicate and rather thin. Kakiemon ware with its refined style of decoration soon won the admiration of the European countries. It was extensively copied by Meissen and other European potteries. Undoubtedly Chantilly produced some of the finest imitations of the Kakiemon style of decoration. See *Imari Ware*; *Hizen Ware*.

Kali A Persian word used to describe a large floor covering; especially one measuring more than 10 feet in length. It is also called a Hali. See *Sedjadeh*.

Kamakura The name given to the Japanese historical period A.D. 1185–1333. See *Japanese Periods*.

Kamashimo Zashi In Japanese arms; a variety of sword presented to a Japanese boy when he first wears his ceremonial dress. The sword is short and has a plain black lacquer scabbard, and is mounted with finely worked fittings. This sword was also carried by men when wearing the kamashimo, or court dress.

Kanamono In Japanese sword mounts; a term which literally means hardware. The term *kanamono* is sometimes applied to sword fittings that are not characteristic and are without recognized names. See *Mitokoromono*; *Soroimono*.

K'ang Furniture In Chinese furniture; a term used collectively for the articles of furniture placed on the k'ang. See *Chinese Furniture*.

K'ang Hsi The name K'ang Hsi is given to a reign of the Ch'ing dynasty in China, 1662–1722. See *Chinese Dynasties*.

Kanō In Japanese art; a Japanese school of painting (Kanō-Ryū) founded in the Chinese tradition by Kanō Masanobu, 1453–1490, who, like Shūbun and Sesshū, was a pupil of the celebrated Chinese émigré-painter Josetsu. Maintained through the generations by several branches of the Kanō family and their disciples, the school suffered a temporary decline when it lost the favor of the Ashikaga shoguns after the death of Masanobu's son Motonobu in 1559. It was reinvigorated by Kanō Tanyū, 1602–1674, and flourished on into modern times under the patronage of the Tokugawa shoguns. The style is characterized by impressionistic india-ink monochrome landscapes, highly calligraphic in style, and by flower, bird and animal subjects in sweeping colors and color washes. See *Tosa*.

Kaolin Or China Clay. In ceramics; kaolin is a necessary ingredient in hard paste porcelain. The French word *kaolin* is derived from the Chinese word *Kao-ling* which is the name of a mountain north-west of the town of Ching-tê-chên in north China where this material was originally obtained. Kaolin is a fine white clay which is the result of the decomposition of feldspar. See *Porcelain*.

Karabagh An Oriental rug belonging to the Caucasian group. It derived its name from Karabagh, a province in Transcaucasia, where it is made. The foundation is of wool; the pile is of wool and of a medium length. The patterns are Caucasian and Persian. The colors in the antique Karabagh are subdued, while they are usually strong in the modern Karabagh. The early rug is also of superior workmanship. See *Caucasian Rugs*.

Kara Dagh An Oriental rug belonging to the Persian classification. The warp and weft are of wool; the pile is of wool and medium in length. One end is selvaged and turned back and the other is selvaged and fringed. The designs are of a Persian-Caucasian blend, with the former predominating. It is decorated with a design of small repetitive motifs. See *Persian Rugs*.

Kara-Geuz Rug See *Hamadan Rug*.

Kara-Kane The Japanese term for bronze, which means Chinese metal. Japan obtained its knowledge of this alloy from China. It is mostly copper with some lead and a little tin. This copper, lead and tin compound has very small quantities of arsenic, anti-

KAKIEMON PLATE

mony and zinc. Japanese bronze is particularly suitable for casting because it has an especially smooth surface and easily develops a rich and beautiful patina. See *Sentoku*.

Karatsu In Japanese ceramics; a glazed pottery made at the town of Karatsu in the Hizen province as early as the 13th century. Many of the potters had been brought from Korea. Korean stoneware and pottery imitations were made, some of which had a black clay body. Chōsen Karatsu is the name applied to the ware of a blue-black clay with an iron brown glaze. Hakeme or brush streaking is applied to a Chōsen Karatsu ware made of blue-black clay having brush strokes of olive green or white over a green, black or brown glaze. E-Karatsu or painted ware is generally crudely and swiftly touched in black or brown. Mishima Karatsu or inlay ware has impressed designs inlaid with a white slip. Kenjo Karatsu is a better quality of ware made for the Prince of Hizen for presentation purposes, since kenjo means presentation. It is made of a fine yellowish or brownish clay and has a transparent crackled glaze. It is generally decorated with mishima work. Karatsu ware is highly prized by the Japanese tea masters for use at the tea ceremony. The ware consists chiefly of tea bowls rather crudely modelled. See *Mishima*.

Kas In Dutch cabinetwork; the cupboard or kas was an important article of furniture in a Dutch household. It was generally an enormous piece of furniture. One characteristic variety was designed as a double-bodied cupboard. The upper section which was recessed was surmounted with a heavy overhanging cornice supported on two columns which rested on the top of the lower section. Each section had two cupboard doors. Another variety was single-bodied and was designed with two long cupboard doors, the base being fitted with a row of two drawers. A distinctive feature of this variety was also its large overhanging cornice. The kas was generally panelled, and it was most frequently mounted on ball feet. The kas

was also frequently found in the houses of the early Dutch settlers in New York and New Jersey. It was often painted in bright and colorful gay designs. See *Cupboard*.

Kasane In Japanese lacquer; a nest of trays. See *Nest of Trays*.

Kashan An Oriental rug belonging to the Persian classification. It derived its name from the city of Kashan, where it is woven. The city of Kashan is noted for its fine rugs, woven chiefly during the 16th century; for its silk rugs and for its fine modern rugs. The foundation of these rugs is cotton, frequently silk or linen. The pile is fine short wool, and frequently silk. As a rule the Kashan is evenly and closely woven. The designs are almost always floral with many connecting vines, done in a rather naturalistic treatment. The details of the designs are carefully executed. See *Persian Rugs*.

Kashgar An Oriental rug belonging to the Turkoman group. It is woven in the vicinity of Kasgar, a city in eastern Turkestan. It is usually coarsely woven. The foundation is cotton; the pile which is rather long is generally of wool and occasionally of silk. The designs are of Chinese origin. See *Turkoman Rugs*.

Kashi A Persian word which was originally applied to all kinds of pottery made in Persia. It is now the accepted term for particular kinds of enamelled tile work, produced in Persia and in sections of Mohammedan India, principally during the 16th and 17th centuries. The enamelled tile work included brick work and tile mosaic work. In the figured tile mosaic designs the shaped tesserae were either cut from an enamelled tile after it was fired or they were cut into shape before they were colored. Included among the favorite kashi designs were conventional designs of flowers, foliage and fruit, interlacing arabesques, an endless variety of geometrical designs and inscriptions in Arabic characters. The colors most frequently used were mustard yellow, brown, purple, cobalt blue, turquoise blue and white.

DUTCH KAS

Kashira In Japanese sword mounts; the cap or fitting on the pommel of a Japanese sword. It was usually made of metal but sometimes of horn. The kashira is elaborately worked with inlaying, chasing or engraving and its decoration usually conforms with or matches that of the fuchi which is on the lower part of the hilt. On a tachi this mount is called a kabuto gane. See *Fuchi*.

Kashmir An Oriental rug woven in Kashmir, India. The modern Kashmir is distinctly a commercial creation. See *India Oriental Rugs*; *Oriental Rug*.

Kashmir Rug See *Soumak*.

Kastrup In Danish ceramics; a pottery manufactory was founded at Kastrup on the island of Amager around 1755 by Jacob Fortling, d. 1761. The best period was from around 1755 to 1762 and the mark was an "F" in manganese. The faïence was in the Strasbourg Rococo manner and was painted in muffle kiln colors. Figure modelling was also practiced. After several changes in ownership it closed in 1814. After 1772 commercial stoneware was made and cream-colored earthenware in the English style.

Kata-Kiri-Bori In Japanese sword mounts; a method of incised chiselling which produces decorative designs of unrivalled beauty. It is frequently used on sword fittings. In this method the worker uses the burin or cutting tool to produce lines of varying width and depth of individual value as an artist uses his brush. The metal worker is required to make the design in one effort, since there is no subsequent retouching or finishing. See *Bori*.

Katana In Japanese arms; the name given to the national sword of Japan. The tachi was the first sword having a curved single-edged blade and it was succeeded centuries ago as a fighting sword by the katana which is precisely similar. The long, slightly curved blade is single-edged. The best of these blades, made by the early celebrated blade-makers, are considered to be the finest steel

KATANA

ever produced. The armorer signed his blade on the tang. The hilt is from 8 to 10 inches long and generally covered with shark skin, same, and occasionally metal. The hilt is nearly always artistically wound with flat braid, cord or whalebone. The protective mount on the pommel is the kashira and the one at the lower part of the hilt next to the guard is the fuchi. On each side at the center of the hilt is a menuki. The tsuba, or guard, is the most important fitting on the sword, and above and below it are usually oval washers, called seppa. The scabbard is almost always made of honoki, a fine-grained light wood of the *magnolia hypolenca*. It is lacquered in black and is frequently decorated with the crest, or mon, of the owner in gold lacquer. At times one or two small sheaths are hollowed out on the sides of the scabbard from the top, and in these are carried the kogai, which is a head pin, and the kozuka, a small knife. At the edge of the sheath for the kogai is a guard or flat piece of metal called the kurikata, and the one for the kozuka is called the uragawara. The kojiri is the metal cap at the tip of the scabbard. These sword mounts were usually elaborately decorated and the best were executed by celebrated artists. See *Wakizashi*; *Dai-Shō*; *Japanese Sword Mounts*; *Watered Steel*.

Katár A Hindu sword which is an elongated form of a dagger with a broad blade and having a handgrip composed of two parallel pieces connected by a crosspiece.

Katchlie Bokhara An Oriental rug belonging to the Turkoman group. Katchlie is an Armenian word meaning cross. This rug derived its name from the bands that divide the field into four sections to form a cross. It is woven by the Tekke tribes. It is also called a Princess Bokhara. See *Turkoman Rugs*.

Kauffmann, Angelica 1741–1807. A well-known painter and decorative artist born at Coire, Switzerland, and working in England from 1766 to 1781. She executed work for the Adam brothers, for whom she designed small-scale pictorial subjects to be used in the painted panel decoration for ceilings. Her work undoubtedly influenced the painted decoration in the Neo-Classic manner used in contemporary English cabinetwork. Her manner of painting, like that of Greuze, displayed a certain sentimental mode associated with one phase of the Neo-Classic movement and seems to have resulted from an idealistic attempt to sentimentalize the ancient classic world. See *Adam, Robert*.

Kayin Rug A coarse form of the Herat rug. See *Herat Rug*.

Kazak An Oriental rug belonging to the Caucasian group woven by the Cossack nomads. *Kazak* is a corruption of the word *Cossack*. The Kazak rug is of a coarse texture due to the use of numerous weft threads after each row of knots. The foundation is of wool. The pile, which is long, is also of wool. The designs consist of bold, geometrical figures. Usually the rug has a silky luster due to tne length of the pile and the extra weft threads, which causes the pile to lie so that the side of the yarn is exposed rather than the end. See *Caucasian Rugs*.

Kebori In Japanese sword mounts; a method of incised chiselling. In kebori or hair-line engraving the lines are of equal depth and width. The decorative designs produced on sword fittings are of remarkable fineness. See *Bori*; *Kata-Kiri-Bori*.

Kellinghusen In ceramics; a faïence manufactory was founded at Kellinghusen, Holstein, Germany, by Carsten Behrens around 1760 and was active until about 1826. At least three other local potteries were operating at Kellinghusen twenty years after Behrens started. They all used the same clay from Ovendorf which was very good. The wares were produced chiefly for a peasant market and were admirably designed and executed. The painted decoration which consisted largely of tulips and carnations was executed in a bold and vigorous manner, giving the wares a singular charm.

Kelsterbach In German ceramics; a faïence manufactory was founded in 1758 at Kelsterbach, Hesse-Darmstadt, by William Cron and Johann Christian Frede. In 1761 the Landgrave Ludwig VIII of Hesse-Darmstadt took over the manufactory and began to produce porcelain. When the Landgrave died in 1768, the manufacture of porcelain ceased and was not resumed until 1789. After 1802 the production was largely cream-colored earthenware in the English style. It closed around 1823. The mark was "HD" in monogram and was used from about 1766. On the faïence wares the "HD" was generally in manganese; on the porcelain in underglaze blue or impressed, and usually under a crown; on the earthenware it was impressed. All varieties of porcelain and faïence wares were made from around 1761 to 1768. They were of fine quality but generally with little originality. However some interesting porcelain figures of excellent workmanship were made during that period. The later wares were of little artistic importance.

Ken In Japanese arms; it is the oldest type of sword used in Japan during historical times. It had a straight, double-edged blade which at times was slightly wider near the point. It is also called a tsurugi.

Kent, William 1685-1748, English architect and decorator. He was also known as a painter, sculptor and furniture designer. He occupied a prominent place in the arts of his day although his merit has never been determined. His influence predominated in the furniture and in the decoration of the large mansions between 1730 and 1745. His furniture designs and style of ornament were most strongly influenced by the Baroque style which prevailed in Italy. The furniture was exuberantly carved and gilded. His designs for chairs and settees were frequently modelled in the style of the French Régence. The form of much of his furniture was of a ponderous and exaggerated nature. His style of ornament was often marred by its cumbrous composition. Very characteristic

MIRROR, AFTER
WILLIAM KENT

of his style were the massive gilt side tables with their florid carvings and with their heavy marble tops. His chief contribution was that he designed furniture to be an ordered part of the architectural scheme of the decoration. He incorporated classic architectural design principles into many pieces of furniture in order that they would harmonize with the classic mansions then being built. This architectural treatment was more pronounced in wall or stationary pieces, such as massive bookcases, secretary cabinets and similar pieces. See *Queen Anne and Early Georgian*.

Kentucky Rifle In arms; a name given to a particular type of early American flintlock rifle which was especially popular among the frontiersmen of Colonial times. It evolved from the original German rifle brought to Pennsylvania by German settlers. The Kentucky rifle was lighter and had a much smaller bore than the German prototype and was usually 5 feet or more in length. The stock was of walnut, maple or cherry and the wood continued almost to the muzzle. The fittings were usually of brass and it was characterized by a brass star-shaped ornament on the left side of the stock, and an inset patch box on the right side with a brass cover. These rifles were always handmade and were produced by the German gunsmiths of Lancaster County, Pennsylvania, from about 1725 to 1820. See *Rifle*; *Patch Box*.

Kenzan, Ogata 1662–1743. In Japanese ceramics; a Japanese potter, painter and poet working in Kyōto. The work of Ogata Shinsho or Kenzan dates from the latter part of the 17th century through almost the first half of the 18th century. He was a younger brother of Ogata-Kōrin who was one of the great lacquer artists of all times. Kenzan studied ceramic technique under Ninsei who excelled in enamelled pottery. His designs, which were bold, free, and sketchy, had a marked simplicity and were painted in sure swift brush strokes. Kenzan's designs of cherry blossoms and maple

CHIPPENDALE KETTLE-SHAPE
SECRETARY CABINET

leaves, of bamboo grass leaves with snow upon them and of prunus boughs with blossoms were included among the favorite motifs that were extensively copied by later potters working in the Kenzan style. He often supplemented his designs with a short poem. He principally made utensils for use in the tea ceremony. Very late in life he retired to the village of Iriya near Tokyo where he produced some of his finest work. See *Ninsei*; *Musashi*; *Kyōto*.

Kermanshah An Oriental rug belonging to the Persian classification. The foundation is of cotton; the pile is of wool and as a rule trimmed rather short. The ends are usually finished with a narrow web and loose warp threads. The texture is firm. The designs principally consist of floral motifs and scrolling floral branches. A center medallion and a special corner composition in each one of the four corners within the border are frequently a feature of design. See *Persian Rugs*.

Kermesse The term originally referred to the mass said annually on the day the church was founded and in honor of the patron saint. This celebration which was indigenous to Holland, Belgium and Northern France was accompanied by feasting, dancing and all kinds of games. It is also spelled kermess and kirmess.

Kettle-Shape In cabinetwork; the name given to the shape of a piece of furniture, such as a chest of drawers, a secretary cabinet or another piece of a similar nature, having the lower portion swelling outward in the front and on the sides. The contour is somewhat similar to bombé, except that all the swelling is concentrated in the lower part of the piece of furniture, giving it a distorted appearance. Kettle-shape is most frequently identified with Dutch and English cabinetwork. The terms *bombé* and *kettle-shape* are sometimes used as if they were synonymous. In American cabinetwork the kettle-shape was sometimes found on secretary bookcases and chests of drawers designed in the Chippendale style from around 1760 onwards; see *Bombé*.

Kettle Stand A stand upon which a tea-kettle is placed. In particular, a silver stand in the form of a shaft resting on a tripod base, being about 27 inches high. It was introduced in England early in the 18th century. In English cabinetwork; see *Teakettle Stand*.

Keyhole Pattern In silver; an openwork flange handle, having one of the openings resembling a keyhole. This type of handle was widely used on American silver porringers.

Key Pattern In ornament; also called Greek Fret. See *Fret*.

Khanda In arms; the sword of India. It is the oldest and most typical form of sword found in India. The single-edged blade, which is sometimes double-edged, is broad and straight, and generally widening towards the usually blunt point. The broad plate guard and wide finger guard on the hilt are padded on the inside and the pommel is rather disc-shaped. The pommel is surmounted with a long spike with a knob at the end.

Khilim A double-sided tapestry-woven rug made in the Orient. It is still much in vogue in the Orient because of its useful and decorative qualities, small bulk and light weight. It is often used in the East as a summer rug. The Khilim represents the tapestry weavings of the East. The designs are generally based upon the rug designs in the respective locality where the rug is woven. See *Tapestry*.

Khiva Bokhara An Oriental rug belonging to the Turkoman group. It derived its name from the city of Khiva, in the province of Bokhara, where this variety of Oriental is produced. The foundation is usually of wool; the pile is of wool and of medium length. The ends are usually finished with a wide colored web and a long loose fringe. The octagon is almost always used, and is quartered by alternating colors. It resembles the Tekke Bokhara, except that it is not as fine,

and the hard division into squares of oblong spaces, which is characteristic of the Tekke Bokhara, is almost always omitted. See *Turkoman Rugs*.

Khorassan An Oriental rug belonging to the Persian classification; so called after the province of Khorassan. The foundation is most frequently cotton but is sometimes wool. The pile is wool and is short or medium in length, and is usually trimmed unevenly. The ends are finished with a narrow web and loose warp threads. The antique Khorassan was woven chiefly at the villages of Dorosch, Birjand and Gahyn. The rug is distinctive for its brilliant coloring, for its soft texture and for its wide variety of motifs which include floral motifs, scrolling branches, human figures and animal and bird figures. Some of the designs are large and showy; other designs are characterized by all the minute patterns used in Persian rug design. See *Persian Rugs*.

Khotan An Oriental rug woven in the vicinity of Khotan, a city in eastern Turkestan, belonging to the Turkoman classification. It is usually coarsely woven. The foundation is cotton; the pile which is rather long is usually of wool and sometimes of silk. The ends are finished with loose warp threads. The designs are generally half-Chinese and half-Persian in origin. See *Turkoman Rugs*.

Kiangnan Ting Ware In Chinese ceramics; an arbitrary name given to a creamy white glazed ware made during the Ming dynasty that more or less resembled Ting yao. The provinces of Kiangsu and Anhwei which were formerly joined under the name of Kiangnan had a number of kilns that produced creamy white wares. It has never been established which one of the kilns made the so-called Kiangnan Ting ware. This ware has a light buff or grey stoneware body with a crackled cream-white glaze, which sometimes has a wrinkled or withered appearance. It has an unusual dull luster and the texture has often been compared to an ostrich egg shell. See *Ting Yao*.

KEYHOLE PATTERN HANDLE

Kian Temmoku In Chinese ceramics; originally the name *kian* was an arbitrary name, which through usage is now given to a variety of Chinese ware that consists chiefly of tea bowls and occasionally vases. It is reputed that these bowls were found near the old Sung kilns at Yung-ho Chên in the Chi Chou district in the department of Kian in south central Kiangsi province. If this location is correct this ware would be the Chi Chou ware mentioned in records and described as being brown, like that of Ting Chou, but thick and coarse. The Kian ware is quite different from the Chien ware. It is a close buff stoneware. The glaze is usually a lifeless black-brown with dabs of brown yellow which result in a tortoiseshell effect. The inside of the bowl is more richly colored. Later in the Sung period these bowls often had birds, leaves, etc., painted in a brown black on the mottled surface. The designs are often barely recognizable and seem more like an accident than a planned design. See *Chien Yao*; *Temmoku*.

Kidderminster Carpet The name given to an ingrain carpet in England, because the city of Kidderminster is the largest manufacturing center for this type of carpet. Ingrain carpets or the principle of double cloth weaving was started at Kidderminster in 1735. See *Ingrain Carpet*; *Brussels Carpet*.

Kidney Table In French cabinetwork; see *Haricot*.

Kiel In ceramics; a faïence manufactory was started at Kiel, Holstein, Germany, in 1763 by J. S. F. Tännich of Strasbourg and was at first owned by the Duke of Holstein. After several changes it finally closed in 1788. It seems that all the finer wares were made in the period from 1763 to 1772. The characteristic faïence of that period painted in enamel colors in the style of porcelain ranks with the best of its type made in Europe. The tin glaze or the tin enamel glaze was of remarkable whiteness and the enamel colors were fresh and strong. The flower painting varied in quality but the finest was equal to Strasbourg. Attractive figure subjects and landscapes in the manner of Dutch painting were favorite motifs. Included among the characteristic wares were bishop bowls, wall fountains, flowerpots with four sides and plates and dishes with pierced basketwork rims or wavy edges. Of especial interest was a variety of pot-pourri having a pear-shaped body mounted on a spreading foot and having a pierced lid richly surmounted with applied fruits, flowers and leaves.

Kiku-No-Go-Mon The Japanese name for the Imperial chrysanthemum crest. See *Chrysanthemum*.

Kilij In arms; the saber of Turkey. The rather crescent-shaped blade is long and narrow with the cutting edge on the convex side. The back of the blade parallels the cutting edge to about 8 or 10 inches from the point then abruptly continues to the point in a straight line. This straight back line has a sharp edge. The hilt resembles a pistol handle composed of two pieces of ivory, horn, bone or a similar material. The slender, straight, crossbar or guard is tipped with either ball or acorn ornaments.

Kimono Tray In Japanese lacquer; the name kimono tray or midare kago is given to a large oblong lacquered tray characterized by its deep sides. It is generally made of a very fine quality of black lacquer and very often the family crest or mon executed in gold appears in the center. The kimono tray is placed on the matted floor or tatami and a tall two-panelled screen is generally placed in front of it. The Japanese lady dropped her kimono and other clothing into this tray which was removed by a servant.

Kindjal In arms; the weapon principally carried by the Cossacks which is similar to the qama of Georgia. It is generally in the form of a broad, double-edged blade with nearly parallel edges which abruptly tapers to a long sharp point. Sometimes the blades are curved. The straight hilt has a broad pommel. See *Qama*.

KIEL POT-POURRI JAR

King's Pattern   In English silver; an early 19th century English silver pattern. The rounded end of the stem of the spoon centered a shell motif and along the broad part of the stem was an elongated double shell motif. Both of these motifs were enclosed in a scroll design from which straight double lines continued to the bowl.

Kingwood   A wood widely used in cabinet-work, a rosewood. It derived its name from the French term *bois du roi* or king-wood, as it was favored by Louis XIV. See *Violet Wood*.

Kin-Makie   See *Japanese Lacquer*.

Kinran-de   In Japanese ceramics; the Japanese term applied to a gold brocaded design, copied from the Chinese, used to decorate porcelain. See *Eiraku*; *Kutani*.

Kiribame   In Japanese lacquer; a variety of lacquer work having small sheets of gold or silver inlaid in the surface of lacquer. See *Japanese Lacquer*.

Kiribame   A Japanese metal art. In kiribame or insertion work the design is completely chiselled in the round in metal and is then fitted into the surface of a different metal which has been exactly cut out to receive the design. In this manner the chiselled design is seen on both sides. For example a box lid ornamented in this manner has the design on its top surface and when opened the inside of the lid has the reverse surface of the design perfectly executed. This process of insertion work was originated and perfected by Suzuki Gensuke. Great skill is required to cut an accurate outline of the design in the metal ground and to solder the ground and design together so that all evidence of the joining is removed.

Kiribame-Zōgan   In Japanese metal art; a decorative process of inserted inlaying. It is a method of chiselling a design in pierced work and outlining the openwork with a veneer of a contrasting metal such as gold to emphasize the outline. For example the metal worker having cut an openwork

floral design in a thin sheet of metal fits a delicate banding of a contrasting metal around each petal of the flowers, producing an effect of transparent flowers outlined in a contrasting metal. This method was developed by Tōyoda Kokō.

Kirman   An Oriental rug belonging to the Persian classification made in Kirman, Persia. It is a closely woven rug. The warp is of cotton and the weft is of wool or cotton; the pile is of a selected wool and is medium in length. The ends are finished with a narrow web and loose warp-threads. The rug is notable for its soft, fine texture and for its excellent coloring and designs. The motifs, which include lotus, palmettes, scrolling floral branches and other foliation, are treated in a more naturalistic manner than those found in any other Persian rug. See *Persian Rugs*; *Lavher*.

Kir-Shehr   An Oriental rug belonging to the Turkish classification; it is named after the town where it is woven. The warp and the weft are of wool; the pile, which is long, is of fine wool. The ends are usually finished with a web and loose warp threads. The rug is thick and durable. See *Turkish Rugs*.

Kis Khilim   Kis is a Perso-Turkish word meaning girl. The name is given to a tapestry rug woven by an Eastern girl for her dowry. See *Khilim*.

Kit-Cat Frame   One of the standard sizes of English carved frames having a sight dimension of 36 inches by 28 inches originally used in portraiture from the early 18th century and later adopted in other branches of painting. It received its name from the Kit-Cat portrait which was one of a widely known series made by Kneller for Jacob Tonson and the Kit-Cat club, which was a club of Whig politicians and men of letters established in the reign of James II. The size of the Kit-Cat portrait was less than half length, but it included the hands. The earliest portrait bearing a date was executed in 1703. It is said that this size portrait was adopted because the walls of the dining

IMARI BOWL WITH
KINRAN-DE DECORATION

room of the club at Barn Elms, a borough of London, north of Waterloo Bridge, were too low for half size portraits.

Kiyōmizu Ware In Japanese ceramics; the name given to a variety of pottery first made around the middle of the 17th century in a district in Kyōto named Kiyōmizu. The term *Ko Kiyōmizu* or old Kiyōmizu is generally reserved for the pottery made at the kilns on the hill of Kiyōmizu. It is a three-colored enamelled pottery comprising blue, green and red. Sometimes gold is added. It has a creamish white clay body. The glaze is cream-colored and is either crackled or not crackled. There were probably more than ten kilns located around the hill in Kiyōmizu making this type of pottery during the latter half of the 17th century. The clay was very plentiful; however, the supply became exhausted and the clay had to be brought from other sections in Japan. At the present time Kiyōmizu ware is commercial, and consists of both pottery and porcelain. There were also kilns located at Kiyōmizu Zaka, the word *zaka* meaning down. This section is down from the hillside of Kiyōmizu and these wares are generally included in Kyōto wares. See *Kyōto*; *Ninsei*; *Awata Ware*.

PISTOL-HANDLE KNIFE

Kloster-Veilsdorf In German ceramics; a porcelain manufactory was started at Kloster-Veilsdorf, Thuringia, in 1760 by Prince Friedrich Wilhelm von Hildburghausen. It was the outstanding Thuringian porcelain manufactory of the 18th century and is still in existence. The mark was "CV" either separated or in monogram in underglaze blue, and after 1797 it was a clover leaf. The best work was done prior to 1780 and was in the Rococo taste. The enamel colors were clear and fresh. Of especial interest was some admirable fruit and flower painting executed in an individual style. Attractive figure subjects and small garlands of flowers in the style of the French painter, Watteau, were also noteworthy. Some of the figure modelling was of excellent quality, in particular some

figures from the Italian Comedy and some draped figures of gods and goddesses. After 1780 the Neo-Classic style was adopted and although the pieces were of finished workmanship, such as the vases, they were lacking in originality.

Kneading Table See *Bread Trough*.

Kneehole Writing Table In English cabinetwork; the name is given to a variety of writing furniture introduced during the William and Mary style. The characteristic form of kneehole writing table had a flat oblong top, over a long drawer, which surmounted a recessed center cupboard flanked by two sets of three drawers each. The deeply recessed center compartment was designed to accommodate the knees of the writer. Each set of drawers rested on four feet which were most frequently of the bracket variety. Variations in design occurred. It is generally accepted that the writing table of kneehole form was found in America as early as 1725. It was made throughout the 18th century in America in the different successive styles. See *Writing Furniture*; *Writing Table*; *Dressing Table*.

Kneeland, Samuel 1755-1828. American cabinetmaker working at Hartford, Connecticut. About 1792 he formed a partnership with Lemuel Adams and in 1798 he moved to Farmington.

Knibb, Joseph One of the most eminent 17th century English clockmakers working around 1670 to 1708. Existing specimens of his work are of the highest quality. He made fine lantern clocks, tall case clocks and bracket clocks. After examining his clocks many regard his work to be of the same fine caliber as the work of Thomas Tompion and Daniel Quare. See *Roman Notation Clock*.

Knife In English silver; the table knife with a silver handle was introduced in England during the 17th century. The pistol handle knife, which derived its name from the shape of the handle, was a popular 18th century variety. The knife with a straight handle was introduced later in the 18th century and the design for the handle conformed to the design for the spoon and the fork with which it was to be used. See *Dessert Knife*; *Fork*; *Spoon*.

Knife Box In English cabinetwork; the mahogany knife box was generally designed in pairs and was placed at each end of the sideboard table in the Georgian dining room. It was of vertical box form and had a sloping lid and a shaped front. The interior was divided into many small oblong partitions. The knives and forks were so inserted that the handles were exposed and the spoons were of the opposite arrangement. It was introduced during the Chippendale style. Adam often designed the pedestal sideboard with a pair of knife boxes on the long side table in addition to the urns on the two pedestals which flanked the side table. The knife box in America was designed in the Hepplewhite style from around 1785 to 1800 and in the Sheraton style from around 1795 to 1810. See *Pedestal Sideboard*; *Knife Urn*; *Pedestal Sideboard Table*.

Knife Urn In English cabinetwork; the early urns as used by Adam were designed as part of his arrangement of a side table flanked by two pedestals. The urns, which were placed on the two pedestals, were usually fitted with lead liners, one was filled with ice water and the other with water for rinsing the silver knives and forks. The practice of rinsing table silver in the dining room continued until the 19th century. Occasionally one of the urns instead of holding water was fitted for the reception of knives. Knife urns as designed by Hepplewhite and Sheraton were separate and movable pieces and were generally made for the reception of knives. Hepplewhite stated that the knife urn should be made of satinwood or some other light wood and that it should be placed at each end of the sideboard or on the pedestals which flanked the sideboard table. The knife urn was often inlaid with vertical stringing lines. The knife urn was

made in America in both the Hepplewhite and Sheraton styles and its dates are essentially similar to those for the knife box. See *Knife Box*; *Pedestal Sideboard*; *Pedestal Sideboard Table*.

Knob Handle In furniture mounts; bronze round and flat knob handles ornamented with rosettes were frequently employed on the drawers of furniture designed in the French Empire style. Ormolu or bronze knob handles were also used on English Regency furniture. Brass knob handles were typical of the Early Empire style in America. Glass knob handles were used in America from about 1820 to 1840. Wooden knob handles were especially identified in America with the Late Empire and Early Victorian furniture.

Knop In ornament; the name given to a small rounded protuberance, especially one used to ornament the stem of a drinking vessel, a chalice, or a candlestick.

Knotted Lace See *Punto a Groppo*.

Knuckle Arm In furniture; on some types of Windsor chairs the terminals or ends of the arms have a carved feature called knuckles. They are smoothly carved grooves cut on the vertically rounded end of the arm. In America the name *knuckle arm* is applied to this type of arm.

Knulling Or Nulling. A convex rounded molding, which slightly projects, consisting of a repetitive pattern very often of waved or upright members separated by indentations. It is more or less between the egg and dart and bead and reel.

Knurling A variety of embossment used by goldsmiths consisting of a repetitive pattern separated by indentations such as on the edges of coins.

Kodōgu In Japanese sword mounts; a term applied collectively to all the mounts on a Japanese sword or knife, with the exception of the tsuba. See *Soroimono*; *Mitokoromono*.

KNIFE BOX

KNIFE URN

Kogai In Japanese sword mounts; the name given to a head pin, or skewer, often carried in a sheath in the scabbard of a sword or dagger. It is usually carried with the waki-zashi or short sword, often with the dagger, and seldom with the katana or long sword. There is no generally accepted explanation for its purpose. The handle was elaborately decorated to match the handle of the kozuka. At times the kogai was finely split lengthwise, from the top of the hilt to the point, forming a pair of hashi or chopsticks, when it was called a wari-kogai. See *Kozuka*.

Kojiri In Japanese mounts; the term applied to the metal tip on a scabbard. Its form varies greatly both in size and shape.

Ko-Katana In Japanese sword mounts; the name sometimes applied to the knife carried in a Japanese scabbard including the handle and the blade; while sometimes restricting the term *kozuka* to the blade only. However, the term *kozuka* is generally given to the blade and handle combined. See *Kozuka*; *Kogai*.

Konieh An Oriental rug belonging to the Turkish classification. It derived its name from the province of Konieh where rug weaving is an important industry. The warp and weft are of fine wool; the pile is of a fine selected wool, medium in length. The ends are finished with a web and selvage, sometimes a fringe. The modern Konieh is inferior to the early Konieh; the former usually being rather heavy and coarsely woven. See *Turkish Rugs*.

Königsberg In German ceramics; a small faïence manufactory was established at Königsberg, East Prussia, by John E. L. Ehrenreich in 1772. After changing hands several times it closed in 1811. The faïence mark was the monogram of Ehrenreich, "HE", impressed with the date added. The forms and decoration were in the Rococo style and the influence of Marieberg wares was evident. The painted decoration was generally done only in blue, which in the best work was a rich vivid tone. Flowers

KOREAN BOWL WITH
INLAID SLIP DECORATION

realistically treated were a favorite motif. Later the manufactory produced a lead-glazed earthenware marked with a "K" impressed. A second manufactory was in operation at Königsberg from around 1775 to 1785, making wares in the style of Wedgwood.

Korai See *Korean Dynasties*.

Korean Dynasties The art works of Korea are identified with the respective period in which they were produced. The Korean periods are designated by the dates of the dynasties. The following is a chronological order of the dynasties: Silla, 1st to the 10th century A.D.; Korai, A.D. 918 to 1392, and Yi, 1392 to 1910. See *Korean Wares*.

Korean Wares In ceramics; Korean wares are generally found in the excavation of tombs. Excavations have revealed that Chinese were living in Korea as early as the Han period and had been buried with their personal belongings such as lacquered wares and pottery. Korean tombs have also shown personal possessions such as pottery. This pottery although it displays Chinese influence has a distinctive Korean character. Included among the wares found in old Korean tombs are celadon, white porcelain of the Ting and Ying Ch'ing types, brown and black glazed wares of the Temmoku type, Ju Chou and Yüeh Chou types. Although these wares are found in Korean tombs it is not a conclusive proof that they were all made in Korea. The subject has caused much controversy as many pieces, particularly the white wares, are said to have been brought from China. The historical periods of Korea are generally known as Silla, 1st to 10th century A.D.; Korai, 918 to 1392, and Yi, 1392 to 1910. The wares of the Silla period usually have a grey color body varying from a rough coarse material to a thin, smooth and well-finished ware, from a soft pottery to a hard stoneware. It is unglazed but at times it has a crude greenish-brown slip glaze. It is decorated with an incised wavy pattern, applied reliefs, wheel-made rings, crude perforations and cross hatching. Korai ware is a porcelaneous stoneware or a coarse porcelain showing a brownish color on exposed parts with a celadon-type glaze which varies from a fine bluish-green to a brownish-green. The wares of the Korai period are generally divided into particular eras. From about 1150 to 1170, which is the best period, the ware is thin and finely made and has a beautiful blue-green celadon glaze. The decoration is usually incised and carved. Some of the wares also resembled Ting Chou ware. The characteristic Korean inlaid decoration was introduced during the following period, 1170 to 1274. It was made by filling in an incised design with white and black clays. Later the method of stamping the design was introduced, which was more elaborate and called mishima by the Japanese. Relief designs were also molded and stamped on the inside of the celadon bowls. This type of Korean ware can be distinguished from the Chinese by the shallow and lumpy base covered with glaze and marred with sand on which it was placed in the kiln, or the marks of the spurs. From about 1274 to about 1350 the green glaze of the celadon becomes coarse and brown and the quality of the ware begins to decline. The decoration of underglaze black was introduced. From 1350 to the Yi dynasty the wares became inferior. The painted wares and mishima decoration are coarse and the designs are trite, and the glaze which had been a beautiful blue-green became a dull brownish color. The wares of the Yi period are usually a rather coarse porcelain having a greyish glaze that is occasionally crackled, and decorated in an underglaze red or a blackish-blue underglaze in a Chinese manner. See *Mishima*; *Celadon*; *Ting Yao*.

Koro The name applied to a Japanese or Chinese incense burner.

Ko'ssu A very fine silk fabric woven in the tapestry weave in China. The designs are elaborate and colorful and are usually partly worked in gold threads.

Koultuk An Oriental rug belonging to the Persian classification. It is also called Zenjan. See *Persian Rugs*.

Kovsh A Russian vessel made of silver, wood or some similar material used for ladling out drinks. It usually has a boat-shaped body and is fitted with a single spatulate handle. It was popular from the 16th to the 18th centuries.

Ko Yao In Chinese ceramics; Ko Yao or elder brother's ware is supposed to have been made by the elder brother Chang at Liu-t'ien in the Lung-ch'üan district of the province of Chekiang in the latter part of the Southern Sung dynasty, A.D. 1127–1280. Chinese records always associate Ko yao and Kuan yao together without making any particular effort to differentiate between the two wares. It was made of the same dark-colored clay and it is believed that the ware had a brown lip rim and an iron foot. It is assumed that the various Kuan glazes were also used on Ko ware. It had both large and small crackle. In fact crackle was a special feature of Ko ware. The imitation of Kuan yao and the making of Ko yao were carried on at Lung-ch'üan at least until the end of the Yüan dynasty. Both wares were widely copied at Ching-tê-Chên from the 18th century. Eventually the term *Ko* was used simply to refer to the various kinds of buff and grey crackle wares without any reference to the original Sung pieces. The glazes are distinctive for their thickness and solidity, sometimes resulting in a soft surface texture like polished marble. The glazes are fat and undulating and often terminate in thick drops. The crackle varies in width and both the small and large crackle are occasionally combined on the same piece. Intentional crackle was obtained by several methods. One simple method was to add a special clay which was a kind of pegmatite to the glaze. Sometimes the crackle is accentuated by rubbing a coarse red or black ink into the fissures. See *Sung*; *Kuan Yao*; *Crackle*.

KO WARE INCENSE VASE

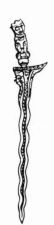

BALINESE KRIS

Kozuka   In Japanese sword mounts; the small knife carried in a sheath in the scabbard of a Japanese sword or dagger. The name *kozuka* is also applied to the blade only, when it is detached from the handle. It has a straight single-edged blade made of kataha plates, produced by welding together a plate of steel and one of iron. The steel side of the blade is flat with a high polish, while the iron side tapers to the cutting edge and is unpolished. Frequently the iron side is inlaid or engraved. The flat metal handle, which is generally about $\frac{1}{2}$ inch in width and slightly less than 4 inches long, is elaborately decorated, and conforms to or matches the kogai if they are made in a pair. See *Kogai*.

Krautstrunk   In German glass; the name given to a tumbler, generally made of green glass, covered with prunts or glass studs. It was introduced during the 16th century. It was similar to an igel, which is a squat glass tumbler, except that the former was taller and the sides were not as bulging. See *German Glass*; *Waldglas*.

Kreussen   In German ceramics; a flourishing manufacture for stove tiles or Hafner ware was in existence at Kreussen, near Bayreuth, Bavaria, during the 16th century. It seems that the manufacture of stoneware which became an important production dated from the late 16th century and was continued at least until 1732. All the artistic stoneware was of the 17th century. The stoneware was covered with a brown salt glaze of varying tone. One variety was decorated only with applied reliefs. In the other principal variety the reliefs were painted with bright opaque enamel colors of blue, red, green, yellow and white, sometimes with touches of gilding. This use of overglaze enamel colors at Kreussen was the first in Europe; the earliest date was recorded in 1622. The enamelled decoration was executed in a similar style to that found on the German enamelled glass and was probably done by the same painters. Included among their productions were four- or six-sided flasks called Schraubflasch and made only at Kreussen, tankards of squat cylindrical forms with pewter lids, bell-shaped tankards and pear-shaped and globular-shaped jugs. The finest reliefs which were made from around 1700 to 1725 were well modelled, large and in rather high relief. The motifs for the reliefs included figure subjects, such as the Apostles, The Family or The Wedding and also coats-of-arms and inscriptions in typical Roman lettering.

Kris   In arms; a Malay knife that is also found in such places as Java and Bali. It originated about the 14th century and its blade and hilt are in many different forms. The blade is either straight, half straight and half wavy, or wavy from hilt to point. The blades vary from 5 inches to 3 feet and have five to fifteen waves. All the blades are characterized by a wide part at the hilt which terminates in a point that is frequently notched to serve as a guard.

Ku   In Chinese bronzes; a vessel used for drinking wine at festivals. It is in the form of a trumpet with a wide flaring lip rim and its slender body tapers to a slightly flaring foot.

Kuan Chün Yao   In Chinese ceramics; see *Chün Yao*.

Kuang   In Chinese bronzes; a vessel used for pouring libations. The body, which resembles a sauce-boat, is rounded and rests either on short feet or a molded base. It contains a loop handle and a pouring lip. A cover, which extends over the top and pouring lip, is usually in the form of a conventionalized tiger or bull.

Kuan Ti   In Chinese art; a Chinese Confucian subject extensively used in Chinese painting, sculpture, textiles and ceramics. He is the god of war and is represented in full armor. He is generally seen seated with his right hand raised, or mounted on his horse or standing near his horse. He has a flowing beard. Until late in the 16th century he was known as Kuan Yü, a famous warrior.

Confucius, K'uei Hsing and Kuan Ti are the three most commonly represented Confucian subjects. See *Chinese Gods*.

Kuan Yao In Chinese ceramics; the term literally means Imperial ware and it could be and was applied to all varieties of porcelains made at the Imperial potteries. The original Sung Kuan, which was called Ta Kuan by later writers, was first made at the Imperial pottery at K'ai-fêng Fu in Honan during the early years of the 12th century. Apparently the Kuan yao potters followed the Imperial court when it fled south in 1127. The northern Sung Kuan was made for only about fifteen or twenty years. According to Chinese records the color of the glaze is described as pale blue, green or grey; moon-white; deep green and bluish or greenish with a tinge of pale red. Much of the ware had both large and small crackle. The body of the original ware is not known. The southern Sung Kuan was made at Hangchow. Other potteries in the vicinity made wares of the Kuan type. The Hangchow Kuan followed closely the northern Kuan glazes. The body was dark brown or red which gave the ware a brown mouth and iron foot. In other words the dark body showed through the glaze when it was thin at the lip rim and the body was exposed at the raw edge of the foot rim.

Kuan Yin In Chinese art; a Chinese Buddhist goddess. The figure of Kuan Yin was extensively produced in ivory, jade and blanc de chine. She is known as the goddess of mercy and is seen at times with an upturned vase, representing the source of water that produces growth. She is also represented as the mother goddess, holding a child or having a child near her. See *Chinese Gods*.

Kuan Yü See *Kuan Ti*; *Chinese Gods*.

K'uei Hsing In Chinese art; a Chinese Confucian subject. He is the god of literature. He is depicted as a demon-faced creature and has one foot placed on the head of a monster which is a fish dragon. He is holding a brush and other implements of writing. See *Chinese Gods*; *Kuan Ti*.

Kuei Kung In Chinese ceramics; the term *kuei kung* or devil's work is often given to the delicate openwork that was characteristic of some of the later Ming porcelains. It was so called because the work was so delicate that it seemed beyond the realm of human skill. See *Ling Lung*.

Kuft Work The name given in India to damascening. See *Damascening*.

Kukri In arms; a knife or dagger of the Gurkas of Nepal. The blade is heavy and curved with the cutting edge on the concave side. The hilt is straight and is occasionally fitted with a disc-shaped guard and pommel.

Kulah Rug An Oriental rug belonging to the Turkish classification. It derived its name from the town of Kulah, in the vicinity of which it is woven. The warp and weft are of fine wool. The pile is a very fine selected wool and is comparatively short. The ends are finished in a narrow selvage with loose warp threads. This rug is of very fine workmanship. A great majority are of the prayer rug variety. The Kulah prayer rug is characterized by its numerous borders and its inner field which is usually filled or partly filled with small designs. See *Turkish Rugs*.

Künersberg In German ceramics; a faïence manufactory was started at Künersberg, near Memmingen, Bavaria, in 1745 by Jacob Küner, a successful merchant, and was active until about 1767. The wares attributed to this manufactory were sometimes marked with the initials "KB" or "Künersberg." Included among their productions which were widely diversified were lobed or gourd-shaped vases, cylindrical tankards, plates with wavy edges and jugs with very slender narrow necks. Figures were also made. Some of the finest German faïence is attributed to this manufactory. It was delicately and minutely painted either in soft high temperature colors or in overglaze enamel colors on a beautiful pure white ground. The most

IVORY FIGURE OF
KUAN YIN

beautiful faïence ascribed to Künersberg was painted in the overglaze enamel colors in the style of porcelain. Gold was much used in this work in the form of delicate lacework and scrollwork borders frequently used around minutely painted landscape panels or chinoiseries. Other favorite motifs included sprays of flowers realistically treated, fruit, birds on branches and coats-of-arms.

Kurdistan An Oriental rug belonging to the Persian classification. It derived its name from the province in which it is woven. The warp and the weft are of wool; the pile is of wool and is of medium length. The ends are usually finished with a narrow web and knotted fringe. The rug is exceptionally firm and durable, due to the fact that a coarse, heavy, two-strand yarn is used as an extra filling between each row of knots. The designs are varied and usually are of a rather mediocre quality. See *Persian Rugs.*

Kurfürstenhumpen In German glass; see *Elector Glass.*

Kurikata In Japanese sword mounts; the term applied to a small projecting fitting on a Japanese scabbard to keep it from slipping through the obi or sash. It is usually decorated like the other fittings, and also serves as a protection at the opening in the scabbard which holds the kogai, in the same manner as the uragawara serves for the the kozuka

KUTANI VASE

Kutani Ware In Japanese ceramics; porcelain was first made around the middle of the 17th century at Kutani in the Kaga province in east Japan. The Kutani kilns were under the patronage of the House of Maeda. Prince Maeda sent Gotō Saijirō to Hizen to study. Ko Kutani or old Kutani displayed a diversity in its designs. In some specimens the designs are copied from late Ming and early Ch'ing wares; in other examples the designs are purely Japanese. The decorative designs reflect at times the influence of Arita ware. In the Akae Kutani the red and green enamels are supplemented by purple, yellow, overglaze blue and sometimes gold and silver. Underglaze blue

is seldom used. Ao Kutani or blue-green Kutani, in which no red enamel is applied, used yellow, blue-green and purple enamels. The enamel colors for Kutani ware are thick. Around the beginning of the 19th century the production of old Ao Kutani was revived, having been interrupted for a number of years. A potter named Iidaya-Hachiroemon developed a kinran-de ware which came to be the most popular and typical of all the wares produced in the Kaga province. In this ware the red ground is solidly applied and the delicate decoration, which is copied from Chinese designs, is executed in gold. See *Kinran-de.*

Ku Yüeh Hsüan In Chinese ceramics; a distinctive ware made partly in the reign of Yung Chêng and partly in the reign of Ch'ien Lung during the Ch'ing dynasty. This ware tries to reproduce in porcelain the soft coloring on the enamelled glass made by Hu, whose studio name was Ku-Yüeh-Hsüan, or ancient moon pavilion. According to the story the emperor expressed his admiration for this glassware and wished that the same effect could be simulated in porcelain. Therefore T'ang Ying set out to make a porcelain resembling glass and to copy the same style of decoration and the same soft coloring. He made a highly vitreous body with a milky texture and a glassy glaze on which the enamelled decoration affected the soft coloring of the original glass. This type of porcelain is highly prized. It is known as Fang Ku Yüeh Hsüan or imitation Ku Yüeh Hsüan.

Kwaiken In Japanese arms; an early form of knife carried by Japanese women and used for ceremonial suicide by severing the veins in the neck. The blade was slightly curved and was either single-edged or double-edged.

Kwangtung Yao In Chinese ceramics; there are many kilns located in the province of Kwangtung, which is the southernmost province in China, and it is reputed that some were operating as early as the T'ang dynasty

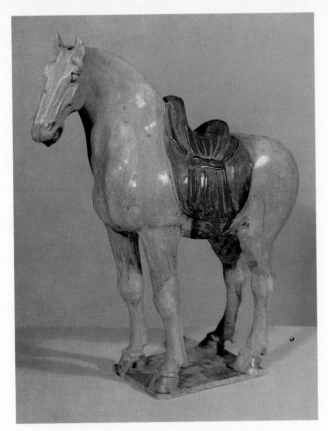

POTTERY HORSE—*Chinese, T'ang Period.*
The Metropolitan Museum of Art, bequest of Edmund C. Converse, 1921.

PORCELAIN SAUCER—*Chinese, Ch'ing Dynasty.*
The Metropolitan Museum of Art, bequest of John D. Rockefeller, Jr., 1960.

PORCELAIN VASE—*Chinese, K'ang Hsi Period.*
The Metropolitan Museum of Art, bequest of Benjamin Altman, 1913.

PORCELAIN PLATE—*Chinese, K'ang Hsi Period.*
The Metropolitan Museum of Art, bequest of John D. Rockefeller, Jr., 1960.

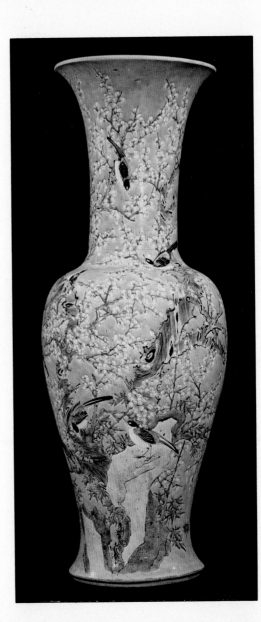

and were making earthenware cooking vessels. The dating of the mottled Kwangtung wares, or Canton stonewares as they are generally called, is a difficult problem. It is certain that they were made at least as early as the late Ming dynasty. They are still made and are exported in large quantities. The kilns at Shekwan West which is close to Fatshan are probably the best known. It is a hard-fired ware and has a dark brown body of reddish tone. The glaze is thick and smooth and is characterized by mottling and dappling. The glaze may be olive-brown, bluish-black or green flecked and streaked with grey-green, white, buff and grey with often bright blue breaking through. At times the brown tone predominates but the most highly prized pieces are those in which the general tone is blue. Occasionally the mottled glazes bear a surface resemblance to the dappled Chün yao. This ware was also made into figures such as the god of war and other deities. The figures are generally covered with either a crimson-red flambé glaze or a celadon type of glaze, except for their faces and hands which are left unglazed. Other types of wares are also attributed to this province.

Kylin A Chinese animal figure. See *Ch'i-Lin*.

Kyōto In Japanese ceramics; a general term applied to the wares produced in Kyōto. The kilns in Kyōto are principally operated by individual ceramists and the artistic wares of Kyōto are chiefly known by the names of the family who owns the kiln. In the time of Kenzan there were about four or five kilns operating in Kyōto. The early ware was pottery with color decoration in the Japanese taste. This decoration reflected the influence of Ninsei's enamelled pottery. After Ninsei's death the tradition of Kyōto ware was carried on by his disciple, Kenzan. At the beginning of the 19th century when porcelain was developed nationally the technique of Arita porcelain was learned by the Kyōto ceramists. Due to the vogue for Chinese porcelain the Kyōto ceramists made imitations of Chinese enamelled porcelain, celadon, blue and white and three-color late Ming and early Ch'ing ware. One of the outstanding makers of Kyōto porcelain was Okuda-Eisen, 1753–1811, who is regarded as the originator of this sort of porcelain. Mokubei, 1767–1833, who was a pupil of Eisen's, excelled in the imitation of enamelled porcelain, blue and white, celadon and three-color Ming ware. He also made fine enamelled pottery. Eiraku, 1795–1854, was skilled in the imitation of Ming three-color, gilded porcelain and blue and white wares. At the present time there are about ten kilns in Kyōto producing artistic wares, which are principally porcelain. Included among these are Rokubei, Chikusen, Eiraku, Kawai and Seifu. See *Awata Ware*; *Iwakura Ware*; *Raku Ware*; *Eiraku Ware*; *Omuro*; *Kiyōmizu Ware*; *Kenzan, Ogata*; *Ninsei*.

KYŌTO CHARCOAL BOWL

L

Labelled Decanter An 18th century English term applied to a glass decanter having an engraved inscription such as *Claret*, *Port* or *Sherry*. Engraved labels on decanters were fashionable in England from around 1750 onwards.

Labelled Furniture In American cabinet-work; occasionally a paper label is found pasted on an article of American furniture. Many times this label is the original label of the cabinetmaker who made the original piece. A label is not always a true indication of the original maker, for it may be the label of a dealer in furniture or a label of a repairer. If it is the label of a repairer it probably was pasted on at a later date. Paper labels could also be removed and pasted on another piece of furniture. See *Ebéniste*.

Laburnum Wood The wood of the laburnum tree, *cytisus laburnum*, which has been cultivated since the 16th century in England. It was extensively used by cabinetmakers during the William III and Queen Anne reigns. It was chiefly used in oystering, which is a kind of veneer work.

Lac-Burgauté In Chinese ceramics; see *Burgauté*.

Lace The art of lace-making has from the earliest times been closely associated with the art of needlework, and it is from the cutwork or openwork embroidery that the origin of lace may be traced. The term *lace*, which is derived from the Latin word *laqueus* meaning loop or noose, is given to a slender openwork fabric made of fine threads of gold, silver, silk, flax or cotton, generally enriched with inwrought or applied designs or patterns. Lace consists of two parts, namely the ground and the pattern. In addition to the honeycomb or network ground which is of various kinds, some laces, points and guipures are simply connected by irregular threads, which are

LACE GLASS PLATE,
VENETIAN

commonly known by the French term *brides*. The design or toile is made simultaneously with the ground or separately, when it is either worked in or appliquéd. The openwork decorative stitches introduced into a design are called jours or fillings. Lace is divided into needle-made and bobbin-made laces, and it is called respectively needlepoint and bobbin lace or pillow lace. See *Needlepoint*; *Bobbin Lace*.

Lace Glass Or Vitro di Trina. In Venetian glass; a type of clear glass having designs of glass threads developed in a distinctive lace-like pattern. It first came into use around the second quarter of the 16th century. See *Venetian Glass*; *Threaded Glass*.

Lacet The French term *lacet* which means braid, is given to the silk or linen braid used to form patterns for laces. The name is also given to the lace made out of this braid.

Lacework In ceramics; lace is reproduced in porcelain by dipping an actual piece of lace in a porcelain "slip". It is then dried and fired so that the lace is burnt away and only the porcelain replica remains. This method for making porcelain lace was introduced at Meissen around 1740, although the credit for the invention is generally given to J. A. Hannong working at the Strasbourg manufactory where it was used around the same time.

La China See *Buen Retiro*.

Lacis A French term meaning network. The name is applied to a darned netting or darned lace, first made in Italy around the 15th century. It was characterized by a foundation of handmade openwork netting, upon which were darned patterns of a stiff or geometrical nature. See *Darned Netting*.

La Courtille In French ceramics; a hard paste porcelain manufactory founded in Paris in 1771 by Jean-Baptiste Locré. This manufactory, which was also called Rue Fontaine-au-Roy, Basse Courtille or Manufacture de Porcelaine Allemande, produced a very translucent porcelain of excellent quality. It is generally believed to have been the most important and productive pre-Revolution factory in Paris. After several changes in ownership it closed in 1840. The mark was crossed torches with the flames pointing upwards in underglaze blue or incised. The forms and painted decoration were in the Neo-Classic style. The wares displayed fine workmanship and were admirable for their refinement and elegance. Especially noteworthy were some well-modelled biscuit figures.

Lacquer   A term given to colored and occasionally opaque varnishes applied to particular objects made of wood or metal. The name is derived from resin lac which is the basic substance for lacquer. The lacquering of wood is practiced extensively in India, Burma and the Far East. In India lacquer work is frequently referred to as Sind lac and is applied to a variety of articles, such as trays, boxes, furniture and similar pieces. In Sind lac work the article is placed on a crude lathe and while it is rotating the worker presses sticks of lacquer against it. The rotating piece produces a friction which causes the lacquer to soften and adhere on the desired portion. Sometimes several layers of colored lacquer are applied and the design is then cut with a sharp tool revealing the color desired. These designs are usually geometrical or floral, worked either in black and gold or in colors. In Europe the term *lacquering* is generally given to the practice of applying a coat of varnish to metal objects, such as those made of tin, brass or pewter, in order to given them a golden luster. The art of lacquering as practiced in Japan and China is different from all other types of lacquer work. See *Japanese Lacquer*; *Chinese Lacquer*; *Vernis Martin*; *Japanning*; *Cinnabar*; *Tsui-Shiu*.

Lacroix, Roger Vandercruse 1728–1799. One of the foremost French ébénistes working in Paris during the 18th century. He produced many fine pieces of cabinetwork for the palaces of Versailles and the Tuileries as well as for the Duke of Orléans and the château of Madame du Barry at Louveciennes. The marquetry work on his furniture is regarded as equal to the finest. His best pieces were made toward the end of the reign of Louis XV in citronnier wood inlaid with ebony.

Lacy Pressed Glass   In American glass; the name given to a variety of pressed glass characterized by patterns and designs of lacy and bead-work combinations covering the entire surface. This type of over-all decoration was emphasized from around 1830 to 1850 which is called the lacy period. See *American Glass*; *Pressed Glass*.

Ladder-Back   In English and American cabinetwork; the ladder-back chair was a popular pattern from about 1750 to 1790. With the exception of slight modifications the chair displayed little variation in its design. In a characteristic Chippendale-style variety the slightly flaring uprights support a serpentine fret-pierced crest rail over three conformingly shaped and pierced cross rails. The quadrangular chamfered legs are connected with plain stretchers. Some of the later English specimens reflected the prevailing Neo-Classic influence in the carved detail, such as carved patera, sometimes appearing on the crest rail as well as in a modification of the shape of the crest rail. The term *ladder-back* is also applied to the earlier slat-back chair. See *Slat-Back Chair*.

Ladik   An Oriental rug belonging to the Turkish classification. Ladik is a corruption of the word Laodicea, the name of the town where this rug is woven. The warp is of a fine wool and the weft is usually a dyed wool. The pile is made of a fine selected wool and is rather short. The ends are usually finished in a broad red web, and short fringe. Traditionally the Ladik is a fine example of workmanship. See *Turkish Rugs*.

AMERICAN LADDER-BACK
CHAIR

Ladle In silver; a kind of spoon displaying some variation in its form. As a rule it had a cup-shape or hemispherical bowl. Occasionally the bowl was in the shape of a shell or some other similar form. It was fitted with a long handle that conformed in design to the contemporary spoon. It was used for soup and for punch. Extant English examples of soup ladles date from the first half of the 18th century. A smaller ladle similar in design to the larger ladle was also made and was used for different sauces and sugar. See *Punch Ladle.*

Lafosse, Charles de 1636–1716. Lafosse was a prominent French historical and decorative painter and holds an important place next to that of Le Brun, de Mignard and de Jouvenet as a foremost decorative artist of the 17th century. During his early life he studied under Le Brun and in 1658 he went to Italy where he continued his studies for five years. Through the offices of Colbert he received a pension from the King.

Lahore Rug An Oriental rug woven at Lahore, India, which was an important rug-weaving centre during the reign of Akbar the Great, 1556–1605. He established at Lahore a royal manufactory. The modern Lahore rug is purely a commercial creation. See *India Oriental Rugs*; *Oriental Rugs.*

Lajoue, Jacques de 1686–1761. French painter and decorative artist. His name is sometimes linked with Meissonier and Pineau as one of the three inventors of the more intensified or accelerated phase of the Rococo dating from around 1730. His work is not generally regarded to be as important in the movement of art as the work of either Meissonier or Pineau. Some of his asymmetrical Rococo designs were especially fantastic and extravagant. His work as a whole belongs in the realm of fantasy.

Lalique Glass A decorative French glass originated by René Lalique of Paris, 1860–1945, working from around the beginning of the twentieth century. The colorless glass was remarkable for the purity of its

SILVER LADLE, ENGLISH

material. The designs, which had a singular elegance, were composed of foliage, flowers, birds and animals, and were molded and pressed as well as engraved with the wheel. His early work was largely restricted to small articles such as scent bottles. Later he made many large and massive pieces such as bowls, vases and figures.

Lambeth In English ceramics; the term *Lambeth* is generally given to the faïence or delftware made in a group of London potteries at Aldgate and in the parishes south of the Thames and outside the City Walls, at Southwark, Vauxhall and especially at Lambeth during the 17th century. The faïence potteries at Lambeth were in existence at least until 1763, and other potteries in the vicinity were active until around the middle of the 19th century, although little faïence was made. No marks were used. Lambeth faïence was essentially influenced by the faïence made at Delft, Holland; however, some distinctively English styles were created around the middle of the 17th century. Some of the wares were also decorated in the tradition of Italian majolica. Included among their productions were globular jugs, ointment-pots, barrel-shaped mugs, plates and dishes, globular narrow-necked wine bottles, candlesticks, salt-cellars and stem-cups copied from silver, puzzle cups and posset-pots. Some of the wares were left entirely unpainted, others were painted in blue or in colors on the tin-glazed or tin-enamelled ground. It is often very difficult to distinguish the later 18th century faïence made at Lambeth from that made at Bristol and Liverpool. The principal inspiration for these wares was the Chinese porcelains exported to Europe. See *Faïence*; *Delft*; *Delftware*; *Bristol*; *Liverpool.*

Lambrequin A term originally meaning pendent draperies applied to a variety of pendent lace-like ornament treated in a formal manner. The motif, which is generally believed to be of French origin, was found in the ornamental designs of such decorative artists as Bérain and Marot workin the Baroque style. See *Rouen*.

Lamellé   In leather work; the term applied to a decorative work on leather. It is a process of cutting slits in a piece of leather, then creating a geometrical pattern by passing slender metal strips, usually of silver, through the slits.

Lamerie, Paul   1688–1751. Noted silversmith working in London from 1703. Lamerie, who was born in Holland, went to London, where in 1703 he was apprenticed to Pierre Platel, a well-known silversmith. He is generally regarded as one of the most celebrated English silversmiths and his pieces of ornamental plate are unexcelled in their perfected workmanship.

La Moncloa   Or Florida. In Spanish ceramics; a rather unimportant porcelain manufactory was established at La Moncloa, near Madrid, by Ferdinand VII in 1817 and continued until 1850. Some of the supplies at Buen Retiro were used here. The productions were chiefly imitations of contemporary French wares. "Moncloa" under a crown, impressed, was the usual mark. The mark "M" or "Md" under a crown was also used, as at Buen Retiro. See *Buen Retiro*.

Lamp   The lamp in which oil was burnt with a wick is of ancient origin. The terracotta hand lamp with a spout, which was a characteristic Roman type, was used for centuries and until the end of the 17th century the usual form of lighting was a wick laid in an open vessel. This type of lamp was often placed in a lantern, or on a candlebeam or chandelier. The majority of improvements in the early oil lamps originated on the Continent where the French produced a self-feeding lamp in the 16th century as well as a plaited cotton wick. Until the latter part of the 18th century oil lamps were not too practical and produced considerable smoke, which accounts for the large consumption of wax candles. In 1782, Aimé Argand, a Swiss, contributed the first important invention in oil lamps with a tubular wick which created an air current both outside and inside the flame. In England Chippendale, Adam and Hepplewhite made many elaborate designs for fixtures to hold oil lamps, and Wedgwood produced many oil lamps of basalt ware and jasper ware.

Lance   In arms; a horseman's spear. The early lance was a plain wood shaft with a steel head. The 14th century lance had two swellings on the shaft for a grip with a guard or vamplate to protect the hand. Lances were from 10 to 14 feet in length and the heads were generally leaf-shaped. The jousting lance had either a blunt head or three blunt points.

Lancet   The Early Gothic style of ornament and architecture in England is also referred to as the Lancet style because the Early English Gothic was characterized by the use of the Lancet arch. The difference between the Gothic or pointed arch and the Lancet arch is that the latter came to a sharper point at its apex. See *Gothic*; *Gothic, English*.

Lancet Clock   An English mantel clock popular from about 1800 to 1850. Apparently it was so called because the form of the top resembled the pointed Gothic arch called a Lancet arch and reflected the prevailing taste or interest in Gothic forms. It was generally decorated with inlaid brass designs and was usually mounted on four brass feet. The sides were frequently provided with brass ring handles.

Landiers   French andirons. This term is now usually reserved for the kitchen andirons of wrought-iron. See *Andirons*.

Langue de Bœuf   A dagger similar to a basilard. It derived its name from the supposed resemblance of its broad blade to the shape of the tongue of an ox. See *Basilard*; *Dagger*.

Lang Yao   In Chinese ceramics; a Chinese term applied to Sang de Bœuf or ox-blood color porcelain. See *Sang de Bœuf*.

SHEFFIELD LAMP, ARGAND TYPE

Languedoc In French Provincial; an old province in southern France, situated between the Loire River and the Pyrenees. The style of provincial furniture of Bas-Languedoc or lower Languedoc essentially has the same characteristics as that of Provence. The style of furniture of Haute-Languedoc or upper Languedoc is closely related to the articles of furniture from Gascogne and the Basque country. See *Provence*; *Gascogne*; *Basque*; *French Provincial*.

Lannuier, Charles Honoré American cabinetmaker working around 1805–1819 at 60 Broad Street, New York City. His work, like that of Duncan Phyfe, is representative of the American Directoire style.

Lantern In English and American accessories; the lantern, which was used in ancient classic times, is defined as a receptacle for a light enclosed by some substance which transmits the light and protects it from a draft. Lanterns were made for outside use and for domestic use. Many portable lanterns served both purposes. The other domestic lanterns were ceiling and wall lanterns. In England, horn was the usual material for the case, at least until the end of the 15th century. Due to the French policy of developing various crafts, glass became more plentiful toward the end of the 17th century and glass lanterns, particularly ceiling lanterns, became very fashionable early in the 18th century. They were made of carved gilt wood, bronze, or brass, and the ornament essentially followed the prevailing 18th century styles. Globular, hexagonal, octagonal and bell-shaped lanterns were included in the popular forms. Lanterns were not used to any great extent in America until early in the 18th century. Of interest were the American portable lanterns made of pierced tin, fitted with a candle or occasionally with a small oil lamp. Later this lantern was fitted with a glass window and sometimes a lantern was found with a horn window. The bull's eye lantern was made with a magnifying glass in the opening. The so-called dark lantern, which was first

BRASS CEILING LANTERN, ENGLISH

imported into America around 1800, was made with two tin cylinders, one fitting closely within another. An opening in the inner cylinder allowed the light to shine through a bull's eye glass, but with a quick turn of the cylinder the light was shut off.

Lantern Clock In English furniture; the name given to a bracket or wall clock, made from about 1575 to 1680. It is also called a bird-cage clock. It was a small rectangular brass clock with four turned brass Doric columns at the corners supporting brass pierced-work crestings on the front and sides of the top. The top was surmounted with a bell suspended from arched brass bands. The front and back were covered with brass plates and the sides with hinged doors. It rested on small turned feet. The shape resembled a lantern or bird-cage. The circular dial, with its Roman numerals, was affixed to the front plate. In the early type the dial extended within the front columns, while in the later type the dial projected beyond the front columns. This type of clock was either hung on the wall or placed on a wall bracket, with the chains holding the weights hanging loosely. See *Clock*.

Larch Wood See *Mélèze Wood*.

Laristan Rug See *Niris Rug*.

La Rochelle In French ceramics; a faïence manufactory was established at La Rochelle, Charente-Inférieure, in 1749, aided by workmen and supplies taken from the faïence manufactory at Marans. It is believed that Pierre Roussencq of Marans was the first manager. It changed hands several times and closed in 1789. Although it is only reasonable that some of the work resembled Marans, the manufactory developed some more or less distinctive interpretations of the painted decoration found in the faïence at Rouen, Strasbourg, Moustiers and Nevers. Of particular interest was the painted decoration in the Nevers style with its strong drawings and clear high temperature colors. No regular factory mark is known; however, various initials and monograms are found.

Two earlier faïence manufactories were active at La Rochelle during the early 18th century. They were relatively unimportant.

La Seynie In French ceramics; see *Petite Rue Saint-Gilles*.

Latch Hook In Oriental rugs; see *Angular Hook*; *Caucasian Rugs*.

Latten The name given to a kind of mixed metal of a yellowish color and closely resembling brass, widely used during medieval times for hanging lights or chandeliers, candlesticks, vessels and other similar articles. Essentially it was a more impure mixture of brass in which unrefined zinc was blended with copper, while in brass the mixture comprised zinc and copper. Latten was much used in England until the 16th century.

Lattice-Back Chair In English cabinetwork; a filling of lattice-work or trellis-work supported on a horizontal bar raised several inches above the seat was a fashionable variation for open chair backs designed in the Sheraton style. This pattern, which permitted a variety of treatment, was remarkably effective and continued to be used in the early years of the 19th century. Chairs designed in the Chinese Chippendale taste around 1760 sometimes had effectively treated lattice-work or trellis-work backs.

Lattice-Work In English furniture; the terms *lattice-work*, *fretwork* and *cutwork* are essentially interchangeable terms for wood cut into designs or patterns. See *Fretwork*. The term *lattice-work* is also given to the tracery of glazing and to trellis-work executed in metal.

Latticinio In Venetian glass; opaque dead-white glass. The term is reserved for the threads and filigrees of opaque white glass, in distinction to white glass which is understood as colorless and transparent. The latticinio chiefly employed in the filigree Venetian Renaissance glass is a glass colored milk-white by oxide of tin or arsenic. The term *latticinio glass* is used to describe glass decorated with opaque white glass threads in a clear matrix. See *Glass Cane*; *Glass*; *Threaded Glass*; *Venetian Glass*.

Laub und Bandelwerk In ornament; a German term which literally means leaf and strapwork. It was a late Baroque style of ornament which was very fashionable on glass, porcelain and faïence during the early 18th century. The laub und bandelwerk ornament of Germany was especially characteristic of German Baroque and was particularly important in ceramic art.

Laurier Aromatique Wood See *Oleander Wood*.

Lavabo The Latin term *lavabo* meaning to wash is applied to an ecclesiastical basin, usually of gold or silver, used for washing the hands of bishops and priests during the celebration of the sacred rites. The custom of washing the hands before putting on the sacred vestments or before praying is most ancient and dates from Biblical times. During the early times not only the priest but also the faithful washed their hands before entering churches. The name *lavabo* is also given to a washing trough used in medieval monasteries. In Europe the basin called a lavabo which was in general use in 18th century houses was placed beneath a wall fountain or a water container provided with a spigot. See *Wall Fountain*. In French cabinetwork; a popular variety of lavabo was copied from an antique Roman tripod and was introduced late in the 18th century. The top of the small circular stand was dished for the reception of a basin and it was mounted on three decorative incurvate supports, which were joined with a smaller circular shelf upon which was placed the pitcher. It was often designed with two slender uprights which supported a mirror and towel rack. This lavabo of antique tripod form was a fashionable article of Empire furniture and it was almost an indispensable companion piece to the coiffeuse. Many of the elegant examples were made of bronze and their decoration was similar to the classic originals.

LAVABO, FRENCH EMPIRE

Lavher Lavher is a corruption of the word *Rawar*, which is the name of the village where the finest Kirman rugs were woven. The term therefore denotes weaving of a very high quality. A very fine Kirman is often referred to as a Lavher Kirman. See *Kirman*.

Lawrence Frame In English accessories; a form of oblong gilded frame with integral spandrels having a somewhat oval sight dimension used in portraiture. It derived its name from Sir Thomas Lawrence, 1769–1830, an English painter who is known for his portraits of royalty, nobility and children, and who is said to have favored this kind of a frame. This frame with its gilded detail made of composition retained its popularity well into the reign of Queen Victoria.

Layette The term *layette* originally referred to a small French Gothic wooden coffre, placed in the large coffre; it was used as a receptacle for small valuable possessions. The tiroir or a drawer in a table, which was first made toward the end of the 15th century in France, was also referred to as a layette.

Lead Glass In English glass; a glass fused with an oxide of lead. See *Ravenscroft, George*; *Flint Glass*; *Glass*.

Lead Glaze In ceramics; see *Glaze*.

Lebrun, Charles 1619–1690, celebrated French decorative artist. He was appointed First Painter to Louis XIV in 1662, and from that time the decorative work in all the royal palaces was under his supervision. In 1667 he was appointed art director of the Manufacture Royale des Meubles de la Couronne or the Royal Manufactory of Court Furniture which was established in the Gobelins. He also held different posts in the Academy of Painting and Sculpture. From 1662 until his death in 1690 he was virtually the arbiter of the arts of France. Lebrun did not recognize any division between the fine arts and the decorative arts; he always endeavored to unite them. He had a wide conception of art and he felt that every detail was a part of a harmonious whole. Although his color and drawings had little merit he did possess great artistic talent. Lebrun's art was notable for its splendor and for its balance. Above all he had the imagination to form conceptions on a gigantic scale and the talent to realize them in the most minute detail. His chief work was the palace of Versailles. Among his more celebrated works were the Apollo gallery at the Louvre and the Mirror gallery at Versailles. Practically all of his compositions were reproduced by celebrated engravers. See *Louis XIV*.

Lectern In English cabinetwork; a form of ecclesiastical desk. It was also used as a domestic desk for reading and writing during medieval times before the portable desk came into general use. Many lecterns were remarkable for their rich and skillfully wrought carved Gothic ornament. See *Desk*.

Leeds In English ceramics; an English pottery manufactory at Leeds, Yorkshire, owned by Humble, Green and Company, which bebecame Hartley, Greens and Company, made much cream-colored earthenware of the finest quality from 1774 to 1820. It was called The Old Pottery, and after 1820 it changed hands several times and continually declined. It finally closed in 1878. The pottery enjoyed a large domestic and export market. The most typical Leeds ware made until 1820 was characterized by a distinctive slightly greenish-yellow tone with a glass-like glaze. Useful wares were principally made. Especially characteristic were the pierced or punched decoration and the twisting handles terminating in flowers or leaves which were distinctive for their delicacy and refinement. Monochrome and polychrome painted decoration were used; however, much of the ware was not painted. The majority of the contemporary Staffordshire wares were made at Leeds. Modelled figures, especially on elaborate centerpieces, were also made. The old Leeds wares were generally not marked; however, the im-

LAWRENCE FRAME

pressed marks of "Leeds Pottery" or "Hartley Greens & Co" over "Leeds Pottery" were occasionally found.

Lefèbvre, François Or Lefèbure. A noted French master goldsmith working in Paris circa 1635. In 1635 he published a book of flowers and foliage for the study of the art of goldsmithing. This important book containing a series of six engravings represented bouquets of flowers and foliage executed in the art of the goldsmith, a variety of motifs of seed pods, and scenes with persons after the manner of Callot.

Lei In Chinese bronzes; the name given to a libation vessel or jar for holding a beverage. It appears in different forms. It is found in the shape of a jar or vase, as well as in the form of an animal, such as an elephant or tiger.

Leleu, Jean François 1729–1807. A French ébéniste who was admitted as a master cabinetmaker on September 19, 1764. It is generally accepted that he was the first to inlay the grooves of flutings such as on commodes with thin brass and to put metal rings around the pilasters and columns. His cabinetwork was representative of the Louis XVI style which displayed large uniform unbroken surfaces and a closer affiliation with Roman architectural details in its decoration. See *Louis XVI*.

Lemon Wood The wood of the tarata tree, *pittosporum eugenioides*, of New Zealand, used in cabinetwork; also the wood of the lemon bearing tree, *citrus limonum*.

Le Pautre, Jean 1618–1682, French architect, designer and engraver. His early work along with the work of Jean Marot, 1619–1679, was characteristic of the reign of Louis XIII in which the Italian Baroque style was developed in a modified form. Their work was carried on by their respective sons, Pierre Le Pautre and Daniel Marot, c. 1662–c. 1752. The prolific designs of these two generations of artists represent a complete repertoire of the prevailing fashions for

furniture and mural decorations during the reign of Louis XIV. They made designs for practically every detail in the interior decoration of a house, such as chimney-pieces, doorways, ceilings, panels for walls, sconces and wall brackets. They designed details of decoration for vases, gold and silver plate and other metal work. They made numerous designs for many pieces of furniture. The work of Jean Le Pautre was often over-elaborated. His style of ornament was characterized by the pronounced use of swags, cartouches, amorini and arabesques. However, although he used the same motifs over and over again, he was especially talented in developing something new each time in his compositions. Daniel Marot was the pupil of Jean Le Pautre. Pierre Le Pautre, c. 1648–1716, was made a dessinateur et graveur at the Bâtiments in 1699, and from that time until his death his decorative work had great influence. He combined in his style of ornament the nobility of the Louis XIV style with the gracefulness of the approaching Louis XV style, which combination is regarded as the essence of the Régence style. His work, which was prophetic, is now generally considered to be an important creative factor in developing the Régence style. See *Marot, Daniel*; *Louis XIII*; *Louis XIV*.

Lesum In German ceramics; a faïence manufactory was established at Lesum, near Bremen, in 1755 by Johann Christoph Vielstich. By 1800 the production of faïence was completely supplanted by that of common earthenware. The factory is still in existence. The faïence was marked with "VI" with painters' initials. Included among their wares were tureens in the form of birds and animals, cylindrical tankards and openwork baskets. The painted decoration was in high temperature colors that were generally rather dull; red was never used.

Letter Rack In English furniture; around the middle of the 18th century small decorative mahogany hanging racks were designed

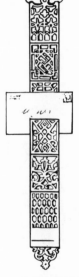

LETTER RACK, ENGLISH

for the reception of letters. They were generally flat and vertical, and were divided into about five sections which could be pulled forward. Each section was about as deep as an envelope but not as wide. Letter racks designed in Chinese and Gothic lattice-work patterns were particularly effective.

Le Vasseur, Etienne A French ébéniste who was admitted as a master cabinetmaker on December 17, 1766. He belonged to that group of cabinetmakers working in the Louis XVI style who used part of their talent to make reproductions of the sumptuous marquetry pieces of André Charles Boulle. In fact some of the Boulle work of the late 18th century was executed with such consummate skill that it was extremely difficult to distinguish the reproductions from the originals unless the latter were signed. The bronzes for these pieces were cast from Boulle models. See *Louis XVI*.

Ley A kind of pewter consisting of tin and lead. The percentage of lead varies, although the general average was about 80 parts tin to 20 parts lead. See *Pewter*; *Black Pewter*.

Li In Chinese bronzes; a vessel used for ritual ceremonies and also as a cooking vessel. The body was either round with three legs or square with four legs, and had two lobes on the rim through which a pole or rod was passed to facilitate carrying when it was hot. The li is of the same form as the ting except that the former has hollow legs. See *Ting*.

LIBRARY STEPS

Library Steps In cabinetwork; a portable set of steps designed as a piece of furniture and used in a library to enable a person to reach books on the upper shelves. In English cabinetwork; library steps were introduced during the first part of the 18th century; however they were not extensively used until about 1750 when libraries in private homes were furnished with book shelves at times reaching the full height of the wall. The steps were made in various heights depending on the height of the shelves in the room. The low type had 3 or 4 steps while the high type had as many as 10 steps.

The steps were usually made to conform in style with the other furniture in the library as well as to serve a utilitarian purpose. The most common variety resembled a step-ladder with hand rails. Sometimes the library steps were ingeniously designed to serve a dual purpose, such as in the form of a bench or a table. Sheraton illustrated in his DRAWING BOOK library steps enclosed in a library table. The top of the table was hinged and the library steps were designed to fold into the frieze. See *Bed Steps*.

Library Table In cabinetwork; a large oblong writing table. The top, inset with leather, is over a frieze fitted with two or three drawers. In English furniture; the term *library table* is particularly applied to a pedestal writing table and is correctly called a library writing table. See *Pedestal Writing Table*; *Writing Furniture*; *Drum Table*.

Lighthouse Clock In American furniture; a shelf clock so named because of its supposed resemblance to the shape of a lighthouse. It was an invention of Simon Willard and was patented in 1822. The brass dial and open works which were surmounted with a bell were enclosed within a dome-shaped glass hood. The glass hood rested on a tapered columnar body that was mounted on an octagonal plinth with a small door. It had a molded base with bracket feet. Variations occurred in the design of the wooden body and base.

Lighthouse Coffee Pot In English silver; the term applied to a coffee pot having a plain circular body tapering towards the top, with a straight spout and hinged lid in the form of a high conical cover. The wooden handle which was fitted into sockets was at a right angle to the spout. This variety which dates from around 1670 is so-called because of its resemblance to the shape of a lighthouse. The form was copied from Chinese porcelain teapot forms which were brought to Europe at that time. A later variety had a domed cover and curved spout.

Lilihan An Oriental rug woven in the Sultanabad district and at Kamarae, in Persia. The foundation is cotton with a wool pile. Its design is based on a modification of the old Persian designs. It is a purely commercial creation. See *Persian Rugs*.

Lille   In French ceramics; the earliest faïence manufactory was started here in 1696 by Jacques Féburier and Jean Bossu and was active until 1802. Another faïence manufactory was started in 1711 by Barthélémy Doréz and Pierre Pélissier and closed in 1820. A third faïence manufactory was begun in 1740 by Jean-Baptiste Wamps and principally made tiles. No factory mark was used by any of these potteries. It is generally believed that their earlier wares resembled Delft and Rouen wares and that their later wares were influenced by the Strasbourg wares. The faïence manufactory founded by Doréz also made a soft paste porcelain. No mark is known to have been used. It is believed the porcelain was similar to that made at Saint-Cloud. A hard paste porcelain manufactory was started in 1784 under the patronage of the Dauphin by Leperre-Durot. It closed in 1817. The accepted mark was a dolphin stencilled in red. The wares had little quality and were of undistinguished Paris types.

Lille Lace   The manufacture of lace at Lille, the capital of French Flanders, is of early origin and dates back to the 16th century. Undoubtedly the beauty of Lille lace was its ground, called fond clair or point de Lille, which was commonly regarded as the lightest and finest, as well as most transparent of all grounds. In this ground two threads were twisted around each other and the remaining two sides were made by a crossing of the threads over each other. In Europe in the 18th century practically two thirds of the lace-workers made this ground under the names of Blonde de Fil and Mignonette. The designs in the bobbin-made Lille laces were marked by a thick thread. Especially characteristic of Lille lace was a rather stiff design with a straight edge. It would seem that Lille laces were not particularly coveted by the 18th century aristocracy, since they never appear in their inventories.

Lille Tapestries   The weaving of tapestries at Lille, France, dates from the 15th century. The most active period was from the latter part of the 17th century into the 18th century. Included among the merchant weavers were François Pannemaker and his son André, working during the late 17th and 18th centuries, and Jan de Melter who established a tapestry atelier in 1688 which was carried on by his son-in-law Guillaume Werniers. See *Tapestry*.

Lily-Pad   In American glass; the name given to a kind of applied decoration. The so-called lily-pad design was shaped or tooled from a superimposed layer of glass. The lily-pad decoration varied in design. One typical variety had a curving stem which supported a rather flat leaf-like ovoid pad.

LILY-PAD PITCHER, AMERICAN

Limbach   In German ceramics; a porcelain manufactory was established at Limbach, Thuringia, in 1772 by Gotthelf Greiner. The early mark was "LB" in monogram or crossed "L's", sometimes with a star added. After 1787 the mark of a trefoil or clover leaf was adopted. Wares for daily use were chiefly painted in blue or in purple and were seldom of fine quality during the 18th century; better work was done during the 19th century. Figure modelling was also practiced. The characteristic figures were dressed in the contemporary fashion. Their faulty proportions and doll-like stiffness seemed to be a part of their singular charm.

Limerick   In Irish needlework; Limerick tambour lace was first established in Ireland in 1829, although if the strict meaning of the term *lace* is observed this tambour work should not be referred to as lace. In tambour work the designs are formed by drawing a floss thread or cotton with a hooked or tambour needle through the meshes of the net. In another variety of tambour work, known as run lace, the designs were run or worked in with a needle on the net ground. Run lace is finer and lighter in character than tambour work. This work became popular after Nottingham machine-made net was developed and was referred to as Nottingham Lace. It was introduced into Ireland by Charles Walker, of Oxfordshire, who started a manufactory at Mount Kennet in Limerick which he conducted until 1841.

Lime Wood   See *Tilleul Wood*.

Limoges   In French ceramics; a hard paste porcelain manufactory was established at Limoges, Haute-Vienne, in 1771 by Grellet, Massié and Fourneira under the protection of the Comte d'Artois. In 1784 it was purchased by the King to make a white porcelain which was later to be decorated at Sèvres. The usual mark was "cd"; "Limoges" with a fleur-de-lis was also recorded as a mark. The decoration was similar in style to that found on Paris and Sèvres porcelain. During the late 18th and 19th centuries the manufacture of porcelain flourished at Limoges, because of the local supplies of kaolin. Limoges was near Saint-Yrieix which was the chief source for kaolin and petuntse in France. Several porcelain manufactories were opened during the late 18th century and numerous ones came into existence during the 19th century. The production when marked had either the name of the place or the maker. During the second half of the 19th century Limoges became one of the largest producing centers for porcelain in Europe. These were simply a commercial product.

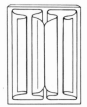

LINEN-FOLD

Limousin   In French Provincial; a former province in central France now in the departments of Haute-Vienne and Corrèze. The provincial furniture of Limousin differs very little from that of Auvergne. The province was the center of iron workers from whose shops came the fine andirons and fire dogs for the French châteaux. Limousin possessed a great wealth of different woods, which were freely employed in cabinetwork. This variety of woods and the use of turning for decorative purposes were features of Limousin cabinetwork. See *French Provincial*.

Linden Wood   See *Tilleul Wood*.

Line-Engraving   A method of engraving on steel or copper plates, in which the line is incised or cut-out; this is the reverse of the method used in the wood-cut, where the line to be printed is made in relief, and the spaces to be left in white are cut-out. To make the impression or print, ink is applied to the plate and then wiped off, leaving the engraved lines filled. Paper is then dampened and laid on the plates, and pressure is applied with a roller. The ink adheres to the paper as it is pressed into the lines. See *Engraving*.

Linen-Fold   In ornament; a carved Gothic motif resembling a scroll or fold of linen. It was a favorite form of decorating panels of furniture, such as the panelled façade of a chest, especially at the end of the 15th and beginning of the 16th centuries. See *Gothic, English*; *Gothic, French*.

Linen Press   In English furniture; a wooden device for pressing flat linens, such as tablecloths, while still damp. The flat pieces were placed between two thick boards and the pressure was controlled by a spiral screw. The movable linen press was known in England around the middle of the 16th century and in all probability it was introduced from Holland. It was about 2 feet in height and less than $1\frac{1}{2}$ feet in width. See *Press*.

Ling Chih   In Chinese ornament; the ling chih fungus, *polyporus lucidus*, is a favorite motif in Chinese ornamental design. It was originally symbolic of good luck and later of longevity. The treatment of this motif was closely similar in appearance to the head of the ju-i scepter, which makes all wishes come true.

Ling Lung   In Chinese ceramics; the term is applied to delicate openwork or pierced work. Cups and bowls of delicate openwork designs were made by potters working in the Wan Li reign of the Ming dynasty. See *Kuei Kung*.

Linnell, John   d. 1796. English cabinetmaker, carver and designer. He succeeded William Linnell at No. 28 Berkeley Square in 1763. He is chiefly known through his numerous designs, many of which are in the Victoria and Albert Museum. He made designs for chairs and settees, beds, commodes, desks, tables, mirrors, sconces, picture frames and many other articles. He supplied large quantities of furniture to William Drake for Shardeloes between the years 1763 and 1768.

Linnell, William   d. 1763. English cabinetmaker, carver and upholsterer working around 1730 to 1763 at No. 28 Berkeley Square. Contemporary accounts describe him as an excellent carver of wood. He refers to himself as a carver such as for picture frames and for various kinds of carved decoration. According to his records he also supplied tables and chairs. Included among his customers revealed by his bills were Sir Richard Hoare at Barn Elms and William Drake at Shardeloes. After his death in 1763 his large and widely diversified inventory was sold at auction. He was succeeded at No. 28 Berkeley Square by John Linnell who was probably related to him.

Lion-and-Ring Handle   In furniture mounts; a form of brass handle consisting of a ring suspended from the mouth of a lion mask. It was used in England toward the end of the 18th century on furniture designed in the Sheraton style and was also sometimes used during the Regency style. See *Bail Handle*; *Loose-Ring Handle*; *Mounts*.

Lion Mask   In ornament; the lion mask was used as a decorative motif in furniture design. It was employed in such styles as the Louis XIV, Empire and Regency. The lion mask was much used as a carved decorative motif on English furniture designed in the Queen Anne and Early Georgian style from

around 1720 to 1735. See *Queen Anne and Early Georgian*; *Lion-and-Ring Handle*.

Lion Mask Furniture   In English cabinetwork; see *Queen Anne* and *Early Georgian*.

Lion Monopodium   In cabinetwork; a decorative support composed of a head and chest of a lion resting on an elongated leg terminating in a lion's paw. It was used as a decorative support on tables in place of a leg and was especially identified with the French Empire and Regency styles.

Lion Sejant Spoon   In English silver; a silver spoon having a lion seated upon the molded end of the handle. It was introduced around the 15th century.

Liseuse   In French cabinetwork; a small 18th century French reading stand or table fitted with open shelves for the reception of books. This type of table was frequently designed with a center shaft in place of legs so that it could revolve.

Lit à Barreaux   In French Provincial cabinetwork; a popular form of bed from around 1820, having a low headboard and footboard consisting of either long spindles or a combination of spindles and balusters extending from the crest rail to the base. It was often designed in the Louis XV style and had valanced side rails as well as valanced headboard and footboard crest rails. The valanced base of the footboard terminated in short cabriole legs.

Lit à Colonnes   In French cabinetwork; a bed with four posts supporting a tester or canopy, introduced before or around 1550. The posts and headboard were elaborately carved. From around the end of the 16th century beds completely covered in rich materials became fashionable and the fabric was affixed to or pasted directly on the carved wood frame. The four-post bed continued in fashion until the end of the reign of Louis XIV, when other forms of beds, such as the lit d'ange and lit à la duchesse, came into vogue, but was revived in the Louis XVI style. Late in the reign of Louis XIV the

LION MONOPODIUM

four-post bed was designed with a footboard and in back of the headboard a piece of rich material the width of the tester was hung flat from the tester against the wall. The Louis XIV style lit à colonnes was monumental in character and was remarkable for its display of rich silk fabrics. In French Provincial cabinetwork; the lit à colonnes of a much more modest quality was a characteristic 18th century bed. Other forms of 18th century provincial beds were the lit clos and the bed built into an alcove.

Lit à Couronne In French furniture; a lit en bateau characterized by a small round or oval crown-shaped canopy with the draperies or bed hangings suspended from the canopy in a soft concave curve over the two ends of the bed which is placed lengthwise against the wall. Sometimes the draperies were secured by curtain holders above the ends of the bed. This couronne or crown-shaped canopy was especially fashionable from the time of the Restoration, 1814-1815, to the end of the reign of Louis Philippe.

Lit à la Duchesse In French furniture; a bed having a flat, oblong, tester extending the entire length of the bed. It was designed without posts and simply had a low headboard. It was introduced in the late 17th century and was especially fashionable during the Louis XV style. It was also designed in the succeeding Louis XVI style. With the general adoption of the duchesse bed and the angel bed, beds once again were made with the wood showing. See *Lit d'Ange.*

Lit à la Polonaise In French furniture; a bed having a headboard and footboard of equal height. Each one of the corners of the headboard and footboard supported an iron rod which curved upward and inward. The four iron rods centered and supported a dome covered in fabric and from which fell four draperies. Each one of the draperies was gracefully fastened to one of the iron rods where they joined the headboard and footboard. It was in vogue during the Louis XV and Louis XVI styles.

Lit à la Turque In French furniture; this form of bed was placed lengthwise against the wall and had a shaped backpiece and two side or end pieces. These so-called Turkish beds, which were actually beds, differed essentially from a sofa only in their dimensions. When the bed was dressed each end was fitted with a rolled cushion. This bed is depicted in French furniture literature with a small and narrow arched canopy extending outward from the wall and with the draperies or bed hangings falling from the canopy in a graceful concave curve extending outward to the two ends of the bed and secured by curtain holders. It was in vogue from around 1755 to 1785.

Lit à l'Impériale In French furniture; a form of four-post bed or a lit à colonnes having a headboard and an arched tester which was generally crown-shaped or dome-shaped with irregular contour. It was introduced in the 16th century. Apparently this type of bed was seldom made in the Louis XV style but was revived in the succeeding Louis XVI style.

Lit Clos In French Provincial furniture; the lit clos or closed bed is especially identified with the furniture of Brittany and is often referred to as a Breton Bed. This type of bed was found in all the colder regions, such as Auvergne, Limousin and Normandy. The lit clos resembled a huge cupboard with its solid panelled sides. The panelled front doors were made with shutters or with spindles or pierced ornament. This unique bed, which was occasionally fitted with an upper berth, assured the occupants of a certain amount of privacy while undressing, since the majority of peasant cottages only consisted of one room. It also served as a protection against the cold damp drafts of that climate. The lit clos was also made without doors, when it was called a lit demi-clos. This variant form was provided with curtains to be drawn together. The lit clos was of early origin and extant examples date from the 16th century.

LIT À LA TURQUE,
LOUIS XV

Lit d'Ange   In French furniture; a bed having a flat oblong tester that did not extend the entire length of the bed. It was designed without posts and had a low headboard and footboard, the latter as a rule being lower than the headboard. It was introduced in the late 17th century and was especially fashionable during the Louis XV and Louis XVI styles. It is also called an angel bed. See *Lit à la Duchesse.*

Lit d'Anglais   In French furniture; a form of bed placed lengthwise against the wall and having a shaped backpiece and two side or end pieces. When the bed was dressed it had the appearance of a sofa and was provided with a roll cushion at each end. It came into vogue around 1750. Essentially it is similar to the lit à la Turque.

Lit Demi-Clos   In French Provincial furniture; see *Lit Clos.*

Lit de Repos   In French furniture; the day bed or rest bed was introduced around 1625 and was designed with either one or two ends and was mounted on either six or eight turned legs. The day bed became more frequent under Louis XIV and from early in the 18th century this category of furniture began to display a variety of types. See *Chaise Longue; Duchesse; Méridienne; Baigneuse.*

Lit en Bateau   In French furniture; the fashionable French Empire style bed deriving its name from its supposed resemblance to a boat. The design was borrowed from models used in classical antiquity for dining and reclining. The bed was designed to be placed lengthwise against the wall. The dossiers or two end pieces were of equal height and usually narrowed toward the top and rolled over. The characteristic lit en bateau had a side piece with a concave line that continued the curve from each end piece in an unbroken line. The lower line of the side piece was straight and close to the floor. The lit en bateau was frequently placed in an alcove. See *Lit à Couronne.*

Lit en Tombeau   In French furniture; a variety of tester bed which was more frequently found from the 17th century onwards. It is illustrated in French furniture literature with a low headboard. The two tall head posts supported a flat tester which continued at a right angle for almost one or more feet and then sloped sharply in a straight line to the footboard. In order to explain the unusual shape of the tester it has been suggested that the bed was designed for a room with a sloping ceiling. Since the bed hangings and the bed are rather modest it apparently was not found in a richly appointed bedroom.

Lithography   In art; the process of reproducing a print from the impression of a design or drawing that was done on the prepared surface of stone or other material. There are two principal types of lithography; one in which the drawing is done on a grained stone with a greasy crayon, called chalk; the other in which the drawing is done on a polished stone with ink. Black and tint lithographs are those done in the chalk process with the addition of several colors although black is the most important. In the process where black is used like other colors, from twelve to thirty stones may be used, depending on the fineness of the work; this is called chromo-lithography; it is necessary to use many stones in order to reproduce the best work of an original painting or other work of art, as one stone is' required for each color. The process of lithography is that of water and grease; an oily compound is applied to the portions of the surface to be printed and the other portions are moistened; when the roller containing the greasy color passes over the part that is oily it receives the grease and when it passes over the moist portion, the grease will not adhere.

Lithophane   In ceramics; the method of casting intaglio designs on thin translucent porcelain so as to produce a picture of light and shade when light shines through. This work is especially identified with the ceramic

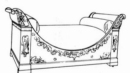

LIT EN BATEAU, FRENCH EMPIRE

work at the Meissen and Berlin manufactories after the second quarter of the 19th century.

Lit Mi-Clos In French Provincial furniture; see *Lit Clos*.

Lits Jumeaux In French furniture; twin beds came into general use in France in the 18th century. The first mention of twin beds appeared in Paris in 1743. Another early record occurred in a Bordeaux inventory, 1755, which listed, "deux lits jumeaux à la duchesse." Twin beds in French furniture literature are sometimes depicted under one large tester extending the entire length or part of the length of the two beds. See *Lit à la Duchesse*; *Lit d'Ange*.

Liverpool In English ceramics; faïence or delftware was made at Liverpool from around 1716 to about 1785. Cream-colored and white earthenware were subsequently made. Transfer printing on pottery was also a large part of their production. The majority of potters making faïence were principally engaged in the American export trade, and, as a result, little attention was given to any artistic productions. Liverpool faïence essentially resembled the faïence made at Bristol; however, the latter was generally superior. Huge punch bowls were a characteristic variety. Ship-bowls were among the best examples of Liverpool delftwares. Cream-colored earthenware, much of it being printed in blue or in black, and other Staffordshire types were produced at several potteries during the latter part of the 18th and 19th centuries. A printed ware manufactory was conducted by John Sadler and Guy Green in Liverpool during the latter part of the 18th century. They decorated by the transfer-printing process Liverpool earthenware and porcelain and also the wares from other parts of England, especially those from Staffordshire. Their earliest recorded work was in 1756. During the second half of the 18th century several of the potters producing faïence wares also made porcelain. Richard

LIVERY CUPBOARD, ENGLISH GOTHIC

Chaffers, d. 1765, a Liverpool potter, made a soapstone porcelain similar to that made at Worcester around 1756. See *Herculaneum*; *Faïence*; *Delftware*; *Bristol*; *Lambeth*.

Livery Cupboard In English cabinetwork; the livery cupboard, also called a bread and cheese or food cupboard, was introduced around the beginning of the 16th century. The word *livery* is derived from the French word *livrée*, which means a delivery or dispensing of clothes, food and other articles by the master to his retainers. The term *livery* is now generally applied to a ventilated cupboard in which food and wine were left to be given out to members of the family, guests and servants. Essentially there were two principal varieties. One kind was a small livery cupboard which was kept in the bedroom and was either hung on the wall or placed on a table. It varied in height from about 2 to 3 feet. The other variety was a large livery cupboard which was generally referred to as a standing cupboard since it rested on its own supports. This cupboard was placed in the great hall. The ventilation was usually provided by pierced or spindled doors. After Charles I, 1625–1649, the tradition of serving liveries was discontinued and was never resumed after the Restoration. See *Panetière*; *Almoner's Cupboard*; *Cupboard*.

Lobby Chest In English cabinetwork; Sheraton states in his CABINET DICTIONARY 1803, that the term refers to a form of half chest of drawers suitable for the use of a small study, lobby or small lodging room. It seems that its height was up to 3 feet and as a rule it was designed with four rows of drawers. Occasionally it was provided with a pull-out writing board beneath the top.

Lochaber Axe In arms; a 16th century Scotch weapon having a long blade attached to a shaft by two collars. A strong hook is fixed in the upper part of the shaft.

Lock, Matthias English furniture designer, cabinetmaker and carver working around 1740 to 1769. His address was given in 1746

as Nottingham Court, Castle Street, near Long Acre, and in 1752 it was near Ye Swan, Tottenham Court Road. At the present time Lock is often referred to as the pioneer of the Rococo or Rocaille style in England because he and his collaborator, Copland, issued several publications of engraved ornament, treated in the Rococo style, in the decade preceding the publication of THE DIRECTOR by Chippendale. The earliest known publication by Lock of engraved ornament was issued in 1740 and was entitled A NEW DRAWING BOOK OF ORNAMENTS. Between 1740 and 1752 he published several other works and then there was a lapse of sixteen years until 1768 when A NEW BOOK OF ORNAMENTS was published. Evidence now suggests that in those intervening years Lock and Copland were retained by Chippendale and that Chippendale was indebted to both designers for a portion of the designs in THE DIRECTOR. In 1769 two new works were published; A NEW BOOK OF PIER FRAMES and A NEW BOOK OF FOLIAGE. The engraved plates of ornament and the designs for furniture contained in these two works were in the Neo-Classic style. Albums and sketch books containing original designs by Lock are now in the Victoria and Albert Museum. He was a skillful draftsman. He is regarded as one of the best and by some as the best draftsman among the designers issuing trade catalogues around the middle of the 18th century whose drawings are extant. See *Chippendale, Thomas*; *Copland, Henry*.

Loc Maria In French ceramics; a faïence manufactory was founded at Loc Maria near Quimper in the department of Finistère by Jean-Baptiste Bousquet in 1690 and in 1743 it was taken over by Pierre-Paul Caussy of Rouen. The finest work was done from about 1743 to 1782 and closely imitated the wares made at Rouen. Around the last quarter of the 19th century, the manufactory began to make imitations of its 18th century productions.

Locust Wood See *Courbaril Wood*; *Acacia Faux Wood*.

Logwood See *Campeche Wood*; *Bloodwood*.

Lohan or Eighteen Lohan In Chinese ornament; the Lohan or Arhat are the enlightened or personal disciples of Buddha. Sixteen are of Hindu origin and two more were added by the Chinese to increase the number to eighteen. Probably the group of 500 Lohan did not appear before the end of the 10th century. The Chinese popularly give the name of Lohan to a wider circle of Buddha's disciples who have been assigned to the retinue of the 500 Lohan. The images of the Lohan are derived chiefly from the art work of one or two painters of the T'ang dynasty and from accounts found in Buddhist records. The Lohan and their attributes have been widely used in Chinese painting, sculpture and the decorative arts. In Japan the name *Rakan* is given to the Lohan and the name *Gohyaku-Rakan* is given to the 500 Lohan.

Long Case Clock In furniture; see *Tall Case Clock*.

Longton Hall In English ceramics; the earliest Staffordshire porcelain was made at Longton Hall, near Newcastle-under-Lyme, from 1751 or earlier. The manufactory was conducted by William Littler and apparently was active until 1760. It seems no factory mark is known to have been used. The identification of this porcelain depends upon its likeness to some salt-glazed stoneware also made by Littler. The stoneware which is marked with crossed *L*'s has not been conclusively identified as the work of Littler; however, the evidence strongly indicates that it was his work. The porcelain wares ascribed to Longton Hall include dishes in the form of folded leaves, plates, sauce boats, butter dishes and tureens. Some figures attributed to the manufactory possess considerable merit. The painted decoration was in underglaze blue of a strong tone and in rather harsh enamel colors.

IVORY FIGURE OF A LOHAN

Looking-Glass See *Mirror*.

Loom, Eastern In Oriental rug weaving; see *Eastern Loom*.

Loop-Back In cabinetwork; the name given to a type of Windsor chair back. In this variety the back is made from a continuous piece of bent wood which is joined to each rear corner of the seat. When this loop-back is made as an armchair the arms were joined to the sides of the loop-back. It is sometimes called a balloon-back or bow-back. See *Windsor Chair*.

Loop Stitch A stitch used in embroidery, similar to a chain stitch, secured at the loop end by a short stitch. It is also called picot stitch. The name is also given to a stitch used in crocheting and tatting.

Loosdrecht In Dutch ceramics; see *Weesp*.

Loose-Ring Handle In furniture mounts; a brass ring handle attached to a round brass or back plate at the top. It was also designed in either oval or octagonal form with a conformingly shaped brass. Articles of furniture designed in either the Sheraton or Regency style were frequently fitted with brass loose-ring handles. See *Bail Handle*; *Lion-and-Ring Handle*; *Mounts*.

Loper In cabinetwork; the narrow strips fitted into the framework of slant-front bureaux, cabinets and other similar pieces, which can be pulled forward by means of small knobs to support the fronts when they are let down.

Lorraine In French Provincial; originally a medieval kingdom and later a province in eastern France, now part of Alsace-Lorraine. The provincial furniture of Lorraine was distinctly French in feeling and was characterized by its restraint and sobriety. It was completely different from that of her neighbor, Alsace. The Louis XV pieces were distinctive for their simplicity and graceful lines. The carved detail which was finely executed was sparingly employed. Oak, walnut and cherry were the favorite woods. The furniture was frequently

LOOP-BACK WINDSOR
CHAIR

mounted with finely made polished steel hinges and keyplates. See *French Provincial*.

Lorraine Lace In lace-making; laces of the province of Lorraine were generally known in the commercial world as les dentelles de Saint-Mihiel, since that town was one of the most important lace-producing centers in Lorraine. The manufacture of lace was flourishing in the province of Lorraine in the 17th century. The early laces were rather coarse; however, they were soon supplanted by more delicate and fine bobbin-made laces of various designs with a mesh ground or réseau. Lorraine laces continued to flourish in the 19th century, their work being essentially similar to Lille and Arras. The town of Mirecourt, which was also an early and important lace center in Lorraine, was very active and successful in the 19th century. See *Cluny Guipure*.

Lotus In ornament; the lotus flower was one of the principal forms of plant ornamentation employed by the ancient Egyptians. It was used in the ornamentation of all kinds of work from enormous Egyptian columns down to the smallest objects. The lotus capital was one of the favorite Egyptian details employed in the French style of ornament late in the 18th century. See *Denon, Baron*; *Egyptian Detail*. The lotus flower was also one of the flowers of the Chinese four seasons, representing Summer. See *Chinese Four Season Flowers*.

Louis XII King of France from 1498 to 1515. See *Gothic, French*; *François I*.

Louis XIII King of France from 1610 to 1643. The style of Louis XIII, which is one of the principal styles of the French Renaissance, corresponds roughly to the first half of the 17th century. It approximately spans that time from the founding of the Bourbon dynasty in 1589 to the establishment of the Baroque Louis XIV style. The art of this period did not possess a strong national character and is full of contradictions and is composed of many incongruous elements. Sometimes this era is further divided into the Henri IV style but this only adds further complexities. During this time French decorative art principally consisted of an assortment of prevailing fashions borrowed from Flemish, Spanish and particularly Italian sources. The French artist gradually assimilated all that he borrowed and he modified it in accordance with his inherent good taste. The result was the emergence of the sumptuous and resplendent Louis XIV style, triumphant in scale and remarkable for the skillful originality of its planning. For about the first four decades of the 17th century the work of the French cabinetmaker reflected the influence of the Netherlands. However, it must be remembered that all branches of Flemish art had been strongly influenced by Italian art through the work of Rubens. Fortunately the French cabinetmaker avoided much of the Flemish excesses in his style of ornament. Some French furniture also displayed evidence of the traditions of the French school of Henri II. The Louis XIII style of furniture was heavy and massive and of solid construction; it was essentially rectilinear in form. Carving and turning were the two favorite methods for decorating the surfaces of furniture. The outstanding characteristic of the Louis XIII style was the use of turning. This method was never more employed than during this period, nor was the best work of this period ever surpassed. Spiral turning was the most common variety and baluster turning had the greatest artistic quality. The turned work was always distinctive for the excellent taste shown in its profile and for the skillful arrangement of its design in order to have the correct play of light and shade. Some pieces of furniture had moldings as their only decoration. The moldings were frequently arranged in geometrical designs. The style of ornament during the reign of Louis XIII was essentially similar to the Flemish Baroque ornament. It was generally characterized by the prominent use of cartouches, elaborate strapwork, banderoles, luxuriant swags composed of fruit and flowers, well-

rounded cherubs or amorini, twisted and curling palm branches, grotesque masks, protuberant and ovoid-shaped shields and elaborate scrollwork. See *Baroque*; *Louis XIV*; *Diamond Point*; *Le Pautre, Jean*; *Rubens, Peter Paul*; *Renaissance, French*; *Henri II*; *François I*; *French Provincial*.

Louis XIV   The name given to the Baroque style of ornament developed in France under the patronage of Louis XIV, 1643–1715. The Louis XIV style furniture was essentially rectilinear, with an increasing use of curved lines. The furniture was majestic, magnificent and massive. Profusely carved and gilded furniture was characteristic of the Louis XIV style. The marquetry of metal and tortoise shell combined with handsome bronze mounts was regarded as the supreme artistic expression of the Louis XIV style. Charles Lebrun, 1619–1690, the French painter, was virtually the arbiter of the arts of France from 1662 until his death in 1690. The early phase of the Louis XIV style which was dominated by Italian influence lasted until 1661 when Louis XIV became of age and assumed the reins of government. The Louis XIV style was unified under Louis XIV's personal rule. The Louis XIV style, which was characterized by its stately and heroic classicism, reached its perfect maturity around 1685–1690. In the final years of the 17th century a new style known as the Régence began to develop. The classic Baroque ornament of the Louis XIV style was notable for the symmetry of its composition and for its rich elegance. The French artists drew deeply for their inspiration from Italian Baroque art; however, they carefully avoided the excesses of Italian Baroque ornament. Heavy heroic Roman ornament and war-like trophies were employed during the early phase of the Louis XIV style. Included among the favorite Louis XIV style classic motifs were arabesques, rinceaux, cartouches, foliated scrolls, shells, acanthus leafage, grotesques of pleasing design, female and animal masks, satyrs, dolphins, cherubs, garlands and festoons,

LOUIS XIV PANEL

and mythological themes devoted in a large measure to the glorification of Louis XIV. Under Louis XIV all the arts were strongly organized and developed, and, as a result, France became a center of great activity and dissemination in all branches of the arts. Her ascendancy in the arts under the Bourbon monarchs was evident to a greater or less extent in the style of ornament and furniture design adopted in continental Europe and England through the remaining four decades of the 17th century and throughout the 18th century. See *Baroque*; *Régence*; *Boulle, André Charles*; *Le Pautre, Jean*; *Marot, Daniel*; *Lebrun, Charles*; *Bérain, Jean*; *Louis XIII*; *French Provincial*; *Macé, Jean*.

Louis XV The name given to the Rococo or Rocaille style of ornament developed in France during the reign of Louis XV, 1715–1774. During the Régence a style of ornament marked by asymmetry was evolved from the Baroque style in France and was widely used by French craftsmen from around 1720 to 1760. From around 1730 the movement was intensified and accelerated in the work of such designers as Oppenord and Meissonier, who were among the principal designers of these more extravagant forms. This extreme phase, which carried the Louis XV style to its culmination, was marked by an extravagant and a more complete and organic use of asymmetry. It is important to remember, however, that asymmetry was not an invariable rule of the style. It is generally accepted that the Louis XV achieved its finest expression in the decorative arts from around 1740 to 1755–1760. The finished and perfected Louis XV style possessed a charming gracefulness and a light and inventive elegance which were typically French. The Louis XV style as interpreted by the gifted French decorative artists was remarkable for its spontaneous gaiety and for its lively and fanciful qualities. These decorative artists also possessed the supreme technical ability to achieve asymmetry without loss of balance. Many

LOUIS XV PANEL

decorative appointments, such as mirrors, sconces and cartels, were given novel and surprising shapes in which the dominant lines were suggested through related curves. In articles of furniture requiring a symmetrical basis, such as commodes and tables, the principle of asymmetry was expressed in the elaboration of surface ornament, which was often in the form of gilded bronze appliqués. Certain natural forms were the foundation of the Rococo style of ornament. Rocks and shells with foliage and flowers dominated the theme of ornament. Bouquets of flowers tied with ribbons and flowers gracefully arranged in baskets were everywhere. Branches of palm and laurel were used in decoration. Plants were selected from the native flora such as endive, parsley and cress leaves. Especially favorite themes were the attributes appropriate to love, music, pastoral life and agriculture. The doll-like figures, chinoiseries and singeries introduced during the Régence were much in favor. Fantastic chinoiseries, such as those invented by Boucher, are closely associated with the style. The Louis XV style furniture was characterized by its curved contour; straight lines were employed only when necessary. Legs of cabriole form were typical of the style. The extravagant use of C-curves and S-curves practically abolished the use of right angles. The Louis XV style furniture was characterized by its graceful suppleness and by the continuity of its parts. This latter feature was particularly evident in chair design, in which each member seemed to flow into one another without any feeling of separation. The final phase of the Louis XV style was marked by a more moderate use of the curved line and by ornament of a less fanciful quality. Finally due to the discoveries at Pompeii and Herculaneum, which resulted in a universal enthusiasm for the antique, the Louis XV style was gradually abandoned. Naturally there was a period of transition during which numerous pieces such as chairs and commodes retained all or some of the curved lines of the Louis XV style but were decorated with Neo-Classic ornament. See *Rococo*; *Caffieri, Jacques*; *Oeben, Jean François*; *Vernis Martin*; *Régence*; *Meissonier, Juste Aurèle*; *Watteau, Antoine*; *Oppenord, Gilles-Marie*; *Ebéniste*; *French Provincial*; *Migeon, Pierre*; *Louis Philippe*; *Boucher, François*.

Louis XVI The name given to the classic style of ornament developed in France during the reign of Louis XVI, 1774–1793. The classic style of ornament in France came into vogue around 1760. There was a period of transition from about 1760 to 1770 in which certain elements of the Rococo or Rocaille style and the Louis XVI were harmoniously combined in furniture design. Finally when the transition was completed the structural lines were chiefly based on the rectilinear and the curve of the circle, oval and ellipse entirely supplanted the sinuous curve of the Rococo style. Cylindrical or quadrangular tapering and fluted legs supplanted the cabriole legs of the Louis XV style. The inspiration for French art after the middle of the 18th century was derived from antiquity. At first during the Louis XVI style the cabinetmaker was content to confine his imitation of antiquity to the borrowing of architectural detail such as pilasters and columns and to decorative classic motifs as interpreted during the Renaissance. Soon the Renaissance motifs were artfully blended with some antique Roman motifs; for example arabesques both ancient and Renaissance were employed. From about 1770 to 1785 Roman architecture and Roman ornament were the dominating factors of the Louis XVI style. Gradually as the taste for the antique became more exacting French designers introduced new motifs derived from the antique art of Rome, Pompeii, Herculaneum and Greece. Greek art was becoming better understood. Gradually the Louis XVI style of classic ornament became more and more buried under this accumulation of new materials for decoration. This pronounced taste for the antique and its closer imitation resulted in the Directoire style which ultimately evolved into the style of the French Empire. The essence of the Louis XVI style was its exquisite refinement and its restrained and graceful elegance. Decorative motifs from Roman art and French flowers were the principal themes for ornament during the Louis XVI style. Running motifs, which were a legacy of ancient architecture, were much used; such as guilloche, leaf bands, bead chains and rows of short flutings. Included among the classic motifs were the following; the head of the ram, cloven hoof feet, human and animal masks, satyrs, dolphins, cherubs, acanthus leaf, rinceaux, arabesques, wreaths, rosettes, lyres, pine cones, floral festoons, draperies, classic urns, often of tripod form, and classic vases. These classic motifs were harmoniously combined with the relatively modern floral arrangements common to the styles of Louis XV and Louis XVI; such as baskets of flowers and bouquets of roses and lilies and sprays of laurel and oak leaves tied with ribbons. Graceful bowknots of ribbons and streamers were very fashionable. Also employed were the different attributes appropriate to war, love, music, pastoral life and agriculture. The Louis XVI style, which reasserted the taste for classic form and ornament, was dominated completely by the principle of symmetry. Only in such incidental details as flowers, ribbons and bowknots was any deviation from the principle of symmetry permitted. See *Classic Revival*; *Louis XV*; *Directoire*; *Riesener, Jean Henri*; *Carlin, Martin*; *Leleu, Jean François*; *Röntgen, David*; *Levasseur, Etienne*; *Weisweiler, Adam*; *Gouthière, Pierre*; *French Provincial*; *Beneman, Guillaume*.

Louis XVIII King of France from 1814 to 1824. In the literature on French cabinetwork, the furniture made during his reign is sometimes known by his name rather than by the more usual connotation of the Empire style. See *Charles X*; *Restoration*; *Empire*.

Louis Philippe The term is given to a style

LOUIS XVI PANEL

of French furniture which was made during the reign of Louis Philippe, 1830–1848. The Louis Philippe style was essentially an exaggerated and coarse version of the Louis XV style. The Louis Philippe style was characterized by cabriole legs having exaggerated curves, by light colored woods and by a profusion of ornate ornament which had little artistic merit. Many of the more costly veneered pieces were decorated with Sèvres plaques and with bronze mounts. This furniture lacked the refinement, the fine proportions and the perfect balance which had always characterized the earlier French cabinetwork. See *Charles X*; *Victorian*; *Biedermeier*.

Lounge A piece of furniture for reclining. A kind of couch usually characterized as having a back and one arm.

Louvre The origin of the palace of the Louvre dates from the 13th century when Philip Augustus, 1180–1223, erected a great fortress defended by a rectangle of fortications. The fortress was demolished by François I, 1515–1547, who commissioned Pierre Lescot, the celebrated architect of the Louvre, to build the portions of the wings of the present palace. The rest of the palace buildings surrounding the great courtyard were built during the reigns of Henry IV, 1589–1619, Louis XIII, 1610–1643, and Louis XIV, 1643–1715. Henri IV established the practice of providing free workshops and apartments in certain parts of the Louvre for painters, sculptors, goldsmiths, cabinetmakers, enamellers and engravers. While these artists did not work exclusively for the crown, they entered into direct relations with it and enjoyed many special privileges. This practice was fully developed under Louis XIV and continued throughout the 18th century. Many of the great French works of art were created in the workshops at the Louvre. See *Macé, Jean*.

Love Seat In English cabinetwork; see *Courting Chair*.

Loving Cup In English silver; a decorative

CHIPPENDALE LOWBOY,
AMERICAN

drinking vessel, generally having two handles, designed either with or without a cover. At the present time the earliest two-handled cup has the hall mark 1533–1534. The second earliest cup is the Arundel cup, having the hall mark 1616–1617. This cup is preserved at Mercers' Hall, London.

Low-Back In cabinetwork; the name given to a type of Windsor chair back. It had a horseshoe-shaped arm rail which centered a flat arched crest section. It is especially identified as an early American form of Windsor chair. See *Windsor Chair*.

Lowboy In American cabinetwork; the lowboy was introduced in America around 1700 and it was a favorite piece of American furniture for almost one hundred years. The term *lowboy*, like the term *highboy*, is purely an American term. In England this article of furniture, which was introduced around 1690, was called a side table or a dressing table. The lowboy essentially followed the design of the lower section of the highboy. It was designed in the William and Mary, Queen Anne and Chippendale styles. The lowboy had a rectangular top over an apron, which was generally valanced and was always fitted with drawers. The arrangement of the drawers varied. It most frequently had one long drawer over a row of three drawers, the two lateral drawers often being deeper. The lowboy designed in the Queen Anne and Chippendale styles was mounted on four legs of cabriole form. See *Highboy*; *Philadelphia Style Lowboy*; *Dressing Table*.

Lowestoft In Chinese ceramics; see *Chinese Lowestoft*.

Lowestoft In English ceramics; a small porcelain manufactory operating at Lowestoft, Suffolk, from 1757 to 1802. The soft paste porcelain made at Lowestoft contained bone ash in its composition and in that respect resembles the soft paste made at Bow. Their productions, which had a rather naïve and unsophisticated charm, consisted chiefly of tablewares, various small objects such as pounce boxes, and also some small figures of cats, dogs and sheep. It seems that many commemorative gift pieces were made for country purchasers, such as mugs, tea caddies and birthday plaques. Dated and inscribed pieces bearing such inscriptions as "A Trifle from Lowestoft" were rather common. Among the finer wares were large well-painted punch bowls. Painted decoration in the Rococo and Chinese styles was especially favored. Much of the ware was painted in underglaze blue and the designs were frequently copied from Worcester patterns. The painted decoration in color was in imitation of the Chinese porcelain exported to Europe by the Dutch East India Company. There was no factory mark; however, the Worcester crescent and the crossed swords of Meissen were frequently copied. See *Chinese Lowestoft.*

Low Post Bed In American cabinetwork; around 1820 the bed designed with low posts and without a tester became quite fashionable. This low post bed was largely superseded around 1830–1840 by a variety of bed having a low headboard and low footboard made with an open frame and filled in with turned vertical members, such as ring-turned or spool-turned members. Many beds of this variety were made around the middle of the 19th century in America. See *Lit à Barreaux.*

Low-Relief See *Relief.*

Lu In Chinese art; a Chinese animal subject extensively used in Chinese sculpture, ceramics and painting. It is a deer and is symbolic of longevity. See *Chinese Animal Figures.*

Lucchese Patterns In textiles; the beautiful and rich designs originated by the Lucchese weavers working in the town of Lucca, Italy, during the 13th and 14th centuries. These designs appeared on velvets, brocades and damasks and were of the finest workmanship.

Ludlow Bottle In American glass; a globu-

lar-shaped bottle varying in color from amber to olive-green, supposed to have been made in the early 19th century, at Ludlow, Massachusetts.

Ludwigsburg In German ceramics; one of the seven most important porcelain manufactories in Germany during the 18th century was established at Ludwigsburg, Württemburg, in 1756, and in 1758 was taken over by Duke Charles Eugene of Württemburg, 1737–1793. It finally closed in 1824. The usual factory mark from 1758 to 1793 and occasionally later was two interlaced "C's" generally under a ducal coronet. Occasionally stags' horns from the Württemburg arms were used as a mark from around 1775; the initials "F. R." generally under a crown were the mark of King Frederick of Württemburg, 1806 to 1816. The finest wares were made between 1764 and 1775. The most important productions of the manufactory were always the figures. Especially fine were some groups of dancers in the Rococo style. However, the chief contribution Ludwigsburg made to the ceramic art of figures were miniature groups made from about 1765 to 1770 in the Rococo style. Some miniature groups were representations of the Venetian Fairs and were replete with stalls and booths as well as buyers, peddlers and attendants. Vases and tablewares in the Rococo style reflected the influence of Frankenthal. The colors were splendid and the painted decoration was of a most finished workmanship. Figures and landscapes in panels, Rococo scrollwork, birds and bouquets of flowers were included among the favorite motifs. Especially noteworthy were some of the painted flowers. In the later years the forms and decorations were in the Neo-Classic and Empire styles. Faïence was also made at Ludwigsburg from 1757 and around 1776 cream-colored earthenware was added to the productions. The latter was of fine quality and frequently copied the porcelain wares.

Lu-hsing In Chinese art; a Taoist deity, who with Fu-hsing are two popular gods.

LOWESTOFT MUG

They are the star gods of longevity, preferment and happiness, and with Shou Lao, who is believed to be a transformation of the founder of Taoism, make up the trinity of Taoism. Both are seen wearing official robes and one has a ju-i sceptre, which grants every wish, and the other is holding a baby who is reaching for a peach in his other hand. See *Chinese Gods*; *Shou Lao*.

Lunette In ornament; a design of half-moon or crescent shape. A radiating lunette or a lunette filled with a radiating fan-shaped design was much employed by Robert Adam in his style of ornament.

Lunéville In French ceramics; a faïence manufactory was started here in 1731 by Jacques Chambrette who also established another branch factory at Saint-Clément. The potteries, after changing ownership several times, remained active throughout the 19th century. The early faïence was generally not marked and the wares were probably in imitation of those made at Strasbourg, Sceaux and Niderviller. Especially well-known are the big faïence dogs and lions which were used in pairs and were generally placed in the halls during the 18th century in France. Lunéville's chief claim to fame is due to the fine biscuit figures and groups. One variety made around 1750 and onwards was of a soft earthenware and the other variety from around 1766 was virtually a true porcelain. These figures were done by Paul Louis Cyfflé who at first was working for Chambrette and then started his own factory in Lunéville in 1766 which he sold in 1780. The best models for these figures were from everyday life and were imbued with a rare intrinsic charm. From 1766 the figures were marked "Terre de Lorraine" or "T.D.L." impressed in relief with a stamp. Cream-colored earthenware in the English style and fine tablewares were also made at Lunéville.

Lung In Chinese art; a mythical animal subject widely used in Chinese painting, textiles, ceramics and sculpture. He apparently belonged to nature worship and is believed to bring beneficial rains. There are various types of dragons such as of the sky, earth and sea and they assume different forms. Probably the best known, which is also the device of the Emperor and the emblem of Imperial power, has a bearded scowling head, straight horns, a scaly serpentine body, with four clawed feet, a line of bristling spines along his back and emitting flames from his hips and shoulders. For the last two hundred years the Imperial dragon has had five claws on each foot, while a dragon with four claws on each one of the four feet represents a prince of lower rank. The dragon is often depicted flying in clouds, rising from the waves or playing with or pursuing a pearl. He is generally regarded as the foremost animal figure in Chinese art. See *Chinese Animal Figures*; *Claw and Ball Foot*.

Lung Ch'ing The Lung Ch'ing reign of the Ming dynasty in China, 1567–1572. See *Chinese Dynasties*.

Lung-Ch'üan In Chinese ceramics; see *Celadon*.

Luster The name given to the drops of cut glass or crystal that ornament a chandelier. The name is also given to a chandelier or candelabrum so ornamented.

Luster Decoration In ceramics; a metallic film either completely covering or used as a design on the surface of pottery. This film of metal is reduced from an oxide or a sulphide. The luster pigment containing silver, copper, gold or platinum is applied with a brush over an already fired glaze. It is refired in the kiln in a reducing atmosphere caused by a smoke-producing material so that the carbon set free in this manner is united with the oxygen in the pigment and leaves a layer of pure reduced metal. There was always a great risk involved in the process. It is stated in 16th century documents that probably only six out of one hundred pieces were successful. When the metallic film was thin it often produced an iridescence of bluish, reddish or purple, or mother-of-pearl reflections. It was this color

MING EWER WITH LUNG
DESIGN

changing that gave the Near Eastern, Spanish and Italian luster painting of the 15th and 16th centuries their great beauty. The Hispano-Moresque lustered wares of the 14th, 15th and 16th centuries were of unrivalled beauty with their golden, tarnished-copper and greenish luster. During the 17th century a hard bright-red copper luster was used and it is still being made at Manisses, a suburb of Valencia. Luster painting in Italy during the 16th century revealed a mastery of ruby red and golden yellow, bluish and mother-of-pearl iridescence of great beauty. Early in the 18th century Böttger at Meissen produced a purplish mother-of-pearl luster which was sparingly used on Meissen porcelain until around 1740. Late in the 18th century certain new processes were introduced in English industrial pottery to make pottery in imitation of copper and silver. This metallic film was rather thick and showed the natural color of the metal. Platinum salts were reduced to produce a silver surface and gold was used to produce a pink or purple luster. When this latter was applied over a red stoneware body it gave a coppery or ruddy gold effect. Much of the English luster ware of these types was made in Staffordshire during the late 18th and first half of the 19th centuries. The pearly luster used at Belleek and Worcester and other places around and after the middle of the 19th century was due to nitrate of bismuth. A similar method was invented in Paris by Gillet and Brianchon. See *Hispano-Moresque*; *Deruta*; *Italian Majolica*; *Gubbio*; *Belleek*; *Valencia*.

Lyonnais In French Provincial; an old province in east central France, now the departments of Loire and Rhône. The provincial furniture made at Lyonnais was essentially similar to the cabinetwork of Bresse. The early furniture made at Lyonnais during the Renaissance was similar to that of Burgundy. See *Bresse*; *Burgundy*; *French Provincial*.

Lyons In French ceramics; it is generally accepted that some of the first French majolica was made at Lyons as early as 1510; however, the artistic productions ascribed to Lyons were from the latter part of the 16th century. Around 1733 the making of faïence was revived when a manufactory was established by Joseph Combe and Jacques Marie Ravier. It was active until 1770. Other faïence manufactories were also operating in Lyons during the 18th century but nothing is known of their history. The styles for Lyons faïence were similar to those of Moustiers. The painted decoration was almost always in high temperature colors. Especially fine were the pieces with pictures of saints and inscriptions.

Lyre-Back Chair In English cabinetwork; an open chair back with a pierced splat which had the outline of a classical lyre. The lyre motif was borrowed from France and was used by several designers. The lyre-back chair was introduced by Robert Adam around 1775. In one variety the lyre-shaped splat was filled with lyre strings made of slender metal rods. Fine designs of lyre-back chairs were executed in the Hepplewhite style. Sheraton showed a preference for splats of either classical vase or lyre form. Duncan Phyfe's lyre-back chairs were especially fine and very characteristic of his work. See *Lyre-Form*.

Lyre-Form In furniture design; a splat, a support or some similar member in the form of a lyre. The lyre-form was used by Sheraton as a decorative feature and it was used by Duncan Phyfe on his articles of furniture designed in the Sheraton style. Sheraton employed the lyre-form especially for splats on open chair backs and he used the lyre-form for trestle end supports on sofa tables. The designers of Regency furniture also employed the lyre-form. See *Lyre-Back Chair*.

Lyre-Form Sofa In English and American furniture design; a variety of sofa deriving its name from the supposed resemblance of the contour of its outscrolled sides, which continue into the seat rail, to that of a lyre. See *Grecian Sofa*.

DUNCAN PHYFE
LYRE-FORM SOFA

M

Macassar A striped ebony wood from Macassar, in the Dutch East Indies, used in cabinetwork.

Mace The name originally given to a medieval weapon of iron or steel used for breaking through armor. It generally had a short shaft and a club-like head that was occasionally spiked. The mace as a ceremonial ensign was first used in France toward the end of the 12th century. The mace in the ensuing centuries became more elaborate. It was usually finely pierced and decorated and was often made of gold and silver.

Macé, Jean French ébéniste working in the style of Louis XIV. He lived at the Louvre from at least 1644 until his death in 1672. He is generally regarded as one of the earliest of French marqueteurs, having learned the art in the Netherlands. He was Marqueteur du Roi.

Ma-Chün In Chinese ceramics; see *Chün Yao*.

Macled In armor; see *Mail*.

Macramé In lace-making; a term of Arabic derivation given to a fringe of knotted thread made of cotton, silk or linen. Macramé was finely developed at Genoa in the 19th century and was notable for its finished workmanship. It was chiefly applied to decorating towels, and it comprised a fringe of thread purposely left at each end which was knotted together in geometrical designs. See *Punto a Groppo*.

Madeira Work A general term given to the fine white embroidery work done on the island of Madeira. This needlework, which was made mostly by the nuns of Madeira, was worked on a fine linen or cambric with white thread, and was essentially similar to Irish embroidery or broderie Anglaise. See *Irish Embroidery*; *Broderie Anglaise*.

SILVER MACE, ENGLISH

Madia In Italian Renaissance cabinetwork; a piece of kitchen furniture used to store loaves of bread. It was a bread cupboard. It was generally fitted with cupboard doors variously arranged and sometimes with a row of narrow drawers above or below the cupboard doors. It was usually raised on legs which varied in height. Occasionally the madia was designed with a hinged lid instead of a fixed top. In a broad sense the madia in its general use as well as to some extent in its general design resembled the English hutch or the French huche.

Madrid Royal Tapestry Factory A tapestry manufactory was established in 1720 at Madrid by Philip V; its first director was the tapestry weaver Jacques van der Goten, with the painter Andrea Procaccini as designer. It closed in 1808 and reopened in 1815. Its greatest productive period was the last quarter of the 18th century when the tapestries woven were based chiefly on cartoons by Goya. See *Tapestry*.

Magdeburg In German ceramics; a faïence manufactory was started at Magdeburg, Hanover, in 1754 by Johann Philipp Guischard. Open basketwork borders were a characteristic decoration for the early faïence wares which closely resembled those made at Münden. They were also marked with an "M" like the Münden wares. In 1786 Guischard was granted a privilege to make cream-colored earthenware in the English style. In a few years his manufactory was one of the largest producers of cream-colored earthenware in Germany. They were marked with "M" or "Guischard", impressed. The factory was active until 1839. In 1791 another manufactory was started by Johann Heinrich Wagener and chiefly made tile stoves. In 1799 Elias Karl Rousset and Georg Schuchard started a manufactory producing cream-colored earthenware in the English style. The wares were marked with the names impressed. It closed in 1865.

Mahal Rug   See *Sultanabad Rug*.

Mahogany   *Swietenia mahagoni*. In English cabinetwork; after 1720-1725 mahogany began to succeed walnut as the wood in common use. In 1733, Sir Robert Walpole repealed the import duty on mahogany, and after that date mahogany became plentiful. Sheraton in his CABINET DICTIONARY of 1803 mentions three kinds of mahogany, namely Cuban, Spanish and Honduras, and states that of these three Spanish is the finest. The use of mahogany in England did not affect the design of furniture to any great extent until around 1740-1750, with the exception of the massive library tables and bookcases designed in an architectural style for the Palladian mansions. As a result of the increased supply of mahogany around 1740 a style of mahogany furniture began to evolve that was indigenous to England. This style, which was based on English principles of design, reflected French influence in its simplified style of carved ornament. This French influence became more pronounced in the form and in the ornament during the Rococo phase, 1745-1765. Mahogany continued to be used, especially for library and dining room furniture, throughout the 18th and early 19th centuries. Veneered mahogany was commonly laid on a framework of red pine. The vogue for mahogany in America extended approximately from 1730-1740 to 1840. See *Satinwood*; *Acajou*; *Queen Anne and Early Georgian*; *Chippendale, Thomas*; *Empire*.

Maidenhead Spoon   In English silver; a silver spoon having the stem of the spoon terminating in the head of a maiden. It was introduced late in the 14th century. See *Spoon*.

Maie   In French Provincial cabinetwork; the *maie* or *pétrin*, which were the French terms for a kneading trough, was a characteristic article of provincial kitchen furniture. A principal type of Louis XV maie

had a flat hinged top which when opened revealed a single or double trough. The panelled trough which was wider at the top than at the bottom generally rested on four turned legs or on a cupboard section fitted with two panelled doors. The Provençal Louis XV style maie was often elaborately carved and its four turned legs were generally joined with a valanced and molded broad box stretcher. Many of the finer models were made of walnut.

Mail   In armor; the chain armor worn during the Middle Ages. Chain armor was superseded by mixed chain and plate armor and finally by plate armor. The term *mail* is also used for armor in a general sense and includes plate armor as well as chain armor. Included among the different types of a coat-of-mail are the following: a ringed coat-of-mail is made of steel rings sewed side by side on leather or on quilted linen. A rustred coat-of-mail is made of steel rings that are oval and are sewed on the material so that they half overlap each other. A macled coat-of-mail is made of small lozenge-shaped, steel plates, sometimes overlapping each other, and sewed on leather or on fabric. A grains d'orge coat-of-mail is made entirely of interlacing riveted rings. A trellised coat-of-mail has a base of fabric or leather, with leather strips forming a trellis design and with each square containing a metal plate riveted on the ground. A scaled coat-of-mail is made of small, scale-shaped, steel pieces, sewed on leather or linen overlapping one another.

Mainfere   In armor; a medieval steel gauntlet to cover the bridle hand of a horseman.

Main Gauche   In arms; a dagger used in dueling during the 17th century. It had a straight, double-edged blade which frequently had prongs near the hilt to catch an opponent's sword. It has a very short grip with a triangular hand-guard and long, straight quillons.

Maître Banc   In French Provincial cabinetwork; a wooden bench with a high back and

LOUIS XV MAIE OR PÉTRIN

arms designed to seat three persons. The back is divided into three sections and the middle section is hinged so that it can be let down and used as a table. The bench was reserved for the use of the master of the house. It is chiefly identified with Basque provincial furniture. See *Settle*.

Maître Ebéniste   See *Ebéniste*.

Majolica   Or Maiolica. In ceramics; the term is applied to all varieties of Italian tin-glazed earthenware. This glaze, which is its distinguishing feature, is a lead glaze to which has been added tin ashes that results in a white and opaque glaze. By extension the term may be applied to all tin-glazed ware made in the Italian tradition character-istically painted in the polychrome majolica colors which are blue, green, yellow, orange and manganese purple. See *Faïence*; *Italian Majolica*.

Makatlik   A Perso-Turkish word meaning a runner. The term is applied to an Oriental runner generally about 2½ to 4 feet in width and about 10 to 20 feet in length. It is used in the Orient as a cover for a low divan or bench placed against a wall.

Maker's Mark   In English silver; see *Hall-Marks, London*.

MAKIMONO

Makimono   In Japanese art; a very long and narrow paper picture scroll. At each end of the makimono is attached a rod of wood or ivory on which it is rolled or unrolled. When it is not in use it is rolled up and usually placed in a box especially provided for it. Picture scrolls existed in China in the Six Dynasty period, A.D. 265–589 and were introduced into Japan sometime later. The primary purpose of a makimono is the illustration of a story. At times the transition of scenes and the passage of time are indicated by beautifully brush-written charac-ters inserted between the pictures. Stories of court life are frequently painted with the human figures, houses, flowers and trees outlined in fine lines and then painted in rich colors. Fukinuki-yatai, or roofless houses,

is the special technique of the makimono painters. In this method the interior and the people in the house are seen obliquely from above as the roof and the ceiling are re-moved so as to make them visible. The makimono scroll unrolls horizontally, the kakemono vertically. See *Kakemono*.

Makkum   In Dutch ceramics; a faïence and tile manufactory was started at Makkum, Friesland, in 1675 by Freerk Jans Tichelaar and is still continued by his family. The principal productions were imitation Delft, crudely painted thick peasant-style dishes and tiles. The modern production has been limited chiefly to imitations of old Delft. A second manufactory conducted by the Kingma family produced only tiles and was active from around 1650 to 1835.

Makri Rug   See *Meles Rug*.

Malaga   In Spanish ceramics; see *Hispano-Moresque*.

Maline   In lace-making; a French term mean-ing Mechlin applied previously to 1665 by the French commercial world to all the laces of Flanders with the exception of Brussels laces and those made with a Point Double or a double ground. See *Mechlin*.

Maltese Lace   The name given to the black and white silk guipures of a fine quality first made at Malta around 1833. It is stated in literature on lace that Lady Hamilton Chichester in 1833 persuaded a woman by the name of Ciglia to copy the lace of an old Greek coverlet. From that time onwards the Ciglia family began to manufacture Maltese lace in which a Maltese cross has been introduced as a distinctive feature. These fine guipures were later extensively manu-factured at Auvergne and at Bedfordshire as well as in Ireland.

Mamori Katana   In Japanese arms; the name applied to a small sword that was first given to a male child of a samurai or fighting man. It was worn by boys who were under five years of age. It was called a charm sword and had the hilt and scabbard covered with brocaded silk with a purse or kinchaku attached to it.

Manchette   The French term for an armpad. All 18th century French armchairs whether upholstered or caned generally had upholstered elbow rests or manchettes. See *Armpad*.

Mandarin   In Chinese ceramics; the name given to a variety of porcelain jar made during the later part of the 18th century. The ware is generally characterized by panels framed in underglaze blue, with figure subjects painted in red, pink and gold. It seems that this ware was copied by many English porcelain manufactories.

Maniple   In ecclesiastical costume; one of the Eucharistic vestments in the Western Church comprising at the present time a strip of material from 2 to 4 feet in length. It is worn hanging from the left arm near the wrist by the celebrant, the deacon or subdeacon. It is said that originally in very early times it was a linen cloth or napkin which might be used as a handkerchief to wipe the tears shed for the sins of the people. The early maniple when it became one of the sacred vestments was extremely narrow and about 4 feet in length with fringed ends. Embroidered crosses were later added to the ends. During the Middle Ages the maniple was often richly designed and was often ornamented with elaborate embroidery and occasionally was decorated with pearls and precious stones.

Mantua Tapestries   Mantua is the oldest tapestry weaving center in Italy, dating from the early 15th century. Its most important work was done during the middle third of the 15th century, from designs by the painter Andrea Mantegna. See *Tapestry*.

Manufacture Royale des Glaces   A French glass manufactory founded in 1665 by Nicolas du Noyer, at the Faubourg St. Antoine, in Paris. It was reorganized in 1668 by Richard Lucas de Nehou. It originally made mirrors, and toward 1679 produced the mirrors for the Galerie des Glaces at Ver-

sailles, at the request of Louis XIV. The factory was removed in 1693 to St. Gobain.

Manufacture Royale des Meubles de la Couronne   Or a Royal Manufactory of Court Furniture. The name was given to a series of workshops and ateliers organized in the Gobelins in 1667 for the production of furniture and furnishings for all the royal palaces of Louis XIV. The establishment was to be filled with "good painters, master weavers, goldsmiths, metal workers, engravers, mosaic workers, lapidaries, enamellers, joiners in ebony and other woods, dyers and other good workers in every kind of art or crafts." The king's First Painter received the title of director of the manufactory. To insure a supply of craftsmen a school was established for sixty children under the king's protection. After a preliminary education they served an apprenticeship of six years and a further period of four years as workmen. At the end of this period of training they were classed as masters of their craft.

Manwaring, Robert   English designer, cabinet and chair maker working around 1760 to 1770 in the Haymarket. In 1765 he published THE CABINET AND CHAIR MAKER'S REAL FRIEND AND COMPANION which had more than one hundred designs for chairs, benches, stools and rustic seats for summer houses. In 1763 he contributed plates to the ONE HUNDRED NEW AND GENTEEL DESIGNS published by the Society of Upholsterers and Cabinetmakers. In 1766 he worked in conjunction with others to bring out a revised edition under the title of THE CHAIRMAKERS' GUIDE.

Maple   The wood of the maple tree, *acer campestre*, used in cabinetwork. It is hard and its color is reddish, veined and wavy. Maple, curly maple and bird's-eye maple were used in American cabinetwork, especially in New England where the maple was plentiful. It was also much favored in America for inlay work. Maple which is not as fine as mahogany or as ordinary as pine

MANCHETTE

was used for furniture coming between these two categories.

Marans In French ceramics; a faïence manufactory was started at Marans, Charente-Inférieure, in 1740 by Pierre Roussencq. Around 1750 some workmen and materials were taken to La Rochelle where a new faïence manufactory was being organized. It is not known how long the factory remained active. Included among the marks are "PR" in monogram and "MR". Included among the surviving examples is a wall fountain having painted decoration executed in a rather coarse version of the Rouen style.

Marbled Ware In English ceramics; the practice of blending together different colored clays to produce a ware resembling marble or agate dates to the ancient Romans during the first century. The English potter, Dwight, working at Fulham during the late 17th century, decorated his stoneware with marbled bands made from white, brown and grey clay. This method was used for the solid agate ware produced at Staffordshire during the second quarter of the 18th century in which white, brown and blue-stained clays were blended to form a marbled pattern. Wedgwood using the same method developed a ware which closely imitated natural agate and which was made into decorative vases. In another kind of marbling the surface of the ware was decorated with colored clay slips that were combed and mingled on the surface to resemble marbling. This method had been practiced on peasant pottery for many years. This marbling with colored clay slips, in which the parts essentially remain separate and distinct, was practiced in Staffordshire and many other places from the late 17th century onwards. In another method the marbling is achieved by using metallic oxides in a fluid lead glaze, producing indefinite splotches of color. The colors used were blue from cobalt, copper green and yellow from iron and violet, purple and brown from manganese. When only manganese brown

MARIEBERG TERRACE VASE

was used in the glaze the ware is sometimes referred to as tortoise shell. This method which had been practiced by Palissy during the 16th century was employed by Whieldon and his followers in Staffordshire during the 18th century. In a fourth type of marbling, which was practiced only at Marieberg near Stockholm, the opaque white tin glaze was marbled with coloring oxides. In Chinese ceramics; fine examples of marbled wares are found in Chinese stoneware from the T'ang dynasty on. See *Agate Ware*.

Marble Slab Or Slab Top. In English cabinetwork; sideboard tables and side tables with marble slabs or marble tops were especially fashionable in England from around 1710 to 1760. They were found on plain walnut and mahogany sideboard tables and also on elaborately carved and gilded side tables. The tables designed for these marble slabs were often referred to as frames for marble slabs or slab frames.

Marbling The name is given to the painting of wood to simulate marble. It was practiced late in the 18th century in interior decoration and occasionally on furniture. Decorative side tables, commodes and pedestals were among the chief types of furniture which were sometimes treated in this manner. The practice of painting wood to simulate marble was occasionally used by Robert Adam. Decorative side tables and pedestals in an Adam designed interior were sometimes treated so that they would harmonize with the background.

Marieberg In Swedish ceramics; a faïence manufactory at Marieberg near Stockholm was started in 1758–1760 by Johann Eberhard Ludwig Ehrenreich and was active until 1788. The factory also made cream-colored earthenware and porcelain; however, it is best known for its faïence. The well-known crown marks were generally found on the faïence after 1763. The better wares were produced during the early years, and had one of three distinctive glazes, namely greysih, violet or marbled. The marbled glaze with its black-violet, grey, and less prominent red, blue, and brown streaks, was almost unique in faïence ceramics and was very effective and pleasing. High temperature colors except for a clear strong blue were rarely used. The enamel colors were particularly fine. Gilding was seldom used. The early wares, 1760–1766, were in the Scandinavian Rococo taste. Included among the productions were knobs in the form of fishes and birds, tureens with shell moldings and richly colored applied fruit, flowers and leaves and the so-called terrace-vases having a base formed of swirling waves or a winding flight of steps. The later faïence in the French Rococo and Neo-Classic styles retained an individual and fine quality. The cream-colored earthen-ware, which was usually marked with "Sten" over "M B" impressed, was decorated either with transfer prints or designs molded in relief. The soft paste porcelain was similar to that made at Mennecy. Especially characteristic were the reeded custard cups with painted floral motifs. The usual mark was an incised monogram "MB". Hard paste porcelain was also made and the painted decoration was often monochrome.

Marks In ceramics; the custom of writing a mark of origin on pottery dates from early times, with signatures of painters occurring on ancient Greek pottery. The practice of inscribing a mark on the base undoubtedly had its provenance in Chinese porcelain. Although these Chinese marks were generally the name of reigning Emperors they were interpreted in Europe as potters' marks, with the earliest fully developed factory mark occurring on 16th century Medici porcelain in the form of the Cathedral dome of Florence. Meissen's adoption in 1724 of the crossed swords as a factory mark established the practice of using factory marks with some degree of regularity in Europe, with other porcelain as well as some faïence factories following the Meissen custom. Finally the custom of marking porcelain was sanctioned by law, and in 1766 French porcelain makers were required

to put on their wares a mark already registered with the police authorities. A regular marking system was developed at such manufactories as Sèvres, Vienna and Frankenthal. However, since the system was never competently protected against imitation and was seldom compulsory, and in that respect different from the marks on silver, it is patent that the 18th century marks were far from reliable evidence as to the source of origin of a piece of pottery. Aside from the factory marks and full names of potters and painters, the latter generally occurring on hausmalerei and special work fabricated outside the manufactory, it was a rather general practice in the 17th and 18th centuries for ceramic workers to add an identifying sign, such as an initial letter or a numeral, to their work. This was added purely for the information of those managing the factory. A mark in color or in gold was used by the painters and gilders, while the throwers and "repairers" used a scratched mark. Occasionally scratched marks were in reference to the composition and impressed or scratched numerals were sometimes used as mold numerals. Included among other marks were the ownership marks, dealers' marks and destination marks. Several methods were employed in making pottery marks, namely by incising or scratching the mark in an unfired soft paste, by impressing the mark in a soft unfired paste with a stamp or stamps, by painting or printing under the glaze in blue until around 1850 when the mark was also made in chrome green, and finally by painting, stenciling or transfer printing over the glaze.

Marlborough Leg In American cabinet-work; although the term *Marlborough* is found in contemporary Colonial accounts, its origin has never been definitely ascertained nor has its ascription been completely clarified. It seems that the term is given to a square or square tapering leg occasionally terminating in an enlarged square or plinth foot. In a broad sense the term apparently may be applied to the straight legs used on

CHELSEA C. 1752–1756

SÈVRES 1754

MEISSEN C. 1740–1760

DERBY C. 1784–1810

CHANTILLY C. 1725–1800

furniture designed in the Chippendale style. It is sometimes referred to in the literature on American furniture as "a refinement and rival of the cabriole."

Marli A term applied to the raised border, which is frequently decorated, of a flat dish or plate. It forms a plane almost parallel to the bottom or center part of the plate.

Marli In French lace-making; Marli, which derived its name from a village between Versailles and St. Germain, was essentially the predecessor of tulle. It was created around 1765 and for the ensuing two decades was extremely fashionable. Marli, which consisted of a bobbin-made mesh ground with an edging of loops, was much favored by Marie Antoinette. The pattern for Marli very often consisted of the small spots of point d'Esprit.

CHAIR, AFTER DANIEL
MAROT

Marot, Daniel c. 1662–c. 1752, French designer, engraver and architect. His work, which was characteristic of the second phase of the Louis XIV style, was distinctive for its splendor and elaboration. He made many designs for André Charles Boulle, especially for tall case clocks and bracket clocks. He migrated to Holland after the Revocation of the Edict of Nantes in 1685 and was taken into the service of William of Orange. Recent research proves that Marot did go to England and that he arrived some time in 1694 and probably left sometime in 1698 to return to Holland. It has not been definitely ascertained that he worked on the interior decoration of Hampton Court Palace. However, the interior decoration and much of the furniture bear unmistakeable traces of certain features characteristic of his engraved designs and arrangements. Marot possessed a profound knowledge of French classical design. His designs for furniture and decorative appointments were remarkable for their lavish display of classical ornament. He published a prolific number of designs for interior decoration and furniture. These books exerted enormous influence on contempor-

ary English taste, and he was undoubtedly responsible for the introduction of new forms and style of ornament from abroad. His later work showed a blending of Dutch and French designs. The general features of his work remained French; however, a Dutch feeling was evident in the treatment of form and in the style of ornament. See *Le Pautre, Jean*; *William and Mary*; *Louis XIV*; *Dutch Furniture*.

Marquetry In cabinetwork; marquetry is a kind of veneer in which shaped pieces of various kinds of very thin wood or other material of equal thickness are combined to form a design and are laid upon a surface with glue. The Dutch were very partial to marquetry work. The reputation of the Dutch marqueteurs was so great that several were engaged to work in Paris at the beginning of the 17th century. Dutch marquetry was distinctive for its birds, scrolls, foliage and floral designs depicted in brilliant colored woods. Marquetry was unknown in England until the Restoration in 1660. It was introduced from Holland and it became a favorite decorative process for expensive furniture. Floral marquetry was fashionable during the Carolean style; seaweed and arabesque marquetry became the vogue during the reign of William and Mary. The marquetry of metal and tortoise shell executed by André Charles Boulle was regarded as the supreme artistic expression of the Louis XIV style. The marquetry of various colored woods was also employed in the Louis XIV style. In order to gain more varied tones the different woods were often shaded and tinted. The shading was commonly done by means of a hot iron and the tinting by chemical washes. The delicate and exquisite floral marquetry executed by François Oeben working in the Louis XV style was unrivalled. The French marqueteurs used almost one hundred different kinds of wood in marquetry work. Jean Henri Riesener, Martin Carlin and David Röntgen working in the Louis XVI style all were celebrated marqueteurs. Marquetry was revived about 1765 in England. The finest English marquetry furniture in the French taste was produced in St. Martin's Lane around 1770 where the shops of Thomas Chippendale and John Cobb were located. The light-colored exotic woods, which were worked in naturalistic designs in the manner of contemporary French floral marquetry, were laid in a ground of mahogany, satinwood or harewood veneer. Later, due to the influence of Adam, marquetry work was treated in a more classic manner and was usually in panel arrangement. See *Inlay*; *Intarsia*.

Marquise In French cabinetwork; a variety of upholstered armchair characterized by a very wide and deep seat and having a back of medium height. It was extremely comfortable and was generally fitted with a loose seat cushion. The marquise was a popular type of 18th century French armchair, and French furniture literature states that it was often used before the fireplace. Essentially it seems to correspond to the English courting chair or love seat. See *Courting Chair*.

Marronnier Wood The wood of the French chestnut tree, *castanea vesca*, used in cabinetwork, especially by the French ébénistes. It is both a hard and soft wood and its color is white.

Marrow Scoop In English silver; a silver spoon used for extracting marrow from the bones. One principal type is about 8 inches long, having at one end a very narrow, elongated spoon bowl and at the other end an even narrower spoon bowl of conforming design. Another variety, less frequently seen, has a normal size spoon bowl at one end and a marrow scoop at the other. It was introduced late in the 17th century.

Marseilles In French ceramics; although some distinctive faïence in the manner of Nevers, Moustiers and Rouen was made at Marseilles during the late 17th and first half of the 18th centuries, the reputation of Marseilles faïence chiefly rests upon the fine enamel-painted faïence made during the third quarter of the 18th century. The earliest faïence of importance was made at Saint-Jean-du-Désert, a suburb of Marseilles, in a factory conducted by Joseph Clérissy, in 1679. There were at least six other large and prosperous and also some minor faïence manufactories operating in Marseilles during the 18th century. However with the exception of the early productions at Saint-Jean-du-Désert it is difficult to separate the Marseilles faïence into factory groups because many of the wares were not marked and the migration of the painters from one pottery to another tended to create a common style. The painted enamel decoration in the Rococo style was executed in a subtle free-flowing manner that imbued it with spontaneity and an effortless charm. It was gay and stimulating. The forms were also in the same easy and graceful French spirit. The enamel colors were of great beauty. Figures were also made in faïence, but they had little originality. The only porcelain of importance made at Marseilles was produced in the faïence manufactory of Joseph-Gaspard Robert from around 1773. His faïence and porcelain were decorated in a similar manner; especially typical were the extravagant Marseilles flowers.

Martha Washington Chair In American cabinetwork; a variety of armchair, which according to tradition is supposed to have been used by Martha Washington at Mt. Vernon. At the present time there is no written evidence to substantiate this claim; however, her name has become associated with both this form of American chair as well as a type of sewing table. This variety of armchair has a tall upholstered back. The top of the back is generally serpentine arched. The scroll-shaped open arms rest on incurvate arm supports. The legs are slightly tapered and are either of quadrangular or cylindrical form, and are often joined with a stretcher. This armchair combined features of design from the Chippendale, Hepplewhite and Sheraton styles.

Martha Washington Mirror In American

MARTHA WASHINGTON
CHAIR

cabinetwork; a colloquial term applied to the Constitution mirror. See *Constitution Mirror*.

Martha Washington Pattern   See *Ingrain Carpet*.

Martha Washington Table   In American cabinetwork; a sewing or work table so named because of its association with Martha Washington at Mt. Vernon. This variety of table has an oval or almost oval top over two or three rows of single small drawers, flanked by ends, which serve as bins and conform in shape to the top. The oval top is either in one piece or is divided into three parts. When it is made in one piece the entire top can be raised. When it is made in three parts the center portion is fixed while the part over each bin can be raised. This variety of sewing table is made in the Hepplewhite, Sheraton and American Empire styles and has a fitted interior with sewing accessories. See *Work Table*.

MARTHA WASHINGTON
TABLE

Maru–Bori   In Japanese sword mounts; the term applied to carving in the round. See *Bori*.

Mascaron   The French word *mascaron* is an architectural term having the same meaning as the English word *mask*. The term is applied to an ornamental representation of a face or a face and neck used in the keystones of arches, in panels and other similar positions. Mascarons were a favorite Renaissance motif and more often represented satyrs or fawns and other animal heads in a grotesque manner rather than human heads.

Mason Ironstone   See *Ironstone China*.

Masulipatam Rug   An Oriental rug woven in Masulipatam, India. The early rugs were usually finely woven and designed. The modern ones are purely commercial creations. See *India Oriental Rugs*.

Mat   In Oriental rugs; see *Yestiklik*.

Mat   In lace-making; a term applied to the closely worked or solid part of a design, especially in bobbin-made lace.

Matchlock   In arms; the matchlock was the earliest form of mechanism used to discharge a firearm. At first it consisted of an S-shaped lever, called serpentine, which was pivoted at its center to the stock. The upper end was forked to hold the match. The match was pushed down into the flashpan which ignited the priming by applying pressure to the lower end of the lever. A further improvement was provided by adding a catch and a trigger. A match is a cord burning slowly and steadily which was employed for igniting the powder in the pan of a matchlock. See *Firelock*; *Wheel-lock*.

Matted   In English silver; a decorative process, also called matted ground, introduced during the latter part of the 17th century. This process, which was of Dutch origin, consisted of delicate evenly spaced punchwork giving the surface of the silver a soft dull appearance. It was popular until the last decade of the 17th century.

Maximinenstrasse   In German ceramics; see *Cologne*.

Mayer, Elijah   An English potter working at Hanley, Staffordshire. During the late 18th and early 19th centuries he made cream-colored earthenware and black basalt and other stonewares of excellent quality. His cream-colored earthenware was generally of the same high standard as that made by Wedgwood. After 1820 the firm was E. Mayer and Son. The mark was "E. Mayer", impressed.

Mayhew, John   In English cabinetwork; see *Ince, William*.

Mazarine   In English silver; during the Late Georgian period large oval silver meat dishes were occasionally provided with a strainer called a Mazarine. They were so-called after Cardinal Mazarin, or a general in the army of Louis XIV by that name. The Mazarine was a flat piece of pierced silver made to fit within the depression of the meat dish, and was used to hold boiled fish and to allow the water to drain through to the bottom of the dish.

Mazarine Blue In Chinese ceramics; it is generally accepted that the phrase *mazarine blue* refers to a brilliant deep blue monochrome glaze introduced during the reign of K'ang Hsi. See *Gros Bleu*. The term *mazarine blue* perhaps so-called from Cardinal Mazarin or the Duchesse de Mazarin was given in England to a deep rich blue and appeared in late 17th century records. The name was also given to the material or the costume of a mazarine blue color.

Maze-Gane A Japanese metal art. In this process two different metals, namely shibuichi and shakudo, are melted individually and then combined after they are sufficiently cool so as not to lose their distinctive character. This results in a beautiful clouded or mottled effect which forms the groundwork for pictorial designs inlaid in gold and silver and chiselled in kata-kiri. This process was used extensively for Japanese sword mounts.

Mazer The term *mazer*, derived from the old High German *masa* meaning spot, was given in England to a very popular type of drinking vessel in common use from the 13th to 16th centuries, made of some kind of wood, correctly a spotted wood and properly spotted maple wood. It was invariably in the form of a shallow bowl having a diameter from about 5 to 9 inches and about $1\frac{1}{2}$ to $3\frac{1}{4}$ inches deep. The mazer was favored by all classes and the finer examples were mounted in silver. The mounts comprised a band attached to the top of the bowl, a circular plate called a "print" embossed with a design depicting an allegorical figure subject, attached to the inside of the bottom of the bowl, and very often a foot. Occasionally the mazer was provided with a loosely fitted cover of wood. When the silver foot is of any unusual height the vessel is referred to as a standing mazer. The term *mazer* was also often given in contemporary records to vessels of mazer-like form made entirely of metal.

Mazerwood A term applied to the wood of the European maple.

McIntire, Samuel 1757–1811. A prominent architect and builder of Salem, Massachusetts. He was also a most skillful carver. At the present time it is generally accepted that he was employed to execute the fine carvings on furniture made by other cabinetmakers, such as by the Sandersons who were well-known Salem cabinetmakers. It is also generally believed that he did make some few pieces of furniture. After his death in 1811, the carving business was carried on by his son, Samuel Field McIntire, whose carved work has often been mistaken for that of his father.

Measures Vessels generally made of metal, with or without a hinged cover, of standard size for measuring liquids, frequently used as drinking vessels. They were made in different shapes and in different capacities. Some were stamped with the capacity. See *Mutchkin*; *Chopin*; *Gill*; *Tappit Hen*; *Noggin*; *Plouk*; *Baluster*.

Meat Dish In English silver; the silver dish or plate for meat was introduced late in the 17th century and was sometimes decorated with a simple gadroon border. This style of ornament prevailed throughout the 18th century. It was generally oval in shape and usually from 10 to 25 inches in length. The dish used for the joint of meat was provided with shallow grooves or channels in the bottom to allow the juice to drain into a deeper well from which it was removed with a ladle. This variety of meat dish is often referred to as a "well-and-tree" plate, since the arrangement of the channels resembles the branches and trunk of a tree.

Mechanical Bank A 19th century small iron coin bank resembling a toy made in different forms. In one type a coin is placed in the hand of a mechanical boy, and by a spring motion is thrown into a slot at the other end, which is in the form of an animal's head with the coin going in the open mouth.

STANDING MAZER

Mechlin In lace-making; a delicate and filmy transparent Flemish bobbin-made lace, executed in one piece and often regarded as one of the prettiest of all lace fabrics. Its distinguishing feature is a bright and silky thread which outlines the design and gives the effect of embroidery, and for that reason the lace is often called Broderie de Malines. Another characteristic feature is the hexagonal mesh of the ground, with its short and finely plaited and twisted sides. Occasionally the early Mechlin lace displayed a decorative ground, such as fond de neige. Floral motifs were much in evidence in the designs. It was made principally at Mechlin, and also at Antwerp, Lierre and Turnhout. It is difficult to trace when it was first made, since practically all of the Flemish laces until 1665 were called Malines. Mechlin lace was fashionable in the 18th century, and it was essentially used as an extra or additional trimming with yards and yards being used for cravats, ruffles and lingerie. It seems from contemporary accounts that much of the lace was made in the manner of modern insertion. See *Maline*.

Médaillier In French cabinetwork; a cabinet having an interior of very shallow drawers or trays for the reception and display of rare medals enclosed within cabinet doors. The médaillier was always an elegant and ambitious piece of cabinetwork and was made in France from the 16th century onwards. In a general sense the term may be applied to similar articles of furniture having especially designed drawers for holding medals. Especially praiseworthy is the celebrated médaillier made for Louis XV by the French ébéniste, Gaudreau, and which is in the Bibliothèque Nationale. See *Medal*.

Medal A piece of metal, generally in the form of a coin, cast or struck with a portrait or effigy of a person, an inscription, or some figure or device to commemorate or honor a person or event. The study and collecting of medals for their historical and antiquarian value as well as those of fine artistic workmanship was an especially fashionable

MEDALLION

practice from the 15th century in Italy, which included the famous Medici collection, and in France from the 16th century. At this time specially made cabinets were used to hold these medals. Medals are principally made of gold, silver, bronze and copper, and many are also engraved. The earliest medals date from ancient Rome, and from the fall of the Roman Empire until about the end of the 14th century it seems that very few if any were made until the practice was revived in the Renaissance. Prior to the 16th century medals were cast, and at the beginning of the 16th century medals began to be struck from engraved dies in the same manner as coins. The medal of Pope Julius II was struck about 1506 and was the first so produced. Many of these early struck medals were fine works of art made by great artists and the most beautiful were produced by Benvenuto Cellini, 1500–1571. In England, although medals were first produced in the reign of Henry VIII, 1509–1547, it was not until the Elizabethan period, 1558–1603, that medals of fine quality were produced by émigré Continental craftsmen. See *Médaillier*.

Medal and Coin Cabinet In cabinetwork; see *Médaillier*.

Medallion In ornament; a large medal or something resembling a large medal, such as a round or oval tablet, having a figure represented in relief, a portrait or a decorative motif. It was a favorite ornament during the Italian Renaissance. The medallion was characteristic of the François I style; it was the head or bust of a man or woman in full face or in profile carved in varying degrees of relief. It was usually enclosed in a round frame fashioned as a wreath of foliage such as the laurel or in a frame made from a turned molding. It was extensively employed in English ornament after 1530 during the Tudor period when Italian Renaissance motifs were freely blended with English Gothic ornament. Medallions of circular or oval form, frequently decorated with classical figure subjects or trophies of armor, especially Roman body armor, were employed by Robert Adam. Portrait medallions were executed in Wedgwood's jasper ware and were remarkable for their beautiful coloring and classical composition. They were occasionally used for the enrichment of fine furniture such as commodes designed in the Adam style. See *Romayne Work*; *Migeon, Pierre, II*; *Della Robbia*.

Medici Porcelain In Italian ceramics; the famous and very frequently beautiful soft paste porcelain which was the first to have been made in Europe. It was known to have been made under the protection of Francesco Maria de' Medici, Grand Duke of Tuscany, from about 1575 to 1587. Accounts relating to its invention are conflicting and some mention that it was made under Francesco's predecessor, Cosimo I. There are still extant about sixty specimens and two dated specimens, almost all of which bear a carefully painted mark of the dome of the cathedral of Florence with the initial "F" beneath. The forms are often similar to Urbino majolica and include pilgrim bottles, vases, dishes with broad flat rims and central convex bosses, ewers, twin flasks for oil and vinegar and small jugs with pinched lip spouts. As a rule the painting was in blue only with occasional touches of purple for outlining, and was inspired by the painted decoration on Chinese porcelains. Chinese motifs were mingled with characteristic majolica motifs such as grotesques and foliage. Painted figure subjects were relatively rare. The glaze was seldom pure white and was generally hazy with minute bubbles.

Medici Tapestry Works A tapestry manufactory was established in 1546 by Duke Cosimo I at Florence, Italy. Its greatest productive period was under Duke Cosimo I. He appointed in 1546 Nicholas Karcher and John Roost as master weavers, and Bronzino, 1502–1572, and Francesco Salviati, 1510–1563, who were both painters, as designers and cartoonists. In the last half of the 16th century John van der Straaten,

1523–1605, became the appointed designer. See *Tapestry*.

Meiji The Meiji period of Japan A.D. 1868–1912. See *Japanese Periods*.

Mei P'ing In Chinese ceramics; the name *prunus vase* or *mei p'ing* is given to a small gallipot having a very small neck and mouth. The vase is used to hold a flowering plum-blossom branch.

Meissen In German ceramics; a German porcelain manufactory was established in 1710 in the fortress of Albrechtsburg, at Meissen, where it remained until 1865, under the protection of Augustus the Strong, Elector of Saxony, with Johann Friedrich Böttger as manager. The Saxon State manufactory is still in existence, producing the porcelain always known in England as Dresden and in France as Saxe. From 1710 until the outbreak of the Seven Years War in 1756 the manufactory enjoyed an almost unrivalled supremacy. Much of the porcelain made during that period possessed the highest artistic merit and had the greatest influence on the history of European ceramic art. The leadership of Meissen passed to Sèvres when the Seven Years War started. Under the management of Count Marcolini, 1774 to 1814, the prosperity of the factory was revived, but it was no longer capable of creating new styles. Much of the success of Meissen was due to Johann Gregor Herold, 1695–1775, who was the art director from 1720 to 1765. He improved the quality of Böttger's porcelain and brought it closer to the Chinese standard for porcelain. Shortly after 1720 he invented a new range of enamel colors and also fine colored enamel grounds. He also created and introduced several new kinds of painted decoration. Of particular interest were the chinoiseries; a new European miniature style with landscapes, especially harbor scenes, and small figures; bird motifs, and versions of Oriental flowers and realistically treated European flowers. The fame of Meissen to a large extent depends chiefly upon its porcelain figures. Johann

MEISSEN VASE

Joachim Kaendler, 1706–1775, the celebrated modeller, was working at Meissen from 1731 to 1775. He with the help of his assistants is virtually regarded as the creator of the European style of figure modelling. The best-known mark was the crossed swords from the Electoral arms of Saxony. It was first used around 1724, and the mark with slight variations such as dots or a star remained the factory mark until World War II. During the so-called Böttger period, 1710–1719, red stoneware and white porcelain were made. In the early Herold period, 1720–1731, chiefly painted wares were produced. Especially typical were the painted chinoiseries freely adopted from the Chinese Famille Verte. From about 1725 to 1730 the Japanese brocaded Imari pattern and the Kakiemon styles were more or less closely copied. The outstanding feature during the Herold and Kaendler or Late Baroque period, 1731 to 1740–1745, was the great development in figure modelling. Chinoiseries in painted decoration were supplanted by a miniature style of landscape painting with small figures. In the succeeding Rococo period, 1740–1745 to 1763, the fashion for Meissen figures reached its height. In the subsequent two periods, 1763 to 1774, and the Marcolini period, 1774 to 1815, the influence of Sèvres was evident and the decoration was in accordance with the contemporary Neo-Classic style. See *Zwiebelmuster*; *Indian Flowers*; *Deutsche Blumen*; *Porcelain*; *Böttger, Johann Friedrich*; *Ozier Pattern*; *Toy*.

CANDLESTICK BY
MEISSONNIER

Meissonnier, Juste Aurèle 1695–1750, French goldsmith, painter, sculptor, architect and furniture designer. He was one of the principal designers whose ideas created the fashion for the Rocaille or Rococo style. He is best known for his numerous collections of designs which were interpreted by the cabinetmakers, metal workers and other craftsmen. He is generally regarded as the most extreme of all the designers working in the Rocaille style. He was popular not only in France but in all the other countries of Europe which adopted the Rococo style of ornament. His best work was imbued with a quality of freedom and pliability that was remarkably striking. Unfortunately much of his work was marred by his fondness for complicated curves. Louis XV appointed him Designer to the Chamber and Cabinet of the King. Another principal designer and architect in the Rocaille style who was also best known for his collection of designs was Gilles-Marie Oppenord, 1672–1742. He was appointed Chief Director of all Architectural and Decorative Work for the Regent. His designs at times retained some of the grandeur of the previous century. Both the work of Meissonier and Oppenord was characterized by the principle of asymmetry, by complicated curves and by the predominance of shell work in their style of ornament. See *Louis XV*; *Rococo*; *Slodtz, René Michel*.

Mélange Campan See *Campan Marble*.

Meles Rug An Oriental rug belonging to the Turkish classification. The warp is wool and the weft is wool or cotton; the pile is wool and rather short. The ends are finished in a narrow web and a loose fringe. The designs are mostly Caucasian in character. The old Meles rug is superior in color and in design to the modern one. It is also called a Makri rug. See *Turkish Rugs*.

Mélèze Wood The wood of the larch tree, *abies larix*, used for inlay and cabinetwork, especially by the French ébénistes. It is hard and its color is yellow reddish.

Melon Foot In cabinetwork; an English bun foot having vertical grooves. See *Bun Foot*.

Melon Support In English cabinetwork; the name sometimes given to an Elizabethan bulbous-shaped support. See *Cup and Cover*; *Bulbous*.

Memoriam Picture See *In Memoriam Picture*.

Ménager In French Provincial cabinetwork; see *Buffet Vaisselier*.

Mendlesham Chair In English furniture; a variety of wood chair, revealing a relationship with the Windsor chair, made in Suffolk. The chair was made by Daniel Day, a wheelwright, working in Mendlesham in the early 19th century. The seat and legs were similar to those found on a Windsor chair, but the back had a straight top rail. The space between the top rail and the lower cross rail was filled in with turned balls, centering a narrow splat.

Mennecy Or Mennecy-Villeroy. In French ceramics; a soft paste porcelain and faïence manufactory protected by the Duc de Villeroy was founded in 1734 and at first was operated in the Rue de Charonne in Paris. It was transferred to Mennecy in 1748 and to Bourg-la-Reine in 1773. These three manufactories essentially form a single manufactory. It was managed from the beginning by François Barbin. Little is known of his productions except for the porcelain. In 1766 the factory was bought by Joseph Jullien and Symphorien Jacques. It was in operation until 1806. For the last twenty years of its existence it chiefly made faïence. The factory mark for the Villeroy porcelain was "DV". In 1773 Jullien and Jacques registered "B R" as a mark for their new factory. Early Mennecy porcelain to some degree imitated the wares from Saint-Cloud and Chantilly. The material, however, soon developed a distinctive character. The characteristic Mennecy glaze was brilliant and shiny, and the color of the finest was milky white. The inspiration for the mature Mennecy style was largely the work at Vincennes. The enamel painting of its finest work was distinctive for its individual treatment of borrowed motifs and for its fresh cool crisp colors. The figure modelling was not always very finished but it did have a charming simplicity. Biscuit figures of the Jullien and Jacques period were rather uninteresting. The porcelain productions at Bourg-le-Reine are difficult to distinguish from the work at Mennecy unless they are marked.

Mentonnière In armor; an extra protection piece worn over the armor for tournaments. It is a tilting breastplate which also afforded protection to the lower part of the face.

Menuiserie The French term for a joiner's work or joinery and also for carpentry and the work of the carpenter. See *Ebéniste*.

Menuisier The French term for a joiner and also for a carpenter and joiner. See *Ebéniste*.

Menuki In Japanese sword mounts; the pair of ornaments placed one on each side of the hilt of a sword or knife. They are usually a matched pair and frequently conform in design to the other fittings. Fine examples of menuki worked in gold and other metals are remarkable for their jewel-like beauty. The menuki are held in place on the hilt either by a projecting pin or by the braid or cord usually wound on the hilt.

Merese In glass; the term is generally applied, especially in English and American glass, to a flat glass button with a sharp edge which joins the bowl and the stem or the foot and the stem of a stemmed vessel, such as a goblet.

MENUKI

Méridienne In French Empire cabinetwork; a day bed having out-scrolled ends of unequal height designed with a back panel. In the majority of examples the back panel was shaped, and curved gracefully downward from the higher to the lower out-scrolled end. The day bed or the couch designed in the antique style was extremely fashionable during the French Empire. See *Grecian Couch*; *Recamier*; *Baigneuse*.

Merisier Wood The wood of the wild cherry tree, *prunus avium*, used for inlay and cabinetwork, especially by the French ébénistes. It is a hard wood and its color is reddish striped.

Mesail In armor; a movable visor used on medieval helmets. The helmets fitted with these projecting pointed visors were called dog-faced or pig-faced basinets.

Meshed Rug An Oriental rug belonging to

the Persian classification. It derived its name from the city of Meshed where it is woven. The foundation is cotton, sometimes wool; the pile is wool and of medium length. The ends are finished with a narrow web and loose warp-threads. Traditionally the Meshed rug is noted for its rich coloring. and for its fine floral and animal designs. The modern Meshed rug is usually very durable; however, it lacks the workmanship of the early Meshed. See *Persian Rugs*.

Metal In glass; the name is given to both the molten material and to the finished material of which glass objects or products are made.

Metope An architectural term applied to one of the square places between the triglyphs in a Doric frieze. A metope can be either plain or sculptured. See *Triglyph*.

Mezza Majolica In Italian ceramics; a term previously applied to the lead-glazed and other Italian pottery which preceded the true tin-glazed majolica. The distinction is erroneous since tin was already present to some extent in the white glaze of the majority of these earlier painted wares. The term was also given to lead-glazed wares with decoration incised through a white clay slip. It is more appropriate that these wares with incised decoration should be called Sgraffiato wares.

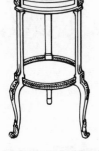

TABLE WITH PORCELAIN PLAQUES, AFTER PIERRE MIGEON II

Mezzo Punto A mixed Venetian point lace or guipure having the needle-made designs of flowers and scrolls outlined in a bobbin-made lace or tape and joined with pearled brides on a coarsely worked mesh ground or réseau.

Mezzo-Rilievo Half relief. See *Relief*.

Mezzotint A method of engraving on a copper plate to produce a print of various tones in black and white, or solid color in light and dark tones. A copper plate is made ready by the use of a tool similar to a chisel, with a short wide blade having a cutting edge and with one side incised with lines, which form teeth. The artist prepares the ground by rocking the tool across the surface of the plate numerous times until it is completely covered with burrs, or minute raised particles of the copper. The ground then resembles the texture of a fine fabric. The design is worked on the ground by scraping with a tool resembling a double-edged knife with a sharp point. The tones of light and dark are produced by the degree of scraping. The finished plate is covered with a thick ink and then wiped off, leaving the proper amount of ink, especially in the darker or raised portions, which require slightly more ink. The design is then impressed on paper. See *Engraving*.

Michelangelo Buonarroti 1475–1564, celebrated Florentine sculptor and painter. He inaugurated a new school of art that marked the beginning of the Baroque, and although he enriched art with unsuspected new effects, his style was pernicious to art and ultimately led to the Baroque. His followers who did not possess his lofty conceptions could not successfully imitate his heroic forms. Michelangelo's influence was evident in furniture design during the Late Renaissance. His love of figures, his skill in creating a race of supermen and his complete mastery of the naked figure as portrayed in the ceiling of the Sistine Chapel inspired the cabinetmaker to decorate furniture with carved human figures having a sculpturesque quality. His influence was also noticeable in the tendency toward boldly modelled moldings, sometimes of exaggerated scale. A more vigorous and agitated style of ornament, often of an increased scale and displaying a greater complexity of curved forms, also reflected his influence. The exaggerated scale and some false architectural features used by Michelangelo in his work ultimately led architecture into the Baroque. See *Baroque*; *Renaissance, Italian, Vignola, Giacoma da*.

Migeon, Pierre, II 1701–1775. French ébéniste. During the style of Louis XV the practice of using porcelain plaques and medallions to enrich certain articles of furniture was introduced. They were found on delicate small pieces of veneered and marquetry furniture used by ladies, such as a variety of small tables and desks. The cabinetwork of Pierre Migeon II is particularly identified with the use of fine porcelain plaques and medallions.

Mignonette In lace-making; a light and delicate bobbin-made lace, also called Blonde de Fil and Point de Tulle, the latter term derived from the resemblance of the ground to that fabric. The lace was made in a variety of widths, but never exceeding 3 inches. It was made of Lille thread, which was bleached at Antwerp, and it was produced in the neighborhood of Paris, Lorraine, Auvergne and Normandy. The lace was also manufactured in Switzerland, Arras and Lille. It was much used in the 17th century and due to its clear ground and lightness it was especially favored for head-dresses and for trimmings. The lace was frequently mentioned in 18th century advertisements and apparently much of it was exported. See *Lille Lace*.

Milan Lace Milan lace is of early origin and one of the earliest dates, recorded in Italian lace-making, 1493, belongs to Milan. It seems that Milan continued to be an active center for the manufacture of fine lace at least until the last quarter of the 18th century. The so-called Punto di Milano or points de Milan were all bobbin-made laces originating at Milan, and although these laces were reproduced at Genoa and Naples, it is generally accepted that the work was inferior to Milan lace. The flowing designs of scrolls and foliage resembled to some degree woven linen, and jours or fillings were sometimes introduced to give it a lighter appearance. In the early lace the designs were joined with bars, and in the 17th century a large mesh was introduced for the ground, which gradually became smaller. Although the mesh ground varied, it most often had four plaited sides to each mesh. In more recent times a torchon lace was made at Milan which was quite popular with the peasants.

Milch Glass Or Milk Glass. In glass; the name given to an opaque white glass made in imitation of porcelain. It was fabricated in different countries. Milch glass was made in Venice around the beginning of the 16th century; in Germany, Bohemia and France toward the end of the 17th century and in England late in the 18th century. See *Glass*; *Venetian Glass*; *Bristol, Chinese Glass*.

Mildner Glass In German glass; the name given to a kind of decoration employed on glass. It derived its name from Johann Mildner, 1764–1808, working in Gutenbrunn, Austria, who used this kind of decoration and who very often signed his work. This decoration, which consisted of one or two medallions, was generally found on slightly conical cylindrical tumblers. The medallions were decorated in such a manner that both the engraved gold decoration on the outside and the engraved silver decoration on the inside received a red background. The medallions on the outside often depicted religious subjects or portraits, while the inside was ornamented with inscriptions. These decorated medallions were fitted in the sides of the glass from which medallions of similar shape had been cut.

Milk Bench In American furniture; see *Water Bench*. In French Provincial; see *Seillage*.

Milk Glass In glass; see *Milch Glass*.

Milkmaid Cup In English silver; a festive drinking or wager cup. These cups were imported into England from Holland during the first half of the 17th century in great numbers. See *Jungfrauenbecher*.

Millefiori In Venetian glass; the term, which means a thousand flowers, was given by the Venetians to a kind of decorative glass first made by the early Romans. In this process slender glass rods of every conceivable color were fused together to form glass canes and then cut crosswise revealing a pattern. These cut sections were placed side by side and fused together and then blown into the

MILDNER GLASS TUMBLER

shape desired. Cups and other articles were made in this manner into designs resembling the surface of stony coral. It seems that the ground color most frequently used was a purple or a violet. The majority of mille-fiori glass pieces were small. The technique was revived during the 19th century in the French manufactories of paperweights. See *Glass Cane*; *Venetian Glass*.

Millefleurs In decorative art; the French term *millefleurs*, or thousand flowers, is given to an over-all decorative design of flower and leaf motif worked in a natural-istic or conventionalized manner. The flower and leaf motif is generally small and delicate in size in comparison to the size of the article which it decorates. The millefleurs work had its origin in China and was introduced into Europe through the Near East. Rich bro-cades, Oriental carpets and French and Flemish Gothic tapestries are included among the different articles that are notable for the exquisite composition of their mille-fleurs decoration.

Mimpei Ware In Japanese ceramics; see *Awaji Ware*.

Mina Khani Motif A design motif used in Oriental rugs, especially in Persian rugs. It usually consists of flowers of open face design, joined by rhomboidal vines so as to form a diamond arrangement.

MING PLATE, HUNG CHIH

Ming The Ming dynasty of China was founded in 1368 with its capital at Nanking. The Ming period, which includes the reigns of seventeen emperors, extended until 1644. The art work of this period is referred to as Ming. In Chinese ceramics; the great imperial porcelain factory was rebuilt at Ching-tê-Chên in the year 1369. Aside from the three-color ware, Ming porcelains are most often painted with a brush either in underglaze blue or red, or in colored enamels on glazed or unglazed porcelain. The painting of enamels on biscuit or un-glazed porcelain was more common during the succeeding dynasty. The colors used on porcelain enamelled on the biscuit were chiefly green, yellow and aubergine with the addition of a colorless flux for white. The designs were drawn in a black manganese pigment and were filled in with washes of transparent enamel. Gilding was also used on Ming porcelains. It was either applied in leaf form or was painted with a brush. The majority of Sung monochromes were copied by the Ming potters. There is little information on the wares of the first Ming reign of Hung Wu, 1368–1398. The wares of the Yung Lo period, 1403–1424, are plain white and are embossed, engraved or decor-ated in color with underglaze red. Fine white eggshell porcelain bowls were made. During the Hsüan Tê reign, 1426–1435, all the Chinese arts flourished. A great variety of porcelain was made. Especially notable are the wares decorated in a brilliant under-glaze red, derived from copper and called Chi Hung. This red was also used as a mono-chrome glaze. Fine white teacups with engraved designs and white altar cups with the character T'an engraved inside the bowl are characteristic types. Colored enamelled porcelain ware was also produced but it did not compare in quality to the Chêng Hua enamelled pieces. A deep cobalt blue monochrome, called Chi Ch'ing, was also made. The porcelains of the Ch'êng Hua period, 1465–1487, are considered to rival those of the Hsüan Tê reign. Especially fine are the on-glaze colored enamelled wares painted in subdued colors and with a pictorial effect. This is generally regarded as the classic period in Ming for this type of work. Enamelled painting on glazed wares had also been practiced during Sung. Wares were also decorated under the glaze with the brilliant sacrificial red. During the Hung Chih reign, 1488–1505, yellow glazes were skillfully used on porcelains. Beautiful white bowls and three-color ware were also made. During the Chêng Tê reign, 1506–1521, yellow monochromes were highly esteemed. The colored glazes in the three-color ware were more transparent and sleek and had lost some of their force and strength. Although earlier individual specimens are extant, the so-called mixed color ware or ts'a ts'ai, the enamelled ware of the red and green family and the polychrome enamelled ware combined with underglaze blue or the five-color ware or wu ts'ai are generally dated from the Chêng Tê period or early 16th century. In the Chia Ching reign, 1522–1566, most of the wares made in the previous reigns were continued. Underglaze red was discontinued and was replaced by an overglaze red. The characteristic monochrome was a deep blue of soft tone having a rather powder-like texture. The greatest variety of porcelains painted in enamels on the glaze were made in the Chia Ching reign. Porcelain was also enamelled on the biscuit. The three-color ware was also made. During the Wan Li reign, 1573–1619, polychrome enamels or five-color ware combined with underglaze blue was produced on a larger scale than in any of the preceding reigns. During the three final reigns of the Ming dynasty there is little to mention except that although the Imperial factory declined due to the chaotic times which preceded the fall of the dynasty, private porcelain factories continued to operate and to produce fine pieces of the highest quality. See *Sung*; *Ch'ing*; *Chinese Gods*; *Five-Color Ware*; *Three-Color Ware*; *Ts'a Ts'ai*; *Ling Lung*; *Blue and White Ming*; *Mohammedan Blue*; *Red and Green Family*; *Blanc de Chine*; *Celadon*.

Miniature The term *miniature* was originally applied to the small picture in a medieval manuscript that was decorated or miniated with red lead, from the Latin word *minium*, meaning red lead. The term is now applied in art to a very small painting, in particular to a portrait. Miniatures are painted in water color, oil and enamel. Fine miniatures were made in enamel from around the middle of the 17th century. In this process the white enamel is applied on gold plate and fired. The colors, which are made of metallic oxides, are painted on, and then slightly fused to the enamel. The finished painting is coated with transparent flux which pro-

duces an enamel surface. This is really not true enamelling work, since vitreous compounds are not used as colors. As a rule miniatures painted in oil are on copper. German and Dutch miniatures were often painted in oil on copper. Ivory miniatures which are painted in water color came into general use in England early in the 18th century. Prior to that time they were chiefly painted on vellum, cardboard or some similar material.

Miniature Tall Case Clock In English furniture; the term generally given to a tall case clock that was of much smaller proportions than the standard tall case clock. It is also sometimes given the colloquial name of grandmother's clock. See *Tall Case Clock*.

Minton In English ceramics; Thomas Minton, 1765–1836, who served an apprenticeship at Caughley and also worked at Spode, founded a pottery at Stoke-on-Trent, Staffordshire, in 1796, which is still carried on by his successors. For the first two years only blue-printed and cream-colored earthenware were made. Porcelain was made from 1798 to 1811. It was started again around 1821 with the help of workers from Derby and became the chief production under Herbert Minton, 1792–1858, who was the son of the founder. From 1836 to 1841 the firm was Minton and Boyle. The present company was formed in 1883. In 1849 Minton was fortunate to secure the services of Leon Arnoux who became art director and remained at Minton until his death in 1902. The early work which was not marked was often admirable. Included among the marks was an "M" between two crossed "S's" in blue enamel from 1820 to 1830; "Minton" impressed after 1865; "HM & Co." impressed for Herbert Minton & Co., 1847–1876. The modern marks are numerous. A great variety of wares were produced at Minton. Some of the later productions from 1820 onwards rank among the best contemporary porcelain. They were admir-

MING GALLIPOT, C. 1500

able for their technical excellence and for their artistic forms and designs.

Mirror It seems evident that the principle of backing a piece of glass with a metallic film was known to the Romans in ancient times, but apparently the technique of silvering glass with an amalgam of tin and mercury was not perfected until around the middle of the 16th century by the Venetians, who had learned shortly after 1500 how to make broad glass. Up to that time mirrors of polished metal were preferred, although glass mirrors of a crude quality, backed by a metallic substance, were made throughout the medieval period, but they were too crude for a satisfactory reflection. Crude glass mirrors were chiefly made in Germany during the 12th and 13th centuries and convex mirrors of crown glass were made at Nuremberg at least by the 15th century. Hand mirrors of polished metal or crystal, set in costly frames, were used as toilet mirrors during the medieval period. The early wall or hanging mirrors, which became fashionable in Italy during the Renaissance, were made of a sheet of highly polished metal with a richly carved giltwood frame. Two sliding wood doors often ornamented with painted designs were used to cover the unattractive surface of the mirror and also to prevent oxidation. Occasionally curtains were substituted for the doors. The manufacture of glass mirrors began to flourish in Venice from after the middle of the 16th century. During the 17th century there was a great vogue for wall mirrors, and France and England acquired the technique for making mirrors. Wall mirrors, which were introduced into England from the Continent, were relatively scarce in England throughout the 16th century. After the Restoration in 1660 they began to figure prominently in interior decoration. The majority of wall mirrors were rectangular and were hung vertically. See *Toilet Mirror*; *Pier Mirror*; *Early Georgian Architectural Wall Mirror*; *Girandole*; *Fretwork Mirror*; *Cheval Mirror*; *Convex Wall Mirror*; *Courting*

MISERICORD, GERMAN
15TH CENTURY

Mirror; *Bilbao*; *Psyché*; *Eglomisé*; *Elliott, John*; *Bronzes, Chinese*; *Bull's Eye Mirror*.

Mirror Black In Chinese ceramics; the name given to the fine Chinese black glaze porcelain of the K'ang Hsi period. The black glaze which has bluish or brownish reflections was made by mixing iron of coffee-brown with the cobaltiferous ore of manganese. It is also called wu chin or black gold.

Mirror Knob In English and American furniture; the fashion for supporting a wall mirror on two small round or oval knobs developed in England during the latter part of the 18th century. Especially pleasing were the knobs decorated in painted enamel. These enamel knobs, which were usually in brass frames, were decorated with landscapes, ships, ladies in contemporary costume and other similar subjects. See *Battersea*; *Bilston*.

Mir Serebend Rug The finest Serebend of pure Serebend design was woven at Mir, a village adjacent to the Fereghan plains, which was destroyed by an earthquake, and is generally referred to as a Mir Serebend. Today many imitations of the Mir Serebend are made. See *Serebend Rug*.

Mirzapur Rug An Oriental rug woven in the city of Mirzapur, India. The early Mirzapur carpet showed a pronounced Hindu character in its designs in distinction from the Persian forms. Today the rug is purely a commercial creation. See *India Oriental Rugs*; *Oriental Rug*.

Misericord In cabinetwork; an English ecclesiastical term meaning compassion or mercy. It is derived from a monastic use of the Latin word *misericordia* which refers to an indulgence or relaxation of the rule. The misericord in church furnishings is a small projecting shelf or bracket attached to the under side of a hinged wooden seat in a choir stall. Its purpose is to give support to a person while standing. Misericords were also provided for chancel seats. They were often elaborately and ingeniously carved.

Miséricorde A medieval dagger which was in use from late in the 12th century. It had a thin, short blade and was the principal form of medieval dagger. It was used to penetrate the armor after the opponent had been unhorsed. See *Dagger*.

Mishima In Japanese ceramics; the small repetitive and radiating designs in the form of stars, circles, semi-circles, conventional flowers and bands. This type of decoration is completely Korean in its origin, and at first it was found only in those Japanese provinces where Korean potters had settled. Later it was used throughout Japan. The designs are generally impressed and are only rarely incised, and are filled with a white slip, sometimes on a grey glaze. The name is derived from the supposed resemblance of these rows of repetitive designs to the rows of characters in the yearly Mishima calendar for which the town of Mishima was famous. See *Karatsu*; *Korean Wares*.

Mission Chair In cabinetwork; the Spanish Renaissance armchair called a frailero or monk's chair was the prototype for the mission chair so profusely and cheaply manufactured in America. However, the mission chair possessed none of the dignity or grace which made the original distinctive. It seems that when the Spanish missionaries settled in California and Mexico, they furnished their monasteries similarly to those at home. However, the furniture was a very poor reproduction of the original pieces. And, as a result, the so-called mission furniture made in America was destined to be a fiasco. See *Frailero*.

Miter In ecclesiastical costume; a covering for the head comprising part of the insignia of a bishop in the Western Church and also worn by certain abbots and other ecclesiastics as a mark of unusual dignity. The miter, which originally was not divided, is now a tall cap deeply cleft at the top. The outline of the front and the back resembles the form of a pointed arch. The early double pointed miter was very low. It is generally accepted that the miter around the 14th century as it became more pointed and enriched achieved its highest perfection in form and elaborate decoration. From the latter part of the 15th century the miter increased in size and in height until it attained its present elevation around the middle of the 18th century. Miters varied in the richness of their decoration. An exceedingly rich form of miter was set with jewels and precious stones or with plates of gold or silver. Other miters were magnificently worked in embroidery with pearls. The material most commonly used for miters has been white silk or linen.

Mitokoromono In Japanese sword mounts; the term means objects for three places. In sword mounts it refers to the kozuka, kogai and menuki, comprising a set having conforming or matching decoration. Many such sets were made by celebrated artists and were often presented by the Shogun to noblemen whom he favored as well as by the noblemen to each other. See *Soroimono*; *Kodōgu*.

Modes In lace making; see *Jours*.

Modillion An architectural term given to a horizontal bracket which was used in a Roman cornice. The outer side is designed as an Ionic volute with its cushion, and the volute on the inner side is larger and reversed. In cabinetwork; the architectural feature of the modillion was sometimes incorporated into the principles of design in an article of furniture. The characteristic 16th century Italian Renaissance credenza was designed with a frieze which generally was fitted with two or three drawers that were separated by modillions.

MODILLION

Mohair In textiles; mohair was sometimes used in the 17th and 18th centuries for upholstery and draperies. Mohair, which was introduced into Spain by the Moors, was originally a kind of fine camlet fabricated from the hair of the angora goat. Later in the 18th century the name was given to a kind of fabric simulating the original mohair and fabricated entirely of silk. Mohair was mentioned in English records as early as the 17th century.

Mohammedan Blue In Chinese ceramics; the Chinese supplies of cobalt blue, which were used in the underglaze blue decoration, were supplemented by a superior blue imported from the Near East known as Mohammedan blue. During the Ming dynasty, 1368–1644, the finest blue and white ware was made from this blue. Supplies of Mohammedan blue were available during the Hsüan Tê reign, 1426–1435, Chêng Tê reign, 1506–1521 and the Chia Ching reign, 1522–1566. Chinese records say that the tone of the blue varied. The blue and white wares were exceedingly fine during the Hsüan Tê period. The blue and white wares of the Ch'êng Hua reign, 1465–1487, are considered inferior to those of the Hsüan Tê period due to an insufficient supply of Mohammedan blue. During the Chêng Tê period the blue and white wares were highly regarded. The Mohammedan blue which was apparently plentiful was a dark color. The body of these wares was thick but of a fine texture. The glaze seemed to be bubbly which gave a kind of hazy effect to the blue. The blue had a soft tone and was applied in heavy outlines that were filled in with flat washes. During the Chia Ching reign the color of the Mohammedan blue was a rich violet blue that was distinctive for its intensity. The supplies of Mohammedan blue were practically exhausted during the Wan Li period, 1573–1619. Most of the Wan Li blue and white ware has a seemingly dull greyish blue. See *Ming*; *Blue and White Ming*.

Mokkō In Japanese sword mounts; a tsuba having four lobes. Tsuba of this form were quite popular and appear frequently.

Mokume-Ji A Japanese metal art which produces a ground resembling grained wood. In this process several thin metal plates are beaten together. The plate is then punched from one side so that the opposite side resembles broken blisters. These blisters

MOKKŌ TSUBA

are hammered down until each produces its own wave effect. Although iron was generally used, the finest work was in shakudo with a gold graining.

Molding In cabinetwork; *molding* is an architectural term for the decorative treatment given to the features of a structure by means of curved forms, which accentuate these features by the effect of light and shade. Moldings of wood and sometimes of metal are used to decorate the surface of furniture. Wooden moldings are either cut on the body of a piece of furniture or are applied. A molding which recedes in from the surface is almost always cut out of the wood; while a molding which projects beyond the surface is almost always applied. In fine cabinetwork moldings are in scale with the piece they decorate as well as with each other. The play of light and shade is effected by the correct use and combination of moldings. Moldings are either plain or are carved with a repetitive design, such as the egg and dart, husk chain or gadrooning. Metal moldings are principally identified with French cabinetwork. They were especially used on marquetry and veneered commodes, tables and other similar articles of furniture. Moldings were sometimes arranged in geometrical designs such as the diamond point motif employed during the Louis XIII style on panelled cupboard doors. See *Cavetto*; *Torus*; *Ovolo*; *Astragal*; *Ogee*; *Bead*; *Dentil*; *Acorn*; *Bolection*.

Molina Rosa Marble See *Garfagnana*.

Momoyama The Momoyama period of Japanese history, 1573–1615. See *Japanese Periods*.

Monatsbecher In German silver; see *Häufebecher*.

Monkey Band In German ceramics; the name given to the original set of Meissen figures made by Kaendler around 1750 to ridicule the Royal orchestra at Dresden. Each figure represents a musician in the form of a monkey. See *Meissen*.

Monk's Chair In cabinetwork. See *Frailero*; *Chair Table*.

Monk's Table In English cabinetwork; see *Settle*.

Monstrance In ecclesiastical art; the term *monstrance* derived from the Latin *monstrare* meaning to show is given to a vessel generally of precious metal in which the Host is exposed. It is also sometimes used as a reliquary or a receptacle for exhibiting relics. The custom of exposing the Host is not very old and it is generally believed that the monstrance was introduced around the end of the 14th century. The early forms of these vessels varied. An early monstrance was in the form of a turret elaborately wrought in precious metal with four openings of crystal. The present form of the monstrance was introduced in the 16th century. It is designed as a circular disc of crystal enclosed in a frame of golden rays and is mounted on a stem and foot.

Monteith In English silver; a punch bowl with a movable rim, which is the only difference between this form of punch bowl and the regular punch bowl. The rim is decoratively scalloped or notched, and it is stated in silver literature that the name for this bowl was derived from a Scotchman named Monteith who wore a cloak with a scalloped border. However, notches were also occassionally found on punch bowls without movable rims. Various explanations have been advanced for the indentations. It has been suggested that the glasses were placed in the bowl with the stems outward in order that they could be carried into the room without breaking or that the glasses were suspended in the bowl for chilling purposes when the bowl was first filled with cracked ice.

Montereau In French ceramics; a manufactory was founded at Montereau, Seine-et-Marne, in 1775 by several Englishmen, Messrs. Clark, Shaw & Cie. It produced white earthenware of the English type. The manufactory prospered and in the early 19th century the manufactory at Creil was united with it. The productions at Montereau, which were numerous and as a rule of a rather ordinary character, were rarely marked.

Montigny, Philippe-Claude 1734–1800. French ébéniste, received master January 29, 1766. He made fine reproductions of the elaborate marquetry pieces of André Charles Boulle. See *Le Vasseur, Etienne*.

Moore, James English cabinetmaker working from around 1708 to 1726. He was in partnership with John Gumley in the Strand until he died in 1726. The several pieces which can be assigned to Moore are of an excellent quality and are distinctive for their exuberant carving and gilded gesso detail. During the first quarter of the 18th century Moore and Gumley ranked with the leading cabinetmakers. Their authenticated pieces which were treated in a Baroque manner had an air of stately grandeur that made them suitable for the Palladian mansions. James Moore left his business to his son, James Jr., who was working from around 1726 to 1734. He was appointed cabinet and chairmaker to the Prince of Wales in 1732 and he died in 1734. See *Gumley, John*.

Moresque In Spanish-Moorish style of ornament. See *Mudéjar*.

Morion In armor; a 16th century open helmet that was the usual headpiece of foot soldiers. The crown often had a high comb and the brim peaked sharply upward in the front and back. It is sometimes called a comb-morion to differentiate it from the Spanish morion. The Spanish morion had a pear-shaped crown without a comb and a narrow brim. Its crown was similar to the cabasset with a tiny horizontal point.

Morning-Star A medieval weapon. See *Holy-Water Sprinkler*.

Morse In ecclesiastical costume; see *Cope*.

Mortise and Tenon In joinery and carpentry; the combination of the mortise and

MONTEITH

tenon or the two parts which fit and complete each other. The mortise or hole, which is generally rectangular in form, is cut in the surface of a piece of wood in order to receive the tenon or shaped projection made on the end or side of another piece of wood. Hence they form a tight and strong joint.

Mortlake In English ceramics; a manufactory making brown stoneware was started at Mortlake, Surrey, by Joseph Kishere in 1800. The pottery was still in existence in 1843. They principally made jugs, mugs and flasks. The usual mark was "Kishere Mortlake", impressed.

Mortlake Tapestry Works A tapestry manufactory was established at Mortlake, England, in 1620, under the proprietorship of Sir Francis Crane, 1620–1636, with Francis Cleyn as art director and Philip de Maecht as one of the head weavers. It continued to operate until 1703. Its finest work and greatest period of productivity was from 1620 to 1636. See *Tapestry*.

Mosaic A decorative art which is a form of inlay work. Mosaic work has been practiced since ancient times. There are different kinds of mosaic work, such as the mosaic of gems laid in ivory for the ornamentation of jewelry. Especially fine were the pictorial designs achieved on mosaic work in which colored marbles and other similar materials were used. Glass mosaic used to decorate pulpits, altars, tombs and other similar marble objects was principally practiced in Italy. Mosaic work was also executed in wood. Although marble, mother-of-pearl, semi-precious stones are all used in mosaic work the principal material is opaque glass. By using glass it is possible to obtain almost every tone or shade of color desired. The different colors are made by mixing various metallic oxides to the melted glass. It is then made into a small square slab and broken into small cubes called tesserae. The broken edge of the tesserae is used for the surface of the mosaic work. Gold and

silver tesserae are made by placing the metal leaf on a thin flat form of transparent glass and then, in a heated condition, applying molten glass, using pressure. The tesserae are then cut out. A floor mosaic of square stones or tiles laid in a geometrical design is called *tessellated*. See *Cosmati Work*; *Inlay*.

Mosbach In German ceramics; a faïence manufactory was started at Mosbach, Baden, in 1770 by Pierre Berthevin under the protection of the Elector Palatine. The marks generally attributed to the factory include "MB" under an Electoral Hat, "MT" in monogram and "T"; the mark "CT" may have been used also. After 1806 the initials of Carl Friedrich, Grand Duke of Baden were found and from 1818 "M" or "Mosbach", impressed, was the usual mark. In a general way the various productions show a resemblance to the wares of Strasbourg. During the latter part of the 18th century gift jugs with inscriptions generally in black letters were made and were similar in style to the jugs made at Durlach.

Mosque Lamp In Islamic glass; lamps from the Egyptian mosques are generally considered to be the most famous specimens of Islamic enamelled glass. These lamps or lanterns containing an oil vessel were designed to be hung from the ceilings of mosques by chains attached to the loops on the shoulder. Frequently the rich and colorful enamelled and gilded decoration was enhanced with passages from the Koran. Although these lamps are associated with the Sultans of Egypt they are of Syrian workmanship. Syria, especially Damascus and Aleppo, deserves credit for perfecting the technique of enamelled glass. It is generally believed that the finest examples of these Egyptian Mosque lamps were made during the late 13th and early 14th centuries.

Mosul An Oriental rug belonging to the Caucasian group. It derived its name from the town of Mosul in Mesopotamia. The warp and weft are usually of wool; however, both can sometimes be cotton. The

MOSAIC

pile is long and soft because a large amount of camels' hair and goats' hair are used in it. Because of the warm yellowish tones so often found in these rugs, they have a tendency to appear glossy. The designs, which are usually striking in character, are numerous and are frequently of Persian origin. See *Caucasian Rugs*.

Mosul Kurd   An Oriental rug belonging to the Caucasian group, woven by the Kurds in the north of Mosul. The foundation is wool and the pile, which is rather long, is also wool. The ends usually have a nomadic web extension and triangular braided mats. The designs are rather coarse and crude. See *Caucasian Rugs*.

Mote Spoon   In English silver; a small silver spoon used to take tea leaves from the teacup. The bowl of the spoon is decorated with a pierced design and the round stem has a pointed end which is barbed. It was introduced late in the 17th century. See *Punch Spoon*.

Mother-of-Pearl   A nacreous inner layer found in several various kinds of large shells. It was cut and polished and was used in the East in a restricted sense as an inlay from around the 16th century. A small portion of mother-of-pearl was occasionally used as an inlay in conjunction with other materials in European cabinetwork, such as in pietra dura and in floral marquetry. Inlays of ivory and bone were sometimes supplemented with mother-of-pearl. During the Late Georgian era in England it was more freely used on such articles as boxes and tea caddies. Papier-mâché furniture, such as sewing tables, made in America during the Victorian era, was occasionally further embellished with mother-of-pearl.

Mother-of-Pearl Glass   See *Satin-Glass*.

Moton   In armor; see *Besague*.

Moulin   The French word *moulin*, or mill, was applied to a small utensil usually having a box-like section surmounted with a metal grinding device of cup-shape form with a horizontal attachment that was rotated by hand. The moulin was used in France from the 15th century for grinding spices and mustard, and from the 18th century for grinding coffee. Although the majority were made of wood with an iron grinding device, many were made of silver and gold and elaborately wrought. A fine example of a coffee mill or a moulin à café was one belonging to Madame de Pompadour which was made of gold and engraved with a coffee tree design.

Mounts   In furniture; the metal ornaments or decorative hardware applied to the surface of furniture, among which are included metal handles, back plates, escutcheons, moldings and appliqués. Since magnificent bronze mounts were an important part of French furniture from the time of Louis XIV through the Empire, the era abounded with great metal workers. These bronze mounts which were often veritable works of art were principally used on marquetry and veneered commodes, tables, writing furniture, tall case clocks and other similar articles. French mounts were used by Chippendale, Adam and Hepplewhite on furniture designed by them in the contemporary French style. See *Cressent, Charles*; *Boulle, André Charles*; *Caffieri, Jacques*; *Gouthière, Pierre*; *Boulton, Matthew*; *Ormolu*; *Bail Handle*.

Mourning Jug   In German ceramics; see *Freiberg*.

Moustiers   In French ceramics; one of the most important centers in France for the manufacture of faïence. Several distinctive styles for the decoration of faïence were created at Moustiers that were extensively copied. The earliest faïence of artistic importance was made in a manufactory established in 1679 by Pierre Clérissy, remaining active until 1852. The blue and white Tempesta style from around 1680 to 1710 and the blue and white Bérain style from around 1710 to 1740 are principally associated with the Clérissy factory. Both styles were original

FURNITURE MOUNTS

MUDÉJAR ORNAMENT

and were of first-rate artistic importance. The subjects for the first style were often copied from the engraved designs by Antonio Tempesta, 1555–1630. The second style is named after Jean Bérain, 1638–1711, whose decorative engravings inspired the designs. It is generally regarded as the most original work produced at Moustiers. The best in this style was remarkable for its smooth milky white tin-glaze ground and for its soft blue decoration. Another manufactory was founded in 1738 by Joseph Olerys and was active until 1790 or later. The work of this factory is chiefly indentified with a "high temperature polychrome" style, named after Olerys and inspired by the faïence made at Alcora, Valencia, and used from 1740 onwards. The high temperature colors were a fine yellow, a soft blue, a green and a brown or violet; red was never used as a high temperature color at Moustiers. Another manufactory was operated from 1718 to 1791 by Jean Baptiste Ferrat. This manufactory adopted the Strasbourg style of colored enamels from around 1770 onwards. The designs were inspired to a large extent by the faïence made at Marseilles. Another manufactory was started in 1779 by Jean Gaspard Féraud and Joseph-Henri Berbegier and was active until 1874. They developed a new style of painting in high temperature colors from around 1779 onwards. The work was well-painted in soft colors and the tin glaze for the ground was extremely smooth and glossy. In addition to these manufactories there were many other minor manufactories. During the 19th century reproductions were made of the earlier styles. See *Faïence*.

Mudéjar In style of ornament; the name given to the fusion of the art of Christian Spain with that of Moorish art. The most distinctive feature of Spanish art during the Middle Ages was the concurrent existence in Spain of two schools of art. This was due to the fact that in the 8th century the Spanish people were conquered by the Mohammedan Moors from across the Straits of Africa.

During the ensuing centuries the Spanish Christians slowly pushed the enemy southward toward the sea, until the rule was terminated with the conquest of Granada in 1492. The Moors, who were supreme ornamentalists and the world's finest geometricians, greatly influenced the artistic taste and customs of Spain. The naturalistic representation of men, animals and plants was forbidden in the Mohammedan style of ornament. This naturally resulted in a development of a conventionalized leaf design, which was often used as a background for inscriptions in arabic characters, and an endless variety of geometrical designs and of patterns worked on a geometrical basis. Mohammedan art was outstanding for its brilliant coloring and for the exuberance of its ornamentation. The ornament was always clearly defined and distinct. The Spaniards accepted from Mohammedan art that which was in harmony with Christian principles. A great many Spanish craftsmen were conquered Moors, who, in designing furniture, incorporated Moorish style of ornament and methods of construction. These oriental precepts in art were so deeply rooted that even after the Moors were finally expelled in 1607 during the reign of Philip III, this Moorish influence was always to a greater or less degree present. This combination of Hispano-Moresque or Mudéjar art was always a distinctive feature in all forms of Spanish art.

Muffineer In English silver; the name given to a small container originally used for sprinkling salt on hot buttered muffins. A muffineer is the same as a caster or dredger except it is smaller. It was introduced into England during the latter part of the 17th century. The early form was cylindrical with a dome-shaped perforated top while the later types followed the prevailing silver styles. The muffineer was later made in sets of three, with one piece being considerably larger than the other two pieces. The larger muffineer was for sugar and the two smaller ones were for pepper, apparently for Jamaica and Cayenne pepper.

Muffle Color In ceramics; an enamel color fired in a muffle kiln. See *Petit Feu*.

Mug A drinking vessel generally cylindrical in form either with or without a handle chiefly made of metal or pottery. In the 18th century mugs were often made to represent a grotesque human face. A silver mug was frequently given as a christening gift to a child. In English silver; small silver mugs with one handle and without a lid, which are commonly regarded as an off-spring of the English silver tankard, came into general use in the late 17th century. Although they varied in shape and in characteristics, in a general sense they retained a cylindrical form with slightly tapering sides. See *Can*.

Mühlenbecher In silver; a festive drinking cup originally made in Holland around the 17th century. It is also called a wind-mill cup. It is a bell-shaped cup surmounted with a wind-mill, fitted with a clock, and having a ladder extending down from the entrance to the wind-mill with a tube running parallel with the ladder. After filling the cup with wine, the one who is to drink the contents blows through the tube, causing the sails of the wind-mill to revolve and the figures of the clock to move. The object is that the cup must be emptied before the sails of the wind-mill stop; otherwise the person must drink the additional number of cups specified on the clock at the first attempt.

Mukade In Japanese sword mounts; a name applied to a centipede. Naturalistic or conventionalized designs of a centipede are often used for decoration on Japanese armor and sword mounts. This is in commemoration of the slaying of the giant centipede by Tawara Toda in the 10th century. Centipede designs are often seen on tsuba in the form of a ring of wire parallel to the edge crossed by short wires.

Mulberry Wood See *Murier Wood*.

Mule Chest In English cabinetwork; the name originally applied to an early 18th century oak chest which was fitted in a low frame or stand designed with a row of drawers and mounted on four relatively short legs. This form of chest made in walnut and later in mahogany was quite popular during the first half of the 18th century and was used for storing blankets, linens and draperies. Many were provided with brass handles on the sides in order to remove the chest from the stand. Slight variations sometimes occurred in the design. Chests of this type mounted on a stand were also popular in America and because they were primarily used as a receptacle for blankets they are commonly called blanket chests.

MULE CHEST, ENGLISH

Mull The name is given in Scotland to a snuff box. It derived its name from a type of machine in which tobacco was ground. Occasionally the large mull was fashioned from the small end of a horn and was decorated with silver.

Münden In German ceramics; a faïence manufactory was started at Münden, Hanover, around 1737 by Carl Friedrich von Hanstein who was granted a privilege in 1755. After 1793 it chiefly produced cream-colored earthenware in the English style. A mark of three crescents from the coat-of-arms of von Hanstein was an accepted mark. Especially typical of their wares were plates with open basketwork rims having forget-me-nots at the intersections of the plaited work and vases with pierced double walls. The painted decoration was usually in high temperature colors.

Munich Tapestries A tapestry manufactory was established at Munich in 1718 by the Duke of Bavaria. It operated until around 1800. Many of the Munich tapestries were designed from the cartoons of the court painter, Christian Winck. See *Tapestry*.

Muntin In furniture construction; a vertical or upright member of a framework having an intermediate or central portion. It is similar to a stile which occupies the outside position. See *Stile*.

Murano   See *Venetian Glass*.

Murier Wood   The wood of the mulberry tree, *morus nigra*, used for inlay and cabinetwork especially by the French ébénistes. It is soft and its color is white and yellow.

Muromachi   The name of the historical period in Japan, 1338–1573. It is called the Ashikaga period. See *Japanese Periods*.

Musashi   In Japanese ceramics; the province of Musashi has a number of potteries almost all of which are near or within the city of Tokyo. The pottery is lacking in any individual characteristics. Records state that the first pottery was built at Akasaka in 1630 by potters from Osaka. Included among the potters working at a later date was the Kyōto potter, Kenzan.

Muscadier Wood   See *Nutmeg Wood*.

Music Stand   In English furniture; the characteristic article of furniture used to support music which is now called a music stand was called a music desk in the 18th century English trade catalogues. These desks or stands to support music were also used to support books and were quite plentiful during the second half of the 18th century. The majority were designed with a tripod base. From around 1760 onwards metal candle branches were often provided on each side of the music stand and from around 1780 the music stand was made with a sliding staff. This staff, which slides into the stem or standard, superseded the earlier ratchet form used for adjusting the top. See *Canterbury*.

Muskabad   See *Sultanabad Rug*.

MUSTARD POT

Musket   A firearm used by the infantry from around the middle of the 16th century. Originally it was clumsy and heavy and was fired from a rest. During the 17th century the musket was improved and the rest was dispensed with. The musket was fired by a matchlock. In a broad sense the term is applied to the firearms that preceded the rifle which came into general use around the middle of the 19th century.

Musketoon   The term is applied to a short musket with a large caliber. It was rather of the blunderbuss type.

Mustard Pot   In English silver; a small silver vessel used at the table to hold mustard. It was usually cylindrical or oval in form with a handle and a movable glass liner. The lid, which usually had a thumbpiece, was nearly always notched for the stem of a spoon. The mustard pot was introduced in the Early Georgian period and the earliest extant example dated 1737 is made of pierced work with a glass liner. In the latter part of the 18th century the mustard pot was often fitted in a frame with cruets and casters.

Mustard Spoon   In English silver; a miniature silver spoon usually formed in the shape of a small sauce ladle. It was introduced at the same time as the mustard pot.

Mutchkin   A Scottish liquid measure equal to one half of a Scottish chopin or three fourths of an English pint. A vessel of this capacity was commonly made in pewter. See *Chopin*; *Measures*.

Mutton-Fat Jade   See *Jade*.

Myall Wood   A hard fragrant Australian acacia wood, *acacia pendula*, used for inlay and cabinetwork, having a reddish or purplish color. See *Violet Wood*.

Nabeshima Ware In Japanese ceramics; Prince Nabeshima established kilns in the Hizen province with Korean potters around 1600. However, porcelain was not made until around 1660. These wares were made for Prince Nabeshima who kept them for his personal use and also gave them as presents. In addition to the colored enamelled porcelain or Iro Nabeshima, which is the finest Nabeshima ware, Nabeshima kilns also made celadon and underglaze blue and white. A characteristic enamelled porcelain shape was a deep plate or a low flat bowl on a rather high foot rim, which very often had a finely drawn "comb" pattern. Included among the motifs were blossoms drawn in a free naturalistic manner and bold and simple geometrical designs. The colors were iron red, a soft fresh green, pale yellow, lilac purple and occasionally turquoise blue or black; these colors were supplemented with underglaze blue. Nabeshima is generally regarded to be the finest Japanese enamelled porcelain. The kilns are still active. When clan control was abolished in 1868, the quality of the ware suffered as quantity became an important consideration. See *Hizen Ware*; *Okochi*.

Nailsea In English glass; glassmaking flourished at the town of Nailsea, which is in the Bristol district, for about 85 years. The Nailsea glass works were opened in 1788 by John Robert Lucas, and, after several changes in ownership, finally closed in 1873. Nailsea produced a wide variety of articles, such as ornamental flasks, bottles, mugs, jugs, bowls, objects of superstition such as witch balls, and many novelty pieces such as rolling pins, pipes, bells and canes. These articles were fabricated from different kinds of glass. Some were made from a bottle glass that ranged in color from a dark green to a dark brown. Their most characteristic decoration was a scattering of spots and irregular splashes of white. Articles were also made from a pale lucid green bottle glass. Many articles were made of a clear glass and were decorated with threads, loops and stripes in white enamel. Other pieces were made of either clear or colored glass and were ornamented with colored and opaque white threads, loops, stripes and spiral effects. As a rule Nailsea glass was inferior in quality and in workmanship to that produced at Bristol. Much of the charm of the typical Nailsea glass was in its rather crude, but striking, primitive decoration. See *Witch Ball*; *Paperweight*.

Namazlik A Perso-Turkish term meaning a prayer rug. A small Oriental rug; it can usually be recognized by the point or niche at one end of the central field, representing the niche of the mosque. Every faithful Mohammedan owns a prayer rug and when he prays he spreads the rug on the ground with the apex of the niche toward Mecca, and prostrates himself in reverence, his head resting in the angle. The width of the prayer rug is from 2 to 4 feet and the length from 4 to 6 feet.

Namban In Japanese sword mounts; a design frequently used for decorating sword fittings. It is usually worked in iron and is characterized by elaborate interlaced scrolls and dragons pierced in openwork designs. When the namban design was used on a tsuba it frequently contained a loose ball, representing the pearl the dragon is guarding, which can be moved through openings that appear less than its diameter. Namban was a popular form of decorative design in the 17th century and the name is also given to the thousand monkey design.

Name Chest In American cabinetwork; a colloquial term given to an early American chest having a name carved or painted on the chest, such as is occasionally found on

NABESHIMA PLATE

some chests similar to a Hadley chest and a Pennsylvania Dutch chest. See *Hadley Chest*; *Pennsylvania Dutch Chest*.

Nanako In Japanese sword mounts; the name *nanako* or fish roe is applied to a surface or background pattern used for the fine mountings for Japanese swords. It is a pattern of minute raised dots executed by a sharply struck cupped punch. The metal most frequently used is shakudo although gold and copper are sometimes used. These minute dots are seldom more than one one-hundredth of an inch in diameter. The technical skill required to execute these various nanako patterns is remarkable since the dots are accurately and perfectly arranged in either straight or concentric lines. In addition to gonome nanako and daimyō nanako there are other intricate patterns. One pattern has a smaller dot raised on each of the regular dots; another has two smaller dots superimposed on each of the original dots; and a third pattern has separated dots with the background space stamped with flowers so minute that they cannot be seen with the naked eye. See *Gonome Nanako*; *Daimyō Nanako*; *Ishime*.

Nancy Tapestries During the first quarter of the 18th century Duke Leopold, d. 1729, established a tapestry atelier near his palace at Nancy. The weavers were from the Gobelins. They were commissioned to commemorate in tapestry the warlike virtues of his father, Duke Charles V of Lorraine, based on the paintings of Charles Herbel, d. 1703. Charles Mitté was one of the manufacturers employed. See *Tapestry*.

Nanking Yellow In Chinese ceramics; a thin pale golden brown glaze that is invariably brownish. It was introduced during the K'ang Hsi reign and was chiefly found in narrow bands or in broad washes, separating or encircling blue designs. It was much used during the last half of the 17th century on wares sent to Europe, such as on small jars, bottles and similar articles.

Nanking Ware In Chinese ceramics; the

PERSIAN NARGHILE

terms *Nanking china* and *Nanking ware* were popularly applied, especially in England and America in the late 19th century, to the Chinese blue and white porcelain that was so enthusiastically collected. It was the blue and white porcelain of the Ch'ing dynasty and especially that made during the K'ang Hsi reign, 1662–1722, which was the finest. This exported ware was usually in the pure Chinese tradition and was seldom made in forms especially for the export trade. See *Blue and White Ch'ing*.

Nantgarw In English ceramics; a porcelain manufactory was started at Nantgarw, Glamorgan, Wales, in 1813 by William Billingsley and Samuel Walker. From 1814 it was transferred to Swansea for a year or two and was reopened before 1817. It closed in 1822. The usual factory mark was "Nantgarw", impressed, which was also used for a while at Swansea. The manufactory made a very translucent soft paste porcelain of a fine white color. Unfortunately it was apt to lose its shape in the kiln. Tablewares were the principal production. The painted decoration was in accordance with the contemporary decoration on Paris porcelain. Various dealers bought much of the porcelain and had it painted in London.

Nara The Nara or Tempyo period of Japan A.D. 710–794. See *Japanese Periods*.

Narghile A smoking pipe with a long, flexible tube in which the smoke is drawn through a bowl containing water. It is oriental in origin. The bowl was originally made from a coconut shell. Later it was made from porcelain, metal and glass. It is also called a hubble bubble and a hookah.

Nashi-Ji In Japanese sword mounts; the term applied to a form of ishime work resembling the texture of the skin of a pear. See *Ishime*.

Nashi-Ji In Japanese lacquer; a form of lacquer work having coats of lacquer at various depths sprinkled with gold or silver, resembling the skin of a pear. See *Japanese Lacquer*.

Nassau Stoneware In German ceramics; see *Westerwald*.

Nautilus Shell Cup In German silver; a decorative standing cup made of the nautilus shell and finely mounted in silver. It rested on a handsomely worked silver stem and foot. Occasionally the shell was made into the shape of an ostrich or a swan. Frequently the body of the cup was made of small pieces of shell worked together with silver and with some enamelling. The cup was introduced around 1550. It was also made in other European countries. See *Standing Cup*.

Near Eastern Ware In ceramics; see *Persian and Near Eastern Pottery*; *Turkish Pottery*.

Nécessaire A French term meaning a small coffre, casket or étui. Nécessaires are mentioned in French records as early as the 14th century and were divided in compartments to carry writing and needlework accessories, articles for the dinner service for traveling and later tea and coffee services. Smaller nécessaires were used for toilet articles. The term is now applied especially to the elaborate and beautiful nécessaires used for traveling or placed upon a table, which were fashionable in the 18th century, particularly in France. The nécessaire was about 4 to 9 inches in height and proportionately wide. The case was often made of striped agate and mounted in finely chased gold. The interior of the case was exquisitely fitted with gold-mounted cut glass scent bottles, a gold-mounted powder box and mirror, a gold thimble, scissors and centimeter rule, together with a spoon, ivory writing tablets and other necessary articles. The name is also given to any small fitted dressing or make-up case carried by a French lady. The difference between a nécessaire and an étui is that the former is always fitted while the latter is an empty case. See *Etui*; *Souvenir*.

Needle Painted The term applied to a picture executed in fine embroidery work. See *Embroidery*.

Needlepoint In lace-making; the name given to lace made with a needle on a parchment pattern in distinction to bobbin lace which is made with bobbins. See *Lace*.

Needlework A general term for work produced by hand, with a needle; in particular, all kinds of handmade embroidery.

Needlework Carpets See *Embroidered Rugs*.

Nef A large and elaborate piece of medieval plate made in the form of a ship. It was principally made of silver and occasionally of gold. Its original purpose was to hold the knives and other table utensils, the goblet and the salt used by the master of the house. It was chiefly used as a table ornament. The costliness of the nef reflected the affluence of its owner.

Neo-Classic In style of ornament; see *Classic Revival*.

Neo-Gothic In cabinetwork; see *Charles X*; *Smith, George*; *Gothic, English, Regency*.

Nephrite See *Jade*.

Nest of Drawers In English cabinetwork; a miniature form of a chest of drawers. The nest of drawers was made throughout the 18th century and its design followed the different successive styles for the chest of drawers.

Nest of Tables In English cabinetwork; the nest of tables was introduced in England rather late in the 18th century. These tables which were small and light in structure were also called quartetto tables since a complete set was composed of four tables. The tables were graduated in size so that each one fitted under another, and were so designed that each table could be drawn out of each other. According to contemporary records these tables were generally found in the drawing room and were used for refreshments. The nest of tables was illustrated in Sheraton's CABINET DICTIONARY See *Table Gigogne*.

Nest of Trays In Japanese lacquer; the name

NAUTILUS SHELL,
SILVER-MOUNTED NEF

nest of trays or *kasane* meaning one over the other, a pile or set, is given to a tier of lacquered trays so designed that each one is stacked upon the other to form a block-like or box-like arrangement. The kasane generally comprises three and occasionally five trays and is furnished with a lid. It is made in a variety of sizes and serves numerous purposes. One of its principal uses is a dining tray or ozen. The small kasane is often finely decorated in either raised or incised lacquer work.

Netsuke In Japanese art; the netsuke is an extremely small sculptured piece, of delicate and exquisite workmanship, made of ivory, wood, metal and sometimes porcelain. The netsuke was attached to the end of the cord and served as a button or catch between the girdle and the kimono to hold an inrō, a money or tobacco pouch. It is believed to have been introduced around the middle of the 16th century, about the same time as the inrō. The most noted netsuke carvers were in Osaka, Kyōto and Edo or Tokyo. The finest workmanship in netsuke carving was achieved during the early part of the 19th century and lasted until the fall of the Tokugawa shogunate in 1867. Netsuke are occasionally classified by the materials used, such as ivory, wood, bone, earthenware, lacquer, metal or stone; or they may be classified according to subjects, such as stage masks or dolls. However, they are chiefly classified according to their form into katabori, kagamibuta, manju and ryūsa. Katabori or figure-carved netsuke represents a human figure, animal form or some similar subject realistically treated. The kagamibuta netsuke comprises a bowl made of ivory or horn designed with a lid or cover of metal. The cord is fastened to the underside of the lid and passes through a hole pierced in the bowl. The cover is finely carved. As a rule the artistic value of this form of netsuke is in the carving on the lid rather than in the carving on the ivory bowl. The manjū or bun-shaped netsuke derives its name from a kind of Japanese cake which is of similar

NETSUKE

shape. It is a round flat piece of ivory, horn, wood or bamboo and is carved. It is made in either one or two pieces. Variations occur and some are square or oval in shape. The ryūsa netsuke is similar to the manjū netsuke, except that the former is made hollow inside by the turning lathe. It is carved in openwork designs of birds, blossoms, insects and arabesques. The sashi netsuke is a long narrow piece, at the end of which is a pierced hole to run the string through, and the other part is put through the girdle. The name *ichiraku* is given to a form of netsuke which is woven with thin rattan or wire into the shape of a gourd or some other object. See *Inrō*.

Neufforge, Jean-François de 1714–1791. French architect, sculptor and engraver. He began publishing an important work in 1757 entitled RECEUIL ÉLÉMENTAIRE D'ARCHITECTURE, which was finally completed in 1772. His work is especially identified with the Classic Revival. He illustrated classic interiors as early as 1761 and made designs for furniture in the early phase of the French Classic Revival around 1768.

Nevers In French ceramics; during the 17th century much fine faïence distinctive for its bold drawings and rich colors was made at Nevers. The eminent position attained by Nevers during the 17th century was lost in the succeeding century. It remained a flourishing productive center but the quality of the decoration declined rapidly. Potteries are still in existence. No factory mark was ever used. Faïence figures were made from the earliest times. It seems that only high temperature colors were used at Nevers, and that the red always gave them trouble. Beautiful colors and strong drawings were characteristic of the Nevers style. A soft manganese purple was always a popular color at Nevers, especially for outline drawing. During the first half of the 17th century borders of continuous figures and later of flowers were much favored. Some of the polychrome painted decoration of this period ranks among the best of French faïence. The so-called Bleu Persan style was introduced during the second half of the 17th century and is probably the most important Nevers creation. The motifs chiefly consisted of foliage and birds of a French or Chinese character painted in opaque white and yellow on a deep blue ground. Sometimes, however very rarely, the blue ground was simply marbled in white. The forms were of Chinese shapes such as double gourd-shaped vases. Painted decoration in blue and manganese colors became fashionable during the second half of the 17th century and practically supplanted the earlier polychrome decoration of the first half of the 17th century. This was due to the vogue created by Chinese porcelains and the faïence made at Delft.

Nevers In French glass; glassmaking flourished in Nevers from the second half of the 16th century. Today Nevers is principally known for the small glass figures made by lamp work which were popular during the 17th and 18th century. Generally no higher than five inches they depicted a wide variety of religious and secular subjects and were prized possessions for the collector's cabinet. Small figure subjects made in Nevers are practically indistinguishable from those made in Paris and elsewhere.

New Canton In English ceramics; see *Bow*.

New England Windsor Armchair In cabinetwork; in this variety of Windsor chair the back and arms are made from a continuous piece of bent wood. See *Windsor Chair*.

New Hall In English ceramics; a company of five Staffordshire potters started a porcelain manufactory at New Hall, Shelton, Staffordshire, in 1782, having in the preceding year bought the Bristol patent for hard paste porcelain and for the sale of china clay and china stone. Simply decorated wares in the manner of the cottage style formerly used at Bristol were typical. Later, from about 1810 to about 1825 when the factory is believed to have closed, a rather glassy bone porcelain was made and was marked

with the name of the factory, "New Hall", printed in red. This later ware was also decorated in a simple cottage style.

Nickel Silver See *German Silver*.

Niderviller In French ceramics; a faïence manufactory was started at Niderviller, Moselle, in Lorraine, in 1754 by Baron Jean-Louis de Beyerlé with the assistance of artists and workers from Strasbourg. Porcelain was also made after 1765. From late in the 18th century faïence fine wares were made. The manufactory is still in existence. Although the early wares were generally not marked, sometimes "JLB" in a monogram was found between 1754 to 1770. Crossed "C's" under a crown was one of the marks used from 1770 to 1793. Included among the late 18th century marks was "Niderviller", impressed. The early wares in the Rococo style are generally regarded to be the most important and strongly reflect the influence of Strasbourg. The painted decoration was executed with admirable skill and taste. Figure painting in crimson monochrome was much favored. After 1770 the so-called Décor Bois decoration was frequently used and it is generally believed to have been an original Niderviller creation. A more individual style of work was attained in their faïence figures which were distinctive for their delicate modelling and coloring. The porcelain figures were frequently in biscuit, and often revealed the same finished and delicate workmanship found in the faïence figures. The later tablewares were rather undistinguished and were decorated in the contemporary Louis XVI style with sprigs of cornflowers and other similar patterns found on Paris porcelain. See *Décor Bois*.

Niello A form of inlay work in which delicate and minute incised designs are made on a highly polished surface and are filled with a black metallic amalgam. Although gold and bronze were occasionally used, silver was the principal metal, since the contrast between the silver and the refined

NEW ENGLAND WINDSOR
ARMCHAIR

and exquisite black designs was the most effective. The art of niello work was practiced as early as the Roman Empire and has survived as one of outstanding arts of the Far East. See *Inlay*.

Nieuwer Amstel In Dutch ceramics; see *Weesp*.

Night Table In English cabinetwork; the night table or pot cupboard as it is referred to in contemporary English furniture literature was introduced early in the 18th century. A popular variety during the second half of the 18th century was similar to the enclosed washing stand of that period. It was a small oblong table provided with a removable tray top, fitted with handgrips, which was over a cupboard with one or two doors. Sometimes a shallow drawer was below the cupboard compartment. It was mounted on four quadrangular tapering straight legs. The close-stool chair was also introduced early in the 18th century. See *Chaise Percée*.

Niku-Bori In Japanese sword mounts; a term applied to carving in relief. The various forms of relief are usu-niku-bori, low relief; chiu-niku-bori, half relief; and atsu-niku-bori, high relief.

Ninsei 1596–1666. In Japanese ceramics; a Japanese painter and potter of Kyōto. His full name is Nonomura Seibei; however, he is better known by his artist name of Ninsei. In pursuing his art career he studied under masters of the two principal schools of Japanese art, namely the Tosa and the Kanō school. He was a skillful painter. Ninsei's influence on Japanese ceramics is immeasurable. It is generally accepted that the secret of decorating in vitrifiable enamels, which was first practiced in Hizen, came into the possession of Ninsei, and that Ninsei imparted this knowledge to others. His earliest work was influenced by Chinese and Korean designs; however, he later created a distinctive style of his own that was entirely Japanese in feeling. He first worked in kilns in the district of Omuro, Kyōto. Later he

IMARI NISHIKI-DE PLATE

traveled all over Japan practicing and teaching his theories and technique. His pieces consisted chiefly of utensils for use in the tea ceremony. The body of his ware was fine and hard and the glaze was characterized by a fine network of crackle. His favorite glazes were a cream color, a grey and a metallic black. His designs were elaborate and executed in fine detail. Ninsei's work reflected his Japanese art heritage by his use of undecorated spaces. His work has always been extensively copied. See *Kyōto*.

Nipt Diamond Waies In glass; a diamond or lozenge-shaped network on glassware, produced by nipping together vertical threads of applied glass.

Niris An Oriental rug belonging to the Persian classification. It is rather coarsely woven. The foundation is of wool; the pile, which is of medium length, is also of wool. The ends are sometimes finished with a web and a loose short fringe, sometimes with a checked selvage. The designs vary. Essentially the rug seems more like a Turkestan product than one of southern Persia. It derived its name from the salt lake Niris, in the province of Laristan, in Persia. See *Persian Rugs*.

Nishiki-de In Japanese ceramics; a variety of porcelain made in Arita with elaborate over-all designs in underglaze blue and colored enamels featuring a prominence of blue, red and gold. These so-called brocade patterns were freely adopted especially at the English porcelain manufactories of Worcester and Derby where they remained fashionable for a long time. See *Imari*; *Chinese Imari*.

Noggin A small cup or mug; it is also a small amount of liquid equal to about one gill. See *Measures*.

Noir Fin Marble See *Belgium Marble, Black*.

Nonsuch Chest In English cabinetwork; a late 16th century oak chest having an inlaid decoration representing the palace of Henry

VIII at Cheam, called Nonsuch. The palace is conventionally portrayed with its many cupolas, dormer windows and towers with lantern-shaped roofs. These chests have been found in England, the Scandinavian countries and Germany. See *Chest*.

Norman, Samuel English cabinetmaker working around 1758 to 1763. Norman and his partners John Mayhew and James Whittle conducted a business on King Street, Covent Garden. They did cabinetwork, upholstery, carving and gilding. In 1759 their shop was burned to the ground. Mortimer's UNIVERSAL DIRECTOR in 1763 refers to Norman as "Sculptor and Carver to their Majesties and Surveyor of the curious carvings in Windsor Castle" and his address is Soho Square.

Normandy In French Provincial; an old province in northern France on the English Channel; it is now the departments of Eure, Seine-Inférieure, Orne, Calvados and Manche. The provincial furniture of Normandy was as distinctly French as that of Provence. It was notable for its fine proportions, for its refined lines and delicate detail and for its rich carved decoration. The armoire was one of their choice pieces. Steel buttress hinges and elongated pierced keyplates were much in evidence; however, they were not as florid as those found on Provençal cupboards. They also made a wide variety of charming small wall shelves. In addition to the native woods, they made some of their fine 18th century pieces of mahogany and ebony. Especially fine were slat-back chairs designed in either the Louis XV or Louis XVI styles. Sometimes these chairs were painted. See *French Provincial*.

Normandy Lace Bobbin-made laces were produced from the beginning of the 16th century in the French province of Normandy and in the 18th century her lace manufacture made rapid progress. The laces of Mechlin, the guipures of Flanders, the black thread laces as well as other varieties were all successfully imitated. Havre, Dieppe, Honfleur, Eu and Fécamp were all important lace centers, producing double and single grounds, guipures and a variety of thick Valenciennes. It seems that after Havre the laces of Dieppe are considered to rank second in importance. The peasant lace-makers at Dieppe liked to give their laces names, such as Dentelle à la Vierge and Poussin. They made a variety of Valenciennes of much more simple design and workmanship.

Northamptonshire Lace The laces of the three English counties of Bedfordshire, Buckinghamshire and Northamptonshire were essentially very similar. The earliest laces of these three counties resembled the old Flemish patterns with a wavy and graceful design and a well-made ground. It seems that some of these designs were worked in with a needle on the net ground. Around 1778 the familiar locally-termed "point" ground was introduced, which date marks the beginning of the regular bobbin-made lace trade of these counties. This ground was praiseworthy for its clearness, and the designs were also of excellent workmanship. Of particular interest was the so-called baby lace with its "point" ground and designs of Lille and Mechlin inspiration. Many other grounds were used, such as trolly and double ground. Insertion lace became popular around 1830. Around 1850 Maltese guipures, "plaited" laces and raised plait were introduced, and the earlier and finer work with a "point" ground became increasingly scarce. See *Regency Point*; *Buckinghamshire*; *Bedfordshire*.

Northern Celadon In Chinese ceramics; see *Celadon*.

Norton, Captain John In American ceramics; a potter of Bennington, Vermont. See *Bennington*.

Nottingham In English ceramics; salt-glazed stoneware was produced at Nottingham from around 1690 to 1800. The most important stoneware was made from around 1700 to 1765. The grey body of the stoneware was concealed by a wash of ferruginous

LOUIS XV HANGING
CORNER SHELVES,
NORMANDY

clay which gave it a warm brown tone and a slight metallic sheen. The wares, which were distinctive for their well-proportioned forms, included cylindrical mugs, large and small jugs, two-handled loving cups, teapots, tea caddies and other similar articles. The decoration, chiefly consisting of geometrical and floral motifs, was generally incised and impressed with small stamps. Sometimes conventional flowers were painted from the dark brown slip used as a wash over the ware. Occasionally a clay grit was sprinkled on the surface to give it a roughened texture. It was used in horizontal bands and on jugs in the form of a bear. After the middle of the 18th century molded decoration was sometimes used, and at a still later date applied reliefs were often employed for decoration.

Nottingham Lace In lace-making; see *Limerick*.

Nove In Italian ceramics; a faïence and porcelain manufactory was established in 1728 at Nove, Venezia, by Giovanni Battista Antonibon. With the exception of a short interval between 1802 to 1824 the manufactory remained in the hands of the Antonibon family until in the 19th century. No regular factory mark seems to have been used on the faïence. The mark of a six- or eight-pointed star in red and more rarely in gold or blue enamel, with or without the word "Nove" was used on porcelain but rarely on faïence until the 19th century when it was commonly used on all wares. Much faïence of good quality was made in the Rococo style and was painted in high temperature colors from around the middle of the 18th century. The later faïence reflected the influence of Sèvres porcelain and was painted in enamel colors. Porcelain is believed to have been made from around 1752 onwards. It seems that the porcelain made at Nove was of a hybrid paste; no examples of hard paste porcelain are known. The best and most individual work belongs to a period from around 1760 to 1780. The

NUPPENBECHER

material was rather opaque and grey and the colors were lively and clean. Especially prominent was a deep glossy red enamel. The forms and painted decoration for the best work were fanciful and typically Italian with masquerade figures, Italian landscapes, peasant scenes and similar subjects. The later work was chiefly copied from Sèvres and other manufactories and had little distinction. Cream-colored earthenware of excellent quality was also made at Nove.

Nunome-Zōgan A Japanese inlay art. Nunome-Zōgan or reticulated inlaying is one of the two principal kinds of Japanese inlaying; the other being Hon-Zōgan. Delicate and elaborate diaper designs are inlaid with gold or silver on an iron surface. This method can consist of about ten processes when the designs are very intricate. The iron surface is heated sufficiently to develop a softness, and then a very thin sheet of gold or silver is hammered into the designs. By varying the proportions of the alloy different tones of gold can be obtained in the same design. See *Sumi-Zōgan*.

Nuppen In glass; an applied drop of glass widely used by the Germans to ornament such drinking glasses as the krautstrunk and roemer. See *Roemer*; *Prunt*; *Nuppenbecher*.

Nuppenbecher In German glass; a small beaker ornamented with applied pads or prunts. It was apparently a popular type of drinking vessel in Germany during the Middle Ages. It was made of an unrefined glass generally of a deep green color. It is one of the basic forms of German waldglas. See *Waldglas*.

Nuremberg In German ceramics; Nuremberg is generally regarded as the most important center for tile-work stoves from the 16th century onwards. Hafner ware jugs and mugs were also made. It seems also that many of the remaining examples of 16th century German majolica were made here. In 1712 two merchants established a faïence manufactory producing some of the most important faïence made in Germany. The best of this faïence was made from around 1715 to 1740 and was in a distinctive German Baroque style. Included among the productions were jugs with narrow necks, cylindrical tankards and plain and reeded dishes. Much of the painted decoration was in blue on a grey or pale blue ground. Other high temperature colors were also used; however, red was relatively rare. Especially fine was some work painted in blue in which web-like designs of Baroque scrollwork or foliage covered the entire surface. Panels with various subjects, such as coats-of-arms, landscapes and religious and mythological figure subjects, were finely painted and were enclosed within Baroque strapwork or scrollwork borders. No factory mark was used until about the middle of the 18th century when "NB" in monogram was used; however, painters' signatures were quite common. After 1770 the manufactory showed evidence of decline. The influence of Meissen porcelain was evident and some of the work was painted in enamel colors. See *Hafner.*

Nuremberg Egg   The term *Nuremberg egg* is often applied to a watch of flattened oval shape. It is reasonable to suppose that this type of watch originated in Nuremberg where it appears to have been made as early as 1600. These watches, which were especially popular from 1610 to 1625, were oval or egg-shaped and the cases were of pierced and engraved silver and brass, with the back and front having hinged covers. The watches were generally worn on a chatelaine.

Nursing Chair   In English cabinetwork; a term sometimes applied to a chair characterized by a low seat. See *Chauffeuse.*

Nursing Lamp   A small early American fluid lamp. See *Sparking Lamp.*

Nutmeg Box   In English silver; a small decorative container or box designed to hold nutmegs and generally fitted with a nutmeg grater. It was made in a variety of shapes, such as in the form of a shell, acorn, egg, miniature urn or oval box. Occasionally it was made of shell such as a mottled cowrie shell and was mounted in silver. Another variety was a hanging grater which was generally demilune or cylindrical in shape. The nutmeg box and grater was introduced in the early 18th century.

Nutmeg Wood   The wood of the nutmeg tree, *myristica fragrans*, of the East Indies, used for inlay and cabinetwork, especially by the French ébénistes. It is hard and its color is red and light yellow. It is also called muscadier wood.

Nymphenburg   In German ceramics; a German porcelain manufactory under the patronage of Prince Max III Joseph of Bavaria, d. 1777, was established in 1753 at Neudeck-ob-der-Au and removed to Nymphenburg in 1761. It is one of the seven great 18th century German porcelain manufactories. From around 1755 to 1767 its productions in the Rococo style were unrivalled for their exquisite decoration and for their modelling of figures. The manufactory suffered a financial crisis in 1767 and never regained its earlier position. It operated as a Bavarian State possession until 1862 when it was leased privately. It still is in existence. The factory mark was the Bavarian shield of arms and it varied in size and shape. The figures in the Rococo style were remarkable for their simplification of form, for their flexible movement and for their flowing rhythmical lines. The models showed a humor and fantasy symbolic of the make-believe spirit of the Rococo. Many of the figures were not painted; however, when color was used it was treated in an original manner that did not disturb the lines. Of especial interest were some biscuit figures, busts and portrait reliefs in the Neo-Classic style. The painted decoration in the Rococo style on tablewares was outstanding for its beautiful color and execution. Naturalistic flowers, fruit, pastoral landscapes and

NUREMBERG EGG

figure subjects were much favored. Especially fine and characteristic were the beautiful gilt, blue and pink borders having a delicate lace-like quality. The tableware made in the Neo-Classic style was of fine quality; however, the painted decoration was in accordance with the prevailing fashion for porcelain and revealed little originality.

NYMPHENBURG FIGURE

O

Oak The wood of the oak tree, *quercus robur*, used in cabinetwork. It is a hard compact wood and its color is yellow white. Oak wood was the principal wood used in making fine furniture during the Gothic period in England and in France. Oak was used in England until the time of the Restoration in 1660, when it was superseded by walnut for making fine furniture. In America it was used later than in England. Walnut gradually began to supplant oak in France from around the middle of the 16th century.

Oberkampf, Philip 1738–1815, a celebrated German cloth printer and dyer. He received his training in his father's workshop. At the age of nineteen he went to Paris and became a French citizen. In 1760 he founded his manufactory for linen and cotton printed fabrics at the village of Jouy, which was near Versailles. The designs were usually of a pictorial nature and were generally done in a single soft French tone on a light or natural-colored ground. His printed fabrics became famous almost immediately and in 1783 Louis XVI made his workshop a Manu-facture Royale. His early prints were chiefly in a deep rose and the designs were princi-pally inspired by Chinese art. His later prints were to a great extent scenes from pastoral life and from allegorical and mythological subjects. Many of his greatest designs were done by Jean Baptiste Huet, a well-known tapestry designer and cartoonist working around 1780 at the Beauvais Tapestry Works. See *Toile de Jouy*.

Occasional Table In cabinetwork; the de-velopment of tables, like all articles of furni-ture, was from the simple to the complex and from the few to the many. In addition to the specialized varieties of tables, such as card, writing, dressing and work tables, there was also a marked need for tables intended for general use as occasions arose.

The term *occasional table* is given to this large variety of tables suitable for many purposes. The occasional table was made in the differ-ent successive styles of furniture and it conformed in form and in ornament to the prevailing fashion in table design. See *Center Table*.

Odjaklik A Perso-Turkish term meaning a hearth rug. The term is applied to a small Oriental rug. It can usually be recognized by the pointed formation of the central field at both ends. In the Orient it is spread before the fireplace on the arrival of a guest. It is usually of the finest workmanship.

Oeben, Jean François c. 1720–1763. It is generally accepted that Oeben was the great cabinetmaker during the reign of Louis XV. He was appointed Ébéniste du Roi in 1754. Oeben was primarily a marqueteur and the bronzes for his furniture were largely exe-cuted by Philippe Caffieri, 1714–1774. His cabinetwork possessed remarkable grace and beauty and was executed in the highest degree of craftsmanship. His delicate and exquisite floral marquetry which was inlaid in a ground of choice woods was unrivalled. Toward the end of his life he favored the classic style and his later work was essentially of a transitional nature between the Louis XV and Louis XVI styles. It is more than probable that he never would have enjoyed such great fame if he had not been commis-sioned by the king, in 1760, to produce the celebrated Bureau du Roi. The Bureau du Roi was completed after his death by his pupil Riesener whose signature appears on it. It is generally believed that Oeben had completed the construction and the designs for the marquetry before his death. See *Bureau du Roi*.

Oeil-de-Perdrix In French ceramics; a re-petitive pattern or a diaper arrangement of dotted circles on various colored grounds.

TOILE DESIGNED BY
OBERKAMPF

It was introduced on Sèvres porcelain around 1760.

Oeil-de-Perdrix Marble   See *Griotte d'Italie Marble*.

Oeil-de-Perdrix Wood   See *Partridge Wood*.

OLD NANKING VASE

Oettingen-Schrattenhofen   In German ceramics; a faïence manufactory was started in 1735 at Oettingen, Bavaria, and moved in 1737 to Schrattenhofen. It was active well into the 19th century. Especially characteristic of their productions were cylindrical tankards with boldly painted Rococo motifs in high temperature colors. They were marked "Schrattenhofen". The more common wares for daily use were not marked. It is generally believed that a brown ware similar to that made at Ansbach and at Bayreuth was also made. Later the manufactory made white and cream-colored earthenware.

Offenbach   In German ceramics; a faïence manufactory was established at Offenbach, near Frankfurt-on-Main, in 1739, by Philipp Friedrich Lay. It seems that the factory was still active in the early 19th century. Included among the marks was an "O" with a double "F" written as one. Tablewares painted in high temperature colors in a peasant style with flowers, fruit, birds and figure subjects were the characteristic productions.

Ogee   A molding in the form of a cyma reversa, which means a molding comprising a continuous double curve that is convex above and concave below. The term is also applied indiscriminately to a molding in the form of a cyma recta, which is concave above and convex below. See *Cyma Curve*; *Molding*.

Ogee Bracket Foot   In cabinetwork; see *Bracket Foot*.

Oil Spot Temmoku   In Chinese ceramics; see *Honan Temmoku*.

Okochi   In Japanese ceramics; kilns were established around 1660 at Okochi, which is about ten miles from Arita in the Hizen province, under the patronage of Prince Nabeshima. Its finest period for Iro Nabeshima was from around 1720 to 1770. Nabeshima wares were imitated at other kilns. See *Nabeshima Ware*.

Old English Pattern   In English silver; a term applied to spoon design introduced in the 1760's. In this design of spoon, which is either plain or ornamented, the end of the stem curves backward instead of forward. This form of silver spoon has continued in fashion from the third quarter of the 18th century to the present time.

Old Nanking   In Chinese ceramics; a name given to the blue and white porcelain made at Ching-tê Chên. See *Ching-tê Chên*; *Blue and White Ming*; *Blue and White Ch'ing*; *Nanking Ware*.

Oleander Wood   The wood of the oleander tree, *nerium odorum*, or laurier aromatique, was widely used for inlay and cabinetwork, especially by the French ébénistes. It is hard and its color is reddish yellow. It comes from the East Indies.

Olivewood   See *Olivier Wood*.

Olivier Wood   The wood of the olive tree, *olea europaea*, used for inlay and cabinetwork, especially by the French ébénistes. It is hard and its color is yellow with brown veins.

Omuro   In Japanese ceramics; a kiln for making colored enamelled pottery was established at Omuro, which is a little north of Kyōto, shortly after the middle of the 17th century. Ninsei was first working at Omuro before he traveled around Japan. The enamelled pottery was similar to that made at Awata and Iwakura. It had a white clay body. The glaze was cream-colored and most frequently finely crackled. It was decorated with overglaze enamels of red, green and light blue. Sometimes gold was used in the decoration. See *Ninsei*.

Onion Foot   In cabinetwork; a flattened ball foot in a form supposed to resemble that of an onion. See *Ball Foot*; *Foot*.

SÈVRES WALL SCONCE—*French, 18th Century.*
The Metropolitan Museum of Art, gift of The Samuel H. Kress Foundation,
1958.

PORCELAIN GROUP—*German, 18th Century.*
The Metropolitan Museum of Art, gift of R. Thornton Wilson,
in memory of Florence Ellsworth Wilson, 1950.

MEISSEN PORCELAIN—*German, early 18th Century.*
BEAKER AND SUGAR BOWL. *The Metropolitan Museum of Art, gift of*
R. Thornton Wilson, 1950, in memory of Florence Ellsworth Wilson.
PLATE. *The Metropolitan Museum of Art, gift of R. Thornton Wilson,*
1954, in memory of Florence Ellsworth Wilson.

SÈVRES POT-POURRI VASE—*French, mid-18th Century.*
The Metropolitan Museum of Art, gift of The Samuel H. Kress Foundation 1958

Onion Pattern   In German ceramics; see *Zwiebelmuster*.

Onolzbach   In German ceramics; see *Ansbach*.

Onslow Pattern   In English silver; a stem used on silver spoons in which the end of the stem terminates in a volute scroll. It was named after a member of Parliament during the reign of George II, 1727–1760.

Onyx   See *Quartz*.

Onyx Marble   See *Alabaster*.

Opalescent Dewdrop Glass   In American glass; see *Hobnail*.

Open Salt   See *Salt-Cellar*.

Openwork   In cabinetwork; any wood carving that is pierced through or perforated, such as an openwork splat in a chair back. See *Fretwork*. The term is also used in lace-making, embroidery, cutwork and crocheting to denote the spaces between the parts which have been closely worked.

Oppenord, Gilles-Marie   See *Meissonier, Juste Aurèle*.

Opus Anglicanum   In needlework; an early form of English embroidery in which certain fine stitches, such as long and short stitches, were worked in such a manner that the finished piece of embroidery resembled a painting. In a general sense the term is applied to English embroidery work of the 12th and 13th centuries. It is also spelled opus anglicum.

Opus Araneum   In lace-making; during the Middle Ages the name was given to darned lace or netting having a spider work appearance. A early form of darned lace or netting was characterized by an open and irregular form of darning that resembled the web of a spider. See *Darned Netting*.

Opus Consutum   In needlework; the name was applied during the Middle Ages to cutwork or appliqué work.

Opus Filatorium   In lace-making; during the Middle Ages the term was given to darned netting or darned lace. See *Darned Netting*.

Opus Tiratum   In needlework; the name was used during the Middle Ages for drawn thread work or drawnwork.

Orange Wood   The French term is *oranger*. The wood of the orange tree, *citrus aurantium*, used for inlay and cabinetwork, especially by the French ébénistes. It is hard and its color is yellow and white.

Orders   In classic architecture; the name used to denote the columns which are composed of a base, shaft and capital with their different subordinate members surmounted by an entablature. The Five Orders are Doric, Ionic, Corinthian, Tuscan and Composite. The last two were added later and are Roman innovations. In England during the 18th century some of the cabinetmakers' trade catalogues included plates of the Five Orders with explanations as to their proportions and principal parts, the purpose being to associate cabinetwork with architecture. See *Pilaster*.

Oribe Ware   In Japanese ceramics; pottery ware made by Furuta Oribe, 1544–1615. He was a tea master of great fame and toward the end of the 16th century he was made a daimyō or feudal lord and had his castle near Kyōto. His pottery consisted of rather crude forms with dented shapes. Among his articles were bowls and fan-shaped dishes which are much favored by tea masters. The designs were of marked simplicity, such as blades of grass, several persimmons and a stalk or two of rice. The Japanese classify Oribe wares as green, red and black. All three types have a portion of the ground in a distinctive green glaze. The so-called red ware has a portion in a reddish brown glaze. The green and black wares have part of the ground covered in a greyish color glaze.

Oriental Alabaster   See *Alabaster*.

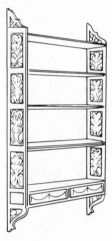

HEPPLEWHITE OPENWORK
HANGING SHELVES

Oriental Lowestoft In Chinese ceramics; see *Chinese Lowestoft.*

Oriental Rug A handmade rug woven in the Near East and Far East. The foundation is a warp of cotton, linen, wool or silk threads. Short pieces of colored wool, camels'-hair, goats'-hair or silk are knotted to each of the warp threads in such a manner that both ends of each tuft project in front. These tufts are tied with one of two kinds of knots; the sehna or the ghiordes knot. After a row of tufts has been completed a weft thread is run across the warp and above the range of tufts. As each row of tufts and weft are made, they are packed closely together by a blunt fork or comb-like instrument. Then the tufts are carefully trimmed to form an even surface. Oriental rugs are divided into six general classifications: Turkoman; Caucasian; Turkish; Persian; Chinese; India. Although it is generally accepted that rugs of some sort have been used since very primitive times little is known of their actual history. It is believed that the rugs used by the ancient Greeks were of a tapestry texture rather than a pile variety. The origin of hand-knotted or pile rugs is shrouded in obscurity. Literature pertaining to Oriental rugs suggests as their provenance the great plateaus of Persia, the plains of central Asia or the highlands of Anatolia. Undoubtedly carpet weaving was practiced from early times both in Persia and Anatolia. It seems a reasonable assumption that hand-knotted rugs were either invented in Persia or introduced in Persia by the nomad tribes from the North at a very early date. Apparently carpet weaving existed in Persia long before the 9th century A.D. The early craft was practiced only as a rural or tribal industry, and it was not until early in the 16th century with the establishment of the Sefavi dynasty in Persia that hand-knotted rugs reached their acme of craftmanship. Oriental rugs possess a remarkable beauty of design. A singular aspect of these designs is the manner in which the same patterns have been repeated

LOUIS XV ORMOLU
WALL SCONCE

again and again in the rugs of a given period, and in many examples have been handed down with little variation from one century to the following century. Geometrical designs have been generally favored by the nomads, while floral designs, especially when realistically treated, are usually associated with a sedentary population having superior technical equipment and the talent to create more ambitious and elegant rugs suitable for use in princely palaces. See *Eastern Loom*; *Sehna Knot*; *Ghiordes Knot.*

Orinak Rug See *Vagireh.*

Orléans In French ceramics; in 1753 a privilege was granted to Jacques-Etienne Dessaux de Romilly to start a faïence and porcelain manufactory at Orléans, Loiret. It was active until 1812. According to contemporary records it seems that considerable faïence and porcelain, presumed to be a soft paste, were produced. However it has always been difficult to identify early Orléans porcelain as well as faïence. It is believed that faïence decorated in the Strasbourg style with colored enamels was made during the early period. The mark registered for porcelain in 1766 was a crowned "O". Later the manufactory also made faïence fine or lead-glazed earthenware in the English style and agate and marbled earthenware also in the English style. These wares were often marked with either the name of the proprietor or the place. Towards the end of the 18th century other porcelain manufactories were also active in Orléans.

Orme Wood The wood of the elm tree, *ulmus campestris*, used for inlay and cabinetwork. It is hard and firm and its color is brown.

Ormolu In metal mounts; the term *ormolu* or ground gold (or moulu) was applied in France from the 16th century to gold leaf or gold that was ground and prepared for gilding bronze or other metals. Although in France the term *bronze doré* is now used instead of ormolu, in England the term *ormolu* has been used since the middle of the 18th century to denote objects of gilded bronze or brass, especially for furniture mounts. Fire gilding has been used since the Middle Ages. It is made by a mercuric process. The mercury is heated to a proper temperature and then the gold is added. The paste is applied to the metal with a wire brush. Then it is subjected to a burning temperature during which the mercury evaporates and only the gold is left on the surface. The metal with its gold finish is polished and burnished. Gilded bronze furniture mounts and appointments such as cartels, sconces and andirons made by the celebrated ciseleurs working in France during the 18th century are of unrivalled beauty and workmanship. In England the mounts on furniture were generally of cast brass until about 1750, and any mounts of the French type which were occasionally employed were imported. However, around 1760 with the advent of the Classic Revival ormolu mounts became fashionable in England and were used to decorate some of the very fine furniture, such as on commodes enriched with marquetry in the French taste. See *Boulton, Matthew*; *Thomire, Pierre Philippe*; *Gouthière, Pierre*; *Caffieri, Jacques*.

Orphrey In ecclesiastical costume; the term *orphrey* derived from the Latin *aurifrisium* meaning gold embroidery is applied to the ornamented bands or borders of gold and rich embroidery affixed to ecclesiastical vestments, such as to the chasuble and cope. The term is also applied to any rich embroidery or to a piece of richly embroidered fabric.

Orrery An instrument which shows the motions of the planets in the solar system by the rotation of balls operated by clockwork. Sometimes an orrery is fitted with a clock dial for telling time. It was invented about 1700 by George Graham and was made for Charles Boyle, the Earl of Orrery. See *Globe Stand*.

Orvieto In Italian ceramics; pottery was made at Orvieto, Umbria, as early as the 13th century. It produced a primitive type of majolica during the 14th and early 15th centuries painted in copper green and manganese purple. This type of green and purple decorated majolica was also made at Siena and Florence in Tuscany and at Faenza; however, Orvieto was probably the earliest center. The forms, which were often clumsy and of poor proportions, included jugs with very wide mouths, small dishes with two handles and other similar articles. The decoration was in relief and distinctly reflected Gothic influence. Thick foliage, starry flowers, animals and masks were much favored for decorative motifs. Crowned figure subjects treated in a Gothic style drawn in outline on a cross-hatched ground were a popular Orvieto decorative manner. See *Italian Majolica*.

Osterbro In Danish ceramics; a third Copenhagen faïence manufactory was founded at Osterbro in 1763 by Peter Hofnagel. He employed workers from other Copenhagen potteries and after a law suit he withdrew in 1769. It seems that the wares were painted in blue or in manganese and occasionally with touches of gilding. The quality of the material in the pieces ascribed to him is rather imperfect.

Ostrich Cup In silver; a tall, decorative standing cup. The body of the cup was made of an ostrich egg and was richly mounted in silver. It rested on an elaborately worked silver stem and foot. It was first made around the 15th century. See *Standing Cup*.

Ottoman Or Turkey Sofa. In English cabinetwork; a very low and long upholstered seat. Sheraton in his DRAWING BOOK refers to it as a fashionable novelty in imitation of the Turkish manner of sitting. He also illustrates an ottoman which extends the entire length of the room.

Ottomane Or Ottoman. In French cabinetwork; a variety of upholstered canapé or settee introduced in the Louis XV style. In this form of canapé the two ends are a continuation of the back which continue to curve around to form two semicircles.

LOUIS XV OTTOMANE

Generally a pillow is placed at each end. It is the same as the canapé à corbeille.

Ottweiler In German ceramics; a faïence and porcelain manufactory was started at Ottweiler in the Rhineland by Etienne-Dominique Pellevé under the patronage of Prince Wilhelm Heinrich of Nassau. Lead-glazed earthenware in the English style was also made from 1784 onwards. In 1794 the models and molds were transferred to Sarreguemines. The faïence was apparently not marked and is difficult to identify. The porcelain is generally marked with an "NS". The hard paste material varied in quality. Tablewares in the Rococo style are the most characteristic productions and are of good quality. Mythological subjects and scenes from the Italian Comedy framed in delicate gilt Rococo scrollwork were much favored and were painted in beautiful colors. The forms of some of the tablewares such as pear-shaped jugs were distinctly of French inspiration. Underglaze blue painting and purple monochrome were also used. The glazed earthenware or faïence fine was not marked. Faïence fine wares generally ascribed to this factory are plain white and are in the French Neo-Classic style.

Oude Amstel In Dutch ceramics; see *Weesp*.

Oude Loosdrecht In Dutch ceramics; see *Weesp*.

Oudenarde Tapestries Tapestries woven at Oudenarde, which is a town in east Flanders. It was an important weaving center during the 16th century. The weaving of tapestries continued at Oudenarde until the last quarter of the 18th century. See *Tapestry*.

Oudry, Jean Baptiste d. 1755, French animal painter. See *Tapestry Furniture Coverings*.

Oushak An Oriental rug belonging to the Turkish classification. It was so named because it was woven in the vicinity of Oushak. The foundation is usually of wool; the pile is of wool and is deep. The old Oushak was of good workmanship, while the modern one is purely a commercial creation. The

Oushak does not follow any special color scheme or design. There are several types of Oushaks; namely the Gulistan, Enile, Yaprak and Sparta. See *Turkish Rugs*.

Oustri-Nan See *Hamadan Rug*.

Overlay Glass See *Cameo Glass*.

Overmantel Mirror In English furniture; at the end of the 17th century in England a mirror was designed to harmonize with the panelling over the mantelpiece. The majority of frames were made of carved gilt wood; occasionally the wood frame was enhanced with japanning and sometimes the frame was of glass. The mirror generally comprised three panels of glass, the center panel being the widest. Occasionally the mirror was of great size and filled the entire space between the chimneypiece and the cornice. The early overmantel mirror was seldom seen in America. One characteristic form of mantel mirror found in America around 1800 was rectangular in form and it had colonettes separating the panels and supporting a cornice.

Ovolo A classic convex molding, which was a part of the Ionic capital, carved with the egg and tongue. It is not to be confused with the echinus molding of the Doric column which was a much larger and more important molding. See *Echinus*; *Egg and Tongue*; *Molding*.

Owl Jug In ceramics; a variety of armorial faïence jug made in the form of an owl and having a removable head forming a cup. It is generally accepted that the original faïence owl jug, of which there are about fifteen surviving examples, was made at Brixen in the Tyrol from around 1540 to 1570 and was used as an archery prize. The feathers were either applied in relief and painted in blue or simply painted on the body. On the breast of the owl was a coat-of-arms applied in high relief and painted in oil colors and in gold. Variations in detail occur. The faïence owl jug was copied in Rhenish stoneware and lead-glazed earthen-

STONEWARE OWL JUG

ware during the 16th century, and at a later time it was also made in other countries.

Ox Blood In Chinese ceramics; see *Sang de Bœuf*.

Oxbow In cabinetwork; a curve which is the reverse of serpentine. It comprises a complete concave curve in the center, with a complete convex curve on each side. It is also called yoke-front. See *Serpentine*.

Ox-Horn Cup A form of drinking vessel. See *Drinking Horn*.

Oyster, Daniel 1764–1845. American clockmaker working at Reading, Pennsylvania, circa 1779. He was the maker of many very fine tall case clocks.

Oystering In English cabinetwork; a veneer used in cabinetwork during the periods of Charles II and William and Mary. The effect produced resembled an oyster in design. The oyster pieces were usually cut from laburnum and walnut saplings. The pieces were either circular or oval and were produced by cutting transversely or diagonally through saplings or small branches of about 2 or 3 inches in diameter. They were joined together as parquetry in the form of irregular polygons and were laid on as a veneer. Oystering was used as a border. It was used as a ground design when accompanied with patterns of simple geometrical inlays of light-colored wood. It was also used as a veneer for the entire ground of a piece of furniture. It is also called plum pudding. See *Parquetry*.

Ozen A Japanese lacquered dining tray. See *Dining Tray*.

Ozier Pattern In German ceramics; relief border patterns presumably designed by Kaendler were introduced at Meissen for tablewares from around and after 1730. These relief border designs were extensively copied by other porcelain manufactories. One design is a zig-zag basketwork pattern called the ordinair-ozier, and the other is a regular woven basketwork pattern with radial ribs, called the alt-ozier. Both patterns were introduced around or slightly after 1730. Around 1742 the neu-ozier design with curved S-shaped ribs was introduced.

MEISSEN BOWL WITH
BASKET WEAVE OZIER RIM

P

CLUB FOOT

2 DRAKE FOOT

SLIPPER FOOT

SNAKE FOOT

Pad Foot In English cabinetwork; several types of feet are here grouped together due to their similarity of form. They are all used on cabriole legs and are especially identified with Queen Anne cabinetwork. However tripod tables in the Chippendale style were occasionally designed with snake feet or other forms of pad feet. These various forms of feet splay outward from the leg and are usually slightly raised from the floor by a small disc-shaped projection, called a cushion or a shoe, as a protection. The pad foot and club foot are disc-shaped and rounded on the bottom. A Dutch foot is shaped as a club foot. The term *Dutch foot* is also applied to various other types, such as a pad foot, disc foot or a flattened hoof foot. The drake foot is a club foot which is cut or cloven so as to have three parts. The slipper foot is very flat and pointed. The snake foot is flat with its tip resembling the head of a snake. See *Foot*.

Padouk Wood A Burmese leguminous tree, *pterocarpus macrocarpus*, which produces a kind of rosewood, commonly called padouk wood. It was used by the French cabinet-makers during the 18th century. See *Andaman Redwood*.

Pagodite In mineral; see *Agalmatolite*.

Pai Ting In Chinese ceramics; see *Ting Yao*.

Pai Tz'u In Chinese ceramics; a Chinese term for the white porcelain ware called blanc de chine. See *Blanc de Chine*.

Paktong See *German Silver*.

Pa Kua Or Eight Trigrams. In Chinese symbols; see *Eight Trigrams*.

Palampore A kind of chintz bed-cover made in different parts of India. Some of these bed-covers with their hand-painted designs were of remarkable beauty. The hand-painted cloths from Masulipatam were made in many beautiful patterns.

Palier In French Provincial cabinetwork; see *Buffet-Vaisselier*.

Palissandre A Brazilian rosewood. See *Violet Wood*.

Palissy, Bernard c. 1510–c. 1590. French alchemist and potter. His reputation as a potter is chiefly predicated on literary sources, especially his own highly-colored writings. It is not possible with any degree of certainty to distinguish between his work and that of his assistants and followers, since the actual work of Palissy is not known to have ever been signed or marked. The outstanding merit of his work so far as it can be identified is in the use of finely colored glazes. After serving an apprenticeship as a glass painter he settled in Saintes around 1540 and began to conduct a series of experiments in ceramics. According to his own writings he succeeded in making a pottery which completely satisfied him. This was the so-called jaspée ware decorated in mingled colored glazes. Shortly after he produced the "rustiques figulines" upon which rested his later reputation as a potter. Around 1556 Catherine de Medici called him to Paris to make a grotto at the Tuileries which she was then having built. In 1574 he was recorded as "grottier et architecte des rustiques figulines du roy et de la royne." These "rustiques figulines" were the familiar pottery wares molded after nature with shells, lizards, snakes, fish, various kinds of leaves, rocks and moss and other natural subjects. The wares were principally decorative, unless they were large enough to be used in a garden or in a grotto, and included oval dishes, ewers, vases, plates and basins. They were remarkable for their skillful application of fine colored glazes of blue, yellow, purple brown and greyish white. Some of the best pottery was admirable for its free spirit and rhythmical designs in producing naturalistic subjects. The jaspée

348

wares were notable for their skillful blending of glazes, either separate or mingled, producing an unrivalled harmony of colors. There is no evidence to prove that Palissy designed the molded forms decorated with fine French Renaissance motifs in which figure subjects were often introduced into the composition of the designs. Palissy's followers and imitators continued to produce wares in the Palissy style for many years.

Palladio, Andrea 1518–1580, Italian architect. Palladio designed a large number of fine buildings, chiefly town palaces and country villas in various parts of Italy. His designs adhered to the fine classic proportions of the buildings of ancient Rome. His work, which was executed with scholarly accuracy, expressed a revolt against the distortion both of proportion and ornament into which the architecture of his time had fallen. His work was notable for its elegant simplicity of line, refined proportions and dignified stateliness. The name *Palladian* is given to designate this style as practiced in England and introduced there by Inigo Jones, in 1620. His architectural designs influenced some of the cabinetwork during the Late Italian Renaissance. The cabinetwork, which was influenced by Palladio, was characterized by a more sparing and concentrated use of ornament and by undecorated moldings and heavy bases. See *Michelangelo*; *Renaissance, Italian*.

Palmer, Humphrey English potter working from 1760 at the Church Works, Hanley, Staffordshire. He was living at the same time as Wedgwood, whose wares he imitated. In 1778 he secured financial aid from J. Neale, his London agent, and the firm was known as Palmer & Neale and Neale & Co. Robert Wilson became a partner in 1786, and after 1802 the factory was carried on by his son, David Wilson. In the 19th century the firm was sold. They made tablewares of porcelain and cream-colored earthenware of good quality. They also made imitations of the fine black and jasper stonewares perfected by Wedgwood. Of particular interest

were some delicately finished figures painted in clear and fresh enamel colors. Included among the marks were "H.P.", "Palmer", "Neale & Co.", "Neale & Wilson", and "Wilson" all impressed.

Palsjö In Swedish ceramics; a faïence manufactory was started at Palsjö, near Helsingborg, in 1765 by Michael Anders Coster. Much of the production was simply painted in blue or in manganese and essentially resembled the wares made at Copenhagen. The mark was "PF" for Palsjö Fabrik.

P'an In Chinese bronzes; a basin used for washing the hands during ceremonial rites as well as for everyday use. It is a basin-shaped vessel which rests on a raised foot rim or base.

Panchetto In Italian Renaissance cabinetwork; a small wooden side chair designed with three legs. It had a small wooden seat supported on three splayed legs and a shaped wooden back, which was generally fan-shaped. It was often decorated with chip carving. It resembled to some extent the sgabello, but it was more crude in both construction and decoration.

Panel In cabinetwork; a panel is defined in architecture and other constructive arts as a compartment or section of a surface either sunk below or projected above the level of the surface and contained in a frame, such as a molding or other border, occasionally of a different color or material. In addition to this general meaning the term *panel* is also applied in cabinetwork to a flush veneered surface, such as a marquetry design arranged within a border and laid into a veneered ground, with the entire surface of the same level. For example, panels of floral marquetry were a feature of William and Mary veneered walnut furniture. The term is also applied to a panel of figured veneer set flush with the surface and framed with a small bolection molding. This form of panel work was a feature of mid-18th century English cabinetwork and was found on the cupboard doors of secretary bookcases.

PANCHETTO

Especially praiseworthy were the panel effects achieved in late 18th century English cabinetwork, when veneered surfaces were the forte of the English cabinetmaker. The term is also applied to painted panels especially characteristic of commodes designed in the Adam style.

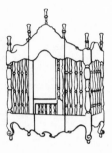

LOUIS XV PANETIÈRE

Panelled-Back Chair In English cabinetwork; see *Wainscot Chair*.

Panetière In French Provincial cabinetwork; the panetière, which was a small livery cupboard, was an interesting and delightful article of provincial furniture. It is generally thought that the panetière had its origin in southern France and in all probability in Provence. Its height, which varied from about 33 to 43 inches, generally exceeded its width by several inches. The characteristic Louis XV style Provençal panetière had an open frame with finely turned spindles surmounted by matching finials. It had a very small central cupboard door which had a finely wrought steel fretwork escutcheon and a buttress hinge. It was designed with a molded and valanced base that curved into short scrolled supports. It was often delicately carved with Rococo foliage and scrollwork motifs. As a rule it was made of walnut. It was either hung on a wall or placed on a table. See *Livery Cupboard*; *Cupboard*.

Panoplie Or Panoply. In ornament; a decorative grouping of pieces of arms and armor arranged as a kind of wall ornament, usually in a symmetrical manner. The term is also applied to the decorative arrangement of such pieces represented in mural panels, tapestry designs and similar works of art.

Pao-Pie In Chinese ceramics; see *Celadon*.

Pap Boat In English silver; a boat-shaped vessel for holding pap, used to feed infants and introduced during the 17th century. In American silver; silver pap boats depicted in American silver literature have a rather shallow circular body with a rounded bottom provided with a wide elongated spout projecting from the rim and a scroll-shaped handle.

Pap Bowl In English and American silver; pap bowls depicted in American silver literature have a bowl-shaped body and a spout that is shorter than that of the pap boat. They are depicted without handles.

Papelera In Spanish cabinetwork; a Spanish term given to any form of a cabinet designed as a receptacle for documents and papers and writing materials. In particular, the term was applied to an oblong Renaissance cabinet, similar to the vargueño, but without a drop-front. The richly decorated interior of small drawers and doors was the façade of the papelera. It was usually mounted on turned ball feet. The papelera was generally placed on a narrow, graceful, trestle table stand with an ornamental wrought-iron underbrace. See *Vargueño*.

Paperweight In glass; it is generally accepted that the art of making glass paperweights achieved its highest development in France. It is believed that paper weights were first made at St. Louis, which is located in the Vosges Mountains, around 1820. The earliest record of a dated and signed paperweight is of those made at St. Louis, which are signed and dated "S.L. 1845". This date is generally accepted as the beginning of the era when paperweights became veritable works of art as is evidenced by those produced at St. Louis, Clichy and Baccarat. The finest paperweights are generally attributed to Baccarat. The colored glass designs which in the finest specimens are remarkable for their intricate and artistic treatment include glass canes, millefiori, filigree, latticinio, fruit, flowers, birds, butterflies, animals, reptiles, fish and portraits. In addition to the glass designs many paperweights were further enriched by cutting and faceting. Sometimes the paperweight was made with overlay or case glass which was beautifully cut through to the clear crystal glass to reveal the decorative designs worked inside. Some paperweights had sulphides incrusted in the glass; the subjects for these sulphide paperweights were frequently portraits or religious and historical medallions. Paperweights with ceramic cameos are still another variety. In England fine artistic paperweights were produced at such places as Bristol, Nailsea, Stourbridge, and at the Whitefriars Glass Manufactory of James Powell and Sons, London. Paperweights were extensively produced in America. Some of the best were made at Sandwich and by the New England Glass Company and at Millville, New Jersey, at the glass works of Whitall, Tatum and Company. See *Glass*.

Papier-Mâché A French term meaning mashed paper, given to a decorative art that had long been practiced in Persia and in the East. The art was practiced in France around the middle of the 18th century, and became popular in England from around 1775 onwards. Papier-mâché was composed of paper pulp, which was made from a specially prepared paper mixed with glue, chalk and occasionally sand. This mixture after being pressed was molded and baked. It was so hard that it could be sawn, and was able to take a very high polish by a process similar to japanning. In addition to such articles as snuff boxes and trays it was occasionally made into small tables and other pieces of furniture of a similar nature. In America some papier-mâché furniture was made during the Victorian era, such as sewing tables. This furniture was distinctive for its colorful quality. Sometimes papier-mâché was molded over the frames of wooden furniture in order to make it more durable. Papier-mâché in the early 19th century was sometimes embellished with paper-thin pieces of mother-of-pearl. See *Clay's Ware*.

Papillon, Jean 1661–1723, a French designer and maker of wallpaper. He introduced the papiers de tapisseries around 1685. These were the first wallpapers to be made in such a manner that their designs could be joined together. His son, Jean Michel Papillon, b. 1698, was also a producer of wallpaper.

Pappenheimer In arms; a type of rapier with a hilt generally having a perforated guard. It is sometimes referred to as a Walloon sword and is named after Marshal Maximilian Pappenheim, circa 1630.

Pap Spoon In English and American pewter and silver; the name given to a spoon used to feed infants. A characteristic 18th century variety consisted of an elongated bowl having a cover hinged in the middle and enclosing the entire bowl except for a small opening at the tip. The stem was in the form of a hollow tube open at both ends and about halfway on the stem was a ring-shaped piece serving as a finger grip. Pap or other similar food was placed in the bowl and was fed to the infant by manipulating the thumb on the opening of the stem. See *Pap Boat*; *Pap Bowl*.

Parcel Gilded Or partially gilded. In cabinetwork; in this form of gilding the carved enrichments on mahogany, walnut or painted furniture were gilded. Parcel gilding was employed both in France and in England during the 18th century. Sheraton in his CABINET DICTIONARY illustrated drawing room chairs in the French taste and recommended that the painted examples be partially gilded to "give a lively effect". He preferred a white ground with gilt enrichments. The term *parcel gilded* is also applied to silver or other metal which has been partially gilded. See *Gilding*, in Furniture.

PARGETTED CEILING

Parget Or Pargeting. In interior design; a decorative plaster-work with the designs executed either in relief or indented used for the ornamentation of walls or ceilings. An English record of 1606 mentions "all the parget carv'd and branched trim with flowers and fruits and winged cherubim". The term is also applied to other forms of ornamental wall work, such as gilding, and an English record of 1569 states "golde was the parget." The art of decorative plaster-work was introduced in England during the reign of Henry VIII, 1509–1547, by Italian craftsmen.

Parian Ware In English ceramics; a variety of hard paste porcelain introduced by the Copeland manufactory at Stoke-on-Trent in 1846. It derived its name from the supposed resemblance of its marble-like paste to that of Parian marble. The usual proportions of kaolin and petuntse found in hard paste porcelain are considerably altered in the Parian porcelain. It was principally used for biscuit figures.

Paris Porcelain In French ceramics; the term *Paris porcelain* is generally reserved for the hard paste porcelain made at numerous factories operating in Paris from around and after 1770. The painted decoration was essentially inspired by the contemporary styles in vogue at Sèvres. The delicate painting in the Louis XVI style was later supplanted by the more formal and severe style of the Empire. It is generally accepted that the manufactories Clignancourt, Rue Thiroux, Faubourg Saint-Denis and the Rue de Bondy, all four of which enjoyed some princely protection, and also La Courtille, which was operated privately, produced the finest Paris porcelains and that some of their best productions were equal to the hard paste porcelain produced at Sèvres. See *Rue de Bondy*; *La Courtille*; *Rue Amelot*; *Clignancourt*; *Petite Rue Saint-Gilles*; *Faubourg Saint-Denis*; *Rue de Crussol*; *Pont-aux-Choux*; *Rue Popincourt*; *Rue de la Roquette*; *Rue Thiroux*.

Paris Touch See *Touch of Paris*.

Parliament Clock In English furniture; see *Act of Parliament Clock*.

Parquetry In cabinetwork; a mosaic of woods used as a veneer on furniture. These pieces of different kinds and colors of woods of simple geometrical form were carefully fitted to one another and applied to a ground. In English cabinetwork parquetry was chiefly used after the Restoration, 1660, in the early period of walnut veneered furniture and often in association with marquetry. Oystering was a form of parquetry. In French cabinetwork parquetry was fre-

LOUIS XV PARQUETRY
PETITE COMMODE

quently employed on such articles as commodes and occasional tables. Cube parquetry was a favorite form during the Louis XV style. See *Tunbridge*.

Partizan In arms; a 16th and 17th century weapon consisting of a long shaft having a broad blade with short, knife-like, up-curving branches at its base. The shapes of the blades vary. The partizan was frequently elaborately decorated and was used, and is still used, by the guards of high dignitaries as a ceremonial weapon.

Partridge, Nehemiah An American craftsman practicing japanning or lacquer work in Boston and advertising in 1712 "all sorts of japan work."

Partridge-Eye Marble See *Griotte d'Italie Marble*.

Partridge-Eye Pattern In French ceramics; see *Oeil-de-Perdrix*.

Partridge Wood The wood from a West Indian tree, *andira inermis*, used for inlay and cabinetwork, especially by the French ébénistes. It is hard and its color is reddish and mottled. It is also called Oeil-de-Perdrix wood.

Pas d'Âne Guard The medieval ring-shaped sword guards, on each side of the sword, below the cross-piece, at the base of the hilt. See *Hilt*.

Passement In needlework; decorative bandings, gimps and needle-made and bobbin-made laces were called passements until the 17th century. Now the term is given to the pricked-through designs on parchment upon which both bobbin and needle-made laces are fabricated.

Passementerie A French term used to describe trimming of gold or silver lace, or of braid or gimp, as well as jet or metal beads and similar materials.

Passglas In German glass; a characteristic and popular late 16th and 17th century communal drinking glass, generally made of green glass. It was cylindrical in form and was decorated with horizontal glass rings which were equidistant. These rings were used to determine the quantity of liquid to be drunk at one time. The bandwurm or tapeworm glass is a variety of the capacious passglas decorated with an applied glass thread which encircles the glass in a spiral manner.

Pastel In art; the process of painting or drawing with dry pigments or colored chalks. The method was also called crayon drawing.

Pastiglia The name given to an Italian Renaissance decorative art. Pastiglia was a surface decoration. In the process of pastiglia work a thin fabric was affixed to the entire surface, both the carved and plain portions, of a piece of furniture, such as a cassone. Then several coats of pastiglia or plaster, which was a thick creamy mixture, were applied to the surface and allowed to harden completely. Then the design, which was usually in low relief, was gradually developed by successive brush applications of pastiglia. The final detail work was done with a knife. Gold was then applied and sometimes burnished. Pastiglia work was chiefly identified with the 15th century, although the process continued to be used for the next two hundred years.

Patch Box The term applied to a small box used by a lady to hold patches for the face. Patch boxes were mentioned in English records as early as 1674. In France the patch box was called a boîte à mouches from the French word *mouche* meaning fly, a patch for the face or a beauty-spot. It was in general use in France in the 17th and 18th centuries and mentioned as early as 1647. The boîte à mouches was made in a variety of forms and was exquisitely executed in gold, silver, enamel and similar fine materials. Many designs for patch boxes were made by famous contemporary artists and designers such as Bérain and Marot.

Patch Box In arms; a small box used to carry patches, and frequently to carry fire-arm accessories, such as extra flints and caps. These small boxes are often elaborately decorated. The bullets for the early rifles were smaller than the bore of the rifle and a piece of greased leather, called a patch, was wrapped around them in order to fit the bore.

Patchwork The art or handicraft known as patchwork was practiced in very early times in Egypt. It was introduced into Europe during the Middle Ages and flourished throughout the succeeding centuries. It was particularly a favorite domestic art in England and in Holland where velvet patchwork was used for such articles as court dresses, wall hangings and bedstead valances. In America the art of patchwork was noteworthy for its fine workmanship and decorative value. This art was brought to America by the first settlers who used patchwork in a utilitarian manner for warmth and comfort by piecing together the odd pieces of material and then quilting them. Patchwork and quilting flourished in America throughout the 18th and 19th centuries. American patchwork quilts are praiseworthy for the great variety of their designs. It is important to distinguish between patchwork and applied work, for in true patchwork the various patches are pieced together, while in the latter the patches are applied to a ground. See *Quilting*.

CHELSEA PATCH BOX

Pâte de Verre In French glass; an ornamental colored glass, having its origin in antiquity, revived around the end of the 19th century by French artist glassmakers. In this technique the glass is made from powdered glass of different colors that are skillfully blended and refined in molds. The designs are generally executed by cutting in facet form.

Pâte Dure In ceramics; the French term applied to hard paste porcelain. See *Porcelain*.

Pâte-sur-Pâte In ceramics; the French term applied to the method of building decoration in low relief by successive layers of slip applied with a brush. The process was developed at Sèvres around the middle of the 19th century. M. Solon who had worked at Sèvres came to work at Minton around 1870, where he remained for thirty-five years. He was very skilled in the pâte-sur-pâte method of decoration. And as a result pâte-sur-pâte is perhaps best known in some of the Minton wares. Pâte-sur-pâte was adopted by all the important European potteries.

Pâte Tendre In ceramics; the French term for soft paste porcelain. See *Soft Paste*.

Paten In ecclesiastical art; a plate or shallow dish, generally circular, made of precious metal, most commonly of silver, on which the bread is laid at the celebration of the Eucharist. It is used as a cover for the chalice. In very early times patens were also made of other materials, such as glass or crystal, and were sometimes enamelled and set with jewels. As a rule extant examples of English patens dating prior to the reign of Edward VI or the year 1547 have an engraved sacred device in the center. Occasionally the circle enclosing the device is slightly sunk from the field of the paten, and sometimes the device is enriched with enamelling and inserted from the back on a detachable piece of metal. According to a church ordinance it was mandatory for every medieval paten and chalice used in the celebration of Mass to be made of gold or silver.

CHARLES I SILVER CHALICE
AND PATEN

Patera In ornament; an architectural term given to the representation of a flat circular dish or disk usually ornamented in low relief to decorate a frieze or some similar part. The name is given in furniture design to a flat circular ornament having some kind of carved, painted or inlaid decoration. The term has been incorrectly extended to rosettes and other almost circular flat embellishments having little resemblance to the original models. Paterae were a favorite enrichment in English cabinetwork for friezes, chair splats and other similar members designed by Adam and in the subsequent styles of Hepplewhite and Sheraton.

Patina The term is applied to a greenish film formed on bronze, caused by long exposure to the atmosphere, or by long burial in the earth. The term is also given to a film similarly formed on other metals. A patina formed by natural causes produces a beautiful color, such as on ancient Chinese bronzes. Artificial patina is produced by treatment with acids. The finest and most beautiful artificial patina is found on Japanese sword mounts made of shakudo and shibuichi. Various other materials, such as wood, stone and marble, also acquire a patina to their surface color and surface texture. See *Bronzes, Chinese*; *Shakudo*.

Patron In arms; a cartridge box having a hinged lid and fitted with vertical compartments. It was used during the 16th and 17th centuries to hold the paper cartridges, called patrons, for pistols and muskets.

Patty Pan In English glassware; see *Jelly Glass*.

Pauldron In medieval armor; the shoulder plate worn to protect the body where the arm-piece joins the cuirass.

Pavis A large convex medieval shield which served as a protection against arrows or other flying missiles and was sufficiently high and wide to protect the entire body.

Paw and Ball Foot In cabinetwork; a foot similar to a claw and ball foot, except that it is designed with an animal's paw in place of a claw. See *Foot*.

Paw Foot In cabinetwork; a foot carved in the form of an animal's paw, such as a lion's paw. Paw feet, especially bronze paw feet, were a feature of the Empire style. They were also used during the English Regency. See *Foot*.

Pax Or Paxbrede. In ecclesiastical art; a small tablet or board (brede) of circular or quadrangular form made of gold, silver, ivory or some similar material bearing a representation of the Crucifixion or other sacred subject produced by engraving, enamelling, painting or carving. The pax, which was generally mounted on a low spreading foot, was provided with a scrolled handle projecting from the under side of the tablet. The sacred subject on the pax was kissed by the celebrating priest at Mass and was then passed to the other officiating clergy and finally to those attending the Mass to be kissed. The pax as a symbolic substitute for the kiss of peace came into practice in the 13th century. Many medieval inventories listed the pax in their articles of church silver.

Peach Bloom In Chinese ceramics; a beautiful and refined porcelain ware first perfected during the K'ang Hsi period. The ware developed from the attempt to rival the Ming sacrificial red obtained from the use of copper to make the color. The Peach Bloom wares comprise seven small classic forms; such as a ring-necked bottle, a chrysanthemum vase with elongated neck, an amphora-shaped vase, a writer's water coupe, a writer's water jar which is shaped like a beehive, a dish and a flat rounded box for vermilion. The body is white and of a fine texture. The glaze is generally thin and even. On these wares that are perfectly formed the color varies from a pink to a liver color and is usually strewn with mottlings and splotches of greenish colors and brown. The mark should be of a clear blue under a very pale greenish white glaze and centered under the foot. The Chinese call these wares chiang tou hung or bean red, p'in kuo hung or apple red, and p'in kuo ch'ing or apple green.

Peachblow In American glass; a late 19th century American ornamental glass. The glass was made of one piece of glass, or with a milk-white under layer. Its decorative coloring generally varied from white to rose, greenish-yellow to red and light blue to pink. Its name was derived from the fine Chinese porcelain ware called Peach Bloom, since this ware was thought to have some resemblance. See *Art Glass*.

Pear Drop In furniture mounts; see *Drop Handle*.

Pearl In lace-making; a minute loop worked on the edges of a design.

Pearl-Tie In lace-making; the term *pearl-tie* is the English equivalent of the French term *bride*, the latter being the more customary term. See *Bride*.

Pearl Ware In English ceramics; a pure white earthenware akin to the cream-colored earthenware was introduced by Wedgwood about 1779 and was called Pearl ware. This ware was made to satisfy a demand for the revived fashion for underglaze blue decoration. The ware was extensively adopted in Staffordshire but did not enjoy the success of the cream-colored ware. See *Cream-Colored Earthenware*.

Pear Motif The name given to a design motif used in Oriental rugs, especially in Persian rugs. It has also been called cone, crown jewel, loop, palm and flame. Its shape rather suggests a pear, and it is now generally so called.

Pear Wood A durable, smooth grain fruitwood, *pyrus communis*, with a reddish tinge, used in English and American cabinetwork. Like the other fruitwoods it was used from the early days for simple country furniture. In America many well-designed pieces were made of both pear wood and apple wood. Pear wood was occasionally stained black to imitate ebony and was sometimes used as a veneer for tall case clocks. See *Poirier Wood*.

Pedestal In English cabinetwork; at the beginning of the Early Georgian period the pedestal was introduced by the architects as a piece of movable decorative furniture. The pedestal, which in classical architecture is the support of a column, was a development of this same substructure. The pedestal consisted of a base, dado and cornice. It was generally used to support a marble or bronze sculpture. The architectural character of the pedestal distinguishes it

PEDESTAL IN THE
NEO-CLASSICAL STYLE

from the candlestand. The Early Georgian pedestals were generally either short and columnar in form or of term shape. Relatively few designs for pedestals were made during the Rococo era because of their classic character. Under the influence of Robert Adam pedestals were again widely used, especially in the interior of homes decorated in the Adam taste. Pedestals were particularly suitable for classical treatment. See *Term*.

REGENCY PEDESTAL
SIDEBOARD

Pedestal Sideboard In English cabinetwork; or a sideboard of pedestal form. It was illustrated in the CABINETMAKERS' LONDON BOOK OF PRICES in 1788. One characteristic variety was designed with a swell-front central section, which was similar in design to the sideboard with deep lateral wine drawers, and which was flanked and joined to the pedestal ends, each having a single cupboard door. Each pedestal end was surmounted with an urn. The central portion was mounted on two tapered legs which continued from the stiles that flanked the central frieze drawer. Sheraton illustrated in his DRAWING BOOK this form of pedestal sideboard as well as the sideboard with the deep lateral wine drawers. They were surmounted with a finely chased brass gallery which served to support plate. The brass gallery was fitted with two or more candle-branches, which when lighted "gave a brilliant effect to the silver ware." At the beginning of the 19th century the sideboard of pedestal form was designed with the pedestal end section flanking a shaped shelf over a row of two drawers. Each pedestal contained a single frieze drawer over a long cupboard door. See *Pedestal Sideboard Table*; *Sideboard pedestals*; *Sideboard*.

Pedestal Sideboard Table In English cabinetwork; it is generally accepted that the arrangement of the sideboard table flanked by pedestals, surmounted with urns, was originated by Robert Adam. The sideboard pedestals surmounted by urns or vases were introduced about 1760. The sideboard table was designed with a frieze and generally rested on six legs. The table was often fitted with a brass gallery for the support of plate. This arrangement of sideboard table, pedestals and urns continued to be used in the spacious dining rooms until the end of the 18th century. The pedestals and urns were generally made of the same material and were designed to accord with the sideboard table with which they were to be grouped. See *Sideboard Pedestals*; *Sideboard Table*; *Knife Box*; *Knife Urn*.

Pedestal Writing Table In English cabinetwork; the massive library or writing table of pedestal form did not come into general use until late in the reign of George I, 1714-1727. The characteristic variety of open pedestal table had an oblong molded flat top, over a row of frieze drawers, supported on a pair of pedestals, each containing a bank of three or four drawers. Each set of drawers generally rested on a molded base, and occasionally on feet. It was decorated on all four sides, since it was generally designed to be placed away from the wall. A smaller form of pedestal table was occasionally used as a dressing table. Numerous designs for the large mahogany writing table of pedestal form appeared in Chippendale's DIRECTOR and in other trade catalogues. The carved decoration was usually in the Rococo or Chinese taste. Occasionally the pedestals were of bombé contour. Less elaborate examples were also designed by Chippendale. It was designed in the successive 18th century styles of furniture. See *Writing Furniture*; *Library Table*.

Pediment In cabinetwork; the term *pediment*, which is the triangular termination in classical architecture at the ends of buildings and over porticoes, is applied in furniture to any part resembling an architectural pediment either in form or in position. In English cabinetwork; a pronounced feature of Early Georgian cabinetwork was the architectural character given to many pieces of furniture. The architectural influence was especially apparent in massive bookcases,

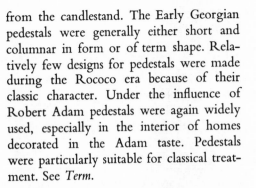

secretary cabinets and other similar pieces which lent themselves especially well to architectural principles. Several different forms of pediments were employed on such pieces. In the broken pediment, the lines are either arched or straight and stop before they reach the apex. The swan neck or scrolled pediment consists of opposed S curves which scroll over at the top and terminate in paterae. In both types there is usually centered in the opening a low plinth which is frequently surmounted with a carved ornament. Another form of pediment is the triangular pediment which is not cleft.

Peg Tankard   In English silver; a variety of tankard. It was so named because the inside was fitted with a row of pegs, one above another from top to bottom. The number of pegs vary depending on the size of the tankard. A two quart tankard is fitted with eight pegs, since there is a gill of liquid between each peg. Each person drank the distance between each peg as the tankard was passed around. It was introduced during the third quarter of the 17th century.

Peking Bowl   In Chinese ceramics; a variety of porcelain bowl made during the Ch'ien Lung reign and the early 19th century. It is reputed that these bowls were especially produced for the Emperor, who used them as gifts. They are characterized by a dull opaque green, blue, yellow or crimson ground with an over-all engraved scroll-work decoration.

Pelletier, John   English carver and gilder working around 1690–1710. From his bill accounts it can be deduced that he made carved and gilded frames for tables, mirrors, screens and other similar articles. There are two sets of stands at Hampton Court Palace which can be accepted as his work on the evidence of his accounts. They are in the Louis XIV style and are distinctive for the fine quality of their design and for their carving.

Pelmet   A decorative piece of fabric such as velvet or damask usually shaped or draped and hung above windows from a wooden case or box. In England in the 18th century the pelmet was known as a cornice and was illustrated in contemporary books of design.

Pembroke Table   In English cabinetwork; a small oblong table with a drop-leaf on each side. The drop-leaves were supported by hinged wooden brackets. The frieze was fitted with a small drawer. The table was supported on four slender legs which were almost always straight. The table of the Pembroke pattern was introduced after the middle of the 18th century. Sheraton states that the table derived its name from the lady who first ordered one and who probably submitted the idea for the table to the cabinetmaker. After 1770 the table was often made of inlaid satinwood and was decorated with painted motifs in the classic taste. The legs were of taper form. The average length of the table when extended was around 3 or $3\frac{1}{2}$ feet. The Pembroke table was always distinctive for its delicate and restrained lines and for its elegant simplicity. It served many purposes, such as a tea or breakfast table. The Pembroke table was popular in America from around 1760 to 1820 and it was made in each of the prevailing styles. See *Harlequin Pembroke*.

HEPPLEWHITE PEMBROKE
TABLE

Pendant   In ornament; a carved, molded or turned ornament chiefly made of wood, brass or bronze that points or projects downward. Pendants were often employed on the valanced aprons of lowboys designed in the Queen Anne style. See *Drop Handle*; *Finial*.

Pennsylvania Dutch   In American folk art; the name given to a group of early settlers who were invited to settle in Pennsylvania by William Penn. They came chiefly from around the Rhine, from Switzerland, Bavaria, Alsace and Holland. Their first ship landed in 1683, and for almost the next one hundred years they came in increasing numbers. They settled in the south-eastern part of Pennsylvania. Due to the tenacity with which they clung to their language and traditions, which had been dear to them in the old country, they developed a peasant or folk art peculiar to them. Much of the early Pennsylvania Dutch furniture essentially resembled European peasant furniture of the 18th and 19th centuries. The furniture, which included wooden chairs, benches, settles, tables, cupboards and chests, was plain and of sturdy construction. Because of their innate fondness for color and decoration the furniture was often painted and brightly decorated with such characteristic motifs as hearts, peacocks, parrots, geometrical designs borrowed from barn signs, pomegranates and tulips in urns. Especially pleasing are the many small wooden pieces with their carved decoration, such as salt and spice boxes, spoon racks and ladles and spoons. They practiced all the different handicrafts necessary for daily living. They made crude pottery for daily use, and as the potter became more adept he ornamented his earthenware with sgraffiato decoration. In addition to such favorite motifs as the tulip, heart and peacock, he recorded on the plates everyday life and manners and both Biblical and secular inscriptions. The terms *Pennsylvania German* and *Pennsylvania Dutch* are now used interchangeably. See *Fractur*; *Taufschein*; *Pennsylvania Dutch Chest*; *Pennsylvania German*; *Stiegel, Heinrich Wilhelm*.

PENNSYLVANIA DUTCH
CHEST

Pennsylvania Dutch Chest In American cabinetwork; the painted Pennsylvania Dutch chest, which was characterized by its crudely designed painted decoration, did not follow any particular period style. As a rule the front of the chest was ornamented with two or three shaped panels which were decorated with painted flowers, fruit, foliage and birds. The tulip was a favorite floral motif. The initials of the owners were often found on these chests. Many of these chests were made as dower chests. The almost primitive quality of these chests in both construction and decoration gave them a singular charm. See *Pennsylvania Dutch*.

Pennsylvania German Or Pennsylvania Deutsche. The term *Pennsylvania German* is now used interchangeably with *Pennsylvania Dutch*, which is the corrupt name for Pennsylvania Deutsche or German. See *Pennsylvania Dutch*.

Peony In Chinese art; one of the flowers of the Chinese four seasons. It represents Spring. See *Chinese Four Season Flowers*.

Pepper Box In arms; the name given to a kind of revolver that was popular during the middle of the 19th century. It does not have a barrel; however, the chambers, which are long, serve as barrels. The pepper box had its hammer either on the top or underneath.

Pepper Caster In English silver; see *Caster*.

Pepper Mill A pepper grinder. The name is given to a small cylindrical device of wood or metal used to hold pepper-corn, which is the dried berry of the black pepper. It is held in the hand, and by a turning motion of the cap or a handle, the pepper is ground and sprinkled on the food.

Percier, Charles 1764–1838, a French architect. See *Fontaine, Léonard*; *Empire*.

Perfume Burner A French essence vase. See *Cassolette*.

Pergolesi, Michele Angelo d. 1801. An Italian decorative artist, engraver and designer working in England prior to 1770. He was much in demand for designing mural decorations and for painting ceilings. In 1777 he brought out a prospectus for his ORIGINAL DESIGNS from his own address at 16 Broad Street, Golden Square. He said that the work would be in two volumes and that each volume would contain twenty-four numbers and that it would be issued in parts. At the time of his death fifteen of the parts had been issued. In this work he related that for a long time he had been a student of antique ornament. His treatment of antique and Renaissance motifs in the Neo-Classic manner is skillful and finished. It is a reasonable assumption that some of the painted and inlaid decoration in the Neo-Classic manner which was being used in contemporary cabinetwork was inspired by the designs of Pergolesi. See *Adam, Robert.*

Périgord In French Provincial; an old division of the former province of Guienne, in south-western France north of the Garonne River. See *French Provincial*; *Gascogne.*

Periwig Chair In English cabinetwork; a high-back carved and turned walnut armchair introduced during the William and Mary period. It derived its name from the elaborately carved and pierced half-hoop cresting which surmounted the back of the chair. The cresting was designed to provide a flattering background for the men's periwigs and for the ladies' head-dresses which were unusually high at the time. A feature of the chair was its fine meshed caning. The chair was also designed as a side chair.

Perpendicular Style The term is applied to the Late Gothic style of ornament and architecture in England. See *Gothic, English*; *Tudor.*

Persian and Near Eastern Pottery In ceramics; Islamic pottery of the Mohammedan period is descended from the ancient wares of the Near East. The oldest and most primitive Islamic pottery is called Gabri ware. The name is derived from the Persian fire worshippers of pre-Mohammedan times. Gabri is a red-bodied earthenware. It is covered with a white slip and it has incised designs covered with a lead glaze. It is a sgraffiato decoration usually with the design remaining in the white slip and with the ground removed showing the red body. The transparent lead glaze has a yellowish tint and is also colored with manganese-purple and green, and at times rarely with ochreous red and yellow. The majority of Gabri wares were probably made from the 10th to the 13th centuries. Gabri ware is also reputed to have been made at Amul, south of the Caspian Sea, which has the ochreous red and yellow colors. Few pieces of early Persian pottery are found intact as

they are excavated. The exceptions are those pieces found buried inside larger vessels. Pottery found at Samarra is a buff-colored faïence similar to Italian majolica. It most frequently has an opaque white glaze turned pinkish grey from burial. It is decorated with designs in dark blue, at times with splotches of green or with luster tones of deep red, golden brown or green. Some Samarra wares have yellow and green glazes in monochrome or are mottled and splotched similar to the Chinese T'ang ware. Similar Samarra type wares are also found at Susa, Rhages, and at Fostat, Egypt. The most common ware of Persia, Egypt, Syria, and Asia Minor has a sandy white body covered with a clear silicious glaze. In this ware a wide variety of decoration is found. In one type the engraved designs covered with a white glaze are colored with blue, green and maganese-purple. In another type the design is carved, engraved or in relief under a monochrome glaze of lapis blue, pale greenish blue, deep purplish blue, opaque turquoise, green and white. Chinese wares had a great influence on those of the Near East just as the Near East wares had in China. In Ming porcelains are found the Mohammedan floral scrolls and the Mohammedan blue. In the later Persian wares are found copied the Chinese blue and white wares as well as the celadons and the monochrome glazes. See *Turkish Pottery.*

Persian Knot In Oriental rug weaving; see *Sehna Knot*; *Oriental Rug.*

Persian Rug Designs In Oriental rugs; included among the designs most frequently used in Persian rugs are the following: Pear, Shah Abbas, Herati, Mina Khani and Guli Hinnai. See *Persian Rugs.*

Persian Rugs A general classification applied to a group of Oriental rugs which are woven in Persia. For centuries the finest rugs have been woven in Persia. The rugs are distinctive for their graceful designs which cover practically every inch of the surface. The motifs consist of blossoms and leaf

BOTTLE-FORM VASE,
RHAGES

scrolls, arabesques, cartouches enclosing inscriptions, cloud bands, various plants, animal figures and similar subjects. The colors which are rich and deep are skillfully blended. This group includes: Tabriz; Sarakh; Shiraz; Herez; Feraghan; Khorassan; Gorevan; Serebend; Serapi; Herat; Kara Dagh; Hamadan; Souj-Bulak; Sehna; Saruk; Koultuk; Kurdistan; Kirman; Kermanshah; Niris; Bijar; Joshaghan; Afshar; Kashan; Lilihan; Meshed; Sultanabad; Yezd; Savalan; Ispahan; Arak; Muskabad; Mahal; Bakhtiari; Bakhshis; Teheran; Vase Rug; Hunting Rug; Animal Rug; Garden Rug. Under the patronage of the first three Sefavi monarchs, namely Shah Ismail, 1500–1524, Shah Tahmasp, 1524–1576, and Shah Abbas, 1588–1629, Persian rugs achieved their acme of workmanship. After a gradual decline the great period came to an end in 1722. A modern revival dates from around 1885. See *Oriental Rug*; *Persian Rug Designs*; *Shah Abbas*.

PERSIAN RUG BORDER

Pesaro In Italian ceramics; potteries were in existence at Pesaro, near Urbino, from late in the 15th century. It was formerly believed that a luster ware similar to that made at Deruta was also made here during the Renaissance; unfortunately there is no evidence to substantiate this claim. This reputed luster ware was Pesaro's chief claim to fame; however, other varieties of majolica of some interest were made here during the 16th century. The manufacture of majolica declined during the 17th century; toward the latter part of the 18th century it was somewhat revived. See *Italian Majolica*.

Petite Commode In French cabinetwork; a very small commode. It usually was designed with three very narrow drawers arranged in three rows, and occasionally with one or two cupboard doors in place of the drawers. Sometimes it had a marquetry top in place of marble. It was mounted on four slender legs. It was a fashionable piece of 18th century French furniture and was used in many rooms for different purposes.

Some were fitted with the necessary accessories for letter writing or for sewing. The petite commode was distinctive for its fine marquetry work and for its delicate bronze mounts.

Petite Desserte In French Provincial furniture; a small table, which was a form of servante, designed with three slender legs and with three circular shelves increasing in size from top to bottom. The top shelf served as the top of the table. It was introduced during the 18th century and it was a relatively plain piece of furniture. See *Dumb-Waiter*.

Petite Rue Saint-Gilles In French ceramics; a hard paste porcelain manufactory was started in 1785 in Paris by François-Maurice Honoré. It was sometimes called the Boulevard Saint-Antoine manufactory. Around 1810 Honoré gave up the factory and acquired another at La Seynie. Early in the 19th century Honoré was associated with Dagoty who had started a manufactory in the Boulevard Poissonnière which remained active until 1867. The productions were principally tablewares decorated in accordance with the contemporary styles fashionable at Sèvres. The manufactories of Honoré and Dagoty chiefly flourished during the French Empire and in the subsequent years. The marked wares all date from the 19th century and generally included in the marks were the names of the proprietors. See *Paris Porcelain*.

Petit Feu In ceramics; the French term for the low temperature required to fire or melt painted decoration executed in vitreous enamel colors into the glaze of porcelain or faïence which has already been fired. In order to have this low melting point a large amount of lead or other flux is added to the glassy colors themselves to increase their fusibility. These enamel colors are fired at a comparatively low temperature of 700° C to 900° C in a muffle kiln. They are often referred to as muffle colors. A much wider range of colors can be obtained in enamel colors than in the so-called high temperature colors or those colors which can stand the heat of the grand feu. See *Enamel*, in Ceramics; *Grand Feu*.

Petit, Nicholas 1732–1791. A notable French ébéniste who received his master in 1761. He executed many fine pieces of cabinetwork for the nobility, especially in marquetry work and in black lacquer decorated in the Chinese taste. One of his most praiseworthy pieces is a commode with fine floral marquetry work which is in the bibliothèque at Versailles.

Petit Point A needlework closely worked in wool or silk on an open mesh material, such as canvas, which is entirely covered by the embroidery. This variety of needlework was used as early as the 15th century and later was extensively practiced in France. The term *petit point* was originally applied to this type of needlework in France. See *Needlework*; *Gros Point*. The name is also given to a stitch in embroidery generally used in petit point. The stitch is also called a tent stitch. See *Tent Stitch*; *Embroidery*.

Petit Poussin A narrow delicate inexpensive bobbin lace principally made by the peasants at Dieppe, France. See *Normandy Lace*.

Pétrin In French Provincial cabinetwork; see *Maie*.

Petronel In arms; the name given to a firearm of the 16th century that was larger than the pistol and smaller than the arquebus. It was a heavy piece and of large caliber. The stock had an exaggerated curve and it was fired by holding it against the chest.

Petuntse In ceramics; the fusible feldspathic ingredient of hard paste porcelain. In China the stone was pulverized at the quarry and sent to the potter in the form of little bricks. In Chinese the term *petuntse* means little bricks.

Peuplier Wood The wood of the poplar tree, genus *populus*, used in cabinetwork. It is light and spongy and its color is white.

Pew Group In English ceramics; the name applied to the charming stylized Staffordshire figures made of salt-glazed stoneware. They are represented as ladies and gentlemen, usually in country attire, seated on a high back settle and occasionally playing musical instruments. These pew groups date from about 1735–1745.

Pewter In English pewter; the name given to an alloy in which the principal part is tin. Without an alloy tin is too soft to work into durable vessels, so a very small portion of lead, copper, brass, bismuth, zinc or antimony, or a combination of two or more of these metals, is added. Each metal added served a purpose. The advantages of a tin lead mixture were its low cost and ease of handling. If it contained a high percentage of lead, the articles were soft, heavy and easily damaged and were characterized by a dull color and a coarse texture. When copper was used as an admixture, the pewter was characterized by greater strength, smoother surface, closer texture and better color. Bismuth tended to harden the alloy; it lowered the melting point and caused a brittleness. An improvement was the substitution of brass, which introduced zinc with the copper. Antimony replaced both bismuth and zinc. It served the same purpose as bismuth, and, in addition, it produced a metal that could take a high polish and did not lower its melting point. Roman pewter consisted of tin and lead alone. During the Middle Ages lead continued to be the principal admixture used. In London around 1348 an ordinance was passed which stated that only the finest grade of pewter could be used in plates, dishes and similar articles. It defined fine pewter as consisting of tin with an admixture of brass, as much as the nature of tin could take, or about 23%. By the same act hollow ware, such as flagons and tankards, were decreed to be made from an alloy of tin and a reasonable amount of copper. Reasonable was defined as 26 parts to 112 parts of tin; however, it varied according to the shapes and purposes of the vessels made.

STAFFORDSHIRE PEW GROUP

Ley, or common pewter, which was used for tankards and wine measures consisted of 80 parts tin and 20 parts lead. A variety of pewter called trifle, which consisted of 83 parts tin and 17 parts antimony, was not included in the first ordinance but it also was a relatively early grade. Since the use of antimony in small articles gave such excellent results, it was later combined with tin and copper in making plate. By the end of the 17th century in England, antimony practically superseded copper in the making of fine pewter. An average specification for fine pewter consisted of 100 parts tin and 17 parts antimony. The finest hard pewter contained over 90% tin and less than 8% antimony and 2% copper. Each country in Europe had its own laws regulating the different grades of pewter. Pewter can be hammered, cast or spun into shape. There were three classes of pewterers in England. The Sadware workers executed their work by hammering. They made plates, dishes and similar articles. The Hollow ware workers did their work by casting. They made all kinds of vessels that were hollow in form. The Triflers chiefly made small articles both for ornamental and domestic use from a variety of pewter called trifle. See *Britannia Metal*; *Sadware*; *Hollow Ware*; *Hammered*; *Trifle*; *Ley*; *Ashbury Metal*; *Touch Mark*; *Touch Plate*; *Black Pewter*.

PHILADELPHIA STYLE
HIGHBOY

Pfalz-Zweibrücken In German ceramics; a porcelain manufactory was established here in 1767 under the protection of Duke Christian IV of Pfalz-Zweibrücken. In 1775 the Duke withdrew his patronage and the manufactory was leased privately. Nothing is known of the productions after 1775; however, it is believed that porcelain and also cream-colored earthenware in the English style were made. The factory mark was "PZ" in a monogram. Tablewares were the principal production. Especially typical was a decoration of small bouquets of flowers in colors. An inferior quality of hard paste porcelain was used for dishes for daily use which were chiefly blue and white.

Pharmacy Vase In ceramics; a variety of drug jar either without a spout for dry drugs or with a spout for liquid medicines. Some of the finest Hispano-Moresque wares and also Italian Renaissance majolica were made in the form of pharmacy jars. It was a custom in Italy during the Renaissance to display elaborate services of drug vases in the pharmacies which were at that time a favorite local rendezvous. See *Albarello*.

Philadelphia Chair In American cabinetwork; the term *Philadelphia chair* is given to describe a method of construction used on chairs designed in the Queen Anne and Chippendale styles. In this method the side rails of the seat were mortised into the rear supports. Although this method is identified with Philadelphia chair making from around 1750 to 1785 some chairs have been found that employed this method which were made in other cities.

Philadelphia Chippendale In American cabinetwork; Philadelphia achieved its high rank in American furniture history during the Chippendale era. It is generally agreed that the finest Chippendale style furniture made in America was produced in Philadelphia. Philadelphia style highboys and lowboys are usually considered to be among the finest specimens of furniture made in America and equalled only by the block-front furniture of Townsend and Goddard. See *Affleck, Thomas*; *Randolph, Benjamin*; *Savery, William*; *Gostelowe, Jonathan*; *Gillingham, James*.

Philadelphia Style Highboy In American cabinetwork; a highboy surmounted with a swan neck or scrolled pediment made in Philadelphia from about 1760 to 1775. It was essentially a more richly carved example of the highboy designed in the Chippendale Rococo style. For example the inner ends of the scrolled pediment terminated in carved rosettes, the stiles were often enriched with quarter-round fluted columns, the carved recessed shells were flanked with foliated scrolls in relief, the valanced apron was often embellished with carved Rococo leaf ornament and the cabriole legs were richly carved with acanthus leafage. The development of the highboy and lowboy in the Philadelphia school of Chippendale furniture has no counterpart in any other country. See *Highboy*.

Philadelphia Style Lowboy In American cabinetwork; a richly carved Chippendale style lowboy made in Philadelphia from about 1760 to 1775 in the Rococo taste. See *Philadelphia Style Highboy*; *Lowboy*.

Phyfe, Duncan 1768–1854, a well-known American cabinetmaker. He was born at Loch Fannich, Scotland. He arrived in America with his family in 1783 and settled in Albany, New York. He was apprenticed to a coach builder or cabinetmaker. He is later listed in the New York city directory of 1792. His first shop was on Broad Street. In 1806, he moved his shop and home to 34 and 35 Partition Street. Later, in 1811, he bought the property at 33 Partition Street. In 1817, Partition Street was renamed Fulton Street. His shop and home were then 168, 170 and 172 Fulton Street. In 1837, the firm name was D. Phyfe and Sons and in 1840, D. Phyfe and Son. In 1847 he retired. Duncan Phyfe did not create a furniture style. He followed the prevailing styles which were fashionable during his career; namely the Sheraton, Directoire and Empire styles. His best cabinetwork was done during the first quarter of the 19th century and displayed many features of the Sheraton and Directoire styles. This furniture was distinctive for its excellent proportions, for its graceful and elegant forms and for its fine decorative details, which were always in good taste. The furniture was made from the highest quality of mahogany. His later work was characterized by large and massive forms and essentially followed the French Empire style. The terms *early* and *late* are often used to distinguish his early and best work from his later and inferior work.

Physician's Model A carved nude reclining Chinese female figure, usually of jade or ivory and elaborately worked. These figures were used by Chinese female patients to indicate the location of their illness or pain to a doctor. They were also used to indicate the illness to a doctor and not disclose the patient's identity for fear of having a poison prescribed. It is also called a doctor's lady.

Picardy In French Provincial cabinetwork; an old province in north-eastern France, east of Normandy, with a sea coast on the English Channel; it is now a part of the departments of Somme, Aisne, Oise, Yonne and Pas-de-Calais. The provincial furniture of Picardy and Artois is essentially the same. The furniture was distinctly French in feeling and was well proportioned. The cabinetwork was light and neatly executed. The favorite style was Louis XV, as it was in the majority of provinces. Transitional pieces which combined both Louis XV and Louis XVI characteristics displayed a pleasing technique in the blending of these two styles. See *French Provincial*.

Pickled Finish The term applied to the surface appearance of light-colored wood such as English deal after the paint has been removed. It is characterized by a whitish patina caused by the remaining particles of white gesso or a plaster-like composition that was used as an original base before painting.

Picot In lace-making; one of the many minute decorative loops worked on brides or cordonnets to enrich the lace.

Pie-Crust Table In English cabinetwork; the name given to a variety of mahogany circular tea table of tripod form designed in the Chippendale style. The edge of the circular top was carved in a series of curves. It derived its name from the supposed resemblance of the carved edge to the edge of a pie-crust. The top of the pie-crust table was cut from a single piece of wood and it generally tilted. The circular top was mounted on a carved shaft which rested on a carved tripod base. A structural feature

CHIPPENDALE PIE-CRUST TABLE, AMERICAN

which was sometimes employed on this variety of table is commonly referred to as a bird-cage. The finest examples of American pie-crust tables were made in Philadelphia. It appears that only relatively few were made in New England. See *Bird-Cage Support*; *Tea Table*; *Tripod Table*.

PIED DE BICHE

Pied de Biche In French cabinetwork; the French term applied to an early form of foot used on the cabriole leg of chairs and tables. It resembles the cloven-hoof foot of a doe or a stag. It was introduced in French furniture circa 1690 during the Louis XIV style. See *Cabriole Leg*; *Hoof Foot*; *Foot*.

Pied de Biche Spoon In English silver; the term also applied to the trifid-end spoon. See *Trifid-End Spoon*.

Pierced In cabinetwork; any carving that is cut through or perforated, such as a pierced splat in a chair back. It is the same as openworked. See *Openwork*.

Pierced Work In needlework; an elementary form of cutwork. See *Cutwork*.

Pier Mirror In furniture; a long vertical mirror designed to be placed on the portion of a wall between two windows or two doors. The term *pier* is an architectural term designating that portion of a wall. As a rule the pier mirror was very large and had a richly carved and molded gilt wood frame. See *Mirror*; *Pier Table*; *Trumeau*.

Pier Table In cabinetwork; the name is given to any decorative side table especially designed to fill a window pier. As a rule it was placed under a large pier mirror and was commonly found in the drawing room. Pier tables and pier mirrors were very fashionable throughout the 18th century. Pier tables designed by Adam were usually in pairs as they were an important feature in the symmetrical architectural treatment of the drawing room. Adam favored a pier table of semi-circular or semi-oval plan. Pier tables designed by Adam were principally made of either inlaid and painted

satinwood or of gilded wood. See *Pier Mirror*.

Pietra Dura In Italian decorative art; a fine variety of inlaid mosaic in which the tesserae were cut and polished semi-precious stones, such as amethyst, lapis lazuli, onyx, agate and jasper. The decorative motifs, which included all kinds of flowers, birds and butterflies, were realistically treated in their brilliant natural colors. Pietra dura was used in cabinetwork, especially on fine cabinets and decorative side tables made of ebony or a dark-toned wood. These pieces of furniture were sometimes further enhanced with inlays of ivory, exotic woods, mother-of-pearl, tortoise shell and various metals, and also with applied gilded bronze mounts. Although pietra dura was highly developed late in the 16th century it did not achieve its greatest perfection until the first half of the 17th century. At that time almost every elegant home in Italy and in Europe contained at least one fine example of pietra dura work. It was much favored for the French court furniture until practically the end of the reign of Louis XIV; in particular for ebony cabinets and for the tops of side tables made of carved gilt wood. The tops of these tables ornamented with pietra dura were generally of black basalt. See *Inlay*.

Piggin In English ceramics; a small shallow pottery vessel with a long handle at one side used for ladling out the liquor brewed in the tyg. It was principally made during the 17th and 18th centuries. See *Tyg*. In English silver; see *Cream-Pail*.

Pike A medieval weapon resembling a spear, having a long wooden shaft with a sharp-pointed steel head. Sometimes it had a sharp-pointed hook at the side of the head. The pike was used by the infantrymen.

Pilaster In cabinetwork; the pilaster, which in architecture is an engaged pier that projects slightly from the wall, was a favorite architectural feature of design employed in cabinetwork. The pilaster has a column and a base and is often fluted like a column. The pilaster was extensively employed as a decorative feature during the Italian Renaissance. During the Georgian period in England architecture was the serious study of the cabinetmaker. Early Georgian bookcases and other similar pieces incorporated architectural features in their principles of design. The stiles were usually ornamented with fluted pilasters adorned with Corinthian capitals and the cornices were surmounted with pediments. Chippendale wrote in the DIRECTOR, "of all the arts which are either improved or ornamented by architecture, that of cabinetmaking is not only the most useful, but capable of receiving as great assistance from it as any whatever. . . ."

Pilgrim Bottle The name given to a flattened vessel which was generally almost circular in shape designed with two loops or rings on the shoulders to hold a cord. As a rule it had a short neck. The body generally rested on a short spreading foot or base. Variations in form occurred. Pottery pilgrim bottles were made in China at least as early as the T'ang dynasty, 618–906. The silver pilgrim bottle was introduced in Europe late in the 16th century. It was finely wrought. It generally had loose silver chains attached from a finial on the stopper to a loop on each side of the shoulder.

Pilgrim Furniture In American cabinetwork; the name sometimes given to the furniture identified with the Pilgrims from their earliest days in America until about 1690. This furniture was essentially simple and crude in character and was undoubtedly similar to what they had been accustomed to in England. It seems that they may have brought a few pieces with them; however, most of this furniture was made in America by the local cabinetmakers who brought with them the traditional methods of English rural cabinetwork.

Pillar and Scroll Clock In American furniture; see *Terry Clock*.

Pillement, Jean 1728–1808. A noted French painter, decorative artist and engraver. During his lifetime he had been painter to Marie Antoinette and to the King of Poland. He was also one of the foremost designers at the Gobelins. He gained great fame for his chinoiserie decorations which were found in many of the great mansions of France. He created a delightful type of chinoiserie in the Rococo style which was very popular in England.

Pillow In Chinese ceramics; the pottery pillow or chên of oblong rectangular form, generally being slightly concave on the top, is of early origin and is among the articles found in ancient tombs. It appears from extant examples dating from the T'ang dynasty that tomb pillows as well as those used in daily Chinese life are rarely more than one foot in length. A passage in the T'ao Shou reveals that the Chinese regarded the use of porcelain pillows as "most efficacious in keeping the eyes clear and preserving the sight, so that even in old age fine writing can be read". It seems reasonable to assume that the existence of this curious belief among the Chinese accounted for much of the usage of porcelain pillows. Pillows were also made of other materials, and were occasionally inserted with porcelain plaques, but the majority by far were made of porcelain.

Pillow Lace In lace-making; see *Bobbin Lace*.

Pillow Sword In arms; a European sword having a straight blade and a straight crossguard. The term is derived from the custom of hanging it at the bedside of the master of the house. It was introduced during the first quarter of the 17th century.

Pimm, John American cabinetmaker of Boston, Massachusetts, who was active from about 1736 until his death in 1773.

Pinchbeck An alloy of 3 parts zinc and 4 parts copper which was much used for such articles as fine watch cases. The alloy derives its name from Christopher Pinchbeck, 1670–1732, a celebrated English watch and clockmaker, who was the inventor of this alloy. He also invented various kinds of astrono-

TZ'U CHOU PILLOW, SUNG

mico-musical clocks. Pinchbeck, which is the color of old brass, becomes a soft and warm golden color when polished.

Pinched Trailing In glass; the name is given, especially in English and American glass, to applied bands of glass that are pinched into wavy lines to give a decorative effect. It is also called Quilling.

Pine It is a straight-grained durable yellow or white wood, genus *pinus*. It varies from hard to very soft, such as in the white pine. Pine was used in English cabinetwork from around the beginning of the 17th century. It was used during the Early Georgian and Chippendale styles for articles of furniture such as mirrors and candlestands which were to be entirely gilded. In America there was an abundance of both the hard yellow pine and the soft white pine. Since the soft pine was easy to handle, the majority of the simpler types of furniture were made of pine. From around the beginning of the 18th century it has probably been more used than any other variety of wood. Walnut and mahogany furniture very often have parts which do not show made of pine. A mahogany or walnut veneer is often applied to an article of furniture made of pine. See *Pumpkin Pine*.

PINEAPPLE CUP

Pineapple Cup In silver; a tall decorative standing cup generally made of silver. The body is in the form of a pineapple or in the form of a cluster of two, three or four pineapples. It is surmounted with a figure, a group of figures or some similar subject. The body generally rests on a figural support, such as Neptune, and occasionally on other forms of supports, such as a tree trunk. The cup was designed with an elaborately wrought spreading base. The cup varies in height, the tallest being about 27 inches. The pineapple cup is principally identified with German silver and was introduced in the latter part of the 16th century. It is also called an Ananaspokal. See *Standing Cup*.

Pineau, Nicolas 1684-1754. A prominent French decorative artist of the 18th century, who is generally regarded as one of the chief pioneers in the Rococo style of ornament. The work of interior decoration that he executed for many of the palaces and châteaux of France rewarded him with a great reputation. In 1716 he was commissioned by Peter the Great to work at St. Petersburg where he stayed until 1727. Among his notable achievements in Russia were his chinoiseries at the Peterhof Palace.

Pinte In German ceramics; a variety of small tankard or cylindrical-shaped mug generally having roll moldings at the mouth and at the foot. The form, which was taken from a wooden prototype, was a characteristic form for Rhenish stoneware during the 16th and early 17th centuries. See *Schnelle*.

Pinxton In English ceramics; a small porcelain manufactory was started at Pinxton, Derbyshire, in 1796 by William Billingsley with the help of John Coke. Between 1796 and 1801 the manufactory made a translucent glassy soft paste porcelain having bone ash as one of its ingredients. The porcelain was often of fine quality; unfortunately it was sometimes misshapen. The forms were essentially simple and the wares were decorated in the current Derby styles. There was no recognized factory mark. In 1801 Billingsley left and in 1804 the business was taken over by John Cutts. An inferior and coarse porcelain that was almost opaque was then made until the manufactory closed in 1813.

Pipe Rack In English furniture; the pipe rack was introduced toward the end of the 17th century. It was designed to hold clay tobacco pipes with long slender stems. This kind of pipe was popularly called a churchwarden. One variety of pipe rack, designed to stand on a table, consisted of a turned shaft which rested on a turned circular base. The shaft was fitted with a disc which was pierced with holes through which the stems of the clay pipes could pass. The base was fitted with one or more spill holders.

Another variety was made to be attached to the wall. It had a solid wooden back to which were attached two rows of slotted rails for the pipes. The bottom was fitted with an open small bin for spills, below which was a drawer for tobacco.

Piqué d'Or   In French decorative art; see *Posé d'Or*.

Piranesi, Giovanni   1704–1784, a celebrated Venetian architect, draughtsman and etcher. He studied art at Rome and was greatly inspired by the classic works of art. He wrote many books; however, his outstanding contribution to furniture and the decorative arts was a book of engravings, entitled DIVERSE MANIERE, published in 1769. This book, which proved to be an endless source of supply and inspiration, was filled with fine classical ornament for mural decorations, for furniture and for such decorative objects as vases and candelabra. It is now generally believed that Piranesi strongly influenced French and English designs in the Neo-Classic style as well as Italian. See *Classic Revival*.

Pistol   It is generally thought that the pistol was first made at Pistoia, Italy. Caminello Vitelli, who was working around 1540, is given credit for inventing the pistol. The earliest pistol was made with a short single barrel and a heavy butt, which was almost at a right angle to the barrel. Shortly afterward the butt was lengthened and was practically level with the barrel. The early pistol was generally made with a wheellock. The pistol made with a metal handle or butt was in general use during the 16th and 17th centuries and was distinctive for its fine workmanship. It was very often mounted in silver. The first pistols made with a double barrel were rather clumsy since the barrels were arranged side by side and required two locks and two hammers. In another type of double barrel pistol only one lock and one hammer were required since one barrel was laid over the other barrel. It was made with a flint lock. See *Dag*; *Duelling Pistols*.

Pistol-Handle Knife   In English silver; a table knife so named because the handle is slightly pistol-shape. See *Knife*.

Pitcher   A large vessel for holding liquids, commonly of earthenware, provided with either a handle or two ears and generally with a lip for pouring out the liquids; a jug or vessel of jug shape or vase shape.

Pi Yü   A Chinese term applied to jade of a dark green color. See *Jade*.

Placcate   In medieval armor; an additional piece of protective steel plate covering the breast.

Placet   In French cabinetwork; a French stool. See *Escabeau*.

Plaited Lace   Italy claims the invention of plaited lace, and since much was made at Genoa it was known as Genoese lace. However, Spain also fabricated much plaited lace and it also was known as Point d'Espagne. The designs, which were geometrical and open, were formed on a pillow with bobbins. Plaited lace was made without a ground. Elaborately wrought gold plaited laces made at Genoa and Spain in the 17th century were especially praiseworthy.

Plaited Stitch   A stitch used in needlework which produces a herringbone effect and frequently receives that name.

Plane Wood   See *Platane Wood*.

Plaque   A decorative plate or tablet of metal, porcelain or some other material of rectangular, round or oval form, either plain or decorated, chiefly intended to be hung as a wall ornament or to be inserted in a fine article of cabinetwork. Sèvres plaques were occasionally inserted in some Louis XV and Louis XVI cabinetwork, such as tables and cabinets, and Wedgwood plaques were occasionally used in English cabinetwork designed in the Neo-Classic style. See *Jasper Ware*; *Migeon, Pierre*; *Louis Philippe*.

Plastron-de-Fer   In medieval armor; the

LOUIS XVI SÈVRES PLAQUE

steel breastplate worn under the hauberk. See *Hauberk*.

Platane Wood   The wood of the plane tree, *platanus orientalis*, used in cabinetwork. It is soft and its color is brown.

Plate   The term *plate*, from the old French words *plate* and *platte*, and the Spanish *plata*, meaning silver, and derived from the Latin *plata* is, in a strict sense, applied to articles of silver. However, the term *plate* is frequently applied to articles made of silver and gold used for domestic, ecclesiastical, or decorative purposes. Sometimes the term is applied to articles of plated ware, that is, metal covered with gold or silver and not of the solid precious metal. The term *plate* is also given to a shallow dish of porcelain, pottery or metal used at the table to hold food or for serving food.

Plate Armor   See *Mail*.

Plateau   A very low and long finely wrought decorative centerpiece for the dining table, generally made of bronze doré or silver and mounted on short feet or a plinth. The plateau, which was fashionable during the second half of the 18th century was usually designed in several parts, in order that its length could be adjusted. In France it was also called a surtout.

Plated Silver   See *Sheffield*.

Plate Pail   In English cabinetwork; the mahogany plate pail was used to carry the plates from the kitchen to the dining room. The more elaborate examples were often octagonal in form and the sides were of pierced fretwork. One of the eight sides was usually left open in order to facilitate the handling of the plates. The pail was fitted with a brass handle. Plate pails were often designed in pairs and were left by the fireplace to keep the plates warm. The plate pail was introduced around the middle of the 18th century.

Plateresque   In Spanish Renaissance ornament and architecture. See *Renaissance, Spanish*.

REGENCY PLATE STAND

Plateresque   In silver; a term applied by the Spanish to the elaborately detailed gold and silver work, which flourished during the late 15th and 16th centuries. See *Renaissance, Spanish*.

Plate Stand   In English furniture; stands designed especially to hold plates were introduced during the second half of the 18th century. These stands, which were rather plain pieces, were supported on either a tripod base or on four turned legs and were usually fitted with casters. Some were designed to hold only plates and the tops were round with a high spindled gallery just large enough to accommodate a stack of plates. The majority of stands were made with a rectangular top having one end rounded with a spindled gallery for the plates while the other end of the top was fitted with divisions to hold knives, forks and spoons. Sheraton in his CABINET DICTIONARY of 1803 states that these stands are among the pieces of cabinetwork termed a Canterbury and were made to stand by a table at supper. See *Canterbury*.

Plate Warmer   In English cabinetwork; the plate warmer in addition to being designed as one of a pair of sideboard pedestals was also designed as a separate piece of furniture. It was in the form of an enclosed mahogany stand. It had a metal-lined interior and was fitted with a heater. It was used in the dining room. It was introduced around the middle of the 18th century. See *Sideboard Pedestals; Chauffe-Assiette; Chauffe-Plat*.

Plinth   In cabinetwork; an architectural term for the lowest square member of the base of a column or pedestal, applied in furniture to the plain and flat base, often enriched with carved moldings, found on such articles as bookcases incorporating architectural features in their principles of design. It is also applied to a block-shaped foot. See *Break-Front Secretary Bookcase; Plinth Foot*.

Plinth Foot   In English cabinetwork; a rectangular block-like foot. It was sometimes used by Adam and by Chippendale around

1760 on chairs and tables having straight quadrangular legs. It was used by Chippendale, especially on the legs of chairs and tables designed in the Chinese and occasionally in the Gothic taste.

Plique-à-Jour A process of enamelling. See *Enamel*.

Plouk A Scottish name given to a small knob or blister, found on the inside near the rim of a liquid metal measure, to denote the place of exact measure. See *Measures*.

Plum Blossom In Chinese art; one of the flowers of the Chinese four seasons, representing Winter. See *Chinese Four Season Flowers*.

Plume Grain In English cabinetwork; see *Feather Banding*.

Plum-Pudding In English cabinetwork; see *Oystering*.

Plum Wood See *Prunier Wood*.

Plymouth In English ceramics; a manufactory producing the first hard paste porcelain in England was active in Plymouth, Devonshire, between 1768 and 1770, when it was transferred to Bristol. The manufacture of hard paste porcelain was due to William Cookworthy, a chemist of Plymouth who discovered the secret for making Chinese porcelain and then after many years of searching found the necessary materials in Cornwall. In 1768 he received a patent and established a manufactory at Coxside, Plymouth. Occasionally the porcelain was of good quality; however, it was often technically imperfect and inclined to be misshapen. The alchemist's sign for tin in underglaze blue, blue enamel, red or gold was the usual mark. The decoration revealed little originality. The painting in underglaze blue had a rather blackish tone. The enamel colors with the exception of a deep red and leaf green were usually impure in tone.

Point In needlework; the French word *point*, used from the 16th century, and the Italian word *punto*, used from the 15th century, refer to work done with stitches with the needle. The term *point* is applied to lace made entirely with the needle; however, the word is sometimes improperly applied to lace in general, as well as to pillow lace imitating lace produced with the needle. Point lace is also called needlepoint and needlepoint lace. The word *point* is often prefixed to the name of particular places where it is made. Point is also used in names of various stitches in embroidery and lace-making; and it is used to describe the small oblong or square designs worked on the net ground of various kinds of lace.

Point à l'Aiguille A French term meaning needlepoint lace. The name is also given to Brussels needlepoint lace. See *Brussels Lace*.

Point Appliqué A needlepoint or bobbin-made lace or a combination of both applied to a net foundation. The foundation usually is a machine-made net. See *Lace*.

Point Coupé In needlework; a French term meaning cutwork; a form of openwork embroidery. See *Cutwork*.

Point d'Alençon See *Alençon Point*; *Lace*.

Point d'Angleterre See *Angleterre*; *Lace*.

Point d'Argentan See *Argentan Point*; *Lace*.

Point de Bruxelles In lace-making; see *Angleterre*.

Point de France In lace-making; the vogue in France for cutwork and lace was due to Italian influence and the Italian fashions in lace were found at an early date in France. Louis XI, 1461–1483, sent to Venice and Milan for lace-workers. In the reign of Louis XIII, 1610–1643, the fine point laces of Italy and Flanders were highly coveted, with gold lace sharing the popularity of thread lace. Due to the vast sums spent on foreign laces it was decided that a lace industry should be established in France which would rival the foreign work. In 1665 a royal ordinance was passed with exclusive privileges for ten years establishing in various towns, such as Alençon, Aurillac,

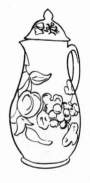

PLYMOUTH CHOCOLATE
POT

Sedan, and Arras, the manufacture of laces in the manner of Venetian and Italian point laces that were to be called collectively Points de France. The royal venture proved successful and Points de France supplanted those of Venice, and France became a lace-making as well as a lace-wearing country. A more moderate price bobbin-made lace was also extensively produced. Alençon made the finest of the needlepoint laces, and it seems that when the ten-year privilege expired in 1675, the name Point de France was given to Alençon alone, which was profusely used in the reign of Louis XIV. In examining contemporary engravings and paintings it seems that during the reign of Louis XIV all of the Alençon lace was of a Venetian character with brides. The term *Point de France* was last found in an inventory of 1723.

Point de Gaze In lace-making; a filmy delicate needlepoint lace made at Brussels in which the pattern and the ground are worked simultaneously by means of the same thread. It is made in small segments and the joining is covered as in early Brussels point laces by leaves, sprigs and similar motifs. Examples of this lace shown in the Paris Exhibition in 1867 were notable for the variety and richness of their fillings or jours and for the clearness of the ground. The cordonnet or outline thread is stitched around the edge or outline of the design, which feature is characteristic of Brussels needlepoint. The toile is worked in such a manner to give the effect of shading.

POINT DE VENISE À RESEAU

Point de Neige Lace worked upon a ground, having a snow-like appearance. Several varieties of Venetian Rose Point lace have grounds of starred threads resembling snowflakes. It is also called Punto Neve. See *Lace*.

Point de Paris In lace-making; from the 17th century lace was extensively made in various localities in the neighborhood of Paris. One early variety was an inexpensive narrow bobbin-made lace. From 1665 onwards until the French Revolution the quality of the designs and the workmanship

were admirable. Of particular interest were the gold and silver laces of Paris, frequently enriched with pearls and generally known as points d'Espagne. They were known throughout Europe and until the Revocation of the Edict of Nantes in 1685 they were an important commercial article. See *Point Double*.

Point de Raccroc In lace-making; a special stitch known to the lace-workers of Brussels and Bayeux. The stitch was known in England as fine joining. See *Vrai Réseau*.

Point d'Espagne In Spanish lace-making; see *Spanish Lace*; *Point de Paris*; *Plaited Lace*.

Point d'Esprit In French lace-making; a delicate bobbin-made tulle embroidered with dots produced in the French province of Brittany and also in Denmark and Genoa. See *Marli*.

Point de Tulle See *Mignonette*; *Lace*.

Point de Venise See *Venetian Point*; *Lace*.

Point de Venise à Réseau A delicate Venetian point lace having a very fine square mesh ground and characterized by a rather flat effect. It has never been determined whether it was made to imitate Alençon or vice versa. However, it is generally accepted that it surpassed both Alençon and Brussels in fineness. The cordonnet or outline thread was stitched to the edge of the design and was worked in a flat manner, and a minute mesh border was worked between the cordonnet and the ground or réseau.

Point d'Ivorie See *Punto Tagliato a Fogliami*.

Point Double In lace-making; the term *point double* was given to a variety of ground which required twice or double the number of threads employed in a single ground. It was also called Point de Paris and Point des Champs.

Pointillé In pewter; the French term given to a decorative work which is done by pricking the pewter with a sharp pointed tool.

Point Lace In lace-making; see *Point*.

Point Plat A French term meaning flat point. A term in lace-making applied to lace without a raised cordonnet or outline cord. The name is also sometimes applied to Brussels bobbin lace. See *Lace*

Point Plat de Venise A name given to the Venetian point laces, which were flat or were executed without any raised work. It is also called Venetian Flat Point, and is in direct contrast to the Venetian Raised Point, which is done in relief of varying degrees. See *Venetian Point*; *Lace*.

Point Plat de Venise au Fuseau A name given to a modern Venetian lace made with bobbins; *fuseau* being the French word for bobbin. Around 1875 bobbin-made polychrome lace was introduced in Venice. The motifs, which included flowers, foliage, fruits, arabesques and birds, were realistically colored. See *Lace*.

Poirier Wood The wood of the pear tree, *pyrus communis*, used in cabinetwork, especially by the French ébénistes. It is very hard and its color is reddish.

Poitou In French Provincial; an old province in western France, on the Bay of Biscay, south of Brittany, it is now mostly in the departments of Deux-Sèvres, Vendée and Vienne. The provincial furniture of Poitou designed in the Louis XIII style was characterized by an abundance and variety of walnut or oak cupboards or armoires. They were generally heavy in construction and rich in ornament, and were finely carved with geometrical decoration, especially the diamond point and star diamond point. Furniture designed in the Louis XV style was well proportioned and was usually simply decorated with rather thin moldings. The pieces were distinctly French in feeling. During the Louis XVI style the furniture was decorated with rather flat carved motifs of classic inspiration. Some of the furniture was made of exotic woods, such as rosewood and amaranth. See *French Provincial*.

Pokal In glass; the German term *pokal* is applied to a large standing cup with a cover; particularly one having fine decoration and artistic merit. Pokal is from the French word *bocal* and the Italian word *boccale*, derived from the Latin word *baucalis*. The term *bocal* was used as early as 1532 in French records.

Poleaxe A medieval weapon; see *Battle-Axe*.

Pole-Hammer A medieval weapon having a long shaft with a steel head resembling a spiked hammer. Sometimes it had a sharp point extending beyond the head. It is also called a war-hammer.

Pole Lantern In Spanish furniture; the Spanish pole lantern, which is also called a farol, was a distinctive Spanish decorative appointment. It was a relatively large many-sided lantern and was made of tin, which was painted and gilded. The tin was cut into elaborate openwork designs and usually had many colored pieces of glass placed in back of or fitted in the openwork. The lantern was mounted on a long red pole or on a pole covered with crimson velvet. Occasionally the lantern was suspended from the ceiling on a long heavy silk cord.

Pole Medallion A design used in Oriental rugs; in particular in the Hamadan and Shiraz rugs. The motif consisted of a medallion with appendant decorative treatment.

Pole Screen In English cabinetwork; a variety of fire screen which came into general use during the first half of the 18th century. It had a small rectangular or shaped frame, which was fitted with a fabric panel and which was attached to a pole or rod. The pole was mounted on a tripod base. The framed panel could be adjusted at any height on the pole. The pole screen was designed in each of the successive 18th century styles of English furniture. The pole screen of tripod form was a popular piece of American furniture and it was designed in the Chippendale, Hepplewhite and Sheraton styles. See *Fire Screen*; *Ecran à Eclisse*.

HEPPLEWHITE POLE SCREEN

Polish In English furniture; there are several principal processes for acquiring a gloss by friction or rubbing and thus enriching the grain and figure of a wood surface. Very often some stain is added to these polishing mediums to improve the color. The earliest method of rubbing with oil, namely nut, poppy and linseed oil, came into general use in the 16th century. In addition to oil rubbing, beeswax and turpentine came into favor. The former, especially on oak, darkened the wood, while the latter gave a light warm golden tone, which did not darken the wood except for any particles of dust adhering to the film of wax. For the fine cabinetwork made of walnut, mahogany and satinwood from about 1660 onwards a lengthy and costly method of rubbing down and polishing with tripoly powder and oil after the surface was varnished came into favor. The less expensive furniture, in particular articles for general use and provincial pieces, was polished with wax or was finished with linseed oil very frequently dyed with alkanet root, which produced a reddish stain. A new method imparting a hard glass-like sheen by covering the surface with a fine film of shellac was introduced from France around 1820 and was called French polish. In this process pads dipped into a solution of shellac dissolved in spirit were rubbed on the surface at regular intervals. This polishing medium is not too satisfactory since it is seriously damaged by heat and wears off with use. See *Varnish*.

Polish Carpet See *Polonaise Rug*.

Polonaise Rug The name given to an early Persian rug first made during the reign of Shah Abbas, 1588–1629. The Polonaise rug was of the same construction as an Oriental. Another type was woven by the tapestry method. The rug was invariably hand-made and it was woven entirely in silk with gold and silver threads for the ground. The provenance of these sumptuous rugs has never been completely solved. Undoubtedly some were made in Persia. Although pile carpets were made in Poland these so-called Polonaise or Polish rugs with silk piles are a mistaken attribution. *See Oriental Rug.*

Pomander The term is derived from the French phrase *pomme d'ambre*, meaning apple of amber. The name is given to a small ball of ambergris or of musk enclosed in a silver container. It was worn on a chain around the neck or hung from the girdle to counteract fevers and offensive smells. The container which was often finely wrought in gold or silver is also called a pomander. See *Vinaigrette*; *Pouncet Box*.

Pome In ecclesiastical art; a ball of gold or silver, containing hot water, placed on the altar during the winter months. It was used by the priest to keep his hands warm and to prevent any accident which might occur from handling the chalice with chilled fingers. The pome, which was often engraved with sacred imagery, was frequently provided with a little dish. It was mentioned in medieval inventories.

Pommel The knob or rounded end on the hilt of a sword, dagger or some similar hand weapon. It was chiefly used to keep the hand from slipping.

Pommier Wood The wood of the apple tree, *pyrus malus*, used for inlay and cabinetwork, especially by the French ébénistes. It is hard and its color is white.

Pomona Glass In American glass; a late 19th century American art glass. It was blown from clear glass, frequently patterned molded, and was made with two entirely different surfaces. One surface was treated with a pale amber tint or stain and the other with etching. Sometimes the piece of glass was further enhanced with a running motif of pale blue stained flowers and straw-color leaves. See *Art Glass*.

Poniard In arms; a small dagger having a blade in section square or triangular. The poniard was useful only for thrusting.

Pont-aux-Choux In French ceramics; a

SILVER POMANDER

manufactory producing white earthenware was started in Paris around 1740. Its reputation is due to the cream-colored earthenware of fine quality and color which they began to produce around 1765. In 1772 it was advertized as a Manufacture Royale. The decoration, which was molded in relief, chiefly consisted of flowers, foliage and other similar motifs and was in imitation of silversmith's work. The fleur-de-lis in gold occurred as a mark; however, the wares were not regularly marked. In 1777 the fleur-de-lis was registered as a porcelain mark by the proprietor of Pont-aux-Choux. However, porcelain bearing this mark is rarely found. See *Paris Porcelain*.

Ponteuse In French furniture; a distinctive variety of 18th century chair similar to the fumeuse with a shaped narrow back. The occupant sits in a reverse position and rests his arms on the wide crest rail. The crest rail is in the form of an oblong box with a lid which when opened was divided into two compartments. The ponteuse was used by persons watching card games and other games of chance and the opened box was used to hold tokens, counters, chips and money. See *Fumeuse*; *Voyeuse*; *Chaise à Accoudoir*.

Pontil Mark Or Punty Mark. In glass; the name given to the mark left on the bottom of blown glass. An iron rod called a pontil was attached to the bottom of the foot of a glass while the bowl was being formed. When the glass was finished the pontil was broken away leaving a rough mark where it was attached. After the middle of the 18th century this mark was ground down to make a smooth depression, and polished.

Pontypool An English term applied to japanning on metal. It was invented about 1660 by Thomas Allgood, at Pontypool, in South Wales. It is also called Pontypool Japan. His son, Edward, continued on with the work and further developed the process. Later the process of japanning on metal

spread to the larger centers in England, such as London and Birmingham. Japanning was particularly applied on tea and coffee pots, tea caddies and trays. Birmingham became the most important center for producing this work. During the middle of the 18th century the Birmingham work was decorated with colors, while the work being done at Pontypool was in gold only, usually with Chinese figures and scenes.

Poplar Wood See *Peuplier Wood*.

Poppy Head In Gothic ornament; a decorative carved finial used on the ends of pews, benches and other similar ecclesiastical furniture. It is occasionally simply cut in the form of a plain fleur-de-lis or in some other similar decorative motif; however, it is very often richly carved with leaves, flowers, figure subjects and other like motifs.

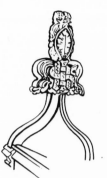

GOTHIC POPPY HEAD

Porcelain In ceramics; true porcelain was made in China as early as the T'ang dynasty, 618–906. The Chinese used the term *porcelain* in a broad sense. In addition to the fine hard white, more or less translucent, vitrified material which is required in the European definition, the Chinese included fine hard dusky and grey materials which had been fired to such a vitrifiable state that they emitted a musical note when struck. The musical note was the principal test of early porcelain in China. In European ceramics; European porcelain falls into two main classes, the true porcelain also called hard paste porcelain or pâte dure and the artificial porcelain known as soft paste porcelain or pâte tendre. True porcelain is made of kaolin or china clay and of petuntse or china stone. Kaolin is a nonfusible silicate of aluminum, and petuntse is a fusible silicate of aluminum, and when these two related materials are fired at a temperature of 1300° C–1400° C they produce a white more or less translucent vitrified material. This material may be glazed with a compound of petuntse with lime or some similar fluxing material. True porcelain or feldspathic porcelain is so hard that ordinary steel will not cut it. The secret for making true porcelain in Europe was discovered by Johann Friedrich Böttger of Meissen in 1708, and in the following year he made a suitable glaze for it. The ware was first placed on the market at Leipzig in 1713. Although the secret became known elsewhere due to a few runaway workmen from Meissen, it was not until after the middle of the 18th century that any considerable number of hard paste porcelain manufactories were established. Unglazed porcelain is called biscuit or bisque. The terms *porcelain* and *china* are synonymous. The artifical or soft paste porcelain was made with glassy substances before Böttger discovered true porcelain. See *Soft Paste Porcelain*; *Parian Ware*; *Bone China*; *Enamel*, in Ceramics; *Glaze*.

PORRINGER
JAMES II, 1685

PORRINGER
AMERICAN, 1725

Porringer   In silver; a two-handled cup generally having a cover used for serving hot drinks made of wine. It is usually about 4 inches high and proportionately wide. As a rule the lower portion of the body is elaborately worked. This cup is closely associated with and is similar to the caudle cup. It was introduced around 1600 and is principally identified with English silver. See *Caudle Cup*. The term *porringer* is also given to a shallow silver bowl having a single flat pierced handle horizontal to the rim. It is similar to the English bleeding bowl but is larger in size. It is principally identified with American silver. See *Bleeding Bowl*.

Porró   Or Porrón. In Spanish glass; the porró was a characteristic 18th century spouted wine vessel peculiar to Valencia and Catalonia. It consists of a low squat-shaped body which curves inwards and tapers to form a long neck. The lip rim is in the form of a disk or an undulating trefoil. A very long drinking spout which tapers almost to a point is attached to the shoulder of the body and slants slightly upward. The porró is still used by the peasants for drinking wine; the wine being emitted from the spout in the form of a stream into the mouth of the drinker.

Porter Chair   Or Page Chair. In English furniture; a tall, commodious, upholstered leather chair having deep wings or side pieces equal to the depth of the seat and continuing to form an arched top, the purpose being to protect the occupant against drafts. It was found in the halls of the stately town houses and country mansions during the 18th century and was used by the manservant whose duty it was to open the door.

Portland Vase   The name given to a Roman glass vase. It is believed to have been made around the first century A.D. It was found in excavations near Rome in the late 16th century. It was in the possession of the Barberini family in Rome, and in 1786 it was acquired by the Duke of Portland. It is also referred to as the Barberini vase. The vase is now in the British Museum in a restored condition, since it had been broken into pieces by a madman. It is cameo glass and it is generally considered to be the finest extant example of that type of work. The ground color is almost black and the designs are of Roman figures in white relief. Wedgwood made reproductions of the Portland or Barberini vase in blue and blue-black jasper ware with relief figures in white. This work was started in 1786 and completed in 1790, and it is believed that about fifty reproductions were made before Wedgwood's death and that not over sixteen pieces exist at the present time. See *Cameo Glass*; *Glass*.

Portobello   In English ceramics; a variety of Staffordshire earthenware made around 1739 decorated with applied reliefs of ships and the figure of Admiral Edward Vernon, with inscriptions commemorating the capture of Portobello, Panama, by him in 1739. This so-called Portobello ware is very characteristic of the wares made by Thomas Astbury. See *Astbury, Thomas*.

Portor Marble   A black Italian marble having gold veins. It is procured from the Porto Venere quarries at Spezia, in Liguria.

CHANTILLY CACHEPOT
c. 1730-1740

CAPO DI MONTE VASE
c. 1780

MEDICI SPOUTED JAR
c. 1580

VINCENNES TUREEN
c. 1753

ST. CLOUD SPICE BOX
c. 1700-1725

SÈVRES VASE
1757

MENNECY WALL FOUNTAIN
c. 1750

Courtesy of the Metropolitan Museum of Art

EUROPEAN PORCELAIN

MEISSEN VASE
c. 1725

CHELSEA CANDELABRA
c. 1765

CROWN DERBY VASE
c. 1784-1811

FURSTENBERG FIGURES
THE MINERS
c. 1760

FULDA FIGURE
A GARDENER BOY
c. 1770-1775

WORCESTER JUG
c. 1770-1775

NYMPHENBURG FIGURE
COLUMBINE c. 1760

LUDWIGSBURG INKSTAND
c. 1760

HOCHST CARTEL
c. 1765

Courtesy of the Metropolitan Museum of Art

MARSEILLES TUREEN
c. 1760

FULDA VASE
c. 1741–1744

ROUEN SUGAR CASTER
c. 1700–1720

STRASBOURG TUREEN
c. 1750

DELFT PLATE
c. 1700–1725

MOUSTIERS EWER
c. 1710–1740

DELFT VASE
c. 1700

SCEAUX JUG
c. 1760

Courtesy of the Metropolitan Museum of Art

ITALIAN AND SPANISH POTTERY

MAJOLICA DISH
Florence or Faenza, c. 1480–1500

MAJOLICA ISTORIATO TAZZA,
LUSTERED AT GUBBIO
Urbino, 1538

MAJOLICA ALBARELLO
Deruta, c. 1510

HISPANO-MORESQUE LUSTERED JAR,
WITH ARMS OF POPE PAUL V
Cataluña, 1605–1621

HISPANO-MORESQUE LUSTERED PLATE,
WITH ARMS OF JOAN PAYO COELLO,
ABBOT OF POBLET
Valencia, 1480–1499

HISPANO-MORESQUE LUSTERED DEEP DISH,
WITH ARMS OF THE GUASCONI FAMILY
OF FLORENCE
Valencia, mid 15th century

*Photographs in first row and second row left
courtesy of the Metropolitan Museum of Art*

Others courtesy of The Hispanic Society of America

WHITE WARE WINE EWER
WITH PHEASANT STOPPER
T'ang

NORTHERN CELADON
SHALLOW BOWL
Sung

TZ'U CHOU AMPHORA-
SHAPED VASE WITH CARVED
DESIGN OF PEONY AND
LOTUS PETALS
Sung

YING CH'ING STATUETTE
OF A SCHOLAR,
PARTLY GLAZED
Sung

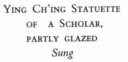

YING CH'ING LOTUS CUP
WITH DRAGON HANDLE
AND BEADED LIP RIM
Sung

LUNG CH'ING FIVE-COLOR
WARE JAR
Ming

Courtesy of Frank Caro, New York

CHINESE PORCELAIN

WAN LI FUKIEN FIGURE
OF KUAN YIN WITH
CREAMY-WHITE GLAZE
Ming

CHIA CHING FIVE-COLOR
WARE JAR
Ming

CH'IEN LUNG KU YÜEH
HSÜAN BOTTLE-SHAPED
VASE *Ch'ing*

YUNG CHÊNG BRUSH JAR
OR PI T'UNG WITH
SEPIA DECORATION *Ch'ing*

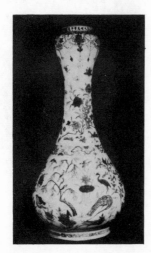

WAN LI FIVE-COLOR
WARE BOTTLE-SHAPED
VASE
Ming

K'ANG HSI CLAIR DE LUNE
AMPHORA-SHAPED VASE
Ch'ing

Courtesy of Frank Caro, New York

KAKIEMON DEEP DISH
17th-18th century

IMARI LARGE BOWL
18th century

KUTANI DISH
17th century

KAKIEMON BOWL
17th century

IMARI BOWL
17th century

NABESHIMA DISH ON A HIGH FOOT
19th century

Courtesy of the Boston Museum of Fine Arts

JAPANESE SWORD MOUNTS

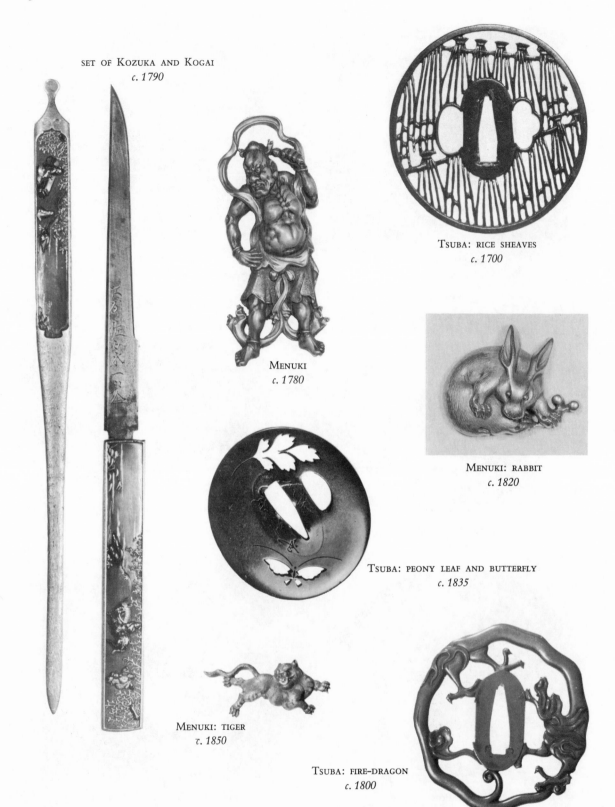

SET OF KOZUKA AND KOGAI
c. 1790

MENUKI
c. 1780

TSUBA: RICE SHEAVES
c. 1700

MENUKI: RABBIT
c. 1820

TSUBA: PEONY LEAF AND BUTTERFLY
c. 1835

MENUKI: TIGER
c. 1850

TSUBA: FIRE-DRAGON
c. 1800

Courtesy of the Cooper Union Museum

GOLD AND HELIOTROPE
SNUFF BOX WITH PORTRAIT
MINIATURE
French, 18th century

GOLD VINAIGRETTE WITH
MINIATURE
French c. 1810

GOLD AND STRIPED AGATE
JEWELLED NÉCESSAIRE
English c. 1760

JEWELLED GOLD SCENT
BOTTLE
French c. 1760

CHASED GOLD ÉTUI
French c. 1780

GOLD AND ENAMEL PATCH BOX
CONTAINING SMALL BRUSH WITH
GOLD HANDLE *French c. 1785*

JEWELLED GOLD AND ENAMEL SNUFF
BOX WITH PORTRAIT MINIATURE
French c. 1775

GOLD AND TORTOISE SHELL
NÉCESSAIRE
French early 18th century

Courtesy of the Metropolitan Museum of Art

ENGLISH SILVER

SILVER CAUDLE CUP
INITIALS E.N.
London, 1682-1683

SILVER TEA CADDY
PAUL LAMERIE
London, 1744-1745

SILVER TEAKETTLE WITH
STAND AND BURNER
INITIALS B.B.
London, 1762

SILVER SALVER
JOHN ROBINSON
London, 1744-1745

SILVER PUNCH BOWL
JOHN EAST
London, 1705-1706

SILVER SOUP TUREEN
PAUL STORR
London, 1806-1808

Courtesy of the Metropolitan Museum of Art

SILVER COFFEE POT
FRANÇOIS THOMAS GERMAIN, PARIS
1756-1757

SILVER MUSTARD POT
ANTOINE BAILLY, PARIS
1758-1759

SILVER SUGAR BOWL
JACQUES FAVRE, PARIS
1779-1780

SILVER SAUCE BOATS
PIERRE ADRIEN DACHERY,
SAINT-QUENTIN
1768-1775

SILVER SUGAR CASTERS
NICOLAS BESNIER, PARIS
1728-1729

COVERED SILVER DISH WITH FLANGE HANDLES
ELOI GUÉRIN, PARIS
1749-1750

Courtesy of the Metropolitan Museum of Art

AMERICAN SILVER

SILVER CHAFING DISH
JOHN BURT, BOSTON
1725-1745

SILVER CAN OR MUG
JOSEPH MOULTON. NEWBURY, MASS.
c. 1750

SILVER TANKARD
SIMEON SOUMAIN, NEW YORK
c. 1725

SILVER TWO-HANDLED CUP
CORNELIUS KIERSTEDE, NEW YORK
Early 18th century

SILVER TEAPOT
PAUL REVERE, JR. BOSTON
1770-1810

SILVER PORRINGER WITH KEYHOLE
PATTERN FLANGE HANDLE
SAMUEL CASEY, NEWPORT
18th century

SILVER SALVER ON A FOOT
JOHN CONEY, BOSTON
Early 18th century

Courtesy of the Metropolitan Museum of Art

AMPHORISKOS
EGYPTIAN
c. 1500–1400 B.C.

Photo: John Kalinich

BLOWN-MOLDED PYXIS
SIDON OR TYRE
c. late 1st Century B.C.

DRAGON-STEM GOBLET
VENETIAN
c. 16th Century

ENAMELLED MOSQUE LAMP
SYRIAN
c. 1350

ENAMELLED GOBLET
VENETIAN
c. 16th Century

POKAL OR GOBLET WITH AN
ENGRAVED HUNTING SCENE
NUREMBERG
c. 1660–1670

Courtesy of the Corning Museum of Glass

GLASS

Photo: Marc Bomse

DUTCH ROEMER WITH DIAMOND
POINT ENGRAVING
NETHERLANDS
17th Century

Photo: John Kalinich

ENAMELLED ARMORIAL BEAKER
GERMAN, PROBABLY SAXON
dated 1671

GOBLET WITH RAVEN'S
HEAD SEAL
LONDON
c. 1676-1678

Photo: Marc Bomse

GOBLET WITH DIAMOND STIPPLE
ENGRAVING
ENGLAND OR NETHERLANDS
Signed F. Greenwood, dated 1746

BLOWN-THREE-MOLD SUGAR BOWL
AMERICAN
c. 1820-1835

LILY-PAD PITCHER, SOUTH JERSEY TYPE
AMERICAN
c. 1840-1860

Courtesy of the Corning Museum of Glass

DRAWNWORK
Italian 16th or 17th century

LACIS OR NETWORK
Italian, late 16th century

**CUTWORK WITH DETAILS
IN NEEDLEPOINT LACE**
Italian 16th century

RETICELLO, NEEDLEPOINT
Italian, late 16th century

GROS POINT DE VENISE
Italian 17th century

POINT DE VENISE À RESEAU
Italian 18th century

Courtesy of the Metropolitan Museum of Art

LACE

TAPE LACE, BOBBIN-MADE
Italian 17th century

GUIPURE LACE, BOBBIN-MADE
a) Italian 17th century
b) Flemish 17th century

ANGLETERRE, BOBBIN-MADE
Brussels, early 18th century

MECHLIN, BOBBIN-MADE
Flemish, 18th century

POINT DE FRANCE, NEEDLEPOINT
French, late 17th century

VALENCIENNES, BOBBIN-MADE
Flemish, 18th century

ALENÇON, NEEDLEPOINT
French mid 18th century

ARGENTAN, NEEDLEPOINT
French, 18th century

Courtesy of the Metropolitan Museum of Art

Portrait Flask In American glass; a glass flask made during the 19th century having the portrait of an American president or some other celebrated or historical personage pressed in the glass. See *Flask*.

Portrait Medallion In ornament; see *Medallion*.

Posé d'Or In French decorative art; the term *posé d'or* is applied to the art of inlaying in a ground of tortoise shell elaborately chased gold designs representing baldachins, arabesques, silhouettes of figures and other similar subjects. This work was often further enhanced by piqué d'or which is the term given to the decoration consisting of tiny gold nails or minute studs driven into the tortoise shell and set closely together. It was worked in designs of flowers, foliage or shell-forms to complete or add detail to the chased gold subjects. When these gold nails were of a slightly larger diameter and were used to give a more bold emphasis to the design the work was called clouté d'or. Posé d'or and piqué d'or work in tortoise shell introduced in the Louis XIV period continued to be a favorite process employed by French artists for ornamenting snuff boxes, étuis and exquisite small objects of virtù throughout the Louis XV period and succeeding styles.

Posset-Pot In English ceramics; a small cylindrical pottery drinking vessel made during the 17th and 18th centuries. The posset-pot was fitted with a cover and two handles and with a small spout projecting from the side of the cup through which the posset was sucked. Posset was an old English drink and is especially associated with Christmas Eve. It is usually a mixture of warm ale or wine with hot curdled milk, sugar, spices and bits of bread or oatcake. During the 17th and 18th centuries there was a penchant for curious drinking vessels in pottery. See *Tyg*.

Potash Glass In glass; a glass having an alkaline flux of potash. See *Glass*.

Potato-Ring In Irish silver; see *Dish Ring*.

Potiche In ceramics; the name given to a vase generally having a polygonal or rounded body of almost cylindrical form with slightly pronounced shoulders. The neck is slightly smaller in width than the body. It is fitted with a cover of conforming design with a finial. This form of vase was widely used in Chinese ceramics.

Pot-Pourri The French term *pot-pourri*, which literally means rotten pot, is applied to a mixture of dried petals of different flowers mixed with spices and kept in a jar or container for its perfume qualities. It was mentioned in England as early as 1749. In ceramics; the name is given to a container designed with a delicate perforated cover used to hold a mixture of pot-pourri. It was made in a variety of forms, such as bowls, jars and vases. Many were made by European potters in porcelain, faïence and pottery.

Potsdam In German ceramics; a faïence manufactory was started at Potsdam, near Berlin, around 1739 by Christian Friedrich Rewend and remained in the Rewend family until 1775. There were several changes in ownership and it was still active in 1800. It has been established that the mark "P" over "R" was occasionally used until 1775. The manufactory did not develop any distinctive style. The wares essentially resembled the wares made at Delft. The painted decoration in underglaze blue and in polychrome in the Delft style was carefully executed.

Potsdam In German glass; a glass manufactory was established at Potsdam, near Berlin, in 1679 under the patronage of Friedrich Wilhelm, Elector of Brandenburg. The work was under the direction of Johann Kunckel, the famous chemist who is generally given credit for the perfection of ruby glass. The early Potsdam glass was of fine quality although it was often affected by crizelling. After 1689 the defect was overcome by additional quantities of chalk similar to the Bohemian glass formula. After the death of the Elector Friedrich Wilhelm

NIDERVILLER POT-POURRI

in 1688 Kunckel's experimental glasshouse was destroyed by fire and shortly thereafter he left the Potsdam factory. In 1736 the Potsdam factory was moved to Zechlin and operated as a State enterprise until 1890. The early production at Potsdam is celebrated for the engraved work of famous artists such as Franz Gondelach, and their hochschnitt cameo relief work. The characteristic pieces of Potsdam included large tankards and well-formed goblets with domed covers resting on heavy baluster stems. Much of the work featured decorative borders of lozenge or circular-shaped cutting. The engraved motifs, which were occasionally gilded, were frequently of a military nature, including armorial devices, trophies of arms, monograms, portraits and allegories. From about 1700 to 1720 the engraved work of H. F. Halter, who often signed his initials, appears on goblets in the form of portraits and landscapes with buildings. See *Cassel*, in German glass; *Hochschnitt*.

LOUIS XV POUDREUSE

Potten Kant In lace-making; a Flemish term, literally meaning pot lace, given to a flowerpot pattern identified with Antwerp lace and symbolical of the Annunciation. In the early representations of the visit of the Angel Gabriel to the Virgin Mary, lilies were either held in his hand, or were arranged in a vase or pot. Gradually all was omitted but the vase of flowers or simply the vase. This vase motif displayed variation in its composition. See *Antwerp Lace*.

Pottery In ceramics; the term was formerly used to describe all kinds of ceramic wares, that is porcelain, stoneware and earthenware. At the present time the term *pottery* is applied only to earthenware and is not applied to porcelain nor to stoneware. The body of pottery is not vitrified. Slipware, majolica, faïence and delftware are all varieties of earthenware. See *Earthenware*.

Pou In Chinese bronzes; the name applied to a ritual vessel which is in the form of a large round deep bowl with a cover, and rests on a raised foot rim.

Poudreuse In French cabinetwork; the toilet table or dressing table called a poudreuse was a fashionable and necessary article of 18th century French furniture. As a rule the poudreuse was designed in the same manner; naturally slight variations occurred. It had an oblong top over a frieze. The top was divided into three hinged parts; the two end sections opened to wells equipped with toilet accessories. These two end sections which opened outward, that is left and right, were used as shelves for the toilet articles. The center section lifted up and was fitted with a framed mirror which moved forward on two grooves. Under the center panel was a pull-out slide beneath which was a drawer. Beneath each end panel there was a false drawer to correspond to the wells and a real drawer. The toilet table is generally considered to be one of the choice articles of 18th century French furniture and it was designed in each of the successive styles. In the more costly examples the wells were lined with silk and the toilet articles were made of fine French porcelain, cut glass or lacquer. By the end of the 18th century the dressing table with its rising mirror was no longer in vogue. The principal Empire mahogany dressing table had an oblong white marble top over a frieze fitted with drawers and was designed either with lyre-shaped supports or with supports of X-form. A miniature Psyché mirror was often placed on the marble top. See *Coiffeuse*.

Pounce Box Or Sand Caster. In English silver; a sand caster or pounce box was one of the essential writing accessories found on the standish or inkstand. It conformed in design to the ink-pot and was provided with a perforated top. This pot or box contained pounce, a fine powder made from pulverized gum sandarac, a resin which exudes from the tree *callitris quadrivalvis* of north-west Africa. It was used to prevent the ink from spreading over an erasure or on unsized paper; it was not used to dry the wet ink. See *Standish*.

Pouncet Box In English silver; a small silver

box provided with a perforated lid introduced during the middle of the 16th century. Gentlemen carried it in the pocket or attached to a black string, until the early part of the 17th century. The box contained a sponge saturated with a pungent aromatic vinegar and it was thought to ward off disease, as well as serving as a protection against offensive odors. See *Pomander*.

Powder Blue Ware In Chinese ceramics; porcelain of the Ch'ing period, especially of the K'ang Hsi reign, which is characterized by a beautiful and rather even ground of bright soft blue with a slightly clouded appearance. As a rule the ground is covered with very close and minute blurry particles; occasionally the ground is not so closely speckled. Since it is not possible to lay an even ground of underglaze blue by means of a brush, it was necessary to devise some other method. It is generally believed that the ground on powder blue ware was applied by blowing on the blue and then carefully applying the glaze after the blue was entirely dried. Sometimes gold or silver decoration was applied over the glaze. When decorative designs were to be painted on the ware a piece of paper was cut in the proper shape and was temporarily laid on the portion to be reserved in white, while the blue was blown or sprayed on. Later the designs in the white portions were painted in underglaze blue, and, after the article was glazed and fired, with overglaze enamels.

Powder Stand In English cabinetwork; the name wig or powder stand was given to a small turned stand which was usually a little over a foot in height. In a broad sense it could be compared to a modern hat stand. The top which was often circular in shape was supported by a short shaft that rested on a circular base. It was used to hold the wig while the owner was not wearing it and to hold the wig while powdering it. The wig stand was chiefly utilitarian and had no special decorative value. Although wearing a wig is of ancient origin, the ladies in England

did not wear them until the 16th century and the men until after the Restoration. See *Basin Stand*.

Pratt, Felix In English ceramics; it is reputed that Felix Pratt and his successors, who were Staffordshire potters, made a variety of pottery from around 1780 to 1820 decorated in relief with figures, fruits, leaves and other motifs painted in orange, green and blue underglaze colors. There is no doubt that this variety, which was rarely marked, was made by other contemporary English Staffordshire potters. Around the middle of the 19th century the manufactory was making wares with a stipple-printed decoration in several different colors. They were marked " F. & R. Pratt".

Prayer Rug An Oriental rug; see *Namazlik*.

Press In English cabinetwork; the name given to a variety of cupboard or ambry with long cupboard doors fitted with shelves for linen or with pegs for clothes. The press was a relatively scarce piece of furniture during the 16th century and was found only in the extremely wealthy homes. See *Ambry*; *Cupboard*; *Clothespress*.

Press Bed In English furniture; a variety of bed designed to fit in a cupboard or wardrobe mentioned in Stuart inventories and continued to be made in the 18th century. The door of the wardrobe turned up to form the tester which was supported by two detached poles placed under it. Hepplewhite in his GUIDE states that he did not illustrate this form of bed, but attracts attention to a wardrobe resembling a press bed which could be adapted for this purpose by making the door open upward to form the tester.

Press Cupboard In American cabinetwork; the term *press cupboard* is given to a form of cupboard resembling the English hall and parlor cupboard which was introduced in England around the middle of the 16th century and until recently called a court cupboard. The press cupboard was first

PRESS CUPBOARD,
AMERICAN

made in America during the second half of the 17th century and was popular in the early 18th century. It was a large rectangular piece in which the upper section had three recessed panels, fitted with one or more cupboard doors, with the end panels often being canted, surmounted with a projecting frieze and cornice which rested on two bulbous form supports. The lower portion was fitted with either drawers or cupboard doors. These oak cupboards were inspired by those of the Jacobean era. The name *press* is applied to these cupboards because it is believed the drawers or compartments served as a clothespress. See *Hall and Parlor Cupboard*.

Pressed Glass In glass; the term applied to glassware which receives its form from a cast iron mold by the pressure of a mechanical plunger which is usually worked by a hand lever. The method of pressing glass was introduced as a means of producing inexpensive glass tableware in imitation of hand-cut glass. The glass receives its design or pattern from the mold in which it is pressed. The practical machine for pressing glass was developed in America in the later 1820's and within a few years was in general use in American glasshouses. See *American Glass*.

Pretender Glass In English glass; see *Jacobite Glass*.

Pricket The name given in the Middle Ages to the spike for securing a candle found on candlesticks and chandeliers. It was later supplanted by a nozzle. The name was also given to the candle or taper itself which was stuck on the pricket.

Prie-Dieu In cabinetwork; the Gothic bedroom generally contained a small prayer stand or prie-dieu. The term *prie-dieu* was not given to a prayer stand until the early part of the 17th century, at which time in France a small room or oratory was sometimes known by the same name. The form of the prie-dieu varied. Essentially it consisted of an upright vertical portion supporting a narrow shelf serving as an arm rest

PRIE-DIEU, ITALIAN

or book rest and a flat portion close to the floor used for kneeling.

Prince of Wales Plume In English ornament; the name given to the Prince of Wales emblem of three ostrich plumes. It was a favorite decorative motif for a chair splat designed in the Hepplewhite style.

Prince, Samuel d. 1778. American cabinetmaker of New York. He had a shop on Cart and Horse Street.

Prince's Metal An alloy consisting of about three parts copper and one part zinc. It is a modified brass and its color resembles gold. The alloy was invented by Prince Rupert, Count Palatine of the Rhine and Duke of Bavaria, 1619–1682.

Princess Bokhara An Oriental rug; see *Katchlie Bokhara*.

Print Rack In cabinetwork; an article of furniture, consisting of an upright frame having two rectangular panels, one on each side. Usually one panel is in a fixed position, and the other is hinged so that it drops down. It is used for holding etchings, engravings and similar prints.

Proskau In German ceramics; a faïence manufactory of considerable importance was established at Proskau, Silesia, in 1763 by Count Leopold von Proskau, d. 1769. It changed hands several times and was active until 1850. The manufacture of lead-glazed earthenware was started in 1788 and in 1793 the manufacture of faïence was abandoned. The best period was from 1763 to 1769. The mark was generally a "P". The productions were essentially a liberal imitation of the faïence made at Strasbourg and were painted in enamel colors. The wares were marked by a pronounced penchant for freely modelled and applied leaves, fruit, flowers and bouquets of flowers. Vases filled with flowers and the lids of tureens heaped with fruit were typical. From 1770 to 1783 the mark was "DP"; the "D" standing for Count Dietrichstein. Essentially the productions of this period were a continuation of the earlier work. Tureens in the form of fruit or vegetables and modelled figures generally in the classical style were made. Chiefly useful wares were made from 1783 and were marked with "Proskau", impressed. The lead-glazed earthenware or steingut principally followed English models. The faïence made between 1783 and 1793 was again marked with a "P" and was in the Neo-Classic style.

Provence In French Provincial; an old province in south-eastern France. It is now formed by the districts of Basses-Alpes, Var, Bouches-du-Rhône and part of Vaucluse. Arles was the principal cabinetmaking center; Avignon and Carpentras also produced a large amount of furniture. Provençal cabinetwork had an air of strength and vigor, and was skillfully executed. Their cabinetwork was characterized by its wide variety of forms and its many different types of pieces. Their ornament, whether of wood or of metal, was exuberant and was notable for its originality. The moldings were firm, clear-cut and rich. Louis XV style panelled pieces such as the buffet bas, armoire and commode were remarkable for the interesting and varied treatment of their moldings which gave them a singular quality of charm and gaiety. An outstanding feature of their cabinetwork was the use of large finely wrought steel buttress hinges and fret-pierced escutcheon plates which often extended the entire length of the cupboard doors. Oak, walnut, chestnut and cherry were the favorite woods. Included among the pieces that were characteristic of Provence were the buffet-crédence, the pétrin, the panetière, many charming small hanging wall shelves for pewter, tumblers and pottery dishes, and the delightful small hanging farinière or flour box and the saloir or salt box. See *Buffet-Crédence*; *Maie*; *French Provincial*.

Provincial, French See *French Provincial*.

Prunier Wood The wood of the plum tree, *prunus domestica*, used for inlay and cabinet-work. It is hard and its color is white with red and reddish veins.

Prunt In glass; an applied drop of glass widely used by the Germans to ornament such drinking glasses as the krautstrunk and roemer. It has the same meaning as the term *nuppen*, although apparently the term *prunt* was generally used by the English glassmaker. The prunt was either smooth or drawn out in one or more points. Sometimes it was impressed with many small dots. See *Roemer*; *Nuppen*; *Nuppenbecher*.

Prunus In Chinese ceramics; a graceful design of blossoms and sprays of the winter flowering prunus (which is a representation of a Chinese and Japanese species *prunus mume*, prunus being derived from the Latin *prunus* meaning plum tree) falling on the ice that is breaking up at the coming of spring. The prunus is reserved in white in a blue ground broken by a network of lines resembling cracked ice. The prunus design, which symbolizes the approach of spring, was a favorite decoration for the ginger jar during the reign of K'ang Hsi. In the fine specimens which are highly esteemed the blue ground is a pure sapphire blue. Hawthorn or the mayflower pattern is often erroneously applied to the prunus design. See *Ginger Jar*.

Psyché In French cabinetwork; a mahogany cheval dressing glass. It was introduced toward the end of the 18th century and it was an important and imposing article of Empire furniture. It had a mirror plate long enough to reflect a person's full length. The mirror was enclosed in a rectangular frame which was attached to columnar supports by swivel screws. The uprights rested on splayed bridge feet. Bronze candle arms were generally attached to the uprights. The psyché was richly mounted in classic bronze appliqués. It was also designed in miniature. These small swinging mirrors were usually placed on different kinds of tables which could serve as dressing tables. See *Cheval Mirror*; *Coiffeuse*.

PRUNUS MOTIF

Puente Stand In Spanish cabinetwork; the name given to a variety of elaborately carved table trestle stand which was especially designed to support the vargueño. It was fitted with two long slides, which, when pulled out, supported the drop-front of the vargueño. The ends of each slide were generally decorated with a carved shell motif or a grotesque animal mask. At each end of the stand were three fluted or spiralled columns which rested on a runner base. The stand was designed with a high arcaded stretcher which connected the middle column of each trestle end support. The term *puente* is frequently applied to any table trestle stand which is used to support a vargueño or papelera. See *Vargueño*; *Taquillón*.

Pulvinated Frieze In cabinetwork; an architectural term applied to a frieze having a convex curve. The pulvinated frieze is found in late Roman architecture as well as in many examples of Renaissance work. The name is derived from the ancient Roman word *pulvinar* meaning a couch or cushioned seat of the gods, and a cushioned seat in the circus. Pulvinated frieze drawers are often found on William and Mary style furniture such as on a cabinet mounted on a stand, and on the Queen Anne style writing cabinet with a fall-front and other similar articles.

Pumpkin Pine The term *pumpkin pine* is sometimes applied to the wood of the northern white pine, *pinus strobus*, which is indigenous to the regions from Newfoundland to Virginia. It has a pale straw color with very thin dark lines, or resin ducts, running parallel to the straight grain. This wood is also known as white pine, soft white pine and cork pine. Great quantities of it were available and because it was easy to work with and was durable and of uniform texture it was extensively used from Colonial times for furniture and structural purposes.

Punch Bowl In English silver; the punch bowl, which was introduced after the Restoration, was a fashionable piece of English silver. The design for the early large

PUNCH BOWL AND LADLE

punch bowl was borrowed from the porcelain models made in China and imported into Europe. It was a wide deep bowl around 11 to 21 inches in diameter, and was without a molding around the rim. It rested on a plain foot rim. Occasionally the large examples had two ring handles. Some of the Early Georgian punch bowls were embossed with fluting. From around 1730 the punch bowl frequently rested on a short cylindrical-shaped stem mounted on a foot rim. Toward the end of the 18th century when hot punch became popular many punch bowls were designed with a conforming tray. In English ceramics; porcelain and earthenware punch bowls largely inspired by Chinese export porcelain were also much favored. Of particular interest were the punch bowls made at Bristol from around 1750 painted with ships, which appear to have been made in some examples for foreign sea-going captains.

Punch Ladle In English silver; a variety of spoon, usually having a cup-like bowl designed with a long handle. Sometimes the handle was made of turned wood. Occasionally the handle was made of whale bone twisted and tipped with silver; this type of handle was frequently used with porcelain punch bowls. The bowls of punch ladles often had coins inserted in the bottom. It was introduced at the beginning of the 18th century.

Punch Lifter In English glassware; an English glass vessel used to serve punch introduced around 1800. It had high shoulders and a decanter-shaped body with a long neck. Its capacity was a glassful of liquor. The lifter was lowered into the punch bowl filled with punch, grog or toddy. The liquor entered a hole in the bottom, and when it was full, the thumb was placed over the mouth. It was then carried to the person's glass. When the thumb was removed from the mouth of the vessel, the contents poured from the hole in the bottom into the glass. The Scottish vessel had a bulbous-shaped body and was used for toddy and it was also called a toddy lifter.

Punch Spoon In English silver; the name frequently given to a type of spoon having a perforated bowl at one end of the stem while the other end of the stem is pointed and barbed. It is used to spear lemon slices and to remove cloves and lemon seeds from the punch bowl. It was made in England during the 18th century in three sizes. The smallest size was introduced in America and was called a mote spoon. See *Mote Spoon*.

Punto In lace-making; an Italian term meaning point or stitch. In particular the term is used to designate different kinds of lace, such as Punto in Aria, Punto a Groppo and like terms. See *Point*.

Punto a Groppo An Italian term applied to a knotted lace first made in Italy during the 15th century. It was made by knotting together fine cords or threads of gold, silver, silk or linen, so as to form patterns, usually of a geometrical nature. The threads were cut into short lengths, and the knots were tied with the fingers and without the aid of the needle or the bobbin. Sometimes when the pattern was completed, the thread ends were permitted to hang loose like a fringe, or else the ends were worked up and cut off. The modern survival of this kind of lace is called macramé. See *Lace*.

Punto a Maglia Quadra An Italian term applied to an early kind of darned netting or darned lace. See *Darned Netting*.

Punto a Relievo See *Punto Tagliato a Fogliami*.

Punto a Reticella A fine variety of Italian needlework fabricated either by drawing the threads of the cloth or producing a lace with the buttonhole stitch on a parchment pattern. See *Reticella*.

Punto Avorio See *Punto Tagliato a Fogliami*.

Punto Gotico An early Venetian point lace having designs of Gothic inspiration executed in a stiff and formal manner. These designs were quite different from the flowing and rhythmic character of the Renaissance motifs found in the Venetian point laces.

Punto in Aria An Italian term meaning stitches in the air. A name given to the first point laces made in Italy and Venice in the 15th century, to distinguish them from the earlier forms of lace, which had a cloth foundation, such as drawnwork or cutwork. These laces are notable for their richness and diversity of design. The patterns were always held together by irregularly arranged pearled brides or ties. See *Venetian Point*; *Lace*.

Punto Neve See *Point de Neige*.

Punto Tagliato In needlework; an Italian term meaning cutwork. The earliest cutwork had for its foundation a coarsely woven linen, upon which were buttonholed patterns and then the linen was cut away. Gradually the patterns became more ornate, and a finer quality of linen was used.

Punto Tagliato a Fogliami The richest and most intricate of all Venetian point laces worked in a similar manner to the Punto in Aria, the difference being that the outlines of the designs were all in relief which was formed by placing cotton or padding threads inside the outlines and then working over the padding with fine needle-made stitches. It was undoubtedly the most complicated of all point laces and was worked sometimes in double or triple relief with exquisite stitches of a wide variety worked on the flowers. The designs, which were chiefly floral and scroll motifs, were held together by irregularly arranged pearled brides or ties. The fine quality of the work often resembled carved ivory in relief. This lace was made of either linen or silk thread and was either white or unbleached. It was known by different names, depending upon the degree of relief and its general character, such as Rose or Raised Venetian Point, Gros Point de Venise, Punto a Relievo, Venetian Raised Ivory Point or Punto Avorio or Point d'Ivorie.

PUNTO TAGLIATO A FOGLIAMI

Punto Tirato In needlework; an Italian term applied to drawnwork, which is one of the oldest forms of openwork.

Punty Mark In glass; see *Pontil Mark*.

Purchase A name applied to a thumbpiece or billet used to raise the lid on a tankard. See *Thumbpiece*.

Puritan Spoon In English silver; a plain variety of silver spoon, having an ovoid bowl and a flat stem with a stumped end. It became popular during the Cromwellian period, 1649–1660. It appealed to the Puritans because of its plainness.

Purl A term in lace-making. See *Pearl*.

Purl A kind of embroidery work, first done during medieval times, which consisted of copper wire covered with fine silk. It was then wound tightly on a needle, and pushed off in the form of a short length of fine coiled tube. These lengths were threaded and then sewn down to the ground. Owing to the type of the material, the designs were limited to conventional scrollwork and floral motifs. Sometimes entire bookbindings were worked in purl; occasionally only the borders were worked in purl. The name is also given to the spiral of gold or silver wire used in lace-making. The term is also applied to a kind of 16th century lace. It is an earlier form of lace, generally in the form of an edging worked in elaborate loops.

Pu-Tai Ho-Shang In Chinese art; a Chinese Buddhist subject. He is the god of children and earthly happiness. He is generally represented with a smiling cheerful face and a fat and unclothed belly, and he is usually in a reclining position resting against bags of money. The subject was widely used in Chinese ceramics. In Japan he is called Hotei. See *Chinese Gods*; *Hotei*.

CANDLESTICK IN THE FORM OF A PUTTO

Putti In ornament; an Italian term which is essentially similar to amorini. The singular is putto. See *Amorini*.

Putz The name applied by the Pennsylvania Germans to the Christmas Nativity art. See *Crèche Art*.

Puzzle Jug In ceramics; a variety of drinking jug generally having pierced openwork around the neck which made it impossible to use in the normal manner. The only way liquid could be drunk was by sucking it through an inconspicuous opening in the spout at the end of a tube which went around the neck and through the handle to the bottom of the jug. Variations in detail occurred. The puzzle jug was of early origin and was known during medieval times. During the 17th and 18th centuries unusual pottery drinking vessels were quite popular and the puzzle jug made in faïence and in earthenware was much favored.

Pyx In ecclesiastical art; a vessel in which the Host or consecrated bread of the sacrament is reserved. Pyxes were made in various forms and materials. Especially early was the pyx in the shape of a dove made of precious metal suspended over the altar by a chain. Another early pyx was in the form of a cylindrical box often with a conical cover surmounted by a cross. This pyx which was often enriched with enamelling was later mounted on a stem and foot. Pyxes mentioned in medieval church inventories are described as made of silver and gilt, lapis lazuli, ivory and enamelling.

Qama In arms; the principal weapon of Georgia from which the kindjal of the Cossacks was copied. The qama does not vary much either in size or in quality. The usual form is a broad, double-edged blade with nearly parallel edges which taper abruptly to a sharp point. Many have fine panels on the blades with their hilts and scabbards beautifully worked with silver often set with coral. See *Kindjal*.

Quaich A Scottish drinking cup, originally made from a solid piece of wood, or of small staves of wood, secured by hoops, in the manner of a cask. It is usually fitted with two flange handles. It varies in size, being from about 4 to 8 inches in diameter. During the 17th century the quaich was first made in silver; it was also made in pewter or brass.

Quare, Daniel 1648–1724. Celebrated English maker of watches and clocks. His reputation in the art of horology is second only to Tompion's and by many he is regarded as Tompion's equal. Around 1680 he produced repeating works for watches from his own designs. He made an outstanding contribution to horological art by producing a clock with a one-year timepiece. One of these clocks is a tall case clock made in 1705 which is in Hampton Court Palace.

Quartetto In cabinetwork; an Italian term applied to a nest of four tables. See *Nest of Tables*.

Quartz A form of transparent and usually colorless silica, which is found in hexagonal crystals. Occasionally it is found in green, rose, yellow and other colors. Of the solid minerals, it is the most common. It is also found in crystalline form having a glassy luster. In the crystalline types there are: rock crystal, which is almost colorless and transparent; rose quartz which is rose colored; false topaz or citrine, a pale yellow; amethystine, which is bluish-violet. Other varieties are called: sardonyx and onyx, which are beautifully banded; agate, which is mottled; jasper, usually red and opaque; smoky quartz, brown color; bloodstone and heliotrope, green with red jasper marks.

Quatrefoil In ornament; a favorite conventional Gothic motif comprising four parts, such as a leaf or flower having four lobes or foils. The term is used in Gothic architecture for the small semi-circular openings or foils introduced in the pierced tracery of windows. See *Trefoil*; *Cinquefoil*.

Quattrocento An Italian term referring to the 15th century. It is especially applied to the 15th century as a period of risorgimento or revival of learning and classical art. It precedes the Cinquecento.

Queen Anne and Early Georgian The name given to the style of ornament and furniture design developed in England from 1702 to 1750. The period was during the reign of Queen Anne, 1702–1714; George I, 1714–1727, and George II, 1727–1760. The furniture was characterized by its use of curvilinear lines and the cabriole leg. The Queen Anne furniture was distinctive for its simplicity, its fine proportions, its graceful curving lines and its richly figured walnut veneered surfaces. The Early Georgian style lies between the style of Queen Anne and the Chippendale style. Its cabinetmakers to a large extent carried on the traditions inherited from the Queen Anne style. The chief difference was in the elaboration of the style of ornament and the more massive character of most of the pieces. Other distinctive features of the Early Georgian style were the use of mahogany from around 1720 and the architectural style given to some massive pieces of furniture such as bookcases. It must be remembered that mahogany did not affect to any great extent the designs for furniture until around 1740–1750, except

QUEEN ANNE SIDE TABLE

for such pieces as massive bookcases and library tables designed for the Palladian mansions. William Kent is associated with one phase of the Early Georgian style. He influenced the furniture and decoration in the great mansions between 1730 and 1745. The ornamentation on Queen Anne furniture was largely limited to the carved shell motif, which was sometimes combined with a husk pendant or acanthus pendant. After the death of Queen Anne the development in fashionable furniture was from the simple to the decorated. The term *Decorated Queen Anne* is often given to the era between 1715 and 1725, when a greater elaboration of carving was employed. Among the motifs commonly employed were included the shell, honeysuckle, rosettes, husk and acanthus pendants, acanthus leafage and various foliated and floriated scrolls. Mask motifs in a variety of forms, such as lion, female, Indian and satyr figured prominently on furniture between 1720–1740. Around 1720 the lion mask became the newest development in fashionable furniture and was of common occurrence until 1735. Lion mask furniture was remarkable for its vigorous and realistic carvings; the lion phase attained its richest development around 1725. The eagle motif, which was contemporary with the lion motif, was particularly prominent from 1725–1745. About 1730 the use of grotesque motifs became more pronounced; the satyr's mask was often employed between 1730–1740. After 1735 the French influence became more apparent. Ornament of French derivation, such as the cabochon and leaf or ribbon motif, became increasingly popular. Much of the finest mahogany furniture from around 1725 to 1740 was parcel gilded, or the carved detail was enhanced with gilding. From around 1745 the influence of the French Rocaille became increasingly evident. See *Kent, William*; *Mahogany*; *Queen Anne Splat-Back Chair*; *Cabriole Leg*; *Pilaster*; *Claw and Ball Foot*; *Club Foot*; *Pad Foot*.

Queen Anne Splat-Back Chair In English cabinetwork; the curved line dominated the form of the characteristic Queen Anne splat-back walnut chair. The spoon-shaped curve was a distinguishing feature of the profile of the back. The cresting was practically eliminated and the corners of the chair back were rounded off. The open chair back was hooped. The uprights were generally ramped or undulating. As a rule the plain solid splat which joined the seat rail was either vase-shaped or fiddle-shaped. The corners of the seat rail were rounded off. It was fitted with a slip seat. The chair rested on cabriole legs which usually terminated in club feet. Around 1710 the cabriole leg was designed with a claw and ball foot. The club foot continued to be used as an alternative throughout the first half of the 18th century. It was designed as an arm chair and as a side chair; the latter being the more common. The Queen Anne splat-back chair was a remarkably comfortable chair. It seems that Queen Anne splat-back chairs were made in America from around 1710 to 1755. See *Cabriole Leg*; *Club Foot*; *Pad Foot*; *Claw and Ball Foot*; *Hogarth Chair*; *Dutch Chair*; *Queen Anne and Early Georgian*.

Queen Anne Style See *Queen Anne and Early Georgian*.

Queen's Pattern In English silver; an early 19th century English silver pattern. The rounded end of the stem of the spoon centered a shell motif and along the broad part of the stem was a motif resembling a fleur-de-lis. Both of these motifs were enclosed in elaborate scrolls which continued along the stem to the bowl.

Queen's Ware In English ceramics; the name was given by Wedgwood to his cream-colored earthenware around 1765 after receiving the patronage of Queen Charlotte. This name was given to the same material at other manufactories. See *Cream-Colored Earthenware*.

Quenouille In French Provincial cabinetwork; a tall slender turned wood support or staff, having a round turned flat base. The top is fitted to hold flax for spinning.

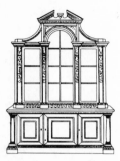

EARLY GEORGIAN
ARCHITECTURAL BOOKCASE

Quilling   In glassware; see *Pinched-Trailing*.

Quillons   In armor; the two projecting arms which together form the cross-guard on the hilt of a sword.

Quilting   In needlework; although the word *quilt* is generally defined as a coverlet consisting of two pieces of material stitched together with something soft between them, quilting was used for a variety of articles. The early Norman hauberk was often made of quilted linen and cotton. During the 17th and 18th centuries quilted doublets and breeches and satin petticoats were fashionable. In the common or traditional type of quilting, the lines of stitches, which were generally running stitches worked in different designs, held the filling in place between the two pieces of materials. In the other principal form of quilting the decorative effect rather than the warmth was of major importance. This type, which was often used on fine wearing apparel, was only partly padded and was worked in a back stitch. Occasionally some of the designs contained no padding between the lines of stitches. In America these two types of quilting were both commonly used. The name *corded quilting* is frequently given to a form of quilting which was also decorative rather than utilitarian. In this work the design was made by two rows of parallel stitches about one quarter of an inch apart, and a cord was inserted between these two rows of stitches. See *Patchwork*.

Quimper   In French ceramics; see *Loc Maria*.

Quiver-Leg   In French cabinetwork; a round and tapered chair leg identified with the Louis XVI style. It was so called because of its supposed resemblance to the case in which the arrows were carried. Sometimes the leg was carved with arrow feathers at the top.

Quodlibetz   In ceramics; the name, meaning *what you please*, is given to a painted decoration in which letters, scissors, playing cards and other miscellaneous articles are casually grouped together without any particular plan and are painted in a manner to cast shadows. This decoration was much favored in late 18th century Royal Copenhagen porcelain.

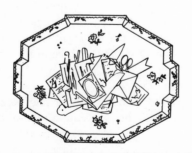

ROYAL COPENHAGEN
TRAY WITH QUODLIBETZ

R

Racinage A process of coloring leather with acids which results in a decorative effect resembling roots of trees, twigs and leaves.

Raden In Japanese lacquer; the name given to an inlay of metal and shell in lacquer work. In this method various shells were used, such as the sea ear, nautilus and similar nacreous shells. See *Japanese Lacquer*.

Raeren In German ceramics; it is generally accepted that the most outstanding of all Rhenish salt-glazed stoneware was made at Raeren, near Aix-la-Chapelle in the Rhineland, from around 1560 to 1600. The material for the earlier wares was always brown. During the first half of the 16th century the influence of Cologne was evident. The wares of the best period were admirable for the perfectly balanced proportions of their forms and for the well-placed friezes or medallions in relief. Of outstanding interest were the huge jugs almost 20 inches high with either double or arcaded friezes of reliefs depicting Biblical and mythological stories, circular pilgrim bottles with finely modelled armorial bearings and foliage in rather high relief, cylindrical pharmacy vases, jugs with long beak-like spouts, large globular Bartmann jugs and tall conical tankards often simply decorated with small medallion reliefs. From about 1580 a grey body ware was introduced; however, it did not entirely supplant the brown body ware until early in the 17th century. The grey body stoneware, which permitted finer relief work, was slightly colored with blue. Probably the greatest figure in the history of Rhenish stoneware was Jan Emens working at Raeren from around 1566 to 1594. Baldem Mennicken, the second great Raeren potter, signed his work from 1575 to 1584. From early in the 17th century there was a growing tendency for over-elaboration in which the elegant and

RAEREN STONEWARE JUG

refined simplicity of the earlier work was lost. See *Rhenish Stoneware*.

Rafraîchissoir In French cabinetwork; the name given to a kind of servante or dumb-waiter, in the form of a small table, used in the dining room to chill the wine. The principal variety had a frieze well, fitted with a metal liner, in which the bottles of wine were chilled. It was designed with two or three undershelves for the reception of additional glasses and plates. It was introduced in France during the early 18th century. It was widely used for intimate supper parties and one was placed at each person's chair. In this manner the guest could serve himself and the presence of the butler could be discreetly dispensed with.

Rail In furniture construction; a horizontal member between two supports, such as the seat rail of a chair. The two ends of a rail were finished as tenons to slide into the mortises cut in the vertical members.

Raised Point A term applied to laces in which the design is raised in relief. They are in direct contrast to the flat point laces. See *Flat Point*; *Lace*.

Raku Ware In Japanese ceramics; a soft, coarse and low fired pottery of a light brown or grey color. The articles made are for use in the tea ceremony, such as tea bowls, small jars, incense burners and flower vases. Much of this ware is made without the potter's wheel; it is shaped or molded by hand into a crude form. One method used in modelling Raku ware is to form the clay into a rope-like shape and coil it upon itself to form the article. Then it is patted and molded into its crude shape by hand, leaving a trace of the rope-like form. Other pieces are made by shaping with the fingers, and the foot is formed by scraping away part of the heavy body. The glaze is either thick and glossy or it is thin. The glaze colors include black, red, brown, grey-white and straw yellow. As a rule the ware is not decorated; occasionally it may have a roughly sketched design in a contrasting glaze color. The ware was first produced by a potter, who settled in Kyōto in the first half of the 16th century, named Ame Ya or Masakichi. The ware is generally marked with a gold seal of the character Raku which means pleasure or contentment.

Ramsay, David Celebrated English horologist. He was clockmaker to James I. He learned his craft in France and was working in London around 1603. He is generally regarded as the most eminent watchmaker of that era. His successor was Edward East.

Randle, William An American craftsman practicing japanning or lacquer work. His notices appear in the Boston News Letter in 1715. His name is also spelled Randal.

Randolph, Benjamin An American cabinetmaker working around 1762–1792 in Philadelphia. He had his shop at the sign of the Golden Eagle on Chestnut Street between Third and Fourth Streets. He was a carver of great skill and made some of the finest furniture in the Chippendale style. See *Philadelphia Chippendale.*

Ranseur In medieval armor; a weapon used by foot soldiers which developed from the partizan. It is composed of a long wooden shaft fitted with a steel head consisting of a long narrow point with a fork-shaped projection on each side at its base which was used to break swords. See *Partizan.*

Raphaelesque In decoration; the term is often applied to a style of painted decoration executed by Raphael in the Loggia of the Vatican. He received his inspiration for this work in the beautiful decorations in painting and in stucco found in the Golden House of Nero. See *Bérain, Jean, the Elder; Grotesque; Urbino; Arabesque.*

Rapier In armor; the name is given to two kinds of swords. The one type, which was used during the 16th and 17th centuries as a dueling sword, consisted of a long double-edged and pointed blade with a wide cup-shaped hilt. It was used chiefly as a thrusting sword in dueling and in fencing together with a dagger. During the 17th century it was succeeded by the so-called small sword. This type has a pointed blade and the cutting edge has been discarded as well as the use of the dagger.

Rappoir A device of the early 18th century made of ivory and used as a tobacco grater. The rappoir is mentioned in English records.

Ratchet Clock In furniture; a clock, usually a wall clock, having a long vertical square-shaped rod, with ratchet teeth cut on both sides. The clock face and works are enclosed in a case attached to the ratchet. The clock is kept running by slowly descending on the shaft under its own weight.

Rat-Tail Spoon In English silver; a pointed prolongation added to the back of the bowl of a spoon, the purpose being to give additional strength to the handle. It was introduced during the last half of the 17th century. See *Spoon.*

Rauenstein In German ceramics; a porcelain manufactory was started at Rauenstein, Thuringia, in 1783 by Christian Daniel, Johann Georg and Johann Friedrich Greiner. Their productions were principally coarse imitations of the contemporary wares made at Meissen. Included among the marks were "R" either with or without a star and "R-n" with or without crossed hoes.

Ravenscroft, George 1618–1681, English glassmaker. In 1673 Ravenscroft, a chemist, with Signor da Costa, an Italian glassmaker, as his assistant, was engaged by the Glass Sellers' Company of London to establish a glasshouse at Savoy in London and another at Henley-on-Thames to undertake research work in glass. In 1674 he was granted a seven-year patent for his invention of "a new sort of crystalline glass resembling rock crystal." This flint glass or crystal glass in which silica was derived from the calcined

PAINTED DESIGN BY
RAPHAEL, VATICAN

flints, with lead oxide as a flux in place of vegetable potash, produced a glass having more refractive brilliance than any glass made prior to that time. It was also heavier, denser, and soft. The first glasses developed a fault called crizelling, which is an interior network of fine cracks producing a cloudy effect and a loss of transparency. In 1676 the formula was corrected and the Glass Sellers' Company announced that their flint glasses were now free from defect and agreed with Ravenscroft that henceforth all his glasses would be marked, or sealed, with a raven's head. In the ensuing decade the process was further improved. By the end of the 17th century nearly one hundred glasshouses were operating in England producing flint glass, and for almost the next one hundred and fifty years England enjoyed a monopoly for world glass trade. See *Glass*; *Flint Glass*; *Sealed Glasses*; *Cut Glass*.

Raven's Head Seal See *Sealed Glasses*.

Rayonnant A term applied to the Middle Gothic style of ornament and architecture in France. See *Gothic, French*; *Gothic*.

Reading Chair In English cabinetwork; a distinctive variety of chair introduced around 1705-1720 for use in the library. The seat was almost pear-shaped, with the narrow part in the rear, and was joined to a shaped narrow back which had a horseshoe-shaped crest rail supporting an adjustable wooden rest or board for reading. The seat, back and arm rest were generally covered in leather. Sometimes beneath the arms were hinged trays with three circular wells, with brass candlesticks folding underneath. There was a drawer in the seat rail. Variations in design occurred. Such chairs with crest rails were popularly associated with cockfighting and were used by the judges; however, there can be no doubt as to their primary purpose. Sheraton in his CABINET DICTIONARY, 1803, observes that these chairs are "intended to make the exercise of reading easy and for the convenience of taking down a note or quotation from any subject. The reader places

READING CHAIR

himself with his back to the front of the chair and rests his arms on the top yoke."

Reading Stand In English cabinetwork; during the second half of the 18th century numerous mahogany tripod stands were made to support books and were designed in accordance with the prevailing fashion. One principal variety of reading stand had an oblong hinged top with a ratchet easel which rested on a turned shaft with a molded tripod base. The reading stand was frequently designed with lateral metal candle arms. See *Music Stand*.

Reading Table In English cabinetwork; see *Architect's Table*.

Recamier In French cabinetwork; a French day bed or couch introduced during the Directoire style. It was designed without a back. The two ends or the head and foot gracefully scrolled outward and were of equal height. The legs were shaped like a top. It derived its name from the painting by Jacques Louis David of Madame Recamier which portrays her sitting on this type of couch. This day bed designed in the antique style supplanted the characteristic chaise longue of the preceding Louis XVI style. Its form was derived from couches used in classical times for sleeping on or for reclining on at meals. See *Méridienne*; *Duchesse*; *Directoire*.

Red and Green Family In Chinese ceramics; a particular group of colored enamels extensively used on porcelains during the Ming dynasty. The enamels used in the Red and Green family are chiefly red, green and yellow, occasionally supplemented with turquoise green. Underglaze blue was omitted. Since this kind of decoration was used on pottery during the Sung dynasty it is therefore possible that it had been used on wares dating from the Hung Wu reign of the Ming dynasty. However, most of the Red and Green family wares in present day collections date from the Chêng Tê reign with the greatest number of examples being found on porcelain of the Chia Ching reign. See *Ming*.

Red Figure Ware In ceramics; see *Black Figure Ware*.

Red Stoneware In ceramics; the name given in Europe particularly to the unglazed red stoneware made in imitation of the Chinese buccaro ware made at Yi-hsing. See *Buccaro Ware*.

Reeding The term *reeding* is applied to a small semi-cylindrical molding or to an ornamentation of this form. The term *reed* is applied to one of a set of these small semi-cylindrical moldings because of their supposed resemblance to a number of reeds placed beside each other. In cabinetwork; a design in which the convex sides of parallel strips of wood are laid side by side. Each strip essentially resembles half of a lead pencil with the rounded side up. It is the opposite of fluting. Reeding may be cut in the wood or applied to the surface. It was used on French furniture designed in the Louis XVI style, especially for the cylindrical legs of chairs and tables. Legs of cylindrical form were often reeded or fluted. It was also used in England on many articles of furniture from the time of the Classic Revival. Fine examples of reeding are often seen on settees designed in the Sheraton style and in the cabinetwork of Duncan Phyfe. See *Fluting*.

Refectory Table In Renaissance cabinetwork; a very long and narrow rectangular dining table. It was so called because it was used in the refectory or dining room in a monastery. The early 15th century refectory table followed the traditional lines of the trestle table, being constructed with truss-end supports which were usually reinforced by a stretcher. Later in place of the truss-end supports the table was designed with four or more sturdy legs which were joined with a continuous stretcher close to the floor. See *Dining Table*.

Régence The term *Régence* is given to a transitional style of ornament and furniture developed in France which retained certain characteristics of the Louis XIV style and displayed some new ones of the Louis XV style. Historically the Régence covers that period of time from 1715 to 1723, when Philippe, the Duke of Orleans, was appointed Regent for Louis XV, who was the great-grandson of Louis XIV. However, the style of the Régence was evident at the beginning of the 18th century and around 1720 the great transformation in furniture to the Louis XV style was completed. An article of furniture is regarded as being in the style of the Régence if it combines some features of the preceding Louis XIV style and some of the incoming Louis XV style. The work of Charles Cressent, 1685–1768, the distinguished French cabinetmaker, sculptor and metal worker, is closely identified with the style of the Régence. During the style of the Régence a whole new world of fabulous figures made their appearance in ornamental design. A large part of these were inspired by Oriental art, such as charming figure subjects, dragons, landscapes and parasols borrowed from Chinese decorative design. This theme of orientalism was further developed by introducing fantastic doll-like figures of Turks, Sultans and Hindus. From the Italian Comedy Watteau created a repertoire of piquant and exquisite figures, such as Columbine, Gilles and the Serenader. Amusing monkey pieces or singeries, which had already been introduced by Bérain in his grotesque compositions, were further elaborated. All these new themes were mingled with the classic motifs of the Louis XIV style which during the Régence were given far more grace and vivacity. The shell motif was constantly employed. An upright shell with acanthus leafage starting from each side of the base of the shell was a favorite motif. The profile of the folded water leaf with its wavy edge and marked ribbings was much used. Mythological themes were largely of a romantic nature. Attributes appropriate to love, pastoral life and music were increasingly evident. Bronze espagnolettes in the

DECORATIVE DESIGN BY
WATTEAU

manner of Watteau were characteristic of the era. The Régence cabinetwork possessed the rich elegance and dignity of the Louis XIV style, but that singular quality of formal grandeur was gone and in its place was an indication of a graceful suppleness which was so characteristic of the Louis XV style cabinetwork. The line of demarcation between the Louis XIV and the Régence, and the Régence and the Louis XV, is not too clearly defined since each is a rather slow and unconscious evolution from one to the other. The Rococo Louis XV style differs essentially from the Baroque Louis XIV style in its lightness and in its avoidance of the characteristic symmetry of the latter. See *Louis XIV*; *Louis XV*; *Rococo*; *Cressent, Charles*; *Watteau, Antoine*; *Chinoiserie*; *Cabriole Leg*.

Regency In history the name *Regency* covers that period from 1811 to 1820 when George, Prince of Wales, acted as regent for his father, King George III. In the decorative arts the name *Regency* is given to an English development of several styles from about 1795 to 1820. This development included a Greek revival, an Egyptian revival and a Chinese revival. Toward the end of the century a revolution in taste was occurring both on the Continent and in England, based upon a closer and more profound classic revival. This new revival fostered the cult of antiquity. It was essentially an archaeological revival in which antique Greek and Roman interior decoration and material remains were copied. On the Continent this resulted in the French Empire style, while in England the term *Regency* seems more appropriate since the English development was not a close version of the French Empire style. Regency furniture was characterized by its eclectic quality. The different types of furniture were based essentially upon a vernacular interpretation of classic ideals; an incorporation of certain features of the French Directoire; a simplification of 18th century tradition, and a coarse version of the French Empire. The early Regency furniture was characterized by its dignified simplicity.

REGENCY CARD TABLE

Many of the early pieces were skillfully designed and admirably executed. The later phase of the Regency was marred by a mania for novelties. As a result the Regency furniture in its later phase became cumbrous and dull, and at times even ugly, and was characterized by its meaningless ornament and distorted lines. Included among the favorite motifs were the hocked animal leg, the lion monopodium, archaic lion masks, Grecian and Roman terms, the swan, lyre, anthemion, Greek palm leaves, acanthus leafage, paterae and rosaces. The Chinese and Egyptian revivals were essentially restricted to the use of decorative details. Among the Egyptian motifs were Egyptian figures, the sphinx, the winged sun disc, lion masks in the Egyptian taste and the lotus flower. The Chinese motifs included such characteristic subjects as pagodas, Chinese figures and landscapes. Applied metal ornaments and metal inlays were extensively employed. The little carving which was used was often gilded in accordance with the prevailing taste for metal mounts. Dark woods such as rosewood and mahogany were generally used. Certain phases of the Regency style can be studied in Sheraton's CABINET DICTIONARY, published in 1803, and in the work of Henry Holland, Thomas Hope and George Smith. Thomas Chippendale Jr., designed and made many pieces of cabinetwork in the style of the Regency. His furniture was of a less extravagant nature and showed the Regency style at its best. During the Regency some English designers renewed their interest once again in the Gothic style. This second Gothic revival in England was stimulated by the considerable amount of building in the "Gothic Castle" style in the first quarter of the 19th century. Cabinetwork in the Regency taste continued to be made in a more or less desultory manner into the reign of Queen Victoria. In America the cabinetwork of Duncan Phyfe exemplified the style of the Regency. See *Classic Revival*; *Directoire*; *Empire*; *Holland, Henry*; *Hope, Thomas*; *Smith, George*; *Greek Revival*; *Gothic, English*.

Regency Point In English lace-making; a bobbin-made lace introduced during the Regency and made in Bedfordshire, Buckinghamshire and Northamptonshire, where the lace industry named it in compliment to the Prince Regent. It was a sturdy, well-designed lace of excellent workmanship, and had toile on the edge. The net ground was admirably clear. See *Northamptonshire Lace*.

Regional Furniture Or L'Art Régional. In French Provincial cabinetwork; the French term *régional* is used in French furniture literature to describe the furniture made in the different provinces displaying regional characteristics or peculiarities associated with that region or province. This local originality was chiefly found in the decorative detail and was more pronounced in some provinces than in others. Regional furniture, which was made by the local cabinetmaker, principally comprises rustique furniture made for the peasant and bourgeois furniture made for the middle class. In America the term *provincial* is the customary designation for all this regional work. It is important to remember that the term *provincial* is correctly applied only to those pieces exhibiting provincial characteristics as distinguished from the work regarded to be national or emanating from the capital. For example, if a piece of furniture is made in one of the large cities and is finely executed and skillfully interprets the prevailing Paris style and displays no local flavor it is no longer a provincial piece. Many provincial pieces were a more or less close interpretation of the prevailing French styles but they were very simply and modestly treated. They were generally made in native solid woods and they had a rather countrified look distinguishing them from the finished and perfected technique of a highly trained cabinetmaker. In other words the furniture should display some provincial character generally held to be distinct from the national character in order to be classified as provincial. See *French Provincial*; *Rustique*.

Reichsadlerhumpen In German glass; the same as Adlerglas. A cylindrical beaker and cover; *humpen* is the generic term for a large cylindrical beaker. See *Adlerglas*; *German Glass*.

Relief In sculpture; the name given to an ornament, a figure, or a similar subject raised from a flat surface of which the sculptured decoration permanently remains a part. Relief work is expressed in three terms depending upon its degree of projection. In high or haut relief or alto-rilievo the sculptured portion is half or more the natural circumference. Sometimes in haut relief the projection is so accentuated that the ornament is almost detached from the ground. In low or bas relief or basso-rilievo the degree of projection is very slight and the sculptured portion is entirely attached to the ground. Half relief or mezzo-rilievo is applied to work executed in degrees of projection between high relief and low relief. The term *bas relief* is now often used to include mezzo relief as well. The term *stiacciato* is used sometimes for very low relief such as is found on coins. In another type of work the ornament is below the surface of the material on which it is cut. This is called hollow relief. It is also called intaglio-rilevato, cavo-rilievo and coelanaglyphic sculpture. See *Bori*; *Intaglio*; *Cameo*.

Relief Decoration In ceramics; various methods are employed to obtain decoration in relief. One method is by free incising or piercing and by freehand modelling. The latter is relatively rare since each piece can never be duplicated. Two common processes are used, either by pressing or casting in molds made from a hand-modelled specimen or from a specimen in some other material such as metal. In pressing, the soft clay is pressed into either plaster or slightly baked clay molds. In casting, a liquid mixture of clay and water is poured into a porous mold which absorbs the water. In another method the relief ornament is stamped or impressed with stamps cut in intaglio and generally made of metal. The

RELIEF SCULPTURE IN
WOOD, ITALIAN

soft clay surface is impressed or pads of clay applied to the surface are impressed. In still another method the molded reliefs are separately made and applied to the surface with slip.

Reliquary In ecclesiastical art; a small box, shrine, chest or other receptacle in which a sacred relic or relics are kept. Relics of saints were objects of such devotion that vessels of the finest workmanship were made to contain them. Medieval inventories reveal their great variety of forms, the rich materials of which they were made and their exquisite designs. Busts of silver mounted on bases, images of saints in silver gilt, monstrances, feretories, tabernacles, small chests of ivory were all included among the many forms of reliquaries containing sacred relics.

Renaissance The name *Renaissance*, which literally means rebirth, is given to a widespread movement of complex character that had its inception in Italy in the 14th century. Its effect on art is identified with the discovery of man as an individual and his inherent human right to enjoy the beauty of this world, and with the revival of classic culture. The earliest manifestation of the Renaissance was in the study of classic literature and in the humanists of the 14th century. After literature, sculpture, architecture and painting, as well as furniture and the other decorative arts, all contributed to this new age of classic culture. The Italians recognized their own national art in this ancient art and returned to it as the only acceptable source of civilization. In architecture the Gothic style was supplanted by the Renaissance style, which employed the Roman Classic Orders which had been in abeyance for almost one thousand years. This revival in classic art began in the first quarter of the 15th century in Florence and spread from Italy into France. Italian Renaissance art was aided by the patronage of the Medici family of Florence and in the 16th century by the papal court of Rome, which became the leading art center during the

HENRI II DRAW-TOP TABLE

16th century and where the art of the High Renaissance culminated.

Renaissance, English England was the last European country to be influenced by the Renaissance, which was established in England during the reign of Queen Elizabeth I. The Elizabethan style, 1558–1603, was a transitional style with Gothic features and Renaissance detail. It corresponded in principle to the French style of François I. After the Restoration in 1660 the furniture design and its style of ornament began to reflect Baroque influence. See *Elizabethan*; *Jacobean*.

Renaissance, French The influence of the Renaissance spread into France during the third quarter of the 15th century. The close contact established with Italy by the recurrent French invasions of Charles VIII, 1483–1498, Louis XII, 1498–1515 and François I, 1515–1547, led to the revelation of the great wealth of classic treasures in Italy and considerably accelerated the flow of Italian Renaissance influence into France. However, due to the vitality of the Flamboyant Gothic style, it was able in the beginning only to modify the decorative details. French Renaissance furniture includes the reigns of François I, 1515–1547; Henri II, 1547–1559; François II, 1559–1560; Charles IX, 1560–1574; Henri III, 1574–1589; Henri IV, 1589–1610, and Louis XIII, 1610–1643. The Renaissance style in France was not one single style; it consisted of several successive styles overlapping one another. In studying the furniture of the French Renaissance it is convenient to divide it into three principal styles, namely François I, Henri II and Louis XIII, for during the reigns of these three kings the greatest changes in the development of French Renaissance art were discernible. Early traces of the Renaissance influence were perceptible during the reign of Louis XII when Renaissance ornament, such as wreathed and medallion heads, mingled with Gothic ornament on Gothic forms. Under François I the Renaissance art made rapid progress. The François I style was essentially a transitional style from the Late Gothic to the Renaissance and it corresponded in principle to the Elizabethan style from the Late Gothic to the English Renaissance. See *François I*; *Henri II*; *Louis XIII*; *Gothic, French*; *Du Cerceau, Jacques Androuet.*

Renaissance, German The early Renaissance in Germany did not have the true characteristics of a national style. It lacked homogeneity both in the principles of design and in style of ornament. The development in the different art centers of Germany was influenced accordingly by Italy, France and the Netherlands, and, as a result, was not unified into a national German style. The accepted dates for the Renaissance in Germany are 1525–1620.

Renaissance, Italian The Renaissance in Italy is usually divided into three periods: Early, 1400–1500; High, 1500–1540; and Late, 1540–1600. Florence, which was in the province of Tuscany, was the cradle of the Renaissance and was the dominating influence in all the arts during the 15th century. Her furniture designs, which were distinguished by simplicity and dignity, became the models which many later art centers tried to emulate. The early furniture was notable for its purity of line and classic proportions; for its sparing but effective use of carving which was generally in low relief, and for the minuteness of detail and the classic purity of its ornamentation. The moldings were few and modest. As a rule all the fine furniture was made of walnut. The High Renaissance represented the culmination of the art movement begun in the 15th century. All the arts achieved their highest degree of perfection. The cabinetmaker expended all his skill in perfecting the proportions for furniture. The ornament was distinctive for the classic purity of its composition. Carving was the preferred method for decorating the surface of furniture. Moldings became more prominent and were often richly carved. Included among the great art centers that flourished during the High Renaissance were Milan, Mantua, Ferrara, Urbino, Venice, Umbria, Bologna, Siena, Verona, Rome, Naples and Liguria. These different centers showed strong individual tastes in their style of ornament and architecture which were reflected in their furniture designs. The furniture of Rome was inclined to be massive and ponderous. It was distinctive for its grandeur and for its vigorously carved moldings and decorative motifs which chiefly consisted of human figures, caryatids and grotesques. Tuscan furniture was distinctive for its dignified simplicity and for the classic purity of its proportions. It was marked by a less frequent use of ornament, especially of human figures. The furniture of Liguria displayed intricate and elaborate carved decoration and was similar to contemporary French designs. Venetian furniture was splendid, graceful and dignified. The ornament was notable for its fine classic designs and graceful rhythmic lines. During the Late Renaissance the furniture was characterized by an excessive use of carving of a sculpturesque and florid quality, by the pronounced use of the human figure as a decorative motif, and by prominent, boldly carved projecting moldings. Although the furniture of the Late Renaissance displayed many excellent qualities of design, the fine classic proportions and the classic purity of ornament of the High Renaissance were very often overlooked. The ornament was of an exaggerated scale and was treated in a heavily ornate manner. The entire alphabet of classic ornament was employed by the Italians during the Renaissance. Repetitive running motifs, which were a legacy of ancient architecture, were much used, such as the guilloche and egg and dart. Included among the favorite decorative motifs were the acanthus leaf, the anthemion, all forms of flowers, fruit and foliage, arabesques, rosettes, roundels, scrolls, vase forms, medallions, swags, paterae, lozenges, cartouches, cornucopiae, banderoles, candelabra and grotesques. Cherubs, cupids, atlantes, terms, caryatids, masks, dolphins, chimeras, satyrs, human and animal figures were all included

RENAISSANCE TABLE,
ITALIAN

among the innumerable classic motifs. Religious subjects, historical, mythological and allegorical stories, as well as garden scenes and marriage processions, were all favorite decorative themes for the painter and carver. During the Late Renaissance there was a marked preference for human figures, grotesques of a less pleasing quality, masks, heraldic devices, banderoles, scrolls, and cartouches. See *Michelangelo Buonarroti*; *Palladio, Andrea*; *Sansovino, Jacopo*; *Baroque*; *Pietra Dura*; *Certosina*; *Pastiglia*; *Intarsia*; *Gothic, Italian*; *Renaissance*.

Renaissance, Netherlands A dual influence has been reflected through the centuries in the architecture and furniture design and also in the other branches of art of the Netherlands. In a very broad sense the work of Belgium was influenced by France and that of Holland by Germany. It was not until around the middle of the 16th century that the Flemish Renaissance style was fully developed. The 16th century Flemish Renaissance furniture essentially followed the French styles of François I and Henri II, but was characterized by a greater freedom and extravagance in design. Walnut was the fashionable wood and carving was the favorite decorative process. The fame of the Flemish wood carver was known throughout Europe, for his carvings were artistic achievements of rare skill. Flemish furniture was always characterized by its great wealth of ornament. Much of their Renaissance furniture was excessively burdened with rich ornament, amounting almost to riotous extravagance. The composition of the ornament was assertively Flemish and as a rule it lacked the refinement of quality for which the Italian Renaissance craftsmen were unrivalled. Late in the 16th century some Flemish furniture was more restrained in its design as well as in its ornamentation and displayed a less frequent use of human figures. This became more apparent in the early 17th century in the Flemish Louis XIII style when the vogue for turning resulted in a further diminishing number

ARMOIRE À DEUX CORPS,
FLEMISH

of carved figures for supports. Since all their furniture was exuberant and ornate it is difficult to ascertain just when the Baroque spirit was felt in Belgium. Undoubtedly an important milestone in the development of Baroque decorative art in Belgium was the completion of Rubens' home in Antwerp in 1620, which reflected strong Italian Baroque influence in its architecture, interior decoration and furniture. The Renaissance appeared later and flourished longer in Holland than in Belgium. The seeds of a distinctive Dutch national style were evident in their architecture and furniture toward the end of the 16th century and became more pronounced in the following century. Included among the favorite Flemish Renaissance motifs were classical heroes, pagan deities, animal figures, birds, grotesques, caryatids, terms, mascarons, arabesques, all kinds of foliage, flowers and fruit, foliated scrolls, C-scrolls, S-scrolls, medallions, swags, strapwork, banderoles, cherubs and winged angels. See *Renaissance, French*; *François I*; *Henri II*; *Louis XIII*; *Rubens, Peter Paul*; *Dutch Furniture*.

Renaissance, Spanish The early phase of the Renaissance from around 1492 to 1556 was known as the Plateresque or Silversmith's style because its ornament resembled the delicate work of the silversmith. This phase of classic architecture in Spain, with its rich decoration, was of a transitional character, since the decorative motifs were usually engrafted on prevailing Spanish Flamboyant Gothic forms and the exuberance of the work reflected Moorish influence. The second phase, which was introduced by Philip II in 1556, was based on the work of the celebrated Italian Renaissance architects Palladio and Vignola. This style is frequently referred to as the style of Herrera, since the architect Juan de Herrera was its chief exponent. The style was characterized by its severe classic forms, plain surfaces and sparse decoration. Due to its coldness and formality the Spaniards did not find it particularly pleasing, and as a result early in the 17th century the Baroque style of ornament began to make itself evident. The architectural style of Herrera prevailed until around 1650 when a reaction against this severe formalism developed. Baroque architecture in Spain is sometimes known as the Churrigueresque style, deriving its name from the architect José Churriguera, d. 1725, under whose influence the style reached a climax of elaboration. This ultra-Baroque style with its overwhelmingly rich decoration remained in fashion until about 1800. The built-in decorations based on Mudéjar principles used in most Spanish interiors made these interiors completely different from those found in any other part of Europe. They consisted of colored tiles or azulejos, a pine-panelled ceiling or artesonado, generally enriched with painted and gilded carved decoration, and carved plasterwork or yesería. Spanish Renaissance furniture was marked by a noticeable absence of such architectural features as cornices, friezes and pilasters. It was even to a large extent devoid of moldings. The simple structure of the furniture was in complete harmony with the simple structure of the room. The intrinsic charm of Spanish Renaissance furniture was in its structural simplicity, boldness of design and vigorous lines. A unique feature of its construction was the frequent use of ornamental wrought-iron under-braces for tables and benches. A striking feature was the limited number of different pieces. The Spanish always seemed satisfied with the more or less basic pieces such as chairs, stools, benches, tables, chests, beds, vargueños and cupboards. Walnut was the principal Spanish wood. Inlay, carving, painting and gilding were all favorite decorative processes. The metal locks, hasps, ornamental bands, braces and decorative nailheads were of the finest artistic quality. Spanish furniture never displayed the wealth of classic motifs found on Italian Renaissance furniture. Her interpretation of the ornament to a large extent was geometrical and conventionalized, for Spain was never completely free of Moorish precepts. Her Baro-

que ornament was less geometrical and stylized and was more profusely employed on furniture. See *Mudéjar*.

Rendsburg In ceramics; a faïence manufactory was established at Rendsburg, Holstein, Germany, in 1764 by Caspar Lorenzen and Christian Friedrich Clar. It changed hands several times and finally closed in 1818. The faïence was chiefly painted in underglaze blue or manganese and only rarely in other high temperature colors. Chinese plants and flowers were much favored for decorative subjects. The wares included such articles as bishop bowls, potpourris, cane handles and snuff boxes. After 1772 the manufactory only produced white and cream-colored lead-glazed earthenware. Much of this ware was unpainted; occasionally the design was picked out in blue. Late in the 18th century the manufactory made some imitation black basalt ware and a red stoneware with a slight glaze. Included among the marks were "CR" joined together and "Ren.I" and "R F"; the last two being for the lead-glazed earthenware.

Rennes In French ceramics; potteries were in existence in Rennes, Ille-et-Vilaine, Brittany, from the 16th century. Two faïence manufactories were active during the 18th century; however, no regular factory mark was used. One factory was started in 1748 by Forasassi, a Florentine, in the Pavé Saint-Laurent, Rue des Capucines. The other factory was started in 1749 by François-Alexandre Tutrel in the Rue Huë. The two manufactories made all types of wares; however, they seldom achieved a high standard in their workmanship. The high temperature colors found on the wares of one factory were characterized by a dull dark green and a bubbled manganese; red was not used.

Rent Table In English cabinetwork; a mahogany writing table of polygonal form which was introduced about 1750 and continued to be made into the early 19th century. Although it served different purposes it

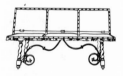

UPHOLSTERED BENCH
WITH HINGED BACK,
SPANISH

was essentially used to keep legal papers concerning the properties of an estate. One characteristic variety had a molded hexagonal top inset with tooled leather over six frieze drawers fitted with bail handles. The top revolved on a quadrangular pedestal fitted with a cupboard door. The drawers were commonly marked with the different letters of the alphabet. The letters were sometimes of ivory and were inlaid. The average diameter was about 52 inches. Variations in design occurred.

Repairer In ceramics; the name given to the ceramic worker who did the molding, joining and finishing of a decorative vessel or figure. As a rule the original model which he used was made by a modeller.

Replica A reproduction, copy or facsimile of a painting, statue or other work of art; properly one that is done by the maker of the original piece and believed to be of equal quality and value.

Repoussé In metal art; the method of making designs in relief upon metal by beating from the reverse side with hammers and punches. The ground remains practically untouched. Bronze, brass, gold and silver are all especially adaptable for repoussé work. Repoussé work has been practiced from very early times. The Greeks, Romans, Assyrians, Phoenicans and others produced repoussé work of the finest quality. See *Crustae*; *Caelatura*.

Reproduction A copy of the original. See also *Replica*.

Rerebrace In medieval armor; the protective steel plate used to guard the upper part of the arm above the elbow. See *Vambrace*; *Cubitiere*.

Réseau A French term meaning net, network. The term is given to the ground of regular uniform meshes that resemble a network. See *Ground*.

Réseau Rosacé In lace-making; a lace ground. This ground is made up of button-hole-stitched hexagons, inside of each is worked a small solid hexagon, joined to the outer hexagon by means of six little ties.

Reserve In decorative processes; the term *reserve* means to retain unaltered; to remain or keep in a particular condition or state, or to leave intact or untouched. For example, the term *in reserve* is frequently used in ceramics to describe a decorative feature or process, such as a piece of blue and white porcelain having the design in reserve. In other words the ground of the design is in blue while the design is in white, which is actually the color of the white body of the porcelain that remained intact or untouched. See *Blue and White Ch'ing*; *Shonzui*.

Resht Work In needlework; during the 18th century in England the name *resht work* was given to a very fine variety of patchwork produced in Persia. This exquisite work was executed in fine, delicate Near Eastern designs, and many examples resembled those found on Oriental carpets. It was true patchwork made of various colored woollen cloth pieces, cut out and sewn together in a manner very characteristic of Oriental workmanship.

Resist In ceramics; a method of decorating pottery by which a resist substance such as wax is used to produce a design. The resist, which is applied on the surface of an object before it is dipped in the colored glaze, is burnt away in the kiln leaving a pattern, generally in white or the color of the body, in reserve on a colored ground. In textiles; the composition applied in calico printing to protect the part of the fabric which is not to be affected by the dye.

Restauration The period following the downfall of Napoleon in 1814. See *Restoration*; *Empire*; *Charles X*.

Restoration A term applied to the English style of ornament and furniture design from 1660 to 1688. It is also called Carolean, Late Jacobean and Late Stuart. See *Jacobean*;

CHINESE VASE WITH
DESIGN IN RESERVE

Jacobean, Late. In French history the term *restauration* is applied to the era following the downfall of Napoleon in 1814, when the Bourbons were restored to the throne of France in the person of Louis XVIII, 1814–1824. In French cabinetwork; see *Charles X.*

Restoration In furniture restoring; the term *restore* means to renew an article of furniture to its original state by the replacement or substitution of parts. A restored piece of period furniture loses much of its intrinsic value. The term *repair* is reserved for those articles of furniture which have been put in good condition without the necessity of substituting or replacing any of the original parts for new parts. Repaired objects retain their intrinsic value. The terms *restore* and *repair* may also be applied to other branches of the decorative arts such as silver, glass and ceramics.

Restoration Chair In English cabinetwork; the name given to a variety of walnut armchair with a high back. It was finely turned and was richly carved and pierced with leaf scrolls and foliations. It had a fine mesh back panel and seat. An elaborate cresting and an ornately carved broad front stretcher were the outstanding features. A crown sometimes held by cupids was often carved in the center of the cresting and in the center of the broad front stretcher. This motif had been copied from the Continent and in England it had the additional significance of complimenting the restored monarchy, 1660. This chair when it was ornamented with a carved crown was popularly called the Restoration chair. It was also called the Charles II or Carolean chair. This chair either with or without a crown was the principal variety of walnut armchair of the Restoration. See *Flemish Chair*; *Jacobean, Late.*

Reticella In Italian needlework; the name was originally given to a drawn-thread linen work, characterized by open squares which were formed by withdrawing threads. In these open squares were worked radiating devices, wheels and similar designs in buttonhole and whip stitches. The name *reticella* was also given to a needlepoint lace which is considered to be the earliest of all laces. It was first made in the late 15th century and it essentially resembled the earlier drawn reticella work. The chief difference was that the lace was made without a cloth foundation and depended entirely upon the needle. As a rule the designs were simple and geometrical, and were arranged in repeated small squares or reticulations. Later the designs, which were in a buttonhole stitch, became more elaborate. It was called Punto a Reticella and Greek lace. See *Needlepoint Lace.*

RETICELLA, ITALIAN

Reval In ceramics; a faïence manufactory was started at Reval, Estonia, around 1775 by Karl Christian Fick of Stralsund and closed in 1792. The wares were chiefly in the Rococo style and reflected the influence of Stralsund faïence. Included among their productions were figures, vases pierced in openwork, tureens applied with flowers and fruit and all other kinds of tablewares. The colored enamels used in the painted decoration had a distinctive and pleasing tone. Of particular interest were some very fine animal figures of dogs, bulls, elephants and tigers. Included among the marks were "Reval Fick" and "RF".

Réveillon J. B. A well-known French designer and maker of wallpaper working in the 18th century. His designs for wallpaper which were in the Neo-Classic taste reflected the influence of the art work found at Pompeii and Herculaneum. His manufactory was made a Manufacture Royale in 1784. Around 1789 he sold his business to Jacquemart and Bénard.

Revere, Paul 1735–1818. American patriot, silversmith and craftsman working in Boston. During his early life he was apprenticed to his father who was a silversmith. His reputation as a master silversmith is evidenced by the many finely wrought specimens bearing his name. These pieces are marked with the name "Revere" either in capital letters or enclosed in a rectangle. In addition to his silver work he carved many frames for oil paintings, and he also acquired a fine reputation as a copper-plate engraver, especially those for coats-of-arms, seals and bookplates. Later in life he was also noted for his work of casting bells.

Reverse Serpentine   In cabinetwork; see *Serpentine*; *Oxbow*.

Revived Rococo   See *Louis Philippe*; *Charles X*; *Victorian*; *Biedermeier*.

Revolving Dish   In silver; a deep oval silver entrée-dish fitted with a strainer and a hot water compartment. It rested on a stand of conforming design. The dish was fitted with an oval shaped cover which could be rolled back. It was introduced during the Victorian era.

Rhages Ware   In ceramics; see *Persian and Near Eastern Pottery*.

Rheims Tapestries   Tapestries were woven at Rheims as early as the 15th century. Its finest tapestries were produced during the first half of the 17th century. Daniel Pepersack, a merchant weaver, was active circa 1627–1647. In his employ was Pierre Damour, a tapestry weaver. Pierre Murgalet, a tapestry designer and cartoonist, worked with Pepersack circa 1630. See *Tapestry*.

Rheinsberg   In German ceramics; a faïence manufactory was founded at Rheinsberg, Brandenburg, in 1762 by Baron von Reisewitz, d. 1763. The factory was bought by Karl Friedrich Lüdicke in 1770, which date marked the beginning of a flourishing manufacture. Around 1786 cream-colored earthenware and black basalt ware in the English style became the principal productions and after 1800 the only productions. The factory remained active until 1866. The mark for faïence after 1770 was "R L" in monogram. The painted decoration on the faïence was generally in polychrome. Much of the productions resembled the wares made at the manufactories at Thuringia. Other

types such as tureens in the form of birds and fruit and vases with pierced double walls show the influence of Münden. The lead-glazed earthenware and the black basalt ware were marked with the name "Rheinsberg", "LRBG" or "R" impressed.

Rhenish Stoneware   In German ceramics; salt-glazed stoneware was made in the Rhineland from late in the Middle Ages; however, it was without artistic importance. From around the middle of the 16th century and for about the ensuing seven decades a salt-glazed stoneware was made at four great centers, namely Cologne, Raeren, Siegburg and Westerwald, that ranks at its best with the finest of German Renaissance art. It has not been determined whether stoneware was first made at Cologne or Siegburg; however, the former was undoubtedly the first of the different leading centers to produce wares having real artistic merit. See *Cologne*; *Raeren*; *Siegburg*; *Westerwald*; *Stoneware*; *Salt Glaze*.

Rhodeswood   The name given to the Jamaica rosewood, *amyris balsamifera*, widely used for inlay and cabinetwork. It is hard and its color is white. It is also called candle wood.

Rhyton   In classical antiquities; a pottery drinking vessel made in a variety of shapes. One characteristic form had the contour of a horn. The lower and narrow portion of the horn was in the form of a head of a deer, a goat or some other animal. The rhyton was fitted with a handle. It could not be set down until it was emptied.

Ribband-Back   In English cabinetwork; the ribband-back was undoubtedly Chippendale's most celebrated design for the mahogany chair with an open back designed in the Rococo taste. Chippendale was exceedingly proud of this design which was of French origin. His ribband-back chairs were executed in the highest degree of delicacy and grace. In this design the splat, which was formed of two long C-scrolls, was interlaced with crisply carved ribbon which

CHIPPENDALE RIBBAND-
BACK CHAIR

was fastened at the top in a bow and tassel.

Ribbed Foot   In English cabinetwork; the name sometimes given to a foot used on the cabriole legs of chairs and tables designed in the Queen Anne style. It is a kind of Dutch foot characterized by grooves. It is also called a Dutch grooved foot. See *Pad Foot*.

Ribbon Work   In embroidery; a variety of embroidery work fashionable in England during the Georgian period. This type of work was found in particular on dresses, work boxes, fire screens and similar articles. Ribbon work was frequently combined with work done on open mesh net. The pieces of ribbon were about one-eighth of an inch wide and were drawn through the fabric by means of a needle.

Ricasso   In arms; the name given to the square-shaped part of the blade on a rapier next to the hilt.

Rice Grain Pattern   In Chinese ceramics; a porcelain having perforated designs. It derived its name from the shape of the perforations which were similar to grains of rice. The perforations were filled with glaze. It was sometimes supplemented with decoration in underglaze blue. The rice grain pattern is characteristic of Ch'ien Lung work, 1736–1795. Perforated decorative designs filled in with glaze were used in western Asia as early as the 12th century.

Riesener, Jean Henri.   1734–1806. He is generally regarded as the greatest cabinet-maker working in the style of Louis XVI. He worked for Oeben and upon the latter's death in 1763 he became foreman of Oeben's workshop. In 1768 he was admitted as a master cabinetmaker. Louis XVI made him Ebéniste du Roi. He finished the celebrated Bureau du Roi which had been begun by Oeben and his name alone was stamped upon it. His early work reflected the classic spirit found in the later work of Oeben. His work became more delicate but retained essentially all the vigor and grace of his earlier pieces. All the qualities of the Louis XVI style such as perfection in proportions, unity of composition and graceful elegance were combined in his work. His marquetry and bronze mounts were of the most exquisite workmanship. His marquetry of dainty garlands, delicate bouquets of flowers, showers of blossoms and draperies with gently flowing curves were imbued with the spirit of French grace. Riesener did much work for Marie Antoinette, and since she loved roses the marquetry decoration on these pieces was a veritable garden of roses. His interpretation of antique detail borrowed from Roman architecture was remarkable for its elegance. See *Louis XVI*.

Rifle   In arms; the name *rifle* is derived from the cutting of spiral grooves in the barrel of a firearm which cause the balls or bullets to rotate on their axis thereby giving more accuracy. The credit for this invention is given to August Kotter Sparr who worked in Nuremberg in the 17th century. The rifle did not come into general use until it was further perfected in the 19th century.

Rigaree   In glass; the name is given to an applied decoration consisting of narrow vertical parallel lines or bands resulting in very small contiguous ribs.

Rimbault, Stephen   English clockmaker of St. Giles, London, working around 1763 to 1785. He specialized in making musical bracket or table clocks with a complex mechanism. The portion above the dial has dancing figures, a party of musicans or some similar group, and when the clock plays different tunes these mechanical figures are automatically set in motion.

Rinceau   In ornament; an ornamental oblong panel design having elaborate leaf scroll-work developed symmetrically on each side of a vertical central part or point, such as a candelabrum, a vase or a cherub's head. It was used during the Italian Renaissance and was widely employed in French decorative designs.   The plural is rinceaux.

Ringed Coat-of-Mail   In armor; see *Mail*.

RINCEAU

Riobitsu In Japanese sword mounts; the name applied to the openings in a tsuba for the handle of the kogai and the handle of the kozuka. These are placed at the sides of the center opening called the seppa dai.

Rising Sun In ornament; see *Sunburst*.

Rittenhouse, David 1732–1796. An American scientist, astronomer, mathematician and clockmaker. He was born in Germantown, Pennsylvania, where he studied and began his noted work of producing technical instruments and clocks. In 1770 he moved to Norriton Township, Pennsylvania, where he continued this work at his shop located on his father's farm. He made many fine tall case clocks and he is regarded as an outstanding figure in the history of American horology.

Roberts, Richard English chairmaker of Air Street, Piccadilly, who was working from around 1714 to 1729. He was probably the son of Thomas Roberts, whom he succeeded in the Royal accounts after 1714.

Roberts, Thomas English cabinetmaker working around 1688 to 1714. During the reigns of William and Mary and Queen Anne he furnished the Royal palaces with chairs and fire screens. In all probability he was the father of Richard Roberts. See *Roberts, Richard*.

Rocaille A style of ornament. See *Rococo*.

Rock Crystal A colorless and transparent quartz. Rock crystal has been used for ornamental purposes from very early times. During the Roman Empire it was carved into vases, drinking vessels and other similar articles. It was often enriched with engraved decoration. The Chinese carved rock crystal into fine figure subjects of Buddhist gods and goddesses. Craftsmen working during the Early Renaissance also executed beautiful objects in rock crystal. See *Quartz*.

Rocking Chair In American cabinetwork; a wooden chair either with or without arms, having rockers fitted to the legs. It became

SLAT-BACK ROCKING
CHAIR

popular as an article of cottage and farmhouse furniture between 1725 and 1750. The slat-back variety was an early and favorite form. The chair was either originally made with rockers or was converted by the addition of rockers. See *Boston Rocking Chair*.

Rockingham In English ceramics; a general pottery from around 1745 to 1842 was located on the estate of the Marquis of Rockingham, Swinton, Yorkshire, and became known by his name because it was located on his estate. From 1826 when the manufactory was financially helped by the heir to the Rockingham estates, the name Rockingham was formally adopted, and the griffin, which was the family crest, was used as the mark. After 1830 the word "Royal" was added to the mark. It is not possible to identify the very early wares. A stoneware was made from around 1765. It was not until after 1778 when the Brameld family became associated with it, that the factory became important. From 1787 to 1806 the factory was in partnership with Leeds pottery. The earthenwares made during this period, which were not marked, cannot be distinguished from the wares of Leeds. After 1806 the Brameld family became the owners and the wares were marked with either "Brameld" or "Rockingham", impressed. Included among the wares made under Brameld were cream-colored and blue-printed earthenware, marbled and tortoise-shell earthenware, black basalt and other stoneware. Especially characteristic was a manganese brown lead glaze known all over England as the Rockingham glaze. Porcelain was included in the productions after 1820. Due to the royal patronage the wares became quite fashionable. They were in a rather ornate revived Rococo style and were often excessively gilded.

Rockingham Glaze In English ceramics; see *Rockingham*.

Rococo The term *Rococo*, which was borrowed from the French, was first used in England to describe any fashion in dress or in art that was antiquated, whimsical or freakish. At the present time the word is used interchangeably with the French word *Rocaille*, meaning rock work or grotto work. The term *Rocaille* was originally applied to describe the artificial grottoes found in French gardens which were decorated with natural stones of irregular outline and stalactites and other ornamentation made of shells. These rocailles or grottoes had been fashionable in France for almost two centuries from the time of Catherine de Medici. The term *Rocaille* or *Rococo* is the name now given to a singular form of asymmetrical ornament evolved from the Baroque in France during the Régence. It was widely used by French craftsmen from around 1720 to 1760. Certain natural forms were used as the foundation of the style which was richly fantastic. It was marked by a profusion of rocks or rocaille and shells or coquillage, with flowers, foliage and fruits. Various forms of ornamental curves, especially C-scrolls, figured prominently. The style was more suitable for interiors and for the decorative arts than for architecture. Included among its chief pioneers were Pineau and Audran. From around 1730 the movement was accelerated and intensified in the designs of such men as Meissonier. This movement, which carried the style in France to its culmination, was marked by an extravagant and a more thorough use of asymmetry. Sometimes the word *Rococo* is restricted in its use to this later and more advanced phase. In France this style of ornament, which reached its finest expression in the decorative arts from around 1740 to 1755-1760, is called the Louis XV style and in the other countries it is called the Rococo style. The Rococo style was very fashionable in England from about 1745 to 1765. Unfortunately the English cabinetmaker lacked the imagination which is the essence of this style to develop the Rococo in a manner similar to the French. Due to the revived interest in classic art a reaction took place in France which resulted in the style of Louis XVI. In England the Adam brothers were the guiding spirit of the Classic Revival. Robert Adam's classic style began to influence the style of ornament and furniture design in England shortly after 1760. See *Meissonier, Juste Aurèle*; *Watteau, Antoine*; *Régence*; *Baroque*; *Louis XV*; *Classic Revival*; *Boucher, François*; *Oppenord, Gilles-Marie*; *Chippendale, Thomas*; *Lock, Matthias*.

Roemer In German glass; a favorite Rhenish wine glass of capacious size which has retained its popularity as a hock glass until the present time. It was generally made of greenish glass varying in shade from a light to a dark green. The characteristic roemer in its most fully developed form, made in the 17th century and later, had a cylindrical bowl resting on a wide and short cylindrical hollow stem decorated with applied drops of glass called prunts or nuppens, and was mounted on a foot formed by the close spinning of a thread of glass around a removable conical core. The applied prunts were either smooth or drawn out to form one or more points. The prunts were also frequently impressed with dots. It is reasonable to assume that the roemer, which is depicted in many Dutch and Flemish genre paintings, was also made in the Low Countries and probably in other parts of Europe. Its high position in contemporary society is well illustrated by the use of diamond point engraving and enamelling found on some of the specimens. The roemer continued to be made in the green glass of the original waldglas long after the method of decolorizing glass was known, for much of the beauty of the roemer lies in its green-colored glass. The origin of the name *roemer* has never been satisfactorily explained. See *Glass*; *German Glass*; *Waldglas*.

Rogers Groups A contemporary term applied to small plaster statuettes or figures that were popular in America during the Victorian era from the third quarter of the 19th century. These inexpensive small figures or Rogers groups were executed by John Rogers, an American sculptor. An almost endless variety of subjects were

ROCAILLE DESIGN BY
FRANÇOIS BOUCHER

employed in these figures which included famous historical and literary persons, Civil War themes and subjects from everyday American life.

Rōiro In Japanese lacquer; the name given to a highly polished black lacquer. See *Japanese Lacquer.*

Roll-Top Desk In cabinetwork; see *Cylinder Desk*; *Bureau à Cylindre.*

Romanesque The name is given to a style of ornament and architecture developed in Europe in the 11th century and attaining its highest development in the 12th century. The principal elements of this style were borrowed from Roman and Byzantine art. The style was characterized by a barbaric vigor, undoubtedly a result of the times in which it grew. This robust quality was especially evident in northern Europe. The Romanesque style spread very quickly into the countries which were formerly a part of the Western Roman Empire, the characteristics of the style changing in each respective country in accordance with the character of the inhabitants. There were also variations within each country. In each French province the Romanesque style fell into separate schools and in Italy there were also different schools. In England the style is generally referred to as Norman and usually dates from the Norman invasion in 1066. The abundant use of carved ornament chiefly consisting of foliage was much in evidence. The Romanesque style was gradually supplanted in the different European countries by the Gothic style which was the glory of the medieval age. The style lingered in some countries longer than in others. In art; the term *Romanesque*, which simply means of Roman origin, is applied to all branches of European art based on Roman art from the fall of the Western Roman Empire in A.D. 475 until the Gothic period. See *Gothic*; *Byzantine.*

ROMANESQUE MURAL ORNAMENT

Roman Furniture European furniture design was borrowed primarily from Roman rather than from Grecian furniture. All branches of Grecian art were continued in Roman art, for Rome through her ascendancy became the logical transmitter of Grecian art. The Romans possessed few artistic ideas, so they simply repeated and elaborated the forms and ornament which the Greeks had developed. When the Roman borrowing began, the art of Greece had lost its perfection, and in its decline had become ornate and over-elaborated. The Romans with their innate love for pomp and splendor understood this ornateness, while the earlier Greek simplicity would not have been appreciated. It is only natural that the Romans carried the ornament and forms toward a greater elaboration. In appraising Roman contribution to furniture design, it did furnish several important innovations, including the couch with a back and several distinctive forms of tables. The study of Roman furniture is derived principally from fresco paintings at Pompeii and Herculaneum, representations on Roman tombstones and sarcophagi and actual examples in marble and in bronze. There were about twenty varieties of woods in common use by the ancients including maple, citron, beech, cedar, oak, fir, holly and lime. The lavish use of veneering, plating and inlay work was a feature of Roman furniture. The Greeks also used veneering and inlay work but in a less pretentious manner. The plating of furniture with silver, gold and bronze became a rather common practice for costly furniture. The folding stool or sella curulis which had been designed by the Greeks and earlier by the Egyptians was often quite graceful, especially when made of bronze. Occasionally the Romans designed it with a low back, which was an interesting contribution in Roman furniture design. See *Grecian Furniture*; *Classic Revival*; *Empire.*

Roman Notation Clock In English furniture; an English tall case clock having Roman numerals on the dial. It is fitted with a large bell and a small bell for striking the hours. This idea was invented by Joseph Knibb, a London clockmaker, about 1700.

The small bell indicates the Roman numeral I, and the large bell indicates the V and X, striking once for the V, and twice for the X. See *Tall Case Clock*.

Roman Work In needlework; a characteristic type of cutwork embroidery known by different names such as Strasbourg work, Venetian work and Ragusa guipure. The fabric was an écru-colored linen or batiste, and the outlines of the design were worked with close and even rows of buttonhole stitches with the outside edge of the stitches always worked on the outline edge of the design. The buttonhole stitches were worked in a matching écru-colored silk. Next the outlines of the pattern were joined with cross bars and buttonhole bars and the large spaces between the designs were worked with wheels. Finally the superfluous cloth between the designs was cut away. This cutwork was often lined with a bright colored silk and was used for pillow covers and similar articles.

Romayne Work An English term used to describe English Renaissance ornament copied from the Italian Renaissance classic motifs. Very characteristic were the wreathed and medallion heads which were referred to as Romayne medallions. See *Medallion*.

Rome Tapestries Tapestries were woven at Rome from the 15th century. The first school was founded by Pope Nicholas V in 1445. See *San Michele*; *Barberini Tapestries*.

Rondache In medieval armor; the French term for a round shield used by foot soldiers.

Röntgen, David 1741–c. 1809, a German cabinetmaker. His principal workshop was at Neuwied, near Coblenz. He had only limited facilities in Paris where he could receive orders and deliver his furniture. He was patronized by Marie Antoinette and was admitted as a master cabinetmaker in 1780. His cabinetwork lacked the delicate execution and finish which was found in the fine French cabinetwork executed by such ébénistes as Riesener and Carlin. However,

his marquetry work was above reproach. The vivid coloring, the expressiveness that he gave to his figures and the quality of his flowers, which he treated in a vigorous and original manner, were truly praiseworthy. Prior to Röntgen the light and shade found in pictures depicted in marquetry were obtained by burning or engraving the wood. He achieved a better effect of light and shade, which gave his marquetry a quality of new depth and vividness, by skillfully arranging the very small pieces of darker woods in the manner of very small stone mosaics or pietra dura work. His favorite subjects for marquetry work were scenes from classical mythology. He produced numerous pieces of furniture for the royalty of Europe. Undoubtedly his great contemporary reputation was due to a large extent to his mechanical genius. Early in his career Marie Antoinette appointed him her Ebéniste-Méchanicien. He was expert in designing harlequin pieces of furniture equipped with many springs and latches which, when set in motion, opened different drawers, doors and panelled sections. Some of his commodes and tables were remarkable for their mechanical precision. See *Louis XVI*.

Rope Stitch A stitch used in embroidery. It resembles the crewel stitch, except that it is worked from the top of the material downward. See *Embroidery*.

Rörstrand In Swedish ceramics; a faïence manufactory was started at Rörstrand, near Stockholm, in 1725 by the Swedish Chamber of Commerce at the request of Johann Wolff. There were several changes in management. Its most flourishing period dates from 1753. Lead-glazed earthenware in the English style, known as flintporslin in Sweden, was included in the productions from around 1773 and by 1800 it had entirely supplanted faïence. From that time the wares had little artistic merit until a modern revival. Marks were rarely found before 1745. They included "Stockholm" or "Rörstrand", occasionally both together

ROMAYNE MEDALLION

either written in full or abbreviated, with the date, approximate price and a painter's mark. The most characteristic work was in the Rococo style from around 1740 onwards. Of particular distinction were the often fanciful Rococo forms and several original designs composed of chinoiseries and Rococo motifs. The practice of painting in opaque white on a greyish blue ground or bianco sopra bianco was much favored. The finest polychrome painted decoration was in high temperature colors. Some of the wares after 1760 reflected the influence of Marieberg and were painted in enamel colors and were decorated with applied fruit, flowers and foliage. The wares were widely diversified and in addition to the tablewares included tea trays, stoves and other very large pieces of faïence.

Rose Campan   See *Campan Marble*.

Rose Glass   In English glass; see *Jacobite Glass*.

Rose Point de Venise   In lace-making; Venetian Raised Point. See *Punto Tagliato a Fogliami*.

Rose Pompadour   In French ceramics; the soft rose-pink enamel ground color introduced at Sèvres around 1757. It remained in vogue until about 1765. In England it is often miscalled Rose du Barry.

Rose Quartz   See *Quartz*.

Rosetta Wood   A wood of the East Indies used for inlay and cabinetwork. It is hard and its color is reddish orange veined with dark markings.

Rosette   In ornament; a rosette is described as a circular ornament having many small designs arranged around its center, or in concentric circles. The rosette motif was found to a greater or less extent in all the historical styles of ornament.

Rosewater Ewer and Dish   In silver; from the 13th to the 17th centuries large basins or rosewater dishes and ewers were in general use in the houses of noble families. The wash-ing of hands at the dining table was a custom for many centuries until the practice of using forks came into general usage, at which time rosewater dishes were superseded by finger bowls placed on the table, one for each guest. The water was poured over the hands from the ewer, which usually contained rosewater, and was caught in the basin. These ewers and dishes were elaborately wrought and were notable for the quality of their craftsmanship. The large dish generally had a raised center portion of the same contour as the foot of the ewer upon which the ewer was placed.

Rosewood   A hard wood, *dalbergia nigra*, used for inlay and cabinetwork. It is dark red streaked with black. Rosewood was used in English cabinetwork as a contrasting wood for veneered border bandings from around 1760 in conjunction with satinwood. This practice continued through the early phase of the Regency. After 1800 rosewood became very popular in England. Many Regency pieces were made entirely of solid rosewood. Rosewood was used in America during the Victorian era from around 1845 to 1860. See *Rhodeswood*.

Rosso Antico   In English ceramics; a contemporary name given to the unglazed red stoneware made by Wedgwood having the same styles and designs found on Wedgwood's basalt or black basaltes stoneware. See *Wedgwood*.

Rouen   In French ceramics; painted faïence of great distinction was made at the numerous factories located at Rouen, Seine-Inférieure, Normandy, from around and after 1670 which had a great formative influence on the faïence styles adopted in France, Germany and Holland. Evidence of decline was perceptible from around 1770–1780. A Rouen innovation introduced late in the 17th century was a decoration of lambrequins and formal scrolls; the term *lambrequin* being used to include all types of formal pendent lace-like ornament. The term *style rayonnant* was given to a charac-

GOTHIC CARVED WOOD
ROSETTE

teristic type of Baroque design because of the radial treatment of its motifs, made from around 1690 to 1740. At its best the painted decoration which included lambrequins, festoons, formal scrolls, flowers, cornucopias, armorial bearings and rarely figure subjects, had a splendid vitality and formality which was typically Baroque in spirit. Blue was the principal color used for this lambrequin style and its variants with their symmetrical radiating formal designs; however, other high temperature colors, especially a dull red, were also found. Rouen developed a distinctive and beautiful polychrome style reflecting Chinese and Baroque influence, 1720–1750. Probably the most beautiful and original Rouen polychrome decoration was in the Rococo style, 1745–1770. The style was remarkable for its ingenious and fanciful treatment of Rococo motifs. Pastoral landscapes, mythological subjects and Chinese motifs were given a new expression that was completely captivating. The simpler types of designs included the familiar à la corne and à la carquois. From around 1770 to 1780 faïence painted in colored enamels and inspired by Strasbourg, Meissen and Marseilles was made. The first French soft paste was made at Rouen. A patent was granted in 1673 to Louis Poterat which included the manufacture of porcelain. It seems that very little was actually made.

Rouet In French Provincial; the rouet or spinning wheel is found in a variety of sizes and forms in the French provinces. It was an important utilitarian article of furniture, and it was found in the homes of the bourgeois as well as the cottages of the peasants. Some of the finest and most interesting rouets were made in Flanders. They consisted of many spindles beautifully proportioned and delicately and finely turned. See *Spinning Wheel*.

Rouge Box In Chinese ceramics; the name given to a small container for holding vermilion which was used for signature seals. The box, which is usually made of porcelain, is circular and is rather flat. The cover

is the same size and shape as the body part which holds the vermilion. The Japanese rouge box is generally made of lacquer.

Rouge Campan See *Campan Marble*.

Rouge de Cuivre In Chinese ceramics; the French name given to the underglaze red, which is a copper color, used during the Hsüan Tê period, 1426–1435. It was used either alone or with underglaze blue.

Rouge de Flandre Marble A marble from Philippeville, Namur, Belgium. The marbles are similar to the St. Rémy marbles in color and in texture. They are somewhat darker but of a richer red, with more numerous white veins.

Rouge Royal Marble A marble from Namur, Belgium. One of the Belgium red marbles. The red ground is not very brilliant, and the white veins are neither well-defined nor clear.

Roundabout Chair In English cabinetwork; see *Corner Chair*.

Roundel In ornament; the name applied to an object which is circular in form; a background for ornamentation, in circular form. Roundels were much used in medieval ornament.

Royal Copenhagen In Danish ceramics; a porcelain manufactory was started around 1771–1772 in Copenhagen by F. H. Müller and is still in existence. A royal privilege was granted in 1775, and around 1779 the manufactory was taken over by the King. Its best period was from around 1780 to 1800. A gradual decline became evident after 1800; however a modern revival dates from 1885. The factory mark was three wavy lines, one under the other, generally in underglaze blue. The hard paste porcelain made from around 1772 to 1779 was generally painted in underglaze blue, purple or iron red. Stylized floral patterns were much favored for this painting. The wares reflected the influence of Meissen and Fürstenberg. From around 1780 the Rococo style

ROUEN PLATE IN
STYLE RAYONNANT

was supplanted by the Neo-Classic style. The painted decoration was in accordance with the contemporary German fashions. Medallion portrait heads in a grey monochrome or in black silhouette were very fashionable. Charming wreaths of small flowers painted in polychrome were also characteristic. A pale gilding was used on the severely classic molded borders. The many figures were essentially copied from the models of other manufactories. Blue and white wares for daily use were also made and were generally decorated with slight formal floral patterns of German origin.

Rubens, Peter Paul 1577–1640, celebrated Flemish painter. The paintings of Rubens influenced the art work of Europe, especially Catholic Europe, for the first half of the 17th century. After studying in Italy and Spain for eight years he returned to Antwerp in 1608 and in the following year he was appointed court painter. During his years of study he had acquired such facility in arranging large scale compositions and of using light and color to increase the general effect of more movement and contrast that he had no rival north of the Alps. His paintings expressed his conception as well as the Flemish conception of the fullness and richness of life. The art of Rubens became very fashionable for it was suitable to enhance the splendor of palaces and to glorify the powers of this world. He accepted commissions from the rulers of Spain, France and Flanders. In so doing he was instrumental in spreading Roman Baroque art through Europe. Rubens devoted much time to the study of antique carvings in which field he became a leading authority. This same vitality, richness, fullness and movement were also evident in his ornament. It is easy to understand why Rubens is regarded as the originator of the Baroque movement in the Netherlands and one of its principal transmitters in Europe. See *Baroque*; *Renaissance, Netherlands*; *Louis XIII*.

RUE DE BONDY EWER AND BASIN

Ruby Back Porcelain In Chinese ceramics; see *Canton*.

Ruby Glass In German glass; Johann Kunckel is generally given credit for perfecting ruby glass in a mass, made with gold chloride, although Dr. Andreas Cassius of Hamburg actually discovered it. It appears that Kunckel working in Potsdam around 1679 first produced ruby glass in a practical manner. Ruby glass toward the end of the 17th century was either cut or engraved in the same manner as colorless glass. The art of producing ruby glass in a mass was lost for some time. Glass of ruby color made in Bohemia around the beginning of the 19th century was a colorless glass with a thin overlay of ruby glass. The method of coloring a mass of glass ruby was rediscovered in 1888 by Rauter working at the glass works in Ehrenfeld. See *Bohemian Glass*.

Rudder Table In cabinetwork; it is another name applied to a butterfly table.

Rue Amelot In French ceramics; a hard paste porcelain manufactory was located on the Rue Amelot in 1786 under the protection of the Duc d'Orléans. The mark "L P" was registered in 1786. It is believed that the manufactory at an earlier time was located in the Rue des Boulets and the Pont-aux-Choux respectively. Essentially the wares were of little artistic importance. Especially typical of its painted decoration was a design of strewn flowers generally of roses. See *Paris Porcelain*.

Rue de Bondy In French ceramics; a hard paste porcelain manufactory was started in 1780 on the Rue de Bondy, Paris, by Dihl with the patronage of the Duc d'Angoulême. In 1795 it was moved to the Rue du Temple and in 1825 to the Boulevard Saint-Martin. It closed in 1829. Tablewares were the principal productions and they varied in decoration from simply painted floral designs to richly painted and gilded elaborate designs. Especially characteristic and charming were the simply decorated wares with sprig patterns of cornflowers. Biscuit figures were also made. Included among the marks were

"A G" in monogram either with or without a crown. See *Paris Porcelain*.

Rue de Crussol In French ceramics; a hard paste porcelain manufactory was started in Paris in 1789 by Christopher Potter, an Englishman. He named it the "Manufacture du Prince de Galles," and operated it until around 1792. Subsequently it changed hands several times. Included among the marks were "Potter", "E B" and "P B" in underglaze blue. The productions were decorated in the contemporary Paris styles. See *Paris Porcelain*.

Rue de la Roquette In French ceramics; a leading center in Paris for the manufacture of faïence and porcelain. A faïence manufactory was conducted by Digne around 1750. Spouted pharmacy vases painted in the Rouen style are ascribed to this manufactory. Another manufactory at a somewhat later date was operated by Ollivier and made principally tile stoves. It is believed that a soft paste porcelain manufactory was conducted here by François Hébert and that the mark of crossed arrows was used. A hard paste porcelain manufactory was conducted here by Souroux who registered "S" as a mark in 1773. From 1774 a hard paste porcelain manufactory was operated by Vincent Dubois. Hard paste porcelain with the mark of two crossed arrows with the points pointing upwards is believed to have been made at Dubois' manufactory. These pieces bearing this mark are similar to the usual Paris types. See *Paris Porcelain*.

Rue du Temple See *Rue de Bondy*.

Rue Fontaine-au-Roy See *La Courtille*.

Rue Popincourt In French ceramics; a hard paste porcelain manufactory was established in 1782 in Paris by J. N. H. Nast. After 1784 it was known as Rue Amandiers Popincourt. The manufactory, which was active until 1835, enjoyed a flourishing business; however, the productions were of little artistic importance. All types of wares were made, including tablewares, clock cases, ink stands and biscuit figures. The mark was "Nast" stencilled in red. See *Paris Porcelain*.

Rue Thiroux In French ceramics; a hard paste porcelain manufactory was started around 1775 by Leboeuf under the protection of Marie Antoinette. The mark registered in 1776 was an "A" and the wares were known as "porcelaine de la Reine." After changing hands several times it was still active in 1869. The 18th century porcelain was admirable for its fine quality and for its delicately and slightly painted floral designs of cornflowers and roses executed in excellent taste. See *Paris Porcelain*.

Rumble Seat In American cabinetwork; see *Wagon Seat*.

Rummer In English glass; an 18th century English drinking glass, usually having a cylindrical or ovoid shaped bowl, resting on a very short stem or knob, with either a square or round molded and cut base.

Runner In Oriental rugs; see *Makatlik*.

Runner Foot In cabinetwork; a horizontal side bar connecting the front leg and rear leg of a chair, and upon which the legs terminate and rest. It is the same as a bar foot. Runner feet were much used in chair design during the Italian Renaissance. These runner feet or side runners generally terminated in carved lion feet. See *Foot*.

RUNNER FOOT

Running Stitch A stitch used in embroidery. It is a small stitch and taken evenly. See *Embroidery*.

Run Work A lace in which the pattern is formed by running a thread with a needle through a net ground. See *Limerick*.

Rush Seat In cabinetwork; a chair seat made of rushes or reeds. The stalks of rushes or reeds must be cut at a particular time of the year and carefully cured, otherwise they would decay. A rush seat was common on turned wood chairs and it was considered to be very durable. See *Splint Seat*; *Flag Seat*.

Russian Imperial Tapestry Works A tapestry manufactory was established in St. Petersburg, Russia, by Peter the Great in 1716, and was discontinued in 1859. Its greatest productive period was under Catherine II, 1762–1796. See *Tapestry*.

Rustique In French Provincial furniture; the term *rustique* is given to the simple farmhouse and peasant type furniture made in the French provinces. Naturally, in a general sense the term *rustique* can be applied to all farmhouse or cottage furniture executed in a country-like or peasant manner in the other countries of Europe as well as in America. The local originality existing in the different French provinces was especially marked in the rustique furniture, giving the work a singular charm. Any semblance of a style, such as the Louis XV style, was more evident in their panelled pieces, such as armoires and buffet-vaisseliers, with their shaped molded panels, than in their tables and chairs with wooden seats. See *French Provincial*; *Regional Furniture*.

Rustred In armor; see *Mail*.

RUSTIQUE ARMOIRE,
BRETON

Sabaton In armor; see *Soleret*.

Saber In arms and armor; a cutting and thrusting weapon which is similar to the broadsword. It has a slightly curved blade about 34 inches in length with the cutting edge on the convex side and a handgrip and a guard to protect the hand. At times the blade is also furnished with a sharp edge on both sides near the point. The saber is used by the cavalry and also as a fencing sword. It developed from a cavalry sword of Oriental origin introduced into Europe by the Hungarians during the 18th century. See *Sword*.

Saber Leg In cabinetwork; a slender quadrangular leg employed on chairs that curves slightly forward in a concave curve. It is so called because of its supposed resemblance to the shape of a saber. In this form of concave leg the foot is not a separate portion from the leg. This form of leg was used in the Directoire, Empire, Sheraton and Regency styles.

Sabicu Wood The hard wood of a tree, *lysiloma sabicu*, of the West Indies used for inlay and cabinetwork.

Sabot In French furniture mounts; a French term given to the decorative bronze appliqué or shoe applied to the foot of an article of French furniture; such as a commode, a table, or some similar article of furniture.

Sack Glass In English glass; a 17th century drinking glass having a stem and foot. It was used for drinking sack, a general name applied to a class of white wines formerly imported into England from Spain and the Canary Islands and mentioned as early as 1536. These sack wines were usually given names relating to their place of origin, such as Canary Sack or Sherry sack; Sherry meaning Xeres the place of origin.

Sacring Bell In ecclesiastical art; a small bell, generally of silver, rung at the elevation of the Host. Little sacring bells of silver and occasionally of gold were listed in medieval church inventories. The bell was in the form of an inverted cup, enriched with engraved decoration, and provided with a handle at the top. Later the sacring bell was made larger although it retained its earlier form, and it was designed with a chime of small bells.

Sacristy Cupboard In Italian cabinetwork; the sacristy cupboard, which was the earliest Italian movable cupboard, was an ecclesiastical piece of furniture. It served as a receptacle for the sacred utensils which were used in church ritual. It was introduced during the Gothic period. The credenza or domestic cupboard essentially resembled the early Renaissance sacristy cupboard. See *Credenza*; *Cupboard*.

Saddle Bag In Oriental rug weaving; see *Hehbehlik*.

Saddle-Cheek Chair In English cabinetwork; a large comfortable upholstered armchair with wide wings or cheeks down the sides to protect the occupant against any draft. The name first appeared in late 17th century trade accounts and was used throughout the 18th century to describe an easy chair with deep wings. Hepplewhite in the CABINET MAKER AND UPHOLSTERER'S GUIDE illustrated a chair of this variety.

Saddle Cover In Oriental rug weaving; see *Semerlik*.

Saddle Seat In English cabinetwork; the shaped wooden seat of a Windsor chair. In this form of seat the wood is slightly cut away in a sloping manner from the center front. The saddle seat was a characteristic feature of design for both English and American Windsor chairs. The majority of

SABER LEG

Windsor chairs had saddle-shaped seats. See *Windsor Chair*.

Sadware In pewter; the trade name applied to the heavier articles made of pewter; such as plates, trenchers and similar articles. The sadware workers executed their work by hammering. See *Pewter, Hammered*.

Saint-Amand-les-Eaux In French ceramics; a faïence manufactory was started at Saint-Amand-les-Eaux, Nord, by P. J. Fauquez. The factory was active until the French Revolution. Around 1800 the factory was acquired by the Bettignies family, who operated it until 1882. Much of the faïence was in imitation of Rouen and Strasbourg. The early painted decoration was in high temperature colors, while during the second half of the 18th century the polychrome painted decoration was in enamel colors. A factory mark of "F's" and "P's" in monogram was sometimes found. Creamcolored and white earthenware in the English style was also made in the late 18th and 19th centuries. Soft paste porcelain was also made from around 1771 to 1778 and was resumed after 1800, principally making copies of Sèvres soft paste porcelain.

Saint Anne Marble A marble from the Basses-Pyrénées, France. The Saint Anne Granit is a closely packed grey marble and derives its name from its grey, granite-like appearance. The Saint Anne Grand Dessin marble is a darker grey. The Saint Anne Rubane is darker than the first two.

Saint-Clément In French ceramics; a faïence manufactory was started at Saint-Clément, Meurthe-et-Moselle, in 1758 by Jacques Chambrette as a branch of the Lunéville factory. It changed hands several times and was active until late in the 19th century. The factory produced a fine enamelled and gilt faïence closely resembling the faïence made at Sceaux. Figures were made in faïence painted in enamel colors, and also in biscuit in the manner of Lunéville. Much creamcolored earthenware of a good quality was also produced. It seems no factory mark was

SAINT-CLOUD TEAPOT

in use until the 19th century when "St. Clément" and "St Ct" were employed.

Saint-Cloud In French ceramics; a soft paste porcelain manufactory, also making faïence, was active at Saint-Cloud, Seine-et-Oise, from before 1678 to 1766. It is regarded as the first important French porcelain manufactory. It was started by Pierre Chicaneau, d. 1678, and letters patent were granted to his family in 1702. Saint-Cloud had a branch manufactory in the Rue de la Ville L'Evêque, Paris. A sun face and a fleur-de-lis were registered as marks in 1696; however, the latter is very rare. The well-known factory mark "St C" over "T", usually in blue and often accompanied by other letters, dots, and crosses, was apparently not used until after 1722. It seems that Saint-Cloud figures never bore the factory mark. Much of the charm of Saint-Cloud porcelain is in the material itself which at its best is a rather warm ivory tone with a distinctive firm and smooth texture. The porcelain often closely resembled the Chinese Blanc de Chine. Of particular interest were the forms with their beautiful and refined lines. Baroque lacework scrolls painted in blue were a favorite decoration and were executed with delicacy and grace. Figures, which were often left unpainted, were admirably modelled. The porcelain from around 1730 to 1750 strongly reflected the influence of Meissen. Chinese Famille Verte porcelain and the Japanese Kakiemon styles were frequently the inspiration for the painted decoration.

Saint-Jean-du-Désert In French ceramics; an early center for French faïence. Italian potters were working at Saint-Jean-du-Désert, which is a suburb of Marseilles, as early as the 16th century. See *Marseilles*.

Saint Mihiel Lace In lace-making; see *Lorraine Lace*.

Saintonge In French Provincial; a former province in western France, bordering Poitou on the north and Guienne on the south. It is now the greater part of the department of Charente Inférieure and a small part of Charente. Their Louis XV cabinet-work was distinctive for its harmonious and graceful lines and for its excellent proportions. A distinctive and effective feature of their panelled furniture designed in the Louis XV style was the frequent use of contrasting woods. For example, the buffet bas and dressoir often had walnut panels framed in cherry or elm framed in walnut. They produced many fine specimens of chairs with straw or rush seats. Some of their fine 18th century pieces were made of mahogany and amaranth. See *French Provincial*.

St. Petersburg In Russian ceramics; the Russian Imperial Porcelain manufactory was established in 1744 under the protection of the Empress Elizabeth. However, it was not until almost twenty years later that the manufacture of hard paste porcelain was successfully conducted. Evidence of artistic decline became perceptible around 1825; however, the manufactory has enjoyed a modern revival. The marks were principally monograms and imperial emblems according to the different reigns. The porcelain made from around 1762 onwards was in the Neo-Classic taste and was in imitation of the contemporary French, Viennese and German styles. It was often lavishly gilded. Sèvres porcelain in the Empire style was later closely imitated. Figures were made in painted enamels and in biscuit. Russian folk types and peasants were popular subjects for the figures.

Saint-Porchaire In French ceramics; a white earthenware with inlaid decoration was made at Saint-Porchaire from around 1525 to 1560. There are about sixty surviving examples. The ware is quite unlike any other ceramic ware both in respect to its extreme fragility and in the unusual technique of its inlaid decoration. The intricate inlaid decoration, comprising French Renaissance motifs, was produced by impressing the soft white clay body with metal stamps and filling the impressions with different colored clays, chiefly brown, black and reddish or ochre yellow. It was covered with a transparent

ivory-colored lead glaze. Some of the elaborate specimens such as ewers, candlesticks and salt-cellars were of architectural forms and were lavishly ornamented with applied Renaissance motifs such as statuettes, cupids, masks, grotesques and cherubs. Occasionally the reliefs were lightly touched with colored glazes of green, purple and blue. The ware is also called Henri Deux or Henri II.

Salade In medieval armor; a helmet introduced early in the 15th century which supplanted the basinet. Essentially it had a low rounded or bowl-shaped crown and a neck guard for the back of the neck. The shape of the salade varied. There was a large difference between those worn by the cavalry and those worn by the foot soldiers. Toward the end of the 15th century the salade was replaced by the armet. It is also spelled sallet.

Salamander Back In American cabinetwork; a variety of slat-back turned chair deriving its name from the supposed resemblance of the slats, which were generally three or four, to the contour of a salamander. It is stated in American furniture literature that they were found in Canada, Vermont and New Hampshire around 1720–1730. See *Slat-Back Chair*.

Salem Secretary In American cabinetwork; the name given to a variety of Sheraton-style secretary bookcase which is also known in New England as a Salem desk. The recessed upper section is designed with four, occasionally only two, glazed doors enclosing bookshelves. The projecting lower section is fitted with two or three rows of drawers. In one type the top center drawer in the lower section is designed with a fall-front writing flap which opens to a fitted writing interior. In another type the lower part of the upper recessed bookcase section is fitted with small drawers and pigeonholes. See *Butler's Sideboard*.

Sallet In medieval armor; see *Salade*.

Salopian In English ceramics; see *Caughley*.

Salt-Cellar A small container or vessel used

SHERATON SALEM
SECRETARY

on the table for holding salt. The name is derived from the term *salte-seller*, the name applied to the vessel in the latter part of the 15th century. The word *seller* was a variant of earlier words such as salsar, salare and selere, derived from the Latin term *salarius*, and the French term *salière* meaning a salt-holder. In English silver; a small salt-cellar or open salt, evolved from the trencher salt, frequently made of pierced work conforming to the prevailing fashion, was popular from about 1760 to about 1790. It was fitted with a blue glass liner for holding the salt. See *Trencher Salt*.

Salt Chair In French cabinetwork; see *Chaise à Sel*.

Salt, Cylindrical Standing In English silver; an elaborately wrought standing salt having a cylindrical shaped body. The upper part of the body flared into a bowl-shaped section. It was fitted with a high domed cover which was generally surmounted with a figure. The body rested on a domed base which was mounted on three feet or supports sometimes in the form of swan neck scrolls. It was introduced during the 16th century. See *Salt, Standing*.

Salt Dish In silver; see *Trencher Salt*; *Salt-Cellar*.

Salt Glaze In ceramics; a thin hard film of glaze made on the surface of stoneware by throwing salt into the kiln at the point of highest temperature during the only firing. The brown color which is so characteristic of salt-glaze ware is made by applying a wash of clay rich in iron oxide to the surface of the stoneware before it is fired in the kiln. Black was also obtained by a wash of ferruginous clay. The colors blue and purple are produced from cobalt and manganese oxides respectively. See *Glaze*.

Salt, Hourglass Standing In English silver; an elaborately worked standing salt. It was so named because of the supposed resemblance of its shape to that of an hourglass. It was introduced during the 16th century. See *Salt, Standing*.

SILVER STEEPLE STANDING
SALT

Saltire Stretcher In cabinetwork; an X-form stretcher. It is also called a cross stretcher. See *X-form Stretcher*.

Salt Spoon In English silver; a miniature silver spoon used to sprinkle salt. The bowls of salt spoons are usually round or nearly round and the stems seem to follow, on a miniature scale, those of the larger contemporary spoons. The salt spoon was introduced in the 18th century.

Salt, Standing In English silver; a massive elaborately wrought salt container. It was made in a variety of shapes; some of the well-known and characteristic shapes included the hourglass, bell, and steeple. It varied in height from around 7 inches to 16 inches. The standing salt was placed in the center of the table. It had a special social significance because it divided the host and his more important guests from the lesser guests, who sat "below the salt." The standing salt was introduced during the 16th century. It was made on the Continent, but it did not achieve the same importance there as in England.

Salt, Steeple Standing In English silver; a standing salt having a shallow cupola, raised on scrolled brackets attached to the rim of the body, in place of a cover. The cupola was surmounted with a steeple-shaped spire. It was introduced toward the end of the 16th century. See *Salt, Standing*.

Salver The term *salver*, derived from the Spanish word *salva*, is applied to a tray or plate on which things, including food and drink, are offered or presented to a person. A small salver is usually called a card tray. The salver was used in England in the 16th and 17th centuries to hold the assay cup when tasting its contents for poison. In English silver; the name is given to a form of tray having a flat circular top and mounted on a foot, which can be held by one hand of the server. Earliest extant salvers are usually of this form and date from the 17th century. The term is also given to a flat silver tray generally mounted on three or more feet used for serving refreshments, letters and similar service. This salver was made in a variety of sizes and also in several different shapes, such as square with incurvate corners, circular either with or without a shaped edge, and in octafoil outline. It frequently had a molded border and the center was often ornamented with an engraved heraldic insignia. In English glass; a rather flat rimmed glass dish mounted on a stem and foot on which jelly is served at the table. It was made in different sizes and often used in conjunction with jelly glasses. See *Jelly Glass*; *Comport*.

Samarkand   An Oriental rug belonging to the Turkoman group. It was woven in the vicinity of the city of Samarkand, which is in eastern Turkestan. The foundation is usually cotton, and the pile which is trimmed medium in length is generally of wool. The designs are essentially of Chinese origin. See *Turkoman Rugs*.

Samarra Ware   In ceramics; see *Persian and Near Eastern Pottery*.

Sambin, Hugues   The Renaissance style of Burgundian furniture was greatly influenced by the architectural work and by a book of designs published around 1570 of Hugues Sambin. His work was characterized by bold and vigorous carvings which were distinctive for their vital and dramatic quality. His carved figures were full of life and were animated with a forceful energy which was very striking. Some examples of Burgundian furniture of fine craftsmanship which combined this style of carving with well-balanced proportions were notable for their singular richness and elegance. See *Henri II*; *Burgundy*.

Same Yaki   In Japanese ceramics; a pottery ware known as Same or shark-skin made in the province of Satsuma. The body is a grey clay. The glaze is minutely granulated and is said to resemble the skin of a shark. These wares were produced at least as early as 1800.

Samian Ware   In ancient ceramics; the name applied to an ancient variety of pottery made of Samian earth or other fine earth. By extension the term is given to the ancient Roman pottery called Arretine ware and terra sigillata. Samian earth is the name given to the fine clay from the island of Samos in the Aegean Sea. See *Arretine Ware*.

Samite   A rich, heavy, silk fabric, usually interwoven with gold, made during the Middle Ages. It was used in the elaborate vestments of the clergy. It was also worn by noblemen and noblewomen on state occasions.

Samovar   A Russian metal urn used for heating water to make tea. It consists of a vertical tube running through the center of the urn which is a container for burning charcoal to heat the water. The somewhat cup-shaped top portion of the tube is used as a place to set a teapot or teakettle to keep it hot.

Sample Chairs   In American cabinetwork; the name given to six chairs which are believed to have been made around 1770 by Benjamin Randolph, cabinetmaker of Philadelphia. They are called sample chairs since they were probably used as models for his fine workmanship as well as an exhibition of his skill. There are five side chairs and one wing chair, all in the Chippendale style. One side chair is relatively plain while the other four display elaborate and masterfully carved detail. The wing chair and one side chair are in the Philadelphia Museum of Art, one is privately owned, and the others are at Winterthur, Williamsburg and Yale.

Sampler   In needlework; the original purpose of a sampler was to preserve a sample of stitches or patterns used in embroidery work. It appears that the early samplers were worked by adults. The later ones were chiefly a decorative display of juvenile skill. It is reasonable to assume that samplers were

RENAISSANCE CUPBOARD,
AFTER HUGUES SAMBIN

made during the Middle Ages in Europe. One of the earliest dated English samplers in existence bears the date of 1644. From around 1750 it became the custom for children to sign their samplers and give their ages. There are in existence a few American samplers made during the 17th century. Until relatively recent times it was customary for every little girl to make a sampler.

Sanctuary Lamp A term applied to a kind of lamp hung in the church usually before the tabernacle. The early sanctuary lamp was generally shaped like a shallow bowl to hold a candle, and hung from the ceiling by three chains.

Sanda In Japanese ceramics; the celadon wares produced at Sanda, in the province of Settsu, are considered among the finest in Japan. About 1800 three potters from Kyōto, Kamesuke, Kamekichi and Shūhei, who were pupils of Eisen, began making celadon wares of fine quality.

Sandalwood A yellowish wood, *santalum freycinetianum*, of the East Indies. It is fragrant and closely grained. It is used in cabinetwork and for drawer and chest linings. Also the red sandalwood, *pterocarpus santalinus*, of India.

Sandarac Wood See *Citron Wood*.

Sand Caster In English silver; see *Pounce Box*.

SANDWICH PRESSED
GLASS CUP PLATE

Sanderson, Elijah 1751–1825. American cabinetmaker working at Salem, Massachusetts, with his brother, Jacob, 1757–1810. They had fine craftsmen working for them at their cabinet shop. It is generally believed that Samuel McIntire, the carver, did some carving on furniture for them.

Sanderswood A name applied to sandalwood or red sandalwood.

Sandwich Glass In American glass; a glass manufactory was founded at Sandwich, Cape Cod, Massachusetts, in 1825 by Deming Jarves. It was called the Sandwich Manufacturing Company. It was incor-

porated in 1826 as the Boston and Sandwich Glass Company. The factory ceased to operate in 1888. The term *Early Sandwich Glass* is generally applied to the glass produced there during the first fifteen years, that is from 1825 to 1840. It is usually accepted that it made blown glass and cut glass from 1825 and that it started to produce pressed glass in quantity as well as lacy and colored glass from around 1830. It made all types of flint glassware for every use, and it employed all the contemporary fashionable methods in its decoration. See *Paperweight*; *Glass*.

Sang de Bœuf In Chinese ceramics; a beautiful red-glazed porcelain of the Ch'ing dynasty, especially of the K'ang Hsi reign. The body of the ware is white or greyish white and is of a fine texture. The red glaze, which is made from copper, is glassy with minute pores and bubbles. There is always a minute delicate crackle that is hardly distinguishable. The red glaze has a tendency to run or fall, and, especially in the K'ang Hsi pieces, forms a welt at the base but does not run over. In many of the later pieces the glaze was allowed to run over the bottom and had to be ground off. The red glaze often slips down from the lip rim and sometimes off the shoulder exposing portions of buff or greenish white. The color appears to be a blend of tiny blotches of blood-colored particles, or at times larger splotches when it is called strawberry red. Many pieces are streaked with grey. Sometimes the ware is the color of ashes of roses or a harmonious blend of red, rose, grey and green. The foot is usually well formed and does not have any red glaze underneath. The glaze under the base is occasionally olive green, clear or mottled. Occasionally it has red or pink splotches, or at times it is a buff or pale green crackle. Usually the inside has a greenish or buff crackled glaze. Sang de Bœuf is also called Ox Blood and Lang Yao. See *Chi Hung*.

Sang de Pigeon In Chinese ceramics; a crimson or liver red porcelain ware commonly called Sang de Pigeon. It is stated that this ware was first made late in the K'ang Hsi reign. However, the only examples known at the present time are of the Yung Cheng reign as well as those produced during the late 19th century. The red glaze is produced from copper oxide and is at times a deep rich color. The texture of the glaze is perfectly even and is usually dull, pitted with minute pores, or at times it is glossy.

San Michele Tapestries The manufacturing of tapestries was revived in 1710 by Pope Clement XI at the Hospital San Michele in Rome. Jean Simonet was the manager, and Andrea Procaccini, the painter, was the art director. Pietro Ferloni was the manager from 1717 to 1770. See *Rome Tapestries*.

Sansovino, Jacopo 1486–1570, Italian architect and sculptor whose architectural forms and style of ornament greatly influenced the design of furniture. He arrived in Venice from Rome in 1527 and designed numerous fine Venetian buildings. His designs provided the initiative for a new style that was the harbinger of the Venetian Baroque. His work was noted for its fine proportions and graceful ornament, sometimes slightly marred by excessive sculptured decoration. However, the quality of the decoration was always distinctive for its beauty and fine craftsmanship. See *Renaissance, Italian*.

San Ts'ai In Chinese ceramics; see *Three-Color Ware*.

Sapan Wood It is obtained from the East Indian sapan tree, *caesalpinia sappan*, and is widely used for inlay and cabinetwork, especially by the French ébénistes. It is hard and its color is red. Also related woods from Brazil, the Antilles and Jamaica. It is also called Brazilwood.

Sapin Wood The wood of the fir tree, *pinus roxburghii*, used for inlay and cabinetwork, especially by the French ébénistes. It is elastic and soft and its color is white.

Saraband Rug See *Serebend Rug*.

Sarakh Rug See *Bijar Rug*.

Sardonyx An ornamental stone which is a type of onyx. It is generally composed of one or more layers of carnelian or sard, which is a brownish red color, alternating with milky white chalcedony. If the layers are of carnelian it is more correctly called carnelian onyx. See *Quartz*.

Sarreguemines In ceramics; a faïence manufactory was started at Sarreguemines, Lorraine, France, around 1770 by Paul Utzschneider which was carried on by his descendants throughout the 19th century. The factory, which was quite active, produced a variety of wares, included among which were cream-colored and white earthenware, lustered and marbled lead-glazed earthenware and stoneware in the Wedgwood style. The wares were usually marked with the name of the town, "U & Cie" in an octagon or "U C" in a triangle.

Saruk An Oriental rug belonging to the Persian classification. It is very finely woven. The foundation is usually cotton, sometimes linen. The pile which is short is of wool. The ends are finished with a narrow web and loose warp threads. The Saruk is distinctive for its rich coloring, for its velvet-like texture and for its great variety of designs. Originally Saruks were woven at the village of Saruk. The modern ones are chiefly woven at Sultanabad. See *Persian Rugs*.

Satin A closely woven silk fabric with a lustrous surface produced by a special manner of weaving, in which the weft threads are floated over several warp threads instead of crossing warp and weft threads regularly. Exported satin from China was found in Europe at least as early as the 13th century. A less expensive quality of satin was made in Europe with a weft of wool and was often referred to as satin of Bruges. Although damask and brocade were more fashionable 18th century fabrics than satin, the latter, either plain or figured, was also much used. During the late 18th century there was a vogue in France for satin with delicately printed decoration. See *Silk*; *Upholstery*.

CARVED WOOD LANTERN WITH SANSOVINO FORMS

Satin Cafard See *Satin de Bruges*.

Satin Damask A silk fabric, in the damask style, characterized by a satin weave background with the designs commonly of taffeta construction. The name is also given to a linen damask in which the designs and background are made with satin weaves. See *Damask*.

Satin de Bruges A fabric, made as early as the 16th century, with a silk warp and a linen or wool weft, woven with a satin weave. During the 18th century it was called satin de Hollande and satin Cafard.

Satin de Hollande See *Satin de Bruges*.

Satin-Glass In American glass; a late 19th century American art glass. It is characterized by an inner layer of opaque glass, ornamented with square-shaped indentations, covered with an overlay of colored glass in the indentations and an over-all layer of clear glass. It was then subjected to acid vapors to produce a satin-like finish. It is also called mother-of-pearl glass. See *Art Glass*.

Satin Stitch A stitch used in embroidery, closely worked in parallel lines over a design, making a satin-like surface. If the design is without padding it is called a flat satin stitch, and with padding, a raised satin stitch. See *Embroidery*.

Satinwood The wood of an East Indian tree, *chlorxylon swietenia*, used for inlay and cabinetwork. It is hard and has a yellow-gold color and is veined and wavy. Also a Florida tree having an orange color, and used for furniture. The red satinwood of the West Indies is red, veined with yellow. In English cabinetwork; from around 1770 the tendency was toward woods of a lighter tone, in particular satinwood and harewood. Mahogany was still used for general household articles and for library and dining room furniture. Robert Adam's preference for satinwood was largely responsible for its popularity and its extensive use by other contemporary designers and cabinetmakers. In fact this era is frequently referred to as the

SATSUMA VASE

Age of Satinwood. Satinwood veneer was much used in conjunction with veneers of other colored and stained woods; such as mahogany, tulipwood, kingwood, rosewood, ebony, harewood and stained holly. Entire articles of furniture such as chairs, tables and commodes were made of satinwood, especially in the furniture designed by Robert Adam. Satinwood continued to be used until around 1820. In American cabinetwork the use of satinwood was restricted to inlay work, such as stringing lines and paterae. See *Rosewood, Sheraton*.

Satsuma Ware In Japanese ceramics; toward the end of the 16th century the feudal prince of Satsuma, after completing a campaign in Korea, brought back with him a number of Korean potters. It seems that one of the Korean potters discovered at Nawashirogawa, which is near Kagoshima, the capital of the province of Satsuma, a clay of remarkable fineness. The White Satsuma was developed from about 1640 on, with its hard fine texture, its even and almost microscopic crackled glaze and soft ivory tint. A similar development occurred at Chōsa in the adjacent province of Osumi. It is believed that the Old Satsuma which is prized by collectors with its nishiki-de or brocade pattern in colored enamels and gold was first developed at Chōsa and was perfected there around 1790. The early wares of this type with their finely crackled ivory-white glaze were moderately decorated. They were delicately painted with some few of the following colors: a dry iron red, a bluish green enamel, a shiny blue, yellow, purple, black and a subdued matt relief gold. The painted decoration chiefly consisted of flowers, landscapes, the phoenix, but not any human figures. After 1850 the tendency was for over-elaboration and all kinds of figure subjects were included. These over-decorated imitations of the Old Satsuma were primarily intended for export. In addition to the Old Satsuma they also made wares with finely crackled monochrome glazes and wares with fluid glazes in two or more layers. Of particular interest was the so-called dragon scale glaze which was marked with spots of milky white. Mishima wares were also produced.

Satyr In ornament; a mythological creature generally represented as half man and half goat, used as a decorative motif. The satyr mask was extensively employed during the Italian Renaissance in furniture design. It was subsequently used in French and English style of ornament. The satyr mask was often used as a decorative motif from around 1730 to 1740 on furniture designed in the Early Georgian style. See *Queen Anne and Early Georgian.*

Sauce Boat In English silver; a vessel, slightly boat-shaped, used to hold sauce for fish, meat and dessert. The shape of the sauce boat varied. Sometimes it had a lip at each end and a small scroll handle at each side and rested on a low molded foot. A favorite form of sauce boat had a wide spout or lip on one side and a scroll handle on the opposite side. It rested on three small feet. Another type of sauce boat is generally called a sauce tureen and was modelled after a large soup tureen. The sauce boat was introduced in the first half of the 18th century.

Saucepan In English silver; the saucepan, which was a vessel for serving hot food, was introduced during the late 17th century. It was in the form of a cylindrical bowl having a cover and a scroll handle and it rested on a low molded foot. Generally the saucepan was without decoration, although occasionally it had an engraved coat-of-arms. The later type of saucepan was of ogee contour, either with or without a cover, and was fitted with a long turned wood handle. See *Brandy Warmer.*

Saucer In English silver; the name originally applied to a small dish or pan in which sauce was served. During the 16th and 17th centuries in England small, shallow silver dishes were used for serving sauces of various kinds. These dishes, which were usually round but occasionally oval, varied in size from about 5 to 8 inches in diameter, and were generally fitted with two handles.

The handles were either in the form of slender scrolls or miniature shells. The name *saucer* as applied to the small dish on which is set a tea or coffee cup is of rather modern usage.

Saunier, Jean-Jacques A French ébéniste who was admitted as a master cabinetmaker in 1752. At the beginning of his career he was an expert marqueteur. His pieces of furniture admirably illustrate the development in French cabinetwork from the use of certain details and motifs borrowed from Roman architecture to the closer imitation of antiquity which ultimately triumphed in the style of the French Empire. See *Louis XVI.*

Savalan Rug See *Sultanabad Rug.*

Savery, William 1721–1787, American cabinetmaker. He had his shop on Second Street in Philadelphia. He is regarded as one of the most outstanding cabinetmakers working in the Chippendale style. See *Philadelphia Chippendale.*

Savoie In French Provincial; a department in south-eastern France that was formed of the old provinces of Savoie, Haute Savoie, the Maurienne and the Tarentaise; on the east it borders Switzerland and Italy. The provincial furniture of Savoie has the same general characteristics as that of Bresse, and the earlier pieces are similar to those of Burgundy. See *Bresse*; *Burgundy*; *French Provincial.*

GEORGE II SILVER SAUCE BOAT

Savona In Italian ceramics; a considerable faïence manufacture was carried on during the 17th and 18th centuries at the Ligurian coast towns of Savona, Albissola and Genoa. However, little exact information is available about their productions which are generally grouped under Savona, probably the leading center. The faïence made at Delft was the principal influence. Chinese, Spanish and French influences were also evident in some of the designs. Included among the characteristic wares were pharmacy vases, vases with two handles, plates and dishes with flat rims and tea table wares.

The early work was only in blue and white. Later other high temperature colors were used and much effective work was achieved in different polychrome styles. The painted decoration was often admirable for its fine drawings. Of particular interest was a variety with cupids, horsemen and other figure subjects depicted against a mountain landscape and painted either in blue or in polychrome on a greenish toned ground. Other equally interesting styles were also developed.

WORCESTER PLATE WITH
SCALE BORDER

Savonarola Chair   In Italian cabinetwork; an early wooden chair of ancient Roman curule form or a folding chair of X-form. It consisted of about seven serpentine X-shaped staves. The lower staves were secured with runner feet while the upper staves or supports were secured by straight arms. It had a flat-arched back rail made of wood, which was joined to the rear ends of the arms. The narrow seat was made of slats and was placed slightly above the intersection of the supports. A loose cushion was usually placed on the seat. The early Savonarola chair was crude and plain; it was not richly ornamented until the end of the 15th century. See *Curule*; *Dantesca Chair*.

Savonnerie Carpet   A hand-tufted, cut pile carpet first made at the Savonnerie manufactory around 1620 at Chaillot, Paris, which was transferred to the Gobelins in 1826. The Savonnerie carpet manufactory was founded by Simon Lourdet and Pierre Dupont. The name *Savonnerie* was derived from the fact that the building in which it was established was formerly a soap factory. It received the patronage of the French crown, and the carpet workers were removed from the Louvre to Chaillot in 1631. The Savonnerie is of the same construction as an Oriental rug. However, it is not as finely woven, and the wool in the pile is heavier. The colors and designs are distinctly French. The designs usually consist of large central oval panels, wreaths of flowers, foliage scrolls and elaborate borders. The name *Savonnerie* is also given to other hand-tufted carpets made in other parts of France. See *Oriental Rug*.

Savonnette, Boîte à   In French silver; see *Soap Box and Sponge Box*.

Saxe   In French ceramics; the term *Saxe porcelain* was the name given in France to Meissen porcelain. See *Meissen*.

Scagliola   A colored composition in imitation of marble. It is made of ground gypsum mixed with glue, having spar, stone or marble dust worked in the surface. Robert Adam effectively used scagliola in cabinetwork to provide a touch of color. It was used for table tops and was occasionally inset in panels in furniture.

Scaled   In armor; a coat-of-mail. See *Mail*.

Scale Pattern   In European ceramics; a diaper arrangement or a repetitive pattern resembling overlapping fish scales. Especially characteristic was the English Worcester scale-blue used from around 1765 to 1785, and the more unusual scale-pink. Similar monochrome patterns in purple, green, yellow and other colors were used particularly for borders on Meissen, Berlin and Vienna porcelain from around and after 1760 and were known as *Mosäik*.

Sceaux   In French ceramics; a porcelain and faïence manufactory was started at Sceaux, Seine, probably as early as 1735 with Jacques Chapelle as manager and later owner, under the patronage of the Duchesse de Maine. The manufactory changed hands several times. The wares revealed little artistic merit after 1810. From late in the 18th century cream-colored earthenware was also added to the productions. It is doubtful that much porcelain was made before 1763. The mark "S X" was submitted for porcelain in 1773. The influence of Mennecy and Sèvres was evident in the porcelain. Flower painting in blue similar to that found on Mennecy porcelain was much favored. Some of the painted decoration was obviously done by the same artists who painted the faïence. The faïence, which was of fine quality, was painted in enamel colors and gilt in the style of porcelain, and ranks among the best of its kind. The early faïence wares reflected the styles of Mennecy and Vincennes. The faïence in the Louis XVI style was distinctive for its refinement and elegant simplicity. The painted decoration included birds, flowers, foliage, cupids and exquisite pastoral scenes executed in the style of contemporary Sèvres painting. Tablewares were the principal production. Finely modelled faïence figures frequently closely copied from Sèvres were also made. Included among the faïence marks were "O P" and "S P", the latter being of a later date.

Scenic Paper In wallpaper; the vogue for scenic wallpapers developed in France late in the 18th century and the most celebrated scenic papers were printed in Paris from around 1804 to 1840. The pictorial designs for these papers chiefly illustrated subjects from history, such as Napoleon's Egyptian campaign, subjects from mythology and other classic literature, and panoramic views of famous cities or countries. Scenic wallpapers were especially fashionable in America and many examples are extant in American homes. Undoubtedly their excellent state of preservation is due to the quality of paper, which was made of fine linen rags, and to the method employed in hanging expensive papers. In this method, the walls were covered with a wooden framework or batten over which canvas was stretched. Then the paper was fixed to the canvas. Occasionally in a less expensive method the wallpaper was backed with canvas or muslin before it was pasted to the wall. The practice of pasting paper directly on the wall was a later and cheaper method. Many contemporary records state that the cost of hanging paper exceeded the original price of the paper which in those days was quite costly. As a rule these scenic papers, which required more than a year in preparing the woodblock engravings, were hung in an unbroken line above the chair rail around a room and were without repetition. Generally they were designed with much sky so that if the ceiling was low they could be cut off without imparing the value of the scene. Undoubtedly the most popular scenic wallpapers in America were printed by the Frenchman Joseph Dufour. The Monuments de Paris and Vues d' Italie, popularly called the Bay of Naples scenes, were especially favored. Dufour at the beginning of his career made a novelty paper called a drapery paper, which was simply a fad of short duration. His most famous series was the Cupid and Psyché series of which some original sets are found in America. The Adventures of Telemachus, also by Dufour, printed in 1825, was highly regarded and Andrew Jackson selected it for the Hermitage. Another popular series by Jean Zuber first printed in France in 1834 was called Scenic America and the recognition implied by France in this series was quite complimentary to a young country who had only recently won her independence. In addition to the printed scenic papers, painted scenic papers were also employed in America, which were less expensive and quite effective, although they lacked the finished details found in the printed papers. See *Wallpaper*.

Schäpergläser In German glass; a variety of glass vessel painted chiefly in black enamel. It derived its name from Johann Schäper, 1621–1670, gifted artist-enameller working at Nuremberg from around 1640 onwards. The details were produced by scratching lines through the black pigment with a needle point to the surface of the glass. The subjects were principally landscapes, generally with ruins, painted in bands around the glass vessel or in circular or oval panels. A glass beaker dated 1660 is the earliest known surviving example. Schäper also did the identical work on German faïence such as jugs. His style of painting was highly regarded by his contemporaries and, as a result, his name is often given to a school of painting carried on by his followers using a similar black enamel technique. See *Schwarzlot*.

Schäper, Johann In German ceramics; see *Schäpergläser*; *Schwarzlot*.

SCHÄPERGLÄSER

Schiavone An Italian name given to a 17th century sword having a basket hilt. It derived its name from the Slavonic guards or Schiavoni stationed in Venice who used this type of sword. See *Sword*.

Schmelz In glass; a German term applied to a variegated or marbled opaque Venetian Renaissance glass. The color was principally a combination of bluish green and purple tints. See *Glass*; *Venetian Glass*.

Schnabelkrug In German ceramics; a Rhenish stoneware jug with a long beak-like spout. It was a very popular form for the Siegburg wares made during the late 16th and first half of the 17th centuries. See *Rhenish Stoneware*.

Schnelle In German ceramics; a tall tankard having straight sides tapering upwards and generally having roll moldings at the mouth and at the foot. The form, which was taken from a wooden prototype, was a characteristic form for Rhenish stoneware during the 16th and early 17th centuries. See *Pinte*; *Rhenish Stoneware*.

Schrattenhofen In German ceramics; see *Oettingen*.

Schraub-Flasch In German ceramics; a four- or six-sided flask made with a metal screw stopper. It is identified with the brown salt-glazed stoneware made at Kreussen, near Bayreuth, during the 17th century. Each corner was marked by a fantastic caryatid or a column and the panels were framed in rope or chain designs executed in relief. See *Kreussen*.

Schrezheim In German ceramics; a faïence manufactory was started at Schrezheim, near Ellwangen in Wurtemberg, in 1752 by Johann Baptist Bux with a privilege from the Prince-Archbishop of Trèves. Evidence of decline was perceptible before 1800. The factory was active until 1862. The mark was a sprig of box conventionalized to resemble an arrow-head. Especially characteristic were tureens in the form of vegetables, fruits and different animals' heads. Helmet-shaped

SIEGBURG STONEWARE
SCHNABELKRUG

ewers, cylindrical tankards, jugs, coffee pots and pitchers were included in their productions. The painted decoration was generally in polychrome; blue and white was seldom found. During the 19th century the manufactory principally reproduced the 18th century wares in a lead-glazed earthenware.

Schwarzlot In ceramics; a German term meaning black lead generally given to a style of painted decoration in black enamel, occasionally with a touch of red, such as for flesh tones, and gilding. This technique was used in window glass painting by the Dutch glass painters and later was first used on faïence by Johann Schäper around 1660. It was later used on Meissen porcelain especially for harbor scenes. Vienna porcelain also used this kind of decoration. Some of the Viennese examples were of incomparable beauty. See *Schäpergläser*; *Stained Glass*.

Schwerin In German ceramics; a faïence manufactory was started at Schwerin, Mecklenburg, in 1753, by Johann Adam Apfelstädt and is still in existence. The wares were sometimes marked with "A Sverin" or "A S" for Apfelstädt-Schwerin. The 18th century productions were essentially without any particular distinction.

Scimitar The name given to all Oriental swords having a curved or crescent-shaped single-edged blade. This Asiatic sword is of undetermined origin. Its crescent-shaped blade was designed to give the utmost cutting power. The Persian scimitar is particuarly noted for its rich and ornate decoration. See *Yataghan*; *Sword*.

Sconce In furniture; a bracket candlestick or two or more bracket candlesticks projecting from a wall plaque. In a broad sense the term is given to any ornamental lightholder which is attached to a wall. Sconces were known on the Continent by the beginning of the 16th century. Until late in the 17th century wall sconces in England were made of metal. During the William and Mary period sconces were often made of carved gilt wood. Contemporary with these carved gilt wood sconces were metal sconces having the backplates fitted with mirrors. Sconces were always an important decorative appointment and were skillfully and handsomely executed in accordance with the prevailing style of ornament. Bronze doré sconces in the Louis XV style were remarkable for their capricious shapes.

Scorpion In arms; the term *scorpion* was given to a variety of different kinds of weapons. In European arms it is applied to a variety of halberd having a long, narrow blade, with spikes on the opposite side. See *Flail*.

Scratch-Back See *Backscratcher*.

Scratch Blue Ware In English ceramics; a salt-glazed stoneware having a nearly white body with incised decoration filled with blue color, made at Staffordshire from around 1748 to 1776. This almost white body was obtained by introducing ground flint as an ingredient into the clay mixture. The incised designs were chiefly patterns of conventionalized flowers. It is thought that this scratch blue ware may also have been made at Liverpool and in other parts of England.

Screen In furniture; the term *screen* has a comprehensive meaning in furniture. Essentially it refers to anything in the nature of a partition which conceals from view, such as a portable covered framework; it also refers to a shield or protection such as a fire screen. See *Fire Screen*; *Candle Screen*. Screens were used in the Middle Ages; however, as a rule, these early screens were generally a permanent fixture, such as a screen built to hang over a fireplace. Many of the 17th century hinged or folding screens were very large and some had as many as twelve panels. In France from the time of Louis XV onwards the folding screen became noticeably smaller and the majority were made with three or four panels. These screens were very often reduced to the proportions of a fire screen. The panels were made of such materials as tapestry, rich

figured silks and painted canvas. The tall hinged or folding type of screen was an important decorative accessory. It did not come into general use in England until after the Restoration, 1660, when lacquered screens were imported in large quantities from the Orient. Occasionally panels of rich fabrics were used in place of the lacquer panels. Around the middle of the 18th century in England there was a vogue for small mahogany folding screens consisting of two sections often fitted with panels of Chinese printed paper. They were mounted on slender straight quadrangular legs. French decorative folding screens were richly carved and were decorated in accordance with the prevailing style. During the Louis XV style the upper part of each panel was occasionally fitted with a mirror. During the second half of the 18th century in both France and England adjustable screens were sometimes fitted into the structure of the backs of small pieces of furniture, such as work tables, small writing tables and petite commodes. See *Table à Ecran*.

Screen, Table Screen or Ink-Screen In Chinese art; a small screen in the form of an oblong, square or circular plaque set in an ornamental stand, generally of wood and occasionally of bronze, having a total height around 12 to 14 inches. The plaques for table screens are made chiefly of jade, ivory, and porcelain, and are praiseworthy for the artistic merit of their decoration. They are elaborately decorated with Chinese motifs consisting of Buddhist and Taoist figures and legends, pavilions, mountain landscapes, lakes, bamboo trees, flowers and animal subjects. The richly carved ivory screens were made principally in the 18th century. Fine examples of porcelain ink-screens are found in private collections dating from the 16th century. K'ang Hsi Famille Verte oblong plaques mounted in crisply carved wood stands are especially typical of the Ch'ing dynasty. It is stated in literature on the Chinese decorative arts that the ink-stick used for making ink in calligraphy was

PORCELAIN INK-SCREEN, K'ANG HSI

rubbed on the ink-stone behind the ink-screen or yen p'ing. It is also observed that the screen protected the writer's work from the splash of the brush. According to the definition of the term *screen*, which means to protect or conceal, either one or both uses seem a reasonable assumption. See *Writing Equipage*.

Scribanne In Dutch and Flemish cabinet-work; a secretary cabinet or a bureau cabinet. The upper section, which was fitted with two doors, was surmounted on the oblong top of a slant-front desk with several rows of long drawers beneath. It generally rested on a plinth base. The slant-front lid opened to reveal a fitted writing interior. Variations in design occurred. It was introduced during the 17th century. See *Commode Secretary*.

Scrolled Pediment In English cabinetwork; see *Pediment*.

Scroll Foot In cabinetwork; a foot carved in the form of a scroll, which may turn either forward or backward. See *Spanish Foot*; *French Whorl Foot*; *Foot*.

Scroll Handle In silver; a handle shaped like the letter S with the lower half smaller. A handle formed of two scrolls is called a double scroll handle.

Scrolls, C and S In ornament; a decorative curve in the form of the Roman capital letter C and S from which each receives its name. C and S scrolls were a favorite Baroque style of ornament. They were also introduced into the structure of furniture designed in the Baroque style, such as in chairs. During the Rococo style C and S scrolls lost their sculpturesque Baroque quality. Decorative curves were a pronounced feature of the Rococo style, with slender and graceful C and S scrolls figuring prominently. See *Scroll-Shaped Leg*; *Flemish Scroll*.

Scroll-Shaped Leg In cabinetwork; a carved leg in the form of some type of scroll or decorative curve. A console or bracket leg having a scroll-shaped profile was a characteristic form of leg for chairs designed in the Louis XIV style. During the reign of Charles II in England, 1660–1685, there was a growing tendency to introduce scrolls into the structure of furniture. Arms, arm-posts, legs and stretchers were often shaped in the form of scrolls. Scrolls were worked in a variety of combinations, the S scroll, C scroll and Flemish scroll being the most commonly employed. Around 1680 scroll-shaped legs were introduced in the characteristic Restoration or Charles II chair. The typical Flemish chair introduced around the middle of the 17th century, with Baroque features, was designed with two front Flemish scroll legs. See *Restoration Chair*; *Flemish Chair*; *Scrolls C and S*.

Scrutoire In cabinetwork; a rare or obsolete term for escritoire. See *Escritoire*.

Sealed In pewter; a term applied to a lid or base frequently found on medieval flagons, which was cast with a hole in the center and which was later inset with a seal of pewter generally having a device in relief. It is called a sealed lid or sealed base.

Sealed Glasses In English glass; the term is applied to glasses having a seal or hall-mark of the glasshouse. The Glass Sellers' Company of London is particularly identified with glasses bearing a raven's head seal which were produced by George Ravenscroft during the latter part of the 17th century. During this time a few other glass-houses marked their glasses, including some for whom the Glass Sellers' Company were agents. See *Ravenscroft, George*; *Flint Glass*.

Seal Top Spoon In English silver; a silver spoon, having a stem terminating in a seal top, scratched or incised with initials. It was introduced during the 16th century.

Seaweed In English cabinetwork; the term *seaweed* or *endive* is given to a form of marquetry which became very popular during the reign of William and Mary. It consisted of an over-all pattern of minute delicate scrolls usually symmetrically arranged. The

SEAWEED MARQUETRY

seaweed pattern represented the culmination of the English marqueteur's skill. The beautiful designs of delicate scrollwork were made from boxwood or holly, and were veneered on a walnut ground. Seaweed marquetry was sometimes combined with oystering or parquetry. It was especially used on such articles as fall-front writing cabinets and tall case clocks. See *Marquetry*.

Secretaire In English cabinetwork; a term, derived from the French *secrétaire*, given to a variety of writing furniture. It is commonly cabinet-shaped and is provided with drawers and pigeon-holes and a writing board. Personal papers are frequently stored in the cabinet portion. It is a bureau or secretary. See *Writing Furniture*.

Secrétaire à Abattant In French cabinetwork; a relatively tall rectilinear French secretary characterized by a drop-front panel which opened to a fitted interior of small drawers, compartments and pigeonholes. The frieze was usually fitted with a long narrow drawer. The lower portion beneath the drop panel was generally fitted with two cupboard doors; occasionally it had drawers instead of the cupboard doors. It was mounted on a base with short feet. It was introduced around the middle of the 18th century and is chiefly identified with the style of Louis XVI. Some of the early examples were made in the Louis XV style and have short cabriole legs. It was generally finely veneered with marquetry combined with applied bronze mounts. It retained its popularity until the time of Louis Philippe, 1830–1848. See *Abattant*.

Secretary In cabinetwork; a form of writing furniture. It is usually provided with drawers and pigeonholes. It is a bureau or a writing desk. See *Writing Furniture*.

Secretary Bookcase In English cabinetwork; the term *secretary bookcase* or *bureau bookcase* is generally reserved for a piece of writing furniture similar to a secretary cabinet. The chief difference was that the upper section was fitted with adjustable shelves for the reception of books. Later the secretary bookcase was always fitted with glazed doors. Such a piece was rather rare until after the middle of the 18th century. See *Writing Furniture*; *Secretary Cabinet*; *Break-Front Secretary Bookcase*.

Secretary Cabinet In English cabinetwork; the secretary cabinet or bureau cabinet was introduced during the William and Mary era. The name *secretary cabinet* is given to a form of double-bodied writing furniture. The upper section was designed as a cabinet and the lower section as a slant-front bureau. The upper portion, which was fitted with two doors and opened to reveal a series of small drawers and compartments, rested on a narrow shelf at the top of the slant-front bureau. The lower portion was designed with a slant-front over two small drawers and three graduated long drawers. The slant-front opened to an interior of pigeonholes and small drawers. Variations in design sometimes occurred. For example, in place of the slant-front it was also designed with a long false drawer, which could be pulled out, and the hinged front of the drawer could be let down to serve as a writing flap. This false drawer was fitted with pigeonholes and small drawers. The characteristic feature of the secretary cabinet during the William and Mary style was the boldly molded double-hooded cornice. The cabinet doors were sometimes fitted with beveled mirror panels. The secretary cabinet was designed in the successive 18th century styles of furniture. The secretary cabinet was commonly designed with a fall-front writing drawer in the Hepplewhite and Sheraton styles. The upper body was recessed and was fitted with two glazed doors. The lower projecting body was often designed with two cupboard doors in place of the three graduated drawers. It is generally accepted that the secretary cabinet was first designed in America in the Queen Anne style. See *Writing Furniture*; *Writing Cabinet*.

Secretary Chest-on-Chest In English cabi-

LOUIS XVI SECRÉTAIRE À ABATTANT

network; an article of writing furniture designed as a chest on a chest. The upper chest in the characteristic variety had a row of three small drawers over three long drawers. The lower chest contained four long drawers and was surmounted on feet or a bracket base. The upper drawer in the lower chest was false and could be pulled out and let down to serve as a writing board. The interior of the drawer was fitted as a desk. The secretary chest-on-chest was introduced around the beginning of the 18th century. It is also called a tallboy bureau.

Sedan Clock A large watch or a small clock usually about 5 to 7 inches in diameter. It was extensively used during the 17th and 18th centuries in England and in Europe to be carried in coaches and carriages. Some were made with a striking movement so as to tell time in dimly lighted coaches. The name *Sedan clock* is derived from Sedan chair since it was widely carried in these chairs and, in turn, the Sedan chair derived its name from Sedan, France, where it was first introduced. It is also called a Coach watch or clock, Traveling watch or clock or a Carriage watch or clock.

Seddon, George 1727–1801. English cabinetmaker. He started in business around 1750 at London House in Aldersgate Street. He carried on a large and successful business during the second half of the 18th century. When a fire destroyed his shop in 1768, a news item stated that he employed eighty cabinetmakers and that he was one of the most eminent cabinetmakers in London. After 1784 he was listed at No. 150 Aldersgate Street, which remained the business address for his sons, Thomas and George, and later his grandsons. The firm maintained a high reputation until about the middle of the 19th century. No other contemporary firm had display rooms or work rooms on so large a scale. Included among the very few authenticated pieces are some painted satinwood chairs made around 1790, which are of good quality and reveal a graceful elegance in their lines. It is a reasonable

GHIORDES KNOT

RIGHTHAND SEHNA KNOT

LEFTHAND SEHNA KNOT

assumption that they did make much fine furniture.

Sedjadeh A Persian word meaning floor covering. The name is given to an Oriental rug of medium size, usually measuring more than 7 feet and less than 10 feet in length. See *Kali*.

Sehna Khilim An Oriental tapestry-woven rug in the Sehna colors and design. See *Khilim*; *Sehna Rug*.

Sehna Knot In Oriental rug weaving; one of the two types of knots used in tying the tufts of pile yarn upon the warp in Oriental rugs. It is so knotted that from every space between the warp threads, one end of the knot projects. It is named after the city of Sehna, in Persia. It is also called the Persian knot. See *Ghiordes Knot*; *Oriental Rug*.

Sehna Rug An Oriental rug belonging to the Persian classification. It is very finely woven and is tied with the Sehna knot. The warp is of cotton, linen or silk, and the weft is of cotton, single-strand wool or linen. The pile is of selected wool and is very short. The ends are usually finished in a narrow web with loose warp-threads. The Sehna rug is distinctive for its fine texture and for the skillful blending of its colors. As a rule the designs are composed of small patterns and diaper arrangements based principally on the Herati and the pear motifs. The Herati motif generally also appears in the border. See *Persian Rugs*.

Seiji In Japanese ceramics; see *Celadon*.

Seillage In French Provincial cabinetwork; a kind of cupboard. It was a form of an étimier. The racks in the lower portion were generally used to hold the buckets of fresh milk. See *Etimier*.

Semainier In French cabinetwork; the term *semainier*, meaning a week, is given to a chest of drawers generally fitted with seven long drawers of equal depth, resting on a base with very short legs or simply feet. It was introduced around the middle of the 18th century. The height and width of the semainier varied.

Semerlik A Perso-Turkish word meaning saddle cover. It is a cover woven exactly like an Oriental rug. It is usually almost square and varies in size from 2½ to 4½ feet. It has an opening at one end for the pommel of the saddle to pass through. See *Oriental Rug*.

Sentoku A variety of Japanese bronze distinctive for its fine golden tones and for the satin-like sheen of its surface. This bronze was first perfected in China during the Ming dynasty. See *Kara-Kane*.

Seppa In Japanese sword mounts; the name applied to sword fittings resembling washers. Their original use was to support the tsuba which was thinner in the center. The larger one, called O-seppa, was placed above the tsuba, and the smaller, or Ko-seppa, was placed under the tsuba. Seppa are usually ornamented like the other mountings. The dai seppa, which was sometimes used on the tachi, is flat and nearly as large as the tsuba and elaborately decorated. It has the same contour as the tsuba and covers the center portion of the tsuba which is plain and undecorated. See *Seppa Dai*.

Seppa Dai In Japanese sword mounts; the name given to the plain, oval, narrow space in the center of a tsuba around the opening for the tang. If the tsuba is signed by the maker, it is found on the seppa dai. The name of the maker is signed on the left of the opening and his residence and date are on the right of the opening.

Serapi An Oriental rug belonging to the Persian classification. The rug derived its name from the village of Sirab in the Herez district. It is referred to as a Herez fabric because it is woven by Herez weavers. The foundation is cotton and the pile is wool and rather short. The ends are usually finished with a narrow web and loose warp threads. It is a light and bright rug, with clear grounds for the display of elaborate vine and floral designs. There are few runners.

As a rule the Serapi rug was generally woven in carpet size. See *Persian Rugs*.

Serebend An Oriental rug belonging to the Persian classification. The warp and weft are of cotton. The pile is of selected wool and is short. The ends are usually finished with a narrow web and loose warp threads. The characteristic design, which is almost always found on the Serebend rug and which is occasionally called the Mir design, consists of a field filled with horizontal rows of small pear motifs alternating in direction. The border stripes are narrow and numerous. The color and the designs are excellently balanced and well-blended. It is also called a Saraband. See *Persian Rugs*.

CHIPPENDALE SERPENTINE
CARD TABLE

Serebend Pattern See *Serebend Rug*.

Serpentine In cabinetwork; the name given to a type of undulating curve. It is composed of a convex curve in the center and a concave curve at each end. It is the opposite of the so-called oxbow or yoke-front. Serpentine curves figured prominently in the Rococo style. See *Oxbow*; *Serpentine Front*.

Serpentine Front In cabinetwork; the front of an article of furniture such as a chest of drawers, a commode or a sideboard that is horizontally of serpentine contour. See *Bow Front*; *Serpentine*.

Serre-Bijoux In French cabinetwork; the serre-bijoux or jewel box resembled a small table of delicate proportions. The top was in the form of a small box-like structure designed with an abattant or drop-front, which, when opened, revealed an interior fitted with small drawers. It rested on four slender legs occasionally connected with an undershelf. Sometimes the box-like structure was fitted with one drawer in place of the drop-front. It was introduced during the Louis XV style.

Serre-Papiers In French cabinetwork; a small article of furniture consisting of several lateral tiers of small shelves and pigeonholes, which were sometimes fitted with small doors, for the reception of papers. It was usually found at either end of the bureau plat and was either detachable or designed as a part of the writing table. Sometimes the serre-papiers was mounted on a stand which conformed in design to the bureau plat and which was placed next to it. It was introduced during the style of Louis XV. See *Bureau Plat*; *Gradin*.

Servante In French cabinetwork; the name given to different forms of tables which enabled the host and guests to serve themselves after the dessert and refreshments had been arranged on the servante by the servants. See *Desserte*; *Dumbwaiter*; *Rafraîchissoir*.

Service Wood See *Cormier Wood*.

Serving Table In American cabinetwork; the name is sometimes given to a plain variety of side table, generally made of mahogany, used in the dining room for the service of meals. It was generally designed with one or two frieze drawers.

Seto Ware In Japanese ceramics; pottery wares produced at the kilns in the Seto district in the province of Owari. It is possibly the oldest of Japanese pottery centers and dates from at least the 9th century. Early wares of the 13th century had incised and embossed designs with a glaze, now called Yellow Seto. It was yellowish-green with a slight blue tone and was an attempt to imitate Chinese celadon. These wares were first produced by a potter named Kato but called Toshiro who had returned from China at the beginning of the 13th century. The term *Yellow Seto* now refers to all Old Seto wares having a yellowish glaze. The first Yellow Seto of the Toshiro kiln had an unrefined grey body with a partly opaque brownish-yellow glaze. In the 15th century the yellow Seto had a transparent glaze that was generally crackled. The earlier wares were articles for the tea ceremony. The later wares were mostly for everyday use, and were decorated with designs of reeds and grass in dark brown brush strokes under the glaze. The best period was from

the second half of the 16th century and the first half of the 17th century. Later the wares included all forms for Japanese use as well as porcelain wares.

Settee In English cabinetwork; a seat for two or more persons having a back and arms. The upholstered settee and sofa were often of similar construction. The term *settee* first appeared in English inventories around the early 18th century. Wooden arms for upholstered settees were reintroduced early in the 18th century and were occasionally found from that time onwards. In addition to the upholstered settees there were also the chair-back settees and caned settees. The upholstered settee was introduced in England early in the 17th century; however, relatively few upholstered settees were made until after the Restoration in 1660. Very few upholstered settees were made in America until the Chippendale style. They became more plentiful in the Hepplewhite and succeeding styles. See *Sofa*.

Settle In English cabinetwork; the oak settle, which was either built into the wall or movable, was characterized by its massive and solid construction. It was introduced during the Gothic period. It usually had a high panelled back with panelled arms and sides. The portion below the seat generally formed a chest, with the seat being hinged to give access to it. It was designed to accommodate several persons. Cushions were usually placed on the seat to afford a little comfort and to provide an air of luxury. During the 17th century the settle grew lighter in form. One variety of settle combined the double purpose of seat and table. This table settle had an oblong rectangular back which extended beyond the uprights. The back worked on pivots and could be pulled forward to rest on the arms. In this manner it served as a table. It was essentially similar in construction and function to the chair table. It is sometimes referred to as a monk's table. See *Chair Table*; *Archebanc*; *Cassapanca*.

EARLY GEORGIAN
SETTEE

Setzbecher In German silver; a kind of small cup. See *Häufebecher*.

Séverin, Nicolas-Pierre French ébéniste, received master July 26, 1757. He made fine reproductions of the elaborate marquetry pieces of André Charles Boulle. See *Le Vasseau, Etienne*.

Seville In Spanish ceramics; the manufacture of pottery was centered at Trina, a suburb of Seville. Ordinary glazed pottery with impressed relief decoration was made as early as the 11th century, comprising water and oil jars and two-handled vases. Of particular interest are the tiles which were made by various processes. It is claimed that tiles impressed with designs in relief and covered with colored glazes were made at Seville as early as 1260. Mosaic tile work or alicatados was made at Seville during the 14th century. In this method the already fired pieces in the different colored glazes were cut into the desired shapes to form the design. Green, white, brown and blue were the principal colors. Another method known as Cuerda Seca or dry cord was introduced around the middle of the 15th century. In this process a dry cord of grease and manganese was painted into the impressed outlines of the design, which kept the different colored glazes separated. After the tile was fired the so-called dry cord left a dull brown line between the colored glazes. Pharmacy vases, dishes and ewers were also decorated in this manner. In another process introduced late in the 15th century, known as Cuenca or cell type, a stamped design having limiting lines in relief served to separate the colored glazes. Early in the 16th century tiles were made in the tradition of Italian majolica. See *Tiles*.

Sèvres In French ceramics; a soft paste porcelain manufactory was established in 1738 at Vincennes under the patronage of Louis XV. In 1753 it was proposed to move the manufactory to Sèvres between Paris and Versailles. In 1769 a hard paste porcelain was made and was marked with a crowned version of the crossed "L's" which were in use from 1745–1753 to 1793. Date letters were first added in 1753. The factory mark from 1793 to 1804 was "R F" or "R F" in monogram for République Française, over "Sèvres." Numerous marks were used during the 19th century, many of which included the word "Sèvres". The factory is still in existence. The so-called Vincennes period dates from 1738 to 1753. During the second period, 1753 to 1772, the finest and most finished soft paste porcelain was made. Much of the reputation of Sèvres is associated with this work. From 1772 to 1804 both hard paste and soft paste porcelain were made. From 1804 to 1830 the style of the Empire prevailed. In 1804 the manufacture of soft paste was abandoned and was resumed around 1850. Many technical improvements and innovations including the pâte-sur-pâte process were introduced around and after the middle of the 19th century. Faïence was also added to the productions. The influence of Meissen was evident in the productions made at Vincennes. However the light and graceful Vincennes style of painted flowers, landscapes, and figure subjects, as well as the simple and graceful forms, had an intrinsic French charm. Perhaps the most important productions were the modelled flowers in vogue around 1750. The figures were all original models. In 1751 a porcelain biscuit was introduced and colored enamel figures were extremely rare after that date. Although some of the Sèvres figures and groups were superb they were seldom as interesting as those made at Meissen and Vincennes. Perhaps the most characteristic of all Sèvres decoration is painting in panels reserved on a colored ground. Turquoise or bleu celeste was introduced in 1752, yellow or jaune jonquille in 1753, a pea green in 1756 and the now famous pink or Rose Pompadour in 1757. The early underglaze dark blue or gros bleu introduced around 1749 was supplanted before 1760 by the strong blue enamel or bleu de roi. These grounds were distinctive for their technical excellence and for their incomparable smoothness. A very

SÈVRES VASE

finely wrought gilding is closely connected with the grounds. Occasionally to soften the brilliance of these grounds repetitive patterns were introduced and were an interesting Sèvres invention. Gilt or colored diaper arrangements of dots, circles, pebbles and other motifs were employed. A late diaper arrangement was the so-called jewelled decoration. High temperature ground colors, including black, yellow, blue, brown and tortoise shell were invented after 1770 and were used either in or on the hard paste porcelain glaze which did not take the earlier ground colors too well. See *Fond Ecaille*; *Oeil-de-Perdrix*; *Caillouté*; *Jewelled Decoration*.

Sewing Table In cabinetwork; it is the same as a work table. See *Work Table*.

SGABELLO

Sgabello In Italian cabinetwork; the sgabello or stool chair was introduced during the 16th century and was a popular variety of Renaissance side chair. It was a relatively small chair and was generally made of walnut. It consisted of a small wooden seat which was often octagonal in shape and which rested on a small square box-like section that was surmounted on a solid front support and a solid back support in place of legs. The chair back, which was practically fan-shaped or almost triangular in form, was usually made from a single piece of wood and slanted slightly backward. Variations in design occurred. Frequently the wooden seat rested directly on the solid front and solid back supports. The sgabello was very often enriched with carved decoration.

Sgraffiato Or Graffiato. In ceramics; an Italian term literally meaning a scratched decoration. There has been a growing tendency in modern times to restrict the use of this word to decoration scratched with a pointed instrument through a coating of slip or engobe to the body beneath, resulting in a design of two contrasting colors. Although according to the etymology of the word this arbitrary usage is incorrect, it does provide a term for a distinctive type of decoration. The term *incised decoration* is used for designs simply scratched in the soft clay without any color contrast. Incised decoration was frequently used on some of the finest Chinese porcelains; however, in Europe its use was almost limited to the simply decorated peasant wares. Sgraffiato decoration is of early origin. Perhaps the most notable early examples are the so-called Gabri wares of Persia, some of which date from the 8th and 9th centuries. The process was widespread both in time and in place. It is also spelled Sgraffato, Sgraffito, and Graffato. See *T'zu Chou*.

Shagreen The name given to a piece of untanned leather originally procured in Persia and Turkey from the hide of a horse or wild ass. The artificial granular or grain-like surface found on early 17th century shagreen was acquired by pressing small seeds into the skins while they were soft and flexible. Later, after several processes, the skins were generally dyed green or black and then permitted to dry, during which time they became very firm. Shagreen was used during the Jacobean period in England to cover small boxes and cases for valuable possessions. In the 18th century shagreen was used in England for knife cases, tea caddies and other similar articles. Later shagreen was made from the highly polished skins of seals, sharks and other fish.

Shah Abbas In Oriental rugs; the name *Shah Abbas* was given to a design motif especially used in Persian rugs. The motif generally consists of the profile of a large flower in not quite full bloom and often framed by the outline of a symmetrical pointed leaf. Shah Abbas was Shah of Persia from 1588 to 1629. He was called Abbas the Great, because Persia flourished under his rule. He was a great patron of the arts. Some of the finest Oriental rugs were woven during his reign. He was the first patron of rugs woven in gold, silver and silk. The term *Shah Abbas* is sometimes loosely applied to a fine antique Persian Oriental rug. See *Oriental Rug*.

Shaker Furniture In American cabinet-work; American furniture made in the communal workshops of the Shakers. The Shakers were members of a religious communistic and celibate sect. They were popularly called Shakers because of movements in dancing that were performed in their worship. The sect had its origin in England in 1747 and came to America in 1774. The principal community of the sect has been at New Lebanon, New York, during recent times. The furniture was of marked simplicity. The various articles of furniture, which were strictly made for utilitarian purposes, were composed of straight lines. The forms were elementary, and the furniture was devoid of any kind of decoration. Chair seats were frequently made of rush.

Shakudo In Japanese metal art; the term applied to an alloy, which is 97% copper and 3% gold, used for the fine, artistically chiselled metal, which is used for Japanese sword mounts. Its natural color is dark copper. It acquires a beautiful satin-like black patina with a violet luster, after being treated. It is boiled in a solution of lye, then rubbed and polished with powdered charcoal. It is dipped in a solution of salt and plum vinegar. Next it is dipped in diluted lye and then placed in water. Finally it is boiled in a mixture of verdigris, copper sulphate and water. Shibuichi is another alloy which serves the same decorative purpose as shakudo. It is composed of three parts copper and one part silver. Its natural color is light gunmetal. After it is treated it becomes a beautiful soft grey with a silver-like luster. Both shakudo and shibuichi produce excellent grounds for the art of inlaying with gold, silver and other metals, as well as for carved decoration.

Shamshir In arms; the saber of Persia. The rather crescent-shaped blade is narrow and thick with the cutting edge on the convex side. Sometimes the blade is engraved with the name of the owner or maker, frequently with the date. The slender hilt is furnished with a cross-guard and a pommel projecting at right angles to the hand grip.

Shaving Dish See *Barber's Basin*.

Shaving Stand In cabinetwork; a variety of small dressing mirror. See *Toilet Mirror*.

Shaving Table In English cabinetwork; a smaller and more compact variety of a dressing table with a hinged box lid provided with a framed mirror rising upward at the rear and designed with compartments for the reception of soap, razors, bottles and other similar toilet accessories. As a rule the portion beneath the top of the table was fitted with one or two rows of shallow drawers and perhaps a shallow cupboard compartment flanked by several rows of small drawers. It was generally mounted on four legs. This type of dressing table became fashionable from around the middle of the 18th century onwards and was called a shaving table in contemporary trade catalogues. Chippendale illustrated a shaving table in the third edition of the DIRECTOR, 1762.

GEORGE III SHAVING TABLE

Shearer, Thomas An English cabinetmaker and designer who was a contemporary of Hepplewhite. He contributed the majority of the 29 plates found in the THE CABINET MAKERS' LONDON BOOK OF PRICES published in 1788. The majority of these plates again appeared in DESIGNS FOR HOUSEHOLD FURNITURE under Shearer's own name, which was also published in 1788. His designs for sideboards, bookcases and other articles of furniture possess a distinctive quality and are well drawn.

Sheffield Plate A term applied to all types of articles both useful and ornamental made of copper and silver by a special process which is no longer used. The name is derived from Sheffield, England, where the process was adopted and perfected. The original process was discovered by Thomas Boulsover, in 1742, by accident. The original process of making the plate was first to cast a plate of copper, having a mixture of brass, into the desired size, then to make its surface even and smooth. Two equal size plates of silver were made even and polished and were fitted on each side of the sheet of copper. A flux of borax was applied to the edges of the three sheets and they were then placed in a furnace. When the silver began to melt, the welded piece was immediately removed and allowed to cool. The desired thickness was acquired by passing the plate several times through rollers. The plate could be embossed only to a certain degree, and it was necessary to apply separately cast embossed decorations. The edgings were soldered on the exposed cut edges of the plate to conceal the red line of the copper. The making of Sheffield plate terminated about the middle of the 19th century, when manufactories began making commercial plate by the electro-plating process.

Shell In ornament; a decorative motif of shell form. It was much used in furniture design. During the Louis XIV style the shell motif was extensively employed and was always symmetrically treated. The shell motif was constantly used during the style of the Régence. It was usually pierced or elaborated in many different ways. The upright shell with acanthus leafage starting from both sides of the base of the shell was typical of the era. A feature of the Rococo style was the excessive use of certain motifs; in particular the shell motif. It was given many fanciful new forms of irregular outline, and it was often pierced. The shell motif was the favorite motif during the reign of Queen Anne. It was introduced from Holland and was generally in the form of a scallop shell symmetrically treated. A large double shell was one of William Kent's most familiar details. See *Rococo*; *Coquillage*.

Shell-Back In English silver; the molded shell motif on the back of the bowl of a silver spoon where it joins the stem. It was introduced during the reign of George II, 1727–1760.

Shell-Work In English decorative art; a fashionable amateur hobby pursued by the English ladies of the 18th century. In this work such articles as boxes, mirror frames and vases were covered with designs made from many minute colored shells. Sometimes this work was supplemented with painted seeds and paper filigree decoration. The collecting and selecting of the shells appeared to be an interesting pastime.

Shemakha Rug See *Soumak Rug*.

Sheraton Style Circa 1790–1805. See *Sheraton, Thomas*.

Sheraton, Thomas 1751–1806. English cabinetmaker and furniture designer born at Stockton-on-Tees in Durham. Biographical information is very meager. He was reared in humble surroundings and was apparently trained as a cabinetmaker. He was a man of much ability and resource and he possessed great artistic talent; however, due to his own eccentric character his life was one of sordid poverty and disappointment. About 1790 he settled in London and it is not known to what extent if any he carried on the business of cabinetmaking. From about 1793 he supported his family by his various publications. From 1791–1794, he published THE CABINET-MAKER AND UPHOLSTERER'S DRAWING BOOK in four parts. In 1803 he published the CABINET DICTIONARY. In 1805, he published the first part of his last and unfinished book, THE CABINET-MAKER, UPHOLSTERER AND GENERAL ARTIST'S ENCYCLOPAEDIA. The popular conception of the Sheraton style as compared with the earlier styles of Chippendale and Hepplewhite is based upon a book of designs entitled THE CABINET-MAKER AND UPHOLSTERER'S DRAWING BOOK. The accepted dates are from about 1790 to 1805. Sheraton's designs in his DRAWING BOOK were remarkable for their refined elegance and excellent proportions; for their light and graceful forms, and for the delicate charm of their ornament. His fine sense of balance was evident in the contour and in the distribution of ornament. The delicate details he introduced in his drawings have never been surpassed in English furniture design. His later designs in the CABINET DICTIONARY incorporated certain features of the French Directoire and French Empire styles. These designs are usually referred to as Late Shera-

CONVEX SHELL

CONCAVE SHELL

DOUBLE SHELL

ton in contrast to the Early Sheraton in his DRAWING BOOK. When the term *Sheraton style* is used it generally refers to the early and fine Sheraton work. Some of his designs in the Directoire taste often had many pleasing qualities, although they could not be compared with his early work. His drawings in the ENCYCLOPAEDIA were of a decadent nature and showed specimens of the French Empire style as developed in England. As a rule the forms were heavy and dull and the ornament was of a fantastic nature. Sheraton also designed some ingenious pieces of harlequin furniture. The contour of Sheraton's early designs was essentially influenced by the classic form of Robert Adam and of the Louis XVI style. He strongly admired the elegance which characterized the Louis XVI style and he constantly endeavored to identify his drawings with that style. Sheraton favored straight lines and his designs were essentially rectangular with emphasis on the vertical lines. He employed the straight tapered leg of either quadrangular or cylindrical form, the latter being more typical. Sheraton's work was characterized by its slender forms. The fragile delicacy which marked Hepplewhite's work became more pronounced in Sheraton's. Mahogany was the principal wood. Satinwood was employed more extensively on Sheraton furniture than in any other style. The decorative processes employed on furniture included carving, gilding, marquetry, veneering, painting, lacquering or japanning. The style of ornament included the classic motifs introduced by Robert Adam and the prevailing motifs of the Louis XVI style. Included among the favorite classic motifs were circular paterae generally filled with rosettes, fans or shells; delicate foliage scrolls; lyre motif; three Prince of Wales' feathers; slender and graceful classic urns often decorated with festooning; pendants and festoons of husks; honeysuckle, and large and small graceful inlaid ovals. Reeding was much used, especially on the legs of chairs and tables. See *Classic Revival*; *Regency*; *Louis XVI*; *Adam, Robert*.

Shibuichi In Japanese metal art; see *Shakudo*.

Shibuichi-Dōshi A Japanese metal art. It resembles maze-gane. In this process two different kinds of shibuichi are combined and a third kind of shibuichi is added. It produces a beautiful clouded effect which affords an excellent ground for the elaborately worked designs. In this type of work the designs seem to float beneath the surface, due to the peculiar feeling of depth created in this kind of ground. See *Maze-Gane*.

Shield In armor; a piece of protective armor used for defense. It is carried on the arm or in the hand and is used to ward off missiles. The shield varies in shape and has been used since ancient times. It is known by various names, such as scutum, ysgwyd, rondache, targe and pavis.

Shield-Back In English cabinetwork; an open chair back so-called because of its supposed resemblance to the shape of a shield. Credit for creating the distinctive shield-back form has been assigned at different times to both Adam and Hepplewhite. Although it has never been conclusively proven who was the originator of the shield-back it can be stated without reservations that Hepplewhite employed the form most successfully and most constantly of all the designers. He used it in a great variety of designs all of which were artistically pleasing. The shield-back was made in two principal forms; namely, one having a pierced splat and the other having banisters. One characteristic shield-back had five slender radial bars or banisters that converged on a segmental rosette patera. The interlaced heart-shaped back naturally evolved from the shield-back. See *Heart-Shaped Chair Back*.

Shingen Tsuba In Japanese sword mounts; a variety of tsuba consisting of either a plate of brass or of iron having silver and copper wires woven over and through it. The name is derived from Takada Shingen, the most powerful daimyō of the middle of the 16th century, who favored this type of tsuba.

SHERATON CHAIR BACKS

Shino Yaki In Japanese ceramics; a pottery ware first made at a kiln known as Shino in the Seto district of the Owari province around 1590. It was made under the supervision of Shino Sōshin who was a famous tea master. The ware was much favored by tea masters. It had a coarse body with a thick semi-opaque white glaze which was bubbly and had a tendency to form a thick crackle. The decoration comprised hasty brush strokes in iron oxide or blue and was revealed by the glaze being partially wiped away from that portion. The term *Grey Shino* was applied to a ware which had a white inlay effect on a grey ground. See *Seto*.

Ship Decanter In English glass; the term *ship decanter* is given to a glass decanter having an especially wide base. It is believed that this variety of decanter was made for use on sailing ships during the 18th century.

Shiraz An Oriental rug belonging to the Persian classification. It derives its name from the city of Shiraz where it is made. As a rule it is rather loosely woven. The foundation is generally of wool. The pile which is medium in length is of wool. The ends are finished with a selvage embroidered in bright colors, and the sides are overcast with yarns of various colors sometimes supplemented by tassels. The pole medallion motif appears frequently in the designs. The colors are bright and strong with blue tones predominating. See *Persian Rugs*.

SHOCHIKUBAI—PINE BAMBOO AND PLUM BLOSSOM

Shirvan An Oriental rug belonging to the Caucasian classification. It derived its name from the district of Shirvan. The foundation is wool; however, in the modern Shirvan it is occasionally cotton. The pile is wool and of short length. The ends are usually finished with a narrow web and either loose or knotted warp threads. The designs are chiefly mosaic and are softened by the use of primitive floral motifs. It is woven only in small sizes. The early Shirvan is greatly superior to the modern Shirvan. See *Caucasian Rugs*.

Shisham A dark brown, compact and durable wood, *dalbergia sissoo*, of the East Indies. When it is correctly treated it has a fine natural polish. It is extensively used in making Bombay furniture. It is also called Sissoo. See *Bombay Furniture*.

Shitogi Tsuba In Japanese sword mounts; an early type of tsuba found on the ceremonial sword, tachi, after it was no longer used as a fighting weapon. The name is derived from the original shape of the shitogi, the ritual rice cake. It is of narrow form, having two long concave sides with a loop of metal attached to these concave sides for additional protection.

Shochikubai In Japanese ornament; the term for the pine, bamboo and plum, which is a set of three lucky symbols widely employed in sculpture, painting, carving, fabric designs, ceramics and lacquer work. This motif had its origin in China. The design is worked in both conventional and naturalistic forms. It is symbolic of strength, longevity and devotion.

Shoe In cabinetwork; a small square piece of plain wood upon which the foot rested. It served as an added protection and was much used in French cabinetwork. For example the Louis XV French whorl foot commonly rested on a shoe. See *Sabot*; *Pad Foot*.

Shoe Piece In English cabinetwork; the name given to the shaped projection joining the splat of an open chair back to the seat rail. Prior to 1700 the splat did not join the seat rail and rested on a crosspiece several inches above the seat rail. This separate member or shoe piece was later discarded in the Hepplewhite shield and heart-shaped chair backs as well as in Sheraton's designs for chair backs. In his designs the splat, the banisters or bars and the trellis work panels were supported on a horizontal crosspiece several inches above the seat.

Shonzui In Japanese ceramics; in 1513 a potter named Gorodayu Go Shonzui went to China to study the art of making and decorating porcelain in underglaze blue. Upon his return to Japan he settled at Arita in the Hizen province where he produced porcelain wares in blue and white. The characteristic Shonzui design known as Kara Kusa has oblique wavy bands of underglaze blue alternating with white bands. The designs on the blue bands are in reserve and consist chiefly of brocade and imbricated patterns. These bands are generally used in combination with landscapes, flowers and plants in the Chinese taste. A favorite style of Shonzui decoration included geometrical designs, especially in the form of circles or discs.

Shorthose, J. English potter working at Hanley, Staffordshire, from about 1785 to around 1823. Included among his principal productions were cream-colored and blue-printed earthenware, black basalt stoneware and porcelain. The marks found on his wares were "Shorthose"; "Shorthose & Heath"; and "Shorthose & Co", impressed or printed in blue, sometimes with two crescents.

Short, Joseph 1771-1819. American cabinet-maker of Newburyport, Massachusetts, whose shop was on Merrimack Street between Market Square and Brown's Wharf.

Shou Lao In Chinese art; a Chinese Taoist subject. He is the god of long life and is generally believed to be a transformation of Lao Tzü who was the founder of the religion. He is represented as an old man with a long beard and he has a large protuberance on his bald head. He is clothed in flowing robes on which is shown the character shou or longevity. He is seen seated and sometimes he is seen riding on the back of an animal or a bird. See *Chinese Gods*; *Lu-hsing*.

Show Case In English furniture; an article of furniture for the display of curios and other valuable possessions. The term is generally applied to those pieces of furniture which do not belong to the category of cabinets. Essentially it was a plain piece of furniture. During the mid-Georgian period the tops of oblong tables were sometimes provided with a block-like superstructure of glass of conforming size for the display of ship models, porcelain and other similar curios.

Shrine In ecclesiastical art; an elaborately wrought small case, chest or other repository to hold the relics of a saint. Also a large structure of rich workmanship and materials in which the relics of a saint are kept, such as that of St. Edward the Confessor in Westminster Abbey. By extension the term is sometimes given to the chapel in which the shrine stands. It is also occasionally applied to a receptacle holding an object of religious reverence and to a recess or niche in which sacred images may be placed. See *Feretory*.

Shu Fu Ware In Chinese ceramics; during the Yüan dynasty, 1280-1368, a porcelain ware was produced at Ching tê Chên known as Shu Fu or Privy Council ware. It is the earliest porcelain known to have been ordered by the Imperial officials. The ware has an opaque glaze of pale bluish-green with relief decoration of lotus flowers and similar flowering plants with the Chinese characters, shu fu, found in the design. Bowls and flat-bottomed plates having square-shaped foot rims are the most common.

Shu-Nuri In Japanese lacquer; the name given to cinnabar or red lacquer. See *Japanese Lacquer*.

Sideboard In English cabinetwork; the sideboard designed with a central shallow napery drawer, usually over a valanced or arched apron piece, flanked by two deep lateral wine drawers or cupboards, was developed during the last quarter of the 18th century. The wine drawers contained divisions for bottles and were lead lined. It generally rested on six slender tapering legs of either cylindrical or quadrangular form. The four front legs continued from the stiles. It was usually veneered in mahogany. Variations in design occurred. From around the end of the century the structure of the sideboard

HEPPLEWHITE SIDEBOARD

became more massive. The wine drawers or cupboards became deeper and in some specimens extended almost to the floor. The long central frieze drawer was often over two cupboard doors. It is reasonable to assume that the sideboard, which was first designed in the Hepplewhite style, became fashionable in America from around 1785. See *Pedestal Sideboard*.

Sideboard Pedestals In English cabinetwork; the sideboard pedestals which flanked the sideboard table and which were surmounted by urns or vases were introduced about 1760. The interior of the pair of pedestals was generally designed for different uses. One of the more common combinations was a plate warmer and a cellarette; the latter having an interior fitted for the reception of bottles. The pair of urns were usually fitted with lead liners, one was used for ice water and the other with water for rinsing the silver knives and forks. Occasionally one of the urns instead of holding water was fitted for the reception of knives. The pedestals and urns were generally of the same material and conformed in design and ornament to the sideboard table with which they were to be grouped. See *Pedestal Sideboard Table*; *Sideboard Table*; *Plate Warmer*.

Sideboard Table In English cabinetwork; a long side table designed for the dining room. It was found in the English dining hall from around the middle of the 17th century. During the first half of the 18th century it was usually designed with a marble top which rested on a valanced frieze. As a rule the frieze was not fitted with drawers. Chippendale illustrated the mahogany sideboard table in his DIRECTOR. It was designed either with or without a marble top which rested on a frieze. The characteristic grouping of the sideboard table flanked by pedestals surmounted with urns was originated by Adam. This arrangement continued to be found in many spacious dining rooms until the end of the 18th century. Hepplewhite illustrated the sideboard table with a frieze and without drawers in his GUIDE.

ADAM STYLE SIDEBOARD TABLE

Sheraton illustrated in his CABINET DICTIONARY the sideboard table with a frieze and without drawers. He refers to these tables "as the most fashionable at present." They were designed in the style of the Regency. It seems that the number of sideboard tables with marble tops made in America was relatively limited. The majority of these tables found in America were made from around 1740 to 1785. See *Pedestal Sideboard Table*; *Sideboard*.

Side Chair The term is generally understood to apply to a chair without arms. However, it has never been satisfactorily explained why the word *side* should indicate an absence of arms. The side table is definitely designed to be placed against a wall or a side of a room and is ornamented accordingly, while a side chair is finished in the back in the same manner as an armchair. In furniture literature various ideas have been advanced for the usage of the term, and although the thoughts are interestingly developed they are not entirely convincing.

Side Table In cabinetwork; a table designed to stand against a wall and ornamented accordingly. It was made in both large and small sizes. The side table was essentially a decorative piece of wall furniture. However, it was also designed as a utilitarian article of furniture as well. The side table was principally made in America in the Chippendale, Hepplewhite, and Sheraton styles and it was generally made of mahogany. The richly decorated English side table and pier table were seldom if ever found in America. Occasionally some of the more decorative American side tables are referred to as pier tables, based on the supposition that they were originally designed to stand between two windows. See *Console Table*; *Pier Table*; *Dressing Table*; *Lowboy*; *Sideboard Table*.

Siegburg In German ceramics; potteries were in existence at Siegburg in the Rhineland from the 14th century. During the second half of the 16th century it was one of the four most important centers for Rhenish salt-glazed stoneware. Its best productions were from about 1550 to 1590. The town was sacked by the Swedes in 1632 and the potteries never recovered. Siegburg made a grey or nearly white stoneware. On the finer specimens the stoneware was almost white and the salt glaze was thin and colorless. Included among the many interesting forms identified with Siegburg stoneware are the Trichterbecher or a cup with a funnel-shaped mouth, a jar with a handle designed as a candle socket, a small jug in the form of an owl, ring flasks, goblets, and the Schnabelkrug or a jug with a beak-like spout. The more richly decorated wares with beautiful applied reliefs of animals, birds, leaf scrolls and Biblical figure subjects date from around 1560. Especially praiseworthy were the tall tapering tankards or Schnellen with reliefs of Biblical subjects arranged in three long strips on the front.

Siena   In Italian ceramics; potteries were in existence at Siena, Tuscany, as early as 1265 and by 1500 Siena was a flourishing center for the manufacture of majolica. Unfortunately only very little majolica can be ascribed to Siena for the 15th and 16th centuries. The painted decoration on some pharmacy vases and dishes attributed to Siena reveal a similarity to that found on a type of Faenza majolica. Ample contemporary records show that majolica was produced throughout the 16th century. A minor revival of majolica occurred during the 18th century. See *Italian Majolica*.

Siena Marble   A marble from Siena, Tuscany. The Convent Siena marble is a rich orange tone having numerous black and purple veins. The term *Siena* is used to designate other marbles having yellow tones. The Yellow Siena marble is a lighter yellow color, with some transparent veins. The Montarenti Dark Siena is a darker yellow with numerous black veins, some making blurred patches and other veins resembling threads. The Montarenti Light Siena is a richer color with clearer black veins and some blurred patches of white.

Signed Furniture   A term applied to fine furniture, which is signed by the cabinetmaker, having either his name or initials. In particular, the French signed pieces, which are stamped with the ébéniste's name and the date when he received his master. See *Ebéniste*.

Silesia Hafner Ware   In German ceramics; during the 16th century a small but significant variety of Hafner ware dishes were made in Silesia. This variety is characterized by the use of lines in the designs incised with a sharp tool which served to keep the different colored tin glazes or tin-enamelled glazes of yellow, green, blue, purple, white and brownish black separated. Occasionally relief decorations were also added. See *Hafner*.

Silhouette   A profile or shadow outline of an object made by projecting the shadow on a sheet of white paper by the light of a candle and the outline then filled in with black. The name is also applied to a profile cut from a piece of black paper with scissors. This variety of design is of ancient origin although the name *silhouette* only dates from about the middle of the 18th century. The name is derived from Etienne de Silhouette, 1709–1767, French Minister of Finance. During his four months in office he proposed many unpopular forms of taxation and strict economy measures which caused his downfall and his name, because of this extreme and unnecessary economy, became a popular term for anything that was of simple or plain form. See *Zopf*.

Silk   The fine lustrous substance woven from the filaments obtained by reeling from the cocoon of various types of silk worms, the cultivated species being the *bombyx mori*. Silk was imported into Europe in the Middle Ages and was regarded as an article of great luxury. It appears that the raising of the silk worm and the spinning of the silk was introduced from China to Constantinople around the 8th or 9th century. The manufacture of silk spread to northern cities in Italy, such as Florence, Milan and Venice,

SIEGBURG STONEWARE
RING FLASK

and from Italy to France. The French king Henri IV, 1589–1610, encouraged the development of the silk industry in France, while in England the silk industry was stimulated by the immigration of Huguenot refugees after 1685. The leading English centers for silks and velvets from around 1690 were Canterbury and Spitalfields. Due to the fact that silk was almost entirely imported the English manufactories specialized in mixed wool and silk. The different cloths made from silk include such fine and beautiful fabrics as brocade, damask, satin, taffeta and velvet. See *Upholstery*; *Lucchese Patterns*.

Silk Rug An Oriental handmade rug. It is very finely woven. The foundation is of silk, sometimes cotton, and the pile is of silk. The ends are usually finished with a web and loose warp threads. Silk rugs were first made in China and later in Persia and India. They are distinctive for their beautiful and delicate designs, for their fine coloring and their natural silky luster. As a rule the finest silk rugs are from Persia. Many are from Kashan in northern Persia. At the present time a much inferior and purely commercial silk rug is woven in Asia Minor.

Silla The name of the Korean historical period from the 1st to the 10th century A.D. See *Korean Dynasties*.

Sillon de Caderas Or Hip Joint Chair. In Spanish cabinetwork; a chair of ancient Roman curule form or a folding chair of X-form. It is probably the earliest type of Spanish chair. It was similar to the Italian Dantesca and Savonarola chairs. It is generally believed to have been of Moorish origin where it was reserved as a seat of honor. As a rule the sillon de caderas was richly decorated with a minute inlay design of ivory, bone and exotic woods. The seat and back panel were generally of leather. By the time of the Spanish Renaissance the chair had lost most of its popularity. See *Curule*.

Silver-Gilt Or Argent Doré. See *Vermeil*.

Silvering In English cabinetwork; from the

SILLON DE CADERAS

time of the Restoration in 1660 English furniture was occasionally silvered. Essentially the methods employed for silvering in cabinetwork are similar to those used for gilding. Silvering is less costly than gilding but unfortunately it discolors more quickly. Because of this tendency to tarnish the 18th century workman sometimes applied a coat of varnish to protect the silvering. Silver leaf covered with a coat of yellow varnish was sometimes used as a less expensive substitute for gold. Elaborately carved side tables and mirror frames were favorite articles for silvering. See *Gilding*, in furniture.

Silver Plate See *Plate*.

Silver-Plated Ware See *Sheffield Plate*.

Sinceny In French ceramics; a faïence manufactory was started at Sinceny, Aisne, France, in 1733 and managed by Denis-Pierre Pellevé of Rouen who brought artists and potters from that city. The factory was active until 1864. From 1733 to 1775 Rouen styles in high temperature colors were made. Essentially this early faïence, which was of fine quality, differed from Rouen faïence only in a whiter tin-enamelled glaze, in a stronger blue, a paler red and a more frequent use of yellow. Figure modelling was also done. During the second period from 1775 to 1795 painters from Strasbourg were working at Sinceny and the painted decoration was in enamel colors in addition to the earlier high temperature colors. This faïence in enamel colors and gilding in the Strasbourg style was seldom as interesting as the earlier work. The letter "S" with a dot on each side is generally recognized as the actual factory mark; "Sinceny" written in full has also been found; "S C Y" was found in the second period.

Sind Lac Sind lac is a variety of lacquer work that is widely practiced in India. In this method layers of colored lac are applied on the surface of an object as it is being turned, as on a lathe. The decorative designs are cut through the layers revealing the various colors. See *Lacquer*.

Singerie In ornament; a French term applied to a decorative grotesque composition in which monkeys and apes were playfully treated. Singeries were introduced by Bérain in his fanciful compositions. These amusing monkey pieces were further elaborated by Watteau and were fashionable in the Rococo style of ornament.

Sissoo A type of wood used in cabinetwork; see *Shisham*.

Six Dynasties In Chinese historical periods; see *Chinese Dynasties*.

Skeleton Clock In furniture; a clock which has the works visible; such as one designed with a glass case. It is also called a squelette clock.

Skewer In English silver; the silver meat skewer was introduced about 1750. Wooden skewers were used to hold the meat on the spit but were replaced by silver skewers for serving at the table. The silver skewers ranged in length from 6 inches to 15 inches and were made in sets. The early skewer was plain and terminated in an oval loop. From around 1760 the loop end was decorated with a shell motif and by 1770 its decoration conformed to that of the silver spoon and fork. See *Attelet*.

Skillet In English silver; a variety of vessel used to serve hot food, dating from the late 17th to the early 18th centuries. It was a plain cylindrical deep bowl provided with a cover hinged to the side. A scroll handle was attached to the side and it rested on three small feet in the form of animals' feet. Skillets of this variety were also made with a long straight handle and a flat bottom without feet.

Skillin A prominent family of wood carvers working at Boston during the 18th century. They were Simeon Skillin, Sr., 1716–1778, John, 1746–1800, Simeon, Jr., 1757–1806, and Samuel. They were particularly known as ship carvers and during their many years of work produced figureheads for sailing ships as well as many other fine figure

carvings in wood. John Skillin has been given the credit of carving the figurehead of Hercules for the American frigate *Constitution*.

Slab Top In cabinetwork; see *Marble Slab*.

Slant-Front Writing Desk In English cabinetwork; the characteristic form of the slant-front writing desk or bureau was introduced around 1700. It was a favorite article of furniture during the early 18th century. It had an oblong top and a hinged slant lid over a central and two small supporting drawers and three graduated long drawers. It rested on a molded base and feet which were usually of bracket form. The slant lid opened to reveal an interior of small drawers, pigeonholes and compartments. Variations in design occurred. During the Chippendale style it was generally designed with four long drawers and the slant lid rested on pull-out slides. The slant-front writing desk was found in America from early in the 18th century and it enjoyed great popularity. During the Federal period the slant-front was frequently enriched with an inlaid American eagle. See *Writing Furniture*; *Bureau à Pente*.

SLANT-FRONT WRITING
DESK, ENGLISH

Slat-Back Chair In English cabinetwork; a high open-back carved and turned chair introduced around 1685. The open back consisted of three or more carved and shaped solid horizontal crossrails or slats. In all probability the design for the later ladder-back chair was inspired by this early slat-back variety. In American cabinetwork; the tall slat-back chair was found in America at the beginning of the 18th century. This turned chair was designed as an armchair and as a side chair. The turned uprights were joined with four, five or six shaped horizontal slats. The legs were connected with turned stretchers. As a rule the American slat-back chair had a rush seat and was made of maple. It was a popular chair, and chairs of the slat-back pattern are still used today in farmhouses and cottages. See *Banister-Back Chair*; *Ladder-Back*.

Sleeping Chair In English cabinetwork; a padded and upholstered chair, with or without arms, having a high back with deep side wings extending the full length of the back. As a rule the back of the chair could be let down with a ratchet. It was introduced during the reign of Charles II, 1660–1685.

Sleepy Hollow In American cabinetwork; a colloquial term given to a type of open armchair introduced around 1830. It had a high raked upholstered back which continued to form a deep upholstered and cushioned seat. Very often the chair was fitted with rockers.

Sleigh Bed In American cabinetwork; a type of veneered mahogany bed of the Empire style popular in America for a few years after 1820. The name is derived from its supposed resemblance to a sleigh. It was rather heavy and ponderous and consisted of a panelled rolled-over headboard and a footboard of equal height having a pronounced outward roll. The design for this type of bed was inspired by contemporary French Empire models. See *Lit en Bateau*.

QUEEN ANNE SLIPPER
CHAIR

Slip In ceramics; clay thinned with water to a liquid or semi-liquid condition. It is used for the decoration of pottery. It is used to join or to lute the several pieces of an unfinished vessel or figure after it is removed in sections from the mold. Slip is used to fix handles, finials and other similar parts to the body of a vessel. The equivalent French term is *barbotine*. See *Engobe*; *Slipware*.

Slipper Chair In American cabinetwork; a term sometimes applied to a chair characterized by a low seat. See *Chauffeuse*.

Slipper Foot In English cabinetwork; an elongated foot essentially similar to a snake foot used on a cabriole leg. See *Pad Foot*; *Foot*; *Cabriole Leg*.

Slip-Stem Spoon In English silver; a silver spoon with a beveled or obliquely cut stem end. The stem was sloped off without a knop. It was introduced during the 15th century. It is also called a slip-top spoon.

Slipware In ceramics; pottery decorated in white or colored clay slips which are applied to a contrasting colored body. Clay slip was also used as a coating to cover the entire body of pottery in order to conceal the color of the body which was usually a buff or reddish color. The use of clay slips for decorating pottery had its origin in antiquity. Probably the finest use of the slip technique was in Egypt during the 13th and 14th centuries. Continental and English slipware was principally the work of peasant potters, who for a daily living made very ordinary crockery. The main centers in England for slipware were Wrotham and particularly North Staffordshire. See *Sgraffiato*; *Mishima*; *Slip*; *Sussex*; *Toft, Thomas*.

Slodtz, René Michel 1705–1764. French sculptor. He was the son of Sébastien Slodtz, 1655–1726, who was also a sculptor and who had been born at Antwerp. René Slodtz, working with his brothers, Antoine, Sébastien and Paul, produced a large number of decorative works for the churches in Paris. Different members of the Slodtz family held in succession the office known as "Dessinateur de la Chambre et du Cabinet du Roi" after Meissonier's death. Their designs in the Rococo style for girandoles, candlesticks, sconces and chandeliers were similar to the designs of Meissonier. However their designs for furniture and panelling were more restrained. The designs of René Slodtz were engraved by C. N. Cochin. See *Meissonier, Juste Aurèle*; *Rococo*.

Slop-Basin The term *slop-basin* is applied to a bowl usually of silver or porcelain used with the tea service for holding slops, or the rinsings of tea. The name *slop-basin* was mentioned in English records as early as the latter part of the 18th century. It is derived from the word *slop* meaning refuse liquid of any kind such as rinsings of tea, coffee or other beverages, or the dirty water of a household.

Smallsword In arms; a sword similar to the rapier except it is shorter and lighter in weight. It superseded the rapier in the third quarter of the 17th century. The blade was often of the colichemarde type and it was fitted with a knuckle guard and very short quillons. The small pas d'âne was protected by two flat oval-shaped shells. It was much used by gentlemen and was usually elaborately decorated. See *Colichemarde*.

Smaltino   In Italian ceramics; a contemporary 16th century term given to a greyish or pale bluish tin glaze used on majolica. A tin glaze of this tone is especially identified with the majolica made at Venice.

Smith, George   An English designer and cabinetmaker. In 1808 he published a COLLECTION OF DESIGNS FOR HOUSEHOLD FURNITURE AND INTERIOR DECORATION. This work contained one hundred and fifty-eight colored plates which included numerous designs for rooms showing the decoration and placing of furniture. He stated that he was guided by the finest ancient specimens of the Egyptian, Greek and Roman styles. He also included ornament in the Gothic and Chinese taste. Unfortunately a large part of his work was inconsistent and completely lacking in harmony. He also published two other books. See *Regency*.

Snake Foot   In English cabinetwork; an elongated foot used on a cabriole leg. See *Pad Foot*; *Cabriole Leg*; *Slipper Foot*.

Snaphance   In arms and armor; an early form of flintlock hand firearm. The snaphance was invented in Germany during the middle of the 16th century. It was operated by a trigger which when released caused a flint to strike a piece of grooved steel, emitting sparks and igniting powder in the pan. See *Firelock*; *Wheel Lock*.

Snuff Bottle   In Chinese art; a very small vessel or container used to hold snuff, generally fitted with a tiny stopper attached to a tiny spoon. Although snuff bottles are known to have been made as early as the K'ang Hsi reign, 1662–1722, they usually date from the Tao Kuang reign and the middle of the 19th century. Snuff bottles were made in a great variety of shapes, sometimes with rounded bottoms having the appearance of smooth stones or little eggs. They were made of jade, glass, porcelain, semi-precious stones, crystal, onyx, agate, amethyst, coral, red lacquer and amber. Those made of porcelain were decorated in the same manner as the other Chinese wares, such as Famille Verte, Famille Rose, Underglaze Red, Underglaze Blue and Tea Dust. Many of the glass snuff bottles were so skillfully made to imitate jade and various stones that it is difficult to distinguish them from the real mineral. Some of the fine glass snuff bottles of plain opaque white and others with exquisite and delicate enamelled decoration bear the mark of Ku Yüeh Hsüan. These pieces are also made with this delicate enamelled decoration on the inside only. See *Ku Yüeh Hsüan*; *Famille Verte*; *Famille Rose*.

Snuff Box   A small box to hold snuff made during the 17th century onwards. It was made of silver, brass, tortoise shell, ivory, horn and other similar materials. Fine specimens were elaborately wrought in gold or silver and were encrusted with jewels. Others were finely decorated with enamel work and miniature paintings. See *Snuff Spoon*; *Snuff Grater*.

Snuffers   Or Candle Snuffers. A device made of metal for cutting off, or snuffing, and holding the charred part of a candle wick. In English silver; the earliest extant snuffers, which date from the 16th century, were in the form of a pair of scissors having capacious cutting pans on each arm, which when closed, resembled the shape of a heart. A tray of conforming design was usually provided for holding the snuffers. Later the cutting pan was made in the form of a small box-like piece and about the middle of the 18th century the underside of the snuffers was provided with three small feet, which raised them above the surface of the tray, making it easier to pick them up with the thumb and forefinger. A later variety of snuffers stand was an upright small box

SILVER SNUFFERS

with a scroll handle resting on a spreading foot. The snuffers were placed in the box section vertically and a hook on the handle held the conical candle extinguisher. In France, snuffers, or mouchettes, are mentioned as early as the end of the 14th century, and those of the 16th century, which resembled the early English examples, were elaborately wrought of gold and silver.

Snuff Grater   A small grater for snuff used from the 17th century onwards. It consisted of a small spoon at one end with a small box at the other end to hold the grated snuff. It was made of metal, ivory and other similar materials. See *Snuff Box*; *Snuff Spoon*.

Snuff Spoon   In silver; the habit of smoking tobacco was followed by the using of snuff which at first was in the form of hard dried rolls and was powdered by the user on a small snuff grater. In England during the last quarter of the 17th century snuff was sold in powdered form and by the beginning of the 18th century it became popular among all classes. A tiny silver snuff spoon with a delicate stem was usually carried in an étui. A very small quantity of snuff was taken from the box with the spoon and placed either on the back of the left hand or between the thumb and forefinger and then sniffed into the nostrils. See *Snuff Box*; *Snuff Grater*; *Etui*.

SOAP BOX AND SPONGE
BOX

Soap Box and Sponge Box   In French silver; a boîte à savonnette or soap box and a boîte à éponge or sponge box made of silver were used in France in the 17th and 18th centuries and formed part of the toilet accessories. The characteristic types were small receptacles of spherical form hinged at the center and resting on a low spreading foot. The sponge box was covered with decorative perforations to allow ventilation, while the soap box was solid. These toilet accessories were often listed in 18th century inventories, such as "a barber's basin, two boxes of silver, one a savonnette and the other a boîte à éponge."

Soda Glass   In glass; a glass having an alkaline flux of soda. See *Glass*.

Sofa   Or Sopha. In cabinetwork; the term *sopha*, which is of Near Eastern origin and referred to the platform in the audience hall on which the Grand Vizier sat in a cross-legged manner, was found in French furniture inventories around 1680. In French furniture literature it is stated that the sofa was a form of canapé with four or six seats. The term *sofa* or *sopha* is found in English inventories around 1700. As the term *sofa* is now understood it appears that the chief difference between an upholstered settee and sofa, since they are often of similar construction, is that the latter is larger, generally has a more overstuffed appearance and may be used for reclining. Sofas are often illustrated in furniture literature with additional loose cushions in the back and at each arm. See *Settee*; *Canapé*.

Sofa à Pommier   In French cabinetwork; the name generally give to a fashionable variety of Empire sofa. It was characterized by a low straight back continuing at right angles to form the sides which were of equal height. As a rule it was a rather massive piece of furniture.

Sofa Table   In English cabinetwork; the sofa table, which was a popular piece of furniture, was introduced late in the 18th century. Sheraton stated that the table was to be placed in front of the sofa. The characteristic variety of Sheraton style sofa table had an oblong top with end drop-leaves over two frieze drawers and rear mock drawers. The drop-leaves which often had rounded corners were supported on hinged wooden brackets. The over-all length of the table was between 5 and 6 feet, the width was about 2 feet and the height was around 27 inches to 29 inches. The legs were designed in different forms. The table was often mounted on a turned pedestal with four splayed supports which were finished with brass paw feet and casters. Sometimes the sofa table was designed with two lyre-form end supports which were joined by a stretcher. The sofa table, designed in the Sheraton style, was first made in America around 1800 and it remained in fashion throughout the American Empire style.

Soft Chün In Chinese ceramics; see *Chün Yao*.

Soft Paste or Soft Paste Porcelain In European ceramics; European porcelain falls into two principal classes; true porcelain or hard paste porcelain made of kaolin and petuntse, and artificial porcelain, known as soft paste or pâte tendre, made with glassy substances. Many successful and artistic imitations of true porcelain were made in Europe during the 17th and 18th centuries by using glass or the materials of glass fused and ground up and mixed with clay or some other ingredient. The ingredients used in soft paste have varied widely over the period of years. Generally the required temperature to fire soft paste is about 1100° C. The glaze was added in a second firing at a lower temperature and lead was freely used as an ingredient in the glaze in order that it would fuse more readily. A clear lead glaze was never used in the usual feldspathic hard paste porcelain of Europe. In reality soft paste is soft in appearance and artistically its decoration is more pleasing in color than true porcelain. Its glaze was easily scratched and was soft. Because of its great production hazards and also because the finished product was not very durable, the making of soft paste was gradually abandoned as the process and materials for true porcelain became better understood. Its production was practically given up in France and England early in the 19th century, the French having been the principal producers of this artificial porcelain. See *Chinese Soft Paste*; *Porcelain*; *Bone China*; *Sèvres*.

Softwood See *Hardwood*.

Soho Tapestries The name given to the tapestries woven in Soho, Birmingham, England. Paul Saunders, d. 1770, an English tapestry weaver was working at Soho. He held the position of Royal Yeoman Arras-

maker working for the Royal Wardrobe from 1761 to 1770. See *Tapestry*.

Soleret In armor; plate armor for the foot that first appeared in the 13th century in the form of strips of metal riveted to leather. Later the plates were riveted to each other in a laminated manner. In the 15th century detachable toe-pieces of excessive length were called à la poulaine. In the 16th century the toe-pieces became very broad and were called sabatons, bear-paw and duck-billed solerets.

Soroimono In Japanese sword mounts; the term, meaning a set of conforming objects, is frequently applied to sword fittings. This soroimono, or set, may consist of any combination of sword mounts, with the exception of the kogai, kozuka and menuki, a set of which is called a mitokoromono. A dai-shō-no-soroimono is the complete set of fittings for a pair of swords, which comprise as many as twenty-four pieces although such sets are very rare. This pair of swords, dai-shō, is the katana and the wakizashi.

Sosuke, Namikawa A kind of cloisonné enamel; see *Cloisonné Enamel*.

Souj-Bulak An Oriental rug belonging to the Persian classification. It derived its name from the city of Souj-Bulak where it is made by the Kurds. The foundation is wool. The pile is wool and medium in length, and is very thick and upright, due to the fact that the yarns are doubled. One end usually has a selvage, the other a selvage and loose warp threads. The Souj-Bulak is compact, strong and serviceable. See *Persian Rugs*.

Soumak An Oriental rug belonging to the Caucasian group; the name is derived from the town of Shemakha. It is woven with a flat stitch and has a flat surface. The method of weaving is a kind of modified tapestry weaving, with many loose threads on the back. Although the rug is not heavy, it is a well-woven rug, and is made entirely of wool. The ends are usually finished with a

SOLERET

heavy knotted fringe. The surface resembles an ordinary herringbone weave, due to the pileless stitch used in weaving it. The designs consist of geometrical motifs. It is also called a Shemakha and Kashmir. See *Caucasian Rugs*.

SOUVENIR

Souvenir   The term derived from the French word *souvenir* meaning memory, and memorandum book or tablet upon which one writes the things to remember, is given to an object of virtù which was fashionable in France during the second half of the 18th century. It is a small fitted case or nécessaire about $3\frac{1}{2}$ inches in length, $2\frac{1}{4}$ inches in width, and $\frac{1}{4}$ inch in thickness. This case, which usually had the name *souvenir* on the front, was fitted with one or more thin ivory tablets, and a porte-crayon or pencil case. One of the earliest references to a souvenir was in 1766 in "l'Inventaire de Mme. de Pompadour" in which were declared and described eight richly made souvenirs. The souvenir was made of gold, or ivory, tortoise shell, enamel and similar materials ornamented with elaborately worked gold. It frequently had a finely executed miniature in the center and was often jewel-encrusted. Recent French literature on the collection at the Louvre classifies this object as étui à tablettes or étui-souvenir. See *Etui*; *Nécessaire*.

Spade Foot   In English cabinetwork; a quadrangular foot that slightly tapers downward from the top. It was often used by Hepplewhite and Sheraton on legs of tapering quadrangular form. The spade foot was most often seen on the legs of chairs and tables. See *Foot*.

Spandrel   The irregular triangular space in architecture formed by the curve of an arch and the angle lines enclosing it, or by two arches. It was a favorite space in architecture for ornament. Spandrels also occur in cabinetwork; such as the arcaded façade of a Gothic chest and other articles having the curve of an arch as a decorative detail. The term is also applied to the triangular spaces at the four corners of the brass dial of a clock outside of the hour circle. By extension the

decorative brass pieces, which fill these spaces on the brass dial, are also called spandrels.

Spangled-Glass   In American glass; a late 19th century American art glass principally made into glass baskets with fancy decorated handles and rims. Flakes of mica were incorporated in the clear glass inner layer, and an overlay of clear tinted glass of various colors was applied. See *Art Glass*.

Spanish Carpets   Spanish handmade cut pile carpets were first made about the beginning of the 16th century. They are of the same construction as an Oriental rug. However, their designs are of European derivation in distinction to the Persian designs. In addition to the cut pile carpets, Spanish carpets of the 17th and 18th centuries are also in needlework, having been worked in the tent stitch or the cross stitch. They also made hand-woven tapestry carpets. See *Embroidered Rug*; *Oriental Rug*; *Tapestry Carpet*.

Spanish Chair   In Spanish cabinetwork; see *Frailero*.

Spanish Foot   In English cabinetwork; a carved scroll foot with vertical grooves. The scroll turns backward in a curve at the bottom. It was especially used in place of the characteristic bun foot during the William and Mary style, in particular for the legs of chairs and sometimes tables. See *Foot*.

Spanish Lace   Spanish lace has in its time often been considered as renowned as the lace of Italy and Flanders. However, it appears that Spain was later in producing lace of an artistic quality than Italy, Flanders or France. Much of the fine Spanish lace was made for ecclesiastical purposes. Point d'Espagne in the customary sense of the word refers to the gold or silver lace occasionally embroidered in colors which was worn by the Spanish noblemen and was so much favored in France in the early years of the reign of Louis XIV. It is doubtful that thread lace of an artistic quality was made in Spain in early times. The heavy white thread lace with its arabesque designs called Spanish point was originally made in Italy and imported to Spain where it was imitated by the nuns in the convents. Barcelona, Talavera de la Reyna, Seville and Valencia were the principal centers for gold and silver lace. The making of silk blonde lace was chiefly limited to Catalonia, especially Barcelona, where the industry was flourishing in the 19th century. It is generally accepted that Spanish silk laces were inferior in workmanship to those made at Bayeux, Caën and Chantilly.

Sparking Lamp In American furniture; an early small lamp, usually of glass, that burned whale oil. It was so named because it was believed to be filled and lighted when a young man visited a young lady, and when the lamp went out it was time for him to leave. It is also called a nursing lamp.

Sparta Rug See *Oushak Rug*.

Sparver In English furniture; an English word meaning a bed curtain, taken from the French word *espervier*. The sparver, which was used as early as the 15th century, developed during the succeeding 16th and 17th centuries into an elaborate hanging suspended over the bed. It generally consisted of tapering strips of silk suspended from the ceiling on a round wooden disk usually brightly painted or gilded and having more or less the contour of a bell tent. The sparver bed differed from the tester bed in that the former did not require bedposts. The term *sparver* was also given to a bed with a tent-shaped canopy, and as a result apparently beds with a tent-shaped canopy may be referred to as a tent bed or a sparver bed. Tent beds were mentioned in English records as early as 1450. See *Field Bed*.

Spatterware In English ceramics; pottery ware in which the ground color was applied by spattering or splashing with a brush. This method of decorating was used at Liverpool and Bristol around 1750. The colors were usually blue, brown, yellow or purple with medallions reserved in the shape

of a shell, a fan, or some other form. It may have been produced to imitate the Chinese wares. See *Powder Blue Ware*.

Spear-Head Spoon In English silver; a silver spoon having the stem of the spoon terminating in the shape of a spear-head. It was introduced around the end of the 14th century and is also called a diamond-point spoon. See *Spoon*.

Spice and Coffee Grinder See *Moulin*.

Spice Box Small silver boxes for spice were first made in England during the 16th century. The early varieties were frequently in the form of a small low box conforming in shape to the embossed escallop shell lid and resting on four tiny cockle-shell-shaped feet. A Continental variety, made of silver, was often of sarcophagus shape mounted on four small feet. It was in three sections and each end had a hinged cover. The center portion was fitted with a receptacle having a hinged cover. One end section was used for allspice. The other end section was divided into two parts; one was for nutmeg and the other was for ginger. The partition which separated the nutmeg from the ginger was of steel and was used for grating the nutmeg. These three ingredients were mixed in the center receptacle according to taste, and were particularly used for flavoring spiced drinks. This variety of spice box was about 5 inches long and 3 inches wide. In France, the spice box, or épicière, which was popular in the 18th century, was a small container, generally of faïence, divided into compartments for holding the spices to be used at the table. There were two principal types. One was in the form of a small open deep dish with divisions for the spices. The other was in the form of a small bowl, with a cover, resting on a spreading foot, and divided into compartments.

Spice Chest In American cabinetwork; the name applied to an article of furniture especially made to hold spices. Some examples of American spice chests made in the 18th century are fine pieces of cabinetwork. One

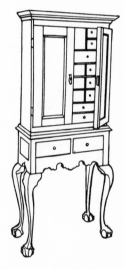

SPICE CHEST, AMERICAN

variety was designed like a chest of drawers mounted on a stand, except that the upper section was fitted with either one or two doors, which, when opened, revealed an interior fitted with many small drawers. The stand, which was mounted on cabriole legs of varying length, was fitted with a row of drawers. Variations in design occurred. Extant examples vary in height from 27 inches to 58 inches. Since spices brought from the East Indies were an expensive luxury in Colonial times these chests were fitted with a lock and key.

GEORGE III SPIDER-LEG TABLE

Spider-Leg Table In English cabinetwork; early in the second half of the 18th century there was a revival of the gate-leg table but in a much lighter form. Due to its very slender turned supports this lighter variety of table of gate-leg construction is usually called a spider-leg table. As a rule it was a rather small table. See *Gate-Leg Table*.

Spider Work In lace-making; the term *spider work* was originally given to an early form of darned lace during the Middle Ages. It was characterized by an open and irregular form of darning having a spider web appearance. See *Darned Netting*.

Spinach Jade See *Jade*.

Spindle In cabinetwork; a member turned on a lathe, generally of slender proportions and tapering toward each end. Turned spindles were employed on such articles as the backs of Windsor chairs, spinning wheels and the spindled galleries occasionally found on some mid-18th century English tea tables of tripod form. Split spindles, which is the name given to spindles cut in half lengthwise, were sometimes applied to the surface of Jacobean oak furniture for decorative purposes. Occasionally the split spindles were stained black.

Spindle Wood See *Fusian Wood*.

Spinet A musical instrument having a keyboard and strings closely resembling the harpsichord in form except it was smaller and contained only one string for each note.

The small case was wing-shaped, and it was placed upon a table or stand since it was designed without legs. The mechanism of the spinet is the same as the virginal, the difference being the shape of the case. The name *spinetta* was used in Italy during the 15th century to describe a virginal of various forms in which the strings were plucked by quills or spines. The spinet or wing-shaped virginal first appeared in England around the middle of the 17th century and was called the triangel virginall. After the Restoration it acquired the name of spinette or espinette when it was copied from the graceful French forms. The spinet was used in England until the middle of the 18th century. See *Clavichord*; *Virginal*; *Harpsichord*.

Spinning Wheel The spinning wheel was an early kind of machine used for spinning raw wool, cotton or flax into thread or yarn. It consisted of a revolving wheel, supported on a stand, driven by hand or by a foot treadle. The wheel rotated a single spindle on which the yarn was spun. After the wheel with an attached treadle was invented, during the second quarter of the 16th century, spinning became a popular occupation for women of all classes. Hand spinning continued as an industry during the entire 18th century. A spinning wheel could be found in almost every farmhouse and cottage. It was usually constructed of several woods. Oak and beech was one of the more frequent combinations in England. The supports and spindles were baluster turned.

Spiral Turning In cabinetwork; see *Turning*; *Twist Turning*.

Spirit Burner The name given to a fluid burner attached to the center of a dish cross. It was used to keep the food hot in the dishes placed upon it. The spirit burner also formed a part of a stand upon which a teakettle was placed. It is also called a spirit lamp. See *Dish Cross*; *Teakettle*.

Spirit Case In English furniture; a finely carved or inlaid 18th century wooden box having a fitted interior for the reception of decanters. The spirit case, which was designed with a hinged lid, was of fine workmanship.

Splat-Back In English cabinetwork; an open chair back having a vertical wooden member centered in the back of the chair and extending from the crest rail to the seat rail or slightly above the seat rail. The splat was either solid or pierced. The outline or contour of the splat varied. See *Queen Anne Splat-Back Chair*; *Lyre-Back Chair*; *Shield-Back*; *Camel-Back*; *Ribband-Back*; *Prince of Wales Plume*.

Splayed In English cabinetwork; the term applied to a member such as a foot or a leg that is raked or flares or spreads outward. For example a splayed foot. *See Pad Foot.* The term is applied to legs that are not vertical. Splayed legs were a feature of Windsor chairs. The two front legs slant to the front and sides and the two rear legs to the back and sides. The American Windsor chair was invariably designed with splayed legs. Splayed supports were employed during the Regency style. Pedestal dining tables in two or more sections with each section mounted on a turned pedestal and tetrapod splayed supports were especially characteristic. See *Drum Table*; *Sofa Table*.

Splint Seat In cabinetwork; the term given to a chair seat made of thin, flat strips of hickory or other wood. A splint seat is also referred to as a bass or basswood seat. Bass is the inner bark of the linden or lime, and the term is sometimes applied loosely to any similar fiber, such as split rushes or straw. This type of seat was made to take the place of the rush seat although it is neither as durable nor as comfortable. It was freely used in American cabinetwork for the plainer types of chairs. See *Rush Seat*; *Flag Seat*.

Spode In English ceramics; a pottery was started at Stoke-on-Trent, Staffordshire, around 1770 by Josiah Spode, 1733–1797, who had previously worked for Thomas Whieldon. His son, Josiah Spode II, 1754–

1827, carried on the business. He introduced porcelain around 1800 and stone-china around 1805. The porcelain was a hybrid bone-ash paste. He is generally given credit for establishing the standard composition for English bone china or bone porcelain. The porcelain made under Josiah Spode II was technically of fine quality; however, the painted decoration and the forms were often ostentatious. Especially typical were ornately gilded vases with colored grounds. Some wares with simplified Japanese designs were generally more pleasing. William Taylor Copeland, who had become a partner in 1813, succeeded to the business in 1833, Josiah Spode III having died in 1829. The firm, which is still in existence, was Copeland and Garrett from 1833 to 1847, and then Copeland, late Spode or W. T. Copeland and Sons. The mark is "Spode". See *Parian Ware*; *Stone-China*; *Bone China*.

SPODE PLATE WITH "JAPAN" PATTERN

Spontoon In arms and armor; a weapon consisting of a wooden shaft with a particular kind of steel spear head. It was used by infantry officers during the 17th and 18th centuries. It is referred to as a form of a halberd or partizan.

Spoon In English silver; the spoon is of ancient origin and dates back to the time of the Egyptians. Until around the middle of the 17th century the bowl of the spoon was more or less fig-shaped, with the narrowest part near the short stem. The stem was generally round or square and terminated in a knop of different forms, such as an acorn, a diamond point or a lion sejant. The bowl of the spoon underwent a gradual change. During the reign of Charles I, 1625–1649, the bowl became broader next to the stem and narrower at the end, and by 1660 the bowl became ovoid. Around 1660 a spoon was introduced which had a flat thin stem. The stem was wider than any of the earlier stems, and the stem end was much wider and thinner than the other part of the stem. The stem end was divided into three parts and the spoon was called a trifid-end spoon. At

SILVER SPOUT CUP,
AMERICAN

the beginning of the 18th century the end of the stem became considerably thicker and rounded but still curved forward. Around the second quarter of the 18th century a spoon was introduced which had the stem end curled back in the fashion of an Ionic volute. This design was called the Onslow pattern. This curving back of the stem end became the general form during the third quarter of the 18th century. However, the stem end was rounded as in the earlier spoons. This pattern is known as the Old English pattern and has continued until the present time. See *Acorn Spoon*; *Diamond-Point Spoon*; *Maidenhead Spoon*; *Lion Sejant Spoon*; *Seal Top Spoon*; *Spear-Head Spoon*; *Apostle Spoon*; *Puritan Spoon*; *Slip-Stem Spoon*; *Trifid-End Spoon*; *Wavy-End Spoon*; *Rat-Tail Spoon*; *Coffin-End Spoon*; *Onslow Pattern*; *Old English Pattern*; *Fiddle Pattern*; *Dessert Spoon*; *Teaspoon*.

Spoon-Back In English cabinetwork; a splat-back chair shaped so as to conform to the shape of a person's back. See *Queen Anne Splat-Back Chair*; *Splat-Back*.

Spooner A spoon holder; a general term applied to an article especially made for the reception of spoons. See *Spoon Rack*.

Spoon Rack In English furniture; the spoon rack was probably first used during the time of Queen Elizabeth I, 1558–1603. The oak spoon rack was chiefly a utilitarian piece and little thought was given to its design. A principal variety toward the end of the 17th century had a solid wooden back to which were attached two rows of slotted rails for spoons and a box beneath for the reception of knives, either with or without a lid.

Spoon-Tray In English silver; a small oval silver dish that became popular in the early part of the 18th century. It was used for the reception of teaspoons, and was placed on the tea table with the teapot and tea cups. These silver spoon-trays were succeeded by small porcelain trays of similar forms.

Spotted Celadon In Chinese ceramics; see *Celadon*.

Spout Cup In English silver; a vessel having a body frequently in the form of a small jug, usually with a cover. It was designed with a long curving spout and generally with a single handle at a right angle to the spout. It was principally used for feeding infants and invalids. It was introduced around 1640 in England. However, it achieved greater popularity in America. It was also called a Feeding Cup.

Sprig In lace-making; a detached needle or bobbin-made lace motif, such as flowers and scrolls, which is later sewn on the net ground. In some lace work, such as Honiton guipure, the sprigs are joined with various needle stitches, cutwork and purlings to form a complete piece of lace. See *Brussels Appliqué*; *Honiton Lace*.

Sprigged Ware In English ceramics; a contemporary English name given to 18th century wares decorated in applied reliefs principally of flowers, foliage, and stems. These applied reliefs were pressed in intaglio molds and were secured to the body of the vessel by a mixture of clay and water or slip. The stems were done in free hand modelling and were also applied with slip. Early examples of this technique were found in Rhenish stoneware and in Astbury and Whieldon earthenwares and salt-glazed stonewares of Staffordshire. The technique was known as sprigging.

Squab A common and contemporary English term applied to a stuffed thick or soft loose cushion in the 17th and 18th centuries. The term is particularly given to a more or less flat, removable cushion used to cover the seat of a chair, settee or sofa. See *Cushion*.

Squelette Clock A French term meaning skeleton. See *Skeleton Clock*.

S-Scroll In ornament; see *Scrolls, C and S*.

Staffordshire In English ceramics; practically all of the information regarding early Staffordshire pottery and the potters working in North Staffordshire is traditional. It has been the custom to associate types of

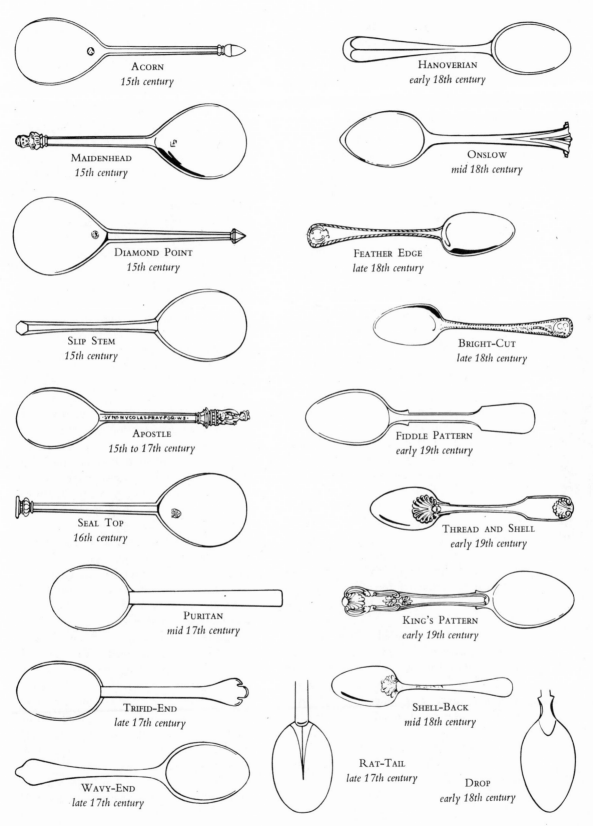

ENGLISH SILVER SPOONS

ACORN
15th century

MAIDENHEAD
15th century

DIAMOND POINT
15th century

SLIP STEM
15th century

APOSTLE
15th to 17th century

SEAL TOP
16th century

PURITAN
mid 17th century

TRIFID-END
late 17th century

WAVY-END
late 17th century

HANOVERIAN
early 18th century

ONSLOW
mid 18th century

FEATHER EDGE
late 18th century

BRIGHT-CUT
late 18th century

FIDDLE PATTERN
early 19th century

THREAD AND SHELL
early 19th century

KING'S PATTERN
early 19th century

SHELL-BACK
mid 18th century

RAT-TAIL
late 17th century

DROP
early 18th century

Staffordshire wares with the names of individual potters; however, these types were undoubtedly made by more than one potter. Marks did not come into anything resembling general use until the latter part of the 18th century, and it has always been difficult to identify the wares of a particular pottery. The tremendous growth of the ceramic industry in North Staffordshire during the 18th and 19th centuries was essentially due to the abundance of clays in the district. The earliest Staffordshire wares of any artistic merit were the slipwares first made during the latter part of the 16th century. Toward the end of the 17th century the Elers brothers produced a red stoneware in imitation of the Chinese buccaro wares. From around 1725 earthenware covered with colored lead glazes in the types associated with Astbury and Whieldon were made concurrently with the solid agate ware and the almost white salt-glazed stoneware in imitation of porcelain. Apparently faïence was never made. Later in the 18th century Wedgwood perfected the cream-colored earthenware with an almost colorless lead glaze. The figures made at Staffordshire in salt-glazed stoneware or in earthenware covered with colored lead glazes have an intrinsic charm. Of particular interest were the so-called pew groups with charming stylized seated figures. From around 1785 the earthenware figures were generally painted in enamel colors. The 19th century Staffordshire figures with their simple modelling and bold colors are an attractive form of peasant art. Toby jugs were a characteristic Staffordshire production. The fine black basalt and jasper stonewares made by Wedgwood were extensively imitated by other contemporary potters. Porcelain was also manufactured at Staffordshire. See *Spode*; *New Hall*; *Minton*; *Davenport*; *Ironstone China*; *Stoke-on-Trent*; *Marbled Ware*; *Agate Ware*; *Tortoise Shell Ware*; *Scratch Blue Ware*; *Crouch Ware*; *Stoneware*; *Wood, Ralph*; *Wood, Enoch*; *Elers*; *Astbury, John*; *Whieldon, Thomas*; *Toft, Thomas*; *Pratt, Felix*; *Cream-Colored Earthenware*; *Wedgwood, Josiah*; *Mayer, Elijah*; *Turner, John*; *Palmer, Humphrey*; *Hollins, Samuel*; *Shorthose, J.*; *Basalt Ware*; *Jasper Ware*; *Adams, William*.

GOTHIC STAINED AND
PAINTED GLASS WINDOW,
AUSTRIAN

Stained Glass The earliest stained glass windows during medieval times were composed of pieces of shaped colored glass arranged in such a manner as to produce a mosaic panel called Opus Sectile, and the colored glass, which received its color in the melting pot, was called pot-metal. This patchwork of colored glass was held together by strips of lead in sections which rather resembled the letter H. The use of paint in the beginning was restricted to an opaque brown, which was employed to close out the light, and in so doing produced lines of detail that defined and outlined the design. Vitreous color pigments were used by the painter. When the pieces of colored glass painted in this manner were put in the kiln and heated the vitreous colors became fused on the surface. Even in the early glass of the 13th century thin painting was often used to indicate shading and to reduce the strong color. Another common practice was to cover the colored glass completely with paint and then proceed to scratch the design out of it. Stippling was often used to soften the tint. And so during the 14th century the method of painting pot-metal glass included shading by stippling made clear by touches of brush work, a limited amount of scratching out of the high lights and cross-hatching the background. During the early Renaissance the outlines of the design still continued to be painted on the colored glass and the rest of the process was based upon the removal of the paint. In this method the entire surface was covered with a dull pale brown. The modelling was obtained by removing the paint with a brush. Sharp lines of light were achieved by scratching away the paint with a needle point or some kind of pointed tool. This work was done much in the same manner as an artist would engrave a plate, since it was sometimes done with a pointed tool. Clear glass was also produced by thinly covering one side with colored glass that was scratched away in a similar manner. In this way red and white or vice versa was made. During the 14th century a method was found of applying a silver compound to glass which would give it a yellow stain. In this manner yellow glass was obtained from colorless glass and green glass from a grey blue glass. This golden yellow glass as well as white glass, as it became more pure, was increasingly used. During the 16th century the work of painting on glass with translucent colors was introduced. The enamel colors were applied to the glass with a brush and then fused to the surface of the glass by heating in a kiln. This method of painting with translucent enamel colors and with the opaque brown was generally applied to all later work. This type of work did not have the richness of the earlier stained colored pot-metal glass but it did permit greater elaboration of detail.

Staining In English furniture; it seems that an oil stain containing a vegetable coloring matter was the earliest form of stain, such as alkanet root producing a reddish stain. Stains were applied to many common woods to simulate ebony, walnut and mahogany. Red and black stains were the most common during the 18th century. As a result of the tendency towards woods of lighter tone for drawing room furniture during the last four decades of the 18th century, a sycamore veneer was stained with a solution of oxide of iron and was known as harewood. Staining was also used in marquetry work. See *Ebonize*; *Marquetry*.

Stalker and Parker In English furniture; from the time of the Restoration, 1660, there was evident an ever increasing appreciation for Oriental lacquer work. Oriental lacquered articles enjoyed great popularity. Practically every home of any importance had an Oriental or English lacquered cabinet mounted on a stand. A further impetus to domestic lacquer work was provided in 1688 by a publication entitled A TREATISE OF JAPANNING AND VENEERING. The authors,

Stalker and Parker, gave their readers full instructions in the art of lacquering. As a result of this publication lacquering became a fashionable hobby. Much of the lacquer furniture was done by amateurs, and although it was decorative and colorful it had little real artistic merit. The vogue for lacquer work reached its peak shortly after the beginning of the 18th century. The taste for lacquer work continued to some extent during the Early Georgian era and was revived intermittently throughout the second half of the 18th century. See *Japanning*; *Chinoiserie*.

Stamped Leather A decorative leather work principally used during the 16th and 17th centuries as wall hangings. In this process silver leaf was applied to rectangular pieces of tanned calf or goat skins. Then the silver leaf was coated with a transparent yellow lacquer which produced a gold-like effect. Designs were embossed or stamped on the leather and painted in rich brilliant colors. It was a costly work. It was regarded as one of the most handsome of wall decorations. It was made chiefly in Spain and in Italy, and later in England and France during the 17th century. See *Gilded Leather*; *Blind Tooling*.

Stand In cabinetwork; a very comprehensive term which denotes almost any kind of support in the form of a frame or a piece of furniture upon which to stand or hang articles. There was an almost endless variety of stands made in cabinetwork, such as stands for candelabra, urns, teapots, trays, wigs, basins, chests, cabinets and many other articles.

Standing Cup In silver; a tall finely wrought decorative cup having a cover surmounted with a finial. As a rule it was mounted on a stem that flared into a circular foot or base. It was introduced around the 14th century. The cup was made of silver or of gold. Frequently it was made of some unusual material, such as the egg of an ostrich or the shell of a coconut, and was richly mounted in silver. The cup varied in height; some

ELIZABETHAN SILVER
STANDING CUP

were as tall as 22 inches. The cup denoted certain social customs and practices. The standing cup was supposed to reflect the affluence of its owner. The cup was often presented as a gift to the royalty of another country. Each company or guild such as the Clothworkers' and Livery Companies generally had its own standing cup. See *Ostrich Cup*; *Coconut Cup*; *Steeple Cup*.

Standish Or Inkstand. In English silver; the name given to the stand to contain the pen, ink and other writing accessories. The term *standish* was in general use from the 15th century, while the term *inkstand* apparently was first used around 1775. The standish made of silver was introduced toward the end of the 17th century and it remained the fashionable material throughout the Georgian period. During the Regency the standish was sometimes made of mahogany or rosewood with bronze mounts. The early standish was fitted with two pots, one for ink and one for sand, the latter having a perforated lid. Later specimens became more elaborate and were fitted with a taper stick, pounce box, wafer-box, penknife and other writing materials and accessories and occasionally with a drawer for quills. See *Pounce Box*; *Wafer-Box*; *Taper Stick*.

INLAID STELLATE MOTIF

Star Diamond-Point In French Provincial cabinetwork; a carved geometrical ornament framed in a square panel. It consisted of eight elongated pyramids, the four center ones being triangular and the four corner ones being quadrangular. The entire eight pyramids had their sharp elongated apexes converging toward the center in which was usually a small round boss. It was characteristic of the cabinetwork from the province of Gascogne. See *Diamond-Point*; *French Provincial*.

Stars In American cabinetwork; stars were a characteristic form of ornament on American furniture. Inlaid or painted stars or markings resembling stars are sometimes used to determine the date of a piece of furniture. The date may be more or less decided since the stars very often indicate the number of states in the Union at the time the piece was made. Stars are occasionally found as decorative motifs on such articles as mirrors, clocks, tables and desks. However, stars are not a positive indication of the date since they were frequently used for decorative purposes only in varying numbers. In addition to the original thirteen states, 1790, those admitted up to and including the year 1821 are: Vermont 1791, Kentucky 1792, Tennessee 1796, Ohio 1803, Louisiana 1812, Indiana 1816, Mississippi 1817, Illinois 1818, Alabama 1819, Maine 1820, Missouri 1821. See *Stellate*.

Steeple Cup In English silver; a tall decorative finely wrought standing cup. It derived its name from the resemblance of its tall finial on the cover to that of a steeple. The design of the finial was copied from English Renaissance architecture. It was introduced around 1600. See *Standing Cup*.

Steingut In German ceramics; the German term for cream-colored or white earthenware with a lead glaze. See *Cream-Colored Earthenware*.

Steinzeug In German ceramics; the German term for stoneware. See *German Stoneware*; *Stoneware*.

Stellate In ornament; star-shaped or radiating from the center like the rays of a star. An inlaid stellate motif was occasionally found on either the top center or on both sides of the top center on English double chests or tallboys and similar articles of furniture designed in the Queen Anne style. This legacy from English furniture was often found on fine American highboys and other similar articles of furniture designed in the Queen Anne style.

Stem-Cup In Chinese ceramics; a small porcelain vessel introduced during the Hsüan Tê reign, 1426–1435. It has a wide, rather shallow bowl, and a tall foot or stem which flares gently toward the bottom. The glaze is a pure white of fatty texture and on the bowl are painted three fishes, or three fruits, in underglaze red. The stem-cup was so much appreciated that it was copied at the Imperial factory during the Yung Chêng reign. This form was later imitated in European ceramic wares.

Sterling A term applied to the lawful standard for articles made of silver. It was established by Edward I in 1300, and stated that silverware must consist of at least 11 oz., 2 pennyweight of pure silver and not more than 18 pennyweight of alloy in every 12 oz., or troy pound. In 1696, according to an Act of Parliament, articles of silver could not be made of less fineness than 11 oz., 10 pennyweight; this higher grade of sterling is known as the Britannia standard. In 1720, the act was repealed and the old standard for sterling of 11 oz., 2 pennyweight, was restored. Since that date both standards are permitted at the discretion of the silversmith. The higher grade of silver is punched with the lion head erased and the full-length figure of a woman, called Britannia; while the standard for the other grade is the leopard's head and the lion passant. For American sterling, see *American Silver*. See *Hall-Marks, London*.

Stiacciato In sculpture; a form of relief. See *Relief*.

Stiegel, Heinrich Wilhelm 1729–1785. American glass manufacturer. He migrated from Mannheim, Germany, to Pennsylvania in 1750. He found employment at the Elizabeth Furnace and soon became part owner. In 1769 he decided to manufacture flint glass tableware comparable to that imported from England. In order to achieve that end he brought skilled glass engravers and enamellers from Europe to the Stiegel Furnace at Manheim, which is near Lancaster, Pennsylvania. His enterprise flourished for a few years. However, in 1774, due to his personal extravagances and competition from abroad he declared bankruptcy. Since his glass manufactory did not use an identifying mark it is not possible with absolute

certainty to identify any glass as real Stiegel. A piece of glass can only be accurately identified as Stiegel type glass or in the Stiegel tradition or characteristic of the supposed Stiegel technique. It is generally accepted that Stiegel type glass is flint glass of clear and thin quality. He is believed to have made every type of glass tableware. Designs attributed to Stiegel are greatly varied and are closely related in their vigorous execution to other contemporary folk art decoration. See *Pennsylvania Dutch*; *Glass*; *Flint Glass*; *Ravenscroft, George*.

Stile In furniture construction; a vertical or upright member of a framework having the side, end or corner position, such as the corners on Gothic chests which were simply extended to form the short legs or feet. See *Muntin*.

Stiletto In arms; a 17th century European dagger only used for stabbing. The blade was very strong and usually of square or triangular section. Many of these stilettos had turned steel hilts.

Stipple Engraving The process of engraving with dots as contrasted to lines. The art of producing light and shade effects, especially in engravings and etchings by means of dots or strokes. See *Engraving*.

Stirrup Cup The name given to the drinking vessel or cup containing wine or some other drink handed to a man mounted on horseback about to depart for a journey as a parting drink. Stirrup cups were mentioned in English literature as early as 1681. The stirrup cup was also proffered to an arriving guest just before he dismounted. It was often a potent drink conveying a warm and cordial welcome. Stirrup cups were made of different materials, such as silver.

Stockelsdorf In German ceramics; a faïence manufactory was started at Stockelsdorf near Lübeck in 1771; it seems that it was probably a continuation of an earlier stove factory. The finer wares upon which the reputation of the factory depends were

STIEGEL TYPE GLASS JAR

probably made prior to 1788 and displayed a high standard of artistic excellence. Stoves were perhaps the most important production and were notable for their artistic merit. They were generally of pyramidal form and were in the Rococo or Neo-Classic style and were decorated with applied flowers, foliage and scrolls. The painting in enamel colors was very fine. Flowers in the Strasbourg style, figure subjects and landscapes were much favored for the painted decoration which was charmingly executed. In one variety the wares were painted in a very powerful blue. Included among the characteristic decorative and useful wares were large trays and tea table tops, wall fountains, four-sided plant containers and helmet-shaped ewers with shell moldings. Included among the marks was "Stff" for Stockelsdorf faïence.

Stoke-on-Trent In English ceramics; the name of a federated town in North Staffordshire. A number of small towns in which the pottery industry of North Staffordshire was originally centered were united to form Stoke-on-Trent. They included Burslem, Stoke, Tunstall, Longton, Longport, Fenton, Shelton, Lane Delph (now Middle Fenton), Lane End, Cobridge and Hanley. See *Staffordshire*.

Stole In ecclesiastical costume; a narrow band of silk or linen occasionally enhanced with embroidery and sometimes even with jewels worn over both shoulders, except by deacons who wear it over the left shoulder only, and hanging down to the knees or lower. Originally the stole in ancient Roman times signified an ordinary long robe, the Latin word being *stola* meaning clothing and hence a robe or garment. It is generally believed that the stole in its present narrow form as an ecclesiastical vestment occurred prior to the 9th century.

Stone-China In English ceramics; a dense hard earthenware having china stone as an

STOCKELSDORF STOVE

ingredient in its composition. Stone-china, which was generally of a greyish or bluish tone, was introduced by Josiah Spode II at his manufactory at Stoke-on-Trent around 1805. He hoped that this ware would supplant the coarse Chinese export porcelain. The painted decoration was generally composed of Oriental motifs which were transfer-printed in blue with touches of red. The ironstone china patented in 1813 by Charles James Mason is supposed to contain pulverized slag of iron; however, it is essentially very similar to Spode's stone-china. See *Ironstone China*.

Stoneware In ceramics; a name given to all types of clay pottery except porcelain having a body fired to a state of vitrification that is non-porous. Stoneware is always hard and is always fired in a high temperature kiln, generally ranging from 1200° C to 1400° C. Vitrified feldspathic stoneware was made in China before the 7th century and is commonly regarded as the fore-runner of porcelain. Kaolinic and feldspathic stonewares are kindred to porcelain, generally lacking only the whiteness and translucency of porcelain, and are sometimes referred to as porcelaneous stonewares. Stoneware was made in certain northern parts of Germany as early as the 15th century. Grey and red stoneware bodies were the most common until around the middle of the 17th century in Europe. The glaze for stoneware has to be a special quality to stand the heat of the kiln. A salt glaze was the most common. Due to the non-porous nature of the material stoneware does not require a glaze. A distinctive variety of an almost white salt-glaze stoneware in imitation of porcelain was made at Staffordshire around the second quarter of the 18th century. The German term for stoneware is *Steinzeug*, and the French is *Grès*. See *Buccaro Ware*; *Elers*; *Fulham*; *Nottingham*; *German Stoneware*; *Salt Glaze*; *Bouffioulx*.

Stool In cabinetwork; the stool, which is defined as a seat without arms or a back mounted on legs, was a familiar article of furniture in classical antiquity. One classical variety had a rectangular seat mounted on four legs, while another type was the folding stool of X-form, which, with its crossed legs, resembled a modern camp stool. During the Gothic period the joint or joined stool was the usual form of seating for all but the master of the house. It was of trestle form and the under-framing was keyed through the solid splayed end supports. Occasionally the under-framing was boxed in to form a shallow chest. Stools were still profusely used throughout the 16th century. Many were still of Gothic construction. Stools were square, round, rectangular and occasionally triangular. They generally rested on truss end supports, on four turned and blocked legs or on plain round columns. Cushions were frequently placed on the stools. Legs for stools essentially followed the designs for chair legs throughout the 17th and 18th centuries. As chairs became more plentiful the necessity for stools greatly diminished. However, in the large 18th century home stools were still much in evidence. See *Escabeau*; *Joint Stool*; *Footstool*; *Tabouret*.

Store Kongensgade Or Delfs Porselins Eller Hollandsch Steentoys Fabrique. In Danish ceramics; a faïence factory was founded in 1722 at Copenhagen and conducted by Johann Wolff. Its best work was from 1727 to 1749. It closed shortly after 1770. The principal mark was "IP" in monogram. The early work was obviously inspired by the blue and white of Delft and Nuremberg. The later work was in the Scandinavian Rococo style. Some later designs were also versions of Chinese plant designs. Painting in blue was the usual style; however, some polychrome painting was also done. The characteristic bishop bowls identified with Baltic ceramics were included in their wares.

Storr, Paul 1771–1844. One of the foremost English silversmiths working in London.

He produced a great amount of silver for domestic use and his work in the style of the Classic Revival was executed with the highest quality of craftsmanship. Many of his finest and most elaborate pieces were executed from the designs by John Flaxman.

Stove In ceramics; see *Hafner*.

Straight Bracket Foot In cabinetwork; see *Bracket Foot*.

Stralsund In Swedish ceramics; a faïence manufactory was established at Stralsund, Pomerania, Germany, in 1756 by Johann Ulrich Giese, of Sweden, to which Stralsund belonged between 1720 and 1814. It was active until 1792. Its best work was made in a four-year period between 1766 to 1770 when the factory was leased to Johann Ehrenreich who had founded the faïence manufactory at Marieberg. The wares made during this period closely resembled Marieberg faïence. The marks included the three nails of the Crucifixion with the initials of the proprietor and painter and the date. Especially characteristic were tureens and vases in the Rococo style decorated with applied reliefs of flowers, birds, small figures and foliage and pot-pourri vases with richly pierced covers and wavy bases. The painting was in enamel colors and was characterized by a prominent use of green. A powerful violet blue and also manganese were employed for shading, especially on openwork dishes and similar pieces.

Strap Handle In silver; a flat narrow handle frequently worked in an S-scroll shape.

Strapwork In ornament; a narrow band that has been folded, crossed or interlaced in many different designs. It was often worked into very elaborate and intricate designs. A characteristic feature of the Flemish Baroque style was its prominent use of elaborate strapwork. See *Laub und Bandelwerk*.

ENRICHED STRAPWORK

Strasbourg In French ceramics; a faïence manufactory was conducted by the Hannong family from 1720 to 1781 at Strasbourg, Alsace, producing some of the finest of French faïence. Shortly before 1750 the practice of painting in enamel colors and gilding which previously had been almost exclusively limited to porcelains was introduced at Strasbourg and established a fashion which was followed at the majority of French and German faïence manufactories. The manufacture of porcelain was started around 1752 but was transferred to Frankenthal in 1755. Around 1766 porcelain was again made at Strasbourg. The wares generally fall into three periods corresponding to the chief proprietors; C. F. Hannong, 1721–1739; Paul Hannong, around 1740–1760, and Joseph Hannong, 1762–1781. The early wares did not have a factory mark; however, the initials of painters were rather common. "P H" in monogram appeared as a faïence mark around and after 1740; the initials "P H" were on the porcelain. From 1762 the monogram "J H" was used plus initials and numerals. Strasbourg faïence was distinctive for its pure and brilliant white glaze and for its magnificent and rich enamel colors. The early faïence was chiefly painted in blue in a style derived from Rouen. The stylized so-called Indian flowers, adapted from Meissen, were introduced around 1740 and were supplanted around 1750 by the naturalistic treatment of flowers or Deutsche Blumen, also from Meissen. However, regardless of the inspiration, the Strasbourg flowers were superb and were copied in practically every faïence factory in France and Germany. The figures included all the characteristic Meissen types. The so-called Trompe l'Oeil wares such as tureens in the form of vegetables and dishes molded with fruits painted in natural colors were made at Strasbourg and were perhaps the finest of their type. From 1762 to 1781 the faïence production was to a great extent a repetition of the middle period; however, the porcelain reflected the influence of the Louis XVI style. See *Faïence*; *Trompe l'Oeil*; *Haguenau*.

STRASBOURG TUREEN

Strawberry Dish In English silver; a shallow circular fruit dish, deeper than a plate. It generally has a scalloped and ribbed border. It was introduced during the 18th century.

Straw Work In decorative art; the practice of ornamenting table tops, boxes, frames of mirrors and other similar articles with straw, which after it is split into the required widths is bleached and dyed and laid in designs with the aid of adhesive on the surface of the article to be decorated. In the more ambitious examples the decoration was in the form of floral marquetry, landscapes and figure subjects. Straw work as a form of decoration was highly developed in Italy, France and Spain during the 17th century. Dunstable seemed to be the chief center of production in England for this type of work during the second half of the 18th century. This craft was greatly stimulated during the Napoleonic wars by French war prisoners skilled in the art of straw work marquetry.

Stretcher In cabinetwork; a horizontal crosspiece in various forms joining the legs of chairs, settees, stools, benches and tables. Essentially the stretcher was used to provide additional strength and it varied from simple to richly ornate forms. Some of the earliest stretchers were found in Gothic tables of trestle construction which occasionally were stretchered, and in the early chairs with stretchers close to the ground, superseding the Gothic chair of box-like form enclosed to the ground. During the cabriole leg period stretchers were generally discarded. Chippendale reintroduced them in his designs for chairs and tables with straight legs. They were also employed in some cabinetwork in the Neo-Classic taste. See *X-Form Stretcher*; *H-Form Stretcher*.

Stringing In English cabinetwork; stringing is a line or a very narrow band of wood or other material employed as an inlay in a contrasting ground for a decorative purpose.

Sycamore, boxwood and other light-colored woods were used for this purpose from the second half of the 16th century onwards. Delicate stringing lines were often inlaid on veneered mahogany surfaces in the Hepplewhite and Sheraton styles. In the succeeding Regency style stringing lines of brass were often employed.

Stuart, Early and Late　The term *Stuart* is applied to the period when the various members of the House of Stuart were the reigning monarchs of England. The term *Early Stuart* refers to the things pertaining to the reigns of James I, 1603–1625, and his son Charles I, 1625–1649. The term *Late Stuart* refers to the reigns of Charles II, 1660–1685, James II, 1685–1688, and also the reign of the latter's two daughters, Mary, 1689–1694, whose husband William of Orange continued to reign until 1702, and Anne, 1702–1714. The House of Stuart was succeeded by the House of Hanover in the person of George I of Hanover in 1714.

Stump Foot　In American cabinetwork; a form of plain quadrangular rear leg with a slight outward curve in which the foot as a separate portion from the leg disappeared and the leg continued directly to the floor. It was found on chairs having front legs of cabriole form. It is especially characteristic of the Philadelphia school of Chippendale furniture.

Stumpwork　A needlework, practiced in the 15th through the 17th centuries, which has the design or most of the design done in relief. The raised designs were produced by a foundation of cotton or wool. See *Needlework*.

Sturzbecher　In German ceramics; a Rhenish stoneware cup having a stem but no foot. The stem was in the form of the figure of a man. When the bowl of the cup was inverted the figure of the man was upright. It is especially identified with the salt-glazed stoneware made at Siegburg during the second half of the 16th century.

Style　In furniture; in the introduction of a style the ornament which is most easily understood appears first and is applied to the prevailing forms. This is generally referred to as a time of transition. Gradually the ornament is perfected and the forms for furniture are designed in the new fashion and are controlled by it. Each one of the great and acknowledged styles of furniture has distinct characteristics peculiar to itself and represents the manner of presenting a design in a given period. The same motifs are often used in the different styles but they vary in manner and treatment according to the prevailing dictates of fashion. For example, a Baroque shell motif is very different from a Rococo shell motif. A true style of furniture like any branch of the decorative arts truthfully and artistically interprets the spirit of the period to which it belongs. The more ambitious and elegant articles of furniture were always made for the very wealthy classes. These pieces expressed in their ornament and design the ultra mode of that particular fashion. The less affluent used furniture of similar design but treated in a more simplified manner. Much of the extant 17th and 18th century cabinetwork belongs to this latter category of which undoubtedly more was originally made.

SIEGBURG STONEWARE
STURZBECHER

Styles of Furniture

Gothic

	A.D.
French	1160–1515
English	1180–1558
Spanish	1200–1520
Italian	1200–1400

Renaissance

Italian	
Early	1400–1500
High	1500–1540
Late	1540–1600
French	
François I	1515–1547

Henri II	1547–1589
Louis XIII	1589–1643
English	
Elizabethan	1558–1603
Early Jacobean	1603–1649
Cromwellian	1649–1660
Netherlands	1520–1643
Spanish	1520–1620

French

Louis XIV	1643–1715
Régence	1700–1720
Louis XV	1720–1770
Louis XVI	1760–1793
Directoire	1793–1804
Empire	1804–1830

English

Late Jacobean	1660–1688
William and Mary	1689–1702
Queen Anne and Early	
Georgian	1702–1750
Chippendale	1745–1780
Adam	1765–1792
Hepplewhite	1780–1795
Sheraton	1790–1805
Regency	1795–1820

American

American Colonial	1630–1789
Jacobean	–1700
William and Mary	1700–1720
Queen Anne	1710–1755
Chippendale	1750–1785
American Federal	1789–1830
Hepplewhite	1785–1800
Sheraton	1795–1820
American Directoire	1805–1815
American Empire	1815–1830

NOTE. These styles are explained in the text of the dictionary under each respective name. The dates in this chart do not necessarily conform to those of the reigning monarch.

See *Baroque*; *Rococo*; *Classic Revival*; *Louis Philippe*; *Victorian*; *Biedermeier*; *Georgian Period*; *Charles X.*

Sucket Fork In English silver; a fork used for sweetmeats during the Tudor period. It has a two-tined fork at one end and a spoon at the other.

SILVER SUGAR TONGS

Sugar Bowl In English silver; the sugar bowl was introduced during the first quarter of the 18th century. An early variety had a hemispherical body resting on a molded circular foot or occasionally on three small feet. The cover resembled an inverted saucer. A later form of sugar bowl had an inverted pear-shaped body. The cover was generally dome-shaped. In the second half of the 18th century a pierced sugar bowl with a blue glass lining was made. It was generally in the form of a classic vase with a high cover or it was shaped like a basket with a bail handle. A basket-shaped sugar bowl without piercing was made late in the 18th century. The sugar bowl was made in other shapes. It more or less followed the form of the teapot and coffee pot which was in accordance with the prevailing style.

Sugar Sifter In English silver; a silver ladle-shaped spoon used to sprinkle sugar. It consisted of a round bowl, which was perforated, with a curved handle. It was introduced in the late 18th century. It is sometimes called a berry spoon or ladle when the bowl was shaped like the bowl of a spoon.

Sugar Tongs In English silver; a small device for serving lumps of sugar from the sugar bowl to the tea cup, introduced during the first half of the 18th century. The early sugar tongs were scissor-shaped with loop handles and scrolled stems terminating in wide flat claws designed as a shell motif. Around 1750 a bow spring variety was introduced consisting of a pair of stems joined by a U-shaped piece with cast silver handles and terminating in claws designed as a shell or acorn motif. Toward the end of the 18th century the stems of the majority of sugar tongs conformed in design to the contemporary spoon.

Sukashi-Bori In Japanese metal art; the name given to pierced, perforated or ajouré chiselling. This type of chiselling is generally used in conjunction with a variety of metal carving in which the designs appear on both sides of the metal or more or less carving in the round. See *Niku-Bori*.

Sulphides In glass; see *Cameo Incrustation*.

Sultanabad Rug An Oriental rug woven in the Sultanabad district in Persia. The foundation is cotton, and the pile is wool and medium in length. The designs are essentially simplified old Persian designs. It is purely a commercial creation. The district of Sultanabad is one of the great commercial centers of modern Persian Oriental rugs. Other varieties of the Sultanabad rug are Savalan, Mahal, Muskabad and Arak. See *Persian Rugs*.

Sumi-Zōgan In Japanese metal art; the name *sumi-zōgan* or ink inlaying is given to a metal inlay work in which the design appears to have been painted on with India ink. It is usually a shibuichi ground inlaid with shakudo. The design is first cut or chiselled out of a small block of shakudo in relief with all the sides of the cuts sloping so that each cut is wider at its base. A block of shibuichi is then cut with grooves or channels which correspond perfectly to the parts of the design. The cut design of shakudo is then laid on and fixed into the grooves of the shibuichi. It is then ground down and polished until the inlaid design and the ground are perfectly blended. This process of metal inlay produces the most unusual and beautiful effects. The most common design subjects, which are typically Japanese, include bamboo, pine, peony, birds and geese or heron in the moonlight. See *Hon-Zōgan*; *Shakudo*; *Zōgan*.

Sunburst In ornament; a decorative motif designed to imitate the sun with its rays. In English furniture literature the term is given to the motif when the rays are either in a full circle or in a segment of a circle. A carved or inlaid sunburst in a deep lunette or recessed semi-circle was a favorite decorative motif on English Queen Anne style tallboys and was centered on the top and bottom center drawers. Sometimes in American furniture literature the term *rising sun* or *sunrise* is given to the sunburst motif when the carved rays are in the segment of a circle. This sunrise motif is more properly called a fan motif in America. A carved fan motif was a characteristic decoration on New England highboys designed in the Queen Anne style.

Sunderland In English ceramics; several potteries were active in Sunderland, County Durham, during the late 18th and early 19th centuries, making a rather inferior quality of cream-colored and white earthenware. The decoration was principally transfer-printed. The potteries were the North Hylton Pottery started in 1762, the Southwick Pottery founded in 1789, the Ford Pottery started in 1800, the Wear Pottery started in 1803 and the Southwick Union Pottery operating in 1802. The marks for the North Hylton Pottery were "Dixon & Co.", "Dixon, Austin & Co." over "Sunderland" and "J. Phillips Hylton Pottery", all impressed. The Southwick Pottery's mark was "Scott" impressed. The Ford Pottery's mark was "Dawson" impressed. The mark for the Wear Pottery was "Moore & Co." impressed. The Southwick Union Pottery's mark was "Union Pottery" impressed.

Sunflower In ornament; the decorative flower carving often found on Connecticut chests. It is also called an aster. See *Connecticut Chest*.

Sung In Chinese ceramics; the Sung dynasty ruled over China from A.D. 960 to 1127 and over the southern half from A.D. 1127 to 1279. The Tartar tribes invaded north China in 1127, and the reigning Sung emperor left his capital at K'ai-Fêng Fu and established his court at Hangchow which became the southern Sung capital. The Sung emperors were patrons of the arts, and all the arts flourished during their reigns. Ceramic art enjoyed one of its most

TZ'U CHOU VASE, SUNG

brilliant phases. T'ang earthenware with its low-fired lead glazes was supplanted by high-fired porcelaneous ware with feldspathic glazes. Porcelain and high-temperature glazes came into vogue late in the T'ang dynasty and by the Sung dynasty the fashion for porcelain was established. The term *porcelain* is used in the broad Chinese sense which includes, in addition to the white translucent body, grey and dusky bodies which have been fired to such a state of vitrification that they emit a musical note when struck. This musical note was the principal test of early porcelains in China. Painting in underglaze blue and overglaze enamels which was so typical of the later wares produced at Ching-Tê-Chên was not in vogue during the Sung period. Monochromes were in vogue and color effects were achieved by mixing coloring oxides in the glaze. In this manner a wide range of delicate and elusive tints were achieved; some were undoubtedly accidental and were chiefly due to the opalescent nature of the bubbly glazes. An important feature was crackle, which in the beginning was accidental but later purposely obtained. The refinement of form and color was a distinctive feature of the Sung monochromes. Potters in the ensuing centuries returned to them again and again for inspiration. The ornament on the Sung wares was obtained by carving, etching, applying stamped reliefs or by pressing in molds. The designs were notable for their free-flowing quality and delightful freshness. The Yüan dynasty, 1280–1368, is generally regarded in ceramics as an extension of the Sung dynasty. See *Chien Yao*; *Chün Yao*; *Ju Ware*; *Kuan Yao*; *Ko Yao*; *Ting Yao*; *Celadon*; *Tz'ū Chou*.

Supper Set   In Chinese ceramics; a number of small ornamental trays which when grouped together form a large tray of varying shape. The trays can be used individually or joined together. Especially praiseworthy are the K'ang Hsi Famille Verte supper sets consisting of 13 petal-shaped trays which form a lotus flower. In another characteristic

SUPPER SET, K'ANG HSI

grouping 4 triangular trays form a circle which is surrounded by 8 other trays forming a rosette.

Supper Table   In English cabinetwork; the term *supper table* is generally given to a variety of a mahogany circular tilting-top tripod table introduced around 1750. It continued to be made until about 1780–1790. The difference between a tea table of tripod form and a supper table was that the top of the latter was divided into compartments which were used to hold plates or cups and saucers for an informal supper. One variety had a shaped molded top fitted with eight circular dished compartments for plates. It was mounted on a turned shaft which rested on a tripod base. In another variety the eight compartments were not completely separated from each other. The circular top had a molded edge of eight scallops and had a raised center portion. The outer edge of the raised center portion was in eight concave arcs. The inner part of the central portion was dished to form a central quatrefoil depression. Sometimes it was designed with ten compartments and had a cinquefoil depression. The average diameter was about 30 inches. See *Tea Table*; *Tripod Table*.

Sureau Wood   The wood of the elder tree, *sambucus nigra*, used for inlay and cabinetwork; it is hard and its color is yellow.

Surtout   The French term given to the ornamental centerpiece for the dining table, fashionable in the second half of the 18th century. These long and low finely wrought surtouts usually made of gilded bronze, silver or porcelain were also in vogue in America and were generally considered essential for state dinners in Boston, New York and Philadelphia. See *Plateau*.

Susa Ware   In ceramics; see *Persian and Near Eastern Pottery*.

Sussex   In English ceramics; during the late 18th and early 19th centuries slipware was made in a number of towns in Sussex. Essentially most of it was rather crude. However, at Brede and Chailey in Sussex and at Bethersden in Kent, a more interesting variety of slipware was made. The designs comprising stars, circles, foliage and formal patterns were incised or impressed and were inlaid with white clay. Included among the wares were pocket flasks and drinking mugs in the form of pigs.

Sutherland Table   In English cabinetwork; a small, oblong, drop-leaf table, having a very narrow top which was only about 7 or 8 inches in width when the leaves were dropped. A principal difference between the Sutherland table and the Pembroke table was that the leaves of the former when raised were supported on legs which swung out rather than on wooden brackets. The Sutherland table was introduced early in the 19th century and was made by such firms as Gillow's and Seddon's.

Suzuri Bako   In Japanese art; the suzuri bako or ink-stone box was designed to hold the ink-stone or suzuri and the small water-dropper or mizu sashi used in writing or painting. The black oblong ink-stone has a flat depressed center portion which slopes slightly toward one end to form a well. The ink, in the form of an ink-stick or sumi, was made by boiling a type of glue or fish oil and pine soot together with some scented material such as musk. In order to make ink a little water is dropped from the water-dropper into the well, called *umi* meaning sea, and the ink-stick is dipped in the water and rubbed on the stone until the desired blackness is attained. This liquid ink is also called sumi. It appears that sumi, which is given the English name of India-ink, was introduced into Japan at a very early date, since Chinese calligraphy was used for the first time in Japan in the 3rd century. The ink-stone box is chiefly made of wood and is very often lacquered. Many of these lacquer boxes are highly prized as collector's items, since the

suzuri bako is one of the several choice articles on which the lacquer worker expended his greatest skill. See *Writing Equipage*.

Swag   In ornament; the swag motif is the same as the festoon motif. See *Festoon*.

Swan Neck   In cabinetwork; the term is applied to a variety of pediment in which the form consists of opposed S-curves that scroll over at the top and terminate in paterae. The center space between the two S-scrolls generally has a low plinth surmounted with some decorative feature, such as a vase. See *Pediment*.

Swan Neck Handle   In silver; a handle which is arched in the form or shape of a swan's neck or S-curve.

Swansea   In English ceramics; the Cambrian Pottery in Swansea, Glamorganshire, Wales, was operating at least as early as 1765 and was active until 1870. The reputation of Swansea rests upon a soft paste porcelain made from 1814 to 1822, having some of the qualities of whiteness and translucency associated with Nantgarw porcelain. Included among the marks were the names of the town, the pottery and the different proprietors. The name "Swansea" was a more or less usual mark for the porcelain; the usual marks for the pottery were "Dillwyn" over "Swansea" and "Dillwyn & Co." The forms for Swansea porcelain were distinctive for their refined simplicity and were in the contemporary Neo-Classic taste. Much of the ware was decorated in London to the order of dealers. The painted decoration executed at Swansea included flowers, fruit, birds, figure subjects and landscapes. As a rule the earthenware had little or no artistic merit. Practically all the different kinds of current Staffordshire wares were imitated, such as cream-colored and white earthenware, blue-printed ware, marbled and black basalt ware. Painting in colors was done and figures were also made. Another pottery called the Glamorgan

SWAN NECK PEDIMENT

Pottery was active from around 1813 to 1839, making earthenware similar to that made at Swansea.

TSUBA WITH
SWASTIKA DESIGN

Swastika In ornament; a primitive symbol or motif in the form of a cross having arms of equal length with equal extensions projecting at right angles from the end of each arm and all projecting in the same direction. There are two kinds of swastikas, namely the right-handed and left-handed swastika. The left-handed is more popular in Japan where it is employed as a symbol of Buddhism, meaning good fortune or luck. It was a characteristic motif in Oriental rug design.

Swatow In Chinese ceramics; the name generally applied to a type of porcelain ware introduced during the Sung dynasty. It is characterized by a rather unrefined finish and a gritty foot rim caused by placing it on sand in the kiln. The ware is most usually found in the form of large bowls made during the Ming period decorated in red and green enamel or in blue and white. Much of this ware was exported to Japan and islands of the Pacific from a southern China port believed to have been Swatow. Much of this ware is found in Japan under the name of gosu-akaye. The enamelled Swatow pieces bear a marked similarity to the red and green ware of the later Ming period. The designs were most frequently arranged in a repetitive manner with panelled borders and the subjects included stylized plants, dragons, animals and birds such as the phoenix. This work was executed with free and swift brush strokes and displays a strong Oriental feeling. The underglaze blue ware, while not having the perfected technique of the Imperial ware, is charming for its freedom of design expression.

Sweet Gum Wood In American cabinetwork; see *Bilsted*.

Sweetmeat Glass In English glass; during the 18th century the sweetmeat glass was generally in the form of a saucer-shaped bowl mounted on a stem and circular foot. This glass is usually but not always called a dessert glass. It was used for serving sweetmeats and comfits.

Sweetmeat Jar In English glass; see *Honey Pot*.

Swell-Front In cabinetwork; see *Bow-Front*.

Swing-Leg In English cabinetwork; the name applied to a type of leg introduced early in the 18th century. This type of leg was found particularly on the Early Georgian drop-leaf dining table. The leg was secured on a pivot which swung out to support the flap. This swing-leg is not to be confused with the stretchered gate-leg. The swing-leg was used on the Queen Anne card table until around 1715 when it was largely superseded by a form of construction called a concertina movement. See *Gate-Leg Table*; *Dining Table*; *Card Table*; *Concertina Movement*.

Swinton In English ceramics; see *Rockingham*.

Swiss Embroidery The name generally applied to the beautiful and delicate white embroidery work made by the peasants of Switzerland during the first half of the 19th century. The work was executed upon fine linen or muslin in satin stitches and other embroidery stitches with white thread. Swiss work resembles Madeira work, Irish work and broderie Anglaise.

Sword In arms and armor; a hand weapon made of metal consisting of a rather long blade and provided with a hand grip or hilt which is usually of a protective nature. Swords were made in a variety of types. See *Rapier*; *Saber*; *Scimitar*; *Smallsword*; *Cutlass*; *Yataghan*.

Sycamore Wood *Acer pseudoplatanus*. In English cabinetwork; the designs for English marquetry were often cut from sycamore wood as well as from holly, box and pear;

in particular for the arabesque foliage designs during the William and Mary style which were done in quieter tones. See *Harewood*.

Syllabub The name given to an English drinking glass made during the late 17th and 18th centuries. An early form of the syllabub glass was the same as a posset cup and had two handles and a spout. It is also called a Whipt-Syllabub glass. A later type largely conformed to the bell-shaped English jelly glass and sometimes had in addition two handles. It was used for serving syllabub, which is an old English drink made of cream or milk that is curdled by adding wine or cider and generally sweetened and spiced.

DROP-LEAF DINING
TABLE WITH SWING-LEG

T

Tabard In medieval armor; a short coat either with short sleeves or without any sleeves worn by knights over their armor. It was generally emblazoned with the arms of the knight. The name is also given to a similar coat worn by heralds and emblazoned with the sovereign's arms.

Tabernacle In ecclesiastical art; a richly worked receptacle or repository for the pyx containing the consecrated Host. It is also often used as a receptacle for relics. An elaborately ornate canopied structure, such as a shrine or tomb, is called a tabernacle. The term is also applied to a canopied niche or recess in a wall holding an image. These canopies over niches were remarkable for their richly carved work or elaborate tracery. Sometimes they were richly cusped and surmounted with crocketed gables, and were often placed in pairs side by side or in a row. In architecture the term *tabernacle work* is given to richly carved tracery, similar to that customary in canopied niches, employed on ecclesiastical screens, pulpits and stalls. Architectural work in which tabernacles are a marked feature is also called tabernacle work.

TABERNACLE MIRROR, AMERICAN

Tabernacle Mirror In American furniture; a rectangular architectural type vertical wall mirror having a cornice and columns at each side. Mirrors of this type, which were commonly gilded, were popular from about 1795 to 1820. The term *tabernacle* has been applied to them because of their supposed architectural resemblance to a tabernacle. Many of these mirrors had acorns or balls attached under the cornice. Above the mirror portion was a smaller panel of either wood or glass enhanced with a decorative painting. The themes for this painted decoration were often of a patriotic nature, such as an American eagle, the American flag, ships, or a naval battle of the War of 1812.

Tabernacle Work In ecclesiastical art; see *Tabernacle*; *Crozier*.

Table In cabinetwork; the table, which is defined as an article of furniture consisting of a flat top of wood or some similar solid material supported on legs or a central pillar, was known in classical antiquity and was principally used for the serving of meals. As a rule each person had his own individual table and it was generally placed next to the couch on which the dinner guest was reclining. One characteristic type had an oblong top resting on three rectangular tapering straight legs. One form of Egyptian table had a round top mounted on a central support. During the Middle Ages the table was principally used for dining and it was usually of trestle form, having a removable top resting on trestle supports. The table with a frame constructed by a joiner came into use during the Middle Ages, although it did not supplant the trestle form table until a later date. The development of the table from medieval times to the 19th century has been one of increasing specialization. Tables for cards and games, for dressing, writing, needlework and for serving tea, as well as side tables, pier tables, sideboard tables, occasional tables and numerous others were all gradually evolved. As in all categories of cabinetwork the 18th century was the great period for table making.

Table à Ecran In French furniture; a French term applied to a table fitted with a screen that rises from a slot along the rear edge of the top. The screen was usually made of silk or India painted paper and was enclosed in a narrow frame. The purpose of the screen was principally to keep the draft of air from blowing the candle flame. It was chiefly found on certain small writing tables, night tables and work tables. See *Screen*.

LOUIS XVI TRIC-TRAC TABLE
French, late 18th century

LOUIS XV CONSOLE
French, c. 1740

RENAISSANCE CENTER TABLE
WITH DOLPHIN SUPPORTS
Italian 16th century

CHIPPENDALE SUPPER
TABLE *English, c. 1755*

CHIPPENDALE CHINA TABLE
English, c. 1760

SHERATON SOFA TABLE
English, c. 1800

LOUIS XVI BOUILLOTTE
TABLE *French, c. 1780*

CHIPPENDALE DROP-LEAF
BREAKFAST TABLE
English, c. 1760

REGENCY DRINKING TABLE
English, c. 1815

LOUIS XV HARICOT
OCCASIONAL TABLE
French, c. 1750

DIRECTOIRE TRICOTEUSE
French, late 18th century

SHERATON DROP-LEAF GAMING
TABLE *English, late 18th century*

CHIPPENDALE TRAY-TOP TEA
TABLE *American, c. 1760*

SHERATON DRUM TABLE
English, late 18th century

LOUIS XVI CABARET
French, c. 1775

EARLY GEORGIAN CARD
TABLE *English, c. 1740*

ADAM PIER TABLE
English, c. 1775

GUARD ROOM TABLE
Spanish, 17th century

QUEEN ANNE CORNER TABLE
WITH A TRIANGULAR DROP-LEAF
American, c. 1730

EARLY GEORGIAN EAGLE
CONSOLE TABLE
English, c. 1735

Table à Gradin In French cabinetwork; see *Gradin*.

Table à Ouvrage In French cabinetwork; the small French work table equipped with the accessories for needlework was distinctive for its delicate and graceful form. It was introduced during the Louis XV style. It was finely veneered and frequently enriched with marquetry, and often had a marble top. One characteristic variety had two or three shallow drawers, and the slender legs were joined with an undershelf. Sometimes the work table had a rising candle screen in the rear. Originally the work table was called a chiffonnière. The French term *tricoteuse*, which refers to a knitter or knitting machine, was applied to a certain kind of work table which had a high wood or metal gallery around the top in order to contain safely the balls of knitting wool. Gradually the term *tricoteuse* was given to other forms of work tables.

Table à Papillon In French cabinetwork; a small French toilet table fitted with a framed mirror and toilet accessories. It was so-called because of its supposed resemblance to the shape of a butterfly. See *Poudreuse*.

Table Chair In English cabinetwork; see *Chair Table*.

Table de Chevet In French cabinetwork; a bedside table. This small table was principally designed with a shallow cupboard compartment, and occasionally with a drawer and cupboard compartment. It was mounted on long slender legs. Frequently the shallow cupboard compartment was fitted with two tambour doors.

Table de Jeu The French term for a card table or a gaming table. See *Card Table*.

Table Gigogne In French cabinetwork; a nest of tables. One variety consisted of four graduated tables so designed that each table could be drawn out of each other. Another interesting variety was made with a circular top mounted on four straight legs joined with a cross stretcher. It was provided with four small tables of equal size having a quadrant-shaped top and three straight legs joined with a quadrant-shaped shelf. The tops of the four small tables were equal to the circumference of the large top, and when they were not in use they were placed under the top of the large table with their shelves resting on the cross stretcher. See *Nest of Tables*.

Table-Pétrin In French Provincial cabinetwork; a dining table having an oblong top extending well over an oblong shallow cupboard or compartment mounted on four sturdy legs. The top was removable and the bin served as a kneading trough or pétrin. It was a characteristic piece of peasant furniture.

Table Tronchin In French cabinetwork; the architect's table was introduced during the Louis XV style. A characteristic variety had an oblong top over a frieze drawer and lateral pull-out slides with leather panels. The leather panelled top was designed as an adjustable writing and drawing board and was supported by a rising easel rest. The table was mounted on four legs. See *Architect's Table*.

Tabouret In cabinetwork; a French term originally applied to a small drum, which this form of seat is sometimes believed to resemble. It is a low seat or stool, without arms or back, for one person. During the Louis XIV style it was principally designed with a square seat and occasionally with a round or oval seat mounted on four straight legs or legs of X-form. The seat of the tabouret was richly upholstered in silk damask, velvet or some similar material. In France the king occupied a chair, and the privilege to sit upon a tabouret or stool in his presence was restricted to the wives of the royalty and nobility. In England from Elizabethan times these same Continental rules were also observed and tabouret etiquette was followed as late as the Court of George II.

LOUIS XIV TABOURET

Tabriz Rug An Oriental rug belonging to the Persian classification. It is of an exceptionally fine weave. The warp is cotton, sometimes linen or silk. The weft is cotton, single-stranded wool or linen. The pile is of a selected wool and is short and very compact. The ends are usually finished with a narrow web and loose warp threads. It is distinctive for its rich colors which are beautifully blended, for its fine texture and for the interesting composition of its designs. See *Persian Rugs*.

Taces In armor; the terms *taces*, *tassets* and *tuilles* are frequently used interchangeably. The taces and tassets, which are similar, are laminated pieces of plate to protect the thighs. The pointed protective pieces for the thighs on Gothic armor are called tuilles.

Tachi In Japanese arms; the earliest type of single-edged Japanese sword. It succeeded the very early ken which was double-edged. The tachi, which was discarded as a fighting sword many centuries ago, is now a state sword. The katana, a similar sword, supplanted the tachi as a fighting sword. The difference between a tachi and a katana is in the manner in which it was carried. The tachi was suspended from the sash by two cords with the blade edge downward, and the katana was thrust in the sash with its edge upward. The fittings on a tachi are of different shapes from those on the usual swords and are known by different names. See *Katana*.

Taffeta The name given to various cloths made with a plain weave, especially a closely woven silk characterized by a fine cross rib and having a smooth and crisp quality. In early times the name was applied to plain woven silks and by the 17th century to silk fabrics with a luster or gloss. Taffeta was used for cushions and bed hangings in England from early in the 17th century. It appears that a watered taffeta in various colors, which was plain, flowered or striped, was rather widely used for different kinds of hangings. See *Silk*.

T'ai Ch'ang In Chinese periods; the T'ai

Ch'ang reign of the Ming dynasty of China, 1620. See *Chinese Dynasties*.

Taka-Bori In Japanese sword mounts; carving in high relief. See *Bori*.

Taka-Makie In Japanese lacquer; the name given to lacquer decoration in relief. See *Japanese Lacquer*.

Takatori In Japanese ceramics; pottery ware was originally produced at Takatori in the province of Chikusen by two potters from Korea during the latter part of the 16th century. These two potters, Shinkuro and Hachizō, were later assisted by Igarashi Jizayemon from Karatsu. Takatori utensils for the tea ceremony are highly esteemed by the tea masters since these early wares were produced under the supervision of Kobori Enshū, 1579–1647, a famous tea master of Fushimi. Takatori wares which are wheel-thrown are made of a fine clay that is generally light grey, nearly white or reddish in color. The glaze is a rich dark brown in which different shades of brown are seen, such as a golden brown, olive brown and a purplish brown. Occasionally a light fawn-color glaze occurs. The wares also include figures of Japanese deities and animals in different colored glazes.

Taka-Zōgan In Japanese sword mounts; the term applied to hon-zōgan inlay when it projects above the surface. See *Zōgan*.

Ta Kuan In Chinese ceramics; see *Kuan Yao*.

Talavera de la Reina In Spanish ceramics; majolica and faïence were made at Talavera de la Reina and at neighboring Puente del Arzobispo in Castile from early in the 16th century, continuing into the 18th century. No factory marks were ever used. They developed an original style of painting remarkable for its vigor but having little refinement. The colors were dominated by a powerful green, a canary yellow and a thick orange, and to some extent by a heavy blue. Horsemen, hunting scenes, buildings, trees, animals, birds, figures and coats-of-arms were much favored as motifs. The

TACHI

distinctive and interesting forms were to a large extent of traditional Spanish shape and included broad flat-bottomed jugs, helmet-shaped ewers, very large basins and dishes and globular jars and two-handled vases. During the 18th century the wares reflected the influence of the faïence made at Alcora. It has also been suggested that the scented red pottery or buccaro made in Central and South America and imported to Spain was also made here.

Tallboy In English cabinetwork; the term given to a double chest of drawers or a chest-on-chest introduced around 1700 in England. The term may also be applied to a chest of drawers on a stand, which was introduced around 1680 and which, when it was designed with drawers in the stand, was similar in design to the American highboy. However, this article is more often referred to in English furniture literature as a chest of drawers on a stand. The double chest of drawers was popular in England until around the middle of the 18th century, when other forms of bedroom furniture, such as the clothespress, were introduced. However, there was some demand for double chests of drawers throughout the 18th century. See *Chest-on-Chest*; *Chest of Drawers on a Stand*.

Tallboy Bureau In English cabinetwork; see *Secretary Chest-on-Chest*.

Tall Case Clock In cabinetwork; the term is applied to any clock having a tall, narrow case which rests upon the floor. In England the narrow, tall case clock first made its appearance about 1660. Prior to this time the clock was suspended by a wall bracket with the weights hanging. The tall case was invented to protect the weights from interference. With the invention of the long and heavy pendulum with its relatively very short swing, about 1670, the trunk of the tall case clock became slightly wider. It not only became an instrument of great precision but also an important piece of decorative furniture. The cabinetmaker expended all his skill in decorating the case. A characteristic English tall case clock is

HEPPLEWHITE TALL
CHEST OF DRAWERS

about $6\frac{1}{2}$ feet high. It is composed of a hood, trunk and base. The hood, which enclosed the movement of the clock, was flanked by colonettes and was surmounted by a frieze and a molded cornice. The slightly projecting hood rested on a long trunk which was fitted with a door. The trunk was mounted on a slightly projecting base. The early case clock was usually panelled and veneered with walnut. The more elaborate examples after 1680 were decorated with marquetry, oysterwood parquetry or lacquer work. The French tall case clock was richly decorated with marquetry and bronze appliqués. Philippe Caffieri, 1634–1716, Jacques Caffieri, 1678–1755, and André Charles Boulle, 1642–1732, are especially famous as the makers of beautiful French tall case clocks. Daniel Marot is well known for his designs of tall case clocks which he made for André Charles Boulle. The tall case clock was first made in America around 1730 and continued in vogue until around 1840. As a rule it was made of mahogany. The tall case clock was not made in any considerable quantity in America until around 1775 when the case clock with a scrolled pediment that centered a low plinth became fashionable. See *Miniature Tall Case Clock*; *Clock*.

Tall Chest of Drawers Or High Chest of Drawers. In English and American cabinetwork; the tall chest of drawers was developed around the middle of the 18th century. The typical variety was designed with a single row of two or three small drawers beneath which were five or six graduated long drawers. It rested on bracket feet. The difference between a chest-on-chest and a tall chest of drawers is that the latter has all its drawers constructed in one section. The term is also given to an earlier variety of tall chest of drawers that rested on a frame or low stand rather than directly on bracket feet. The stand which was without drawers was commonly designed with rather short cabriole legs. This type is more commonly found in American cabinetwork. See *Chiffonier*, in French cabinetwork; *Tallboy*.

Tambour Desk In English and American cabinetwork; a general term applied to a desk having a form of tambour construction. The favorite type of tambour desk in America had a hinged writing lid which was before a low oblong superstructure fitted with two lateral tambour slides and a central solid cupboard door. The slides and cupboard door opened to fitted small drawers and pigeonholes. The hinged writing lid was over two rows and occasionally three rows of drawers which were mounted on slender tapered legs. Occasionally the lower section was designed with four graduated drawers and was mounted on bracket feet. It was made in the Hepplewhite and Sheraton styles. See *Cylinder Desk*.

Tambour-Front In cabinetwork; the term applied to a form of sliding door used on cabinets, cupboards and writing desks, during the latter part of the 18th century. It consisted of slender strips of wood, with convex surfaces, glued vertically and adjoining each other on a canvas backing. The door would slide along the sides of the interior. The top on a cylinder desk was constructed in the same manner except that the slats were affixed horizontally and opened in an upward sliding manner. See *Tambour Desk*; *Bonheur du Jour*.

Tambour Lace A variety of embroidery work of Near Eastern and Far Eastern origin which in more recent times has been called tambour lace. It was unknown in Europe until the middle of the 18th century when it was introduced in Saxony and Switzerland, and in England about 1820. It derives its name from the tambour frame on which it is worked. This frame consists of two hoops, one fitting within the other, on which the material is stretched in the manner of a drum or tambour top. The designs which are copied from a drawing on paper are worked on a net ground material, in a cotton or floss thread which is drawn through the net with a hooked or tambour needle. See *Limerick*.

Tambour Stitch A decorative stitch used in embroidery, resembling the links of a chain.

It is similar to the chain stitch. See *Embroidery*.

Tanagra Statuette A small terra cotta figure or statuette found in large numbers at Tanagra, Greece. Tanagra figures were used as household gods or ornaments and were placed in temples or buried in tombs. Genre figures and statuettes or graceful girls in standing or seated positions made during the 4th and 3rd centuries B.C. are particularly noted for their charm and artistic quality. Many of these figures have painted decoration.

Tang In arms; the part of a knife, sword or edged tool that is inserted in the handle or hilt. In Japan the armorers signed their blades for knives, spears and swords on the tang.

T'ang The T'ang dynasty of China, A.D. 618 to 906, has been called the great age of Chinese art and literature. Sculpture, painting and the lesser arts flourished during T'ang times. In Chinese ceramic art; T'ang pottery reached a high plane of development. T'ang pottery in collections is mostly from the tombs as was the pottery of the Han period. Included among the specimens of T'ang articles are bowls, dishes, ewers, jars, figures in costume and armor, horses and camels. Numerous models buried with the dead are of objects that surrounded them in life. The body of T'ang ware varies from a soft pottery to a porcelaneous ware. It is usually a soft white material similar to plaster of Paris and varies in color from white to pinkish white to buff. Although some figures are unglazed, they usually have a neutral glaze that has a tendency to yellow, and both types are decorated with unfired colors. The same glaze, which is colored with blue, green and brownish-yellow, is used on the finer figures. The decoration was more or less of simple technique. It consisted of pressing in molds, incising with a pointed tool and stamped reliefs appliquéd on the surface. Frequently the ground was cut away with a knife, leaving the design in relief. The stamped reliefs

SHERATON TAMBOUR DESK, AMERICAN

were usually medallions or palmettes, frequently having intricate designs. Stamped reliefs also included small figures of animals, rosettes and occasionally human figures. Another incised ornament has the design outlined with a pointed instrument with the enclosed spaces covered with variously colored glazes. High-fired glazes such as celadon green, chocolate brown, cream white, flambé and grey were introduced during the T'ang period. The lead glaze on T'ang pottery colored with oxides that produce green, blue and brownish yellow differs from the Han glaze in that it has a paler hue, since it is applied on a light colored body or on a white slip.

Tankard Originally the term was applied to the hollowed logs bound with iron which were used to carry the water from the city conduits. Later the term was applied to drinking vessels formerly made of wooden staves and bound with metal, and now in particular to a tall jug or mug provided with a handle chiefly made of pewter, stoneware, earthenware and to some extent of silver, sometimes fitted with a lid and principally used for drinking beer. In English silver; in an early form of English tankard the body was made of a section of ox horn and was mounted with a silver base, bands, handle, cover and thumbpiece. Extant examples of horn tankards with silver mounts date from 1567. The tankard tapering slightly upward, resembling the section of an ox horn, and the cylindrical straight-sided tankard made of silver were introduced late in the 16th century. The silver tankard was provided with a lid, thumbpiece and handle and rested on a flat base. These capacious drinking vessels, which displayed several variations in shape, retained their popularity throughout the 18th century. See *Peg Tankard*.

Tanto In Japanese arms; a variety of dagger fitted with a guard or tsuba. The blade is slightly curved like the Japanese sword, but sometimes it is straight, and is rarely over 12 inches in length. The tanto is generally mounted with all the fittings used on the swords, which are usually elaborately decorated. See *Aikuchi*.

Tanzenmann The name given to a Swiss drinking vessel, generally made of wood. It was carved in the standing figure of a peasant who carried a large basket on his or her back which was used as a drinking cup. The basket, which was detachable, was edged with a wide silver band. It was introduced during the 17th century. In Germany this type of cup is called a *Buttenmann*.

Tao Kuang In Chinese periods; the Tao Kuang reign of the Ch'ing dynasty, 1821–1850. See *Chinese Dynasties*.

Tape Guipure Or Tape Lace. In lace-making; tape guipures or tape laces comprised much of the coarse bobbin-made laces produced in Italy, Spain and Flanders in the 17th and 18th centuries. They were chiefly characterized by flowing designs formed by decorative or plain braids or tapes about one eighth of an inch in width and joined together with either brides or a coarse réseau. They were worked in an endless variety of designs but they essentially retained a striking and flowing quality in their patterns formed of braids or tapes. Some lace centers in the 19th century, such as Devonshire, made large quantities of a coarse and inexpensive tape lace in the form of collars and cuffs.

Tape Lace In lace-making; see *Tape Guipure*.

Taper Box In English silver; a device used to seal letters with wax. It consists of a small cylindrical box, having a chimney-shaped top, through which the end of the taper coil passes. The coil of taper wax itself is contained in the box.

Taper Jack In English silver; a device used to seal letters with wax. It was made in several different shapes. One characteristic variety consists of a small pear-shaped silver frame standing on a spreading foot. It rests on a small flat tray with a handle. A horizontal spindle, through the center of the frame, supports a coil of wax taper, the end of

CARVED WOOD
TANZENMANN

which passes through a narrow opening at the top of the frame, in which it is secured when lighted. It was introduced around 1700.

Taper Stick In English silver; a miniature candlestick used for melting wax to seal letters. The taper stick was intended for use on the writing table. Sometimes it was secured to an inkstand, or it formed the top part of the lid for the small box which held the wafers. It was introduced around 1680. See *Wafer-Box*.

Tapestry In textiles; a hand-woven fabric. The weft threads do not run from selvage to selvage, but form the pattern, each one being worked with a bobbin back and forth over the warp threads, only where its particular color is needed. In this manner the warp threads are completely covered and are apparent only as ribs. Therefore a tapestry is a bobbin-made ribbed fabric with the surface consisting entirely of weft threads. It is exactly alike on both sides except for irregular loops of thread on the back. In this it is unique. The wefts are soft and the warps are coarse, open slits being left where colors meet parallel with the warps. As a rule tapestries have ribs, hatchings and slits. The ribs form horizontal lines, the hatchings vertical lines and the slits diagonal lines. It is this line contrast which is the basis of tapestry texture. The most apparent feature and the most distinguishing feature of tapestries are the open slits. Tapestries are of early origin. The oldest extant tapestries are Egyptian. Tapestry wall hangings are generally divided into Gothic, Renaissance, Baroque, Rococo and Neo-Classic. The subjects are chiefly pictorial and are developed in accordance with the prevailing style of ornament. The subjects for the tapestries are chiefly religious, historical, allegorical, mythological and romantic. It is generally accepted that the finest tapestries were woven in France. The art of tapestry weaving was perfected during the 14th century at Arras and Paris, which were great tapestry centers. The technique of tapestry weaving as displayed in Gothic tapestries has never been surpassed. François Boucher, 1703–1776, the celebrated French painter and decorative artist, was undoubtedly the greatest tapestry designer of the 18th century. Tapestries woven from his cartoons at Beauvais and Gobelins are referred to as Beauvais-Boucher and Gobelins-Boucher. Also notable are the fine wall tapestries woven at Gobelins after the designs by Charles Antoine Coypel, 1694–1752. Especially outstanding are his series of twenty-eight designs illustrating Cervantes' story of Don Quixote. See *Brussels Tapestries*; *Tournay Tapestries*.

Tapestry Carpet In textiles; a hand-woven carpet of tapestry weave. It is woven exactly like a tapestry wall hanging. As compared to a wall tapestry the tapestry carpet is coarser, heavier and of simpler design. It has a ribbed surface that is comparatively flat. A tapestry carpet requires a heavy lining. See *Aubusson Carpet*; *Polonaise Rug*; *Khilim*.

Tapestry Furniture Coverings Hand-woven tapestries used in upholstery work were woven at all the important tapestry weaving centers in Europe. The 18th century in France was the great century for tapestry furniture coverings and much of the fine furniture was so upholstered. The fine sets for furniture coverings were woven at the Gobelins, at Beauvais and at different manufactories located in the city of Aubusson. The illustrations of La Fontaine's fables by Oudry inspired a large majority of the designs for the tapestry furniture coverings. His animal designs were superb. Jean Baptiste Oudry, d. 1755, was a well-known French animal painter. He was a designer of tapestries and was working at Beauvais in 1726 and at the Gobelins in 1733. Also much favored for furniture coverings were Boucher's delightful pastoral scenes with shepherds and shepherdesses.

Tappit Hen In pewter; a Scotch term applied to a pewter drinking vessel made with or without a lid. The body is cylindrical with the middle part slightly concave. It is fitted with a handle. Specifically the tappit hen contains a Scotch quart. By extension

PEWTER TAPPIT HEN

the name is given to any pewter vessel having the form of a tappit hen but of varying capacity. For example, if a mutchkin or a chopin is shaped like a tappit hen it is generally so called.

RENAISSANCE TAQUILLÓN
WITH VARGUEÑO

Taquillón   In Spanish cabinetwork; the name given to a characteristic variety of base designed to support a vargueño. The taquillón was surmounted on feet and was approximately of the same dimensions as the vargueño. It was designed in four equal compartments, being fitted with two upper drawers and two lower cupboard doors, or four of each. Above the compartments were two slides, which, when pulled out, supported the drop-front of the vargueño. The front of the taquillón was richly but not as lavishly designed as the interior of the vargueño. It was frequently inlaid with bone or ivory ornament and was decorated with gilded moldings or was carved with rosetted panels and lozenge motifs. The designs were invariably geometrical in character. See *Vargueño*; *Puente Stand*.

Taracea   In Spanish furniture; Spanish inlay work composed of minute dots of ivory. It was sometimes called granos de trigo because of its resemblance to grains of wheat.

Tarata Wood   See *Lemon Wood*.

Targe   Or Target. In armor; a shield. In particular, the round wood and leather buckler of the Highland clans which was studded with metal bosses and has a large spike extending from the center boss. Targe is also the name given to the small medieval tilting shield used by a horseman.

Tassets   In armor; see *Taces*.

Tassie, James   1735–1799, a Scottish gem engraver and modeler. Later he became associated with Dr. Quin in Dublin, and together they developed an enamel of a fine hard quality. From this enamel, Tassie made gems and medallions which are now called Tassie gems. In 1766 he moved to London where he produced his beautiful impressions of antique gems. He also pro-

duced many large profile medallion portraits. The medallions were cast in a white enamel paste. Some of his portrait medallions were made with just the head in enamel, with a background of tinted ground glass, which received its color tone from a colored paper placed beneath. After his death in 1799, his nephew, William Tassie, 1777–1860, who was also a gem engraver and modeler, continued James Tassie's business. He was successful in executing important pieces and in enhancing the famous collection of casts and medallions.

Tatting   In lace-making; the name given to a knotted lace made with a fine linen or cotton thread wound on a small shuttle. Generally it is delicate, light and lacy in texture. See *Lace*.

Taufschein   A German term correctly applied to a baptismal certificate. In America it is also frequently applied to a birth certificate of the Pennsylvania Germans, although the proper term for a birth certificate is *geburtsschein*. See *Fractur*.

Tavern Glass   In English glassware; heavy and sturdy drinking glasses made during the 17th and 18th centuries were generally known as tavern glasses.

Tavern Table   In English and American cabinetwork; the name given principally to a small table of the Jacobean style. The top is rectangular, octagonal, round or oval and extends well over the deep apron which is sometimes fitted with a drawer. The legs, which are connected with a box stretcher close to the floor, are frequently splayed.

Tazza   The term *tazza*, derived from the Italian word *tazza*, is in turn derived from the Persian word *tas*, meaning a goblet. The word is now commonly given to a type of decorative drinking vessel having a wide circular shallow or saucer-like bowl properly mounted on either a stem and foot or on a foot. It was made of silver, Limoges enamel, Venetian glass and other similar materials. Especially distinctive were the beautifully wrought tazze made in the 16th century.

TAPESTRY—*Flemish, 15th Century, School of Arras.*
The Metropolitan Museum of Art, gift of Mr. and Mrs. Frederic B. Pratt, 1935.

EMBROIDERED CHASUBLE—*Spanish, early 15th Century.*
The Metropolitan Museum of Art, The Cloisters Collection, Purchase 1953.

DETAIL FROM EMBROIDERED SKIRT—*English, 18th Century.*
The Metropolitan Museum of Art, Rogers Fund 1961.

NEEDLEPOINT POLE SCREEN—*English, 18th Century.*
The Metropolitan Museum of Art, Rogers Fund 1952.

Tcherkess Rug See *Circassian Rug*.

Tchetchen Rug See *Tchichi Rug*.

Tchichi Rug An Oriental rug belonging to the Caucasian classification. It derived its name from a tribe of wandering mountaineers who weave them. The foundation is wool, and the pile is of a fine wool, medium in length. The ends are usually finished with a narrow web and with a fringe of loose warp threads. The patterns are a combination of Caucasian and Persian designs and are generally worked in a repetitive manner over the field to form a trellis design. Invariably the main border stripe consists of heavy parallel bars, diagonal to the side, separating pointed rosettes. It is also called Tchetchen or Tzitzi. See *Caucasian Rugs*.

Tea Caddy In English furniture; a small box or case to hold tea. The word *caddy* is believed to have been derived from the Malay word *kati*, or the Chinese word *catty*, which means a measure of weight equal to about one and one third pounds avoirdupois, and signified the small box in which the tea was sent to Europe. During the 18th century in England tea caddies were made in a great variety of materials, such as wood, porcelain, pewter, ivory, tortoise shell, brass and silver. However, the favorite materials were various woods, such as mahogany, rosewood and satinwood. The tea caddy was fitted with a lock and key for originally tea was an expensive commodity. The interior of the tea caddy was either partitioned and lead-lined for black and green tea or was fitted with canisters for the two types of tea. Wooden tea caddies were commonly square, oval, oblong, hexagonal and octagonal. Hepplewhite illustrated tea caddies of oblong, circular and oval form and recommended that the ornament be inlaid in various colored woods or painted. The tea caddy was distinguished by the high quality of its craftsmanship. Its contour and style of ornament were in accordance with the taste of the period. From an artistic standpoint those of the late 18th century with their delicate inlays and refined and graceful lines were especially pleasing and elegant. See *Tea Chest*.

Tea Canister See *Canister*.

Tea Chest In English furniture; an early name for a tea caddy which was still in common use around the end of the 18th century. In Chippendale's DIRECTOR, 1754, tea chests are listed among the pieces made by Chippendale. Hepplewhite's GUIDE, 1788, used both the names *tea chest* and *tea caddy*, and in Sheraton's CABINET DICTIONARY, 1803, he mentions that different kinds of tea chests are now called caddies. See *Tea Caddy*.

Tea Dust In Chinese ceramics; a glaze on porcelain ware developed during the Ch'ien Lung period which was a yellowish green or yellowish brown color sprinkled with a tea-green color.

Teakettle In English silver; the teakettle was generally made in the shape of the contemporary teapot, the chief difference being the position of the handle and the spout. The stand upon which the kettle rests is provided with a spirit burner. It was introduced at the beginning of the 18th century.

Teakettle Stand In English cabinetwork; the introduction of tea tables at the end of the 17th century led to the designing of small mahogany stands for the silver teakettle and its burner. An early variety which undoubtedly served many other purposes had a small circular top mounted on a turned shaft which rested on a tripod base. A characteristic variety of a mahogany kettle or urn stand in the Chippendale style had a small quadrangular top with a raised rim. The front of the shallow frieze was fitted with a small pull-out slide to hold the teapot. It rested on four slender legs. The width of the table averaged around 12 to 15 inches. Variations in design occurred. It was designed in the successive 18th century styles. By the end of the century the teakettle or urn stand was no longer fashionable. Although the early teakettle stand was found

VENEERED TEA CADDIES

in America in the Chippendale style the majority were made in the Hepplewhite and Sheraton styles.

Teakwood The wood of the East Indies teak tree, *tectona grandis*, which is widely used in cabinetwork. It is a strong, durable and hard wood and its color is yellowish brown. It is widely used for Indian furniture. Teakwood is often erroneously ascribed to Chinese cabinetwork, but it is never found in any traditionally proper pieces of Chinese furniture. See *Chinese Furniture*; *Tzu T'an*.

Teapot In English silver; it seems that tea, coffee and chocolate were first introduced in England around 1650. Coffee was never as popular as tea, and chocolate was chiefly considered to be a morning drink. The early English teapot, circa 1670, was tall. It had a tapering cylindrical body and spout, a conical cover, and a scrolled wooden handle fitted into silver sockets. Toward the end of the 17th century the teapot became shorter and the spout resembled a swan's neck. At the beginning of the 18th century the contour of the body was pear-shaped and it was fitted with a domed lid. Gradually the neck of the body was lengthened and the lower part of the body became more bulbous. Early in the 18th century a teapot was designed with a globular shaped body, being flattened at the top and bottom and resting on a molded foot. The teapot of globular form was followed by the teapot having the outline of an inverted pear. During the last quarter of the 18th century the form of the teapot was influenced by the Neo-Classic style. It was often oval or octagonal and had vertical sides and a flat base, and a straight tapering spout. It was frequently designed with a small stand mounted on four small feet. Variations occurred in all the forms of these teapots.

Teapoy In English furniture; a small tray-top table generally supported on three legs or on a central shaft resting on a tripod base. George Smith, who illustrated the teapoy in his HOUSEHOLD FURNITURE, stated that "they are used in the drawing room to prevent the

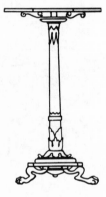

TEAPOY

company rising from their seats when taking refreshments." Because the word *tea* appears in the word *teapoy* it has been erroneously associated with tea. Due to this imagined connection with tea the term is sometimes given to a tea chest, fitted with canisters, mounted on legs or on a stand.

Tear In glass; the air bubble enclosed within glass for a decorative purpose. Sometimes it was produced accidentally but more frequently it was done purposely as a decorative feature. In English glass the tear first appeared in the stem. From around 1715 to about 1760 a cluster of more or less comma-shaped or spherical-shaped tears were found in the base of a bowl, a knop or a finial. See *Air Twist*.

Tea Service The accessories or utensils needed for a tea table which include the teapot, cream pitcher and sugar bowl. The addition of the coffee pot, teakettle and slop-basin is optional. Sometimes included are the cups and saucers and spoons. In English silver; in the first half of the 18th century although teapots, sugar bowls and cream jugs were made in the same contemporary style, complete tea services, or tea sets, which included the various pieces of the same style and date did not appear until the latter part of the 18th century. See *Tray*.

Teaspoon In English silver; a spoon usually holding half the amount of a dessert spoon. It was introduced late in the 17th century. The dessert spoon originated at the same time. Both the teaspoon and dessert spoon followed the pattern of the large spoon. See *Spoon*.

Tea Table In English cabinetwork; tables principally made for the serving of tea came into general use around the end of the 17th century. However, due to the popularity of tea gardens among the fashionable society in the first half of the 18th century, tea tables did not become plentiful until around the middle of the 18th century when

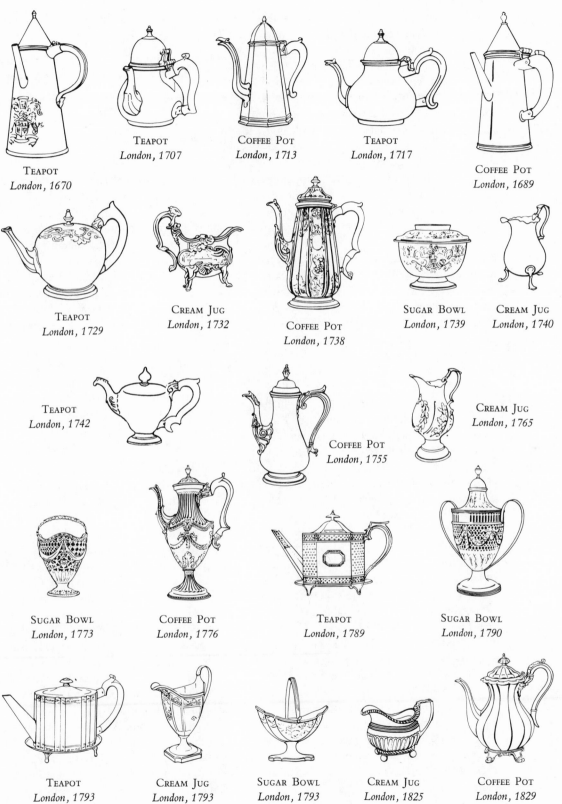

TEAPOT
London, 1670

TEAPOT
London, 1707

COFFEE POT
London, 1713

TEAPOT
London, 1717

COFFEE POT
London, 1689

TEAPOT
London, 1729

CREAM JUG
London, 1732

COFFEE POT
London, 1738

SUGAR BOWL
London, 1739

CREAM JUG
London, 1740

TEAPOT
London, 1742

COFFEE POT
London, 1755

CREAM JUG
London, 1765

SUGAR BOWL
London, 1773

COFFEE POT
London, 1776

TEAPOT
London, 1789

SUGAR BOWL
London, 1790

TEAPOT
London, 1793

CREAM JUG
London, 1793

SUGAR BOWL
London, 1793

CREAM JUG
London, 1825

COFFEE POT
London, 1829

the social custom of inviting friends for tea at one's home resulted in the designing of numerous suitable decorative mahogany tea tables in the Chippendale style. The principal variety was of tripod form and had either a shaped oblong or circular top mounted on a carved shaft which rested on a carved tripod base. The top was made with a carved raised edge or with either a delicately pierced gallery of fretwork or a gallery of baluster form spindles. Sometimes the circular top was carved with the so-called pie-crust edge. The top generally tilted so that the table could be placed against a wall when not in use, and it very often revolved. The cirular top having an average diameter of between 25 and 30 inches was very popular. A structural feature which was sometimes employed on this variety of table is commonly referred to as a bird-cage. Another characteristic variety of a mahogany tea or china table was designed in the Chinese taste. It had an oblong top with a delicately pierced fretwork gallery over a conformingly pierced frieze which rested on four straight quadrangular legs. Frequently the legs were joined with a serpentine X-shaped stretcher. Occasionally the top lifted off and could be used as a separate tray. The average length of the table was around 33 inches. The tea table of tripod form became fashionable in America around 1760. It seems that the English tripod table with its spindled gallery or pierced fretwork gallery was not made in America. During the Hepplewhite and Sheraton styles the Pembroke table became the fashionable form for the tea table. An early 18th century form of walnut tea table made in England and in America had an oblong molded and tray-shaped top over a frieze which was supported on four cabriole legs. Its average height was about $2\frac{1}{2}$ feet. The Chippendale style china table with an oblong top was also made in America and was designed with either a pierced or a solid gallery. See *Bird-Cage Support*; *Pie-Crust Table*; *Pembroke Table*; *Tripod Table*; *China Table*.

CHIPPENDALE TEA TABLE

Tea Tray In English furniture and silver; see *Tray*.

Tea Urn In English silver; a large urn-shaped vessel fitted with a lid and two looped handles. It usually rested on a base mounted on four small feet. It is generally used to hold the tea previously brewed or to hold the hot water for replenishing the teapot. It was introduced around 1760.

Teheran An Oriental rug belonging to the Persian classification. It derived its name from Teheran, a city in Persia. The foundation of the rug is cotton and the pile is wool and short in length. The Teheran rug varied in quality. In the finest Teheran the quality of the wool is excellent and the texture is compact. The designs, which are intricate, are copied from old Persian motifs. Rug weaving at Teheran is not an old industry. See *Persian Rugs*.

Tê-Hua In Chinese ceramics; a location in the Ch'üan-Chou district of the province of Fukien noted during the later part of the Ming period for the beautiful pure white porcelain known as Blanc de Chine. See *Blanc de Chine*; *Ming*.

Tekke Bokhara An Oriental rug belonging to the Turkoman classification. It is so named because it is woven by the Tekke Turkoman tribes of nomads. It is generally considered to be the finest of the Turkoman group. It is finely woven. The foundation is wool and the pile is fine wool and short in length. The ends are usually finished with a deep red web and a long fringe of loose warp threads. As a rule the pattern is composed of elongated octagons, each one being divided into four parts by lines. These lines of demarcation are heavy and hard and as true as those of a checkerboard. Each quartering is diversified by geometrical motifs. A conventionalized diamond-shaped motif fills the spaces between the octagons. All colors in the design are subordinated to the reds. The designs of the prayer rug made by the Tekkes are entirely different. See *Katchlie Bokhara*; *Turkoman Rugs*.

Telescopic Dining Table In English cabinetwork; Richard Gillow in 1800 patented a device to extend the length of a dining table. It consisted of slides operated with or without rollers that would operate on various types of grooves. These slides could be extended to the desired length and then the table boards or leaves were placed upon them. See *Gillow, Robert*.

Temmoku In ceramics; a comprehensive term given to a large variety of Chinese pottery, stoneware and semi-porcelain with a rich thick glaze in which predominate bluish, purplish-black or reddish-brown colors. In particular the term applies to one variety called Chien yao. See *Chien Yao*; *Honan Temmoku*; *Kian Temmoku*. The term *temmoku* is also a Japanese term, and it is the name given to these tea bowls of the Chien yao type having mottlings or fine streaks like the breast of a partridge or the fur or a hare. During the Ming period these bowls were much favored by the Japanese due to the importance of the tea ceremony. By extension the term is now given to tea bowls with a dark brown glaze.

Tempera The Italian term applied to the process of painting in the tempera medium; that is, powdered colors tempered or held in solution by the yolk of eggs. This method requires precision of touch and great skill in drawing because it does not permit corrections to be made easily. When correctly applied the colors are more brilliant and richer than work done in oil. The work in tempera of the Venetian painter Carlo Crivelli, c. 1430–c. 1493, has never been rivalled. Although the method is not entirely different from distemper, the term *tempera* is principally restricted to work in the fine arts, while *distemper* is usually reserved for work done on theatrical scenery, wall decoration and cartoons for tapestries. See *Distemper*.

Temperantia Salver In pewter; a finely decorated pewter salver characterized by a central boss which depicts in relief the figure of a woman representing Temperance with an inscription reading Temperantia. The salver is richly worked in delicate motifs. François Briot is reputed to have made the first temperantia salver, circa 1600.

Tempyo The Tempyo or Nara period of Japan; A.D. 710–794. See *Japanese Periods*.

Tent Stitch A short slanting stitch, which is used in needlework. It is done in even lines from left to right. It is the stitch commonly used in petit point. See *Embroidery*.

Tereh In Oriental rugs; a Perso-Turkish word meaning design. It is generally placed before the name of a design used in Oriental rugs; such as tereh Herati.

Term Or Terminal Figure. In cabinetwork; a term usually consisted of a quadrangular pillar which often tapered downward and was adorned with the figure of a head or the upper part of the body. The term originated in classic antiquity and was originally used to mark the limit or extent of anything, especially boundaries. The pedestal of term shape originated on the Continent. The characteristic gilt terminal pedestal consisted of a small molded top which rested on a classical female bust mounted on a quadrangular pillar. The pillar, which generally tapered downward, rested on four ornately scrolled feet or on a molded square plinth. Terms were mentioned in England as early as 1640. See *Pedestal*.

Terrace Vase In Swedish ceramics; a distinctive Rococo vase identified only with the wares made at Marieburg. The body of the vase was mounted on a base formed either of swirling waves or a winding flight of steps. Sometimes a rabbit or some other kind of animal was at the foot of the steps. See *Marieburg*.

Terra Cotta In ceramics; a hard-baked clay material that varies in color from deep red to a drab or pale buff depending upon the clay. It can be colored and also glazed; for example, the famous tin-enamelled terra cotta works of the della Robbias. A variety of articles are produced from terra cotta,

GILTWOOD TERM

such as statuettes, sculptured figures and architectural relief ornaments. Many fine terra cotta sculptures and reliefs were produced from early Greek and Etruscan times.

Terra Sigillata Ware In ancient ceramics; see *Arretine Ware*.

Terre de Pipe In French ceramics; a French term for a lead-glazed soft earthenware having a white body. See *Cream-Colored Earthenware*.

Terry Clock In American furniture; a rectangular form of bracket or mantel clock. It derived its name from Eli Terry, 1772–1852, who was the maker. It was an inexpensive clock. Eli Terry by using wooden works instead of the customary brass works was able to produce a cheaper clock. As a rule the mahogany Terry clock was characterized by a scroll-top case which generally centered a low plinth. The glass door was flanked by slender round pillars. It had a painted white wooden dial. The lower part of the glass door had an oblong painted panel. It had a valanced base finished in very slender bracket feet. The majority of Terry clocks were made between 1815 and 1837. The later date marked the beginning of the production of machine-made clocks with brass works. Terry style clocks were made by others as well as by Eli Terry and his family. Seth Thomas, who was in partnership with Eli Terry for a year in 1809, bought the rights to make similar clocks.

GLASS MUG WITH
APPLIED THREADING

Tessellated See *Mosaic*.

Tester In English cabinetwork; the canopy extending over a bed supported by the posts or suspended from the ceiling. See *Canopy*; *Bed*; *Field Bed*; *Lit à Colonnes*.

Tête-à-Tête In French cabinetwork; a French term, meaning a private conversation, given to a small upholstered canapé or settee for two persons. It was introduced in the latter part of the 18th century and was frequently placed on an angle to the fireplace forming a semi-circle with another tête-à-tête or a fauteuil for the persons or person seated opposite, or vis à vis.

The Hague In Dutch ceramics; a porcelain manufactory was started here around 1773 by Anton Leichner and was active until 1790. The mark which was the emblem of the city was a stork with a fish in its beak. It is thought that prior to 1776 the manufactory operated simply as a decorating establishment. The painted decoration was technically fine and showed finished workmanship; however, it was lacking in originality. Birds, flowers, cupids, and landscapes, sometimes with figure subjects, were characteristic motifs. The forms were in the early Neo-Classic style. Two faïence manufactories producing faïence in the Delft style were also operating at The Hague during the second half of the 16th century.

Thistle Glass In English glass; a glass of thistle shape which became popular during the reign of George I, 1714–1727. It had a shouldered, knopped or plain baluster stem.

Thomas, Seth 1785–1859. In American furniture; an American clock-maker. He was born at Wolcott, Connecticut. In 1809 he entered the partnership of Terry, Thomas and Hoadley. By 1813 he had his own business at Plymouth Hollow, Connecticut. See *Terry Clock*.

Thomire, Pierre Philippe French ciseleur working in the Louis XVI style. He produced metal work of the finest quality. Later in his career he worked in the Empire style. Some of his bronze appliqués for furniture designed in the Empire style were remarkable for their jewel-like quality. See *Gouthière, Pierre*.

Thread and Shell In English silver; see *Fiddle and Thread*.

Thread Circuit In English glass; a thin trail of applied glass or applied threads of glass chiefly used to decorate and encircle the rim of a bowl or the neck of a glass vessel. In American glass it is generally called threading and was a favorite form of applied decoration.

Threaded Edge In silver; a decorative

pattern used for edges and rims consisting of an engraved thread line. It was introduced early in the 19th century in England.

Threaded Glass In glass; threaded or filament glass was first made by the Romans, and was rediscovered and perfected by the Venetians around the beginning of the 16th century. It is a principal method for decorating glass. In this method threads of colored glass are ingeniously treated to form various patterns, such as plaited or reticulated patterns, lace glass or filigree glass. Vases with colored threads and filigree decoration are composed of many small colored glass canes. A filigree vase or bowl is fabricated from canes of colored filigree and of clear transparent glass. The glassmaker selects canes of various colors and patterns to form different combinations of filigree. After various processes the vase is produced and each cane, either colored or with a filigree pattern, serves to form a stripe. If during the course of fabrication the vitreous mass is given a slight twist the stripes, instead of being in a straight line, have a spiral direction. This spiral treatment is often seen in specimens of Venetian glass. See *Latticinio*; *Glass Cane*; *Venetian Glass*; *Glass*.

Three-Color Ware Or San Ts'ai. In Chinese ceramics; porcelain and sometimes stoneware or earthenware decorated on the biscuit with colored glazes used in washes over the designs set in a single colored ground. In order to confine the various colored glazes within their given spaces three different processes were employed. In one method the designs are outlined with threads of clay with the details in slight relief. In another method the designs are outlined by incised lines. Incising or sgraffiato work had been employed by the T'ang potter. In the third method the designs are carved in relief and are usually supplemented with openwork. The glazes include turquoise, yellow, purple, green and a dark violet blue. Occasionally a neutral colorless glaze is used for white; frequently, however, certain parts, especially the face and the hands, are unglazed. Although the ware is called Three-Color ware, in reality it is not confined to three. The early 15th century glazes were rather thick and were inclined to be opaque while the later or 16th century glazes became more transparent and smoother. These glazes were also used as monochromes during the Ming dynasty. The turquoise blue was especially effective. Evidence indicates that some Three-Color ware was made during the Hsüan Tê reign, 1426–1435. During the Ch'ing dynasty some porcelain ware was decorated with washes of colored glazes. The colors were principally green, yellow and aubergine and the glazes were transparent and sleek. Sometimes the glazes were applied in patches resulting in a spotted effect. This was often called egg and spinach glaze. See *Ming*.

Thumb Glass In English glassware; a late 18th century English drinking glass having indentations or impressions that fit the finger ends, so that the glass would not slip from the hand of an unsteady drinker.

Thumb-Nail In cabinetwork; a molding that slants downward in a concave curve to a narrow edge. It was often employed around the edge of the top of a lowboy or some other similar article.

Thumbpiece The name given to a metal protuberance attached to the lid and next to the handle of a drinking vessel such as a tankard by means of which the lid is raised by a person's thumb. It was designed in a variety of shapes; such as a lion, deer, dolphin, acorn, knuckle, twin pomegranates or some similar subject. It is also called a purchase or a billet.

Thurible In ecclesiastical art; see *Censer*.

Thuringia In German ceramics; a number of faïence and porcelain manufactories were situated in the forest region of Thuringia during the 18th century. Although some of the faïence produced here was of a very high standard, especially that produced in certain potteries having princely protection, the majority of faïence had little artistic importance. Essentially the manufacture

THUMBPIECE ON A
CHARLES II TANKARD

ELIZABETHAN TIGER
WARE JUG

catered to the middle class. The painted decoration was distinctive for its vigor, but had very little refinement. Especially characteristic was the use of strong, powerful high-temperature colors, which included a bright blue, a dry red, a greyish green, all tones of yellow and manganese. Cylindrical tankards were characteristic productions. Among the motifs which were conventionally treated were birds, trees, figure subjects and coarse chinoiseries. A number of porcelain manufactories were started here around 1770, essentially due to a plentiful supply of local clay. The porcelain industry is still flourishing. The rather coarse and greyish tone hard paste porcelain was produced by a cheaper process. Most of it had little artistic merit. Some of the factories were principally engaged in producing porcelain for the middle class market. These wares often closely imitated Meissen, even to the Meissen mark. See *Dorotheenthal*; *Erfurt*; *Abtsbessingen*; *German Porcelain*; *Gotha*; *Kloster-Veilsdorf*; *Limbach*; *Rauenstein*; *Groszbreitenbach*; *Volkstedt*; *Ilmenau*; *Wallendorf*.

Thuyawood The fragrant wood of an African tree, *callitris quadrivalvis*, used for inlay and cabinetwork. It is fine and hard and its color is brown spotted. It is also called thuja.

Tickenhall In English ceramics; some very early English slipware, perhaps of the 16th century, is generally attributed to Tickenhall, Derbyshire. The pottery is very hard and has a red body covered with a dark brown glaze. The rather primitive designs are made from small flat pads of white clay in the form of flowers, animal heads and similar motifs. A characteristic and popular form was a tall cylindrical mug having two loop handles near the base.

T'ien Ch'i In Chinese periods; the T'ien Ch'i reign of the Ming dynasty in China; 1621–1627. See *Chinese Dynasties*.

T'ien Shun In Chinese historical periods; the T'ien Shun reign of the Ming dynasty of China; 1457–1464. See *Chinese Dynasties*.

Ties In lace-making; see *Brides*.

Tiffany Glass In American glass; Tiffany or favrile glass was made by Louis C. Tiffany, 1848–1933, American artist and designer of decorative glass. He was president and art director of the Tiffany Glass and Decorating Company. See *Favrile*.

Tiger Skin Ware In Chinese ceramics; see *Hu P'i*.

Tiger Ware In ceramics; a contemporary English term given to Rhenish stoneware having a mottled brown glaze, because of the supposed resemblance of the glaze to the skin of a tiger. It was made during the 16th and 17th centuries and is particularly identified with the stoneware made at Cologne and Frechen. Especially characteristic were tiger ware jugs, frequently richly mounted in silver. See *Rhenish Stoneware*.

Tiles In ceramics; the use of pottery tiles for wall decoration had its origin in the Near East; the earliest specimens dating from the ninth century. Seville was an important center for the production of tiles made by various processes. Mosaic tile work or Alicatodos, which was a Moorish style, was very fashionable in Seville at the beginning of the 15th century. Valencia produced numerous blue-painted and occasionally luster-painted tiles during the latter part of the 15th century. Late in the 15th century painted tiles were made in Italy employing the Italian majolica technique and were of great beauty. Practically all the tiles made in Italy were used in pavements and only rarely for ceilings and never for wall decorations. The Italian majolica technique spread to Spain and to the Netherlands at the beginning of the 16th century where it was used as wall decoration. They developed in the majolica technique a style of pictorial painting over a large number of tiles which had never been done in Italy. The pictures made in Spain and Portugal were in imitation of the tapestries. France, Germany and Switzerland also adopted the technique of majolica tiles. The great development of

Dutch tiles in the form of small tiles and in large pictures dates from the 17th century and was principally active in Rotterdam and Friesland. A special feature in Dutch tiles during the 17th century was the gradual abandonment of polychrome painting in favor of monochrome painting in either blue or manganese purple. Chinese motifs were relatively rare. A charming variety of small figure subjects such as horsemen, soldiers, cavaliers, ladies, peasants and children were much favored. Especially fine and important were the sets of tiles painted to form pictures. The making of so-called Dutch tiles spread to England, France and Germany. During the 18th century throughout Europe the style of painted decoration was in accordance with the prevailing fashion; the Rococo style being later supplanted by the Neo-Classic style. See *Seville*.

Tilleul Wood The wood of the linden tree, *citrus medica*, formerly called lime, used for inlay and cabinetwork especially by the French ébénistes. It is soft and its color is pale yellow.

Tilting Chest In English cabinetwork; a medieval chest with carved decoration depicting scenes of tournaments and honors of the field of combat. See *Chest*.

Tilting-Top Table In English cabinetwork; see *Tea Table*; *Supper Table*; *Pie-Crust Table*; *Bird-Cage Support*.

Time Lamp The name given to a 17th century oil lamp used to indicate time. It consisted of a slender shaft resting on a dished base with a handle. The shaft supported a projecting wick cup which was surmounted with a clear glass oil cistern. The glass cistern contained marks to indicate time as the oil was consumed.

Ting In Chinese bronzes; the ting, which is a type of cauldron, was used in ritual ceremonies and also served as a cooking vessel. The body was round with three legs and sometimes square with four legs. It was provided with two lobes on the rim through which a rod or pole could be passed in order to carry the ting when it was hot. See *Li*.

Tin Glaze or Tin Enamel Glaze. In ceramics; a lead glaze made white and opaque by the addition of oxide or ashes of tin. The glaze may also be colored blue, brown, purple, black and other colors by the addition of metallic oxides. It is used on majolica and faience. Tin glazes, which had their origin in antiquity, were probably known in Spain as early as the 11th century and were used in Italy during the 14th century. See *Faïence*; *Majolica*; *Glaze*.

Ting Yao In Chinese ceramics; a white ware first made at Ting Chou. Although it was probably made as early as the T'ang dynasty it was perfected during the Northern Sung period. After the Sung court fled south in 1127, Ting ware was also made in the neighborhood of Ching-tê Chên. However, the production of Ting ware continued in the original locality. The fine plain white Ting ware had tear stains, lei hên, or straw-colored patches, generally on the outside of the bowls, caused by a thickening of the glaze. Chinese writers refer to the Ting ware with engraved decoration as hua hua, impressed decoration, yin hua, and painted decoration, hsiu hua; however, no specimen of the latter has been found. The three favorite motifs were the lily, the peony and the phoenix. The finer white Ting wares are distinguished by the names fên ting, or flour ting, and pai ting or white ting. The fine Ting wares had a close-grained greyish-white porcelaneous body with a smooth ivory white glaze that was beautifully mellowed. The name t'u ting or *earthy ting* was given to a coarser ware with a thicker and more yellow glaze that was finely crackled. As a rule the Ting bowls had a raw edge, as though placed in the furnace in an inverted position. This edge was commonly concealed with a metal band. The different Ting wares were widely copied in other localities during the Sung period as well as in the succeeding periods.

FAIENCE TILES, DUTCH

Tinja In Spanish ceramics; a large globular or pear-shaped pottery jar used for water, oil or wine. These big oil and water jars were a characteristic production of Seville and were often decorated with impressed reliefs of repetitive patterns, heraldic devices, Arabic inscriptions and similar subjects.

Toasting Glass In English glass; a drinking glass of fine quality having a deep conical bowl and a tall, exceptionally thin stem.

Toastmaster Glass In English glass; a tall stemmed drinking glass having an unusually thick bowl to magnify its capacity.

Tobacco Box In English silver; a small silver box to hold tobacco introduced during the 17th century. It was generally oval in form with a loose lid and it was somewhat larger and deeper than a snuff box. As a rule the tobacco box was plain except for an engraved insignia or a coat-of-arms.

Tobacco Grater See *Rappoir*.

Tobi Seiji In ceramics; see *Celadon*.

Toby Jug In English ceramics; a characteristic pottery beer jug first made around 1769 by the Ralph Woods, father and son, working in Staffordshire. It was in the form of a seated man usually holding a pipe, with the handle attached to his back. The three-cornered hat which he wore was very often detachable and formed a lid. The front corner of the hat also served as a pouring spout. It is very probable that the name as well as the form was taken from undated engravings of Toby Philpot who was the subject of a song called The Brown Jug, published in 1761. Many jugs of similar form with different subjects were made such as The Thin Man and The Planter. The toby jug is a very characteristic Staffordshire production and has been endlessly imitated since it was first made. See *Staffordshire*; *Wood, Ralph*.

Toddy Lifter In glass; see *Punch Lifter*.

Toft, Thomas English Staffordshire potter. He and his brothers, James, Charles and

STAFFORDSHIRE TOBY JUG

Ralph, were working in North Staffordshire during the late 17th and early 18th centuries. Due to the fact that some very fine surviving examples bear the name of one of the Toft family, it became the practice at one time to apply the name of Toft loosely to all the different kinds of slipware made in Staffordshire. The type of slipware bearing the name of Toft was distinctive for its skillfully executed designs. Slips of reddish brown, dark brown and olive green were cleverly counterchanged under a yellow lead glaze. Inscriptions, trailed lines and diamond-shaped and other repetitive patterns were skillfully manipulated. Sometimes the slip was impressed with stamps. Large signed platters have designs of Adam and Eve, grotesque borders, lions, foliage and other similar motifs. The signed Toft wares seldom have a date. See *Staffordshire*.

Togidashi In Japanese lacquer; an unusually beautiful form of lacquer work in which the design is built up with many coats of lacquer in gold or silver and colors and then rubbed down to reveal them. The term is also applied to black and gold lacquer work. See *Japanese Lacquer*.

Togidashi-Zōgan A Japanese inlay art. The term *togidashi-zōgan* or ground-out inlaying is given to a variety of metal inlay work which is distinctive for the exquisite character of its inlaid designs. In this process which is very intricate and tedious the designs seem to be coming from under the soft metal surface and appear to be floating in atmosphere. See *Zōgan*.

Toile A French word meaning cloth; a pattern of flat texture found in some laces resembling woven cloth, as distinguished from the mesh ground. By extension, the pattern in general, as contrasted with ties or brides and meshes or réseaux. See *Treille*.

Toile de Jouy In textiles; a French term meaning fabric of Jouy. Originally the name was given to a linen or cotton printed fabric made at Jouy, France, in a manufactory established by Philip Oberkampf in 1760.

The subject of the design was usually pictorial and was generally done in a single soft French tone on a light or natural colored ground. Now the name is loosely applied to any printed fabric having similar designs. See *Oberkampf, Philip.*

Toilet The term *toilet* is derived from the French *toilette*, the diminutive form of the French *toile* meaning cloth. The name *toilette* was originally given to the square piece of linen laid on a table and on which was placed the different articles used in beautifying the face and hair. After these different beauty aids and preparations had been used, they were wrapped in the toilette and kept in the chest or coffre de nuit. The early linen toilettes were soon superseded by toilettes made of colorful and rich fabrics. An English record of 1683 mentions a "toilet of blue velvet with gold and silver fringe." The term *toilet* was also used for the articles and the box to contain them and later to the table especially designed to hold the toilet accessories. An English record of 1662 applied the term to the accessories and mentions a "toilet of beaten and massive gold." And in 1724 the toilet is defined as "the dressing box wherein are kept the paints, pomatums, essences, patches, etc., the pin-cushion, powder-box, brushes, etc., are esteemed parts of the equipage of a lady's toilet." See *Dressing Table.*

Toilet Mirror In English cabinetwork; the toilet mirror or dressing table mirror was not in general use until late in the 17th century. The principal type was the mirror in the silver toilet set which came into fashion after the Restoration. The mirror was enclosed in a silver frame and was supported by a brace. Some of the finest silver toilet sets were made by Huguenot refugees. Around 1700 the swinging toilet mirror on a box stand was introduced. The mirror was enclosed in an upright frame which was attached to two uprights by swivel screws. The uprights were secured to a stand. The design for the stand varied. A characteristic stand was designed with a row of three drawers. The toilet mirror was designed throughout the 18th century in all the prevailing styles. The toilet mirror designed in the Hepplewhite style generally had a shield-shaped or oval frame. The uprights were curved to harmonize with the contour of the frame. During the Sheraton style the frame was oblong and its width generally exceeded its height. In another late 18th century variety of toilet mirror the principles of design were similar to those in the cheval mirror. The swinging toilet mirror on a box stand is also called a shaving stand. This type of mirror was popular in America throughout the 18th century and it was also designed in the American Empire style. See *Psyché*; *Dressing Table*; *Mirror.*

Toilet Table See *Dressing Table*; *Toilet.*

Tokmak An Oriental rug belonging to the Turkish group. This rug is one of the Konieh variety. See *Konieh Rug*; *Turkish Rugs.*

Tokugawa In Japanese historical periods; the Tokugawa or Edo period in Japan, 1615–1867. See *Japanese Periods.*

Tôle In furniture; sheet metal, usually tin, which is painted. Tôle is used for making lanterns, shades for candle holders and oil lamps, and other articles of a similar nature. During the French Empire period many vases and jardinières were often made of tôle painted in the antique classical manner. Articles of tôle, particularly lamps and lanterns, were greatly favored in Italy and Spain during the earlier periods. See *Pole Lantern.*

Tompion, Thomas 1638–1713. Celebrated English clock and watch maker. He is often referred to as the father of English watchmaking. The pre-eminent position held by England in the history of horological art for about one hundred years, beginning with the last quarter of the 17th century, is generally credited to Tompion's work. He was clockmaker to Charles II and was the maker of many fine clocks for William III. He was closely associated during his career with Dr. Hooke and Rev. Edward Barlow and

HEPPLEWHITE TOILET
MIRROR

he was able to develop skillfully some of their theories. Several important inventions are credited to Tompion. He made some of the first watches with balance springs. The work which he had so ably started was carried on by his immediate successors.

Tonder Lace Especially characteristic of Danish needlework is a particular kind of embroidery or drawnwork in linen or muslin which was extensively used in Denmark before the art of lace-making was introduced from Flanders in the 16th century. Lace-making as an industry was found only in the province of North Schleswig, since this art of fine needlework was not pursued throughout Denmark as a means of livelihood. Until around 1830 their handmade laces which were inspired by European patterns were praiseworthy for the excellent quality of their workmanship and for their fine flax or silk thread. The fashion for drawn linen or muslin lace continued to prevail in Tonder. In this work handmade laces were cleverly simulated. It is made by drawing out the threads of fine muslin, then reuniting and dividing the threads to make elaborate designs, such as arabesques, floral and scroll motifs. Sometimes a thin cordonnet is introduced to outline the pattern.

Tongue and Groove In joinery and carpentry; the projecting tongue or tenon on the edge of a board joined or fitted into the groove or mortise cut in the edge of another board. See *Mortise and Tenon*.

Tonlet In armor; a wide, flaring and rather long bell-shaped skirt of plate armor having wide vertically fluted folds. It was especially used for fighting on foot as well as when jousting at the barrier. This medieval skirt of armor was also called a base, lamboy or jamboy.

Tooled Leather See *Stamped Leather*.

Toranj In Oriental rugs; the name is commonly given to all prominent medallion designs employed in Oriental rugs. It is also spelled turunji.

LOUIS XIV TORCHÈRE

Torchère The term is generally reserved for a tall slender decorative stand with a small top used for the reception of a candelabrum. It was generally designed in pairs. French carved and gilded torchères were made in the prevailing styles from the middle of the 17th century. Chippendale in his DIRECTOR illustrated designs for torchères in the Rococo taste. Adam's designs for torchères were close adaptations of the many tall and slender metal tripods found at Pompeii and Herculaneum and were notable for their fine classic design and ornamental detail. In this variety the small top, instead of resting on a long shaft, rested on three long slender supports or legs which often rested on a molded plinth. The legs were frequently headed with an animal's head, such as the favorite ram's head. See *Guéridon*; *Candlestand*.

Torchon In lace-making; a coarse bobbin lace first made in the 16th century. It was worked in simple designs upon a coarse mesh ground, and was made by the peasants in almost every European country. See *Lace*.

Toro, Bernard 1672–1731. French ornamental sculptor born in Toulon and working like his father as a carver at the Arsenal. In 1719 he succeeded to the post of master sculptor of the Arsenal at Toulon. Much of his earlier fame depended on carvings believed to have been executed by him, but are now regarded to be the work of others. At the present time he is best known for his drawings and engravings which display a remarkable verve and fantasy often touched with the grotesque. Many features in his work are dependent on the decorative work of Bérain.

Tortoise Shell In cabinetwork; the shell of certain tortoises, especially that of the hawk's-bill turtle, which is semi-transparent, brilliant and finely mottled, was extensively used in ornamental work. It was sometimes used in conjunction with other inlays in pietra dura work. Especially praiseworthy was the marquetry of metal and tortoise shell executed by André Charles Boulle.

During the 18th century it was sometimes tinted green or yellow and used as a veneer on boxes, tea caddies and other similar articles. See *Boulle, André Charles.*

Tortoise Shell In American glass; a late 19th century ornamental glass characterized by a pale brownish amber color with splashes of a darker tone. It derived its name from its supposed resemblance to tortoise shell. It is believed that much of this tortoise shell glass was made at Sandwich. See *Art Glass.*

Tortoise Shell Ware In English ceramics; earthenware made at Staffordshire around the middle of the 18th century having a lead glaze mottled with manganese brown and occasionally with other colors to produce a tortoise shell effect. See *Staffordshire; Whieldon, Thomas.*

Torus The name given to a large convex molding which is generally a semi-circle. See *Astragal; Molding.*

Tosa A Japanese school of painting, Tosaryū, founded by Fujiwara Tsunetaka in the 13th century in the tradition of the 9th century Kose-ryū, the 10th century Kasugaryū and the 11th century Yamato-ryū. It was so-named because this Fujiwara became vice-governor of Tosa province. That the line of demaracation between the successive schools of traditionally indigenous painting is vague is illustrated by the expression "Tosa no Sampitsu" or "The Three Brushes of Tosa", which refers to Fujiwara Motomitsu, founder of the Kasuga-ryū, Tosa Mitsunobu, 1435–1525, and Tosa Mitsuoki, 1617–1691. The Tosa-ryū, which has maintained its position as a basic school of Japanese art up to the present time, remained aloof from continental influence and retained its indigenous spirit. While the Tosa artists were eclectic in their adoption of a wide choice of styles, the school is characterized by its realistic treatment of genre and historical subjects in bright, flat colors outlined in india-ink, and by its meticulous detail. See *Kanō.*

T'o T'ai In Chinese ceramics; see *Eggshell.*

Tou In Chinese bronzes; a ritual vessel used for sacrifices and at funerals and banquets. It is a deep round vessel or bowl having a cover and resting on a high stem with a spreading foot.

Touch Box In arms; a small box or case to hold the fine priming powder with which the pan and touch-hole were filled in early types of firearms. It resembled a powder flask, but it was much smaller. The name is also given to a small box to hold lighted tinder to kindle the match on a matchlock gun.

Touch Mark In pewter; the maker's mark incised on an article made of pewter. See *Pewter; Touch Plate.*

Touch of Paris A term applied to gold which is 19 1/5 carats fine. It was the first lawful standard for gold articles and was introduced in 1300.

Touchpiece A gold medal or talisman. The medal or coin was originally the angel coin of England and the angelot of France, which had a figure of St. Michael on one side and a three-masted ship on the other. It was first used in England in the 14th century by Edward III, and in France by Louis IX, or Saint Louis, in the 13th century. It was a coin given by European monarchs, especially French and English, to sufferers of the King's Evil, a disease known as scrofula. The king would touch his subject and then present the coin. The disease was believed to have been curable by the king's touch. Touching was practiced until the first half of the 18th century.

Touch Plate In English pewter; in 1503 an act was passed making it mandatory for pewterers to put their touches on all pewter ware made by them. The pewterers were obliged to strike their personal touches at the Guild headquarters upon an official plate which became known as a touch plate. Today there are only five touch plates in existence, covering a period from 1640 to

TOU, LATE CHOU PERIOD

1824. Many of the early touch marks contained only the maker's initials within a simple device. Between 1670–1697 some makers struck their name in full, and generally after 1697 the full name was used due to Guild regulations. See *Pewter*.

Touchstone The purity of gold and silver plate was tested in early times by making a mark with the piece on the touchstone. The color of the mark was compared with the color marks already on the touchstone that were made by gold or silver pieces of accepted purity.

Touraine Tapestries The weaving of tapestries at Tours, France, dates from the 16th century. It was active in the production of fine tapestries during the 17th century and into the 18th century. See *Tapestry*.

Tournay Or Tournai. In Flemish ceramics; a soft paste porcelain manufactory was started in 1751 at Tournay in Flemish Doornik, Belgium, by F. J. Peterinck, with a privilege from the Empress Maria Theresa. Evidence of decline became perceptible around 1800. From around 1817 to 1850 the factory was principally engaged in making forgeries of Sèvres, Chelsea and Worcester. In the beginning the wares were marked with a tower taken from the Tournay coat-of-arms; however, after 1760 it was found only on the finer grades of porcelain. The more general mark from 1756 to 1781 was the crossed swords with crosses in the angles; it was used on all types of wares. Many of the very fine pieces from around 1780 to 1800 were unmarked. This manufactory is generally regarded as one of the most important 18th century manufactories for soft paste porcelain. From around 1755 the porcelain was technically of a fine quality, having a not unpleasant slightly yellowish tone. Much of the decoration was in imitation of Meissen and Sèvres. The most common of all Tournay porcelain is in blue and white; the so-called Meissen onion pattern was much favored. The shapes and forms for the tablewares were in the Rococo

TOURNAY GLAZED WHITE
PORCELAIN GROUP

style but showed a certain restraint and simplicity that was pleasing and original. German flowers, exotic birds in the Sèvres style, figure painting and landscapes in Sèvres or Meissen style were of fine quality and were carefully painted. The figures were generally unmarked; in style they showed a strong resemblance to those of Chelsea, Worcester and Mennecy. The majority were in glazed white porcelain. During the last two decades of the 18th century the Louis XVI style was adopted.

Tournay Tapestries The weaving of tapestries at Tournay, Flanders, dates from the 14th century. Its most important period was during the middle of the 15th century. Tournay gothic tapestries are renowned.

Towel Horse In English furniture; a utilitarian article of furniture consisting of a light wooden frame mounted on feet with two or more turned crosspieces constructed either in one panel or in two or more panels folding in a manner similar to a folding screen. It was introduced around 1750 and was regarded as a necessary article after the introduction of the washing stand. The piece was without artistic merit, since its purpose was strictly utilitarian. See *Washstand*; *Basin Stand*.

Townsend, Christopher 1701–1773. American cabinetmaker of Newport, Rhode Island, working circa 1740–1773. He was the brother of Job Townsend and father of John Townsend. See *Goddard, John, I*.

Townsend, Edmund 1736–1811. American cabinetmaker of Newport, Rhode Island. He was a son of Job Townsend.

Townsend, Job 1699–1765. American cabinetmaker of Newport, Rhode Island, working circa 1725–1765. He was a brother of Christopher Townsend, and father of Job Townsend, Jr., 1726–1818, who was working circa 1760–1818.

Townsend, John 1721–1809. American cabinetmaker of Newport, Rhode Island. See *Goddard, John, I*.

Toy In ceramics; the name given in England to porcelain scent bottles, étuis, snuff boxes, patch boxes and other similar small objects made in the Rococo style in the fanciful and delightful forms of miniature figures, fruits, animals and other similar forms. This variety of so-called toys was originally introduced at Meissen. Especially delightful and charming were the toys made at Chelsea and at Mennecy.

Tracery Work In ornament; the great tracery windows were first developed in Gothic architecture. Tracery work is the name given to the decorative openwork in a Gothic window. Traceried windows were such a dominating influence in Gothic architecture that the character of the stone framing was chiefly instrumental in the naming of the different Gothic styles, such as Rayonnant and Flamboyant. Tracery work, either solid or pierced, was extensively employed by the wood carver in decorating Gothic furniture and was copied from the traceried windows. It was used to decorate the panels on the façade of a chest and it was used to decorate the panelled backs of chairs and settles and other similar articles.

Trailed Circuit In glass; the name is given, especially in English glass, to a kind of applied decoration. It consisted of two thick applied threads that were nipped together to form a chain. It is also called Guilloche or Chain.

Trailed Ornament In English glass; see *Colored Looping*.

Traite In French Provincial cabinetwork; the name sometimes given to a long low cupboard of marked simplicity. The traite was frequently designed with as many as five or six cupboard doors. Very often the center portion was open and consisted of two rows of shelves. This center portion was flanked at each end by a cupboard section. See *Etimier*.

Transfer Printed Decoration In ceramics; a method first used in England by which an impression from an engraved metal plate brushed with enamel colors is made on a thin piece of paper and transferred to the surface of pottery or porcelain and melted into the glaze. The method was used as early as 1753 on Battersea painted enamels. It has never been conclusively ascertained who invented the process. Several different persons claim the invention, among whom were John Sadler and Guy Green of Liverpool who operated a successful printed ware manufactory from 1756. At first the printing was done over the glaze in red, purple and black. From around 1760 the method was used for underglaze printing in blue. The underglaze blue-printed method was much used at Staffordshire and other centers producing English white earthenware during the early 19th century. A process known as bat printing was introduced late in the 18th century. Sometimes, especially from around 1825, the outlines of the design in black, grey or pale purple were transferred and the painted decoration was filled in by hand. Other methods of transfer printing were also developed, such as transfer printing in gold, transfer stippling in several colors and lithographic transfers of birds, pictorial subjects and other motifs in natural colors in imitation of painting. The practice of transfer printing was slowly taken up by the other European countries. Transfer printed decoration generally produces an inferior quality of decoration. See *Bat Printing*.

Trauschein A German term meaning a marriage certificate. The term is frequently used to describe the certificate given at the time of marriage by the Pennsylvania Germans. See *Fractur*.

Travailleuse In French cabinetwork; a lady's work table. See *Table à Ouvrage*.

Tray In English furniture; the wooden tray was known as early as the Middle Ages. The social custom of tea drinking made necessary the designing of suitable decorative wooden trays. Chippendale in his DIRECTOR illustrated designs for decorative mahogany trays. The tray was generally

GOTHIC PIERCED
TRACERY WORK

oblong and had a finely pierced fretwork gallery with two scrolled handgrips. Trays designed at a later date in the Adam style were frequently oval. Circular trays were relatively rare. Lacquer trays were popular throughout the 18th century. Shortly after the middle of the 18th century plain, oblong, sturdy, mahogany trays were made for the butler's use and were set upon folding stands of X-form. Designs for the wooden tea tray of oval form were given in Hepplewhite's GUIDE. It was generally fitted with brass handgrips. Hepplewhite stated that the tops were to be inlaid in various kinds of colored woods or were to be ornamented with painted decoration. The silver tray was generally oblong and occasionally oval. One variety which was designed with a pierced silver gallery and hand grips very often had a turned mahogany base in place of silver. See *Tray Stand*; *Spoon-Tray*.

Tray Candlestick In English silver; see *Chamber-Candlestick*.

Tray Stand In English cabinetwork; toward the middle of the 18th century a small tripod stand was introduced which was especially designed to support the silver tray on which the tea and coffee service were placed. The circular top, which usually tilted, was notched to receive the feet of the silver tray. It rested on a turned shaft which was supported on a tripod base. The tripod tray stand was slightly over 2 feet in height. See *Tripod*; *Tripod Table*; *Tray*.

Treen The term *treen* was commonly used in England until the end of the 18th century to describe a wide variety of small useful articles made from wood, the term being derived from *tree*. The word is frequently found in the 16th and 17th century records referring to spoons, bowls, mugs, trenchers and other similar articles as services of treen. During these early times when the use of glass, silver and china was restricted to the wealthy houses, small articles made of a variety of different woods were in common use.

TREE OF LIFE MOTIF,
PERSIAN

Tree of Life Motif In decorative art; an ornamental design of ancient origin. It is usually characterized as a conventionalized tree growing from a vase and sustained by the Water of Life. Although its ancient origin is obscure it is identified with Oriental and Sanskrit mythology. This motif is frequently found in the decorative art of the Far East and Near East on such articles as Oriental rugs, pottery and sculpture. In America the Tree of Life motif was a very popular design of the Pennyslvania Germans on such articles as fracturs.

Trefoil The term *trefoil* derived from the Latin word *trifolium* meaning three leaf, is applied to any plant with trifoliate leaves. In ornament; a decorative figure resembling a trifoliate leaf composed of three foils or lobes which was a favorite Gothic motif. In architecture; an ornament composed of three lobes or sections formed by the spaces or openings divided by cusps so as to suggest the figure of a three-lobed leaf. See *Cinquefoil*; *Quatrefoil*.

Treille In lace-making; a French term applied to the net grounds of needlepoint and bobbin laces to distinguish them from the pattern. See *Lace*; *Toile*.

Trellised In armor; a variety of coat-of-mail. See *Mail*.

Trencher An English term applied to a plate in the form of, or used as, a trencher. In England during the Middle Ages food was eaten from trenchers which were commonly thick slices of bread. The joint of meat was brought to the table on a charger and portions of meat were placed on these trenchers of bread, cut into pieces and passed to the mouth with the fingers. Later the trencher was a flat square piece of wood, and in the 16th century was made of wood or metal, generally circular in form. In the 18th century a flat earthenware plate with a narrow rim was made and generally called a trencher plate.

Trencher Salt In English silver; a small salt-cellar, open salt or salt dish in the form of an open bowl. It was so named because it was placed near each person's trencher or plate. Extant English examples date from around 1600. See *Salt-Cellar*.

Trestle Table In cabinetwork; the characteristic Gothic dining table was of trestle construction. It had a massive oblong removable top of oak which rested on truss end supports that were usually reinforced with a single stretcher connecting the end trusses. The truss ends were generally made of wood, occasionally of iron or brass, and frequently folded. Toward the end of the 15th century the trestle table became more finished in detail and the trusses became more elaborately carved. The primary function of a table during the Gothic period was for dining. Occasionally the trestle table was made in smaller sizes and served different purposes. See *Dining Table*; *Joint Stool*; *Banc*; *Table*.

Triangular Pediment In cabinetwork; see *Pediment*.

Trichterbecher In German ceramics; a Rhenish salt-glazed stoneware cup having a funnel-shaped mouth. Although it was made in different centers producing stoneware in the Rhineland during the 16th and 17th centuries, it is a particularly characteristic form for the salt-glazed stoneware made at Siegburg.

Tricoteuse In French cabinetwork; a work table. See *Table à Ouvrage*.

Tric-Trac Table In French cabinetwork; a table designed for tric-trac which is the French word for backgammon. It was introduced around the middle of the 18th century. The characteristic tric-trac table had an oblong removable top which frequently centered an inlaid checkerboard. The reverse side of the top was inset with green baize. The frieze was designed with a well and two end drawers. The well contained an inlaid tric-trac or backgammon board. The drawers opened on opposite sides of the table for the convenience of the

players. The table was mounted on four legs. The average length of the table was around 45 inches. See *Card Table*.

Tridarn Cupboard In English cabinetwork; the tridarn, or three section, cupboard is of Welsh or Welsh Border origin. It was introduced during the second half of the 17th century, and with slight variation in design was made throughout the 18th century. It was essentially similar in design to the Hall or Parlor Cupboard designed with a closed upper portion and a closed lower portion. It had an additional third section which surmounted the closed upper portion. This additional third section consisted of a canopy which rested on a turned or carved support at each front corner. The back was panelled and occasionally the sides were panelled. The additional shelf space formed by the canopy was used for the display of pewter vessels. The middle section was straight-fronted and had three panelled cupboard doors and the lower section had the two cupboard doors. The tridarn cupboard was simply decorated along English traditional lines. See *Hall and Parlor Cupboard*; *Cupboard*.

Trifid-End Spoon In English silver; a spoon having the end of the stem notched in two places. The clefts vary. Sometimes it is divided into almost three equal parts, in others the center portion is much wider. It was introduced around 1660. Also called a pied de biche spoon. See *Spoon*.

Trifle In pewter; a name given to a variety of pewter containing 83 parts tin and 17 parts antimony. It was chiefly used for small articles, such as buckles, buttons and small domestic utensils. See *Pewter*.

Triglyph An architectural term for a member or ornament in the Doric order, comprising a block or tablet with three vertical grooves or glyphs, actually two complete grooves and a half groove on each side, repeated at regular intervals along the frieze. Triglyphs were sometimes employed as a decorative architectural detail in furniture

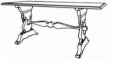

TRESTLE TABLE, ITALIAN

DIRECTOIRE BRONZE
TRIPOD

design, such as on the frieze of a table or a commode. They were frequently found in the Louis XVI style of cabinetwork. See *Metope*.

Tripod In classical antiquities; any utensil or article of furniture having three feet. In particular the name is given to either a seat or table having three legs or to a stand which held the cauldron used for cooking or for heating water. Antique Greco-Roman bronze tripod stands were widely copied during the Classic Revival of the 18th century for such articles as torchères and decorative center tables. See *Athénienne*; *Torchère*; *Basin Stand*; *Tripod Table*.

Tripod Table In English and American cabinetwork; the name is given to a form of table having a top which is supported on a central shaft that rests on three feet or a tripod base. It is generally accepted that Chippendale was instrumental in developing the vogue for mahogany tripod tables in England which began around 1755. As a rule the top was made to tilt and frequently it revolved. The size of these tables varied. The larger ones were generally used for afternoon tea while the small ones were chiefly used as candlestands. The tea table of tripod form became fashionable in America around 1760. See *Pie-Crust Table*; *Tea Table*; *Supper Table*; *Candlestand*; *Bird-Cage Support*; *Tray Stand*.

Triptych See *Diptych*.

Trivet A metal stand for holding a kettle, pot or a similar vessel. The characteristic variety is made with three very short legs and has a handle of turned wood. The top of the trivet was of pierced brass and the legs of iron. See *Footman*.

Trofei In Italian ceramics; a contemporary Italian term for a decoration used on Italian Renaissance majolica. It consisted of attributes or symbols such as armor, weapons and musical instruments that were appropriate to war and music respectively. It was much favored at Castel Durante and Faenza. See *Trophies*.

Trolle Kant In lace-making; an early Flemish bobbin-made lace dating from the 16th century having the pattern outlined with a thick thread or cordonnet. *Kant* is the Flemish word for lace. In England this variety of lace, with a heavy cordonnet which is called gimp or trolly, is known as trolly lace. See *Trolly Lace*.

Trolly Lace It is generally accepted that the origin of trolly lace is derived from the Flemish *trolle kant*, in which the designs were outlined by a thick thread. It is reputed that trolly lace was introduced at Devonshire, England, by Normandy peasants who sought refuge in England at the time of the Revolution. Devonshire trolly lace was made of a coarse British thread and with larger and heavier bobbins. The manufacture of trolly lace was continued in the English Midlands.

Trompe l'Oeil The term which means deceive the eye or fool the eye is applied to a school of painting that goes back to the legendary Greek Zeuxis who was reputed to have painted grapes so realistically that birds swooped down to pick at them. Roman and Pompeiian decorators employed this style of painting for murals to give the illusion of spaciousness to small rooms. During the 17th and 18th centuries this technique was given to cards, scissors and other similar articles by realistic painters. Although the articles were painted on the canvas they were executed in such vivid perspective that they appeared to be pasted on. In ceramics; the term is given to 18th century faïence wares such as tureens in the form of vegetables, fruits, birds, boars' heads and other similar natural objects and dishes molded in a similar manner with vegetables and fruits painted in natural colors. The tureens were a Meissen innovation while the latter were a Strasbourg innovation. It is generally accepted that this style had its origin in the Italian della Robbia school. These so-called trompe l'oeil wares were very popular and were produced at many faïence manufactories. Perhaps nowhere was the style more aptly interpreted than at Strasbourg. See *Décor Bois*; *Quodlibetz*.

Trophies In ornament; attributes or symbols appropriate to pastoral life, love, music, war, hunting, fishing, science, agriculture and astronomy were employed as decorative motifs. Trophies of love included bows, arrows, torches and quivers; pastoral emblems such as crooks and the large straw hats of shepherdesses, and attributes of war such as body armor. All these symbols were especially favorite themes for ornament during the Louis XV and Louis XVI styles. "Trofei" were also a characteristic form of decoration for large Italian majolica plates made during the 16th century.

Trophy Cup The term *trophy cup* is applied to a two-handled cup awarded as a token or evidence of victory, skill or valor. In English silver; the earliest extant two-handled cup bears the hall-mark of 1533–1534 and the second earliest is the Arundel cup hall-marked 1616–1617. In the 17th century this form of cup became more plentiful and from the reign of Queen Anne a large number of two-handled cups began to appear. This was due to the popularity of horse-racing and these cups were adopted as trophies to be awarded to the winning horse or rider. Two-handled cups used as trophies bear hall-marks dating as early as 1702.

Trotter, Daniel American 18th century cabinetmaker working in Philadelphia. He produced fine pieces in the Chippendale style. See *Philadelphia Chippendale*.

Trousse A French term meaning packed in a receptacle or a collection of things, applied to a set of implements carried in a sheath, during the 16th century and later. It consisted of a hunting knife, knives and forks, and sometimes instruments used for cutting up game. In China the trousse consisted of a sheath containing a long slender knife, a pair of long chopsticks, toothpick and pickle spear. Many of the Chinese variety are elaborately decorated with jade or ivory handles on the knives, and the sheaths were often lacquered and mounted with silver.

Truckle Bed See *Trundle Bed*.

Trumeau In French furniture; the name given to a pier mirror. Mirrors were in vogue in France from around the middle of the 17th century. They were magnificent and plentiful. The abundant use of mirrors was one of the special features of the Louis XIV style. The trumeau was designed in accordance with the prevailing style of ornament. Especially characteristic of the Empire style were imposing pier tables beneath large mirrors. See *Pier Mirror*.

Trumpet Leg In English cabinetwork; the name given to a variety of turned leg identified with the William and Mary style. It was used on chairs and settees and on highboys and lowboys. It was so named because of its supposed resemblance to a trumpet. See *William and Mary*.

Trundle Bed Or Truckle Bed. In English and American cabinetwork; a low bed on wheels which was trundled under the large bed when not needed. It was in use in England from the late Middle Ages until the middle of the 18th century.

Ts'a Ts'ai Or Mixed Colors. In Chinese ceramics; enamelled porcelain decorated with many combinations of two colors, such as blue designs with a yellow ground, green and yellow, aubergine and yellow, red and yellow, blue and green, red and green, and red and gold. This variety of ware was made in the Chêng Tê period, 1506–1521, of the Ming dynasty. However, there is evidence to support the belief that it was also made in the 15th century. See *Ming*.

Tsêng In Chinese bronzes; the name given to a ritual vessel or a deep pot used for food. It is a large pot-shaped vessel with lobes on the rim through which a rod or pole is passed for carrying.

Tsuba In Japanese sword mounts; the guard on a Japanese sword or knife. It is the most

LOUIS XVI TRUMEAU

important fitting. The tsuba is a metal plate which is generally elliptical, although many resemble a rectangle with gently curving sides and rounded corners. The majority of tsuba are made of steel or iron, and the finest are of shakudo or shibuichi or a combination of both. The center of the tsuba has a specially shaped opening through which the tang passes and around this opening is a plain narrow space called seppa dai. If the tsuba bears the signature of the artist it is found on the seppa dai. The tsuba may also have an opening at either side of the seppa dai called riobitsu for the kogai or kozuka to pass through, or two riobitsu when both are used. The artists who produced the best of these tsuba and other sword fittings developed the art of metal work to the highest point it ever achieved. They executed these pieces in every variety of technique such as inlaying, carving, piercing and engraving. With an almost endless repertory of subjects and themes they have produced a story of Japan through several centuries, portraying her historical, religious, legendary, mythological, and contemporary customs. See *Japanese Sword Mounts*.

SHERATON TUB CHAIR

Tsui-Shiu A Chinese lacquer work in which several layers of colored lac are revealed by carving. The Japanese work is called Guri.

Tsun In Chinese bronzes; a ritual vessel used for holding a beverage. It consists of a cylindrical body with a flaring lip rim and rests on a slightly flaring foot.

Ts'ung In Chinese ceramics; a ritual vessel used in the worship of the earth. It was supposed to contain the divining rods. It was in the form of a rather tall rectangular vase with a circular foot rim and neck rim. A set of the Pa Kua symbols was molded in relief on each side of the body. Sometimes vertical ribs extended the length of the vessel. See *Eight Trigrams*.

Tsurugi In Japanese arms; see *Ken*.

T'u In Chinese art; a Chinese animal subject widely used in Chinese ceramics and art. It is represented as the hare that is seen in

the moon where it is mixing an imaginary liquid of an elixir to prolong life. See *Chinese Animal Figures*.

Tub Chair In English cabinetwork; Sheraton in his CABINET DICTIONARY, 1803, in writing about an easy chair of tub shape observes that they are "stuffed all over and intended for sick persons, being both easy and warm for the wide wings coming quite forward keep out the cold air." In English furniture literature it seems that the term is applied to an easy chair having the wings and back made in a semi-circle and upholstered as a continuous unit. See *Easy Chair*; *Barrel-Back Chair*. By extension the term is commonly given to a form of upholstered chair having a low, arched horseshoe-shaped back continuing to form the arms and characterized by its rounded appearance. It is mounted on straight quadrangular or cylindrical tapering legs. The sides and back are rounded about the seat and are upholstered as one unit. See *Gondola-Back Chair*.

Tucker In American ceramics; William Ellis Tucker started a kiln in Philadelphia about 1825 or 1826 to produce a hard bone china and pottery. In 1828 the mark was "Tucker and Hulme, Philadelphia", frequently with "China Manufacturers" added. In 1832 the partnership was with Judge Joseph Hemphill. Tucker appears to have withdrawn and his son Thomas continued on with Hemphill. The pottery continued until 1837. They employed workers from Europe and made many imitations of Sèvres wares. The decoration included portraits of famous men, such as George Washington, family coats-of-arms and monograms.

Tudor In English style of ornament; the term is applied to the last phase of the Gothic style in England. Its accepted dates are 1485 to 1558. The name is derived from the English House of Tudor whose reigning members during this period were Henry VII, Henry VIII, Edward VI and Mary. It was characterized by the Tudor arch or four-centered arch and also by the Tudor rose. In interior decoration it was identified by wainscot walls generally divided into small rectangular panels and by plasterwork ceilings introduced during the reign of Henry VIII by Italian craftsmen. It was essentially a time of transition. The form was Late Gothic and the style of ornament consisted of Gothic and Renaissance motifs blended together. From 1530 onwards Renaissance motifs as interpreted by the Italian school were used in conjunction with Gothic motifs. Wreathed medallion heads were a favorite carved decoration borrowed from the Italian Renaissance style of ornament. The term *Tudor* is also applied to the things pertaining to the House of Tudor when their members were the reigning monarchs. The last Tudor to sit upon the English throne was Queen Elizabeth I, 1558–1603, during whose reign the early Renaissance was established in England. See *Gothic, English*; *Elizabethan*.

Tudor Period   1485–1603   See *Tudor*.

Tudor Rose   In English ornament; the Tudor rose was designed as a decorative motif in 1486. It was symbolic of the uniting in marriage of Elizabeth of York and Henry VII of Lancaster at the close of the War of Roses. In the design the Tudor rose was always open and generally consisted of five petals conventionally treated.

Tufft, Thomas   An American cabinetmaker working in Philadelphia around 1750 to 1793. He had his shop on Second Street. He produced fine articles of furniture in the Chippendale style. See *Philadelphia Chippendale*.

Tuilles   In armor; see *Taces*.

Tulip Ware   In American ceramics; the name given to a variety of earthenware with sgraffiato decoration or with decoration scratched through a coating of slip, made during the 17th and 18th centuries by the Pennsylvania German potters. The ware is characterized by a stylized design of tulips and leaves symmetrically arranged. Tulips were always a favorite motif in all kinds of Pennsylvania German decoration. See *Sgraffiato*; *Pennsylvania Dutch*.

Tulipwood   The soft white wood of the North American tulip tree, *liriodendron tulipifera*, used in cabinetwork. It becomes yellowish with age and was frequently used in inlay work in America. Also the Brazilian rose-colored wood, *physocalymma floribundum*, of very fine grain used in European cabinetwork. The name *tulipwood* is also given in a general sense to several species of wood that are finely streaked and have beautiful markings in different colors.

Tulle   In lace-making; a variety of lace having a very fine and delicate bobbin-made net ground without any ornament. It is generally accepted that the name was derived from Tulle, the principal town in the department of Corrèze, in France, where this lace work is reputed to have been first fabricated in France. Both tulle and marli were much favored by Marie Antoinette.

Tulwar   In arms; the saber of India. Tulwar is the name applied to all of the curved swords of India. The blades vary greatly in curvature, size and quality. The hilts are usually furnished with a disc-shaped pommel and heavy quillons.

Tumbler   In English glass; the name was originally given to a drinking vessel with a convex or pointed base. It could stand only when inverted. The term is now given to a plain cylindrical glass drinking vessel that rests on a flat base and is without either a handle or a stem.

Tumbler Cup   In English silver; a small drinking vessel. It was so named because it has a rounded bottom. It rocks and tumbles but will not fall over on its side since the silver is hammered in such a manner that the bottom is thicker and heavier than the sides. It was introduced during the late 17th century.

PLATE WITH SGRAFFIATO
TULIP DECORATION

Tunbridge In English furniture; a form of parquetry work perfected during the early 19th century. It was so called because it was made at the English town of Tunbridge, in Kent. The mosaic-like patterns were made by cutting slender strips of different natural-colored woods into the desired minute checker sizes and then by gluing them together. They were then cut with a saw and applied as a thin veneer to the surface of the article. After the veneered piece was laid on it was polished to a high gloss. By making the veneer in this manner many veneers of the same design were produced. Due to the fact that only natural-colored woods were used great skill was required to find all the contrasting colors necessary to form the geometric patterns. This Tunbridge work was applied to boxes, trays, tea caddies and some small articles of furniture, such as the tops of work tables. "English mosaics," as Tunbridge ware was called, achieved its height of popularity during the Early Victorian era, when its most ambitious work was produced. Evidence of decline became increasingly apparent after 1850. See *Parquetry*.

Tung Yao In Chinese ceramics; see *Celadon*.

Tunicle In ecclesiastical costume; a vestment proper to subdeacons worn over the alb and also by bishops between the alb and the dalmatic at the celebration of the Eucharist. It is essentially similar to the dalmatic, although in a correct sense the tunicle should not be cut as generously as the dalmatic and the sleeves should be narrower. The tunic in ecclesiastical costume has the same meaning as the tunicle. See *Dalmatic*.

Tureen In English silver; during the late 17th century it became the custom to serve soup from a large bowl placed either on the dining table or on a side table. The Early Georgian soup tureen was in the form of a large oval bowl with a loop handle at each end of the bowl and it was provided with a domed cover fitted with a fixed C-scroll handle. The bowl rested on four feet and it was generally elaborately wrought. The

GEORGE III SILVER SOUP
TUREEN

later 18th century soup tureen designed in the Neo-Classic style was in the form of an urn and it rested on a high spreading base. In European ceramics; especially praiseworthy were the many faïence and porcelain tureens made in Europe during the 18th century. See *Trompe l'Oeil*.

Turkey Work In English needlework; the name given to a form of needlework imitating Oriental carpets woven with a knotted pile in the Near East in such countries as Persia and Turkey, from which it undoubtedly derived its name. Turkey work, which was used for the coverings of chairs and cushions and occasionally for rugs, was done in two principal methods. In one form the wool was drawn through a canvas ground and knotted to form a pile. In the other method the technique employed was similar to that used for Oriental rugs. Turkey work was fashionable in England from around early in the 16th century to around the middle of the 18th century. See *Oriental Rug*.

Turkish Knot In Oriental rug weaving; see *Ghiordes Knot*.

Turkish Pottery In ceramics; the wares of Turkey, which date from the 15th century, are a whitish-colored earthenware. In the early period the body was covered with a fine white slip usually containing tin-ashes. These early specimens are mostly in blue and white with floral designs and inscriptions. However, some pieces had the designs outlined in black and filled in with blue, red and green. About the second half of the 16th century the ware was a tin-glazed earthenware, and although blue and white continued, much of it was decorated with enamel colors on a white ground. Its artistic development seems to follow that of the beautiful Turkish wall tiles, and the designs, such as those on plates, were finely executed in either a symmetrical or asymmetrical arrangement. These designs consisted of natural or conventionalized flowers, especially the tulip and the rose, leaves, plants and fruits as well as Persian scrolls, arabesques, geometrical patterns and human and animal figures. Many plates are found with an imbricated or scale pattern. The colors include blue, red, persimmon, green, yellow and turquoise. Turkish wares were generally in the form of plates, mugs, jugs and also narghiles. The plates have flat rims which are decorated with designs in the form of a running pattern of leaves or some similar subject. Many of these rims have designs displaying a Chinese influence with cloud-bands and waves and conventionalized volutes drawn with a thin line. During the 17th and 18th century blue and white wares seemed to be more popular than those with more colors. See *Persian and Near Eastern Pottery*.

Turkish Rugs A general classification applied to the Oriental rugs woven in Asia Minor. Especially notable are their fine prayer rugs. The colors are warm and have a tendency to soften the rather angular treatment of many of their designs. There is a great difference between the early and the modern Turkish rug. The latter is purely a commercial creation. It is generally heavy, loosely woven and of almost any design. However, it does give excellent service. This group includes: Ghiordes; Kulah; Demirdji; Oushak; Ladik; Bergamo; Meles; Anatolian; Makri; Kir-Shehr; Kaba-Kara-man; Yuruk; Ak-Hissar; Gulistan; Enile; Yaprak; Sparta; Herek. See *Oriental Rug*.

Turkman Rug See *Guendje*.

Turkoman Rugs A general classification applied to a group of Oriental rugs, which are woven by the Turkomans in Russian central Asia, east of the Caspian Sea. They are notable for their rich red colors. Their patterns are rectilinear, with octagon motifs and other polygonal shapes, based on the designs of marble tiled and inlaid floors. They usually have a wide web. The rugs of Eastern and Russian Turkestan are predominantly Chinese in design and texture, but geographically they are classed with the other Turkoman rugs. Belonging to this group are: Tekke Bokhara; Afghan Bokhara; Khiva Bokhara; Katchlie Bokhara;

Princess Bokhara; Beluchistan; Yomud; Beshir; Samarkand; Kashgar; Yarkand; Khotan. See *Oriental Rug*.

Turner, John d. 1786. An English potter working at Stoke from around 1755 and at Lane End from around 1762, Staffordshire. He made cream-colored earthenware and stonewares which were equal in quality to those made by Wedgwood. Of particular interest were his fine white and buff-colored stonewares and his blue jasper wares. His factory was quite active and enjoyed a good reputation. He exported wares to Holland. The business was carried on until 1803 by his sons, John and William. The marks were "Turner" or "Turner & Co," impressed.

Turning In cabinetwork; to form or shape a piece of wood by cutting with some instrument while the wood is revolving on a lathe. There are many various types of turning. As a rule the particular kind of turning received its name from its supposed resemblance to the object whose name it had; for example, spool, ring, spiral, ball, knob, vase, bead and reel, baluster and bulbous turnings. An outstanding characteristic of the French Louis XIII style was the use of turning. Never was this method more often employed than during this style, nor was the best work of this style ever surpassed. Legs of tables, the entire framework of chairs, ornamental finials and pendants, decorative corner columns on cupboards were all favorite subjects for the cabinetmaker's lathe. The most common variety was spiral. Baluster turning had the greatest artistic value since the outlines could be executed in an endless variety in accordance with the skill of the craftsman. The turned work of the Louis XIII style was always distinctive for the excellent taste shown in its outline or profile and for the skillful arrangement of its design in order to have the correct play of light and shade. In English cabinetwork; late in the Elizabethan style and in the following Early Jacobean style baluster turnings were frequently applied to the surface of furniture

C. 1660

C. 1700

as a decorative detail. They were often stained black. Turning was a fashionable decorative process during the Late Jacobean style. Spiral and baluster turnings were the favorite types. Turning was also popular during the William and Mary style. Inverted cup-shaped, trumpet- and vase-shaped legs were typical for the legs of chairs and settees and tallboys designed in the William and Mary style. Turning was not much used during the Queen Anne and Early Georgian and Chippendale styles. Turning was still used for the shafts of tripod tables and for the baluster-form spindled galleries for tripod tables. Veneered surfaces were typical of late 18th century cabinetwork. See *Twist Turning*.

Turquoise   In French cabinetwork; the name given to a kind of day bed introduced during the Louis XV style. The turquoise, which was designed without a back, had end pieces of equal height. The seat was fitted with a thick and flat loose oblong cushion somewhat resembling a mattress. A round bolster was placed at each end and if the turquoise was placed against a wall there were generally two additional square cushions to rest against the wall.

LOUIS XV TURQUOISE

Turtle-Back   In ornament; see *Boss*.

Tuscany   In Italian ceramics; the rapid growth of Italian majolica during the 15th century was due principally to the potters working in Faenza and Tuscany, the chief centers at the latter being Siena and Florence. Of particular interest was a Tuscan variety of majolica, probably of Florentine derivation and dating from around 1410, painted principally in rich translucent green within outlines of manganese purple or brownish black. Heraldic lions, foliage, figures and busts were among the favorite motifs. Especially outstanding and dating from around 1430 were the well-known Florentine jars or vases painted in blue and sometimes known as oak leaf jars from the conventionally treated leaf motifs. The original inspiration for the leaves as well as much of the painted decoration on Tuscan wares until about 1475 was derived from Valencian earthenware dishes and tiles which were exported in large quantities to Italy and particularly to Pisa during the 15th century. This imitative phase was brought to a close around 1475 by the rich and magnificent Gothic foliage of typically coiled leaves. This original treatment of Gothic leaves is especially identified with the majolica made at Tuscany and Faenza during the last quarter of the 15th century. See *Italian Majolica*.

T'u Ting   In Chinese ceramics; see *Ting Yao*.

Twin Beds   In cabinetwork; see *Lits Jumeaux*.

Twin Bottle   In glass; see *Gemel Bottle*.

Twist Turning   In English cabinetwork; turning was a popular decorative process from about 1660 to 1700. Spiral or twist and baluster turned members were especially favored and they were effectively used in many various combinations. Single twist or single-rope twist resembling a twisted rope and double twist or double-rope twist resembling two ropes twisted about each other were sometimes combined on the same article of furniture. For example the uprights of the chair back and the front legs were double twisted and the rear legs and stretchers were single twisted. See *Turning*; *Barley Sugar Turning*.

Tye and Dye   In textiles; a method of printing a design by hand. Usually small parts of the material are taken and are tied with thread according to the design, and then dipped into the various colored dyes. If the knot is exceptionally tight the color cannot penetrate, leaving a ring of the ground color. If it is loosely tied the color penetrates and a blurred effect results. With this method some very interesting and colorful patterns can be obtained.

Tyg   In English ceramics; a pottery drinking vessel made in great numbers at the various English pottery centers from the beginning of the 17th century. It was a very large cup or mug, generally designed with three or four handles on the side in order that it could easily be passed from one person to the other. These tygs were often decorated with names, quaint inscriptions, mottoes and emblems. See *Posset-Pot*; *Piggin*.

Tzitzi See *Tchichi Rug*.

Tzu Chin In Chinese ceramics; crackled ware of the K'ang Hsi period varying in colors from a pale grey to brown tones and sometimes nearly black. The most noted ware is known as tzu chin, or lustrous brown, which includes various colors such as golden brown, golden black, café-au-lait and chocolate brown. It is also called Batavian ware. The glaze is sometimes in varying effects, such as brown mottled with black or a mottling and shading of brown with a harmonizing color. During the later part of the K'ang Hsi period and in the Yung Cheng and Ch'ien Lung times a decoration of Famille Rose color in panels was used on a ground of the café-au-lait color. See *Batavian Ware*.

Tz'u Chou In Chinese ceramics; a wide variety of wares were made at Tz'u Chou, which was a pottery center as early as the Sui dynasty, A.D. 589–618. Especially characteristic were the shapely vases with their strong, free-flowing designs that were painted in black slip, incised or carved. Tz'u Chou pottery had a buff-grey, buff or grey stoneware body which often had porcelaneous quality. Occasionally it had a light reddish or reddish-buff stoneware body. The body was covered with a dressing or wash of white slip. Numerous potteries made wares of the Tz'u Chou type. Different methods were employed in decorating the Tz'u Chou wares. The following are the characteristic kinds of decoration. In one variety of Tz'u Chou wares the designs were painted in black or black brown slip under a creamy or transparent glaze that was sometimes minutely crazed. Occasionally the black slip decoration had sgraffiato details. In another variety the designs were painted

in black under a colored glaze of pale blue or turquoise or deep green that was sometimes finely crazed. Sgraffiato was another type of Tz'u Chou ornament. In this type the stoneware body was covered with a thick black, brown or creamy glaze and the ornament was formed by cutting away the ground around the design and exposing the color of the body. Sometimes the design was engraved in outline and filled in with a black glaze through which the details were scratched. Another kind of Tz'u Chou ware was painted in red and brown or black slips under a usually transparent glaze that was sometimes crazed. The painted slip decoration frequently had sgraffiato decorations. A kind of Tz'u Chou ware had enamelled decoration. The decoration was painted in black or brown slip and in three colored enamels, that is, iron red, green and yellow. In another late technique actual leaves were applied to the body. After it had been washed in slip, the leaves were removed and then the piece was glazed and fired.

Tzu-T'an The name given by the Chinese to a hard and compact wood used in Chinese cabinet-work from at least the 8th century. It is more commonly called red sandalwood or palissandre. It has little or almost no figure and varies in color from a reddish brown to red. The genus of this wood is a matter of controversy. Tzu-t'an is generally identified as either *pterocarpus santalinus* or *dalbergia*, probably *dalbergia benthamii*. The latter is indigenous to China, while the former is imported and is found in the tropical forests of India as well as in other places. It seems reasonable to assume that both genera, which are closely related, were used. Early extant examples made of this wood are found at the Shosoin at Nara, Japan. These pieces were imported to Japan from China prior to the second half of the 8th century. Through the centuries tzu-t'an acquires a beautiful patina and becomes a deep violet color, ranging from a brownish to a blackish violet tone. Undoubtedly the Chinese prefer tzu-t'an above all other woods. See *Chinese Furniture*.

TZ'U CHOU GALLIPOT

U

UKIYO-E

Ukiyo-e In Japanese art; "Pictures of the Drifting World," the genre wood-block prints of the Japanese, are generally considered to have originated with Iwasa Matabei, 1577–c. 1650, son of the Daimyō of Itami, who jettisoned the traditions of the Tosa school of painting, adopted a style of mundane realism, and translated it to two-color India-ink and ochre wood-block prints. As the wood-block medium developed with the multiplication of blocks and colors, it became a poster art of temporal and theatrical life and scenery, which failed to attract cultural recognition in Japan until its values were assessed by early foreign academic and commercial residents such as Fenellosa and Bing in the 19th century. Originally a flat art which punctuated its message by relative size and position of details, ukiyo-e gradually adopted occidental perspective in the 18th century, with a resultant loss of force and orientalism as it became more photographic and water-color in style.

Underglaze Blue In ceramics; blue pigment color painted on the clay body of the ware under the glaze before firing. In Chinese ceramics; the blue and white wares of the Ming and Ch'ing dynasties are considered to be the finest ever produced. See *Underglaze Red*; *Blue and White Ming*; *Blue and White Ch'ing*.

Underglaze Red In Chinese ceramics; red pigment colors painted on the clay body of the ware under the glaze before it was fired. It is said to have originated in China. Decoration in underglaze red reached its highest development during the Hsüan Tê period, 1426–1435, and the reign was famous for this ware. Of particular importance are the white porcelain stem-cups decorated with three fishes in underglaze red of this period. During the K'ang Hsi reign and later in the Ch'ing period an underglaze red was called Rouge de Cuivre. It was then used either singly or with underglaze blue. See *Rouge de Cuivre*; *Underglaze Blue*; *Ming*.

United States Pottery In American ceramics; see *Bennington*.

Upholstery In English and American crafts; the term *upholstery* is defined as the work of the upholsterer or the materials, in particular the textiles and materials employed in the covering and stuffing of furniture. It includes such interior fittings of a house as window and bed draperies, cushions and similar articles. It is generally accepted that upholstered furniture dates from the reign of Queen Elizabeth I, although isolated examples of upholstered chairs and stools are mentioned in the inventories of Henry VIII. After the Restoration in 1660, which ushered in an era of luxurious furniture introduced from the Continent, upholstery began to figure more prominently. A great variety of materials are used in upholstery and in practically every period some of these coverings were of needlework, which has been a fashionable as well as a practical pastime for women for many years. Because imported textiles, such as silk velvets, brocades and damasks from Italy, were so costly the principal material used during the so-called age of walnut was needlework on canvas worked in gros point or petit point. Crewel work and turkey work were also popular. After 1770 gros point needlework was largely superseded by tapestry coverings and light weight silks. During the 18th century, when upholstery reached its zenith, cut silk velvets, brocades, brocatelles, damasks, French tapestry, satins, taffetas, Spanish leather, horsehair, chintz and other printed cottons and linens were included in the fashionable textiles. The general tendency for the last four decades of the 18th century was towards textiles of lighter weight and of more delicate designs and colors. Uphol-

496

stery in America essentially followed the prevailing fashions in textiles employed in England. During the 18th century imported textiles from France and England, such as velvets, brocades and damasks, were extensively used. Some of the earliest furniture was covered with needlework on canvas. English and French chintz were freely used in America and were advertised in newspapers as early as 1712. Other cotton and linen printed fabrics, such as toile de jouy, were very popular. Dimity was much favored both in England and in America for window and bed draperies during the last quarter of the 18th century. See *Tapestry Furniture Coverings*.

Uragawara In Japanese sword mounts; the protective fitting or guard on a Japanese scabbard at the opening in which the kozuka is carried. See *Kurikata*.

Urbino In Italian ceramics; Urbino is generally regarded as the most important center for the manufacture of Italian majolica around and after the middle of the 16th century. It was under the patronage of the Duke of Urbino. Castel Durante and Gubbio are also included in the Duchy of Urbino. Although potteries were in existence at Urbino from 1477, the manufacture of majolica did not achieve any artistic importance until around 1520 when Guido Pellipario, the son of Nicola Pellipario working at Castel Durante, settled at Urbino. He adopted the name of Fontana, and his pottery in addition to one conducted by his son, Orazio Fontana, were the two most important during the best period for Urbino majolica. Especially associated with Urbino majolica is the istoriato or pictorial style of painting developed by Nicola Pellipario while working at Castel Durante and the decoration of grotesques on a white ground with a pronounced use of modelled decoration. Nicola Pellipario was also working at Urbino from around and after 1528. The istoriato style of painting was in vogue in Urbino from around 1530 to 1580. Around 1570 the decoration of grotesques inspired by Raphael's painting in the Loggia of the Vatican began to appear and finally supplanted the istoriato style. These Urbino grotesques were accompanied by an increasing use of modelled decoration such as handles in the form of dolphins, figures modelled in the round, applied reliefs of masks and other similar kinds of plastic decoration. This type of work was continued into the 17th century. Practically nothing is known about Urbino majolica during the second half of the 17th century. See *Italian Majolica*; *Castel Durante*; *Raphaelesque*; *Istoriato*.

Urn Stand In English cabinetwork; see *Teakettle Stand*.

Usu-Niku-Bori In Japanese sword mounts; a term applied to carving in low relief. See *Bori*.

Utrecht Velvet A velvet with a cut pile made either of worsted mohair or mohair and cotton, used as a covering for furniture and for hangings or draperies. See *Velvet*.

URBINO PLATE

V

Vagireh Rug An Oriental rug belonging to the Persian classification, generally of the Bijar variety. The rug is about 3 feet by 5 feet. It is a small sample weaving and it is used by the weavers as a guide in making a large carpet. It is also called an Orinak. See *Persian Rugs*.

Vaisselier In French cabinetwork; see *Buffet-Vaisselier*.

Vaisselier-Horloge In French Provincial cabinetwork; the name given to a buffet-vaisselier having a tall case clock centered in its open shelves. The trunk and base of the tall case clock extended the height of the shelves and the hood of the clock was above the cornice. The vaisselier-horloge was a unique article of furniture and was particularly identified with the regional furniture of Bresse. See *Buffet-Vaisselier*; *Tall Case Clock*.

Valance In upholstery work; the name given to the border of drapery attached to the canopy of a bed, to the border of drapery above the window, or to the short curtain around a bedstead from the mattress to the floor serving to screen or conceal the space underneath. The early meaning was the valance beneath the canopy of a bed. Valances having this connotation were mentioned in English inventories as early as 1547. The various kinds of valances were made in an almost endless variety. Window valances were sometimes skillfully made of wood and were painted to match the fabric of the window hangings.

Valencia In Spanish ceramics; Valencia has been a principal center for Spanish pottery including blue and white, lustered and other earthenwares from the 13th century until the present day. The fame of its lustered productions was apparently well established around the beginning of the 15th century. The greater part of these beautiful Hispano-Moresque lustered wares were made during the 15th century and later at Manisses, a suburb of Valencia. Lustered wares of incomparable beauty were produced during the 15th and early 16th centuries. During this time they received princely and aristocratic patronage not only in Spain but also and especially from the Pope and Papal Princes in Italy. Especially praiseworthy were the armorial dishes of that period. The luster varied from a soft golden or greenish tone to a reddish purple similar to tarnished copper, sometimes having bluish or mother-of-pearl reflections. Later in the 16th century the luster was inclined to be a brownish yellow golden tone which was not as desirable and in the succeeding two centuries it was a rather hard bright reddish color like polished copper, which was even less desirable. The lustered earthenware comprised such pieces as vases, dishes, pharmacy jars and bowls. Coats-of-arms, arabesques, interlacements, starry flowers, trefoil leaves, vine leaves arranged in bands or in concentric circles, repetitive patterns of small circles, rosettes and small flowers, Arabic script and many other motifs were included in the decorative designs. Blue and white wares were made concurrently with the lustered wares; however, they were seldom as fine. Beautiful blue and white Valencia tiles were also made from the 15th century. See *Luster Decoration*; *Tuscany*; *Hispano-Moresque*.

Valenciennes In lace-making; although it is not known when lace was first produced at Valenciennes, it is accepted that their finest laces were made from around 1725 to 1780. The lace made within the city was referred to as Vrai Valenciennes and was regarded as the most choice. It was made of the finest quality of flax, and because of the almost unbelievable number of bobbins used in its fabrication it was extremely costly. The designs were remarkably rich

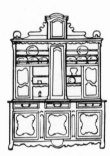

LOUIS XV
VAISSELIER-HORLOGE

498

and elegant, and the mesh ground was either square or diamond-shaped with closely plaited sides. The last important piece of Vrai Valenciennes was a headdress presented by the city to the Duchesse de Nemours when she was married in 1840. The technique of making Valenciennes lace was introduced into Flanders in the 17th century, and it was made at Ypres as early as 1656. This lace was admirable for its elaborate workmanship, with as many as two to three hundred bobbins being used on the same pillow for a piece of lace less than 2 inches in width. There was little variation in this lace until 1833 when a Ypres manufacturer, Duhayon Brunfaut, introduced a clear ground of twisted thread in place of the earlier thick ground, with striking flower designs which became immediately fashionable. Other leading centers producing this lace were Bruges, Courtrai, Menin, Alost and Ghent. All Valenciennes lace manufactured outside of the city itself was called Fausses Valenciennes.

Vambrace In armor; the protective plate armor for the forearm which, in the early 13th century, was worn under the hauberk and later in the century was worn over it. The name is also used to include the plate armor covering the forearm, elbow and a short upper section.

Varangian In cabinetwork; see *Harvard Chair*.

Vargueño In Spanish cabinetwork; an oblong walnut cabinet which was principally designed as a receptacle for documents and other valuables and could also be used as a desk. It was Spain's most distinctive and finest piece of cabinetwork. It was notable for its skillfully executed and exuberantly rich decoration. The vargueño was designed with a hinged drop-front which opened to disclose a richly ornamented interior of drawers and cupboard doors. In the earlier vargueño the interior was usually intricately inlaid in geometrical patterns of bone or ivory. This ivory was often brilliantly

painted in red, blue, green and gold and the pieces in white were often etched with designs in black. Later due to the influence of the Italian Renaissance the interior usually displayed an architectural façade incorporating colonettes and pilasters made of ivory or carved and gilded. The small doors and drawers were handsomely carved and brilliantly painted and gilded with classic motifs or richly inlaid with exotic woods or ivory. As a rule the only exterior decoration of the vargueño was the exquisite wrought-iron mounts which were sometimes gilded. These usually consisted of delicately pierced wrought-iron appliqués generally backed with crimson velvet, and an elaborate lock, hasp and pulls. Also at each end were drop handles. See *Puente Stand*; *Taquillón*; *Cabinet*.

Varnish In English furniture; in this practice the gloss is acquired by varnish rather than by a polishing medium, such as oil or beeswax, rubbed into the surface. The body of varnish is composed of a base of oil or a spirit and a resinous substance, such as lac. This process essentially consists of applying successive coats of varnish and of rubbing or cutting them down after about every three coats. After the last one or two coats are applied the surface is finally polished by friction or rubbing. From around 1820 French polish supplanted the use of varnish. See *Polish*.

Vasa Murrhina In American glass; a late 19th century American art glass, characterized by an inner layer of colored glass, with various colored metals, in flake or dust form, fused in it. It is covered with an overlay of clear glass. See *Art Glass*.

Vase Rug An early Persian Oriental rug of the 16th century. The rug derives its name from a representation of a Chinese vase filled with flowers that is seen at widely separated intervals within a profusion of leaves and flowers and is therefore often difficult to find. See *Persian Rug*.

Vasse, François-Antoine 1681–1736. French sculptor working in 1708 as a decorative

VARGUEÑO ON PUENTE
STAND, SPANISH

sculptor at Versailles. In 1715 he became Dessinateur Général de la Marine. At the present time his designs are generally considered to be a vital creative force in developing the Régence style as well as contributing to the creation of the Rococo. He was especially active from around 1715 to 1730.

Velvet In textiles; a silk warp pile fabric; the term *warp pile* meaning that the pile has an extra warp added to the usual ground warp and weft threads. The pile yarns are lifted over cutting wires which cut the pile as the wires are withdrawn, producing a cut pile fabric. In a loop pile velvet the wires do not cut the warp pile. Velvets are either plain or figured. In a plain velvet the entire surface is covered with a short and even pile. There are several varieties of figured velvets which are produced by using different methods of weaving. One form of figured velvet is produced by using a warp pile of different lengths. Another type combines both a cut and uncut warp pile. In another form the designs are in cut velvet worked on a satin ground or a brocaded ground. The Italian cities of Lucca, Genoa and Florence were the earliest centers in Europe and they were flourishing from around the 13th century. They produced magnificent figured velvets during the Renaissance. The Flemish city of Bruges was a leading center during the 16th century. Also noteworthy are the late 17th century Venetian figured velvets with their brilliant and elaborate designs and the late 17th and 18th century French velvets. During the second half of the 18th century the vogue for velvets declined in favor of lighter weight textiles. See *Silk*; *Lucchese Patterns*; *Ciselé*; *Upholstery*.

Vendée In French Provincial; a department in western France that was formed from the old province of Bas-Poitou. The provincial furniture of Vendée was characterized by an abundance and variety of massive Louis XIII style armoires or cupboards made of oak or walnut and decorated with the diamond-point design. As a rule the Louis XV furniture was simply decorated with

VELVET DESIGNS,
ITALIAN

moldings that were rather thin. The Louis XVI cabinetwork was characterized by its simple flat carved decoration which was of classic inspiration. Much of the cabinetwork was of a transitional nature for although the ornament was in the style of Louis XVI the forms retained the graceful curving lines of the Louis XV style. See *French Provincial*.

Veneering In cabinetwork; a decorative process in which a thin layer of wood generally having fine markings is laid upon a wood surface. By the veneering of woods of a fine quality on a common framework it is possible to produce surfaces remarkable for richness of figure and of color. Then, too, by selecting woods of pronounced markings the veneered surface can be artistically arranged to form fine decorative effects. Veneering was practiced in England only to a very limited extent before the Restoration, 1660. However, its possibilities were quickly appraised by the cabinetmakers during the reign of Charles II. Veneered surfaces were a feature of William and Mary cabinetwork, and oystering, which is a distinctive form of parquetry employed in English cabinetwork, was used during the William and Mary style. Undoubtedly the esteem accorded Queen Anne furniture' is due to some extent to its richly figured veneered walnut surfaces. The use of contrasting veneers was a special talent of the later 18th century cabinetwork and it attained a high degree of excellence. Richly toned satinwood and mahogany veneered surfaces were freely inlaid with decorative veneered bandings and borders of contrasting wood, such as rosewood, tulipwood, satinwood and mahogany. Graceful oval panels of richly figured veneers were especially characteristic of Sheraton's work. Broad veneered bandings, panel borders and stringing lines laid in a contrasting veneered surface were also popular during the Regency. Veneering was practiced in America from around the reign of William and Mary and was freely employed on the Hepplewhite and Sheraton styles. Veneering was a fashionable decorative process in France in the Louis XV style and was praiseworthy for its fine workmanship. Due to the characteristic undulating surface of the Louis XV style more skill was required than in the succeeding Louis XVI style. The Continental practice of laying sandbags over the undulating surfaces until the glue was fixed was occasionally employed in some English veneered work with curving surfaces. See *Parquetry*.

Venetian Blind   See *Jalousie*.

Venetian Flat Point   See *Point Plat de Venise*.

Venetian Glass   It appears that glassmakers were in Venice as early as the 11th century and that by the 13th century the industry of glassmaking was well established, although the work possessed little artistic distinction before the 15th century. Due to the increasing fire hazard an edict was passed in 1291 transferring the industry to the neighboring island of Murano. The Venetians rediscovered the technique of decolorizing glass with manganese resulting in the *cristallo*, so called because of its resemblance to rock crystal. Much of the early glass was also colored in rich tones of purple, blue and green. Venetian glass, which was a soda-lime glass, was remarkably ductile and plastic, permitting the development of many fanciful forms such as fruit, flowers and birds. Venetian Renaissance glass, which maintained its supremacy from late in the 15th century for almost the next two hundred years, was distinctive for its elegant and slender forms and for its exquisite and delicate decoration. Enamelling, which had been employed in the Near East with unrivalled skill, became one of the most important methods for decorating Venetian glass during the last quarter of the 15th century. The gilding on the enamelled glass possessed a singular soft and warm quality. Millefiori, aventurine, latticinio, schmelzglas, lace glass, fondi d'oro and milch or milk glass were all included in the typical Venetian types. The use of glass threads embedded in the glass

was the basis of many exquisite designs. Engraving with a diamond point was occasionally used from around the third quarter of the 16th century onwards. Venetian glass was exported throughout Europe and more was made by emigrant Italian workmen. Probably the most famous center outside of Italy was at Antwerp where craftsmen from Murano were recorded as early as 1541. From around late in the 17th century onwards Venetian glass began to show a gradual decline. Chandeliers and mirror frames decorated with a multitude of modelled flowers were characteristic later pieces. In the 18th century due to the vogue for cut and engraved decoration developed by the Germans and Bohemians, the Venetians also produced work in this medium, but unfortunately their soda-lime glass was not suitable for this form of decoration. Venetian Renaissance styles were revived around the middle of the 19th century. See *Glass*; *Mirror*; *Threaded Glass*.

Venetian Painted Furniture   Undoubtedly Italy's finest contribution in cabinetwork during the Rococo style was her charming painted Venetian Rococo furniture. The most exquisite pieces were made around the middle of the 18th century. Venice was the leading art center in Italy during the 18th century and she made much fine furniture during that period. The painted Venetian furniture was admirable for its graceful curving lines, for its unrivalled harmonious colors and velvet-like texture, and for the composition of its rich decoration which was made more interesting with exotic birds, flowers and chinoiseries. The painted furniture was made in numerous pieces based on the Louis XV style prevailing forms. Especially outstanding were the commodes, generally fitted with marble tops, and many delightful small pieces such as hanging cabinets and bookshelves and mirrors and boxes for dressing tables. The furniture was often painted in water colors for economical reasons. When done in water colors the surfaces first received a

VENETIAN GLASS
DRAGON-STEM GOBLET

coat of gesso, a plaster-like material, which gave the surface a velvet-like texture and absorbed the water colors exceptionally well. Then a coat of varnish was applied to make it more durable. Although the work done in water colors was not as permanent as work done in oil paints, it excelled oil paints in its freshness of color and its velvet-like texture.

Venetian Point   Venice has long been celebrated for her needlepoint laces first made in the 15th century. Fringes of Venice, "gold of Venice," white silk, black silk, silver and white thread of Venice were mentioned in English inventories from early in the 16th century. However, it was not until around the middle of the 16th century that Venetian laces and cutwork embroideries were found to any appreciable extent in England and France. Venetian laces were in great demand in France until 1665 when Colbert established the Points de France. There were many various kinds of laces made at Venice, probably around twenty different types, such as knotted and plaited laces, lacis, punto a reticella, Venetian flat and raised points and Venetian points with a mesh ground or réseau and a mixed Venetian guipure or mezzo punto. See *Burano Lace*; *Italian Lace*.

VENETIAN ROCOCO
SECRETARY COMMODE

Venetian Raised Ivory Point   See *Punto Tagliato a Fogliami*.

Venetian Raised Point   See *Punto Tagliato a Fogliami*.

Venetian Rose Point   See *Punto Tagliato a Fogliami*.

Venetian Velvet   In textiles; around the 14th century the Venetians developed a velvet in which the designs were in slight relief above the ground, both being in cut silk velvet. As a result the term is often applied to a figured cut silk velvet. See *Velvet*.

Venice   In Italian ceramics; it is generally accepted that majolica was not made in Venice before 1525. As a rule the tin glaze did not have as much tin oxide as was gener-

ally used in the glazes for majolica, and as a result it was partially transparent. Perhaps the most characteristic tin enamelled glaze for Venetian majolica had a bluish or greyish tone, given the contemporary name of Smaltino. The earliest Venetian majolica reflected Oriental inspiration, due to the trade relations existing with Oriental countries. Lotus flowers and scrolled foliage in the Chinese style were typical. The close trade relations between Venice and Nuremberg in the 16th century resulted in a distinctive class of great beauty having armorial bearings of important Nuremberg families. Another 16th century variety was in the istoriato Urbino style with pictorial subjects. Another type had coiled foliage and flowers painted in colors reserved on a blue ground with panels containing figure subjects or busts. Of particularly interest was a late 17th century thinly potted resonant variety of majolica with a smaltino glaze. It had molded decoration of flowers, foliage, cupids, and masks, apparently taken from silver models, with landscapes painted in colors often enclosed in painted Baroque scrolls. Other distinctive varieties of majolica ware were also made during the 16th and 17th centuries, such as one variety with a rich decoration of luscious fruits. During the 18th century one of the porcelain manufactories produced faïence with painted flowers. See *Italian Majolica*; *Faïence*.

Venice   In ceramics; there were three porcelain manufactories operating in Venice during the 18th century. They were conducted by Francesco and Giuseppe Vezzi, c. 1720 to c. 1740; by Nathaniel Friedrich Hewelcke, 1757 to 1763, and by Geminiano Cozzi, c. 1764 to 1812. The porcelain attributed to the Vezzi manufactory was a true porcelain of varying quality. It is presumed that the marks were "Venezia", "Ven a" or "V a". The painted decoration included figures from the Italian Comedy, charming naturalistic flowers and motifs of Chinese and Japanese inspiration. Underglaze blue painting of a clean quality was also found. The wares comprised globular shaped teapots, small bowls, saucers and cups without handles. The porcelain attributed to Hewelcke, who was a dealer from Dresden, was marked with a "V" and was not free from imperfections. Much of the porcelain ascribed to this factory had an unusual primitive charm. The porcelain made at the Cozzi manufactory was a hybrid soft paste porcelain with a thin glaze, generally marked with an anchor. The productions chiefly consisted of tablewares, vases and figures and were frequently in imitation of Meissen. Especially admirable were the fine colors including a rich red, a beautiful bluish purple and a clear emerald green. The gilding was of fine quality and soft in tone. The painted decoration in the Rococo style was often distinctive for its fanciful Italian interpretation. Their versions of Meissen Rococo border patterns had an abandon that was entirely delightful. Of outstanding interest were some delicately modelled white glazed and biscuit figures and groups showing an unusual and frequently very charming miniature style.

Ventail In armor; a protection for the face. The word has various meanings and in the 14th century in the form of *aventail* it was used to describe a piece of mail hung from a basinet. In the 16th century the name was given to a part of a visor, on a closed helmet, which is an upper beaver.

Vermeil The term *vermeil*, meaning gilding, is taken from the French word *vermeil*. The term *vermeil* also means silver-gilt and gilt bronze. A French dictionary of 1839 states that "vermeil is a liquid which gives lustre and fire to the gold and makes it resemble ormolu". In the work of the goldsmiths and silversmiths the term *vermeil* is applied to articles of silver-gilt in which the vermeil, or rouge, is mixed with the gold amalgam and applied on silver plate to give a warm rich rose tone to the gold. Vermeil or argent doré or silver-gilt is mentioned in French inventories as early as 1316 onwards and in important inventories such as those of Charles VI in 1383 and of the Louvre in 1420.

Vernis Martin In French lacquer work; European lacquer work was done in an essentially different method from that practiced in the Orient. Apparently the imitation of Eastern lacquer work was started in Europe at least as early as the 17th century. The vogue for this kind of decoration in Europe received an early important stimulus through the Dutch East India Company who were successful importers of Oriental lacquer wares. The taste for chinoiseries with their subjects taken from an imaginary Chinese fairy-tale world had been strongly developed under Louis XIV. In France, where lacquer work achieved a remarkable standard of excellence, workshops were allocated in the Gobelins Manufactory in the 17th century to improve this medium of decoration. In the 18th century the Martin brothers who were members of a distinguished family of French artists-artificers were successful in producing exquisitely executed lacquer work. There were four brothers, namely Guillaume, Simon Etienne, Julien and Robert, 1706–1765. It is generally accepted that Robert Martin produced the most artistic work. Originally they were fine coach painters. The term *vernis martin* has been given to the varnish which they perfected, since the word *vernis* is the French word for varnish. They did not invent the varnish, but they perfected it and improved the methods for applying the varnish which they jealously guarded. They imitated every variety of Chinese lacquer. They made a large amount of exquisite lacquered furniture. Especially notable were their tables, desks and commodes enhanced with bronze Rococo appliqués. Their famous lacquer work was regarded as the acme of magnificent decoration. By 1748 they had at least three manufactories in Paris which were incorporated into a Royal Manufactory of Lacquer in the Chinese Manner. The taste for lacquer work continued until the Revolution. See *Lacquer*.

LOUIS XV VERNIS
MARTIN ENCOIGNURE

Verre de Fougère　In glass; the French name given to waldglas. See *Waldglas*.

Verrier　In French Provincial cabinetwork; the name generally given to a set of open hanging wall shelves which were used for the reception of drinking glasses.

Vert Antique Marble　Or Verde Antico. A marble from Larissa, Thessaly, Greece. It is a brecciated serpentine type of marble, being mottled or spotted like a serpent's skin. It is found in three varieties; light, intermediate and dark green. The brecciated pieces are nearly black with a bright green ground. Its beauty is derived from the formation of clouded colors caused by small patches of calcite.

Vert Campan　See *Campan Marble*.

Vicar and Moses　In English ceramics; the name given to a popular and well-known pottery figure group first made around 1770 by the Ralph Woods, father and son, of Burslem, Staffordshire. The group portrays a parson asleep in the pulpit with his good friend and parish clerk Moses delivering the sermon.

Victorian　Victorian furniture did not possess the characteristics of a true style. It was an incongruous assortment of many styles marred by a mania for tasteless novelties. The Victorian era extends approximately from the time Queen Victoria ascended the throne in 1837 until her death in 1901. The Victorian era both in England and in America is frequently divided into three phases; Early Victorian, 1837–1850; mid-Victorian, 1850–1875, and Late Victorian, 1875–1901. The early Victorian furniture is generally regarded as the best. It was usually made of rosewood or mahogany. The Louis Philippe style was fashionable in France around 1840. This return to the Rococo was evidenced in the contemporary Victorian furniture in its profuse and exaggerated curves and in its abundant naturalistic fruit and flower carvings. Especially

VICTORIAN CHAIR

characteristic were the American black walnut chairs designed in that fashion. From around 1840 to 1860 John H. Belter produced numerous Victorian pieces of furniture made of rosewood which were of fine quality. Daniel Pabst, a Philadelphia cabinetmaker working around 1860, also produced some fine walnut Victorian pieces. During the two later phases black walnut generally supplanted rosewood and mahogany. A strong preference for Renaissance forms marked the mid-Victorian furniture. Charles Locke Eastlake, an English architect, published a book in 1868 with furniture designs borrowed from the Jacobean style. The designs for Victorian furniture were borrowed from all the recognized styles. Almost every piece was either an adaptation of some single style in which the best features of that style were ignored or which was a tasteless blending of several styles. Sometimes the designers added a few novelties of their own. The designs for Victorian furniture, with a few exceptions, were without artistic merit, but the quality of materials and workmanship was commendable, particularly in the cabinetwork executed for the rich Victorians. The desire for lavish display which characterized all phases of Victorian decorative art was also apparent in the richly tufted, draped and corded upholstery work. Probably the most appropriate inclusive label for the art of the Victorian period is the word Romanticism. The art of Romanticism was chiefly a retrospective art, displaying a love of the past, especially of the medieval past. It was also an art of sentiment. It worshipped the beauties of nature. This frame of mind with its romantic trend became successively dominant during a great part of the Victorian age. See *Belter, John H.*; *Louis Philippe*.

Vide-Poche　In French cabinetwork; the term *vide-poche*, or pocket-emptier, was given to a small dressing table used in the bedroom. It was introduced during the Louis XV style and was made in various forms usually of delicate construction with very slender and graceful legs. The vide-poche was frequently designed with a rectangular top over two very small frieze drawers and was fitted with a rising panelled candle screen. Sometimes the vide-poche had a small circular top with a raised edge.

Vienna In Austrian ceramics; a hard paste porcelain manufactory was established at Vienna in 1719. It was the second European hard paste porcelain manufactory, the first being at Meissen. The productions generally fall into three groups: 1719 to 1744 under the management of Claudius Innocentius Du Paquier; 1744 to 1784 under the Austrian State; 1784 to 1864 under the management of Konrad von Sorgenthal, d. 1805. Evidence of decline became perceptible after 1805 and the factory closed in 1864. No factory mark was used during the early period. A shield mark with the arms of Austria was adopted after 1744, the form varying considerably. After 1749 the shield mark was in underglaze blue. After 1783 in addition to the shield mark the last two numerals of the year were generally impressed, and after 1800 the last three numerals. The early wares were notable for beautiful specimens in the Baroque style. The Baroque decoration included interlacing scrolls and foliations, pendent swags of drapery, and palmettes which often covered the entire surface with a delicate web of decoration. The beautiful Vienna iron-red was also prominent in these early wares. During the second period the tablewares were in the Rococo style and to a large extent were in imitation of Meissen and Sèvres. Of particular interest were the figures and groups which showed an individual quality although the types were of Meissen inspiration. The best figures were executed in a lively and vivacious style that was completely captivating. The third period is notable for its superb tablewares in the Neo-Classic style painted in miniature style and richly gilded. They were remarkable for their great refinement and perfection of workmanship. The forms were distinctive

for their elegant simplicity; urn-shaped vases were especially typical. Perhaps the principal innovation was a style of highly wrought gilding in relief. Interesting new ground colors of technical perfection also contributed to the refinement of the wares. Practically all the figures were of biscuit and were chiefly copied from Sèvres. The material had a warm white tone that was pleasing. See *Schwarzlot*.

Viennese Hand-Tufted Carpet See *Hand-Tufted Carpet*.

Vieux Paris In French ceramics; porcelain wares made by the various manufactories in Paris particularly during the 18th century. The term *Vieux Paris*, or *old Paris*, is given to those wares that are without an accepted identifying mark but which are known to have been produced in the Paris kilns because of their colors and decoration which are characteristic of Paris wares.

Vignola, Giacomo da 1507–1573. One of the foremost late Renaissance Italian architects. In 1550 he was appointed Papal architect to Pope Julius III. After the death of Michelangelo in 1564 he succeeded him as architect in charge of the Basilica of St. Peter. Vignola together with the Italian architect Della Porta erected the church of the Gesù in 1570, which is the principal church of the Jesuit Order in Rome. This church with its gorgeously decorated interior of colored marbles, bronzes, sculptures and masses of gilding, furnished the model for the sumptuous style called the architecture of the Jesuits. Because he was the designer of the extravagantly rich interior decorations Vignola is generally identified with the beginning of the Baroque movement in Italy.

Vile, William d. 1767. Celebrated English cabinetmaker to the King working from around 1750 until he retired in 1765. He and his partner, John Cobb, carried on a large and successful business under the name of Vile and Cobb at No. 72 St. Martin's Lane on the corner of St. Martin's Lane and

LOUIS XV VIDE-POCHE

Long Acre. At the beginning of the reign of George III the firm of Vile and Cobb ranked pre-eminently among the cabinetmakers to the Crown. This was chiefly due to the elegant quality of the cabinetwork and to the distinctive character of the designs. In the first decade of the reign of George III the work of Vile was unrivalled. None of the known pieces of Chippendale working in the Rococo was a worthy challenge for the cabinetwork of Vile. He also supplied much furniture to the aristocracy. He supplied furniture to Horace Walpole which is revealed in the Strawberry Hill accounts from 1760 to 1771. Authenticated pieces by Vile, which date from the early years of the reign of George III, are superbly finished and reveal an individuality in design. Some of the pieces are remarkable for their exuberant carvings which are vigorously executed and skillfully finished. The veneered mahogany was carefully selected for fine and brilliant markings. The pieces are notable for their well-balanced lines and correct proportions. Especially outstanding is the fresh and original quality found in the principles of design and in the treatment of the decorative detail. It is impossible to estimate the degree of individual responsibility of Vile and Cobb for this cabinetwork. Suffice it to say that Vile was the senior partner and the known pieces for which Cobb was responsible are in the Neo-Classic style and are decorated with marquetry work. Literature on English furniture by authorities has fully recognized the singular ability of these two partners. See *Cobb, John.*

SILVER VINAIGRETTE

Vinaigrette   In English silver; the name given to a small decorative box, generally of gold or silver, having a hinged lid and an inner perforated cover. It contained a tiny sponge which was saturated with aromatic vinegar. It was used by the ladies to dispel any feeling of faintness. Occasionally it was fitted with a ring through which a chain could be passed. It was made in a variety of forms such as a book, purse, egg or some similar form. It was introduced during the 18th century and was a more recent adaptation of the 16th century pomander, which it partially superseded. See *Pomander.*

Vincennes   In French ceramics; a hard paste porcelain manufactory was established at Vincennes, near Paris, in 1765 by Pierre-Antoine Hannong. In 1777 a heraldic label showing the patronage of Louis-Philippe, Duc de Chartres, was registered. The factory changed hands, and after 1788 there is no further record of its productions. The wares were similar in form and in painted decoration to the current fashions for Paris porcelains. The important soft paste porcelain manufactory was moved to Sèvres. See *Sèvres.*

Vinovo   In Italian ceramics; a porcelain manufactory was started at Vinovo, near Turin, by Giovanni Vittorio Brodel and Pierre-Antoine Hannong in 1776 under Royal patronage. It was active until 1820. Included among the marks were a cross over a "V", sometimes accompanied by the initials "D G"; occasionally the cross was used alone. The material for the porcelain resembled a soft paste, actually it was of a hybrid composition. Generally it had a rather warm and pleasing creamy tone. The decoration was in the late 18th century French style, comprising such typical motifs as small bouquets, sprigs of cornflowers and classical scrolls. The enamel colors were of a good quality; especially fine were the soft warm tones of yellow and brown. The figures were admirable for the texture of the material. Essentially they were nicely finished but revealed little originality. They were in white glazed and unglazed porcelain as well as in painted enamel colors.

Violet Wood   The name given to any of various hard woods having reddish or purplish color, such as palisandre, kingwood, rosewood, myall wood and acacia.

Virginal   A musical instrument having strings and a keyboard. The case was not provided with legs as it was placed upon a table or a stand. The mechanism consists of a jack or upright piece of wood at the end of the key-lever having a thin piece of wood attached by a pivot and to which is affixed a leather or quill point. By pressing the key the rising lever causes the quill point to pick the string as it passes, making the tonal vibration, and when falling passes the string freely due to the pivot action. The early virginal had a rectangular case resembling a clavichord and was called a clavicordium virginale since it was frequently found in convents as well as a favorite ladies' instrument. In Italy during the 15th century the case appeared in other forms such as wing-shaped, harp-shaped and trapezoid and because the quill, or spine, had replaced earlier materials used for a pick it was called a spinetta. In England the name virginal was used for all these shapes during the 16th and early 17th centuries; about the middle of the 18th century the name *virginal* was applied only to the rectangular form. See *Clavichord*; *Spinet*; *Harpsichord*.

Virtù Or Vertu. The term *virtù*, derived from the Italian word *virtù*, and the French word *vertu*, is applied to a curio, an antique, or other work of the fine arts. An object or article of virtù is one in which virtuosos are interested. The term *virtù* is also applied to an interest in, or a knowledge of, the fine arts; a taste for curios or works of art.

Visor In armor; the term given to various kinds of protective armor for the eyes, and when made in one piece to protect the face. A movable visor hinged to the helmet was introduced in the 14th century. The salade of the 15th century had a visor which joined the beaver at the lower part of the face. In the 16th century the close helmet had a visor which is commonly called a beaver. It is made in three sections, namely, a visor with slits, an upper beaver or ventail, and a lower beaver or chin piece. See *Beaver*.

Vitrine In French cabinetwork; the name given to a form of cabinet introduced during the Louis XVI style. It was designed with one or two glazed doors and was fitted with shelves. The vitrine was especially designed to hold and display the fine porcelain and other small objects of art. As a rule it was a rather plain article of furniture so that it would not detract from its contents. The vitrine was designed in different sizes. The very small vitrine was sometimes placed on a table or on a commode.

Vitro di Trina In Venetian glass; lace glass. See *Venetian Glass*.

Vitruvian Scroll In ornament; a classic repetitive pattern of wave scrolls. This wave motif consisted of a series of scrolls forming a continuous or running pattern. It has a resemblance to the waves. It was widely used in English cabinetwork by the architectural designers, working in the Early Georgian style, especially as a decoration for the friezes on various types of side tables.

Volant In armor; a detachable piece of plate armor used to reinforce the front of a helmet. The name is also applied to various pieces used in tilting armor, such as a piece covering the breast, left shoulder and lower part of the face in the 16th century.

Volkstedt In German ceramics; a soft paste porcelain manufactory was started in 1760 by Georg Heinrich Macheleid at Volkstedt, Thuringia. The mark was a hay-fork from the Schwarzburg arms. Shortly after, Macheleid obtained a privilege from the Prince of Schwarzburg-Rudolstadt to make hard paste porcelain. The factory changed hands many times and is still in existence. During the 19th century it obtained a bad reputation for making forgeries. The early mark was one or two crossed hay-forks; the latter mark was drawn to resemble the crossed swords of Meissen, who protested. In 1787 it was changed to either a single fork or crossed forks with incurvate prongs and having a line at the point where they crossed; however, the former mark apparently continued to be used. Around 1799 the letter "R" was used as a mark. The early porcelain was not free from imperfections and relief decorations were often used to conceal these defects. Meissen wares were freely copied,

VIRGINAL MOUNTED ON A STAND

and the majority of their productions were essentially a coarse version of Meissen. Among their finer productions were tablewares and vases with excellent painted decoration in the Rococo style of figure subjects enclosed in Rococo scrollwork and of naturalistic flowers. The figures were executed in the manner of peasant art and were sometimes imbued with a singular charm. See *Thuringia*.

Volute In ornament; a spiral scroll-shaped ornament. During the Louis XIV style the open arm on the characteristic Louis XIV style chair almost always terminated in a volute. During the Louis XV style the majority of cabriole chair legs terminated in a small volute or whorl.

Vorschrift A handwritten manuscript of the Pennsylvania Germans. See *Fractur*.

Voulge In arms and armor; the earliest and most primitive medieval cutting and thrusting weapon. It consists of a long wooden shaft with a steel head attached in the form of a cleaver extending to a long point. See *Halberd*; *Gisarme*; *Ranseur*; *Partizan*.

Voyder The name given to an early form of large dish or tray mentioned in medieval English records. It was used by the servants to collect the scraps of food left on the trencher or plate while dining. Although the material used for the early voyder is not known, pewter voyders are mentioned in 16th century English records.

LOUIS XVI VOYEUSE

Voyeuse In French cabinetwork; a form of upholstered chair having a narrow flaring back of medium height continuing to form a rolled-over padded crest rail. In this form of chair the occupant sat in a reverse position and the crest rail served as an arm rest. It was in vogue in France from around 1740 to 1780 and was designed in the Louis XV and Louis XVI styles. It is stated in French furniture literature that the chair was especially used by persons watching card games and games of chance. Sheraton in his CABI-

NET DICTIONARY, 1803, illustrates the French voyeuse and refers to it as a conversation chair. See *Conversation Chair*.

Vrai Réseau In lace-making; a French term given to a fine handmade bobbin net ground which was the real Brussels ground when it succeeded the bride ground later in the 17th century. It was made in small strips of an inch in width and was joined together by a special stitch called point de Raccroc, known in English as fine joining. Vrai réseau was remarkable for its fineness which was made possible by the extraordinary fineness of its thread. In Flanders vrai réseau is called droschel. See *Brussels Lace*.

Vries, Jan Vredeman de Born circa 1527. In Dutch and Flemish Renaissance ornament; de Vries was a Dutch painter, architect, sculptor and designer of furniture. His designs and those of his son, Paul, were a dominating factor in decorative art until the Baroque style was developed by Peter Paul Rubens. In 1577 Jan de Vries published a book on designs and style of ornament in Antwerp. He incorporated many architectural features in his designs for furniture. His interpretation of Italian Renaissance motifs lacked refinement. Typically characteristic of his work was the use of elaborately carved consoles; heavy cornices; richly carved pilasters; rich scrollwork; twisting curves; the use of human figures, animal figures, caryatids and grotesques, and pierced crestings and strapwork. De Vries' book of engravings also had wide influence in England and contributed to the development of the Elizabethan style. See *Renaissance*, *Netherlands*.

Vulliamy, Benjamin Lewis 1780–1854. He was a member of a prominent family of clockmakers who settled in London early in the 18th century, having originally come from Switzerland. Different members of the family held office as clockmakers to the Crown. Benjamin Vulliamy made numerous clocks and watches for George III.

Wafer-Box In English silver; a small box generally made of silver and occasionally of glass or porcelain to hold the wafers which were used to seal letters. The wafer, which was an adhesive disk of dried paste, was made of flour, gelatin or some other material to which coloring matter was added. See *Taper Stick*; *Standish*.

Wager Cup A silver drinking cup. See *Jungfrauenbecher*.

Wag-on-the-Wall Clock In American furniture; the name popularly given to the dial and works of a tall case clock which was hung on the wall. These works were intended to be put in a tall case and many were hung temporarily on the wall until the case was finished. See *Tall Case Clock*.

Wagon Seat In American cabinetwork; a form of early American settee called a rumble seat or a wagon seat, found in the country districts. It is believed to have been used both as a seat in the house as well as on the wagon. The back of the settee was generally of slat-back construction or in the form of a chair-back settee. It was of sturdy construction and was without decoration.

Wainscot The term was originally used during the Middle Ages as a shipper's term for bundles of wood shipped to England from Baltic ports to be used in the construction of wagons or wains. In the 17th century the English gradually applied the word to wood to be used for furniture and for panelling. It is also spelled wagenshot, and wageschot. Panel-work or wainscot of oak or other wood was used to line the walls of a room. The term *wainscot* is particularly applied in interior decoration to the panel-work lining the lower part of the walls of a room, the panelled wooden dado.

Wainscot Chair In English cabinetwork; the name is principally applied to a variety of oak armchair having a panelled back with open arms and legs. The legs were joined with a continuous stretcher close to the floor. This variety of armchair was first introduced during the Elizabethan era and was the principal armchair of the Elizabethan style. It continued to be made throughout the 17th century. There was little variation in the shape of the chair. It was rectilinear in form and was solid and massive in construction. The arms on the earlier chair were flatter and straighter, while the arms on later chairs had a downward curve. The surface of the chair was decorated with carving and sometimes with a combination of inlay work and carving. It is also called a panelled-back chair.

Wakizashi In Japanese arms; the name given to the shorter of the two swords carried by a Japanese samurai, or fighting man. The wakizashi is similar to the long sword called katana; however the mounts are usually more elaborately decorated. The slightly curving blade is about 18 inches in length. The wakizashi was usually fitted with both the kogai and kozuka, while the katana seldom had the kogai and frequently had neither. The wakizashi was carried as a supplementary weapon as well as for ceremonial suicide. See *Katana*.

Waldenburg In German ceramics; potteries were in existence at Waldenburg, Saxony, as early as the Middle Ages. A salt-glazed stoneware having a grey or light brown body with a brown surface was made here from around the middle of the 16th century. This early stoneware had little artistic merit, and it was not until later in the 16th century that more richly decorated wares were found. Their principal productions were all kinds of drinking vessels of distinctive form decorated with reliefs, such as circular wreaths, medallions, and allegorical figure subjects.

WAGON SEAT, AMERICAN

Waldglas In German glass; the term *waldglas* or forest glass is applied to utilitarian vessels, such as drinking glasses and flasks, of a rather simple form produced during the medieval period by glasshouses located in German forests, the ash of beechwood serving as a source for the potash alkali. Although some pieces made of waldglas dating from the 14th century have been found as far south as Spain, the largest production was in the north and did not start until late in the 15th century. It is an unrefined glass and is characteristically green in color due to the many impurities, especially iron, found in the available raw materials. Much of the decoration found on waldglas vessels is in the form of applied nuppens or prunts. The waldglas of northern Europe was made in many places in France, Germany and the Netherlands, and in recent years there has been an increasing appreciation for this common greenish glass.

EAGLE WALL BRACKET, AMERICAN

Wall Bracket In English cabinetwork; the detachable wall bracket served as a shelf or ledge to support some object as a vase, clock, bust, candelabrum or statuette. The carved wood wall bracket, which was generally gilded or painted, was introduced into England from France. It did not come into general use until the time of William and Mary when it was principally used to display porcelain from China and Delft ware from Holland. Many of these early brackets were very French in taste and mirrored the influence of Daniel Marot in their elaborate carved ornament. Wall brackets were an important decorative accessory throughout the 18th century. The wall bracket carved with a spread eagle was characteristic of the Early Georgian style. Chippendale illustrated designs for gilded or painted wall brackets enhanced with such favorite motifs as C-scrolls, stalactites, exotic birds and pagoda tops. Another variety was made of mahogany and was composed of delicate pierced fretwork. This type was generally used for the reception of porcelain figures and vases and was especially popular. Under the influence of Robert Adam wall brackets were later designed in the classic taste. Designs for wall brackets in Hepplewhite's GUIDE were usually of carved and gilded or carved and painted soft wood.

Wall, Dr. In English ceramics; the name frequently attached to the early period of Worcester porcelain, 1751–1783, since Dr. Wall was one of the founders. Although Dr. Wall died in 1776 the period is generally extended to 1783, which date marks the death of William Davis, who was the first manager and who is commonly credited with the early productions. See *Worcester*.

Wallendorf In German ceramics; a porcelain manufactory was started at Wallendorf, Thuringia, in 1764 by Johann Wolfgang Hammann. It was conducted by the same family for many years and in 1898 was formed into a company. Originally the mark was a "W" made to resemble the crossed swords of Meissen; after 1778 it was simply a small "w". The productions were principally useful wares for a middle class market. The painted decoration was largely in imitation of Meissen; the so-called Meissen onion pattern was a very popular design. The figures, which were generally not marked, included all kinds of subjects; many were copied from Meissen models. Of particular interest were some charming figures in contemporary dress executed in the manner of peasant art. They had the same naïve charm associated with the somewhat primitive figures made at Limbach.

Wall Fountain In furniture; the wall fountain, which was usually affixed to the wall, was a container for holding water with a spigot at the bottom. It was generally made of pewter, copper or pottery and the lavabo or wash basin, which was placed beneath it was made to match it. In the Spanish home the wall fountain and lavabo were made of colorful pottery and were invariably placed in a niche lined with colored tiles. They were often in the dining room and provided a striking and colorful note to the décor of the room. Large wall fountains and basins were a distinctive accessory of French provincial furniture. They were chiefly found in the dining room. Especially colorful were the ones made of faïence. Later they were sometimes made of tôle. Frequently the wall fountain and lavabo were attached to a kind of tall and narrow panelled cupboard stand. The stand had a tall narrow back panel to which the wall fountain was attached, while the basin rested on the cupboard portion which was fitted with a single cupboard door. See *Lavabo*.

Wallpaper   In the decorative arts; wallpaper was a European development originating in France. Its development was chiefly inspired by the vogue for Chinese paintings on paper imported to Europe in large quantities during the 17th century, as well as by the necessity to reproduce in a less costly manner the tapestries, silks and velvets used for wall coverings. The earliest wall-papers were the so-called illuminated papers found in France and also in England late in the 16th century. The vogue for wallpaper was not firmly established until early in the 18th century when illuminated papers, with their designs inspired by the contemporary painted and printed cotton and linen textiles used in upholstery, became extremely fashionable in France. Around 1750 in France the method of making wallpapers printed in colors from wood blocks was developed and as a result the illuminated papers with their painted decoration done by hand became obsolete. The process of printing in colors from several superimposed wood blocks was generally adopted in England, Germany and Holland from around 1765–1770. Flock papers with their wool powder colors were also fashionable for a certain period in both England and France. Hand-painted papers from China were always highly prized and were considered to be a great luxury. These papers generally depicted either flowering shrubs with birds and butterflies or scenes from Chinese life,

such as lantern processions. Wallpapers of Chinese inspiration referred to as Franco-Chinese and Anglo-Chinese were made in these two respective countries to meet the demand for Chinese painted papers. Also much favored were the chinoiseries made in France from the engraved designs of such gifted French artists as Boucher. Paper in imitation of painted panels executed on wood or canvas found in overdoor panels and overmantel panels was also made and frequently used in France. At the end of the 18th century the vogue for scenic paper was firmly established. In America the early wallpapers were imported from England or France and the prevailing European fashions in wallpaper were essentially observed in America. It is generally accepted that the first manufactory for wallpaper was founded in Philadelphia in 1739 by Plunket Fleeson. See *Flock Paper*; *Illuminated Paper*; *Scenic Paper*.

Wall Pocket   In ceramics; a decorative object made of faïence, porcelain or pottery, having the shape of a vase, with one side being flat so that it can be hung on a wall. It is also called a wall vase.

Walnut   The wood of the walnut tree, *juglans regia*, was widely used in cabinet-work. It was much favored because of its warm color and smooth texture. Walnut was the principal wood in English cabinet-work after the Restoration in 1660. The vogue for walnut continued in England until the advent of mahogany. There was evident in French cabinetwork an increasing number of articles made of walnut from around the middle of the 16th century. French Provincial cabinetmakers throughout the 18th century liked to work in walnut. All the fine Italian furniture was made of walnut during the Renaissance. Walnut was also the favorite wood of Spanish cabinetmakers during the Renaissance. In American cabinetwork walnut was also much favored for fine furniture and it continued to be used even after mahogany became the prevailing wood. The white

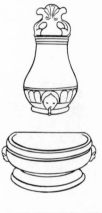

WALL FOUNTAIN AND
LAVABO

and in even larger quantities the black or Virginia walnut were exported to England from Virginia and also from Maryland, Pennsylvania and New York. See *Mahogany*; *Oak*; *Queen Anne and Early Georgian*; *Dutch Furniture*.

Wan Li In Chinese periods; the Wan Li reign of the Ming dynasty in China, 1573–1619. See *Chinese Dynasties*; *Ming*.

Warburton, John In English ceramics; a family of potters making wares at Hot Lane, Cobridge, Staffordshire, during the second half of the 18th century. He and his successors were among the first potters to make cream-colored earthenware. A Jacob Warburton, 1740–1826, was a partner in the New Hall Porcelain Company. The mark "Warburton", impressed, was used, but it was extremely rare.

Wardrobe In cabinetwork; the terms *wardrobe* and *garderobe* have similar meanings. During medieval times in both France and England the terms referred to the small room adjoining the bedroom in very wealthy homes which was used for dressing and for the reception of clothes and other possessions. Later the terms included the tall massive cupboards in which the clothes were kept. See *Cupboard*; *Wing Wardrobe*.

War-Hammer In arms; a medieval weapon consisting of a shaft mounted with a hammer head balanced on the opposite side by a pick. It was carried by horsemen. This type of weapon was often used for fighting on foot in tournaments of the 15th century.

Wari-Kogai In Japanese sword mounts; a kogai split lengthwise. See *Kogai*.

Warwick Frame In English silver; the name given to a variety of cruet stand, introduced around 1750. The base of the stand was in the form of a cinquefoil plate and it was mounted on three scrolled supports. It was designed with a central rod and handle. It generally had a cartouche enclosed in scrolls for the coat-of-arms.

Washstand In English and American cabinetwork; the washstand was not designed as a special piece of furniture until about the middle of the 18th century in England. A principal variety was the mahogany circular tripod basin stand designed in the Chippendale style. Other later designers such as Hepplewhite and Sheraton made numerous designs for this category of furniture. The washing stand was often designed as a piece of harlequin furniture. When it was closed it frequently resembled a small night stand or table. The principal variety of washing stand found in America was the corner washing stand. The front of the triangular top was generally rounded. The two straight sides of the top were generally surmounted with a shaped wooden back piece which served as a protection for the wall. The frieze and median shelf, the latter being often fitted with one or two drawers, conformed in shape to the top. It was designed with three or four legs. The center of the top was often cut for the reception of the washing bowl. See *Basin Stand*.

Wassail Bowl The name given in England to a medieval bowl generally made of gold or silver in which wassail was served. Wassail is a drink made of wine or ale, seasoned with sugar, spice and roasted apples. It was a feature of medieval Christmas celebrations.

Water Bench In American furniture; a piece of kitchen furniture used by the Pennsylvania Dutch during the first half of the 19th century. Its form resembled that of a dresser having a deeply recessed open superstructure with the top used as a shelf over a row of three small drawers and resting on the projecting lower section. This lower portion is provided with two cupboard doors and rests on bracket feet. Pails of fresh water were placed on the top of the lower section and the milk pails were kept in the cupboard portion. It is also frequently called a milk bench or bucket bench. See *Seillage*.

Watered Steel In arms; the term *watered steel* is frequently used to describe the blades used on weapons of the East which have peculiar markings in their steel. It is known

WATER BENCH, AMERICAN

by a variety of names including Damascus, which was an important caravan center and from where this watered steel first reached Europe. In early times steel was produced in the same manner everywhere, in small furnaces like a blacksmith's forge. The results were irregular, producing a mass having from the bottom up, cast iron, hard steel, soft steel, wrought iron and burnt iron. This was broken into small pieces and the qualities selected by eye were welded and then forged into the desired article. In Europe almost all the qualities were usable for one article or another while in the East iron and steel were much less used for general purposes and therefore a wide selection of the desired qualities was possible. The blade maker could then produce almost any variety he desired by welding the hard and soft pieces, then doubling and welding them several more times. Such a finished product when etched is called watered steel. Later they were able to make recognizable patterns by mixing selected qualities, welding and doubling the bars in such a manner that controlled the watering. Usually the patterns of watered steel are not visible until the surface is lightly etched. The most common etching substance is a hot solution of an impure native ferric sulphate applied with a rag. Watered steel, which was not made in Europe, is peculiar to Turkey, Persia, India and Japan. The finest steel ever produced is found in many of the old Japanese sword blades. The fine Japanese blades contain from 32,000 to 64,000 layers; the very finest were produced by Masamune, 1265–1358, the famous blade makèr and other celebrated makers. The process comprised four bars, and by carefully welding and doubling almost twenty times, they produced their finest pieces having over four million layers to the quarter of an inch.

Waterford In Irish glass; the name *Waterford* is applied to the fine articles of glass made at the city of Waterford in Ireland during the last quarter of the 18th century

and the first half of the 19th century. A glasshouse was operated at Waterford by John Head from 1729 until 1740. Then in 1783 William and George Penrose founded the world famous Waterford glasshouse. In 1799 it passed to Ramsey, Gatchell and Barcroft. In 1811 it was owned by Jonathan Gatchell and in 1823 it was called Gatchell and Walpole. From 1835 until it closed in 1851 it was known as George Gatchell and Company. It was a very large factory and produced a great amount of fine articles of glass for table service as well as decorative pieces. In particular it is noted for its fine crystal glass prism lusters and faceted lusters used on handsome chandeliers. See *Glass*.

Water Leaf In ornament; a decorative motif resembling an ivy leaf. The profile of the folded water leaf with its wavy edge and strongly marked ribbings was a favorite decorative motif during the Louis XV style.

Water Pipe See *Narghile*.

Watteau, Antoine 1684–1721, a celebrated French painter. Watteau was the founder of a new school of painting which marked a revolt against the stately and heroic classicism of the Louis XIV style and which initiated the Louis XV style. Watteau was to influence French art until the return of classical antiquity when French art was completely dominated by the painter, Jacques Louis David, 1748–1825. Among the followers of Watteau were Lancret, Pater, Boucher, and Fragonard. Watteau lived most of his life during the reign of Louis XIV. He gained much of his knowledge of decorative art and ornamental design in the atelier of the brilliant painter and decorative artist, Claude Gillot, 1673–1722. Gillot introduced the decorative fêtes champêtres, in which he was later excelled by Watteau. The ornamental designs of Watteau and Gillot were undoubtedly inspired to some extent by the work of Bérain; however, they imparted far more vivacity to their work. The use of numerous curves in the work of Gillot and Watteau anticipated the Rocaille or Rococo style.

DECORATIVE DESIGN BY
ANTOINE WATTEAU

Especially fashionable were their chinoiseries and singeries and their decorative designs of ingenious compositions in which Turks and other quaint doll-like figures from the Italian Comedy figured prominently. See *Régence*; *Louis XV*; *Rococo*; *Bérain, Jean, the Elder*.

Wavy-End Spoon In English silver; a spoon having a stem end which resembled the trifid-end spoon but the clefts were omitted and the end was waved. It was introduced at the end of the 17th century. See *Trifid-End Spoon*; *Spoon*.

Wax Jack In silver; see *Taper Jack*.

Weaver, Holmes 1769–1848. American cabinetmaker of Newport, Rhode Island, working circa 1790–1848.

Web Foot In English cabinetwork; a foot used during the style of Queen Anne. It was used on cabriole legs and generally had three toes. It derived its name from its supposed resemblance to a web foot. See *Foot*.

Webb and Scott American cabinetmakers working circa 1790–1800 at Providence, Rhode Island. Their shop was on Benefit Street and they are recorded as makers of Chippendale style pieces having motifs of the Hepplewhite style.

Wedgwood, Josiah 1730–1795. Celebrated English potter and founder of the manufactory at Etruria, Staffordshire, which is still in existence. Numerous potters having the name of Wedgwood were working in Staffordshire from the 17th century. After the death of his father in 1739, who operated the Churchyard Pottery at Burslem, Josiah Wedgwood began to work in the family pottery. He served an apprenticeship from 1744 to 1749. He joined Thomas Alders, a potter at Stoke, and in 1754 he joined Thomas Whieldon at Fenton. In 1759 he started a new pottery of his own in the Ivy House, Burlsem, making all the current Staffordshire types including salt-glazed stoneware. In 1764 he moved to

WEDGWOOD BLUE
JASPER WARE VASE

larger premises in the Brick House Works, later called the Bell House. In 1768 he had as his partner Thomas Bentley, a Liverpool merchant, who inspired in Wedgwood an appreciation for the antique. They completed a new factory in 1769 which Wedgwood named Etruria. In 1780 Bentley died, and in 1790 Wedgwood formed a partnership including his three sons and a nephew. Undoubtedly Wedgwood's early productions were of the Whieldon type. While working with Whieldon he perfected a green glaze used especially on teapots and other vessels known as cauliflower and pineapple wares. Wedgwood always paid great attention to detail. He perfected cream-colored earthenware and an almost colorless glaze for it. Around 1765 he named it Queen's Ware. Ranking among his important and characteristic work were his marbled, onyx, agate and pebbled vases which he made by mingling different colored clays. In addition to the basalt or black basaltes stoneware, which he introduced around 1769, he also made cane-colored and red stoneware; the latter being named rosso antico. His jasper wares were remarkable for the exquisite quality of the workmanship. Sometime around 1779 Wedgwood introduced a white earthenware which he named pearl ware. From around 1792 to 1810 platinum or silver, gold or pink and copper luster painting were employed at Etruria. Included among the productions was a bone china made from 1812 to 1816. The pre-Etruria wares were seldom marked. From 1769 to 1780 the marks included "Wedgwood and Bentley" and "W & B". From 1771 the name "Wedgwood" was found on useful wares and after 1780 on all varieties of wares. See *Staffordshire*; *Basalt Ware*; *Jasper Ware*; *Cream-Colored Earthenware*; *Pearl Ware*; *Luster Decoration*; *Wheildon, Thomas*.

Weesp In Dutch ceramics; the first successful porcelain manufactory in Holland was established at Weesp in 1759 by Count Gronsfeldt-Diepenbroek. Weesp hard paste was very white and of fine quality. It was similar in form and in decoration to the contemporary German wares. Figures were also made and they were of fairly good quality. The accepted mark was a version of the Meissen crossed swords with three dots around them in underglaze blue. In 1771 the manufactory was bought by Johannes de Mol, d. 1782, and transferred to Oude Loosdrecht. A new mark was adopted; "MOL". The production was essentially similar to the earlier wares. The quality of the porcelain was fine. It flourished until 1782 and in 1784 it was moved to Oude Amstel near Amsterdam. After another change in ownership it was removed to Nieuwer Amstel in 1809. It ceased to operate around 1820. The wares produced at Oude Amstel and Nieuwer Amstel are rather undistinguished. The style of decoration was influenced by the contemporary wares of France as well as of Germany.

Weisweiler, Adam French ébéniste, received master March 16, 1778. Much of the cabinetwork of Weisweiler who worked during the Louis XVI style forecast the Directoire and Empire styles. He often designed the supports for his tables and desks in the form of delicate and elegant bronze caryatids and canephoroi. He specialized particularly in small choice pieces of furniture. See *Louis XVI*; *Classic Revival*.

Well-and-Tree Plate In English silver; see *Meat Dish*.

Welsh Dresser In English cabinetwork; the oak dresser was a popular piece of 18th century cottage furniture. It was often called a Welsh dresser since it was especially identified with Wales and the border counties. The sideboard portion of the dresser was usually surmounted with a recessed superstructure of shelves. The sideboard portion was designed with a row of three drawers. Occasionally below the drawers were three cupboard doors. See *Dresser*.

Welsh Ware In English ceramics; see *Combed Ware*.

Westerwald In German ceramics; an important district for the production of Rhenish salt-glazed stoneware during the 17th and 18th centuries. The stonewares produced in the three principal towns, namely Höhr, Grenzau and Grenzhausen, did not achieve any artistic importance before 1590. As a rule it is difficult to separate their productions. Westerwald stoneware is often erroneously referred to as Nassau ware, since the towns were not incorporated in the Duchy of Nassau until the 19th century. The white stoneware made at Höhr around 1590 was difficult to distinguish from the later Siegburg wares. Several potters from Raeren settled at Grenzhausen, and the style was essentially a continuation of the Raeren wares. Large grey stoneware jugs with reliefs and impressed patterns painted in blue were typical of all the Westerwald wares. There was a general tendency for over-elaboration in the use of excessive applied and impressed ornament. During the second half of the 17th century new kinds of decoration were introduced, including a manganese-purple coloring. The use of dots in relief, clustered to form flowers, birds and rosettes, was a familiar decorative method around 1680. Around 1700 white salt-glazed stoneware was re-introduced. Essentially these later wares were an interesting form of peasant art. Figures in contemporary costume, lion salt-cellars, vessels in the form of birds were made. In a new method of decoration the lines were cut in such a manner as to keep the blue and purple colors separate. White coffee pots and teapots enriched with traditional Rhenish carved decoration were very fashionable. See *Rhenish Stoneware*; *Stoneware*.

Whale Oil Lamp An early fluid lamp that burned whale oil. It was fitted with a burner, having a tin cap containing one or two wickholders. The wicks entered the font through holes in a piece of cork under the cap.

What-Not In English cabinetwork; the term was applied during the Regency to a small open-shelf stand which was derived

WELSH DRESSER

from the French étagère. It was designed with slender uprights which supported the two or more shelves. It was popular in England during the 19th century and was used for displaying various small objects, such as small pieces of china and ivory. See *Etagère*.

Wheat-Ear   In ornament; a decorative motif resembling ears of wheat. The pierced splat of the shield-back chair designed by Hepplewhite was often carved with the wheat-ear motif.

Wheel-Back   In English cabinetwork; the name given to a variety of open chair back designed by Robert Adam. It derived its name from its supposed resemblance to a wheel having spokes and a hub.

Wheel-Lock   In arms and armor; the name given to a type of firing mechanism on a hand firearm. The wheel-lock is an improvement on and superseded the earlier matchlock. It was invented in Nuremburg, Germany, in 1517. It was introduced into England in 1530 and continued to be extensively used until about 1660. It consisted of a grooved steel wheel which extended into the priming pan. In order to fire the gun the lock was wound up with a key. A cock, which had a spring and contained a piece of iron pyrites, was let down onto the priming pan, with the iron pyrites touching the wheel. When the trigger was pressed the wheel spun rapidly and caused sparks to ignite the powder in the priming pan. See *Firelock*; *Snaphance*.

WHORL FOOT

Whieldon, Thomas 1719–1795. English Staffordshire potter. He started a pottery at Fenton Low or Little Fenton in 1740. He was one of the outstanding potters of his time and he made practically every type of current Staffordshire ware. His name is especially associated with a variety of pottery having mingled colored lead glazes. In order to produce this effect he dusted the cream-colored body of the pottery with various coloring oxides which were more or less irregularly absorbed into the thick lead glaze, producing indefinite patches of color running into one another. The colors were distinctive for their beauty and included green, yellow, purple, grey and dark brown. These same colored glazes were used over relief decorations. Sometimes Whieldon mottled only with manganese brown, producing a ware which is sometimes called tortoise shell ware. Unfortunately Whieldon never marked any of his wares. Included among his earlier productions were teapots and other vessels in the natural form of vegetables and fruit and known as pineapple and cauliflower wares. Josiah Wedgwood was in partnership with Whieldon from 1754 to 1759. See *Staffordshire*.

Whipt-Syllabub   An English drinking glass. See *Syllabub*.

Whitebeam Wood   See *Alisier Wood*.

White Granite   In ceramics; a hard white pottery. It is also called Ironstone China. See *Ironstone China*.

White Iron Ware   A term applied to articles made from a metal commonly called sheet-tin. It was first used in Scotland early in the 17th century and was another successor to pewter. It did not achieve popularity until the first quarter of the 18th century. Articles made from old sheet-tin bear a strong resemblance to articles made from pewter. It was cheaper and lighter to handle than pewter. This old sheet-iron was thick and heavily coated with tin. It was extensively used in Germany. In England and America a similar ware was called block-tin. By the 19th century the character and method of tinning had changed to such an extent that articles made from sheet-tin bore little resemblance to pewter.

White Jade   Camphor Jade. See *Jade*.

White Silver   See *German Silver*.

Whorl   In ornament; the term, meaning a turn or volution of a spiral scroll, given in the decorative arts to a spiral scroll. In cabinetwork it occurred in the French whorl foot, in the mid-18th century English chair splat with acanthus whorls and in the whorled terminals of the so-called cupid's bow crest rail.

Wicker Chair In English furniture; wicker chairs made of twigs or osiers probably by the local basketmakers were found in cottages and farmhouses as early as the 16th century. Wicker armchairs provided with wings and a hood, undoubtedly serving as a protection against drafts, are mentioned in farm inventories as early as 1571. Because of their perishable quality they have long since disappeared. See *Guérite*.

Wiederkomm In German glass; a cylindrical German glass drinking vessel made during the 16th and 17th centuries. It very often held as much as a quart of liquid. It was usually richly ornamented with enamelled decoration depicting favorite landscapes and buildings and armorial devices. See *Adlerglas*; *Willkom*.

Wig Stand In English cabinetwork; see *Powder Stand*; *Basin Stand*.

Willard, Simon 1753–1848, an American clockmaker of Roxbury, Massachusetts. He was the inventor of the banjo clock which he patented in 1802. See *Banjo Clock*.

Willett, Marinus 1740–1830. American cabinetmaker working in New York City in the late 18th and early 19th centuries. His shop was at "the upper end of Maiden Lane near the new Oswego market, at the sign of the Clothes press." In advertisements of 1773 and 1774, he stated, "every article in the Cabinet or Chairway may be had on the shortest notice and executed in the best manner by Willett and Peasey."

William III Prince of Orange, and King of England from 1689 to 1702. He reigned jointly with his wife, Mary II, who died in 1694. The style of furniture from 1694 to 1702 is sometimes called William III. See *William and Mary*.

William and Mary The term applied to the style of ornament and furniture design in England during the reign of William, d. 1702, and Mary, d. 1694, from 1689 to 1702. This style which is the second and last of the picturesque English Baroque fashions of the 17th century was largely under foreign tutelage. The two outstanding influences were Dutch and French, with the former being the paramount influence. During this era English cabinetwork in veneered and solid walnut developed along almost parallel lines with contemporary Dutch work. A fuller French influence was more apparent in this style than in the preceding Carolean style. An impetus to the French influence was provided by the migration of highly skilled Huguenot craftsmen who fled France after the Revocation of the Edict of Nantes in 1685. Undoubtedly the most celebrated of these Huguenot craftsmen was Daniel Marot, who sought refuge in Holland and whose later designs show a blending of Dutch and French influences. The furniture of the William and Mary style may be divided into several categories. The English royalty had much of their furniture designed in the style of Louis XIV, especially carved and gilded chairs and settees. Also included in the ambitious pieces of cabinetwork were cabinets and chests of drawers veneered in walnut and skillfully decorated in seaweed marquetry. Lacquered furniture comprised another important group. Contemporary with the gilded, marquetry and lacquered furniture was a large quantity of plain, well-designed, useful furniture made from veneered and solid walnut, which was chiefly used by the prosperous middle class. Finally there was furniture made of oak, constructed and decorated along English traditional lines, which was chiefly found in the farmhouse and cottage. The molded and fluted tapering quadrangular pillar leg with its boldly gadrooned capital was typical of the style of Louis XIV. In English cabinetwork turning was very often substituted. The wide flaring capital was turned in the form of an inverted cup and the turned tapering leg was frequently vase-shaped or

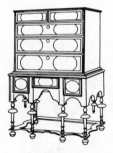

WILLIAM AND MARY
CHEST OF DRAWERS ON
STAND

trumpet-shaped. Around 1700 the cabriole leg was introduced. The vogue for china collecting resulted in the designing of special pieces of furniture for the displaying of china, such as wall brackets and tiered shelves. China cabinets with glazed doors became more numerous. Lacquered articles enjoyed great popularity. The kneehole writing table and tallboy were introduced. The furniture was essentially rectilinear with a tendency to introduce curvilinear lines, such as in the hooded and double hooded tops on secretary cabinets, in the valanced aprons on tables and in the shaping of the chair backs. Among the decorative processes employed on furniture were turning, carving, gilding, marquetry, oystering, parquetry, veneering and lacquering. The ornament was not as over-elaborated as during the preceding Carolean style. Many of the favorite classic motifs were borrowed from the French. Included among them were ornamental drapes, pendants of husks, female masks, acanthus foliage and scrolls and arabesque foliage. See *Marot, Daniel*; *Stalker and Parker*; *Seaweed*; *William III*; *Louis XIV*; *Dutch Furniture*.

WILLOW PATTERN FROM
SPODE PLATE

Willkom In German glass; a capacious cylindrical drinking vessel used in Germany during the 16th and 17th centuries. It was a salutation glass and was used by the host to greet a guest upon arrival. This glass was frequently richly decorated in enamel. It is also spelled Willkommen. It is also sometimes called in England a Wiederkomm. See *Wiederkomm*.

Willow Pattern In English ceramics; a decorative design executed in a pseudo-Chinese manner introduced at the Caughley manufactory around 1780. It is reputed that this design, which was employed for underglaze blue transfer-printing on English porcelain and pottery, was engraved by Thomas Minton. The design was copied and adapted by many other potters in both France and Germany as well as in England. It is probably the best-known of all transfer-printed designs depicting a river with a bridge across

it and trees along the bank. The two birds associated with the scene in its later characteristic form are, according to legend, supposed to represent the souls of two lovers flying away from an irate father.

Wilson, Robert In English ceramics; see *Palmer, Humphrey*.

Wilton In English carpets; the town of Wilton has been known since the reign of Queen Elizabeth I for the manufacture of carpets. Due to the Revocation of the Edict of Nantes in 1685 many émigré carpet weavers settled in England, and in 1701 King William III granted a charter to the carpet weavers at Wilton to manufacture carpets in the French manner. The charter was renewed in 1706 and 1725. Unfortunately little is known about the history of carpet weaving at Wilton until around the middle of the 18th century. In 1740 Lord Pembroke at Wilton introduced the method of weaving carpet with a pile using the same principles employed in weaving velvet. Carpet woven in this manner with a looped pile is known as Brussels carpet, deriving its name from the place of origin. Ingrain carpet or the principle of double cloth weaving, which was started at Kidderminster in 1735, was also introduced at Wilton around 1750. Although both Brussels and double cloth carpets are not hand-knotted they are generally not regarded to be a strictly machine-made product until steam power was applied to the looms in 1850. The name *Wilton* is applied to a form of carpet similar to Brussels carpet, but differing in having a cut pile. According to records there was quite a demand for Wilton carpets in America, and the Pennsylvania Gazette in 1773 advertised "fine broadcloths, cassimers, saggathies and Wiltons." When the manufactory at Axminster for hand-knotted carpets closed in 1835, the looms were transferred to Wilton.

Wincanton In English ceramics; see *Bristol*.

Winckelmann, Johann 1717–1768, a famous German archaeologist. He went to

Rome in 1755 and studied Roman antiquities and gradually acquired an unrivalled knowledge of ancient art. He was a prolific writer and his books covered all phases of ancient Roman and Grecian art. Scholars gained their first real information about the treasures excavated from Pompeii and Herculaneum from his books. French and English classic designs were greatly indebted to Winckelmann's archaeological researches. See *Classic Revival*.

Windmill Cup In silver; a kind of Dutch drinking cup. See *Mühlenbecher*.

Window Bench In cabinetwork; any seat or bench made to be placed in the recess of a window. Robert Adam was very partial to long benches and window seats for he felt that they added to the formal effect of the drawing room. The characteristic window bench designed by Robert Adam had outscrolled sides and rested on slender tapered legs.

Windsor Chair In English and American cabinetwork; the Windsor chair which has been popular in England since the beginning of the 18th century was first made in Buckinghamshire in the 17th century. The Windsor chair is characterized by its slender turned spindles, its wooden saddle seat and turned splayed or raked legs which are usually joined by an H-form stretcher. The back of the Windsor chair was designed in several characteristic varieties. One of the earliest types is now usually referred to as the comb-back type of Windsor chair. The term *hoop* or *bow* back is given to another type of back which was designed during the first half of the 18th century. At a later date the form of the back displayed further variations. The frame of the chair was generally of yew while the seat was of elm and the spindles of either birch or ash. It is generally accepted that the American Windsor chair was first made in Philadelphia around 1725. In addition to the comb-back and hoop-back the other principal types included the low-back, fan-back, New England armchair and loop-

back. The various bent parts as well as the spindles were usually of either oak or hickory. The seat was made of pine and the legs and stretchers were of either maple or birch. The type of Windsor chair depends entirely upon the construction of the back. The chief difference between the English and American Windsor chair was the pierced splat. The English Windsor chair was commonly designed with a pierced central splat between the spindles, while the back of the American Windsor was composed entirely of spindles. During the first half of the 18th century the English Windsor chair sometimes had legs of cabriole form, while the legs of the American Windsor were invariably splayed or raked. See *Low-Back*; *Comb-Back*; *Hoop-Back*; *Fan-Back*; *New England Windsor Armchair*; *Loop-Back*; *Saddle Seat*; *Splayed Leg*.

Wine Cistern In English silver; it appears that a portable vessel or cistern for holding bottles of wine during meals was known from early times and was in use from the 15th century. These early cisterns for wine bottles, or wine coolers, were made of latten, copper, brass or other similar metals. From around 1680 to 1720 low oval silver cisterns of massive size and great weight were made. Especially characteristic of this form of silver cistern was its capacious oval body provided with two handles and resting on a large spreading base. Water and broken ice were put in the cistern to keep the wine bottles cool as well as to refresh and chill the wine glasses.

LOW-BACK WINDSOR
CHAIR

Wine Cooler Or Wine Cistern. In English cabinetwork; the wine cooler or wine cistern was made of various materials, such as marble, silver, pewter, bronze, copper and wood. The wooden wine cooler or wine cistern lined with lead came into use around 1730 and was made of mahogany. Chippendale illustrated several designs for wine coolers. The mahogany wine cooler with its lead lining was often tub-shaped or oval and was mounted on four legs. Its average height was slightly less than 2 feet. The wood was bound with wide brass bands. It was fitted with two side bail handles and a lower drain cock. Mahogany wine buckets of coopered construction were also used. The round tapering bucket, which was bound with brass bands, was fitted with two side bail handles. The wine cooler was generally placed under the sideboard table or sideboard. It seems that when the wine cooler was furnished with a cover it could also be used as a case for bottles or a cellarette. Sheraton in his CABINET DICTIONARY of 1803 did not make any distinction between a wine cooler, a wine cistern or a cellarette.

GEORGE III WINE COOLER

Wine Cooler   In English silver; a large vessel or container, generally urn-shaped, resting on a foot and fitted with two handles, designed to hold a single bottle of wine. It was intended to stand on the dining table. Frequently the center was fitted with a removable jacket which held the wine bottle, the space between the jacket and the wall being packed with ice. It was introduced around 1700. See *Wine Fountain*; *Wine Cistern*.

Wine Fountain   In English silver; a tall, massive vase-shaped vessel fitted with a small tap from which the wine was drawn. It was designed with a cover and was introduced around 1700. See *Wine Cooler*.

Wine Funnel Stand   In English silver; in the 18th century silver funnels were used for filling bottles with wine. A low circular silver stand or tray was sometimes used to hold the funnel when not in use. These stands, usually having slightly tapering sides, were made with a domed center over which the funnel was placed.

Wine Glass Cooler   In English glass; a glass vessel that resembles a finger bowl, the chief difference being that it has one or two lips in the rim. It was introduced around the middle of the 18th century.

Wine Table   In English cabinetwork; another name for the drinking table. See *Drinking Table*.

Wine Taster   In English and French silver; a shallow bowl used to aid the vintner in testing the color as well as the flavor of the wine. The wine taster was made in a variety of forms in the different countries. Included among the more common forms were a shallow bowl about 3 inches in diameter fitted with two looped handles and decorated with a punched design of flowers and leaves; a small shallow bowl fitted with an open-work flange handle; and a small shallow bowl having sloping sides and having the center of the bottom dome-shaped. The wine taster dates from the 17th century.

Wine Wagon   In English silver; the name given to a variety of decanter stand, usually fitted for two or more bottles, mounted on small silver wheels, having a handle attached for wheeling it around the dining table. It was introduced around 1790. See *Decanter Stand*.

Wine Waiter   In English cabinetwork; the name frequently given to different forms of small tables or cupboards of slightly less than average table height, mounted on casters to facilitate their circulation in a Georgian drawing room. Of particular interest was an open wine wagon fitted with a fixed tray provided with partitions for bottles and a tall handgrip in the center. It is often thought that these tables were of Irish origin.

Wing Chair   In English cabinetwork; the tall wing chair or winged armchair, which is an upholstered easy chair, was introduced during the reign of Charles II, 1660–1685. The wings were undoubtedly intended to protect the occupant against the drafts which were plentiful in the homes of those times. It was designed in all successive styles throughout the 18th century. The arms in both the Hepplewhite and Sheraton styles extended to the back of the seat and the wide wings rested on the arms. In the earlier 18th century styles the arms generally extended only to the wings; the arm and wing having the appearance of one continuous piece. This feature of design afforded a more pleasing and graceful line. The contour of many examples of the Queen Anne and Early Georgian wing chair is especially fine. Hepplewhite in the GUIDE recommended the wing chair to be upholstered in leather or horsehair, or a "linen case to fit over the canvas stuffing." It is generally believed that the wing chair was first designed in America in the Queen Anne style early in the 18th century. It was a popular piece of American furniture and it was designed in the prevailing 18th century styles. See *Bergère*; *Confessional*; *Easy Chair*.

Winged Lion Leg In cabinetwork; a special feature of design during the French Empire style was a mixture of strange creatures used as supports for chairs and decorative tables such as winged sphinxes and winged lions. It was also employed during the English Regency. The winged lion leg was a favorite form of support for sofas designed in the American Empire style.

Wing or Winged Wardobe In English cabinetwork; a large wardrobe introduced in the second half of the 18th century comprising a clothespress flanked by two slightly recessed narrow cupboards. The upper section of the clothes press portion was fitted with two doors which opened to reveal six or seven clothespress shelves; each shelf was generally made about 6 inches deep. The lower section was fitted with three graduated long drawers. Each one of the slightly recessed cupboard sections or wings was fitted with a long cupboard door and was used for hanging clothes. The wardrobe rested on a molded plinth. Variations in design occurred. Sheraton illustrates this type of wardrobe in his DRAWING BOOK. The term *wing* is apparently a recent name for this type of wardrobe and it seems reasonable to assume that it may be derived from Sheraton's description of this variety of wardrobe given in his DRAWING BOOK in which he refers to the slightly recessed cupboard sections as wings.

Winslow, Kenelm 1599–1672, an American cabinetmaker of Plymouth, Massachusetts.

He made early oak furniture. See *Disbrowe, Nicholas*.

Winthrop Desk In American cabinetwork; see *Governor Winthrop Desk*.

Wistarberg In American glass; a glass manufactory known as Wistarberg was started by Caspar Wistar in 1739 in Salem County, New Jersey. He made window glass, lamp chimneys and simple bottles, dishes, pitchers, etc. Green glass or bottle glass was generally used. After Wistar's death the glassworks was operated by his son Richard until it closed in 1780. Wistarberg and other nearby glasshouses are credited with the development of the so-called South Jersey style in American glass. The most characteristic decorative feature which was employed until the middle of the 19th century was the lily-pad.

WISTARBERG SUGAR BOWL

Witch Ball In English glass; a colored hollow glass ball splashed with bright colors, often made at Nailsea. It was sometimes as large as 7 inches in diameter. It was hung in the windows of the homes and was intended to ward off evil spirits. Witch balls were made in America during the early 19th century. They were more commonly of green glass and used as stoppers for jars and as floaters for fishermen's nets. See *Nailsea*.

Wood Engraving Or Woodcut. The process of cutting lines on a block of wood so that the design is in relief. This process of wood cutting originated in China, and dates from the 15th century in Europe. In the early form of woodcut the outline was strong and distinct, and the shading lines were not so thick. Lines of cross hatchings were not used but black patches were used at times in forming such things as a shoe or a cap. During the 16th century the cross hatchings were used for shading. During this time the method of woodcut was executed in a rather conventionalized manner; however, it reached its greatest expression through this simple form by the work of such great artists as Dürer and Holbein. The woodcuts of the 17th and 18th centuries continued to follow the conventionalized form by shading with straight lines or simple curves. See *Engraving*.

Wood, Enoch 1759–1840. English modeller and potter working at Burslem, Staffordshire. In 1783 he was working in partnership with his cousin, Ralph Wood, at Burslem. The firm was known as Enoch Wood & Co., in 1790, and in the same year was changed to Wood and Caldwell. This partnership with James Caldwell continued until 1818. The pottery was known as Enoch Wood & Sons until 1846 when it ceased to operate. They made practically every kind of Staffordshire pottery including cream-colored and blue-printed earthenware, black basalt and jasper stoneware and perhaps porcelain. Enoch Wood was a modeller and he modelled numerous busts; especially familiar are the busts of John Wesley and George Whitefield, the preachers. His numerous pottery figures were generally painted in enamel colors. Included among the marks are "E Wood", "Wood and Caldwell" and "Enoch Wood & Sons".

Wood, Ralph 1715–1772. English Staffordshire potter, he and his son Ralph, 1748–1795, also a potter, were working at the Hill factory, Burslem. The marked Ralph Wood pottery wares are chiefly toby jugs and figures. Toby jugs in the form of a seated old man holding a pipe were first made by the Ralph Woods and have been extensively imitated. He also employed the technique of mingled colored lead glazes associated with the wares of Thomas Whieldon. However, his glazes differed from the latter in that the patches were kept more distinct, which produced more of a painted effect. Of course the blurred edges and streaked colors obviously showed that the colors were not actually painted. See *Whieldon, Thomas*; *Staffordshire*; *Toby Jug*.

Worcester In English ceramics; a porcelain manufactory was established at Worcester in 1751, and in the following year it absorbed Lowdin's porcelain manufactory at Bristol.

VICAR AND MOSES BY THE RALPH WOODS

During the first forty years of its existence it was the most productive English porcelain manufactory. It ranks second only to Chelsea in artistic importance. There were many changes in the management. The name of Dr. John Wall is frequently attached to the early period of Worcester porcelain, 1751–1783, since Dr. Wall was one of the founders. Although Dr. Wall died in 1776 the period is generally extended to 1783, which date marks the death of William Davis, who was the first manager and who is commonly credited with the early productions. In 1783 the manufactory was bought by Thomas Flight, who was the London agent for the firm, for his sons John and Joseph. In 1792, a year after the death of John Flight, Martin Barr was taken into the company. From 1792 to 1807 the partnership was called Flight and Barr and in 1807 it became Barr, Flight and Barr and in 1813 Flight, Barr and Barr. In 1840 it was amalgamated with the Chamberlain pottery of Worcester and in 1852 it was called Kerr and Binns. In 1862 it became the Royal Worcester Porcelain Company and is still in existence. For a long time the factory did not have any regular mark, although a script "W" was sometimes used. The crescent was used enough to be regarded as a factory mark. From around and after 1790 there were numerous marks. The early Worcester porcelain was a kind of soft paste porcelain containing soapstone or steatite. The early productions were principally tablewares of practical and plain forms, technically well finished. Underglaze blue painting was much used for almost fifty years. The process of transfer printing was largely adopted around 1756 and the underglaze blue around 1760. The so-called Worcester-Japan patterns which were free adaptations of the Japanese Imari and Kakiemon styles were made almost from the beginning and remained in vogue for a long time. More ambitious pieces began to appear from around 1770. Colored grounds imitated from Sèvres were made, including turquoise, apple-green and lavender. The plain dark blue was occasionally marked with the scale pattern, which can virtually be regarded as a Worcester innovation. The scale blue as well as the less common scale pink were fashionable from around 1765 to 1785. The gilding was of excellent quality and was frequently finely chased. Probably the painting of exotic birds in panels on a colored ground is the best known of all Worcester decoration. Chinoiseries in the Chelsea style and landscapes in panels on colored grounds were also favored. In the middle period, which extends from around 1783 to 1840, the decoration was in accordance with the successive styles, the early Neo-Classic being supplanted by the Empire. See *Scale Pattern*; *Transfer Printed Decoration*.

Work-Box A fitted box used by ladies to hold such articles as needles and threads necessary for sewing and needlework. It was introduced around the 17th century and was often covered with silk and richly ornamented with embroidery work. The work-box was generally portable; however, occasionally it formed the top of a table. In English cabinetwork; when work tables came into general usage the work-box lost much of its popularity. In the majority of extant composite examples, having a work-box mounted on a stand and dating from around 1760, the box was generally treated in a utilitarian manner and the stand was the most interesting feature.

Work Table In English cabinetwork; the term *work table* is generally applied to a small delicate table fitted with the accessories for needlework. It was introduced during the second half of the 18th century and was distinctive for the elegance of its design. The work table was usually designed with one or two small shallow drawers or with a top which lifted up to reveal a well. It rested on four slender legs. The pouch variety was a characteristic and favorite type. It was fitted with a fabric work bag which was suspended under the top of the table and in which the ladies could keep

their fancy needlework. Many varieties of work tables were made by the cabinet-maker during the late 18th century. Some were fitted with a screen with a fabric panel which pulled up at the rear of the table. Sheraton gave considerable prominence to work tables in his DRAWING BOOK. His designs for the pouch variety of work table having a silk work bag attached to a pull out frame were especially elegant. Although the work table was made in America in the Hepplewhite style, the majority by far were in the Sheraton and Empire styles. It was fashionable in America from around 1800 to 1830–1840. See *Martha Washington Table*; *Table à Ouvrage*.

Wriggled Work In pewter; a decoration in the form of a broken line pattern, produced by the rocking motion of the tool. See *Pewter*.

Writhing In English glass; the term is given to swirled ribbing or fluting. It was often used to decorate the bowl or stem of a piece of glass. The term is also applied to surface twisting. It is also spelled wrything.

Writing Arm In cabinetwork; a very wide flat arm on a chair used as a board for writing. It is particularly found on some Windsor chairs.

Writing Cabinet In cabinetwork; the tall, rectilinear double-bodied writing cabinet was a favorite form of writing furniture. It was introduced during the 15th century in Italy. The upper body had a drop-front which when let down revealed many ingeniously designed small drawers and compartments. Occasionally it was designed with two doors in place of the drop-front. The lower portion was designed with two doors; the interior being fitted with either shelves or drawers. Late in the 16th century the lower body was designed simply as a stand upon which the upper body rested. The Italian craftsman exerted all his skill in designing and decorating the surface of these cabinets made of walnut and ebony. A great demand for these cabinets spread through-

SHERATON WORK TABLE

out Europe. The early writing cabinet was often decorated with certosina work. The interior was often richly embellished with intarsia work. During the Late Renaissance it was often decorated with pietra dura work. See *Secrétaire à Abattant*; *Vargueño*; *Writing Furniture*.

Writing Cabinet In English cabinetwork; the name is generally given to an oblong cabinet with a fall-front, which when opened, reveals a series of pigeonholes, drawers and secret compartments. The fall-front when let down serves as a writing flap and is often inset with a leather panel. The cabinet rests on a stand, table or chest of drawers. Sometimes the upper section is designed with two doors in place of the fall-front. This variety is generally fitted with a pull-out writing board beneath the cabinet portion. It was introduced during the reign of Charles II and the early examples were supported on turned stands. Around 1685 the oblong cabinet was frequently mounted on a chest of drawers and was decorated with floral marquetry. During the William and Mary style it was sometimes decorated with seaweed marquetry or oyster-wood parquetry. See *Secretary Cabinet*; *Writing Furniture*.

GEORGIAN SPOON-BACK
WRITING CHAIR

Writing Chair In cabinetwork; the term *writing chair* is given to one of several varieties of occasional chairs. As a rule the majority have a rather low back. Especially characteristic is the French chaise à bureau and the English corner or roundabout chair. Another characteristic Early Georgian variety of writing chair, which was originally made in walnut, had a plain, cartouche-shaped, solid wooden, spooned back with open scrolled arms which looped into incurvate supports. The seat rail was circular and was fitted with an upholstered slip seat. The cabriole legs had scrolled brackets beneath the seat rail and terminated in claw-and-ball feet. The knees of the two front cabriole legs were boldly carved with shell motifs combined with acanthus pendants.

Writing Equipage In Chinese ceramics; since calligraphy and painting are considered by the Chinese among the highest accomplishments, the potter expended great skill in creating and decorating the various writing accessories. The following comprise the principal writing equipage. The pencil brush or pi was provided with a fine porcelain handle or pi kuan. The brush rest or pi ko was given many delightful forms. Especially characteristic was a miniature range of mountains in the form of three or five hills. A brush pot or jar or pi t'ung, generally cylindrical in form, was designed for the brush to stand in and a bed or pi ch'uang for the brush to recline on. The brush bath or the vessel for washing the brush or pi hsi was generally in the form of a shallow bowl and occasionally it was shaped like a lotus flower, chrysanthemum or blossom. There was also a handrest or chên shou and a paperweight or chên chih in the form of a coiled lizard and other fanciful forms. In order to make the ink or mo there was an ink-pallet or mo yen and an ink-cake, which was also given a bed or mo ch'uang. Ink-stones made of pottery or porcelain with a depression to form a well and an unglazed space for rubbing the ink-stick were not as efficient as real stones with a fine and smooth texture. The ink-stick was rubbed on the ink-stone behind the ink-screen or yen p'ing. The water-dropper or shui ti was given various ingenious shapes, such as a peach. Especially typical was the water-dropper modelled in the form of a frog. The small water pot or shui ch'êng with its miniature ladle was also given many unusual shapes. Finally the seal vermilion was kept in a seal box or rouge box or yin sê ch'ih which was generally circular or square and occasionally octagonal or multi-foil. The decorative handles for the seals were of an endless variety and included handles modelled in the form of dragons, lions and turtles. Many of these writing accessories were also made in other materials such as jade, ivory and metal. See *Screen, Table Screen or Ink-Screen*; *Handrest*; *Suzuri Bako*.

PORTABLE DESK
c. 1605

WILLIAM AND MARY WRITING
CABINET WITH A FALL-FRONT,
MOUNTED ON A STAND
Late 17th century

DESK-ON-FRAME
Early 18th century

QUEEN ANNE WRITING CABINET,
MOUNTED ON A CHEST OF DRAWERS
Early 18th century

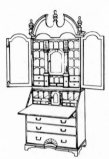

QUEEN ANNE SLANT-
FRONT SECRETARY
CABINET
Early 18th century

QUEEN ANNE KNEEHOLE
WRITING | TABLE
Early 18th century

QUEEN ANNE BACHELOR CHEST
WITH FOLDING TOP FOR WRITING
Early 18th century

CHIPPENDALE SLANT-FRONT
WRITING DESK
Mid 18th century

CHIPPENDALE SECRETARY
CHEST-ON-CHEST
c. 1750

CHIPPENDALE CHEST OF DRAWERS
WITH TWO WRITING SLIDES
c. 1760

CHIPPENDALE RENT
TABLE *18th century*

CHIPPENDALE BREAK-FRONT SECRETARY
BOOKCASE, WITH A CENTRAL FALL-
FRONT FITTED WRITING DRAWER
Mid 18th century

SHERATON WRITING TABLE
Late 18th century

SHERATON CARLTON HOUSE DESK
Late 18th century

SHERATON
WRITING
CABINET

Late 18th century

CHIPPENDALE ARCHITECT'S TABLE,
WITH THE DRAWER ENCLOSING A
LEATHER-LINED WRITING PANEL
18th century

SHERATON LADY'S WRITING
TABLE *c. 1800*

SHERATON SECRETARY
BOOKCASE *c. 1800*

REGENCY TAMBOUR CYLINDER
DESK *Early 19th century*

REGENCY PEDESTAL WRITING
TABLE *Early 19th century*

Writing Furniture In cabinetwork; there are many forms of writing furniture. Included among the English writing furniture are the following varieties: Bureau, Desk, Secretary, Secretary-Bookcase, Secretary Cabinet, Break-Front Secretary Bookcase, Carlton House Desk, Escritoire, Cylinder Desk, Roll-Top Desk, Writing Cabinet, Kneehole Writing Table, Pedestal Writing Table, Slant-Front Writing Desk, Tambour Desk, Architect's Table, Writing Table, Secretary Chest-on-Chest. Included among the principal varieties of French writing furniture are the following: Bonheur du Jour, Bureau à Cylindre, Bureau à Dos d'Ane, Bureau à Pente, Bureau Plat, Cabinete-Secrétaire de Cylindre, Secrétaire à Abattant, Serre-Papiers, Table Tronchin.

Writing Table In cabinetwork; the term *writing table* is essentially restricted to a piece of writing furniture having a flat top which is often inset with a panel of leather. The under portion is fitted with one or more drawers to hold papers. In English cabinetwork; it seems that tables primarily designed for writing were not made in England until around the end of the 17th century, when, after the Restoration, 1660, writing tables and bureaux were introduced from France. The small portable desk and the oblong writing cabinet with a fall-front were essentially the only furniture designed for

writing during the Carolean era, 1660–1688. See *Writing Furniture*.

Wrotham In English ceramics; a variety of English slipware was made at Wrotham, Kent, during the 17th and 18th centuries. Tygs with many handles, mugs with two handles, possets-pots and candlesticks were especially characteristic productions. The slipwares were decorated with applied and stamped reliefs in white clay, comprising rosettes, fleur-de-lis, stars, masks and similar motifs. Applied and stamped inscriptions were also found.

Wrought Iron The term *wrought iron* or *malleable iron* is applied to iron which is comparatively soft, very tough or tenacious and fusible at a very high temperature. At a red heat it is capable of being rolled or hammered into any shape required. It differs from cast iron which is hard and brittle and fusible at a low temperature. The term *wrought* is applied to metals beaten out or shaped with a hammer or other tool. *Wrought* is also applied to that which is constructed or made by means of labor or art, or that which is molded, formed or created, such as a gold or silver box having elaborately wrought decorative detail.

Wu Chin Ware In Chinese ceramics; see *Mirror Black*.

Wu Ts'ai Yao In Chinese ceramics; see *Five-Color Ware*.

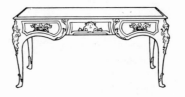

RÉGENCE BUREAU PLAT
OR WRITING TABLE

X-Form Chair In cabinetwork; a folding chair of X-form. See *Curule*.

X-Form Stretcher In cabinetwork; a stretcher which joins the legs in such a manner as to form an X. Serpentine X-form stretchers often centering a decorative finial were particularly characteristic for chair design during the William and Mary style and the Louis XIV style. The principal William and Mary style settee was designed with six legs and they were generally joined with two serpentine X-form stretchers, **each** very often centering a finial. It is also called a saltire stretcher or a cross stretcher.

X–FORM STRETCHER,
WILLIAM AND MARY
SIDE TABLE

Yaprak Rug See *Oushak Rug*.

Yard of Ale In English glass; the name given to an unusual type of glass drinking vessel of the 18th century. It was a long glass tube which was generally fashioned to resemble a coach horn. It was so named because of its length. It is also called an ale-yard. They were mentioned as early as 1685.

Yarkand An Oriental rug belonging to the Turkoman group. It is woven in the vicinity of Kashgar, a city in Eastern Turkestan. The foundation is cotton and the pile, which is rather long, is generally wool and occasionally silk. As a rule it is rather coarsely woven. The designs are of Chinese origin. See *Turkoman Rugs*.

Yataghan In arms and armor; the name given to a type of sword that is one of the special Asiatic varieties common to the Mohammedan world. It consists of a double curved blade, concave toward the grip end and convex toward the point end. The back of the blade is almost straight. It does not have any hand guard or quillons although the pommel is usually elaborately ornamented. See *Sword*.

Yatsushiro In Japanese ceramics; a kiln location in the province of Higo. Yatsushiro ware is noted for its use of mishima decoration on pottery, particularly that made during the 17th century. It had a reddish clay body. The impressed designs, which were executed in the typical Korean manner, were generally inlaid with white and occasionally with black. See *Mishima*.

Yesería In Spanish decorative art; a carved plasterwork extensively employed in Spanish Renaissance interior decoration. Yesería was particularly used as a frieze on the walls of a room and as a border or banding around the openings of doorways and windows. This form of carved plasterwork was highly colored in the Moorish houses, while it was white in all of the Spanish Christian houses. The decorative motifs, which were either of Moorish inspiration or displayed an Oriental flavor in their interpretation of Renaissance ornament, were very often remarkable for their fine composition and finished detail. Yesería, as well as the use of colored tiles or azulejos and the painted wooden ceiling or artesonado, were based on Mudéjar principles and made the Spanish interiors entirely different from those found in any other part of Europe. The most exotic interiors were found in the south of Spain where the Moorish influence survived the longest. At a later time the yesería was cast in molds. See *Renaissance, Spanish*.

YESERÍA

Yesteklik A Perso-Turkish term meaning mat. A small Oriental rug usually less than 4 feet in length and of proportionate width. In the Orient it is chiefly used to cover the pillows on the couch.

Yew Wood See *If Wood*.

Yezd Rug An Oriental rug belonging to the Persian classification. It derived its name from a city in central Persia. See *Persian Rugs*.

Yi Dynasty The name of the Korean historical period from 1392 to 1910. See *Korean Dynasties*.

Yi Hsing Yao In Chinese ceramics; an unglazed stoneware produced at Yi-hsing-hsien in Kiang-su province. It is a reddish or brownish stoneware. Its greatest productive period was during the latter part of the Ming dynasty and during the Ch'ing period. The articles most commonly produced were usually small and dainty and included teapots, wine cups, tea cups, bottles and dishes. This ware was taken to Europe by the Portuguese traders in large quantities where it was given the name of buccaro. See *Buccaro Ware*.

Ying Ch'ing In Chinese ceramics; an arbitrary name given to a ware made during the Sung dynasty. One theory advanced by some modern collectors is that the Ying Ch'ing wares should be regarded as of the Ju type. This ware has a hard white body that is highly translucent and burns brown where exposed. The glaze is thick and generally full of bubbles which gives it a soft effect. The glaze is white with a faint bluish tinge which is darker where the glaze runs thicker. The glaze is sometimes crazed. The lip rim of the bowl was generally glazed and the bottom was often not glazed and sometimes revealed the marks of the ring on which it was fired. Unglazed lip rims were relatively rare. Some of the specimens were very skillfully potted and were sometimes worked as thin as eggshell porcelain. The quality of this ware varies widely; this is due to the variety of locations where it was made. It is believed that much of this ware was made in Honan since the decorative designs have a strong similarity with those designs on Northern celadon. Some of the ware was without decoration. When decoration was added it was incised, carved or molded in relief by pressing the object in an intaglio mold. The decoration was covered with a transparent glaze. Included among the favorite motifs were boys among flowers, lotus flowers, ducks and fishes. Beautiful vase forms and ewers were especially distinctive. See *Sung*; *Ju Ware*.

Ying-Hsuing In Chinese ceramics; a term meaning bear and eagle. The name was given to a form of vase made during the Ming period that consisted of two cylindrical vases of conforming shape joined together with the figures of a bear and an eagle linking the vases on one side. These vases were reputed to have been presented to soldiers for heroic deeds.

Yin Yang In Chinese symbols; a circle divided by a wavy line. It is a symbol of the dual powers of nature or symbol of Creation, yin representing the female and yang the male element. See *Eight Trigrams*.

Yōdansu In Japanese lacquer; the term *Yōdansu* meaning in a general sense a cabinet or chest is given to a beautifully lacquered rectangular cabinet with two small cupboard doors enclosing a nest of drawers. Its average height is about 13 inches, width about 15 inches and depth about 12 inches. The drawers and the interior of the cupboard doors are also finely lacquered in characteristic Japanese motifs. The cabinet is mounted with chased brass hasps and a lock plate, and the drawers are fitted with back plates and loose-ring handles. Although it is a decorative object it also serves several useful purposes, such as a dressing case for jewelry, handkerchiefs and other small articles. It seems that the form of the yōdansu was borrowed from the Chinese who have a similar piece made of choice wood and enriched with brass hasps and a lock plate.

Yoke-Elm Wood See *Charme Wood*.

Yoke-Front In cabinetwork; see *Oxbow*.

Yomud Rug An Oriental rug belonging to the Turkoman classification. It derives its name from the Yomud tribe of Turkomans, who weave them. The foundation is wool or goats' hair. The pile is either fine wool of medium length or goats' hair. The side selvage of two ribs, because of its different colors, forms a checkerboard effect. The ends are finished with a wide web which is sometimes striped and a fringe of loose warp threads. The designs are both Turkoman and Caucasian. Usually the field of the rug is covered with diamond forms in the Turkoman manner, but with Caucasian latch hook variations. The border also shows further Caucasian influence. See *Turkoman Rugs*; *Caucasian Rugs*.

Yorkshire Chair In English cabinetwork; see *Derbyshire Chair*.

Youghal In Irish lace-making; a school was opened at the Presentation Convent at Youghal, County Cork, in 1852 for making needle-made laces. Irish point lace owes its origin to this convent school and is also indebted to its lace-workers who were instrumental in spreading their art of fine needlework to other parts of Ireland. A marked feature of Youghal lace was that it was entirely made with the needle. See *Irish Point*.

Ysgwyd In armor; an ancient British oblong shield similar to the shield used by the Romans. See *Shield*.

Yu In Chinese bronzes; the name given to a ritual libation vessel. The yu appears in various forms. One form resembles a pot-bellied jar fitted with a cover and a bail handle and rests on four feet. Another appears in the likeness of a bird.

Yü In Chinese bronzes; the name given to a large and deep ritual food pot.

Yü A Chinese term applied to jade. See *Jade*.

Yüan The Yüan period or dynasty of China, 1280–1368. See *Chinese Dynasties*.

Yüeh Yao Or Yüeh Chou yao. In Chinese ceramics; celadon wares made at the kilns in the old district of Yüeh, which is now called Shao-Hsing, in the province of Chekiang. Yüeh ware was first produced during the period of the Six Dynasties and was fully perfected during the T'ang period. The body is a hard light grey porcelaneous stoneware that burns deep orange or reddish-brown where exposed. It is covered with a beautiful transparent glaze of various tones of green although greyish-greens and olive greens predominate. Yüeh ware was beautifully proportioned in classic forms. The decoration which was also executed in a refined and classic manner included incising, delicately molded appliqués and modelling in low relief. A variety of articles were made, such as vases, bowls, small plates, wine pots, teapots and small boxes.

Yung Chêng In Chinese periods; the Yung

YŌDANSU

Chêng reign of the Ch'ing dynasty in China, 1723–1735. See *Chinese Dynasties*.

Yung Lo   In Chinese periods; the Yung Lo reign of the Ming dynasty in China, 1403–1424. See *Chinese Dynasties*.

Yuruk Rug   An Oriental rug belonging to the Turkish group. The foundation is either brown wool or goats' hair. The pile which is long is made of fine wool and is sometimes mixed with goats' fleece. The ends are usually finished with a narrow brown web and short fringe. Yuruk means mountaineer, and these rugs are woven by shepherds as they watch their flocks. The rug is sturdy and gives excellent service. See *Turkish Rugs*.

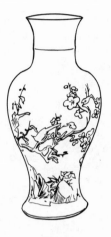

YUNG CHÊNG VASE

Z

Zara Maki In Japanese sword mounts; a form of ishime work imitating stone. It was much used as a surface decoration for a background on sword fittings. See *Ishime*.

Zenjan Rug See *Koultuk Rug*.

Zerbst In German ceramics; a faïence manufactory was started in 1720 at Zerbst, Anhalt, by Johann Caspar Ripp and Daniel van Keyck under the patronage of the Prince of Anhalt-Zerbst. The manufactory changed hands several times and remained active until 1861. Occasionally the wares were marked with a "Z"; painters' marks were quite common. Decorative and useful tablewares were the principal productions, which were sometimes of a good quality but were lacking in any distinctive style. The painted decoration, which was either in high temperature polychrome colors or in blue and white, followed the successive fashionable styles during the 18th century. From around and after 1805 cream-colored and white earthenware in the English style was the chief production.

Zōgan In Japanese sword mounts; the term applied to inlay work. It is especially used in executing the elaborate decorative designs on sword mounts. See *Gomoku-Zōgan*; *Hon-Zōgan*; *Kiribame-Zōgan*; *Nunome-Zōgan*; *Togidashi-Zōgan*; *Sumi-Zōgan*.

Zopf In German decorative art; the term, literally meaning pigtail, is given to a German phase of the Classic Revival, characterized by silhouette portraits and the serious and solemn painting of figures in contemporary costumes. See *Silhouette*.

Zucchi, Antonio Pietro 1726–1795. A Venetian artist who received great acclaim for his painted decoration. When Robert Adam toured Italy in 1754 he was accompanied by Zucchi. In 1766 he came to England at the request of Robert Adam. He was employed by Adam at Osterley and other well-known English houses. Contemporary items commenting on his work are praiseworthy. These articles say that he was a painter of great eminence and that his painted decoration on ceilings was elegantly executed. In 1781 he married Angelica Kauffmann, and they returned to Italy in 1782. See *Adam, Robert*.

Zurich In Swiss ceramics; a porcelain and faïence manufactory was founded at Zurich in 1763 by a company. From around and after 1790 faïence and lead-glazed earthenware were the principal productions. The manufactory changed hands several times and remained active until the end of the 19th century. The mark was a "Z" with or without dots. A soft paste porcelain was made for the first two years. Hard paste porcelain was made from around 1765, and in the ensuing decade the manufactory produced porcelain of great beauty, admirable for its extremely delicate enamel painting. The principal productions were tablewares in the Rococo style and they were of the most finished workmanship. Minutely painted Swiss landscapes and scenes with figures were much favored and are the best known. The coloring was distinctive for its subdued richness and for the manner in which it fused into the brilliant glaze almost as in soft paste porcelain. This beautiful coloring was found in their treatment of Meissen flowers and fruits. The more common wares were largely in imitation of the so-called onion-pattern identified with Meissen. The porcelain figures were principally inspired by Ludwigsburg models. The glaze had the same smoky tone found in the table-

GLASS TUMBLER WITH
ZOPF DECORATION

wares. The figures included musicians, peasants, soldiers and other subjects in contemporary costume. The best of the figures were notable for their charming simplicity. The faïence was decorated in a manner similar to the porcelain. The lead-glazed earthenware or faïence fine was decorated with transfer printing.

Zwiebelmuster In German ceramics; a German term literally meaning onion pattern. The design was of Chinese inspiration and was composed of formal flowers and foliage and conventionalized peaches mistaken for onions which they did resemble. The decoration was generally in underglaze blue and occasionally in purple. It was introduced at Meissen around 1739 as a decoration for common blue and white wares for daily use, and was much copied by other manufactories.

Zwischengoldglas In glass; the method of laminating a layer of gold between two glass surfaces. See *Fondi d'Oro*; *Doppelwandglas*.

ZWISCHENGOLDGLAS
TUMBLER

CLASSIFIED LIST

OF SUBJECTS AND TERMS

CLASSIFIED LIST OF SUBJECTS AND TERMS

Although the alphabetical arrangement of a dictionary has its obvious advantages, it is certainly more useful to the student that words and terms which are related within particular fields of research or study be grouped together. Therefore, the various topics are arranged alphabetically on the following pages, and the terms under each topic in turn listed alphabetically.

Arms and Armor

Ailettes	Cuirass	Kilij	Ranseur
Allecret	Cuisse	Kindjal	Rapier
Anelace	Cutlass	Kris	Rerebrace
Arbalest	Dag	Kukri	Ricasso
Armet	Dagger	Lance	Rifle
Arquebus	Deringer	Langue de Boeuf	Ringed Coat-of-Mail
Backsword	Dirk	Lochaber Axe	Rondache
Barbute	Dragon	Mace	Rustred
Basilard	Duelling Pistols	Macled	Sabaton
Basinet	Epaulière	Mail	Sabre
Battle-Axe	Estoc	Mainfere	Salade
Beaver	Falchion	Main Gauche	Sallet
Besaque	Fauchard	Matchlock	Scaled
Bill	Firelock	Mentonnière	Schiavone
Blunderbuss	Flail	Mesail	Scimitar
Braguette	Flanchard	Miséricorde	Scorpion
Brayette	Flintlock	Morion	Shamshir
Broadsword	Framea	Morning Star	Shield
Buckler	Genouillière	Moton	Smallsword
Burgonet	Gisarme	Musket	Snaphance
Byrnie	Glaive	Musketoon	Soleret
Cabasset	Godendag	Pappenheimer	Spontoon
Caliver	Gorget	Partizan	Stiletto
Camail	Grains d'Orge	Pas d'Ane	Sword
Carbine	Greave	Guard	Tabard
Casque	Gurkha	Patch Box	Taces
Catchpole	Halberd	Patron	Targe
Chain Mail	Half-Pike	Pauldron	Tassets
Chanfron	Harquebus	Pavis	Tonlet
Chausses	Hauberk	Pepper Box	Touch Box
Cinquedea	Heaume	Petronel	Trellised
Claymore	Helm	Pike	Tuilles
Coat-of-Mail	Helmet	Pillow Sword	Tulwar
Colichemarde	Hilt	Pistol	Vambrace
Colt	Holy-Water	Placcate	Ventail
Comb	Sprinkler	Plastron-de-Fer	Visor
Corselet	Jack	Plate Armor	Volant
Couter	Jamb	Poleaxe	Voulge
Creese	Jambeau	Pole-Hammer	War-Hammer
Crinet	Jambiya	Pommel	Watered Steel
Crossbow	Katár	Poniard	Wheel-Lock
Cross-Guard	Kentucky Rifle	Qama	Yataghan
Cubitiere	Khanda	Quillons	Ysgwyd

Carpets and Rugs

CHINESE:	Derbend	Shirvan	Amritsar
Chinese Hand Tufted	Genghis	Soumak	Delhi
Chinese Oriental Rug	Guendje	Tcherkess	Fathpur
CAUCASIAN:	Kabistan	Tchetchen	India Oriental
Baku	Karabagh	Tchichi	Kashmir
Cabistan	Kashmir	Turkman	Lahore
Caucasian	Kazak	Tzitzi	Masulipatam
Chichi	Mosul	INDIA:	Mirzapur
Circassian	Mosul Kurd	Agra	PERSIAN:
Daghestan	Shemakha	Akbar the Great	Afshar

Carpets and Rugs (*continued*)

Aiyin
Animal Rug
Arak
Ardebil
Bakhshis
Bakhtiari
Bibik-Abad
Bijar
Burujird
Djushaghan
Feraghan
Garden Rug
Gorevan
Hamadan
Herat
Herez
Hunting Rug
Ispahan
Joshaghan
Kara Dagh
Kara-Geuz
Kashan
Kayin
Kermanshah
Khorassan
Kirman
Koultuk
Kurdistan
Laristan
Lilihan
Mahal
Meshed
Mir Serebend
Muskabad
Niris
Orinak
Oustri-Nan
Persian
Polonaise
Saraband
Sarakh

Saruk
Savalan
Sehna
Serapi
Serebend
Shiraz
Souj-Bulak
Sultanabad
Tabriz
Teheran
Vagireh
Vase Rug
Yezd
Zenjan

TURKISH:
Ak-Hissar Mohair Rug
Anatolian
Bergamo
Demirdji
Enile
Ghiordes
Gulistan
Herek
Kaba-Karaman
Kir-Shehr
Konieh
Kulah
Ladik
Makri
Meles
Oushak
Sparta
Tokmak
Turkish
Yaprak
Yuruk

TURKOMAN:
Afghan Bokhara
Beluchistan
Beshir

Bokhara
Kashgar
Katchlie Bokhara
Khiva Bokhara
Khotan
Princess Bokhara
Samarkand
Tekke Bokhara
Turkoman Rugs
Yarkand
Yomud

OTHER RUGS:
Alpujarra
Aubusson
Axminster
Brussels
Cross-Stitch
Djijim
Embroidered
French
Hand-Tufted
Hooked Rug
Ingrain
Khilim
Kidderminster
Kis Khilim
Needlework
Oriental Rug
Polish Carpet
Savonnerie
Sehna Khilim
Silk Rug
Spanish
Tapestry
Viennese Hand-Tufted
Wilton

CARPETS AND RUGS:
       Related Terms
American Eagle Pattern

Angular Hook
Barber Pole Stripe
Cloud-Band
Eastern Loom
Ghiordes Knot
Guli Hinnai Motif
Hali
Hearth Rug
Hehbehlik
Herat Border
Herati Motif
Kali
Latch Hook
Lavher
Loom, Eastern
Makatlik
Martha Washington
   Pattern
Mat
Mina Khani Motif
Namazlik
Odjaklik
Pear Motif
Persian Knot
Persian Rug
   Designs
Pole Medallion
Prayer Rug
Runner
Saddle Bag
Saddle Cover
Sedjadeh
Sehna Knot
Semerlik
Serebend Pattern
Shah Abbas
Tereh
Toranj
Tree of Life Motif
Turkish Knot
Yesteklik

Ceramics: Chinese

Altar Cup
Apple Green
Armorial Ware
Aubergine
Batavian Ware
Black Gold Ware
Blanc de Chine
Blue and White Ch'ing
Blue and White Ming
Boccaro
Bowl
Brinjal Bowl
Brush Jar

Buccaro Ware
Bulb Bowl
Burgauté
Cachepot
Canton
Cash Pattern
Celadon
Chi Chou Yao
Chien Yao
Chi Hung
Chinese Export Porcelain
Chinese Imari
Chinese Lowestoft

Chinese Soft Paste
Ch'ing
Ch'ing Ho Hsien
Ching tê Chên
Chrysanthemum Vase
Ch'ü Chou
Chü-Lü Hsien
Chün Yao
Clair de Lune
Company Porcelain
Coupe
Crab's Claw Crackle
Crackle

Crazing
Cup Stand
Devil's Work
East India Porcelain
Egg and Spinach Glaze
Eggshell
Famille Jaune
Famille Noire
Famille Rose
Famille Verte
Fên Ting
Fish Roe Crackle
Five Color Ware

Ceramics : Chinese (*continued*)

Flambé	Kuan Yao	Pai Tz'u	T'ang
Fukien	Kuei Kung	Pao-Pie	Tea Dust
Gallipot	Ku Yüeh Hsüan	Peach Bloom	Tê-Hua
Ginger Jar	Kwangtung Yao	Peking Bowl	Temmoku
Granary Urn	Lac-Burgauté	Pillow	Three Color Ware
Han	Lang Yao	Potiche	Tiger Skin Ware
Hare's Fur	Ling Lung	Powder Blue Ware	Ting Yao
Hawthorn	Lowestoft	Prunus	Tobi Seiji
Hill Jar	Lung-Ch'üan	Red and Green Family	T'o T'ai
Ho Chou	Ma-Chün	Rice Grain Pattern	Ts'a Ts'ai
Honan Celadon	Mandarin	Rouge Box	Ts'ung
Honan Temmoku	Mazarine Blue	Rouge de Cuivre	Tung Yao
Hu p'i	Mei P'ing	Ruby Back Porcelain	T'u Ting
Imperial Ware	Ming	Sang de Boeuf	Tzu Chin
Imperial Yellow	Mirror Black	Sang de Pigeon	Tz'u Chou
Incense Burning	Mohammedan Blue	San Ts'ai	Underglaze Blue
Accessories	Nanking Yellow	Shu Fu Ware	Underglaze Red
Iron Red	Nanking Ware	Soft Chün	Writing Equipage
Jesuit Ware	Northern Celadon	Spotted Celadon	Wu Chin Ware
Ju Ware	Oil Spot Temmoku	Stem Cup	Wu Ts'ai Yao
Kiangnan Ting Ware	Old Nanking	Sung	Yi Hsing Yao
Kian Temmoku	Oriental Lowestoft	Supper Set	Ying Ch'ing
Ko Yao	Ox Blood	Swatow	Ying-Hsuing
Kuan Chün Yao	Pai Ting	Ta Kuan	Yüeh Yao

Ceramics: European, Near Eastern and American

Abtsbessingen	Bat Printing	Bristol	China Clay
Adams, William	Bayreuth	Brunswick	China Stone
Agate Ware	Bear Jug	Buccaro	Cistercian Ware
Albarello	Bellarmine	Bucchero Ware	Clignancourt
Alcora	Belleek	Buen Retiro	Coalbrookdale
Alicatados	Bellevue	Bunzlau	Coalport
Alla Castellana	Bennet Pottery	Byzantine	Cold Colors
Alla Porcellana	Bennington	Cabaret	Cologne
Amberg	Berettino	Cadogan Teapot	Combed Ware
American Pottery	Berlin	Caen	Copeland
Company	Bianco Sopra Azzurro	Caffaggiolo	Copenhagen
Amstel	Bianco Sopra Bianco	Cailloutages	Corne, à la
Amul Ware	Bird Tureen	Caillouté	Cornflower
Ansbach	Biscuit	Callot Figure	Costrel
Aprey	Biscuit Figure	Cambrian Pottery	Crabstock Ware
Apt	Bishop Bowl	Candaliere	Cream-Colored
Apulian Ware	Bisque	Cane-Colored Ware	Earthenware
Arcanist	Black Basaltes	Capo di Monte	Creil
Arnheim	Black Figure Ware	Carpet Bowls	Crinoline Group
Arras	Bleu-de-Roi	Carquois, à la	Cries of Paris
Arretine Ware	Bleu Persan	Cassel	Criseby
Astbury, John	Blind Earl's Pattern	Castel Durante	Crolius
Aumund	Blue-Dash Charger	Castelli	Crouch Ware
Bacini	Bone China	Castleford	Crown-Derby
Baden-Baden	Bordeaux	Castor Ware	Cuenca
Barbeaux	Böttger, Johann	Caughley	Cuerda Seca
Barber's Basin	Friedrich	Cavetto	Davenport
Barbotine	Bouffioulx	Chantilly	Décor Bois
Bartmann Jug	Bourg-la-Reine	Chelsea	Delft
Basalt Ware	Bow	China	Delftware

Ceramics: European, Near Eastern and American (*continued*)

Della Robbia
Demi Grand Feu
Derby
Deruta
Deutsche Blumen
Doccia
Don Pottery
Dorotheenthal
Douai
Dresden
Durlach
Dwight, John
Earthenware
Eckernförde
Eigelstein
Elers
Enamel
Enghalskrug
Engine Turned
   Decoration
English Porcelain
English Soft Paste
Engobe
Erfurt
Escudelles ab Orelles
Etruria
European Soft Paste
Faenza
Faïence
Faïence Fine
Faïence Parlante
Ferronnerie
Faubourg Saint-Denis
Faubourg Saint-Lazare
Feathered Ware
Feldspar
Feldspathic Glaze
Figuline
Finger Vase
Flintporslin
Florence
Florida Porcelain
Flörsheim
Fond Ecaille
Frankenthal
Frankfurt-on-Main
Frechen
Freiberg
French Porcelain
Frit
Frog Mug
Fuddling Cup
Fulda
Fulham
Fürstenberg
Gabri Ware
Gaudy Dutch

Gera
German Flowers
German Porcelain
German Stoneware
Gilding
Glaze
Goat and Bee Jug
Göggingen
Göppingen
Gotha
Graffiato
Grand Feu
Grenzhausen
Grés
Grés de Flandre
Greybeard
Gros Bleu
Groszbreitenbach
Gubbio
Guelder Rose Vase
Habaner Ware
Hafner
Hague
Haguenau
Hanau
Hard Paste
Harlequin China
Hausmalerei
Henri Deux Ware
Herculaneum
Herend
Herreboe
High Temperature
   Color
Hispano-Moresque
Höchst
Höhr
Holitsch
Hollins, Samuel
Hound-Handled Pitcher
Hull
Ilmenau
Indian Flowers
Ironstone China
Istoriato
Italian Majolica
Jackfield
Jasper Ware
Jaune Jonquille
Jersey Porcelain and
   Earthenware Company
Jewelled Decoration
Joseph Jug
Kaolin
Kashi
Kastrup
Kellinghusen

Kelsterbach
Kiel
Kloster-Veilsdorf
Königsberg
Kreussen
Künersberg
Lacework
La China
La Courtille
Lambeth
La Moncloa
La Rochelle
La Seynie
Laub und Bandelwerk
Lead Glaze
Leeds
Lesum
Lille
Limbach
Limoges
Lithophane
Liverpool
Loc-Maria
Longton Hall
Loosdrecht
Lowestoft
Ludwigsburg
Lunéville
Luster Decoration
Lyons
Magdeburg
Majolica
Makkum
Malaga
Marans
Marbled Ware
Marieberg
Marks
Marli
Marseilles
Mason Ironstone
Maximinenstrasse
Mayer, Elijah
Medici Porcelain
Meissen
Mennecy
Mezza Majolica
Minton
Monkey Band
Montereau
Mortlake
Mosbach
Mourning Jug
Moustiers
Muffle Color
Münden
Nantgarw

Nassau Stoneware
Near Eastern Ware
Nevers
New Canton
New Hall
Niderviller
Nieuwer Amstel
Norton, Captain John
Nottingham
Nove
Nuremberg
Nymphenburg
Oeil-de-Perdrix
Oettingen-
   Schrattenhofen
Offenbach
Onion Pattern
Onolzbach
Orleans
Orvieto
Osterbro
Ottweiler
Oude Amstel
Oude Loosdrecht
Owl Jug
Ozier Pattern
Palissy, Bernard
Palmer, Humphrey
Palsjö
Parian Ware
Paris Porcelain
Partridge-Eye-Pattern
Pâte Dure
Pâte-sur-Pâte
Pâte Tendre
Pearl Ware
Persian and
   Near Eastern Pottery
Pesaro
Petite Rue Saint-Gilles
Petit Feu
Petuntse
Pew Group
Pfalz-Zweibrücken
Pharmacy Vase
Piggin
Pinte
Pinxton
Plymouth
Pont-aux-Choux
Porcelain
Portobello
Posset-Pot
Pot-Pourri
Potsdam
Pottery
Pratt, Felix

Ceramics : European, Near Eastern and American (*continued*)

Proskau
Punch Bowl
Puzzle Jug
Queen's Ware
Quimper
Quodlibetz
Raeren
Rauenstein
Red Figure Ware
Red Stoneware
Relief Decoration
Rendsburg
Rennes
Repairer
Resist
Reval
Rhages Ware
Rheinsberg
Rhenish Stoneware
Rockingham
Rockingham
  Glaze
Rörstrand
Rose Pompadour
Rosso Antico
Rouen
Royal Copenhagen
Rue Amelot
Rue de Bondy
Rue de Crussol
Rue de la Roquette
Rue du Temple
Rue Fontaine-au-Roy
Rue Popincourt
Rue Thiroûx
Saint-Amand-les-Eaux
Saint-Clément
Saint-Cloud
Saint-Jean-du-Désert

St. Petersburg
Saint-Porchaire
Salopian
Salt Glaze
Samarra Ware
Samian Ware
Sarreguemines
Savona
Saxe
Scale Pattern
Sceaux
Schnabelkrug
Schnelle
Schrattenhofen
Schraub-Flasch
Schrezheim
Schwarzlot
Schwerin
Scratch Blue Ware
Seville
Sèvres
Sgraffiato
Shaving Dish
Shorthose, J.
Siegburg
Siena
Silesia Hafner
  Ware
Sinceny
Slip
Slipware
Smaltino
Soft Paste or
  Soft Paste Porcelain
Spatterware
Spode
Sprigged Ware
Staffordshire
Steingut

Steinzeug
Stockelsdorf
Stoke-on-Trent
Stone-China
Stoneware
Store Kongensgade
Stove
Stralsund
Strasbourg
Sturzbecher
Sunderland
Susa Ware
Sussex
Swansea
Swinton
Talavera de la Reina
Terrace Vase
Terra Cotta
Terra Sigillata Ware
Terre de Pipe
The Hague
Thuringia
Tickenhall
Tiger Ware
Tiles
Tin Glaze or
  Tin Enamel Glaze
Tinja
Toby Jug
Toft, Thomas
Tortoise Shell
  Ware
Tournay
Toy
Transfer Printed
  Decoration
Trichterbecher
Trofei
Trompe l'Oeil

Tucker
Tulip Ware
Turkish Pottery
Turner, John
Tuscany
Tyg
Underglaze Blue
United States Pottery
Urbino
Valencia
Venice
Vicar and Moses
Vienna
Vieux Paris
Vincennes
Vinovo
Volkstedt
Waldenburg
Wall, Dr.
Wallendorf
Wall Pocket
Warburton, John
Wedgwood, Josiah
Weesp
Welsh Ware
Westerwald
Whieldon, Thomas
White Granite
Willow Pattern
Wilson, Robert
Wincanton
Wood, Enoch
Wood, Ralph
Worcester
Wrotham
Zerbst
Zopf
Zurich
Zwiebelmuster

Ceramics: Japanese and Korean

Arita Ware
Awaji Ware
Awata Ware
Banko Ware
Bizen
Brocade
Eiraku Ware
Hagi-Yaki
Hirado Ware
Hizen
Imari

Iwakura
Izumo
Kairaku-en
Kakiemon
Karatsu
Kenzan, Ogata
Kinran-de
Kiyōmizu
Korean wares
Koro
Kutani

Kyōto
Mimpei Ware
Mishima
Musashi
Nabeshima
  Ware
Ninsei
Nishiki-de
Okochi
Omuro
Oribe Ware

Raku Ware
Same Yaki
Sanda
Satsuma
Seiji
Seto Ware
Shino Yaki
Shonzui
Takatori
Tobi Seiji
Yatsushiro

Decorative Art Processes and Methods

Alto-Rilievo
Atuajía
Bamboo-Turned

Banded
Barley Sugar Turning
Bas-Relief

Basse-Taille
Basso-Rilievo
Bead Work

Bidri
Blind Tooling
Bori

Decorative Art Processes and Methods (*continued*)

Bronze Doré
Caelatura
Cameo
Carving
Cavo-Rilievo
Certosina
Champlevé Enamel
Chasing
Chinese Lacquer
Chinkinbori
Chip Carving
Cinnabar Lacquer
Cloisonné Enamel
Clouté d'Or
Coelanaglyphic
Coromandel
   Lacquer
Cosmati Work
Criblé
Cross-Banded
Crustae
Damascening
Distemper
Ebonize
Eglomisé
Embossing
Enamel
Encaustic Painting
Endive Pattern
Engraving
Etching
Feather Banding
Filigree

Filigree Paper
   Decoration
Flat Carving
French Polish
Fresco
Friesian
Fundame
Gilded Leather
Gilding
Gouache
Graining
Guri
Half-Relief
Haut-Relief
Herringbone
   Banding
High-Relief
Hira-Makie
Hirame
Hollow Relief
Hon-Zōgan
Incising
Inlay
Intaglio
Intaglio-Rilevato
Intarsia
Japanese Lacquer
Japanning
Kin-Makie
Kiribame
Knurling
Kuft Work
Lacquer

Lamellé
Line-Engraving
Low-Relief
Marbling
Marquetry
Mezzo-Rilievo
Mezzotint
Mosaic
Nanako
Nashi-Ji
Niello
Nunome-Zōgan
Ormolu
Oystering
Papier-Mâché
Parcel Gilded
Parquetry
Pastiglia
Pietra Dura
Piqué d'Or
Plique-à-Jour
Plume Grain
Plum-Pudding
Polish
Pontypool
Posé d'Or
Racinage
Raden
Relief
Repoussé
Reserve
Rōiro
Scagliola

Seaweed
Shell-Work
Shu-Nuri
Silver-Gilt
Silvering
Sind Lac
Sosuke, Namikawa
Spiral Turning
Stained Glass
Staining
Stalker and Parker
Stamped Leather
Stiacciato
Stipple Engraving
Straw Work
Stringing
Sumi-Zōgan
Taka-Makie
Taracea
Tempera
Togidashi
Tooled Leather
Tortoise Shell
Tsui-Shiu
Tunbridge
Turning
Twist Turning
Varnish
Veneering
Vermeil
Vernis Martin
Wood Engraving
Zōgan

Ecclesiastical Art and Vestments

Alb
Almoner's Cupboard
Alms Dish
Amice
Ampulla
Apostle Spoon
Apparel
Aquamanale
Baldachin
Baptismal Basin
Burse
Calamus
Canister
Cannula
Censer
Chalice

Châsse
Chasuble
Chrismatory
Christmas Nativity Art
Ciborium
Communion Cup
Cope
Corporal Case
Coster
Crèche Art
Crozier
Cruet
Cumdach
Dalmatic
Diptych
Dole Cupboard

Dossal
Faldstool
Feretory
Flabellum
Frontal
Glastonbury Chair
Incense Boat
Lectern
Maniple
Misericord
Miter
Monstrance
Morse
Orphrey
Paten
Pax

Pome
Poppy Head
Prie-Dieu
Putz
Pyx
Reliquary
Sacring Bell
Sacristy
   Cupboard
Sanctuary Lamp
Shrine
Stole
Tabernacle
Thurible
Triptych
Tunicle

Embroidery

Appliqué or
    Applied Work
Assisi Work
Bargello
Basket Stitch
Berlin Wool Work
Black Work
Blanket Stitch
Broderie Anglaise
Broderie de Nancy
Chain Stitch
Chinese Embroidery
Couching
Crewel Stitch
Crewelwork

Cross-Stitch
Cutwork
Drawnwork
Embroidery
Fagoting
Feather Stitch
Gobelin Stitch
Gros Point
Hemstitch
Herringbone Stitch
Hungarian Work
India Embroidery
Irish Embroidery
Irish Stitch
Japanese Embroidery

Limerick
Loop Stitch
Madeira
Needle Painted
Needlework
Opus Anglicanum
Opus Consutum
Opus Tiratum
Patchwork
Petit Point
Pierced Work
Plated Stitch
Point
Point Coupé
Punto Tagliato

Punto Tirato
Purl
Quilting
Resht Work
Ribbon Work
Roman Work
Rope Stitch
Running
    Stitch
Sampler
Satin Stitch
Stumpwork
Swiss Embroidery
Tambour Stitch
Tent Stitch

Furniture and Cabinetwork: English and American

Acorn Chair
Act of Parliament Clock
Affleck, Thomas
Alcove Cupboard
Allison, Michael
Almoner's Cupboard
Ambry
Andirons
Antique Furniture
Apron
Architect's Table
Arm Pad
Arrow Back
Ash, Gilbert
Astrolabe Clock
Astronomical Clock
Aumbry
Baby Cage
Bachelor Chest
Back Plate
Back Stool Chair
Backgammon Board
Backman, Jacob
Bag Table
Bail Handle
Bale Handle
Ball and Claw
Ball Foot
Balloon-Back
Balloon Clock
Bandy Leg
Banister
Banister-Back Chair
Banjo Clock
Bar-Back
Barber's Chair
Bar Foot
Barometer

Barrel-Back Chair
Basin Stand
Bass Seat
Beau Brummel
Bed
Bedstead
Bed Steps
Bell Seat
Belter, John H.
Beman, Reuben, Jr.
Bench
Bible Box
Bilbao
Billiard Table
Bird Cage
Bird-Cage Clock
Bird-Cage Support
Blackamoor
Blanket Chest
Block-Front
Bonnet Top
Bookcase
Book-Rest
Boston Rocking Chair
Boulton, Matthew
Bow-Back
Bow-Front
Box
Box Stretcher
Brace-Back Chair
Bracket
Bracket Base
Bracket Clock
Bracket Foot
Bradburn, John
Bradshaw,
    George Smith
Bradshaw, William

Brand Dogs
Brasses
Bread and Cheese
    Cupboard
Bread Trough
Breakfast Table
Break-Front
Break-Front Bookcase
Break-Front Secretary
    Bookcase
Brewster Chair
Buhl
Bulbous
Bull's Eye Mirror
Bun Foot
Bureau
Bureau Bookcase
Bureau Cabinet
Bureau Dressing Table
Bureau Table
Burgomaster Chair
Burjier
Burling, Thomas
Butler's Sideboard
Butler's Table
Butterfly Table
Cabinet
Cabinetmaker
Cabriole Leg
Camel-Back
Candle-Board
Candle Box
Candle Screen
Candle-Slide
Candlestand
Caned
Canopy
Canted

Card Table
Canterbury
Carlton House Desk
Carolean Chair
Carver Chair
Caster
Cat
Celestial Globe Stand
Cellarette
Center Table
Chair
Chair-Back Settee
Chairmaker
Chair Table
Chamfered
Chandlee
Chapin, Aaron
Charles II Chair
Cheese Coaster
Chest
Chest-Bench
Chest of Drawers
Chest of Drawers
    on a Stand
Chest-on-Chest
Chest-on-Frame
Cheval Fire Screen
Cheval Mirror
Cheveret
Chiffonnier
Child's Chair
Chimney Glass
China Cabinet
China Table
Chinese Chippendale
Chinese Railing
Chippendale, Thomas
Chippendale, Thomas, Jr.

Furniture and Cabinetwork: English and American (*continued*)

Claw and Ball Foot
Clay, Charles
Clay's Ware
Clock
Close-Stool
Clothespress
Cloven Hoof Foot
Club Foot
Cluster Leg
Cobb, John
Cobirons
Cockfighting Chair
Coffer
Cogswell, John
Comb-Back Windsor
   Chair
Commode Dressing
   Table
Concertina Movement
Connecticut Chest
Console Table
Constitution Clock
Constitution Mirror
Conversation Chair
Convex Wall Mirror
Copland, Henry
Corner Cabinet
Corner Chair
Corner Cupboard
Corner Table
Couch
Counter Table
Court Cupboard
Courting Chair
Courting Mirror
Cradle
Creepers
Crest Rail
Cricket Stool
Cricket Table
Croft
Cromwellian Chair
Crossrail
Cross Stretcher
Crozier-Back
Cruciform Stretcher
Crunden, John
Cup and Cover
Cupboard
Curio Cabinet
Cylinder Desk
Darly, Mathias
Davenport
Day Bed
Deception Bed
Demilune
Derbyshire Chair

Desk
Desk-on-Frame
Dining Table
Disbrowe, Nicholas
Disc Foot
Dished
Divan
Dole Cupboard
Doll House
Dossier
Double Chest
Dovetail
Dowel
Dower Chest
Drake Foot
Draw-Top Table
Dresser
Dressing Mirror
Dressing Table
Drinking Table
Drop-Front
Drop Handle
Drop-Leaf
Dropped Seat
Drum Table
Duck Foot
Dumb-Waiter
Dunlap
Dutch Foot
Eagle Console Table
Early Georgian Archi-
   tectural Wall Mirror
East, Edward
Easy Chair
Elbow Chair
Elfe, Thomas
Elliott, John
Envelope Table
Equation Clock
Escutcheon
Evans, David
Exercising Chair
Faldstool
Fall-Front
Fan-Back Chair
Fancy Chair
Farthingale Chair
Fender
Fiddle Back
Fiddle-Shaped Table
Field Bed
Fireback
Fire Dogs
Fire Grate
Fire Plate
Fire Screen
Fire Tools

Flag Seat
Flower Box
Folwell, John
Food Cupboard
Foot
Footman
Footrail
Footstool
Form
Four-Poster
Franklin Fly Whisk
Fretwork Mirror
Frieze
Fromanteel, Ahasuerus
Frothingham, Benjamin
Gallery
Gaming Table
Garderobe
Gate-Leg Table
Gates, William
Gautier, Andrew
Gilding
Gillingham, James
Gillow, Robert
Girandole Mirror
Glastonbury Chair
Globe Stand
Goddard, John, I
Goddard, John, II
Goodison, Benjamin
Gostelowe, Jonathan
Gouty Stool
Governor Winthrop
   Desk
Graham, George
Grandfather's Clock
Grandmother's Clock
Grecian Couch
Grecian Sofa
Grendey, Giles
Gumley, John
Hadley Chest
Haig, Thomas
Hains, Adam
Halfpenny, W. and J.
Hall and Parlor
   Cupboard
Hall Chair
Hall Settee
Hallett, William
Handkerchief Table
Handle and Back Plate
Hanging Corner
   Cupboard
Hanging Shelves
Hanging Wall Cabinet
Harland, Thomas

Harlequin
Harlequin Pembroke
Harvard Chair
Heart-Shaped
   Chair Back
Hepplewhite, George
H-Form Stretcher
Highboy
High Chest of Drawers
Highdaddy
Hinge
Hitchcock Chair
Hitchcock, Lambert
Hocked Animal Leg
Hogarth Chair
Hood
Hooded
Hoof Foot
Hoop-Back
Horse Dressing Glass
Horse Fire Screen
Horseshoe Back
Hunter's Table
Hunting Board
Hunting Chair
Hunt Sideboard
Hutch
Ince, William
   and Mayhew, John
Irish Chippendale
James, Edward
Jensen, Gerreit
Johnson, Thomas
Johnston, Thomas
Joined
Joiner
Joint Stool
Jones, William
Kettle-Shape
Kettle Stand
Kneading Table
Kneehole Writing Table
Kneeland, Samuel
Knibb, Joseph
Knife Box
Knife Urn
Knob Handle
Knuckle Arm
Labelled Furniture
Ladder-Back
Lancet Clock
Lannuier, Charles
   Honoré
Lantern Clock
Lattice-Back Chair
Lectern
Letter Rack

Furniture and Cabinetwork: English and American (*continued*)

Library Steps
Library Table
Lighthouse Clock
Linen-Press
Linnell, John
Linnell, William
Lion and Ring Handle
Lion Mask Furniture
Lion Monopodium
Livery Cupboard
Lobby Chest
Lock, Matthias
Long Case Clock
Looking-Glass
Loop-Back
Loose-Ring Handle
Loper
Lounge
Love Seat
Low-Back
Lowboy
Low Post Bed
Lyre-Back Chair
Lyre-Form
Lyre-Form Sofa
Manwaring, Robert
Marble Slab
Marlborough Leg
Martha Washington
    Chair
Martha Washington
    Mirror
Martha Washington
    Table
Mayhew, John
McIntire, Samuel
Medal and Coin Cabinet
Melon Foot
Melon Support
Mendlesham Chair
Milk Bench
Miniature Tall Case
    Clock
Mirror
Mirror Knob
Misericord
Monk's Chair
Monk's Table
Moore, James
Mortise and Tenon
Mounts
Mule Chest
Muntin
Music Stand
Name Chest
Nest of Drawers
Nest of Tables

New England Windsor
    Armchair
Night Table
Nonsuch Chest
Norman, Samuel
Nursing Chair
Occasional Table
Ogee Bracket Foot
Onion Foot
Openwork
Ottoman
Overmantel Mirror
Oxbow
Oyster, Daniel
Pad Foot
Panelled-Back Chair
Parliament Clock
Partridge, Nehemiah
Paw and Ball Foot
Paw Foot
Pear Drop
Pedestal
Pedestal Sideboard
Pedestal Sideboard
    Table
Pedestal Writing Table
Pelletier, John
Pembroke Table
Pennsylvania Dutch
    Chest
Periwig Chair
Philadelphia Chair
Philadelphia
    Chippendale
Philadelphia Style
    Highboy
Philadelphia Style
    Lowboy
Phyfe, Duncan
Pickled Finish
Pie-Crust Table
Pierced
Pier Mirror
Pier Table
Pilgrim Furniture
Pillar and Scroll Clock
Pimm, John
Pipe Rack
Plate Pail
Plate Stand
Plate Warmer
Plinth Foot
Pole Screen
Porter Chair
Powder Stand
Press
Press Bed

Press Cupboard
Prince, Samuel
Print Rack
Quare, Daniel
Queen Anne
    Splat-Back Chair
Rail
Ramsay, David
Randle, William
Randolph, Benjamin
Ratchet Clock
Reading Chair
Reading Stand
Reading Table
Refectory Table
Rent Table
Restoration
Restoration Chair
Reverse Serpentine
Ribband-Back
Ribbed Foot
Rimbault, Stephen
Rittenhouse, David
Roberts, Richard
Roberts, Thomas
Rocking Chair
Roll-Top Desk
Roman Notation Clock
Roundabout Chair
Rudder Table
Rumble Seat
Runner Foot
Rush Seat
Saber Leg
Saddle-Cheek Chair
Saddle Seat
Salamander Back
Salem Secretary
Saltire Stretcher
Sample Chairs
Sanderson, Elijah
Savery, William
Sconce
Screen
Scroll Foot
Scroll-Shaped Leg
Scrutoire
Secretaire
Secretary
Secretary Bookcase
Secretary Cabinet
Secretary
    Chest-on-Chest
Seddon, George
Serpentine
Serpentine Front
Serving Table

Settee
Settle
Sewing Table
Shaker Furniture
Shaving Stand
Shaving Table
Shearer, Thomas
Sheraton, Thomas
Shield-Back
Shoe
Shoe Piece
Short, Joseph
Show Case
Sideboard
Sideboard Pedestals
Sideboard Table
Side Chair
Side Table
Skeleton Clock
Skillin
Slab Top
Slant-Front
    Writing Desk
Slat-Back Chair
Sleeping Chair
Sleepy Hollow
Sleigh Bed
Slipper Chair
Slipper Foot
Smith, George
Snake Foot
Sofa
Sofa Table
Spade Foot
Spanish Foot
Sparver
Spice Chest
Spider-Leg Table
Spirit Case
Splat-Back
Splayed
Splint Seat
Spoon-Back
Spoon Rack
Squelette Clock
Stand
Stile
Stool
Straight Bracket Foot
Stretcher
Stump Foot
Style
Supper Table
Sutherland Table
Swell-Front
Swing-Leg
Tabernacle Mirror

Furniture and Cabinetwork : English and American (*continued*)

Table
Table-Chair
Tallboy
Tallboy Bureau
Tall Case Clock
Tall Chest of Drawers
Tambour Desk
Tambour-Front
Tavern Table
Tea Caddy
Tea Chest
Teakettle Stand
Teapoy
Tea Table
Telescopic Dining Table
Terrestrial Globe Stand
Terry Clock
Tester
Thomas, Seth
Tilting Chest
Tilting-Top Table
Toilet
Toilet Mirror

Toilet Table
Torchère
Tompion, Thomas
Tongue and Groove
Towel Horse
Townsend, Christopher
Townsend, Edmund
Townsend, Job
Townsend, John
Tray
Tray Stand
Trestle Table
Tridarn Cupboard
Tripod
Tripod Table
Trivet
Trotter, Daniel
Truckle Bed
Trumpet Leg
Trundle Bed
Tub Chair
Tufft, Thomas
Tunbridge

Twin Beds
Urn Stand
Varangian
Vile, William
Vulliamy,
   Benjamin Lewis
Wag-on-the-Wall
   Clock
Wagon Seat
Wainscot
Wainscot Chair
Wall Bracket
Wardrobe
Washstand
Water Bench
Weaver, Holmes
Web Foot
Webb and Scott
Welsh Dresser
What-Not
Wheel-Back
Wicker Chair
Wig Stand

Williard, Simon
Willett, Marinus
Window Bench
Windsor Chair
Wine Cooler
Wine Table
Wine Waiter
Wing Chair
Wing or Winged
   Wardrobe
Winged Lion
   Leg
Winslow, Kenelm
Winthrop Desk
Work Table
Writing Arm
Writing Cabinet
Writing Chair
Writing Furniture
Writing Table
X-Form Stretcher
Yoke-Front
Yorkshire Chair

Furniture and Cabinetwork: French

Abattant
Alsace
Andiers
Angel Bed
Angoumois
Annular Clock
Archebanc
Armoire
Armoire à Deux Corps
Armoire d'Encoignure
Artois
Athénienne
Auvergne
Avril, Etienne
Backgammon Table
Baigneuse
Bahut
Banc
Bancelle
Banquette
Bas d'Armoire
Basque
Basset
Beaujolais
Beneman, Guillaume
Bergère
Bibliothèque
Boat Bed
Boîte à Farine
Boîte à Gaufre
Boîte à Sel

Bombé
Bonheur du Jour
Bonnetière
Borne
Bosse, Abraham
Boudeuse
Bouillotte Lamp
Bouillotte Table
Boulle, André Charles
Bout de Pied
Bresse
Bretagne
Breton
Breton Bed
Brittany
Bronze Doré
Brûle Parfum
Buffet
Buffet à Deux Corps
Buffet à Glissants
Buffet Bas
Buffet-Crédence
Buffet-Vaisselier
Buhl
Bureau
Bureau à Cylindre
Bureau à Dos D'Ane
Bureau à Pente
Bureau du Roi
Bureau Ministre
Bureau Plat

Burgundy
Cabaret
Cabinete-Secrétaire
   de Cylindre
Cabriolet
Caffieri, Jacques
Canapé
Canapé à Corbeille
Cantonnière
Capucine
Caquetoire
Carlin, Martin
Cartel
Cassolette
Causeuse
Chaise à Accoudoir
Chaise à Bec de Corbin
Chaise à Bureau
Chaise à Capucine
Chaise à Poudreuse
Chaise à Sel
Chaise à Vertugadin
Chaise de Femme
Chaise Encoignure
Chaise Percée
Chaise Longue
Champagne
Chantourné
Chauffe-Assiette
Chauffe-Plat
Chauffeuse

Chenets
Chiffonnier
Chiffonnière
Classeur
Coffre
Coiffeuse
Commode
Commode-Desserte
Commode Secretary
Confessional
Confidente
Cornucopia Leg
Crédence
Crédence Table
Cressent, Charles
Dauphiné
Delanois, Louis
Demoiselle à Atourner
Desmalter, Jacob
Desserte
Diamond Point
Dossier
Dressoir
Dubois, René
Duchesse
Duchesse Brisée
Ebéniste
Ebénisterie
Ecran à Coulisse
Ecran à Eclisse
Ecran à Eventail

Furniture and Cabinetwork : French (*continued*)

Egouttoir
Encoignure
Encoignure
  à Deux Corps
Enfilade
Escabeau
Escritoire
Escudie
Espagnolette
Essence Vase
Estagnié
Etagère
Etimier
Fauldesteuil
Fauteuil
Flandre
Flâneuse
Forme
Franche-Comté
French Bracket Foot
French Whorl Foot
French Provincial
Fumeuse
Garde-Manger
Garnier, Pierre
Gascogne
Gaudreau,
  Antoine-Robert
Gondola-Back Chair
Gondola-Shape
Gouthière, Pierre
Gradin
Guéridon
Guérite
Guienne
Haricot
Huche
Jacob, Georges
Jardinière
Joubert, Gilles
Kidney Table

Lacroix, Roger
  Vandercruse
Lafosse, Charles de
Landiers
Languedoc
Lavabo
Layette
Lefèbvre, François
Leleu, Jean François
Le Vasseur, Etienne
Limousin
Liseuse
Lit à Barreaux
Lit à Colonnes
Lit à Couronne
Lit à la Duchesse
Lit à la Polonaise
Lit à la Turque
Lit à l'Impériale
Lit Clos
Lit d'Ange
Lit d'Anglais
Lit Demi-Clos
Lit de Repos
Lit en Bateau
Lit en Tombeau
Lit Mi-Clos
Lits Jumeaux
Lorraine
Louvre
Lyonnais
Macé, Jean
Maie
Maître Banc
Maître Ebéniste
Manchette
Manufacture Royale des
  Meubles de la Couronne
Marquise
Médaillier
Ménager

Menuiserie
Menuisier
Méridienne
Migeon, Pierre, II
Montigny,
  Philippe-Claude
Normandy
Oeben, Jean François
Ormolu
Ottomane
Palier
Panetière
Perfume Burner
Périgord
Petit, Nicolas
Petite Commode
Petite Desserte
Pétrin
Picardy
Pied de Biche
Placet
Poitou
Ponteuse
Poudreuse
Prie-Dieu
Provence
Provincial, French
Psyché
Quenouille
Quiver-Leg
Rafraîchissoir
Recamier
Regional Furniture
Riesener, Jean
  Henri
Röntgen, David
Rouet
Rustique
Sabot
Saintonge
Salt Chair

Saunier, Jean-Jacques
Savoie
Secrétaire à Abattant
Seillage
Semainier
Serre-Bijoux
Serre-Papiers
Servante
Séverin, Nicolas-Pierre
Signed Furniture
Sofa à Pommier
Star Diamond-Point
Table à Ecran
Table à Gradin
Table à Ouvrage
Table à Papillon
Table de Chevet
Table de Jeu
Table Gigogne
Table-Pétrin
Table Tronchin
Tabouret
Tête-à-Tête
Thomire,
  Pierre Philippe
Traite
Travailleuse
Tricoteuse
Tric-Trac Table
Trumeau
Turquoise
Vaisselier
Vaisselier-Horloge
Vendée
Vernis Martin
Verrier
Vide-Poche
Vitrine
Voyeuse
Wall Fountain
Weisweiler, Adam

Furniture and Cabinetwork: Italian, Spanish and Others

Arca
Armadio
Armario
Arqueta
Bancone
Bent-Wood
Bombay Furniture
Cassapanca
Cassone
Chatônes
Chinese Furniture
Credenza
Credenzina

Curule
Dagobert
  Chair
Dantesca Chair
Dutch Chair
Dutch Furniture
Espetera
Faldistorium
Flemish Chair
Flemish Furniture
Frailero
Fresquera
Friar's Chair

Garden Seat
  or Barrel-Shaped Seat
Grecian Chair
Grecian Furniture
Guard Room Table
K'ang Furniture
Kas
Madia
Mission Chair
Panchetto
Papelera
Pole Lantern
Puente Stand

Quartetto
Roman Furniture
Sacristy Cupboard
Savonarola Chair
Scribanne
Sgabello
Sillon de Caderas
Spanish Chair
Taquillón
Vargueño
Venetian Painted Furniture
Writing Cabinet
X-Form Chair

General Subjects and Terms

Agalmatolite
Alabaster
Amethystine Quartz
Amphora
Aquamanale
Aquarelle
Aquatint
Argand Lamp
Armillary Sphere
Astral Lamp
Audubon, John James
Backscratcher
Baldachin
Balsamaria
Bambocciata
Battersea
Bellows
Bell Pull
Betty Lamp
Bibelot
Bilston
Black Jack
Bloodstone
Blue John
Bobêche
Bobéchon
Boggle
Bombard
Bonbonnière
Bougeoir
Brazier
Bric à Brac
Bronze
Bronzes, Chinese
Brummagem
Bull's Eye Lamp
Buttenmann
Camphor Jade
Candelabrum
Candlebeam
Candlestick
Canister
Carnet de Bal
Carriage Clock
Cellini, Benvenuto
Chair Rail
Chandelier
Chia
Chiaroscuro
Chih
Chio
Chiu
Christmas Nativity Art
Chueh
Chu-Posts
Citrine
Clavichord

Coach Watch
Corona
Couronne
Crèche Art
Cresset
Cries of London
Cruzie Lamp
Cumdach
Curio
Currier and Ives
Curtain Holder
Cushion
Dado
Derbyshire Spar
Dinanderie
Dining Tray
Diptych
Doctor's Lady
Domino Paper
Etui
Ewer
Fabergé, Carl
False Topaz
Fan
Fei-Ts'ui Jade
Figurestone
Fire Mark
Fire Pan
Fire Plate
Flagon
Flock Paper
Fractur
Geburtsschein
Genre
German Silver
Gesso
Girandole
Go
Goblet
Grisaille
Guadamací
Handrest
Hand-Screen
Harpsichord
Heliotrope
Hibachi
Ho
Hookah
Hsien
Hu
Hubble-Bubble
Hurricane Glass
Hurricane Lamp
I
Illuminated Manuscript
Illuminated Paper
Incense Box

Ink-Stone Box
In Memoriam Picture
Inrō
Ivory Carving
Jack
Jade, Chinese
Jadeite
Jalousie
Japanese Fan
Japanese Wood-Block
    Print
Jasper
Jug
Kakemono
Kanō
Kara-Kane
Kasane
Kermesse
Kimono Tray
Kit-Cat Frame
Koro
Ku
Kuang
Lamp
Lantern
Latten
Lawrence Frame
Lei
Li
Lithography
Luster
Makimono
Mazer
Mechanical Bank
Medal
Memoriam Picture
Miniature
Mother-of-Pearl
Moulin
Mull
Mutton-Fat Jade
Narghile
Nécessaire
Nephrite
Nest of Trays
Netsuke
Nickel Silver
Nuremberg Egg
Nursing Lamp
Onyx
Onyx Marble
Oriental Alabaster
Orrery
Ozen
Pagodite
Paktong
P'an

Papillon, Jean
Paris Touch
Pastel
Patch Box
Patina
Pelmet
Pennsylvania Dutch
Pennsylvania German
Physician's Model
Pilgrim Bottle
Pinchbeck
Pitcher
Pi Yü
Pou
Pouncet Box
Pricket
Prince's Metal
Putz
Quartz
Rappoir
Replica
Reproduction
Réveillon, J. B.
Rhyton
Rock Crystal
Rogers Groups
Rose Quartz
Samovar
Sardonyx
Scenic Paper
Scratch-Back
Screen, Table Screen
    or Ink-Screen
Sedan Clock
Sentoku
Shagreen
Silhouette
Snuff Bottle
Snuff Box
Snuff Grater
Souvenir
Sparking Lamp
Spice and Coffee Grinder
Spinach Jade
Spinet
Spinning Wheel
Spooner
Squab
Stirrup Cup
Surtout
Suzuri Bako
Tanagra Statuette
Tankard
Tanzenmann
Tassie, James
Taufschein
Tea Canister

General Subjects and Terms (continued)

Time Lamp
Ting
Tobacco Grater
Tôle
Tosa
Tou
Touch of Paris
Touchpiece

Trauschein
Treen
Trencher
Triptych
Trousse
Tsêng
Tsun
Ukiyo-e

Venetian Blind
Virginal
Virtù
Voyder
Vorschrift
Wall Fountain
Wallpaper
Water Pipe

Whale Oil Lamp
White Jade
White Silver
Work-Box
Wrought Iron
Yōdansu
Yu
Yü

Glass

Adlerglas
Agata
Air-Twist
Ale Glass
Aleyard
Almorratxa
Altare
Amberina
Amen Glass
American Glass
Annealing
Art Glass
Aurene
Aventurine
Baccarat
Balloon Glass
Baluster Stem
Bandwurm Glass
Barberini Vase
Black Glass
Blacking Bottle
Blown-Molded
Blown Three Mold
Bohemian Glass
Bone Glass
Bottle Glass
Brandy Snuffer
Bristol
Broad Glass
Broken Swirl
Bull's Eye
Burmese
Cameo Glass
Cameo Incrustation
Canadella
Cántaro
Càntir
Captain Glass
Carafe
Case Bottle
Case Glass
Casing
Cassel
Chain
Champagne Glass
Checkered-Diamond

Chestnut Bottle
Chinese Glass
Clichy
Coaching Glass
Coin Glass
Colored Looping
Comport
Constable Glass
Cordial Glass
Crimping
Crizelling
Crown Glass
Cruet
Crystal Glass
Cup Plate
Cut Glass
Daisy-in-Hexagon
Daum Frères
Decanter
Dewdrop
Diamond Daisy
Diamond Pattern
Diamond Point
    Engraving
Dobbin
Doppelwandglas
Dram Glass
Drawn Stem
Dutch and Flemish Glass
Elector Glass
Enamel
Engraved Glass
Etched Glass
Favrile
Fiat
Filigree Glass
Finger Bowl
Finger Glass
Firing Glass
Flashing
Flask
Flemish Glass
Flint Glass
Flip
Flowered Glass
Flute

Fondi d'Oro
Free Blown Glass
Fuddling Glass
Gallé, Emile
Gemel Bottle
German Glass
Gin Glass
Glass
Glass Cane
Glass Sellers' Company
Gondelach, Franz
Green Glass
Grog Lifter
Hall-Marks, Glass
Hand-Blown Glass
Hanoverian Glass
Hobnail
Hochschnitt
Hock Glass
Hogarth Glass
Honey Pot
Humpen
Ice Glass
Igel
Iridescence
Islamic Glass
Jacobite Glass
Jelly Glass
Joey Glass
Krautstrunk
Kurfürstenhumpen
Labelled Decanter
Lace Glass
Lacy Pressed Glass
Lalique Glass
Latticinio
Lead Glass
Lily-Pad
Ludlow Bottle
Manufacture Royale
    des Glaces
Merese
Metal
Milch Glass
Mildner Glass
Milk Glass

Millefiori
Mosque Lamp
Mother-of-Pearl Glass
Murano
Nailsea
Nevers
Nipt Diamond Waies
Nuppen
Nuppenbecher
Opalescent Dewdrop
    Glass
Overlay Glass
Paperweight
Passglas
Pâte de Verre
Patty Pan
Peachblow
Pinched Trailing
Pokal
Pomona Glass
Pontil Mark
Porró
Portland Vase
Portrait Flask
Potash Glass
Potsdam
Pressed Glass
Pretender Glass
Prunt
Punch Lifter
Punty Mark
Quilling
Ravenscroft, George
Raven's Head Seal
Reichsadlerhumpen
Rigaree
Roemer
Rose Glass
Ruby Glass
Rummer
Sack Glass
Salver
Sandwich Glass
Satin-Glass
Schäpergläser
Schmelz

Glass (*continued*)

Sealed Glasses	Tavern Glass	Tortoise Shell	Waterford
Ship Decanter	Tear	Trailed Circuit	Whipt-Syllabub
Soda Glass	Thistle Glass	Trailed Ornament	Wiederkomm
Spangled-Glass	Thread Circuit	Tumbler	Willkom
Stiegel,	Threaded Glass	Twin Bottle	Wine Glass Cooler
Heinrich Wilhelm	Thumb Glass	Vasa Murrhina	Wistarberg
Sulphides	Tiffany Glass	Venetian Glass	Witch Ball
Sweetmeat Glass	Toasting Glass	Verre de Fougère	Writhing
Sweetmeat Jar	Toastmaster Glass	Vitro di Trina	Yard of Ale
Syllabub	Toddy Lifter	Waldglas	Zwischengoldglas

Japanese Sword Mounts

Aikuchi	Japanese Sword	Kwaiken	Shibuichi-Dōshi
Aoi Tsuba	Japanese Sword	Mamori	Shingen Tsuba
Ashi	Mounts	Katana	Shitogi Tsuba
Bori	Jimigaki	Maru-Bori	Soroimono
Daimyō Nanako	Kabuto Gane	Maze-Gane	Sukashi-Bori
Dai Seppa	Kabuzuchi	Menuki	Sumi-Zōgan
Dai-Shō	Kamashimo Zashi	Mitokoromono	Tachi
Dai-Shō-No-	Kanamono	Mokkō	Taka-Bori
Soroimono	Kashira	Mokume-Ji	Taka-Zōgan
Fuchi	Kata-Kiri-Bori	Mukade	Tang
Gama Ishime	Katana	Namban	Tanto
Gomoku-Zōgan	Kebori	Nanako	Togidashi-Zōgan
Gonome Nanako	Ken	Nashi-Ji	Tsuba
Gozame Ishime	Kiribame-Zōgan	Niku-Bori	Tsurugi
Guri Bori	Kodōgu	Nunome-Zōgan	Uragawara
Hari Ishime	Kogai	Riobitsu	Usu-Niku-Bori
Hira-Zōgan	Kojiri	Seppa	Wakizashi
Hon-Zōgan	Ko-Katana	Seppa Dai	Wari-Kogai
Ishime	Kozuka	Shakudo	Zara-Maki
Itō Sukashi	Kurikata	Shibuichi	Zōgan

Lace

Alençon Point	Bone Lace	Couronne	Fond Chant
Angleterre	Bride Bouclée	Crochet	Fond de Neige
Antwerp Lace	Bride Epinglée	Curragh	Fond Simple
Application Lace	Bride Picotée	Darn	Genoa
Argentan Point	Bride Tortillée	Darned Netting	Gimp
Argentella	Brides	Dentelle	Gold Thread
Arras Lace	Brides Ornées	Dentelle à la Vierge	Greek Lace
Aurillac Lace	Brussels Appliqué	Devonshire	Gros Point de Venise
Baby Lace	Brussels Lace	Droschel	Ground
Bayeux Lace	Buckinghamshire Lace	Duchesse	Gueuse
Bedfordshire Lace	Burano Lace	English Point	Guipure
Binche	Buttonhole Stitch	Engrêlure	Guipure de Flandre
Bisette	Campagne	Filet Brodé à Reprisés	Hollie-Work
Blonde de Caën	Carrickmacross Lace	Filet Guipure	Honiton Lace
Blonde de Fil	Cartisane	Fillings	Irish Point
Blonde Lace	Chantilly Lace	Flanders Lace	Irish Rose Point
Blonde Mate	Cluny Guipure	Flat Point	Italian Lace
Bobbin Net	Coraline Point	Fleur Volante	Jours
Bobbin Lace	Cordonnet	Fond	Knotted Lace

Lace (continued)

Lace
Lacet
Lacis
Lille Lace
Lorraine Lace
Macramé
Maline
Maltese
Marli
Mat
Mechlin
Mezzo Punto
Mignonette
Milan
Modes
Needlepoint
Normandy Lace
Northamptonshire Lace
Nottingham Lace
Openwork
Opus Araneum
Opus Filatorium
Passement
Pearl
Pearl-Tie

Petit Poussin
Picot
Pillow Lace
Plaited Lace
Point
Point à l'Aiguille
Point Appliqué
Point d'Alençon
Point d'Angleterre
Point d'Argentan
Point de Bruxelles
Point de France
Point de Gaze
Point de Neige
Point de Paris
Point de Raccroc
Point d'Espagne
Point d'Esprit
Point de Tulle
Point de Venise
Point de Venise à
  Réseau
Point d'Ivorie
Point Double
Point Lace

Point Plat
Point Plat de Venise
Point Plat de Venise
  au Fuseau
Potten Kant
Punto
Punto a Groppo
Punto a Maglia
  Quadra
Punto a Relievo
Punto a Reticella
Punto Avorio
Punto Gotico
Punto in Aria
Punto Neve
Punto Tagliato
  a Fogliami
Purl
Raised Point
Regency Point
Réseau
Réseau Rosacé
Reticella
Rose Point de Venise
Run Work

Saint Mihiel Lace
Spanish Lace
Spider Work
Sprig
Tambour Lace
Tape Guipure
Tape Lace
Tatting
Ties
Toile
Tonder Lace
Torchon
Treille
Trolle Kant
Trolly Lace
Tulle
Valenciennes
Venetian Flat Point
Venetian Point
Venetian Raised Ivory
  Point
Venetian Raised Point
Venetian Rose Point
Vrai Réseau
Youghal

Marble

Altissimo Marble
Belgian Marble, Black
Bleu Turquin
Breccia
Brèche
Campanini
Campan Marble
Carrara Marble

Fior di Persica
Fleur de Pêcher
Fleuri
Garfagnana Marble,
  Rosso
Griotte d'Italie
Griotte St. Rémy
Isabelle Campan

Mélange Campan
Molina Rosa
Noir Fin Marble
Oeil-de-Perdrix
Partridge-Eye
  Marble
Portor
Rose Campan

Rouge Campan
Rouge de Flandre
Rouge Royal
Saint Anne
  Marble
Siena Marble
Vert Antique
Vert Campan

Ornament and Related Subjects

Acanthus
Acorn
Acorn Molding
Acroterium
Albertolli, Giocondo
Amorini
Anthemion
Applied Decoration
Appliqué
Arabesque
Arcaded
Architrave
Artesonado
Aster Ornament
Astragal Molding

Atlantes
Audran, Claude
Azulejos
Ball-Flower
Baluster
Banderole
Bead
Bead and Reel
Bell Flower
Bérain, Jean, the Elder
Bernini, Giovanni
Bocage
Bolection
Boss
Boucher, François

Bowknot
Broken Arch
Broken Pediment
Buddha
Cabochon
Candelabrum
Canephora
Card-Cut
Cartouche
Caryatid
Cavetto
Caylus, Anne Claude
  Philippe, Comte de
Chambers, Sir William,
Chair Rail

Cherub
Ch'i-Lin
Chimera
Chinese Animal Figures
Chinese Four Season
  Flowers
Chinese Gods
Chinese Symbols
  and Emblems
Chinoiserie
Chrysanthemum
Cinquefoil
Cipriani,
  Giovanni Baptista
Clodion, Claude-Michel

Ornament and Related Subjects (*continued*)

Periods, Styles and Related Subjects

Adam, Robert
American Colonial
American Directoire
American Empire
American Federal
Ashikaga
Baroque
Biedermeier
Byzantine
Carolean
Charles X
Ch'êng Hua
Chêng Tê
Chêng-T'ung
Chia Ching
Chia Ch'ing
Ch'ien Lung
Chien Wên
Chinese Dynasties
Chinese Taste
Ch'ing
Ching T'ai
Chippendale Style
Ch'ung Chêng
Churrigueresque
Cinquecento
Classic Revival
Colonial Style
Commonwealth
Cromwellian
Directoire
Dutch Colonial
Early Georgian Style
Edo

Elizabethan
Empire
English Decorated
  Style
Etruscan
Federal Style
Five Dynasties
Flamboyant
François I
Fujiwara
Georgian Period
Gothic
Gothic, English
Gothic, French
Gothic, German
Gothic, Italian
Gothic, Spanish
Gothic Taste
Greek Revival
Han
Heian
Henri II
Hepplewhite Style
Herrera, Juan de
Hispano-Moresque
Hsüan Tê
Hung Chih
Hung Hsi
Hung Wu
Jacobean
Jacobean, Late
Japanese Periods
Jogan
Kamakura

K'ang Hsi
Korai
Korean Dynasties
Lancet
Louis XII
Louis XIII
Louis XIV
Louis XV
Louis XVI
Louis XVIII
Louis Philippe
Lung Ch'ing
Meiji
Ming
Momoyama
Moresque
Mudéjar
Muromachi
Nara
Neo-Classic
Neo-Gothic
Perpendicular
Plateresque
Quattrocento
Queen Anne and
  Early Georgian
Queen Anne Style
Rayonnant
Régence
Regency
Renaissance
Renaissance, English
Renaissance, French
Renaissance, German

Renaissance, Italian
Renaissance,
  Netherlands
Renaissance,
  Spanish
Restauration
Restoration
Revived Rococo
Rocaille
Rococo
Romanesque
Sheraton Style
Silla
Six Dynasties
Stuart, Early and Late
Styles of Furniture
Sung
T'ai Ch'ang
T'ang
Tao Kuang
Tempyo
T'ien Ch'i
T'ien Shun
Tokugawa
Tudor
Tudor Period
Victorian
Wan Li
William III
William and Mary
Yi Dynasty
Yüan
Yung Chêng
Yung Lo

Pewter

Ashbury Metal
Baluster Measure
Biberon
Black Pewter
Block-Tin Ware
Britannia Metal
Brunkessi
Burette

Cardinal's Hat
Chopin
Cymaise
Gill
Guernsey
Hammered
Jersey
Kaiserteller

Ley
Measures
Mutchkin
Noggin
Pewter
Plouk
Pointillé
Sadware

Sealed
Tappit Hen
Temperantia Salver
Touch Mark
Touch Plate
Trifle
White Iron Ware
Wriggled Work

Silver

Acorn Spoon
Ajouré
Alms Dish
American Silver
Ananaspokal
Anathema Cup
Animal Cup

Apostle Spoon
Argyle
Asparagus-Tongs
Assay Cup
Attelet
Bacon Dish
Baltimore Assay Marks

Baptismal Basin
Basket
Basting Spoon
Bayonet Fastener
Beaded
Beaker
Bell Salt, Standing

Berry Spoon
Biggin
Billet
Bird-Cup
Bleeding-Bowl
Bougie-Box
Bouilloire

Silver (continued)

Bouillotte
Brandewijnkom
Brandy Warmer
Bratina
Bright-Cut
Britannia Standard
Butter Dish
Caddy-Spoon
Can
Canapé Dish
Candle Extinguisher
Candle-Snuffers
Cann
Carafe
Card Tray
Caster
Caudle Cup
Chafing Dish
Chalice
Chamber-Candlestick
Charger
Charka
Chocolate Pot
Cistern
Coaster
Coconut Cup
Coffee Pot
Coffin-End Spoon
Coin Silver
Communion Cup
Continental Silver
Cow-Creamer
Cream-Pail
Cream Jug
Cruet Stand
Cut-Card Work
Date-Letter
Decanter Stand
Dessert Knife
Dessert Spoon
Diamond-Point Spoon
Dish Cover
Dish Cross
Dish Ring
Dopskal
Double Cup
Double Scroll Handle
Double Spoon
Dram Cup
Dredger
Drinking Horn
Drop
Ecuelle
Egg Cup Frame
English Silver
Entrée Dish
Epergne

Eponge, Boîte à
Ewer
Feather Edge
Feeding Cup
Fiddle Pattern
Fiddle and Thread
Fine Silver
Fish-Server
Fish-Slice
Folding Spoon
Fork
Freedom Box
Globe Cup
Hall-Marks,
   English Provinces
Hall-Marks, Irish
Hall-Marks, London
Hall-Marks, Scottish
Hanap
Hanoverian Pattern
Hansel in the Cellar
Hansje in den Kelder
Häufebecher
Hawk's Beak Spout
Helmet-Form Creamer
Helmet-Form Ewer
Hollow Ware
Honey Pot
Hot Milk Jug
Hot Water Jug
Hot Water
   Vegetable Dish
Incense Boat
Inkstand
Jug, Hot Milk
Jug, Hot Water
Jungfrauenbecher
Kettle Stand
Keyhole Pattern
King's Pattern
Knife
Kovsh
Ladle
Lamerie, Paul
Lighthouse Coffee Pot
Lion Sejant Spoon
Loving Cup
Maidenhead Spoon
Maker's Mark
Marrow Scoop
Matted
Mazarine
Mazer
Meat Dish
Milkmaid Cup
Monatsbecher
Monteith

Mote Spoon
Muffineer
Mug
Mühlenbecher
Mustard Pot
Mustard Spoon
Nautilus Shell Cup
Nef
Nutmeg Box
Old English Pattern
Onslow Pattern
Open Salt
Ostrich Cup
Ox-Horn Cup
Pap Boat
Pap Bowl
Pap Spoon
Paten
Peg Tankard
Pepper Caster
Pepper Mill
Pied de Biche Spoon
Pineapple Cup
Pistol Handle Knife
Plate
Plateau
Plated Silver
Plateresque
Pomander
Porringer
Potato Ring
Pounce Box
Pouncet Box
Punch Bowl
Punch Ladle
Punch Spoon
Purchase
Puritan Spoon
Quaich
Queen's Pattern
Rat-Tail Spoon
Revere, Paul
Revolving Dish
Rosewater Ewer
   and Dish
Salt, Bell Standing
Salt-Cellar
Salt,
   Cylindrical Standing
Salt Dish
Salt,
   Hourglass Standing
Salt Spoon
Salt, Standing
Salt, Steeple Standing
Salver
Sand Caster

Sauce Boat
Saucepan
Saucer
Savonnette, Boîte à
Scroll Handle
Seal Top Spoon
Setzbecher
Sheffield Plate
Shell-Back
Silver Plate
Silver Plated Ware
Slip-Stem Spoon
Skewer
Skillet
Slop-Basin
Snuffers
Snuff Spoon
Soap Box and
   Sponge Box
Spear-Head Spoon
Spice Box
Spirit Burner
Spoon
Spoon Tray
Spout Cup
Standing Cup
Standish
Steeple Cup
Sterling
Storr, Paul
Strap Handle
Strawberry Dish
Sucket Fork
Sugar Bowl
Sugar Sifter
Sugar Tongs
Swan Neck Handle
Tankard
Taper Box
Taper Jack
Taper Stick
Tazza
Teakettle
Teapot
Tea Service
Teaspoon
Tea Tray
Tea Urn
Thread and Shell
Threaded Edge
Thumbpiece
Thurible
Tobacco Box
Touchstone
Tray Candlestick
Trencher Salt
Trifid-End Spoon

Silver (*continued*)

Trophy Cup	Wager Cup	Well-and-Tree Plate	Wine Fountain
Tumbler Cup	Warwick Frame	Windmill Cup	Wine Funnel Stand
Tureen	Wassail Bowl	Wine Cistern	Wine Taster
Vinaigrette	Wavy-End Spoon	Wine Cooler	Wine Wagon
Wafer-Box	Wax Jack		

Textiles

American Tapestries	Damask	Ko'ssu	San Michele Tapestries
Armorial Tapestry	Deshilado	Lille Tapestries	Satin
Arras Tapestry	Dimity	Lucchese Patterns	Satin de Bruges
Aubusson Tapestry	Drap d'Or	Madrid Royal Tapestry	Satin Cafard
Barberini Tapestries	Dublin Tapestry	Factory	Satin Damask
Barcheston Tapestries	Works	Mantua Tapestries	Satin de Hollande
Batik	Enghien Tapestries	Medici Tapestry	Silk
Baudekin	Faubourg St. Antoine	Works	Soho Tapestries
Bayeux Tapestry	Faubourg St. Germain	Mohair	Taffeta
Beauvais	Faubourg St. Marceau	Mortlake Tapestry	Tapestry
Berdelik	Felletin Tapestries	Works	Tapestry Furniture
Brocade	Ferrara Tapestries	Munich Tapestries	Coverings
Brocaded Damask	Flemish Tapestries	Nancy Tapestries	Toile de Jouy
Brocatelle	Fontainebleau Tapestries	Oberkampf, Philip	Touraine Tapestries
Brussels Tapestries	Fringe	Oudenarde Tapestries	Tournay Tapestries
Calico	Fulham Tapestries	Palampore	Turkey Work
Cartoon	Genoese Velvet	Passementerie	Tye and Dye
Chenille	Gobelins	Rheims Tapestries	Upholstery
Chintz	Hand Block Printing	Rome Tapestries	Utrecht
Ciselé Velvet	Hôpital de la Trinité	Russian Imperial Tapestry	Valance
Counterpane	Horsehair	Works	Velvet
Cretonne	Indiennes	Samite	Venetian Velvet

Woods

Abricotier	Aulne	Cherry	Elder
Acacia Faux Wood	Baywood	Chestnut	Elm
Acacia Wood	Beechwood	Chestnut Wood, French	Epine-Vinette
Acajou	Bilsted	China Tree Wood	Erable
Agal	Birch	Circassian Walnut	Fir
Agalloch	Birdseye Maple	Citron	Frêne
Ailanto	Bloodwood	Citronnier	Fruitwood
Alder	Bog Wood	Copaïba	Fumed Oak
Alisier	Boxwood	Corail	Fusain
Almond	Brazilwood	Coral Wood	Guaiac
Aloes	Buis	Cormier	Gumwood
Amandier	Burl	Courbaril	Hardwood
Amaranth	Calambac	Crape Myrtle	Harewood
Amboina	Caliatour	Crotch Mahogany	Hawthorn
Amboise	Camagon	Curly Maple	Hêtre
Amboyna	Campeche	Cypress	Hickory
Andaman Redwood	Cannelle	Cytise	Holly
Anise	Cedar	Deal	Holy-Wood
Apple	Cerisier	Eaglewood	Horn-Beam
Apricot	Charme	Ebénier des Alpes	Houx
Ash	Châtaignier	Ebony	If

Woods (*continued*)

Jacaranda
Kingwood
Laburnum
Larch
Laurier
  Aromatique
Lemon
Lime
Linden
Locust
Logwood
Macassar
Mahogany
Maple
Marronnier
Mazerwood
Mélèze
Merisier
Mulberry

Murier
Muscadier
Myall
Nutmeg
Oak
Oeil-de-Perdrix
Oleander
Olivewood
Olivier
Orange
Orme
Padouk
Palissandre
Partridge
Pear
Peuplier
Pine
Plane
Platane

Plum
Poirier
Pommier
Poplar
Prunier
Pumpkin
  Pine
Rhodeswood
Rosetta
Rosewood
Sabicu
Sandalwood
Sandarac
Sanderswood
Sapan
Sapin
Satinwood
Service
Shisham

Sissoo
Softwood
Spindle
  Wood
Sureau
Sweet Gum
Sycamore
Tarata
Teakwood
Thuyawood
Tilleul
Tulipwood
Tzu-T'an
Violet Wood
Wainscot
Walnut
Whitebeam
Yew
Yoke Elm

BIBLIOGRAPHY

BIBLIOGRAPHY

A selected reference bibliography for students who wish to explore the different phases of the decorative arts beyond the purpose and the function of a dictionary. These books will indicate important sources and will suggest lines for further study. Many of these books will be useful in more than the one classification to which it has been assigned. The bibliography does not attempt to include the many reference works used by the writers, especially those in foreign languages and also the innumerable monographs of the present century. It is simply offered as a preliminary guide to the available literature on the Decorative Arts.

Source Reference on Furniture and Ornament

ACKERMANN, RUDOLPH. *Repository of Arts, Literature, etc.* London, 1809–1828.

ADAM, ROBERT AND JAMES. *Works in Architecture.* Began publishing in parts in London, 1773, and printed for the authors, 1778–1822

ADAM, ROBERT. *The Ruins of the Palace of the Emperor Diocletian at Spalatro in Dalmatia.* London, 1764.

ALBERTOLLI, GIOCONDO. *Ornamenti diversi inventati, disegnati ed eseguiti da Giocondo Albertolli.* Milano, 1782.

BÉRAIN, JEAN LOUIS. *Oeuvre de J. Bérain.* Paris, 1711.

BÉRAIN, JEAN LOUIS. *Oeuvres de J. Bérain contenant des ornaments d'architecture.* Paris, 1711.

BÉRAIN, JEAN LOUIS. *Ornaments Inventés par J. Bérain.* Paris, 1711.

CAYLUS, ANNE CLAUDE PHILIPPE, COMTE DE. *Recueil d'Antiquités; Egyptiennes, Etrusques, Grecques, Romaines, et Gauloises.* 7 vols., Paris, 1756–1767.

CHAMBERS, SIR WILLIAM. *Designs for Chinese Buildings and Furniture.* London, 1757.

CHIPPENDALE, THOMAS. *The Gentleman and Cabinet-Maker's Director, being a collection of the most Elegant and Useful Designs of Household Furniture in the most Fashionable taste.* First edition published in 1754; second edition in 1755 and the third edition in 1762, London.

CRUNDEN, JOHN. *Convenient and Ornamental Architecture.* London, 1770.

CRUNDEN, JOHN. *The Joyner and Cabinet-Makers Darling or Pocket Director.* London, 1765.

DARLY, MATHIAS AND EDWARDS, GEORGE. *A New Book of Chinese Designs.* London, 1754.

DARLY, MATHIAS. *The Compleat Architect.* London, 1770.

DENON, DOMINIQUE VIVANT, BARON DE. *Voyage dans la Basse et la Haute Egypte.* 2 vols., Paris, 1802.

DOSSIE, ROBERT. *The Handmaid to the Arts.* 2 vols., London, 1758. A second edition with improvements and additions in 1764.

HALFPENNY, W. AND J. *New Designs for Chinese Temples, Garden Seats, etc.* Published in parts between 1750–1752 in London.

HAMILTON, SIR WILLIAM. *Collection of Etruscan, Greek and Roman Antiquities from the Cabinet of the Hon. Wm. Hamilton.* par F. Morelli. Naples, 1766.

HAMILTON, SIR WILLIAM. *Collection of Engravings from Ancient Vases mostly of pure Greek Workmanship discovered in Sepulchres in the kingdom of the Two Sicilies . . . 1789 and 1790. Now in the possession of Sir W. Hamilton. With remarks on each vase by the author.* 3 vols., Naples, 1791–1795.

HEPPLEWHITE, A. AND CO. *The Cabinet Maker and Upholsterer's Guide.* First edition in 1788; second edition in 1789, and third edition in 1794, London.

HOPE, THOMAS. *Household Furniture and Interior Decoration.* London, 1807.

Household Furniture in Genteel Taste, published by the Society of Upholsterers and Cabinet-Makers. First edition, London, 1760.

INCE, WILLIAM AND MAYHEW, THOMAS. *The Universal System of Household Furniture.* Published in parts between 1759 and 1763 in London.

JOHNSON, THOMAS. *One Hundred and Fifty New Designs for Carver's Pieces, Frames, Candlestands, Candelabra, Tables and Lanterns.* Issued in monthly parts between 1756–1758, with a second edition in 1761, London.

JOHNSON, THOMAS. *Twelve Girandoles.* London, 1755.

JONES, WILLIAM. *The Gentlemen's and Builders' Companion.* London, 1739.

LOCK, MATTHIAS AND COPLAND, HENRY. *A New Book of Foliage.* London, 1769.

Source Reference on Furniture and Ornament (*continued*)

LOCK, MATTHIAS AND COPLAND, HENRY. *A New Book of Ornaments, consisting of Tables, Chimnies, Sconces, Clock Cases, etc.* London, 1768.

LOCK, MATTHIAS AND COPLAND, HENRY. *A New Book of Pier Frames.* London, 1769.

LOCK, MATTHIAS AND COPLAND, HENRY. *A New Drawing Book of Ornaments.* London, 1740.

MANWARING, ROBERT. *The Cabinet and Chair Maker's Real Friend and Companion.* London, 1765.

MANWARING, ROBERT. *The Chair Makers' Guide.* Revised edition, London, 1766.

MAROT, DANIEL. *Oeuvres du Sieur D. Marot, architecte de Guillaume III, Roi de la Grande Bretagne.* Amsterdam, 1712.

MAROT, DANIEL. *Receuil des planches des sieurs Marot, père et fils.* Amsterdam, 1712.

MEISSONNIER, JUSTE AURÈLE. *Oeuvre de Juste Aurèle Meissonnier, peintre, sculpteur, architecte et dessinateur de la chambre et cabinet du roy.* Paris, 17–.

PERCIER, CHARLES AND FONTAINE, PIERRE FRANÇOIS LEONARD. *Choix des Plus Cèlebres Maisons de Plaisance de Rome et des Environs.* Paris, 1809.

PERCIER, CHARLES AND FONTAINE, PIERRE FRANÇOIS LEONARD. *Palais, Maisons et autres Edifices Modernes Dessinés à Rome.* Paris, 1798. New edition 1830.

PERCIER, CHARLES AND FONTAINE, PIERRE FRANÇOIS LEONARD. *Recueil de Décorations Intérieures, Meubles, Bronzes, etc.* Paris, 1812.

PERGOLESI, MICHELE ANGELO. *Original Designs on Various Ornaments.* The plates were issued separately between 1777–1791 in London.

PIRANESI, GIOVANNI. *Diverse Maniere D'Adornare I Cammini.* Roma, 1767.

RICCOBONI, LOUIS. *Histoire du Théatre Italien.* Paris, 1728.

SHEARER, THOMAS. *Designs for Household Furniture.* London, 1788.

SHERATON, THOMAS. *Designs for Household Furniture exhibiting a Variety of Elegant and Useful Patterns in the Cabinet, Chair and Upholstery Branches on eighty-four plates, by the late T. Sheraton.* London, 1812.

SHERATON, THOMAS. *The Cabinet Dictionary, containing an explanation of all the terms used in the Cabinet, Chair and Upholstery Branches, with directions for varnishing, polishing and gilding.* London, 1803.

SHERATON, THOMAS. *The Cabinet-Maker, Upholsterer and General Artist's Encyclopaedia.* Unfinished. Part I published in London, 1805.

SHERATON, THOMAS, *The Cabinet-Maker and Upholsterer's Drawing Book.* Published in four parts from 1791–1794.

SMITH, GEORGE. *A Collection of Designs for Household Furniture and Interior Decoration.* London, 1808.

SMITH, GEORGE. *A Collection of Ornamental Designs after the Manner of the Antique.* London, 1812.

SMITH, GEORGE. *The Cabinet-Makers' and Upholsterers' Guide, Drawing Book and Repository of New and Original Designs for Household Furniture.* London, 1826.

STALKER, JOHN AND PARKER, GEORGE. *Treatise of Japanning and Varnishing.* London, 1688.

The Cabinet Makers' London Book of Prices and Designs of Cabinet Work, THOMAS SHEARER AND OTHERS. First edition 1788 and second edition 1793. London.

WINCKELMANN, JOHANN JOACHIM. *Histoire de l'antiquité.* Paris, 1764.

WINCKELMANN, JOHANN JOACHIM. *Monuments antiques inédits.* Paris, 1766.

WINCKELMANN, JOHANN JOACHIM. *Réflexions sur l'imitation de l'art grec.* Paris, 1754.

Furniture

ADAMS, LOUIS G. *Decorations Intérieures et Meubles des Epoques Louis XIII et Louis XIV; Reproduits d'Aprés les Compositions de Crispin de Passe; Paul Vredeman de Vries; Sébastien Serlius; Bérain; Jean Marot; De Bross; etc.* Paris, 1865.

BAILLE, G. H. *Watchmakers and Clockmakers of the World.* London, 1929.

BAJOT, EDOUARD. *Profils et Tournages; Recueil de Documents de Styles . . . Gothique, François I, Henri II, Henri III, Henri IV, Louis XIII, Louis XIV, Louis XV, Louis XVI, Empire.* 2 vols., Paris, 1898–1903.

BELL, J. MUNROE. *The Furniture Designs of Chippendale, Hepplewhite and Sheraton, arranged by J. Munroe Bell.* New York, 1938.

BODE, WILHELM, VON. *Italian Renaissance Furniture.* Translated by Mary E. Herrick. New York, 1921.

BRACKETT, OLIVER. *English Furniture Illustrated, A Pictorial Review of English Furniture from Chaucer to Queen Victoria.* Revised and edited by H. Clifford Smith. London, 1950.

BRACKETT, OLIVER. *Thomas Chippendale.* London, 1924.

BRITTEN, FREDERICK JAMES. *Old Clocks and Watches and Their Makers.* Third edition; London, 1911.

BYNE, ARTHUR AND BYNE, MILDRED STAPLEY. *Provincial Houses in Spain.* New York, 1925.

BYNE, ARTHUR AND BYNE, MILDRED STAPLEY. *Spanish Interiors and Furniture.* 3 vols., New York, 1921.

CESCINSKY, HERBERT. *English Furniture of the Eighteenth Century.* 3 vols., London, 1909–1911.

Collection de L'Art Régional en France (A Survey of Provincial Architecture). *L'Habitation Provençale,* R. DARDE; *L'Habitation Basque,* L. COLAS; *L'Habitation*

Furniture (continued)

Bretonne, J. BOUILLE; *L'Habitation Landaise*, H. GODBARGE. Paris, 1925.

Collection de L'Art Régional en France (A Survey of French Provincial Furniture). *Le Mobilier Lorrain*, CHARLES SADOUL; *Le Mobilier Basque*, LOUIS COLAS; *Le Mobilier Breton*, PAUL BANÉAT; *Le Mobilier Provençal*, HENRI ALGOUD; *Le Mobilier Bas-Breton*, JULES GAUTHIER; *Le Mobilier Alsacien*, PAUL GÉLIS; *Le Mobilier Bressan*, ALPHONSE GERMAIN; *Le Mobilier Normand*, LÉON LE CLERC; *Le Mobilier Flamand*, V. CHAMPIER; *Le Mobilier Auvergnat*, JULES GAUTHIER; *Le Mobilier Vendéen et du Pays Nantais*, JULES GAUTHIER. Paris, 1924.

DILKE, LADY. *French Decoration and Furniture in the Eighteenth Century*. London, 1901.

DOWNS, JOSEPH. *American Furniture, Queen Anne and Chippendale Periods*. New York, 1952.

ECKE, GUSTAV. *Chinese Domestic Furniture*. Peking, China, 1944.

FÉLICE, ROGER, DE. *Little Illustrated Books on Old French Furniture*, 4 vols.; Vol. I, *French Furniture in the Middle Ages and Under Louis XIII*, Translated by F. M. ATKINSON, London, 1923. Vol. II, *French Furniture under Louis XIV*, Translated by F. M. ATKINSON, New York, 1923. Vol. III, *French Furniture under Louis XV*, Translated by FLORENCE SIMMONDS, New York, 1920. Vol. IV, *French Furniture under Louis XVI and Empire*, Translated by F. M. ATKINSON, New York, 1921.

HAVARD, HENRY. *Dictionnaire de L'Ameublement et de la Décoration Depuis le XIII Siècle Jusqu'à Nous Jours*. 4 vols., Paris, 1887–1890.

HEAL, SIR AMBROSE. *London Furniture Makers, From the Restoration to the Victorian Era, 1660–1840*. London, 1953.

HORNOR, WILLIAM MACPHERSON. *Blue Book of Philadelphia Furniture, William Penn to George Washington*. Philadelphia, 1935.

JOURDAIN, MARGARET. *English Decoration and Furniture of the Early Renaissance, 1500–1650*. London, 1924.

JOURDAIN, MARGARET. *English Decoration and Furniture of the Later XVIII Century, 1760–1820*. London, 1922.

JOURDAIN, MARGARET. *English Interior Decoration, 1500–1830*. London, 1950.

JOURDAIN, MARGARET. *Regency Furniture, 1795–1820*. Revised and Enlarged Edition. London, 1948.

JOURDAIN, MARGARET. *The Work of William Kent*. London, 1948.

JOURDAIN, MARGARET AND EDWARDS, RALPH. *Georgian Cabinet-Makers*, second edition, London, 1946.

JOURDAIN, MARGARET AND ROSE, T. *English Furniture, The Georgian Period, 1750–1830*. London, 1953.

KIMBALL, FISKE AND EDNA DONNELL. *Creators of the Chippendale Style*. Metropolitan Museum Studies, May and November, 1929.

LENYGON, FRANCIS. *Furniture in England from 1660 to 1760*. London, 1915.

LE PAUTRE, JEAN. *Collection des plus Belles Compositions de Le Pautre*. par Decloux et Dowry. Paris, 18–.

LITCHFIELD, FREDERICK. *History of Furniture; From the Earliest to the Present Time*. Seventh edition; revised and enlarged, London, 1922.

LOCKWOOD, LUKE VINCENT. *Colonial Furniture in America*, 2 vols., Third edition, New York, 1926.

LONGNON, HENRI AND HUARD, FRANCES WILSON. *French Provincial Furniture*. Philadelphia, 1927.

MACQUOID, PERCY. *A History of English Furniture*. 4 vols., London, 1904–1908. Vol. I, *The Age of Oak*, 1904; Vol. II, *The Age of Walnut*, 1905; Vol. III, *The Age of Mahogany*, 1906; Vol. IV, *The Age of Satinwood*, 1908.

MACQUOID, PERCY AND EDWARDS, RALPH. *The Dictionary of English Furniture, from the Middle Ages to the Late Georgian Period*. Revised and enlarged by Ralph Edwards, 3 vols., London, 1954.

MAILLARD, ELISA. *Old French Furniture and Its Surroundings, 1610–1815*. Translated by MacIver Percival, London, 1925.

MCCLELLAND, NANCY VINCENT. *Duncan Phyfe and the English Regency, 1795–1830*. New York, 1939.

MILLER, EDGAR GEORGE, JR. *American Antique Furniture*. 2 vols., Baltimore, 1937. An abridgement of the two volume work, New York, 1950.

MILNE, JAMES LEES. *The Age of Adam*. London, 1947.

MOLINIER, ÉMILE. *Royal Interiors and Decorations of the 17th and 18th Centuries*. 5 vols., Paris, 1902. Vol. I, *Louis XIV*; Vol. II, *Régence and Louis XV*; Vol. III, *Régence and Louis XV*; Vol. IV, *Louis XVI*; Vol. V, *Louis XVI*.

NUTTING, WALLACE. *Furniture of the Pilgrim Century, 1620–1720*. Revised edition, Massachusetts, 1924.

NUTTING, WALLACE. *Furniture Treasury*. 2 vols., in 1928 and a 3rd. vol. in 1933. Massachusetts.

NUTTING, WALLACE. *The Clock Book*. New York, 1924.

ODOM, WILLIAM M. *A History of Italian Furniture from the fourteenth to the early nineteenth centuries*. 2 vols., New York, 1918.

OPPENORD, GILLES MARIE. *Oeuvres de Gille Marie Oppenort*. Paris, 18—.

PALMER, BROOKS. *The Book of American Clocks*. New York, 1950.

RICCI, SEYMOUR DE. *Louis XIV and Regency Furniture and Decoration*. New York, 1929.

RICCI, SEYMOUR DE. *Louis XVI Furniture*. London, 1913.

RICHTER, GESELA MARIE AUGUSTA. *Ancient Furniture; A History of Greek, Roman and Etruscan Furniture*. Oxford, 1926.

ROGERS, JOHN C. *English Furniture*. Revised and enlarged by Margaret Jourdain. London, 1950.

SALVERTE, COMTE FRANÇOIS DE. *Les Ebénistes du XVIII Siècle, Leurs Oeuvres et Leurs Marques*. Paris, 1937.

SALVERTE, COMTE FRANÇOIS DE. *Le Meuble Français d'après les ornamenistes de 1660 à 1789*. Paris, 1930.

Furniture (continued)

SCHMITZ, HERMANN. *The Encyclopedia of Furniture; an Outline History of Furniture Design.* London, 1926.

SINGLETON, ESTHER. *Dutch and Flemish Furniture.* London, 1907.

SINGLETON, ESTHER. *French and English Furniture.* New York, 1903.

SYMONDS, ROBERT WEYMSS. *English Furniture from Charles II to George II.* 2 vols., London, 1929.

SYMONDS, ROBERT WEYMSS. *Masterpieces of English Furniture and Clocks; a Study of Mahogany and Walnut Furniture.* London, 1940.

SYMONDS, ROBERT WEYMSS. *Thomas Tompion, His Life and His Work.* London, 1951.

General Repertory of Ornament

BERLINER, RUDOLF. *Ornamentale Vorlage-Blätter des 15. bis 18. Jahrhunderts.* 4 vols., Leipsig, 1924–1926·

DESTAILLEUR, HIPPOLYTE ALEXANDRE GABRIEL WALTER. *Recueil d'estampes relatives à l'ornementation des apartments aux 16e, 17e et 18e siècles.* 2 vols., Paris, 1863–1871.

GUILMARD, D. *Les Maîtres Ornemenistes.* 2 vols., Paris, 1880. Vol. I, Planches, Vol. II, Texte.

JESSEN, DR. PETER. *Der Ornamentstich.* Berlin, 1920.

JESSEN, DR. PETER. *Meister des Ornamentichs.* Berlin, 1923.

SPELTZ, ALEXANDER. *Styles of Ornament, from Prehistoric Times to the Middle of the XIXth Century.* Translated from the second German edition. Revised and edited by R. Phene Spiers. London, 1910.

SPELTZ, ALEXANDER. *The Coloured Ornament of All Historical Styles.* Leipsig, 1915. Part I, Antiquity; Part II, Middle Ages; Part III, Modern Times.

Ceramics: English, European and American

BARBER, EDWIN ATLEE. *Pottery and Porcelain of the United States.* New York, 1901.

BARRETT, FRANKLIN A. *Caughley and Coalport Porcelain.* London, 1951.

BARRETT, FRANKLIN A. *Worcester Porcelain.* London, 1953.

BEMROSE, GEOFFREY. *Nineteenth-Century English Pottery and Porcelain.* London, 1952.

BRINCKMANN, JUSTIUS. *Führer Durch die Sammlungen Zugleich ein Handbuch der Geschichte des Kunstgewerbes.* Hamburg, 1894.

CAMBRIDGE UNIVERSITY. *Catalogue of the Glaisher collection of pottery and porcelain in the Fitzwilliam Museum, Cambridge* by BERNARD RACKHAM. 2 vols., Cambridge, 1935.

CHAFFERS, WILLIAM. *Marks and Monograms on European and Oriental Pottery and Porcelain.* Edited by Frederick Litchfield. 2 vols.; fourteenth issue; London, 1932.

COX, WARREN E. *The Book of Pottery and Porcelain.* 2 vols., New York, 1944.

DIXON, JOSEPH LAWRENCE. *English Porcelain of the Eighteenth Century.* New York, 1952.

GARNER, FREDERICK HORACE. *English Delftware.* London 1948.

HANNOVER,, EMIL. *Pottery and Porcelain; a handbook for collectors.* Translated from the Danish of Hannover; edited with notes and appendices by Bernard Rackham, 3 vols., London, 1925. Vol. I, Europe and the Near East Earthenware and Stoneware; Vol. II, *The Far East*; Vol. III, *European Porcelain.*

HONEY, WILLIAM BOWYER. *English Pottery and Porcelain.* Third Edition, London, 1947.

HONEY, WILLIAM BOWYER. *European Ceramic Art, from the end of the Middle Ages to about 1815.* 2 vols., London, 1949–1952.

HONEY, WILLIAM BOWYER. *French Porcelain of the Eighteenth Century.* London, 1950.

HONEY, WILLIAM BOWYER. *German Porcelain.* London, 1947.

HONEY, WILLIAM BOWYER. *Old English Porcelain, a handbook for collectors.* New Edition, London, 1948.

HONEY, WILLIAM BOWYER. *The Art of the Potter.* London, 1946.

HONEY, WILLIAM BOWYER. *Wedgwood Ware.* New York, 1949.

HONEY, WILLIAM BOWYER. *Dresden China; An Introduction to the Study of Meissen Porcelain.* New York, 1955.

LANE, ARTHUR. *French Faïence.* London, 1948.

LEACH, BERNARD. *A Potter's Book.* London. 1940.

LITCHFIELD, FREDERICK. *Pottery and Porcelain; a guide to collectors.* Fifth edition; enlarged and completely revised by Frank Tilley. New York, 1951.

Ceramics : English, European and American (*continued*)

NEURDENBURG, ELIZABETH. *Old Dutch Pottery and Tiles.* Translated by Bernard Rackham. London, 1923.

POUNTNEY, WILLIAM J. *Old Bristol Potteries; an account of the old potters and potteries of Bristol and Brislington between 1650 and 1850.* Bristol, 1920.

RACKHAM, BERNARD. *A Key to Pottery and Glass.* London, 1940.

RACKHAM, BERNARD. *Early Staffordshire Pottery.* London, 1951.

RACKHAM, BERNARD. *Italian Maiolica.* New York, 1952.

RACKHAM, BERNARD. *Medieval English Pottery.* New York, 1949.

RACKHAM, BERNARD AND READ, HERBERT. *English Pottery; its development from early times to the end of the eighteenth century.* London, 1924.

RAMSAY, JOHN. *American Potters and Pottery.* New York, 1939.

SPARGO, JOHN. *Early American Pottery and China.* New York, 1926.

VAN DE PUT, A. *Hispano-Moresque Ware of the XV Century.* London, 1904.

Ceramics: Chinese, Korean and Japanese

BOWES, JAMES L. *Japanese Pottery.* Liverpool, 1890.

BRINKLEY, CAPTAIN FRANK. *Japan and China, their history, arts and literature.* Vol. VIII, *Japan Ceramic Art,* London, 1904; Vol. IX, *China Ceramic Art,* London, 1904.

BUSHELL, S. W., LAFFAN, W., AND CLARKE, T. B. *Catalogue of the Morgan Collection of Chinese Porcelains.* New York, 1904–1911. Vol. I, reprinted in 1907 by the New York Metropolitan Museum of Art.

BUSHELL, STEPHEN W. *Description of Chinese Pottery and Porcelain, being a translation of the T'ao Shuo by Chu Yen.* Oxford, 1910.

BUSHELL, STEPHEN W. *Oriental Ceramic Art,* illustrated by examples from the collection of W. T. Walters. Text and notes by S. W. Bushell. New York, 1897–1899.

David, Sir Percival Victor, Collection. *A Catalogue of Chinese Pottery and Porcelain in the collection of Sir Percival David,* by R. L. HOBSON, London 1934.

Eumorfopoulos, George, Collection. *The George Eumorfopoulos collection; a catalogue of the Chinese, Corean and Persian pottery and porcelain,* by R. L. HOBSON. 6 vols., London, 1925–1928.

GRAY, BASIL. *Early Chinese Pottery and Porcelain.* London, 1953.

HETHERINGTON, A. L. *The Early Ceramic Wares of China.* London, 1922.

HOBSON, ROBERT LOCKHART. *Chinese Art.* Revised by Soame Jenyns; second edition, London, 1952.

HOBSON, ROBERT LOCKHART. *Chinese Pottery and Porcelain; an account of the potter's art in China from primitive times to the present day.* 2 vols., New York, 1915.

HOBSON, ROBERT LOCKHART. *Handbook of the Pottery and Porcelain of the Far East.* Third edition, London, 1948.

HOBSON, ROBERT LOCKHART AND HETHERINGTON, A. L. *The Art of the Chinese Potter from the Han dynasty the end of the Ming.* New York, 1923.

HOBSON, ROBERT LOCKHART. *The Later Ceramics Wares of China.* London, 1925.

HOBSON, ROBERT LOCKHART. *The Wares of the Ming Dynasty.* London, 1923.

HONEY, WILLIAM BOWYER. *Corean Pottery.* London, 1947.

HONEY, WILLIAM BOWYER. *Guide to the Later Chinese Porcelain Periods.* London, Victoria and Albert Museum Guide, 1927.

HONEY, WILLIAM BOWYER. *The Ceramic Art of China, and other countries of the Far East.* London, 1945.

HUISH, MARCUS B. *Japan and Its Art; including pottery and porcelain, lacquer, enamels, textiles and embroideries, etc.* Third edition, London, 1913.

JENYNS, SOAME. *Later Chinese Porcelain. The Ch'ing Dynasty, 1644–1912.* London, 1951.

JENYNS, SOAME. *Ming Pottery and Porcelain.* London, 1953.

KÜMMEL, OTTO. *Kuntsgewerbe in Japan.* Berlin, 1919.

LAN, P'U. *Chinge-tê-chén T'ao-lu;* or *The Potteries of China.* A translation with notes by Geoffrey R. Sayer. London, 1951.

MONKHOUSE, W. COSMO. *A History and Description of Chinese Porcelain.* London, 1901.

MORSE, EDWARD S. *Catalogue of the Morse Collection of Japanese Pottery.* Boston, 1901.

OKUDA, SEIICHI. *Masterpieces of pottery and porcelain in Japan.* Kyōto, 1934.

TOKYO, SAIKO-KWAI. *Kakiyemon and Nabeshima Wares.* Tokyo, 1929.

WATANABE, KOI. *Collection of famous examples of Kutani, Nabeshima and Kakiyemon ware.* Osaka, 1933.

WATANABE, KOI. *Collection of famous examples of old Japanese Pottery.* Osaka, 1933.

Silver, Sheffield and Pewter

BIGELOW, FRANCIS HILL. *Historic Silver of the Colonies and its Makers.* New York, 1917.

BOESEN, GUDMUND and BOJE, CHR. A. *Old Danish Silver,* Copenhagen, 1949.

BRADBURY, FREDERICK. *Guide to Marks of Origin on British and Irish Silver Plate, 1544–1946. Old Sheffield Plate Makers' Marks, 1743–1860.* Seventh edition; Sheffield, 1947.

BRADBURY, FREDERICK. *History of Old Sheffield Plate.* London, 1912.

CARRÉ, LOUIS. *A Guide to Old French Plate.* London, 1931.

COTTERELL, HOWARD HERSCHEL. *Old Pewter: Its Makers and Marks.* London, 1929.

COTTERELL, HOWARD HERSCHEL. *Pewter Down the Ages.* London, 1932.

ENSKO, STEPHEN G. C. *American Silversmiths and Their Marks III.* New York, 1948.

FREDERIKS, J. W. *Dutch Silver.* The Hague, 1952.

HAVARD, HENRY. *Histoire de l'Orfèvrerie Française.* 2 vols., Paris, 1896.

HUGHES, BERNARD AND THERLE. *Three Centuries of English Domestic Silver—1500–1820.* London, 1952.

JACKSON, SIR CHARLES JAMES. *English Goldsmiths and Their Marks.* Second edition revised and enlarged, in two parts. London, 1921.

JACKSON, SIR CHARLES JAMES. *Illustrated History of English Plate, ecclesiastical and secular.* 2 vols., London, 1911.

JONES, E. ALFRED. *Old Silver of Europe and America, From Early Times to the Nineteenth Century.* London, 1928.

KERFOOT, J. B. *American Pewter.* Boston, 1924.

MASSÉ, H. J. L. J. *Chats on Old Pewter.* Edited and revised by Ronald F. Michaelis. New York, 1949.

MASSÉ, HENRI JEAN LOUIS JOSEPH. *Pewter Plate, a historical and descriptive handbook.* London, 1910.

OMAN, CHARLES CHICHELE. *English Domestic Silver.* London, 1947.

VEITCH, HENRY NEWTON. *Sheffield Plate. Its history, manufacture and art with makers' names and marks, also a note on foreign Sheffield plate.* London, 1908.

WATTS, WILLIAM WALTER. *Old English Silver.* London, 1924.

WENHAM, EDWARD. *Domestic Silver of Great Britain and Ireland.* London, 1935.

WYLER, SEYMOUR. *The Book of Old Silver.* New York, 1937.

WYLER, SEYMOUR. *The book of Sheffield plate with all known makers' marks including Victorian plate insignia.* New York, 1949.

Glass

BERGSTROM, EVANGELINE H. *Old Glass Paperweights.* New York, 1947.

BUCKLEY, FRANCIS. *A History of Old English Glass.* London, 1925.

BUCKLEY, WILFRED. *European Glass.* London, 1926.

DILLON, EDWARD. *Glass.* London, 1907.

GARNIER, ÉDOUARD. *La Verrerie et l'Emaillerie.* Tours, 1886.

HARTSHORNE, ALBERT. *Old English Glasses, an account of glass drinking vessels in England.* 2 vols., London, 1897.

HAYNES, E. B. *Glass through the Ages.* London, 1948.

HONEY, WILLIAM BOWYER. *Glass, A Handbook and a Guide to the Museum Collection, Victoria and Albert Museum.* London, 1946.

KNITTLE, RHEA MANSFIELD. *Early American Glass.* New York, 1927.

LEE, RUTH WEBB AND ROSE, JAMES H. *American Glass Cup Plates.* Northborough, 1948.

LEE, RUTH WEBB. *Early American Pressed Glass.* Enlarged and revised. Pittsford, 1931.

LEE, RUTH WEBB. *Victorian Glass.* New York, 1944.

MCKEARIN, GEORGE S. AND HELEN. *American Glass.* New York, 1941.

SCHMIDT, ROBERT. *Das Glas.* second edition. Berlin, 1922.

THORPE, W. A. *A History of English and Irish Glass.* London, 1929.

Textiles, Tapestries and Oriental Carpets

COLE, ALAN S. *Ornament in European Silks.* London, 1899.

DILLEY, ARTHUR URBANE. *Oriental Rugs and Carpets, a comprehensive study.* New York, 1931.

FLEMMING, ERNST. *An Encyclopaedia of Textiles.* London, 1928.

GÖBEL, HEINRICH. *Tapestries of the Lowlands.* New York, 1924.

HAWLEY, WALTER A. *Oriental Rugs, Antique and Modern.* New York, 1937.

HUNTER, GEORGE LELAND. *Decorative Textiles.* Philadelphia and London, 1918.

HUNTER, GEORGE LELAND. *The Practical Book of Tapestries.* Philadelphia and London, 1925.

KENDRICK, A. F. AND TATTERSALL, C. E. C. *Hand-Woven Carpets, Oriental and European.* London, 1922.

Textiles, Tapestries and Oriental Carpets (continued)

LEJARD, ANDRÉ. *French Tapestry*. Paris, 1947.

MARILLIER, HENRY CURRIE. *Handbook of the Teniers Tapestries*. London, 1932.

MARTIN, FREDRIK ROBERT. *A History of Oriental Carpets before 1800*. London, 1906.

MUMFORD, JOHN KIMBERLY. *Oriental Rugs*. New York, 1929.

Lace and Needlework

ASHTON, LEIGH, *Samplers*. London, 1926.

BOLTON, ETHEL STANWOOD AND COE, EVA JOHNSTON. *American Samplers*. Boston, 1921.

HEAD, MRS. R. E. *The lace and embroidery collector; a guide to collectors of old lace and embroidery*. New York, 1922.

HENNEBERG, FREIHERR ALFRED VON. *The Art and Craft of Old Lace*. New York, 1931.

JONES, MARY EIRWEN. *British Samplers*. Oxford, 1948.

JONES, MARY EIRWEN. *The Romance of Lace*. London, 1951.

JOURDAIN, MARGARET. *Old Lace, a Handbook for Collectors*. London, 1909.

JOURDAIN, M. *The History of English Secular Embroidery*. London, 1910.

KENDRICK, ALBERT FRANK. *English Needlework*. London, 1933.

LEFÉBURE, ERNEST. *Embroidery and Lace; their manufacture and history from the remotest antiquity to the present day*. Translated and enlarged with notes by A. S. Cole. London, 1888.

LOWES, EMILY LEIGH. *Chats on Old Lace and Needlework*. London, 1919.

PALLISER, MRS. BURY. *A History of Lace*. Revised, re-written and enlarged by M. Jourdain and Alice Dryden. Fourth edition, London, 1902.

SELIGMAN, G. SAVILLE AND HUGHES, TALBOT. *Domestic Needlework*. London, 1926.

SYMONDS, MARY AND PREECE, LOUISA. *Needlework Through the Ages*. London, 1928.

Far East Art

AUDSLEY, GEORGE ASHDOWN. *The Ornamental Arts of Japan*. 2 vols., in nine sections, London, 1882. Vol. I, *Drawing, Painting, Engraving, Printing, Embroidery, Textile Fabrics, Lacquer*; Vol. II, *Incrusted-work, Metal-work, Cloisonné Enamel, Modelling and Carving, Heraldry*.

BISHOP, HEBER REGINALD, Collection. *Investigations and Studies in Jade*. Metropolitan Museum of Art, 2 vols., New York, 1906.

BOLLER, WILLY. *Masterpieces of the Japanese Color Woodcut*. Boston, 1949.

BUSHELL, STEPHEN W. *Chinese Art; including jade, bronze, lacquer, ivory, porcelain, pottery, textiles, enamels, etc*. 2 vols., second edition revised; London, 1909.

Eumorfopoulos, George, Collection. *The George Eumorfopoulos collection; catalogue of Chinese and Corean bronzes, sculptures, jades, etc*., by W. PERCEVAL YETTS. 3 vols., London, 1929–1932.

GOETTE, JOHN. *Jade Lore*. New York, 1937.

GUNSAULUS, HELEN C. *Japanese Sword Mounts in the collection of Field Museum*. Chicago, 1923.

HAWKSHAW, J. C. *Japanese Swords Mounts*. London, 1910.

HILLIER, J. *Japanese Masters of the Color Print*. London, 1954.

INN, HENRY. *Chinese Houses and Gardens*. Revised edition, edited by Shao Chang Lee. New York, 1950

JOURDAIN, MARGARET AND JENYNS, SOAME. *Chinese Export Art in the eighteenth century*. London, 1950.

KANDA, MATUNOSUKE. *Japanese Lacquer*. Tokyo, 1941.

KOIZUMI, G. *Lacquer Work*. London, 1923.

KOOP, ALBERT J. *Early Chinese Bronzes*. London, 1924.

LAUFER, BERTHOLD. *Jade, a study in Chinese archaeology and religion*. Chicago, 1912.

NOTT, STANLEY CHARLES. *Chinese Jade*. London, 1936.

Pageant of Japanese Art. Edited by staff members of the Tokyo National Museum, Tokyo, 1952. Vol. II, *Painting*; Vol. III, *Sculpture*; Vol. IV, *Ceramics and Metal Work*.

POPE-HENNESSY, UNA. *Early Chinese Jades*. London, 1923.

Sassoon Collection. *Catalogues of Chinese Ivories*. 3 vols., New York, 1950.

SÉGUY, E.-A. *Les Lacques du Coromandel*. Paris.

STRANGE, EDWARD F. *Chinese Lacquer*. London, 1926.

The Arms and Armor Club of New York. *Catalogues of Japanese Sword Fittings*. New York, 1921 and 1922.

The Romance of Chinese Art. Completed by a group of authors. New York, 1936.

VETLESEN, MRS. GEORG, Collection. *Chinese Jade Carvings of the XVIth to XIXth Century*. 3 vols., New York, 1939.

WHITLOCK, HERBERT P. *The Story of Jade*. New York, 1949.

Miscellaneous Subjects

ASHDOWN, CHARLES HENRY. *British and Foreign Arms and Armor.* London, 1909.

BAINBRIDGE, HENRY CHARLES. *Peter Carl Fabergé.* London, 1949.

BAKER, OLIVER. *Black Jacks and Leather Bottells.* London, 1921.

BOEHN, MAX VON. *Miniatures and Silhouettes.* Translated by E. K. Walker, London, 1926.

BOLTON, THEODORE BOLTON. *Early American Portrait Painters in Miniature.* New York, 1921.

CUNYNGHAME, HENRY H. *European Enamels.* London, 1906.

DEMMIN, AUGUSTE. *An Illustrated History of Arms and Armour.* London, 1877.

HILBURGH, W. L. *Medieval Spanish Enamels.* London, 1936.

HUGHES, THERLE AND BERNARD. *English Painted Enamels.* London, 1951.

KUNZ, GEORGE FREDERICK. *Ivory and the Elephant in Art.* New York, 1916.

LAKING, SIR GUY FRANCIS. *A Record of European Armour and Arms through Seven Centuries.* 5 vols., London, 1920–1922.

LEMBERGER, ERNST. *Meister-Miniaturen aus Fünf Jahrhundersten.* Stuttgart, 1911.

LONG, BASIL S. *British Miniaturists working between 1520–1860.* London, 1929.

REYNOLD, GRAHAM. *English Portrait Miniatures.* London, 1952.

SNOWMAN, A. KENNETH. *Carl Gustavovich Fabergé, 1846–1920.* London, 1953.

STONE, GEORGE CAMERON. *A Glossary of the Construction, Decoration and use of Arms and Armour.* Portland, 1934.

TWINING, E. W. *The Art and Craft of Stained Glass.* London, 1928.

VIOLLET-LE-DUC, EUGÈNE EMMANUEL. *Medieval Stained Glass.* A translation. Atlanta, 1946.

WEHLE, HARRY B. *American Miniatures, 1730–1850.* New York, 1927.

WERCK, ALFRED. *Stained Glass.* New York, 1922.

WILLIAMSON, GEORGE C. *The Book of Ivory.* London, 1938.

SUPPLEMENT

Foreword to the Supplement

The nearly 700 terms selected for the second and enlarged edition of THE DICTIONARY OF ANTIQUES AND THE DECORATIVE ARTS are based on the English Arts and Crafts Movement, l'Art Nouveau and the Modern Movement and the Twentieth Century, with selected terms of the American Victorian period of interest to collectors. The general content and over-all plan of the first edition of the DICTIONARY have proved so well adapted to the needs of its users that it seemed advisable to follow the essential form and character in the presentation of the new material incorporated as a supplement at this time. Cross references are to entries within the Supplement unless a page reference to the main text is given.

LOUISE ADE BOGER

VICTORIAN

WESTWARD HO COMPOTE
GILLINDER & SONS GLASSWORKS

THONET BENTWOOD
CRADLE, *c. 1895*

CUT GLASS PLATE, PARISIAN PATTERN
C. DORFLINGER, *c. 1890*

SILVER SPOON, ALHAMBRA
PATTERN, *Mid-19th century*

REGISTRATION MARK
For October 22, 1857

HISTORICAL BLUE PLATTER
Mid-19th century

CANTON CHINA CANISTER
Mid-19th century

BELLEEK SWAN DISH
CERAMIC ART CO., *c. 1890*

GOTHIC CHAIR
JOHN JELLIFF, *c. 1840*

COFFEE TABLE
E. W. GODWIN, *c. 1870*

CHAIR
JOHN BELTER, *c. 1850*

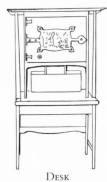

DESK
C. F. A. VOYSEY, *1896*

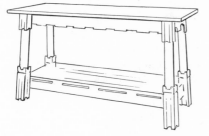

TABLE
PHILIP WEBB, *c. 1870*

CARCEL LAMP
c. 1850

SOFA
CHARLES L. EASTLAKE, *c. 1880*

Aalto, Alvar b. 1898. Finnish architect and designer; famed for his sanatorium at Paimio. He adapted the spring-support principle used by Breuer in his tubular steel chair to bent laminated plywood, and was the first to apply this principle to domestic furniture of laminated plywood. He also experimented with curving plywood to fit the human shape. In 1934 he introduced a chair having a continuous seat and back bent in sweeping curves and formed from a single sheet of plywood, suspended within a bent cut-out plywood frame. The chair was ingeniously designed so that the curves made use of the natural springiness of plywood.

Adam, Henri Georges b. 1904. French engraver, designer and painter; began sculpture in 1940. He was one of the most important sculptors of his generation. His first works in tapestry in 1947 introduced a new technique using black and white. In his tapestries Adam discovered his true dimension, and it is in a spirit of architectural understanding that he can successfully integrate his work to the wall.

Adams and Company In American glass; in 1851 Adams, Macklin and Company took over the old Stourbridge Flint Glass Works established by John Robinson at Pittsburgh in 1823. They manufactured flint glass tablewares, pressed, engraved, and later, lime glasswares. They were noted for their fine cut glass. At the Philadelphia Centennial Exhibition, 1876, they exhibited flint and opal wares. They established a large export business and were still operating in 1889.

Adams, Mark b. 1925. American weaver-turned-designer; specializes in tapestries which are woven in Aubusson, France. He originates his designs in découpage, using countless pieces of colored paper. His tapestries are primarily architectural in scale and concept and are notable for their striking colors.

Aesthetic Movement In England the *l'art pour l'art* movement was much in evidence in decorative art from the 1870's until the trial of Oscar Wilde, the leading aesthete, in 1895, which resulted in his banishment. The aesthetes were enchanted by the artistic charm of Japan, the medievalism of Morris and Rossetti, the ideals of Ruskin, the elegance of Wilde and the free treatment of artistic ways of expression followed by Whistler. The symbols of the movement – the lily (purity), peacock (beauty) and sunflower (constancy) – were much in evidence. Other manifestations associated with the movement include "blue and white" (Nanking ware) introduced from Paris to London by Whistler, consciously disposed fans, spidery bamboo chairs and all kinds of wickerwork furniture. The force of the movement did much to promote a general interest in art and design. See *Whistler, James McNeill.*

Albany Slip In American ceramics; a rich, dark brown clay, found near Albany, New York, used sometimes as a glaze and after c. 1800 as a lining for salt-glazed stoneware vessels.

Albers, Anni b. 1899. American, born in Germany, designer-weaver; studied at the Bauhaus in Weimar and Dessau. She is known for her work in the textile field as an artist, designer for industrial production, lecturer and teacher. Her weaving is notable for the imagination with which she selects new and experimental materials. She is married to Josef Albers, also Bauhaus-trained, a painter and designer.

Allesch, Marianne von b. 1886. American, born in Germany, designer of glass tableware.

American Art Nouveau　See *Tiffany, Louis Comfort*.

American Craftsmen's Council　Established by Mrs. Vanderbilt Webb in 1943 and was chiefly responsible for the renaissance of craftsmanship in America. More than 125 of the leading craft organizations in America are affiliated as members with the Council, whose aim it is to provide education in the crafts and to stimulate public interest in and appreciation of the work of handcraftsmen. The Council conducts the Museum of Contemporary Crafts, founded in 1956, New York, and publishes CRAFT HORIZONS magazine. As part of the program to find new horizons of expansion for the American craftsman the Council maintains a close relationship with America House in New York, the leading marketing outlet for craftsmen in America. The Council also has a similar relationship with the School for American Craftsmen, originally founded by the Council in 1945 and a division of the Rochester Institute of Technology since 1950. The Council, following the trail blazed by William Morris, has enforced, within the new order of things, a respect for the handmade product and has secured the recognition of the individual artist-craftsman.

American Organ　See *Harmonium*.

American Tapestries　The weaving of tapestries in America is especially identified with the production of two manufactories. The first tapestry atelier in America was started by William Baumgarten in New York City in 1893. Weavers were brought over from France, chiefly from Aubusson. Under the management of M. Foussadier from the Royal Windsor Tapestry Works in England, the factory soon gained an excellent reputation for its high standard of creative artistic work. The other atelier, also noted for its excellent workmanship, was begun by Albert Herter in 1908 on East 33rd Street in New York City.

Anderson, William C.　American glassmaker, designing for Libbey. See *Libbey Glass Company*.

André, Emile　1871-1933. French architect and furniture designer of the Nancy School. His furniture around 1900 notably reveals a complete fusion of Art Nouveau and Neo-Rococo traditions.　See *Nancy School*.

Antimacassar　In the Victorian era; a small auxiliary covering for chair or sofa made to protect upholstery from contact with the head of the sitter. The name derives from the former practice of using Macassar Oil as a hair dressing. The earliest examples were of starched white crochet. Later the antimacassar became the tidy.　See *Tidy*.

Antiques Law　Effective February 1, 1967. By Public Law 89-651, objects 100 years old are designated as "antiques." The law affects objects arriving in the United States from abroad and frees them from duty. It supersedes the earlier rule setting 1830 as the date before which an object became "antique." The 1967 law relieves importers of customs duty on glass, porcelain, silver plate, tables, case furniture and chairs. See *Antique Furniture*, page 15.

Ariel　See *Swedish Glass*.

Arikawa　Modern Japanese artist-potter; working near Tajimi in the Gifu Prefecture. He typifies that group of Japanese artist-potters who have made it their life work to revive and continue some of the traditional Japanese pottery styles. Arikawa is identified with the Shino style. His tea bowls made by methods and materials used in the area for several hundred years are highly prized by collectors.　See *Seto Ware; Rosanjin, Kitaoji*.

Arita　In Japanese ceramics; an important center in the Saga Prefecture for handcrafted pottery. Arita ware is popularly called Imari ware because in the Edo period it was shipped to various parts of the country from the port of Imari, which is near Arita. Pottery has been virtually its only industry since the 17th century. Li-Sanpei, a naturalized Korean, discovered china clay of a fine quality in Izumiyama, Arita, and succeeded in making the first white porcelain of native materials in 1615. This discovery opened a new dawn for Japanese ceramics, and since then many beautiful articles have been made in this town.   See *Hasami; Japanese Contemporary Pottery.*

Art Glass   See page 22.

Art Moderne   A style brought into existence by the Paris Exposition of 1925, which stood for modern decorative and industrial art. The French art of 1925, called New Art or Art Moderne, was not strictly new. Apart from a marginal interest in Art Nouveau, the new style essentially took up French classicism, especially geometric forms associated with the Empire style; but it was now interpreted according to the ideals and philosophy of the 20th century. Such designers as Jacques Ruhlmann, Jules Leleu, Louis Suë and André Maré typified the best in Art Moderne at the Paris Exposition.

Art Nouveau   A significant movement possessing the desire to break with the past, to start anew. It flourished between 1895 and 1905, and was in full bloom around 1900. In spite of its international character it was a markedly national style and was not the same in two countries. Though it extended itself into all realms of artistic activity, it belonged foremost to the decorative arts. It possessed the merit, as did the English Arts and Crafts Movement, of reviving handicraft; it was the 19th century's final reaction against the machine. Its most important contribution to the arts of interior decoration was to re-establish a sense of unity in interior design, conceiving of a room and its contents as a unified whole. Art Nouveau, acclaimed as New Art, was never free from the bondage of the historical past. It reveals features from earlier traditional styles, especially the Gothic, Rococo and Baroque. Each in its own way contributed to mold Art Nouveau – the first in theory and to some extent in ornament, especially the Flamboyant Gothic with its flame-like and leaf-like tracery; the second with its application of asymmetry; and the third with its

plastic conception of form. It also found inspiration in the highly linear and colorful art of Japan. In part it was an inspired return to nature; sensuous undulating lines studied from the movement of growth are a striking feature. The sinuous whiplash curve became Art Nouveau's typical contour, embracing the arts of decoration with forms reminiscent of plants and flowers. Straight lines are erased wherever it is feasible, while structural divisions are no longer definable and flow into one another to maintain a continuous linear movement. Art Nouveau at its best, rich in linear rhythm, reveals a harmony of line which is noteworthy in the history of decorative art.   See *French Art Nouveau; Jugendstil; Gaudi, Antonio; Proto-Art Nouveau; Glasgow School; Tiffany, Louis C.; Secession; Dutch Art Nouveau; Belgian Art Nouveau.*

Art Nouveau   In American ceramics; around 1900 the influence of the French-inspired Art Nouveau became evident. Among the most important potters working in the new style were Grueby, van Briggle, Tiffany and the group of decorators working for the Rookwood, Weller and Newcomb potteries. Some of the most advanced of these designs were the work of van Briggle.   See *Grueby, William H.; Briggle, van, Pottery Company; Tiffany, Louis C.; Weller Pottery.*

Artist-Craftsman   The name given to the creative individual who both designs and executes useful and decorative objects in his medium, whether in ceramics, wood, glass, textiles or metal. Exceptions occur in some cases where it is quite normal for the designer and craftsman to collaborate, as, for example, tapestry-making.   See *Designer-Craftsman.*

Artist-Potter   In ceramics; a craftsman who designs as well as makes his pots.   See *Artist-Craftsman.*

Arts and Crafts   An inclusive title for the arts of decoration and handicraft; that is, all those that contribute to the making of the house beautiful. The title is also identified with the movement usually understood as the English revival of the decorative arts, which began about 1875. During the 1880's England built up an artistic vitality which affected all Europe. This was the decade when the English guilds for arts and crafts were founded and produced some of their best work. See *Arts and Crafts Movement*.

Arts and Crafts Exhibition Society In English arts and crafts; many beautiful pieces, especially furniture, were presented at the exhibitions of the Arts and Crafts Society from 1888 to 1914. The original furniture of designers such as Ernest Gimson, M. H. Baillie Scott, George Walton, Charles Ashbee, Charles Voysey and the Barnsleys was admired for its good taste and reticence. This Arts and Crafts style, an extremely simple and constructive one, was frequently called Style Liberty or Style Inglese on the Continent, where it had considerable influence. Once again England became a leader in artistic cabinetwork. See *Arts and Crafts Movement; Voysey, Charles; Walton, George; Baillie Scott, M. H.; Ashbee, Charles; Cotswold School; Mackmurdo, Arthur; Sachlichkeit*.

Arts and Crafts Movement The title, originating in England, came into general use when the Arts and Crafts Exhibition Society was founded in 1888 with the aid of William Morris. The Arts and Crafts Movement was, in the words of Morris, "to help the conscious cultivation of art and to interest the public in it." It brought a revival of artistic craftsmanship. Between 1880 and 1890 five societies for the promotion of artistic craftsmanship were started: Century Guild, 1882; Art Workers' Guild, 1884; Home Arts and Industries Association, 1884; Ashbee's Guild and School of Handicraft, 1888; Arts and Crafts Exhibition Society, 1888. See *Morris, William; Arts and Crafts Exhibition Society; Design and Industries Association; Arts and Crafts; Craft Centre of Great Britain; English Contemporary Arts and Crafts; Council of Industrial Design; Mission Furniture*.

Art Workers' Guild In English arts and crafts; founded in 1884. Walter Crane and Lewis F. Day were its leading originators. See *Arts and Crafts Movement*.

Ashbee, Charles Robert 1863–1942. English architect, designer and writer; in 1888 he founded in the East End of London the Guild and School of Handicraft, with himself as chief designer. In 1902 Ashbee moved to Chipping Campden, in the Cotswolds, in his attempt to revive handicraft far from the center of modern living. Here he started the School of Arts and Crafts, which lasted from 1904 to 1914. The Guild itself functioned until 1908. He designed furniture, metalwork and jewelry and also a few embroideries and wallpapers. His leading claim to fame remains his Chipping Campden experiment. See *Arts and Crafts Exhibition Society*.

Associated Artists In American decorative arts; the Louis C. Tiffany Company, Associated Artists, formed in 1879, followed the trail blazed by William Morris and his followers. It was launched as a guiding hand to improve taste in the decorative arts and to restore an interest in them. The group comprised Candace Wheeler, 1827–1923; John La Farge, 1835–1910; Lockwood de Forest, 1850–1932; Samuel Coleman and Louis C. Tiffany, 1848–1933. They decorated interiors for many private homes and public buildings, including the White House, in 1882–1883. See *Arts and Crafts Movement; Tiffany, Louis C.*

Aurene Glass In American glass; an iridized glass created by Carder in 1903, somewhat similar in appearance to Tiffany's Favrile. It was a metallic glass, that is, glass having a high metal content, usually silver or gold, which remained in suspension so long as it was subjected to the oxidizing flame, but on contact with a reducing flame precipitated to the surface to form a shiny, semi-opaque metallic layer. By combining metallic and non-metallic glasses, Carder obtained exotic iridescent hues, glistening surfaces alternating with the deep colors of ordinary glass, pieces somewhat related to painting in their effects and to sculptural modelling in their method. Frequently the final surfaces were sprayed with a solution of stannous chloride, giving them the sensuous velvet-like touch which

was so typical of Aurene. See *Carder, Frederick; Art Glass*, page 22.

Austrian Art Nouveau   See *Secession*.

Austrian Werkbund   See *Deutscher Werkbund; Oesterreichischer Werkbund*.

B

Baggs, Arthur   See *Binns, Charles F.*

Bailey, Banks and Biddle Company   In American silver; jewelers and silversmiths of Philadelphia, Pennsylvania, founded by Joseph T. Bailey, jeweler, in 1833. Known as Bailey and Kitchen, 1839–1846, when Andrew B. Kitchen joined the firm. Became Bailey and Company in 1846. George Banks and Samuel Biddle joined with Joseph T. Bailey, Jr. and the firm became Bailey, Banks and Biddle before 1904. See *Caldwell, J. E., and Company*.

Baillie Scott, Mackay Hugh   1865–1945. English architect and designer. He was perhaps the best-known of all English designers on the Continent, especially in Germany, where he decorated the palace of the Grand Duke of Hesse at Darmstadt. One of his favorite devices was to decorate the flat surfaces of his basically simple but rather massive forms of furniture with elaborate stylized natural motifs executed in colored woods, mother-of-pearl, ivory and pewter, and modelled in relief. His work was notable for its sound craftsmanship and fresh approach. See *Arts and Crafts Exhibition Society*.

Baker Furniture Inc.   In American furniture; established by Siebe Baker at Allegan, Michigan, in 1890. The factories were moved to Holland, Michigan, in 1933. From 1931 to 1941 the company was especially known

for its 18th century mahogany reproductions. At the present time it is probably best known for its reproductions of French and Italian cabinetwork. The Baker Furniture Museum, Holland, Michigan, and the Baker Museum and Craft Shop, Grand Rapids, Michigan, were established by this company for the furtherance of public interest in the art of cabinetmaking. See *Grand Rapids Furniture*.

Baker, John   b. 1916. English stained glass artist and teacher; worked on the restoration of ancient glass, Canterbury Cathedral, 1947–1950. He specializes in stained glass windows for modern churches. See *English Contemporary Arts and Crafts*.

Bakewell, Pears and Company   In American glass; the Pittsburgh Flint Glass Works was known under several names, including B. Bakewell and Company; Bakewell, Page and Bakewell; and Bakewell, Pears and Company. See *Bakewell's Glass Works*.

Bakewell's Glass Works   In American glass; the best known of the glasshouses of the Pittsburgh area. It was established in 1808 by two Englishmen, Benjamin Bakewell and Benjamin Page. It is generally accepted that this was the first company to make cut glass on a commercially successful scale. This company, which had the longest life of any American glasshouse (1808–1882) produced flint glass of excellent quality. In 1817 President Monroe ordered an important service engraved with the arms of the United States from Bakewell's.

Ball, Tompkins and Black In American silver; this firm like Tiffany and Company, was a fashionable New York City store. Henry Ball, Erastus O. Tompkins and William Black were the partners. They were successors to Marquand and Company in 1839 and were succeeded by Ball, Black and Company in 1851. See *Black, Starr and Frost, Ltd.; Marquand and Company.*

Bamboo In English ceramics; many objects made in unglazed cane-colored ware were modelled in the form of bamboo shoots and were known as Bamboo ware. See *Cane-Colored Ware*, page 79.

Bandbox In American accessories; by the 1820's and early 1830's the production of printed or stenciled papers for bandbox coverings had become an integral part of the wallpaper manufactories' output. Though actual wallpaper was occasionally pasted to these boxes, which were made of either cardboard or thin wood and were used for storage or transportation of clothing, the majority by far were covered with papers especially printed for this purpose. Among the early fashionable motifs, all of which were in the classical taste, were the charioteer motif and variations of the romantic temple landscapes. Some bandbox papers showed contemporary scenes, such as the balloon ascent of the 1830's, and for this reason have considerable historical interest. See *Wallpaper*, page 511.

Bang, Jacob E. See *Danish Contemporary Arts and Crafts.*

Barcelona Chair See *Rohe, Ludwig Miës van der.*

Barnsley, Edward b. 1900. English designer-craftsman; son of the cabinetmaker Sidney Barnsley of Cotswold School fame. He is the unquestioned leader of the group of craftsmen who have continued the Gimson tradition of fine handcrafted furniture. His workshop is at Petersfield. See *Cotswold School.*

Barnsley, Ernest Arthur 1863–1926. English architect and designer. See *Cotswold School.*

Barnsley, Sidney 1865–1926. English architect and designer-craftsman. See *Cotswold School.*

Barovier and Toso In Italian glass; the Barovier family, among the most ancient in Murano, goes back to the 12th century. During the 19th century a glassworks was founded with the name Barovier, later modified in 1939 into the present one under the artistic management of Ercole Barovier. Its participation in the renewal of Murano artistic glass since 1925 has been remarkable. This is due to Ercole Barovier, who has been one of the few Italian artists who have succeeded in creating genuinely modern forms. Ercole's son Angelo, a painter and designer of contemporary glass, also works in the manufactory. See *Venini, Paolo; Murano Glass.*

Bar-Tal, Ariel b. 1920. Israeli, born in Budapest, glass artist; came to Israel in 1950 and at once began to make glass sculpture, abstract compositions he modelled with the aid of glass tubes and a Bunsen burner. He continued his experiments in glass, inspired by the classic shapes and sheens of ancient glass in the Haaretz Museum. In 1960 Baroness Bethsabée de Rothschild, patroness of the arts of Israel, arranged for a special showing of Bar-Tal's work at Tiffany and Company, New York. His glass was well received and Tiffany commissioned him to create a second collection in 1961. His work shows the influence of the ancient glass of Palestine, 1st to 4th centuries A.D. He has realized many of the ancient forms in his free-blown urns, vases and bowls, applying by hand a lovely patina of muted pastels that blend into each other, giving an effect of translucence and iridescence reminiscent of old Roman glass.

Bates, Kenneth F. b. 1904. American enameller, writer and teacher; has been one of the guiding forces in the design program at the Cleveland Institute of Art, where he has taught since 1927. He is the author of ENAMELING, 1951, and BASIC DESIGN, 1960. His work, always small in scale, is varied in form. His approach to subject matter, mainly flowers and religious themes, ranges from realistic rendering to stylization influenced by synthetic cubism and complete abstraction.

Baudouine, Charles A. American cabinet-maker working in New York City from 1845 to 1900. He was perhaps best known as a successful emulator of Belter's laminated furniture. He avoided infringement of Belter's patent by making laminations with a seam down the center instead of from a single panel.

Bauhaus In Weimar, 1919, a new school and workshop, the Staatliches Bauhaus, was opened under the directorship of Walter Gropius to teach experimental methods of designing for the machine. It was also established at Dessau and Berlin. The school's chief workshop at Dessau, designed by Gropius, was one of the important buildings of the 1920's. Closed by the National Socialists in 1933, the Bauhaus was pre-eminent in establishing internationally a style of design related to the requirements of machine production. Its theories are often summarized in the slogan of functionalism: form should follow function, creation for use. The functional solutions were expressed in geometric forms influenced by De Stijl's ideas. Many Bauhaus designs were acquired by industry for mass production. Most of the products were made by hand, but the precision and clarity of their geometric contours imbued them with a machine-made appearance. Among the Bauhaus innovations in furniture design were the employment of metal tubes, highly polished surfaces made more interesting by textures rather than decoration, stacking furniture to facilitate storage. Bauhaus

textile designs emphasized the architectural character of fabrics as used in modern buildings. Their geometric patterns and textural effects have extensively influenced 20th century textile design. See *Weimar School for Arts and Crafts; Modern Movement; De Stijl; Breuer, Marcel; Rohe, Ludwig Miës van der.*

Bazel, Karel Petrus Cornelis de 1869–1923. Dutch architect, designer and graphic artist; he, with Dijsselhof, Nieuwenhuis, Lauweriks and several other artists, created the Dutch version of Art Nouveau. His woodcuts around 1894 show the impact of Symbolism in Holland, and his book illustrations reveal some Egyptian influence. See *Dutch Art Nouveau.*

Beardsley, Aubrey Vincent 1872–1898. English graphic artist and illustrator; one of the very important and influential graphic artists of Art Nouveau. His illustrations for Malory's *Morte d'Arthur*, 1892, reveal the influence of William Morris and the Pre-Raphaelites. In his illustrations for Oscar Wilde's *Salomé* he attained his own fully matured style. Beardsley was a prolific producer. An important early collector of Japanese art, he adapted Japanese ideas and transformed them into an artistic language, thus creating his own personal expression.

Behrens, Peter 1868–1940. German architect, painter and graphic artist; one of the leading artists in the Munich School. He first worked as a designer of glassware, jewelry, porcelain and furniture in 1898. He was an original member of the artist colony of Mathildenhöhe from 1899 to 1903. His first building was his own house in the artist colony, 1901, for which he also designed the interior decoration and furniture. Here his style began to turn away from Jugend's linear rhythm to the more simple and geometrical. He was active in all aspects of architecture and interior design, and he became a pioneer in modern construction. In 1936 he taught advanced architecture to the Prussian Academy of

Art in Berlin. Among his pupils were Le Corbusier, Gropius and Miës van der Rohe. See *Jugendstil; Munich School; Mathildenhöhe.*

Belgian Art Nouveau Generally regarded as the epicenter of Art Nouveau. In Belgium as in France the Neo-Baroque and Neo-Rococo clearly influenced the new style. The plastic and noticeably three-dimensional treatment found in Belgian Art Nouveau presents a far more heavy and ponderous impression of the new art than any that appeared in France. See *Horta, Victor; Velde, Henry van de; Serrurier-Bovy, Gustave; Hankar, Paul; Wolfers, Philippe; Art Nouveau.*

Belgian Contemporary Arts and Crafts At the present time, as in many countries, Belgian arts and crafts are dominated by ceramics. Especially notable is the brilliant ceramic work of Pierre Caille, one of Europe's leading artists; Olivier Strebelle, whose unique ceramic sculptures are in many collections; and Octave Landuyt. Charles Leplae and Oscar Jespers, sculptors in their own right, have made ceramic pieces of great poetic intensity. The works of Pierre Paulus are noteworthy. Belgium is rich in enamellers. Kurt Lewy, Odette Grégoire and Martha Velle represent various approaches to this art. Participating in the renaissance of the art of tapestry in Belgium are artists Floris Jespers, Edgar Tytgat, Rodolphe Strebelle, Anto Carte, René Vanden Neste, Marcel Baugniet and Georges Devêche. They have been remarkably well assisted by two Mechlin manufacturers, that of Manufacture Royale de Tapisseries d'Art Gaspard De Wit and Manufacture Royale de Tapisserie Bracquenié. At the present time there are highly talented Belgian artists who have availed themselves of the improvements that modern technique has brought to the art of glass staining, while remaining faithful to the character and purpose of the medium. E. Yoors shows a perfect understanding of the art in his wide stained glass windows of a religious character. J. Hendricks and J. Wouters, both artists and craftsmen, have produced works of secular art which are

sturdy in composition and perfect in execution. Michel Martens is among the avant-garde craftsmen working in stained glass. The goldsmith's craft in Belgium is heir to the art of metalwork that reached an extraordinary development in the Middle Ages, when Liège and the Meuse valley were the centers of production of religious items in gold and silver. In the field of religious art the goldsmith F. Jacques is pre-eminent.

Belleek Ware In ceramics; a glazed Parian ware first popularized by McBirney and Armstrong of Belleek, Ireland, in 1863. It is characterized by a pearly luster which is colorless or tinted, the most common colors being pastel pink or green. The ware is very translucent and has a natural ivory-color body that is easily scratched. The early mark is a round tower with an Irish harp on the left and an Irish wolfhound on the right. Under this is a ribbon with the name *Belleek* and a shamrock. Belleek was shown in the United States at the Philadelphia Centennial Exhibition in 1876 and was greatly admired. By 1882 Ott and Brewer produced the first piece of Belleek porcelain made in the United States; it was in the form of a square tray. Lenox produced a shell-shaped dish in 1887. Perhaps the best-known American Belleek ware was produced by Knowles, Taylor and Knowles and known as Lotus ware.

Belter, John H.   d. 1863. American, born in Germany, cabinetmaker; working in New York from about 1840 to 1860. Typical of his work are ornate rosewood chairs and settees in the revived Rococo taste with pronounced curves and elaborate open-worked frames profusely carved with flowers, fruit and foliage. In order to avoid shrinkage and to obtain strength the wood was built up in several thin layers with the grain of the wood in every other layer running in the opposite direction, or laminated, as the method is called; it was then glued together and cut out. Pieces made by Belter are notable examples of a local style.

Bennett, Edwin, Pottery Company In American ceramics; organized in Baltimore, 1890. The printed mark adopted for all their semi-porcelain wares was a globe, pierced through the United States by a sword, on the guard of which appear initials of the company, EBPC. The motto forming part of the mark is "Bona Fama Est Melior Zona Aurea." See *Bennett Pottery*, page 40.

Bennett, Ward American sculptor and designer of furniture and interiors. In 1938 he was apprenticed to Le Corbusier, who has had a profound influence on his work. He prefers to work with a total design environment; architecture, landscape and interiors.

Benson, William Arthur Smith 1854–1924. English architect and designer; foremost metalworker of his time. Though he was the only metalworker personally associated with William Morris, he broke away from Morris's insistence on handcraftsmanship and as early as 1880 began to employ machine techniques as a means of making simple cheap domestic articles, mainly in base metals. He influenced such later workers as Arthur Dixon of Birmingham and Llewellyn Rathbone of Liverpool, both of whom specialized in simple vessels of copper and brass.

Bergh, Elis See *Swedish Modern Glass.*

Berkey and Gay In American furniture; in 1860 Julius Berkey with Alphonso Hamm established a small cabinet shop at Grand Rapids. The partnership was of short duration. In 1862 Berkey formed a partnership with Elias Matter; the company was known as Berkey and Matter. By 1865 the name was changed to Berkey Brothers and Company. In 1867 it was known as Berkey Brothers and Gay, through the addition of George M. Gay to the firm. The firm was incorporated as the Berkey and Gay Furniture in 1873. The

company grew rapidly due to Messrs. Berkey and Gay who possessed the characteristics required for success in furniture manufacturing. At one time it was the largest furniture company in Grand Rapids. Closed in 1948. See *Grand Rapids Furniture.*

Berlage, Hendrik Petrus 1856–1934. Dutch architect and furniture designer. In the 1890's he produced a sober unornamented kind of furniture in which the constructive problems were of first importance; it was similar in character to and paralleled only by the furniture of designers working in England in the Arts and Crafts Movement. There were no traces of Art Nouveau in his work. See *Dutch Art Nouveau; Nieuwenhuis, Th.*

Berndorf Electroplate Manufacturing Co. In Austrian silver; established at Berndorf, lower Austria, in 1843, by the German Herman Krupp together with the Austrian Alexander Schoeller for the manufacture of silver and silver-plated ware. Their production was chiefly silver-plated cutlery. In 1957 it was merged with the Aluminum Company of Ranshofen, when the name was changed to Vereinigte Metallwerker Ranshofen, Berndorf A. G. The company makes chiefly cutlery with an aluminum base; it also makes stainless steel and silver-plated ware.

Bertoia, Harry b. 1915. American, born in Italy, sculptor and designer; settled in the United States in 1930. He is noted for his chrome-plated steel wire mesh armchair which he designed for Knoll Associates, 1952. The seat cradle of this Bertoia classic is suspended by triangular side braces over the base. This gives the chair flexibility, automatic adjustment to two positions by means of an effortless shift of body weight. Now he devotes his time exclusively to sculpture.

Billington, Dora M. English artist-potter, writer and teacher; comes from a family who have been potters for at last three generations. Her hand-thrown pots are notable for their simplicity and purity of form. She is head of the art department at the Central School for Arts and Crafts, London. She is the author of THE ART OF THE POTTER, 1937.

Bing and Grøndahl In Danish ceramics; a porcelain manufactory founded in 1853 at Copenhagen. In the 1930's and 1940's it was one of the two large porcelain manufactories, Royal Copenhagen being the other, which developed a perfect glazing technique for stoneware that benefited the Danish stoneware production as a whole.

Bing, Samuel (or **Siegfried**) See *Maison de l'Art Nouveau.*

Binns, Charles Fergus 1857–1934. American, English-born, educator, technologist and potter; the most influential figure in American ceramics during the first quarter of the 20th century. In 1900 he was made the first director of the New York School of Clay Working at Alfred University, which later became the New York State College of Ceramics. During the 35 years he directed this pioneer school of ceramics it became the leading institution for ceramic education and research in the U.S. His book THE POTTER'S CRAFT, 1922, was for many years the standard work in the field. He worked exclusively in high-fired stoneware, fired in a coal-burning kiln which he constructed at Alfred. Many important ceramists and educators were his students, including Charles E. Cox, Arthur Baggs, John F. McMahon, Marion L. Fosdick and Charles Harder. This group spread the idea of the individual potter, in complete command of both process and design. Binns' pieces were severely simple; he turned to China, especially the Ching Dynasty, for his inspiration, rather than to Art Nouveau.

Black Milk Glass In American glass; milk glass of so deep an amethyst color that it looks black unless held up against the light. See *Milk-White Glass.*

Black, Starr and Frost, Ltd. In American silver; this New York City firm traces its history to Marquand and Paulding who began their partnership in Savannah, Georgia, c. 1801. Other firms which succeeded in a direct line or were related include Marquand and Company; Ball, Tompkins and Black; Ball, Black and Company. Became Black, Starr and Frost in 1876; the "Ltd." was added in 1962. See *Ball, Tompkins and Black.*

Blenko Glass Company In American glass; in 1922 William Blenko, English glassmaker, and his son William established a glassworks at Milton, West Virginia, which still perpetuates the handicraft tradition of glassblowing. At Blenko the machine is nonexistent; they use the same methods and tools that the master craftsmen in Europe used hundreds of years ago. The table and decorative ware depend for appeal on simple forms, color and the organic (freehand) irregularities resulting from handwork and lacking in machine-work. In 1947 Winslow Anderson was made design director. See *Myers, Joel.*

Blount, Godfrey 1859–1937. English artist, poet and designer-craftsman. In 1896 he set up the Haslemere Peasant Industries for weaving, embroidery, simple furniture and other popular crafts. He founded the Peasant Arts Society. See *Hand-Loom Weaving.*

Blumenau, Lili American designer for woven fabrics, born in Germany; teacher, writer and lecturer; came to America in the late 1930's. She believes and practices that creative invention in weaving is based on understanding the character of the individual elements of yarns so that the craftsman knows their possibilities as he develops textures and patterns in cloth. She is the author of THE ART AND CRAFT OF HAND WEAVING, 1959.

Boehm, Edward Marshall b. 1912. American sculptor-ceramist: started a pottery studio in 1949 at Trenton, New Jersey. Recognition came to him in 1951 when he made his first bird glazed in color; since then he has received numerous commissions. In

1961 the Democratic party of New Jersey commissioned him to make an eagle, which was presented to President John F. Kennedy.

Bojesen, Kay 1888–1956. Danish designer-craftsman; had the greatest influence on the functional trend in Danish silver in the 1930's. A number of Bojesen's silver pieces made in his own workshop in the late 1930's are today modern classics. For many years he designed silver for Georg Jensen, where his early work showed the decorative ornamentation which once so definitely characterized Jensen's silver. He also designed glass objects and such wood accessories as bowls and platters. See *Jensen, Georg.*

Boston and Sandwich Glass Works See *Sandwich Glass,* page 414.

Boulton, M., and Company In English silver; located at Soho, near Birmingham, this firm was the most important manufacturer of Sheffield plate in this area. Ceased to operate in 1848. See *Elkington, George Richards; Boulton, Matthew,* page 55.

Bouvier, Michel Parisian-trained cabinetmaker; settled in Philadelphia in 1815. His business was dissolved in 1861. A contemporary of Quervelle, he enjoyed similar success, being patronized by Joseph Bonaparte, brother of Napoleon, and the Philadelphia merchant Stephen Girard. He was the great-great-grandfather of Jacqueline Bouvier Kennedy, widow of President John F. Kennedy. See *Quervelle, Anthony G.*

Brangwyn, Frank b. 1867. English painter, graphic artist and designer; the son of W. Curtis Brangwyn, an architect and designer who took a leading role in the Gothic revival under Pugin. From 1882 to 1884 he was an assistant to William Morris, making detailed drawings for tapestries. He travelled extensively. He designed tapestries, textiles, stained glass, rugs and carpets for S. Bing for Art Nouveau in Paris, 1895–1896, and designed his first complete set of furniture and decoration in 1900. After a period of time devoted entirely to fine art, Brangwyn

designed furniture, pottery, metalwork and complete decorative schemes during the late 1930's. He was knighted in 1941.

Brass In furniture; an innovative material in furniture design shown at the Great Exhibition, 1851, in a bed made by R. W. Winfield at Birmingham, England. Even brass drawing room furniture was exhibited. Brass beds became widely popular later in the 19th century.

Brauwers, Joseph Parisian cabinetmaker, working in New York from 1815 to c. 1825. Brauwer's label on a card table reads "No. 163 William Street, New York. (Ebenist From Paris) Cabinetmaker. With the Richest Ornaments just imported from France."

Breuer, Marcel b. 1902. American, born in Hungary, architect and designer; studied at the Bauhaus, 1920–1924, where he invented the first tubular steel chair. He became internationally famous for the cantilevered tubular steelchair in which he applied a new design principle by substituting a double S-shaped support for the conventional four legs. See *Bauhaus.*

Briggle, van, Pottery Company In American ceramics; started in 1891 by Artus van Briggle at Colorado Springs, Colorado. The art pottery wares were characterized by originality of treatment in the modeled ornamentation and a peculiar, soft dull glaze. Designs were modeled in relief before the ware was fired. The incised mark consists of a monogram, the name of the projector and the date, the latter being changed each year. See *Rookwood; Art Nouveau,* in American ceramics.

Briggs, John English contemporary cabinetmaker; trained under Edward Barnsley and has been working independently in Wiltshire since 1932. See *English Contemporary Arts and Crafts.*

Brilliant Period In American glass; the name given to cut glass made from c. 1880 to c. 1905, distinguished for its fine line cutting, which became known as brilliant cutting. This glass is heavy and crystal-clear and is characterized by deep curved miter cuttings called splits, and by such design motifs as hob-star, notched prism and fan. Glass of the Brilliant Period is easily recognized. It is deeper cut than the earlier cut glass and the cuttings are more intricate and elaborate.

Broadloom A term applied to carpets woven in widths of 54 inches or greater, as distinguished from narrow loom widths of 27 or 36 inches. The term does not encompass the type or construction.

Brocard, Joseph French glassmaker; made enamel-painted Islamic glass, first exhibited in 1867.

Brooklyn Flint Glass Works In American glass; in 1823 John L. Gilliland formed John L. Gilliland and Company which in 1843 became the Brooklyn Flint Glass Works. Through the years they were the recipient of numerous medals. In 1864 Amory Houghton and his son Amory, Jr., who had been in the Union Glass Company, obtained controlling interest. In 1868 the business was moved to Corning, New York.

Brooks, Thomas 1811–1887. American cabinetmaker listed under the name of Thomas Brooks & Co. in the Brooklyn directories from 1856 to 1876. Probably best known for his work in the Victorian Renaissance style.

Brouwer, William Coenraad 1877–1933. Dutch sculptor and potter; in 1901 established a pottery manufactory in Leiderdorp which in time became a successful business, producing countless decorative terra-cotta sculptures for buildings in Holland, including the Peace Palace in the Hague.

Brown, Ford Madox 1821–1893. English painter and designer. Though he associated with the artists of the Pre-Raphaelite movement and especially with Rossetti, he did not join the Brotherhood. He designed furniture both under Morris's direct inspiration and also on his own. See *Morris Firm Furniture; Pre-Raphaelites*.

Bryce Brothers In American glass; originally called Bryce, McKee and Company, this glasshouse was active at Pittsburgh, Pennsylvania, 1850–1900. They showed pressed and cut flint glasswares at the twenty-sixth exhibition of the Franklin Institute, 1858. The firm was known as Bryce Brothers by 1886.

Burger, Edwin Austrian-born 20th century glassmaker, working in Milan. Noted for his technique of cutting and engraving glass into sculptured forms.

Burges, William 1827–1881. English architect, designer and writer. His designs for furniture and decoration of all kinds were based on his enthusiasm for medieval work dating from the 13th and 14th centuries. Except for a few pieces, all Burges's furniture both for his own use and his clients was simple and sturdy in construction, uncarved and elaborately painted to conform with his early-medieval ideas. He was one of the earliest collectors of Japanese prints in England, and Japanese motifs appear occasionally on his otherwise Gothic-inspired work. See *Meubles Parlants*.

Burne-Jones, Sir Edward 1833–1898. English painter and designer. From 1861 until the time of his death he designed tiles, large quantities of stained glass and tapestries for Morris and Co. He became Rossetti's pupil in 1856, and later his brilliant disciple. He was the life-long friend and artistic comrade of William Morris. His influence in the wide field of decorative design has been immense. See *Morris, Marshall, Faulkner and Co; Pre-Raphaelites; Morris Firm Tapestries*.

Burton, John American glass artist; has worked in glass since the mid-1930's. He creates only small objects; none of his pieces, such as vases and bottles, are more than 10 or 11 inches high. Burton has a superb instinct for color, form and texture. He takes particular delight in creating in the style of the ancient Egyptian and Phoenician glass-workers, even using a secret process which he developed to impart the textured and pitted "patina of time."

Burton, William and Joseph English ceramists; the Burton brothers of Pilkington's Tiles in Lancashire were inspired by some of their successful tile glazes to produce in 1904 a range of pottery which showed a remarkable variety of glaze effects. In 1906 Pilkington's began producing luster-painted pottery by a number of well-known artists, including Gordon Forsyth and Richard Joyce. See *Pilkington's Tile and Pottery Company; Moore, Bernard.*

C

Caldwell, J. E., and Company In American silver; jewelers and silversmiths of Philadelphia, Pennsylvania, since 1839. See *Bailey, Banks and Biddle.*

Campavias, Estella b. 1918. English, born in Spain, artist-potter; started a pottery in 1955. See *English Contemporary Arts and Crafts.*

Camphor Glass In American glass; a type of glass having a white, cloudy appearance. It was blown-molded and pressed. See *Pattern Glass.*

Canadian Tapestries The province of Quebec is one of the few centers on the American continent where artists are currently designing and weaving their own tapestries. Prominent in this field are such French-Canadian artists as Mariette Rousseau-Vermette, Paul Lacroix, Thérèse Lafrance and Micheline Beauchemin, as well as the work of the Quebec School of Fine Arts.

Cane In American furniture; this organic material, which is the stem and tendril of a climbing palm growing in the East Indies, was used in the latter part of the 19th century in the production of furniture. Cane chairs, settees, benches and beds are especially typical. The steamed cane was woven around frames made from white oak or hickory. A cane chair was exhibited by John Tuph of New York at the Great Exhibition, 1851. Also called Wicker or Rattan.

Canton Ware In Chinese ceramics; a type of blue and white export porcelain. It was not made at Canton but at potteries near Canton as well as at Ching-tê-Chên to the north, although much of the painting was done at the port of Canton where families, including the children, did the work. American trade with China began in 1785, and almost immediately Chinese porcelain tableware was imported directly from Canton, the first port visited. Therefore the term *Canton Ware* become common when speaking of this tableware. It was brought continuously to America in ship's cargoes until the Communist regime. It was heavy, which made it useful as ballast, and it was cheap, so it could be sold at home for common dishes. The charm of Canton is the endless variation of the design. In the pattern there are always willow trees, a tea house, bridge, a flight of birds and a landscape. Never in the true Canton is there a person on the bridge. However, Nanking, which looks like Canton, has one, two or three people on the bridge. That and the border is the great difference in the pattern of Nanking and Canton china. People on the bridge is also a typical motif of the Willow pattern made in England. The Canton china has a lattice or network border in solid blue, dark or light, with scalloped lines above. Canton made before 1890 is better quality than later ware; even before that date deterioration had begun when the great demand was to meet orders sent out from America and

England. Though the Chinese knew the method of transfer printing, they continued to decorate their ware by hand, hence the variation of pattern and color. See *Canton* page 81; *Ching-tê-Chên*, page 104.

Captain's Chair In American cabinetwork; a low-back Windsor. It has a horseshoe-shaped arm rail which centers a flat arched crest section. The portion between the seat and rail is filled in with turned spindles.

Caramel Glass See *Marble Glass*.

Carcel Or mechanical lamp. Invented in France, 1800, by Carcel. The Argand burner was still utilized but was provided with a small pump run by clockwork which raised the oil from the base of the lamp to the wick holder, keeping the wick uniformly submerged in oil. These lamps were costly and only a small number were made in the United States. See *Argand Lamp*, page 18.

Carder, Frederick 1864-1963. American, born in England, glass artist; one of the most inventive and productive experimentalists in glassmaking techniques. He was essentially the founder of modern American glass. It was through his ceaseless research that the gamut of expression for the contemporary glass craftsman was decisively widened. The founder of the Steuben Glass Works in 1903, Carder created the famed Aurene glass in the early part of the century. Later he explored the possibilities of enamelling, the Venetian millefiori method and acid-etching. In the 1920's, simultaneously with Maurice Marinot and other French craftsmen, Carder boldly explored the possibilities inherent in a bubbly non-refined glass heavily acid-etched with geometric designs. Often the glass incorporated bits of metal or of enamel between its layers, achieving an opalescent, rustic matrix. Toward the end of his career as art director for Corning Glass Works, he thoroughly investigated the casting process, devoting most attention to the lost-wax process. Vast architectural ornaments were executed under his direction. After his

formal retirement in 1933 Carder continued to work in his private laboratory and further perfected the lost-wax process. It was developed to the point where, for the first time, the most intricate of glass forms could be executed by a method very similar to the one used with metals. Giving the name *Diatreta* to a variation of this technique (in memory of those intricate 4th century Roman carved cups), Carder created a full range of vases with high reliefs which in appearance were closely akin to the Roman pieces. He will always be remembered as the man chiefly responsible for a new and stimulating period in the art of American glassmaking. See *Aurene Glass*.

Cardew, Michael English artist-potter; was a pupil of Bernard Leach at St. Ives, 1923-1926. Here he studied to produce a well-conceived, simple and artistic type of ware that would attract by its appearance, could be acquired by the public at a reasonable cost, and would fulfill its purpose as a household necessity for daily use. The result was his slipware and galena-glazed pottery, for which he is well known. At his small pottery near Winchcombe in the Cotswolds he produced lead-glazed pottery for cottage and kitchen use, including among other things casseroles, bowls, beer and cider jugs and mugs, all having a racily native character. His large cider jars are his triumph. Cardew succeeded in reviving lead-glazed earthenware in the English style. In 1942 he took over from Harry Davis the pottery school connected with the Achimota College in West Africa. After the craft part was closed he set up his own workshop and kiln at Vumé on the Volta River, some one hundred miles away. There Cardew made stoneware, some of which is among the most beautiful to come from the hands of modern potters.

Carnival Glass In American glass; made in imitation of Tiffany and Aurene iridescent Art glass, from around 1910 to the 1920's. During this time vast quantities were produced in shades of gold to red, which is sometimes described as marigold and was the most popular color. It was also produced in a blue-green, purple, amethyst, blue, green and other colors. All of it was iridescent and most was pressed, although some cut glass motifs were used. Much of the Carnival glass was made by companies in western Pennsylvania, West Virginia and Ohio. Of these, the most important were Imperial Glass Company and Northwood Glass Company. It was known as Carnival glass because it was given as prizes at fairs and carnivals. Also called Taffeta glass as its iridescence displayed a luster or gloss reminiscent of that fabric. Poor Man's Tiffany was still another name. See *Northwood, Harry; Iridescent Glass.*

Cartier, Inc. French jewelers and silversmiths. Founded in Paris in 1847 by Louis François Cartier. His grandson, Pierre Cartier, established the New York firm in 1908. Their jewelry and silver have always been noted for fine quality, craftsmanship and creative designs.

Cast Iron Furniture A marked feature of Victorian design was the reproduction of things familiar in one material by means of another newly developed or unused one. Cast iron beds were shown at the Great Exhibition, London, 1851. Of these the ART JOURNAL says that they had become general only "within the last five years." The manufacture of cast iron furniture for interiors and for garden use started in the United States in the 1840's. Of shorter duration for interior use, the manufacture of garden pieces continued into the beginning of the 20th century.

Caster In American silver; the silver-plated revolving caster was a table ornament in general use in the second half of the 19th century. The rotary caster was patented in 1862. These condiment holders generally consisted of six bottles set in a base with either a pedestal or four feet, with an elaborate handle in the center. The bottles were of pressed or cut glass.

Castleford-Type Wares In English ceramics; tea ware made by a number of potters, 1800–1825, in white, translucent stoneware with relief molded designs, often with blue borders. The teapots frequently had sliding or hinged covers. Although traditionally attributed to David Dunderdale and Company, only a few examples are marked "D.D. & Co. Castleford Pottery".

Castle, Wendell b. 1932. American designer-craftsman and teacher; one of America's leading furniture-makers. His furniture, which is notable for its fine handcraftsmanship, is often given unusual forms, such as a chest in the form of an apple.

Centura Tableware In American glass; by developing methods for strengthening glass chemically, Corning in 1962 found a way to make glass five times stronger, on a laboratory scale, than ever before possible – glasses so strong they can be bent or twisted. Among the products made by these processes is Centura tableware. See *Pyrex; Glass-Ceramics.*

Century Guild In English arts and crafts; the Century Guild was formed in 1882 by Arthur Mackmurdo and Selwyn Image. Its aim was "to render all branches of art the sphere no longer of the tradesman, but of the artist. It would restore building, decoration, glass-painting, pottery, wood-carving and metal to their right place beside painting and sculpture." Mackmurdo started HOBBY HORSE, the Guild's magazine, in 1884. See *Mackmurdo, Arthur; Arts and Crafts Movement.*

Century Vase In American ceramics; designed by Karl Müller and exhibited at the Philadelphia Centennial of 1876. The vase is ornamented with painted and Parian relief scenes that depict different aspects of American history and industry. The two handles are in the form of bison heads, and a medallion of George Washington crowned by an American eagle with thunderbolts is the forceful decoration on the front of the vase. See *Union Porcelain Works.*

Ceramic Art Company In American ceramics; established in 1889 at Trenton, New Jersey, by Jonathan Coxon Sr. and Walter Scott Lenox, who had learned the process of manufacturing Belleek when employed at Ott and Brewer. The factory excelled in Belleek, and the swan dish made around 1890 was one of its celebrated pieces. In 1906 the company was renamed Lenox Inc. The Belleek swan dish is still being made by Lenox. Characteristic marks include *The Ceramic Art Co. Trenton, N.J.* enclosed within a wreath, and *CAC* enclosed within a circle with a painter's palette and brushes above to the left and the word *Belleek* printed in red below this stamp over the glaze.

Challinor, Taylor and Company In American glass; a firm in Tarentum, Pennsylvania, active in the 1870's and 1880's in the manufacture of marble glass which they originally termed "Mosaic" glass. They made a great variety of pressed glass animal dishes. See *Marble Glass.*

Chaplet, Ernest 1835–1909. French potter; noted for his stoneware and porcelains. He started a school, L'Art du Feu; among the pupils was Auguste Delaherche.

Charles, Richard English designer who first made his appearance in 1860 with the publication of THE CABINET MAKERS' MONTHLY JOURNAL OF DESIGN. Some of his designs with their Gothic motifs and joined and plank construction of medieval times bear a marked resemblance to the work of his better known contemporaries Eastlake and Talbert. See *Talbert, Bruce J.; Eastlake, Charles L.*

Charpentier, Alexandre 1856–1909. French sculptor, graphic artist and furniture designer; active in the early 1890's in the decorative arts. In 1895 Charpentier, along with the decorator and designer Félix Aubert (b. 1866), the architect Tony Selmersheim (b. 1871), the potter Moureau-Nélaton, and Jean Dampt (1854–1946), formed the group in Paris called Les Cinq. When the architect Charles Plumet (1861–1925) joined the group in 1896, the name became Les Six. They all worked in the Art Nouveau style. Charpentier's furniture at first was simple and rectilinear, clearly influenced by the English Arts and Crafts Movement. From around 1900 he adopted all the Art Nouveau decorative elements; as a sculptor he often added carved reliefs of nude figures. See *Parisian Art Nouveau.*

Chelsea and Dedham In American ceramics; the Chelsea Keramic Art Works, started by Alexander W. Robertson, was active from 1872 to 1889 at Chelsea, Massachusetts. This art pottery was developed by Hugh C. Robertson, brother of the founder, from 1891 as the Chelsea Pottery and from 1895 as the Dedham Pottery.

Chikusen c. 1915. Japanese artist-potter; the present Chikusen family is the fourth generation to operate the kiln at Kyōto. Production is limited to underglaze blue and white porcelain. (Japanese blue and white porcelain is second only to Chinese blue and white.) The underglaze blue and white wares such as bowls, vases and cups made by the different members of this family have always been highly prized by the Japanese. See *Kyōto,* page 279.

Chinese Export Porcelain See *Chinese Lowestoft,* page 104.

China-Trade Porcelain See *Chinese Lowestoft,* page 104.

Chow, Fong b. 1923. American, born in China, artist-potter; came to the United States in 1943 and studied art, concentrating on ceramics. He designed for Glidden Pottery from 1954 to 1957 and was appointed assistant curator of Far Eastern art at the Metropolitan Museum of Art in 1958. Chow has strong admiration for the work of the potter Shoji Hamada. He believes that simplicity is not poverty of expression but the discarding of the non-essential. This is evident in his pottery.

Choy, Katherine Pao Yu 1929–1958. American, born in Hong Kong, artist-potter; in 1952 became assistant professor of art and head of the ceramic department at Newcomb College, New Orleans. While here, until her untimely death, she was very productive in the creation of her own unique pieces of pottery.

Christofle Silver, Inc. In French silver; founded in 1837 at Paris by Charles H. Christofle who introduced a silver-plating process that produced an especially bright finish, which was an immediate success. Moved to St. Denis at a later date. Although Christofle make sterling ware, their world renown is due to their silver-plated flatware. Essentially "Christofle" and "silver-plated" are synonymous in France.

Cire Perdue (Lost-Wax) The art of casting in bronze. Casting is perhaps the most primitive of metal processes. It has passed through three phases; the first was solid casting, in which the mold was formed of clay, sand or stone and the metal was poured in until the hollow was full. In the second phase in casting bronze an iron core was introduced, no doubt to save the cost of the more valuable metal. In the third and final phase a core, usually of clay, was used, around which the metal was cast in a mere skin, only thick enough for strength without waste of metal. In this method, now called *cire perdue*, if a statue was to be cast the figure was first roughly modelled in clay; over this a thin skin of wax was laid and worked by the sculptor with modelling tools to the required form and finish. Then a second skin of clay was formed all over the wax, fitting perfectly into every line and depression. Soft clay was then laid on to strengthen the mold, until the entire statue looked like a shapeless mass, around which iron hoops were bound. Next it was placed in a hot oven which baked the clay both of the rough core and the outer mold and melted the wax which ran out through small holes made for that purpose. The relative positions between the core and mold were preserved by various small metal rods previously driven through from the outer mold to the rough core. Then the melted bronze was poured in. After slowly cooling, the outer mold was broken away and the core was broken up and removed as much as possible, perhaps through a hole in the foot. Finally the projecting rods of bronze were cut away.

Clark, Kenneth English, born in New Zealand, ceramist and lecturer; in 1953 he set up his own studio which he shares with his wife, Ann Wynn Reeves, ceramist and painter. See *Reeves, Ann Wynn; English Contemporary Arts and Crafts.*

Clark, T. B., and Company In American glass; located in Honesdale, Pennsylvania. They bought the Maple City Glass Company in 1904. Much of their production was in standard cut glass patterns on blanks of good quality. Their trade-mark was "Clark". See *Cut Glass, American.*

Clarke, Geoffrey b. 1924. English stained glass artist; works also in iron, bronze and silver. His religious sculpture is notable. From 1952 to 1957 he executed three 70-foot-high stained glass windows for the new Coventry Cathedral. See *English Contemporary Arts and Crafts.*

Coalbrookdale In English ceramics; a term referring to porcelains decorated with modelled flowers in relief, which were produced mainly between 1820 and 1840. Minton was the chief maker of these flower-encrusted porcelains but there are also examples from Coalport, Derby, Rockingham and Spode. Some pieces are marked, in blue, "Coalbrookdale", "C.D.", "C. Dale" or "Coalport", which may be why the general name *Coalbrookdale* is given to all porcelains of this type.

Cockerell, Sydney b. 1906. English bookbinder and teacher; learned his craft from his father. He runs his hand-bindery in Hertfordshire under the name of Douglas

Cockerell and Son, specializing in the repair and binding of valuable books and manuscripts and the making of marbled papers. See *English Contemporary Arts and Crafts.*

Coil Spring In the mid-19th century the coil spring was introduced as a major innovation in creating comfort in furniture. Because of the coil spring the art of the upholsterer ultimately found its acme of achievement toward the end of the 19th century in the so-called Turkish-frame type. See *Turkish-Frame Type.*

Cole, Sir Henry 1808–1882. English author; played an important role in shaping the new course of English decorative arts. He was a prime mover in the Great Exhibition of 1851; he was chiefly responsible for the success of the South Kensington Museum, the ancestor of the Victoria and Albert Museum. See *Summerly's Art Manufactures; Great Exhibition of 1851.*

Colenbrander, Theodorus A. C. 1841–1930. Dutch pottery and textile designer; one of the leaders of the modern decorative art movement in Holland. By the mid-1880's he had originated his distinctive Javanese batik-inspired style. See *Dutch Art Nouveau.*

Collage First introduced in Paris, early 20th century; a picture or visual arrangement made in part or entirely of pasted pieces of paper, wallpaper illustrations, photographs, or any other textured or figured material. The Cubists were the first to use this method as a serious form of expression, one which will no doubt remain a permanent part of the technical vocabulary of art. Later, collage grew more ambitious and extended its range in scale and materials to include such novel elements as string, nails, watch springs, train tickets. In the course of time, artist-craftsmen embraced collage and with characteristic enthusiasm have created a lively body of work that offers new insights into the possibilities of concept. See *Découpage.*

Collingwood, Peter English weaver; started his own workshop in 1952. See *English Contemporary Arts and Crafts.*

Colonna, Eugène French decorative artist; designer of textiles, pottery and furniture. Colonna designed and produced fine examples of Art Nouveau furniture, notable for their austerity. See *Parisian Art Nouveau.*

Columbian Art Pottery In American ceramics; established by Morris and Willmore at Trenton, New Jersey, for the manufacture of table and toilet wares in a Belleek body, in 1893, the year of the World's Columbian Exposition at Chicago, hence the name. Among their accepted marks is the name of the company.

Commemoratives See *Historical Blue.*

Cooper, Francis b. 1906. English goldsmith; his father was one of the leading craftsmen of his day. Apprenticed to his father from 1924 to 1927, Cooper restarted the workshops at Betsom's Hill, Westerham, Kent, in 1946. He has a particular interest in all branches of gold and silver that include modelling and chasing. His work covers a wide range, including jewelry, stone-carving, brasses, lettering, etc. He has had numerous commissions, both ecclesiastical and secular. See *Cooper, John Paul.*

Cooper, Hans b. 1920. English, born in Germany, artist-potter; came to England in 1938. He started working in ceramics with Lucie Rie in 1947. See *English Contemporary Arts and Crafts.*

Cooper, John Paul 1869–1933. English architect, silversmith and jeweler; under the influence of Henry Wilson he took up metalwork in 1897, reviving the use of shagreen. He gave up his professional practice and made the handicrafts his main interest. In 1907 he set up a workshop at Maidstone; in 1911 he moved to Betsom's Hill, near Westerham, where he built a house, studio and workshops for his own use. See *Cooper, Francis; Wilson, Henry.*

Copier, Andries Dirk See *Leerdam*.

Cornelius, Christian A leading American manufacturer of Argand lamps. In 1812 he established a firm in Philadelphia known successively as C. Cornelius and Son; Cornelius and Company; and finally Cornelius and Baker. By 1845 this company was the largest lamp manufacturer and ornamental founder in the country. Its renown and importance continued until the end of the 19th century. See *Solar Lamp*.

Corning Flint Glass Works In American glass; established by Amory Houghton and Amory Houghton Jr. at Corning, New York, 1868. Noted for their fine cut glass. Later they formed the Corning Glass Company. See *Union Glass Company; Brooklyn Flint Glass Works; Corning Glass Works*.

Corning Glass Works In American glass; one of the oldest industrial firms in the United States; it traces its origin to a glass business established in 1851 by Amory Houghton and others in Somerville, Massachusetts. Since 1868 its headquarters have been at Corning, New York. It has been primarily a supplier of technical and specialty glass and produced the first incandescent bulb blanks for Thomas A. Edison. It is a leader in products for the cooking, serving and storing of food, such as Pyrex, Corning Ware, Centura tableware and Pyroceram. The Corning foundation supports The Corning Museum of Glass which has in its collection important examples of glassmaking from earliest times to the present. See *Steuben Glass; Pyrex; Glass-Ceramics; Centura Tableware; Corning Flint Glass Works*.

Cotswold School In English arts and crafts; in the early 1890's Ernest Gimson and Sidney and Ernest Barnsley moved their furniture manufactory from London to Gloucestershire in the Cotswolds, where it seems that craftsmanship survived with more vigor than in other parts of England. The Cotswold School of furniture designers was the link between the English rural traditions of craftsmanship and the ideas of William Morris. Gimson and the Barnsleys believed that furniture design must come out of a close knowledge of the processes of production and a respect for the materials used. Although Gimson never executed any of his designs and made nothing himself except turned ash chairs, he worked closely with his craftsmen. Simplicity of form, sound construction and an unerring judgment in the choice of woods are the main features of Gimson's work. The oak furniture made by the Barnsleys clearly reveals their debt to Philip Webb and foreshadows the more rustic side of the Cotswold movement. In 1902 Gimson and Ernest Barnsley opened workshops at Daneway House, Sapperton. After Gimson's death in 1914 the Daneway House workshops were closed, but craftsmen to this day keep his traditions alive in the Cotswolds. See *Arts and Crafts Exhibition Society*.

Cottage Furniture In American furniture; the name given to a class of painted furniture considered appropriate for use in country houses. A. J. Downing's THE ARCHITECTURE OF COUNTRY HOUSES, 1850, was much interested in the style and furnishings of these houses. A marked feature of cottage furniture is the persistence of earlier classical designs. Flowers, such as those on chests of drawers, are painted naturalistically in the Victorian taste. Williams and Jones, in their book BEAUTIFUL HOMES, 1878, write, "The cottage suites of enamelled wood are exceedingly pretty, particularly for country houses or children's chambers."

Cotton Printing In American textiles; despite the English ban on colonial manufacturers, cottons and linens were printed on a limited scale in America during the 18th century. Essentially the textile industry had its initial beginnings in the last quarter of the 18th century. Philadelphia was perhaps the leading colonial center of calico printing, and it was here that John Hewson, 1744–1821, a London calico printer, encouraged by Benjamin Franklin, established a manufactory for printing fabrics around 1772. It is generally accepted that the first successful cotton mill was started at Pawtucket, Rhode Island, in 1793, by Samuel Slater, an Englishman, who had worked for years with one of Arkwright's partners in an English mill. As the English textile machinery was carefully guarded against piracy, Slater had to reconstruct the Arkwrights' complex spinning frame from memory. Apparently the production of the mill was limited to checks, ginghams and chambrays. Francis Cabot Lowell, after staying in Lancashire from 1810–13, successfully reconstructed and introduced the power loom in America at Waltham, Massachusetts. The owners of the Waltham Company which manufactured sheets soon expanded their production to the manufacturing and printing of calicoes. The Merrimack Manufacturing Company, started at Lowell in 1822, continued toward this end. Messrs. Thorp, Sidall and Company of Philadelphia introduced printing from engraved copper rollers imported from England in 1809, and by 1822 engraved copper rollers for calico printers were being made at Philadelphia by Mason and Baldwin, the latter of locomotive fame. Shortly thereafter, excellent printed calicoes were manufactured because of the technical advances that were constantly being introduced. See *Calico*, page 76.

Council of Industrial Design   Established in England in 1944 to bridge the gap between designer and industry, to encourage manufacturers to use the service of good designers and to educate the public taste so that their work will be appreciated.   See *Design and Industries Association*.

Crackle or Ice Glass   In American glass; originally produced by the Venetians, this glass was copied in the last two decades of the 19th century when all kinds of novelty glass, or Art glass, was so fashionable. The Boston and Sandwich Glass Company produced for a short period a crackle glass, more commonly known as overshot glass. In contrast to the sharply rough outer surface

that almost has a crystalline look, the inner surface was smooth. It was not a true pattern although they made it in a full line of tableware. A large amount of crackle glass was made by glasshouses in Pennsylvania and the Midwest. It was also made in pastel colors, such as green and pink. None of it was comparable in quality to the Venetian glass and later European crackle glass.   See *Ice Glass*, page 244.

Craft Centre of Great Britain   The national exhibition center for the crafts, which was brought into being in London, 1950, by the combined efforts of the five main British craft societies. The oldest of these, the Arts and Crafts Exhibition Society, was formed in 1888 by a small group of artists and craftsmen which included William Morris. The main purpose of this society was to hold regular exhibitions of creative work in the whole range of crafts. The Red Rose Guild of Craftsmen, a society with roughly similar aims but centered in the north of England, came into being in 1920. The other three societies, the Senefelder Club, the Society of Wood Engravers and the Society of Scribes and Illuminators, are concerned with the specialized crafts of lithography, wood engraving and calligraphy. During World War II these five societies realized the importance of cooperating to form a single body that could be considered to represent the opinions and standards of work of the best designer-craftsmen in England. *Fine craftsmanship* as a term is used by the Centre to define the work of a man who designs as well as makes, and who excels at both.   See *Arts and Crafts Exhibition Society; English Contemporary Arts and Crafts.*

Crane, Walter   1845–1915. English designer painter, book illustrator and writer on art: the most popular of the disciples of William Morris. A promoter of the Art Workers' Guild, he was its first president. Many of Crane's wallpapers and ceramics from the 1870's and 1880's bear inscriptions.   See *Art Workers' Guild; Meubles Parlants.*

Cros, Henri 1840–1907. French glassmaker. Revived pâte de verre technique, a composition of powdered glass which can be colored and molded.   See *Pâte de Verre*, page 353.

Custard Glass   See *Marble Glass*.

Cut Glass, American   It is possible that cut glass was made in the United States toward the end of the 18th century. From about 1820 most glasshouses producing fine glassware were also operating their own glass cutting works. The so-called Middle Period of cut glass manufacture extends from around 1830 to 1880, a time when methods of manufacture changed and many new glasshouses were started. Cutting motifs were fairly simple, the flute cutting being the most characteristic. The peak of cut glass production extended from about 1880 to 1905, the so-called Brilliant Period. At this time, due to progress in manufacturing techniques, American cut glass was surpassed by none. Outstanding names in fine cut glass include James Gillinder and Sons; C. Dorflinger and Sons; T. G. Hawkes and Company; Libbey Glass Company; H. C. Fry Glass Company; T. B. Clark and Company; J. Hoare and Company; Tuthill Glass Company; Pairpoint Corporation. See *Brilliant Period; Cut Glass*, page 138.

Czechoslovak Contemporary Glass   Reveals the great vitality of this glass-producing area (one-time Bohemia) and the extra-ordinary skill of its glassblowers and designers. At the present time their work in glass, apart from traditional 18th century reproductions, shows the fruition of design trends which emerged in the 1920's. This glass is usually in warm, deep colors: dark green, dark red and dark blue. These models, especially vases and goblets of simple form, are cut with large geometrical facets, forming lines parallel to the main contour, resembling those designed around 1915 by Cornelius de Bazel for Leerdam. Czechoslovak glass in this geometrical style was chiefly the work of the architect-designers Kotera, Rozsypal and Hofmann, and the sculptor Horejc. Some of these designers are still active. Included among the outstanding designers of today are Jan Koula, Jan Kotik, Oldrich Lipa and Pavel Hlava. New techniques are exploited; for instance, the sandblasting of Ladislav Oliva, whose abstract patterns hewn out of the glass create sparkling lustrous prisms contrasting with plain surfaces and clean beveled or round rims. A few artists, such as René Rouibeck, have a desire to create at the furnace, to capture the instantaneous quality of glass as it freezes under the skilled craftsman's hand. This marks a release from the traditional central European approach of cutting and engraving to reveal hidden optical effects, unsatisfied with the result of the material itself when it emerges from the annealing furnace as a wonder of optical depth.

D

Dahlskog, Ewald   See *Swedish Modern Glass*.

Dalpayrat, Adrien-Pierre b. 1844. French ceramist; the firm Dalpayrat et Lesbros in Bourg-la-Reine specialized in pottery with sculptured forms and very highly developed glazes.

Dammouse, Albert Louis 1848–1926. French sculptor and glass artist; surrendered to the attraction of *pâte de verre*, which he made in delicate pastel shades and molded into exquisite bowls and dishes often in the shapes and colors of flowers. This outstanding artist working within the genre revealed amazing skill and sensitivity.

Danish Contemporary Arts and Crafts   Denmark is an important Scandinavian country in the field of progressive and experimental modern design. The emphasis on furniture is especially strong. Danish modern ceramic art is foremost a glazing art; artists are chiefly interested in the color possibilities and the textural effects of glazing. This great interest in glazes is related to the impression made by Japanese stone-ware, which first became known in Europe late in the 19th century. The Danish tradition for glazes on stoneware can be traced to the spade-work done in the early 20th century by Patrick Nordström at Royal Copenhagen. In the 1930's Nathalie Krebs, in collaboration with various artists, especially Eva Staehr-Nielsen, created a standard production of perfect stoneware with fine mat glazes at her well-known workshop, Saxbo. Among the chief glassworks making the first-quality glass are Holmegaards Glass Works, with Per Lutken as chief designer, and Kastrup Glass Works, with Jacob E. Bang as chief designer. The field of textile design includes such names as Gerda Henning, weaver, and Marie Gudme Leth, textile printer, both pioneers in their respective work, and Lis Ahlmann and Paula Trock, two weavers who contributed to the renaissance of the art of weaving in the 1930's. Jens Harald Quistgaard, well known as a designer in silver and stainless steel, has in recent years also become interested in glass, pottery and cast iron. See *Danish Modern Furniture; Jensen, Georg; Bojesen, Kay.*

Danish Modern Furniture The groundwork for the light modern Danish furniture was laid in the 1930's when Danish cabinetmakers employed the leading contemporary Copenhagen designers to free them from the mire of derivative styling. Toward the end of the 1940's, as a result of the fruitful collaboration between designers and cabinetmakers, a few simple types of handmade furniture had been created which were to become the nucleus for production by more industrialized methods. The basic frames are machine-made, but the plastic shaping of the arms and legs, the intricate joinings and soft

oil rubbings are by hand. The Danish mania began in America around 1948. The interest in Danish furniture created among American designers a new respect for the manner in which woods of various colors and grains are combined. In contrast to the handcrafted, sculptured quality of their wood furniture, a few manufactories make furniture using purely industrialized methods in which such modern materials as light metals and plastics are exclusively employed. Typical examples are Arno Jacobsen's two chairs in upholstered plastic, the "egg" and "swan," 1958. Paul Kjaerholm's furniture, which has its roots in a tradition stemming from Miës van der Rohe's steel furniture of the late 1920's, is mostly a combination of steel and natural materials. See *Klint, Kaare; Juhl, Finn; Wegner, Hans.*

Darricarrère, Roger b. 1912. American, born in France, stained glass artist; works with stained glass, leaded stained glass and faceted stained glass in concrete. His work is primarily architectural in scale and use.

Daum Frères Auguste Daum, 1854–1909, and his brother Antonin; French glass manufacturers of the Nancy group, which was started by Emile Gallé. Enthusiastic admirers of Gallé, they managed to absorb his influence while retaining their own character and style. After World War I, Paul (d. 1944), the son of one of the Daum brothers, continued the family business. Two of his sons carried on after World War II. In 1946 the family glassworks was renamed Cristalleries de Nancy, the artistic designer being Michel Daum. Attached to the Cristalleries de Nancy is the Daum museum, which houses a fascinating collection of glass made by three generations of the Daum family, who contributed much to the development of modern glass. Their work is greatly admired in Europe. Michel Daum has developed his own style, entirely different from that of the two preceding generations. It well expresses the spirit of the present day. One of the remarkable features of Daum glass is the superb quality of its crystal. All Daum pieces, even the biggest, are free blown.

Davis, Alexander Jackson 1803–1882. American architect and designer of furniture; perhaps the most active designer of Gothic furniture in the 1830's and 1840's. He designed chairs, tables, pulpits and organs for churches, as well as pieces for the many houses which he built along the Hudson and in upper New York state and Connecticut. In 1838 Davis began work on a Gothic mansion for the Pauldings in Tarrytown, New York, known as Lyndhurst.

Day, Lewis Foreman 1845–1910. English designer, writer and lecturer. In 1870 he set up his own business and designed textiles, wallpapers, stained glass, embroidery, carpets, tiles, pottery and book covers. He was a founder member of the Arts and Crafts Exhibition Society, 1888. He wrote numerous books on ornament and design. See *Art Workers' Guild; Arts and Crafts Exhibition Society.*

De Distel In Dutch ceramics; an earthenware manufactory operating in Amsterdam, 1895–1923. Th. Nieuwenhuis designed pottery for the manufactory.

Deck, Theodore 1823–1891. French artist-potter; generally regarded as the first of the studio-potters. Early in his career he began to undertake research into the character of Persian and Turkish pottery of the 16th and 17th centuries, which enjoyed success at the Paris Exhibition of Arts and Industries in 1861. Later his research was directed to Chinese monochrome glazes. In 1887 his book LA FAÏENCE was published in Paris. In 1888 he was appointed director of the Sèvres manufactory.

Decorative Art Society Founded in New York in the late 1870's by Candace Wheeler, who desired to establish an American counterpart of the societies being started in England, such as the Royal School of Needlework. It had a twofold character: the fostering of good taste in needlework and artistic production, and the encouragement of talent in women, as well as providing a means of remunerative employment for their gifts in this direction. The four largest branches or schools of the Decorative Art Society (New York, Philadelphia, Boston and Chicago) were under the direction of English teachers and followed closely the excellencies of the English schools. Other kindred societies founded in America, such as the Women's Exchange, the Needlework Society, the Household Art Society and the Blue and White Industry, stemmed from the same English root and followed the English example to make needlework their chief object of interest.

Décorchemont, François Emile b. 1880. French glass artist; surrendered to the attraction of *pâte de verre*. His work, however, looks far from delicate and suggests strength and vigor. His forms are almost geometrically austere, the finely modelled relief decoration modest and generally abstract. He composed and blended his colors with singular skill; with the help of these strikingly beautiful hues he displayed the pure beauty of his shapes and emphasized the organic necessity of the decorative motifs. Very little of the work of this great artist seems to be extant. A few examples are in important glass collections.

Découpage Flourished in the early 18th century in France, where it received its name, meaning *paper cut-outs*. Later it became a fashionable pastime in England. Essentially, découpage is a form of collage. While most of the present-day work in découpage is purely decorative and made to hang on the wall, a surprising amount is applied to cover the surface of trays, boxes, tops of tables, panels of screens, etc. No doubt the queen of découpage in the United States was Caroline Duer (b. 1865). She is recognized as having influenced perhaps more than anyone else the revival in the United States of this charming craft. Her work is notable for the amount of fine detail in the cutting and application of her compositions. See *Collage*.

Dedham Pottery See *Chelsea and Dedham*.

Delaherche, Auguste b. 1857. One of the foremost French potters of Art Nouveau; he was associated with S. Bing at various times.

Denver China and Pottery Company See *Lonhuda Pottery*.

Design and Industries Association Established in England in 1915; it acknowledged the program developed by the Werkbund and stated in its JOURNAL, 1916, that it was "accepting the machine in its proper place, as a device to be guided and controlled, not merely boycotted." See *Arts and Crafts Exhibition Society; Deutscher Werkbund; Council of Industrial Design*.

Designer-Craftsman Used interchangeably with *artist-craftsman*. The modern designer-craftsman often gives part of his time to designing for mass production, and his influence in that field is very healthy. The designer-craftsman, in contrast to the industrial, places special value on handwork for its own sake. The fundamental difference between handicraft and machine production is clearly recognized; however, the two come together under the banner of design. See *Artist-Craftsman*.

De Stijl A movement originated by Dutch painters during World War I; flourished from around 1917 to 1928. It restricted the elements of composition to independent rectangles and circles; it employed freely asymmetrical balance in place of traditional symmetry. De Stijl principles left their imprint on later work at the Bauhaus. The theories put forth by De Stijl artists and writers still furnish the essential formal aesthetic of a large part of modern architecture and much modern design. See *Rietveld, Gerrit*.

Deutsche Werkstätten In 1897 Obrist, Pankok, Paul and Riemerschmid founded the Münchener Vereinigte Werkstätten für Kunst in Handwerk. In 1898 a similar organization, the Dresdener Werkstätten fur Handwerkskunst, was started in Dresden under the management of Karl Schmidt. Both organizations aimed to create a national German art, with no tinge of stylistic imitation and on a sound constructive basis through cooperation between artist and artisan. In 1906 the Deutsche Werkstätten in Dresden produced its first machine-made furniture, designed by some of the best German architects. They prided themselves on developing the style of furniture from the spirit of the machine. At that time, except for Germany, there were scarcely any prominent artists or architects working for industrial design. Next they approached the problem of standardization of parts. Their first unit furniture, designed by Bruno Paul, was shown in 1910 as *Typenmobel*. The idea originated in America, where it had been in use for a while for bookcases. See *Schmidt, Karl; Sachlichkeit; Deutscher Werkbund*.

Deutscher Werkbund Similar ideas to those held by the Deutsche Werkstätten guided the activities of the Deutscher Werkbund, established in 1907 to coalesce the various individual experiments into a world-wide recognized style. This association comprising manufacturers and designers was formed to promote high standards of craftsmanship and industrial design by encouraging a closer cooperation between architect, designer, manufacturer and workman. From the beginning this group felt no horror of the machine. The program developed by the Werkbund – the acceptance of the machine in its proper place – was adopted by other countries' associations: the Austrian Werkbund, 1910, the Swiss Werkbund, 1913, the English Design and Industries Association, 1915, etc. See *Deutsche Werkstätten*.

Diehl, Edith d. 1953. American hand-binder, teacher, collector, lecturer and author; recognized as the dean of American hand-bindery. She was a source of inspiration to all American binders for her wide knowledge of the subject and her superior skill as a craftsman. She is the author of BOOKBINDING: ITS BACKGROUND AND TECHNIQUE.

Dijsselhof, Gerrit Willem   1866–1924. Dutch painter; leading designer in the sphere of decorative art in the 1890's; foremost among the artists inspired by Japanese design. The special batik-inspired Dutch Art Nouveau made its appearance in his work. His great work in this style, the so-called Dijsselhof Room, 1891–1892, now in the Gemeentemuseum at the Hague, is decorated with materials in batik technique with Japanese-inspired designs. The furniture, of simple, clean-lined construction, reflects the influence of the English Arts and Crafts Movement.   See *Dutch Art Nouveau*.

Dixon, Arthur Stansfield   1856–1929. English architect, designer and metalworker; a friend of Morris. He started a series of evening classes for instruction in beaten metalwork and other handicrafts in 1893. Two years later this grew into the Birmingham Guild of Handicraft. Dixon designed the base metals which constituted the Guild's greatest output.   See *Benson, William*.

Dixon, James, and Sons Ltd.   In English silver; established in Sheffield, 1806. They were the leading makers of Britannia and silver-plated wares imported into the United States from the 1830's to the 1860's.

Dolmetsch, Carl Frederick   b. 1911. English musical instrument maker; trained by his father, Arnold Dolmetsch, in ensemble music and the study of the violin. He gave concerts on both sides of the Atlantic. The present workshop, in Haslemere, Surrey, where he makes his own instruments, was founded in 1917 by his father, who had been making instruments since 1890. Leslie Ward, musical instrument maker, began working for Dolmetsch in 1921 and subsequently was made a partner. The Dolmetsch instruments have been distributed all over the world. See *English Contemporary Arts and Crafts*.

Dorflinger, Christian   1828–1915. Alsatian-born, settled in the United States 1846. He established the Greenpoint Glass Works on Commercial Street, Brooklyn, in 1860. In 1865 he established his glasshouse at White Mills, Pennsylvania, which in 1873 he named the Wayne County Glass Works. When his sons, William, Louis and Charles were made partners in 1881, the firm became C. Dorflinger and Sons. Eventually it became one of the largest in the country and Dorflinger cut and engraved glass gained world renown because of its quality and beauty. Among the skilled glassmakers in his employ at various times were Nicholas Lutz and Charles Northwood.   See *Cut Glass, American*.

Doughty, Susan Dorothy   1892–1962. English ceramist whose work with birds and the exquisitely modelled flowers and plants with which they are usually identified has become a collector's item in the United States. She started producing her ceramic birds in 1936 for the Royal Worcester Porcelain Company. She made a speciality of American birds; in recent years she also brought out models for an English bird series.

Dovecote   The Scottish tapestry manufactory of Dovecote, located in the village of Corstorphine near Edinburgh, was sponsored by the 4th Marquis of Bute in 1910. At its inception two artist-weavers were installed from Merton Abbey, the workshop of William Morris. Closed during World Wars I and II, Dovecote reopened in 1946 under the Edinburgh Tapestry Company, and was directed by members of the Bute family. Among the contemporary English artists whose designs have been woven on the Dovecote looms are Frank Brangwyn, Henry Moore and Graham Sutherland.

Drerup, Karl   b. 1904. American, born in Germany, a painter, artist-craftsman and teacher; came to the United States in 1937. Recognized as one of the foremost creative enamellers and one whose work has been profoundly influential. His enamels combine the best use of traditional techniques with a fresh approach to subject matter. For Drerup, enamels are an intimate medium, small in scale. The forms he uses are bowls, trays and other simple shapes that afford ample surface for decoration. Among the techniques he employs are grisaille and cloisonné.

Dresser, Christopher 1834–1904. English, born in Glasgow, designer and writer. His first book on design, THE ART OF DECORATIVE DESIGN, published in 1862, was followed by numerous others on botany, design and Japanese art, and a number of articles and lectures. Dresser visited Japan in 1876 as an official representative of the British government. He started the Art Furnishers' Alliance in 1880. He was a tireless worker and produced a great number of designs in practically all media – pottery, furniture, metalwork, etc. – and in styles ranging from the purely functional to the most daring and unusual.

Durand, Victor American glassmaker, born in France. First employed by Louis C. Tiffany c. 1889 and later joined the Vineland (N.J.) Flint Glass Company which became the firm of Kimball and Durand. His son, Victor Durand Jr., was mainly responsible for the iridescent Art glass known as Durand, made between 1912 and 1924 by the Durand Art Glass Works in Vineland, New Jersey, which were taken over by the Kimball Glass Company after Victor Durand Jr.'s death in 1935. See *Iridescent Glass*.

Durbin, Leslie b. 1914. English goldsmith and silversmith; apprenticed to Omar Ramsden, artist-goldsmith, in 1929, and worked with him as a journeyman until 1938. Durbin started his present workshop in partnership with Leonard Moss and three assistants in 1946. His work shows his personal preference for simplicity and plain surfaces. Design, to Durbin, is a simplicity of form that preserves the character of the tools. He has had numerous special commissions, both ecclesiastical and secular. In 1942 he was awarded the M.V.O. by King George VI in recognition of the Stalingrad sword which he had made. See *English Contemporary Arts and Crafts*.

Dutch Art Nouveau In architecture and furniture Holland was comparatively untouched by the mainstream of Art Nouveau. The outstanding feature of Dutch artists in their conscious efforts to free themselves from Historicism is the notable similarity with the English Arts and Crafts Movement. However, in the art of the illustrators and painters there are several essential features which have a great deal in common with Art Nouveau and might even correctly permit the designation Dutch Art Nouveau. It is also characteristic that such Art Nouveau as is to be found is notably two-dimensional. This is in part due to the influence of batik, such as batik-inspired textiles for furniture coverings and wallpapers. See *Nieuwenhuis, Th.; Berlage, H. P.; Bazel, Karel de; Dijsselhof, Gerrit; Lauweriks, Johannes; Art Nouveau*.

E

Eames, Charles b. 1907. American industrial architect-designer; in 1945 he introduced his shock-mounted chair, with two separate pads of molded plywood serving as a back and seat and a skeleton-like steel tubing frame. Making use of the springiness of both tubular steel and laminated plywood, this chair with its rubber shock mounts electronically welded to the wood and steel is a notable product of machine technology. Apart from his almost indestructible molded plywood chair, known and used around the world, and his 1951 version of a molded plastic shell chair, he introduced a molded wire mesh chair in 1951. Eames, together with his wife, Ray, was awarded the first Kaufmann International Design Award in 1960.

East Liverpool Pottery Company In American ceramics; this firm, located in East Liverpool, Ohio, manufactured "Waco" china and decorated wares, mainly in a white granite body. The first mark, a modification of the British Royal Coat of Arms, was found on souvenir china made for the Presidential campaign of 1896. Later marks had the name "Waco" in combination with the company's monogram.

Eastlake, Charles Lock 1836–1906. English architect and writer; his widely read book HINTS ON HOUSEHOLD TASTE, 1868, had great influence in England and in America. The furniture he favored possessed a vaguely traditional rural character deriving from early English forms, somewhat Elizabethan and early Jacobean, uncomfortable but marked by good materials and sound joinery. A debased Gothic style having nothing to do with his principles became known as the Eastlake style in England and America.

Eckhardt, Edris American designer-craftsman and teacher. In 1953 she developed a gold-glass process that successfully reproduced the rare and beautiful gold glass of the Egyptian and Byzantine glassworks. Her remarkable rediscovery of a lost art, a process by which gold leaf is fused between layers of glass, contributed important new techniques to this most difficult plastic medium.

Eckmann, Otto 1865–1902. German painter, graphic artist and designer; after 1894 gave up painting and concentrated on decorative art. He belonged to the Munich School of Art Nouveau. He was an important early collector of Japanese wood-block prints; the influence of these is evident in the floral and plant fantasies he did for the magazines PAN and JUGEND. He was the leader of the German floral style. He also designed tapestries, metalwork and furniture. See *Jugendstil; Munich School.*

Edwardian Relating to Edward VII (b. 1841) of England and his reign, 1901–1910.

Eisch, Erwin b. 1927. Bavarian glassmaker; in the early 1960's won international recognition among craftsmen for his original and often evocative blown glass. The son of a glass engraver, and chief designer for his family's glass manufactory at Frauenau, Eisch brings to his one-of-a-kind pieces a feeling for the extreme ways in which molten glass will move.

Ekman, Johan See *Swedish Modern Glass.*

Electroplating In American silver; a method of silver-plating by electrolysis in which the silver is decomposed in a bath of potassium cyanide and deposited on a base metal surface, such as copper, Britannia, white metal and German nickel. In 1837 J. O. Mead of Philadelphia went to England and learned this process. In 1845, William and Asa Rogers, in partnership with J. O. Mead, manufactured electroplated silver in Hartford, Connecticut, as Rogers and Mead until 1846. Among the best known early companies making silver-plated wares were Rogers Brothers; Meriden Britannia Company; Reed and Barton. See *Elkington, George Richards; Rogers Brothers; Sheffield Plate,* page 429.

Elkington and Company See *Elkington, George Richards.*

Elkington, George Richards 1801–1865, founder of the electroplating industry in England. Apprenticed to his uncles, who made Sheffield plate in Birmingham, he became owner of the business on their death. Later he made his cousin Henry Elkington a partner. The science of electro-metallurgy was then in its infancy, but the Elkingtons were quick to appraise its possibilities. They already had certain patents for the application of electricity to metals when in 1840 John Wright, a Birmingham surgeon, discovered the valuable properties of a solution of cyanide of potassium for the purposes of electroplating. Immediately the Elkingtons purchased and patented Wright's process, subsequently buying the rights of other processes and improvements. In 1841 they opened large new works for electroplating and electrogilding at Birmingham. In 1842 Josiah Mason, English pen manufacturer, knighted in 1872, became a partner. This new method was a blow to the Sheffield industry from which it never recovered. Electroplating was both cheaper and more adapted to the ornate decorative treatment favored by Victorian designers. See *Sheffield Plate*, page 429.

Email Ombrant In English ceramics; a kind of decoration taken over by Wedgwood in the 1860's from France, using a design impressed in intaglio and flooded with translucent glaze, generally green. It makes a design in light and shade; the most deeply impressed parts appear darkest. The principle is the same as in the popular lithophanes made at Berlin and Meissen from 1827 onwards.

Embroidery, Late Victorian and Edwardian In English needlework; the second half of the 19th century witnessed a great revival in the art of embroidery. William Morris and Sir Edward Burne-Jones were the first to cast aside the influence of Berlin wool work and the needlework picture so fashionable in Early Victorian times. Embroideries made by Morris owed a great deal to 17th century English crewelwork, but the introduction of figure subjects into these designs was his innovation. Of great importance and owing to Morris's influence was the starting of the Royal School of Needlework. See *Royal School of Needlework*.

Empoli In Italian glass; a small town near Florence with a tradition of glassmaking. Empoli's glassworks are family enterprises, comparatively small and rather primitive, sustained by the tradition of good craftsmanship. The glass of Empoli is an expression of folk art, of traditional shapes and colors. See *Italian Contemporary Arts and Crafts*.

E.N.A.P.I. (Ente Nazionale Per L'Artigianato E Le Piccole Industrie) The organization of handcraftsmen in Italy. Its headquarters are in Rome, with branches in other cities, including Florence and Milan. See *Italian Contemporary Arts and Crafts*.

End-of-Day Glass In American glass; a late 19th century Art glass, so called because it was supposed to have been made from leftovers in the furnace at the end of the day's work. This has become a misnomer for marble glass.

Endell, August 1871–1925. German architect and designer; strongly influenced by Obrist in Munich, where he belonged to the Münchener Vereinigte Werkstätten. His two great works in the Jugend style are the Atelier Elvira, 1898, and the Sanatorium auf Föhr, 1900. His ornamentation has an Obrist-like and Japan-inspired character. Also designed textiles and furniture. See *Munich School; Obrist, Hermann*.

English Contemporary Arts and Crafts The effects of the Industrial Revolution upon the British Isles were earlier and more ravaging than in other European countries. It was left to a sprinkling of isolated craftsmen to hold on to the main traditions of English craftsmanship with their fingertips until the late 19th century revival of the crafts under the intellectual stimulus of John Ruskin. The group of men that followed him, led by William Morris, understood the significance of creative craftsmanship and attempted to relate this to a way of life. The solutions they proposed for the problems of society are still a matter of argument, but in the process of reaching them they saved the crafts. The modern craftsman respects his materials and takes pleasure in the skillful use of hand and tool. Often he gives part of his time to designing for mass production, and his influence in that field is very healthy. Since the 1890's each craft has had a full history of its own. The Gimsons and the

Barnsleys in furniture, Bernard Leach in pottery, Omar Ramsden and Leslie Durban in silversmithing, the Dolmetsch family in musical instrument making – these and many others have enriched the traditions of their own crafts and have trained successors to match their own high standards. Among the craftsmen are John Briggs, John Baker, Estella Campavias, Kenneth Clark, Geoffrey Clarke, Sidney Cockerell, Peter Collingwood, Francis Cooper, Hans Cooper, Carl Dolmetsch, Margaret Hine, John Hutton, Margaret Kaye, Stefan Knapp, David Leach, Heber Matthews, Henry Moore, Keith New, William Newland, Michael O'Connell, John Piper, Katherine Pleydell-Bouverie, Roger Powell, Ann Wynn Reeves, Patrick Reyntiens, Lucie Rie, Graham Sutherland, Margaret Traherne, Nicholas Vergette and others. See *Craft Centre of Great Britain*.

English Glass from 1860 The 1860's witnessed the start of an intellectual movement toward the plastic forms and furnace decoration advocated by Ruskin as suitable to the material. In 1861 a milestone was reached when William Morris commissioned his friend the architect Philip Webb to design for his use, at the now famous Red House at Bexley Heath, the first modern drinking-glass service, which was executed by James Powell and Sons of the Whitefriars Glass Works. One of the oldest in England, this firm was founded in 1680 by members of the Powell family; their first glasshouse was in Whitefriars, from which it derived its name. Throughout the late Victorian and Edwardian periods the taste for simply-formed glassware continued to increase under the influence of the Arts and Crafts Movement. Much of the best work was made by Whitefriars. In time, however, Whitefriars and other venerable firms such as Brierly Hill and Thomas Webb went back to the safe mediocrity of pseudo-classic models. Now all English glassworks also make modern pieces, but the work lacks freshness and vitality.

Esherick, Wharton b. 1889. American painter, sculptor and designer-craftsman; noted for his furniture, which he began making in the late 1920's. A sculptor as well as a craftsman, he creates furniture forms that reveal the beauty of the wood in shapes that would not be logical in any other material. Collectors treasure an Esherick chair or table, accessories such as ladles and bowls. All of these objects are characterized by tactile qualities, making them things to be handled, as well as by their visual, sculptural qualities.

F

Faulkner, Kate b. 1898. English artist and designer; sister of Charles Faulkner, one of the original partners in the Morris firm. She worked for the firm from early days, painting tiles and executing gesso work. She designed four wallpapers for Morris and Co.

Federoff, George b. 1906. American, born in Alaska, designer-craftsman; works with wood and ivory to create simple and original carved accessories such as bowls and candelabra at his workshop in Sitka, Alaska. He always chooses exotic woods that display the greatest variety and richness of figure. Especially notable are his wood bowls accented with stringing lines of inlaid ivory that enrich their sculptured forms.

Feure, Georges de 1869–1928. French decorative artist, designer of interior decoration, textiles, pottery and furniture. He designed and produced some of the finest examples of Art Nouveau furniture, notable for its refined elegance, being more in the tradition of the Louis XVI style. See *Parisian Art Nouveau*.

Finnish Contemporary Arts and Crafts
Finland, like Sweden, has always had a vital folk art, various arts and crafts being practiced by practically the entire population. In 1875 the Finnish Society for the Arts and Crafts was founded, and in 1879 the Friends of Finnish Arts and Crafts also appeared. By 1900 a general artistic revival had taken place in Finland. Today, whether industrial or in arts and crafts, the influence of Finnish designs is noticeable the world over. Finland ranks among the leading "glass countries." Tapio Wirkkala, who joined the Karhula-Iittala Glass Works in 1947, is one of the world's great glass designers. Timo Sarpaneva, who joined Karhula-Iittala in 1950, is a great force in Finnish glass. His work is more abstract. Another Finnish artist whose work is much admired both in glass and pottery is Kaj Franck of the Wärtsilä group, the oldest art industry in the country, founded in 1793. There is also Helena Turpeinen of the Riihimaki Glass Works, and A. Salmenlinna. A brilliant woman was the late Gunnel Nyman (d. 1948), a versatile artist with a fine sense of form. The quality of her work was recognized by Karhula, Riihimaki and Notsjö, rival glassworks for whom she worked simultaneously. Kyllikki Salmenhaara is perhaps Finland's foremost ceramist, and Rut Bryk's unique ceramic plaques with their narrative content and beautiful glazes are world-famous. Dora Jung, the dean of studio weavers, is best known for her linen damask tapestries. Also excellent are the tapestries by the designer-weaver Martta Taiple. Eva Brummer enjoys a fine reputation for her hand-knotted rya rugs. The high quality of design of the leading Finnish artists, their admirable craftsmanship, owes much to their belief that beauty is an essential element of life. Finland's leadership in today's Scandinavian arts and crafts is generally recognized. See *Aalto, Alvar; Wirkkala, Tapio.*

Fisher, Alexander 1864–1936. English goldsmith, painter and sculptor; the revival of interest in fine enamelling in England from the 1880's onwards was mainly due to Fisher's efforts. In 1884 he studied the techniques of enamelling in Paris and on his return set up a workshop. He exhibited extensively in England and on the Continent.

Flashed Glass In American glass; a term applied to glass with a thin coating of colored glass over a layer of clear glass. Ruby, in imitation of Bohemian glass, was the most favored color. See *Flashing*, page 186.

Fleming, Baron Erik 1894–1954. Swedish goldsmith artist; began his career in metalwork in 1921. He made many beautiful pieces in gold and silver at his atelier Borgila in Stockholm. He executed commissions for the King of Sweden. His influence in the art of silversmithing extended beyond Sweden.

Flint Enamel In American ceramics; a popular glaze used on Bennington pottery, so named because of its resemblance to enamel. The process was a new one, patented in 1849 by Christopher Webber Fenton under the name *Fenton's Enamel*. In this method the biscuit piece was given a coat of transparent glaze before the powdered color was sprinkled on, through holes perforated in a small box, over the surface of an article, in quantity to produce lighter and darker shades and leaving part of the body to show through. When the piece was fired the powdered colors melted and fused with the underglaze, flowing and spreading over the surface of the article. See *Bennington*, page 40.

Fort Pitt Glass Works In American glass; established at Pittsburgh in 1827 by Curling and Price. Became R. B. Curling and Sons by 1831. They manufactured flint glasswares, cut, pressed, molded, of every description. By 1863 they discontinued the manufacture of tableware and produced lighting glassware. In 1867 they advertised oval and royal lamp chimneys and silver glass reflectors.

Fourdinois, Henri French cabinetmaker working in the Second Empire (1852–1870) for Napoleon III and the nobility. His cabinetwork, based on Renaissance styles, was notable for its fine workmanship. See *Second Empire*.

Frampton, George James 1860–1928. English sculptor and designer-craftsman. He studied architecture and stone and wood carving at the Royal Academy Schools, 1881–1887. He worked in Paris in 1888; shortly after his return he took up metalwork. He designed and produced a number of important presentation pieces made of silver. He was knighted in 1908.

Franck, Kaj See *Finnish Contemporary Arts and Crafts*.

Frankl, Paul T. 1878–1962. American, born in Vienna, architect, writer, interior and furniture designer; as a young man he was especially attracted by the artistic culture of Japan and the dynamic force of industry in America. He went to Japan, where he learned the tremendous appeal and force of simplicity, and finally abandoned the Academic European standards to work out his own ideas on the principles of selection he had absorbed. His so-called skyscraper furniture of the 1920's, deriving its name from the architecture which influenced it, was designed on severely simple perpendicular lines with all superfluous ornament removed.

Fratelli Toso In Italian glass; a glassworks established in 1854, making it the oldest glasshouse now operating in Murano. It took part in the 19th century revival movement. At the present time it is managed by Ermanno and Aldo Toso and avails itself of the artistic cooperation of Giusto and Renato Toso. See *Murano Glass; Venini, Paolo; Salviati and Company*.

French Art Nouveau See *Nancy School; Maison de l'Art Nouveau; Art Nouveau; Parisian Art Nouveau*.

French Contemporary Arts and Crafts A renaissance of tapestry, ceramics, stained glass and bookbinding began in France after the conclusion of World War II. The successful revival of the French tapestry industry through the efforts of Jean Lurçat has had an international impact. Instead of reproducing old designs, the celebrated weavers of Aubusson now execute designs by leading contemporary French artists. Modern French tapestries have stimulated the production of tapestry designers and weavers in many countries. Decorative wall hangings in various techniques have now become one of the most diversified and important forms of expression for artist-craftsmen in Europe and America. Among the prominent designers are Mathieu Matégot, who designs in the abstract-expressionist style and is one of the most productive, Fernand Léger, Maurice André, Marc Petit, Marc Saint-Saëns and Jean Picart Le Doux. Ceramics is another significant medium for French craftsmen. The best-known center of ceramics in France is Vallauris, which is greatly indebted to Picasso for its new life. Of particular interest are the works of the ceramists Jean Derval, Gilbert-Portanier, Georges Jouvé and R. Perot (the last two show talent for utilitarian ceramics). In the craft of stained glass, France has been elevated to a position of leadership through the windows of Jean Barillet. Also well known are Max Ingrand and Gabriel Loìre. French bookbinding is still unexcelled. Contemporary French bindings are notable for the originality of their designs and the technical perfection of their work. France remains the only country where a binding is executed by a group of craftsmen, each performing a special function. This alliance of highly skilled craftsmen produces superb works. Included in this distinguished group are the binders Paul Bonet, Pierre Lucien Martin, Henri Mercher, Claude Stahly and Georges Leroux. The movement responsible for much of today's fine glass began in France at the close of the 19th century in the work of such men as Gallé, Daum, Lalique, Dammouse, Martinot, Thesmar and Décorchemont.

Frosted Glass See *Camphor Glass*.

Fry, H. C., Glass Company In American glass; established by Henry Clay Fry, at Narberth, Pennsylvania, in 1900 and in operation until 1924. Fry was a recognized leader in the cut glass industry. At its finest Fry glass was notable for its clarity and color, for its sharp and precise cutting, and for its originally conceived designs. See *Cut Glass, American.*

G

Gaillard, Eugène French decorative artist, interior decoration and furniture designer. One of the foremost furniture designers of Art Nouveau; his work is notable for a certain plastic and dynamic quality. In this respect his work has a certain affinity to that of Majorelle. See *Parisian Art Nouveau; Majorelle, Louis.*

Gallé, Emile 1846–1904. French furniture designer and pioneer in glass-making; one of the most interesting of all Art Nouveau designers as well as France's outstanding naturalist. Gallé's furniture almost always remained to a certain extent in the French stylistic tradition. The decoration, both inlay and carving, is floral in character and blossoms freely over all the surface. See *Meubles Parlants; Nancy School; Majorelle, Louis; Gallé, Emile,* page 199.

Galusha, Elijah 1804–1871. American cabinetmaker; around 1830 settled in Troy, New York, where he opened a cabinetmaker's shop. His fine furniture was highly esteemed throughout upstate New York.

García, Juan José c. 1885. Spanish artist-craftsman; one of the great master-craftsmen of Europe working in silver. His distinguished work shows the development from traditional designs to modern.

Gardener, Benjamin Noted American manufacturer of Argand lamps. Around 1812 he established at Philadelphia the bronze-casting company of Fletcher and Gardener. Between 1827 and 1845 he managed his own company in New York. Many of his lamps bear a bronze label, "B. Gardener, New York." See *Cornelius, Christian.*

Gate, Simon See *Swedish Modern Glass.*

Gates, John Monteith b. 1905. American architect and designer. See *Steuben Glass.*

Gaudi, Antonio y Cornet 1856–1926. Catalonian architect and designer of interior decoration and furniture; with rare imagination he successfully brought together most of the style elements of the 19th century, namely, Neo-Gothic, Neo-Rococo, Neo-Baroque and the most fanciful naturalism, into a decorative, rhythmic whole. His chairs and interiors with their markedly plastic shapes and their flowing undulating lines admirably exemplify his distinctive Art Nouveau style. Casa Mila, Barcelona, 1905–1907, represents his mature architectural style. See *Art Nouveau.*

Gehlin, Hugo See *Swedish Modern Glass.*

Gerlach, Gerhard b. 1907. American, born in Germany, bookbinder and teacher; studied hand-bindery from the time he was sixteen years old. He passed his master examination in hand-bookbinding, given by the Leipzig Bookbinders Guild in 1931. Gerlach is generally recognized as the foremost binder working in the United States. He works as a team with his wife Kathryn at his workshop in South Shaftesbury, Vermont.

German Art Nouveau See *Jugendstil.*

SILVER SPOON
HENRY VAN DER VELDE, *1902-3*

WHIPLASH MOTIF, EMBROIDERY
HERMANN OBRIST, *c. 1895*

CARVED
SCREEN
EMILE GALLÉ, *1900*

REVOLVING
MUSIC STAND
ALEXANDER CHARPENTIER
1901

ARMCHAIR
RICHARD RIEMERSCHMID, *1899*

VASE
ROZENBURG, *c. 1905*

TULIP FAVRILE VASE
LOUIS C. TIFFANY, *c. 1910*

LEADED GLASS TABLE LAMP
LOUIS C. TIFFANY, *c. 1910*

TRIPOD
TABLE
HECTOR GUIMARD
c. 1908

SILVER CUP
GOLDSMITH'S & SILVERSMITH'S CO.
London, 1900

OAK CHAIR
CHARLES RENNIE
MACKINTOSH, *1897*

CHAIR
EUGÈNE COLONNA, *c. 1900*

SETTEE
EUGÈNE GAILLARD, *c. 1911*

EMBROIDERED FLOWER MOTIF
M. H. BAILLIE SCOTT, *c. 1900*

SIDEBOARD TABLE
SERRURIER-BOVY, *c. 1900*

German Contemporary Arts and Crafts
The national organization of craftsmen in the Federal Republic of Germany is called Arbeitsgemeinschaft des Deutschen Kunsthandwerks, with main offices in Cologne. Munich is the center of Bavarian handicrafts. German ceramics range from traditional forms to the more experimental. Working in this field are such well-known potters as Ingeborg and Bruno Asshof, Signe and Klaus Lehmann, Celine von Eichborn, Karl Scheid and Hubert Griemert. German metalworkers are also proficient. Spurred by the recent church-building program, goldsmiths and silversmiths have been given many commissions to create the necessary appointments for the new churches. Among these are Karl Schrage, Hein and Gertrude Wimmer and Hermann Jünger. Outstanding in this medium is Elizabeth Treskow, whose work is remarkable for its refinement in the use of precious materials.

Gil, David b. 1922. American potter; designs a variety of production pieces, including tiles and dinnerware, for his company, Bennington Potters, Vermont, which he bought in 1948.

Gilbert, Leigh Marks 1861–1905. English silversmith and metalworker. After working in a firm of manufacturing silversmiths from 1871 to 1878, he set up his own workshop, where he did everything by hand. From time to time he worked in collaboration with Sir George Frampton.

Gilbert, Sir Alfred 1854–1934. English sculptor and metalworker. The revival of interest in metalwork in England in the mid-1880's was mainly stimulated by Gilbert's experimental work in that medium.

Gillinder, James, and Sons In American glass; established in 1860 at Philadelphia, Pennsylvania, by William Gillinder, an English glassworker who settled in the United States in 1854. The original name of the firm, Franklin Flint Glass Company, was first changed to Gillinder and Bennet and later to Gillinder and Sons. In 1912 the brothers William T. and James purchased a flint glasshouse known as Brox and Ryal in Port Jervis; operations there were under the name of Gillinder Brothers. The Philadelphia glass works closed in the 1930's. At the Philadelphia Centennial Exposition, 1876, the Gillinders built a glassworks on the fair grounds, with the glassworkers demonstrating the varied techniques of decorating glass. Thousands of fascinated visitors gazed with awe at the exciting performance. Gillinder glass, cut or pressed, is noted for its fine quality of craftsmanship and design. Expert in the technique of frosting, the firm became famous for its Westward Ho pattern in frosted glass, the covered pieces of which had as a finial a finely sculptured model of an Indian. The Lion is another of the famous frosted glass patterns. Many of the pieces made at the Philadelphia Centennial bear the Gillinder name and occasionally the date as well. See *Pattern Glass; Cut Glass, American.*

Gimson, Ernest William 1864–1919. English architect and designer. See *Cotswold School.*

Girard, Alexander American architect, interior and industrial designer. His exhibition in 1949 at the Detroit Institute of Arts, called For Modern Living, was given national acclaim as the first good design show. Since 1952 he has been designing furniture, fabrics, etc., for Herman Miller.

Glasgow School In Scottish arts and crafts; the name generally given to the group of architects and designers who were all students of the Glasgow School of Art during the latter part of the 19th century. In 1893 Francis Newberry, principal of the school, organized a series of lectures on arts and crafts. In the following year, as a result of this stimulus, a number of students under the leadership of Charles R. Mackintosh assembled an exhibition of furniture, metalwork and embroidery of an entirely original character. Their work made a notable impression. Mackintosh and his wife, Margaret, and Herbert and Frances MacDonald McNair subsequently exhibited as a group – The Four, as they are often called – with the Vienna Secession, and at the Glasgow Exhibition in 1901, the Turin Exhibition in 1902, and in Budapest, Dresden, Munich, Venice and Moscow. Essentially, the Glasgow School is the English corollary to the Continental Art Nouveau. See *Mackintosh, Charles R.; Spook School; MacDonald, Margaret.*

Glass-Ceramics In American glass; in 1957 the Corning Glass Works announced development of a new family of crystalline materials made from glass and trademarked *Pyroceram.* These super-strength glass-ceramics, used to make Corning Ware cooking utensils, missile radomes, etc., were hailed as one of the greatest technological advances in glass research since the discovery of heat-resistant borosilicate glass. See *Pyrex; Centura Tableware.*

Gol, José Maria Spanish glass artist working in the period of Functionalism, 1915–1940. He followed the tradition of old Spanish glass and also did some interesting work in enamel-painting.

Godwin, Edward William 1833–1886. English architect and designer; one of the earliest designers to be influenced by Japanese art. He was a member of Whistler's circle and designed the White House of Whistler. He decorated his own house in the Japanese style in 1862. From 1868 onwards he designed furniture, wallpapers, carpets and textiles. With respect to furniture, Godwin produced forms which, with their light rectilinear structure combined with a carefully calculated balance of form, were conditioned by Oriental precepts. In his book ART FURNITURE, WITH HINTS AND SUGGESTIONS ON DOMESTIC FURNITURE AND DECORATION, 1877, Godwin included numerous pieces of furniture in what he called Anglo-Japanese, all distinctive for the same rectilinear construction.

Goodden, R. Y. b. 1903. English architect; divided his time between architecture and industrial design, especially in glass and silver, until 1939. He received the award of Royal Designer for Industry in 1947. Goodden's designs in gold and silver include work for the Corporation of the City of London. He was commissioned to design the silver altar candlesticks presented to the Washington National Cathedral by King George VI.

Gorham Corporation In American silver; in 1818 Jabez Gorham, born 1792, in Providence, Rhode Island, started a small manufactory that since 1865 is known as the Gorham Corporation. Around 1841 Gorham, recognizing the advantages of machinery, was among the first to introduce factory methods to augment handcraftsmanship in the production of silverware. In 1868 they adopted the sterling standard of 925/1000 fine silver. At the same time the family trade-mark, a lion, an anchor and a capital "G", was adopted for use on all sterling articles. Since 1868 flatware year markings have also been used. In the late 19th century Art Nouveau designs executed by the English artist William J. Codman were introduced under the name "Martele". In all periods Gorham has been well known for the excellent quality of its die work, for the fine design and finishing of its wares.

Gothic Revival, English In response to a growing romantic tendency, the Gothic revival began in England around 1750 as a variation on the Georgian. The interest lay in its picturesqueness, in its details, not in its principles and construction. Under the Regency another attempt was made to revive the Gothic. During the Victorian period the Gothic style was partly inspired by the literary vogue set by Sir Walter Scott, but chiefly by the religious movement to "Christianize" church architecture. Augustus Pugin, who became the champion of the Catholic Gothic revival after the publication of his influential CONTRASTS, in 1836, favored English medieval. The second phase of the Gothic revival was chiefly inspired by the writings of John Ruskin. It derived its details notably from medieval Italian architecture eulogized by Ruskin in THE STONES OF VENICE, 1851–1853. In one chapter, "The Nature of Gothic," Ruskin expresses some of his most important ideas. (An alternative was French medieval, brought into fashion by the writings of Viollet-le-Duc.) William Morris completes the triad of the Gothic revival in England. It was through him that the basic principles formulated by Pugin and developed by Ruskin acquired actuality. See *Pugin, Augustus; Morris, William.*

Goupy, Marcel b. 1886. French glass designer working for Rouard, Paris, 1918–1936.

Graal Glass The name given to the technique employed by Orrefors in the making of colored glass, whereby the cutting of the pattern is only an intermediate stage and the glass receives its final form in the furnace. See *Swedish Modern Glass.*

Grand Rapids Furniture In American furniture; in a general sense the history of the Grand Rapids Furniture industry is divided into three periods: the pioneer period from the time of William Haldane (known as Deacon Haldane), who opened a cabinet shop in his house in 1836, to the coming of machinery around 1850; the organization period from around 1850 to about 1890; and from 1890 into modern times. By far the most important was the organization period, as it set the tempo of the furniture industry throughout the United States wherever furniture was made. The manufacturing business as it is understood today was established by Julius Berkey in 1860. The Philadelphia Centennial Exposition, 1876, was a milestone in Grand Rapids furniture history as it marked their debut as a national furniture center. Three enterprising Grand Rapids furniture manufacturers, one of whom was Berkey and Gay, displayed furniture in the prevailing style of the time,

the so-called Victorian Renaissance. The Grand Rapids display became one of the sensations of the exhibition. For the first time the attention of eastern buyers was focused on western Michigan. By January 1878 enough of them came to Grand Rapids from the East to warrant the simultaneous presentation by all local furniture makers which has been known since as "the market." The Grand Rapids City Directory for 1908 listed forty-nine furniture manufacturing companies. The halcyon days were from about 1890 to 1925. During the first three years of the depression, three of the largest furniture companies went out of business. Several smaller companies also closed; all that survived had a struggle to keep in business. The struggle, however, marked a turning point in the city's furniture-making career. It was during the depression decade around 1938 that the general level of Grand Rapids furniture design took an upward trend and merged with a new character more akin to the Grand Rapids furniture industry of today. Baker Furniture, Inc., has been a fruitful influence. See *Berkey and Gay; Baker Furniture, Inc.*

Granite Ware or White Ware In American ceramics; such names as Granite Ware, White Granite, Opaque Porcelain and Flint China were given to a heavy-grade ware similar to ironstone that was a staple product of American potteries from around 1860 to 1900. Hotel China and Semi-Porcelain appeared around 1885. See *Ironstone China,* page 249.

Grasset, Eugène 1841–1917. French, born in Switzerland; architect, graphic artist and designer. Grasset went to Egypt in 1869 and to Paris in 1871. Here he studied Viollet-le-Duc and Japanese art assiduously. He published books and articles on ornament; in theory he advocated respect for materials and utility of objects, but he considered decoration necessary and used motifs derived from nature. He worked in various fields of the decorative arts. He was one of the originators of poster design, which emerged as an art at the end of the 1880's and the beginning of the 1890's.

Great Exhibition of the Works of Industry of All Nations, 1851 The first international exhibition ever held; opened May 1, 1851, closed to the public October 11, 1851, final closing ceremony October 15, 1851. Built on a Hyde Park site, the Crystal Palace was the outstanding example of mid-19th century iron and glass architecture because of its great size (1851 feet long, much longer than Versailles) and the absence of any other material. The purpose of the Great Exhibition was to present a living picture of the point of development at which the whole of mankind had arrived and a new starting point from which all nations would be able to direct their further exertions. It was one of the few great undertakings in the 19th century that proved an unqualified success. In the decorative arts it was a stimulant to reform. See *Cole, Sir Henry*.

Gregory, Mary In American glass; a decorator for the Boston and Sandwich Glass Company, working around the 1870's or 1880's. Her painted decoration is always in white on transparent glass, either clear or colored. She recorded her love of children in an artistic manner and in that respect her work is reminiscent of the illustrator Kate Greenaway.

Greenpoint See *Union Porcelain Works*.

Griffen, Smith and Hill In American ceramics; operated a pottery at Phoenixville, Pennsylvania; became widely known for their Etruscan majolica, 1879–1890. Among their popular patterns were the maple leaf, shell and seaweed, and cauliflower. The mark was an impressed monogram *GSH*, sometimes surrounded by a band with the words *Etruscan Majolica*. The monogram alone is also used and, sometimes, *Etruscan Majolica* impressed in a horizontal line.

Gropius, Walter Adolf George b. 1883. American, born in Germany, architect, writer and designer; a foremost pioneer of modern design. In 1937, the year he came to the United States, he was appointed Professor of Architecture in the Graduate School of Design, Harvard University. In the following year he was appointed chairman of the department of architecture. He retired in 1952, becoming Professor of Architecture, Emeritus. See *Bauhaus*.

Grotell, Maija American, born in Finland, artist-potter and teacher; came to the United States in 1927. She works chiefly in stoneware, understands good potting. Some of her pieces have considerable charm.

Gruber, Jacques French architect and furniture designer of the Nancy School; his Art Nouveau furniture was notably influenced by the Louis XV style. See *Art Nouveau*.

Grueby Faïence Company In American ceramics; an art pottery established in Boston in 1897. The pieces were modeled by women artists who signed their monograms in addition to the impressed mark of the pottery, which was *Grueby; Grueby Pottery, Boston, U.S.A.;* or *Grueby, Boston, Mass.* These pieces were sold at Tiffany, and Tiffany glass shades were first fitted on Grueby pottery lamps. When the Grueby works closed, Tiffany began to make his own pottery lamps.

Grueby, William H. American ceramist; in 1894 he began to produce bricks and tiles with a dull mat glaze that quickly became popular and had an almost immediate effect on the entire production of American pottery. In 1897 he began to make vases hand-thrown and hand-carved with the same mat glazes he used on his tiles. He was one of the most important potters working in the French-inspired Art Nouveau. Tiffany was attracted by the superb quality of Grueby pottery and ordered Grueby bases for some of his lamps. In 1907 Grueby went out of business. See *Art Nouveau, in American ceramics; Rookwood Pottery*.

Guild and School of Handicraft   See *Ashbee, Charles; Arts and Crafts Movement.*

Guimard, Hector   1867–1942. French architect and furniture designer; the foremost French architect working in Art Nouveau. His three chief architectural works are Castel Béranger, 1894–1898; the cast-iron entrances to the Paris Métro stations, 1900; and the Humbert de Roman Building, 1902. The principles of his style have derived from nature, with decorations that are functional parts of construction. His furniture possesses a similar harmony of design; each piece is a sophisticated play of details placed with great refinement. See *Parisian Art Nouveau.*

Gullaskrufs   See *Swedish Modern Glass.*

H

Habermeier, Konrad   b. 1907. German glassmaker working chiefly in engraved glass.

Haile, Thomas Samuel   d. 1949. English artist-potter; working in stoneware. Though he found his expression in techniques relating to the early wares of China and Japan, he succeeded in infusing into his work an altogether modern spirit. He worked for a time in the United States, first in New York at the Henry Street Settlement House, then spent a year at Alfred and taught at the University of Michigan. He returned to England, where he met an untimely death. His influence in America has been considerable.   See *Murray, William S.*

Hald, Edward   See *Swedish Modern Glass.*

Hall, John   American designer; the final interpretation of the Empire style was recorded by John Hall of Baltimore in his CABINET MAKER'S ASSISTANT, 1840. A heavier debased interpretation of basic French Empire designs, Hall illustrated massive scroll supports in monotonous repetition for every imaginable position for sofas, tables and the like. They were well adapted for cutting with a bandsaw and were intended for the maker who wanted to promise inexpensive furniture which was made possible by the introduction of machinery.

Hamada, Shoji   b. 1894. Japanese artist-potter; working exclusively in high-fired stonewares. He is perhaps the best-known of modern Japanese potters. He came to St. Ives with Bernard Leach in 1920, and he built his own kiln in the pottery village of Mashiko, Japan, in 1931. His pottery reflects the ease and complete mastery he brought to his work; with no waste of motion Hamada expresses everything simply, effortlessly. His work has had a strong influence on other Japanese potters as well as on the development of studio pottery in Europe and the United States.   See *Mashiko; Leach, Bernard; Chow, Fong.*

Hampshire Pottery   In American ceramics; started in 1871 in Keene, New Hampshire, and run by Messrs. J. S. Taft and Company. They made ordinary ware and later "majolica". They specialized in souvenir pieces for summer resorts, often using transfer printed designs, frequently in black.

Hand-Loom Weaving   In English arts and crafts; the revival of hand-loom weaving in the 20th century dates from the founding under Ruskin's inspiration of the Langdale Weaving Industry, initiated by Albert Fleming in 1883 for the production of simple homespun cloths. This afforded the stimulus for other enterprises such as Annie Garnett's Windermere Spinnery, 1891, and

Katie Grasett's London School of Weaving, 1898, which made more deluxe fabrics. See *Blount, Godfrey.*

Handel, Philip J. American glassmaker; in 1885 he founded the Handel Company in Meriden, Connecticut. By 1900 he had started a branch factory in New York City. He made a wide variety of decorative glass pieces, including acid-cut-back cameo vases in Art Nouveau flower and plant designs. Owing to the increasing popularity of gas and electric lamps in the early years of the 20th century, lamps became the company's staple product. Many are similar to the Tiffany lamps made at the Tiffany Studios. However, they were always less costly. The Handel Company, a victim of the Depression, closed in the 1930's.

Hankar, Paul 1859–1901. Belgian architect and designer of furniture; a leading architect of the 1890's. Orientalism played an important role in his work, and in decorative art he was greatly influenced by the English work. He began to design furniture in 1891. It was very simple, rather ponderous, and revealed a marked interest in new constructive solutions. Some of his furniture both in shape and construction is Japanese in feeling. Art Nouveau features are not the most important ones in his work. See *Belgian Art Nouveau.*

Hansen, Johannes See *Wegner, Hans.*

Harder, Charles See *Binns, Charles F.*

Hardoy Chair A kind of chair adapted from a folding wood and canvas chair used by Italian officers in North Africa during the Libyan campaign. This non-folding adaptation with a metal rod frame and leather was done by three Argentinians: Antonio Bonet, Juan Kurchan and Jorge Ferrari-Hardoy. A most inexpensive and practical easy chair, it is nothing more than a continuous metal frame on which four pocket-like corners of a length of leather are slipped over the two uprights of the back and the two front corners of the seat.

Harker Pottery Company In American ceramics; established at East Liverpool, Ohio, by Benjamin Harker Sr. in 1840, when the manufacture of yellow and Rockingham wares was begun. From 1847 to 1850 or later, the firm was Harker, Taylor and Company, when they produced such Rockingham pieces as hunting and hound-handled pitchers. From 1885 white granite and semi-porcelain were the staples produced. In 1890 the Harker Pottery Company was incorporated. Among the marks is a bow and arrow with the name "Harker" or initials of the company, "H.P.", which was used for a number of years.

Harmonium A wind keyboard instrument, a small organ without pipes, provided with free reeds. Essentially it is the adaptation of the ancient Chinese free-reed to the mechanism of the modern keyboard. The musical tones for both the harmonium and its subsequent development, the American organ, are produced by tongues of brass technically called vibrators. The vibrator or reed, which swings backwards and forwards like a pendulum while vibrating, is set in periodic motion by impact of a current of air from bellows operated by the feet of the player. An essential difference between the harmonium and the American organ is the direction of the necessary pressure of wind or air current. In the former the wind apparatus forces the current upwards; in the latter, it sucks it downwards. Therefore the American organ has exhaust instead of force bellows. The harmonium is used as a substitute for the pipe organ which it resembles particularly in having a number of stops which produce a variety of tone colors. It developed in the early 19th century from G. J. Grenie's Orgue Expressif (1812; suggested by the Chinese mouth organ, Sheng). Experimental forms led to the first real harmonium patented in Paris, 1840, by Alexandre Debain. He even patented the name *harmonium*, which obliged later experimenters to shelter their improvements under other names. For this reason the venerable name of organ became associated with an inferior instrument which eventually necessitated the distinction, reed and pipe organs. The "expression stop" which permits the player to produce gradations of intensity by foot control (regulation of the pressure in the bellows) was invented in 1854 by Mustel (Mustel organ). The American organ has a softer tone but lacks the expressive stop of the harmonium. The principle of this organ, originating in France, was developed by Estey in Brattleboro, Massachusetts, 1856, and by Mason and Hamlin, Boston, 1861.

Hasami   In Japanese ceramics; an important center in the Nagasaki Prefecture for handcraft pottery. Since it was near Arita, in the Saga Prefecture, pottery-making spread to Hasami. However, while Arita potters produced very colorful designs, the potters in Hasami produced mostly simple blue and white designs and their wares were limited to Japanese-style tea utensils.   See *Japanese Contemporary Pottery; Arita*.

Hawkes, T. G., and Company   1890–1962. Founded by Thomas G. Hawkes at Corning, New York, in 1880. Hawkes glass at its best is magnificent and unrivalled, particularly when cut on Corning blanks or on the blanks of the Steuben Company. Hawkes himself personally created and patented some of the best designs of the Brilliant Period. See *Cut Glass, American*.

Heal, Sir Ambrose   1872–1959. English furniture designer; in 1893 entered firm of Heal and Son, the only commercial firm closely associated with the Arts and Crafts Movement. From 1896 onwards all the firm's furniture was designed by Sir Ambrose.

Heaton, Clement J.   1861–1940. English designer and craftsman in stained glass and metals. He was the son of Clement Heaton, the founder of Heaton, Butler and Bayne, stained glass manufacturers and general decorators. He was practically the sole English craftsman to work in cloisonné enamel at that time; he established his own

company, Heaton's Cloisonné Mosaics, Ltd. He went to Switzerland in the early 1890's and settled in Neuchâtel, carrying out a number of important commissions for stained glass and cloisonné. He patented in Switzerland a process for the manufacture of embossed wallpaper, which he designed. In 1912 he settled in America.   See *Heaton, Maurice*.

Heaton, Maurice   American, born in Switzerland; designer-craftsman. He came to the United States in 1914, working first for his father, making stained glass windows for churches. He developed his technique for fusing enamel to glass in 1947.   See *Heaton, Clement J.*

Heesen, Willem   See *Leerdam*.

Henderson, D. and J.   See *Jersey Porcelain and Earthenware Company*, page 259.

Herkomer, Hubert von   1849–1914. English, born in Bavaria; painter, etcher, metalworker and enameller. In 1883 he founded the Herkomer School of Art at Bushey and directed it until his retirement in 1904. He became interested in metalwork and enamelling in 1896.

Hine, Margaret   See *Newland, William*.

Historical Blue   In American ceramics; the name given to transfer printed Staffordshire pottery depicting American historical events, views of cities and towns, pictures of heroes and other notable persons, patriotic emblems such as the Eagle of the United States Seal, Arms of the States and the like. There was a total of about 800 subjects. The dark blue printed ware of the 1820's was supplanted in the 1830's and 1840's by light colors, that is a light blue or the familiar "pink" Staffordshire, black, sepia and green, and occasionally in two colors. The ware comprised tea services, dinner services, sets of plates, jugs and the like. Also called Old Blue. Of these so-called Anglo-American printed wares a much later class of blue-printed ware was the Commemoratives, made around 1900 of entirely new subjects produced to meet the wide demand for Historical Blue. Also included in the Anglo-American wares, though not fundamentally American, were the picture pot lids showing great English houses, scenes from literature and other similar subjects. See *Pot Lids; Printed Wares*.

Historical Glass In American glass; chiefly flasks and pressed glass, decorated with portraits of famous people or emblems illustrating national or local events. See *Flasks*, page 186.

Hoare, J., and Company In American glass; originally known as Hoare, Burns and Dailey, this firm moved in 1863 from their South Ferry Works in New York to the Greenpoint Flint Glass Works. In 1873 they moved to Corning, New York. Their designers and craftsmen were among the best of that time and were notable for their cut glass patterns. The trade-mark was "J. Hoare & Co., 1853, Corning". See *Cut Glass, American*.

Hobbs, Brockunier and Company In American glass; in 1863 Hobbs, Burnes and Company of Wheeling, West Virginia, became Hobbs, Brockunier and Company. The firm arranged a fine display of glass at the Philadelphia Centennial Exposition, 1876. They were an important center for the manufacture of Peachblow. Their Peach-blow was a case glass, usually made with a mat or dull finish, the outside shaded from a deep red to a yellowish hue and with a milk-white lining. See *Peachblow*, page 355.

Hoffmann, Josef 1870–1955. Austrian architect, graphic artist and designer; played an important role in the founding of the Vienna Secession, 1897. He contributed to VER SACRUM, the Secession magazine. Though his early work included examples in the curvilinear vein, his work on the whole stresses geometric forms. This was apparent in his designs for architecture, furniture and decorative objects, paralleling the work of

Mackintosh in Glasgow but retaining his own distinctive style. He was more interested in constructional problems than in ornament. The simple geometric ornament, the square and the circle, which he and the architect Olbrich developed in the late 1890's, was sparingly employed and was subordinate to a strict ornamental order. Hoffmann favored the square motif, Olbrich the circle. The simpler relationships of flat surfaces preferred by Hoffmann showed the way to the next generation's stylistic ideals of undecorated geometric form. Due to the work of Hoffmann, Olbrich and others such as Adolf Loos, Vienna quickly gained recognition as one of the most progressive centers of the new movement in Europe. Hoffmann was a brilliant teacher and had a great influence throughout central Europe. He founded with Moser and others the Wiener Werkstätte in 1903. The Palais Stoclet, Brussels, 1905–1911, was one of his important early works in architecture, for which he did the interior decorations and furnishings. He continued to practice and teach until a few years before his death. See *Secession; Wiener Werkstätte; Klimt, Gustav*.

Holmgaard Glass Works See *Danish Contemporary Arts and Crafts*.

Home Arts and Industries Association In English arts and crafts; particularly interested in rural crafts. Started in 1884, it established village classes in wood-carving, metalwork, weaving, pottery, needlework and the like. See *Arts and Crafts Movement*.

Horn Furniture See *Staghorn Furniture*.

Horta, Victor 1861–1947. Belgian architect; the country's most important architect at the turn of the century. He was the first to achieve a fully developed mastery of Art Nouveau. It is generally accepted that Horta launched the new style in his house designed for Professor Tassel, No. 12 Rue de Turin in Brussels, completed in 1893. His dynamic and plastic forms were in part of Neo-Baroque inspiration. In 1902 he won the first prize at the Turin Exhibition with a rather heavy suite of furniture. Around 1905 Horta gave up the Art Nouveau style.   See *Belgian Art Nouveau*.

Hubbard, Elbert   American furniture manufacturer who founded the Roycrafters in the United States. Like his contemporary, Gustav Stickney, he produced Mission-style furniture of good design.   See *Stickney, Gustav; Mission Furniture*.

Huber, Patriz   1878–1902. German architect and designer; one of the original seven artists invited to Mathildenhöhe. He was one of the most characteristic of the Darmstadt artists; an interior designed by him in 1899 shows the Jugend style in full bloom. See *Jugendstil; Mathildenhöhe*.

Hultberg, Paul   b. 1926. American enameller; well known for his enamelled architectural wall panels. A bold and colorful abstractionist, his murals are notable for their freshness and vitality.

Hunt, William Holman   1827–1910. English artist.   See *Pre-Raphaelites*.

Hutton, John   b. 1906. English, born in New Zealand, glass engraver and mural painter; in 1959 made an engraved glass screen 70 feet high and 40 feet wide for the West Wall of the new Coventry Cathedral. See *English Contemporary Arts and Crafts*.

I

Ice Water Pitcher   In American silver; the tilting ice water pitcher made in silverplate was patented by the Meriden Britannia Company in 1854 but was also made by several other firms. The earliest pieces, holding two to four quarts, sat on a stand or tray with one matching goblet. Later pieces, of more ornate design, had two or more goblets.

Idoux, Claude   b. 1915. French painter also noted for his stained glass, some of which he created for the church of Baccarat in collaboration with Le Normand and others. Since 1945 Idoux has participated in the renaissance of tapestry in France. See *Le Normand, Albert*.

Image, Selwyn   1849–1930. English designer and illustrator.   See *Century Guild*.

Imperial Glass Company   See *Carnival Glass*.

Inscriptions on Furniture   See *Meubles Parlants*.

International Silver Company   In American silver; incorporated in 1898 by a number of independent silversmiths whose family backgrounds began in early colonial times, the International Silver Company of Meriden, Connecticut, has become the world's largest manufacturer of silverware. The quality of its silver has gained world renown. Among the many independent companies which became part of the International Silver Company were Meriden Britannia Company, established at Meriden, 1852; Forbes Silver Company, Meriden, 1894; Holmes and Tuttle, Bristol, 1851; Middletown Plate Company, Middletown, 1864; Rogers Brothers, Hartford, 1847; Rogers, Smith and Company, Hartford, 1854; Wilcox Silver Plate Company, Meriden, 1867; and numerous other companies. See *Meriden Britannia Company; Rogers Brothers*.

Iridescent Glass   In American glass; the exquisite iridescence on ancient glass was the result of corrosion after centuries of being buried in the earth. The modern method of coating colored glass with metallic stains to achieve iridescence probably originated with Lobmeyr in Vienna. Iridescent glass was first displayed in the United States at the

Philadelphia Exposition, 1876. After much experimentation Louis C. Tiffany produced his glowing Tiffany or Favrile glass. By 1904 Carder had perfected Aurene. One of the first imitations of Tiffany glass was called Quezal. Iridescent glass was first mass-produced around 1910. See *Tiffany, Louis C.; Aurene Glass; Durand, Victor; Carnival Glass; Kewblas; Quezal.*

Ironstone China In English and American ceramics; a dense hard earthenware patented by Charles James Mason in 1813, which he introduced at his pottery at Lane Delph, Staffordshire. It was supposed to have pulverized slag of iron as an ingredient in its clay composition. Essentially it was similar to the stone china introduced by Spode around 1805. A staple of American potters from around 1860 to 1900, it was given such names as White Granite, Opaque Porcelain and Flint China, the so-called Hotel China and Semi-Porcelain appearing about 1885. See *Granite Ware.*

Italian Contemporary Arts and Crafts Italy, noted for its creative artistry – an exact duplicate is difficult to find – is a fertile land for new ideas. Italian influence in contemporary design and crafts is undeniably great. Color is everywhere. In the textile arts, which have always been among the principal expressions of Italian skill, the use of color and texture is outstanding. The work of Geiga Bronzini and Renata Bonfanti is commendable. In the art of enamelling, which has had a long history in Italy, the name of the enameller Paoli de Poli is well known. In contrast to the elegant surfaces of de Poli's enamels are the exciting effects Tonino de Laurentiis achieves in the champlevé technique. Luigi Martinotti is known for his pictorial enamels. The art of *pietra dura* – a fine variety of inlaid mosaic flourishing in Italy in the first half of the 17th century in which the tesserae were cut from semi-precious stones – has been successfully explored by Richard Blow, a gifted American designer, at his Montici

workshop. A parallel revival has occurred in the field of mosaics. Another exacting technique, also peculiarly Italian and early, is intarsia, an inlay of many colored woods. Enrico Bernardi's intarsia work is notable. Glassware produced in the island of Murano still is of a superior quality. A secondary source for glass is Empoli and its vicinity in Tuscany. See *Murano Glass; Italian Contemporary Ceramics; E.N.A.P.I.; Empoli.*

Italian Contemporary Ceramics The dominant position of the faïence technique in Italian ceramics has never been seriously challenged. So strong is this native tradition than even today the high-fired wares and those influenced by the glaze techniques of the Far East, which dominate the work of the artist-potter in other countries, play a comparatively minor role here. Italian ceramics, generically a low-fired faïence, are vigorous and colorful and are based chiefly on an earthy, forthright and popular concept of the art. This basic quality is perhaps brought to its highest perfection in the work of Guido Gambone of Florence (b. 1909), who creates and commands the world of fantastic shapes. His work recalls the vigor and fantasy of Etruscan figure pottery, while unmistakably contemporary in form and feeling. The result is semi-abstract ceramic sculpture of the first order. The work of the ceramic sculptor Luccio Fontana of Milan is a tour de force of super-impressionist virtuosity based on Baroque themes. The peculiar abstract qualities resulting from the construction of forms out of sheets of clay rather than by molding or mass modelling gives a unique character to the bowls and figures created by the sculptor Melotti of Milan. Pietro Cascella of Rome, who is typical of the versatility of the Italian artist, is a potter, ceramic sculptor and mosaicist. His abstract designs show an explosive imagination that is at times startlingly effective. Other distinguished ceramists are Agenore Fabri, Aligi Sassú, Marcello Fantoni, Zaccagnini, Victor Cerrato, Rosanna Bianchi, Salvatore Meli and Giovanni

Battista Valentini. Ceramic tiles by Ugo Lucerni and Annamaria Cesarini Cascella (wife of Peter Cascella), and the ceramic painting of Aligi Sassú exemplify other possibilities in the medium. See *Italian Contemporary Arts and Crafts*.

Italian Modern Furniture In the years following World War II, a group of Italian architects around Milan brought forth some new furniture, looking handcrafted and sculptured to pin-point delicacy. Essentially it was a mélange of antique, Baroque and Rococo with a touch of Bauhaus and Art Moderne. A marked characteristic was the floating look, an almost weightless appearance. For example, chair legs that had formerly extended from the seat frame to the floor were cut off in mid-air. Beneath the truncated legs a concealed stretcher supported the "floating" seat. It presaged the doom of the block-like look which up to that time meant *modern* in the United States. At the present time the trend in contemporary furniture is toward glass and metal, used either alone or in conjunction with wood. Experimental designs by the architect and designer Carlo Molino (b. 1905) illustrate a definitely Italian sense of the aesthetic quality of these materials. The tables, seating equipment and occasional pieces made by Guglielmo Pecorini show a thorough understanding of the decorative possibilities of wood framing combined with natural and plastic fibers. See *Italian Contemporary Arts and Crafts*.

J

Jack, George 1855–1932. American architect and designer; about 1890 became chief furniture designer to Morris and Co.; in 1900 took over the work of Philip Webb. Many of his furniture designs were of semi-traditional forms to be made in mahogany with elaborate inlay and metal mounts. See *Webb, Philip; Morris, Marshall, Faulkner and Co.*

Jacobsen, Arne Danish architect, interior decoration and furniture designer; in 1957 he introduced two chairs in upholstered plastic, the "egg" and the "swan." See *Danish Modern Furniture*.

Jacquard In textiles; in 1805 Charles Marie Jacquard invented a draw loom with an overhead mechanism that made it possible to lift a few warps of thread at a time, instead of small successive groups as in the shaft system. The intricate Jacquard mechanism worked by means of perforated cards pressed against needles connected with the heddles. The card perforations in the Jacquard system represent the design. At each pick, a card pressed against the needles, lifting the appropriate warps. To make a design using this mechanism, it was necessary only to make a new set of cards. This loom was an important advance from draw loom slavery where heddles were lifted by hand at the direction of a foreman.

Japanese Contemporary Pottery Before the Meiji Restoration, 1868, Japanese pottery was made only for home consumption according to traditional Eastern methods of production. After the Restoration, manufacturers started to make export pottery to fill demands from the Western countries. German teachers contributed significantly to the introduction of Western methods of ceramics to Japan. In present-day Japan the two kinds of industry, traditional handcraft pottery (bowls, dishes, tea utensils and the like) and export industrialized pottery (Western style dinnerware) are proceeding each in its own way, without being mixed.

Many pieces of Japanese handcrafted pottery are functional for the Western as well as for the Japanese manner of living and are suitable for quantity commercial production. Among the most important centers for handcrafted pottery are Seto, Tokoname, Mino, Yokkaichi, Shigaraki, Mashiko, Kyōto, Kutani, Tobe, Arita and Hasami. Export pottery is common to a greater or lesser extent to all these areas but it is not their speciality, with the exception of Yokkaichi. Most of the industrialized Western style dinnerware is made in or around Nagoya. Japanese pottery is produced mostly in the western half of Japan; Mashiko is one of the exceptions. See *Tokoname; Mino; Yokkaichi; Shigaraki; Mashiko; Kasaoka; Kyōto; Kutani; Tobe; Arita; Hasami.*

Japanism　The art of Japan was first made known to the Western World in 1859, the year Japan was opened to trade. Japanese art delights in all the subtleties of line, in all the brilliant caprices of color; it disdains symmetry and paints and carves animals with a realism still unrivalled in the Western World. It gave Europe the opportunity to discover what she was seeking and though it was not the father it was the godfather of the Modern Movement. It preached the gospel of simplification as no other art has ever preached it and taught that organic integrity within the work of art itself is fundamentally a law of beauty. The lessons that had travelled so far were first assimilated by decorative art; they gave it instruction in the treatment of lacquers, ceramics and enamels, but above all they helped it to throw off the trammels of tradition. No foreign influence has affected 20th century Western designer-craftsmen to the same extent as the arts of Japan. See *Aesthetic Movement; Whistler, James MacNeill; Mackintosh, Charles R.; Godwin, Edward; Burges, William; Voysey, Charles; Art Nouveau; Beardsley, Aubrey.*

Jekyll, Thomas　1827–1881. English architect and designer, one of the earliest designers to be influenced by Japanese art. A member of Whistler's circle, he decorated several houses in the Japanese taste and designed ornamental ironwork, embroidery and interior decoration. See *Godwin, Edward.*

Jelliff, John　1813–1893 American cabinetmaker who was active in Newark, New Jersey, from 1836 until his retirement in 1890. He was noted for the quality of his furniture, which was in accordance with 18th century traditional cabinetmaking.

Jensen, Georg　1866–1935. Danish sculptor; began his silversmithing as an art form in 1904 when he opened his shop in Copenhagen. In 1906 he started collaborating regularly with Johan Rohde, a creator of forms that for refinement are unrivalled. Both men were quite conservative, each in his own way. Rohde based his forms on classic shapes but lifted them to fresh heights. Jensen's ornament was behind the times too. It was in this atmosphere, safe from progressive design, that the art of Jensen and Rohde flourished and matured. Jensen's ornament of tight clusters of flowers or fruit juxtaposed with swelling hand-hammered surfaces influenced design generally. Rohde's serene light forms and restrained details were beyond the reach of imitators. Even after the deaths of Rohde and Jensen in 1935, the firm's silver continued to be accepted throughout the world as an achievement in craftsmanship, and today it is still in the forefront of accomplished design and workmanship. Later designers include such well-known names as Jorgen and Soren Georg Jensen, Sigvard Bernadotte of the Swedish Royal family, Henning Koppel, who was the first aggressively modern designer, and Magnus Stephensen, the gifted architect. A great innovation was the introduction of stainless steel in flat and hollow forms as a regular part of Jensen production. See *Stainless Steel; Bojesen, Kay.*

Jersey City Pottery Company　In American ceramics; around 1828 David Henderson took over the Jersey City Pottery Company at Jersey City, New Jersey, and renamed it the American Pottery Manufacturing Company. Around 1840 the name was changed to the American Pottery Company. See *American Pottery Company*, page 11.

Jones, Owen d. 1874. English designer, writer and architect; published with Sir Matthew Digby Wyatt the monumental GRAMMAR OF ORNAMENT, 1856. During the latter part of his life he was mainly engaged on designs for interior decoration for wealthy clients; he also decorated the drawing room for George Eliot at The Priory, 21 North Bank, Regent's Park, London.

Jugend   See *Jugendstil*.

Jugendstil or Jugend Style   A name Art Nouveau quickly acquired in Germany. It derived from JUGEND, a ribald and lively periodical first published in Munich in 1896, in which Otto Eckmann charmed his readers with Art Nouveau vignettes. The title, according to the editors, meant *youth*. The Jugend style had two principal centers,

one in Munich and a second somewhat later at Mathildenhöhe in Darmstadt. In these two towns, which played an important role in its development, Jugend enjoyed a brief but golden age before it was abandoned in the first years of the 20th century by the leading artists, who cast aside its linear rhythm in favor of the ruler and the compass. See *Munich School; Mathildenhöhe; Art Nouveau; Maison de l'Art Nouveau; Deutsche Werkstätten; Sachlichkeit.*

Juhl, Finn b. 1912. Danish architect and furniture designer; he designed a teakwood open-armed chair with a molded sculptured frame for the cabinetmaker Niels Vodder in which he emphasized the separation between seat and frame. This ingenious way of shedding weight is one of his characteristic design principles and occurs in some of his case pieces such as chests of drawers that reveal a similar independence between drawers and frame. This so-called floating device was freely adopted in America after his work became more widely known. See *Wegner, Hans; Danish Modern Furniture.*

K

Kanishebe   Modern Japanese artist-potter; belongs to that group of famous potters who have directed their work along traditional paths. His work is identified with Bizen, one of the wares most highly prized by tea masters. He rediscovered the methods and materials which had been used to produce the great Bizen pots of the Monoyama period. His best pieces are scarcely distinguishable from Bizen masterpieces of the past. His work is highly respected by the Japanese.   See *Rosanjin, Kitaoji.*

Karasz, Mariska   1898–1960. American, born in Hungary; self-taught embroiderer and

writer; came to the United States in 1914. She is the author of several books, the best-known being ADVENTURES IN STITCHES, 1949, in which she states that "a needle is a woman's traditional instrument of self-expression." She pioneered in the creative use of stitches. As a result of over 50 one-man shows held between 1948 and 1960, she became one of the best-known artist-craftsmen in the United States. In a period of little more than ten years she liberated embroidery from traditional design and function, and inspired countless individuals to find in it a means of expression harmonious with other contemporary arts.

Karhula-Iittala See *Finnish Contemporary Arts and Crafts.*

Kasaoka In Japanese ceramics; an important center in the Okayama Prefecture for hand-crafted pottery. The origin of pottery in Kasaoka is very old, but the making of it is not always successful. The present manufacturers built their kiln at Kasaoka in 1907 and called their wares Kibi Yaki; they make artistic traditional vases, plates and tea utensils. See *Japanese Contemporary Pottery.*

Kastrup Glass Works See *Danish Contemporary Arts and Crafts.*

Kasuba, Aleksandra b. 1923. American mosaicist; her mosaics chiefly comprise marble tesserae in combination with Venetian glass tesserae. She occasionally introduces into her mosaic murals various materials such as pebbles, marble chips, slate, terra-cotta and glass because of their textural impact. Her designs show her preference for either a realistic or completely abstract treatment.

Kato, Hajime Modern Japanese artist-potter; belongs to that group of famous potters who have directed their work along traditional paths. A versatile potter; he works in different techniques and has achieved a mastery over them all. His son, Tatsumi, is also a ceramist. See *Rosanjin, Kitaoji.*

Kaufmann, Edgar Jr. b. 1910. American critic, writer, lecturer, designer and editor; studied painting in New York, Vienna, Florence and London. He was apprenticed to Frank Lloyd Wright. Kaufmann served as director of the Department of Industrial Design at the Museum of Modern Art, New York, from 1946 to 1948 and directed their Good Design Exhibitions from 1950 to 1955. He has been an influential friend of modern design.

Kawai, Kanjiro b. 1890. Japanese artist-potter; his stoneware reveals great variety in shape and finish. Much of his work is hand-built rather than thrown. His son Hiroshi works with him. In Japan his work is highly prized. See *Kyōto.*

Kaye, Margaret b. 1912. English designer-craftsman; specializes in stained glass and embroidered pictures. She has developed an individual collage style of needlework.

Kewblas In American glass; a kind of iridescent Art glass produced by the Union Glass Works, Somerville, Massachusetts, in the 1890's. It was an opaque colored glass that was more opalescent than iridescent. See *Iridescent Glass.*

King, Jessie Marion 1876–1949. Scottish illustrator, designer, bookbinder and fabric printer; designed mural decorations for schools in Lanarkshire and specialized in book illustration and jewelry. She designed and made hand-painted pottery and batik work.

Kirk, Samuel, and Son, Inc. In American silver; in 1815 Samuel Kirk, who was born in 1793 at Doylestown, Pennsylvania, opened a shop in Baltimore and established the oldest surviving silver firm in the United States. It is generally accepted that Samuel Kirk introduced the elaborate and widely imitated repoussé decoration to America in 1828. Even though the silversmiths of other cities were doing similar work, Kirk and the Baltimore group brought great skill to this style of ornamentation, and for this reason it is often referred to as "Baltimore silver." Repoussé decoration attained its full flowering in the 1840's.

Klimt, Gustav 1862–1918. Austrian painter; studied mosaics, glass painting and ceramics in Vienna. He was one of the founders of the Vienna Secession, 1897, and he collaborated with the Wiener Werkstätte. He was the principal exponent of Art Nouveau painting in Vienna; his sphere of influence extended beyond Central Europe. He created the wall decorations for Josef Hoffmann's Palais Stoclet in Brussels, 1905–1911; various aspects of his interior decoration link this house to Art Nouveau. See *Secession; Hoffmann, Josef.*

Klint, Kaare 1888–1954. Danish architect and furniture designer; exercised great influence through his appointment in 1924 to lead the newly created class in furniture design at the Royal Academy's School of Architecture. He was the first Danish furniture designer to found his system on purely rational principles. See *Danish Modern Furniture.*

Knapp, Stephan b. 1921. English, born in Poland; enameller, sculptor and painter. He is noted for his architectural wall panels. See *English Contemporary Arts and Crafts.*

Knowles, Taylor and Knowles Company In American ceramics; established in 1872 at East Liverpool, Ohio. A considerable amount of Belleek ware was made by this company in the 1880's. Later it developed a similar ware known as Lotus Ware, probably the finest porcelain made in America. Each piece was an individual design. The mark was "Knowles, Taylor and Knowles" enclosed in a circle surrounding a crescent and star, and "Lotus Ware" below the circle.

Koepping, Karl 1848–1914. German painter, etcher and glass designer; he developed an extremely delicate style of glass design in which he transferred the Japanese technique of fusing various colored glazes from earthenware to glass. In a great many Jugend-inspired glasses of extreme delicacy, he exploited the possibilities of his material almost to breaking point in straw-like forms. See *Jugendstil.*

Kosta See *Swedish Modern Glass.*

Krejci, Luba b. 1925. Czechoslovakian master-designer in lace construction; noted for her unique "murals in lace" in which her figural work reveals her understanding and fondness for people and nature. The hair of her figures is often made out of tassels. Her material is usually hand-woven hemp or flax, as well as machine-made string which the artist herself dyes, soaks and boils. She has adapted lace to her needs and has given it a new lease on life with her original techniques and wealth of invention.

Kroll, Boris b. 1913. American textile designer; in 1934 began his own firm, Boris Kroll Fabrics, Inc., designing and producing hand-woven upholstery and drapery fabrics. In 1939 he added power looms and in 1945 formed the Boris Kroll Jacquard Looms and Research and Testing Laboratories.

L

La Farge, John 1835–1910. American painter, craftsman, lecturer and writer. His immediate effect on his own generation was due to his help in reawakening the decorative arts in collaboration with his close friend Henry Richardson. See *Associated Artists; Richardson, Henry.*

Lalique, René 1860–1945. French jewelry designer; the foremost French Art Nouveau artist working in jewelry, gold and silver and contributors to modern glass. His experiments with glass, making imitation precious stones of glass shaped like uncut cabochons and mounted in a most original manner, eventually brought him to the art of glassmaking, to which he devoted the remainder of his life. His glass was represented at the opening of S. Bing's shop L'Art Nouveau in 1900 and was enthusiastically acclaimed; he became one of Bing's regular contributors. In 1909 he bought a modest glassworks not far from Paris, where he made extremely costly and beautiful scent bottles to defray his expenses while he carried on his experiments in glass, gradually perfecting the designs and techniques that were to bring him world-wide fame. He founded a larger glassworks at Alsace in 1921 with his son Marc as manager. Lalique was the first to use glass for abstract sculpture. He truly belonged to the 20th century, for he did not share the craftsman's horror of mechanization and used the machine wherever it was possible, to make his designs available to the general public. Possibly more than any other individual he made the modern world aware of decorative glass. Like his father, Marc Lalique models his own molds, and all the glass made at this genuinely modern glassworks is cast in molds except for the bowls of drinking glasses, which are blown. While following the technique his father evolved, Marc has developed his own personal and contemporary style.

Landberg, Nils See *Swedish Modern Glass.*

Larsen, Jack Lenor b. 1927. American textile designer and producer; in 1952 formed the fabric firm Jack Lenor Larsen, Inc., which designs, manufactures and distributes upholstery, drapery and casement fabrics. He has brought a fresh viewpoint to virtually every facet of fabric design for the home and industry.

Laughlin, Homer, China Company In American ceramics; established in East Liverpool, Ohio, in 1874 by Homer and Shakespeare Laughlin. They produced chiefly white granite; in later years semi-vitreous china and higher grade wares were manufactured to some extent.

Lauweriks, Johannes L. M. 1864–1932. Dutch decorative artist and designer; the interest in Egyptian art which was especially pronounced in Holland in architecture as well as in decorative art was best expressed in Lauweriks' work. In the 1890's he produced woodcuts in a style clearly revealing Egyptian influence, as well as furniture with Egyptian features. In his silverwork, traces of Art Nouveau are evident.

Leach, Bernard b. 1887. English artist-potter, born in Japan; studied drawing, painting and etching in London, 1903–1907. He returned to Japan in 1911 and studied pottery under Kenzan VI. He met Shoji Hamada, who accompanied him on his return to England in 1920 and remained in England for three years. Hamada helped Leach to set up his pottery at St. Ives, which had a wood-burning fire kiln patterned after the Japanese chamber kiln. Leach began to make high-fired stoneware. His pottery was never a one-man shop, but rather made use of the creative and productive energies of several people. His influence has been effective not only through his pottery and the work of his students but also through his book, A POTTER'S BOOK, 1940, in which he strongly states his philosophy of pottery-making and gives a vivid description of the Oriental approach to technique. Essentially it became the potter's bible and focused the attention of potters on Chinese and Japanese values in pottery, and on stoneware as a perfect medium for the expression of something individual and yet universal in ceramics. See *Mashiko; Tomimoto; Hamada, Shoji; English Contemporary Arts and Crafts.*

Leach, David English artist-potter; apprenticed to the Leach pottery under his father, Bernard Leach, 1930–1933. He managed the Leach pottery for some years. After supervising a monastic pottery at Aylesford Priory, he established his own in Devonshire. See *Leach, Bernard; English Contemporary Arts and Crafts.*

Lebeau, Joris Johannes Cristiaan 1878–1946. Dutch decorative and graphic artist; outstanding among glass designers. He specialized in designs for industrial art, textiles, glassware and posters. He learned his batik technique from Dijsselhof.

Le Corbusier (pseudonym for Jeanneret-Gris, Charles Edouard) 1887–1965. French, born in Switzerland; architect, painter and designer. His furniture is notable for a mastery of plastic form and calculated proportion. One of his typical architectural devices, lifting the main part of a building off the ground by columns of markedly sculptural quality to imbue it with a weightless look, is evident in his classic chrome-plated steel chaise longue with an adjustable back. In this instance the design minimizes the strength it takes to support a relaxed human being.

Leek Embroidery Society In English needlework; established about 1879 by the wife of Thomas Wardle of Leek. The designs, generally repeating patterns, were printed on the material, and the embroidery silks were dyed at Leek. The gold thread was brought in from China. The society made both ecclesiastical and domestic embroideries. Among the designers were Thomas Wardle, J. D. Sedding and R. Norman Shaw.

Leerdam The most stimulating period of the Royal Netherlands Glass Works, Leerdam, came after World War I and is indelibly associated with Andries Dirk Copier (b. 1901), who made the glassworks famous. He joined the staff as a designer in 1917. From the beginning the simplicity and the purity of his work were as outstanding as its character. Though each piece he created was different, it was always Dutch, for he believed that in spite of world-wide tendencies in modern art, each country should preserve its own inherent national character. Very soon Copier was appointed artistic director of the Royal Leerdam Glass Works. He designed numerous models for drinking glasses for mass production, thereby making it possible for people with good taste and modest means to buy this beautifully designed and excellently manufactured glass. Copier continued his experiments with new forms and new techniques for his artistically important pieces. He created new models either for his now world-famous Unica (single pieces for wealthy collectors and museums) or for the Serica (limited series of a given model, sold at prices within the reach of many glass-lovers for whom the

Unica is generally too costly). In the span of almost half a century Copier has shown himself to be one of the great contemporary glass designers, one whose ideas and imagination appear inexhaustible. Copier has attracted important young designers to Leerdam. Of these Sybren Valkema (b. 1916) is the oldest and the only one not trained at the Leerdam Glass School. Most of Valkema's work is characterized by abstract forms, closely related to contemporary sculpture. Much of the glass of Floris Meydam (b. 1919) is sold abroad. Willem Heesen (b. 1925) has given new life to old techniques and has succeeded in combining them with modern shapes. Gerard Jacobus Thomassen (b. 1926) specializes in drinking services. Lodewijk Jacobus Franciscus Linssen (b. 1936) has become known for his experiments in new shapes. Austrian-born Brigette Altenburger (b. 1942) had already shown herself as a versatile artist before coming to Leerdam in 1963. See *Netherlands Contemporary Arts and Crafts.*

Leleu, Jules See *Art Moderne.*

Le Normand, Albert b. 1915. French painter and stained glass artist; collaborated with Claude Idoux, Paul Reynard and Denise Chenay on the stained glass windows of the church of Baccarat, 1952–1955. Since 1945 he has also been designing tapestry. Le Normand has made drawing an important element in all his work.

Lenox Company In American ceramics; in 1889 Walter Scott Lenox came to Trenton, New Jersey, to establish a pottery company which was named Lenox in 1906. It remains the undisputed master in the making of fine porcelain dinnerware in America. See *Belleek.*

Lethaby, William Richard 1857–1931. English architect, designer, teacher, lecturer and writer on architecture and art; a leading designer before and after the turn of the century. He designed furniture, metalwork (chiefly fireplaces) and embroideries, painted pottery and tiles, woodwork and leadwork. He was greatly influenced by Philip Webb. His furniture is mainly characterized by a respect for the material and a deep understanding of the construction problems involved. Lethaby was a founder of the Art Workers' Guild, president of the Arts and Crafts Exhibition Society and a founder of the Design in Industry Association.

Libbey Glass Company   In American glass; William A. Libbey bought the New England Glass Company at East Cambridge, Massachusetts, in 1878. His son Edward moved the factories to Toledo, Ohio, in 1888. Libbey glass was generally heavy and deeply cut. The majority of their designs were original and protected by patents. Libbey glass was noted for its excellent color and crystal purity and for the execution of the patterns by the most skillful craftsmen. Their intaglio cut glass was also notable. Joseph Locke, while employed by Libbey, invented Amberina, 1883, Pomona, 1885, Peachblow and Agata.   See *New England Glass Company; Cut Glass, American; Art Glass*, page 22.

Liebes, Dorothy   b. 1899. American weaver and textile designer; frequently called First Lady of the Loom. Her color palette is as notable as her textural creativeness.

Lime Glass or Soda Lime Glass   See *Pattern Glass*.

Lindstrand, Vicke   See *Swedish Modern Glass*.

Littleton, Harvey K.   American artist-potter and glassblower; well established as a potter before he abandoned this craft in the late 1950's to work in glass. By 1960 he had begun research in glass, and shortly afterwards he set up a workshop near his country house at Verona, Illinois. Littleton is recognized as a leading revivalist of creative glassblowing in the United States.

Lobmeyr   In Austrian glass; the J & L Lobmeyr Company of Vienna is one of Europe's oldest and most important glassworks and has produced such eminent designers as Josef Hoffmann, Oswald Haerdtl, Stefan Rath, Vally Wieselthier, Ena Rottenberg and Jaroslav Horejc.

Locke, Joseph C.   See *Libbey Glass Company*.

Lonhuda Pottery   In American ceramics; established at Steubenville, Ohio, in 1892, by Messrs. Long, Hunter and Day. The name was derived from the first syllables of their names. Later the company moved to Zanesville, Ohio. Products were underglaze slip-painted wares with shaded and blended grounds. The mark first used was the company's monogram. Later marks included an Indian head, a shield, and the initials of the decorators. At a later date, W. A. Long went to Denver, Colorado, where he organized a new company, the Denver China and Pottery Company, which produced Lonhuda ware.

Loos, Adolf   1870–1933. Austrian architect and designer; in a series of articles, 1897–1898, protesting against the extravagance of Art Nouveau, he recommended trying "to find beauty in form instead of making it rely on ornament." In furniture he preferred the functionally sound examples of English and American design, and furniture designed by him in 1898 was without ornament. In respect to the Modern Movement he was one of the first architects (the others being Van de Velde, Sullivan, Wagner and Wright) to admire the machine and to understand its essential character.   See *Secession; Mission Furniture*.

Losanti Ware   In American ceramics; a kind of art pottery, a hard paste porcelain developed by M. Louise McLaughlin in Cincinnati, Ohio, and exhibited at the Paris Exhibition of 1878. The following year Miss McLaughlin founded the Pottery Club of Cincinnati. A member of the club was Mrs. Marion Longworth Storer who founded her own pottery, Rookwood, in 1880. The name *Losanti* was derived from the former name of the city, Losantiville.   See *Rookwood Pottery*.

Lotus Ware See *Knowles, Taylor and Knowles Company.*

Low Art Tile Works In American ceramics; a factory in Chelsea, Massachusetts, that was making tiles from 1877. In 1883, under the title of J. G. & J. F. Low, the factory produced tiles commercially for mantel facings, panels and stoves. In its employ was Arthur Osborne, whose excellent paintings in relief served to establish Low's reputation. In 1884 Low put out a catalogue of its art tiles.

Lundin, Ingeborg See *Swedish Modern Glass.*

Lurçat, Jean b. 1892. French painter and tapestry designer, considered a pioneer of modern tapestry. In 1945 he helped to found the Association of Tapestry Cartoon-Painters.

Lutz, Nicholas American born in France; glassmaker. After learning the art of glassmaking in France, Lutz came to the United States and in 1869 began to work for the Boston and Sandwich Glass Company, where he stayed until it closed in 1888. From there he went to the Mount Washington Glass Company and then to the Union Glass Works at Somerville, Massachusetts. Lutz is especially noted for the striped glass which he produced at Sandwich and also for his threaded glass. He specialized in fruit paperweights that show tiny apples, cherries or pears with green leaves against a white latticino background. While at Sandwich, Lutz created the strawberry paperweight.

Lyman, Fenton and Company See *Bennington,* page 40.

M

MacDonald, Frances 1874–1921. English designer and metalworker, educated at Glasgow School of Art; worked at times with her older sister, Margaret. She married Herbert McNair and collaborated with him in the design of furniture and stained glass. From 1907 she taught gold- and silversmithing, metalwork and enamelling at the Glasgow School of Art. See *MacDonald, Margaret.*

MacDonald, Margaret 1865–1933. English designer, metalworker and embroiderer; educated at Glasgow School of Art. In 1900 she married Charles R. Mackintosh; she collaborated in all his works and had a marked influence on his decoration. See *MacDonald, Frances; Mackintosh, Charles R.; Glasgow School.*

Mackintosh, Charles Rennie 1868–1928. Glasgow architect, designer and watercolorist; the most powerful exponent of the Glasgow School. He developed an individual style in architecture, interior design and furniture in the 1890's and became the leader of the well-known group called The Four (Herbert McNair, Margaret and Frances MacDonald and himself). The Four explored the decorative arts, developing into the Glasgow style, the English corollary of Art Nouveau. Mackintosh's brief architectural career included several tea-rooms for Miss Cranston, 1897–1910; Windy Hill, 1899–1901; Hill House, 1902–1903; Glasgow School of Art, 1897–1909; and the Scottish Pavilion at the Turin Exhibition in 1902. Later he devoted his time to furniture design and decoration. His furniture made in the 1890's was the most original of any at this time. His chairs with extremely tall backs, often 6 feet 6 inches high, exemplify his peculiar inventiveness. Especially typical of his style are very simple pieces with broad plain surfaces contrasted with comparatively small controlled areas of rich pattern. He had an aversion for rich and heavy upholstery. The light and airy quality that predominates in Mackintosh's interiors reveals the importance of Japanese influence on his work. See *Glasgow School; Voysey, Charles; Spook School.*

Mackmurdo, Arthur Heygate 1851–1942. English architect and designer; one of the leading personalities of the Arts and Crafts Movement. His best designs for furniture were his simplest; his most original designs were without ornament, depending for their beauty on the strong contrast of verticals and horizontals. See *Arts and Crafts Movement; Arts and Crafts Exhibition Society; Century Guild.*

Maison de l'Art Nouveau The name Art Nouveau, which was finally accepted in the majority of countries (the notable exception being German-speaking countries, where it was called Jugendstil) derives from S. Bing's first shop, Maison de l'Art Nouveau at 22 Rue de Provence, Paris. Bing, who was an early important collector of Japanese art, opened his shop in December, 1895; shortly afterward the name began to take root. A contemporary description of the orange-colored sign on the front of Bing's shop reads: "Above two enormous sun aureoles with their round discs violently exaggerated without taste and style can be read these two words with their delightful modesty: Art Nouveau." Little did Bing realize that his shop was destined to become the focal point and Paris the main center of the new style. Of the shop and its name Bing observes, "At its birth Art Nouveau made no claim to rising to the distinction of a generic term. It was simply the name of an establishment opened as a meeting ground for all keen young artists anxious to demonstrate the modernness of their tendencies." See *Nancy School; Parisian Art Nouveau.*

Majolica In English ceramics; the word *majolica*, spelt with a "j", was used in the 1860's to designate pottery with relief decoration and colored glazes. It was widely made in a number of European countries and also in England, notably by Minton and Wedgwood. It was also popular with American potters and included many novelties as well as a full line of tableware. See *Griffen, Smith and Hill.*

Majorelle, Louis 1859–1926. French furniture designer. After attending the Académie des Beaux Arts in Paris from 1877, he returned to Nancy in 1879 to take over his father's business, which specialized in period furniture. In the 1880's he produced work in the Louis XIV, Louis XV and Louis XVI styles. In the 1890's he worked mainly in the Neo-Rococo style until about 1897, when he adopted the Art Nouveau style under the influence of Gallé. Majorelle followed in Gallé's footsteps, but he is less bound by tradition in his construction and more plastic in his decoration. The most striking feature of his work is the dynamic line. He is regarded as the leading furniture designer of the Nancy School; upon its decline he returned to classicism. See *Nancy School; Gallé, Emile.*

Mallard, Prudent 1809–1879. American cabinetmaker born in France; came to New York City in 1829 and opened a cabinet shop in Royal Street in New Orleans in 1838. In accordance with the dictates of fashion Mallard worked chiefly in the Victorian Rococo and Baroque styles.

Maloof, Sam b. 1925. American designer-craftsman of modern furniture; his workshop is in Alta Loma, California. Especially distinctive is the strength conveyed in the light, fluid and simple lines of his furniture, where he carries out his belief that joinery is an aesthetic part of design. His seat furniture has a minimum of upholstery.

Marble Glass In American glass; a kind of opaque pressed glass popular in the late 19th century which originated as an imitation of mosaic pottery. It was generally made in shades of opaque purple blended with opaque white in a marbleized effect. Also called Purple Slag and, erroneously, End-of-

Day. Opaque glass in a brown and white mixture was called Caramel or Custard glass. See *Challinor, Taylor and Company*.

Marinot, Maurice 1882–1960. French painter and glass artist; showed his first glass creations at the Salon des Indépendants in 1912. One of the few glass designers who made all his work entirely himself. In his fully developed style the forms are simple and without decoration. Within the material called glass – heavy, thick, in several layers of uneven thickness – air bubbles and garlands with exotic colors, which the changing light affected, were recreated by Marinot, each piece being a fragment of some strange deep-sea vegetation. His influence was enormous on several younger glass artists, such as Barovier and Copier. This great but modest glass artist still exerts wide influence on glass designers throughout the world.

Marlboro Street Factory In American glass; active at Keene, New Hampshire, 1815–1850. It was the oldest flint glasshouse in New England, except for those in the Boston area. Among its products were flasks and blown three mold. It was especially noted for its blown three mold decanters and inkwells.

Marquand and Company In American silver; noted silversmiths and jewelers, active in New York City, 1834–1839. Frederick Marquand, Joseph P. Marquand and Erastus O. Tompkins were the partners. See *Ball, Tompkins and Black; Black, Starr and Frost, Ltd.*

Martin Brothers English artist-potters; in the 1870's Robert Wallace and his brothers Edwin and Walter set up a pottery at Southall using salt glaze stoneware for individual work. They learned the craft from the firm of Doulton of Lambeth and were probably the first to experiment in this medium. The joint work of the Martin Brothers has enjoyed notable fame in recent years, and they are often referred to as the first masters of modern English pottery. Their best work was done after they attended the Paris Exposition, 1900, where they saw the finer Japanese wares, which guided them to simple shapes and to more subtly wrought indefinite slips and glazes. See *Artist-Potter; English Contemporary Arts and Crafts*.

Martin, Edith Park b. 1918. American embroiderer; her work is noted for its great artistry and lively creativity. Recipient of the Gold Thimble awarded by the AMATEUR NEEDLEWORK OF TODAY in 1959 and 1963.

Mathildenhöhe In 1899 the Grand Duke Ernst Ludwig of Hesse-Darmstadt invited seven artists to live as a group in the artist colony of Mathildenhöhe in Darmstadt. The original group, "Die Sieben," comprised the architect and designer Peter Behrens of the Munich Schools; architect and designer Joseph Olbrich, one of the founders of the Secession in Vienna; designer Hans Christiansen; architect and designer Patriz Huber, 1872–1902; sculptors Ludwig Habich, b. 1872, and Rudolf Bosselt, 1871–1938; and painter Paul Bürck, b. 1878. The colony was officially opened in 1901 with an exhibition called A Document of German Art. The activity of the group was dominated by Behrens and Olbrich. See *Jugendstil; Behrens, Peter; Olbrich, Joseph*.

Mashiko In Japanese ceramics; an important center for handcrafted pottery. Mashiko is a small farming town about 50 miles north of Tokyo with a population of 25,000. About 40 families, mostly part-time workers of the farming community, are engaged in making pottery. Each family has its own kiln and bakes pottery only once every month or two. Clay deposits suitable for pottery-making were discovered near Mashiko in 1853. The people began trying in a very primitive way to supply low-grade kitchen utensils to the Tokyo market. However, in 1924, a young potter named Shoji Hamada, who is at the present time one of the leaders in Mingei-type (folk art)

handcrafted pottery, settled down in Mashiko and started his life work. Through his
influence Mashiko potters improved in
making Mingei-type pottery, which is the
speciality of Mashiko. The famous English
potter Bernard Leach visited the town on
several different occasions to study Mashiko
pottery.   See *Japanese Contemporary Pottery;
Hamada, Shoji; Leach, Bernard; Yanagi,
Soetsu.*

Mason, John   b. 1927. American ceramist;
has executed numerous commissions of
architectural ceramic wall reliefs and ceramic
sculpture.

Mathsson, Karl Bruno   b. 1907. Swedish
architect and designer; occupies a singular
position for his laminated wood-frame contour chairs, which he has been continually
developing and refining over a period of
more than 20 years.

Matthews, Heber   b. 1905. English ceramist,
studied painting and design at the Royal
College of Art; subsequently concentrated
on the study of pottery under the tuition of
William S. Murray. Matthews was one of
the early exponents of English contemporary
ceramics and was adviser to the Council of
Industrial Design. He exhibited widely all
over the world.   See *English Contemporary
Arts and Crafts; Murray, William S.*

McCobb, Paul   American designer; his sensitivity to the enduring elements of design
and his positive belief in the contemporary
way of life are reflected in his lasting contributions to contemporary design. Through
his understanding of the machine and
materials he has achieved in his work an
original concept which has been greatly
felt in creating new design trends. Beyond
his reputation for furniture design, he also
designs such products as television sets,
radios, pottery, glassware and kitchens.

Mead, J. O.   See *Electroplating.*

Meeks, Joseph, and Sons   An important
American cabinetmaking firm, 1797–1868,
who had a "Manufactory of Cabinet and
Upholstery Articles" at 43 and 45 Broad
Street, New York. In 1833 Endicott and
Swett printed a colored lithograph for the
firm which illustrated forty-one furniture
designs and three drapery designs. It was the
first American publication to show complete
furniture designs, which essentially with their
large plain surfaces, projecting columns and
scroll supports were in the American Empire
style.

Meriden Britannia Company   In American
silver; organized in 1852 by H. C. Wilcox
and Company, at Meriden, Connecticut,
for quantity production. Their first products
were Britannia hollow wares. By 1855
silver-plated wares were included. In 1862
the Rogers Brothers moved to Meriden and
the 1847 Rogers Brothers trade-mark was
an important addition to the Meriden
Britannia Company whose officers were
instrumental in the formation of the International Silver Company in 1898.   See
*Wilcox, H. C., and Company; Rogers Brothers;
International Silver Company.*

Meydam, Floris   See *Leerdam.*

Middle Period   See *Cut Glass, American.*

Meubles Parlants   In English cabinetwork;
decorative symbolism expressed by means
of an inscription, painted or inlaid, is a
medieval idea. It was reintroduced by Gothic
revivalists, such as Bruce Talbert and William Burges, working in the 1870's and
1880's. Later inscriptions were widely
employed by the artists of the Arts and
Crafts Movement. The use of quotations to
convey a mood or to reveal the function of
furniture stemmed from the strong literary
attitude which was widespread in England
in the second half of the 19th century. This
fashion for the use of texts on furniture was
not confined to England. In the early 1890's
the French designer Emile Gallé created a
number of pieces of furniture which bear
inscriptions – the so-called meubles parlants,
with quotations from Hugo, Maeterlinck,
Ruskin, Morris and others. The vogue for
inscriptions was by no means limited to

furniture; they appeared in other media such as ceramics and wallpapers. See *Crane, Walter; Summer, George H.*

Milk-White Glass or Milk Glass In American glass; originally called Opaque White, it was developed in imitation of porcelain. A few examples of hand-blown milk-white glass exist from the early part of the 19th century. It was first pressed on a large commercial scale in the 1870's and the 1880's; its great popularity continued until c. 1900. This glass was characterized by a translucent quality and although it was white, the white had a bluish tinge. These two marked features are evident when a piece is held up to the light. The most familiar articles in milk-white glass are the covered animal dishes. See *Opaque Colored Glass; Black Milk Glass; Milch Glass*, page 319.

Millais, Sir John Everett 1829–1896. English painter. See *Pre-Raphaelites.*

Miller, Frederick A. b. 1920. American silversmith; through his work as designer and teacher has become well known as a silversmith in the United States. His name is most commonly associated with hollow ware. The technique he most frequently employs is called stretching, an early process that Miller was among the first to use in the United States for free-form bowls. See *Stretching.*

Mingei See *Mashiko.*

Mino In Japanese ceramics; one of the most important centers for handcrafted pottery. In the Mino district, which covers the southeast part of Gifu Prefecture, there are many towns, such as Tajimi, Toki and Mizunami, which chiefly produce pottery and since they are located near each other their products have common characteristics. Potters migrated to this district from Seto in the 16th century. However, the traditional Mino pottery (Shino, Oribe and Kizeto) was made in this district first and transferred

to Seto later. See *Seto; Japanese Contemporary Pottery.*

Mission Furniture In American cabinet-work; a development around 1900 which was essentially an offshoot of the English Arts and Crafts Movement. It was inspired by the rustic aspect of the English Cotswold group and featured severely straight and simple lines, vertical slat backs, "weathered oak" finishes and leather upholstery. See *Cotswold School; Arts and Crafts Movement; Society of Arts and Crafts; Stickney, Gustav.*

Mocha Creamware or Banded Creamware In English ceramics; a lathe-turned work found chiefly on mugs and jugs, with bands of decoration colored in combed or seaweed designs, popular around 1790–1850 and widely exported to America. A small amount of "Moca" ware decorated with bands of spattered slip was made in America.

Modern Movement The name universally recognized for the trend which was to become the basis for the philosophy and artistic ideals of the 20th century. The Modern Movement, which removed all ornament and permitted a structural form to emerge, freed from petty structural conceits, gave full attention to the qualities of the material and honesty in the use of it. The shapes that most obviously suggest the 20th century are generally geometric, precisely finished, smooth and lacking the elaboration and variety of detail usually associated with the craftsman's handwork. Functionalism exerted the greatest influence in and also through architecture. Each of the important originations of modern furniture design has been the work of a modern architect. They were compelled to design not only furniture but all kinds of equipment and furnishings for their buildings, since little suitable furniture existed. The best modern work is marked by three qualities; precision, economy and simplicity, which the functionalists claim achieves a perfect beauty free from what they refer to as the mannerisms of past styles. See

Wagner, Otto; Loos, Adolf; Velde, Henry van de; Sullivan, Louis; Wright, Frank Lloyd; Bauhaus; Sachlichkeit; Japanism; Modern Style.

Modern Style Essentially a period style, having a peculiar preference for certain kinds of form, a functionalist care for efficiency in use, a rational dislike of unnecessary ornament. That it is a true period style is shown by the fact that its mannerisms may be copied and abused in the so-called modernistic style, which is a degraded burlesque, without regard either for tradition or the requirements of use.

Modernistic See *Modern Style.*

Modular Furniture A development of the early 1950's in which several components such as seating and storage units share a common metal or wood base or frame and can be rearranged as need dictates.

Molded Wares In American ceramics; mass-produced, factory-made pottery shaped in molds, as opposed to earlier forms thrown on the potter's wheel, which arrived after c. 1830, a product of the Industrial Revolution. See *Parian Ware; Rockingham.*

Monart Glass In English glass; the name given the glass made by Salvador Ysart, a glassmaker from Barcelona, who joined the Scottish firm of John Moncrieff in Perth, 1922, and did a series of decorative pieces oxidized with colored marble-like effects in the Venetian-Mediterranean tradition.

Moncrieff, John See *Monart Glass.*

Moore, Bernard English artist-potter; working in North Staffordshire. The most striking feature of English pottery in the early years of the 20th century was a preoccupation with glaze technique and a widespread vogue for pottery with no decoration other than that of colored or figured glazes. Moore's thrown pots are characteristic of the interest of the more specialized potters in glaze technique. His forms and glazes were in emulation of Far Eastern pottery.

In the first two decades of the 20th century he achieved a remarkable control of high and low temperature glazes. Especially notable was his "rouge flambé."

Moore, Henry b. 1898. English sculptor and designer; noted for the massive archaism of his work in stone and bronze, and for the power of his draftsmanship. Tapestries and wall hangings designed by Moore are also distinctive for the same style of draftsmanship. See *English Contemporary Arts and Crafts.*

Morgan, William de 1839–1917. English potter and novelist; in the early 1860's made the acquaintance of Morris, Rossetti and Burne-Jones. He was the chief exponent of Morris's craft movement in pottery. Despite his grievously imperfect technique he was perhaps the most outstanding of all the artist-potters of the late 19th century. His pottery falls into two principal types: that painted in "Persian" colors (blues and greens) and that painted in luster colors.

Morris Chair See *Morris Firm Furniture.*

Morris Firm Furniture In English cabinetwork; it is usually accepted that Morris himself had little interest in the design of furniture. Probably the only pieces in which he had a direct hand, namely the settles and cabinets made for Red Lion Square and Red House, were chiefly designed to furnish large areas to be painted by Burne-Jones and himself. Except for some very plain greenstained bedroom furniture designed by Ford Madox Brown, all the early designs made by the firm were the work of Philip Webb. The principal influence of the firm on furniture design came not so much through the newly designed pieces by Webb as through its popularization of the light rush-seated furniture adapted from models found on farms in Sussex and an armchair with an adjustable back bar, the so-called Morris chair. See *Morris, Marshall, Faulkner and Co.; Morris, William; Webb, Philip; Jack, George.*

Morris Firm Tapestries In English textiles; Morris's most ambitious undertaking was the revival of tapestry-weaving along medieval lines. Except for the tapestries made by the Royal Windsor Works, 1876–1897, Morris's productions were the first tapestries to be woven in England since the early 18th century. In 1879 Morris made his first tapestry experiments; however, it was not until 1881 when the large high-warp looms were installed at Merton Abbey that Morris was able to tackle large tapestry panels. The most ambitious tapestries attempted by Morris and Co. were the Adoration and the Holy Grail series, both originally designed by Burne-Jones. See *Morris, Marshall, Faulkner and Co.; Morris, William.*

Morris, Marshall, Faulkner and Co., Fine Art Workmen in Painting, Carving, Furniture and Metals The establishment of this firm in 1861 by William Morris marks the beginning of a new era in the decorative arts, for it was through this firm that the influence of Morris and his associates, such as Burne-Jones, Rossetti, Ford Madox Brown, and Webb, was chiefly exercised. The firm started business at 8 Red Lion Square, London; in June 1865 it moved to 26 Queen Square. In 1875 it was reorganized as Morris and Co.; in April 1877 showrooms were opened at 264 (later 449) Oxford Street; in June 1881 the workshops were transferred to Merton Abbey. In the 1920's the showrooms were moved to 17 George Street, Hanover Square, London; in 1940 the firm went into voluntary liquidation. See *Morris, William; Morris Firm Furniture; Morris Firm Tapestries; Pre-Raphaelites.*

Morris, May 1862–1938. English designer and embroiderer, daughter of William Morris, from whom she received her artistic education; designed wallpapers and textiles for Morris and Co. In 1910 she lectured in England and the United States on embroidery, jewelry, pattern-designing and costume. She was one of the founders of the Women's Guild of Arts, 1907.

Morris, Talwin 1865–1911. Scottish architect and designer, a prolific designer of book bindings and covers; designed some furniture, metalwork and stained glass. His work was closer to the English arts and crafts than it was to the Glasgow School and Charles R. Mackintosh.

Morris, William 1834–1896. English designer, craftsman, poet and socialist. The influence of Morris on the decorative arts in England and eventually abroad was so deep and far-reaching that there is scarcely a late 19th century designer who is not indebted to it. Morris's entire life was a crusade against the worthless standards of mid-Victorian mass production, which he traced to the influence of machine manufacture and the disappearance of honest and satisfying handcraftsmanship. His own special contribution to design was in the field of flat pattern-making, in which his output was profuse and his genius unrivalled. This principle he applied to printed and woven textiles, tapestries, wallpapers, carpets and rugs. It is generally believed that except perhaps for a few pieces for his own use, Morris never designed furniture or any three-dimensional objects such as pottery or metal. Morris was a painter, designer, scribe, wood-engraver, illuminator, dyer, weaver, and finally a printer and papermaker. He mastered each of these crafts so that he could successfully direct and criticize the work of others. See *Morris, Marshall, Faulkner and Co.; Gothic Revival, English; Pre-Raphaelites; Arts and Crafts Movement; Webb, Philip; Morris Firm Tapestries; Morris Firm Furniture; Burne-Jones, Sir Edward; Embroidery; Morris, May.*

Moser, Koloman 1868–1918. Austrian painter, designer and graphic artist; a founding member of the Vienna Secession, 1897. He began teaching in 1899 and became an influential figure in the Austrian decorative art movement, working in illustration, stained glass, textiles and glassware. He established the Wiener Werkstätte with Hoffman and Wärndorer, 1903. He was

Austria's closest parallel to the French and Belgian exponents of curvilinear form. See *Secession.*

Mt. Washington Glass Company In American glass; active in South Boston and New Bedford, Massachusetts, 1837–1894, making blown, cut and pressed glass. They had a fine display of cut glass at the Philadelphia Centennial Exposition, 1876. They made a ware called Peachblow showing pastel shades of pale blue and rose-pink. They also made Amberina and in 1885 they patented a ware called Burmese that shaded from rose-pink to yellow. See *Pairpoint Corporation; Art Glass,* page 22.

Müller, Karl See *Union Porcelain Works; Century Vase.*

Münchener Vereinigte Werkstätten für Kunst in Handwerk See *Deutsche Werkstätten; Riemerschmid, Richard.*

Munich School The name generally given to a group of seven artists living in Munich and working in the Jugend style: Otto Eckmann, Hermann Obrist, Richard Riemerschmid, Bernhard Pankok, August Endell, Bruno Paul and Peter Behrens. The last-mentioned subsequently settled in Darmstadt, 1899. The furniture designed by this school is markedly constructive; its wealth of joints, curving ribs, struts and the like is reminiscent of the work of Serrurier-Bovy and van de Velde. In the opening years of the 20th century, both in furniture and interior design, this group began to turn away from the curvilinear Jugend style to the more simple and geometrical. Stimulated by the writer Hermann Muthesius, they experimented with construction and function, working more along the principles of the contemporary English arts and crafts designers. See *Jugendstil.*

Murano Glass Most of the fine Italian (Venetian) glass comes from Murano. The glasshouses on this island, which have won for Italy its enviable position in the world of glass, are small independent glassworks and in that respect are unlike the large Continental glass manufactories. See *Venini, Paolo; Barovier and Toso; Salviati and Company; Seguso Verti D'Arte; S.A.L.I.R.; Fratelli Toso.*

Murray, William Staite English artist-potter and teacher; began working in high-fired stoneware in the 1920's. He was interested in Far Eastern techniques, especially glaze effects. He possessed a remarkable genius for pottery and produced many unique pieces. His forms have an extraordinary subtlety and suggestiveness, well indicated by the titles he gave them, such as "The Fawn" or "Autumn Wind and Rain." The pots do not imitate the forms or effects named, but the mood suggested by the title comes through in the form, color and surface quality. Often the manner of his masterly brushwork or incised decoration projects the mood further still. Chief among his pupils were Sam Haile, Heber Matthews, Constance Dunn and Henry F. Hammond. His influence through his pupils has been great.

Muthesius, Hermann 1861–1927. German writer; served as a connecting link between the English style of the 1890's and the German in the 1900's. He propagated the ideas set forth by Wagner, Loos, van de Velde, Wright and Sullivan. An ardent advocate of reason and simplicity in architecture and art, he soon became the recognized leader of a new trend towards sachlichkeit. See *Sachlichkeit.*

Myers, Joel American glassworker and potter; currently design director for Blenko Glass in Milton, West Virginia. See *Blenko Glass Company.*

N

Nakashima, George American architect and designer-craftsman; spent several years in architectural offices in America, Europe and Asia, especially in Japan and India. He returned to America and after World War II settled in New Hope, Pennsylvania. He gave up architecture to become a furniture designer and woodworker, and started his own one-man shop in 1947, gaining fame for his fine handcrafted work. His chairs, tables and cupboards, which reveal his feeling for woods, have exerted wide influence on the work of other craftsmen.

Nancy School In France, where Art Nouveau became firmly established and retained its popularity the longest, Rococo exerted the strongest influence on the new art. Two distinct centers developed: one in Paris around Bing and his shop, the other in Nancy. The closest affiliation between Rococo and Art Nouveau existed at the latter, because under the reign of Stanislas Leszczynski the center of Nancy had been transformed by Rococo façades and sinuous grillwork into a maze of linear fantasies. Artists such as Gallé and Majorelle working in Nancy with its magnificent 18th century Place Stanislas perhaps came closest to the gracefulness of Rococo design in their Art Nouveau forms. The Nancy School started to develop around 1890 under the aegis of Gallé; it reached its peak around 1900; after Gallé's death in 1904 its vitality declined. See *Gallé, Emile; Majorelle, Louis; Vallin, Eugène; André, Emile; Gruber, Jacques; Maison de l'Art Nouveau; Parisian Art Nouveau.*

Natzler, Gertrud and Otto American, born in Austria, self-taught artist-potters; always work as a team. The Natzlers opened their first workshop in Vienna in 1933. They first won public recognition at the World Exposition in Paris, 1937, when they received a silver medal for a group of their ceramics.

They came to the United States in 1939. The Natzlers reduced their art to its basic elements of throwing and glazing, refined these techniques to a high degree and united their separate efforts to a single end. Each piece is hand-thrown on the potter's wheel by Gertrud and bisque-fired in preparation for glazing. Glazes, developed by Otto, are applied by brush and fired.

Nelson, George b. 1908. American architect, industrial designer and author. Along with Howard Myers, Henry Wright and Paul Grotz, he established ARCHITECTURAL FORUM as a major critical force in design and architecture. While still at FORUM he and Wright developed the storage wall system. In 1947 he became design director for Hermann Miller. As such he developed the Comprehensive Storage System (CSS group) in 1959, the sling sofa and the Catenary Seating Group in 1964, and in 1965 the Action Office. His Comprehensive Storage System comprises floor-to-ceiling poles on which can be suspended a wide selection of stacking drawers, shelves, sliding doors, drop-front desk and many other storage and accessory components.

Netherlandish Contemporary Arts and Crafts The awareness of the importance of contemporary design and craftsmanship in Holland finds expression in the collections of the Stedelijk Museum in Amsterdam. At the present time Holland commands an important position as a center of fabric designing and printing. An outstanding fabric designer is Hans Polak, who heads a studio called Het Paapje in Voorschoten. Noteworthy among the weavers are Greten Neter-Kähler, Ria Van Oerle Van Gorp and Edmond de Cuendt. Various churches are enriched by the embroidered hangings of Gerda Becker. Glass, another important Dutch industry, is centered at Leerdam; A. B. Copier is head designer at the Leerdam Glass Company. The dean of potters in Holland is Meindert Zaalberg, a third-generation potter whose studio at Leiderdorp is named Raku Yaki. Among the many others who have achieved distinction in ceramics are Johan Van Loon, one of the most interesting of the younger group, Jan Van der Vaart, and the husband-and-wife team Jonny Rolf and Jan de Roode. One of Europe's leading craftsmen, the goldsmith Leo Brom, lives in Utrecht. See *Leerdam*.

New England Glass Company In American glass; established at Cambridge, Massachusetts, by Deming Jarves and associates in 1818 and remained active until c. 1880. It was one of the leading producers of all kinds of fine glassware, including blown three mold, free-blown, cut, engraved, pressed glass and paperweights. One of the best-known types made there in the 1850's was Bohemian glass, which was inspired by the elaborately engraved wares imported from Bohemia, Germany and Austria. Layers of different-colored glass, sometimes as many as four, were applied over the clear glass, and designs were cut and engraved on the surface so that the underlying colors showed through. The name "overlay" is often given to this type of glass. One of the main engravers for this kind of glass working here was Louis Vaupel. This company outranked all other companies in the production of Art glass. It produced a ware called Peachblow and a variation of Peachblow called Agata, Amberina and Pomona. See *Libbey Glass Company; Art Glass*, page 22.

New England Pottery Company In American ceramics; established in East Boston, Massachusetts, 1854, by Frederick Meagher for the manufacture of common white ware. In 1875 Thomas Gray and L. W. Clark took over the works and maintained the name. From c. 1878 to c. 1893 early ironstone china bore the mark of the Great Seal or Arms of the Commonwealth of Massachusetts. In 1886 the firm began to make a semi-porcelain ware in colored bodies

which was artistically decorated and given the name "Rieti" ware. This was first marked with a mailed hand holding a dagger.

New, Keith b. 1927. English stained glass artist and teacher; in the 1950's executed three 70-foot-high stained glass windows for the new Coventry Cathedral. See *Clarke, Geoffrey; English Contemporary Arts and Crafts*.

Newberry, Francis H. See *Newberry, Jessie R.; Glasgow School*.

Newberry, Jessie R. b. 1864. Scottish designer, embroiderer and teacher; studied at the Glasgow School of Art. In 1889 she married Francis H. Newberry, principal of the Glasgow School of Art, and she taught embroidery in the school from 1894 to 1908. In addition to her embroidery, she did some textile design, including damask linen. See *Glasgow School*.

Newcomb Pottery In American ceramics; the Rookwood approach to pottery was already in effect at Newcomb College in New Orleans in 1895 at the newly formed ceramic department of the Newcomb Art School. In 1897 Newcomb pottery appeared on the market and in 1900 was awarded a bronze metal at the Paris International Exposition. Its popularity continued until 1915. See *Rookwood Pottery; Art Nouveau, in American ceramics*.

Newland, William b. 1919. English, born in New Zealand, artist-potter and teacher; married Margaret Hine, an artist-potter. See *English Contemporary Arts and Crafts*.

Nieuwenhuis, Th. 1866–1951. Dutch graphic artist, designer and potter; a pupil of the architect P. J. H. Cuypers, 1827–1921. He was active in the Dutch Art Nouveau movement with Lion Cachet and Gerrit Dijsselhof. Among the main influences on Dutch artists in the 1890's were the English Arts and Crafts Movement, Japanese art, and the batik technique originating in the East Indies. Nieuwenhuis's work mirrors these influences in emphasizing the linear with designs of peacock feathers, long narrow fishes, and others taken from nature. See *De Distel; Dutch Art Nouveau.*

Noguchi, Isamu b. 1904. American sculptor; well known for doing sculpture in relationship to open areas and to architecture. He casts his sculpture in bronze, aluminum, iron, stone, marble and granite. He also designs glass, pottery and furniture.

Nordström, Patrick See *Danish Modern Ceramic Art.*

Northwood, Harry American glassmaker. Founded the Northwood Glass Company in 1888, located variously at Martin's Ferry, Ohio; Indiana, Pennsylvania; Wheeling, West Virginia, where he first featured iridescent glass. The mark was "N" underlined and later "N" inside a single or double circle. See *Carnival Glass.*

Notsjö (Nuutajärvi) See *Finnish Contemporary Arts and Crafts.*

O

Obrist, Hermann 1863–1927. Swiss sculptor and designer, a founding member of the Münchener Vereinigte Werkstätten; from 1888 devoted himself to decorative art, in 1892 founded an embroidery workshop in Florence which he moved to Munich in 1894. His decorative motifs are derived from nature with stylized but very creative shapes. A series of his embroideries was published in PAN. His embroidery possessed much of the refinement of Japanese art. See *Munich School; Riemerschmid, Richard.*

O'Connell, Michael English fabric printer and designer; specializes in textile murals in a resist-dyeing technique. He has worked in Australia and Africa and now is settled in Hertfordshire. His works include a large hanging for the 1951 Festival of Britain and a proscenium curtain for the Shakespeare Memorial Theatre, Stratford-on-Avon. See *English Contemporary Arts and Crafts.*

Odelqvist-Kruse, Anna-Lisa b. 1925. Swedish designer and embroiderer; noted for her ecclesiastical textiles and embroidery. Since 1954 she has been artistic director of Librarie Limited, which was started at the beginning of the 20th century and originally called Licium Textile Workshop.

Oesterreichischer Werkbund In Austrian arts and crafts; established in 1916. Craftsmen in Austria are well organized through the efforts of this organization. Its offices are in Vienna, and its outlet Wiener Handwerk is a showcase for Austrian handicrafts. See *Wiener Werkstätte; Deutscher Werkbund.*

O'Hara Glass Works In American glass; established by James B. Lyon and Company at Pittsburgh, 1848. Closed 1890. They manufactured flint glass tablewares, blown, cut, engraved, pressed and gilded. In later years they made lime glasswares, for which they received an award at the Philadelphia Centennial Exposition, 1876. Became the O'Hara Glass Company in 1875.

Ohrström, Edvin See *Swedish Modern Glass.*

Olbrich, Joseph Maria 1867–1908. Austrian architect, draftsman and designer; began his career as an illustrator, contributed to *Ver Sacrum.* Olbrich was a leader of the Vienna Secession, which he helped found in 1897. He was invited to the artist colony at Mathildenhöhe in 1899, where he designed practically all of the buildings. See *Secession; Hoffmann, Josef; Mathildenhöhe.*

Old Blue   See *Historical Blue.*

Onondaga Pottery Company   In American ceramics; established in 1871 in Syracuse, New York, to manufacture white granite ware. Among their marks were the Arms of New York State, 1874–1893, for white granite ware; the "Imperial Geddo" mark was used for the first chinaware made by this company; semi-porcelain ware was marked "Semi Vitreous", 1886–1898, and after 1897 the "Syracuse China" mark was used. Became the Syracuse China Corporation.

Opaque Colored Glass   In American glass; similar to milk-white glass or opaque white glass but entirely colored and less translucent.   See *Milk-White Glass.*

Opaque White Glass   See *Milk-White Glass.*

Orrefors   See *Swedish Modern Glass.*

Ott and Brewer Company   In American ceramics; operated the Etruria Pottery at Trenton, New Jersey, from 1863 to 1893, under the direction of William Bromley Sr., from the Belleek factory at Belleek, Ireland. The pottery is especially remembered as a maker of American Belleek in the 1880's. Characteristic marks used by the company include *Manufactured by Ott & Brewer Trenton N.J., U.S.A.*, and a crown pierced by a sword with *Belleek* above and *O &B* below.

P

Pabst, Daniel   American cabinetmaker working in Philadelphia around the mid-19th century. He is known especially for pieces such as sideboards in the Victorian Renaissance style.

Pairpoint Corporation   In American silver and glass; organized in 1880 at New Bedford, Massachusetts, it became one of the country's largest manufacturers of silver-plated ware. Also an outstanding name in fine cut glass. In 1894 the Mt. Washington Glass Company became part of the Pairpoint Manufacturing Company. In 1900, owing to financial difficulties, they merged to form the Pairpoint Corporation.

Palmqvist, Sven   b. 1906. Swedish glassmaker, joined Orrefors 1936. In late 1940's invented so-called "Ravenna" glass, a heavy glass, generally of a transparent tint into which are inlaid simple non-representational patterns in jewel-like colors.

Parian Ware   In American ceramics; unglazed porcelain, believed to have been made first at the United States Pottery, Benning-ton, Vermont, 1847. Within a few years it became a favorite practically everywhere. Chiefly used for pitchers, vases, statuettes and animals. All-white or blue and white examples are the most common. See *Parian Ware*, page 332.

Pankok, Bernhard   1872–1943. German designer and graphic artist; a founding member of the Münchener Vereinigte Werkstätten. He furnished a room at the Paris Universal Exposition of 1900, and he contributed to JUGEND. From 1913 to 1937 he was director of the Staatliche Kunstgewerbeschule in Stuttgart.   See *Munich School; Riemerschmid, Richard.*

Parisian Art Nouveau   Centered about S. Bing, who gathered around him a number of young artists who were to become foremost representatives of Art Nouveau. They designed some of the finest examples of Art Nouveau furniture. In contrast to the Nancy School their furniture was lighter, more refined and austere; the nature-inspired decoration was more stylized and frequently confined to small areas. The three most prominent furniture designers who worked for Bing were Georges de Feure, Eugene Gaillard and Eugène Colonna. In 1900 they designed S. Bing's L'Art Nouveau pavilion at the Paris Universal Exhibition when Art Nouveau was in full bloom. When they and other Parisian artists were confronted with the extravagant excesses of the style they made a subtle retreat and returned to a restrained form of Art Nouveau, more closely allied to French traditional styles. In this final phase, lasting until about 1910, the best work in furniture was achieved. See *Art Nouveau; Nancy School; Charpentier, Alexandre; Lalique, René; Guimard, Hector; Maison de l'Art Nouveau.*

Parrott, Alice Kawaga b. 1929. American designer-weaver; her weaving takes many forms, from rugs to wall hangings, upholstery fabrics and costume. The majority of yarns used are those which she has dyed.

Pattern Glass In American glass; a kind of pressed glass, so called because it was produced in large sets which provided almost everything for the table. It began to be popular in the 1830's and tried to imitate the design and appearance of cut glass. At first the designs were quite simple and copied diamond points and flutes from cut glass. Then patterns became more complex and included circles, ovals and elliptical patterns. The glass was heavy, bell-like when struck, and usually of a high quality. In the 1860's at the New England Glasshouse a formula was developed which permitted soda-lime glass to be pressed. Up to this time only flint glass, also called lead glass, was used; when struck it responds with a bell-like ring. Soda-lime glass, in which lead is omitted from the basic ingredients, responds with a dull sound when struck. In order to conceal the imperfections of soda-lime glass, which is of an inferior quality, more ornate designs were developed which covered the entire surface. This glass was made in enormous quantities throughout the latter part of the 19th century. Frosted, or camphor, glass, in which the glass surface is treated with an acid finish, was one of the most successful wares in the 1870's. The Gillinder family of Philadelphia is noted for its frosted glass wares.

Paul, Bruno b. 1874. German architect, printmaker and decorative artist; a founding member of the Münchener Vereinigte Werkstätten and a contributor to JUGEND. Paul furnished industrial designs for the Deutsche Werkstätten. He was exhibited at the International Exposition of Art in Industry sponsored by R. H. Macy, New York, 1928. See *Munich School; Riemerschmid, Richard; Deutsche Werkstätten.*

Pauline Pottery Company In American ceramics; a firm active in Edgerton, Wisconsin, from 1888 to about 1894, making underglaze decorated art wares. This pottery was originally established by Mrs. Pauline Jacobus in Chicago, 1883. The mark, impressed in the earlier pieces and printed in black on the later ones, consisted of a crown with the letter "C," for Chicago. Characteristic colors of Pauline pottery are vivid yellow, peacock blue and green, and soft creamy tints.

Perkins, Charles Callahan 1823–1886. American lecturer and art critic; an influential friend of the decorative arts.

Petri-Raben, Trude American potter born in Germany; in 1929 designed for Royal Berlin an entire service which is the prototype of modern white dinnerware. The service includes a "perfect" teacup; the delicacy of the bowl is complemented by the handle, the shape of which is easy to grasp and is primarily determined by the bowl.

Pilkington's Tile and Pottery Company In English ceramics; a pottery established at Clifton Junction, near Manchester, in 1892. Pilkington pottery was made under the close supervision of William and Joseph Burton. Some of the glazes were formulated by them, others by Abraham Lomax. The throwing was done by Edward Radford. See *Burton, William and Joseph.*

Piper, John b. 1903. English painter and designer; working at first as a landscape painter and returning to this field towards the end of the 1930's after a period of abstract work. The romantic, nocturnal quality of much of his work has contributed to the striking success of his designs for the stage and more recently for stained glass. In 1959 he designed stained glass for the Baptistery at the new Coventry Cathedral. See *Reyntiens, Patrick; English Contemporary Arts and Crafts.*

Pittsburgh Flint Glass Works In American glass; the name formally given to the glasshouse established by Benjamin Bakewell in 1808 and generally simply called "Bakewell's." See *Bakewell's Glass Works; Bakewell, Pears and Company.*

Pleydell-Bouverie, Katherine English artist-potter; specializes in stoneware with wood ash glazes. Her pottery is more or less similar in character to the work of Bernard Leach and William S. Murray. Simplicity and purity of form predominate and, as if in the interest of form, the glazes are generally sober in color—grey, olive, russet, buff and brown. See *English Contemporary Arts and Crafts.*

Ponti, Gio b. 1891. Italian architect and interior designer, teacher and writer; founder and director of DOMUS, internationally known architectural magazine. One of Italy's foremost architects and designers, Ponti has organized many of the famous Triennale exhibitions in Milan.

Poor, Henry Varnum b. 1888. American painter and muralist; later tried his hand at pottery. He was one of the exponents of figure decoration on pottery.

Portuguese Contemporary Arts and Crafts The tradition of the folk crafts promises a great deal for the future of handicraft tradition in Portugal, where the ever-increasing number of artist-craftsmen adapt more of the traditional techniques to their needs. Today in Lisbon, where countless buildings are decorated inside and out with colored tiles, the ceramic panels of Manuel Cargaliero are a sensitive adaptation in abstract terms of the traditional decorated tile idiom. Among the potters working in the contemporary vein in Portugal are Marie Louise Fragosa, Cecilia Alves de Sousa, Maria de Lourdes Castro and Jorge Barradas. An important potter is Beatriz Campos, who is also a painter. Decoration for her pottery has a spontaneous and natural charm that substantiates her reputation as a skillful modern painter. The French tapestry designer Lurçat helped to revitalize the Portuguese tapestry weavers of Oporto by furnishing them with designs. Among the native tapestry designers who are creating good designs distinctly Portuguese in color and feeling are Thomas de Mello, Antonio Lino, Maria Keil and Lima de Freitas. In glass the work of Thomas de Mello and Maria Helena Matos is outstanding.

Pot Lids In English ceramics; small pottery boxes, generally round, with transfer printed covers, were made in great quantities in the second half of the 19th century and were used for packaging cosmetics and foods such as fish pastes and honey. The art of transfer printing on pottery with colored pictures was perfected by Jesse Austin in 1846, working at the Messrs. Pratt's Pottery, Fenton, Staffordshire. Pictures were printed on various types of tableware but chiefly on pot lids. They included portraits of famous people, historical scenes and buildings, rural scenes and the like, in great variety. See *Historical Blue.*

Powell, Roger English bookbinder; worked with the firm of Douglas Cockerell and Son, becoming a partner in 1936. He set up his own bindery in Hampshire, in 1947. In addition to modern decorated binding, he specializes in the repair of early printed books and manuscripts. Recently he was commissioned to repair and rebind the BOOK OF KELLS. See *English Contemporary Arts and Crafts.*

Pre-Raphaelites In English art; late in 1848 three friends, the English painters Millais, Hunt and Rossetti, initiated the famous Pre-Raphaelite movement in art. They were joined in time by five others, all together comprising the Pre-Raphaelite Brotherhood. It was formed to rescue the great school of English portrait painters of the 18th century from the academicism into which they had fallen and, in general, to rescue English painting from a phase of triviality. The Pre-Raphaelites saw in Raphael an apostate from the ideal and a high priest of academicism. They fashioned themselves after Botticelli and Mantegna. The Brotherhood was allied with the Gothic revival, and like it eloquently defended by Ruskin. Artists such as Rossetti, Hunt, Burne-Jones and Brown designed and/or painted furniture at some time in their career. Their influence stemmed from the workshop of Morris, where they worked in direct collaboration with Morris and where cooperation between artist and artisan became the watchword of the day. See *Burne-Jones, Sir Edward; Brown, Ford Madox; Rossetti, Dante Gabriel; Morris, William; Morris, Marshall, Faulkner and Co.*

Pressed Glass In American glass; a process whereby molten metal is poured into a patterned mold and a plunger is then inserted, forcing the glass into all parts of the mold and in this way impressing the pattern on it. As the plunger is smooth the corresponding surface of a piece of pressed glass is also smooth. In 1827 Deming Jarves, who established the Boston and Sandwich Glass Works in 1825, perfected a mold and a hand-operated machine. With these he produced a tumbler which marked a great revolution in glassmaking. A drawing of this first pressed glass tumbler is still extant, which shows that it was a simple bull's eye pattern between two pillars. Like blown three mold, pressed glass was in imitation of cut glass, and as the cut glass patterns at this time were of a simple nature, so were the early pressed glass patterns. The perfection of the machine led to the production of a variety known as Lacy glass that had a delicacy and intricacy which would not have been possible to attain in cut glass. Examples included all kinds of tableware, lamps, candlesticks and vases. Eventually it was produced in a variety of colors: blue, green, vaseline, amethyst, as well as translucent and opaque white. The Boston and Sandwich Glass Company of Sandwich, Massachusetts, 1825–1888, was pre-eminent as makers of pressed glass. Two hundred and seventy-nine pressed glass patterns, with additional variations, have been identified. From about 1850 onwards, pressed glass is generally referred to as pressed pattern glass or simply pattern glass. See *Milk-White Glass; Black Milk Glass; Marble Glass; Pattern Glass.*

Prestini, James b. 1908. American, born in Italy, engineer and designer-craftsman; well known for his "art in wood," his wood bowls, trays and platters. The forms he creates on the lathe are notable for their classic simplicity and his highly developed sense of design. The magical thinness of his work, designed without fear of its shattering in the process, is dependent upon his technical knowledge of wood characteristics.

Printed Wares In American ceramics; the development of printed pottery was cut short in the United States owing to the tremendous quantity and the almost endless range of attractive patterns and colors produced and exported by the Staffordshire and Liverpool potteries. It is generally accepted that American printed wares were first made around 1839. See *Historical Blue; Transfer Printed Decoration*, page 485.

Proto-Art Nouveau The name given to an English stylistic phenomenon that occurred about 20 years before the Continental movement in the 1890's to which the name Art Nouveau has been given. These English trends dating up to the mid-1890's are not all Art Nouveau but possessed several of the most important elements which were to form an essential part of the style and directly

THE MODERN MOVEMENT AND THE TWENTIETH CENTURY

CHANTARELLE
VASE
TAPIO WIRKKALA,
20th century

BRASS FLOOR LAMP
1950

SWEDISH GLASSES
ORREFORS, *20th century*

SILVER SPOON
HEMMING KOPPEL, *1957*

TEACUP
TRUDE PETRI-RABEN, *1929*

PEDESTAL CHAIR
EERO SAARINEN, *1957*

PLYWOOD CHAIR
CHARLES EAMES, *1946*

STEEL WIRE CHAIR
HARRY BERTOIA, *1952*

TUBULAR STEEL CHAIR
MARCEL BREUER, *1925*

PLYWOOD CHAIR
ALVAR AALTO, *c. 1934*

HARDOY CHAIR
1938

BARCELONA CHAIR
MIËS VAN DER ROHE, *1929*

BLANKET CHEST
WENDELL CASTLE, *c. 1965*

BED
KAARE KLINT, *mid-20th century*

ITALIAN CERAMIC JAR
GUIDO GAMBONE, *20th century*

foreshadowed the later international style. It remained an English phenomenon, an off-shoot of the Arts and Crafts Movement with emphasis on linear and floral decoration. Art Nouveau itself failed to develop in England due to the vigor of the Arts and Crafts Movement. See *Art Nouveau; Arts and Crafts Movement.*

Prouvé, Emile Victor b. 1858. French sculptor, graphic and decorative artist; a pupil and then later a friend and collaborator of Gallé. He decorated some of Gallé's work with inscriptions. See *Meubles Parlants; Gallé, Emile.*

Pugin, Augustus Welby Northmore 1812–1852. English architect, designer and writer; first started to design in the Gothic style at the age of fifteen, making furniture designs for Morel and Seddon. From 1837 until his death he wrote numerous books and pamphlets and designed large quantities of stained glass and metalwork (mostly for church use) and also furniture, wallpapers, textiles and jewelry. His great achievement rests in his writings; as a theorist among Victorians his position is indisputable. In CONTRASTS, 1836, he writes, "The great test of beauty is the fitness of design for the purpose for which it was intended." He despised the trade Gothic furniture, "cheap deceptions of magnificence," resulting from the style that he and his father, A. C. Pugin, had done so much to foster. See *Gothic Revival, English.*

Purple Slag See *Marble Glass.*

Pyrex In American glass; in 1908 the Corning Glass Works developed the first glass capable of withstanding sudden jolts of heat or cold. These borosilicate glasses (so called because of the large amounts of borax used in the formula) were first used to make railway signal lanterns, later became well known to millions of housewives as Pyrex, a brand of glass ovenware and kitchenware. See *Glass-Ceramics; Centura Tableware.*

Q

Quervelle, Anthony G. 1789–1856 Parisian-born cabinetmaker who was disseminating his native Empire style in Philadelphia before 1817. Competent and successful, this cabinetmaker was widely patronized not only by immigrant French aristocrats but also by the White House. Quervelle's label on a secretary made around 1835 reads "Cabinet and Sofa Manufactory, South Second Street, a few doors below Dock, Philadelphia." See *Bouvier, Michel.*

Quezal In American glass; one of the first imitations of Tiffany iridescent glass. It was named after the quetzal bird of Central America, noted for its long feathers of iridescent golden-green. The short-lived Quezal Art Glass and Decorating Company was listed in the Brooklyn directory from 1916 to 1918. See *Iridescent Glass.*

R

Ramsden, Omar 1873–1939. English artist, goldsmith and silversmith; about 1898 set up partnership with Alwyn C. E. Carr. They specialized in ceremonial pieces of gold and silver, but also worked in wrought iron and pewter. Ramsden exhibited extensively in England and abroad. See *English Contemporary Arts and Crafts.*

Randall, Theodore A. b. 1914. American artist-potter, sculptor and teacher; has done extensive research in ceramics, discovering or perfecting innumerable bodies, slips and glazes for artist-potters. He was elected a Fellow of the American Ceramic Society in 1960.

Rathbone, Richard Llewellyn Benson 1864–1939. English metalworker; early study of metalwork possibly was under the influence of William Benson, a relative. At various times Rathbone had workshops at Liverpool, the Menai Bridge, Wales, and in London, mostly turning out objects in base metals. After he came to London he was increasingly interested in the making of unit metalwork. See *Benson, William.*

Rattan See *Cane.*

Ravenna Glass See *Palmqvist, Sven.*

Rebekah at the Well Teapot In American ceramics; made in brown or Rockingham glaze, this teapot was designed and modeled by Charles Coxon at the E. & W. Bennett Company of Baltimore in 1852. He adapted it from an earlier model produced by S. Alcock and Company of Burslem, England, the original being a Parian jug with a blue ground and a raised figure of Rebekah in white. Subsequently Rebekah at the Well teapots were made at a number of potteries.

Rayon The first man-made fiber; designed to imitate silks. It was developed in Europe at the end of the 19th century; the first rayon manufactory was built in the United States in 1910. See *Synthetic Fibers.*

Red Rose Guild of Craftsmen See *Craft Centre of Great Britain.*

Redware In American ceramics; lead-glazed utility wares ranging in color from pinkish buff to reds and reddish browns. Also called Red-clay Pottery.

Reed and Barton In American silver; perhaps the earliest Britannia metal ware in the United States was made by Babbitt, Crossman and Company, organized in 1827 at Taunton, Massachusetts, who were the forerunners of Reed and Barton. By either 1840 or 1847 Britannia metal was produced which bore the name Reed and Barton. By 1848 Reed and Barton was focusing its attention on silver-plated ware. Solid silver services were added to their production in 1889.

Registration Mark From 1842 to 1883 a maker working in glass, metal, wood and pottery could register a design or shape with the London Patent Office as a protection against piracy by other manufacturers for an initial period of three years. These were given a diamond-shaped device with code letters and numerals in the corners of the diamond, from which the exact date of registration can be determined. They appeared in two cycles, 1842–1867 and 1868–1883. From January 1884 registered designs were numbered successively and these numbers appear on wares with the prefix "Rd. No." or "Rd."

Reich Mark In German silver; the Reich silver mark is the quarter moon and crown, which came into use in 1886. It was stamped on pieces only of a specified silver content. The pieces are 800 parts pure silver and 200 parts base metal. This quality is less than the English sterling standard of 925 parts silver per thousand.

Rekston See *Stockton Art Pottery.*

Reeves, Ann Wynn b. 1929. English ceramist and oil painter; shares a studio with her husband, silversmith and ceramist Kenneth Clark. She specializes in colored glazes with a majolica technique and has completed several large architectural ceramic murals. See *Clark, Kenneth; English Contemporary Arts and Crafts.*

Reynal, Jeanne b. 1903. American designer-craftsman; one of the leading modern mosaicists. She has freed mosaics from the Byzantine tradition of fitting the stones tightly together, using an arrangement which permits space around each stone for "breathing," so that each stone counts for itself, as an entity. For her free-standing mosaics she uses the same armature for both sides.

Reyntiens, Patrick b. 1925. English stained glass artist; apart from executing his own designs, he collaborated with John Piper on the great baptistery window, Coventry Cathedral, and eight windows for Eton College Chapel. See *Piper, John; English Contemporary Arts and Crafts.*

Rhodes, Daniel b. 1911. American designer-craftsman, teacher and writer; has achieved eminence as a potter. As a writer of pottery and design his influence has been significant. He is the author of STONEWARE AND PORCELAIN: THE ART OF HIGH-FIRED POTTERY, 1959.

Richardson, Henry Hobson 1838–1886. American architect. He also did furniture design; much of it was integral with the interior woodwork of the churches, libraries and other public buildings he designed. Extant movable pieces reveal their simple and sound construction; most of them are related to the contemporary furniture made by the Morris firm. See *La Farge, John.*

Rie, Lucie b. 1902. English artist-potter born in Austria, trained in the Vienna Arts and Crafts School; settled in England in 1938. She became one of the most accomplished potters working in England. Clarity of outline and precision of detail characterize her work. See *English Contemporary Arts and Crafts.*

Riemerschmid, Richard 1868–1957. German architect and designer; a founding member of the Münchener Vereinigte Werkstätten Für Kunst in Handwerk, with Obrist, Pankok and Paul. His designs for furniture around 1900 are of a distinctly simple and functional style. He became one of the leaders of modern German decorative art. From 1912 to 1924 he was director of the School of Applied Arts in Munich. See *Munich School.*

Rietveld, Gerrit b. 1888. Dutch architect; one of the best-known exponents of De Stijl. He also designed furniture. In a wood armchair designed in 1917, Rietveld attained an effect of relative weightlessness by separating supporting and supported parts, painted blue, red and black. Horizontal elements avoid each other by means of a bypass and do not rest directly on their vertical supports. In this manner the chair seems to be held together by magnetism, since the actual connection is hidden. See *De Stijl.*

Riihimaki Glass Works See *Finnish Contemporary Arts and Crafts.*

Rika, Eliahu b. 1938. Israeli glass artist born in Syria; came to Israel in 1949. Went to work in a glassworks, where he was taught to turn glass tubes. In his spare time he began to turn waste glass tubes into very charming vases. At present he is working for the Crafts Center Batsheva in Tel Aviv, making and designing his own models, inspired by ancient Israeli, Phoenician and Egyptian glass, yet with a character all his own. The majority of these models are decorated with glass ribbons, threads, prunts, etc., in the manner of Islamic glass.

Robineau, Adelaide Alsop d. 1929. American artist-potter of Syracuse, New York; began as a china painter. She founded the magazine KERAMIC STUDIO, which became the official mouthpiece of an organization for china painters. One of the earliest artist-potters in America, she started to make and decorate pottery about 1903 and later learned to throw on the wheel. Her individual porcelains won international honors; her Scarab Vase is her most celebrated piece.

Rocking Chair In American furniture; it is generally accepted that rocking chairs were not made before 1800; if the chair was made prior to that date the rockers were added later.

Rockingham In American ceramics; a brown glazed pottery from which many household items were made. This kind of ware was first produced in Swinton, England, at the private pottery owned by the Marquis of Rockingham. Also made there and known today as Rockingham were many fine porcelain tea sets. In America, however, Rockingham generally denotes a coarse ware with a brown tortoise-shell mottled glaze. The solid brown Rockingham was not produced in as large amounts as the mottled type. From around 1840 to 1900 almost every sizable pottery in America produced Rockingham. The brown color in American Rockingham is inherent in the glaze itself. It is seldom marked, and it is incorrect to give the generic name Bennington to this ware, as most of it was made elsewhere. See *Bennington*, page 40; *Rockingham*, page 400.

Rogers and Mead See *Electroplating*.

Rogers Brothers In American silver; about 1843–1844 the Rogers Brothers began to experiment with the electroplating process and in 1847, at Hartford, Connecticut, Asa Rogers Jr., with his brothers William and Simeon, produced and distributed silver-plated spoons bearing the Rogers Brothers' trade-mark. They offered for sale the first successful electroplated wares in the United States. Owing to the increasing volume of business they organized a new company, Rogers Brothers Manufacturing Company, in 1853. William Rogers left the company in 1856 and with George Smith, manufacturers of silver-plated hollow-ware, established Rogers, Smith and Company. In 1861 the two companies were consolidated. In 1862 the Meriden Britannia Company bought the tools and dies of the company. William Rogers joined the Meriden Britannia Company to direct the manufacture of the 1847 Rogers Brothers wares. Other later companies with which the Rogers brothers were affiliated include: William Rogers Manufacturing Company, Hartford, Connecticut, 1865; Rogers and Brother Company, Waterbury, Connecticut, 1858; Rogers Cutlery Company, Hartford, 1871. All became part of the International Silver Company in 1898. See *Electroplating*; *Meriden Britannia Company*; *International Silver Company*.

Rohde, Johan See *Jensen, Georg.*

Rohe, Ludwig Miës van der b. 1886. American, born in Germany, architect and designer; succeeded Gropius as director of the Bauhaus. He was one of the great innovators of chromium-plated steel furniture. His Barcelona chair, which entrusts the sitter's weight to cantileverage, has become a classic. This steel chair with supporting leather straps and tufted leather cushions received its name from the International Exposition at Barcelona, 1929, where Miës's pavilion for the German government won world acclaim. The best qualities of his work, economy of line, beauty of proportion and extreme simplicity, are revealed in this chair. See *Bauhaus*.

Rookwood Pottery In American ceramics; in 1880 Mrs. Marion Longworth Nichols Storer established her own pottery at Cincinnati, Ohio, and named it Rookwood. Ten years later Mrs. Storer withdrew, but by then the pottery was a successful company. In 1892 the manufactory was moved to a group of buildings near the Cincinnati Art Museum where it still operates in a limited way. The decoration and shapes of these wares were strongly influenced by orientalism and Proto-Art Nouveau. Vases were the principal product. Among the most outstanding decorators working at Rookwood before 1900 were Albert R. Valentien, A. van Briggle, Matthew E. Daly, Kataro Shirayamadani and E. P. Cranch. Characteristic marks are: from 1880 to 1882 an overglaze painted "Rookwood Pottery, Ohio"; from 1882 to 1886 an impressed mark, "Rookwood" and the year; in 1886 the monogram mark consisting of a reversed "R" and "P" was adopted. In 1887 a flame point was placed above the monogram and one point was added for each year thereafter. Therefore the mark for 1900 had fourteen flames. In 1901 the same mark was used with the addition of a Roman numeral below to indicate the first year of the new century. Since that time the mark comprises the monogram, the fourteen flames and the Roman numeral of the particular year of the 20th century in which the object was made.

Rosanjin, Kitaoji 1883–1959. Japanese artist-potter; belongs to that group of potters who devoted their life work to the revival and continuation of some of the traditional Japanese pottery styles. In this manner they have enriched, preserved and continued the classic styles. His wares show a deference to such traditional styles as Bizen, Oribe, Shino and Kizeto. See *Seto*.

Rose Medallion In Chinese ceramics; the name given to a green enamelled dinner ware with medallions of people, pink flowers, birds and butterflies that became a popular export ware from late in the 18th century. Its popularity continued throughout the 19th century. Much of the ware was decorated at Canton and shipped from that port. See *Canton Ware; Canton*, page 81.

Rossetti, Dante Gabriel 1828–1882. English poet and painter; an impassioned medievalist. In all matters of taste Rossetti's influence has been enormous. He may be said to have rejuvenated the decorative arts both directly and indirectly. See *Pre-Raphaelites; Burne-Jones, Sir Edward*.

Rousseau, Eugène 1827–1891. French glass designer specializing in faïence work. He made designs for glass models, 1867, and later entered partnership with Appert Frères at Clichy. A pioneer in modern Art glass, his most original contribution was a technique of inlaying streaks of contrasting colors and textures.

Royal School of Needlework In English needlework; established in 1872, the school had a twofold purpose: it was a center for producing and selling art needlework, and a training school for students. The school commissioned designs from Morris, Burne-Jones, Crane, Image and other prominent designers. Other similar bodies were founded: Leek Embroidery Society about 1879, Ladies' Work Society about 1875, the Decorative Needlework Society, 1888, and the Embroiderers' Guild, 1906. See *Embroidery*.

Roysher, Hudson c. 1912. American designer-craftsman; noted for the liturgical objects he has produced in silver and brass. His simple, straightforward forms designed to be used in worship are in constant demand. All through his professional life he has divided his time between industrial design and silversmithing. His commissions include the Syracuse University Charter Mace of sterling silver with carnelian and lapis lazuli, 1959.

Rozenburg Pottery Company In Dutch ceramics; active c. 1894–1916 at the Hague. Its first foreign showing was at the Paris Exposition, 1900. Of a number of pottery firms whose decorated wares became one of Holland's most characteristic contributions to Art Nouveau the best known was Rozenburg. T. A. C. Colenbrander was the company's most outstanding designer. Also notable were the forms designed by J. Juriaen Kok and decorated by J. Shelling for Rozenberg.

Ruhlmann, Jacques 1869–1932. French interior designer; his work exercised a wide and beneficial influence on interior decoration in France. His furniture relied for its beauty on the general harmony and balance of lines. Some of his chairs and cabinets have the legs partly included as part of the body of the piece itself, a device initiated by Ruhlmann and much imitated. See *Art Moderne*.

Rumford, Count See *Thompson, Benjamin*.

Ruskin, John 1819–1900. English writer and critic. See *Gothic Revival, English*.

Russell, Sir Gordon b. 1892. English industrial designer; an outstandingly successful figure in the field of design for both hand-made and machine-made furniture. Russell began with furniture in the Gimson tradition, later also developing factory production of well-designed furniture. He was also largely responsible for the design of "utility" furniture during World War II, when there was a timber shortage. The result was to provide the public with a complete range of furniture of good construction, simple and attractive lines, at a reasonable price. A director of the Council of Industrial Design of Great Britain, he was elected one of the forty Royal Designers for Industry in 1940 and a First Fellow of the Society of Industrial Artists in 1945.

S

Saarinen, Eero 1910–1961. American, born in Finland, architect-designer; in 1946 he introduced a molded plastic shell armchair. The capacious shell, upholstered in foam rubber, was held up cradle-fashion in a skeleton-like tubular steel framework mounted on four conventionalized steel legs. This skillfully designed easy chair offered such pleasant protection to the occupant that it was dubbed the "womb chair." In 1957 he introduced his molded chalice-like pedestal chair; it was designed with a single stem and base in place of the customary four legs.

Sachlichkeit A development which followed the short-lived Jugendstil in Germany. The term, which has no English equivalent, became the slogan for the ever-expanding Modern Movement. Partisans of Sachlichkeit admired the comfort and cleanness of English work of the 1890's. From the modern designer they asked perfect and pure utility, creation for use; practical undecorated furniture in smooth polished light forms. Some of the earliest results of this campaign were revealed at an industrial art exhibition in Dresden, 1906. As a whole the furniture was neat and comfortable, of a simple classical character with all gingerbread removed. It was not revolutionary but reasonable; the style was created for the machine. See *Muthesius, Hermann.*

S.A.L.I.R. In Italian glass; a glassworks established in 1923 and managed by Giuseppe d'Alpaos and Decio Toso. S.A.L.I.R. specializes in the decorative techniques of engraving, cutting, gilding and painting. See *Murano Glass.*

Salviati and Company In Italian glass; a glassworks established in 1866 by Antonio Salviati, who wanted to revive the glory of the ancient Venetian art of glassmaking on the island of Murano, with its subtle technical skills and superb craftsmanship. The work turned out to be unmistakably mid-19th century. Salviati's descendants were most successful in making beautiful modern glass. See *Venini, Paolo; Murano Glass.*

Sanders, Herbert b. 1909. American artist-potter and teacher; his work includes decorative and utilitarian pottery and porcelain forms. Many of these are glazed with the crystalline glazes for which he is especially well known. He is the author of POTTERY AND CERAMIC SCULPTURE, 1964.

Sarpaneva, Timo See *Finnish Contemporary Arts and Crafts.*

Scheier, Edwin and May American artist-potters; most of their pieces are made on the wheel and are notable for their simplicity. As a rule the principal decoration is the simple and effective striping which follows the motion of the wheel, a characteristic of Scheier pottery. On their ambitious pieces the decoration is generally incised or modelled or both. Bold primitive figures, contemporary in idiom, are typical.

Schmidt, Karl 1861–1948. German designer, trained as a cabinetmaker; in 1898 started a furniture workshop in Dresden. Here from the first he employed modern architects and artists as designers. He began under the influence of the English Arts and Crafts Movement, but soon his interest became chiefly inexpensiveness and production by machinery. See *Deutsche Werkstätten*.

School of Arts and Crafts See *Ashbee, Charles R.*

Schwartz, June b. 1918. American enameller; specializes in the art of basse taille enamel work. Her pieces, chiefly bowls, boxes and plaques, are small in scale and possess the jewel-like quality usually associated with this craft.

Scrimshaw An American whaling folk art developed early in the 19th century by New England whalers. The term is given to the object created and also to the method of carving or etching on whale's teeth or whalebone by the whalers. The art was peculiarly American, and was adapted no doubt from the earlier folk art of carving in ivory on elephant and walrus tusks. Extant examples of Scrimshaw date from 1827 and 1828; the former shows a slave ship and a slave. Probably two of the most common kinds of Scrimshaw are the busk and the jagging or crimping wheel. The busk made of whalebone was the bodice stay in the corsets worn by ladies, while the crimping wheel was a kind of device that made a design along the edge of a pie. Among the wide variety of Scrimshaw articles were workboxes, napkin rings, canes, spool holders, clothespins and the like. In this folk art the design was generally outlined on the surface. Frequently a picture from a book was pasted on the surface and the detail was transferred by pricking in the outlines. The use of ink to complete the work was the usual practice. Colored ink afforded fine touches for the design. Though the work was often crude, notable examples were produced in this folk art medium.

Scroddled Ware In American ceramics; occasionally called lava ware or solid agate ware; often confused with the more easily made marble ware, which was never produced at Bennington and has surface decoration only. Scroddled ware comprises different-colored clays (generally brown to reddish-brown and grey) mixed with cream-colored clay. The different-colored clays were mixed together in such a way that the striations went through the entire piece and were visible outside and inside. The article was given a clear glaze and then fired. The variegated clay fused together, not unlike a marble cake, with a solid body of different mixed striations. Scroddled ware was not produced in quantity at Bennington because the demand was small and the process costly. See *Bennington*, page 41.

Secession The Austrian version of Art Nouveau; a term deriving from the union of advanced Viennese painters and sculptors founded in 1896 under the name Wiener Sezession. It is irrevocably connected with the architects Josef Hoffmann and Joseph Olbrich. Though the early work of the Secessionists includes examples in the curvilinear vein, even before 1900 they began – especially Hoffmann, Olbrich and Loos – to create a style confined to the refined and rational development of architecture and furniture design that bypassed Art Nouveau and led directly to the Modern Movement with its completely new stylistic ideals. The Secession was almost entirely concentrated in Vienna. Its headquarters was in Olbrich's cube-shaped building; its publication was VER SACRUM, begun in 1898 and notable for its square format. Vienna rapidly became an international center for new directions in art and design which were spread across Austria and Europe through the Wiener-Werkstätte. See *Hoffmann, Josef; Olbrich, Joseph; Wiener Werkstätte; Klimt, Gustav; Moser, Koloman; Loos, Adolf; Wagner, Otto; Art Nouveau.*

Second Empire 1852–1870. In French furniture; all the ingredients of the style, both form and decoration, were taken from the previous styles extending over a period of 500 years. However, underlying its incongruous appearance, a distinctive richness, sumptuousness, brilliance and vivid colors gave it an undeniable unity that offset its mode of imitation. For this reason the Second Empire left a deep impression on the art of furniture making. The ambitious furniture was well constructed and made from the finest materials. Oak was restricted to Neo-Renaissance or Revived Renaissance, where carving played an important role which continued to be reproduced almost without a break from 1835 to 1900. Violet wood and ebony were most fashionable as they provided a superb background for the ornamentation. On less costly pieces fruitwood was dyed black in imitation of ebony. Often in seat furniture no wood was visible under a wealth of upholstery, plain stuffed upholstery being supplanted by button upholstery. The Louis XIV style also had its devotees, with copies of André Charles Boulle's work much in evidence. The Second Empire ébénistes found Rococo very attractive; Louis XV style enjoyed a great vogue around 1855 onwards. A few years later the Neo-Pompeiian style was glorified, while from around 1865 the Empress Eugénie embraced everything connected with Marie Antoinette as pseudo-Riesener furniture had its hour of glory. Among the best ébénistes of the Second Empire period were Grohé, Fourdinois and Tahan. See *Victorian.*

Secrest, James and Philip c. 1920. American ceramists; two brothers who work as a team. Their individual pieces are similar—they both use the same bodies, glazes and firing techniques—but they can be distinguished by different approaches to finish and decoration. James' pottery usually incorporates graphic effects achieved with brush, tool or stamp, while Philip's forms are usually amplified with textural or all-over surface treatment. They are best known for their footed stoneware jars, casseroles and other utilitarian vessels, such as mugs, pitchers, plates and bowls.

Sedding, John Dando 1838–1891. English architect and designer; in 1874 established himself in London as an architect and a designer of wallpapers, embroidery and church metalwork. After meeting Ruskin in 1876, he placed himself under his guidance.

Seguso Verti D'Arte In Italian glass; a glassworks founded in 1932 under the direction of Angelo and Bruno Seguso, with Flavio Poli as artistic director until 1963. It is one of the most skillful renovators of Murano glass in the field of contemporary forms. See *Venini, Paolo; Murano Glass.*

Seignouret, François b. 1768. Born in France; settled around 1815 in New Orleans, where he had a cabinet shop on Royal Street until his return to France in 1853. Seignouret was regarded as New Orleans' most fashionable cabinetmaker. Especially notable is his so-called Seignouret chair of gondola form with a splat back, and his massive armoires, which he made for plantation houses of consequence.

Selbing, John See *Swedish Modern Glass.*

Serrurier-Bovy, Gustave 1858–1910. Belgian architect and designer of interior decoration and furniture; his refreshingly simple furniture was inspired by the Arts and Crafts Movement. English influence is evident in the constructive striving and lack of decoration. A marked feature of his furniture, but one not borrowed from England, is slightly curved supports giving the effect of a series of arches, which he freely placed, always diagonally, where they were or were not needed. These slightly arched trusses were adopted and transformed by Van de Velde, becoming one of his most characteristic design principles. See *Belgian Art Nouveau.*

Shaw, Richard Norman 1831–1912. English architect and designer, born in Edinburgh; in the early 1860's designed small quantities of furniture in the Gothic style. From around 1882 he designed stained and painted furniture.

Shigaraki In Japanese ceramics; an important center for handcrafted pottery, located near the old capitals of Nara and Kyōto. There is a good clay deposit in Shigaraki; the clay is suitable for making large objects such as charcoal braziers, jardinières and garden ornaments. The history of Shigaraki pottery is very old. Roof tiles were baked at Shigaraki in the 8th century, when the Emperor Shomu built a villa nearby. See *Japanese Contemporary Ceramics*.

Silver Glass In American glass; in 1855 the New England Glass Company secured a patent for a curious Victorian novelty called silver glass, which had great popularity in its day. Silver glass was made in two layers. The clear glass was blown first, then the nitrate of silver was blown into the hollow space between the layers, through a hole in the base. The base was then sealed. Nitrate of silver came in many colors.

Silver-plate See *Electroplate*.

Sinclaire, H. P., and Company In American glass; Sinclaire cut glass was of fine quality and included many excellent original patterns and forms designed by Sinclaire himself. Some of the finest intaglio work ever done was made by this company. Their trade-mark was "Sinclaire" or "S" in a wreath. This distinguished company closed in 1929 shortly after the death of Mr. Sinclaire. See *Cut Glass, American*.

Sinumbra Literally, without shadow. The name given to a type of lamp that is synonymous with astral. This lamp was widely popular in America from around 1830 to 1850. See *Astral Lamp*, page 23.

Society of Arts and Crafts An American national society founded in Boston in 1897 stemming from the English Arts and Crafts Movement. As the Arts and Crafts Exhibition Society, established in 1888, this society held exhibitions to stimulate public appreciation for the work of American craftsmen.

Soda-Lime Glass See *Pattern Glass*.

Solar Lamp Patented by Cornelius and Company of Philadelphia in 1843. Constructed to burn lard oil and built on the general principle of Argand's, it had an oil font under the burner, a round wick and a bulb-shaped glass chimney. The latter, its special feature, created a kind of hot air chamber in which the free carbon was consumed. This gave a brilliant, clear, steady light that was far superior to any lamp made up to that time. They were widely popular simultaneously with astral lamps in the 1840's and the 1850's. See *Argand Lamp*, page 18.

Soldner, Paul b. 1921. American artist-potter; constantly experimenting. His most recent work has been with Raku pottery, a low-fired soft pottery with a thick lead glaze, created in Kyōto, Japan, in the second half of the 16th century and valued first by the devotees of the tea ceremony. Soldner's work has had a considerable influence on American artist-potters.

Solon, Louis Marc 1835–1913. French ceramist, outstanding among 19th century artists. He worked first at Sèvres, perfecting the process of pâte-sur-pâte introduced there in 1847. In 1870 Solon moved to England and was employed by Minton until 1904. He is known not only for his magnificent work in the pâte-sur-pâte or cameo style but also for pieces with sgraffiato or incised decoration. See *Pâte-sur-Pâte*, page 353; *Sgraffiato*, page 428.

Sowers, Robert b. 1923. American stained glass artist and writer; studied stained glass techniques in England from 1950 to 1953. Since that time he has designed a great number of stained glass windows and other compositions for buildings throughout the United States. He is the author of THE LOST

ART: A SURVEY OF ONE THOUSAND YEARS OF STAINED GLASS, 1954, and STAINED GLASS: AN ARCHITECTURAL ART, 1955.

Spanish Art Nouveau   See *Gaudi, Antonio.*

Spook School   The name often given in England to the group of designers working with Charles R. Mackintosh, because his furniture forms—especially his chair backs—as well as his motifs were markedly elongated, having an eerie quality.   See *Mackintosh, Charles R.*

Staatliches Bauhaus   See *Bauhaus.*

Staghorn Furniture   A suite of staghorn furniture comprising seating pieces and tables made in Hamburg was exhibited at the Great Exhibition of 1851. Planned for a hunting lodge or baronial mansion, these grotesque pieces attracted the sentimental. The furniture also charmed Queen Victoria, who ordered a suite for Balmoral made from trophies of Prince Albert's prowess. The taste spread to the United States, as may be seen in extant pieces of horn furniture dating from the late 19th or early 20th century.

Stahly, Claude (signs **Claude**)   French bookbinder; a distinguished binder since 1934, known for her singular mosaic technique in leather. In recent years she has explored the fields of collage and tapestry. Her collages in mural format have given origin to her tapestries, which essentially bring together these two expressions.

Stainless Steel   The introduction of stainless steel alloys in Germany and England shortly before World War I furnished an important impetus to the development of new forms for cutlery. These alloys made available for the first time a relatively inexpensive metal whose exceptional corrosion-resistance and hardness made it ideally suitable for tableware. In the late 1920's a number of European designers and manufacturers began to pioneer development of quality stainless steel flatware in simple forms appropriate to such a tough metal. In the United States stainless steel knives, forks and spoons were not accepted as quality products in their own right until after World War II.

Stenberg, Marianne   See *Swedish Modern Glass.*

Steuben Glass   In American glass; for centuries the world's glassmakers had tried to produce a flawless, transparent "crystal," that is, a colorless but brilliant glass which would possess the sparkling clarity of natural rock crystal. In 1932 a chemical formula for pure crystal achieved without discoloration was perfected at the Corning Glass Works. In the following year Arthur A. Houghton founded a "new" Steuben Glass for the purpose of exploiting the artistic possibilities of this exciting new material. As director of design he engaged the architect John Monteith Gates, who in turn called in the sculptor Sidney Waugh as chief designer. In 1937, at the Paris Exposition, Gates met the celebrated painter Henri Matisse, who was so impressed with the potentialities of design inherent in the matchless crystal that he offered to make a drawing for Steuben, to be engraved in crystal. Next Gates commissioned drawings to be engraved by Steuben craftsmen from a group of well-known American and European artists. Twenty-seven separate pieces by 27 contemporary artists had been executed by 1940 in editions of six examples of each design. This collection of works of art in crystal is notable for the effective collaboration of artist and craftsman, and after World War II this practice of commissioning artists to design models was continued. Under the tutelage of Gates and Waugh, such talented Steuben designers as George Thompson, Don Weir and John Dreves have all created original work which evokes fully the special brilliance of the pure crystal glass. Steuben also makes presentation pieces for particular occasions such as the visits of royalty and heads of state.   See *Carder, Frederick.*

Stickney, Gustav   American furniture designer, manufacturer and publisher active in the early years of the 20th century. His Mission-style oak furniture which he called

Craftsman was known for its good design. Also published THE CRAFTSMAN MAGAZINE. He subscribed to the theories of William Morris and the Arts and Crafts Movement. See *Hubbard, Elbert; Mission Furniture.*

Stocksdale, Bob b. 1913. American designer-craftsman; specializes in wood bowls, trays, plates, etc., which he turns on a lathe. His creative pieces, made of exotic hardwoods carefully selected for beauty of form and color, are notable for their paper-like thinness, the mark of perfection in this kind of work.

Stockton Art Pottery In American ceramics; a firm active in Stockton, California, 1891-1902, and originally called the Stockton Terra Cotta Company. They were noted for a special art ware which they called "Rekston." This was characterized by heavy colored glazes on enamels and included such pieces as jardinières, umbrella stands and vases.

Strengall, Marianne American, born in Finland, weaver and designer, teacher and writer; an important figure on the American textile scene who has introduced elements of Scandinavian tradition to the United States. She was head of the department of weaving at Cranbrook Academy of Art from 1942 to 1961. Working for industry has been a steady occupation for her, and experimenting with new yarns and fabrics has been an important part of that job.

Stretching In silver; the forming method called stretching is particularly suited to the development of free-form design in silver hollow ware. Known from early times, its use as a craft technique in the United States is recent. Stretching is achieved by beating a relatively thick disc of metal to thin it to the desired shape, striking chiefly on the inside of the developing form. The distinguishing mark that sets stretched silver apart from other forms of hollow ware is the rim, which is a thick strong edge tapering gracefully up out of the body of the piece and making it look, feel and wear better. In the stretching method, which is ideal for irregular shapes, the metal really flows under the blows of the hammer. Stretching is not practical for all forms of hollow ware. A combination of stretching and raising (done by beating a relatively thin sheet of metal so as to contract and thicken it into shape, striking mostly on the outside of the form) is often a more flexible solution to a design problem in hollow ware. See *Miller, Frederick A.*

Strömbergshyttan See *Swedish Modern Glass.*

Studio-Craftsman The individual artist-craftsman. See *Artist-Craftsman.*

Style Inglese See *Arts and Crafts Exhibition Society.*

Style Liberty See *Arts and Crafts Exhibition Society.*

Suë et Mare See *Art Moderne.*

Sullivan, Louis 1856-1926. American architect; an important pioneer of modern design. In his ORNAMENT IN ARCHITECTURE, 1892, he says, "Ornament is mentally a luxury, not a necessity." He was one of the first to believe in the machine and to understand its essential character. His most illustrious pupil was Frank Lloyd Wright. See *Modern Movement; Wright, Frank Lloyd; Loos, Adolf; Wagner, Otto; Velde, Henry van de.*

Summer, George Heywood Maunoir 1853-1940. English designer, archaeologist, painter and etcher; joined the Art Workers' Guild and was associated with Arthur Mackmurdo and the Century Guild. Summer was also a specialist in sgraffiato work and a designer of stained glass. *The Chase* by Summer is among the later tapestries produced by Morris and Co. He designed a music cabinet in 1889 on the door of which appears the text "The Charm of Orpheus." See *Meubles Parlants; Morris Firm Tapestries.*

Summerly's Art Manufactures In English decorative arts; started in 1847 by Felix Summerly (a pseudonym for Sir Henry

Cole). Cole believed that it would promote public taste if well-known painters and sculptors could be persuaded to produce designs for manufactured articles of daily use. This interesting enterprise, directed entirely toward improving contemporary industrial products, lasted for about three years. See *Cole, Sir Henry*.

Sutherland, Graham b. 1903. English painter and designer who began painting in 1930; has since exhibited widely and has been strikingly successful with his plant forms, portraits and religious subjects. He designed a giant tapestry, *Christ in Majesty with the Evangelists*, for Coventry Cathedral. See *English Contemporary Arts and Crafts*.

Swedish Contemporary Arts and Crafts Sweden, like Finland, has always had a very vital folk art, various arts and crafts being practiced by virtually the entire population. In 1845 the Society for the Promotion of the Arts and Crafts was founded and in 1899 the Swedish Home Crafts Association appeared. Since 1912 all local arts and crafts societies have been under a single national association called Svenska Hemslöjdsforeningarnas Riksförbund (shortened to Hemslöjds). The renaissance in Swedish arts and crafts strongly influenced contemporary designer-craftsmen. In the field of ceramics Wilhelm Kage, one-time art director of the modern Gustavsberg Porcelain Manufactory, is often called the grand old man of Swedish ceramics. His successor Stig Lindberg is well known for the flair and distinction he brings to his contemporary designs. At Rörstrand, Carl-Harry Stalhane (b. 1920) is the art director and chief designer. The designers Louise Adelberg and Gunnar Nylund pioneered in mass-produced functional wares, a development of the 1930's and 1940's. Sweden's great weaver was Märta Mass-Fjetterström (d. 1941), who had her own workshop in the little town of Bastad. Departing from traditional designs, she brought a lively creativity and a superlative color sense to Swedish weaving. Her influence in the art of handweaving extended far beyond Sweden. Sigvard Bernadotte, a member of the royal family, is well known as an artist-craftsman, designing in silver, textiles and bookbinding. See *Swedish Modern Glass; Swedish Modern Furniture; Fleming, Baron Erik*.

Swedish Modern Furniture In the 1920's the movement toward aesthetically improving machine-made products was accelerated in Sweden. Steeped as they were in handicraft tradition, the Swedish nevertheless believed and practiced that beauty and quality could be achieved through the furniture architect, as he is called in Sweden, and the manufacturer. Though Swedish modern has such famous designers as Carl Malmsten, Elias Svedberg, Karl Mathsson and Captain G. A. Berg, generally regarded as the apostle of contemporary Swedish, it is predominantly in the tradition of anonymous furniture. In this respect as well as in its standards of usefulness and sparse simplicity it is not unlike Shaker furniture. After its spectacular success at the New York World's Fair, 1939, it enjoyed a great vogue. Many Swedish pieces of graceful and modest design, such as chairs displaying the separation of the frame and upholstery, chairs with spindled backs, wood seats and turned legs and stretchers, cane-panelled low cupboards and slender sideboards, have had a fruitful influence on American furniture. See *Mathsson, Karl Bruno*.

Swedish Modern Glass Orrefors and Kosta are the two best-known glassworks in Sweden, one of the great centers for contemporary glassmaking. Orrefors, under the direction of the Ekman family since 1913, became one of the chief contributors to the modern glass movement. By 1917 two great designers, Simon Gate (1883–1945) and Edward Hald (b. 1883), joined the glassworks to direct the art policy. They were to make the name of Orrefors famous. In 1927 they were joined by John Selbing and, in 1935, Nils Landberg and Sven Palmqvist. In 1947 Ingeborg Lundin joined the glassworks. The sculptor Edvin Ohrström is the designer responsible today for most of the Ariel glass, deriving its name from Shakespeare's spirit of the air, characterized by air bubbles in which the light is glitteringly reflected. Orrefors has made a world-wide reputation for itself because of the excellent quality of its crystal and the purity of its designs, now imitated in most countries. Kosta's best-known designers include Ewald Dahlskog, Elis Bergh and Vicke Lindstrand. There is also the Gullaskrufs Glassworks, founded in 1927; its best designers are Marianne Stenberg and Hugo Gehlin. One of the smaller glassworks is A. B. Strombergsshyttan near Orrefors; Gerda Stromberg produces most of the designs for her son's justly famous manufactory, which produces luxury and drinking glass.

Synthetic Dyes The discovery of synthetics had its origin in the invention of a new dye-stuff in 1856 by an Englishman, William Henry Perkin. He discovered a coal-tar dye to replace the vegetable matter which had been used from ancient times. The new dye was much cheaper than natural coloring. Shortly after, German science and industry produced alizarin and other important synthetic dyes to meet world-wide demand.

Nearly all synthetic dyes are derived from one or other of the five hydrocarbons: naphthalene, benzene, toluene, xylene and anthracene, the most convenient source of which is coal tar. See *Synthetic Fibers*.

Synthetic Fibers In textiles; the history of synthetic fibers began around the mid-19th century; it parallels the development of the dyes with which they are associated. The first step in synthetic fiber-making converted plant cellulose into a liquid, imitating the silkworm's process with its food, the mulberry leaf. Next a machine was developed that changed liquid wood pulp into thread by forcing or pushing it out through fine tubes. The first time a man-made fiber, artificial silk, was shown to the public was at the Paris Exposition, 1899. The practical manufacture of artificial fibers started after World War I when huge supplies of cellulose and chemicals were available. These were converted into the new product rayon. Some time later, after chemists perfected rayon, other new synthetics were created: nylon, orlon, saran, Dynel, etc. See *Synthetic Dyes; Rayon*.

Syracuse China Corporation See *Onondaga Pottery Company*.

T

Taffeta Glass See *Carnival Glass*.

Talbert, Bruce J. 1838–1881. English designer and writer; produced designs for furniture chiefly in the Gothic and Jacobean styles. In 1865 he moved to London, where he became the leading furniture designer of his generation. In 1867 he published GOTHIC FORMS APPLIED TO FURNITURE and in 1876 EXAMPLES OF ANCIENT AND MODERN FURNITURE, in which he discarded the Gothic for the Jacobean style. He designed in different media, including metal. Talbert was among

the first to be strongly influenced by Japanese art; this Anglo-Japanese taste is seen in his wallpapers. See *Meubles Parlants*.

Tawney, Lenore b. 1925. American weaver; has given new freedom and dimension to weaving. See *Woven Forms*.

Taylor, Howson English artist-potter; experimented in glaze technique from 1898 onwards in his Ruskin pottery at Smethwick, near Birmingham. See *Moore, Bernard*.

Terra-Cotta In American ceramics; the use of terra-cotta in architecture is linked in America with the search for a fireproof material. Chicago, New York, Boston and Perth Amboy had the most important plants producing terra-cotta. Ornaments designed by architects such as James Renwick, Thomas Hastings, Louis Sullivan and Bernard Maybeck were made from molds and were supplied to builders in cities throughout the United States. From the office of Adler and Sullivan in Chicago came the most effective designs. Glazed terra-cotta and fire bricks for interior use were a speciality of the Boston Terra-Cotta Company.

Thesmar, André Fernand b. 1843. French painter and glass artist; became interested in the ancient art of enamelling and gave up painting in order to devote his entire time to *les émaux cloisonnés* in the manner in which the Japanese before him had adapted this art to glass. He became a master in making glass objects. The underlay was generally opaque glass decorated with a relief of flowers and plants in exquisite colors. It is evident from the quality, the elegance and the colors of his work that Thesmar was a great artist within a limited field. Clearly influenced by Japanese artists, he was nevertheless completely French and Art Nouveau in his style.

Thompson, Benjamin 1753–1814. Noted chemist and physicist born in Woburn, Massachusetts, and raised in colonial America. Better known by his title, Count Rumford, which he received from the Elector of Bavaria in 1791. Invented several lamps based on Argand's and was a recognized authority on all matters pertaining to the science of lighting. Also perfected the cast iron range or stove.

Thompson, George b. 1913. American architect and designer; engraving and glass designer for Steuben Glass. See *Steuben Glass*.

Thonet Bentwood Furniture In 1856 the German-born Michael Thonet, 1796–1871, perfected a process by which solid lengths of beechwood could be steamed and bent to form long curved rods. He used Carpathian beech because of its singular tight grain; other woods not possessing this quality are apt to splinter at the point of greatest strain. Bentwood made it possible to produce chairs without complicated carved joints and contours, and paved the way for the first mass production of standardized furniture. One piece of bentwood could be used to form both the open back and rear legs, as in the familiar "Vienna" café model. Countless thousands of bentwood chairs by the Austrian firm of Gebrüder Thonet have been sold throughout the world.

Thorn-Prikker, Johan 1868–1932. Dutch painter and decorative artist; produced batik-inspired textiles for wallpapers and designs for marquetry. He also designed furniture which was of a simple character with arched stretchers in the manner of van de Velde. In 1904 Prikker settled in Germany, where he spent the rest of his life. See *Dutch Art Nouveau*.

Tidy A small piece of decorative fabric for covering the back and arms of upholstered furniture to prevent soiling. See *Antimacassar*.

Tiffany and Company, Inc. In American silver; established in 1837 by Charles L. Tiffany with John B. Young, under the name Tiffany and Young. Most of their silver was purchased from John C. Moore who began the manufacture of silverware in 1827. He was later joined by his son, Edward C. Moore. Called Tiffany, Young and Ellis in 1852; became Tiffany and Company in 1853. Tiffany was incorporated in 1868 and the Moore silverware factory became part of the organization. From then on, until Edward Moore's death, the silverware made in the factory bore the mark Tiffany and Co. and the letter "M." Ever since, the initial of the incumbent company president and the name "Tiffany and Co." appear on all Tiffany-made silver. In 1852 Tiffany introduced the English sterling silver standard to the United States, which standard was later adopted by the United States government.

Tiffany, Louis Comfort 1848–1933. American glass designer and jeweler; America made her chief contribution to Art Nouveau in the work of Tiffany, who after turning to the decorative arts, experimented first with glass. His earliest ornamental windows in opalescent glass date from 1876 and by 1880 he had applied for the patents on the metallic iridescent glass for which he became well known. In 1879 he formed the Louis C. Tiffany Company, Associated Artists, which decorated interiors for many houses and public buildings. In 1885 Tiffany Glass Co. was incorporated, concentrating on stained glass windows and related interiors. Tiffany's ornamentation embodying Art Nouveau motifs in glass and mosaics had developed into an original and entirely contemporary style. Upon completion of a new glass manufactory in 1892, Tiffany specialized in blown glass vases and bowls. This glass bore the trademark Favrile, meaning "handmade," and was notable for its shapes and iridescent, brilliant colors. The influence of Far and Near Eastern art was also evident. Tiffany glass was extensively imitated in Europe, especially by Bohemian glassmakers. One of his "lily-cluster" lamps was awarded a grand prize at the Turin Exhibition in 1902. The characteristics of Tiffany's art glass, like Gallé's, originated in technique. Gallé cut decorations from layers of colored glass superimposed on each other; Tiffany's technique was to control the manner in which layers of colored glass flowed either transparently or opaquely over each other, so as to achieve an abstract play of line and color. Most of the forms he used were as uniquely inventive as the iridescent colors with which they were decorated. The artistic expression of Tiffany's style was reflected in the products of many American manufactories such as Rookwood and Grueby, but Tiffany remained pre-eminent in this American style. See *Associated Artists; Tiffany Studios.*

Tiffany Studios In 1878 Louis Comfort Tiffany organized a group under the firm name of Louis C. Tiffany Company, Associated Artists, to promote the decorative arts in the United States. Out of this association grew Tiffany Studios, which developed into the leading concern of its kind in the country. Operated in connection with Tiffany Studios were the Tiffany Glass and Decorating Company at Madison Ave. and 45th St., New York, a large cabinet shop on Second Avenue, and a glassworks (Tiffany Furnace) at Corona, Long Island. Tiffany thus was able to undertake everything connected with the decorating and furnishing of a structure, whether a cottage, mansion, yacht, church, theater or public building. The scope of the undertakings of this firm was truly amazing. Handwork of all kinds was accomplished on a large scale. In workshops, dyeing and printing rooms, and designing studios, workmen made furniture, manufactured lighting fixtures, cast ornamental bronzes, hammered wrought iron, designed and executed hand-tooled leather wall coverings, made windows and mural mosaics of Favrile glass. Rugs and textiles were woven to order and dyed to match interior color schemes. No firm of the time influenced decorating trends more than Tiffany Studios. There was no connection between Tiffany Studios and the older firm of Tiffany and Company, founded in 1837 by the goldsmith and jeweler Charles Louis Tiffany (the father of Louis C. Tiffany) with his friend John B. Young. Tiffany Studios was discontinued in 1933.

Tiles In American ceramics; the decorative painting of tiles had been done in Trenton, New Jersey, before the Centennial Exhibition; after 1876 in Chelsea, Massachusetts, a new ceramic art industry arose. The first in the field was Hugh Robertson, but much more successful was John G. Low. To a large degree, the superior quality of Low tiles is the result of the work of Arthur Osborne, whose ceramic paintings or "plastic sketches" in relief created effects of depth that still receive the highest admiration.   See *Low Art Tile Works*.

Tobe In Japanese ceramics; an important center in the Ehime Prefecture for hand-crafted pottery. Tobe Yaki was first produced in 1775 by order of the feudal lord of Tobe. The potters were invited from Arita, where pottery had already been made from early days by using Amakusa china clay. A china clay similar to Amakusa could be obtained nearby and Tobe learned from Arita the use of such material. At the present time very interesting tea utensils and vases are being made in Tobe.   See *Japanese Contemporary Pottery*.

Tokoname In Japanese ceramics; one of the most important towns for handcrafted pottery, which has been produced there since the 8th century. From one section around this small town a special fine dark salmon-colored clay named Shudei can be obtained. This clay was in demand for making much-admired Japanese tea utensils from early times.   See *Japanese Contemporary Pottery*.

Tomimoto b. 1896. Japanese stoneware potter; one of the leaders of the Folk Art Movement. A close associate of Bernard Leach during the latter's first stay in Japan, he is best known for his beautifully brushed patterns on stoneware. Tomimoto is venerated in Japan as one of the great contemporary potters.   See *Leach, Bernard*.

Toulouse-Lautrec, Henri de 1864–1901. French painter and printmaker. One of the most outstanding figures in the development of French Art Nouveau.

Towle Silversmiths In American silver; Towle and Jones was established at Newburyport, Massachusetts, in 1857 by Anthony F. Towle and William P. Jones. In 1873 A. F. Towle and Sons, successors to Towle and Jones, bought the business of William Moulton IV and Joseph Moulton IV, who in turn were successors to the Newburyport

silversmith William Moulton II (1664–1732). In 1882 the company became incorporated as Towle Silversmiths. In 1890 the well-known "T" enclosing a lion was used for the first time as a trade mark. Towle Silversmiths manufacture both sterling and silver-plated ware.

Traherne, Margaret b. 1919. English stained glass artist, embroiderer and textile designer; has executed numerous windows for churches and school chapels and has received secular commissions from large corporations. She also designs modern embroideries and textiles. Her commissions include embroidered panels for the 1951 Festival of Britain.   See *English Contemporary Arts and Crafts*.

Traquair, Phoebe Anna 1852–1936. Irish mural decorator, enameller, illuminator, painter and embroiderer; educated at the Dublin School of Art. In 1873 she married Ramsay H. Traquair, Keeper of the Museum of Science and Art, Edinburgh. She designed and executed furniture decoration and metalwork, some in collaboration with Sir Robert Lorimer, and she exhibited widely in Europe and the United States. She attained a notable mastery of fine enamelling.

Turkish-Frame Type In American furniture; the name given to a kind of seat furniture in which the structure of the piece was entirely invisible and only the upholstery was seen. The entire form was made from wire bundles and then completely upholstered. A closely related type was composed of wire bundles, but thicker iron rods formed the support for the frame above the seat.   See *Coil Spring*.

Tuthill Cut Glass Company In American glass; active 1900–1923 at Middletown, New York. One of its outstanding specialties was the exquisite form of decoration known as "intaglio cut," a deeply carved engraving that gave a three-dimensional effect. The frosty, silvery finish and minutely graduated incisions imbue it with notable appeal.   See *Cut Glass, American*.

U

Union Glass Company In American glass; in 1851 Amory and Francis Houghton established a glass factory at Somerville, Massachusetts. In 1860 the company failed. Before 1864 a reorganization took place and the Union Glass Company was incorporated with Amory Houghton as treasurer. In 1864 Amory Houghton and Amory Houghton Jr. acquired controlling interest in the Brooklyn Flint Glass Works and left the Union Glass Company. Noted for its fine cut glass, the company remained active until 1924.

Union Porcelain Works In American ceramics; a factory for the production of soft paste porcelain was begun in 1847 by Charles Cartlidge at Greenpoint, Brooklyn, New York, an important center for porcelain. Its best-known piece was a pitcher whose body consisted of oak leaves and acorns with the raised design picked out in gold. Josiah Jones, who was the outstanding modeller for the company, designed the pitcher. The mark "Greenpoint" sometimes was used by this firm, which closed in 1856. Between the years 1857 and 1861, the factory was re-opened and operated by William Boch and Brothers. In 1861, Thomas C. Smith took over the company and renamed it the Union Porcelain Works. During the 1870's Karl Müller, a sculptor, joined the company and was responsible for designing some of the most noted pieces of American porcelain. Of these the Century Vase which he designed for the Philadelphia Centennial of 1876 is the most celebrated. The wares of this company are noteworthy for their design and the high quality of workmanship. The company remained active until the turn of the century. Its pieces frequently bore the mark "Union Porcelain Works Greenpoint N.Y." See *Century Vase*.

Unit Furniture See *Deutsche Werkstätten*.

Utility Furniture See *Russell, Sir Gordon*.

V

Vallin, Eugène 1856–1925. French architect and furniture designer of the Nancy School; the entire conception of his furniture is markedly Neo-Rococo Art Nouveau. See *Nancy School*.

Velde, Henry van de 1863–1957. Belgian painter, architect, writer and designer; has been considered the creator and theoretical founder of Art Nouveau, apart from his important role in the Modern Movement. Absorbed in the doctrines of Ruskin and Morris, he was perhaps the most prolific writer on Art Nouveau and the leading theoretician among the men of the 1890's. Van de Velde made his debut as a decorative designer in 1893, stressing functional unity in his interiors and furniture. He built and furnished his own house at Uccle near Brussels; it served as a model to demonstrate his theories of design. Typical of his style is the undecorated furniture at Uccle, depending for its strength and beauty on the movement of the lines. To van de Velde line was everything. In 1901 he accepted an invitation from the Grand Duke of Saxe-Weimar to head the Weimar School for Arts and Crafts, where he introduced his own methods of art instruction. He remained there until the outbreak of World War I. He also took part in the founding of the Deutscher Werkbund in 1907. He was an important pioneer of modern design, one of the first to admire the machine and to understand its essential character. In his own words, "The powerful play of their iron arms will create beauty as soon as beauty guides them." See *Belgian Art Nouveau; Loos, Adolf.*

Venini, Paolo 1895–1959. The most important among contemporary Italian glass designers; descendant of a glassblower's family from Como. A lawyer by profession, he gave up his career about 1920 to devote himself to the art of glassmaking. He bought himself a partnership in the Murano glassworks of Giacomo Cappelin in 1921 and shortly afterward bought Cappelin out. Venini's insight and artistic gifts, coupled with his determination to cooperate with outstanding designers—men like Gio Ponti, Napoleone Martinuzzi and the Swedish designer Tyra Lundgren—made him the leading personality in Italian glassmaking practically overnight. From 1923 on, Venini glass won first prizes at all international exhibitions. Confronted with Venini's success, other Murano manufacturers also decided to make beautiful modern glass. Among the most successful in this attempt were Salviati's descendants, Barovier and Toso, and the Seguso Glass Works. Since Venini's death the glassworks has been carried on by his widow and his son-in-law, the architect Ludovico de Santillana. See *Murano Glass; Salviati and Company.*

Ver Sacrum See *Secession.*

Vergette, Nicholas b. 1923. English ceramist and teacher who studied painting initially, then turned to pottery and mosaics; well known for his ceramic enamel and ceramic mosaic architectural wall panels. He was invited to teach on a year's grant at the School for American Craftsmen, Rochester Institute of Technology, New York, in 1958. He settled in Illinois in 1959.

Verlys In French glass; started c. 1931 by the Société Anonyme Holophane of Les Andelys,

for many years manufacturers of prismatic lighting glassware. Verlys, essentially a decorative novelty glass, being either blown or molded, is in most instances a lime glass. Verlys of America was a product of the Verlys division of the Holophane Glass Co., Newark, Ohio, which in turn was associated with the Société Anonyme Holophane. This company, which produced molded glass only, differs slightly from Verlys of France; as they used the designs and molds of the French Company. American Verlys is hand signed, the name Verlys being scratched with a diamond point, while the French Verlys is commonly marked with a molded signature.

Victorian The Victorian period in England and America is often divided into three phases: early Victorian, 1837–1851; mid-Victorian, 1851–1875, dating from the Great Exhibition of 1851 in London; and late Victorian, 1875–1901. The age of Victoria bears the indelible stamp of revivalism. The forms and ornament were freely adapted (and often used simultaneously) from the Classic, Baroque and Rococo styles that preceded it. From around 1820 furniture showed a progressive coarsening of the declining Empire and Regency styles, and the earliest Victorian furniture is virtually inseparable from that which preceded it. In furniture design, the early Victorians also inherited a Gothic tendency which, with its meretricious carved ornament, seeped into many Victorian homes. The influence of the Revived Rococo in France, where it was known as the Louis Philippe style, 1838–1848, became apparent in Victorian furniture in the 1840's. Profuse and blown-up curving lines and the abundant use of naturalistic fruit and flower carvings characterized this work. In America John Belter's chairs and settees are notable examples of this taste. A strong preference for furniture in the Renaissance style marked the mid-Victorian period. In the third and final phase Victorian furniture and the decorative arts mirrored the ideas propagated by Ruskin and Morris.

See *Arts and Crafts Movement; Morris, William; Pugin, Augustus; Eastlake, Charles; Pre-Raphaelites; Aesthetic Movement; Japanism; Cotswold School; Mission Furniture; Second Empire.*

Viollet-le-Duc, Eugène-Emmanuel 1814–1879. French architect and writer on archaeology; his chief interest was in the art of the Gothic period. He was employed to restore some of the main medieval buildings of France, including Notre Dame de Paris. As a writer on medieval architecture and related arts he is pre-eminent. The influence of his writings can scarcely be over-estimated. See *Gothic Revival, English.*

Vodder, Niels See *Juhl, Finn.*

Volkmar, Charles American painter and artist-craftsman, studied in Paris under Harpignies and others; known for his paintings of landscape and cattle. While in Paris he became interested in the Limoges process of underglaze painting. In 1879 he returned to the United States and built a kiln at Greenpoint, Long Island, where he made vases and tiles. In 1895 he established the Volkmar Keramic Company. His wares were decorated with underglaze blue designs of historical buildings and portraits of persons prominent in America. Later, with Kate Cory, Volkmar opened a pottery at Corona, New York, and in 1903 he founded a pottery at Metuchen, New Jersey, where his production included tiles and lamps.

Volkmar, Leon b. 1879. American artist-potter and teacher, born in France; son of Charles Volkmar, the well-known painter. Regarded as one of the most fundamental of modern potters, he always tried for simple forms with fine color and texture. Near East influence was strong in his work.

Voulkos, Peter b. 1924. American ceramist; first established a reputation in the United States and Europe for his vigorous and masterfully thrown pots and jars, generally finished in iron-reds or resist patterns in dark slips under mat glazes. In 1957 he turned in a radically new direction characterized by sculptural forms put together from thrown or slab units and coated with rough glazes or slips. The impact of his work has been strongly felt by the younger generation of potters.

Voysey, Charles Francis Annesley 1857–1941. English architect and designer; generally regarded as the most important designer before and at the turn of the century. He designed furniture, textiles and wallpapers. His furniture, like the interiors of the houses he designed, was light and airy and puritanically plain, revealing the importance of Japanese influence on his work. The simple beauty and sober quality of his work furnished the initial inspiration for such designers as Charles R. Mackintosh, M. H. Baillie Scott and George Walton. See *Arts and Crafts Exhibition Society.*

Wagner, Otto 1841–1918. Vienna's most progressive architect at the turn of the century; Hoffmann and Olbrich were his students. In his influential publication MODERNE ARCHITEKTUR in 1896 he expounded the relationship between modern life and modern forms, for example: "Nothing that is not practical can be beautiful." In respect to the Modern Movement he was one of the first architects to admire the machine and to understand its essential character. See *Secession; Loos, Adolf.*

Walton, George 1867–1933. Glasgow architect and designer; moved to London in 1897. He designed and decorated a number of houses; his work owes something to the Glasgow School but much more to the English School. His furniture forms, pleasantly simple, show a penchant for constructive elements and an economy of ornament. See *Arts and Crafts Exhibition Society*.

Warwick China Company In American ceramics; organized in 1887 in Wheeling, West Virginia, for the manufacture of semi-porcelain table and toilet goods. The first stamp was a helmet and crossed swords. From 1893 to 1898 the "Warwick Semi-Porcelain" mark was used and from 1898 "Warwick China."

Waugh, Sidney 1904–1963. American sculptor and designer. See *Steuben Glass*.

Webb, Aileen Osborn (Mrs. Vanderbilt Webb) b. 1893. The person most responsible for the burgeoning crafts movement in the United States at the present time. See *American Craftsmen's Council*.

Webb, Philip 1831–1915. English architect and designer; designed most of the early furniture produced by the Morris firm. His name is associated with a particular type of austere and undecorated farmhouse furniture chiefly made of unpolished or ebonized oak. In Webb's furniture medievalism is reflected not in the ornamental details but rather in the honest joinery and use of materials, in its simplicity and solidity. Furniture of this character, freed from false values, possessed the spirit of the Middle Ages, according to Morris's standards. See *Morris, William; Jack, George; Cotswold School*.

Wegner, Hans b. 1914. Danish architect and furniture designer; especially notable is one of his designs for a chair inspired by a Chinese Ming chair, having a solid splat and an arched horseshoe-shaped crest rail. Both he and the architect Finn Juhl belonged to a small group of artists who did the pioneer work of the 1930's, of which today's industry is gathering the fruits. See *Danish Modern Furniture*.

Weimar School for Arts and Crafts In 1901 the Grand Duke of Saxe-Weimar invited Henry van de Velde to become head of the school. With the outbreak of World War I in 1914 his post was taken over by Walter Gropius, who began to prepare plans for reorganizing the school. The new school, combining an academy of art and a school of arts and crafts, opened in 1919; it was named the Staatliches Bauhaus. See *Bauhaus*.

Weir, Don b. 1903. American painter, teacher and illustrator; engraving and glass designer for Steuben Glass. See *Steuben Glass*.

Weller Pottery In American ceramics; an art pottery established at Zanesville, Ohio, producing wares similar to those made at Rookwood.

Wells, Reginald English artist-potter; began making pottery at Coldrum Farm, West Malling, Kent, probably about 1904; subsequently moved to Chelsea. He experimented in glaze technique. See *Moore, Bernard*.

Wheeler, Candace 1827–1923. American embroiderer; founded the Decorative Art Society, New York, in the late 1870's. Greatly interested in textiles and needlework, she gave her best to the art of embroidery. See *Associated Artists; Decorative Art Society*.

Wheeling Pottery Company In American ceramics; organized in 1879 in Wheeling, West Virginia; in 1887 a second company was formed, under the same management, called La Belle Pottery Company. The two companies joined in 1889. They made white granite ware, plain and decorated, and La Belle factory made "Adamantine" china. They also introduced "Cameo" china, a thin china decorated with designs in various colors and in blue and gold.

Whistler, James Abbott McNeill 1834–1903. American artist; spent most of his professional life in London. The Japanese influence found in Impressionism is strong in Whistler. Many externals in his paintings are Oriental, but much more significant is the delicacy, the sense of selection and economy that pares each canvas down to a few exquisitely arranged accents. Such extreme simplification outraged public taste in England and involved Whistler in his celebrated lawsuit with Ruskin in 1878. To men like Beardsley he was most important and was probably the principal intermediary between Japanese art and Art Nouveau. See *Aesthetic Movement.*

Whistler, Laurence b. 1912. English poet and author; began to engrave glass in 1936 and is generally regarded as the leading exponent of the art in England. One of his most distinguished pieces is an exquisite glass box engraved for King George VI as a present from his consort, Queen Elizabeth. He has been commissioned by Steuben Glass to make designs for engravings.

White Granite See *Ironstone China.*

Whitefriars Glass Works See *English Glass.*

Wicker See *Cane.*

Widdicomb Furniture Company In American furniture; in 1865 William Widdicomb started a small cabinet shop at Grand Rapids; shortly afterward he was joined by his brothers Harry and John. In 1869 Theodore F. Richards became a partner and the firm was known as Widdicomb Brothers and Richards. In 1873 the company was incorporated as the Widdicomb Furniture Company. Widdicomb quality became a trade word. In 1911 the Widdicombs severed their connection with the business. See *Grand Rapids Furniture.*

Wiener Werkstätte Founded in Vienna in 1903 by Josef Hoffmann in conjunction with Koloman Moser and others; under the leadership of Hoffmann these workshops continued the line of the English Arts and Crafts Movement, were more interested in form and materials than in ornament. See *Secession; Arts and Crafts Exhibition Society; Deutsche Werkstätten; Deutscher Werkbund; Oesterreichischer Werkbund.*

Wilcox, H. C., and Company In American silver; established by Horace C. and Dennis C. Wilcox to market the Britannia ware made at Meriden, Connecticut, which became one of the great centers for Britannia metal. This company was a forerunner of Meriden Britannia Company. See *Meriden Britannia Company.*

Wilde, Oscar Fingal O'Flahertie Wills 1856–1900. English author, born in Dublin. See *Aesthetic Movement.*

Wildenhain, Frans b. 1905. American designer-craftsman born in Germany; studied at the Bauhaus in Weimar; a potter whose work is characterized by great variety. He came to the United States in 1947. Whimsical shapes, functional forms and ceramic sculpture are all within the scope of his work.

Wildenhain, Marguerite b. 1898. American artist-potter born in France, teacher and writer; received her art training at the Bauhaus in Weimar. She came to the United States in 1940 and settled in California as a potter, ultimately opening her own school at Pond Farm, Guerneville. She is the author of POTTERY: FORM AND EXPRESSION, 1959.

Willets Manufactory Company In American ceramics; established at Trenton, New Jersey. The factory is noted for Belleek pieces made during the late 1880's and 1890's. Many of Willets' forms were reproductions of the shell and coral forms of Irish Belleek. The characteristic mark was a snake coiled to form a *W* with *Belleek* above and *Willets* below.

Wilson, Henry 1864–1934. English architect, sculptor, metalworker, jeweler and silversmith; he is typical of a number of architects who first took up metalwork as incidental to their professional practice but later made it their chief interest. His interest in metalwork began about 1890 and resulted in his setting up a workshop about 1895. John Paul Cooper occasionally came to work with him. Wilson was one of the leading artist-craftsmen of his day. See *Cooper, John Paul.*

Wirkkala, Tapio b. 1915. Finnish designer-craftsman, sculptor and graphic artist; already had made a name for himself with sculpture and drawings when he became interested in wood, silver and pottery. His laminated hand-carved plywood pieces such as bowls first became known internationally in 1951 at the Triennale in Milan. His interest spread to glass and in 1947 he joined the Karhula Iittala Glassworks. Like many other great artists, Wirkkala found his inspiration in nature, and it is most interesting to see how he interpreted this inspiration in his beautiful and completely unique glass creations. *Chantarelle*, a small glass vase decorated with ribbed-line cutting, was his first great success in glass. Today he is recognized as one of the world's foremost glass designers.

Wolfers, Philippe 1859–1929. Belgian goldsmith and jeweler; since 1850 the family firm represented the chief line in the development of Belgian gold and silver work. Neo-Rococo with traces of Japanese dominated Wolfer's work from the mid-1880's until 1895, when his work was completely transformed to Art Nouveau of a floral and plant-like character. In the 1890's the most fashionable material among Belgian goldsmiths was ivory from the Belgian Congo. Working in this medium Wolfers created brooches, combs and decorative objects of the highest refinement. He frequently used insects as motifs in his jewelry designs. After 1900 his style became more abstract; by 1905 he had abandoned Art Nouveau.

Woman's Exchange An American philanthropic organization founded more than a hundred years ago in Philadelphia; the original slogan, "To help women help them-selves" explains its purpose. It provides an outlet for work that women in need of money make in their own homes. The New York Exchange for Woman's Work was started in 1878 by Mrs. William H. Choate.

Womb Chair   See *Saarinen, Eero.*

Wood, Beatrice   American artist-potter; one of the foremost ceramists in the United States; has been making pottery from about 1939. The aesthetic value and charm of her work springs from her independence from currently accepted traditions. She is, however, capable of producing a Bauhaus piece or achieving a subtle Chinese or Japanese glaze effect. Because of her open receptivity, her work is always filled with fresh excitement. In her pottery decorations and modelled clay figures appears a fantasy sometimes reminiscent of Klee, sometimes of Chagall, but always characteristically Beatrice Wood.

Wooley, Jackson and Ellamarie b. 1910; 1913. American designer-craftsmen specializing in enamels on copper, a medium with which they started working in 1947. Their architectural wall panels, murals and reliefs are for both interior and exterior uses. Smaller in scale are panels commissioned by private individuals.

Wooten Patent Desk   In American furniture; produced by the Wooten Desk Manufacturing Company of Indianapolis, Indiana, and patented by William S. Wooten, October 4, 1874. These desks were conceived as a complete office and very likely were used as such by most owners, whether in their own house or a commercial establishment. Closed, the desk resembles a cylinder-top desk with two cupboard doors below; opened, it is provided with a fall-front writing board and a variety of compartments, including a forty unit filing section on the right hand and on the left hand a letter box surrounded by pigeonholes and small shelves. Several of these desks are extant that belonged to important people: those of Spencer F. Baird,

Secretary of the Smithsonian Institution; Ulysses S. Grant, President of the United States; John D. Rockefeller, and Joseph Pulitzer.

Wormley, Edward b. 1908. American furniture designer; has been designing furniture for the Dunbar Furniture Company of Berne, Indiana, since about 1931. His work achieves a classic clarity that is notable. He often pays tribute to some aspect of the past such as Sheraton, Shaker, Regency or Empire, but in his hands it is given a sense of the present.

Woven Forms In American weaving; the creation of sculptural shapes of interlaced threads woven on the loom. In these hangings the form is determined by distortion of the set pattern of the warp and weft while the piece is still on the loom. The weaver's search for form is reflected in the finished hanging. The development of weaving in three dimensions has been difficult for many weavers, because in extending the bounds of the woven piece beyond two dimensions it is necessary not only to bend or twist the material into volumetric shapes, but to conceive of the hanging itself as enclosed in space rather than defining a planar limit. Among today's weavers who have successfully created woven forms on the looms are Leonore Tawney, Sheila Hicks and Claire Zeisler.

Wright, Frank Lloyd 1869–1959. American architect; one of the first architects to believe in the machine and to understand its basic character and its effects on the relation of architecture and design to ornamentation. These ideals were expressed in his manifesto, THE ARTS AND CRAFTS OF THE MACHINE, 1901. See *Modern Movement; Wagner, Otto; Loos, Adolf; Velde, Henry van de; Sullivan, Louis.*

Wright, Russell b. 1904. American industrial designer; the range of his art in industry includes tableware, glassware, furniture, wallpapers, rugs, fabrics and flatware. He pioneered the change to a more modern style of tableware design. In 1938 he designed and produced at Steubenville a set of earthenware which was simple, functional, undecorated and employed solid colors rather than decals. This modern dinnerware was an immediate success.

Y

Yanagi, Soetsu Japanese art critic and lecturer, tea master, specialist in the fields of fine arts. Appreciation of Japanese Folk Art begins with Yanagi; he discovered it. In 1935, after Yanagi had been collecting early examples of Folk Art for a number of years, a well-known philanthropist and art lover, Magosaburo Ohara, offered to build a Folk Art museum in Tokyo to house Yanagi's collection of "people's art." As soon as the public had the opportunity to appraise the charm of Folk Art, a great demand developed, which led to its revival. Yanagi set down precisely what Japanese Folk Art was and what its qualities were. First of all, artists and geniuses were not a part of folk art; it was done by anonymous craftsmen for the use of the common people. It was unpretentious, everyday craftsmanship. According to Yanagi, the greatest thing was living beauty in daily life; in bringing beauty into life, crafts must play a vital part. The quality of extravagance that is always associated with deluxe art objects was absent, and any excess of decoration was considered objectionable. Folk art had to be simple in shape, in color and design. Finally, he believed people's art was normal art, that nothing was healthier than normal things. See *Mashiko*.

Yellow Ware In American ceramics; utility ware comprising baking dishes, molds and the like, of cream or buff clays with transparent glaze ranging from pale straw-color to deep yellow. When given a mottled brown manganese coating it became Rockingham. Widely made c. 1830–1900.

Yokkaichi In Japanese ceramics; in the 18th century a rich merchant in the town of Kuwana, which is across the bay from Nagoya, started making tea utensils, learning the techniques from Kyōto. He named the product Banko ware. In the 20th century the town of Yokkaichi, adjacent to Kuwani, developed as an industrial town and potters gradually moved there. At present Yokkaichi has become the center of Western style export ware; only a few potters make traditional-type Banko ware. See *Japanese Contemporary Pottery*.

Ysart, Salvador See *Monart Glass*.

Z

Zeisel, Eva American designer, born in Hungary; she developed in collaboration with the Museum of Modern Art, New York, a formal porcelain dinner set, 1941–1945, produced by Castleton China Co. Showing a trend toward simpler and more functional shapes, the set was a landmark in tableware design. Zeisel has also worked in glass, metal, wood and plaster.

Zwobada, Jacques b. 1900. French sculptor, one of the best-known sculptors of the Ecole de Paris; recognized among the several great artists of contemporary France who are master designers. Zwobada recently applied his unique values of black and white to tapestry.

BIBLIOGRAPHY

ALBERS, ANNI. *On Designing*. Middletown, 1961.

ARGIRO, LARRY. *Mosaic Art Today*. Scranton, Pennsylvania, 1961.

ARMITAGE, E. LIDDALL. *Stained Glass*. Newton, Massachusetts, 1959.

ASHBEE, CHARLES R. *Modern English Silverwork*. London, 1909.

ASLIN, ELIZABETH. *Nineteenth Century English Furniture*. New York, 1962.

BAHR, HERMAN. *Sezession*. Vienna, 1900.

BARBER, EDWIN A. *The Pottery and Porcelain of the United States*. Second edition, New York, 1901.

BINNS, CHARLES F. *The Potter's Craft*. Third edition, New York, 1922.

BLOMFIELD, PAUL. *William Morris*. London, 1934.

BLUMENAU, LILI. *The Art and Craft of Hand Weaving*. New York, 1955.

BØE, ALF. *From Gothic Revival to Functional Form*. Oslo, 1957.

BOGER, H. BATTERSON. *The Traditional Arts of Japan*. New York, 1964.

BOGER, LOUISE ADE. *Furniture Past and Present*. New York, 1966.

BUTLER, JOSEPH T. *American Antiques 1800–1900*. New York, 1965.

CLARK, KENNETH. *The Gothic Revival*. London, 1928.

COBDEN-SANDERSON, J. T. *The Arts and Crafts Movement*. London, 1905.

CRANE, WALTER. *William Morris to Whistler*. London, 1911.

DANIEL, DOROTHY. *Cut and Engraved Glass, 1771–1905*. New York, 1950.

DIGBY, GEORGE W. *The Work of the Modern Potter in England*. London, 1952.

DRESSER, CHRISTOPHER. *Japan—Its Architecture, Art and Art Manufacture*. London, 1882.

EASTLAKE, CHARLES L. *Hints on Household Taste*. London, 1868.

FARLEIGH, JOHN. *The Creative Craftsman*. London, 1950.

FRANKL, PAUL T. *New Dimensions*. New York, 1928.

GAUNT, WILLIAM. *The Aesthetic Adventure*. Reprint Society. London, 1945.

GAUNT, WILLIAM. *The Pre-Raphaelite Dream*. Reprint Society. London, 1943.

GODWIN, EDWARD. *Art Furniture*. London, 1877.

GROPIUS, WALTER. *The New Architecture and the Bauhaus*. London, 1935.

HAMILTON, W. *The Aesthetic Movement in England*. London, 1882.

HETTES, KAREL. *Glass in Czechoslovakia*. Prague, 1958.

HIORT, ESBJØRN. *Modern Danish Ceramics*. New York,

HIORT, ESBJØRN. *Modern Danish Furniture*. New York, 1956.

HOWARTH, THOMAS. *Charles Rennie Mackintosh and the Modern Movement*. New York, 1953.

IRONSIDE, ROBIN. *Pre-Raphaelite Painters*. New York, 1948.

JANNEAU, GUILLAUME. *Modern Glass*. London, 1931.

JOEL, DAVID. *The Adventure of British Furniture, 1851–1951*. London, 1953.

KARASZ, MARISKA. *Adventures in Stitches*. New York, 1949.

KOCH, ROBERT. *Louis C. Tiffany, Rebel in Glass*. New York, 1964.

LEACH, BERNARD. *A Potter's Handbook*. Seventh edition, London, 1956.

LEACH, BERNARD. *A Potter in Japan, 1952–1954*. London, 1960.

LEACH, BERNARD. *A Potter's Portfolio*. London, 1951.

LENNING, HENRY F. *The Art Nouveau*. The Hague, 1951.

LICHTEN, FRANCES. *Decorative Art of Victoria's Era*. New York, 1950.

MADSEN, STEPHEN TSCHUDI. *Sources of Art Nouveau*. English translation by Ragnar Christophersen. New York, 1956.

MAKI, O. *Designers of Today*. Helsinki, 1955.

MARYON, HERBERT. *Metalwork and Enamelling*. Fourth edition, London, 1959.

MCCLINTON, KATHERINE MORRISON. *Collecting American Victorian Antiques*. New York, 1966.

MUSEUM OF MODERN ART, NEW YORK. *Art Nouveau*. Edited by Peter Selz and Mildred Constantine. New York, 1959.

MUSEUM OF MODERN ART, NEW YORK. *Introduction to Twentieth Century Design from the Museum's Collection*. Edited by Arthur Drexler and Greta Daniel. New York, 1959.

PEARSON, J. MICHAEL and DOROTHY T. *American Cut Glass*. New York, 1965.

PEVSNER, NIKOLAUS. *High Victorian Design*. Ipswich, Great Britain, 1951.

PEVSNER, NIKOLAUS. *Pioneers of Modern Design from William Morris to Walter Gropius*. New York, 1949.

PLATH, IONA. *The Decorative Arts of Sweden*. New York, 1948.

PLAUT, JAMES S. *Steuben Glass. A Monograph.* New York, 1951.

POLAK, ADA. *Modern Glass.* New York, 1962.

POOR, HENRY VARNUM. *A Book of Pottery.* New Jersey, 1958.

POWELL, H. J. *Glassmaking in England.* Cambridge, 1923.

RAINWATER, DOROTHY T. *American Silver Manufacturers.* Hanover, Pennsylvania, 1965.

RAMSAY, JOHN. *American Potters and Pottery.* Clinton, Massachusetts, 1939.

READ, SIR HERBERT. *Art and Industry.* Third edition, London, 1952.

REYNAL, JEANNE. *The Mosaics of Jeanne Reynal.* Text by Dore Ashton, Lawrence Campbell, Elaine de Kooning, Bernard Pfriem, Parker Tyler and Jeanne Reynal. New York, 1964.

RHODES, DANIEL. *Clay and Glazes for the Potter.* New York, 1957.

RHODES, DANIEL. *Stoneware and Porcelain: The Art of High-Fired Pottery.* Arts and Crafts Series. Philadelphia, 1959.

SKELLEY, LELOISE DAVIS. *Modern Fine Glass.* New York, 1937.

SCHRIJVER, ELKA. *Glass and Crystal, from 1850 to the Present.* New York, 1964.

SOWERS, ROBERT. *The Lost Art: A Survey of 1000 Years of Stained Glass.* New York, 1954.

SOWERS, ROBERT. *Stained Glass: An Architectural Art.* New York, 1965.

STEWART, JANICE S. *The Folk Arts of Norway.* University of Wisconsin Press, 1953.

STINNETT-WILSON, R. *The Beauty of Modern Glass.* London, 1958.

SULLIVAN, LOUIS HENRY. *Kindergarten Chats and Other Writings.* New York, 1947.

SYMONDS, R. W. and WHINERAY, B. B. *Victorian Furniture.* London, 1962.

TALBERT, BRUCE J. *Gothic Forms Applied to Furniture.* London, 1867.

TEAGUE, WALTER D. *Design This Day.* American edition, 1946.

UNTRACHT, OPPI. *Enameling on Metal.* Arts and Crafts Series, New York, 1957.

UPJOHN, WINGERT, MAHLER. *History of World Art.* Second edition, revised and enlarged. Oxford University Press, 1958.

WALLANCE, DONALD W. *Shaping America's Products.* New York, 1956.

WEBB, RUTH LEE. *Nineteenth Century Art Glass.* New York, 1952.

WETTERGREN, ERIK. *The Modern Decorative Arts of Sweden.* English translation by Tage Palm. Malmö Museum, 1926.

WHEELER, CANDACE. *The Development of Embroidery in America.* New York, 1921.

WILDENHAIN, MARGUERITE. *Pottery: Form and Expression.* Enlarged edition, New York, 1958.

WRIGHT, FRANK LLOYD. *On Architecture. Selected Writings, 1894–1940.* New York, 1941.